THE
Women's Book
OF
World Records
AND
Achievements

AN INFORMATION HOUSE BOOK

THE
Women's Book
OF
World Records
AND
Achievements

EDITED BY
Lois Decker O'Neill

ANCHOR BOOKS
ANCHOR PRESS/DOUBLEDAY
GARDEN CITY, NEW YORK
1979

The Women's Book of World Records and Achievements is published simultaneously in hard and paper covers.
Anchor Books Edition: 1979
ISBN: 0-385-12733-2

Acknowledgments

So many people helped in so many ways with suggestions, research, and checking for this book that we can only include them in the following blanket acknowledgment:

Thanks to all mothers, fathers, grandparents, husbands, daughters, sons, nieces, nephews, aunts, uncles, lovers, friends, casual acquaintances made on planes, trains, and buses; business associates; employees of magazines, newspapers, radio and TV networks and stations, libraries (especially the heads of sections at the Library of Congress), churches, schools, colleges, and universities (especially Ms. D. J. HUDSON, assistant secretary to the Warden, the Rhodes Trust, Oxford, England); trade associations, embassies in Washington, D.C. (especially Ms. FRAN O'NEILL, librarian, the Canadian Embassy); the staff of the United Nations Food and Agriculture Organization's Washington office, and the staff at the George Meany Center for Labor Studies in Washington, D.C. Also, both employers and employees in a number of U.S. congressional offices and innumerable helpful bureaucrats in U.S. government offices, including particularly the Women's Bureau of the Department of Labor, the *Newsletter* staff of the Department of State, and lots of people at the Beltsville (Maryland) Agricultural Research Center of the Department of Agriculture, the National Science Foundation, the National Aeronautics and Space Administration, and the White House.

Information House Books research assistants who contributed to this book included Pacita Abad, Anne Brink, Stephanie Franks, Joann Lawless, Carol Polsky, Beverly Savage, Marguerite Ulmer, Susan Weiman, and Madge Williams. I wish to thank them for their efforts. I particularly wish to acknowledge the intelligent work and patient support through crisis after crisis provided by Information House Books editorial assistant RHODA BODZIN. The women's logo was designed for Information House Books by ALYSSA ZAMIR. JEANNETTE

DOWLING, JOANN MATTISON, RITA WHITE, and HARRIET WERBELOWSKY did a great deal of often very difficult typing, always under deadline pressure.

At Anchor Press, HARRIET RUBIN, editorial assistant, backed us up in ways too numerous to describe, for which I am also grateful. DEELDA ELWOOD led a team of copyeditors whose careful checking and astute questions spared us many errors.

Most of all, I wish to thank LORETTA BARRETT, editorial director of Anchor Press, for the pleasure of her company in this effort. She was the first among us to discern the significance of "firsts" in our epoch of women's history.

L.D.O'N.

Washington, D.C.
July 1978

Contents

Introduction

Firsts, Heroes, and the Rest of Us

By Lois Decker O'Neill

In the course of researching and writing this book, we—the authors and editors—made a discovery. Our original idea had been to look for women with provable records of one sort or another, including "firsts," and to combine them with others generally acknowledged as leaders within particular fields of endeavor to produce a book celebrating women's world records and achievements in the late 19th and the 20th centuries. That remains the idea behind the 17 chapters that follow.

But what emerged, somewhat unexpectedly, was considerable evidence that today's women, the world over, live in an epoch of firsts. In one line of work after another, in sports, and in almost every country, barriers to female participation have been falling at what becomes, when one looks at the changes against the sweep of history, a fairly astonishing rate. Admittedly, many of these first women—and they are usually first to say so—have been tokens in worlds that up to now have been reserved for men. But

though they may have been hired in response to pressures from the women's movement or in conformity with new laws enforcing equality of opportunity, these "first women" have generally succeeded in proving their worth and have been followed by seconds and thirds. Not always. But often. And it seems to us important to remember that there has to be a first before there can be 20 or a 100 or 1,000 women in the top jobs, the formerly closed professions, the forbidden territories.

Our hope is that 50 years from now a book like this could not be put together. We like to think that this epoch of firsts will be over, that there will be few, if any, things left for a woman to do that some other woman hasn't already done —or nobody has done. If in 2028 a woman is first to bake a pie on a space shuttle, may she be not just the first woman but the first person to accomplish that unlikely (it now seems) feat!

Had this book been written 50 years

ago, certain chapters could not have been included in it. Outside the cloister and the parochial schoolroom there were not enough women in religion to fill a chapter. Female nurses and a female surgeon had appeared on the battlefields of the American Civil War, and World War I had seen women handling military support jobs for almost all the warring powers—but not enough such women to make a chapter.

Fifty years ago some other chapters would have reflected what they show today: For instance, that women in agriculture, still the world's basic industry, remain largely anonymous, and conversely, that women have been active and actively publicized in many of the arts and in the entertainment industry for many years. Because of the difficulties of identifying firsts within these fields —and the greater difficulty of selecting, from a seemingly endless list of star achievers, which painters, dancers, singers, writers to include, which to reluctantly omit—"Women in the Arts and Entertainment" had to depend on the subjective judgment of the author, her panel of special advisers, and the editors more than any other chapter in the book.

Fifty years ago the chapters on women in science, in medicine, in education, and in the labor movement would have included many of the same women, born in the 19th century, working early in the 20th, who remain important firsts in their fields. But to them the authors have added many others—in biochemistry and nuclear engineering, in urology, in women's studies, and in union management.

The 1920s were another epoch of firsts for women. That fact shows in several chapters. Particularly in the United States, politics and government was then a newly opened, exciting field for women. Unfortunately, U.S. women have not continued to gain in these activities at the rate that might have been expected, looking back to the '20s: as our

chapter shows, they have been outstripped by women ministers, diplomats, and other officials in a number of other countries. (Nowhere, sad to say, have women held their gains or—in some instances—acquitted themselves well as heads of governments.) The 1920s—as later the '30s and '40s—were also a good time for women in communications, particularly in the new and burgeoning broadcast industry. The arrival of TV opened up many additional jobs for women that did not exist earlier. Over and over again, however, the stories of women in communications make it clear that with each new stage of growth they have had to fight hard for the chance to prove themselves, just as NELLY BLY did before she was hired by the *New York World* in 1887.

This venturesome woman reporter, whose exploits are described in the chapter "Women in Communications," was one of my heroes when I was a little girl. I can't remember where I first read about her, but I do know that she was responsible for my growing up wanting to be a newspaperwoman, which was not something anybody in my family had ever been. Both my grandmothers worked outside their homes in addition to raising good-sized families—one alongside her husband in the fields and barn of their Pennsylvania-German farm, the other taking over and making a go of the real estate business that she and her husband, Irish immigrants, had just begun to build up before his early death. My mother's service as a yeoman (F) in the Navy in World War I, which we children loved to hear her tell about, impressed me greatly. But it was Nelly Bly who really fired my imagination.

Her influence was reinforced by that of an anonymous reporter I saw in the city room of the *New York Times* when the staff of the *Curtin Jr. Citizen* was escorted through it during a field trip with the Pennsylvania School Press Association one Easter vacation. A beautiful blonde wearing a red hat and a gray flannel suit as she sat at her typewriter, she was the woman I wanted to be (rather like CANDICE BERGEN, according to an interview in the *Washington Post* not long ago, wanted to be "Brenda Starr, black orchids and all"). Eight years later, when I was just out of college, that woman, described by me in response to the question "Why do you want to work here?" actually got me a job on the *New York Times*. (I didn't stay long, but that's another story, having to do with wartime, love, and the inescapable tension between the pleasures of domesticity and the pull of professional life, with which all of us women and men alike have to cope.)

My excuse for this excursion into the personal has to do with heroes. In 1977, SUSAN JACOBY, free-lance writer who speaks só well so often to the concerns of women today, had a column reprinted in the *Washington Star* under the headline, "When Will Women Ever Be the Kinds of Heroes Who Set You Free?" In it she described how she spent much of her time between the ages of 7 and 10 dreaming of the day when she would follow in the footsteps of her hero and play second base for the Chicago White Sox. Not all her childhood heroes were sports figures, she went on to say, but all of them were men. And when she questioned her women friends about their childhood heroes, "an extraordinary number insisted that they never had any" and the others agreed that theirs too had all been men. One woman claimed MARGARET SANGER, but on closer examination her memory proved faulty; she was actually in college before hearing of the leader of the birth control movement. A later canvassing of 10-to-12-year-old girls elicited the name of just one woman hero: BILLIE JEAN KING.

This column of Ms. Jacoby's astonished me. I couldn't believe it. Did none of the women remember ELEANOR ROOSEVELT (her husband, Franklin D. Roosevelt, was on Ms. Jacoby's list) as a hero? Or BABE DIDRIKSON ZA-

HARIAS? Or ANNE FRANK, whose death qualified her as a hero under the derivation of the word from Greek religion as "a dead man or woman of note given reverence or actual worship as quasi-divine" (Columbia Encyclopedia)? Did none of the girls mention NADIA COMANECI or JANE FONDA or that growing cult figure, AMELIA EARHART, whose presumed death in the Pacific in 1937 added a classic Greek element to her qualifications?

It is 50 years since Amelia Earhart first flew the Atlantic Ocean as a passenger, the first woman in history to do so, before flying it solo as a pilot, again the first woman to do so. All these years later, Pete Hamill tells us, his daughter at the age of 10 found "something about Amelia [that] touched her in a deep, crucial way." She "fulfilled some need in us for the heroic spirit," he concludes, (*Ms.*, September 1976).

"There are people who think the end of the traditional hero would produce more realistic men and women," Susan Jacoby writes. "I doubt it. . . . Doing well under extreme pressure was an important element in my fantasies, and that idea is certainly suitable for any 'realistic' adult."

I couldn't agree more wholeheartedly. But then she concludes: "Things ought to have changed by now, but it seems that barriers to women are more formidable in the world of heroes than in union hiring halls or executive suites."

This is where Susan Jacoby and I really part company. I think that there are plenty of women heroes around. There are a lot of them, including all those mentioned above, in this book. A possible explanation for the apparent absence of women heroes in the days of Susan Jacoby's youth (though it should not really apply to the youngsters she interviewed) emerges in the eulogy SHEILA TOBIAS gave at a memorial service in 1976 for ESTHER MANNING WESTERVELT, described in the chapter "Woman in Education, Social Sciences, and the Humanities":

"There is a missing generation of women in American life. In my historical research, I have been trying to trace that group who but for the Depression, World War II, and the Feminine Mystique of the 1950s would have been in positions of leadership and authority now and during the past ten years. Esther belonged to that generation, but unlike most, she survived the pressure not to succeed. For the women coming after, the women my age, there were few who could direct and inspire us."

Yet as the introduction to the chapter "Women in the Home and Community" reminds us, with startling statistics, for some years far more American women have worked outside the home than is generally supposed. Many have done so out of necessity, being single, or widowed, or divorced, or because they have found that their families could only survive or live as comfortably as they wished in two-paycheck households. But surprisingly large numbers of these women have long since risen, without much notice or fanfare, to positions of leadership and authority. The problem is that they have gone too often unrecognized.

Unsung as they were, records of their achievements are hard to come by. "The Search," contributing editor-writer BARBARA TUFTY dubbed her effort to identify achievers for her chapter, "Women in Science and Technology." Often it was terribly frustrating to get information. Nonetheless, we did find many formerly unidentified "firsts" and record-breakers of other kinds—women of authority and accomplishment, "role models," if you will. Real-life heroes, many of them. There is much to celebrate.

As we searched, we were struck by the roughly revealed patterns of difficult times and breakthrough times for women in many different fields. The pace and the pattern differ markedly from chapter to chapter and division to division within each chapter. For example, the section on women in architecture, in "Women in the Arts and Entertainment," gives a clear impression of what's been happening, and not happening, in this field since SOPHIA HAYDEN, aged 22 and the first woman architecture graduate of Massachusetts Institute of Technology, designed the Women's Building for the Columbian Exposition in Chicago, 1892–93. To emphasize these patterns and the informal sense of history that they give, we have arranged material chronologically as much as possible within chapters and divisions of chapters.

Readers may find that some women appear under unexpected headings—a lawyer in religion, for instance, a doctor in the military, a physicist in medicine, a cabinet member in the chapter on the labor movement, one of America's top women newspaper publishers not where one might first look for her, in the chapter, "Women in Communications," but in the chapter "Women in Business, Industry, and Finance," where she belongs. Some superachievers or others whom fate—or choice—has cast in highly unusual or multiple roles appear in the final chapter, "Far-Out Women." Where there has been reason to mention a woman in more than one chapter or in connection with another woman, we have provided cross references. Occasionally, the names of women who do not have full write-ups in the book appear on lists of record holders or prizewinners, or they may be mentioned in chapter introductions.

With the steadily growing interest in women's studies and the establishment of such institutions as the Schlesinger Memorial Research Library on Women at Radcliffe, women's records in future should be easier to come by. Meanwhile, we hope that this book conveys a sense of what women have been up to in the fields it covers both in the United States and in other nations.

Read on.

LOIS DECKER O'NEILL, *formerly a senior editor, director of the Washington office, and member of the editorial board of Praeger Publishers, since 1976 has been an associate editor of the* Wilson Quarterly, *published by the Wilson International Center for Scholars, the Smithsonian Institution. Ms. O'Neill has worked for newspapers and as a free-lance* writer-editor *and teacher since she was graduated from Swarthmore College, Pennsylvania, in 1942,* summa cum laude *in English and history, Phi Beta Kappa. She and her husband, Edward A. O'Neill, a former journalist, spent the years 1955–63 in India where he served with the U. S. Embassy in New Delhi. They are the parents of a son and daughter.*

1

Women in Agriculture and the World Food Movement

By Barbara Raskin

Alice F. Skelsey, consulting editor

Farm women are a growing political force in the United States. More than 8,000 of them during the past few years have joined newly formed state and local groups that attempt to educate the public about farm issues. They also lobby legislators on pending bills. Each day these women become more politically vocal and publicly visible.

A national umbrella organization named American Agri-Women is perhaps the fastest-growing of all these organizations. It was formed to confederate independent state groups that had sprung up during the controversial price freeze and consumer beef boycott of 1973. On November 11, 1977, 220 women delegates from 33 states, representing more than 3,000 members, attended the third annual American Agri-Women convention in Green Bay, Wisconsin.

"All these women . . . have worked in the fields, pastures, and stock pens beside their husbands for years. They keep the books, buy the supplies, share in decisions, and help deal with bankers to get the monumental loans needed to keep a

modern farm running," the *New York Times* reported.

There were three days of meetings that covered a number of subjects vital to America's small farmers. The women want to "assure the survival of the family farm as a way of life, which they consider threatened by hard times, low prices, and high debts," according to the *Times*. They believe that as women they can promote unity among farmers, thus helping them to become more effective in fighting for favorable farm legislation." JOAN ADAMS, of Oklahoma, was elected to replace SHARON STEFFENS of Michigan as American Agri-Women national coordinator.

Other farm women's groups in the United States have also held conferences recently. WIFE (Women Involved in Farm Economics) met in Sidney, Nebraska, in October 1977. JOAN O'CONNELL, of Sidney, one of the original organizers, told how their group "grew just like a prairie fire." In January 1976 only nine women showed up for the first meeting; a year later WIFE had

5,000 members and chapters in 10 states. Another group doing similar work in Kansas is called Fight for the Family Farm. Still another is Women for the Survival of Agriculture in Michigan.

The members of all these groups enjoy telling how their local organizations got started and which issues gave them impetus to organize. KAREN SMITH, of Burlington, Colorado, one of the early organizers of Partners in Action for Agriculture, which has chapters in Colorado, Kansas, and Oklahoma, says, "We have to be willing to fight for what we believe is a good way of life. The family farm is not only important to us but to the whole country."

Concerned Farm Wives was spontaneously organized by a group of women attending a baby shower. As KATHRYN HELSEL of South Haven, Kansas, tells it, "We started out by responding to editorials in farm journals that said everything was just fine down on the farm. We didn't feel they were being realistic about what was really happening—the falling price of wheat and increasing crop input costs."

In December 1977 the *New Yorker* magazine devoted several columns of its "Talk of the Town" to a delegation of Concerned Farm Wives of South Central Kansas, who were in New York to promote the interests of small farmers. The women carried press kits containing materials about various problems. They set up a display booth at the World Trade Center and embarked upon one of their program objectives—educating the public about farm life and agricultural problems.

DONNA HARPER, a Concerned Farm Wife from Sedgwick, Kansas, told a *New Yorker* reporter:

"We think it is important for the consumer to understand our situation. We feel that the family farm is the most efficient kind of farm, and right now it's in trouble. We feel that the farmer at least ought to be able to make a living. May I tell you how the Concerned Farm Wives got together? There was a farm tour that was sponsored by a local farm cooperative early this year. They needed some women to fix food. Well, we were talking amongst ourselves, and we decided that since there was some important legislation coming up in Washington this spring, rather than just sit around and complain, we should do something. So we formed the Concerned Farm Wives—about two hundred women are in it, but we don't have a formal membership. Local individuals, bankers, machinery dealers, cooperatives, agribusiness people, and the Kansas Wheat Commission pay some of our expenses, but we pay a lot ourselves, out of our own pockets. We went to Washington and gave away bread on the steps of the Capitol last spring. . . . We want people who consume what we grow to know what we do and to support legislation that helps the family farmer, because the family farmer's whole heart and soul are in his farm and he wants to be there and till the soil and raise his children there and he wants to pass it on to the next generation better than it was when he found it."

Today, scholars of both sexes concede that traditional HIStories and standard reference materials have systematically excluded the stories of outstanding women in all areas of human endeavor who rightfully deserved recognition. Thus it was not surprising to find a scarcity of names and a lack of information about farm women who have established records or made unusual contributions to U.S. agricultural history. Although the U. S. Department of Agriculture extols the family farm, it has gathered only the most general kind of material on the historic and economic roles played by women in the development of American agriculture. The most easily obtainable names were those of women who have made achievements in agricultural research or who work within U.S. or international farm agencies. Perhaps the new political consciousness of farm women will spur one or more of the new women's research organizations into keeping—and attempting to retrieve —records on individual women whose achievements on the land remain obscured.

Finding and identifying outstanding rural women from other parts of the world presented an even greater research problem. An estimated half of the rural women living in developing countries today are primarily employed in agricultural work. They labor in anonymity. Banding together to publicize their difficulties is not an option open to them as to U.S. farm women. These women struggle for survival in a world that ignores their primitive working and living conditions. Although they labor in the fields, others own the land. Although they harvest the crops, others manage, distribute, and sell them. Tragically, these women seldom have enough money to buy back sufficient amounts of the food that they produce to eat adequately themselves or to keep their children from malnutrition.

An increasing number of activists and writers in what has lately come to be termed the World Food Movement are calling attention to the plight of rural women in developing countries. The Food and Agricultural Organization of the United Nations in a bulletin entitled *The Missing Half* (1975) notes that for the rural woman "life is a grueling affair. . . . Despite . . . frequent pregnancies and often chronic mal- and undernutrition, she has to perform most of the exhausting and time-consuming unskilled tasks involved in running an unmechanized agriculture (including casual labor and transport of the cash crops for the men). She fetches water from distant wells, collects and carries heavy loads of firewood, and performs the tiring chore of pounding rice and palm fruit, as well as cooking on primitive hearths and looking after the children. . . . Naturally enough, this woman's productivity in farming is low, since she has no training

. . . and her vigor is often impaired. . . . She is always restricted in her movements and sometimes segregated. Her labors, too, are not rewarded. Her rights to own property or retain her earnings are not guaranteed either by law or custom. Her life expectancy is for all these reasons lower than man's. And, unkindest cut of all, her status is consistently lower."

In the attempt to assemble names of women engaged in agricultural activities around the world for inclusion in this chapter, researchers approached foreign embassies in Washington, D.C. Some responded to the request with detailed lists. The Iranian Embassy, for example, contributed 12 names, ranging from:
Her Imperial Majesty the Shahbanou, FARAH PAHLAVI, who was nominated "because of her devotion to the cause of Iranian rural development" and active involvement in "many projects concerned with the education and well-being of the rural population," to
KHORSHID MOFTAKHARI "for her development of ten hectares of rice and wheat land in Mozandaran, which she received under the Land Reform Program."
Other governments submitted responses that exemplified the historical neglect of women agricultural workers. From the Office of the Permanent Secretary of the Ministry of Agriculture, Food, and Consumer Affairs in St. Michael, Barbados, came this reply: "I am directed to inform you that this Ministry is not aware of the name of any woman in Barbados who has contributed significantly in agriculture."

Still other government officials, though unable to supply specific names, went to extraordinary lengths to affirm the agricultural achievements of their national women. Japan's Assistant Secretary of Agriculture telephoned personally from Tokyo. He said that his government had only scanty records on rural women, who traditionally work on small family farms run by their husbands, but asked if his

Embassy in Washington might provide photographs that would symbolically represent all the anonymous farm women of Japan. The Embassy of Sri Lanka responded similarly.

It is to these unidentified women and the millions more like them—the unnamed, unrecognized, and generally unrewarded female farm workers of the world, to whom everyone is indebted—that this chapter is respectfully dedicated.

BARBARA RASKIN *is a novelist* (Loose Ends, The National Anthem, *and* Out-of-Order) *and journalist. Her articles and reviews have appeared in the* Washington Post, *the* Washington Star, *the* Washingtonian *magazine, the* Washington Monthly, Boston *magazine, the* Nation, *and the* New Republic. *A graduate of the University of Minnesota and the University of Chicago, she has taught at Ameri-*can University, George Washington University, and Catholic University. She lives in the District of Columbia with her husband, Marcus Raskin, and their three children.*

Consulting editor ALICE F. SKELSEY, *regional information officer stationed at the U. S. Department of Agriculture's Beltsville (Maryland) Research Center, is a graduate of the University of Colorado. She won a federal internship to study professional administration and management in government. A prolific writer, she was for six years the author of a thrice-weekly nationally syndicated column, "For Women Who Work," and has published six books on working women and on gardening—the most recent,* Every Room a Garden, *in 1977. Married and the mother of four, Ms. Skelsey lives in Annandale, Virginia.*

WOMEN IN AGRICULTURE AROUND THE WORLD— A SAMPLING

Canada's Wheat Crop Wonder Woman

Born in 1861, E. CORA HIND lived to the age of 81, carving out a career in agriculture that has made her name famous among scientists concerned with feeding all the world's people. She grew up in the province of Ontario and after finishing high school moved to Winnipeg, where she got a job as the first typist west of the Great Lakes at $6.00 a week. In 1898, asked by the Maclean Publications to check out the effects of recent heavy rain on the wheat crops, she bought a train ticket in order to survey the fields around Winnipeg through the window. Thus began her long career as an agricultural journalist. In 1901 she was hired by the *Free Press* and became a recognized authority on prairie agriculture in general and wheat in particular. E. Cora Hind was a phenomenal estimator of the size of wheat harvests and in 1905 estimated the wheat crop at 85,000,000 bushels; it turned out to be 84,506,857. In 1907 she estimated 71,259,000 bushels; it was 70,992,584. In 1909 she estimated 118,109,000; it was 118,119,000 bushels. In 1932 the *Morning Post* of London wrote: "It would be strange enough if a man of great experience could soberly and accurately forecast the crop . . . but that such a faculty would be centered in a woman—this for some reason seems extraordinary." E. Cora Hind was awarded an honorary degree from the University of Alberta before her death.

Farm Woman Founder of the Federated Women's Institutes of Canada

ADELAIDE SOPHIA (HUNTER) HOODLESS (1857–1910) was born on a farm near St. George in Brant County, Ontario, and in 1881 married John Hoodless, with whom she had three children. In 1897 she made a speech at a meeting of the Farmers Institute in Stoney Creek, suggesting that farm women form their own institute to study homemaking. Within a few days, the first Women's Institute was organized at Stoney Creek, the beginning of a movement that became worldwide and is now incorporated in the 8-million-member Associated Country Women of the World. Ms. Hoodless also helped found and became the first treasurer (1893–1901) of Canada's National Council of Women, fought successfully for domestic science classes in Canadian schools, and established the Ontario Normal School of Domestic Science and Arts in Hamilton.

She Worked Forty Years for Country Women of the World

LILLA RUSSELL, who represented the viewpoint of rural women in the United Nations, was born in New Zealand, grew up in Australia, and later, with her husband, a member of the Indian Educational Service, lived in India, Ceylon, and Burma. After he was killed in World War I, she moved to England with her two daughters, was active in the Women's Institute for many years, and in 1934 became interested in Associated Country Women of the World (ACWW). She was secretary of the handicraft subcommittee, and after World War II became chairwoman of the executive committee, working to consolidate the ACWW's role in the United Nations. In 1950 she was elected a vice-chairwoman of the Bureau of Non-Governmental Organizations' Conference of the Economic and Social Council, and—by then a grandmother of five and great-grandmother of two—worked with the United Nations' appeal for children. In 1962 she was British delegate to the International Conference on Social Work in Brazil, having represented ACWW on the liaison committee of Women's International Organizations since 1943 and served on the executive committee of the Institute of Rural Life. She was made a member of honour of ACWW at the Dublin Conference in 1965 and remained active until her death in 1977 at 92.

Frenchwoman Who Runs a Major Vineyard

Madame LALOU BIZE-LEROY took over her father's vineyard in 1957 at the age of 23. By 1977 her Romanée-Conti, highest-priced and among the most highly regarded of all French wines, was being offered at all three-star restaurants, according to the *Washington Post*. Mme. Bize-Leroy remembers how terrified she was 20 years ago when her father fell ill and she had to go to Norway in his place to advise Norwegian royalty on purchases for their cellar. The family's representative put her to the test by offering her a wine from another vineyard to taste; she correctly identified it. Mme. Bize-Leroy hopes that her young daughter will one day take her place in the family business.

Royal Horticulture Society's First Woman Council Member

British horticulturalist and journalist FRANCES PERRY, influenced as a child by noted plantman E. A. Bowles, studied at Swanley Horticultural College and at one time worked with Amos Perry, known for his plant introductions and hybrids. During the 1950s she became the first woman organizer of agricultural education and the first woman council member of the Royal Horticultural Society. The author of many articles and books on horticulture, including *Flowers of the World*, for which the Garden Club of America presented her an award in 1973, she is also well known for her lectures and radio and television appearances and is a fellow of the Linnaean Society.

Italian Rural Women's Representative

MARIA PIA MANCINI, born in 1941 on a farm at Grosseto, Italy, was elected national delegate of the Rural Women's Section by the National Confederation of Direct Farmers (CNCD) in September 1977. Ms. Mancini, whose understanding of the role of women in rural life, home economics, and agriculture stems from years of work on her family's farm, in 1959 volunteered to assist the provincial rural women's section, organizing first the women of her town and then of her region. She arranged seminars, helped develop home industries, and obtained government aid in improving production, recreation, and ecology in rural areas.

Top Bulgarian Plant Geneticist

RAINA GEORGIEVA, one of the first graduates of the Agronomy Department at Sofia University in Bulgaria, in 1951 became a professor and chairperson of the genetics and selection department at the G. Dimitrov Higher Agricultural Institute. Ms. Georgieva was responsible for the development of new plant cultures including tobaccos resistant to mosaic virus, varieties of flax, and winter foliage barley. She has published many scholarly works documenting her research on specific plant hybridization techniques.

India's Leading Woman in Agricultural Research

The head of the Department of Zoology at the University of Bangalore, Bangalore, India, A. R. KASTURI BAI, a zoologist, has done agricultural research on silkworms, weed control of paddy fields by beetles, and studies of the honeybee. Born in Bangalore in 1925, Dr. Bai received her B.S. degree in 1943, her M.S. in 1944, and her Ph.D. in 1947. She has held a merit scholarship at the University of Mysore, a Mysore University Research Fellowship, and a National Research Fellowship from the government of India. Trained in Germany as well as in India, Dr. Bai also worked on safety aspects in industrial applications of radiation sources and has more than 60 research works and publications to her credit.

Israeli Agricultural Training Director

Russian-born MINA BEN-ZVI, director since its founding in 1961 of the Mount Carmel International Center for Community Training (MCTC) in Haifa, moved with her parents to Israel as a child in 1921. Educated in Palestine and the United States, she served with the British Army in Egypt (1942–46) and became the first commander in chief of the Women Corps of the Israel Defense Army, 1948–49. In 1947 and again from 1950 to 1952 she helped settle immigrants in rural Israel. For two years, 1958–60, she headed the Department for Home Economics Extension of the Settlement Department and the Ministry of Agriculture. When Foreign Minister GOLDA MEIR (see "Women in Politics and Government," p. 46) toured Africa she saw the enormous need for advancing the status of rural women there. Although Western countries, including Israel, had provided technical skills programs in developing countries, African women seldom attended such courses due to reasons of illiteracy and lack of encouragement. Under the leadership of Golda Meir and INGA THORSSON, a Swedish MP, and with the support of 66 women leaders from 23 African and Asian countries who met in Haifa in 1961, the Center was founded and Mina Ben-Zvi named its director. The first students were rural women with little education, but the program was later redesigned for better-educated students who could train others back in their home countries. All of the students attending the Center in 1977 had 12 years' education and three to five years' work experience. In the 1970s, the Center, at first open only to women, began accepting male students also. Mount Carmel offers two eight-month curricula, one for teachers on early childhood education and the other on rural community development. There are also summer courses in such subjects as the promotion and marketing of handicrafts for home industries and small businesses. A Center school in Machakos, Kenya, to train rural social workers has become part of the College of Administration, Nairobi, and 142 of its graduates plus 159 Haifa graduates from Kenya are now working in their country.

Japan's Internationally Recognized Researcher in Complex Sugars

Chemist KIMIKO ANNO, of Japan, is internationally recognized for her studies on complex polysaccharides. A graduate of the Tokyo Women's Higher Normal School, the Tokyo University of Science and Literature (now Tokyo University of Education), and the Tokyo University Graduate School, she taught at the Tokyo Women's Higher Normal School in 1944 and at the Ochanomizu Women's University in 1952. She also received a degree of Doctor of Agriculture in 1949 and studied for three years at Ohio State University.

Dairy Farmer in Portugal

A native of the Bronx, who graduated from the High School of Music and Art and took a B.S. and M.A. from City College before teaching industrial arts in New York high schools for five years, JOAN SEGAL CATELA in 1970 visited Portugal, where she met and married the owner of an agricultural equipment firm. In 1972 she bought Monte da Laginha (Little Stone Farm) in the heart of the Alentejo farming region. She knew nothing about dairy farming or cattle breeding but learned a great deal by talking to specialists and reading farmers' publications. Today Ms. Catela drives a tractor, bales hay, cuts grass, weighs calves, and does electrical and plumbing repairs on her farm. During the 1974 revolution, her Portuguese neighbors, apparently out of respect for her labor, did not confiscate her land.

Lapland Farm Wife

A member of the Federation of Swedish Farmers, and one of Sweden's 112,000 farm women, ANN-MARIE KNUTSSON, in a series of broadcasts dealing with the day-to-day life of the farmer, has described the special pleasures of farming near the Arctic Circle. On the 77-acre farm in Lapland, which she runs with her husband, the growing season starts late in May, but throughout the months when there is light almost 24 hours a day, work is pursued aggressively. It is often difficult to get the grass cut and

into the drier before it outgrows itself. By the end of the season in October, the Knutssons have harvested 17 acres of potatoes and are ready to turn their attention to some 385 acres of forest land. During the summer months, Ann-Marie Knutsson relaxes from field work by tending her own garden, in which she raises vegetables, herbs, flowers, and great quantities of black currants. "It's nice to see things grow," she says.

U. S. FARM WOMEN

Iowa's Farm Bureau Internationalist

RUTH SAYRE, born in 1896 in Iowa, has dedicated much of her life to improving the living standards of rural women everywhere. She began her Farm Bureau activities in 1920 and climbed up the organizational ladder until her work took on international dimensions. Ms. Sayre first served as chairperson of the Iowa Farm Bureau's Women's Committee at the county, district, and state levels. Later she became midwest regional director, vice-president, and then president of the Associated Women of the American Farm Bureau Federation. President Eisenhower appointed her to his Agricultural Advisory Commission. "Most of the people in the world are still engaged in agriculture . . . in most cases a peasant agriculture," Ms. Sayre says. She worked "to get rural women organized in other countries to help them improve their standards of living through education." She also served for six years as president of the Associated Country Women of the World (headquartered in London) and traveled extensively, meeting with government officials to promote the implementation of educational programs that would help primitive rural societies adjust to a rapidly changing world.

First Agri-Women Coordinator

The first coordinator of American Agri-Women, elected in 1974, was SHARON STEFFENS, of Grand Rapids, Michigan.

Editor of the national organization's bimonthly newsletter, Ms. Steffens has five children and is a partner with her husband in a 140-acre fruit-growing operation. From 1973 to 1975 she chaired Women for the Survival of Agriculture in Michigan and was the first-place winner in 1974 of the Chevron Chemical Company's "Spokesman of the Year" contest. A music major graduate from Western Michigan University in Kalamazoo, Sharon Steffens is a 4-H leader. "I'm a city gal who married a farmer, and I love it," she says.

Organizer of Oregon Farm Women's Crisis Strategy

LINDA BARNES, of Junction City, Oregon, was one of the organizers of Women for Agriculture in 1970. Her story illustrates how a crisis situation caused the politicalization of a group of farm women. When the Oregon governor ordered a ban on straw-burning in the Willamette Valley, Linda Barnes, wife of a grass seed producer, organized other women in the valley to lobby the Oregon state legislature and to explain to the residents of Eugene how vital grass straw-burning was for farmers. The women also requested Oregon State University to investigate ways of controlling the pollution from straw-burning and to find other uses for the straw so that it would not have to be burnt at all. The potential conflict between the farmers and the city residents was partially resolved through the organizing efforts of Linda Barnes and the education program that she and her colleagues launched.

Organizer for Apple Picketing

Many farm women becoming active in politics are using dramatic tactics during crisis situations to draw attention to their needs and problems. The success of New York State's 1972 Great Apple Sauce War has been an incentive to women from other rural regions. One of the organizers of the first round-the-clock picket lines set up in that effort by the New York Women for the Survival of Agriculture was JACKIE FURBER of Wayne County. In a 1975 interview in *American Farmer,* she said, "Our women's peaceful picket worked. As a result our Farm Bureau marketing negotiators got a 50-cent increase. That meant an extra $2 million for growers of processing apples in our part of New York."

Militant Michigan Fruit Grower

A Michigan fruit grower and one of the founders of Women for the Survival of Agriculture (WSA), LAURA HEUSER won the "Spokesman of the Year" award in 1973 and has continued using her speaking talent to educate consumerists and politicians about the problems facing fruit and vegetable growers when prices fall below the cost of production. When WSA was accused by then-Secretary of Agriculture Earl Butz of being too militant, Laura Heuser responded for her organization. "If being militant means we are indignant, determined and aggressive, then we are. And we recommend it to any farmer. . . ."

At the 1977 Green Bay American Agri-Women convention, Ms. Heuser, a horticultural graduate of Michigan State University, said, "I see us as a dominant power source in American agriculture." Ms. Heuser, who describes herself as Agri-Women's "chief evangelist," travels the lecture circuit to speak about women's roles in agriculture and keeps her audiences laughing with earthy witticisms while spurring them on to organize in behalf of the small farmers of America.

Farmers Union Textbook Critic

While working a 350-acre cotton farm in West Texas with her partner-husband and four children, NAOMI CHANDLER wrote a study of economic textbooks used in U.S. colleges, which revealed the systematic academic denigration of family farmers. Her study was widely distributed as was her photographic slide presentation, "Natural Fibers and the Environment," which demonstrates the ecological and economic advantages of cotton, flax, and wool over synthetic fibers made from fossil fuels. A director of women's activities in her local National Farmers Union, Ms. Chandler also works and lobbies for better farm legislation.

First Woman to Be Registered as Farmers Union Lobbyist

The first woman to be registered as a lobbyist for the National Farmers Union since its inception in 1902 is RUTH KOBELL, who has served as a legislative assistant with the organization since 1975. The National Farmers Union, a bipartisan group with a membership of 250,000 farm and ranch families, maintains lobbies in Washington to promote not only farm policy legislation but also other bills with broad social implications which the union considers important. Ms. Kobell first joined the Farmers Union in 1939 while working a small wheat farm in Montana—the state where she was born to homesteading parents in 1918. In 1951 she became an NFU staff member and in 1974 was named director of administrative services.

Farming and Protecting the Land

While working a 1,200-acre grain and livestock farm in central Kansas in partnership with her husband, WANDA NELSON has risen to prominence as an activist for environmental protection and land policy planning. "Women have a valid place in leadership roles in agriculture. They are as involved in farming op-

erations as their husbands," she says. With other women of the Farmers Union, Wanda Nelson travels to Washington, D.C. to lobby Congress for land protection legislation.

Oral Rural History

One of the first anthropologists to study the nature of the American agricultural system through the lives of farm women is LEMBI KONGAS (Ph.D., University of Michigan). In 1975, armed with a tape recorder, she canvassed six rural counties to find and document personal accounts, by farm women of all ages and viewpoints, for her research project: "How does farm life look through the eyes of Michigan farm women actually living it?"

Founders of the New England Small Farm Institute

On August 15, 1977, four young women, CHRISTINA PLATT, PAT SACKREY, NANCY GALLAND, and JUDY GILLAN, who founded the Northampton Massachusetts-based Women in Agriculture, an

outgrowth of the Massachusetts Governor's Commission on the Status of Women, presented plans to a group of trustees for the development of a New England Small Farm Institute. They proposed converting the former Belchertown State School farm into a farmer training institution and prepared feasibility studies on converting the unused farm buildings into dormitories and classrooms for the new Institute. Their design called for a two-year program to train 25 students a year. The federal Environmental Protection Agency was enthusiastic about the project since the Institute planned to train farmers in New England farming techniques that stressed ecologically sound fertilizers and insect control practices. The curriculum is designed to develop a variety of farming skills.

The Changing Role of U. S. Farm Women

The role of the U.S. farm woman has been an integral part of the nation's economy and growth since its beginning 200 years ago. The delineation of that role has varied from generation to generation, but the farm husband and wife have always worked together for survival.

There is, however, a major difference in the working relationship between the farm husband and wife as it existed in the beginning and as it has evolved. Today it is a partnership with joint interest and association in a business enterprise—often a corporation, with the farm wife legally a partner. The early farm "team" began to change in the mid-19th century as manufacturing and urban con-

centration increased and farming became a speculative business with price fluctuations added to the already existing risks of weather conditions. Around 1840, some farm women chose to leave the farm and work in the cities, either in factories or as schoolteachers. Others introduced new industrial occupations into the home, such as the sewing of shoes, the plaiting and sewing of straw and palm-leaf hats and bonnets, and the production of men's clothing.

The organization of the anti-slavery movement, the Married Woman's Property Act passed by the New York legislature in 1848, and the granting of equal guardianship of children to mothers and certain property rights to widows in New

York in 1862 presaged further changes in the farm wife's position. But it was with the Civil War in 1861–65, when men went to war and women stepped in to manage the farms themselves and produce food and fiber for the struggling nation and its soldiers, that their role was altered markedly. When the first farm organization, the National Grange of the Patrons of Husbandry, was formed in 1867, it gave women equal membership and voting power with their husbands. (TEMPERANCE BALDWIN LANE, wife of the founder of the Grange, and her niece, CAROLINE HALL, deserve to be ranked with the founders of that order.)

In 1875 farmers comprised about 48 percent of the U.S. population. Now they were moving westward, seeking new land for new farms, opening up the Western frontiers, settling the prairies. The Homestead Act had a great impact on this exodus; and the farm wife pressed westward, shoulder to shoulder with her husband. She helped fight off Indians, claim jumpers, and grasshoppers. She coped with prairie fires, plagues, blizzards and tornadoes, as well as epidemics of smallpox, cholera, typhoid fever, diphtheria, and malaria. She rose at dawn to stoke the fire in the hearth or cookstove, haul water, cook breakfast, and bake the day's bread. She made her own soap and candles, helped her husband "break" new sod and plant new crops, fed livestock, milked cows, and educated her own children until schools were built. Her babies (she bore an average of six to eight, of which three to five might grow to adulthood) were delivered without benefit of a doctor.

Although it was not until 1920 that the 19th Amendment giving women suffrage was ratified, by 1900 the territories of Wyoming, Utah, Colorado, and Idaho had granted their women the right to vote. Even though the Women's Movement began in the East, particularly in New York, it was, interestingly, in the Western territories, where farming and farm women were of critical importance, that women first won recognition of their equality.

With improved power machinery and equipment, U.S. farm life got easier. The farm wife spent less time in the fields and more time in the house and in other pursuits—social, cultural, and civic. Washing and sewing machines added new dimensions to her homemaking role, and her life expectancy increased to forty-five or fifty years. By 1955 agriculture had more money invested in machinery, buildings, and lands than any other major U.S. industry. Farmers moved into specialized crops and now comprised only 15 per cent of the population. As the individual farm enlarged, the farm wife's role more closely resembled that of the emerging suburban wife. The farmer was more likely to hire farm hands seasonally and his wife was less likely to be actively, physically, and personally involved.

In 1978 less than 4 percent of the population was engaged in farming, but the efficiency of American agriculture keeps increasing. The farm wife is very much a part of farm life—knowledgeable in a wide range of subjects. Some farm women are political activists, promoting agriculture and lobbying before legislators or on television for what they consider fair crop prices and regulations. More are partners in daily operations. A recent poll of 12,000 *Successful Farming* magazine readers found that three fourths of the wives participate in farm business decisions. Among the two million U.S. farm wives, a "new breed" has emerged. —*Adapted from an article by* MARJORY F. HART, *U. S. Department of Agriculture (p. 29).*

First Woman Dairy Editor

The first woman dairy editor ever hired in the 100-year history of the *Farm Journal*, CATHY MACHAN, since 1973 has worked a farm with her husband. Both are active with the Adams County (Wisconsin) Farm Bureau and the Bureau's

Young Farmers. After her graduation from the University of Wisconsin College of Agriculture and Life Sciences, Ms. Machan embarked upon a writing career that has included service with the *Cheese Reporter,* the National Newspaper Association, and the National Milk Producers Federation.

American Farmer Cover-Story Woman

ELAINE DAVIS was selected as a "cover story" by the *American Farmer* magazine, March 1975. Living in rural Willcox, Arizona, with her husband and four children, Elaine Davis runs her home, works in the fields of their 1,000-acre farm, of which 850 acres are cultivated, and, at the time the story ran, was getting up at 4 A.M. two or three days a week to make a 200-mile round-trip drive to Tucson for classes in atmospheric science, Old English, history, and creative writing at the University of Arizona. Explaining how she managed to do schoolwork besides housework and farmwork, Ms. Davis said, "You can't be a woman in this day and age . . . without feeling that you'd like to do some things that are personally rewarding." As for running heavy agricultural equipment: "New farm machinery is powerful; the operator doesn't have to be muscular to handle it. The smallest person can easily

learn to handle the largest tractor or combine."

Master Farm Homemaker

Farm homemaker, teacher, lecturer, writer, and mother of five children, BEVERLY EVERETT has been honored by the state of Iowa for her busy, productive life with the Master Farm Homemaker Award. President of the Iowa chapter of the American Association of University Women, Ms. Everett was a leader of the World Food Forum at the 1974 Triennial Conference of the International Federation of University Women in Tokyo and Kyoto, Japan. She served as national topic chairperson of the AAUW, directing the global interdependence topic study and action for the 185,000-member organization. Ms. Everett has been the featured speaker at many national conferences and conventions, including the American Agricultural Editors Asociation and the Cooperative Marketing Association. She was also the director of the "Feed the World" seminar at the AAUW convention in 1975, a member of the State Extension Advisory Council and the Advisory Council to the Iowa State University College of Agriculture, and has received the Iowa State University Distinguished Alumni Home Economics Award.

From Family Farm to Agribusiness Acreage

The sizes of American farms span an enormous spectrum, but it is not so much the "amount of acreage" as the approach that distinguishes the "new" kind of farm from the old-style one. Although there are still many small independent family farms of the traditional kind that Americans imagine produce their country's food, many of these have been swallowed up by giant agribusiness corporations. These "factories in a field" have a highly technocratic food production chain—from seed to supermarket. In California, a Census Bureau report based on 1974 data reveals that large

agribusiness firms now produce the major portion of the state's food. Approximately 60 per cent of California's agricultural products come from 3,000 farms that average 3,000 acres in size.

According to the U. S. Department of Agriculture, 50 per cent of farm families (compared with 39 per cent of non-farm families) earned less than $10,000 in 1973. Only 9 per cent, of both groups, earned $25,000 or more that year. Many independent farmers have incorporated and mechanized their farms, adopting the more "industrial" approach of the large agribusiness corporations. "More and more family farms have reduced their hired hands, gone heavily into debt to expand and mechanize, and emerged as highly specialized businesses. As the number of such operations grows, more of the total food supply is being produced by large farms; in 1973 farms with $100,000 or more in annual sales accounted for nearly half of the nation's food and fiber marketing, up from only 17 per cent in 1960."

Family Farm Women

The Moravits farm, one of the most progressive family operations in southwestern Wisconsin, is run by DARLENE MUELLER, who was widowed in 1973 but has since remarried, and her five children. Ms. Mueller, president of the Grant County Farmers Union, state director of the Farmers Union Milk Marketing Cooperative, and president of the area FUMMC local, took over the running of the farm after her husband's death. In 1976 she and her children planted 503 acres of corn, 250 acres of small grain, and 250 acres of hay. Heifers are kept for herd replacement and the steers are marketed. The family farrows 400 litters of pigs each year and recently built a huge hog house, which features some of the newest management and technical improvements for increasing pork production efficiency.

CATHERINE HOWELL and her 74-year-old husband, James, are believed to run the oldest commercial farm still operated by direct descendants of the original owner in the Pennsylvania, New Jersey, Delaware, Maryland, and West Virginia area. The New Jersey property is now worked by her son and grandchildren, the 10th and 11th generations of the original Sayre family. There have been no gentleman farmers on the place during its 280 years; the Howells are dirt farmers. "We've never made much," Catherine Howell told the *New York Times* in 1977, "but we managed to put three boys through college at the same time."

"Going Dutch" Dairy Farmer

JEANNE HANSON, a widowed mother of three, runs an 80-cow dairy farm in Massachusetts in partnership with a neighboring herd owner named Don Roberts, who also has three children. They plant 60 acres of corn each year, and chores are divided. Roberts does most of the field work and feeding and Hanson tends to the milking, an arrangement that suits them both. Asked about possible expansion, dairyman Roberts in 1975 told *American Agriculture*, "Well, they always used to say don't grow a bigger garden than your wife can take care of. I'd say don't get a bigger herd than your partner can milk."

Farm Businesswomen

Like three quarters of America's 2 million farm wives, LUETTA HARDNER, of Mountain Lake, Minnesota, is taking an active part in the policy-making, business end of her family farm enterprise. Ms. Hardner has moved away from the physical labor of running a successful turkey operation with her husband and assumed the role of business coordinator. Now she does office work, orders machinery parts, handles promotion, and manages public relations.

ELAINE WATKINS, of Welsh, Louisiana, who in past years had the task of cooking for and feeding 25 farms hands, now goes out "flagging" instead. "Flagging" is the art of guiding in low-flying planes to plant, spray, or fertilize fields, and Ms. Watkins guides the planes that have replaced the hired hands in the rice paddies of her farm.

SALLY KINNEBERG, of Spring Grove, Minnesota, calls herself a "businesswoman" because she helps keep the books for the $100,000-a-year livestock business and farm she runs with her husband. Ms. Kinneberg is upset that city families blame farmers for high food prices. "Some people drive out in the country and say: The farmer can't be poor, he can afford to buy that big machinery." She then goes on to explain that the machines are bought on credit. "Some of us pay as much interest a year as people in the city earn. Last year we paid $6,000 interest on cattle, hogs, and machinery." She agrees with government claims that rising food prices are due to rising production, transportation (fuel), and labor costs.

Iowa's First Master Pork Producer

A licensed artificial inseminator who also serves as "midwife" to the hogs she and her husband raise, DEE VAN DE WALLE, of Chelsea, Iowa, was the first woman to receive the Iowa Master Pork Producers Award in 1974. Author of a newspaper column called "Let's Talk Pork" and producer of a slide show that demonstrates her own swine-raising operation, Dee Van De Walle participated in the City-Farm Swap sponsored by the Agriculture Council of America. She was hostess to a family from Chicago who visited her farm to become acquainted with rural life-styles.

Mink Rancher of the Year

Named Mink Rancher of the Year in 1972, PHYLLIS WATT WUSTENBURG first started raising minks at the age of 10 on her father's mink ranch in Oregon. After receiving a bachelor's degree from Oregon State College in fish and game management and a master's in nutrition and biochemistry from Oregon State University, she took control of the family breeding ranch, the largest then in operation. In 1955 she and her husband started their own breeding ranch with 800 breeder females. A former president of the Mink Farmers Research Foundation, she has been a frequent contributor

to *Fur Rancher* magazine and coordinator of a project for the Great Lakes Mink Association.

Top Woman in Ham Packaging

Some of her employees once presented her with a gold pig engraved "BETTY SHINGLER TALMADGE—America's Greatest Pig Woman." She may be. Two-term first lady of Georgia and longtime senatorial wife before she was divorced from her husband, Betty Talmadge has turned a small ham packaging business into a large corporation. Her sales organization has recently associated with Linder International and now exports meat products to Japan. During the early years of her participation in the Talmadge family ham business, she checked to see that each ham had the right salting, spices, and sugar formula rubbed into it and worked in every capacity in the company—as an unsalaried president, secretary, treasurer, salesperson, bookkeeper, manager, and janitor. Better known for much of her life as an official hostess, in 1977 she published a cookbook entitled *How to Cook a Pig and Other Back-to-the-Farm Recipes.* In 1978 she announced her intention to run for the U. S. Congress.

Hundred-and-Five-Percenter

CONNIE GRIEG, the first woman ever elected to the executive board of the Iowa Beef Improvement Association, is, in the opinion of U. S. Department of Agriculture officials, one of the most successful calf-breeders in the United States. She started her business by buying 20 cows about to be sold for slaughter and putting them to graze on 80 acres of land she had purchased previously as an investment. The first spring she had a 105 per cent calf crop (one cow had twins). Her Little Acorn Ranch now has 106 acres of grazing land, 160 breeding cows and 58 replacement heifers, 18 bulls and 8 horses, plus more new calves every year. Ms. Grieg runs the spread herself

—with assistance from her husband, two young sons, and a few hired hands.

"Pork Pusher"

DONNA KEPPY is a partner with her husband in the operation of a 235-acre Iowa farm that supports 2,000 hogs. She shares all the chores, markets the pigs, and does the farm's paperwork. A former president of the Iowa Porkettes (the women's auxiliary of the National Pork Producers Council), she helped establish a group of "pork pushers," farmers who promote the uses of pork and explain the problems of pig farmers. Ms. Keppy, whose parents and grandparents were also farmers, "represents the type of farm wife we're going to see more of in the future," the director of agricultural promotion for the Iowa Development Commission told a *Wall Street Journal*

reporter. "That's the only way the family farm is going to make it."

First Farrower

The first woman to manage a farrowing house for the American Hog Company is THELMA BALLINGER of Wiggins, Colorado. Since 1970 she has run the 840-sow feeder pig unit and, according to the AHC president, outperforms male managers in the cleanliness and care of her pigs. Although four men work full time for her, Thelma Ballinger told a reporter that hog farmers "have more genuine interest in sanitation. I've cleaned some pens two or three times before I was satisfied. And I think it bothers me more than it does a man to knock a pig in the head. I give pigs more tender loving care."

Farm Wives for Equitable Estate Taxes

Springfield, Nebraska, farm wife DORIS ROYAL, who has organized farm wives all over the United States to fight outmoded estate tax laws, became involved some years ago when she and her husband, Lloyd, attended a University of Nebraska Extension Service course in estate planning. The Royals were stunned to learn that if a husband dies first, property held in joint tenancy is assumed to belong entirely to the husband and is subject to estate taxes (if the wife dies first, her husband does not owe a cent). Further, land values had escalated rapidly since the tax deduction was set in 1942—the Royals' 240 acres, purchased for $72,000 in 1960, were worth $100 an acre in 1942, $1,300 an acre in 1977 (nearly $300,000)—and operating expenses had increased much faster than their profit. Doris Royal, who spent years "working alongside my husband on the farm," would then have owed $32,000 in estate taxes, and if she died, her children, both of whom "worked long and hard to make the farm pay,"

would then have had to mortgage the farm or sell so much land they would no longer own a viable unit.

By 1977 Doris Royal had filed 231,261 signatures from 49 states with Congress; in 1976 her work was covered by the *New York Times,* the *Wall Street Journal,* and farm magazines across the country, and she was interviewed on national TV and asked to testify before House and Senate committees. One farm wife wrote to Doris Royal that a woman may work and scrimp all her life, then have to pay inheritance taxes on an "enormous gift"—of property to which she devoted her whole life. "In my opinion she cannot inherit it because it is already hers. She earned it!"

The International Women's Year Commission report cited the example of rancher MARY HEATH, Cody, Nebraska. She worked beside her husband, Floyd, for 33 years raising cattle and hogs and assisting with haying. With their children they built their ranch to 3,395 acres. When Floyd Heath died in 1974, leaving the property in both their names, Mary Heath found she owed $25,000 in taxes, because it was considered his alone. She inherited a $40,000 debt and borrowed $5,000 to make her first tax payment. Then 55, Ms. Heath was too young for Social Security. Noting that full partnership in marriage was a goal of the Seneca Falls women's conference in 1948, the IWY Commission asked that taxation be eliminated on all property transfers between husband and wife when either dies, and on all gifts made between them.

Wheat Insurance Agency Owner

Born in Elk City, Oklahoma, in 1936, and raised on a farm near Durham, FLORISSA BURTNETT attended college at Abilene Christian College and Panhandle A&M in Goodwell, Oklahoma. After marrying, she and her husband operated a 360-acre farm where they raised beef cattle and wheat. When her husband died suddenly in 1968, Florissa Burtnett, a 31-year-old widow with two small children, decided to take over the Oklahoma Farmers Union Insurance agency which her husband had also run. With great determination she learned the insurance business and has now made her company one of the largest agencies in northwest Oklahoma. Besides running her business, she also started a Farmers Union Youth program which teaches children about economic and legislative matters relating to agriculture. In 1976 there were 30 students between the ages of 6 and 18 who attended the program. Ms. Burtnett has been secretary-treasurer of her local Farmers Union group for 15 years and secretary-treasurer of the Farmers Union county group for 12 years.

Viticulture Firsts

"Half a hundred" women executives, actively involved on the decision-making level in the wine industry, were discovered by *Wines and Vines: The Authoritative Voice of the Wine Industry* in 1976.

Among women leaders in this field were Dr. ANN C. NOBEL, the only woman on the faculty of the Department of Viticulture and Enology at the University of California at Davis. Dr. Nobel is a specialist in flavor chemistry and has a Ph.D. in food science.

In the business end of the industry MAUREEN MCCAIN was cited. Ms. McCain, who grew up in Sonoma County, California, now lives in Three Lakes, Wisconsin, where she owns a 10,000 gallon fruit winery, in which she makes wine out of the cranberries so plentiful in that area.

MARGARET SHAHENIAN is the first woman named a member of the board of directors of the Wine Institute in California. Currently the vice-president and secretary of Guild Wineries and Distilleries, the largest U.S. wine- and brandy-producing cooperative, she entered the wine business in 1947. In 1961 Ms. Shahenian ran a 2,500-acre vineyard through the harvest season.

Until 1975 LOLLY MITCHELL handled public relations for the Architects Collaborative in Cambridge, Massachusetts, and ran her own travel agency. Then she obtained the first commercial wine-making license ever issued by the state of Rhode Island and her life took a totally new direction. She and her husband Jim planted 35 acres of grapes, which they now cultivate at Sakonnet Vineyard in Little Compton on the Rhode Island coast. Their first wines became available in 1977. During the past three growing seasons they have employed seven or eight helpers (including two nuns on sabbatical), but so far the heavy work of planting and pruning has been divided between Lolly and Jim Mitchell—Rhode Island's first licensed vintners.

Llama Lady

North of San Francisco is the River Hold Llamasary, where SALLY TAYLOR has developed one of the first herds of llamas in North America. After three years of effort, she and her husband increased their single pair of llamas into a herd of 7 males, 19 females—and a thriving business. Llamas are good pack animals (a typical 300-pound male can carry up to 100 pounds 20 miles a day). Llama wool, which is combed rather than clipped like sheep wool, sells for $1 an ounce. So many Californians drop by to see the llamas that Sally Taylor had to post a "visit by appointment only" sign on her unusual ranch.

Country Women Tour Leaders

Country Women DORIS BREENER and her 24-year-old daughter, PAM, of Hopkins, Michigan, have developed a farm-home business arranging group tours. With their "travel families" they have made one-day, overnight, weekend, and long journeys to Switzerland, Nova Scotia, New Orleans, Hawaii, Vermont, and Nashville. The Breeners' business began when Doris was asked to plan a one-day trip for members of the Allegan County Extension Council. The trip was so successful that the Breeners turned their talent into a business and the Council now receives some of the business's profits for College Week scholarships and county programs. Both Doris and Pam enjoy traveling with groups, who range in age from 11 to 80, and all of whom get ready to leave on time each morning. "I've decided no one really gets old, just better; and I've met some of the betterest," says Pam, who graduated from Western Michigan University in 1974 and worked as a short-term missionary in Brazil and Haiti before returning to Michigan. The Breeners plan their trips so as to avoid traveling during corn-planting or haymaking seasons and alternate leading the groups so that one of them can always be home on the farm.

Organic Apple Butter Producer

One of America's most successful organic farms—Walnut Acres in Pennsylvania—got its start in 1946 when BETTY KEENE and her husband Paul decided to sell homemade apple butter. The Keenes had left college teaching to become organic farmers and out of necessity turned to their unsprayed apples for some quick income for their family. When the *New York Herald Tribune* published a column about the farm, mail orders began to pour in. Currently the Keenes employ 100 cooks and tractor drivers—nearly one fourth the population of nearby Penns Creek village—and have turned their 4,000-acre farm into a cooperative. Since 1963 everyone associated with the farm has shared both the work and the profits. Walnut Acres now boasts a gristmill and a store, and produces hundreds of natural foods from its whole grains, vegetables, and fruits. Its 500-item catalogue goes to 40,000 mail-order customers throughout the United States and abroad. The Keenes hope to teach Americans the importance of natural foods and to demonstrate how to live and work cooperatively "in harmony with nature."

The Changing Woman Rancher

Owner and co-operator of the Grass Valley Ranch in Lander County, Nevada, MOLLY FLAGG KNUDSTEN has lived in Grass Valley since 1942. She came to Nevada after completing her education in the East and at the University of London. An accomplished judge of horses and cattle, an authority on recent Nevada history, and an anthropologist of the region, in 1973 she received an honorary doctor of science degree from the University of Nevada in Reno. Besides running the large and successful Grass Valley Ranch with her husband, Molly

Knudsten is vice-chairman of the Board of Regents of the University of Nevada System, a trustee of the Nevada State Museum, a member of the College of Agriculture Advisory Board, and the author of *Here Is Our Valley* (1975).

In a chapter entitled "The Changing Role of Women on Ranches," Molly Knudtsen describes some of her neighbors: "There is an American tradition, particularly cherished in the West, of woman as a frail, fluttery flower, so dependent as to verge on imbecility. The Basque tradition [strong among Nevada's sheep raisers] is otherwise. It has respected the rights of women to inherit property and manage financial matters since time immemorial. It may be for this reason that Basque women when widowed or orphaned have been able to carry on the business of their deceased husbands or fathers. . . . Just over the Toiyabe Mountains from Grass Valley live DOLLY ANSOLABEHERE and her niece, MARY JEAN. The story of their operation must surely be unusual, even when compared to the efforts of other Basque women to operate ranches after the death of the head of the household.

"It was in January of 1968 that Big John Ansolabehere was found dead in his pickup truck. He apparently had suffered a heart attack. . . . The Ansolabehere ladies did not sell. They kept the ranch. They ran it. Sometimes they hired help and sometimes they ran it alone . . . it is not a small ranch that can be run without some hired help. Technocracy has come to the ranches as it has come to the rest of the world, and women are physically able to do work that only a few years ago would have been impossible for them. Mary Jean Ansolabehere cleans her ditches with a backhoe, she brands her calves on a calf table, she puts up her hay with the aid of sophisticated, modern haying equipment. It is only when dealing with ranch labor that she finds herself at a disadvantage because of her sex.

"Women's lib may be an accepted way of life in the urban areas of the country, but women's lib has not reached the ranches of Nevada. Traditionally ranching is a man's world and woman's place is in the kitchen, feeding the chickens, and helping raise the leppie calves and lambs. Mary Jean and Dolly have a good deal of trouble with their hired hands. But just as she copes with everything else, Mary Jean seems able to cope with that, too. One irrigator was particularly difficult and refused to do what she wanted. When she insisted, he grew abusive. Reasonable methods of persuasion having failed, Mary Jean felled the man with a well-aimed blow of a shovel, marched to the house, called the sheriff, and had him carted off to jail."

"BILLIE FILLIPINI, MARY PARSONS, PAULINE INCHAUSPE, and KATHIE HOLBROOK are all better than average hands. . . . None of these girls bear any resemblance to the long-suffering ladies in . . . cartoons, whose only function in life is to open gates for their husbands to drive through. But then fiction has a way of lagging behind fact."

First "First Lady" Cattle Rancher

First listed in *The World Who's Who of Women* as "U.S.A. Former First Lady," LADY BIRD JOHNSON is next identified as "Co-Owner, Operator, Radio-TV Station KTBC, Austin, Texas" and then as "Cattle Rancher." While overseeing the management of her prize cattle on the famous LBJ Ranch at Stonewall, Texas, Lady Bird Johnson stays active in the communications world through her radio and television station. She also serves as an adviser to the staff of the LBJ Library at the University of Texas, and to various conservation and beautification programs.

She Raised Peanuts and a President

"MIZ LILLIAN" CARTER, mother of the 39th President of the United States, took an active role in managing the family peanut-farming business before selling out her share to her now famous son. A trained nurse, Miz Lillian also provided medical care to the sick people of Plains, Georgia, and delivered many of the babies born there. She worked as a college housemother before signing up to spend two years with the Peace Corps in India as she neared 70 years of age. In March 1978 the Rome-based Food and Agriculture Organization (FAO) of the United Nations announced that Lillian Carter had been selected to have a Ceres Medal (see pp. 39–40) cast in her honor.

Women Homesteaders

Changing social attitudes during the 1960s and 1970s in America led many young women, urban-born and -raised, to seek new lives in rural areas. Wanting to live closer to nature and to support themselves in simpler, more satisfying ways, they renounced sophisticated city living and moved out to small towns and farmsteads. Many of these women became serious farmers and undertook to learn about the land and its related industries.

Country Women: A Handbook for the New Farmer was written by JEANNE TE-TRAULT and SHERRY THOMAS, two Easterners who moved west to homestead after college. The authors use the term "homestead" to mean "a small, primarily not commercial, diversified, and, hopefully, self-sustaining place." While learning about agriculture, Jeanne Tetrault joined a feminist collective and helped produce a new magazine called *Country Women,* which was the seed from which the *Handbook* grew. Both she and Sherry Thomas still write and edit for the magazine.

Another set of new homesteaders, KAY FISHER and MAGGIE FESSARD, after several years of teaching school in upstate New York, left their jobs to take over the Fisher homestead, Gray Rock Farm. In addition to caring for their herd of cows they board horses, give riding lessons, and plant an annual crop of corn. Part-time help is required only for assistance with field work.

THERESE MACHOTKA HESS has left an active urban life (in Washington, D.C.), after a rural childhood, to return to the land. With her husband, Karl Hess, with whom she worked on urban agriculture and appropriate technology projects in Washington, she is now building a farmhouse under a hillside in West Virginia. Together they poured the slab floor, hoisted the timbers, stacked cinder blocks, and used unusual inventive materials in creating their new homestead. The house, scooped out of the side of a hill, is naturally insulated against seasonal weather shifts, and Therese Hess grows herbs in the living-room floor all year round. The entire farmhouse cost $800 to build—plus a lot of loving labor from a woman who has found and returned to her roots.

Senior Gurus of Homesteading

HELEN KNOTHE NEARING, born in 1904, grew up in suburban New Jersey and studied the violin in Amsterdam and Vienna. Interested in meditation, she went to India in the early 1920s and then spent several years in an Australian commune learning yoga. When she returned to the United States she met Scott Nearing, an economics professor twenty years her senior, who had been ostracized by the academic world and blacklisted as a lecturer and writer because of his political views during and after World War I. Following their marriage, the Nearings sold all their possessions and in 1932 moved to Vermont, where they supported themselves by maple sugaring —working four hours a day, six months a year—so they could spend the remaining time writing, reading, enjoying music, lecturing, and traveling around the world. In 1952, after their Green Mountain neighborhood had become a ski resort, they bought and moved to a blue-berry farm in Penobscot Bay, Maine. "From being a trained violinist I turned to stonemasonry and have . . . done the stonework on more than a dozen build-ings," said Helen Nearing at 73. "The latest house . . . is a two-story 34′×54′ building in which I laid every stone my-self, along with a stone-floor living room, fireplace, and four-flue chimney." Although their books, *Maple Sugar* (1950) and *Living the Good Life* (1954), attracted little notice when they first appeared, the Nearings have become known as the "senior gurus" of home-steading. Some 2,000 back-to-the-land pilgrims visit their farm each year, and they are in great demand as speakers.

Junior Gurus of Homesteading

In the fall of 1968, when SUSAN LAWRENCE COLEMAN was 23, she and her husband Eliot used $2,000 of their $5,000 savings to buy 40 acres of wooded coastland in Maine from their neighbors, HELEN and Scott NEARING. Planning to develop a self-sufficient or-ganic farm within five years, the Cole-mans slept in a three-foot-wide home-built camper body while building a one-room house and clearing land for a gar-den, orchard, and pasture. Inspired by the Nearings' book *Living the Good*

Life, the Colemans became vegetarians and took occasional part-time jobs to supplement the income from their small garden. With customers coming from 50 miles away, they have increased their vegetable and fruit sales to $2,400 a year, which covers their expenses ex-cept for fuel bills and health insurance. Now the mother of two small daughters, Susan Coleman hauls water from a brook, cooks on a wood stove, hand-grinds wheat for flour, operates a pedal sewing machine, and has become an ex-pert at gardening and milking goats. The Colemans have added another room onto their house and built some sheds, a workshop, and an open-air stand for selling produce. "Homesteading is a chal-lenging way to live, involving and de-manding the whole person," Susan says. In 1977 she and her husband won a $2,500 prize in a *Mother Earth News* contest for an essay on how they became self-sufficient in food. While Eliot teaches biological agriculture and leads tours to European organic farms, Susan uses the help of apprentices to run the farm and continues to be "deeply satisfied by farm work and the simple life there." Gradu-ally the Colemans are becoming known as the "junior gurus" of American home-steading.

4-H Scholarship Winners

4-H is a youth education program of the Cooperative Extension Service and is jointly managed for boys and girls of rural communities by the U. S. Depart-ment of Agriculture, the state land-grant universities, and local county governments. More than 80 other coun-tries around the world have modeled youth organizations after America's suc-cessful 4-H program, in which, to pro-vide incentives and reward achievements, scholarships for continuing education, trips to special events, and awards are offered to participants in more than 50

program areas. During 1976, 2,370,311 girls, between the ages of 9 and 19, participated in various 4-H activities.

One of the six national winners in the 1976 4-H dairy program, LINDA KUCK, 17, of Petaluma, California, received a $1,000 scholarship. Despite the fact that a cow once broke Linda's leg, she per-severed in her dairy career and built up a herd of more than 32 Holstein cows, heifers, and calves. In 1976 she was also named an outstanding exhibitor at the California Exposition.

MARY SIMON, **20, of Sedalia, Missouri,**

who plans to become an agronomist and horticulturist because she seeks "an opportunity in adulthood to be creative and to apply scientific principles to practice," received an $800 agribusiness career scholarship.

DEBBIE FLANIGAN, 16, of Frederick, Maryland, won in the swine program division for attempting to raise taller, bigger-boned swine. Debbie also judged livestock shows and learned how to identify and judge various cuts of meat.

Seventeen-year-old CUBA HEARD, of Roff, Oklahoma, studied the scientific aspects of herdsmanship during her high school years. She also helped her family introduce artificial insemination techniques on the Heard farm and assisted with the construction of a double-10 herringbone milking parlor, which significantly reduced the amount of manual labor needed on their farm.

DEBORAH SMITH, 17, of Brookings, Oregon, was honored with a forestry award for having identified 80 different species of trees during field trips she made through her home state.

LESTA JEAN PETTY, 17, of Hot Springs, South Dakota, raised 509 lambs and sold 7,072 pounds of wool. The proceeds from her sheep business, plus the scholarship which she won, will help defray costs for a college veterinary science degree.

ALICE ELIZABETH SLIPPEY, 18, of Duncansville, Pennsylvania, won a 4-H entomology program scholarship, which she will use to pay some of her expenses while she studies medical technology in college.

JEAN ANN HASTON, a 17-year-old Crossville, Tennessee, student, was rewarded for saving a farmer's entire herd of cattle through an article that she wrote on silage sickness—an infection caused by feeding molded silage that had caked around the top outer edge of a silo. Jean had also done research and issued a report, useful to local farmers, on leptospirosis disease that helped in the planning of a vaccination program.

She plans to put her scholarship toward a college education in veterinary medicine.

University of Minnesota freshman MARGARET BENSON, of Okabena, Minnesota, bottle-fed a set of quadruplet lambs which survived to become a part of her flock. Profits from her sheep business will aid in paying college expenses while she studies veterinary medicine.

LINDA FANCONI, a student at California State University in Fresno, was honored for her management of a herd of 25 registered Shorthorns. During her five years in the 4-H beef program, Linda maintained extensive management and production records on her steers and production records on her heifers and cows while increasing her herd from one animal to 25. She also worked with the meat grader at a local locker plant to learn how to identify various grades and cuts of meat.

JOCELINA SANTOS, a 20-year-old Mississippi State University coed, hopes to apply science and technology to the processing, packaging, and distribution of food products from the farm to the consumer. She also hopes to be able to synthesize new foods, develop foods that are acceptable to people in different cultures and improve existing food products. "By doing these things, I will be able to help my fellow man in his struggle to survive."

First Future Farmers National Officer

The first female to serve as a national officer of the Future Farmers of America, which did not admit girls until 1969, was JULIE SMILEY of Mt. Vernon, Washington, FFA national vice-president.

"Star Farmer of Kansas"

The first woman ever to be named "Star Farmer of Kansas," LORENA CROUCHER, 18, was so honored in 1977 by the Kansas Future Farmers of America for being "the state's most enterprising farmer."

Women in Agricultural Schools

General attendance at American agricultural schools has tripled since 1963. In the 72 U.S. institutions which offer agricultural programs there are 98,183 undergraduates and 23,654 graduate students according to the National Association of State Universities and Land-Grant Colleges. In 1975, 28 per cent of these students were women and 59 per cent came from urban areas. Concern about the environment, ecology, and world food production are some of the explanations offered to account for the unusual composition of agriculture students. Good employment possibilities are another positive incentive. Women graduating from agricultural schools are entering all areas of the food industry including marketing and sales, service, education, research, agricultural science, veterinary medicine, and government. While some animal science curriculums now have 50 per cent women, other very popular fields include biological science, ornamental horticulture, floriculture, wildlife, fishery science, recreation, parks administration, economics, food technology, and agricultural journalism.

U. S. WOMEN IN GOVERNMENT AGRICULTURAL POSTS

First and Only USDA Agency Chief

The first woman to become chief of a major USDA agency was LOUISE STANLEY, who was appointed head of the Bureau of Home Economics by Secretary Henry C. Wallace in 1921. Dr. Stanley, who had a doctorate from Yale University and had taken graduate work in chemistry, physics, and biology, was then chairman of the Home Economics Department of the University of Missouri and chairman of the American Home Economics Association's legislative committee, which had been urging all members to promote legislation to ensure the teaching of home economics in public schools. Her salary, while she was chief of her bureau, 1923–43, ranged to $7,500 and was the highest salary received by any woman in the Department of Agriculture.

USDA's First Woman Assistant Secretary

The first woman to attain the rank of assistant secretary in the U. S. Department of Agriculture's more-than-100-year history was DOROTHY H. JACOBSON, who served as Assistant Secretary of Agriculture for International Affairs from 1964 to 1968. A native of Herman, Minnesota, Ms. Jacobson worked for Orville L. Freeman when he was governor of Minnesota and came to Washington when he was appointed Secretary of Agriculture in 1961. She traveled to the Middle East and Southeast Asia in 1961 with the Secretary to study national agricultural programs and to evaluate the Food-for-Peace Program. In 1963 she was on a study team that visited the Soviet Union and other Eastern European nations. Her detailed reports of both trips became the basis for evaluating policies and programs. From 1964 to 1969 she served as executive director of the Population Crisis Commission, from 1969 to 1970 with the American Freedom from Hunger Foundation, and in 1970 became executive secretary of the International Development Conference. Recently she has served as vice-chairman of Greenbelt (Maryland) Consumer Services, a cooperative.

First Woman and First Black Assistant Secretary for Administration, USDA

JOAN S. WALLACE, assistant secretary for administration, the U. S. Department of

Agriculture, directs the Department's management programs, including personnel, equal opportunity, administrative law, contract appeals, operations and finance, and safety and health. Nominated by Secretary of Agriculture Bob Bergland for this prestigious post, she was sworn in December 2, 1977. Dr. Wallace was born in Chicago, obtained her bachelor of arts degree in sociology from Bradley University, Peoria, Illinois, her master's from Columbia, and her doctorate in social psychology from Northwestern University. She also studied management at the Harvard Business School. Before joining the Department of Agriculture, she was director of the School of Social Work at Western Michigan University. In addition, she has held management positions at Morgan State University, Baltimore, Maryland, at Howard University in Washington, D.C., and at the University of Illinois, has directed Afro-American studies at Barat College, Lake Forest, Illinois, and taught and served as a social work analyst at the University of Illinois and the University of Chicago, respectively.

Food Stamp Director

The March 31, 1976, appointment of NANCY SYNDER as director of the Food Stamp Division of the Food and Nutrition Service of the U. S. Department of Agriculture made her one of the highest-ranking career women with the Department. Prior to this appointment, Ms. Synder was associate director for the Coal Mine Workers' Programs with the U. S. Department of Labor, where she directed the Black Lung Program. Before joining the Labor Department in 1966, she served with the Peace Corps. Besides running the USDA food stamp program, Nancy Synder also manages a 75-acre family cattle farm in West Virginia.

Peace Corps Rural Programmer

Special assistant to the director of the Peace Corps and Coordinator for Women in Development, DEBORAH A.

HARDING, 37, has a doctorate in anthropological linguistics from UCLA and has been with the Peace Corps since 1962. In various capacities she has been responsible for programming and training Peace Corps volunteers and delivering qualified trainees to worldwide Peace Corps and UN programs. She has also evaluated and monitored long-range policy objective and administered programs with as many as 30 staff and 150 trainee and volunteer members. A UNESCO Upper Volta, West Africa, project, in which women Peace Corps volunteers work to encourage increased participation of village women in agriculture and forestry projects, is described by Ms. Harding: "The Voltaic social workers and the volunteer work together through village visits, community meetings, and demonstrations to explain agricultural methods that are relevant to their capabilities and needs. In the case of village tree planting projects, the social worker plans and arranges village meetings, while the volunteer provides technical expertise. In one village, approximately two acres near a market place were planted with 400 fast-growing shade trees. The volunteer supervised the fencing of the plantation while the village chief directed the planting and maintaining of the trees. Eighty per cent of the trees survived through the rainy season. After this project and as a result of a survey in the village, 700 fruit trees were ordered for the next planting season."

AID Women-in-Development Coordinator

The coordinator for the Agency for International Development's Office of Women in Development is ARVONNE S. FRASER. She was born into a farm family in 1925, attended the University of Minnesota, married Donald Fraser, who became a Minnesota congressman, and had six children. A treasurer and project director for the Women's Equity Action League, she also served as Democratic presidential campaign coordinator in

1976 for Iowa, Wisconsin, and Minnesota. Sworn in as AID/WID coordinator on June 27, 1977, Ms. Fraser is charged with overseeing the administration of bilateral foreign aid programs in terms of integrating women into the national economies of foreign countries so as to improve their status. She is also responsible for compliance with a 1973 AID policy directive that demands clear statements, in all project proposals how women in developing countries will be involved in the development programs. Ms. Fraser also works with international and voluntary institutions, which frequently collaborate in overseas programs, to ensure the role of women in development.

Food-for-Peace Coordinator

Appointed coordinator of the Office of Food for Peace in the Agency for International Development in January 1977, KATHLEEN STUDDAR BITTERMANN had previously served as deputy and associate coordinator since 1972. Born in Graceville, Minnesota, in 1916, Kathleen Bittermann worked in various economist/statistical positions in the USDA, the Public Health Service, and the Office of Price Administration from 1943 to 1948. In July of 1948, when the Marshall Plan was started, she joined the Food and Agriculture Division, Economic Cooperation Administration, as a GS-9 statistician. Involved in food aid programs for Europe in the postwar period, she has been closely associated with the Food-for-Peace program since its inception in 1954. In addition to fulfilling humanitarian purposes, Food-for-Peace programs are meant to promote economic development, particularly in agricultural production, to develop and expand markets for U.S. agricultural commodities, and to promote the foreign policy of the United States.

First Woman Rural Development Deputy Assistant Secretary

On June 17, 1977, HENRIETTA DUNCAN McARTHUR, former assistant vice-president of Citizens and Southern National Bank in Atlanta, Georgia, was named Deputy Assistant Secretary of Agriculture for Rural Development. Her office directs the operations of the Farmers Home Administration, which is the largest federal credit agency serving rural people; Rural Development Service, which coordinates all rural development programs; and the Rural Electrification Administration and Rural Telephone Bank, which provide about $4.8 billion a year for electric and telephone service in rural areas. Born in Vidalia, Georgia, in 1945, Ms. McArthur is a 1967 graduate of the University of Georgia. She worked on the Carter-Mondale transition team, helping to establish a talent bank for the presidential personnel office.

First Woman Area Director of the USDA Science and Education Administration

The first woman to be named an area director of the USDA Science and Education Administration, MARY E. CARTER is also the first U.S. woman to receive a doctorate (in chemistry) under a Rockefeller grant from the University of Edinburgh. As director of the Southern Regional Research Center in New Orleans, Louisiana, she oversees investigations of new uses for farm products. Her previous experience involved her in several textile-related projects for both industry and government, including an evaluation of protective clothing for gaseous or bacterial warfare and studies of fiber finish and fiber blends. A member of the Fiber Society, an organization whose membership is limited to those who have made an outstanding contribution to the knowledge of fibers, Carter's original research is covered by more than 35 patents. She is the author of many technical publications as well as *Essential Fiber Chemistry,* published in 1971, which examines ten commercially important fibers ranging from cotton to acrylics and spandex.

Only Female FAS Attaché

In July of 1974, ROSINE PLANK became the assistant agricultural attaché on the U. S. Mission to the European Communities (Common Market) staff in Brussels, Belgium. Her continuous on-the-scene role was to assist in the American effort to maintain and expand access for U.S. agricultural products to the nine Common Market nations. Since joining the Foreign Agricultural Service's International Trade Policy Division in 1971, her major interest has been the effect of the Common Agricultural Policy of the European Community on U.S. agricultural exports to the Common Market member countries. A graduate of Georgetown University (B.S., 1971), with a major in foreign service, Ms. Plank said: "More and more women are being trained for service in developing countries, as evidenced by the growing number of young professional women who are training in Arabic and other Third World languages. . . . It's very important that more and more women acquire professional positions in FAS and other international agencies. As more professional women train for overseas assignments, their presence will cease to be a novelty. Only then will we be able to say that the attaché service and other branches of the diplomatic corps are truly open to women. Progress in bringing women into the field has been made by FAS and other government agencies, but there is still much to be accomplished."

First Female FAS Division Director

Now a research associate with the International Food Policy Research Institute, BARBARA HUDDLESTON was the acting director of the Foreign Agricultural Service's Trade Negotiations Division in 1975 when she received the FAS Certificate of Merit for Special Achievement for "outstanding and creative contributions to the shaping and articulation of U.S. international agricultural policy in a period of world tension over food supplies and agriculture trade." The first woman to become a division director in the FAS, Ms. Huddleston was also working on a Ph.D. at George Washington University at the time she was honored for her government service. Born in New York in 1939, she studied international affairs at Wooster College in Ohio and the Johns Hopkins School of Advanced International Studies in Washington. She was a Fulbright scholar at the Free University of West Berlin before joining the Foreign Agricultural Service.

International Marketing Specialist

The only woman international trade fair manager in the Foreign Agricultural Service, "BILLIE" TOVELL is a marketing specialist in the Export Trade Services Division of FAS, where she locates foreign markets for U.S. farm products. Before joining FAS in 1969 as an agricultural trade fair manager in the International Trade Fairs Division, she had 12 years' experience as director of special activities for the Southeastern Fair Association. She also worked as a buyer for a department store and an office manager in an Atlanta, Georgia, construction company.

Cotton-Picking Analyst

As a commodity industry analyst in the U. S. Foreign Agricultural Service, BERNICE M. HORNBECK helps the United States meet stiff cotton competition from other countries. By traveling to major textile-producing countries, studying foreign production, analyzing trade and other tariff factors, she determines the impact of imports on the U.S. cotton industry. Ms. Hornbeck also serves as a technical adviser on textiles and man-made fibers.

Area Resource Conservationist

The only female Ph.D. serving in the Soil Conservation Service in 1976 was

Dr. CAROL A. ANDERSON, an area resource conservationist. After attaining her M.S. and Ph.D. in genetics from the University of Arizona, Dr. Anderson started her career in the Soil Conservation Service in Portland, Oregon. Eventually she moved to Pocatello, Idaho, in 1974 to work with committees, county and city planners, and/or zoning commissions in planning for the conservation and orderly development of the area's natural resources.

Agricultural Engineer

The only GS-9 agricultural engineer on duty in the Soil Conservation Service in 1976 was SUSANNE M. LECKBAND, who has an agricultural engineering degree from California State Polytechnic College. Awarded a Special Achievement award in May 1975, she is involved in the planning, design, construction, and evaluation of the engineering phases of the Home Supply Watershed Project.

Top Woman Forester

The highest-ranking and only woman forester to serve on a regional forester's staff is GERALDINE LARSON of the U. S. Forest Service. With a B.S. in forestry and an M.S. in botany from the University of California, Ms. Larson is an environmental review specialist on the Land Use Planning staff and an environmental coordinator for the California region. Her responsibilities include interpreting national policy and directing the development and preparation of environmental impact statements. Born in New York in 1930, "Geri" Larson today has three college-age children and is chairman of the Bay Area Chapter of the Society of American Foresters.

A Forest Service First

The first woman to hold the coveted post of staff director in the U. S. Forest Service is JANE WESTENBERGER, now director of the Office of Information in San Francisco, California. As a non-forester information director, Ms. Westenberger develops new national environmental programs, selects and trains personnel, teaches workshops, coordinates Forest Service environmental education programs with other agencies, and acts as a consultant on environmental education for Forest Service field stations. Before assuming her post, Jane Westenberger had army experience, 12 years of school teaching and administration, and the job of chief of the Environmental Education Branch of the USDA Forest Service.

First Woman Forest Service Pilot

The first woman pilot in the national Forest Service is MARY BARR, who is the lead plane and general assignment pilot with the North Zone Air Unit based in Redding, California. Experienced in everything from aerial coyote hunting to glider towing, she was first licensed in 1946 and flew more than 11,000 hours before joining the Forest Service. Mary Barr currently holds licenses as an A&P mechanic, FAA chief flight instructor, commercial flight instructor, and airline transport pilot. In between flights, Mary Barr has earned an A.A. degree in environmental science from Lassen Junior College in 1973 and has subsequently completed 34 more units at the University of California at Berkeley and Santa Barbara.

U. S. Forest Service Archaeologist

The first archaeologist ever hired (at 30) by the U. S. Forest Service to work in Region Six (25 million acres including Oregon and Washington) is LESLIE WILDESEN. Ms. Wildesen examines soil, vegetation, and aboveground artifacts in hopes of preserving them. "We're supposed to locate all the historic and archaeological sites, but the problem is we don't know where they are; perhaps 90 per cent haven't been found." With an M.A. in anthropology and a Ph.D. in archaeology, Leslie Wildesen sets up procedural guidelines and educates foresters on methods of conservation.

She Quarantines Plants

As a plant quarantine inspector for the U. S. Department of Agriculture, MARGUERITE HU TAKEDA checks aircraft and vessels arriving in Hawaii for plant and animal products that may carry plant pests and animal diseases. She also checks materials leaving Hawaii bound to the mainland for diseases and pests indigenous to Hawaii. One of a small group of women quarantine inspectors in the U.S.A., she earned her master's degree in horticulture.

Crop Insurance Sales Fieldperson

HILDA S. GRIFFIN is the fifth top salesperson out of 83 in the Federal Crop Insurance Corporation Sales Center in Raleigh, North Carolina. Along with selling crop insurance to producers to protect their investments, Ms. Griffin also develops sales presentations and maintains contacts with agriculture-related organizations, community leaders, banks, and civic groups. She received the Sales Incentive Award for 1972 and 1973.

Seed Marketing Specialist

As officer-in-charge at the Sacramento, California, USDA Agricultural Marketing Service, VERA COLBRY is responsible for the enforcement of Federal Seed Act provisions with respect to labeling and advertising agricultural and vegetable seeds in interstate commerce over a 13-state area. A nationally renowned seed technologist, Ms. Colbry received a B.S. in education from Oregon State Agricultural College and an M.S. in botany from George Washington University. She writes extensively about her field.

Home Economist

Group leader of the Family Economics Research Group at the former Agricultural Research Service (now part of the USDA Science and Education Administration), Dr. FRANCES M. MAGRABI, who retired in 1977, was a home economist and resource person for federal agencies on the subject of family consumption economics. A member of the U. S. FAO Interagency Committee from 1973 to 1977, Dr. Magrabi was responsible for the development of fundamental information on levels and patterns of expenditure and consumption by rural families. This information is used as a basis for appraising levels of living under varying economic situations. She developed an index for measuring the economic status of rural families that provides an inexpensive method to estimate the total money value of goods and services consumed by a household and also designed three computer programs for professional use in aiding families with budgeting problems.

The Agricultural Extension Service

"To aid in the diffusing among people of the United States practical and useful information on subjects relating to agriculture and home economics . . . and to encourage application of the same . . . to persons not attending colleges . . ." was the charge made by the 1914 Smith-Lever Act, which created the Cooperative Extension Service, which came to be known as "the largest adult education enterprise in the world." Although the Extension Service was originally designed as an outreach program for rural farm families, it later ran various programs in American towns and cities as well. Senior citizens, public housing residents, and public welfare families are now also involved in specially designed education programs. In early 1978 the Extension Service, along with the Agricultural Research Service, was made part of the USDA's new Science and Education Administration. Its old home is now part of agricultural history, but its functions continue.

One of only several women in the Agriculture Department to achieve the grade of GS-16, OPAL H. MANN in 1973 became an assistant administrator of home economics in the Extension Service. Involved in making over-all program policy decisions, Ms. Mann provides national leadership to government home economists. She holds a Ph.D. from Ohio State University and was appointed to her post after 18 years of Extension Service experience and 6 years of high school teaching.

The first woman to serve as a New York State Cooperative Extension agricultural agent was KATHRYN BROWN. Raised on a Holstein-Friesian dairy farm, Kathryn Brown has always been interested in agriculture and was graduated from the New York State College of Agricultural and Life Sciences at Cornell.

Working at the University of Minnesota's St. Paul campus horticultural clinic is agent JANE PRICE MCKINNON, who, with a staff of energetic students, answers some 36,000 inquiries about trees, plants, flowers, vegetables, and herbs during each growing season. From an Extension Service background (her father was a county agent for 40 years in Mississippi), Jane McKinnon says, "I was extremely lucky to have been able to pursue an interest in horticulture by being admitted in the first place to the University of Minnesota Graduate School and then to be invited to do this job when it was created in 1970."

DEBBIE KING, Connecticut's first woman Agricultural Extension agent, joined the cooperative Extension Service at the age of 23. A graduate of the University of Connecticut, she became a management trainee for a farm cooperative while completing requirements for certification to teach vocational agriculture.

A plant pathologist for the University of Hawaii College of Tropical Agriculture, ANNE MAINO ALVAREZ was the first female plant pathologist in the Cooperative Extension Service as well as

the first one employed in Hawaii's Plant Disease Clinic, which diagnoses and prescribes treatment for Hawaii's disease-ridden plants and vegetables. Dr. Alvarez learned about tropical plant disease firsthand while exploring the Amazon, studying bacterial disease of beans in Costa Rica, and teaching plant pathology at the University of Neuquen in southern Argentina.

Exension Service women have also served in foreign countries. BERYL BURT, from the 4-H staff in Arizona, went to Nicaragua in 1971 to help plan and present a national in-service training conference for Extension home economists and Ministry of Education employees in the areas of educational methods and nutritional information.

The first woman to serve as a deputy assistant administrator in a non-home-economics program unit of Extension Service was RHONWYN LOWRY, who started her career as an assistant home demonstration agent 25 years ago. Responsible for making over-all policy and program decisions in the 4-H Youth Development Programs, she is also a top staff specialist in 4-H-type expanded food and nutrition programs for youth across the nation.

Farmers Home Administration County Supervisor

One of two female county supervisors, SUSAN GATES, of Morrisville, Vermont, reviews applications for program assistance, advises applicants and borrowers on the selection of farms, houses, land development, soil and water improvements, adoption of approved farm practices, construction, repairs and the maintenance of buildings. She received her B.S. and M.S. degrees in horticulture from the University of Vermont. As a Farmers Home Administration county supervisor, she administers department programs related to rural problems stemming from local agricultural or economic conditions.

Agriculture Attorney

The first woman to be elected to the Board of Trustees in the 101-year history of Loyola University was WINIFRED D. MOLONY, assistant regional attorney in the office of the general counsel of the Department of Agriculture. Based in the Chicago regional office, Ms. Molony handles litigation in the Grain Storage Program of the Commodity Credit Corporation, the Grain Price Support Program, the Federal Food Stamp Program, and other Agriculture Department programs. A graduate of Loyola University and Loyola University Law School, Ms. Molony has had 33 years of federal service.

USDA Federal Women's Program Coordinator

Coordinator of the Department of Agriculture's Federal Women's Program is MARJORY F. HART, who is responsible for ascertaining that "women receive equal treatment in all phases of their employment, including placement in jobs and levels for which they are qualified, advancement in accordance with their abilities, training, and opportunities for upward mobility." Ms. Hart joined the USDA as a program clerk in Idaho in 1962 and is active in the American Society for Public Administration and other professional organizations. She represented the USDA at the International Women's Year Tribune in Mexico City in 1975.

Two Agricultural Historians

Once an archivist at the National Archives, VIVIAN WISER has worked as a historian at the U. S. Department of Agriculture in Washington, D.C., since 1956. One of the authors of *Century of Service: the First 100 Years of the U. S. Department of Agriculture,* she focused attention on the role played by American women in the development of farming and related industries in the United States in a widely distributed

speech given at the Freer Gallery in 1975. In 1962 Vivian Wiser received a Certificate of Merit from the U. S. Department of Agriculture for her work.

Another co-author of *Century of Service* was GLADYS L. BAKER, who now serves as historian in the Agricultural History Group. She was born on a corn-livestock farm near Beaconsfield, Iowa, and received her Ph.D. from the University of Chicago in 1939. Joining the Department of Agriculture as an assistant agricultural economist, she became head of the Department's War Records Project in 1942. In 1961, when the historical research work was organized into a branch, Ms. Baker became head of the Historical Research Section. She is also co-author of *The Department of Agriculture,* published in 1972.

Technocratic Librarians

MAYDELLE STEWART, MARIA WORONIAK, and JEANNE HOLMES of the National Agricultural Library have made significant literature available to the agricultural community by means of on-line access to, and printed products derived from, the Library's computerized Cataloging and Indexing (CAIN) data base.

Jeanne Holmes, who was born in Dayton, Ohio, in 1922, formulates, directs, and coordinates policy and programs for cataloguing and indexing library materials. She also determines long-range and current Library policies and programs. With 27 years of federal service, she frequently represents the Library at various meetings.

Maydelle Stewart, who indexes agricultural literature for the CAIN data base and suggests indexing changes to improve on-line retrieval, received a master's degree in drosophila genetics and worked at the USDA Plant Industry Station from 1941 to 1943 on cytogenetics of ornamentals before entering the library world.

Maria Woroniak is a native of the Ukraine who entered the United States under the Displaced Persons Act after

World War II and has traveled extensively and worked frequently with international organizations. After 15 years of government service, she now directs the development and compilation of a comprehensive index to the world literature of agriculture and related sciences for computerized input and retrieval.

Capitol Hill Counsel

The only woman serving as a chief counsel to a House or Senate agricultural subcommittee is CAROL FORBES, who graduated from American University's College of Law in 1947 at the age of 34 and immediately became the first counsel of the 150-member Congressional Rural Caucus. In 1975 she organized the Congressional Clearing House for Women's Rights and served on the staff of the Family Farms and Rural Development Subcommittee. In January of 1977 she became chief counsel to the Dairy and Poultry Subcommittee. Ms. Forbes conducts oversight hearings, drafts legisla-

tion, writes agricultural policy statements, and advises the chairman and subcommittee members on procedure.

Farmer Congresswoman

Owner and operator of a wheat ranch in Nebraska, VIRGINIA SMITH (R., Neb.) was elected to Congress in 1974 and 1976 from one of the largest congressional districts in the nation, one which encompasses 61 counties and 307 towns. Ms. Smith had enormous experience working on agricultural issues before she began to represent this large farming area. She was national chairperson of the American Farm Bureau Women, the women's branch of the country's largest voluntary organization of farmers and ranchers, from 1955 to 1974; member of the Presidential Task Force on Rural Development, 1971–72; member of the National Livestock and Meat Board, 1955–58; and deputy president of the Associated Country Women of the World, 1962–68.

WOMEN IN AGRICULTURAL RESEARCH, U.S.A.

Frozen Food Pioneer

Teacher, director of research, and consultant, MARY E. PENNINGTON is recognized for her pioneering work on food preservation, which led to her original research on frozen foods. Before becoming a private consultant, Mary Pennington was chief of the Philadelphia Food Research Laboratory of Chemistry with the U. S. Department of Agriculture and later manager of the research and development division of the American Balsa Company. During this time she wrote extensively on the chemistry and bacteriology of foods and food processing. Dr. Pennington was born in Nashville, Tennessee, in 1897 and received her Ph.D. in chemistry at the University of Pennsylvania. She held several fellowships and became director of the Chemistry Laboratory of the Women's Medical College of Pennsylvania as well as bacteri-

ologist in charge of the Philadelphia Bureau of Health. She was one of the first dozen women to join the American Chemical Society and in 1940 received the Garvan Medal (see the chapter "Women in Science and Technology," p. 164). She remained active in food-related industrial and government work until her death at 81.

First Woman Honored by Cereal Chemists

An authority on the chemistry of wheat proteins and the chemistry and biochemistry of the technology of baking, ELIZABETH SULLIVAN in 1948 became the first woman to receive the Osborne Medal, the highest honor of the American Association of Cereal Chemistry. Dr. Sullivan worked for the Russell-Miller Milling Company in Minneapolis while earning her Ph.D. in biochemistry from the University of Minnesota. Except for one year's study in France, at the University of Paris and the Pasteur Institute, she continued working with the milling company, eventually becoming vice-president and director. Later she worked for the Peary Flour Mills and after retirement became president of Experience, Inc. Dr. Sullivan has published some 40 technical papers on determination of moisture in wheat and flour and on the role of certain amino acids in relation to the processing of flour. She has held many positions with organizations such as the American Chemical Society, AACC, and the National Research Committee on Foods. Her awards include the Outstanding Achievement Award from the University of Minnesota and the Garvan Medal.

Cotton Chemistry Champion

The first woman to receive the Southern Chemist Award and the only woman to win the Southwest Chemist Award was RUTH R. BENERITO. Seeking new and improved end-uses for cotton through chemistry, Dr. Benerito contributed to modifications that made cotton crease-, oil-, dust-, and water-resistant. With three patents granted and eleven pending, she is recognized as a pioneer in the development of wash-and-wear cotton. Twice awarded the Agriculture Department's highest award for distinguished service, she serves as head of the Physical Chemical Research Group at the U. S. Department of Agriculture in Louisiana and also as adjunct professor in the Department of Biochemistry at Tulane University Medical School. Named as one of the "Most Important Women in the United States" by the *Ladies' Home Journal* in 1971, Dr. Benerito also received the Garvan Medal of the American Chemical Society.

First in Chemistry Bureau to Receive USDA's Distinguished Service Award

After 35 years of service at the Northern Regional Research Center of the USDA,

Dr. ALLENE R. JEANES was honored by her colleagues upon her retirement in 1976. Dr. Jeanes received her B.A. from Baylor University in Waco, Texas, her M.A. from the University of California at Berkeley, and her Ph.D. from the University of Illinois. In 1953 Dr. Jeanes received the USDA's Distinguished Service Award for research on dextrans and development of a blood-volume expander from these biopolymers—the first woman in the Bureau of Agriculture and Industrial Chemistry to receive the highest honor USDA can bestow. In 1955 she was a member of the Dextran Team that received the USDA Distinguished Service Award. In 1956 she was the winner of the Garvan Medal of the American Chemical Society as the outstanding woman chemist of the year and in 1962 was the first woman in USDA to receive the Federal Woman's Award for her pioneering chemical research on starches and microbial polysaccharides. Her recognition of the value of microbes as sources of carbohydrate polymers that could be used industrially to replace traditional seaweed and seed gums has led to the development of a new fermentation industry—the production of extracellular microbial polysaccharides. Author of over 60 publications and 10 patents in the field of carbohydrate chemistry, Dr. Jeanes's assistance and advice has been continually sought by other research groups in government, industry, and academic organizations.

Female Reproduction Research Chemist

Winner of the 1965 USDA Distinguished Service Award, the 1970 Federal Woman's Award, and the 1972 Arthur S. Flemming Award, Dr. B. JEAN APGAR is a research chemist with the U. S. Plant, Soil, and Nutrition Laboratory in Ithaca, New York. Her recent work involves the study of effects of zinc deficiency and undernutrition on female reproduction. Born in 1936 in Tyler, Texas, Dr. Apgar attended Texas Woman's University for a degree in food and nutrition and then went on for an M.S. and Ph.D. at Cornell. She has worked in biochemistry since 1957.

She Bugged Space

Chief of the Chemical and Biophysical Laboratory at the Beltsville (Maryland) Agricultural Research Center, DORA HAYES has, among many other honors and accomplishments, the distinction of being the first U.S. scientist to send earth insects into outer space for observation aboard Skylab 4. Earlier, Dr. Hayes received an outstanding performance appraisal for her work as a chemist at the U. S. Army Biology Division at Dugway Proving Ground, Dugway, Utah, from 1961 to 1965. She has been studying the metabolism of silkworms in cooperation with RADHA PANT, a woman biologist working in Allahabad, India.

Beetle Fighter

A research chemist for the U. S. Department of Agriculture in Illinois, ODETTE SHOTWELL has conducted a lengthy study of the chemistry of the Japanese beetle in an effort to develop a bacterial disease as a biological control of beetles. The Department's nominee for the Outstanding Handicapped Federal Employee Award in 1969, Dr. Shotwell has also made contributions to the knowledge of aflatoxin, a cancer-producing toxin produced by molds, and is chairman of the mycotoxin committee of the American Association of Cereal Chemists. Her many community activities have included service as co-chairman of the Peoria (Illinois) NAACP education committee, consultant on an inner-city education program, president of the Peoria chapter of the League of Women Voters, board member of a local arts and science center, and chairman of the Truth Corps of the Mayor's Commission on Human Relations.

USDA's Mold Microbiologist

For more than 30 years, DOROTHY I. FENNEL, a microbiologist with the USDA's former Agricultural Research Service (now the Science and Education Administration) has conducted studies on agriculturally, militarily, and industrially important molds, particularly those of the genera *Aspergillus* and *Penicillium* and related fungi. Dr. Fennell's scientific career began at the Northern Regional Research Laboratory in 1942 when she worked on a pencillin project with a team which won the USDA Distinguished Service Team Award in 1947. The importance of her work in the scientific world is attested to by the fact that a new species of *Penicillium* was named *Penicillium fennelliae* in her honor. She won the Federal Woman's Award in 1976.

Research Food Technologist

MAURA BEAN is a project leader and supervisor of a 15-member research unit at the test baking laboratory in the Western Regional Research Center, Albany Area, Berkeley, California. A research food technologist with the Science and Education Administration, she has made significant contributions to the nutritional well-being of food aid recipients, to the stability of foreign wheat trade, and to the control of baking product manufacturing. Ms. Bean received her B.S. in home economics from New York State University and an M.S. in food and nutrition from Michigan State University. Her research contacts extend around the globe.

Poultry Research Chemist

A member of the Regional Poultry Research Laboratory in East Lansing, Michigan, LUCY LEE is working on the control of Marek's disease in commercial poultry flocks. A research chemist with USDA's Science and Education Administration, she is recognized throughout the world as an authority in the biochemistry of the Marek's disease virus. Born in China in 1931, she came to the United States in the 1940s and obtained her citizenship here. She earned a B.S. degree in biology at St. Mary of the Springs College, Columbus, Ohio, in 1953, an M.S. in zoology at the University of Maryland in 1959, and a Ph.D. in biochemistry at Michigan State University in 1967. Married, with two daughters, she speaks Chinese, Japanese, and Spanish.

Veterinarian's Chain of Firsts

Born in Hazlehurst, Georgia, in 1926, Dr. Lois E. HINSON chalked up a chain of "firsts" in her career as a veterinarian. She was the first woman graduate of the University of Georgia College of Veterinary Medicine, the first woman supervisor in the USDA Federal Meat Inspection Division, the first woman inspector in charge of the USDA Federal Meat Inspection Division, the first woman veterinary staff officer at the USDA Headquarters of Federal Meat and Poultry Inspection, the first woman chief staff veterinarian in the U. S. Department of Agriculture, the first woman elected national president of the National Association of Federal Veterinarians, and the first woman delegate to the American Veterinary Medical Association House of Delegates.

Animal Oncology Expert

Her current research on leukemia in cattle has established Dr. JANICE MILLER as an outstanding international expert in the field of animal oncology. Her study of bovine leukemia began in 1964 at the University of Wisconsin, where her discovery of C-type virus particles in lymphocyte cultures from leukemic cows provided the basis for recent advances in this research area. Born in Kansas in 1938, Dr. Miller received a Ph.D. in veterinary science from the University of Wisconsin in 1961 and the Burr A. Beach Award for the outstanding graduate student in veterinary science.

Wildlife Research Biologist

Since 1956 LUCILLE FARRIER STICKEL has been a biologist with the Patuxent Wildlife Research Center at Laurel, Maryland. Born in Hillman, Michigan, she received her B.A. at Eastern Michigan University and her M.S. and Ph.D. at the University of Michigan. Since joining the Patuxent Wildlife Research Center she has been engaged in the pioneering field of pesticide research in which she developed original methods for determining pesticide residue levels in wildlife, including the significance of residues in animal brain tissue as indications of lethal levels. Dr. Stickel serves as assistant to the director of the Patuxent Center in planning and guiding the pesticide research program and evaluating research designs. Often a participant at national conferences on wildlife and pesticides, she has published numerous research papers and articles.

Aquatic Biologist

A co-investigator of aquatic and wetlands plants in the Southwestern United States, HELEN B. CORREL is presently a collaborator at the Fairchild Tropical Garden, Miami, Florida. Born in Providence, Rhode Island, in 1907, Dr. Correl holds a B.A. (1928) and M.A. (1929) from Brown University and a Ph.D. from Duke University (1934). Her professional career as a biologist includes research at Cold Spring Harbor and Woods Hole Biological Stations as well as at the Texas Research Foundation, where she worked from 1956 to 1971. An instructor at Wellesley College and an associate professor at Maryland State Teachers College, Dr. Correl has written several scientific papers as well as co-authoring *Aquatic and Wetland Plants of Southwestern United States,* published in 1971.

Fruit Breeder

At Rutgers University's Department of Horticulture, where she has been since 1948, Dr. CATHERINE H. BAILEY is a member of a team working on the development, through hybridization, of new cultivars of peaches, processing peaches, nectarines, apples, and pears. So far she has introduced 39 new varieties of fruit to the industry. In 1969 she was a joint recipient of the Annual Recognition Award presented by the National Peach Council for outstanding contributions to the peach industry and in 1974 delivered a paper at the XIX International Horticultural Congress in Warsaw, Poland, on "Genetics and Plant Breeding."

Mother of Balboa Park: First Woman Meyer Medal Winner

KATE OLIVIA SESSIONS (1857–1940) was a San Francisco-born horticulturalist and nursery woman who leased 30 acres from San Diego in 1892 and founded Balboa Park. Traveling across the world, she brought back such new plants as the palm *Erythea,* queen palm, flame eucalyptus, Chinese twisted juniper, camphor tree, various acacias, bougainvilleas, Pride of Madeira, and many vines, aloes, and succulents for the park. In 1939 she became the first woman to receive the Meyer Medal from the Council of the American Genetic Association for distinguished service in the introduction of foreign plants.

Botanist-Zoologist Keeper of Cornell's Hortorium

Still hard at work at 85 in 1975 mounting specimens for the Liberty Hyde Bailey Hortorium, named for her famous horticulturist father and housing his collection of wild and cultivated plants and seed and plant catalogues dating back to 1800, ETHEL BAILEY vowed to keep on going as long as she is able. Until her retirement 18 years ago, Ms. Bailey was curator of the Hortorium, well known to plant lovers and researchers throughout the world. She has worked since then as a volunteer, processing between 3,000 and 5,000 specimens a year. A 1911 graduate of Smith College with a degree in zoology, she became equally competent as a botanist under her father's tutelage.

Kauai Horticulturist

Ms. BETTIE E. LAUCHIS has been horticultural director at Olu Pua Gardens, Kalaheo, Kauai, Hawaii, since 1965, where, through her efforts and expertise, over 4,000 species of tropical plants have been collected. A student of horticulture at Kent State University and Western Reserve University in Ohio, Bettie Lauchis taught horticulture in the adult education system in Cleveland and offered a plant propagation course through the University of Hawaii Extension Service. A horticulturist for 20 years, she is a member of the Board of Directors of the American Horticultural Society, a member of the Advisory Board to the College of Tropical Agriculture, University of Hawaii, a member of the American Association of Botanic Gardens and Arboreta, and a member of the International Plant Propagators' Society.

"Tomorrow's Scientists and Engineers" Winner

A winner of the "Tomorrow's Scientists and Engineers" award in 1971, JULIA HALBERG, 22 in 1978, studies the circadian rhythms of plants and animals at the Chronobiology Laboratories in the Department of Pathology and Laboratory Medicine at the University of Minnesota. After traveling in Europe and India, she recognized the priority of world food needs and returned to the United States to work on optimizing the utilization of food by timing its ingestion according to rhythm. "Tomorrow's Scientist" is already hard at work.

THE WORLD FOOD MOVEMENT

Agricultural experts have long known that the world produces sufficient food to feed everyone a nutritionally adequate diet. However, political and economic forces have interrupted the natural and equitable distribution of food so that often it is the agricultural workers of less-developed countries who receive the least nourishment and who often die of starvation. The 1974 world food crisis proved that food had become a commodity rather than a human right.

In recent years women from many different nations have stepped forward to assume leadership in the struggle against starvation. Various private, public, and international organizations have instituted programs that attempt to adjust the imbalance between the world's food producers and its consumers. To stop scarcity and starvation, women scholars and activists are attempting to locate and limit the factors which cause world hunger. The *New York Times* has estimated that there are currently several hundred local and national organizations in the United States that address themselves to the world food issue.

Professor of Food Policy

EMMA ROTHSCHILD, born in London in 1948, has been influential in showing how the world distribution of food is controlled by political and economic forces rather than by humanitarian considerations. Now a resident of New York City, Ms. Rothschild taught an undergraduate course at Yale in 1976 entitled "Food and U. S. Foreign Policy." Her magazine articles, "The Politics of Food," which appeared in the *New York Review of Books* (May 1974), "World Food Economy," which ran in the *New Yorker* (May 1975), and "Food Politics," which appeared in *Foreign Affairs* (January 1976), became standard reference materials for politicians and policymakers involved in agricultural legislation. Her new book, dealing with American food exports, will be published in 1979.

Sharecroppers' Supporter

After writing her thesis, "Land Ownership and Inequality in Appalachia," and receiving her B.A. in rural development from the University of California at Santa Cruz in 1975, CYNTHIA GUYER went to work for the Rural Advancement Fund/National Sharecroppers Fund in Charlotte, North Carolina. The central mission of this organization is to improve the "social and economic conditions of America's rural poor through agricultural skill training, adaptation and demonstration of appropriate agricultural technology, the advancement of community-based cooperative organizations, and the promotion of national legislation which provides realistic financing and technical support to small farmers and community-based, non-agricultural rural development programs." Cynthia Guyer worked with the RAF staff to develop training and community outreach ideas into concrete programs.

World Food Writer-Analysts

Speaker and writer FRANCES MOORE LAPPE is one of the founders of the new World Food Movement. Her book *Diet for a Small Planet* (1975) sold 1.5 million copies. She is co-author of *Food First: Beyond the Myth of Scarcity* (1977). Frances Lappe travels across the country speaking to the growing number of Americans interested in fighting famine. They are, she says, "puzzled by the coexistence of the abundance of food they see around them and the continuing fact of hunger and malnutrition. These are the kinds of really basic questions people are asking about food, not how to create a better sauce Béarnaise."

A Smith College graduate who has lived in Paris for the past 20 years, Susan George is now completing a doctorate on agribusiness at the École des Hautes Études en Sciences Sociales. In a counterreport to the Rome World Food Conference in 1974, SUSAN GEORGE and other members of the Transnational Institute developed their thesis on how the technology and trading systems of the developed world contributed to world hunger. She expanded this analysis into a book, *How the Other Half Dies: The Real Reasons for World Hunger* (1977), in which she describes the historical and economic forces that cause half the world's population to live in a state of undernourishment and suggests new approaches to alleviating the problem.

CATHERINE LERZA, a 1971 graduate of the University of California College of Agricultural Sciences, is an agriculture/food editor and writer currently working with *The Elements* magazine at the Public Resource Center in Washington, D.C. Co-editor of *Food for People, Not for Profit* (1975) and a contributing author to *Managing Your Personal Food Supply* (1977), she has written articles on the development of regional agricultural systems, urban food production systems, federal agricultural programs, agribusiness, and international food politics.

Agriculture/Rural Development Anthropologist

A staff member of the Rockefeller Foundation, 31-year-old SUSAN ALMY is in charge of program development for women in agriculture. Dealing with the conquest of hunger, education for development, and population and health, she researches and develops conferences in the sociological and anthropological aspects of agricultural/rural development programs. With a B.A. from Swarthmore College (1968) and an M.A. and Ph.D. from Stanford University in anthropology, Susan Almy speaks Spanish, Portuguese, French, Ki Meru, Ki Swahili, and German.

Urban Agriculturist

Having grown up on a commercial organic nursery in Maryland and been graduated from American University in 1964, MIRANDA SMITH pursued her interest in agriculture. After working in Canada for 10 years (her last job was with the Rooftop Gardens Project, which researched and developed rooftop technologies) she took a position with the Urban Agriculture Project of the Institute for Local Self-Reliance in Washington, D.C. This group investigates the food production capacity of urban areas and provides technical assistance on various aspects of urban agriculture. While trying to develop community gardens, the project also stresses the integration of urban food and waste systems, economic development and low-energy technologies. Recently Miranda Smith became involved in the technical assistance component of the Bronx Frontier Development Corporation's Composting and Greening operation which is composting 3,000 tons of vegetable waste weekly to provide a high-grade growing medium with which to revitalize the many acres of vacant land in the Bronx area.

Food Fair Founder

LINDSAY JONES of St. Charles, Illinois, was graduated from Smith College in 1969 as a history major in East Asian studies. From 1972 to 1974 she was the director of the Circle Pines Center, a 40-year-old consumer cooperative in Delton, Michigan, before moving to Tennessee, where she was the principal organizer of the first Nashville Food Fairs in 1975. Having formed the Agricultural Marketing Project, a student-initiated, non-profit service/research organization to administer the Food Fairs, at Vanderbilt Medical Center in Nashville, Ms. Jones began to promote her idea. Food Fairs are markets situated in convenient urban areas, such as church parking lots, where farmers can sell loads of produce directly from their trucks to the consumers. During the summer of 1977, Food Fairs were held in 26 Tennessee, Alabama, and Mississippi cities.

Agribusiness Watchdogs

"As a nation, the United States is the largest exporter of food in the world and a significant importer. We are also the leading innovators in the field of agricultural technology. As a result American solutions to agricultural problems have tended to dominate thinking around the world. American corporations are also the leaders in numerous markets spawned by our technology: farm machinery, fertilizers, seeds, pesticides, and the marketing of food itself. Thus the ability of the United States to respond humanely to the food crisis is important to the future of hungry people."

For many of these reasons which she stated, SUSAN SECHLER, now a special assistant to the director of the Economic Budget and Analysis Section of the U. S. Department of Agriculture, went to work for the Agriculture Accountability Project. This Project, the first Nader-like, non-profit, non-partisan public interest group in the country to monitor the food economy, was formed in 1971. During the next five years, Susan Sechler, along with a group of other young women in their mid-twenties—SUSAN DeMARCO, MARTHA HAMILTON, JEAN DANGERFIELD, LINDA KRAVITZ, and NANCY MILLS—wrote books, organized campaigns, testified before congressional committees, and issued press statements about U.S. agricultural policies.

Pro small-farmer, farm worker, environment, and consumer, they focused attention on agribusiness behavior and its effects upon the country. Independently or collectively they participated in the research and or writing of *Hard Times, Hard Tomatoes; The Failure of the Land Grant College Complex; The Fields Have Turned Brown: Four Essays on World Hunger; The Great American Grain Robbery; Who's Minding the Coop? A Report on Farmer Control of Farmers' Cooperatives;* and *Sowing the Till.*

President of the Children's Foundation

A 1962 graduate of the University of Maryland, BARBARA BODE in 1972 became president of the Children's Foundation—a national, non-profit, anti-hunger advocacy organization that develops projects and strategies to bring about full participation in national food programs through educational efforts. When she took over, the Foundation had almost no funding. She taught herself how to be a fund raiser, completely reorganized the staff and board, sharpened the operational focus, and developed new programs. The Foundation today monitors all the domestic federal food assistance programs for children and their families: school lunch, school breakfast, food aid to children's residential institutions, summer food, supplemental food for low-income pregnant women, food stamps, and donated commodities. "Our monitoring," Ms. Bode says, "consists of following legislative developments; educating congressional staffs; working to shape regulations and policies at the federal, state, and local levels . . . and generally working . . . to end inequities in these and other social welfare programs."

FAO WOMEN

B. R. Sen Award Winner, 1977

Winner of the 1977 B. R. Sen Award for outstanding contributions to the work of the United Nations' Food and Agriculture Organization (FAO) in developing countries, Ms. JEAN RITCHIE was cited by the 1977 FAO conference for her "outstanding contribution" as field officer in teaching home economics, developing innovative training courses for women, in the "training of trainers," and in the planning and direction of nutrition, population, and rural family programs in various African nations. Ms. Ritchie, who was born in England in 1913, worked for the FAO Headquarters and Regional Office for Asia and the Far East from 1947 to 1963 and has been associated with African field projects since 1961. She has directed national workshops in 19 countries. In her work with the FAO Programmes for Better Family Living, Ms. Ritchie has played a major role in helping to introduce and integrate the population/family life education component into multidisciplinary programs and assisting in the identification of potential projects in a number of African nations. Her 1950 book *Teaching Better Nutrition* was reprinted in English, French, and Spanish, as was a later book *Learning Better Nutrition*. Trained at Edinburgh, Boston, and the University of Chicago, Ms. Ritchie is a member of many honorary associations and societies.

International Agricultural Economist

A Lebanese agricultural economist, AIDA EID is deputy chief of the Europe, Near East, and Latin America Service of the FAO/IBRD (International Bank for Reconstruction and Development) Cooperative Programme. Born in Jerusalem in 1930, she speaks Arabic, English, Italian, French, and Spanish. Working with the FAO since 1958, she has lectured on project analysis and evaluation besides holding various posts with the organization. She was an economist with the economic analysis division for Latin America, 1962–64, and an area coordinator for the Near East and Europe Cooperative Programme 1969–72. Educated at the University of London and the University of Rome, she received degrees in economics, agricultural economics, and statistics.

FAO Home Economist

Since 1968 LUDMILLA MARIN, an American with a Ph.D. in home economics from the University of Wisconsin, has served as the chief of home economics and social service programs for the UN Food and Agriculture Organization at their main headquarters in Rome, Italy. Prior to assuming this position she was director of the Home Economic Rural Development Program of the American International Association in Venezuela from 1948 to 1958, a member of the Inter-American Institute of Agricultural Science in Costa Rica from 1958 to 1960, an assistant professor of adult education in the College of Education at the University of Wisconsin from 1962 to 1966, and an associate director of the Human Resources Program in the Research and Development Section of Avco Corporation from 1966 to 1968.

Guatemalan FAO Rural Development Expert

For more than 10 years ANA LAURETTA DIAZ has been collaborating in the planning and implementation of extension, home economics, applied nutrition, and community development programs in Latin America. A member of the UN FAO, initially serving with the Home Economics Division and since 1973 attached to the Cooperatives and Other Farmers Organizations Group within the Human Resources, Institutions, and Agrarian Reform Division, Ms. Diaz is responsible for the promotion and technical support of programs concerned with the involvement of women and families in organizations, cooperatives, and other mutual aid activities aimed at the improvement of the economic and social conditions of rural families. She has worked with such national and international agencies as the Institute of Nutrition of Central America and Panama, the Inter American Institute of Education and Ministry of Education in Guatemala, the Interamerican Institute of Agriculture Sciences, OAS-Regional Offices in Montevideo, Uruguay, and Lima, Peru, the International Development Agency Pilot Project in Chile, and the Ministry of Agriculture Extension Service in Chile. Ms. Diaz, born in 1924 in Guatemala, studied at the University of Río Piedras in Puerto Rico and received her bachelor's and master's degrees in home economics and extension from Michigan State University, as well as a diploma in cooperatives and management education from the University of Wisconsin in Madison.

FAO Agricultural Commodity Expert

A Ph.D. from the London School of Economics, GERDA BLAU was born in Austria in 1910, became a British citizen, and now lives in Rome, Italy. Known as a leader in the field of agricultural commodities, she is an economic consultant specializing in international commodity problems. Until her retirement from the FAO in 1969, Dr. Blau had served in the FAO Economics Division (since 1946) as chief of the Fibers Section, chief of the Commodities Branch, director of the Commodities Division, secretary of the FAO Committee on Commodity Problems, and director of Special Studies. Under her early leadership and foresight, the foundation was laid, and extensive and varied approaches developed, for FAO work in agricultural commodities. Her numerous publications have been published in many languages.

Primitive Wheats Researcher

Irish-born ERNA BENNETT (Derry, 1925) has been responsible for genetic conservation and plant exploration in the Genetic Resources Unit of FAO for 10 years. After studying in Ireland, at the University of London, and at the University of Durham, where she specialized in botany and genetics, she joined the FAO in 1967. Ms. Bennett has conducted explorations for primitive wheats and other cereals and food crops in Afghanistan, Iran, Iraq, Turkey, Greece, and Cyprus. During expeditions to more than a dozen other countries, she has distributed seeds from remote areas to other agricultural nations where they could be used for experimental purposes connected with world food needs. In 1971 Ms. Bennett was awarded the Mayer Memorial Medal of the American Genetic Association for her contributions to plant introduction and genetic conservation.

Ceres Medal Women

For a number of years the United Nations Food and Agriculture Organization has cast medals in honor of women who share with others "a vision of a world free from hunger and want." Although not all the women invited to represent Ceres are directly connected with food or agriculture, each represents the ideal to which the FAO is dedicated.

Indira Gandhi
India
Coretta Scott King
U.S.A.
Angela Christian
Ghana
Olave Baden-Powell
Great Britain
Sophia Loren
Italy

Germaine Tillion
France
Sonia Javas
Nicaragua
Marie-Thérèse Basse
Senegal
Margaret Mead
U.S.A.
Mother Teresa
Yugoslavia
Iris Murdoch
Great Britain
Matsuyo Yamamoto
Japan
Kathleen Kenyon
Great Britain
Attiya Inayatullah
Pakistan
Michèle Morgan
France
Irene de Borbon de Parma
The Netherlands
Jacqueline Auriol
France
Shirley Temple Black
U.S.A.

Dechhen Wangmo Wangchuck
Bhutan
Aziza Hussein
Egypt
Gloria Steinem
U.S.A.
Thangam Philip
India
Julia Ojiambo
Kenya
Margot Fonteyn de Arias
Great Britain
Barbara Ward
Great Britain
Alva Myrdal
Sweden
Vittoria Nuti Ronchi
Italy
Dr. Pauline Jewett
Canada
Lillian Carter
U.S.A.
Farah Pahlavi
Iran

Ceres Medal Women Directly Involved in Agriculture

Senegal's Leading Food Technologist

As director of the Institute of Food Technology in Dakar, MARIE-THÉRÈSE BASSE participated in her institute's successful development of *pain de mil* or millet bread, which uses a high proportion of locally grown millet instead of imported wheat flour. Since African countries bordering the Sahara Desert have been seriously affected by droughts since 1968 and suffered severe livestock and crop losses in 1973 and 1974, the development of the *pain de mil* was a crucial breakthrough in the battle to combat food crises. FAO and the World Food Program honored Marie-Thérèse Basse for her work in meeting emergency food needs.

Japan's Pioneer Rural Extension Worker

Home economist MATSUYO YAMAMOTO is director of Tokyo's Research Institute for Home-Family-Community Living. The Ceres medal cast in her honor was designed by her husband, president of the Japan Artists' Association, and was presented to her by the FAO in 1974. Born in Japan in 1909, Matsuyo Yamamoto attended the Tokyo Woman's Christian College and then did graduate work at Washington State University because women were not allowed to attend Japanese higher colleges or universities at that time. Her graduate scholarship, obtained through the Tokyo YWCA, stipulated that she study home economics, and though her primary interests were in psychology and educational philosophy, Matsuyo Yamamoto found the U.S. scientific approach to the study of household subjects (which in Japan meant only cooking and sewing) unexpectedly fascinating. Returning to Tokyo in 1937, she became head of the Home Economic Division of the YWCA School, where she taught family dietetics and cooking science. Following World War II, Ms. Yamamoto was asked by the Ministry of Education to run their new homemaking education program in the Japanese school system. In 1948 she joined the Ministry of Agriculture and Forestry. As the first of seven female section chiefs appointed by the Japanese Government in a postwar push toward sexual equality, Ms. Yamamoto started the Home Economics Extension Service. Combating her Ministry's tendency to concentrate only on agricultural production, she recruited 68 female home economists to serve as field workers for some six million Japanese farm families. By 1965, when Matsuyo Yamamoto left the Ministry to join the UN FAO as chief of the Education and Training Section of the Home Economics unit in Rome, the Seikatsu-Kaizen Movement, dedicated to the improvement of living conditions for rural families, had grown to a strength of 360,000—including 3,000 home advisers, supervisors, and specialists. For the FAO Ms. Yamamoto supervised field workers in the South Pacific, Asia, and various African countries.

Archaeologist of Ancient Agriculture

British archaeologist KATHLEEN KENYON has led numerous archaeological explorations in Britain and the Middle East. It was during her excavations in Jericho that Ms. Kenyon discovered evidence proving that the establishment of permanent settlements in ancient times was dependent on the development of agriculture. Kathleen Kenyon's work threw new light on the practice of farming 10,000 years ago when neolithic people first began to raise wheat and barley and domesticate goats, sheep, pigs, and cattle.

Italy's Chief Plant Researcher

Professor of genetics in the Agriculture Department of the University of Pisa and chief researcher for the Italian Research Council, VITTORIA NUTI RONCHI is an expert on plant tissue. Dr. Ronchi's research deals with nucleic acid synthesis as it relates to the mechanism of tissue differentiation in plants. Her studies of *Nicotiana* species have led to a better understanding of the underlying factors in tumor formation. For the past 20 years, Dr. Ronchi has also been active in social work projects benefiting young women.

Agricultural Aviator

Distinguished French pilot JACQUELINE AURIOL holds many aviation records as well as the Ceres Medal award. She was one of the first women to break the sound barrier and to fly the supersonic Concorde. Mme. Auriol, who works at the Ministère de la Coopération, makes use of her technological skills to assist in agricultural development. By use of a new technique of remote sensing, she gathers information on the earth's resources—locating water for irrigation, spotting plant disease, and mapping various crop species.

Holland's Royal Worker

A member of the royal family of the Netherlands, IRENE DE BORBON DE PARMA is also a Ceres Medal woman. Active on behalf of migratory workers in France, the princess also has made major contributions to the relief of hunger in West Africa.

Royal Worker from Bhutan

Another FAO Ceres Medal princess is DECHHEN WANGMO WANGCHUCK of Bhutan, who at 27 became the world's youngest head of a national Ministry of Development. Responsible for Bhutan's health, education, agriculture, and public works, the princess is also president of the Food Corporation of Bhutan and a member of the National Planning Commission. Princess Dechhen Wangmo Wangchuck founded the National Youth Association of Bhutan while she was still attending school and has continued to use her royal position to assist her people in subsequent years.

Sudanese Minister

H.E. Fatima ABDEL MAHMOUD, Minister of Social Affairs of the Democratic Republic of Sudan since 1976, is involved in several other official duties as assistant general secretary of the Sudanese Council for Peace, Solidarity and Friendship, co-member of the Sudanese Parliament, president of Sudanese National Council for Social Welfare, general secretary for Women in the Ruling Party, and president of the Mother and Child Care Committee. Dedicated to the activities of Sudanese women in agriculture, Dr. Mahmoud has written several books and articles on population, family planning, and women's affairs.

Animal Geneticist

A world expert in animal genetics, Dr. HELEN NEWTON TURNER of Australia was invited to donate her portrait for an FAO Ceres Medal in recognition of her long-time work and study of sheep breeding. She has written several textbooks and published over 100 scientific papers covering her research on sheep production, and given seminars and lectures on her specialty all over the world. Of particular importance in Dr. Turner's work is selection in the breeding of Merino sheep.

An Italian Shepherdess

An unnamed Italian shepherd girl provided the inspiration for the November 1977 Ceres Medal issued by the Food and Agriculture Organization of the United Nations. The shepherd girl, from Ponte Legno in the mountains of northern Italy, so moved the artist with her "sweetness and grace" that he used her as a model for the medal. The reverse side shows people seated around a poor, roughhewn table and the inscription "Fiat Panis" (Let there be bread).

2

Women in Politics and Government

By Alice Lynn Booth

U.S. Congresswoman Patricia (Pat) Schroeder, consulting editor

The 1970s proved to be breakthrough years for women in politics and government. No decade in history has had more significant gains, or "firsts," for women in public life.

The movement of an unprecedented number of women into political positions in the 1970s is easily explainable. Convinced that no one would hand them political power, women organized on their own behalf to claim it. The declaration of International Women's Year and Decade was evidence that the movement supersedes ideologies, economies, geography, race, and religion. The status quo has been upset. "The drive for participation by women is now rooted," said New York State's Lieutenant Governor MARY ANNE KRUPSAK. "It is not just a fad. The political establishment clearly reads this."

Here are some of the '70s breakthroughs:

•Sweden's Prime Minister Thorbjörn Fälldin appointed five women to his 20-member Cabinet, including Foreign Minister KARIN SÖDER. In France, FRANÇOISE GIROUD was named Secretary of State on the Condition of Women, the only post of its kind in the world.

•MARGARET THATCHER became the first woman party leader in British history. As prime minister of the shadow cabinet, she could become Britain's Prime Minister if the Conservatives win the next election.

•ANNEMARIE RENGER became President of the German Bundestag; Japan chose its first female diplomat of ministerial rank as head of the Japanese Mission to the United Nations; Iran's first was a woman provincial governor; BERNADETTE OLOWO of Uganda became the first woman ambassador to the Vatican in 1975, breaking a 900-year tradition that kept female envoys out of the Holy See.

•The first female cabinet member in

Italy, TINA ANSELMI, took over the portfolio of the Ministry of Labor, one of the toughest posts in that economically shaken country.

And in Switzerland, where women were not permitted to vote until 1971, in 1977 a woman was selected from among the members of the National Council to serve for a year as its president—an office equivalent to the U. S. Speaker of the House and the highest office held by a woman in the Swiss Confederation.

In the United States in the '70s:

• For the first time in the history of the Department of State, women employees organized to demand an end to discriminatory practices. Their successes included the withdrawal of a rule that forced a woman to resign from the Foreign Service when she married.

• In 1971, four feminist leaders— Congresswoman BELLA ABZUG, GLORIA STEINEM, BETTY FRIEDAN, and FANNIE LOU HAMER—announced the formation of the National Women's Political Caucus, an organization dedicated to thrusting women into positions of power at all levels of government. "No one gives political power," said Gloria Steinem (see the chapter "Women in Communications," p. 479). "It must be taken and we will take it." Women were going to stop making coffee and start making policy.

• Nineteen seventy-four became "the year of the woman in politics" when ELLA GRASSO was elected governor of Connecticut, the first woman governor in U.S. history who did not follow her husband into office. MARY ANNE KRUPSAK's victory as lieutenant governor of New York State was another historic first. So was JANET GREY HAYES's victory as mayor of San Jose, California, which in turn infused LILA COCKRELL with the confidence to run for mayor of San Antonio, Texas, and win. More U.S. women ran for office in 1974 than in any previous year, and the number of women in state legislatures jumped by 26 per cent.

• Nineteen seventy-four was also the year when Republican MARY LOUISE SMITH, a grandmother, was named chairman of the Grand Old Party, a first; ANNE ARMSTRONG became the first woman ambassador to the Court of St. James's; and the feminist caucus of the Democratic National Committee showed its stuff at the Democratic mini-Convention. Party leaders were shocked to discover that women were the best-organized group there.

• By 1976, U.S. presidential candidates couldn't ignore women. Every serious contender made sure he had women in visible positions on his campaign staff. President Jimmy Carter named two women to his Cabinet, another historic first, and more women were appointed to high-ranking administration jobs than ever before.

• That same year, the Women's Campaign Fund (WCF) proved that women will empty their pocketbooks to elect women candidates. The biggest handicap facing women candidates is lack of money. WCF grew out of MAYA MILLER's Senate campaign in Nevada in 1974, when it was recognized that to overcome the handicap, women would have to help one another.

But though these firsts are the symbols of a new consciousness that, at this time in history, the contribution of women in politics and government is sorely needed, the fact remains that men still run the world. Women have not achieved anything like their potential as policy-and decision-makers, administrators, and diplomats. Women's thoughts, beliefs, experience, and intellect remain barely a whimper in the halls of state around the world.

During the 1970s only five nations had women as heads of government. Today none of those women is in power. In no country today do women come near to sharing power with men. Even the progressive Scandinavian countries have filled only about one fifth of their parliamentary seats with women. Participation by women at the United Nations General Assembly was a staggeringly low 8.8 per cent in 1975. In 26 out of 30 years, representation on the UN Security Council has been an absolute 100 per cent male. The United States's record of political participation by women is about average. Some nations are worse, a few are better. Whether or not a nation is industrialized or developing, the patterns are similar.

Here are some indicators of the long road ahead in the United States: Nationwide, in 1977, women held less than 7 per cent of all elective offices. None of the 100 U.S. senators was a woman. This situation changed temporarily in 1978 with the appointment of MURIEL HUMPHREY to the Minnesota seat vacated by her husband's death, followed by the appointment of MARYON ALLEN as senator from Alabama in her late husband's place. Ms. Humphrey soon announced that she would not run in her own right; Ms. Allen said that she would. (In history, only three U.S. women have been elected to a full Senate term.) Only 18 of 435 members of the House of Representatives in 1978 were women, about the same as 40 years ago. There has never been a woman on the U. S. Supreme Court, and only 5 out of 507 cabinet heads have been women.

The obstacles to genuine participation are enormous. In the United States, women who run for office most often run as outsiders—without established political support and the money that such support generates. Every race is an uphill battle. And everywhere, men who hold power are still reluctant to bring women into positions of responsibility. Legal remedies may bring legal relief but don't automatically bring change. For women to participate fully as political equals, the social fabric of all nations will have to stretch. Such cultural adaptations take struggle and time. Still, the 1970s held the promise that women's voices will become increasingly audible and, eventually, inextinguishable.

With each new accomplishment by a woman in politics, another woman develops the will to try. Colorado's Representative PATRICIA ("PAT") SCHROEDER proved that a young wife and mother with young children could win election to Congress, and keep her family intact while serving. She also proved by her participation on the male-dominated Armed Services Committee that a female voice can make a difference in formulating military policy. Her inspiration will reverberate into the next decade. "Women have been told so often they can spectate and not participate, that they have thought they are not capable of participating," she says. "But, yes, we are."

ALICE LYNN BOOTH, *the author of* Careers in Politics for the New Woman *(1978), is a graduate of the University of California at Berkeley (1965) with a B.A. in political science. She began her career as a newspaper reporter in Chicago and has since reported in the United States and free-lanced abroad for newspapers, radio stations, and magazines. Her articles have appeared in the* Washington Post *and the* Washington Star, *the* Chicago Sun-Times, Philadelphia Inquirer, Glamour, Cosmopolitan, MS, *and* Juris Doctor *magazines. She specializes in politics, women's issues, and problems of contemporary life. In 1977 she became press secretary to Congressman Paul Tsongas (D., Mass.).*

Consulting editor PATRICIA ("PAT") SCHROEDER *is a member of the House of Representatives, U. S. Congress, from Colorado (see p. 72).*

HEADS OF GOVERNMENT

World's First Female Prime Minister

SIRIMAVO BANDARANAIKE ran for the prime ministership of Sri Lanka (Ceylon) for the first time in 1959 to replace her husband after he was assassinated. Journalists joked that the newly widowed Ms. Bandaranaike, who burst into tears every time her late husband's name was mentioned, wept her way into office. She soon stopped crying, however, and ran Sri Lanka with a strong hand until defeated in the 1965 elections. She won office as Prime Minister again in 1970. Her second administration was beset by severe food shortages and other serious problems. In 1971 she imposed emergency rule in an attempt to control corruption and allied abuses. In recent years she has been accused of misuse of power and criticized for nepotism in giving positions of importance to a nephew, her son, and daughters SUN-ETHRA (an official adviser to her mother) and CHANDRIKA (head of the board that controls Sri Lanka's tea and rubber plantations). When elections were held again in July 1977, Mme. Bandaranaike's Freedom Party was overwhelmingly defeated at the polls, she was out again as Prime minister, losing to the United National Party's Junius Richard Jayewardene.

First Woman Prime Minister of Israel

On April 10, 1974, when GOLDA MEIR, Prime Minister of Israel since 1969, announced her resignation, no one knew if it was a gesture to prolong her position or actually the end of a long, turbulent political career. But there was no doubt that her motive was, as it had always been, Israel's well-being. The action reflected the strength of will and tough-minded realism characteristic of Goldie Mabovitch of Milwaukee, Wisconsin, who in 1921 pushed her husband Morris Myerson into going to Palestine. (She had in fact made the move a condition of accepting his proposal of marriage.) By 1928 she was secretary of the women's labor council; soon after, she was a power in the Histadrut, Israel's labor federation, representing the council on the executive board of the Histadrut and at international meetings. She also became active in the World Zionist Movement, was elected a delegate to the World Zionist Congress, went on missions to the United States and Europe during the '30s on behalf of the Zionists, and joined the Jewish self-government organization under the British Mandate. In 1940 she became head of Histadrut's political department dealing with foreign relations.

On May 14, 1948, Golda Meir was one of the signers of Israel's Declaration of Independence, the only signatory to have immigrated to Israel from the United States. She became the only woman member of its first provisional legislature, and in September went to Moscow as Israel's first Minister to the Soviet Union. In January 1949 she was elected to the first Knesset (Parliament) as a Mapai (Labor Party) candidate. Prime Minister David Ben-Gurion later appointed her Minister of Labor and Social Insurance and in 1956 (the same year the widowed Golda Myerson changed her name to its Hebraized version, Meir) made her Minister of Foreign Affairs. In both positions, she was the only woman member of the Cabinet; from 1953 to 1966 she also served as chairman of Israel's delegation to the United Nations. On the sudden death in office of Prime Minister Levi Eshkol, Golda Meir was chosen to be interim Prime Minister and sworn in on March 17, 1969, as the fourth—and first woman —Prime Minister of Israel. She was 71 years old. In the general elections in October 1969, she won the office in her own right. Even after her resignation, during a turbulent crisis of parties and personalities in the aftermath of the October War of 1973, she continued to be viewed as the single figure in the Israeli leadership who could serve as a rallying point for the country.

First Woman Prime Minister of India

INDIRA GANDHI, only child of Jawaharlal Nehru, the first Prime Minister of India (1947–64), in 1966 succeeded Lal Bahadur Shastri as head of the government when he died suddenly in Tashkent. A group of old Congress Party leaders, believing that they could use Nehru's daughter as their instrument, selected her. But Ms. Gandhi was her own woman, then as later, and chose her Cabinet and ruled independently. That she would do so should have been no surprise to anybody. Her independence had deep roots in a lonely childhood and an untraditional, non-arranged marriage that did not prove very happy. And she had been schooled well in her father's official residence in New Delhi, where she acted as his hostess and closest adviser for many years. The results of the general election of 1967 placed her firmly in power; she consolidated this power three years later when she called the parliamentary elections scheduled for 1972 to be held a year early and won by an enormous margin —the Indian masses turning out to give the Congress Party the largest number of votes ever polled in a free election in history.

The years that followed were turbulent. The war with Pakistan over Bangladesh was followed by the worst period economically for India since independence. As her problems mounted, Indira Gandhi came to count more and more heavily on the advice of her younger son, Sanjay, much as her father had once depended on her. In 1975, apparently at his urging, she declared a state of emergency and abrogated many of the freedoms guaranteed by the Indian Constitution. As opposition to her mounted during the following 18 months, there were increasing numbers of arrests of her political enemies. Once again she called for an early election. This time, in the last week of March 1977, she was badly defeated. Since leaving office, she has been under investigation for the political excesses of "The Emergency" and Sanjay has been jailed for his role. Ms. Gandhi has formed a new opposition party, splitting the old Congress Party; her faction is called Congress I (for Indira).

First Woman Prime Minister of the Central African Republic

In December 1974, Mme. ELIZABETH DOMITIEN was appointed Prime Minister of the Central African Republic, bringing to the government nearly 25 years of political experience. She was chosen for the post by President Bokassa, who came to power through a coup d'état in 1966 when he abrogated constitutional rule. Bokassa had been raised by Mme. Domitien's father, a family connection that served her politically. Although her position as Prime Minister was to carry out the President's mandate, she was more than Bokassa's flunky; her political influence and power had been independently earned. Mme. Domitien joined the political movement for her country's independence in 1951, when she was about 20 years old. A fiery speaker in her native Sangho, she could arouse the masses and was active as head of the party's women's organization and the national women's federation and particularly important to Bokassa in winning support from women. She is credited with helping to create a sense of national identity, but she was not considered effective as a statesperson, because she did not speak French and could not take part in diplomatic affairs. She was removed from her post in December 1976, after Bokassa declared himself Emperor and established a constitutional monarchy—a move Mme. Domitien opposed. She was placed under house arrest. It is believed that she is not allowed to leave the country or engage in political activities, but can move freely about.

First Woman President in the World

MARÍA ESTELA M. DE PERÓN, a former professional dancer, on July 1, 1974, became the first woman President in the world, following the death of her husband. Argentina's two-time dictator, Juan Perón. Isabel Perón, as she is more often known, had been elected Vice-President nine months earlier, when Juan Perón was returned to power after eighteen years' exile. On his death, the military junta placed her in power, but a bitterly divided Peronist movement eventually led to violence and a political struggle in which, two years later, she was removed from office by the military and jailed.

REIGNING ROYALTY

Queen of England

ELIZABETH II became head of the British Commonwealth of Nations on February 6, 1952, following the death of her father, King George VI. Her official title is Her Most Excellent Majesty by the Grace of God, of the United Kingdom of Great Britain and Northern Ireland and of her other Realms and Territories, Queen, Head of the Commonwealth, Defender of the Faith. A twist of fate made the second Elizabeth the sixth woman to occupy the throne in her own right. Her father's elder brother, the Duke of Windsor, was heir apparent. His abdication brought her father to the throne, and she became "heir presumptive" (the title of heir apparent being withheld in case a male heir might be born). The princess, who was born April 26, 1926, endeared herself in her radio broadcasts to the beleaguered people of Britain during the darkest days of World War II, and there was much rejoicing when she was crowned on June 2, 1953. Queen Elizabeth and her husband, Prince Philip (Lieutenant Mountbatten when they were married July 10, 1947), have four children—Prince Charles, Princess Anne, Prince Andrew, and Prince Edward— and one grandchild, born in 1977.

The Queen of England is said to be one of the richest women in the world and enjoys many privileges that seem anachronistic in hard-pressed contemporary Britain. But she is a woman of great charm and common sense who has never stopped working hard at very real duties. The love the people of the Commonwealth, and especially Londoners, have for her was evidenced anew during the celebration of her 25th Jubilee in June 1977. Even the leftist *New Statesman* commented that "the present queen . . . has moved sufficiently to make the crown compatible with a more democratic, egalitarian, and irreverent society."

Queen of Denmark

MARGRETHE II, daughter of King Frederik IX of Denmark, in 1960 went to Cambridge University in England to study archaeology, which became a passion with her. She has contributed articles to archaeological journals. "I would have become an archaeologist had I not been a princess," she said. "I have always had a dread of becoming a passenger in life." She was born April 16, 1940, and succeeded to the throne on January 15, 1972, the day after her father died. Denmark's first Margrethe ruled as a powerful regent in the late 14th and early 15th centuries but never received the formal title of Queen because the right of female succession did not exist. It was not established until 1953. Thus Margrethe II is the first real Queen of Denmark. A wife and mother of two children, Margrethe has a traditional point of view about the role of women. "I see no reason why, when some day I must officially take first place," she said in 1968, "I will not be able to take second place in our marriage at the same time."

Queen of Holland

Queen JULIANA LOUISE EMMA MARIE WILHELMINA, reigning sovereign since September 6, 1948, of the Kingdom of the Netherlands, was born April 30, 1909. She became the ruler when her mother, Queen Wilhelmina, who had spent half a century on the throne, abdicated. A constitutional and hereditary monarch, she may be consulted by the government, but political decisions are made by the Cabinet and Parliament. Juliana and her husband, Prince Bernhard, have four daughters. One of them, Princess BEATRIX, has had three sons, the eldest being the first male heir to the Dutch throne in three generations.

LEADING POLITICIANS AND CABINET MEMBERS, WORLDWIDE

First Female President of Germany's Bundestag

The first woman President of West Germany's Bundestag, ANNEMARIE RENGER, was elected to her country's Number Two political position on December 13, 1972. Ms. Renger served as Bundestag President until December 1976, when the Christian Democratic Party assumed power. A member of the Social Democratic Party (SPD), Ms. Renger is now Vice-President of the Bundestag, and remains one of West Germany's most prominent politicians. Ms. Renger was born in Leipzig, 1919. She became an active member of the SPD and was in charge of the party's office in Berlin until 1963 and elected to the Bundestag in 1953. As chairperson of the SPD's Federal Women's Committee, she is an outspoken advocate for women's rights, particularly in the areas of housing, broadcasting, retail trade, banking, and insurance. In January 1977 she became a regular member of the Committee for Foreign Relations. For 10 years, she was a member of the Consultative Assembly of the Council of Europe and of the Assembly of Western Union.

First Woman to Head a Major Political Party in Great Britain

When MARGARET THATCHER was selected to head the Conservative Party in Great Britain on February 11, 1975, Britain's male-dominated political establishment was struck a major blow. The first woman to head a major political party and the first potential female Prime Minister in some 700 years of British parliamentary history, Ms. Thatcher was no flaming feminist. Her victory against four male opponents was a revolt by Tory backbenchers fed up with leader Edward Heath. "Her historic victory deals a mortal wound to the assumption that male chauvinism and political conservatism must inevitably go together," an editorial in the *New York Times* noted. London's *Economist* described her as having "steel in her, an amiability, a way with people . . . combative skill . . . above all, courage."

An elitist, Ms. Thatcher advocates what she considers the traditional British way of life, an attitude that seems increasingly popular with the British public (although her policies as Secretary of State for Education and Science, 1970–74, when she supported independent schools and moved to increase the price of school lunches and eliminate free milk rations, led to schoolyard taunts of "Ms. Thatcher, milk snatcher." Born in a flat above the family grocery store on October 13, 1925, and an early achiever who was always head of her class and leader of sports teams, the future politician received a master's degree in science from Oxford and became a research chemist, at the same time she involved herself in the affairs of the Conservative Party, for which, encouraged by her father, she had begun running errands at the age of 10. She so impressed the party chairman that he asked her to run for Parliament in 1950. Defeated then and again in 1951, the same year she married and began studying law, she was finally elected to the House of Commons in 1959, four years after her twins were born and she had begun the practice of tax law. Margaret Thatcher does not regard herself as a feminist but once observed, "In politics, if you want anything said, ask a man; if you want anything done, ask a woman."

First Canadian Woman Speaker of the Senate

RENAUDE LAPOINTE was appointed by Prime Minister Pierre Trudeau to serve as Speaker of the Canadian Senate on September 16, 1974. A well-known Quebec journalist, who was appointed to the Senate in 1971, in 1965 she became the first woman member of the editorial board of *La Presse* in Montreal. In 1970 she joined the Department of Indian Affairs and Northern Development and was a member of the Canadian Delegation to the United Nations in 1970, '71, and '72. In the Senate, she has served on the External Affairs Committee and the Committee on Legal and Constitutional Affairs. Senator Lapointe was born in Disraeli, Quebec, 1912.

First Woman President of the National Council of Switzerland

Dr. ELISABETH BLUNSCHY-STEINER, born July 13, 1922, in the city of Schwyz, which gave Switzerland its name, was elected President of the Swiss National Council on May 2, 1977. She retired at year's end from the rotating office of the Council, Switzerland's equivalent of the U. S. House of Representatives. First elected to the Council in 1971—the year women were finally granted the vote in Switzerland's federal elections—Dr.

Blunschy-Steiner is an attorney who has been active in women's organizations and has spent most of her legal life advising women on marital problems. This experience has determined her philosophy, so liberal on 90 per cent of social issues that it has earned her a reputation for being radically left in the conservative, farmer-oriented canton of Schwyz, where she also serves as vice-president of the canton's Democratic Christian Party. Establishing equality of men and women in Switzerland is her main feminist goal. Although she is opposed to a liberalization of the abortion policy, Dr. Blunschy-Steiner wants to change Switzerland's patriarchal family law, which now gives men the final say over their wives' assets, income, right to work, and children.

First Woman in British Empire to Achieve Cabinet Rank

Ms. MARY ELLEN SMITH (1862–1933), the first woman to attain cabinet rank in the British Empire, was appointed Minister Without Portfolio in British Columbia in 1921. Ms. Smith, a native of England, who emigrated to British Columbia in 1891, was married to a politician who was a member of the legislature and, when he died in 1917, was Minister of Finance. Ms. Smith succeeded her husband into the legislature and then was appointed to the Cabinet. Although she resigned her ministerial post in 1922, she continued as a member of the legislature until 1928.

Britain's Minister of State for Overseas Development

In February 1977, JUDITH HART was appointed Great Britain's Minister of State for Overseas Development—a position she held in the Labour Party shadow government 1970–74. Elected to Parliament first in 1959, she held several ministerial positions in the Labour administration of 1964–70: she was first Joint Parliamentary Under-Secretary of

State at the Scottish Office; then Minister of State for Commonwealth Affairs; in July 1967, she became Minister for Social Security and a Privy Counsellor; in November 1968, took up the post of Paymaster-General, with a seat in the Cabinet; and in October 1969 became Minister of Overseas Development. She has been a member of the National Executive of the Labour Party since 1969. A sociologist, she published *Aid and Liberation: A Socialist Study of Aid Policies* in 1973, and was closely involved in the negotiations between the European Community and African, Caribbean, and Pacific countries leading to the Lome Convention.

Canadian Minister of Communications

The Honourable JEANNE SAUVÉ, Canada's Minister of Communications since December 1975, was elected to the House of Commons in 1972 and appointed Secretary of State for Science and Technology that same year. In August 1974 she became Minister of the Environment. Ms. Sauvé, who was born in Ottawa, 1922, worked for the Canadian Broadcasting Corporation as a journalist and broadcaster from 1952 to 1972. Her husband, Maurice Sauvé, was a Member of Parliament, 1962–68, and served as Minister of Forestry and Rural Development, 1964–68. They have a son. Outspoken in her support of women's rights, Ms. Sauvé at a conference on women in Canada and the law pointed out some of the unfair limits placed on women. "Some of the put-downs look at first glance like privileges. What about the Criminal Code? If a man and his accomplice are being pursued by the police and the wife helps them to escape, she is not held criminally responsible. Under a proposed change in the Act, [she] will be held responsible for aiding the accomplice. The older concept was demeaning. It perpetuated the idea of the woman as appendage, a non-person. That kind of favor we don't need."

Canada's Minister of National Revenue

The Honourable MONIQUE BÉGIN, born 1936 in Rome, Italy, was appointed Canada's Minister of National Revenue in September 1976, after serving as Parliamentary Secretary to the Secretary of State for External Affairs for nearly one year. She was elected to the House of Commons in 1972. Ms. Bégin is a founding member and was the first vice-president of the Women's Federation of Quebec and from 1965 to 1967 a member of the Canadian Human Rights Foundation. She held a variety of positions before entering politics, including Director of Research for the Royal Commission on the Status of Women in Canada. In 1970 she joined the Canadian Radio-Television Commission as administrator in its research branch.

Canada's Minister of State, Fitness, and Amateur Sport

The Honourable IONA CAMPAGNOLO was appointed Canada's Minister of State, Fitness, and Amateur Sport in September 1976. She was first elected to the House of Commons in July 1974. The following September she was named Parliamentary Secretary to the Minister of Indian Affairs and Northern Development. Ms. Campagnolo was born on Galiano Island, British Columbia, in 1932, and had a long career in radio broadcasting before entering politics. In 1972 she was elected alderman in Prince Rupert. In that role she served as Chairman of the Athletic Committee and was a member of the Information Services Committee. For her contribution to the community she was awarded the Order of Canada.

Sweden's Stateswoman for the World

ALVA REIMER MYRDAL, the first woman to hold a high-ranking job in the United Nations (principal director of the UN Department of Social Affairs, 1949–50), Sweden's first woman ambassador to India, 1955–61, a twice-appointed Minister, 1966–73 (for Disarmament and for Church Affairs), has also served as chairperson of Sweden's Delegation to the Disarmament Conference in Geneva, 1962–73, and as a member of Sweden's delegation to the United Nations in the same years. Her extraordinary career as diplomat, politician, educator, sociologist, and writer makes her one of the world's few female stateswomen. Her relentless struggle for a world that is more human and offers more equal opportunities makes her life a shining answer to the question: What can one woman do to nudge progress along the road from bad to good? She has pioneered reforms in education and housing, and worked to ameliorate inequalities between sexes, generations, classes, and countries. Her living room was the underground center where intellectuals-in-exile planned postwar Europe. Her

speeches and writings have been ideological blueprints for shaping modern Swedish society. Most recently, she has castigated the superpowers in her new book *The Game of Disarmament* (1976). She was born in 1902 in a small Swedish town, where only boys could attend high school. Her father and grandfather were dedicated Social Democrats deeply interested in society's problems. Her mother was unhappily burdened with five children, and Alva, the eldest, knew early that she wished to avoid a future like her mother's. She was 17 when she met Gunnar Myrdal, whom she married. He is a renowned economist and author. Their careers have often overlapped, but Alva Myrdal has never been less than herself. "I think fighting is much more fun than being accepted—socially accepted," she says.

In the Ministries, Sweden's Big Six

First Woman Foreign Minister

The first female Minister for Foreign Affairs in Sweden's history, KARIN SÖDER, was appointed October 8, 1976, one of five women cabinet ministers in the government of Prime Minister Thorbjörn Fälldin. On receiving her appointment, Ms. Söder said she would continue Sweden's traditional foreign policy of "active neutrality." A former teacher and M.P. since 1971, Ms. Söder has been Second Vice-President of the Center Party since 1971 and is a member of the Standing Committee on Local Government and of the Council of Europe. She was born in 1928 in Frykerud in the province of Värmland, is married, and has three children. Her leisure interests include mountain trekking, skiing, flower growing, and family life.

Minister of Housing and Physical Planning

Sweden's Minister of Housing and Physical Planning, ELVY OLSSON also was appointed to the Cabinet of Prime Minister

Thorbjörn Fälldin on October 8, 1976. A farmer's wife, Ms. Olsson has been a member of the Swedish Parliament since 1965. She is chairman of the standing committee on Local Government and a member of the governing bodies of the Board of Urban Planning. First vice-chairwoman of the Center Party's Women's Federation and a member of the Center Party Executive, Ms. Olsson, born in 1923, is married and has two children.

Deputy Minister of Education and Cultural Affairs

Sweden's Deputy Minister of Education and Cultural Affairs, BRITT MOGÅRD, also appointed to the government of Prime Minister Thorbjörn Fälldin on October 8, 1976, has been a member of the Swedish Parliament since 1969 and a member of various cultural, educational, and environmental committees. President of the women's association of the Moderata Samlingspartiet, she has published numerous articles on educational and cultural problems, dealing particularly with the family and the situation of Swedish women. Ms. Mogård was born 1922 and has taught high school.

Deputy Minister of Housing and Physical Planning

The Deputy Minister of Housing and Physical Planning in Prime Minister Thorbjörn Fälldin's Cabinet, BIRGIT FRIGGEBO, born 1941, appointed October 8, 1976, has been a member of the Housing Court since 1975 and has held office in the traffic council and the environmental protection council. Ms. Friggebo joined the Liberal Party in 1956, was chairman of the organization of Liberal Thinking Youth in 1963–64 and helped draw up the Liberal Party's housing policy. In 1971 she became a member of Stockholm's County Council, where she pursued matters relating to housing, politics, and mass transit. Ms. Friggebo is a consultant and section head in the rent negotiations division of SABO, the non-profit housing corporations' coordination agency, which she joined in 1969.

Deputy Minister of Health and Social Affairs

The fifth of the female ministers and deputies in the Cabinet of Prime Minister Thorbjörn Fälldin, INGEGERD TROEDSSON, the Deputy Minister of Health and Social Affairs, appointed October 8, 1976, has a master's degree in political science and has held many official positions within the Conservative Party. She was elected a Member of Parliament in 1973. Born in 1929, Ms. Troedsson is married and has five children.

Undersecretary of State, Ministry for Foreign Affairs, and Chairman of Sweden's Disarmament Delegation

INGA THORSSON, the one-woman "Strike for Peace" in Sweden, who turned her nation around on the issue of nuclear weapons, is the Undersecretary of State in the Ministry of Foreign Affairs, and

at the Disarmament Talks in Geneva, chairman of Sweden's Disarmament Delegation. Ms. Thorsson served as ambassador to Israel 1964–66 and is also a member of the Swedish Parliament. Her international assignments have ranged from delegate to the United Nations General Assembly, the Population Commission, and the Board for the UN Environment Program. She is the head negotiator for Sweden on issues of international population, technical and scientific cooperation, and environmental issues. A writer who has published widely in the field of disarmament, she has written most recently *For Sweden in the World.* She was born in 1915 in Malmö Sweden.

World's First Secretary of State on the Condition of Women

FRANÇOISE GIROUD, the world's first Secretary of State on the Condition of Women, was named to this unique post in France by President Valéry Giscard d'Estaing in August 1974. "What I do is very difficult because the administrative bureaucracy is very heavy and hard to move. But I think if one is obstinate, one can succeed," she said. Mme. Giroud has been obstinate and has succeeded eventually in most of her life. A screenwriter, editor of a highly successful women's magazine, and, for more than 20 years, editor-in-chief of *L'Express,* the most respected news magazine in France, Mme. Giroud dropped out of school at 15, knew such famous men as André Gide and André Malraux early, worked as a script girl for Jean Renoir in the great film *Grand Illusion,* was at one time on the edge of suicide, bore an illegitimate son, and was imprisoned under the Nazis. Her son was born during the German occupation of France, when she could neither marry nor have an abortion. He died in a mountaineering accident in 1972. After the war, she married and had a daughter, and was divorced. As a journalist, Mme. Giroud has shrewdly observed virtually every great personage of our time. When Giscard d'Estaing was running for President and campaigning as a man of the people, she asked him on television the price of a Paris subway ticket. The embarrassed candidate did not have the faintest idea, and he abandoned his campaign approach for a loftier one. Mme. Giroud wrote and voted against him. She accepted her Cabinet post presumably on her own terms but with reservations. She wrote that it seemed absurd to treat women as "another category," a kind of enclave within the nation. No matter how benevolent, she said, the post would be shocking if it meant segregation. She described that kind of attitude as "Let's be kind to the natives." In 1976 she was appointed Secretary of State for Culture in the Cabinet of Jacques Chirac.

When Giscard d'Estaing formed his second Cabinet in March 1977, Mme. Giroud was not reappointed. The office of Secretary of State on the Condition of Women was downgraded and retitled "Delegate for the Condition of Women." NICOLE PASQUIER was named to the new post. "The President," said a female official of the French Embassy in Washington, "believes we have become equal."

First Woman Minister of France

The first woman to achieve the rank of Minister in France, SIMONE VEIL, Minister of Health and Social Security, was appointed on May 28, 1974. One month to the day after assuming the office, she pushed through legislation that greatly liberalized access to contraception. Six months later, on November 29, 1974, at 3:45 A.M., Simone Veil stepped from the French National Assembly exhausted after a dramatic 30-hour debate. The Minister of Health had just won the right to abortion for all French women by a vote of 284 to 189, making France the first nation of Latin and Catholic background to legalize abortion. Although French feminists had fought for a liberalized abortion law for five years, there is

no doubt that Mme. Veil exemplified what a skilled and determined woman placed in a position of power can accomplish to benefit the lives of all women. When a deputy announced that the Order of Doctors would never tolerate abortion, she replied: "Let me remind you, sir, that no one is above the laws of the Republic." Born in Nice in 1927 of Jewish parents, Ms. Veil was sent to Auschwitz in 1944 with her mother and one of her sisters. She and a sister survived the Nazi camps; the rest of her family perished. She married in 1956 and after 10 years of studying law, the birth of three children, and frequent moves dictated by her husband's career, she gave up the law and took the qualifying exams for civil service in the judiciary. Her long career in the Ministry of Justice brought about judicial and prison reform. Eventually, she was put in charge of a special council that advised the President of the Republic on important legal issues; she handled, for example, the petitions requesting commutation of death sentences. With no expertise on health issues, she accepted the appointment as Minister of Health, because "It was an honor I couldn't refuse." She says she is not interested in elective office (she has never joined a political party) but she has headed popularity polls and has been mentioned as a future head of government.

France's Secretary of State for Universities

ALICE SAUNIER-SEITE, the first Secretary of State for Universities in France, was appointed on January 12, 1976. She was born in 1925 in Saint-Jean-le-Centenier and after completing teacher training began her career in vocational high schools. While working for her doctorate in geography, she joined the National Center for Scientific Research where she did research in geography and became a member of the standing committee. She founded a laboratory for climatology and later a laboratory for Celtic studies. After receiving her doctorate, she joined the staff of the Faculté des Lettres at Rennes. In 1969 she became dean of the Collège Littéraire Universitaire in Brest. In 1973 she was vice-president of the Université de Paris-Sud, and that same year, she was appointed director of the university at Reims, the position she held when named to the Cabinet.

Secretary of State to France's Minister of the Economy and Finance for Consumer Affairs

CHRISTIANE SCRIVENER, the first Secretary of State to the Minister of the Economy and Finance for Consumer Affairs in France, was named to this newly created post in the Cabinet of Jacques Chirac on January 12, 1976. Born in Mulhouse, 1925, Ms. Scrivener studied law and literature at the Université de Paris and linguistics at Springfield College in Massachusetts. She earned a degree from the Harvard Business School. A senior civil servant, active in initiating exchange programs between leading engineers and other experts in France and abroad, in 1958 she founded the Association for the Organization of Training Programs, and in 1961 the Association for the Organization of Technical Cooperation Missions. The work of these bodies is combined in the Agency for Technical, Industrial, and Economic Cooperation, under the Department of Foreign Economic Relations. Ms. Scrivener was director of this agency before her cabinet appointment.

First Woman in the Italian Cabinet

The first woman to serve in the Italian Cabinet, TINA ANSELMI, was initiated into politics as a student in a Roman Catholic girl's school during World War II when she joined the partisan movement and ran messages for Catholic partisans fighting the Fascists. Those wartime connections with the then-underground Christian Democratic Party led her into the trade union movement, her springboard to a political career. She has served in the Italian Parliament since 1969. On July 30, 1976, she was picked by Premier Giulio Andreotti to serve as Labor Minister in strike-prone Italy, where the Christian Democratic Party depends on the Communist Party for its survival. Her credentials appeal to both Catholics and leftists. Although she is against abortion reform, she has fought the feminist battle within the Italian Parliament.

First Woman Health Minister in Germany

ELISABETH SCHWARZHAUPT was appointed Health Minister of West Germany in 1961; it was the first time a woman held the position and the first time a woman had held a cabinet position in the country. During her five years in office Ms. Schwarzhaupt, a lawyer, worked on such problems as air, water, and noise pollution and was a staunch advocate of health education.

Germany's Minister for Economic Co-operation

On December 15, 1976, MARIE SCHLEI received her letter of appointment as fifth Minister for Economic Cooperation from German Federal President Walter Scheel. Ms. Schlei, a political leader from Berlin, is following in the footsteps of the President himself, who served in the same job, 1961–66. A member of the German Federal Parliament since 1969, Ms. Schlei was Parliamentary State Secretary to the Federal Chancellor from May 1974 until 1976. Chancellor Helmut Schmidt said of her appointment: "Anyone who is as devoted as she is to fighting for the rights of those who are particularly dependent upon social solidarity, and who also has her spontaneity and warm heart, will continue to be an asset to the German Government." Ms. Schlei was born in 1919 in Reetz near Stargard. Her father was a plumber, her mother a factory worker. She left school after completing the sixth grade to become a temporary shop assistant and later a post office clerk. Her first husband was killed in World War II. In January 1945 she fled with her three-year-old son from Soviet troops and lived for almost three years with relatives near Hanover. She attended evening classes in Berlin to train as a teacher, taught in a working class area of Berlin, had two children by a second marriage, and became a headmistress and school inspector. She joined the Social Democratic Party in 1949, did ground work on social issues, workers' welfare, and the role of women, and in 1972 was elected to the Executive Board of the party's Parliamentary Group.

Germany's Minister for Youth, Family Affairs, and Health

ANTJE HUBER, Germany's Federal Minister for Youth, Family Affairs, and Health, was appointed to the post on December 16, 1976. She is a member of the German Bundestag who was first elected in 1969 and reelected in 1972 and in 1976. Ms. Huber was born in Stettin in 1924, trained as a journalist, and became an editor. In 1948 she joined the Social Democratic Party. In 1961–62 she studied social policy at the Social Academy and later tutored there. She became a member of the SPD Federal Executive in November 1975.

Germany's Minister of State in the Foreign Office

The second-highest-ranking political official in Germany's Ministry of Foreign Affairs, Dr. HILDEGARD HAMM-BRÜCHER, the Minister of State in the Federal Foreign Office in Bonn, is a member of the German Parliament and a leader of the Free Democratic Party (FDP) caucus. She has been a member of the FDP Executive since 1953 and deputy chairman from 1972 to 1976. In her cabinet post, Dr. Hamm-Brücher conducts negotiations with foreign countries, represents the Foreign Minister before the Parliament, and stands in for the Foreign Minister whenever necessary. She was State Secretary in the Federal Ministry for Education and Science from 1969 to 1972. A doctor of chemistry, Dr. Hamm-Brücher studied at Harvard University from 1949 to 1950. She was born in Essen, 1921.

First Woman Minister in Austria

The first woman member of the Austrian Government, GRETE REHOR, was appointed Minister of Social Administration in 1966 and served until April 21, 1970. She set up a Division of Women's Affairs within the Ministry in 1966. Born on June 30, 1910, Grete Rehor was active in the trade union movement and the Austrian People's Party. She was a member of the federal party executive until 1970 and received the Grand Medal of Honor of the Republic of Austria. She died in a car accident in 1972.

Austria's Federal Minister of Science and Research

Austria's Federal Minister of Science and Research, Dr. HERTHA FIRNBERG, was born in 1909, the daughter of a Lower Austrian rural district doctor, and has been active in Socialist politics since her school days. After obtaining a Ph.D. in three subjects, Dr. Firnberg in 1959 sat in the Upper House of the Federal Parliament as a representative of the Socialist Party. In 1963 she was elected to the Lower House. She was invited to join the Federal Government of Austria on April 21, 1970. As a delegate to the Council of Europe, Dr. Firnberg is vice-president of the commissions for Health and Social Affairs and Refugee and Population Affairs.

Austria's Secretary of State for Family Affairs

ELFRIEDE KARL rose from a typing job with a trade union to Secretary of State for Family Affairs in Austria's Federal

Chancellery in only 11 years. Ms. Karl, born 1933, was appointed to the post on November 4, 1971. A member of the Austrian Federal Trade Union and the Austrian Socialist Party, she worked as a secretary for the Social Academy of the Chamber for Workers and Employees 1960–61, and from 1961 to 1971 held successively more responsible jobs in the Chamber, in Salzburg.

Poland's and Denmark's First Female Cabinet Ministers

NINA BANG, who held the Education portfolio in the Danish Cabinet 1924–26, was the first female Minister in Denmark and second in the world—after Poland's IRENE KOSMOWSKA, who was briefly Vice-Minister of Social Welfare for her country in 1918. Ms. Bang, schoolteacher, was elected a member of the Upper Chamber of the Danish Parliament in 1918. As Minister for Education, Ms. Bang was the first woman member of the first Social Democratic government. She worked for school reform laws, and took an active interest in the Danish National Museum. She was born in 1866 and died in 1928.

Denmark's Mother-Daughter Ministers

DORTE BENNEDSEN, former Minister of Ecclesiastical Affairs for Denmark, and a prominent educator and activist for consumer affairs, has fought for extended sex education and the liberalization of abortion laws. An ordained minister, who served as a Navy chaplain in Copenhagen in the 1960s, Ms. Bennedsen was secretary-general of the Danish Youth Council before joining the government. Her mother, BODIL KOCH, was the first woman ever named Church Minister in Denmark, and held that post for 13 years (1953–66).

Denhark's Most Recent Woman Minister for Education

Ms. RITT BJERREGAARD, born 1941, was appointed Denmark's Minister for Edu-cation on February 25, 1977, in the Cabinet of Prime Minister Anker Jørgensen. Ms. Bjerregaard is a Social Democrat who was elected to Parliament in 1971. A teacher with postgraduate training, she was Teachers' Council Chairman from 1968 to 1970. She served as Minister for Education in 1973 and in 1975. She is the author of several textbooks.

Denmark's Minister for Social Affairs

EVA GREDAL, a member of the Social Democratic Party in Denmark, was appointed Minister for Social Affairs in Prime Minister Anker Jørgensen's Cabinet on February 25, 1977. A social worker, who was chairman of the National Association of Social Workers 1959–67, Ms. Gredal was elected to Denmark's Parliament in 1971. She was Minister for Social Affairs in 1971 and 1972–73, vice-chairman of the National Association of Mental Health from 1967 to 1971 and member of the Advisory Committee on Social Affairs during the same period; and a member of the committee on Sexual Education 1964–69. She is married and has four children.

Denmark's Minister Without Portfolio, Ministry of Foreign Affairs

LISE ØSTERGAARD, Denmark's Minister Without Portfolio in the Ministry of Foreign Affairs, was appointed to her post by Prime Minister Anker Jørgensen, whose Social Democratic government was formed on February 25, 1977. Dr. Østergaard is a professor of psychology well known for her scientific articles and books. She was a member of the Danish UNESCO National Commission 1970–73, and president of Danish Refugee Aid from 1974. Dr. Østergaard was born in 1924 and received her Ph.D. in 1962.

Norway's Minister of the Environment

Dr. GRO HARLEM BRUNDTLAND, Norway's Minister of the Environment since

January 14, 1976, is considered a possible future Prime Minister. Her current post grows in political importance as the North Sea oil boom turns environmental protection and planning into major political issues in Norway. Dr. Brundtland, born 1939 in Oslo, took her medical degree in 1963. After a year's study at Harvard University, she qualified as a Master of Public Health. She has been actively involved in political youth work, as vice-chairman of the Senior Secondary Schools' Socialist Association and the Student's Association of the Labor Party. She was first appointed a member of Trygve Bratteli's second Labor Government as Minister of the Environment in 1974. In 1976 she was reappointed by Odvar Nordli.

Norway's Minister of Social Affairs

Norway's Minister of Social Affairs, RUTH RYSTE, born 1932, was appointed on January 14, 1976. Her career has been based on trade union and political activities in the National Union of Government Employees. After service as chairman of the Telemark branch of the National Association of Social Insurance Workers from 1968, she was elected secretary to the Association from 1970. In the autumn of 1973, she was appointed political secretary in the Ministry of Consumer Affairs and Government Administration. In autumn of 1974, she took over as secretary of the Confederation of Civil Servant Unions. In all these positions, she has had a special responsibility for matters relating to social welfare policies. She has been a member of the Central Executive of the Norwegian Labor Party.

Norway's Minister of Consumer Affairs and Government Administration

Ms. ANNEMARIE LORENTZEN was appointed Norway's Minister of Consumer Affairs and Government Administration on January 14, 1976. She was elected a Member of Parliament in 1969 and during the period 1969–73 served on the Standing Committee on Defense. She was appointed Minister of Communications in the Labor Government of Trygve Bratteli in 1973. A member of the National Executive of the Labor Party from 1961 to 1969, Ms. Lorentzen is now chairman of the Secretariat of the women's branch of the Labor Party. She taught secondary school from 1947 to 1969.

Norway's Minister of Justice

INGER LOUISE ANDVIG VALLE, Norway's first consumer ombudsman, was appointed Minister of Justice on January 14, 1976, following five years as a cabinet member. She was Minister for Family and Consumer Affairs from 1971 to 1972; Minister for Consumer Affairs and Government Administration from 1972 to 1973; and Minister of Justice in the Labor Government of Trygve Bratteli from 1973 until she was reappointed in 1976. Ms. Valle, a lawyer, who was born in Oslo in 1921, was executive and head of the Consumer Affairs' Council from 1958 to 1971. She has been chairman of a municipal committee on protection of the environment and a member of a series of committees on law and chairman of a Nordic Committee on Consumer Affairs.

Finland's Minister of Social Affairs and Health

A new government in Finland, appointed on May 15, 1977, included one female minister, PIRKKO ANNIKKI TYÖLÄJÄRVI, Minister of Social Affairs and Health. A Member of Parliament since 1972, Ms. Työläjärvi became vice-chairman of the Finnish Social Democratic Party in 1975. She was Minister at the Ministry of Social Affairs and Health in 1975–76, a job now held by a man; acting economic manager of Rauma Regional Hospital 1970–71 and office manageress at Rauma City Tax Office since 1971. She was born in 1938.

Finland named its first female cabinet member, MIINA SILLANPAA, early, in 1926, and was the first country in the world to have female members of Parliament—19 in 1907.

Soviet Women in Government

According to *Women of a New World,* an official Soviet publication issued in 1969, approximately 875,000 women (43 per cent of the total number of deputies) were elected to local government bodies in Russia in 1967. There were 425 women (28 per cent) in the Supreme Soviet elected in 1966, and 2,983 (more than 30 per cent) in the Supreme Soviets of Union and Autonomous Republics elected in 1967. More recent figures are not available.

At that time, YEKATERINA FURTSEVA, long-term Minister of Culture of the U.S.S.R. was the highest-ranking woman in the Soviet Government. (She still is.) There were four women in the Presidium of the Supreme Soviet of the U.S.S.R.: ZOYA PUKHOVA, a textile worker; ANNA KASATKINA, chairman of a collective farm; ANNA NUTETEGRYNE, chairman of the Chukotka National Area Executive Committee; and YADGAR NASRIDDINOVA, president of the Presidium of the Supreme Soviet of Uzbekistan, and one of the first Uzbek women to become an engineer. Five women were presidents (more or less the equivalent of governors) in the Autonomous Republics: YEFIMIA YASHKINA, a Mordovian, whose people 50 years ago had no written language of their own; TAMARA KHETAGUROVA, of the North-Ossetian Soviet, who is an outstanding economist; ALEXANDRA OVCHINNIKOVA, of the Yakut A.S.S.R., who worked for many years as a road-building technical engineer; BAIKARA DOLCHANMAA, of the Tuva A.S.S.R., born into a family of nomad shepherds; and SAKINA ALIYEVA, president of the Presidium of the Supreme Soviet of the Nakhichevan A.S.S.R. There were also at the time the book was published, 13 women vice-presidents of Presidiums in different republics, 10 vice-chairmen of Councils of Ministers, and 27 ministers of Union republics.

Ireland's First Woman Parliamentary Secretary

Twenty-six-year-old MARIE GEOGHEGAN QUINN became the first woman ever to hold so high a post in the Irish Government when Prime Minister Jack Lynch on July 5, 1977, named her Parliamentary Secretary to the Minister of Industry and Commerce. Ms. Quinn, a member of the ruling Fianna Fail, Eire's second largest political party, is a schoolteacher from Carna in County Galway, married, with a two-year-old son. Elected to Parliament in 1975, she took over her father's seat following his death.

Of the five women now serving in the Republic of Ireland's 146-seat Parliament, Marie Quinn is one of two young politicians from families in which political participation is a tradition: the other is SILE DE VALERA, 22, daughter of Eamon de Valera, former President of Ireland.

Australia's First Female Cabinet Member with Portfolio and First Female Ambassador

The Honourable Dame ANNABELLE RANKIN was a member of the Australian Parliament for twenty years before her appointment as the first woman in Australian history to administer a federal department. She was named Minister of Housing on January 26, 1966. She was also Australia's first woman ambassador in 1971, when she was appointed high commissioner to New Zealand. Born in Brisbane on July 29, 1908, Dame Rankin was active in World War II as an assistant commissioner attached to the Army in charge of welfare work for all women's services. After the war, she was organizer of the Junior Red Cross in Queensland. Her parliamentary career began in 1946 when she was elected to the Senate. From 1947 to 1949, she was Opposition Whip in the Senate and Government Whip from 1951 until her appointment as Minister for Housing.

Australia's Minister for Social Security

Of six female members of the Australian Senate, only one is a Minister. She is the Honourable MARGARET GEORGINA CONSTANCE GUILFOYLE, a member of the Liberal Party, who was named Minister for Social Security on December 22, 1975. She was elected to the Senate in 1970 and reelected in 1974. She became Minister for Education on November 12, 1975, but after the election of December 13, 1975, was named Minister for Social Security. Born in 1926, in Belfast, Northern Ireland, she came to Australia as a child. An accountant, who was a licensed auditor of public companies before her election to Parliament, she has been active in the women's section of the Liberal Party. Senator Guilfoyle is married and has three children.

Fiji's First Ministerial Woman

Member of Parliament and government whip of the Parliament of Fiji, national secretary of the Fijian Association Political Party, and Assistant Minister for Urban Development, Housing and Social Welfare, ADI LOSALINI DOVI worked her way up through the ranks. She began as a stenographer in Fiji's civil service, was private secretary to Ratu Sir Lala Sukuna (the "Father of Modern Fiji"), and became a member of the legislative Council (1966–70). A widow, with four children, she was awarded the Fiji Independence Medal (1970).

First Woman of Cabinet Rank in Mauritania

The first woman to attain cabinet rank in the Islamic Republic of Mauritania, TOURE AISSATA KANE, was appointed Minister for the Protection of the Family and for Social Affairs on August 22, 1975. A teacher and pioneer in the movement for women's liberation in this Islamic Republic, Ms. Kane began the women's movement in her country in 1963. In 1969 she was secretary of information in the National Movement for Women, and director of the movement magazine called *Marienou*. In 1970 she served as president of the Superior Women Council. She was born at Dar El Barka.

Unified Vietnam's First Minister of Education

The top negotiator for the Viet Cong at the Paris Peace talks in January 1973, NGUYEN THI BINH, known as the "flower and fire of the revolution" to her people, has been a Communist Party leader for 30 years and member of the top echelon of the National Liberation Front since its formation in 1960. She served as Minister of Foreign Affairs after North Vietnam defeated the South in April 1975. When the two Vietnams were unified on July 2, 1976, she was appointed Minister of Education. Ms. Binh was born in Saigon in 1927. Her family was middle-class and French-educated; her grandfather Phan Chu Trinh was a nationalist leader. Ms. Binh joined the student movement when she was studying for her bachelor's degree. After participating in demonstrations against the French, she was arrested in 1951 and spent three years in prison where she reportedly was tortured "with water and electricity." She chaired the Women's Liberation Association of the NLF from 1963 to 1966 and organized and recruited peasant women to serve as spies, political agitators, soldiers, and health officers. *L'Express* called her "a sort of Joan of Arc of the rice paddies." "If you asked us who is the winner, we would like to say, peace is the winner," she said a few days after the peace agreement was signed.

Other Female Minister "Firsts"

Belgium's RIKA DE BACKER-VAN OCKEN, June 1977, Minister for Flemish Cultural Affairs; Marguerite de Reimacker-Legot, 1965, Minister of Family and Housing.

Colombia's ESMERALDA ARBOLEDA DE CUEVAS CANCINO, Minister of Transport, 1960–62, also the first Colombian woman to be elected to the Senate, also ambassador to Austria and Yugoslavia, 1966–68.

East Germany's MARGOT HONECKER, Minister of Education since 1963, wife of the head of state and Communist Party president Erich Honecker.

India's Rajkumari AMRIT KAUR, (1889–1964), Minister of Health in the new government of the republic from independence in 1947 to 1957, also founder and president until her death of the Indian Red Cross, also a founder of the All-India Women's Conference in 1926.

Indonesia's Ms. MARIA ULFAH SANTOSO, Minister of Social Affairs, 1946–47.

Malaya's TAN SRI FATIMAH, holder of the Portfolio for Social Welfare, 1973.

New Zealand's MABEL HOWARD, Minister of Health and Child Welfare, 1947.

Nicaragua's OLGA NUÑEZ DE SASALLOW, Deputy Minister of Public Education, 1950–56, also first woman in Nicaragua to get a law degree.

Norway's KIRSTEN MOE HANSTEEN, first Minister Without Portfolio, June–November, 1945.

Portugal's MARIA TERESA CARCOMO LOBO, first woman to hold a cabinet-level post, Undersecretary of State for Welfare, August 21, 1970, to November 7, 1973; MARIA MANUELA MOR-GADO, Undersecretary of State for Public Investments, December 1975 to July 1976; Secretary of State for Finance, July 29, 1976, to March 25, 1977, appointed Secretary of State for Treasury on March 25, 1977, and holds this post concurrently with that of Secretary of State for Finance; MARIA MANUELA SILVA, Secretary of State for Planning, July to October 1977; MARIA DE LOURDES PINTASSILGO, Secretary of State for Social Security, May 15 to July 17, 1974, Minister of Social Welfare, July 11, 1974, to March 26, 1975; MARIA ISABEL CARMELO ROSA, Secretary of State for Consumer Protection, December 1975 to July 1976.

Romania's ANA PAUKER, Minister of Foreign Affairs, 1944.

Venezuela's AURA CELINA CASANOVA, Minister for Development, 1969.

Zaïre's LUSIBU Z. N'KANZA, at 26 named Minister of State responsible for Social Affairs in what was then called the Democratic Republic of the Congo, a job in which she served 1966–71.

Pakistan's First Woman Governor

The most influential woman in the history of Pakistan's modern government, BEGUM LIAQUAT ALI KHAN, a professor of economics, led the Pakistan delegation to the United Nations in 1952 and served as ambassador to the Netherlands in 1954. In 1973 she became the first woman in Pakistan to be governor of a state (Sind). Always active in the women's movement, she has formed many women's organizations, including Pakistan's Women's National Guard.

TOP DIPLOMATS, WORLDWIDE

Except for the unusual instances of Switzerland and Soviet Russia, the foregoing pages do not include many of the hundreds of women, worldwide, who have been elected or appointed governors of states within nations or elected or appointed to their countries' legislatures. They are far more numerous than the example of the United States, which follows (pp. 65ff.), would lead one to guess. The numbers of women who have been first to represent or currently represent their governments abroad as ambassadors or high commissioners (the British Commonwealth equivalent title) are fewer and more manageable, however. Some notable examples follow:

Australia's RUTH DOBSON, first career ambassador, to Denmark, 1974; ANABELLE RANKIN, first woman to head a diplomatic mission, high commissioner to New Zealand, appointed 1971; MARIS KING, third woman in Australian history to head a mission and second career diplomat to do so, a specialist on the South Pacific region who worked her way up in the service from clerk-typist and in January 1977 was named Australia's high commissioner to Naura.
Belgium's E. DEVER, ambassador to Stockholm since 1973.
Brazil's current and recent woman ambassadors (about 12 per cent of the Brazilian foreign service is female): MARIA DE LOURDES CASTRO E SILVA DE VINVENZI, appointed ambassador to Costa Rica in 1974; DORA VASCONCELOS, ambassador to Canada and Trinidad and Tobago, 1965–66; BEATA VETTORI, ambassador to Ecuador and Senegal, 1969, and first woman ambassador to the European Economic Community, 1959–60.
Colombia's ESMERALDA ARBOLEDA DE CUEVAS CANCINO, first woman ambassador, to Austria and Yugoslavia, 1966–68; ELENADE CROVO, Minister of Labor in 1976, now ambassador to Mexico.
Denmark's BODIL BEGTRUP, 1959–68, ambassador in Berne, 1968–73, in Lisbon; NONNY WRIGHT, since 1976 ambassador to Peru.
Finland's first female ambassador, in Oslo, 1958–65; EEVA-KRISTINA FORSMAN, to Belgium 1975–76, and Greece since 1976, rising from the position of trainee in foreign affairs in 1956 to an assignment as attaché in Washington, D.C., to her present rank of ambassador; RIITTA ORO, ambassador to India, Bangladesh, Singapore, Sri Lanka, and Nepal, various dates from 1974–75, up from a trainee's job in 1959.
France's CHRISTIANE MALITCHENKO, ambassador to Bulgaria since 1975.
Germany's ELLINOR PUTTKAMER, first ambassador to Council of European States, 1969, MARGARET HUTTON, ambassador to El Salvador, 1972; Dr. HILDEGUNDE FLEINER, accredited to the European Council in 1975, has also served in Sri Lanka and Singapore.
Ghana's AMONNO WILLIAMS, ambassador to Luxembourg, 1972.
Great Britain's ambassador to Denmark Ms. A. M. WARBURTON, serving in 1977.
India's high commissioner in Ghana, Ms. C. B. MUTHAMMA; Mrs. K. RUKMINI MENON, ambassador in Italy; Ms. MANORAMA GHALLA, ambassador in Peru. (See also ambassador to the United Nations, Ms. VIJAYALAKSHMI PANDIT, p. 63.)
Indonesia's Ms. LAILI RUSAD, 1959, became first woman ambassador for Belgium and Luxembourg; 1967, ambassador to Austria.
Ireland's ambassador MARY TINNEY, to Sweden, 1973.
Israel's ESTHER HERLITZ, ambassador to

Denmark in 1977. (See also GOLDA MEIR, p. 46.)

Japan's SAKADO OGATA, first female diplomat of ministerial rank, 1976.

Jordan's first and only female ambassador, LAURICE HLASS, a Palestinian who lost her home in 1948 and took refuge in Amman, becoming a Jordanian citizen, appointed ambassador in 1969 after many years in the diplomatic corps and represented Jordan at three sessions of the UN General Assembly.

Paraguay's first woman with diplomatic rank, ISABEL ARRUA VALLEJO, attaché of the Embassy of Paraguay to Brazil, 1945–48.

Philippines' Ambassador to Romania LETICIA RAMO SHAHANI, also chairman of the UN Commission on the Status of Women.

Sweden's AGDA RÖSSEL, ALVA MYRDAL, and INGA THORSSON (see also pp. 64, 51, 53).

Uganda's (and the world's) first woman ambassador to the Vatican, BERNADETTE OLOWO, who broke a 900-year tradition that kept female envoys out of the Holy See.

Venezuela's IDA GRAMCKO, ambassador to the U.S.S.R. in 1948.

WOMEN IN THE UNITED NATIONS

First Woman President of the United Nations General Assembly

On September 15, 1953, H.E. Ms. VIJAYALAKSHMI PANDIT of India became the first woman elected president of the United Nations General Assembly. (Only one other woman, Dr. ANGIE BROOKS of Liberia, has been elected to the office since.) The first woman to hold a cabinet position in India, Ms. Pandit was Minister for Local Government and Health in 1937. At the time of her UN election, Ms. Pandit said she did not want to be regarded as "Exhibit A from India." Nor did she care to have undue emphasis placed on her election as the first woman to head the annual meeting of the then 60 member states. "All my political training has taught me to look on myself as an individual, not essentially as a woman. I don't care for this emphasis on women as women. It is an honor for my country rather than an honor for a woman. The principles and purposes of the United Nations Charter belong to human beings, not to men or women." Ms. Pandit, prior to her election, served as her country's ambassador to the United States and Moscow and on several Indian delegations to earlier UN Assembly meetings. She won an inter-

national reputation in the 1930s and '40s fighting for India's independence at the side of her brother, former Prime Minister Jawaharlal Nehru. The daughter of a noted Indian lawyer, Motilal Nehru, educated privately at home except for a few years in Switzerland, imprisoned for civil disobedience three times, a member of the Parliament of India who held many political posts, Ms. Pandit regards her most rewarding work as Minister of Health in the Province of Uttar Pradesh. A graceful, silver-haired, sari-clad woman of 53 when she was elected Assembly president, Ms. Pandit, famous for her fiery speeches on behalf of countries stirred by strong nationalistic tides, said she saw India's transition from colonial status to independence as a lesson for the rest of the world. ("We fought the British Colonial system but we never developed hatred for the British people: as soon as the system ended, India stretched out the hand of welcome") but declared that as UN President, she would disassociate herself from the Indian delegation and act to discharge her new duties with complete impartiality. Most observers agreed that she did just that throughout her year of service.

First Woman to Head a Permanent Delegation to the United Nations

On August 8, 1958, AGDA RÖSSEL of Sweden, became the first woman to head a delegation to the United Nations. She had represented her nation at the United Nations for seven years and had served on the UN commissions on Human Rights and the Status of Women. She was appointed permanent representative with the rank of ambassador and was president of the Commission on the Status of Women, 1956–57. In 1964 Ms. Rössel was appointed Sweden's ambassador to Yugoslavia. Born in Gällivare, Sweden, 1910, she learned to be sensitive to the needs of others at an early age. She was compelled to leave school when she was quite young because her mother became critically ill, and she took care of a household of seven people. She went on to study nursing, and after World War II Ms. Rössel became chief of international activities of the Swedish Save-the-Children Federation. In this capacity, she went to displaced persons' camps in Austria and Germany, set up vocational guidance hostels for young people, and helped to bring 10,000 refugees to Sweden. She also helped organize the Swedish Central Organization of Salaried Employees in the early 1940s. As a member of the UN Commission on Human Rights she disagreed with opinions voiced by Eleanor Roosevelt (see "Women Activists, Heroes, and Humanitarians," p. 738) and by Mme. HANSA METHA of India that the word "women" should appear in an article dealing with the right to "just and favorable conditions of work." In opposition, Ms. Rössel maintained that women were protected by the covenant that reads "without distinction of any kind such as race, color, sex" and were better off not being singled out. She also objected to the statement that working women cannot be good mothers.

Liberia's First Woman Lawyer and the World's Second Woman President of the UN General Assembly

The first woman to practice law in Liberia, Dr. ANGIE BROOKS was the second woman elected president of the UN General Assembly. Her election in 1969 came 16 years after Ms. VIJAYALAKSHMI PANDIT's. Dr. Brooks's election represented the culmination of more than 40 years' work as a lawyer, activist, stateswoman, and humanitarian. Always a champion of the rights of women and the concept of public education for all, she helped establish Liberia's first law school and succeeded in breaking down the traditional exclusion of women from the Liberian Bar Association. She was the first woman in Liberia to hold a cabinet post, and later, after leading numerous delegations to conferences and commissions around the world, she became assistant to the Liberian ambassador to the UN. On his resignation, she was named ambassador. She was Assistant Secretary of State of Liberia from 1958 to 1973, served as ambassador-at-large, 1973–75, is Liberia's permanent representative to the United Nations, and, in 1975, she was also named ambassador to Cuba. Angie Brooks's achievements would be remarkable for any woman, but viewed in the light of her back-country origins, they become astounding. At the time of her schooling, the cost of education in Liberia's class-structured society was prohibitive. The determined Ms. Brooks, however, worked her way through high school as a typist for the Treasury Department and later as a stenotypist for the Justice Department, where her interest in lawmaking was fostered. At that time aspiring attorneys gained their experience through apprenticeship. No woman had ever been accepted as an apprentice until Angie Brooks convinced Clarence L. Simpson (later Liberia's Foreign Minister) to take her on. Unfortunately his liberal attitudes were not shared by many; at her first court appearance Ms. Brooks was ridiculed by judges and observers alike. A law career still her objective, she began to petition Liberian President William Tubman to take an interest in her plight. Impressed by her sincerity and determination, he granted her passage money to the United States, where she worked her way through college and received a B.A. degree from Shaw University in North Carolina and later an LL.B. and M.S. from the University of Wisconsin. She followed these studies with a stint at the University College Law School of London to steep herself in international law before returning home. Not just a lawyer and stateswoman decorated by 19 nations, Angie Brooks in her great lifetime has managed to raise and put through school 47 foster children.

First Woman President of the UN Security Council

JEANNE MARTIN CISSÉ made history on November 15, 1972, when she was elected to preside over the UN Security Council, the first woman ever to do so. Ms. Cissé is not only the only woman ever elected president of the Security Council, she is also the only woman in Security Council history to serve as a representative on the Council. (Two other women have served as alternates: Señora ANA FIGUEROA of Chile in 1952 and Señora EMILA CASTRO DE BARISH of Costa Rica in 1974. Ms. Cissé was also the first woman ever appointed as a permanent delegate to the United Nations, from Guinea, and presented her credentials on August 2, 1972. Prior to her UN assignment, Ms. Cissé was Sec-

retary-General of the Conference of African Women, an international non-governmental organization, 1962–72, and the First Vice-President of the Guinean National Assembly. Born April 1926, she began her career as a teacher and became director of a school from 1954 to 1958. She held numerous trade union, political, and governmental positions, including First Secretary and Second Vice-President of the National Assembly. Ms. Cissé is married and has six children.

Highest-Ranking Woman at the United Nations

The highest-ranking woman in the UN Secretariat, Finland's HELVI LINNEA SIPILA, took up her duties as Assistant Secretary General for Social Development and Humanitarian Affairs, on September 1, 1973. She came to the post as Secretary-General for International Women's Year and the World Conference of the International Women's Year, with broad experience as a lawyer and leader in national and international affairs in fields of equality, development, and peace. She was born on May 5, 1915, in Helsinki, Finland, and graduated from the faculty of Law of the University of Helsinki in 1939. The second woman in Finland to found a law office, she has held leadership positions in many national and international non-governmental agencies. She was a member of the Finnish Delegation to the General Assembly from 1966 to 1971, becoming chairman of the Third Committee in 1971, and was chairman of the UN Commission of the Status of Women. She is married and has four children.

LEGISLATORS, U.S.A.

First (and Oldest) Woman to Serve in the U. S. Senate

The first woman to serve in the U. S. Senate, REBECCA LATIMER FELTON, a

Democrat, got there by appointment and served only one day—November 21–22, 1922. The then 87-year-old outspoken and highly political woman, who had worked long and hard for female suffrage, was appointed as a token gesture to win support from women by a Georgia governor who had opposed the suffrage movement. "The word 'sex' has been obliterated from the Constitution," she said on accepting her appointment. "There are now no limitations upon the ambitions of women." Ms. Felton was born in Decatur, Georgia, on June 10, 1835, and died in Atlanta on January 24, 1930.

Women Elected or Appointed to the U. S. Senate

Hazel Hampel Abel (R., elected 1954)
Eva Bowring (R., appointed 1954)
Vera Cahalan Bushfield (R., appointed 1948)
Hattie Wyatt Caraway (D., elected 1931)
Elaine S. Edwards (D., appointed 1972)
Rebecca Latimer Felton (Ind. D., appointed 1922)
Dixie Bibb Graves (D., appointed 1937)
Muriel Humphrey (D., appointed 1978)
Rose McConnell Long (D., appointed 1936)
Maurine Brown Neuberger (D., elected 1960)
Gladys Pyle (R., appointed 1938)
Margaret Chase Smith (R., elected 1948)

All 11 women senators were first elected or appointed to Congress to fill the unexpired terms of members who resigned or died in office. Margaret Chase Smith (opposite) was first elected to the House of Representatives to complete the term of her husband, who died in office. Six other women senators were elected or appointed to complete their deceased husbands' Senate terms. Only three women—Hattie W. Caraway (below), Maurine Neuberger (p. 67), and Margaret Chase Smith were elected to full six-year terms in the Senate.

First Woman Elected to the U. S. Senate

Despite a traditional background and beliefs making it unlikely that she would arrive at such historic firsts, Democrat HATTIE WYATT CARAWAY became the first woman elected to the U. S. Senate, the first to chair a committee, the first to conduct Senate hearings, and the first to preside over Senate sessions. As the wife of a senator, Ms. Caraway had adhered closely to the theme "a woman's place is in the home" and rarely made public or even social appearances. After the women's suffrage amendment passed, she is said to have remarked, "After suffrage, I just added voting to cooking and sewing." But although she had promised the governor of Arkansas, who appointed her to her husband's seat on his death, that she would retire at the expiration of his term, she abruptly decided to run for a full term on her own. She had enjoyed a brief taste of power and wished to continue. Senator Huey Long of Louisiana became her political mentor, providing the surprise ingredient that brought her victory at the polls in 1932. She won the election with a vote that equaled her six opponents' combined. A populist like Long, Hattie Caraway was against big business, particularly "Wall Street," and she showed a strong interest in farm relief, flood control, legislations against lobbies, and safety in commercial aviation. She was defeated in 1944 by J. William Fulbright.

Longest Incumbent Woman in Congress

MARGARET CHASE SMITH, born in Skowhegan, Maine, on December 14, 1897, served in the U. S. Senate for 23 years (January 2, 1949, to January 3, 1973) and the House for nine years (June 10, 1940, to January 3, 1949), which distinguishes her as having the longest incumbency of any woman senator and the third longest of any woman to serve in the U. S. Congress. Mrs. Smith succeeded to her husband's seat in the

House after his death, but she far surpassed him politically. Although she voted at least 95 per cent of the time along party lines, she was a gutsy individualist and the first Republican to attack Wisconsin Senator Joseph McCarthy on the floor of the Senate at a time when, as she later said, "the then junior senator from Wisconsin had the Senate paralyzed with fear that he would purge any senator who disagreed with him." Smith announced her intention to capture her party's presidential nomination on January 27, 1964, saying: "When people keep telling you you can't do a thing, you kind of like to try it." She received more delegate votes than any candidate except the nominee, Barry Goldwater. Her perfect attendance record, for which she is admiringly remembered, proved her downfall when, at age 74, she was defeated by a much younger opponent. She made it a practice never to campaign when the Senate was in session, and despite her history as the state's biggest vote-getter, 1972 was not a good year for seniority.

Oregon's Woman in the Senate

It was no surprise that MAURINE BROWN NEUBERGER should succeed her late husband, Richard Neuberger, as senator from Oregon after his death. She was elected senator in 1960 and began her one term on January 3, 1961. A former two-term member of the Oregon House of Representatives, she was a seasoned campaigner and politician, and an advocate of the liberal Democratic policies also espoused by her husband. She and her husband were the first husband-and-wife team to serve in both chambers of a state legislature; she was elected to Oregon's House when her husband was a member of its Senate. Senator Neuberger's interests revolved around consumer legislation, health and education, conservation, and implementing the metric system for use in the United States. She was never fearful of controversy.

She took on the tobacco industry in a nationwide antismoking campaign, and is responsible for the slogan that appears on all cigarette packages and in cigarette advertising warning about health dangers. Like so many women in politics, she was disadvantaged by a lack of funds in running for office and decided against vying for a second term in 1966.

First Woman Elected to the U. S. House of Representatives

The first woman elected to the U. S. House of Representatives, Republican JEANETTE RANKIN got there four years before the 19th Amendment gave women across the United States the right to vote. A native of Missoula, Montana, born 1880, she was elected in 1916 from her home state, which had already passed a suffrage amendment. A peace advocate as well as a suffragette before her election, Miss Rankin was the only member of Congress to vote against U.S. entry into World War I. She noted that the war was being fought for democracy and urged that women be granted their "small measure of democracy." Defeated in a bid for the Senate in 1919 because of her antiwar stand, her inability to get the Republican nomination, and suffragette leader Carrie Chapman Catt's failure to support her, Miss Rankin continued to work for peace and consumer causes as a lobbyist, and returned to Congress for one term in 1941. This time, she distinguished herself as the only member to vote against U.S. entry into World War II. This vote ended her political career. In 1968 she led a group of women (named the Jeannette Rankin Brigade in her honor) in a protest against the Vietnam War on the Capitol steps. Jeannette Rankin died on May 18, 1973.

Longest Incumbent Woman in Congress

There's no doubt that EDITH NOURSE ROGERS, who served the longest incumbency of any woman in Congress, became more prominent than her husband, whose death prompted her entrance into politics. Even in the special election held after his death, she outpolled his vote of the preceding fall. Her first term began on December 7, 1925. She served 19 terms until her death on September 10, 1960. A Republican from Massachusetts, she left an outstanding record in vet-

erans' affairs, an interest that stemmed from service during World War I with the Red Cross and the YWCA. She eventually became chairman of the Veterans Affairs Committee and sponsored a law that appropriated $15 million to begin a network of veterans' hospitals. She also sponsored bills creating women's branches in the armed services.

Women Who Have Chaired Congressional Committees

Seven women have chaired congressional committees to date. The first, MAE ELLA NOLAN, who was elected in 1923 as the widow of Representative John Nolan (R., Calif.), chaired the House Committee on Expenditures in the Post Office Department in the 68th Congress; she retired after one term to devote more time to her 10-year-old daughter, calling politics "entirely too masculine to have any attraction for feminine responsibilities." HATTIE W. CARAWAY (see p. 66) chaired the Senate Committee on Enrolled Bills in the 73rd–78th Congresses; MARY TERESA NORTON (opposite) chaired the House District of Columbia Committee from the 72nd Congress, until June 22, 1937, in the 75th Congress, the House Labor Committee from June 22, 1937, in the 75th Congress through the 79th Congress, and the House Administration Committee in the 81st Congress; Caroline O'Day (D., N.Y.) chaired the House Committee on the Election of the President, Vice-President, and representatives in Congress from June 24, 1937, in the 75th–77th Congresses; EDITH NOURSE ROGERS (see p. 67) chaired the House Veterans Affairs Committee in the 80th and 83rd Congresses; MARTHA W. GRIFFITHS (see p. 70) chaired the Select Committee on the House Beauty Shop in the 90th–93rd Congresses; and LEONOR K. SULLIVAN (see p. 69) chaired the House Merchant Marine and Fisheries

Committee in the 93rd and 94th Congresses.

First to Serve as a State Party Chairman, First to Chair a National Party Platform Committee, First to Chair Three Committees in Congress

If politics is an inborn talent, then MARY TERESA NORTON, a woman with many political "firsts" to her credit, needed only to be discovered to skyrocket to political success. The protégé of New Jersey City boss Frank Hague, she was the first woman to serve as a state party chairman (head of the Democratic Party in New Jersey); first to chair a national party platform committee; first to be elected a freeholder in New Jersey; first to chair three House committees; and first elected to Congress from the East (slightly ahead of Edith Nourse Rogers, whose special election in Massachusetts the regular New Jersey election preceded). Ms. Norton served from December 7, 1925, to January 3, 1951. She could have been the first woman nominated for Vice-President in 1932 but turned down the suggestion, knowing she would be a token since the real nominee was already selected. As chairman of the House Labor Committee, she steered President Franklin D. Roosevelt's wage and hour bill through an unsympathetic House of Representatives. A champion of human rights and the cause of welfare, she is credited also with passage of the Fair Labor Standards Act of 1938.

First Congresswoman to Visit the War Theater in World War II

In 1944, under extremely hazardous conditions, Representative FRANCES BOLTON, Republican, of Ohio visited the war theater, the first woman in Congress to do so. The second-longest-serving woman in Congress (29 years), Ms. Bolton was admired for her enthusiasm, hard work, and fervor for what she considered important. She was born in 1885 into a wealthy Cleveland family and as a debutante assisted public health nurses. In the House of Representatives, where she took over her husband's seat but stayed to become one of the nation's most accomplished legislators in her own right, and one of the most colorful women ever to serve in the U. S. Congress, public health became a major preoccupation of hers. She was also an ardent champion of nursing programs and responsible for creation of the army nursing corps. In the 1940s she spoke out against segregation in the military, arguing that black nurses should be given full opportunity to prove themselves. In the 1950s she advocated that women be drafted as well as men. During the Civil Rights debate, when she was in her 80s, she fought to include women in antidiscrimination legislation. Never content with secondhand analyses, and intensely interested in foreign affairs, she traveled hundreds of thousands of miles to see what the world was like and became an expert on Africa. Ms. Bolton was defeated in her final campaign in 1968, at the age of 83.

First Movie Star Elected to the U. S. Congress

One of the most impressive records compiled by a three-term member of Congress belongs to HELEN GAHAGAN DOUGLAS, the first movie star elected to the House of Representatives. A Democrat from California, Ms. Douglas (wife of the actor Melvyn Douglas) served from January 3, 1945, to January 3, 1951. She was defeated in a bid for the U. S. Senate in 1952 by former President Richard M. Nixon, who ran a smear campaign against her, charging she was "soft on Communism." The talented actress and opera singer was born in Boonton, New Jersey, in 1900. Her conversion to politics began in the late 1930s when she became appalled at the conditions of migratory agriculture workers and began speaking widely for New Deal programs. In Congress, Representative Douglas pushed legislation to continue the Marshall Plan and to support NATO. An ardent civil libertarian, she also introduced legislation on women's rights, advocated abolition of the poll tax, and introduced the first bill to protect the rights of citizens appearing before congressional committees. *Liberty* magazine editorialized about her: "You could count on your fingers the congressmen better versed in world affairs and social economics." And the Book of Knowledge cited her as one of the "12 smartest women in the world."

Woman Who Put "Truth-in-Lending" Act on the Books

Representative LEONOR K. SULLIVAN is credited with launching numerous campaigns for consumer protection and was responsible for many of the consumer laws now on the books, including the "truth-in-lending" Consumer Credit Protection Act. The only woman in Congress to vote against the Equal Rights Amendment, she perplexed women's groups because she had also co-sponsored the Equal Pay Act of 1963 and had worked hard for other women's rights legislation during her tenure. Ms. Sullivan began her political career as an administrative assistant to her husband, who was serving his fourth term in the House when he died. Her succession to his seat on January 3, 1953, as the only woman ever to represent Missouri, challenges the view that widows slide easily into political office. A Democrat, she received tremendous resistance from party leaders, who said: "We don't have anything against you, we just want to win." Ms. Sullivan returned to Washington, worked for a year and saved enough money to run her own primary just before the general election, and without party support won against six men. Shrewdly spurning advice to forget the party and run as an independent, she said, "When you run as an independent, you come in as a zombie, because Congress is organized along party lines." She served in Congress for 24 years, retiring on January 3, 1977. Her explanation for voting against the equal rights amendment—"ERA says you are equal . . . I think I'm a whole lot better"— included the opinion that the amendment presaged the beginning of the breakdown of family life.

She Put "Sex" in the Civil Rights Act

A ten-term Democatic congresswoman from Michigan, MARTHA WRIGHT GRIFFITHS is credited with the incredible task of shepherding the Equal Rights Amendment through the House of Representatives, where it had been defeated in past years. But even before her long fight for the ERA, Ms. Griffiths presented the argument for including "sex" in the 1964 Civil Rights Act, which she considers an even greater achievement. Few women in Congress have done as much to advance the cause of women as Martha Griffiths, who served from January 5, 1955, to January 3, 1975. The victim of discrimination herself, shunned by her own party and by Labor, she turned political disadvantage to advantage and entered Congress with unusual independence and used that independence to move through controversial legislation including the ERA, reform of pension laws, social security, and tax reform. "You were supposed to take orders . . . the truth was . . . I had a brain

and I could speak and I could get something done," she has said, explaining the power structure's animosity toward her.

First Japanese-American Woman Elected to Congress

The first Japanese-American woman elected to the United States Congress, from the new state of Hawaii, PATSY MINK, took her seat on January 4, 1965. As a minority group member and a woman, she had two strikes against her but gained a strong reputation in her 12 years in the House, where she wrote and sponsored the Women's Educational Equity Act, which passed in 1974, and championed equal credit opportunity, child care legislation, and bills to end discrimination against women in tax laws. Ms. Mink, born in Paie, Hawaii, on December 6, 1927, is a graduate of the University of Chicago Law School. Always outspoken, she protested the treatment of women delegates at the 1972 Democratic Convention, as she had earlier engaged in a widely reported dispute with a prominent fellow Democrat who said women shouldn't be promoted in government because "hormonal influences would hamper their judgment." In 1976 Patsy Mink gave up her House seat to run for nomination to the Senate but failed to get party and labor backing and was unable to compete with her opponent for funds. President Jimmy Carter in 1977 appointed her Assistant Secretary of State for Oceans and International Environmental Affairs. Thirteen months later she announced her resignation from the job, complaining that she could accomplish little or nothing in it. Shortly thereafter, she was elected president of the Americans for Democratic Action.

First Black Woman Elected to the U. S. Congress

Unbought and Unbossed is the title SHIRLEY CHISHOLM, Democrat of New York, first black woman elected to Congress, chose for her political autobiography. This feisty woman, whose unflinching commitment to racial and sexual equality has been in evidence since January 3, 1969, when she arrived in Washington to take her seat, was a New York City schoolteacher and director of a day nursery. She began her political career in clubhouse politics and was elected first to the New York State Assembly. Ms. Chisholm gave domestic workers their first spokesperson in Congress, fighting for 15 months to get this invisible group protected by the minimum wage law. She also has sponsored legislation dealing with environmental health, day care, food stamps, national home health care, full employment, and women's rights. She seriously pursued the Democratic nomination for the presidency in 1972 and received 154 delegate votes at the Convention, despite the opposition of many blacks and liberals. Responding to critics who charged that she was too pushy for a black woman, she said: "Yes, it's true. I had the nerve to dare to say that I'm going to run for the presidency of the United States." Acknowledging that some of her critics were black men, she said, "Black women are not here to compete or fight with you, brothers. If we have hangups about being male or female, we're not going to be able to use our talents to liberate all of our black people. Black women must give what they have in the current situation."

Battling Bella Abzug

From 1970, the year she was first elected to Congress, she was "Battling Bella." Her loud voice, brash manner, and unflinching commitment to women's rights and to ending the Vietnam War made Bronx-born (1920) New York Congresswoman BELLA ABZUG the scourge of conservatives as well as a subject of frequent ridicule. Yet by 1976 she was also one of the most respected members of Congress. In April 1976 her colleagues voted her the third most influential member of the entire House of Representatives, ranked only behind the two top Democratic leaders, the Speaker and the Majority Leader. What happened in those five years? "I came out of the peace and women's movement," she told a reporter. "They thought I was a lunatic. Now these causes are supported by the majority of people . . . everybody else has caught up." A founder of Women Strike for Peace and a labor lawyer for 25 years before she ran for Congress, Ms. Abzug quickly developed political skills such as marking up bills in committee session and horsetrading to get her legislation passed. She wrote bills on equal credit, mass transportation, welfare reform, women's issues, and she held hearings on covert and illegal activities of the CIA, FBI, and other federal agencies. She was one of six members who first discussed on the House Floor the possible impeachment of Richard Nixon. In 1976 she gave up her House seat to run for the Senate but was defeated, although she proved her political strength by raising as much money as her prime male contender—a real feat for a female candidate. Later she lost a bid for the New York City mayoralty. President Carter in 1977 appointed her to head the National Commission on the Observance of International Women's Year—a job in which she has remained politically highly visible.

First Polish-American Congresswoman

BARBARA MIKULSKI, the spunky congresswoman from a working-class district in Baltimore, Maryland, came to national attention in 1974 as chairperson of the Democratic Party's Commission on Delegate Selection and Party Structure. A two-term member of Baltimore's City Council, Mikulski brought her negotiating skills to national party politics and came up with a compromise in rules that was acceptable to feminists and blacks clamoring for more representation, as well as to old-line party leaders who feared a threat to their traditional power. A staunch feminist and spokesperson for women, the working class and the elderly, Ms. Mikulski grew up in a Polish section of Baltimore. She turned her profession as a social worker into a political career by organizing her community and then using the community organization as a political base when she became frustrated with the role of outside activist. Turning to elective politics as a means of more effective advocacy, she won a city council victory in 1971 against the local political powers that was "the equivalent of a 100-year flood," according to one observer. By the time she ran for reelection in 1974, she had the support of many of her original opponents. Elected to the House of Representatives in November 1976, with 76 per cent of the vote, she is the first Polish-American woman in Congress and the first woman to serve on the House Interstate and Foreign Commerce Committee.

First U. S. Congresswoman from Colorado

PATRICIA (PAT) SCHROEDER was 31 and the mother of two preschoolers (one in diapers) when she decided to run for Congress in 1972. Her husband suggested she should. Despite his own political ambitions, he believed she would make the better candidate. And although she outraged political leaders who thought she should seek a lesser office first, she beat an incumbent congressman with a margin of over 8,000 votes, becoming the first congresswoman from Colorado. Ms. Schroeder admits to some difficulty overcoming the tradition that a mother with young children can't have a demanding career. "Twenty-odd years of cultural conditioning tells you you can't do it," she says. "The amazing thing is that you find out there isn't any reason why you can't." Since taking her seat, Ms. Schroeder, a native of Oregon and a graduate of Harvard Law School, has become a role model for other young

mothers interested in pursuing careers in politics. She has also shaken up Congress' greatest bastion of machismo, the House Armed Services Committee, to which she fought for appointment. "I chose that committee because that is where the money is," she explains. "Defense people say they are protecting women and children. As a woman with children, I want to be able to say there are other things we can do to protect us besides build bases."

Youngest Woman Ever Elected to the U. S. Congress

Brooklyn's ELIZABETH HOLTZMAN, elected to the House of Representatives at the age of 32, the youngest woman ever to take her seat in the U. S. Congress (January 3, 1973), was 11 months younger than Pat Schroeder when she arrived from Colorado. Ms. Holtzman unseated Congressman Emanuel Celler, who had represented Brooklyn for 48 years, and was a former chairman of the House Judiciary Committee and one of the most powerful members of Congress. Immediately after her surprise election, she obtained a seat on the House Judiciary Committee, one of the most influential committees in the House, and participated as a committee member in the deliberations on the impeachment of former President Richard Nixon. Her legal acumen apparent throughout the hearings, covered live on television, won her national attention, and helped solidify public acceptance of women in politics. Concerned about the excesses of intelligence gathering, Representative Holtzman wrote the first legislation enacted since 1949 to restrict the CIA. Together with House Judiciary Committee Chairman Peter Rodino, she introduced legislation to counter the Arab boycott of American businesses that are owned by or employ Jews or that trade with Israel. A graduate of Radcliffe College and Harvard Law School, and a founder of the Brooklyn Women's Political Caucus, "Liz" Holtzman has said that women workers contributed to her political success by forming the backbone of her campaign.

First Black Woman from California to Serve in Congress

The first woman to have a child while serving in Congress, YVONNE BRAITHWAITE BURKE, born in Los Angeles, California, 1934, was also the first black woman ever elected from California. She came to the House of Representatives on January 3, 1973, and gave birth to a daughter, Autumn Roxanne, while in her first term. An attorney, who was a member of the California State Assembly before her election to the U. S. Congress, Burke recalls not being able to find a place to live in the state capital, Sacramento, because she was black. She has chaired the Congressional Black Caucus and was vice-chairperson of the 1972 Democratic National Convention in Miami Beach. An activist legislator, Ms. Burke has introduced more than 20 bills and major amendments since her election, including legislation to provide funds for planning a comprehensive West Coast Mass Transit System, extended federal aid for the mentally retarded, equal opportunity in construction of the Trans-Alaskan pipeline, federal part-time employment for homemakers and the elderly, improved outpatient care facilities in undersupervised areas, and the establishment of a National Center for the Prevention and Control of Rape. In mid-1978, tired of commuting to Washington, she entered the race for attorney general of California and won the primary.

First Black Woman Elected to Congress from Texas, First to Give Keynote Address at Democratic National Convention

When Congresswoman BARBARA JORDAN stepped up to the podium at the 1976 Democratic National Convention, the first black and the first woman to give the keynote address, the room shook with applause and then fell expectantly silent. The congresswoman's eloquence was already firmly established in the minds of most Americans. As a member of the House Judiciary Committee during the impeachment hearings, she had distinguished herself as a brilliant orator: "My faith in the Constitution is whole, it is complete, it is total," she had said, "I am not going to sit here and be an idle spectator to the diminution, the subversion, and the destruction of the Constitution." The first black woman elected to Congress from the Deep South was born in Houston, Texas, on February 21, 1936, the daughter of a Baptist minister. "I, Barbara Jordan, am a keynote speaker, and notwithstanding the past, my presence here before you is one additional bit of evidence that the American Dream need not forever be deferred," she told the Convention that nominated a Georgian, Jimmy Carter, for President.

She has always been ambitious. "I never intended to be a run-of-the-mill person," she said. Shortly after graduating from Boston University Law School, she ran twice for the Texas legislature and lost. In 1966 she ran for the state senate and won, the first black to serve since 1883. She was elected to Congress in 1972, winning 81 per cent of the vote. Ms. Jordan is known as a consummate politician who plays the power game; at times she has been criticized by both blacks and women for neglecting their interests. But most agree that her eloquence serves all Americans. When she announced, in late 1977, that she would not run again for the House (saying she had no "hidden agenda"), friends, colleagues, and sometime critics were united in voicing the hope that her strong voice in U.S. politics would not be stilled.

PARTY LEADERS, U.S.A.

First National Party "Chairman" and First Woman Director of a Presidential Campaign

JEAN WESTWOOD, the first U.S. woman to chair a national political party and manage a presidential campaign, spent 30 years in politics before her election on July 14, 1972, as "chairman" of the Democratic National Committee (DNC). Ms. Westwood had worked with Senator George McGovern's Commission, seeking reform of party rules to include more women, minorities, and young persons. As "co-chairman" of McGovern's 1972 presidential campaign, she was responsible for primary campaigns in more than 14 states. After his nomination as the party's candidate, McGovern asked her to chair the party. During her tenure, she presided over the first selection in history of a replacement nominee for national office (Vice-President). After McGovern's defeat, there was a movement to bring more moderate leadership to the party's top job. Although Ms. Westwood won a narrow vote of confidence at the party's meeting in December 1972, she was narrowly defeated as chairman in a contest with Robert Strauss. She was campaign director for Terry Sanford's presidential campaign in 1976. Jean Westwood was born in Price, Utah, 1923. Her parents were descendants of early Utah pioneers. She and her husband Richard started a five-acre mink ranch on a shoestring in the early 1940s; it became a highly successful business operation. The Westwoods have 2 children and 12 grandchildren.

First Woman "Chairman" of the RNC

The first woman "chairman" of the Republican National Committee (RNC), MARY LOUISE SMITH, was 60 years old when Gerald Ford picked her for the post. "If someone told me that I would be party chairman I don't know if I would have known what they were talking about," she said. "You see, there is no way anyone can ever tell a woman . . . 'If you do this and so, you'll be this.'" She was elected on September 16, 1974. No one believed she could survive a year, but she maintained the leadership position until after the 1976 presidential election, when she resigned. Although she worked her way up the party ranks and was always a loyal Republican, Mary Louise Smith also helped to organize Iowa's Women's Political Caucus. "There's nothing revolutionary about being a feminist," she says. "It's the natural thing." A native of Eddyville, Iowa, she received a B.A. in social work in 1935 at the University of Iowa, where she met and married Dr. Elmer M. Smith. He stayed home during her three years in Washington chairing the party. "Sure, he minds," she says, "but he is a remarkable man." Ms. Smith is the mother of three and a grandmother.

Longest-Serving DNC Secretary—First Woman to Hold the Job

Party chairmen come and go, but DOROTHY VREDENBURGH BUSH is a Democratic Party institution, whose gavel pounding at national conventions began in 1940, when she became the first woman Secretary of the Democratic National Committee (DNC). Her entry into politics was as Alabama's National Committeewoman for the Young Democrats, a post she held until 1950. The woman who has called the roll at nine national conventions, Ms. Bush is known as "always poised amid the din." She also makes, keeps, and coordinates every major record for the conventions. During sessions, her knowledge of procedure makes her an invaluable consultant on parliamentary matters. In 1964 Ms. Bush was a White House coordinator for the *Lady Bird Special*, the train that took Ms. Lyndon B. Johnson on her historic trip through eight southern states.

Instigator of the Democratic National Committee's Feminist Caucus

In 1968 KORYNE HORBAL turned the Minnesota Democratic Party on its ear when she organized its feminist caucus, which took over the party. On October 19, 1973, she attempted to infuse the feminist movement into the Democratic National Committee by organizing its first feminist caucus. The task was more difficult. "It's the most frustrating thing I have ever done," said Ms. Horbal, a housewife who began in politics by ringing doorbells, and was considered a safe, establishment politician until her election as state chairman in 1968. "Many women on the Democratic National Committee arrive there through men and don't identify with the women's movement. They [did not] have their own agenda." Still, she had some immediate successes. Women proved the best-organized group at the party's mini-Convention in 1974, and Ms. Horbal rounded up votes to ensure that the 1976 Convention would not be held in a state that had not passed the ERA. A hardworking, effective politican, she is greatly admired by feminist colleagues and is considered an irritant to some party leaders: "I could have been the woman who climbed up the ladder and pulled it up after me. But I saw what happened to me beginning at the precinct level and I couldn't close my eyes to that."

First to Chair the National Convention of a Major American Political Party

Representative LINDY BOGGS, the first congresswoman from Louisiana, was also first woman to chair a major party's national convention in the United States. She presided over the Democratic Na-

tional Convention held in July 1976. She was first elected to Congress in 1973 in a special election to fill the vacancy created by the disappearance of her husband Hale Boggs, former Majority Leader of the House, who was lost in a flight over Alaska in October 1972. She had managed her husband's campaigns and been active in the Democratic Party for over 30 years. She was seated on March 27, 1973, and reelected in 1974. A staunch supporter of opportunities for women, Ms. Boggs amended the Small Business Act to prohibit discrimination against women in granting SBA loans and assistance.

Only Woman to Serve as Convention Director of a Major National Political Party

"I got into politics by accident," says JOSEPHINE L. GOOD, known to all as "Jo," whose organizational talents have held together six Republican National Conventions over the past 20 years. As Convention Director of the Republican National Committee, the only woman to hold that job in either party, Ms. Good is responsible for handling, planning, and organizing her party's conventions. "I volunteered for the campaign of 1952, and proved I could work 24 hours a day," says Good, whose status as a Republican Party institution is second only to that of the elephant. "In politics, you have to work every day, every night, and every weekend. I do it for the money and because I like my work." During World War II, Ms. Good enlisted in the U. S. Coast Guard Women's Reserve, and served almost three years, attaining the rank of Chief Yeoman. Later she worked on a congressional staff for six years. She met Arthur Summerfield when she was a volunteer at the Republican National Committee and he was committee chairman. When he was appointed Postmaster General, she became his administrative aide, and in 1956 joined the RNC staff.

STATE AND LOCAL OFFICIALS, U.S.A.

First Woman Governor

The first woman elected governor in the United States, NELLIE TAYLOE ROSS (1876–1977) of Wyoming, was catapulted into politics after the death of her husband, Governor William B. Ross, in October 1924. Democratic Party leaders persuaded her to run. She agreed but declined to campaign and won largely because of the sympathy of Wyoming voters. She was defeated for reelection in 1926 partly because women's rights advocates felt that she had failed to support their efforts. Although she was elected the same day that Ma Ferguson won the governorship of Texas, Wyoming gained the distinction of having the first woman governor because the state held its inauguration three weeks before Texas did. Nellie Tayloe Ross was also the first woman director of the U. S. Mint (1933–53). On her 100th birthday, November 29, 1976, she was quoted as saying that her career marked "a milestone in the battle for women's equality."

First Woman Governor Who Didn't Follow a Husband into Office

ELLA TAMBUSSI GRASSO had 21 years of political experience behind her when she took office as governor of Connecticut on January 8, 1975—the first woman in the nation's history to win election as governor who did not follow her husband into office. Known as a shrewd politician who worked her way up the political ladder, Governor Grasso thought about running for many years, but: "Women weren't candidates. You remember John Bailey's famous statement—that he would run a woman when he thought she would lose. He would say that and chortle, 'Ho, ho, ho.'" (Bailey was the Democratic State Party Chairman from whom Ms. Grasso learned the political ropes.) Ella

Tambussi was born in Windsor Locks, Connecticut, on May 10, 1919. Her yearbook in her senior year in high school predicted she would be the first woman mayor of Windsor Locks. "I was horrified. Politics! I mean, I aspired to something eminently greater," she said. But she entered her first primary when her youngest child was 18 months old and was first elected to the Connecticut General Assembly in 1952, when she was 33 years old. By 1955 she was floor leader in the state legislature; in 1959 she was elected Secretary of State, an office she held until 1970 when she became a congresswoman. She served two terms in the House of Representatives, retiring in 1974 to run for governor. Despite her proved vote-getting ability, she had to fight for the nomination, lining up the votes that guaranteed her the nomination as well as her winability with Connecticut voters. She and her husband, a retired schoolteacher whom she calls her "best friend," have two children.

First Woman Governor of the State of Washington

DIXY LEE RAY, the first woman governor of Washington State, had never run for a political office before her election as a governor in November 1976. But she has never followed convention. A college professor who taught marine invertebrate zoology for 24 years at the University of Washington, Ray lived in her mobile home in the country outside the District of Columbia during her two years in Washington when she served as chairperson of the Atomic Energy Commission (1973) and briefly as an Assistant Secretary of State (1975). She quit the latter post in disgust, saying later, "I saw the things that led to Watergate—like too much power. And I decided that people deserve better than that." In Washington State, she was shunned by political leaders and did everything wrong by traditional political standards. Yet she beat her Republican opponent by 129,000 votes, spending slightly more than half what he spent. To the voters, the 62-year-old biologist was a fresh spirit. She dresses in men's shirts over slacks or occasional skirts, continues to live in her mobile home parked at the edge of Puget Sound. Although her greatest love is nature, she is no hero to environmentalists. "The people who beat their breasts and call themselves environmentalists—I think they are a very small percentage of the population," she says. "The only way they like the earth is when it has no people on it."

New York State's First Woman Lieutenant Governor

MARY ANNE KRUPSAK never took a back seat during her eight-year tenure in the state legislature of New York, and she has not let the usually ceremonial position of lieutenant governor push her into the background. Without that determination Ms. Krupsak never would have become the first woman in New York State to win a major party nomination for statewide office. Party leaders offered her two positions held by Republican incumbents who couldn't be beaten. She refused, announced her candidacy for lieutenant governor, and ran a low-budget campaign from her Manhattan apartment. She beat two men in a three-way primary. Her campaign slogan: "She's not just one of the boys." After her election on November 5, 1974, Lieutenant Governor Krupsak launched investigations of state agencies and opened a handful of offices around the state to serve constituents. In 1978 she announced her candidacy for the governorship. Mary Anne Krupsak was born in Amsterdam, New York, on March 26, 1932. She received a law degree from the University of Chicago.

First Woman Lieutenant Governor of Kentucky

THELMA L. STOVALL, elected in 1975 the first woman lieutenant governor of Kentucky, has had more than 25 years of elective politics in Kentucky. A native Kentuckian, who was born in Munfordville, Hart County, 1919, Thelma Stovall took secretarial training at the Mary Rose Kelly Secretaries School in Louisville, and worked at the Brown and Williamson Tobacco Company, where she was secretary of the Tobacco Worker's International Union Local 185 for 11 years. The first woman to hold elective political office in Jefferson County (Louisville), like most male politicians, she worked her way up the political ranks over a long period of time. She served in the state legislature 1950–55, in 1956 was the first woman elected president of the Young Democrats of Kentucky, and was also elected secretary of state that year. She served as secretary of state for three terms, and as state treasurer for two terms. Lieutenant Governor Stovall presides over the senate of the Kentucky general assembly, the first woman ever to officially preside over that body. Her biography states: "She is a Baptist and a Democrat, in that order."

First Woman Lieutenant Governor of Mississippi

Even in Southern Belle country, a woman can overcome and achieve a political career equal to any man. One who has succeeded, EVELYN GANDY, after 28 years in politics, became Mississippi's first female lieutenant governor on January 14, 1976, and the third woman in the United States elected to her state's second-highest office. Ms. Gandy decided early that she would run for state office. Eighteen years before her election as lieutenant governor, she told a newspaper: "Since my early youth, I have been preparing myself for the day when

I could ask the people of Mississippi to give me the opportunity of serving them in public life." Born and reared on a farm in Hattiesburg, Mississippi, she made her first political speech when she was 15 and worked in her first campaign at 16. Ms. Gandy attended the University of Mississippi Law School where she began a long lists of "firsts" as first woman president of the Old Miss Law School and first woman editor of the Mississippi Law *Journal.* In 1947 she became the first woman elected to the state legislature from Forest County. She was her state's first woman assistant attorney general, first commissioner of public welfare, and first commissioner of insurance. In 1959 she was elected state treasurer, the first woman in Mississippi's history to win statewide office.

First Woman to Win Election to a Statewide Office

The first U.S. woman to win election to a statewide office, KATE BARNARD, was elected commissioner of charities and corrections by the electorate of Oklahoma in 1907, and reelected in 1910. Ms. Barnard, who was born on May 23, 1875, in Geneva, Nebraska, and died in Oklahoma City on February 23, 1930, retired from public life in 1914 although she was sought after by unions who wanted her to lobby for them. Ms. Barnard was a champion of the cause of pension benefits to widows, attacked the use of convict labor, and protested the blacklisting of unionists.

First Black Woman Elected to a State Legislature

CRYSTAL BIRD FAUSET, the first black woman elected to a state legislature in the United States, was elected to the Pennsylvania legislature in 1938. Born in 1894, Ms. Fauset was prominent in Democratic Party politics. She was an adviser to Mayor Fiorello La Guardia of New York and to President Franklin D. Roosevelt. She died in 1965.

First Avowed Homosexual to Win Election to a State Office

ELAINE NOBLE, the first avowed homosexual to win a state office in the United States, was elected to the Massachusetts general assembly in 1974 when she was 28 years old. A feisty community activist who took her neighbors' problems to city hall and the state house, Ms. Noble was asked to run by the voters in her Boston community. Her victory was due largely to elderly citizens who were particularly grateful when she spoke up for their needs; she sees herself as representing people who can't represent themselves. A miner's daughter, she put herself through college and graduate school at Harvard and became a college professor. She never planned a political career. "In the 1960s I didn't know the difference between city hall and the state house. If anyone had told me I would run for office, I would have said they were a released mental case." She didn't skirt the issue of her homosexuality. Instead, she announced her candidacy and her sexual preference at the same time. But she never campaigned as a gay candidate. "I was a candidate who was gay, not a gay candidate." Some of her colleagues were apprehensive when she arrived at the State House—in fact, some members refused to sit near her—but after a few months in office even the most skeptical respected her hard work and dedication. In 1978 Ms. Noble, whose seat was abolished in the redistricting of Massachusetts, announced her candidacy for the U. S. Senate.

First Woman Mayor of San Juan

The woman who ran San Juan's city hall fcr 22 years, 1946–68, Doña FELISA VDA. DE GAUTIER, helped found Puerto Rico's Popular Party in 1940 with the country's first elected governor, Luis Muñoz Marín. In 1929, when women won the right to vote, she was fifth in line to register—over the protests of her father, who finally acquiesced "when he saw I was determined." In 1944 she turned down the post of city manager because of protestations by her husband and father. But two years later she accepted and never listened to objections after that. She played a motherly role in city hall, holding open house for her constituents with personal difficulties. A member of the upper class, whose principal concern has always been with the poor, she believes that middle-class women could do more to help society.

First Woman Elected Mayor of a Large U. S. City

JANET GRAY HAYES defeated six men in a tough election campaign that included a primary and a runoff to become mayor of San Jose, California, in January 1974—the first woman elected mayor of a large U.S. city. Hayes was elected to the city council in 1971 and was elected vice-mayor in 1973. The wife of a physician and mother of four children, she was spurred into politics by frustration with the workings of the government. When her children were in kindergarten, Ms. Hayes spent more than two years trying to get a crossing guard at their street corner. That led her into PTA and the local League of Women Voters leadership, but neither organization went far enough. "They say dissatisfaction fuels the engine of progress," she says. "Women don't want to be in the kitchen washing coffee cups anymore. We want to be where the decisions are being made." Ms. Hayes, who was born on July 12, 1926, in Rushville, Indiana, and earned a master's degree in social work from the University of Chicago, believes that her understanding of citizens' problems and needs based upon her own experience qualified her for office.

Mayor of the Nation's Largest City Governed by a Woman

On May 1, 1975, LILA COCKRELL defeated nine male opponents to become mayor of San Antonio, Texas, the nation's 10th largest city (pop. 750,000) and the largest governed by a woman. Her chief opponent outspent her three to one. Ms. Cockrell aggressively sought the mayoralty after Janet Gray Hayes's victory in San Jose, California, convinced her that a woman could be elected a big-city mayor. In 1970, after she had served on the city council for seven years, Cockrell, as mayor pro tem, was told that she would make a great mayor if only she were a man and discouraged from running. Mayor Cockrell, 53 years old when she was elected, is married and has two daughters. Her political life began with the League of Women Voters.

Mississippi's First Black Woman Mayor

A community organizer and civil rights activist who once cropped cotton for $3.00 a day, UNITA BLACKWELL got the town of Mayersville, Mississippi, incorporated and became its mayor—first appointed in 1976 and then elected on June 7, 1977. The town of Mayersville has 500 residents, no police department, schools, or doctors, and few jobs. Its population is 80 per cent black. There are 10 black mayors in Mississippi. The first black woman mayor, Ms. Blackwell, a 44-year-old divorcée, spent 11 days in a Jackson, Mississippi, jail for demonstrating for the right to vote for blacks, and helped organize the Mississippi Democratic Freedom Party.

Sausalito's Surprising Mayor

SALLY STANFORD was 72 years old when the people of Sausalito, California, elected the retired brothelkeeper mayor. It was a sweet victory for the woman who ran for the city council seven times between 1962 and her election as mayor in 1972. Mayor Stanford, born Marcia Busby on a farm in Oregon, was a bootlegger and ran a speakeasy in Ventura County during the 1920s before her debut as San Francisco's Madam Sally Stanford (she borrowed the name from the University). In 1949 she decided that San Francisco was "too full of squares" and that it was time to go legitimate. She opened the Valhalla Restaurant on Sausalito's waterfront, soon began to speak out at city council meetings, and in time turned square enough herself to supply instruments for a school band, even sponsor a Little League baseball team.

First Woman President of the League of Cities

PHYLLIS LAMPHERE, the first woman president of the National League of Cities, and first non-mayor to head the organization since 1941, was elected to the Seattle city council in 1967 by a landslide. Some political leaders told her not to run because the token "woman's seat" was already filled, but Ms. Lamphere (born Phyllis Lee Hagmoe) ran anyway, and won. In the autumn of 1977, with her family campaigning for her, she tried for Seattle's top municipal job, the mayoralty, but lost.

WOMEN IN THE WHITE HOUSE

First to Serve as a Spokeswoman for a President

The first to serve as a spokeswoman for the President, ANNE W. WHEATON, was associate White House press secretary under President Dwight D. Eisenhower's Press Secretary James C. Hagerty for four years—from April 1957, until the end of Ike's second term in 1961. She found her position "rugged." Five months after assuming her job, she summed up for the *New York Times:* "The responsibility to weigh words carefully, at least you try to—knowing that you have the responsibility at all times for reflecting opinions and positions of the President or the Administration in the best possible way. And also you want to do the finest job you can for the news corps because they are reporting it to the people." A close friend of Mamie Eisenhower, Ms. Wheaton served as her personal press representative in the 1952 presidential campaign. She was born in Utica, New York, moved to Albany at the age of 14 when her father, the late John Williams, was named New York State labor commissioner. After attending Simmons College in Boston, she returned to Albany, where she became a reporter for Albany's *Knickerbocker Press*. She was one of the first women political correspondents at the state capitol. Anne Wheaton died in March 1977.

First to Direct the White House Office of Communications

MARGITA WHITE was a summer intern who assisted Vice-President Nixon's press secretary Herbert O. Klein in 1959. On June 18, 1975, she succeeded Klein as director of the White House Office of Communications. The first woman to hold that position, she was appointed by President Gerald Ford. A native of Sweden (she became a U.S. citizen in 1955), Ms. White earned a master's degree in political science and a Woodrow Wilson Fellowship and then worked in several national Republican campaigns. In 1973 she became assistant director of the U. S. Information Agency. She was sworn in as an FCC commissioner on September 23, 1976, the third woman to sit on the commission. She and her husband, an attorney, have two children.

First Woman Assistant to the President

MARGARET "MIDGE" COSTANZA, the first woman to hold the title of Assistant to the President, got into politics in 1959 when she became an Executive Committee member of the 22nd Ward of Rochester. The only woman in President Jimmy Carter's original White House inner circle has always been a bit of a maverick. In 1968 she set up a one-person office for presidential aspirant Robert Kennedy when the party regulars were supporting Hubert Humphrey. She did everything from washing the walls and cleaning the floors to answering the telephones and canvassing voters. She was elected to the Rochester City Council in 1973 with the biggest plurality of any candidate. Despite the tradition that the highest vote-getter becomes mayor, she was appointed vice-mayor. "It was my first run-in with sexism," she says. Ms. Costanza met Jimmy Carter in 1974. When he announced his candidacy for President, she became co-chairman of his New York State campaign.

Second Woman Presidential Assistant

ANNE WEXLER, former Deputy Undersecretary of Commerce for Regional Affairs, in May 1978 became the second woman named assistant to the President in the Carter administration. Ms. Wexler is generally regarded as one of the savviest women in politics today. As a political volunteer in Westport, Connecticut, in the early 1960s, Ms. Wexler pushed for reform of Connecticut's Democratic Party, then joined the movement for reform of the national party as chief consultant to the Commission on Party Structure and Delegate Selection from 1969 to 1972. She was a member of the Charter Commission of the Democratic National Committee in 1974–75. She was also a member, during the 1976 campaign, of the Carter/Mondale campaign's steering committee, and worked as a floor leader for Jimmy Carter at the Convention. Prior to joining the Commerce Department, Ms. Wexler was associate publisher of *Rolling Stone* magazine. She is married to Joseph D. Duffy, who in July 1977 was named chairman of the National Endowment for the Humanities. They have two sons.

The Youngest White House Source

CLAUDIA TOWNSEND, 25, is one of six associate White House press secretaries who speak for the President when reporters call at any hour of the day or night. She and her five colleagues work at this job a week at a time. Ms. Townsend is a Georgian with a B.A. in journalism from the University of Georgia, a onetime, part-time researcher for Ralph Nader, and a local and Washington reporter for the Atlanta *Constitution* and the Cox newspapers, which own the *Constitution*. She came to President Carter's staff in January 1977 as editor of the daily news summary provided by the White House Press Office to the President and other senior officials. In October 1977 she moved into her new $40,000-a-year job. She says that after eight years of the Carter Administration, she may go to law school.

Top Woman on National Security Council Staff

Those who know her were not surprised that JESSICA TUCHMAN should become— at the age of 30—a key adviser to President Carter on nuclear proliferation, conventional arms control, human rights, and the law of the sea. As the top staff person on the National Security Council's "global issues" unit, Ms. Tuchman, who began her job on January 15, 1977, is one of the most important women in the Carter Administration. When asked if she were an overachiever, she replied: "That's a terrible question. I come from a very compulsive pair of parents. They are both very hard workers." Her mother is historian Barbara Tuchman, twice winner of the Pulitzer Prize (see "Women in Education, Social Sciences, and the Humanities," p. 418). Her father is a physician. Her great-uncle was Henry Morgenthau, Jr., Secretary of the Treasury under President Franklin D. Roosevelt for 12 years. "I just always assumed that I was supposed to do the same sort of thing." Her political career goes back to 1968 when she was 21 and became assistant campaign manager to Senator Eugene McCarthy, who was running on an antiwar platform. Three years after McCarthy's defeat she emerged from the Massachusetts Institute of Technology (MIT) with a Ph.D. in biochemistry and the itch to return to the political world. She received a fellowship to work in Congress and spent two years on Representative Morris Udall's Subcommittee on Energy and the Environment. When Udall sought the Democratic presidential nomination in 1976, she went to work as his issues adviser, working 16 to 18 hours a day seven days a week for a year. When Udall's campaign was over, the congressman had three people he thought would be "good for Jimmy Carter and for the country. Jessica was one of them," he said. Working 60 hours a week in 1977, she said, "I couldn't conceive of going on like this for four years. There is a fearsome price you pay. I try to remember the government got along 200 years without me."

Women in the Presidents' Cabinets

President	Secretary	Department	Date
F. D. Roosevelt	Frances Perkins	Labor	1933–45
Eisenhower	Oveta Culp Hobby	HEW	1953–55
Ford	Carla Hills	HUD	1975–77
Carter	Patricia Roberts Harris	HUD	1977–
Carter	Juanita M. Kreps	Commerce	1977–

Because cabinet members—women and men alike—are chosen by Presidents not only for political reasons but also because of their achievements in their own professional fields, the five women above, who have served in the highest executive positions yet accorded to U.S. women, appear in other chapters: Ms. Perkins on p. 331 of "Women in the Labor Movement and Organizations"; Oveta Culp Hobby, who also served as the first director of the Women's Army Corps, on p. 534 of "Women in the Military"; Carla Hills and Patricia Harris, both lawyers, who have both also served in other jobs in government, on pp. 365 and 368 of "Women in the Law"; Juanita M. Kreps, an economist and academic administrator, on p. 409 of "Women in Education, Social Sciences, and the Humanities."

TOP JOBHOLDERS IN THE DOMESTIC AMERICAN BUREAUCRACY

Highest-Ranking Woman in Treasury Department History

BETTE B. ANDERSON of Savannah, Georgia, was sworn in as Undersecretary of the Treasury on April 14, 1977, the first woman to attain such a high-level post in the Treasury's 200-year history. Ms. Anderson started a banking career at the age of 18 as a bank-teller trainee. She progressed through the ranks of the Citizens & Southern National Bank of Savannah, Georgia, and became a vice-president in 1976. She was president of the National Association of Bank Women until she accepted the Treasury Department post. As Undersecretary, Ms. Anderson has responsibility for the department's administration and enforcement, operations and tariff affairs, as well as providing management guidance over many of the department's operating bureaus, including the Bureau of Alcohol, Tobacco and Firearms, the Bureau of the Mint, and the U. S. Customs Service.

Treasurer of the United States and Director of the Mint

On June 7, 1977, President Jimmy Carter announced the nomination of AZIE T. MORTON as treasurer of the United States and director of the Mint. The woman who signs the money was special assistant to the chairman of the Democratic National Committee from 1971 to 1977, when she became staff assistant to the U. S. House District Committee. She was deputy convention manager for the 1976 Democratic National Convention. Ms. Morton has played an active role in the movement for equal opportunity in employment and housing and was director of social services for the Wichita, Kansas, Model Cities Program from 1968 to 1971.

Director of the Office of Revenue Sharing, Department of the Treasury

BERNARDINE NEWSOM DENNING, director of the Office of Revenue Sharing, a lifetime member of the National Association for the Advancement of Colored People, who has taught or been an administrator at the secondary and university levels, is one of three women holding top-level jobs within the Department of the Treasury. Dr. Denning was named to her post on April 28, 1977. She administers two programs of federal fiscal assistance to states and local government: general revenue sharing and antirecession fiscal assistance. Through these programs, nearly $8 billion in federal funds are being returned each year to approximately 39,000 states, counties, cities, towns, townships, Indian tribes, and Alaskan native villages throughout the United States. Before coming to Washington, Dr. Denning was manager of the Title IV Civil Rights Office of the Detroit Public School system since 1975.

Treasury Personnel Official the First Woman Sent Overseas by Ford Foundation

Another of the three highest-ranking career women in the Department of the Treasury, ESTHER C. LAWTON, who was appointed deputy director of personnel on June 23, 1972, is a specialist in position classification and salary administration, and a widely known teacher in that field. Ms. Lawton, who has been with the Treasury Department since 1936, began as a clerk. She has been involved with the reorganization of the U. S. Secret Service and the Customs Office and in 1965 was the first woman consultant to be sent overseas by the Ford Foundation. Ms. Lawton advised the government of Lebanon on modernization of its civil service system. In 1968 she was sent to Jordan on a similar mission. She is the only person to be elected president of the International Society for Personnel Administration for two terms.

Treasury's First Female GS-18

When ANITA F. ALPERN became the U. S. Treasury's first woman GS-18 civil servant on April 29, 1975, only eight other women throughout the federal service had reached that level before her. GS-18 is the highest grade in the Civil Service. Fifty-five-year-old Ms. Alpern, who was appointed assistant commissioner for Planning and Research in the Internal Revenue Service, began her government service in 1942 as a P-1 (now GS-5) economist with the U. S. Employment Service. She joined the Internal Revenue Service in 1960 as a management analyst. Prior to her appointment as Assistant Commissioner, Ms. Alpern, a 1975 Federal Woman's Award winner, had been deputy assistant commissioner with the rank of GS-17.

Deputy Undersecretary of the Interior

The appointment of BARBARA HELLER, a 28-year-old female environmentalist, to the high post of Deputy Undersecretary of the Interior put Secretary of the Interior Cecil D. Andrus out on a limb. Ms. Heller's youth, sex, and lack of "proper" credentials upset the department's establishment. But her background and intelligence got her the appointment, which was announced on May 10, 1977. One of 15 persons who briefed President Jimmy Carter on energy issues after his nomination, Ms. Heller was a member of the energy policy staff of the Environmental Policy Center in Washington, D.C., from 1972 until her appointment. She has served on the Federal Energy Administration's environmental advisory committee, on the Office of Technology Assessment's energy conservation advisory committee, and as a consultant to the OTA on offshore oil technology. A graduate of Boston University (1970), Barbara Heller was a teaching assistant and seminar leader at the John F. Kennedy Institute of Politics at Harvard, 1972–73.

First Woman Assistant Secretary of the Interior

The first woman to serve as Assistant Secretary of the Interior, JOAN M. DAVENPORT, was nominated as Assistant Secretary for Energy and Minerals by President Jimmy Carter on March 30, 1977. The 34-year-old woman, who served as director of the Office of Environmental Assessment in the Federal Energy Administration before her appointment, was acting director of the Office of Technical Analysis of the Environmental Protection Agency from 1974 to 1975.

Twice Director of the Office of Territorial Affairs of the Interior

RUTH G. VAN CLEVE drafted statehood legislation for Hawaii and Alaska in the 1950s; it is not altogether inconceivable that this remarkable woman might some day draft legislation making the Moon the 51st state. On April 21, 1977, Van Cleve was reappointed director of the In-

terior Department's Office of Territorial Affairs, a position she held from 1964 to 1969. Her office has jurisdiction over all U.S. "territories," including the Moon, the Virgin Islands, Guam, American Samoa, and the Trust Territory of the Pacific Islands, together with a few, largely uninhabited Pacific islands under the U.S. flag. In 1972 Ms. Van Cleve, an attorney and most recently assistant general counsel of the Federal Power Commission, published *The Office of Territorial Affairs*, a book in which she describes the little-known, small-sized, but politically and historically important agency of the government, responsible for all matters involving the territories, particularly in their movement toward internal self-government. Ms. Van Cleve's husband is also a government lawyer, and they have two sons. She was born in Minneapolis in 1925 and received her law degree from Yale University. She joined the Interior Department as attorney-adviser in the solicitor's office specializing in territorial affairs after leaving Yale in 1950.

Assistant Secretary of Commerce for Administration

Assistant Secretary of Commerce for Administration ELSA A. PORTER had a long career in government before her appointment to this high position on March 15, 1977. Ms. Porter, who was born in 1928, is married, and has six children, was formerly chief of the Analysis and Development Division in the Bureau of Personnel Management Evaluation of the U. S. Civil Service Commission. In 1971 she was chief of the Manpower Planning and Staffing Branch in the Office of Personnel and Training of HEW. She has an M.P.A. from Harvard University.

First Woman Deputy Assistant Secretary of Commerce for Tourism

JEANNE WESTPHAL, sworn in as Deputy Assistant Secretary of Commerce for Tourism on June 15, 1977, the first woman appointed to that position, was previously the first woman to head a United States Travel Service field office abroad. From 1962 to 1965, Ms. Westphal served as regional travel promotion officer with USTS in charge of northern South America. Ms. Westphal, who was born in New York City and attended New York University and was graduated from the New York School of Interior Design, has also served as president of her own public relations firm.

Commerce Department's Chief Economist

Appointed Chief Economist of the Commerce Department on March 25, 1977, Dr. COURTENAY SLATER had earlier served as senior economist with the President's Council of Economic Advisers (CEA) and the Joint Economic Committee of Congress (JEC). As chief economist, Dr. Slater is the principal economic adviser to the Secretary and departmental liaison with the CEA. She also supervises the work of the Bureau of the Census and the Bureau of Economic Analysis, both parts of the Commerce Department. Dr. Slater, who received a Ph.D. from American University in 1968, served with the JEC from 1969 to 1977. She is 43, married, and has three sons.

First Woman Examiner-in-Chief, Board of Appeals, U. S. Patent and Trademark Office

BRERETON STURTEVANT was sworn in as examiner-in-chief of the Board of Appeals, U. S. Patent and Trademark Office, Department of Commerce, on August 24, 1971, the first woman appointed in the 110-year history of the Board. She was an attorney in private practice who specialized in patent and trademark litigation from 1957 to 1971. A former research chemist, Ms. Sturtevant, born in 1921, was the first woman law clerk in the Delaware Supreme and Superior Courts in 1950.

Highest-Ranking Classified Civil Servant in HEW

Ms. MARIE D. ELDRIDGE, the administrator for the National Center for Education Statistics, is the highest-ranking woman in the classified civil service in HEW. Ms. Eldridge was appointed to this Grade-18 position on November 20, 1975. As director of NCES, she is responsible for collecting, analyzing, and disseminating statistics on all aspects of education in the United States. The 1976 NCES budget was $13 million. Before joining HEW, Ms. Eldridge was director of the Office of Statistics and Analysis at the National Highway Traffic Safety Administration. She joined the federal government in 1954, when she was appointed an analytical statistician with the Department of the Navy. She was born in Baltimore, Maryland, in 1926 and is the mother of two children.

Assistant Secretary for Public Affairs, HEW

Her by-line was a familiar one to the economic and business community before President Carter chose EILEEN SHANAHAN as Assistant Secretary for Public Affairs for the Department of Health, Education, and Welfare. Ms. Shanahan, who was confirmed on March 29, 1977, had covered national economic policy, antitrust and business regulations for the *New York Times*'s Washington bureau for 15 years. Whenever she had the opportunity, she also wrote about the women's rights movement in the capital. Ms. Shanahan, born in Washington, D.C., in 1924, began her journalism career as a copy aide at the *Washington Post*, later moving to the United Press Washington Bureau as a reporter. She was the official spokesperson for the Treasury Department on tax matters until she joined the *Times* in 1962. In 1966 she received the Business Journalism Award of the University of Missouri School of Journalism and in 1972 was named Newspaper Woman of the Year by the New York Women in Communications. She and her husband, John V. Waits, Jr., are parents of two daughters.

Assistant Secretary for Human Development, HEW

The Assistant Secretary for Human Development under HEW Secretary Joseph Califano, ARABELLA MARTINEZ, who was confirmed on March 23, 1977, began a career as a social worker with the Alameda County Welfare Department in Oakland, California, in 1959. Since receiving a master's degree in social welfare from Berkeley in 1966, Ms. Martinez has worked in the Spanish-speaking community in the areas of community development, economic opportunity, leadership training, and housing. From 1969 until 1974 she was executive director of the Spanish-Speaking Unity Council of Oakland, California, and later a self-employed social program consultant in the areas of organization, staffing, program, resource, and community support development. She was honored with a John Hay Whitney Fellowship in 1965 and the Rosalie M. Stern Award in 1974.

HEW Regional Director

BERNICE LOTWIN BERNSTEIN, special assistant to the Secretary of the Department of Health, Education, and Welfare in New York City, directed the widespread operation of HEW's Region II, covering New York, New Jersey, Puerto Rico, and the Virgin Islands, from 1966 to 1977. The most complicated and difficult region to administer in the nation, Region II serves a population of almost 30 million people and had an estimated cash flow of about $20 billion in 1977. Ms. Bernstein began her federal career as an attorney with the National Recovery Administration in 1933. With the exception of five years, Mrs. Bernstein has been associated with HEW and its prede-cessor agencies since 1935. She is married to an attorney and has three daughters.

Highest-Ranking Woman, National Science Foundation

ELOISE E. CLARK joined the National Science Foundation in 1969 as program director for developmental biology. Since then she has steadily been promoted and in 1976 was named assistant director of Biological, Behavioral, and Social Sciences—the first woman to be appointed to such a post in a major research directorate of the Foundation. Dr. Clark completed her Ph.D. in zoology at the University of North Carolina and continued postdoctoral research in physical biochemistry at Washington University in St. Louis and at the University of California at Berkeley and taught biology, physiology, and biochemistry at Columbia University and at the Woods Hole Marine Biological Laboratory. She recently was elected to the Board of Directors of the American Association for the Advancement of Science.

First Female Administrator of the National Highway Traffic Safety Administration

JOAN CLAYBROOK, the first woman to head the National Highway Traffic Safety Administration, was sworn in on April 8, 1977. The nation's leading advocate of auto safety standards after her former boss, Ralph Nader, she became both Nadar's and the auto industry's chief target after assuming the job. A lawyer and chief lobbyist for Nader's myriad public interest organizations, she began her political career as a congressional staffer in 1965 when she was an American Political Science Fellow, and worked on the auto safety bill that created the agency she now heads. From 1966 to 1970 she was special assistant to the agency's first administrator, went to work for Nader's Public Interest Research Group in 1971, and headed up his Congress project in 1972. Joan Claybrook comes from a family that always fought for human rights, and was willing to work at a subsistence salary so she could carry on what Nader calls "full-time citizenship." Because she believed that a woman has greater credibility if she has a law degree, she decided in 1969 to become a lawyer and attended Georgetown Law School at night for four years. A skilled lobbyist, she has been a leading proponent of the "air bag, which the auto industry has consistently fought.

First Woman to Run a President's Transition, Now Deputy Administrator of EPA.

Deputy administrator of the Environmental Protection Agency BARBARA DAVIS BLUM, sworn in on March 11, 1977, ran the transition from President Ford to President Carter, an unprecedented job for a woman. A social worker, businesswoman, and environmentalist, Ms. Blum is most definitely a politician as well. She was deputy political director of Carter's primary campaigns and deputy director of the Carter/Mondale presidential campaign. An Atlanta resident, Ms. Blum earlier held numerous voluntary positions in the areas of health, land use planning, leadership training, and conservation. From 1972 to 1976, as chief lobbyist for SAVE (Save America's Vital Environment), the organization which serves as the lobbying arm of Georgia's conservation movement, she was effective in getting legislation passed dealing with land use, planning, and parks and helped to procure appropriations in the millions of dollars.

Federal Woman's Award Winners

The Federal Woman's Awards Program was established in 1960 to recognize six distinguished women in the federal career service annually for their outstanding contribution to government. In

First Female Peace Corps Director

Director of the Peace Corps CAROLYN R. PAYTON, a psychologist and former director of Howard University's Counseling Service, was nominated by President Jimmy Carter on September 7, 1977. She is the first woman to hold the job in the Corps's 16-year history. Ms. Payton, who worked for the Peace Corps from 1964 until 1970, recalls that in those years it sent volunteers abroad who did not have expert skills to teach but had "a volunteers motivation to transmit human qualities and understanding. I would like the Peace Corps to get back to that level," she has said. Ms. Payton has encouraged the recruitment of more blacks and other minorities and aims at revitalizing the international volunteer program.

Highest-Ranking Woman at the Veterans Administration

DOROTHY L. STARBUCK, who was appointed chief benefits director of the Veterans Administration on May 6, 1977, one of the very few women in the federal service to reach so high a level in general management, joined the Veterans Administration in 1946 as a clerk. She advanced steadily, becoming an assistant manager of the Baltimore Regional Office, manager of the Denver Regional office (the first woman to manage a regional office) and area field director in Washington. Prior to her current job, Ms. Starbuck was the line official in charge of the Western Area of the Department of Veterans Benefits, comprising 15 field stations in 13 western states and Manila.

1976, for the first time, eligibility was extended to women in the legislative and judicial branches of the government. Federal department and agency heads and committee chairmen nominate can-

...he winners are selected by a
... judges composed of representa-
...om the private sector, academe,
...overnment. Those chosen to date
ha... been:

1961

Beatrice Aitchison
Post Office Department
Ruth E. Bacon
Department of State
Nina Kinsella
Department of Justice
Charlotte Moore Sitterly
Department of Commerce
Aryness Joy Wickens
Department of Labor
Rosalyn S. Yalow
Veterans Administration

1962

Katharine W. Bracken
Department of State
Margaret H. Brass
Department of Justice
Thelma B. Dunn
Department of Health, Education, and
Welfare
Elelyn Harrison
U. S. Civil Service Commission
Allene R. Jeanes
Department of Agriculture
Nancy Grace Roman
National Aeronautics & Space Admin-
istration

1963

Eleanor L. Makel
Department of Health, Education, and
Welfare
Bessie Margolin
Department of Labor
Katharine Mather
Department of the Army
Verna C. Mohagen
Department of Agriculture
Blanche W. Noyes
Federal Aviation Agency
Eleanor C. Pressly
National Aeronautics & Space Admin-
istration

1964

Evelyn Anderson
National Aeronautics & Space Admin-
istration
Gertrude Blanch
Department of the Air Force
Selene Gifford
Department of the Interior
Elizabeth Messer
U. S. Civil Service Commission
Margaret W. Schwartz
Department of the Treasury
Patricia G. Van Delden
U. S. Information Agency

1965

Ann Z. Caracristi
National Security Agency
Elizabeth B. Drewry
General Services Administration
Dorothy M. Gilford
Department of the Navy
Carol C. Laise
Department of State
Sarah E. Stewart
Department of Health, Education, and
Welfare
Penelope H. Thunberg
Central Intelligence Agency

1966

Fannie M. Boyls
National Labor Relations Board
Stella Davis
U. S. Information Agency
Jocelyn R. Gill
National Aeronautics & Space Admin-
istration
Ida Craven Merriam
Department of Health, Education, and
Welfare
Irene Parsons
Veterans Administration
Ruth G. Van Cleve
Department of the Interior

1967

Elizabeth Ann Brown
Department of State

Barbara Moulton
Federal Trade Commission
Anne Mason Roberts
Department of Housing and Urban Development
Kathryn Grove Shipp
Department of the Navy
Wilma Louise Victor
Department of the Interior
Marjorie J. Williams
Veterans Administration

1968

Ruth Rogan Benerito
Department of Agriculture
Mabel Kunce Gibby
Veterans Administration
Frances M. James
Executive Office of the President
Ruby Grant Martin
Department of Health, Education, and Welfare
Lucille Farrier Stickel
Department of the Interior
Rogene L. Thompson
Department of Transportation
Nina Bencich Woodside
Government of the District of Columbia

1969

Mary Hughes Budenbach
National Security Agency
Edith N. Cook
Department of Labor
Eileen R. Donovan
Department of State
Jo Ann Smith Kinney
Department of the Navy
Esther Christian Lawton
Department of the Treasury
Dorothy L. Starbuck
Veterans Administration

1970

B. Jean Apgar
Department of Agriculture
Margaret Pittman
Department of Health, Education, and Welfare

Naomi R. Sweeney
Executive Office of the President
Sarah B. Glindmeyer
Government of the District of Columbia
Valerija B. Raulinaitis
Veterans Administration
Margaret Joy Tibbetts
Department of State

1971

Jeanne Wilson Davis
Executive Office of the President
Florence Johnson Hicks
Government of the District of Columbia
Juanita Morris Moody
National Security Agency
Essie Davis Morgan
Veterans Administration
Rita Rapp
National Aeronautics & Space Administration
Joan Raup Rosenblatt
Department of Commerce

1972

Lois Albro Chatham
Department of Health, Education, and Welfare
Phyllis Dixon Clemmons
Government of the District of Columbia
Ruth M. Davis
Department of Commerce
Mary Harrover Ferguson
Department of the Navy
Ruth Mandeville Leverton
Department of Agriculture
Patricia Ann McCreedy
Agency for International Development

1973

Bernice Lotwin Bernstein
Department of Health, Education, and Welfare
Marguerite S. Chang
Department of the Navy
Isabella L. Karle
Department of the Navy

Marilyne E. Jacox
  Department of Commerce
Janet Hart
  Federal Reserve System
Marjorie Rhodes Townsend
  National Aeronautics & Space Administration

1974

Henriette D. Avram
  Library of Congress
Edna A. Boorady
  Agency for International Development
Roselyn Payne Epps
  Government of the District of Columbia
Brigid Gray Leventhal
  National Cancer Institute
Gladys P. Rogers
  Department of State
Madge Skelly
  Veterans Administration

1975

Anita F. Alpern
  Department of the Treasury
Beatrice J. Dvorak
  Department of Labor

Evans V. Hayward
  Department of Commerce
Wilda H. Martinez
  Department of Agriculture
Marie U. Nylen
  Department of Health, Education, and Welfare
Marguerite M. Rogers
  Department of the Navy

1976

I. Blanche Bourne
  Government of the District of Columbia
Carin Ann Clauss
  Department of Labor
Dorothy I. Fennell
  Department of Agriculture
Marian J. Finkel
  Department of Health, Education, and Welfare
M. Patricia Murray
  Veterans Administration
Joyce J. Walker
  Office of Management and Budget

1977

(No awards were made in 1977.)

THE U. S. STATE DEPARTMENT AND FOREIGN SERVICE

First Woman U. S. Foreign Service Officer

LUCILE ATCHERSON CURTIS, born 1894, on December 5, 1922, became the first woman in U.S. history to enter the career Foreign Service. Having passed the Foreign Service examinations, she served in the Department of State's division of Latin American Affairs until 1925, when she was posted to Berne, Switzerland, as Third Secretary of the U.S. Legation. After two years there, she was sent to Panama. Ms. Curtis resigned in 1927. Her daughter, Charlotte Curtis, has had a distinguished career in journalism (see "Women in Communications," p. 466).

First U. S. Woman Ambassador

It was President Harry S. Truman who appointed EUGENIE MOORE ANDERSON

as his ambassador to Denmark in 1949. The first woman ambassador in U.S. history, she served from 1949 to 1953. She later became the first American woman to serve as chief of mission to an Eastern European country (U.S. minister to Bulgaria, 1962–65). Ms. Anderson, who was born in Adair, Iowa, in April 1909, was appointed special assistant to the Secretary of State in 1968.

First Woman Career Ambassador Had Five Firsts

FRANCES E. WILLIS, in 1927, the third woman to enter the Foreign Service, during her 37-year career achieved five firsts. She was the first woman appointed the highest rank in the Foreign Service. As U.S. career ambassador to Switzerland, 1953–57, to Norway 1957–61, and to Ceylon, 1961–64, she was also the first woman to assume charge of a post, the first career Foreign Service woman to be appointed ambassador, the first to be appointed career minister, and the first to be appointed ambassador to more than one country. She retired in 1964. On November 16, 1973, she was honored with the Foreign Service Cup by the American Foreign Service Association for her "outstanding contribution to the conduct of foreign relations of the United States." Ms. Willis was born in Metropolis, Illinois, 1899, was graduated from Stanford University in 1920, and received her Ph.D. from Stanford in 1923.

First U. S. Woman Named Minister to a Foreign Country

RUTH BRYAN OWEN (1885–1977) was appointed by President Franklin D. Roosevelt on April 13, 1933, as U.S. minister to Denmark, the first woman minister from the United States to a foreign country. Ms. Owen, the daughter of famed three-time presidential candidate William Jennings Bryan, of Illinois, inherited political drive, becoming the first woman to win a seat in the U.S. House of Representatives from the Deep South. Divorced after her first marriage and then widowed early in her second, Ruth Bryan Owen was left with four children to support by lecturing and free-lance writing. A member of Congress from Florida serving from April 15, 1929, to March 4, 1933, she was defeated in her bid for the Democratic nomination for a third term because she continued to support her father's lifelong stance as a Prohibitionist, which had lost its popularity with the voters.

"Call Me Madame" Minister

PERLE MESTA, 1893–1975, the first U.S. woman minister to Luxembourg, served from 1949 to 1953. She was appointed by President Harry S. Truman, during whose tenure she became famous for her lavish Washington parties. The wife of George Mesta and daughter of William B. Skirvin, Perle Mesta inherited considerable wealth. During the Kennedy and Johnson administrations, she continued to entertain on a spectacular scale. Ms. Mesta inspired Irving Berlin's musical *Call Me Madam* and its line "hostess with the mostes'."

First Woman Ambassador to a Major Power

CLARE BOOTHE LUCE had already distinguished herself as playwright, author, war correspondent, congresswoman, and political activist when she was appointed by President Dwight D. Eisenhower to serve as U.S. ambassador to Italy, the first American woman ambassador to a major power. She served from March 1953 to December 1956, when she was forced to resign due to ill health. Also the first woman elected to Congress from Connecticut, she was encouraged by Republican Party leaders to run for the seat once held by her stepfather. Her political talents included rhetorical abilities, as well as brilliance and beauty, and she won the nomination over six opponents. A hardworking congresswoman known for controversial positions, she introduced a proposal for a non-aggression pact with European nations (later realized by NATO), a resolution calling for racial equality in the military and creating international machinery for the control of arms and atomic energy. She also introduced a bill to establish a bureau in the Department of Labor to ensure workers equal pay for equal work. Clare Boothe Luce was born in New York City in 1903. She is the widow of Time-Life founder Henry Luce.

The Longest Reigning Passport Chief

At 72, FRANCES G. KNIGHT, still resisting, finally gave up her fiefdom over the U. S. Passport Office. She had controlled the Passport Office for 22 years, beginning in May 1955, and relinquished it unwillingly only when President Jimmy Carter demanded that she do so in June 1977. Ms. Knight is credited with bringing efficiency to the office but is remembered also for her tendency to use a passport as a political instrument. In the '50s she became the cutting edge of government policies that restricted the travel rights of Communists and members of other parties proscribed by the Internal Security Act. She was also known for a readiness to offer the resources of the Passport Office to official investigations keeping tabs on traveling Americans who happened to disagree with their government's views on such matters as the Vietnam War.

First Woman to Head a State Department Bureau and First Black to Hold So Senior a Position

The first woman and the first black to head a State Department Bureau with the rank of assistant secretary, BARBARA WATSON, administrator of the Bureau of Security and Consular Affairs, was spurred to high achievement by her late father, James B. Watson, the first black elected to a judgeship in New York. She was chosen the most outstanding law student in New York and graduated third in her class at New York University's Law School, "It's a good thing Father was not alive. He would have expected me to be first," she later said. Ms. Watson was executive director of the New York City Commission to the United Nations, before she was named administrator of the Bureau of Security and Consular Affairs in August 1968. She held the State Department post until December 1974 and was reappointed to it by President Carter.

Women's Action Organization of the Department of State

Until 11 women employees took action, the U. S. Department of State and its related foreign affairs agencies seemed not to be aware that women employees had any problems. The Department presented 13 task force reports in 1970 recommending streamlining and reform measures. Not one mentioned any of the serious problems affecting its women.

That made the 11 women angry enough to put their careers on the line. They personally had experienced or viewed such discriminatory practices as: forced resignation of married women from the foreign service; discrimination in assignments to certain countries and in policy-making jobs; inequities in shipping or housing allowances during service abroad; inequities in rates and promotion of women; and consistent imbalance in the ratio of men to women accepted as Foreign Service officers. They also sympathized with the plight of Foreign

Service wives, who were virtually denied their own personal lives and whose "performances" were evaluated in their husband's personnel reports.

The 11 women who assembled—for the first time in State Department history —to consider ways to overcome these discriminatory policies and constituted themselves the Women's Action Organization (WAO) were:

Bernice Baer
Barbara Good
Terry Healy
Jean Joyce
Marguerite Cooper King
Mildred Marcy
Mary Olmstead
Mildred Pitts
Idris Rossell
Eliann Savage
Dorothy Stansbury

As a result of their actions, managemen was made aware of the extent of the feeling of discrimination women experienced in the foreign affairs agencies. Some steps were taken to correct the most blatant inequities. They can be summed up in three policy directives: (1) calling for equality in assignments, forbidding discrimination against women for any job, at any level, in any country; (2) allowing women to have both marriage and a career in the Foreign Service, where women with dependents will have equal opportunities to serve abroad if they wish; (3) establishing professional status and standards for secretaries, recognizing them as career professionals entitled to certain rights and treatment.

WAO also lent support to another policy directive for which it was not directly responsible, recognizing the Foreign Service wife as a private individual with personal and career interests.

Although women entrants into the career service have risen to 21 per cent from the static 7 per cent before WAO acted, the group continues to push for women's equality within the department. "Much remains to be done," says WAO president Marguerite Cooper King. "Changes in the regulations do not necessarily mean implementation; some group must ensure that the new policies are carried out. Old male-dominant attitudes persist; our gains can be lost unless all women and friends of women act together in keeping watch on our continual progress."

First U. S. Woman Ambassador to Africa

JEAN WILKOWSKI was sworn in as ambassador to the Republic of Zambia on July 5, 1972, the first woman ambassador to Africa, after having served since 1970 as consular of the U. S. Embassy in Rome. She was born on August 28, 1919, in Rhinelande, Wisconsin, was graduated from St. Mary's of the Woods College in Indiana in 1941, and received an M.A. degree from the University of Wisconsin in 1944. She entered the Foreign Service in 1945 and resigned in April 1976.

State First Woman Security Officer

Reporting to duty as the State Department's first woman security officer on May 22, 1972, may have been as thrilling for PATRICIA MORTON as climbing southeast Asia's Mount Kinabalu peak (13,455 feet), which she did on New Year's Day, 1971. Patti Morton was known as "the girl with the long blond hair who runs up hills" during her two-year tour of duty at the American Embassy in Nepal, where she served as protocol officer and as a secretary. A secretary with the Department for seven years when the higher-ups decided to train her as an investigator in the Washington Field Office, a breakthrough for women in the State Department. She had served as deputy post security officer during an earlier assignment in Kinshasa and earned a meritorious step increase for outstanding work. Ms. Morton holds a B.A. degree in Economics. She joined the department in 1965.

First Woman Executive Director of a Regional Bureau at State

JOAN CLARK, director of the Bureau of European Affairs of the Department of State, 1972–77 was the first woman to head a regional bureau. In 1977 Ms. Clark, a career Foreign Service officer, became director of Management Operations, a position with rank equivalent to assistant secretary. Joan Clark was born in Ridgefield Park, New Jersey, and joined the State Department in 1945.

First Woman to Act as Official Spokesperson for the United States Government in Foreign Policy Affairs

On January 18, 1973, SIMONE A. POULAIN, a public affairs specialist for the

Department of State, became the first woman to act as official spokesperson for the United States Government in foreign policy affairs. She conducted the State Department's daily briefing for newspersons. Ms. Poulain, who has served in the department's Public Affairs Office off and on since 1951 and specializes in liaison with TV networks and various news organizations, handled a wide range of questions at her first briefing. In 1964 she was detailed to the White House and served on Ms. Lyndon Baines Johnson's staff for five years.

State's First Woman Courier

SUSAN SHIRLEY CARTER joined the Foreign Service in 1963 and became the first woman appointed a diplomatic courier in October 1973. A former resident of Florida, Ms. Carter was previously assigned to duties at posts in Paris, Dacca, Mexico City, and the Hague. Her two-year "excursion" tour made her available for courier service to the Western Hemisphere and the West Coast of Africa.

First Woman Director of the U. S. Foreign Service; First Woman Assistant Secretary of State, and First Ambassador to Marry Another Ambassador En Poste

The highest-ranking woman in Foreign Service history, CAROL LAISE, was sworn in as director general of the Foreign Service on April 10, 1975, the first woman to hold that powerful job. As director general, Ambassador Laise, until her retirement at the end of 1977, was in charge of personnel policy, recruitment, training, assignment, and promotion of almost 7,000 Foreign Service officers. In her acceptance speech, she recalled an earlier assignment to England, when her hosts were shocked that a woman was sent. "I might say that we survived the shock—they and I—and it was an experience worth going through. However,

it's not something I want to repeat again." Carol Laise was born in 1917 in Winchester, Virginia. She began her government service with the Department of Agriculture in 1938 at grade level 4 and entered the Foreign Service in 1945. From October 1973 until April 1975, she served as Assistant Secretary of State for Public Affairs, the first female Assistant Secretary of State in the nation's history. In 1967, when she was serving as ambassador to Nepal, Ambassador Laise married Ambassador Ellsworth Bunker. Later, Ambassador Bunker was assigned to Saigon and they rotated visits every month, taking turns making the 2,000-mile trip between Kathmandu and Saigon. As ambassador to Nepal, Carol Laise rode on an elephant in a ceremonial procession as dean of the diplomatic corps, climbed steep mountain trails, and traveled by helicopter to remote regions of the country. Ms. Laise retired at the end of 1977.

First Woman Chief of Protocol in U. S. History

SHIRLEY TEMPLE BLACK gave such a convincing performance as first U.S. woman ambassador to Ghana that President Ford recalled her in June 1975, and made her the first woman chief of protocol in U.S. history. For Ms. Black, Hollywood's darling at the age of three (she earned more than $3 million before the onset of puberty) and one of the few young stars to survive a Hollywood childhood unscathed, the new post was the culmination of nearly a quarter century of public service. As a housewife in suburban Bethesda, Maryland, in the early 1950s while her husband was in the Navy, she developed a yen for politics. When the Blacks moved back to California, she became a GOP precinct captain. In 1967 she ran for Congress and was defeated. During the next few years, she raised nearly $1 million for the Republican Party; as a reward, President Nixon named her a representative to the UN

General Assembly. "People were eager to discount her as a dilettante and a featherbrain," one UN observer said later, "but she took the job very seriously, did her homework, and was highly regarded." As the ambassador to Ghana, she was an outspoken advocate of black self-determination in Africa and was made an honorary deputy Fanti tribal chief before a cheering throng of 20,000 Ghanaians. As chief of protocol, she carried the rank of Assistant Secretary of State and commanded a staff of 44. She was responsible for escorting visiting heads of state around the Capital, squiring them to luncheons, receptions, teas, wreath-layings, and all the ceremonials that official ingenuity can devise. "The rest of the time, I go to every national day every country has. There are 126 a year," she said.

First U. S. Ambassador to Papua, New Guinea

MARY SEYMOUR OLMSTEAD, a career Foreign Service officer who began her diplomatic life in 1945 as a junior economic analyst in Montreal, reached the top rank on December 22, 1975, when she was named the United States' first ambassador to Papua, New Guinea. Ms. Olmstead is most admired for her role in advancing the cause of equal opportunity for women within the State Department and Foreign Service in 1970, when she and 10 other women organized the Women's Action Organization to improve conditions of women employees at the Department of State, AID, and USIA and to eliminate discriminatory policies (p. 92). Ms. Olmstead had the highest rank of all WAO members. Her commitment and clout undoubtedly gave the organization credibility and helped win its successes. She was named deputy director of Personnel for Management and Service in 1971—a position that involved her directly in ensuring equal treatment for all Foreign Service personnel. Mary Olmstead was born on September 28, 1919 in Duluth, Minnesota, and received her M.A. in 1945 from Columbia University.

First Woman Ambassador to the Court of St. James's

When President Gerald Ford on February 19, 1976, swore in ANNE L. ARMSTRONG as ambassador to the Court of St. James's, he accomplished two goals: he demonstrated his commitment to women's equality and rewarded a trusted political ally. At the swearing-in ceremony, President Ford said: "Betty is always needling me a little bit that I should appoint qualified, highly competent women to positions of great responsibility." Ms. Armstrong expressed her own and BETTY FORD's (see the chapter "Women in the Arts and Entertainment," p. 594) excitement "about this tremendous new opportunity for women," to be the "first Chief of State to have the confidence in women to name one as ambassador to one of the world's most prestigious diplomatic posts." Anne Armstrong was born in New Orleans, Louisiana, 1927, and was graduated from Vassar College (Phi Beta Kappa) in 1949. Her husband is wealthy rancher Tobin L. Armstrong. They have five children. Long active in Republican politics, starting as a precinct worker in Texas, in 1971, she became the first woman to serve as co-chairman of the Republican National Committee. In 1972 President Richard Nixon asked her to join the White House staff as Counselor to the President with cabinet rank, the first woman with such rank since the 1950s. Under her direction, the first office of Women's Programs was established in the White House. She left the White House in 1975, and left the American Embassy in London when Ambassador Kingman Brewster, Jr., former president of Yale, succeeded her in 1977.

Highest-Ranking Woman in State Department History

LUCY WILSON BENSON, born in New York in 1927, a former president of the League of Women Voters, was sworn in as Undersecretary of State for Security Assistance, Science, and Technology, on March 28, 1977. As the highest-ranking woman in the State Department's history, Ms. Benson has the awesome charge of controlling arms sales and the proliferation of nuclear arms. Her appointment came as a surprise because she had had no experience in the technical field of arms control (although many of her predecessors were equally inexperienced). Ms. Benson was national League of Women Voters president, 1968–74, and is credited with making the league a strong political force. During the last days of her presidency, men were admitted as full voting members, a historical precedent. Also League president in Massachusetts, and secretary of Human Resources for the Commonwealth of Massachusetts in 1975, she was appointed by the Speaker of the U. S. House of Representatives as a member of the Special Commission on Administrative Review in 1976.

First Woman Ambassador to Belgium

The first woman ambassador to Belgium, ANNE COX CHAMBERS, is a political ally of President Jimmy Carter, who named her to the post in April 1977. Ms. Chambers is a director of Cox Enterprises, Inc., which owns Atlanta Newspapers and the Cox Broadcasting Corporation, director of the Fulton National Bank, and also a director of several educational, civic, and welfare organizations. She was born in Dayton, Ohio, 1919, and attended Finch College and Miss Porter's School in Connecticut. She is married to Robert W. Chambers. They have three children.

Senior Adviser to the Secretary of State and Coordinator for International Narcotics Matters

MALTHEA FALCO was 33 years old and special assistant to the president of the Drug Abuse Council when she was appointed by Secretary of State Cyrus Vance as his senior adviser and coordinator for International Narcotics Matters on February 5, 1977. Ms. Falco, who graduated *cum laude* from Radcliffe in 1965 and attended Yale Law School, earned a J.D. degree in 1968. She was born in Alabama in 1944.

First Woman Ambassador to Cameroon

The U.S. ambassador to Cameroon, MABEL MURPHY SMYTHE, was appointed on April 25, 1977, by President Jimmy Carter. Dr. Smythe was a U.S. delegate to the 13th General Conference of UNESCO in Paris in 1964 and a member of the U.S. National Commission for UNESCO, 1965–70. Before accepting the ambassadorship, Dr. Smythe was vice-president of the Phelps-Stokes Fund. She served as scholar in residence with the U.S. Commission on Civil Rights in 1973–74.

First Woman Ambassador to Finland

The first U.S. woman ambassador to Finland, ROZANNE L. RIDGWAY, is a career Foreign Service officer who was Deputy Assistant Secretary for Oceans and Fisheries of the Department of State with the rank of ambassador before her nomination as ambassador to Finland by President Jimmy Carter in May 1977. She was deputy chief of mission in Nassau, the Bahamas, 1973–75. She received the department's Honor Award in 1966 and 1975 and the Meritorious Honor Award in 1970.

"'You've Come a Long Way, Baby'—Well, Is That All? Is This the 'Expanded' History of Women in Diplomacy?"

By STEPHANIE SMITH KINNEY*

I am a woman and I work for the Department of State. That in itself is not a problem, although there are those who might disagree with me. The problem arises when one must speak both as a woman and as an individual.

Let me give you an example. The department has just published a new book called *Women in American Foreign Affairs,* and the department is terribly excited about it . . . Now that the book has been published, the [Department of State] *Newsletter* wants to know what I think of it—it's about women, you understand—and I am faced with a political decision: should I be a grateful and kindly hypocrite, or a critical ingrate subject to charges of chronic faultfinding? I do not want to be either . . .

Not the "expanded history of women and their place in American foreign affairs" promised, the book is copiously documented with primary sources which appear to be drawn mainly from departmental archives and records, plus news articles and interviews of Women's Action Organization activists, conducted by JEAN JOYCE for the Schlesinger library at Radcliffe . . . [It] is refreshingly devoid of rhetoric and ideology, but it is also devoid of any conceptual framework more stringent than "You've come a long way, baby."

The department has established an affirmative action program for women, celebrated an annual Women's Week, complete with films and a message from the Secretary . . . appointed and hired women to serve as senior officials at home and abroad . . . even taken to hiring married women (many of them married to departmental employees) with some regularity, and, of course, it no longer holds it against a woman if she gets married after she gets employed. To show you how much things have changed, today there's not a man in the department who would dare suggest publicly that women are not suited to serve as officers in certain regions of the world for political and social reasons, and no one would embarrass himself, as many once did, by suggesting that "in some areas of the world climatic conditions are too adverse for women [officers] to withstand." (For some reason these conditions were never too adverse for women clerks and spouses) . . .

I do not discount the importance of women being allowed on the team in order to be able to play the game, but is this all there is to record? I still am not sure whether women have a history in American foreign affairs or not. Perhaps this is the point: there isn't a history of women in American foreign affairs—and there should be.

* Ms. Kinney works on program coordination in the office of the director general of the Foreign Service. Her review of *Women in American Affairs* by Homer L. Calkin (Department of State, 1977) is excerpted from the Department of State *Newsletter,* December 1977.

3

Women in the Home and Community

By Louise Edie Kerrigan
(contributing editor-writer)

A homemaker may list herself as "just a housewife" and, like Therese Carter in Studs Terkel's *Working* (1972), acknowledge that "You don't have to have any special talents. . . . A housewife is a housewife. . . . Low on the totem pole. I can read the paper and find that out." Yet, with Therese, she may add that "Deep down, I feel what I'm doing is important . . . I love being a housewife."

Despite its difficulties and putdowns, homemaking remains the occupation of choice for most of the United States' 35 million housewives—even for a majority of those who are working outside the home—and for women in other nations. But pressures of many kinds are forcing women to reassess the premises on which they have based their lives. There are 12 million widows in the United States alone. The divorce rate continues to accelerate in many countries. As an increasing number of women find themselves financially stranded, the most conservative housewives are becoming aware of the dangers of economic dependency.

In the United States today, a third of women 55 to 64 years old are single,

widowed, or divorced, and along with younger "displaced homemakers" are ineligible for any of the following benefits: welfare (unless disabled or the mothers of children under 18), unemployment payments, Medicare, Social Security (unless married 10 years, effective 1979, and of retirement age), and workmen's compensation. They often lose health insurance and pension benefits and may find themselves expected to pay heavy inheritance taxes not required of widowers. Moreover, single women are frequently responsible for families. In 1977 the Bureau of Labor Statistics listed 40 million women in the work force (41 per cent); the number of married women working had tripled in 25 years to 22.4 million, and nearly 29 million children under 18 had mothers who worked outside the home (with those under 35 increasing most rapidly).

In the decade ending in 1975, single-parent families headed by women increased ten times as fast as two-parent families: the *New York Times* reported that in 1975 such families totaled more than 13 per cent but made up 40 per cent of the poor and included more than half the children living below poverty level; women and children were worse off than the aged, and among the aged, women were far worse off than men (47 per cent of women over 65 received less than $2,000 yearly; only 12 per cent had incomes of more than $5,000). The *Times* noted that together adult women and children under 18 made up two thirds of the United States' population.

Aware of their precarious economic position as never before, American women of many viewpoints have united behind legislation for equitable Social Security, divorce, pension, and inheritance rights, national displaced homemaker laws. They have received a sympathetic hearing from many legislators (who have felt that a vote against them would be like a vote against their own mothers) and some advances have been made. Equal credit has already been won. Displaced homemaker centers have been established. The Martha Movement supports the status of homemakers and seeks recognition of women as equal partners of men, entitled to half the family income and benefits. Other groups all over the country, such as New York's Catalyst and Washington, D.C.'s Wider Opportunities for Women, are assisting women returning to school and to work. Mindful that the average American woman actually works 25 years outside the home, they are also promoting the concept of part-time and flexi-time jobs, and calling attention to the need for improved day care for the benefit of working mothers and their children. And everywhere resourceful homemakers (and their families) are turning crises into creative opportunities just as enterprising women before them, confronted with dire necessity, have put their skills to use in the outside world.

U.S. women moved permanently into serious activity beyond their homes after the Civil War. Some found their way to college. One of these, the first woman graduate of the Massachusetts Institute of Technology, ELLEN H. SWALLOW RICHARDS founded the profession of home economics. Many followed her into this new endeavor, and it remains a field in which women in developing countries are still pioneering.

In the late 19th century women also banded together in clubs of their own—a rapidly spreading grass-roots movement called the "school of the middle-aged woman" by Sorosis co-founder JANE CROLY. In 1904 SARAH PLATT DECKER, the newly elected president of the General Federation of Women's Clubs, exhorted its members to volunteer for service in their communities: "Ladies . . . Dante is dead . . . and I think it is time that we dropped the study of his *Inferno* and turned our attention to our own." The Federation by 1914 had more than 1 million members, and its impact had already been felt in many fields, including pure food and drug regulation, juvenile justice, education, parks and playgrounds, passage of the Mann Act, sweatshop and child labor reforms.

For many women, volunteer community work led to full-time careers, unpaid or paid. A notable early representative (unpaid) was MARY PARKER FOLLETT, (see "Women in Business, Industry, and Finance" the nation's first management expert. ELLIE SMEAL, U.S. housewife-president of the National Organization for Women (NOW), is probably today's most important (paid) example. But there have been and there are many, many others. Some of those whose volunteer activities have been associated with particular movements appear in the chapters on "Women in the Labor Movement and Organizations," "Women in Agriculture and the World Food Movement," "Women Activists, Heroes, and Humanitarians," or elsewhere in this book. This chapter includes an additional sampling of women all over the world who have contributed significantly to their communities and enriched their own lives while learning new skills as volunteer workers.

This chapter also takes note of the strong role that women of the world have played in helping to revive handicrafts and in setting up cottage industries and craft schools, or simply in practicing traditional crafts in their homes and selling their articles on a small scale or through large cooperatives. Other chapters cover women whose work in weaving and ceramics is primarily commercial (see especially the Scandinavian designers in "Women in Fashions and Home Furnishings") or fiber artists like SHEILA HICKS (see "Women in the Arts and Entertainment"). The following pages include pioneer American settlement worker KATHERINE PETTIT, who traveled rough Appalachian backwoods trails to found Hindman and Pine Mountain schools; LUCY MORGAN, who started Penland, probably the oldest and largest summer craft school in the United States; and AILEEN WEBB, whose efforts in Putnam County, New York, burgeoned into the American Crafts Council and the World Crafts Council—the latter bringing together craftspeople from many parts of the world. Here, too, are RUTH DAYAN, of Israel's Maskit; JOICE NANKIVELL LOCH, who revived rug-making in Greece; and traditional weaver-dyer AYANO CHIBA, honored by Japan as a "Living National Treasure."

In the area of crafts and related "domestic" skills, a number of women have won fame and fortune imparting to others their knowledge of needlework, cooking, and gardening. Many others have founded businesses on their kitchen tables or in their basements or garages that have grown to employ hundreds of people. Often motivated by financial necessity, as was LYDIA PINKHAM (1819–83) when she began to sell her wildly successful Vegetable Compound after her husband went bankrupt in 1873, house-

wives have launched such successful enterprises as the Nelly Don dress company and Maidenform (see NELL DONNELLY REED and IDA ROSENTHAL, pp. 259 and 257 in "Women in Fashions and Home Furnishings"). Madam C. J. WALKER, millionaire developer of hair straightener (see p. 512 in "Women in Business, Industry, and Finance"), was another. More recently, MARGARET RUDKIN of Pepperidge Farm fame and BETTE GRAHAM of Liquid Paper have built big businesses beginning at home and based on ideas unlikely, at the time, to have occurred to men.

Even as women have been seeking new ways to make not only homes for their families but also a place for themselves in wider worlds, new possibilities for men to develop their potential in homemaking, nurturing, and cultural roles as well as in traditional jobs have opened up. Additionally, by 1978 a new movement along lines promoted by women's employment experts was beginning to offer both men and women increasing opportunities for part-time, flexi-time, and shared work. Industry and government were looking seriously at such arrangements for those individuals who prefer more free time to more money, including not only working women who must care for children but also the elderly, the handicapped, and mobile younger people who want to see their productivity on the job, their leisure, and their family lives enhanced.

Whether they were working at part-time or full-time jobs, nearly half of American couples in 1976 were earning two paychecks. Their two-paycheck households were offering both men and women insurance against unemployment as well as expanded mutual interests and real options in changing careers or returning to school.

LOUISE EDIE KERRIGAN, *educated at Vassar and the Columbia Graduate School of Journalism, was a general news reporter and suburban editor for the* White Plains *(N.Y.)* Reporter-Dispatch, *general news reporter for the* New York Times, *and women's editor, the* Telephone Review, *in New York City before marriage to a Foreign Service officer took her to Germany, Norway, Canada, Turkey, and Israel. Now divorced, she reentered journalism as*

editor of a citizens' newsletter, the Annapolis Alert, *covering the Maryland General Assembly, and has since worked as a free-lance writer and editor. She appears again in this book as co-author of "Women in Fashions and Home Furnishings," p. 236. Ms. Kerrigan has a daughter who works for an engineering firm and a son in college.*

HOUSEWIVES AND MOTHERS

She Combined Job and Twelve Children

Consulting engineers LILLIAN MOLLER GILBRETH (1878–1972) and her husband Frank were internationally famous as pioneers in time-motion research. They were even more widely known as the parents in *Cheaper by the Dozen* (1948), a best seller written by two of their children and later made into a movie. As an engineer, Mrs. Gilbreth charted ways to save waste and human motion in the office, factory, hospital, and home. She conducted private industrial engineering seminars from her home before universities became interested, and later served on the faculties of Purdue, Rutgers, and the Newark College of Engineering. When she married Frank in 1904, they planned a family of 12— half boys and half girls—and managed them when they had them with the same efficiency they displayed in their engineering partnership. Decisions were made by family council, they answered mail by a family newspaper, a "birthday gift buyer" remembered all the birthdays and bought the presents, and jobs went to the lowest "bidder." After her husband's sudden death in 1924, Mrs. Gilbreth sailed to Europe to keep his speaking engagements at the London Power Conference, the World Congress of Scientific Management, and the Masaryk Academy (Prague). During the Depression she served on two presidential unemployment committees. In World War II, she was educational adviser to the American Council of Education, the Office of War Information, and the War Manpower Commission; she was also industrial consultant to the Navy and, active into her 80s, developed new concepts in devices for the disabled. A prolific writer who won many awards, she was the first woman commencement speaker at the University of California in 1902 and received her master's in literature there, her doctorate in industrial psychology from Brown in 1915, and honorary degrees from California, Brown, Smith, Rutgers, and others. She died at 93, still maintaining that "Age needn't determine what one is able to do." Among her legacies to American homes: kitchens with work surfaces adjusted to height, step-on trash cans, refrigerators with shelves in the doors.

Mothers of the Year

Every year the American Mothers Committee, Inc., celebrates Mother's Day with a luncheon at the Waldorf-Astoria Hotel, New York City, honoring the Mother of the Year. In recent years, they have been:

1968 E. Grossman Bodine
      North Dakota
1969 E. Peterson LeTourneau
      Texas
1970 Dorothy Lee Wilson
      Tennessee
1971 Betty Anthony Zahn
      Oklahoma
1972 Esther Hunt Moore
      North Carolina

1973 Ruth Youngdahl Nelson
      Minnesota
1974 Phyllis Brown Marriott
      District of Columbia
1975 Josephine Wainman Burson
      Tennessee
1976 M. Garnett Grindstaff
      New Mexico
1977 Gloria Berry Langdon
      Oklahoma

First Woman Chosen as "Unsung Heroine of the Year"

Her strengths as a mother and family leader were among the attributes that won RITA DABERTIN, 43, the honor of being named the first "Unsung Heroine of the Year" by the *Ladies' Home Journal* in 1977. Ms. Dabertin, of Whiting, Indiana, one of the 21.7 per cent of U.S. women who are heads of households, was nominated by one of her six children. Widowed while pregnant with her sixth child, she managed her money carefully until her youngest was old enough for kindergarten and she was down to her last $100. After trying several jobs, she decided she preferred factory work to more traditional women's jobs, and joined the American Oil Company as a materials handler. Over the years she made her small budget cover books, music, vacations, and a canoe for her sons. Because of the canoe, she became involved in ecology. When plans were made to drain Indiana's Lake George, she fought to make it a state conservation project, and won. Rita Dabertin has one married daughter, working for her master's in speech therapy. Of her sons, one is a college graduate, two were in college in 1977, and two in high school.

Two Kennedy Mothers

Widow of the assassinated Robert Kennedy, ETHEL KENNEDY despite her husband's death and that of her brother-in-law President John F. Kennedy, has said that she still thinks politics is "the most noble profession." She spends considerable time working for the Robert F. Kennedy Memorial Foundation but most of her life revolves around her family of 11 children and, now, a grandchild. Motherhood, she believes, is "the most important job there is and the most re-warding thing a woman can possibly do, to raise children into adults."

Ethel Kennedy's mother-in-law, ROSE KENNEDY, long regularly voted one of the world's most admired women, mother of nine, grandmother and great-grandmother, has carried on dauntlessly through the death of her husband and the earlier tragic losses of four of her children and the retardation of one. The daughter of Boston politician Mayor "Honey Fitz" Fitzgerald, she has always been a politically active woman, and in her mid-80s, still vital, fashionably dressed, and outspoken, remains so.

Spokeswomen for Stepmothers

When TV reporter JEANNETTE LOFAS married financial consultant Bob Greene in 1972, she left her job to become full-time wife, mother to her son Lars, and stepmother to four daughters. Although her stepdaughters had treated her as a friend before the wedding, their visits afterward became uncomfortable, and her husband began to favor his daughters and overcriticize her son. Ms. Lofas discussed the situation with an old friend, RUTH ROOSEVELT; their co-authored book *Living in Step* (1976) was the result. While they were researching, the National Institute of Mental Health encouraged them to organize the Step Family Foundation. The SFF, incorporated in 1975, now serves as a clearinghouse for information (for a potential 40 million parents "living in step"), conducts workshops, and provides telephone counseling and speakers for meetings. Suggestions: Give the children time; talk to them privately; establish "house rules" that both parents agree to enforce.

SOME PIONEERING HOME ECONOMISTS

**First Female MIT Graduate,
Founder of Home Economics, and
Pioneer Sanitary Chemist**
ELLEN H. SWALLOW RICHARDS (1842–1911) once said, "Home life . . . has been robbed by the removal of *creative* work. You cannot make women contented with cooking and cleaning, and *you need not try.*" This woman, who was the first of her sex to be graduated

from the Massachusetts Institute of Technology and became a world-renowned sanitary chemist, was also the founder of home economics as both science and profession. She completed two years at Vassar College, then entered MIT, not realizing that she was admitted without charge lest there be a fuss over her being a woman. ("Had I realized, I would not have gone," she later said.) She won a welcome by performing such "womanly duties" as dusting and mending, received her B.S. in chemistry in 1873, and a master's from Vassar the same year, then in 1875 married Professor Robert H. Richards, who had taught her mineralogy, and began a career of remarkable accomplishments:

—Through her efforts MIT opened a Women's Laboratory where women could learn chemistry (1876); she taught there until it was torn down after women were admitted directly into MIT in 1878.

—In 1879 she reported adulterations in foods that led to passage of the Massachusetts Food and Drug Act and began a large private practice in sanitary chemistry, examining air, food, and water, and testing wallpapers and fabrics for arsenic content.

—In 1884 she helped set up the world's first laboratory in sanitary chemistry and was in charge of it for 27 years, teaching engineers who set up similar laboratories throughout the world. Also, as chemist for a fire insurance company she exposed the danger of spontaneous combustion of oils in commercial use. She discovered how to clean wool with naphtha and designed the science section of a correspondence school for women.

—In 1893 she became famous for the Rumford Kitchen, which she set up at the Chicago World's Fair for the U.S. Department of Agriculture. It served meals with menus describing the foods nutritionally (carbohydrates, "proteids," etc.). Out of this project came a school lunch program in Boston feeding 5,000 high school pupils daily.

—From 1894 on she acted as dietitian and home economist—establishing these professions—for many hospitals and institutions. When the American Home Economics Association was founded in 1908, she was its first president, serving until 1910. The new profession of home economics decisively influenced agriculture and the food industries, establishing orange juice as a breakfast item and reducing the consumption of starches and fatty meats.

—In her own home, Ellen Richards served simple meals, used plants and washable curtains instead of heavy draperies at the windows, replaced carpets with rugs, and adopted the vacuum cleaner, gas for cooking, showers, and the telephone.

Pioneering Home Economics College Professors

MARTHA VAN RENSSELAER (1864–1932), a secretary and instructor for New York State's Department of Public Instruction at the Chautauqua Summer School, and county school commissioner from 1893–99, in 1900 was asked to organize an extension program for farm wives at Cornell. In 1903 she began teaching homemaking, the first resident accredited home economics course at Cornell, and in 1907 she and FLORA ROSE, a Kansas State Agricultural College graduate, became co-chairwomen of a new Department of Home Economics in the College of Agriculture. Ms. Van Rensselaer received her bachelor's degree from Cornell in 1909, and the two co-chairwomen were made professors in 1911. Their program became a four-year degree course. In 1925 they became co-directors of the newly created State College of Home Economics. Ms. Van Rensselaer was president of the American Home Economics Association, 1914–16, an editor for *Delineator*, 1920–26, home economics chairwoman of the Association of Land-Grant Colleges and Universities, 1928–29, and in 1930 assistant director of the White

House Conference on Child Health and Protection.

Home Economist, First Southeast Asian Chairwoman of the UN Commission on the Status of Women

HELENA Z. BENITEZ, home economist, educator, and international leader, received her B.A. (1933) and a B.S. in education (1934) from Philippine Women's College (now University), and her M.A. from George Washington University, Washington, D.C. (1939). She became dean of home economics at PWU and founded the Home Economics Association (1939) to do community extension work. During World War II she founded the Volunteer Social Aid Committee (1942) and received a Philippine Legion of Honor (1954) for her work with prisoners and wounded. After the war she worked to rebuild PWU and became executive vice-president there; she also founded the Family Life Workshop, the Bayanihan Folk Arts Center, and the America-Philippines Society (New York). She represented her country at 26 world conferences and became the first Southeast Asian chairperson of the United Nations Commission on the Status of Women. In 1966 she succeeded her mother as president of PWU. Ms. Benitez has won many honors for her work, including the Ramón Magsaysay Award for the Advancement of International Understanding.

Home Science Founder of the First Girls' Vocational School in Ghana

ROSAMOND MANCELL, born 1919 at Cape Coast in present-day Ghana, West Africa (then called the Gold Coast), was educated at Wesley Girls' High School and taught home science and dressmaking in Cape Coast from 1928–32. In 1938 she and her husband moved to the city of Kumasi. Noting the lack of vocational training available for girls, she was able in 1942, after some difficulty, to get permission to start a school. Her first six students ranged in age from 12 to 25,

and their classroom was the shade of a tree. Today the school is called the Mancell Girls' Vocational Institute, has approximately 900 students, and occupies modern buildings. To date the emphasis has been on dressmaking, pattern-making, designing, and catering, but the Institute hopes to establish an academic department to prepare students for the certificate granted by the West African Examinations Council. A mark of the Institute's success has been the establishment of at least nine additional girls' vocational centers throughout Ghana started by alumnae.

First Woman Department Head at Sierra Leone University

PAMELA THOMPSON-CLEWRY, head of the Home Economics Department at Njala University College in Sierra Leone, became the first woman department head there in 1971 and is also the first Sierra Leone woman to receive a degree in science and to train as a nutritionist. She obtained her B.Sc. in pure science at Fourah Bay College (1961), an academic postgraduate diploma in nutrition at Queen Elizabeth College, London University (1964), and a M.Sc. in home economics at the University of Illinois (1969). She became assistant lecturer in home economics at Njala in 1964. Coordinator of the Sierra Leone Home Economics Association, Ms. Thompson-Clewry was assistant director for regional activities of the American Home Economics Association-International Family Planning Project (1974–75) and then became regional coordinator for West Africa for the Project. A participant in many conferences around the world on home economics, family planning, and developing countries, Ms. Thompson-Clewry has written two textbooks and 14 handbooks on nutrition, and extensive articles and research papers.

Home Economist for the Elderly

Executive director of the American Home Economics Association (1967–

74), DORIS E. HANSON in 1974 founded HomeCall, Inc., a novel support service for elderly persons who want to live independently in their own homes. Ms. Hanson received her B.S. in home economics in 1949 from Washington State University; her M.A. in home and family life (1958) and an Ed.D. in administration (1964) from Columbia Teachers College. An extension agent in Colorado for two years, she was assistant director of test rooms and associate editor for *McCall's* magazine, 1951–59; served as adviser to the Oklahoma-Pakistan Home Economics Project, Dacca, 1959–62; taught two years at Columbia Teachers College; and was assistant dean of the School of Home Economics at Purdue University, 1964–67. While she was head of AHEA, paraprofessional jobs were becoming important, domestic workers were scarce, and the U. S. Labor Department's Women's Bureau suggested that home economists organize badly needed home services for children and the elderly. "I said I guess that *is* our bag," Ms. Hanson recalls. The Maryland-based nationwide business she now heads offers franchises (and new careers) to professional home economists and social workers, who employ and train young people and experienced adults to assist the elderly. HomeCall provides help with yard work, cleaning, chauffeuring, and cooking.

ORGANIZERS FOR HOMEMAKERS WHO NEED HELP

The Mother of Day Care

NETTIE PODELL OTTENBERG, who organized the National Child Day Care Association and became known as "the mother of day care" for her lobbying activities, was born in Russia and came to the United States at the age of five. She grew up on New York's Lower East Side, where, when she was 16, she found a starving woman in a neighborhood tenement. Shocked at the hostility then prevalent against the poor, she decided to become a social worker and was graduated in the first class of the School of Philanthropy (later part of Columbia University). In 1908, when she was 21, she became a suffragist. Later she began lobbying for day care as she saw more and more mothers entering the work force. When she was in her 70s, she testified before the Senate and obtained the first public money ($50,000) ever allotted to day care in the federal city. Now in her 90s, she continues to work for medical screening for day care children, for the NCDCA's $1.5 million showcase program in the District of Columbia, for therapy for slow learners in public schools and a 1979 conference on slow learners, and for a "granny patrol" paying "kids in gangs" a small amount to be escorts for old people. Nettie Ottenberg practices yoga and swims daily, and during winters at Miami Beach walks several miles a day.

Founder of Catalyst

FELICE N. SCHWARTZ, president and founder in 1962 of Catalyst, Inc., national non-profit organization that assists women in choosing and developing their careers, was graduated from Smith College, then founded the National Scholarship Service and Fund for Negro Students (NSSFNS), which counsels an average of 50,000 black students a year. Ms. Schwartz was executive director of NSSFNS for six years and now serves on its board of directors, as well as on the board of directors of the Planned Parenthood Federation of America, Inc. As head of Catalyst, Felice Schwartz interprets the needs of the job market to a national network of 150 women's resource centers and to advisers of undergraduate women, and offers extensive guidance to

In many parts of the world, female farm laborers continue to work, as they have worked since planting and harvesting began, with their hands. Here, Sri Lankan women husk coir (left) and check the paddy crop (right), while Japanese women (below) pick *mitsuba*. (Courtesy of Victor Sumathipala, Department of Information, Sri Lanka)

Farm Women, U.S.A.

During the Depression of the 1930s, DOROTHEA LANGE (1895-1965) photographed impoverished farmers in America's drought-stricken "Dust Bowl" for the federal Farm Security Administration. This study, one of many that earned for her Edward Steichen's accolade as "the United States' greatest documentary photographer" (see "Women in the Arts and Entertainment"), shows an anonymous young woman of that era—the most heartbreaking in the annals of American agriculture. (Courtesy of the Library of Congress)

In vivid contrast, CATHY MACHAN, dairy editor of the *Farm Journal,* in the mid-1970s drives a tractor on the farm that she and her husband own and operate together in Wisconsin. (Courtesy of *Farm Journal*)

MOLLY FLAGG KNUDTSEN, proprietor of Grass Valley Ranch, in Nevada, is seen riding her pony Lollypop in the East Meadow, where purebred cows graze. (Jonas Dovydenas photo)

PHYLLIS WATT WUSTENBERG, named Mink Rancher of the Year for the Great Lakes region in 1972, fondles one of her valuable animals.

Agricultural Scientists

ETHEL BAILEY, daughter of the founder of the Bailey Hortorium at Cornell University, has continued daily in retirement—as she did during her many years as curator—to prepare plant specimens for the world-famous collection. (*The Chronicle*, Ithaca, New York)

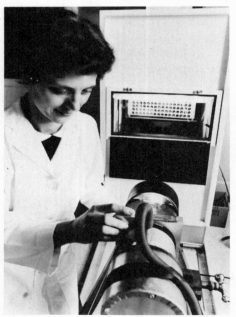

Chemist DORA K. HAYES, chief of the Chemical and Biophysical Laboratory, U. S. Agricultural Research Center, adjusts a color filter in equipment that she uses to study the effects of light and temperature changes on insects. Dr. Hayes, whose experimental insects were rocketed off the earth in November 1973 aboard Skylab IV, is known as "the first woman to bug space."

Diplomat on the Job

As United States Ambassador to Italy, CLARE BOOTHE LUCE, with then Secretary of State John Foster Dulles (behind her, to the right), was photographed making a formal call at the Vatican. In the course of a life full of achievements, Ms. Luce has also been a highly successful playwright, war correspondent, and was the first woman elected to the U. S. Congress from Connecticut. (Courtesy of the Library of Congress)

BETTE B. ANDERSON, the highest-ranking woman in the U. S. Treasury's 200-year history. As Under Secretary of the Treasury (the No. 2 job), she guides the management of many of the Department's operating bureaus, including the Bureau of the Mint, headed by AZIE T. MORTON.

A woman who holds two titles and signs America's paper currency. AZIE T. MORTON is Treasurer of the United States and director of the Mint, a post to which she was appointed by President Carter.

CAROLYN R. PAYTON, above, a psychologist from Howard University and the first woman to serve as director of the Peace Corps. Ms. Payton has, among other things, been encouraging the recruitment of more blacks and other minorities.

Governor of Connecticut ELLA TAMBUSSI GRASSO is the first woman in U.S. history to win election as a governor who did not follow her husband into office. Ms. Grasso, who had been in politics for 21 years when she took office as governor in 1975, entered her first primary when her youngest child (she has two) was 18 months old.

PATRICIA ("PAT") SCHROEDER, a graduate of Harvard Law School, was 31 and the mother of two children when her husband suggested she run for Congress in 1972. She did, beating an incumbent congressman to become Colorado's first woman member of the U. S. Congress. She fought for appointment to the House Armed Services Committee, "because that is where the money is," won that, too, and is often a lone dissenter proposing cuts in the military budget. (Photo by Steve Gascoyne)

Associate White House Press Secretary in the Carter White House CLAUDIA TOWNSEND at 25 years of age became the youngest White House spokesperson. She started as editor of the news summaries and moved up to associate press secretary in less than a year. (Photo by Bruce Reedy)

women returning to work in mid-life or just launching their careers. Married to Dr. Irving L. Schwartz, and the mother of three grown children, she is co-author with MARGARET H SCHIFTER and SUSAN S. GILLOTTI, also of Catalyst, of *How to Go to Work When Your Husband Is* *Against It, Your Children Aren't Old Enough, and There's Nothing You Can Do Anyhow* (1972), a career Baedeker. Felice Schwartz, who also writes "Careerscope" for *Family Circle* magazine, received the Smith College Distinguished Alumna Medal in 1971.

Co-Founders of Wider Opportunities for Women

MARY DRAPER JANNEY and JANE PHILLIPS FLEMING, co-founders in 1965 of Washington (now Wider) Opportunities for Women (WOW), met in the 1940s as economics majors at Vassar College (Poughkeepsie, New York) and studied for their master's degrees at Yale University. Ms. Janney then worked in community organization in Iowa, directed New York City's only interracial civilian defense council, and taught nine years and headed the history department at Washington's Potomac School. Ms. Fleming was active in the civil rights movement and worked in politics and urban planning.

Married, with families, when they met again in Washington, they were only vaguely aware of the economic inequality of women but identified with the problems of educated women returning to work or college. They launched WOW, considered by some observers "the real start of the Women's Movement in Washington," with a questionnaire sent to 3,000 college-educated women in the area. Replies established a strong need for part-time jobs and study opportunities for women. They opened their pioneer center in 1965 with a WOW Desk at the United States Employment Service (now the D.C. Manpower Administration), then led 100 volunteers "working out of somebody's basement" at researching and compiling *Washington Opportunities for Women: A Guide to Part-Time Work and Study in the Washington, D.C., Area for the Educated Woman* (1967); it sold some 10,000 copies.

In 1967 D.C. Manpower contracted with WOW for an Information and Referral Service for women; its innovative programs have since included training and placing inner-city schoolteachers and part-time caseworkers, preparing poverty-level job seekers (eventually including women probationers) for non-traditional jobs such as meat packing, appliance repair, social service, and paramedic work (with A.A. degrees). Among the results of WOW's work was Civil Service accreditation of professional-level volunteer work as valid experience for paid employment.

By 1977 the non-profit, tax-exempt organization had grown from an all-volunteer program to a multifaceted community organization with 25 paid employees, some 40 flexi-time volunteers, and a $450,000 budget. It had served 3,000 employers and more than 30,000 women of all economic brackets in need of morale building and practical assistance such as information, day care referrals, and special training; started an Information Center for Handicapped Children; established a Talent Bank of job seekers with master's degrees or better; conducted guidance courses for college and high school students and for older women and federal employees. In 1972 the Department of Labor funded a project in which WOW assisted women in six other cities in starting comparable programs. From 1974–76 the organization published a bimonthly magazine, *Women's Work* now privately owned, the first national magazine for this special audience.

St. Louis Women "in the Home and Outside"

A group of St. Louis mothers in their 30s who wanted to combine homemaking and work formed the Association of Family Women (AFW) in 1974 so that they could be "in the home and outside." They organized adult classes for women desiring to enter the job market, a pamphlet on starting cooperative child care centers, and a hot line for housebound mothers. In addition, said spokesperson CATALINE ALVAREZ, a wife, full-time law student, and mother of seven, they are "a kind of Ralph Nader group" and "anti-defamation league" for family women.

They Launched the First Center for Displaced Homemakers

TISH SOMMERS and LAURIE SHIELDS, co-coordinators since 1976 of the NOW Task Force on Older Women, surprised themselves and the entire California legislature in 1975 when they lobbied the country's first Displaced Homemaker Act into law in just 121 working days. They are now also national co-coordinators of the Alliance for Displaced Homemakers —an unstructured grass-roots "coalition" of active feminists and traditional church-women's groups across the country.

Tish Sommers attended San Francisco schools and left the University of California (Berkeley) in 1933 to study dance in Germany, returning with "a well-developed social conscience." She received her bachelor's degree from UCLA and her master's in Hispanic studies from the University of Wisconsin, and served as intercultural activities director in Los Angeles during World War II. Then came 23 years as a non-paid "faculty wife," homemaker, and community organizer for the poverty program, civil rights, and the Women's Movement. After her divorce at 57 she moved to Oakland and became a full-time activist for older women. "Organize, don't agonize," she says in *The Not So Helpless Female—How to Change Things Around Even If You Never Thought You Could* (1973). Ms. Sommers was named "one of the Bay Area's Most Distinguished Persons" in 1974 by the *San Francisco Examiner* and was recently appointed to the California Commission on Aging.

Midwesterner Laurie Shields, a journalism graduate with substantial experience in her field, was writing a book with her husband, Arthur Shields, on Ireland's Abbey Theatre and the careers of himself and his brother, Barry Fitzgerald, when he died in 1970. She continued work on the book in Ireland, but had to return to the States in 1974 when her mother became ill. She tried to find a job but was told she was "overqualified." Then, at a workshop, she met Tish Sommers, who was national coordinator of NOW-TFOW, had initiated the drafting of the first displaced homemaker bill by attorney BARBARA DUDLEY, and had helped form the ADH. She asked Ms. Shields to be its director. After the $200,000 California bill passed, ADH raised funds for a campaign to interest women across the country in state and federal bills. Ms. Shields travels the States in "in and out in 24 hours" visits addressing meetings arranged by local organizations.

Founder of the Martha Movement

After three years as a full-time housewife, JINX MELIA, mother of two preschoolers, returned to work as a management specialist, carrying with her a "deep feeling of grievance" over the plight of women in the home. She researched their problems and in May 1976 founded the Martha Movement for all who consider homemaking their primary role but "want to feel better about it." Deploring the isolation, lack of positive feedback, and "unending lack of relief" at home, she and the Marthas have organized "child care entertainments" at shopping centers, hot lines, assertiveness programs, and a newsletter, *Martha Matters*. They are working for better volunteer, business, and government jobs (with credit given for their administrative skills) and demanding TV programs and magazine articles featuring smart, feisty housewives who play important parts as consumers and community leaders. Most important, they favor laws guaranteeing financial protection and "non-dependence"—economically, marriage "is a business partnership; the family income belongs equally to husband and wife." Thousands of America's 63 million homemakers have joined the movement, which gets its name from the Bible story of Martha, who complained as she worked in the kitchen, "cumbered with much serving," while her sister Mary relaxed at Jesus' knee. He admonished her, saying Mary "hath chosen that good part, which shall not be taken from her" (Luke: 10:38–42). Ms. Melia was born in Chevy Chase, Maryland, and grew up the only girl in a family of boys. She was graduated from Trinity College (Burlington, Vermont) looking forward to marriage and motherhood, and has a master of education in counseling from George Mason College. She is president of Jinx Melia Associates, doing career training for women; is an adjunct professor for career development at Georgetown; and recently wrote a major study of women executives for the Department of Health, Education, and Welfare. Although she views her years at home as "the most terrible experience of my life," she wants to return to full-time homemaking "when the working conditions improve."

Flexi-Time Advocate

VIRGINIA H. MARTIN, noted for her activities as a promoter of part-time and flexible-hour employment believes that workers who have some say in their working hours make better parents and more productive employees. For many years Ms. Martin was a volunteer in Junior League and political campaign work; then she took a job on a strict 9–5 schedule and found herself not only having difficulty managing her family life but also losing on-the-job productivity. Volunteering in 1973 to be the first chairperson of the District of Columbia Junior League's Volunteer-to-Career Committee, sponsoring local part-time job development, and becoming as well the co-chairperson of the Women's Equity Action League Task Force for Part-Time and Flexible Hours Employment, she found there was little data available to persuade employers of the value of flexi-time employment. After taking her M.B.A. at George Washington University's School of Government and Business Administration, she helped to found the Committee for Alternative Work Patterns, which sponsored a national conference in 1976, and herself became a part-time consultant-on-call on alternative work arrangements for Arthur D. Little, Inc.

Their Marriage Contract Is in the Textbooks

When HARRIET CODY and Harvey Sadis of Seattle, Washington, were married in 1972 they signed a marriage contract that made page one of a local newspaper and was reprinted in the June 1973 *Ms.* and in several textbooks. In July 1977 *Ms.* asked the couple how the contract had worked out. Both gave it a strong "yes" vote. They have reread and renewed the contract (with no basic changes) every year, with one major addition—an annual separate vacation of at least one week. Harriet Cody reports that the contract "has reinforced for me my own absolute responsibility for my life," and adds, "I feel very lucky to be living with a man who shares the nurturing, the responsibility, the emotional support fifty-fifty." Harvey Sadis says the contract "has given me more options about work." (It enabled him to take a year's leave from teaching.) He likes the fact that after house and food expenses are paid, his money is his own, and he enjoys "the freedom of defining my own role in the relationship"—cooking, having time alone, his own vacations, his own friends, and his own identity. The marriage has been "a lot of work" and has survived, he says, because with the contract "we can both be winners."

Next step, when needed: a child-contract amendment. They know a child will change their lives and that "this change is a joint undertaking."

CLUB AND VOLUNTEER WORKERS

Founder and First President of PTA

ALICE MCLELLAN BIRNEY (1858–1907) was born in Marietta, Georgia, and grew up in a comfortable southern family during the Reconstruction period. She attended nearby schools and in 1875 went to Mt. Holyoke Seminary for one year. As the mother of three daughters, Ms. Birney was disturbed by the lack of information available on raising children; she read widely on psychology and education and in 1895 addressed a Chautauqua, New York, summer school on the importance of child care education, drawing the support of educators and community leaders. In 1897 2,000 women met at a "mothers' congress" in Washington, D.C.; they formed the National Congress of Mothers—since 1924 the National Congress of Parents and Teachers—with Ms. Birney as first president. In two years, membership reached 50,000. Alice Birney, widowed in 1897, resigned as president in 1902 and devoted her remaining years to writing.

Second PTA President, Pioneer for Juvenile Justice, and First Woman to Speak Before the Canadian Parliament

HANNAH KENT SCHOFF (1853–1940) was born in Upper Darby, Pennsylvania, and educated privately and at Waltham (Massachusetts) Church School. The mother of seven children, in 1897 she attended the first National Congress of Mothers in Washington, became vice-president, 1898–1902, founded the second state branch in Pennsylvania, and was elected national president in 1902. Fron 1906 to 1920 Ms. Schoff edited the NCM journal *Child Welfare* (it became the *National Parent-Teacher* in 1934), led the way in forming parent-teacher organizations in schools and in lobbying for child labor and other family welfare legislation, and organized and participated in several international child welfare conferences. When she retired as president in 1920, membership was 190,000 and thirty-seven states had branches. During the same years Hannah Schoff was deeply concerned about children jailed as criminals (at one time 500 were imprisoned in Philadelphia, some merely at their parents' request). In 1899 she obtained the release of an 8-year-old girl jailed for arson and saw her rehabilitated in a foster home. She drafted bills setting up juvenile courts, detention homes for children awaiting trial, and probation for young offenders; the bills were enacted in Pennsylvania in 1901. She also served as president of the Philadelphia Juvenile Court and Probation Association, 1901–23, led other states in establishing juvenile courts, and became the first woman asked to speak before the Canadian Parliament. In 1909 the U. S. Bureau of Education made her head of the American Committee on the Causes of Crime in Normal Children; she surveyed thousands of prisoners in eight states and published the interviews in *The Wayward Child* (1915).

Her Lobbying Secured Passage of the Pure Food and Drug Act

ALICE LAKEY, who led a quiet life at home until she was 46, mobilized the power of the nation's women's clubs behind a campaign that secured passage of the Pure Food and Drug Act in 1906. Ms. Lakey was born in Shanesville, Ohio, in 1857; her mother died when she was six. She gave up a singing career in 1888 because of poor health and became interested in pure food while living in Cranford, New Jersey, with her father, who was fussy about what he ate. She asked Dr. Harvey W. Wiley, chief of the Bureau of Chemistry (Department of Agriculture) and a pure food enthusiast, to speak at the Cranford Village Improvement Association and soon after began to organize the women's clubs of the United States to write letters and ring doorbells. She presented a traveling display of adulterated food to the clubs, and at the 1904 convention handed out stacks of literature. A pure food committee was formed. In 1905 she and five others personally persuaded President Theodore Roosevelt to support the bill, passed after millions of women deluged Congress with letters. Ms. Lakey continued to work for social reforms. In 1919 she called on women's clubs to fight for life insurance for widows and their children. In 1924 Secretary of Commerce Herbert Hoover appointed her a member of the First National Conference on Street and Highway Safety. In the 1930s when a new pure food and drug movement began, she revived her earlier American Pure Food League and was

again its executive secretary. She died in Cranford in 1935.

Founders of the Junior League

In 1901 when MARY HARRIMAN RUMSEY and her friend NATHALIE HENDERSON heard Professor VIDA SCUDDER of Wellesley appeal to students to work in the slums, they led 85 New York debutantes in forming the Junior League for the Promotion of Settlement Movements (later the Junior League of New York) to promote voluntarism "as a means of expressing the feeling of social responsibility for the conditions which surround us."

The daughter of railroad tycoon Edward Henry Harriman and sister of Averell Harriman, Mary Harriman Rumsey received her degree from Barnard College in 1905 in sociology and eugenics; a devoted alumna, she served as a trustee from 1911 until she died in 1934. In New York City during World War I she supported the Community Councils formed under the Council of National Defense and worked to continue the cooperatives after the war. President Franklin D. Roosevelt named her chairwoman of the Consumers' Advisory Board of NRA in 1933; she worked to protect cooperatives from price discrimination. Mary Rumsey, widowed in 1922, fell from her horse in a fox hunt in 1934, contracted pneumonia, and died a month later.

When the Association of Junior Leagues of America was incorporated in 1921 with 24 Leagues in the United States and Canada, DOROTHY WHITNEY STRAIGHT was elected its first president. Youngest child of financier William C. Whitney (Secretary of the Navy under President Grover Cleveland), she married Willard Straight, with whom she founded the *New Republic*. Widowed, she married Leonard Elmhirst and moved to a 2,000-acre medieval manor in Devonshire.

From Urban League to Junior League

It "shows how far the two leagues have come, and how serious is the Junior League's commitment to effecting positive change," a colleague commented when the Association of Junior Leagues, Inc. hired the Urban League's Georgia-born JEWELDEAN (DEAN) JONES LONDA as its executive director in May 1977. Ms. Londa was director of camping and director of the teen-age program of the YWCA for 12 years, then worked for the National Urban League for 18 years. Starting as field representative for the executive director in 1959, she developed funds and liaison with labor, news media, and community leaders through the turbulent 1960s and '70s, and became national director of social welfare in 1974. Dean Londa predicts a bright future for voluntarism in the Junior league, now a 120,000-member organization in 233 communities increasingly involved in advocacy rather than service-oriented volunteering.

Founder of Lighthouses for the Blind

WINIFRED HOLT (1870–1945), pioneer in work for the blind, was born in New York City and attended Brearley School. She went to Italy in 1894 and studied sculpture, later continuing lessons with Augustus Saint-Gaudens and becoming a skilled portrait sculptor. In 1901 she and her sister EDITH saw some young blind students absorbed in a concert in Italy; in 1903 they opened a Ticket Bureau for the Blind in New York and in 1905 started the New York Association for the Blind in their home. An association committee working to prevent blindness later became the National Society for the Prevention of Blindness. Winifred Holt devoted herself to employment, education, and recreational work with the blind, opening the first "Lighthouse" in New York City in 1923. During World War I France asked her to organize her first foreign Light-

houses; others followed until there were Lighthouses in 34 countries. Winifred Holt received a gold medal from the National Institute of Social Sciences in 1914 and became a chevalier of the French Legion of Honor in 1921; she also held medals from Belgium, Italy, and France.

Founders of the YWCA

GRACE DODGE, the first women ever to serve on the New York Board of Education, guided the formative years of the Young Women's Christian Association (YWCA) in the United States. The "Y," which was started in England in 1855, opened its American branch in 1906 after Grace Dodge settled early factional disputes. She served as the first president of the National Board, helping to make many decisions about the ecumenical nature of the Association.

Co-Founder of Camp Fire Girls

In 1910, together with her husband, Dr. Luther Halsey Gulick, and William Chauncy Langdon, both educational and recreational leaders who helped plan the Boy Scouts of America the same year, CHARLOTTE VETTER GULICK founded the Camp Fire Girls—the first national, non-sectarian, interracial organization for girls in the United States. As a bride, Ms. Gulick had studied medicine with her husband for one year, planning to assist in the missionary career he then planned. Later she helped found a mothers' club to study child development, and wrote many magazine articles on child life, including a pioneer article on sex instruction for children, published in the *Ladies' Home Journal*. For 20 years ending in 1907, the Gulicks conducted a large family camp at Gales Ferry, Connecticut. In August 1908 they returned from a child-welfare congress in Europe, bought property in South Casco, Maine, and planned a new girls' camp "so we could keep our family together." Ms. Gulick thought their more successful summers had been built around a theme; in 1910 she decided on Indian lore and ceremonials, and named the camp Wo-HeLo (for Work, Health, Love)—later Sebago-WoHeLo Camp. A motherly woman with a son and three daughters (a fourth died in 1909 at 17), she welcomed 17 novice campers at the Camp Fire camp in 1910.

Founder of the Girl Scouts of America

JULIETTE GORDON LOW (1860–1927), born in Savannah, Georgia, studied painting in private schools and maintained a lifelong interest in playwriting and sculpture. In her early 20s, she traveled extensively through Europe. In England she met William Mackey Low, who was also from Savannah; they married in 1886. Widowed in 1905, Juliette Low in 1911 met General Sir Robert Baden Powell, the founder of the Boy Scouts; with his encouragement she formed the first American unit of the Girl Guides on March 12, 1912, organizing sixteen Savannah girls into two patrols. In 1915 the renamed Girl Scouts of America became a national organization with Juliette Gordon Low as its first president.

One of "Miss Daisy's" Original Girl Scouts

MARIAN ASLAKSON of Bethesda, Maryland, honored in 1977 as a member of the first Girl Scout troop founded in the United States in 1912, likes to amaze Scouts with the fact that she was in "Miss Daisy" Low's original group at Nina Pate's day school in Savannah, Georgia. The troop, called Girl Guides for the first three years, was divided into pink carnation and white rose sections, learned to tie knots, make peppermint drops, blaze a trail, and light a fire with one match to pass the tenderfoot test. Ms. Aslakson is still active in scouting at 77, talks at Scout activities, served on the governing council, and sponsored a leaders' course at Columbia University.

Traveling with her husband, she organized a troop in Peru, half Peruvian and half American. When the two did not mix, she threatened to dissolve the troop, until they "realized they had been missing something" by not making friends, she recalls.

World Chief Guide

OLAVE ST. CLAIR, Lady BADEN-POWELL (1889–1977) was born in Derbyshire, England. She made her debut at 18, and met Lieutenant General Sir Robert Baden-Powell (32 years her elder) aboard ship on a West Indies trip in 1912; they married after a whirlwind romance. Lord Baden-Powell had founded the Boy Scouts in England in 1908; the Girl Guides in 1910. Lady Baden-Powell, a capable organizer, rose through scouting ranks and in 1930 was appointed World Chief Guide by the World Association of Girl Guides and Girl Scouts. The Baden-Powells retired to Kenya in 1938; he died in 1941 there, and the following year she returned to England and scouting for another 35 years. She became Dame of the Grand Cross of the Order of the British Empire (1932) and received many other honors from Britain and other countries.

President of First Women's Club in Indian Territory

ROBERTA CAMPBELL LAWSON was born in Alluwe, Indian Territory (later Oklahoma), in 1876. Her father, merchant/cattleman E. J. Campbell, came from a Virginia pioneer family and was a founder of the Indian College at Bacone, Oklahoma—the United States' only college for Indians for many years. Her mother was Emeline Journeycake, daughter of the Reverend Charles Journeycake, last chief of the Delawares. Married at 23, Roberta Lawson lived in Nowata, where she helped organize and was president of the first woman's club (and first federated club) in the territory, and later president of the

Oklahoma Federation of Women's Clubs. Her husband's oil interests brought the Lawsons a fortune and they moved to Tulsa, where she was a director of the Oklahoma Historical Society, only woman trustee of the University of Tulsa, and a member for thirteen years of the Board of Regents of the College for Women at Chickasha. She was a member of the Women's Clubs' first World Friendship Tour in 1933 and presented several programs of Indian music in costume in Czechoslovakia. Elected first vice-president, then president (1935–38) of the federation, she helped found the national Academy of Public Service to prepare students for government jobs. Roberta Lawson's books on Indian history and her collection of Indian artifacts are displayed at the Philbrook Art Center, Tulsa.

She Organized Britain's WVS and Postwar Women's Home Industries

STELLA CHARNAUD ISAACS, Baroness SWANSBOROUGH (1894–1971), born to a diplomatic family in Constantinople and educated privately, was active in the Red Cross during World War I, then went to India (1925) to become secretary to Lord Reading, viceroy from 1921–26. Lord Reading's wife died in 1930, and a year later he married Ms. Charnaud. He became Foreign Secretary, then died in 1935. With the approach of World War II in 1938 she was asked to organize British women for civil defense; work of the 1,250,000-member Women's Voluntary Services (model for America's wartime WAVS) expanded to all emergencies, including evacuation of children and hospitals. Lady Reading directed her volunteers—known as "spinach and beets" because of their green uniforms and burgundy blouses—from her sandbagged Westminster office. They operated in all theaters of war. When peace came, Lady Reading organized the nonprofit Women's Home Industries, Ltd.

(1947) to promote recovery by selling women's handicrafts. Her other work included aiding British women overseas, exchange students, the unemployed and the aged, and working for housing and slum clearance. The first woman member of the Ullswater Royal Commission on Broadcasting and a member, governor (1946–51), and vice-chairman (1947–68) of British Broadcasting's advisory council, she received many British and American honorary degrees. She became Dame of the Grand Cross of the Most Excellent Order of the British Empire, 1944, Dame of Justice and Grace, Order of St. John of Jerusalem, 1951, and in 1958 was made Baroness Swansborough, a life peer.

B'nai B'rith Firsts

MIRIAM ALPERT, a native of Chicago, joined B'nai B'rith Young Adults in 1940 as a volunteer, became its first national president in 1946, and in the same year joined the staff of B'nai B'rith Women when the national office opened in Chicago. In 1952 she became assistant director and in 1959 executive director of B'nai B'rith Women, overseeing the organization's human rights programs, Jewish education, community service, and youth activities. Miriam Alpert died in 1976 in Washington, D.C.

ANITA PERLMAN, chairwoman of the B'nai B'rith Youth Commission (BBYC), is the first woman to head a B'nai B'rith Commission in the organization's history. A past international president of B'nai B'rith Women, a member of its executive board, its first youth chairwoman, and the first national BBW chairwoman of B'nai B'rith Girls, she is also a founder of the BBYC, a member of the executive committee of the B'nai B'rith Youth Organization from its inception, the first woman to receive the BBYC Legion of Honor Award (1947), and the first adult honorary life member of Aleph Zadik Aleph, teen-age boys branch of BBYO. BBG and B'nai B'rith Young Women established a scholarship fund in her name. She initiated B'nai B'rith Women's "Operation Stork" for prenatal care in cooperation with the National Foundation-March of Dimes, winning the Lane Bryant Citation (now the National Volunteer Award) and a citation from the City of Chicago. Anita Perlman was national BBW chairwoman for the Anti-Defamation League and is the only woman life member of the ADL Commission. With her husband, Louis L. Perlman, she received an ADL award (1972). Earlier the Perlmans also received the B'nai B'rith President's Medal and the Hagana Tribute.

Established Eye-Bank

AIDA DE ACOSTA BRECKINRIDGE (1884–1962), founder and executive director of the Eye-Bank for Sight Restoration, Inc. in New York, was born in Eberon, New Jersey, and educated at Sacred Heart Convent in Paris. In 1903 she flew solo over Paris in a balloon dirigible; her mother ordered her home forthwith, managing to keep the adventure quiet until 1932. In 1908 she married Oren Root and had two children; the Roots were later divorced. During World War I she sold $2 million of Liberty Bonds, persuading Enrico Caruso to sing on Wall Street for the cause. She later served on the American Committee for Devastated France; was volunteer executive and public relations expert for organizations including the 1939 World's Fair fine arts committee and (in World War II) the National War Fund; initiated the naming of May Day as Child Health Day, 1928; and persuaded advertisers to plug the Red Cross free in national ads. After she developed glaucoma in one eye in 1922, and an operation saved the other eye, she raised $5 million and in 1929 established the Wilmer Ophthalmological Institute (named for her surgeon) at Johns Hopkins University.

She founded the l collect tissue for ey

She Originated Call

ELLEN SULZBERGER and national chairpe tion, was born in 1 from Horace Mann Smith College (1945). Ms. Straus married R. Peter Straus, now president of Straus Broadcasting (including WMCA), in 1950; they have four children. In 1963 Ms. Straus founded WMCA Call for Action, a unique service combining telephone referrals with radio broadcasting; volunteers respond to citizen complaints, call back to see that the problem is solved, then may broadcast a documented report if service has been unsatisfactory. In 1969 Call for Action went national, expanding to 50 cities in which some 2,500 volunteers may handle 360,000 calls in one year. Ms. Straus, a dedicated "volunteer professional," says her organization serves a deep need in urban life, offering individuals a grievance system backed by media clout, and providing an early warning system on societal ills. In 1972 she founded WMCA Call for Action Volunteer Professional Consultants, serving on the board of both CFA organizations as well as the boards of the Fund for the City of New York, Mount Sinai Hospital Nursing School, and the Plaza Hotel. Her paid jobs have included assistant public information work for the Atomic Energy Commission, Northeast; news correspondent from Switzerland and Washington, D.C., for an upper New York State chain of papers; and contributing editor, McCall's. As a volunteer Ellen Straus has won many honors: Woman of Conscience, National Council of Women (1970); Louise Waterman Wise Award, American Jewish Congress (1971); Smith College Medal (1971); Hannah G. Solomon Award, National Council of Jewish Women (172); and Woman of the Year—1973, Ladies' Home Journal.

under of Reading Is FUNdamental

When former teacher MARGARET C. MCNAMARA became a teacher-aide in Washington, D.C.'s inner-city schools in 1966, she found the fifth-graders working with "See Jane run" primers. She raided her own three children's bookshelves and took a Jules Verne adventure to a boy who supposedly "couldn't" read: He finished it and was overwhelmed when Ms. McNamara wrote his name in it and gave it to him. This led to Ms. McNamara's founding Reading Is FUNdamental (RIF), which the Ford Foundation agreed to finance as a pilot program providing quality paperbacks to 61 D.C. schools serving families earnless than $5,000. As she had hoped, where complicated teaching techniques had failed, giving students books of their own choice is succeeding.

In 1971 the Advertising Council approved RIF for free magazine and TV ads; in 1976 the United States Office of Education earmarked nearly $4 million in matching funds for RIF; the number of RIF projects in the nation topped 600 in 48 states in 1977. Sponsored by colleges, service organizations, and business firms, the projects let children choose several free books a year; book sales and library use have risen and publishers have been nudged toward books relevant to the children's daily lives. *Foxfire* editor Eliot Wigginton has assigned all royalties for *I Wish I Could Give My Son a Wild Raccoon* (1977) to RIF.

Chairwoman McNamara, who travels the country to promote RIF, was graduated from the University of California (Berkeley) and taught biology and health education in California secondary schools before she married former Secretary of Defense, now World Bank president, Robert S. McNamara in 1940. She is a trustee of Chatham College (Pittsburgh), a member of the boards of the Eugene and Agnes Meyer Foundation and of Smithsonian Associates, and served with the League of Women Voters (1945–60), Michigan's Juvenile Court (1950–60), the White House Conference on Children and Youth (1959), and the National Advisory Council of the Office of Economic Opportunity (1964–68). She received the American Library Association's Clarence Day Award (1975), Doctor of Humanities degrees from Stillman College (Tuscaloosa, Alabama) and Chatham (both 1976), and in 1977 was a *Ladies' Home Journal* Woman of the Year.

"Better to Light One Candle Than to Curse the Darkness"

GRACE POWERS MONACO, who helped found Metropolitan Washington Candlelighters in 1969 after she learned her own first child had cancer, was born in 1938 in Union City, New Jersey. She received her bachelor's degree from College Misericordia (Dallas, Pennsylvania) in 1960, was graduated first in her class from Georgetown University Law Center, and married a classmate, Lawrence A. Monaco, in 1963. She began her legal career in the Justice Department honors program, and during her husband's army service worked as a legal research assistant for a professor at the University of Virginia. She joined the firm of Wheatley & Miller in 1967 after the birth in 1966 of a daughter. In 1968, one month after the first of her three sons was born, Grace Monaco's daughter was diagnosed as having acute lymphocytic leukemia. She was treated at Children's National Medical Center, D.C., and died in 1970. Ms. Monaco was first president as well as a founder of the Metropolitan Washington Candlelighters. The peer self-help program for parents of young cancer patients holds monthly meetings in parents' homes, offers one-to-one help when needed, disseminates information and educational materials, and lobbies for consistent and adequate federal support for cancer research. National liaison chairperson of Candlelighters since 1973, Ms. Monaco also is president of the Candlelighters Foundation, formed in 1976, and serves on several national committees on cancer.

Singer Becomes Fighter for Cerebral Palsy

JANE PICKENS LANGLEY, formerly one of the Pickens Sisters singing group, became a worker for cerebral palsy and the underprivileged when her daughter was born with the handicap. Ms. Pickens devoted herself to the annual fund-raising telethon for United Cerebral Palsy and in 1968 received a Distinguished Volunteer Service Award at the White House. Born in Macon, Georgia, Ms. Pickens grew up in Atlanta and studied at the Curtis Institute of Music, Philadelphia, Pennsylvania; the Juilliard School, New York City; and in Paris; and starred on television's "Jane Pickens Show" and in the musical *Regina* (1949).

National Volunteer Awards

In 1970, Lane Bryant, Inc., which started making National Volunteer Awards in the 1940s, transferred its award program to the National Center for Voluntary Action, a non-profit, privately funded organization established that year under then Secretary of Housing and Urban Development George Romney. Germaine Monteil Corporation, which had presented a Beautiful Activist Award to more than 800 volunteer women since 1970, in 1976 joined NCVA in its award presentations. More than 300 Voluntary Action Centers are affiliated with NCVA, which supports outstanding, innovative volunteer work throughout the country. Some typical award winners follow.

Founder of "Handicapables"

Born with cerebral palsy, NADINE CALLI-GIURI of San Francisco, California, won a 1972 award for her work in starting the "Handicapables"—a word she first heard in 1965 while attending a retreat for the handicapped in Sacramento. She founded the organization in San Francisco with a membership of 25; by 1972 it included groups throughout the Bay area and all over the state. They work to draw the attention of the Federal Housing Authority to the need for housing facilities with safety features for the handicapped.

Reading Improvement Volunteer

DIANE PUNELLI of Des Moines, Iowa, who dropped out of high school in 1957 with an incomplete only in economics (she was graduated in 1971 with an A+), threw herself into work with children learning to read. "Reading changed my life," says Diane, who was asked to become chairwoman of PTA Project RISE (Reading Improvement Services Everywhere) and worked to make remedial services available to all Des Moines schoolchildren. She set up a remedial reading program in which 200 volunteers completed an intensive 10-week course, and with an $1,800 check from the Polk County Board of Education, instituted "Hooked on Books," a program in which 10th-graders go to a bookstore to buy two paperbacks of their choice to read and exchange. Her work won her an award in 1972.

Fighter for Shatter-Proof Eyeglasses

Blinded in 1964 when her eyeglasses shattered in a minor car accident, BARBARA JOAN DAWSON of West Medford, Massachusetts, mounted a successful fight for legislation requiring that all eyeglass and sunglass lenses be shatterproof. Ms. Dawson worked with state and national legislators and the Massachusetts and national Societies for the Prevention of Blindness. Her efforts resulted in Food and Drug Administration regulations (1971). In 1972 she joined 40 ophthalmologists, optometrists, and industry representatives in plans for new legislation needed because of changes in optical technology. Ms. Dawson also worked with the Commonwealth of Massachusetts on a school eye safety program to ensure that children in industrial arts, science, and other classes wear protective lenses. She won a 1973 award.

Tax Consultants for the Elderly

BERYL GRAEFF and her husband Charles, of Harrisburg, Pennsylvania, won a 1974 award for a senior citizens' free tax service, which they conducted in their home. Noticing that many elderly people needed help with property tax or rental rebates, they worked seven days a week from 9 A.M. to 9 P.M., absorbing all costs, including that of a second telephone. By phone, mail, and in person, they gave direct aid to 2,000 people, preparing tax forms that led to rebates for 1,000 in 1974 alone. Cash returns totaled more than $150,000. They also sent for food stamp information and forms, gathered information on other social service agencies needed by their clientele, and worked with the Retired Seniors Volunteer Program (RSVP) assembling kits for similar projects.

Braillist Volunteer

MAGDALENE MUELLER of Burlington, Wisconsin, Braille chairman of the Volunteer Services for the Blind and Visually Handicapped, Milwaukee Public Library, won a 1976 award for years of dedicated service to the blind. Ms. Mueller Brailled more than 20,000 pages at home (winning a sapphire pin from the Library of Congress); since 1965 she has worked once a week at the library, assigning reading materials to 27 other Braillists and teaching Braille to new volunteers. With her husband William, she has created illustrations for Braille books and for the library's Summer Reading Program. The Muellers have made more than 100 bingo boards for the Badger Association for the Blind.

Victim Advocacy Coordinator

JUDITH C. STUTMAN of Denver, Colorado, 1976 NVA winner, became involved in the prevention and treatment of sexual assault in 1974. Coordinator of the Victim Advocacy Program at Denver General Hospital, she helped develop an emergency room program for sexual assault victims. She teaches five-week volunteer training courses and supervises the program, which involves giving medical and legal information, talking to victims' families, and accompanying victims to court. In 1975 Ms. Stutman worked on Colorado assault law revisions; she also has served as chairperson of the NOW Sexual Assault Task Force, president of the Sexual Assault Council (1976), and chairperson of the Western Regional Conference on Sexual Assault (May 1976).

Help for Abused Wives

PEGGY ANNE HANSEN of Bethesda, Maryland, founder and coordinator since 1974 of the Marriage, Divorce, and Family Relations Task Force, Montgomery County, won the highest National Volunteer Award in 1976 for her work with battered women. Ms. Hansen and a corps of volunteers use their home phones for a 24-hour, 7-day-a-week hot line for abuse victims. They developed a network of "underground housing" (kept secret lest husbands harass their wives further), and provide counseling, transportation, and employment and legal information. Ms. Hansen has coordinated and promoted the efforts of police, clergy, health centers, and other

The Home and Community

agencies to aid battered women and their children.

Founder of Women's Residence

Appalled at what she saw during an inner-city field trip she made with her students, VERONICA MAZ, Georgetown University sociology professor, quit her job and opened a soup kitchen, "So Others May Eat" (SOME), in the District of Columbia. When she learned that the District's destitute women (unlike men) have no temporary residence to turn to, she established the House of Ruth for homeless women and children. In an old Victorian mansion on Massachusetts Avenue, opened in 1976, Dr. Maz provides beds and meals for as many as 30 a night, counseling, and assistance in finding jobs and apartments. Starting with much faith and no money, Dr. Maz has worked with whatever donations she could get (during 1977 10,000 people gave) and served more than 1,200 women, and opened an annex that has sheltered 300 battered wives. Soroptimists International has named the House of Ruth its Outreach Service Center, offering assistance for five years, and for her work Veronica Maz received a 1977 Washington-area National Volunteer Award.

First Black President of Girl Scouts

GLORIA DEAN SCOTT, assistant to the president for Educational Planning and Evaluation at Texas Southern University, Houston, in 1975 was elected to a three-year term as president of the Girl Scouts of America. First black to hold the national presidency, Dr. Scott has been a Scout since her youth in Houston, holding local, regional, and national posts. She joined the national board in 1969, chaired the National Program and Training Committee, and was a member of the Human Resources and Services Committee and of the Task Group on Race Relations. Dr. Scott helped plan the 1970 Conference on Scouting for Black Girls, became first vice-president of the Girl

Scouts, 1972–75, and is working to bring poor and minority children into scouting. Dr. Scott, born 1938 in Houston, received bachelor's and master's degrees in zoology from Indiana University (1959 and 1960), and her Ph.D. in higher education in 1965. In 1964 she received the Governor's Award as Outstanding Black Student in the State of Indiana. She serves on the Board of Trustees of the National Urban League and the U. S. Department of Health, Education, and Welfare's National Advisory Committee on Black Higher Education and Black Colleges and Universities. From 1973–75 she headed the post-secondary education unit of HEW's National Institute of Education. In 1977 she received an honorary doctor of laws from Indiana University and in 1976 and 1977 was appointed to the International Women's Year Commission.

Founder of Bangladesh Housewives Association

Ms. TAYYEBA HUQ, born in 1921 in Dacca, is the wife of the Foreign Affairs Adviser to the President of Bangladesh and mother of two sons. Interested in the problems of homemaking in Bangladesh, Ms. Huq organized a work-oriented informal education program, founded the Housewives Association (which published a journal for housewives (1962–70), and is now running an experimental school for young children with the cooperation of neighborhood mothers. She is the author of three books in Bengali on household affairs, home and living, and the home in world perspective.

She Won Flight Privileges for the Handicapped

PATRICIA JOAN THOBEN (1933–77) was born in Anderson, Indiana, paralyzed from the waist down. She was graduated from St. Mary's College of Notre Dame, Indiana received her master's in clinical psychology from De Paul University, and was a caseworker for handicapped patients and their families with the Illinois Department of Public Welfare until she moved to Arlington, Virginia, in 1961 to work with the Public Health Service and later with the Rehabilitation Services Administration of the Department of Health, Education, and Welfare. After thirteen years with HEW, she became a senior program assistant in the Office of Selective Placement Programs of the Civil Service Commission, administering policies concerning handicapped employees, and developed a proposal for an appeals system for handicapped federal employees and applicants. Although she traveled extensively to represent the federal government at conferences, in 1974 two airlines refused to accept Patricia Joan Thoben as a passenger because she could not leave the plane unassisted in case of an emergency. Resultant criticism led to Federal Aviation Administration regulations effective May 16, 1977 (a month before Ms. Thoben died of cancer), requiring airlines to accept as many physically handicapped passengers as possible and to establish procedures for handling them in emergencies.

President of North American Indian Women's Association

MARY JANE FATE, an Athabascan Indian, is a native Alaskan who has been very active in community affairs in addition to managing a home with four children in it. She is president of the North American Indian Women's Association, a member of the Advisory Committee to the Commissioner of Indian Affairs on Foster Children, first vice-president of the Tundra Times Publishing Company,

chairperson of the Fairbanks Native Association, and a board member of the Alaska State Museum Advisory Board, the Fairbanks Community Hospital Foundation, and the Eskimo Indian and Aleut Printing Company.

New York Big Brothers' Mother

JOYCE M. BLACK became first woman president of Big Brothers, Inc. of New York City in 1976, ten years after a past president asked her to join its board because the group needed "a family image." In taking charge as mother of 590 Little Brothers and Sisters (8 to 16 years old) and their matching adults, Ms. Black said she felt "very strongly there should be a woman's view—someone who might bring in a perspective of a mother, how she would feel about a fatherless child." Ms. Black's considerable volunteer experience also includes five years as president of the Day Care Council of New York, and membership on the boards of 45 national, state, and city organizations. When Mayor John V. Lindsay set up the Mayor's Voluntary Action Council of New York City in 1966, she became co-chairperson. In 1973 Governor Nelson A. Rockefeller appointed her to represent consumers on the State Banking Board, which regulates the banking industry; Governor Malcolm Wilson appointed her to the State Temporary Commission of Child Welfare; and she became the first woman trustee of the New York University Medical Center in 1969. Formerly Joyce MacWhatty of Ridgewood, New Jersey, she married lawyer Hiram D. Black in 1948 and has a grown daughter, Suzy.

First Housewife, First Paid President of NOW

ELEANOR (ELLIE) CUTRI SMEAL of Pittsburgh, Pennsylvania, in 1977 became the first housewife to be president of the National Organization for Women (NOW),

as well as NOW's first paid president ($17,500 a year). Ms. Smeal was born in 1939 in Ashtabula, Ohio, to an Italian immigrant family; was graduated from

Strong Vincent High School, Erie, Pennsylvania, in 1957; made Phi Beta Kappa and received a B.A. in political science and public administration from the University of Florida in 1963; completed all her Ph.D. work except her thesis; and in 1971 decided NOW was more important than a doctorate. Mother of a boy and a girl, she joined NOW with her metallurgist husband Charles in 1970; in 1971 she was a member of the first Nominating Committee of the Founding Conference of the National Women's Political Caucus.

First president of the Pittsburgh South Hills chapter of NOW, 1971–73, she was convener and first president of Pennsylvania NOW, 1972–75, and rose through a series of important positions to be national chairperson of the Board in 1975 and president two years later. Busy since her election working for passage of the Equal Rights Amendment and the regaining of government-paid abortion rights, Ms. Smeal is also seeking to upgrade women's jobs to obtain "equal pay for work of equivalent value" (she cites bus drivers' earning more than registered nurses and notes that such inequalities discriminate against average- and lower-income families in which the housewife works). An effective homemakers' bill of rights providing for insurance, employment, and pension benefits and independent Social Security accounts is another of Ellie Smeal's objectives.

Ellie Smeal emphasizes that housewives are often most aware of the inequalities that women face and are among the most active in working for better opportunities for women. She is bothered, however, by the parents of a girl permitted to play Little League ball because of a NOW suit who say, "But we're no Women's Lib," or the professional woman who declares that she is certainly glad to be a doctor, lawyer, Indian chief but she has no time for that feminist nonsense.

"We fought for her to be that," declares Ellie Smeal, "and I won't be happy until I hear her say, 'I believe in the full rights of women under the law and I will fight to the death for the right of another woman to take my place when I am through.'"

CRAFTSPEOPLE

Canadian China Painter, First Artist-Potter in Nova Scotia

In 1887 ALICE MARY EGAN HAGEN (1872–1972) was commissioned to decorate twelve plates for the Women's Art Association of Canada, which presented them to Lord and Lady Aberdeen on his retirement as governor-general. In 1898 she rented a studio in Halifax and began teaching china painting, then was an instructor at the Victoria School of Art and Design. Her husband's work with a British cable company took the family to Jamaica for twelve years. There Ms. Hagen and her pupils gave the money they earned to the Red Cross, and she received bronze and silver Musgrave medals from the government. The Hagens returned in 1916 to Halifax, where she again taught china painting and luster-decoration. In 1930 Ms. Hagen went to Europe with her husband; there she saw Near East lusterware at the Persian Art Exhibit in London, visited the Staffordshire Potteries, saw French war veterans making pottery, and went home to set up a studio and kiln in her home at Mahone Bay and become the first artist-potter in Nova Scotia. She devoted the rest of her life to teaching pottery and working with local clays and glazes. The Art Gallery of Mount St. Vincent University, Halifax, exhibited her work in 1976.

Craftworkers in Birthplace of Appalachian Handicraft Revival

Berea College, founded in Berea, Kentucky, in 1855 by abolitionists who wanted to provide education for low-income young people of all races, is generally acknowledged as the cradle of the Southern Highlands handicraft revival. When Dr. William Goodell Frost became president of the college in 1893 and began "extension" trips into the mountains to find students, he discovered fine homespun coverlets which he began to accept as "barter for larnin'."

MARY ANDERSON, who learned weaving at 14 in Tyner, Kentucky, began sending her work to the college about 1897, on order from the dean of women, JOSEPHINE A. ROBINSON. Ms. Anderson, carrying her baby, rode horseback 25 miles to obtain supplies; she later moved to Berea and began weaving to order. Around the turn of the century, Berea established the first school in the Highlands for teachers of the arts and in 1911 Swedish-born ANNA ERNBERG, then teaching weaving in New York City, was placed in charge of what was then called Fireside Industries; she led the school to a prominent position in American handicrafts. Outside of Berea, women also led the way in founding craft organizations elsewhere in Appalachia.

Founders of Hindman and Pine Mountain Settlement Schools

When a traveling library formed by the Kentucky Federation of Women's Clubs in 1898 proved successful, the Federation sought "gentlewomen" to work with mountain families. KATHERINE PETTIT (1868–1936) of Lexington, who had attended the Sayre Female Institute in her hometown, and MAY STONE of Louisville, a Wellesley graduate, volunteered to conduct camp meetings each summer from 1899 to 1901. In 1902 they opened the Hindman Settlement School with money they had raised the previous winter. Fire destroyed their buildings in 1905–6 and in 1910, but the Hindman people helped them to rebuild and to raise $5,000 for a 65-acre farm. By 1911 200 students were enrolled, studying household skills and handicrafts.

Leaving May Stone in charge of Hindman, Katherine Pettit next founded Pine Mountain Settlement School in Harlan County in 1913 (she was co-director until her resignation in 1930). "Uncle William" Creech, an unschooled mountaineer, donated 250 acres of land to the school for "as long as the Constitution of the United States stands," and two years later, 40 students were studying health care, ballad singing, folk dancing, poultry raising, and crafts lessons.

Founder of Allanstand Cottage Industries

In 1895 FRANCES LOUISA GOODRICH of Britain's Cove, North Carolina (near Asheville), started a revival of the old crafts of the area, emphasizing weaving as a means of relieving the monotony of the solitary lives of mountain women. Ms. Goodrich, a social worker in Presbyterian mission schools in the area, and the mountain women collected some 70 coverlet drafts and set up Allanstand Cottage Industries. They pioneered in encouraging the continued use of native dyes, and worked to the high standards set by ELMEDA MCHARGUE WALKER, master weaver of coverlets until she was past 80. Ms. Walker, who lived a few miles away in Tennessee, wove the upholstery fabric for the Mountain Room planned for the White House by Mrs. Woodrow Wilson in 1913. Ms. Goodrich published *Mountain Spun* in 1931 and that same year presented Allanstand Cottage Industries to the Southern Highland Handicraft Guild.

Leaders of Pi Beta Phi's Arrowmont

EVELYN BISHOP was first head resident and for many years director of Pi Beta Phi Settlement School, founded in Gatlinburg, Tennessee, in 1912 to educate mountain children and encourage home industries. By the 1930s an expert weaver was supervising some 40 looms in mountain homes; the craftwork was exhibited and sold at the Arrow Craft Shop. Aunt Lydia Whaley, one of the best-known Highland craftswomen and basketmakers, worked with crafts at the school; a Gatlinburg pioneer, she spun and wove her family's clothing, made their shoes, ran her own gristmill, plowed and raised crops, hunted, and served her neighbors as nurse, preacher, doctor, and undertaker. She died at 86 in 1926. The settlement school is now the Arrowmont School of Crafts, which draws 1,000 craftspeople to its summer classes.

Penland Pioneer Who Founded Country's Largest Summer Crafts School

Weaving instructor LUCY MORGAN in 1923 launched the Penland Weavers in North Carolina, the beginning of what is probably the largest as well as oldest summer crafts school in the United States. In 1928 the Penland Fireside Industries added ceramics equipment and became the Penland Weavers and Potters, and in 1930 Ms. Morgan established the Penland Weaving Institute for her mountain weavers—six years later there were 116 students. Ms. Morgan and her Blue Ridge weavers risked borrowed money on the chance that customers at the Chicago World's Fair in 1933 would buy coverlets and scarves from their Log Cabin, and found their products in great demand. By 1937 some 40 Penland homes were involved in the work, which not only yielded income but provided social opportunities for mountaineers at the Weavers' Cabin, the community house they built. Lucy Morgan

was a leader in founding the Southern Highland Handicraft Guild (1930), first discussed in 1928 at the Weavers' Cabin. She retired in 1962 as director of Penland, which now covers 370 acres of mountain land and teaches weaving, pottery, woodwork, glassblowing, metal, stonework, photography, and graphics drawing. A faculty of 70 craft experts instructs in return for room, board, and travel pay.

Founder of Churchill Weavers

ELEANOR FRANZEN CHURCHILL, founder in 1922 of Churchill Weavers, Inc. in Berea, Kentucky, was born in Worthington, Minnesota, and was graduated from Hartford Public High School (1906) and from Wellesley College, Massachusetts (1911). She taught at Miss West's School for Girls, St. Joseph, Missouri, 1911–12, then took charge of the School for Boys, Bombay, India. In 1914 in southern India she married David Carroll Churchill. As designer for Churchill Weavers, 1922–46, Ms. Churchill was noted for skillful design and styling and her excellent sense of color. David Churchill, an outstanding textile engineer, designed looms, and together the Churchills trained many mountain youths to weave.

Two Women Launched Biltmore and Tryon Woodworking Industries

The Southern Highlands revival began with weaving; other crafts soon followed. Woodcarvers ELEANOR P. VANCE and CHARLOTTE L. YALE took a cottage on the Biltmore Estate near Asheville, North Carolina, in 1901. Little knowing she was launching the first of the Biltmore Industries, Ms. Vance started a woodcarving class for four boys who had been watching her work. In 1915 Ms. Vance and Ms. Yale moved to Tryon, North Carolina, and established the Tryon Toy-Makers and Wood-Carvers, beginning with woodcarving classes for children. Soon the industry was producing shelves and tables, carved and joined Gothic benches and many other special-order items, and handmade toys reflecting Blue Ridge Mountain life and biblical times.

Grande Dame of World Crafts

AILEEN OSBORN WEBB, acknowledged leader of world crafts, was born on June 25, 1892, in Garrison, New York. She studied at Miss Chapin's School and in Paris, made her debut at 18, and at 20 married future lawyer Vanderbilt Webb. Her commitment to crafts developed by chance: During the Depression she organized Putnam County Products to sell local produce and crafts; this led to the Handcraft League (1929) and to America House (1940), first major retail outlet for handmade objects, and *Craft Horizons,* its then-mimeographed newsletter. Crafts had declined as a result of mass production, and craftspeople worked in isolation, scattered throughout the country; Ms. Webb promoted a craft explosion when she founded the American Craftsmen's Educational Council (now the American Crafts Council) as a national clearinghouse for information (1943) and started the School for American Craftsmen (now at the Rochester Institute of Technology) (1946), the Museum of Contemporary Crafts (1956), and the World Crafts Council (1964). The first Craftsmen's Conference met at Asilomar, California, in 1957 and the first world crafts exhibit was presented in Toronto in 1974. Herself a watercolorist, woodcarver, enam-

elist, and ceramist, Ms. Webb is the mother of four, grandmother of 18, and and a great-grandmother. She retired as WCC president in 1974 and as ACC chairwoman in December 1976; as honorary chairwoman of both she remains active, organizing marketing programs for craftspeople in 86 WCC member nations.

Mother of Canadian Crafts

ADELAIDE MARRIOTT, mother of crafts in Canada, was born in Sarnia and graduated from the Royal Conservatory of Music, where she studied piano. She married chemical engineer Francis Marriott, who joined the staff of McGill University in Montreal. There the work of the city crafts guild impressed her greatly, and when the Marriotts returned to Toronto, she persuaded the newly formed Handicrafts Association of Canada (established in 1931) to become the Ontario branch of the much older Canadian Handicrafts Guild, dating from 1906. In 1932 Eaton's College Street store offered the group a corner of its ground floor rent-free is a sales outlet, in return for a small percentage of profits. Today Toronto has a Guild Shop, a crafts gallery, and a showroom where new work is displayed each month, but Adelaide Marriott is still busy working to expand, upgrade, and define Canadian craft work. In 1973, in her 90th year, she received an honorary degree from York University for her dedication to crafts.

World-Famous Makers of Black Pottery

First woman (and second person) to win the United States' Indian Achievement Award and matriarch of four generations of potters is MARÍA MONTOYA MARTÍNEZ, born in 1887 at San Idlefonso Pueblo, New Mexico. She and her husband Julian first made their world-famous black-on-black pottery in 1909. That year the Pueblo couple found black

shards at archaeological excavations in Frijoles Canyon. María Martínez made the coil-built pots by hand; Julian painted them with more refractory clay, often using designs he copied from archaeological sources, and baked the pots to a shiny coal-black in a controlled, open fire smothered with horse manure. María Martínez was invited to demonstrate at world's fairs up to World War II, was greeted at the White House by four Presidents, laid the cornerstone of New York City's Rockefeller Center, and is the recipient of honorary doctorates and international awards. Because of arthritis, she can now work only on pots that can be held in one hand; her sons Popovi Da and Adam, Adam's wife SANTANA, their daughter ANITA and daughter-in-law PAULINE, and the Martínez great-granddaughters RACHEL and BEVERLY now produce the Martínez pottery.

Mexico's celebrated DOÑA ROSA (ROSA REAL DE NIETO), a potter all her life, accidentally scratched a dry but unfired pot with a stone in 1952, fired it, and saw that the scratched area had turned a deep black. Doña Rosa had found the ancient method by which the Zapotec Indians had made lustrous blackware from the gray clay of Coyotepec, in the Oaxaca region of Mexico. Today her black *cántaros* (round water jugs) and other pottery are in collections all over the world; she has won many awards. In her 70s, Doña Rosa moved from her cottage to a new home where she produces pottery for tourists and tradesmen.

Australian Bush Child Started Rug Industry in Greece

JOICE NANKIVELL LOCH, born in 1893 in Australia, grew up as a bush child in the outback not far from Melbourne, where she attended the university. In 1918 she went to England as a free-lance journalist for the *Melbourne Evening Herald* and there married author Sydney Loch. In 1922, after working with Quaker relief in Poland, the Lochs moved on to the Quaker mission in Thessalonica, Greece, where 1.5 million Greeks from Turkey were being resettled. In the peasant community of Posforion, where they lived, Joice NanKivell Loch served as a lay doctor/nurse dispensing medicines, and became fascinated with rug making. Despite village skepticism, she insisted that the local rugs should be woven in natural wool. When th[e] prize at Thessalonica's firs[t] fair, orders for them poure[d] Loch developed many vegetab[le] other natural dyes for the weavers. D[ur]ing World War II, the Lochs left their village in 1939 to work again with Polish refugees, moving to Bucharest, Constantinople, Cyprus, and Palestine. After the war they returned to find rug making at a standstill. Ms. Loch solicited orders from a few foreigners, sold five rugs that had been saved in the monasteries, ordered wool, and turned the industry over to the Queen's Fund, concerned with village industries in Greece, as a permanent support for Posforion.

Award-Winning Latvian-Canadian Weaver

Canadian weaver VELTA VILSONS was born in Latvia, where she attended agricultural college because her farmer-father wished it ("Nothing grows for me," she says). But her home, like most in Latvia, contained a loom and she was interested in weaving. Ms. Vilsons, then a widow with two small children to support, emigrated to Sweden in 1944, and in 1952 moved to Montreal, where she worked for the Karen Bulow Studio. In 1955 she and a partner opened the Toronto Handweaving Studio; they sold mainly fabrics, draperies, and upholstery. Ms. Vilsons made her first important screen for the new city hall in Toronto and has won several international awards; she opened her own Vilsons Weaving Studio in 1965, and became a teacher at George Brown College when it started a weaving course a few years ago. Toronto's Ontario Hydro Building commissioned four large two-sided screens from Ms. Vilsons. She won a scholarship to Haystack Summer School (Maine) in 1962, studied at Penland (North Carolina) in 1964, and received two Industrial Design Awards in 1967. Velta Vilsons works in her house with studio near Niagara-on-the-Lake.

ese rugs won first international in. Ms. and

askit, Is-
as born in
1917, and
s a young
rming to the
the mass im-
Dayan noted
rom Europe,
India, Tunisia
(70 coun.... .....luded many expert craftswomen. ... studied crafts in London, 1950–53; headed the Crafts Department of the Ministry of Labor, 1953–54; and became director of Maskit when it was established by the government in 1954 to encourage and safeguard crafts and to provide a marketing outlet for the diverse skills of Israeli immigrants. The organization began with 60 workers in two villages; 20 years later it employed 700 craftspeople. A new gallery, Maskit Shesh, has been opened in Tel Aviv, and an international showroom in New York. Sales have topped $3 million a year and private business interests have taken over the once government-subsidized enterprise. Ruth Dayan became president of the Israel Designer-Craftsmen's Association. She married General Moshe Dayan in 1935; they had three children, and were divorced in 1972.

Among the noted craftswomen who have contributed to the wide variety of work sold by Maskit are:

HANNA CHARAG-ZUNTZ, born 1915 in Germany. She studied pottery from 1935–40 in Germany, Florence, Teplitz-Schönau, and Prague and went to Israel in 1940. Hanna Charag-Zuntz teaches, and designs industrial pottery. Her award-winning work has been exhibited.

HANA KRALOVA, who came to Israel in 1965 from Czechoslovakia, where she had studied interior textile design at the University for Applied Art (Prague). She was chief designer in bobbin lace at the Center for People's Art (Prague) and has exhibited at Montreal's Expo '67 and in Europe.

SHULAMIT LITAN, who traveled to Israel from Poland the year she was born, 1936. Self-taught, she designs textiles, working with batik, appliqué, and needlework; she has also done quilting and printing.

SIONA SHIMSHI, born in 1939 to a Lithuanian family in Tel Aviv. She works as textile designer, ceramist, painter, or sculptor according to her need. She studied at the Academy of Fine Arts in Tel Aviv and at Alfred University and Greenwich House Pottery, New York.

LIDIA ZAVADSKY, born in 1937 in Poland. She obtained a master's in law before coming to Israel in 1961, then studied ceramics at the Bezalel Academy of Art and Design in Jerusalem, and established a studio in 1965. She exhibited at Expo '67 and the International Competition of Artistic Ceramics, Italy. She won two prizes in 1969 at the Competition for Designing Ceramic Lamps, and in 1971 was elected titular member of the International Academy of Ceramics, UNESCO.

Nigerian Master Potter

Nigeria's LADI ("born on Sunday") KWALI (the name of her hometown) started making pots at age six. British potter Michael Cardew discovered her magnificent casseroles, water pots, bowls, and huge storage jars, all incised with geometric designs or stylized figures from nature, in 1950. About a year later Cardew started a Pottery Training Centre in Abuja. Ladi Kwali had always coiled and built her pots by hand, using clay from the ground and open fires. At the Centre she learned quickly how to throw by wheel and use glazes, but she still handbuilds some of her large jars and jugs.

Ladi Kwali has traveled internationally to demonstrate her masterful work.

Production Potter of Penland

Functional potter CYNTHIA BRINGLE became interested in art in junior high school, and after a year at Southwestern College in her native Memphis, Tennessee, entered the Memphis Academy of Arts to study painting. She took pottery as a required subject and soon was devoting her leisure hours, including summers at Haystack Mountain School of Crafts, Maine, to ceramics. She received her B.F.A. in 1962 and an M.F.A. from Alfred University (Alfred, New York) in 1964, and opened a pottery studio in Eads, Tennessee, the following year. She taught briefly at the Penland School of Crafts, North Carolina, in 1963 and has conducted summer sessions there since 1964; in 1970 she moved to the mountains a mile from Penland. An energetic production potter, Cynthia Bringle makes pots of many different kinds—her shop displays stoneware, porcelain, raku works, salt-glazed, and lustered.

Canadian Ceramics Master

Ceramist ANN MORTIMER of Newmarket, Ontario, a graduate of Georgian College's Material Arts Program, a registered nurse, and a former Air Canada stewardess, returned to college in 1968 and is now teaching master of design arts at Georgian's Barrie campus. She has exhibited widely in Canada and the United States, and in Czechoslovakia, and has taught a number of workshops on clay and glass techniques, including sessions at the Banff Centre School of Fine Arts and at Calgary Seminars, both in Alberta. Ms. Mortimer was chairwoman of one-man shows for the Canadian Guild of Potters, 1968–70, and its president, 1974–75. She was named a director-at-large of the Canadian Crafts Council in 1976 and chairwoman of the Council's education committee.

World Crafts Councilwomen in Canada

Canadian crafts leader JOAN CHALMERS, born in 1928 in Toronto, was graduated from the Ontario College of Art in Interior Architecture and Design in 1948. She was writer and assistant art director for *Canadian Homes and Gardens,* 1948–52, and from 1952 to 1966 art director for *Mayfair, Canadian Bride, Canadian Homes and Gardens,* and the first woman art director in Canada of *Châtelaine,* the country's largest-circulation magazine. Ms. Chalmers became a director of the Canadian Guild of Crafts (CGC)/Ontario in 1967, served on the Council of the Ontario College of Art, 1968–72, was exhibition chairwoman for CGC/Ontario, 1969–72, and became the organization's first woman president in 1974. She was a national committeewoman for CGC/Montreal, 1970–74 and a key figure in bringing the first world crafts exhibition, "In Praise of Hands," to Toronto in 1974. In 1975 she was appointed secretary of the World Crafts Council and that same year became founding president of the Ontario Crafts Council, a merger of the CGC/Ontario and the Ontario Craft Foundation.

As crafts consultant for Ontario's Sports and Recreation Bureau and vice-president of the North American World Crafts Council, MARY EILEEN HOGG took on the enormous task of organizing the 1974 Toronto World Crafts Council Conference. Ms. Hogg has been Canadian co-director of the World Crafts Council with Joan Chalmers, and a director of the Canadian Crafts Council and the Ontario Crafts Council.

Successor to Aileen O. Webb

BARBARA ROCKEFELLER, who succeeded AILEEN O. WEBB (p. 124) as head of the American Crafts Council in 1976, was a trustee of ACC for four years and chairman of its Board for one. She studied English literature and art at Wellesley

College, married Rodman Rockefeller
(Nelson Rockefeller's eldest son), and is
the mother of four children. Ms. Rockefeller has worked with a number of arts
groups and hopes to promote participation in crafts and world respect for
craftspeople and their work. She finds
American crafts among the "most expressive" she has seen. Barbara Rockefeller has herself studied woodworking,
drawing, and pottery and is a firm
believer in the ability of crafts to give its
practitioners "the power of the sense of
self."

Viennese Teaches Pottery to Washingtonians

VALLY POSSONY, Viennese potter, born
in 1905, studied her craft for five years,
first with an Austrian master who had
been influenced by Asian culture, then
in Holland, Amsterdam, and Berlin. She
fled Austria with the approach of World
War II, reached Paris in 1938, and arrived in New York City in 100-degree
heat in 1940 with "no luggage except
two dogs." In 1942 she went to Washington, D.C., where her daughter Andrea was born in 1944, and returned
to pottery only when she visited Walter
Reed Hospital as a Red Cross volunteer in 1948 and agreed to teach the
veterans there and to train nurses to
teach pottery. She also taught at Catholic
University, has instructed retarded children, and now conducts four classes a
week at her home in a converted barn in
Falls Church, Virginia. She estimates she
has had at least 2,000 students, and
has served as a judge and given demonstrations in many museums, including
the Smithsonian. Ms. Possony enjoys
country living surrounded by handmade
furniture and ceramics—"My pottery is
functional—I like simple lines and earth
colors," she says. Vally Possony maintains large flower and vegetable gardens
and an immaculate shop with 14 wheels.

One of her students: JOAN MONDALE,
wife of the Vice-President (see "Women
in the Arts and Entertainment.")

She Switched to a Second Career

CAROL RIDKER of Bethesda, Maryland, a
sociologist who changed to a career in
pottery, attended the University of Wisconsin (1952–55); married American
economist Ronald G. Ridker in Oslo,
Norway (1955); received her bachelor's
degree from Washington University, St.
Louis, Missouri (1957); and studied for
her doctorate in sociology at Syracuse
University (1964–65). As the mother of
two small children, she worked at the
Brookings Institution, Washington, D.C.,
until the day she chanced to walk past
the Corcoran Art Gallery, wandered in,
and signed up for pottery lessons with
Japanese ceramist Teruo Hara. She completed the four-year Corcoran School of
Art in two years, then taught there,
1966–67. Compared with sociological
research work, which involved a long
wait before the results appeared in book
form, pottery provides more "instant
gratification (or instant failure)" she
says, and allows her to lead a "more harmonious life" working at home with her
family. Her income also easily equals
what she would have made as a sociologist. Carol Ridker's pottery has taken her
on study/lecture/demonstration trips to
Norway, Mexico, Japan, Thailand, India,
Greece, Indonesia, Singapore, England,
Sweden, Colombia, and Peru. She does
both one-of-a-kind porcelain and stoneware pieces and production pottery and
is internationally known for her glazes—
bright copper reds (like the ancient Chinese *sang de boeuf*), celadon (a pale
green), and *temmoku* brown (a plum
brown). Carol Ridker became adjunct
professor of ceramics at American University in 1976. She takes apprentices,
including several who have followed her
example in switching from other professions.

Craftswomen Honored at White House Luncheon

Launching a campaign to bring 20th-century arts into the White House, ROSALYNN CARTER was hostess on May 16, 1977, to a luncheon for Senate wives in honor of contemporary American craftsworkers. Pottery, glassware, wrought-iron napkin rings, honeysuckle and white oak baskets filled with cornshuck and woodshaving flowers, and handmade book favors decorated the luncheon tables. The project was coordinated through major crafts organizations by ELENA CANAVIER of the National Endowment for the Arts; craftspeople created the objects in less than six weeks, not knowing they were for the White House.

Craftswomen represented included: pottery—ROBERTA BLOOM (Marblehead, Massachusetts), CYNTHIA BRINGLE (Penland, North Carolina), DORA DE LARIOS (Culver City, California), BARBARA GRYGUTIS (Tucson, Arizona), CATHARINE HIERSOUX (Kensington, California), ANNE B. SHATTUCK (Eastham, Massachusetts), HARRIET COHEN (Amherst, Maine); glassware—NANCY FREEMAN (Olivebridge, New York); baskets—NANCY CONSEEN (Qualla Arts and Crafts Mutual, Cherokee, North Carolina); cornshuck flowers, by Shuckery and Wood Pretties Center—LILA MARSHALL, and PHYLLIS COMBS (all of Nickelsville, Virginia).

After the luncheon the crafts were exhibited at the Renwick Gallery.

Living National Treasure

The only country in the world to designate its best craft artists as Living National Treasures ("holders of Intangible Cultural Properties") is Japan, where dyer/weaver AYANO CHIBA was named a Treasure in 1955. (The cultural protection law was passed in 1950, and by 1973 37 Living National Treasures representing 31 crafts had been designated.) Tiny Ayano Chiba is the only remaining person who knows the 2,000-year-old art of spinning and weaving hemp, then dyeing it with indigo; she watched her grandparents and parents as a child, learned early to spin, and began dyeing 50 years ago, working on her own with indigo since age 34. Ms. Chiba enthusiastically tells visitors her work is "lots of trouble"; she wakes up at 4 A.M. to be about her business, assisted by her daughter, who has learned to plant *ai* (indigo). The indigo leaves are gathered and stored until January, when it is cold enough to prepare the dye. Designs are stenciled on cotton hemp, which is dyed, then rinsed in the river (the fish nibble off the paste). The indigo-dyed material is absolutely fast. A kimono made of it can last 100 years. The only way to learn her craft is "to do it," Ayano Chiba says. Like the other Treasures, Ayano Chiba is supported by the government, which sponsors public exhibits and training courses for successors in the traditional crafts.

SEWING AND STITCHERY INSTRUCTORS

Sewing Teacher for Millions

MARY BROOKS PICKEN, born 1886, has taught sewing to millions through direct teaching (at the beginning of her career) and (over the past fifty years) through correspondence school sewing courses, the *Singer Sewing Book,* and as a magazine sewing editor. Ms. Picken has written more than 90 books, which have been purchased by well over 1 million people in 87 countries: among the most popular have been *A Dictionary of the*

Language of Fashion (first published in 1939), *Modern Dressmaking Made Easy* (1940) and *Sewing Magic* (1952).

Grande Dame of American Needlework

GEORGIANA BROWN HARBESON, grande dame of American needlework, was born in 1894 in New Haven, Connecticut, attended the Pennsylvania Academy of Fine Arts and Moore Institute, married John F. Harbeson in 1916, and had three sons. Ms. Harbeson designed theater ballets and costumes for the Provincetown (Massachusetts) Players and Paramount films (1928–30) and, with a strong background in painting, became an outstanding designer of needlepoint and crewel embroidery. She exhibited and lectured widely, wrote and designed for magazines, designed 60 models for the first American Needlepoint Line for Minerva (1935–37), and was founder-president of the American Needle Arts Society in 1938—the same year she published the definitive *American Needlework: The History of Decorative Stitchery and Embroidery from the Late Sixteenth to the Twentieth Century* (4th edition, 1970). Ms. Harbeson also was chairperson of arts for the Women's International Exposition of Arts and Industry in Grand Central Palace, 1941–42, taught at Ballard School, New York, 1942–47, and helped organize an American Red Cross/Museum of Modern Art project supplying artist/teachers for hospitalized World War II soldiers. In 1949 she opened the Georgiana Brown Harbeson Studio for hand arts design in New Hope, Pennsylvania, and during the 1950s she did extensive ecclesiastical work, designing needlepoint for the National Episcopal Cathedral in Washington, D.C., and other churches. Active in numerous artistic and press organizations, in 1966 she was named to the Executive and Professional Hall of Fame, and 10 years later was still exhibiting in her 80s.

Leader of the Stitchery Renaissance

One of the needle artists responsible for the stitchery renaissance in the United States was MARISKA KARASZ (1898–1960), who was born in Hungary, immigrated to America as a teen-ager, and became a clothes designer. She wrote books on design and sewing and was guest needlework editor of *House Beautiful* for two years. At first traditional in her approach, she began to use backgrounds and threads never before used for embroidery and "to see stitches in their structural forms—the wrong side sometimes as beautiful as the right!" She tried working on both sides of the fabric, obtaining new textures, and created techniques using all manner of innovative materials including paper, metals, shells, sand dollars. Her work became increasingly abstract and spontaneous, yet of outstanding quality, as she opened new avenues for the "painter in thread." Mariska Karasz's *Adventures in Stitches* (1949) received an Institute of Graphic Arts prize. The Contemporary Crafts Museum gave a one-person retrospective exhibit of her work.

Fine Appliqué Embroidery Craftswoman

Californian JEAN RAY LAURY BITTERS, born in 1928 in Louisiana, received a B.A. from Northeast Louisiana University and an M.A. from Stanford University. One of the United States' most skilled embroiderers, she does fine, intricate appliqué work finished with meticulous care. Her designs are suggested by nature and her colors by each subject. Her books include works on appliqué, quilts and coverlets, dollmaking, and *Handmade Rugs* (1971).

Crewel Best Seller

ERICA WILSON, whose needlework empire quadrupled in the 1970s into a million-dollar industry, was born in England and attended the Royal School of

Needlework in London, where she then became an instructor. In 1952 she came to the United States to teach crewelwork to private pupils and at the Cooper Union Museum in New York. She soon started a correspondence course and became nationally known for her books on embroidery and two series on public television. In 1957 Erica Wilson married German-born furniture designer and manufacturer Vladimir Kagan, whose business sense and drive had helped promote Erica Wilson, Inc. In 1962 she published *Crewel Embroidery,* which at 500,000 copies became the best-selling craft book; she has written some ten books since. Now in her late 40s, she writes a thrice-weekly syndicated news column, lectures, has designed 100 needlework kits, owns embroidery shops in New York, Southampton, and Nantucket, and is director of the Erica Wilson Creative Needlework Society. In 1977 she began needlework cruises; her plans for 1978 included two-week tours of British castles.

Creative Knitting and Macramé Specialist

The author of *Step-by-Step Knitting* (1967), MARY WALKER PHILLIPS was born in Fresno, California, in 1923 and received her B.F.A. and M.F.A. from the Cranbrook Academy. She then demonstrated that knitting need no longer be limited to useful woolens for the family. Her knitted objects are of a special beauty belonging to fabric art. Ms. Phillips came to New York City at 40 and teaches creative knitting at the New School for Social Research there. Her *Step-by-Step Macramé* (1970) has sold a million copies; *Creative Knitting: A New Art Form* (1971), 300,000 copies in the United States.

COOKBOOK AUTHORS

Producer of the "Kitchen Bible"

FANNIE MERRITT FARMER (1857–1915), author of the *Boston Cooking School Cook Book* (1896), did more than any American woman except Ellen H. Swallow Richards (see p. 103), founder of home economics, to make homemaking a profession. Her well-known contribution: the use of explicit directions and level measurements in recipes so that dishes turn out the same each time they are made. Fannie Farmer was born in Boston, Massachusetts, and was stricken with paralysis in her left leg at age 16. She completed high school in Medford and became a mother's helper for a friend whose daughter asked her to define such terms as "a pinch" or "a lump," used in the recipes of the day. In 1887 she enrolled in the Boston Cooking School, completed a two-year course, remained as assistant principal, and became head of the school in 1894. She took her carefully tested recipes to Little, Brown, and paid for the first edition of her cookbook, which was immediately successful and has sold 4 million copies in 11 revisions since. In 1902 she founded the Miss Farmer School of Cookery, where she gave weekly demonstration lectures for homemakers and professional cooks. Her interest turning to diets for the sick and convalescent, she next began teaching nutrition to nurses, hospital dietitians, and Harvard Medical School students, and encouraged Dr. Elliott P. Joslin to persevere in studying the role of sugar in diabetes. In 1904 she published *Food and Cookery for the Sick and Convalescent,* which she considered her most important work. A vivacious redhead with bright blue eyes, who wore pince-nez, Fannie Farmer continued to lecture to women's clubs even after two strokes put her in a wheelchair.

Editor of Best-Selling Cookbook

"I just added the parsley," MYRNA JOHNSTON, 76-year-old retired editor says of the team effort that produced the *Better Homes and Gardens New Cook Book*, third hardback best seller ever (19 million copies). Ms. Johnston learned to cook at home as a child, went on to a home economics degree and many awards at the Iowa State Fair. As a graduate student at the University of Chicago art school, she worked with color photos, first used in the book in 1937. Myrna Johnston, who has traveled, by her estimate, a good million miles in search of recipes for cooks of every degree of skills, remembers condiment recipes in the first edition of the cookbook in 1930, "before Heinz was in there pitching." She still serves as a consultant for the cookbook she brought from its early days before frozen foods up to the microwave era.

The "Joy of" Cook

IRMA (VON STARKLOFF) ROMBAUER, whose book *The Joy of Cooking* was for many years the best seller by an individual cook, was born in St. Louis on October 30, 1877. She attended boarding schools in Lausanne and Geneva and married Edgar Rombauer, a lawyer, in 1899. He taught her to cook. After his death in 1930 she began to collect recipes from around the world. Her book, written at the request of her married son and daughter, remains one of the clearest and most accurate guides to cooking available and is filled with charming asides ("A turnip is not necessarily a depressant"). When she completed it in 1931, she published it at her own expense, sold 3,000 copies, then rewrote it for publication by Bobbs-Merrill (1936), adding step-by-step listing of ingredients as recipes are mixed—a feature of all later editions. She wrote *Streamlined Cooking* (Bobbs-Merrill, 1939), and combined this with her first book in 1943; the volume sold 1.3 million copies in its first decade. *The New Joy of Cooking* (1951), a revised edition including new processing methods, was written in collaboration with her daughter, MARION ROMBAUER BECKER. Ms. Rombauer died in 1962 at the age of 86.

The Reader's Cook

MARY FRANCES KENNEDY ("M.F.K.") FISHER, born in 1908 in Michigan, combined two great loves—reading and cooking—to become America's foremost gastronomical writer/philosopher. She spent her childhood in Whittier, California, where her father edited the local newspaper, and studied at Illinois College, Occidental College, UCLA, and the University of Dijon in France, from which she was graduated in 1931. Her first book, *Serve It Forth,* appeared in 1937 and was immediately hailed for its witty, evocative writing. *Consider the Oyster* (1941) followed, then *How to Cook a Wolf* (1942), her famous guide for wartime cooks trying to cope with food shortages; *The Gastronomical Me* (1943); and *Here Let Us Feast* (1946)—a symposium of great thoughts on eating and drinking through the ages, including excerpts from Plato, Rabelais, and Ovid. The first books were combined in 1954 in *The Art of Eating,* recently reissued in paperback. Also among her works are a brilliant translation of gastronome Jean Anthelme Brillat-Savarin's *The Physiology of Taste* (republished 1971), and *The Cooking of Provincial France,* part of Time-Life's world cooking series. Her memoirs, *Among Friends* (1971), describes the tantalizing dishes of her childhood and her fascination with such "forbidden treats" as mashed potatoes with catsup and watercress and her pet passion, peanut butter and potato chips. *A Considerable Town,* a travel-and-food book about Marseille, was published in 1978. Mother of two daughters, M. F. K. Fisher now lives in the Sonoma vineyard country of northern California.

America's Most Popular French Chef

JULIA CHILD, whose cookbooks and prize-winning TV program have brought the *cuisine bourgeoise* of France into millions of homes, was born in Pasadena, California, on August 15, 1912. Graduated from Smith College with a major in history, she joined the Office of Strategic Services (OSS) in World War II and was assigned to Ceylon. There she met Paul Cushing Child, also with the OSS; both were reassigned to China, and in 1946 they were married. When Paul Child, a gastronome ("I married a hungry man interested in food"), was sent to Paris with the U. S. Foreign Service in 1948, his wife entered the Cordon Bleu cooking school. In 1951, with two Frenchwomen (below) she opened L'École des Trois Gourmandes in Paris, and later established branches in Marseilles, Bonn, and Oslo, the Childs' other posts. The three women also set to work on a three-year project, Volume I of *Mastering the Art of French Cooking,* a book hailed as a masterpiece when it was published in 1961. Paul Child retired that year and the couple moved to Cambridge, Massachusetts, where Julia, carrying her copper bowl and huge balloon whisk, appeared on WGBH-TV to promote her cookbook. She was a sensation. Since 1963 "The French Chef" has been bringing the joy of French cooking to nationwide audiences fascinated by the gusto and side comments of its 6'2" star. ("Keep your knives sharp" and "Never apologize," she admonishes.) The program won the George Foster Peabody Award in 1965, an Emmy in 1966, and the French Ordre du Mérite Agricole in 1972. Volume II of the cookbook appeared in 1970, and Ms. Child has also published *The French Chef Cookbook* (1968) and *From Julia Child's Kitchen* (1975).

The French Partners of Julia Child

SIMONE SUZANNE RENÉE MADELEINE (SIMCA) BECK FISCHBACHER, born in 1904 at Tocqueville en Caux, Normandy, developed her passion for cooking in childhood. She studied with Henri-Paul Pelleprat, *maître* at the Cordon Bleu cooking school. In 1948 a friend (LOUISETTE BERTHOLLE, now Comtesse de Nalèche) asked her to collaborate on a French cookbook for Americans. In 1951 the two decided to seek American help, and found JULIA CHILD, then studying cooking in Paris. "Simca" (a name given her by her husband, Jean Fischbacher) also co-authored (with PATRICIA SIMON, American writer who met her in Provence in 1969) *Simca's Cuisine* (1972) and is working on a book covering the three cuisines that most influence her cooking: that of Normandy, where she lived 18 years with her family, and which has the best French apples, butter, and cream; that of Alsace, her husband's home province; and that of Provence, where the Fischbachers own a working farm that produces a rich variety of herbs and vegetables.

Definitive Canadian Cook

Canadian cooking, which combines French and English traditions with American, would be little known were it not for the work of one prolific writer, researcher, and broadcaster, JEHANE BENOIT. Mme. Benoit, who mingles her knowledge of history with love for traditional recipes, recently published *Enjoying the Art of Canadian Cooking.* She is also the author of *The Encyclopedia of Canadian Cooking, The Canadian Cookbook* and *The Best of Mme. Jehane Benoit,* and has devoted more than 20 years of radio, TV, and other public appearances to discussing and demonstrating Canadian cookery. In 1974 she was made an Officer of the Order of Canada, one of the country's highest honors.

GARDENING EXPERTS

She Brought the French Impressionist Touch to English Gardens

GERTRUDE JEKYLL, born in 1843 in England, studied art in London and Europe and applied her trained artist's eye to replacing the stiff patterns of formal English gardens with flowers planted to produce masses of color; with William Robinson, she pioneered the garden of today. In an article published in 1889, Ms. Jekyll deplored the "bedding-out," which had started in large gardens and almost submerged the "beauties of the many little flowering cottage plots of our English waysides." She translated the color harmonies of the French Impressionist painters into her gardens, and with Robinson, ELLEN WILLMOTT, and others firmly established the herbaceous border in England by the turn of the century. Her taste is clearly expressed in her own garden at Munstead Heath, Surrey, as in other gardens she designed throughout England before her death in 1932.

First Woman to Receive Highest U. S. Gardening Award

LOUISE BOYD YEOMANS KING (1863–1948) a pioneer in the American garden club movement, was born in Wilmington, Delaware, studied art and literature at private schools, and was married in 1890 in Orange, New Jersey, her childhood home. She learned garden skills and soil management from her mother-in-law, who maintained formal gardens in Elmhurst, Illinois, and started her own first garden in Alma, Michigan, in 1902. She corresponded with gardeners around the world, in 1910 began writing magazine articles on gardening, and in 1915 published *The Well-Conditioned Garden*, followed by nine more books in the next 15 years. The mother of three, Ms. King was a founder of the

Garden Club of America in 1913, president of the Garden Club of Michigan, 1912–15, and first president of the Woman's National Farm and Garden Association, 1914–21. After her husband died in 1927, she moved to South Hartford, New York, and started the state's first plowing contest. She was a vice-president of the Garden Club of London and a fellow of the Royal Horticultural Society; in 1921 she became the first woman to receive the George White Medal of the Massachusetts Horticultural Society, the highest garden award in America; and in 1923 she won the Medal of Honor of the Garden Club of America.

She Combined Cabbages and Roses

CONSTANCE SPRY (1886–1960) who arranged the flowers for the weddings of the Duke of Windsor, the Duke of Gloucester, and Queen Elizabeth, as well as the Queen's coronation flowers, was born in Derby, England, spent her childhood in Ireland, and was educated at Alexandra School and College, Dublin. She turned to flower arranging while a social worker in northern England during World War I, combining weeds, grasses, leaves, branches, fruits ("If it's beautiful, why not?") with even the choicest flowers. Her arrangements took their inspiration from great Dutch painters. Bond Street's Atkinson's asked her to design their windows; her fresh approach drew crowds, and at age 42 she opened her own London shop, driving to Covent Garden each morning with oddments from her home garden, including cabbages along with roses. Ms. Spry opened her New York shop in 1938, wrote for *Vogue, Harper's Bazaar, House and Garden*, and *Ladies' Home Journal*, and published 12 books. In 1953, she was appointed to the Order of the British Empire.

Champion of Plants, Indoors and Out

THALASSA CRUSO HENCKEN, whose forthright manner on public television has made her the "Julia Child of the plant world," was born in Guildford, Surrey, where she "grew up taking gardens and gardening for granted." She studied archaeology and anthropology at the London School of Economics, graduating with honors in 1931, and worked on excavations at several sites in the British Isles. Assistant keeper of the costume and 19th-century collections at the London Museum, 1931–35, she married Hugh Hencken in 1935 and has since lived in Boston. Wherever she has lived, she gardened, as "part of the general pattern of everyday life" in her family. Since 1967 her nationwide programs on WGBH-TV, Boston ("Making Things Grow," 1967–69; "Making Things Work," 1970), have delighted U.S. audiences. Another show, "Small City Garden," was seen in Boston (1972) and on the BBC, 1975 and 1977. Her books are *Making Things Grow* (1969), *Making Things Grow Outdoors* (1971), *To Everything There Is a Season* (1973), *Making Vegetables Grow* (1975), and *Calendar* (1976). She has also been a regular columnist for the *Boston Sunday Globe, McCall's,* and *Country Journal.* Ms. Hencken says that "People suffer if they are consistently deprived of contact with nature. Plants still carry on the old cycle of rest, rejuvenation, and fulfillment." But she urges gardeners to "have fun with your plants and refuse to allow them to take over your life." A mother and grandmother, she is a fellow of the Society of Antiquaries of London, an accredited horticultural judge, and has received the Garden Club of America Medal of Merit (1969) and Distinguished Service Medal (1970) and been cited by the Horticultural Society of New York (1970).

BUSINESSWOMEN WHO BEGAN AT HOME

Founder of Pepperidge Farm Bakeries

MARGARET FOGARTY RUDKIN, bakery executive who made her first loaf of bread at the age of 40, was born in 1897. She was valedictorian of her class in Flushing, New York, and married broker Henry Albert Rudkin in 1923, moving from New York in 1929 to Fairfield, Connecticut, where they purchased a house with an old pepperidge tree in the yard. Ms. Rudkin started baking homemade bread for her children and soon was providing it for her neighbors as well. In 1937 she placed some loaves in local stores and in 1938 launched her famous multimillion-dollar baking company. In its first year, Pepperidge Farm, Inc., produced 4,000 loaves a week and expanded to an unused service station in Norwalk. Its products sold on their own merits, with little advertising, because of Ms. Rudkin's insistence on high-quality ingredients, whatever the price (flour used was stone-ground, slow-aged, and unbleached; bread was cut and kneaded in small batches, by hand; only sweet creamery butter was allowed, and no yeast foods or commercial shortenings). With Ms. Rudkin handling production and personnel and her husband, finances and marketing, the company continued to grow rapidly, adding melba toast, pound cake, and later rolls, stuffing, cookies, and frozen pastries. In 1955 Ms. Rudkin received the distinguished award for an individual from the thirty-second Women's International Exposition of the Women's National Institute. The author of *The Margaret Rudkin Pepperidge Farm Cookbook* (1963), she died in 1967.

Bread Baker Only Woman Selected for New Millionaires Book

Founder and board chairman of Brownberry Ovens, Inc., CATHERINE T. CLARK was the only woman selected by *Wall*

Street Journal editors in 1961 for *The New Millionaires and How They Made Their Fortunes.* She told women that the best way to reach the top is to do it as she did—by starting her own business and appointing herself president. A native of Whitewater, Wisconsin, Ms. Clark began baking bread after her marriage to banker Russell J. Clark in 1932. Then the mother of two small daughters, she bought a recipe from a small-town baker and in 1946, with the aid of her household helper, fired up a secondhand oven in an empty grocery in Oconomowoc, Wisconsin. She started with two loaves—white and whole wheat—made with fresh natural ingredients. Using an old beer truck for deliveries, she made a first-year profit of $68. In 30 years she was making 14 kinds of bread, six types of rolls, and croutons, with annual sales of $25 million in two plants (in Wisconsin and Ohio). In 1972 she sold her company for $5.5 million to the Peavey Company, Minneapolis-based agribusiness, where she is the first woman member of the Board of Directors and still active in product development. In the '70s she began a syndicated news column on breadmaking and now writes on "Endangered Food Species"—homemade dishes that may be forgotten in a day of store-bought foods. The Clarks moved to San Francisco in 1960 and weekend at a ranch in Sonoma County.

Welding Executive

BERNICE M. MCPHERSON, 4'11" president of her own welding and construction firm in Gaithersburg, Maryland, was born in 1901 in Carlsbad, California. She became fascinated with welding as a child watching the family blacksmith, but went on to a nursing career. Then she changed her mind and had been welding for years when she moved to Gaithersburg in 1941. During World War II, she won a U. S. Navy award for developing a welding process for weapons sights that greatly reduced production costs. In 1946 she and her husband Maynard founded the B&M Welding Works in Gaithersburg, beginning in a small workshop in their garage. Eventually the firm had 30 employees working on major building projects, with Ms. McPherson also working as a welder at the construction sites. The first woman member of the Washington section of the American Welding Society and later its chairman, in 1970 she received their A. G. Bissell Memorial Award. A mother and grandmother, she died at her summer home on Cobb Island, Maryland, at 75.

Inventor of Liquid Paper

BETTE CLAIR NESMITH GRAHAM, founder of the Liquid Paper Corporation, developed the idea of "painting out" typing errors in 1956 in her kitchen in Dallas, Texas. An executive secretary and artist, she set up the Mistake Out Company, producing Mistake Out and soon Special Match Correction Fluid (for colored papers) at home with the aid of her son and other available assistants. The company expanded to her garage, then to a 10-by-26-foot portable building in which seven employees mixed the fluids, filled bottles, trimmed brushes, and packed orders, all by hand. In 1962 Bette Nesmith married Robert Graham, who helped her market her correction fluid; the company became the Liquid Paper Corporation in 1968 and the portable building is a museum on the grounds of its international headquarters in Dallas. The Liquid Paper subsidiary, L. P. Child Development Corporation, opened its first full-day child care center for working parents in late 1976, the same year Ms. Graham resigned as chairwoman of the Board to become a full-time Christian Science practitioner.

The World's Most Successful Dieter

JEAN SLUTSKY NIDETCH, who in 1963 founded the world's most successful diet business, Weight Watchers, Inc., was born on October 12, 1923, in Brooklyn, the daughter of a cab driver and manicurist. As she frequently tells her followers, she received food as a consolation as a child and became a compulsive eater. She dropped out of City College of New York soon after her father died in 1942, and in 1945 met Martin Nidetch. ("We ate together," she later said of their two-year courtship.) After a few years in Oklahoma and Pennsylvania, the Nidetches and their three children in 1952 moved to Little Neck, Queens. Highly gregarious, Jean Nidetch joined and headed numerous organizations at the same time she was becoming a "professional dieter." When she reached size 44 and 214 pounds, she went to the New York City Health Department's obesity clinic, followed the diet, but secretly ate sweets at night—until she called friends to join her. The diet group grew rapidly, and in October 1962 she reached her goal weight, 142, and quit the clinic. The following year, she founded Weight Watchers. In groups led by women who have lost weight and maintained their loss, the organization emphasizes weekly meetings of peers who encourage each other in sticking to sensible food habits. Jean Nidetch, now divorced and a platinum blond, enthusiastically boosts her multimillion-dollar program on radio and TV and in her books. The business has expanded to include diet foods, a magazine, summer camps, and has many inspired imitators. In 1973 Bob Hope and Pearl Bailey entertained a reunion of 16,000 Weight Watchers at Madison Square Garden. Ms. Nidetch is an honorary Kentucky colonel and was the Long Island Advertising Club's "Man of the Year" in 1972.

Corn Cob Jelly Makers

When the What Cheer (Iowa) sewer pipe company closed down in 1964, a local newsman dreamed up a cottage industry, Corn Cob Products, for the unemployed, and a half-dozen volunteers set to work making corn cob jelly in their kitchens. Today CARRIBELLE WITT of What Cheer boils off a batch each morning, and AUDREY FRITZ of North English, the Corn Cob secretary, treasurer, and manager, makes up batches according to quantities needed. The little company, which grossed $8,400 in 1976, pays its two dozen stockholders a dividend each year. Besides the jelly ("it tastes a little like apple jelly," Ms. Fritz says), the company produces corn cob syrup, spicy apple syrup, and corn cob candy. They sell to summer tourists and through outlets throughout Iowa; Miss Iowa has given corn cob jelly to sister contestants in the last three Miss America contests; a New Zealand cruise ship served the jelly with a "Classic Iowa Breakfast." Without advertising, the company has gained customers all over the United States and abroad.

Model Agent

When JOAN SOLOMON graduated from the University of Minnesota in 1968 and started job hunting, she found her degree in speech pathology leading nowhere. In desperation she registered at the only model agency in her community, and soon noticed that lack of competition had caused the agency to lose its creativity. Knowing the market potential to be enormous, with a number of large corporations in town, she decided she could make a profit on her own. She opened her agency, Dimension Talent, in her apartment with an investment of $500, and six years later found herself a success. Besides managing a model agency (including actors to do commercials), she organized a photography studio and handled national rock tours and trade fairs. In 1976 she sold her business to enter marketing and production, and founded the U. S. Communications Corporation, which has projects ranging from dinner theaters and radio spots to Swing-into-Spring golf balls. She and her partner now have their eyes on a Los Angeles office and production for network television. Joan Solomon strongly urges women to use their intuition in launching ventures of their own.

Problem Solver

BEVERLY HARPER, who founded the Philadelphia consulting firm Portfolio Associates, Inc. in 1969, started out with a post office box and an answering service, making all appointments outside the office because that office was her apartment. She emphasized excellent graphics in making her sales pitch, and by 1977 had 5 full-time employees and nearly 15 consultants, and was doing a gross business in six figures, with state and federal agencies and top corporations. Formerly a federal Manpower administrator, she is especially proud of the material Portfolio published for the Pennsylvania Committee for the International Women's Year, and of the five-state Black Film Festival she initiated and coordinates each year. Portfolio has also conducted attitudinal surveys and studied the mobile home industry and minority businesses. Beverly Harper also is a National Academy of Science task force head and a member of the National Advisory Committee to the Secretary of Transportation.

Business Consultant

MARGARET T. SHAFFER, president and chief executive officer of Paradigm Corporation, a consulting firm in Potomac, Maryland, received her bachelor's degree at the Eastman School of Music (Rochester, New York), and a master's in experimental psychology from Southern Illinois University (1964). After six years as a consultant in other firms, she started her own business at home in 1970 with an old portable typewriter, instant-print letterhead and cards, and a desk "made from an old door." One of the few women in her field at that time, she was strongly motivated by a need to support her family (she has two children), and she built her business rapidly, contracting with other professionals for assistance as her work increased. Margaret Shaffer has investigated non-traditional jobs for women (once spending several hours in a telephone company "cherry picker"), tested reactions to airport noise in major cities, evaluated sales training at Xerox, analyzed community attitudes toward crime-reduction programs; lists as clients such firms as Westinghouse, American Telephone & Telegraph, the American Bankers Association, the National Association of Women Business Owners, and Amtrak; and lectures at Small Business Administration seminars on how to start a business.

At-Home Magazine Publisher

Feeling isolated when she moved to Golden, Colorado, in 1970, and turned down by a local news editor because she had a four-month-old baby, PATRICIA (PATSI) BALE-COX decided to use her college magazine experience in starting a women's magazine at home. A local woman publisher helped her find advertising and the result was the bimonthly *Colorado Woman Digest* (circ. 10,000). Concerned that the Women's Movement, which she believes helps all women, has been portrayed as highly divisive, Ms. Bale-Cox features articles useful to women of all shades of feminism—facts on money management, suggestions about life problems, explanations of different views on the Equal Rights Amendment.

Los Angeles Home Bakeries

NADINE KORMAN of Los Angeles left her job in 1972 when her literary agent-boss told her her salary was frozen "forever," and went into business selling "mousse pies" made in her apartment. She sold the pies door-to-door until the health department received an anonymous letter and closed her down. In 1973 she moved to a new location where she employs 24 people producing 1,000 or more mousse, cheese, and pecan pies every week. The mousses, all 14 flavors, come in crusts of crushed chocolate wafer crumbs and butter, and the egg whites and whipped cream are folded in by hand. Customers include restaurants, Jack Lemmon, Sidney Poitier, and others.

Another Los Angeles home bakery thriving on today's demand for homemade food is Delights by Denis which HELEN BERCOVITZ and her son Denis operate. Ms. Bercovitz explains that Denis, who is spastic and deaf, learned professional baking knowing he could work for a city bakery that hired the deaf, but before he finished training it closed. The Bercovitzes set to work in their kitchen (always in fear of the health department), with Denis selling door-to-door for four years until they could open their own place in 1973. They began with some 45-cent days, now gross $1,500 to $3,000 daily. Helen Bercovitz makes sweets; Denis makes nine different quiches (the main-stay at $2 to $9.25), apple strudel, cheese cake, Coca-Cola cakes and (at Christmas) bourbon cakes. But "sugar is lousy for you," the Bercovitzes say. Desserts are "on the way out." They plan a restaurant with carry-out service one of these days.

Affirmative Action Director

Philosophy major SARAH W. RISHER worked as a reporter, in an employment agency, on Capitol Hill, and as leader of a recreation unit in South Korea until 1973, when she began working for a communications training firm and decided to start her own business. Today she directs Resources for Women, a consulting firm which plans and manages affirmative action programs. Working from an office in her home, she has completed contracts for clients including the telephone company, Federally Employed Women (FEW), the National League of Cities, the Center for Human Services, and Wilson College. She has also designed racial awareness sessions for children in Montgomery County schools. Ms. Risher, a divorcée with two children, is a member of the Department of Agriculture graduate school faculty and of the American Society for Training and Development.

Nursing Home Head Won 1977 Small Business Award

MARY BELLE CLEAMONS GRAHAM, who worked as a maid 25 years ago, today owns a corporation running three nursing homes in Taylorsville, North Carolina, and was named her state's Small Business Person of the Year for 1977. Ms. Graham resigned as housekeeping supervisor of the Alexander County Hospital in 1961 in order to care for her mother at home. With three daughters to support, she took in five more senior citizens and after two years borrowed money to build a home next door for five more. Ms. Graham, who had gone through fifth grade, returned to school in her 50s to improve her basic skills, pass her driver's license exam, and learn to do forms and keep books; in her 60s she went to night school to become a nurse's aide. In 1969 she borrowed $10,000 to buy 19.5 acres of farmland, and friends helped her borrow $150,000 more to build Belle's View Rest Home. Completed in 1974, it houses 34 residents, all indigents referred by county social service departments. "Mamma never dreamed she'd get to shake hands with the President," daughter SARAH ABBOTT, corporation secretary, said when her mother learned she would receive awards from Governor Jim Hunt and President Jimmy Carter dining at the White House with other Small Business Administration (SBA) winners. Sarah Abbott and two other daughters, MARY LOU WELLMAN, supervisor, and CATHERINE CONNOR, head cook, operate Belle's View with their mother and share ownership of the corporation's stock.

4

Women in Science and Technology

By Barbara Tufty
(contributing editor-writer)

Until a few years ago, many qualified women in science and technology had low profiles. They were not very well known, were allowed less access to research facilities than their male counterparts, had fewer job opportunities, carried heavier teaching and work loads, were paid less, published less, and received fewer awards and recognition. Said to have less incentive than males, they were faulted for not finishing their science degrees or, if equipped with doctorates, for not aggressively seeking out responsible employment or for abandoning their careers in favor of marriage and motherhood.

Some women students found their college years bitter and filled with antagonistic encounters. For others, these years proved rich and fulfilling. BETSY ANCKER-JOHNSON, associate director for physical research at the Argonne National Laboratory, and former Assistant Secretary of Science and Technology in the U. S. Department of Commerce, recalls her undergraduate days at Wellesley College as "idyllic." But, she continues, in a paper she prepared for the panel on "Women in Physics" at the 1971 meeting of the American Physical Society, "as a result, I was totally unprepared psychologically for what followed. During my first year of graduate school (at Tübingen University in Germany) what seemed to me like an infinite number of professors, teaching assistants, and colleagues, none of whom were women, told me that women can't think analytically and I must, therefore, be husband-hunting. . . . The resultant discouragement was as great or greater than any I've known since, hence the solid determination with which I emerged with my Ph.D. to go on in research. It needed to be solid because . . . a woman in physics must be at least twice as determined as a man with the same competence in order to achieve as much as he does."

For many women scientists and engineers, finding employment is traumatic, and the first job or jobs, once found, may seem to be leading nowhere. A man's career development "is often handed to him," the U. S. General Services Administration's top woman project engineer, EILEEN DUIGNAN-WOODS, contends: "He gets the right assignments and works on the right projects. In my first jobs in private industry, I was given routine calculations, design details—the 'garbage' jobs. I wasn't allowed to go out in the field, which is an essential part of being an engineer in building and construction" (*Science Digest*, December 1975).

More problems, particularly the sudden breaks and extended gaps that often adversely affect a woman scientist's or engineer's career, may come with marriage—the famous example of the Curies notwithstanding. According to research studies by Dr. MARGARET ROSSITER, professor of science history at the University of California at Berkeley, such "inevitable" things as a woman's shifting of location to follow her husband, being unable to find a job in the new setting or finding herself a victim of nepotism, which forbids members of the same family working at the same establishment, may lead a woman either to turn her scientific career into a hobby or to contribute her skills to support and enhance his career. In her research, Dr. Rossiter found that marriage to a fellow scientist had significant positive effects on the *husband's* career; as assistant to her husband, a wife educated in science provided invaluable support in the way of keeping notes, contributing significant ideas, and following through behind the scenes while her husband gave the lectures, attended noteworthy meetings, published papers, and received honors.

Childbearing can bring additional trials. For three months before her first child's birth, Dr. Ancker-Johnson was not allowed to enter the lab building to hear a talk or to get a book from her office without special permission from the lab director. "In order for a man to understand something of how I felt," she said, "he would have to have an advanced case of leprosy." Conditions were

somewhat more relaxed for the next child. Says Dr. Ancker-Johnson, "My second baby was born while I was employed in a research lab of an industry that possessed reasonably enlightened management. My paycheck stopped eight weeks before delivery (a company rule) and resumed six weeks after (a state law). However, no one cared that I went right on working. I must say I thought it a bit perverse, though, when the wife of one of my assistants had a baby a few weeks later and he was given a week's leave *with pay*." (Dr. Ancker-Johnson now has four children.)

In science and technology, as in other areas, the question of zeal or enthusiasm for work—some call it competition, or vigor, or aggressiveness—is a tough one. Dr. Ancker-Johnson has words on this subject also: "I do research and management for fun, but nevertheless, I compete vigorously. And here again a woman is in trouble. She's damned if she does and damned if she doesn't. If she does not compete, it proves women can't do physics; if she does compete, she isn't feminine, and hence, presumably, is some sort of freak."

Statistics show that times are changing, that women worldwide have more opportunities to earn advanced degrees and find careers as scientists or engineers. One interesting recent survey describes certain patterns or sets of circumstances that contribute toward a woman's finding her place under science's sun: More women succeed if they can avoid the imposition of stereotyped sex roles when they are children and get support rather than ridicule or scolding from their parents, teachers, and peers; women have a better chance for a satisfying science if they attend a small college and if they get personal encouragement from women professors or inspiring 'role models'; if they remain single, are divorced, or are married to an enlightened husband who takes his wife's career as seriously as his own—and helps with the housekeeping.

Most important, for women as for

men, the survey showed (it didn't really need to), is the unpredictable presence of good luck—of being at the right place at the right time with the right chance to prove oneself. The pages that follow describe some of the records set and achievements made by a wide range of scientists and engineers who have been lucky enough to have the right chance and women enough to seize it. They are the true inheritors of such pioneers as MARIA MITCHELL, first director of the Vassar College Observatory and discoverer on October 1, 1847, of a comet named for her.

"I was born of only ordinary capacity but of extraordinary persistency," Miss Mitchell, a Quaker, said of herself. One of Vassar's greatest teachers, she inspired many young women to continue work in astronomy. Her students included ELLEN SWALLOW (see the chapter "Women in the Home and Community," p. 103) and 25 other women noted in Who's Who in America. Born on Nantucket, where "people quite generally are in the habit of observing the heavens," she was a librarian there for 20 years, and spent many evenings in the observatory her father erected on top of the Pacific Bank building. Later, at Vassar,

she pioneered in daily photography of sunspots and faculae, of solar eclipses, and of changes on the surfaces of planets. Miss Mitchell, who died in 1889, founded the Association for the Advancement of Women, was the first woman elected to the American Physical Society, and the first woman member of the American Academy of Arts and Sciences of Boston.

BARBARA TUFTY, *who doubled as writer and consulting editor for this chapter, has been writing and editing science stories for much of her life. A botany graduate from Duke University in 1945, she has written hundreds of articles for newspapers and magazines in the United States and abroad. When not free-lancing, she has worked on the staff of Science Service, the National Academy of Sciences, and now is with the National Science Foundation. She has written several young-adult books about natural disasters and biological cells, and was the first woman to be awarded honorary life membership in the Bombay Natural History Society of India. Married to an engineering editor and publisher, she is the mother of three grown children.*

SCIENTISTS

bel Prize—awarded to the
outstanding achievers in
erse as science, peace, and lit-
as been conferred on women
six times since its inception in
190..

The first woman ever to be awarded this prize was France's internationally renowned Madame MARIE CURIE, who in 1903, with her husband Pierre Curie and colleague Henri Becquerel, received the Nobel Prize for Physics for the discovery of "radioactivity," a term she coined. In 1911, receiving the second prize ever awarded to a woman and becoming the first person ever to receive two Nobel awards, Madame Curie alone was awarded the Nobel Prize for Chemistry for the isolation of pure radium.

IRÈNE JOLIOT-CURIE, a physicist and assistant to her famous mother, whose work she carried on, and in turn working with her husband Frédéric, discovered a technique for making certain elements artificially radioactive. This was an important step toward releasing the energy of the atom. For this discovery, she and her husband were awarded the Nobel Prize for Chemistry in 1935.

In 1947 American biochemist GERTY T. CORI (see the chapter "Women in Medicine and Health Care," p. 219) and her husband, Carl, received the Nobel Prize for Physiology and Medicine, for their research into carbohydrate metabolism, a method by which the body uses its fuel supply of starches and sugars, and the relation of this mechanism to certain hormone secretions.

It was not until 1963 that another woman was awarded the Nobel Prize. German MARIA GOEPPERT MAYER, a doctor of theoretical physics who spent the whole of World War II in America working on isotope separation for the atomic bomb project, received the Nobel Prize for Physics jointly with J. Hans Jensen and Eugene Wigner for their work on the unusual stability of various nuclear structures. Previously, in 1955, she and Jensen had written *Elementary Theory of Nuclear Shell Structure*, which provided the basis for much research and scientific discovery that was to follow.

In 1964 chemist DOROTHY HODGKIN of Great Britain was awarded the Nobel Prize for Chemistry for determining the structure of biochemical compounds essential in combating pernicious anemia.

And in 1977 ROSALYN S. YALOW (see "Women in Medicine and Health Care," p. 222), distinguished medical researcher and professor, shared the Nobel Prize for Medicine and Physiology with Roger Guillemin of the Salk Institute and Andrew Schally of the New Orleans Veterans Administration for her discovery of the radioimmunoassay.

U. S. Women Elected to the National Academy of Sciences

1925	Florence Rena Sabin (d. 1953) Anatomist	1958	Chien-Shiung Wu Physicist
1931	Margaret Floy Washburn (d. 1939) Psychologist	1961	Libbie Henrietta Hyman (d. 1969) Zoologist
1944	Barbara McClintock Botanist	1967	Berta Vogel Scharrer Anatomist
1948	Gerty T. Cori (d. 1957) Pathologist, Biochemist	1968	Rita Levi-Montalcini Neurobiologist
1956	Maria Goeppert Mayer (d. 1972) Physicist	1970	Ruth Patrick Biologist, Ecologist
1957	Katherine Esau Plant Morphologist	1970	Rebecca Craighill Lancefield Bacteriologist

1971	Mildred Cohn Chemist	1975	Frederica Annis de Laguna Anthropologist
1971	Eleanor Jack Gibson Psychologist	1975	Dorothea Jameson Psychologist
1972	Gertrude Scharff Goldhaber Physicist	1975	Margaret Mead Cultural Anthropologist
1972	Elizabeth Shull Russell Geneticist	1975	Rosalyn S. Yalow Medical Physicist
1973	Beatrice Mintz Medical Geneticist	1976	Charlotte Friend Oncologist
1973	Helen M. Ranney Hemoglobin Biologist	1976	Julia Robinson Mathematician
1973	Helen Brooke Taussig Pediatric Cardiologist	1977	Elizabeth Florence Colson Anthropologist
1974	Estella Bergere Leopold Research Botanist	1977	Elizabeth Fondal Neufeld Biochemist
1974	Sarah Ratner Biochemist	1977	Ruth Sager Geneticist
1975	Gertrude Mary Cox Statistician	1977	Evelyn Maisel Witkin Geneticist

ANTHROPOLOGY/ARCHAEOLOGY

Anthropology's Poet-Pathfinder

A pathfinder in uniting the science of anthropology with sociology, psychology, and philosophy, RUTH BENEDICT (1887–1948) was the originator of the controversial concept of "patterns of culture"—an idea that in determining cultural aspects, human beings throughout the world should be viewed as psychiatric and psychological groups rather than as individuals. In her undergraduate days at Vassar, she became deeply impressed with the writings of Walter Pater and his notion that each individual should burn with a "hard gem-like flame" and tend it at the expense of everything else. She was first known as a poet, publishing in *Poetry, The Nation,* and other magazines, but anthropology became her burning flame. After receiving her Ph.D. from Columbia in 1923, she directed her energies to studies of primitive religion, mythology, and folklore. Her fieldwork took her among Pueblo Indians, the Apache, and the Blackfoot tribes. She was a dynamic

inspiration to her students—MARGARET MEAD among them—who traveled along her path, but farther, to New Guinea, Samoa, Fiji, Africa, and South America. Dr. Benedict's 1934 book *Patterns of Culture* stirred controversy. *The Chrysanthemum and the Sword: Patterns of Japanese Culture,* which she published in 1946, two years before her death, caused the Office of Naval Research to give a grant to Columbia for research in contemporary cultures presided over by Dr. Benedict—the most ambitious program of anthropological research the United States had yet seen.

Best-Selling Anthropologist

MARGARET MEAD, teacher and anthropologist, has helped shatter one cultural myth after another. One of the first to do fieldwork in the Pacific Southwest and bring back eyewitness accounts of primitive peoples, Dr. Mead won her first great acclaim with the publication in 1928 of *Coming of Age in Samoa,* a scholarly, unbiased, and sympathetic account of the Samoan people, which made her—at 27—a best-selling author. Following that, she worked with various tribes in New Guinea and (with her third husband) published a photographic study of the people of Bali. As curator emeritus of ethnology at the American Museum of Natural History she has been most concerned with the problems of world hunger and of youth. Her deep involvement with the restless young people of the 1960s resulted in *Culture and Commitment,* published in 1970 and republished in 1978. Only a year younger than the century, she appears to be as vigorous as ever, and goes everywhere, supporting herself with a tall serviceable, wooden staff. When she appeared on stage at a well-attended meeting, one young anthropologist was heard to call her "the mother of us all." It has also been said that communication between Planet Earth and extraterrestrial beings will happen only if a "Margaret Mead of the universe" comes striding through the stars to search out earthlings—just as the young scholar walked through the jungles of Samoa, New Guinea, and other South Pacific islands to discover the ways of human beings little known or understood by the "civilized" world.

First Woman Member of the U. S. National Science Board

From 1950, the year the U. S. Government's National Science Foundation (NSF) was established, until 1957, SOPHIE D. ABERLE served as the first woman member of the National Science Board, which is the NSF's policy-making body. Dr. Aberle received her Ph.D. in anthropology from Stanford in 1927 and her medical doctorate from Yale in 1930. She became well known for her research with the Pueblo Indians, and from 1935–44 was the general superintendent of the United Pueblo Indian Agency, Department of the Interior. She then worked with the division of medical sciences of the National Research Council until 1949. Since that time she has been active on the staff of many organizations and has written books and many professional articles. Dr. Aberle is now research director at the University of New Mexico.

First Woman to Hold Harvard's Norton Fellowship for Archaeology

Archaeologist HETTY GOLDMAN, named professor emeritus at the School of Historical Studies of the Institute for Advanced Study in Princeton, in 1948 was one of the pioneering women excavators in Greece and the Near East, and the first woman to hold Harvard's Norton Fellowship. In 1966 she was awarded the Archaeological Institute of America's gold medal for distinguished archaeological achievement. After earning her master's degree and Ph.D. from Radcliffe, she was at the American School of Classical Studies at Athens, Greece, where she began her excavations with two sites in Boeotia. She then crossed the Aegean Sea to Colophon and to Tarsus. Dr. Goldman has also taught at Hunter College and at the Johns Hopkins University. President MARGARET THOMPSON called Dr. Goldman "a pioneer in many fields and many lands—the first to appreciate the ties between Greece and the Orient and to explore them with unbiased scholarly curiosity."

First to Find the Olduvai Ancient Skull

Although Louis B. Leakey took full credit and won world fame for discovery of what was the oldest manlike creature, the "missing link" in man's evolution from the apes, it was his wife, MARY LEAKEY, who actually bent down and saw the two bulges of brown fossilized molar teeth protruding from a skull buried in the ground of Olduvai Gorge, Tanzania, in July 1959. The discovery created a sensation, for until then, man as we know him today was believed to have evolved in Asia only a few hundred thousand years ago. This skull, at first thought to be 600,000 years old, later proved to be some 1.75 million years old, and from a branch, not the main line, of man's evolution.

Unlike her dynamic husband, who had been searching East Africa for 35 years for clues to the "oldest human," and talking a great deal about it, Dr. Mary Leakey is quiet. In the past, content to work long hours sifting earth for fossils beside her husband and to let him enjoy the fame and honors heaped upon him, after his death in 1972 she stayed on at Olduvai and has herself become a leading authority on prehistoric technology. She has found and identified a remarkable variety of tools that help to show human biological and cultural development. At the Louis Leakey Memorial Institute for African Prehistory, research efforts into man's origin, behavior, and survival are carried on by scientists of several nationalities, including American Richard Leakey, one of the three sons of Louis and Mary.

Excavator of Sites on Cyprus

EDITH PORADA, born in Vienna, holder of the Arthur Lehman chair of art history and archaeology at Columbia University, enjoys a high international reputation for her studies of the ancient civilizations of the Near East. Her major contributions have been in discoveries of cylinder seals and analyses of the significance they held in religious and social life. Her diggings on Cyprus also have unearthed evidences of close commercial ties between Cyprus and the Greek islands during the Late Bronze Age, about 1500 B.C. Dr. Porada received her Ph.D. from the University of

Vienna in 1935 and became a U.S. citizen in 1945. Author of many monographs, as well as articles and reviews in professional journals, she taught at Queens College and was visiting assistant professor at Barnard College before becoming a member of the Columbia faculty in 1958.

First Woman to Investigate the Olmec Culture

As a member of the Smithsonian Institution-National Geographic Society archaeological expeditions, MARION STIRLING and her husband, Matthew, from 1939 through 1946 undertook the first scientific investigation of the Olmec culture in Mexico. This culture is now generally recognized as the earliest civilization in the New World, dating from about 1500 B.C. to the last century before Christ. The Stirlings discovered many valuable artifacts, including eight stone heads 5 to 10 feet high, elaborately carved huge stone altars, a stone sarcophagus, a serpentine mosaic mask five and a half feet square, and many pieces of jade—the most precious substance in pre-Columbian Mexico. They also discovered a monument recording the date of November 4, 31 B.C.—at the time of discovery, the earliest known bar-and-dot inscription in the Mayan style. The Stirlings, looking for contacts between Mesoamerica and South America, also undertook archaeological expeditions in Panama, Ecuador, and Costa Rica. In 1975 Ms. Stirling received the gold medal of the Society of Woman Geographers for outstanding geographic achievement.

Six "Firsts" in Anthropology

FREDERICA DE LAGUNA holds many "firsts." As field director of the University Museum in Philadelphia, she was one of the first fellows of the Arctic Institute of North America, and led the first anthropological and archaeological survey in Cook Inlet and Prince William Sound. From her observations and research in this Alaskan area came the first chronology of the Pacific Eskimo cultures— from about the second millennium B.C. to the present. It was she who first found and copied the Eskimo rock paintings in that area. In 1975 Dr. de Laguna and Margaret Mead were the first women anthropologists chosen to become members of the National Academy of Sciences. After receiving her Ph.D. in anthropology from Columbia University, Dr. de Laguna participated in the first scientific survey of ancient sites in Danish West Greenland. Her major work, however, has been in Alaska; in 1949 she started her famous expeditions in areas never before surveyed. The result of her work was a pioneering and comprehensive three-volume opus called *Under Mount Saint Elias, The History and Culture of the Yakutat Tlingit.* Dr. de Laguna has held many fellowships and won many awards from institutions such as Bryn Mawr, Columbia University, Rockefeller, Viking Fund, the American Association for the Advancement of Science, the American Anthropological Association, and the Rochester Museum of Arts and Sciences; and has been a research associate of the University of Pennsylvania Museum and the Museum of Northern Arizona.

Observer of Social Change in Africa and the American Northwest

For many years anthropologist ELIZABETH FLORENCE COLSON has paid particular attention to methods by which social order among groups of people is maintained in rapidly changing situations. Her studies show how environmental factors, particularly rainfall, affect social, political, and religious organizations and how the introduction of cash crops affects marriage and patterns of family life. For more than a quarter century, she has been observing the resettlement of thousands of Tonga tribes-

people displaced by the building of the Kariba Dam in Central Africa. She also has studied aspects of the Makah Indians of the U. S. Northwest, showing the effect these Indians have had upon white people—a different point of view from the conventional studies on the impact of whites upon Indians. After receiving her master's degree and Ph.D. from Radcliffe, Dr. Colson conducted research at Harvard, the Rhodes-Livingston Institute, and with the African Research Program of Boston University, and has taught at Goucher College, Brandeis University, and the University of California at Berkeley, written several books, and been a fellow for the Center for Advanced Study in the Behavioral Sciences at Stanford, the American Anthropological Association, the African Studies Association, the British Association of Social Anthropologists, and the Royal Anthropological Institute.

She Combined Anthropology with Medicine and Nutrition

With her master's degree and Ph.D. from the University of Michigan, NANCIE LOUDON GONZALEZ was visiting lecturer of anthropology at the University of California at Berkeley. She then taught for many summers at the University of San Carlos in Guatemala, where she made significant contributions to nutritional and medical anthropology. She later was researcher at the Institute of Nutrition of Central America and Panama and taught at the Boston University and the universities of New Mexico and Iowa. She is a fellow of the American Anthropology Association, president of the Society for Applied Anthropology, the author of several books, and was the first woman program director in social sciences at the National Science Foundation. In 1977 she became vice-chancellor of academic affairs at the University of Maryland—the first woman to hold the post.

World Authority on Chimpanzees

One of the most extensive studies attempted on the behavior of chimpanzees in their natural habitat, and on the possible relation of their behavior to that of human beings, made English ethologist JANE GOODALL famous. Ms. Goodall, who was born in 1934 and grew up in a traditional atmosphere of high school secretarial courses and a job, was always fascinated by the world of animals. Invited by a friend to Kenya, she met the famed anthropologist Louis Leakey and was the first of several women researchers inspired and encouraged by him to work on innovative studies of primates. (Later, SHIRLEY STURM took up studies of baboons; DIANE FOSSEY studied gorillas; and BIRUTE GALDIKAS-BRINDA-MOUR studied orangutans.) As assistant secretary at the Museum of Natural History in Kenya, Jane Goodall spent fourteen months by herself tracking down chimpanzees, living with them in their natural surroundings on the shores of Lake Tanganyika, and eventually having them overcome their shyness and accept her presence. Her studies were the first to show that chimpanzees are intelligent social animals able to communicate with one another through gestures, sounds, facial expressions; indulge in many kinds of play; and modify and use objects as tools. (They also are non-strict vegetarians.) Later admitted to Cambridge University, where she earned her doctorate in ethology, the study of primate behavior, she has since returned to continue her work at Gombe Stream Research Center in Tanzania.

First American Indian Ph.D. in Folklore

A member of the Cherokee tribe of Oklahoma, RAYNA DIANE GREEN was the first American Indian to get a Ph.D. in the field of folklore and American studies, from Indiana University. As director of the project on Native Americans in Science at the American Association for the Advancement of Science, she has been involved developing programs and projects for American Indians in science, social science, health, natural resources, and engineering. Her major areas of interest include the folklore of native Americans, women, blacks, and people of the South, Southwest, and New England. She has been book review editor of the *Journal of American Folklore,* and general editor of a five-volume collection of obscene folklore, published by the University of Illinois Press. Dr. Green has taught at Yale, George Washington University, the universities of Maryland, Massachusetts, and Arkansas, and at the Federal City College of Washington.

ASTRONOMY

First Woman Elected an Officer of the American Astronomical Society

As a young girl ANNIE JUMP CANNON used candlelight to record observations of the stars in her family's makeshift observatory in their Dover, Delaware, attic. She also was intrigued by the rainbow spectra of light cast by the prisms from candelabra. Later, as a student at Wellesley, her interest in astronomy was nurtured and strengthened by the dynamic Dr. SARAH F. WHITING, professor of physics and astronomy, who set up the first science laboratory in the United States for women, at Harvard. After special studies at Radcliffe, Dr. Cannon worked at the Harvard College Observatory, studying the characteristics of the light of a star photographed through a prism. Her real achievement, however, was as a "census taker" of the sky. She classified about 400,000 stellar bodies according to their temperature—from the hottest to the coolest. A determined young woman, she was the first female to receive an honorary doctor of astronomy degree from the University of Groningen in the Netherlands. She also received an honorary doctorate of science from Oxford, was named an honorary member of the Royal Astronomical Society, and was the first woman elected an officer of the American Astronomical Society. By 1938 she was one of the first women to hold a titled corporation appointment at Harvard, as the William Cranch Bont astronomer. Dr. Cannon died in 1941.

Bright Years for Women Astronomers

ANNIE JUMP CANNON was one of several women who reached high levels of achievement under the liberal encouragement of Edward C. Pickering, director of the Harvard Observatory for more than 40 years. The significant research of women astronomers blossomed as a result of Pickering's open-minded fairness to them: He treated them as equals; he guided and encouraged their work, and helped promote them. Many women became well known during this period in the last quarter of the 19th century and the beginning of the 20th. A few were outstanding:

WILLIAMINA PATON FLEMING (1857–1911) became a permanent member of the Harvard Observatory staff in 1881 and then one of the best-known women astronomers in the world. She became curator of astronomical photographs—the first such corporation appointment of a woman at Harvard—and in 1906 the Royal Astronomical Society elected her an honorary member. Wellesley made her an honorary fellow in astronomy, and she received the gold medal of the Astronomical Society of Mexico.

ANTONIA MAURY (1866–1952), termed the "most original as well as the most elusive" of the Harvard Observatory group, aided Pickering in confirming his discovery that the star zeta, sixth brightest star in the constellation Ursa Major, was a double star—the first such sighted. She then detected a second double star, β Aurigae, that same year.

HENRIETTA LEAVITT (1868–1921) made significant discoveries particularly on the photographic brightness of circumpolar stars and also helped others toward important discoveries. She discovered and classified hundreds of variable stars, most in the Large Magellanic Cloud. In studying 25 stars in the Small Magellanic Cloud, she made the important discovery of the relation between a star's magnitude and its period of luminosity. Known as the "period-luminosity law" (the brighter the star, the longer the period of light), this was the basis on which astronomer Harlow Shapley made the first sound estimates of the scale of the universe.

MARGARET HARWOOD, born in 1885, was the first to receive the Astronomical Fellowship Award of the Nantucket Maria Mitchell Association; and also was the only woman to hold a position as director of an independent observatory—the Maria Mitchell Observatory at Nantucket.

First Woman Permitted to Observe the Universe at Palomar

Palomar Observatory perches high on a lonely peak in California. The observatory room is cold, solitary, with dimmed lights, and the observer sits on a five-to-six-story-high solitary mechanical chair that, like other parts of the Observatory, can be synchronized to the movements of the heavens as the earth turns beneath the observer. There in that chair in 1965, for the first time officially, sat a woman

—VERA C. RUBIN. Now a staff member of the Department of Terrestrial Magnetism of the Carnegie Institution of Washington, Dr. Rubin has long been interested in the structure and dynamics of the earth's galaxy, and of galaxies beyond. The author of some 60 research papers, for the past several years she has been making an intensive study of the Andromeda galaxy. Dr. Rubin has also been a lecturer in numerous universities and observatories in the United States, Canada, Mexico, Chile, and Europe; associate editor of the *Astronomical Journal;* and member of several astronomy committees of the National Academy of Sciences, the American Astronomical Society, and Harvard.

Astronomer Daughter of Astronomers and Working Partner of Astronomer Husband

The daughter of two astronomers and wife of another, MARJORIE MEINEL has herself been an active astronomer for many years. Her mother was the first woman awarded a Ph.D. from the University of Chicago, in 1917. Her father held prestigious positions at Mount Wilson and Palomar Observatory for 40 years. Her husband became director of Kitt Peak Observatory and later director of the Optical Sciences Center of the University of Arizona. As helpmeet to her husband, Dr. Meinel collaborated with him in his work and together they became a research associate at the University of Rochester when he was teaching there. They co-authored a number of papers and spent some time in India establishing an observatory. Dr. Meinel, who has raised seven children, has few regrets and many positive memories. "I always looked up to the stars," she writes.

First Woman to Chair Astronomy Department at Harvard

Born in England at the turn of the century, CECILIA HELENA PAYNE-GAPOSCHKIN, one of the leading contemporary astronomers of the world, received her A.B. at Cambridge, England, and that same year joined the Harvard College Observatory. In 1925 she earned her Ph.D. in astronomy at Radcliffe and started the many studies that have made her famous: discovering the exploded nova of Hercules and taking photographs of the fragments; devising new techniques for determining stellar magnitudes from photographic plates; and working in particular on variable stars, stellar atmospheres, spectroscopy, and the structure of galaxies. In 1938 she became the Phillips astronomer at Harvard Observatory. In 1956 she became professor of astronomy—one of the first few women professors at Harvard at that time—and was appointed the first chairwoman of the astronomy department. In 1965 she was appointed astronomer at the Smithsonian Astrophysical Observatory, where she continues her research. The most distinguished honor of the American Astronomical Society, the Russell Lectureship, was presented to her in 1977. Throughout her busy life, she has maintained that a woman needs a balanced life of career and homemaking. "I say that a career and homemaking and motherhood may be thoroughly compatible through the exercise of common sense and making of intelligent adjustments."

Observer of Fifty Years of Solar Flares

For the past fifty years, HELEN DODSON PRINCE has closely observed solar activity, particularly the outbreak of solar flares, and studied the effects of such activity on the interplanetary medium and the earth's magnetic field. With her M.S. and Ph.D. in astronomy from the University of Michigan, and an honorary Sc.D. from Goucher College, Dr. Prince has served on the faculties of Wellesley College, Goucher, and the University of Michigan, where she is now professor emeritus of astronomy. She has spent three summers at the astrophysical branch of the Paris Observatory and held research posts at MIT's Radiation Laboratory and the McMath-Hulbert Observatory.

Chief of NASA's In-Flight Space Program

As chief of the In-Flight Sciences Manned Space Program of the National Aeronautics and Space Administration (NASA), JOCELYN R. GILL has been instrumental in devising and executing scientific experiments that have contributed greatly to the success of U.S. space probes—from the first unmanned launches through the Apollo moon flights. After receiving her master's degree in astronomy and astrophysics from the University of Chicago and her Ph.D. from Yale in 1959, Dr. Gill taught at Mount Holyoke College, Smith College, the University of California at Berkeley, and Arizona State College. She also has been a staff member of the radiation laboratory at the Massachusetts Institute of Technology. She joined NASA in 1961. For her outer-space work she has received the Woman's Federal Award and the Achievement Award of Wellesley College. Dr. Gill is a member of the American Astronomical Society, the Nantucket Maria Mitchell Association, the Washington Philosophical Society, and the American Association of the Variable Star Observers.

Prizewinning Sighter of Returning Comets

Professor of astronomy and researcher at the Lunar and Planetary Laboratory of the University of Arizona, ELIZA-BETH ROEMER was the first to receive the Apthorp Gould Prize from the National Academy of Sciences. The award for her "contributions to cometary astronomy, particularly for her consistent success in first sighting comets as they return toward the sun" recognized her years of studying asteroids and periodic comets. In 1965 a minor planet was named Roemera after her by its discoverer, P. Wild, in appreciation of her "untiring and successful efforts to advance the knowledge of the motions and physical properties of comets and minor planets." After receiving her Ph.D. jointly from the University of California at Berkeley and the Lick Observatory in 1955, Dr. Roemer taught astronomy in the Oakland public schools and at Berkeley. She also has worked as an astronomer for the Lick Observatory and the Yerkes Observatory of the University of Chicago. She has been responsible, all together, for sighting 79 comet reentries during the years 1953–76.

Kitt Peak Assistant Director

By the time she attended a high school for girls in New Orleans, astronomer BEVERLY TURNER LYNDS knew that her interests were science. She went on to receive her B.S. degree magna cum laude from Centenary College, a small Methodist liberal arts college, where she received "the invaluable benefit of personal friendship and inspiration of several competent and dedicated scholars." Turned down for a graduate fellowship by Cal Tech because she was the "wrong sex," she received offers from the University of Chicago and from the Lick Observatory of the University of California at Santa Cruz, where she worked as assistant and received her Ph.D. Dr. Lynds set her priorities early in her marriage to a fellow astronomer: Homemaking came first, science second. But she did not give up her own astronomy. Moving where her husband moved, she found part-time work for herself—in

Canada, at Green Bank in West Virginia, and at the Astronomy Department of the University of Arizona. ("As most academic part-time persons know," she writes, "a part-time job is part-time in salary only.") She took her first full-time professional position at Kitt Peak in Arizona in 1971. As assistant director, she spends about 30 per cent of her work time on research and about 70 per cent on administrative duties.

Satellite Programs Initiator

Studying the Milky Way and other galaxies by using satellites and other space-age equipment is the special concern of NANCY G. ROMAN, chief of the astronomy and astrophysics satellite and sounding rocket program of the National Aeronautics and Space Administration since 1960. She is responsible for the initiation of the successful series of Orbiting Solar Observatories, as well as the development of the Geodetic Satellite Program, and the first gamma ray satellite. Her satellite programs of the early 1960s provided scientists with the base of knowledge about planet surfaces that brought about the successful Viking landings of the 1970s. Dr. Roman earned her Ph.D. in astronomy at the University of Chicago in 1949. Her long list of achievements includes being one of three Americans invited by the U.S.S.R. Academy of Sciences to attend the dedication of the Bjurakan Astrophysical Observatory. She also has been an invited visitor to major observatories in Chile and Canada and has received honorary doctor of science degrees from Russell Sage, Hood, and Bates colleges. In 1973 she was elected fellow of the American Astronautical Society.

Noted Solar Physicist

ELSKE V. P. SMITH, born in Monte Carlo, Monaco, obtained her Ph.D. in astronomy from Radcliffe College by doing research at Harvard's Boyden Station, in Bloemfontein, South Africa.

Deeply involved in observing the sun, particularly solar flares and the chromosphere, she spent seven years as a research fellow at the Sacramento Peak Observatory in New Mexico, with her husband and two sons. The family then moved to Boulder, Colorado, where she held one of the first visiting fellowships at the Joint Institute for Laboratory Astrophysics. When they moved to the Washington, D.C., area, she joined the faculty of the new astronomy program at the University of Maryland, where since 1973 she has been assistant provost of the Division of Mathematical and Physical Sciences and Engineering while still retaining her faculty position teaching astronomy. She continues her work in solar physics, occasionally traveling to the Kitt Peak National Observatory for special observations with the McMath solar tower. The author of several professional papers, Dr. Smith also has been a fellow at the Lowell Observatory at Flagstaff, Arizona.

First Woman Director of Royal Greenwich Observatory

British astronomer ELEANOR MARGARET BURBIDGE in 1972 was appointed England's first woman director of the Royal Greenwich Observatory. She stayed for one year and then returned to the University of California at San Diego, where she is currently on the faculty. She was recently elected president of the American Astronomical Society—the first woman. Awarded the Warner Prize for research in 1959 in the field of astrophysics, Dr. Burbidge with her husband Geoffrey and astronomers William Fowler and Fred Hoyle co-authored a research paper famous in the history of astrophysics. It presented a totally new explanation of how elements are formed in the fiery nuclear evolutions of the stars. Acting director of the University of London Observatory, a research fellow and later associate professor at Yerkes Observatory of the University of Chicago, she has also taught at the California Institute of Technology and the University of California at San Diego. She is also a member of the Royal Society of London.

Discovery of Pulsars: Her Story

In 1967 JOCELYN BELL BURNELL, a 24-year-old graduate student in radioastronomy at Cambridge, England, was monitoring a four-and-a-half-acre telescope at Jodrell Bank which she had helped to design and build. She was collecting material on radio galaxies for her thesis and noticed the appearance of an unknown signal from outer space—"a bit of scruff," she called it. Her report set in motion a search for the source that resulted in the discovery and classification of a novel class of stellar objects—pulsars, which send out pulses of radio waves. Controversy centered around the fact that Antony Hewish, Ms. Burnell's immediate supervisor, received the Nobel Prize for this discovery, but Ms. Burnell was not included. Without question, Hewish was instrumental in the ultimate identification of these signals, but scientists around the world have argued that the crucial step may have been Ms. Burnell's identification of the source of the signals.

Only Woman "Czar" of Apollo Telescope Mount Program

ADRIENNE F. TIMOTHY was born in England and obtained her Ph.D. from London's University College, where she worked for a time as research assistant at the Mullard Space Science Laboratory. She later crossed the Atlantic to join Harvard College Observatory as technical associate. She then became staff scientist with American Science and Engineering (AS&E) in Cambridge, Massachusetts, where she worked with the soft X-ray solar telescope on the Skylab Apollo Telescope Mount. Her duties included definition of the AS&E role in the Apollo Mount joint observing program, and the development of the data reduction and analysis system for photographic and digital data. During the Skylab Mission, Dr. Timothy was the only woman "czar" elected by the Apollo Mount researchers, and as such, had the authority to speak for numerous experimental teams in observational and operational matters. In 1974 she joined the National Aeronautics and Space Administration (NASA) as program scientist for the Apollo Telescope Mount Data Analysis and Solar Physics Spacelab Payloads in the Office of Space Science. A year later, she was appointed chief of solar physics. Dr. Timothy is particularly interested in the structure of the inner solar corona, coronal holes, and their relationship with the solar wind.

Rising Star in Stellar Spectroscopy

ANNE P. COWLEY, spectroscopist at the University of Michigan, graduated from Wellesley and the University of Michigan, where she and her husband both received their Ph.D.s in 1963. Dr. Cowley spent summers at the Harvard Observatory and did additional research at Yerkes Observatory before she returned to the University of Michigan, where she now studies stellar spectroscopy. She also visits Kitt Peak National Observatory for observation, and recently spent two years studying the spectra of X-ray sources and interacting binary stars at the Dominion Astrophysical Observatory in British Columbia. Dr. Cowley believes that women scientists "need to develop the self-confidence to say that we can do it and that we want to do it, and then we need to go ahead and do it."

Helping Discover Superclusters of Galaxies

CHRISTINE JONES-FORMAN was the only woman in a team of astronomers at the Harvard-Smithsonian Center for Astrophysics that in 1977 discovered what appear to be "superclusters" of galaxies bound together by a very hot and tenuous gas with a mass many times that of the galaxies themselves. The team suggests that the X-ray emission is most likely produced by a hot gas, primarily hydrogen and helium, existing in such quantities that it may represent the remains of the initial explosion that created the universe, and hence may be a possible source of the universe's "missing mass." The important feature of this gas is that the mass required to produce the X-ray emission is five to ten times greater than all the material seen at other wave lengths and is itself sufficient to gravitationally bind the clusters in the supercluster. With her M.A. and Ph.D. (1974) from Harvard, Dr. Jones-Forman is at present a Harvard junior fellow, primarily studying celestial objects in our galaxy that emit X rays. She has studied several binary (having two parts) X-ray sources including Cygnus X-1, which is believed to be a binary system in which a black hole orbits a normal star. She also optically identified the X-ray source of the celestial object named 341700-37, and discovered its binary nature.

BIOLOGY

Her Rare Flower Halted a $1.3 Billion Dam

The first rare and endangered plant (something like a snapdragon) to halt construction of a proposed $1.3 billion hydroelectric project was originally discovered and identified by KATE FURBISH, a botanist born in 1834, whose life was dedicated to collecting, classifying, and recording the flora of Maine.

Miss Furbish attended schools in Brunswick, Maine, and from there her enthusiasm for plants took her on foot, on hands and knees, on mail stages, rafts, logs, and in rowboats in and out of some of the most inaccessible streams, bogs, fields, and crags of Maine. An inexhaustible explorer, she recorded every type of plant she could find in accurate watercolors. She turned out to be one of those amateurs whose perfectionism helped to advance descriptive plant sciences in their early days. At her death in 1931 at age 98, she left 16 large folio volumes of watercolors and some 4,000 sheets of dried plants to various museums and research centers.

Two plants she discovered were named after her: *Pedicularis Furbishiae*, and *Aster cordifolius l.*, var. **Furbishiae**. The former, commonly known as the Furbish lousewort, made front-page news in 1976 when a botanist announced to the Army Corps of Engineers that the plant, thought to have been extinct for 30 years, had been rediscovered on a bank of the St. John River in northern Maine—an area where the Corps planned to build the Dickey-Lincoln pair of dams, which would inundate the plant's habitat. Because the plant was classified as endangered and hence due to receive federal protection, the plans were halted—amid furor raised by determined environmentalists and outraged engineers.

Outstanding Literary Ornithologist

As a young girl, FLORENCE A. BAILEY developed an intense interest in nature, particularly birds at her country home in New York state. In the early 1900s, she began publishing articles and then books on birds and bird lore, and soon came to be considered the most literary ornithologist of her time. Working with her husband, a field naturalist with the U. S. Biological Survey, she researched many varieties of birds throughout the South, the West, the Pacific Northwest, and the

Dakotas—and published the first thorough report on birds of the Southwest. She was the first woman to receive the Brewster Medal of the American Ornithologists' Union and the University of New Mexico awarded her an honorary LL.D. degree. She continued contributing sections on birds to some of her husband's books and to other publications until her death in 1948.

First Woman Ph.D. from Heidelberg and First in the American Physiological Society

With a degree in physiology from Cornell, IDA H. HYDE was invited to study zoology at the University of Strassburg, Germany. However, the strong prejudice against women prevented her from getting a Ph.D. there, so she obtained it from the University of Heidelberg—the first woman to do so. She worked in Naples, then in Switzerland, became the first woman to conduct research in the laboratories of Harvard Medical School, and went on to teach at the University of Kansas, at Woods Hole Oceanographic Institution, and at the University of Heidelberg. She persisted in following her main interests in different phases of physiology, including the circulation, respiration, and nervous system of animals. In 1902 she became the first woman to join the American Physiological Society. She died in 1945.

First Japanese Woman to Receive a Ph.D. in Science

A graduate of Tokyo Women's Higher Normal School, botanist KONO YASUI stayed on at her alma mater to teach. In 1911 she was the first Japanese woman to publish a treatise in the *Annals of Botany.* During the early World War I years she studied in the United States, then returned to the Tokyo Women's School, where she became a professor in 1919. In 1927 she was the first Japanese woman to receive the degree of doctor of science—for her research on the structure of Japanese coal.

World-Famous Authority on Invertebrate Organisms

LIBBIE H. HYMAN (1888–1969) conducted most of her life work at the American Museum of Natural History in New York City, where she was a researcher on animals without backbones, such as insects, mollusks, worms. She is world-famous for her monumental work called *The Invertebrates,* the most comprehensive work of its kind to appear in English. The series covers the entire field of invertebrate zoology, with special reference to anatomy, embryology, physiology, and ecology. After Dr. Hyman's death, the final volumes were completed by scientists at Oregon State University. Dr. Hyman earned her Ph.D. in 1915 from the University of Chicago and stayed on as research assistant in the zoology department there for 16 years before moving to the Museum. Her real love was for the little ones among the invertebrates—the one-celled protozoa, the sponges, coelenterates (jellyfishes), and turbellarians (flatworms). She published some 145 papers for professional journals, received three doctorates of science and one LL.D., and was the first woman to be awarded the Daniel Giraud Medal from the National Academy of Science for meritorious work in zoology and paleontology, the gold medal of the Linnean Society of London (highest honor of that famed society), and the gold medal of the American Museum of Natural History.

Crusading Scientist with a Lyric Pen

In 1962 marine biologist RACHEL CARSON, with her eloquent book *Silent Spring,* aroused the English-reading world to the destructive effects of man-made pesticides and started a controversy that is still hotly debated. Miss Carson, with 15 years as a scientist and writer with the U. S. Fish and Wildlife Service behind her, had already published *Under the Sea Wind* and *The Sea Around Us,* books that won her awards and an enthusiastic following. *Silent Spring* brought her more followers and also powerful enemies who tried to discredit her attack on chlorinated hydrocarbons and other highly toxic pesticides cycled into the environment and food chain. Eventually her writings resulted in curtailment of some pesticides including DDT and in stronger efforts to develop natural biological controls for insects harmful to man. Rachel Carson died in 1964.

Microbiologist and College President

A "geneticist with nest-building experience" is how microbiologist and educator MARY BUNTING, past president of Radcliffe (1960–72), describes herself. Distinguished as a scientist for her discoveries on the effects of radiation on bacteria and dedicated to halting the waste of gifted educated women, Dr. Bunting, herself the mother of four children, says, "A happy home is not enough. . . . I am convinced the road that lies ahead for women is a dual one of motherhood and career." With her M.S. and Ph.D. from the University of Wisconsin, Dr. Bunting taught at Bennington, Goucher, Yale, Wellesley, and Rutgers before going to Radcliffe, where she founded the Institute for Independent Study. It provides older women whose careers have been postponed or cut by marriage with grants for continuing their education. In 1964 she took a year's leave of absence and became the first woman on the Atomic Energy Commission, where, among other things, she worked to make opportunities for women more visible.

Seasheller for the Blind

TWILA BRATHCHER, an active scuba diver, is the world's leading authority on *Terebra,* a genus of shells. She has

named 13 of these shells previously unknown to science, and in 1974 two other terebra shells were named for her. Her love for exotic shells and her love for children led her in 1956 to devise a way blind children could learn about shells. She mastered Braille, enlisted the aid of the Pacific Shell Club of Los Angeles to supply her with shells, and began putting together boxes of shells, each labeled in Braille; these boxes have been used in almost every school for the blind in the English-speaking world.

First Woman Elected to Council of Biophysical Society

RITA GUTTMAN, a member of the biology department of Brooklyn College of the City University of New York since 1936, in 1967 became the first woman member elected to the Council of the Biophysical Society. Dr. Guttman is known for her application of physics principles to the study of nerve membrane behavior; she has been especially interested in excitation, which, she explains, involves the question of what triggers a nerve to respond when it is stimulated. In 1962 she was a member of the first expedition of the National Institutes of Health to the University of Chile to study the nerve cells of the giant squid of the Humboldt Current. Dr. Guttman, who earned her master's and Ph.D. from Columbia University, was elected the first chairperson of the Caucus of Women Biophysicists at an annual meeting of the Biophysical Society in Toronto, Canada, in 1970, and also at that time was appointed first chairperson of the Society's Committee on Professional Opportunities for Women.

Restorer of Research Center

Senior staff scientist at the Roscoe B. Jackson Laboratory of Bar Harbor, Maine, ELIZABETH SHULL RUSSELL made a permanent mark for herself in the history of genetics research centers after a forest fire destroyed the famous Laboratory in 1947. Thousands of carefully bred mice for genetic research were killed in the fire; she was responsible for rebuilding the supply of pedigreed specimens. Research centers from different parts of the world shipped her special samples, and from these, within 10 years, Dr. Russell was able to help the Laboratory once again function as a vital research center. Dr. Russell, who held a master's from Columbia and her Ph.D. from the University of Chicago (1937), came to the Jackson Laboratory as an independent investigator trying to determine the role of genetics in hair pigmentation of guinea pigs. She has held Finney Howell and Guggenheim fellowships as well as one from the American Association of University Women. She is also a fellow of the American Academy of Arts and Sciences.

Expert on Plant Tissue Structure

Russian-born KATHERINE ESAU has markedly increased knowledge of the structure of plant tissues and the processes involved in differentiation of tissues through her research in plant anatomy and the physiological effects of certain virus diseases in plants. Dr. Esau initiated fundamental investigations of the specific plant transport system called phloem, in which these diseases are manifested early, and she is now generally recognized as the outstanding expert in this field. As a young woman she studied in Moscow and Berlin, then came to the United States in 1923 and was naturalized in 1928. She received a Ph.D. from the University of California in 1931, a D.Sc. from Mills College in 1962, and an LL.D. in 1966. After working as a plant breeder for Spreckels Sugar Company in California, she went on to teach botany at the University of California. A member of the Guggenheim Foundation, the American Academy of Arts and Sci-

ences, the Botanical Society (of which she has been president), and the American Philosophical Society, in 1957 she was elected a member of the National Academy of Sciences.

Inventor of the Diatometer and Winner of World's Richest Prize for Scientific Achievement

Limnologist RUTH PATRICK has spent much of her life wading through hundreds of streams in the Americas—including the Amazon River—to study the aquatic life and ecology of freshwater rivers and lakes. She has become one of the world's experts on diatoms, a family of microscopic one-celled algae whose changing, responding characteristics in relation to the environment help scientists determine the presence and nature of water pollution. Dr. Patrick, a lover of the fascinating shapes of diatoms since she first looked through her father's microscope at the age of seven, was the first to discover their use as a simple, informative aid in the detection of pollution. Her findings, and her invention of the diatometer, a small device that identifies the type of diatom existing in the water, are today used by scientists throughout the world. With a master's degree and Ph.D. from the University of Virginia, Dr. Patrick became a full professor at the University of Pennsylvania, first chairwoman of the Board of the Academy of Natural Sciences in Philadelphia, and the first female director at Du Pont. Dr. Patrick has received numerous honorary degrees and in 1975 was awarded the world's richest prize for scientific achievement—the $150,000 John and Alice Tyler Ecology Award. The prize money, she said, will be used to continue her fieldwork and to put together a significant book about rivers.

World Expert on the Flea—and the Way It Jumps

In August 1977 MIRIAM LOUIS A. ROTHSCHILD, British zoologist, marine biolo-

gist, entomologist, parasitologist, and the world expert on fleas, hosted the first international flea conference on her country estate in Northamptonshire, England. More than 100 flea experts from 15 countries presented papers and exchanged information on parasites—fleas primarily, but also on ticks, mites, and fruit flies.

Dr. Rothschild was the first person to analyze the flea's amazing powerful jumping mechanism with a camera capable of recording 10,000 frames per second—and deduced that a flea's leaping ability would be the same as that of a man's to jump over the local post office tower some 30,000 times without becoming winded. She also once noted that a jumping rabbit flea developed acceleration twenty times greater than that of a moon rocket reentering the earth's atmosphere.

Because her family strongly objected to higher education for females, she received no formal degrees, but has been awarded an Honorary Fellowship of St. Hugh's College at Oxford, an Honorary D.Sc. degree and professorship of biology at London University. She has published more than 200 natural history and science papers, worked on seven volumes of the catalogue of the British Museum, and—while having a baby—co-authored a book, *Fleas, Flukes, and Cuckoos.* Over the past two decades she has catalogued her father's 10 thousand species of fleas and produced six large illustrated volumes. Like many naturalists, she has a few species named after her—a worm and a flea.

This remarkable woman has not restricted her energies just to a narrow field: She has innovated humane methods of handling livestock and was an early advocate in curtailing the use of toxic insecticides. Born in 1908, Dr. Rothschild has four children of her own, and two she has adopted.

She Saw Hazards in DNA Research

Now head of a research section on nucleic acid enzymology at the National Cancer Institute, MAXINE F. SINGER was one of the scientists in 1973 to alert the National Academy of Sciences to the fact that, although new techniques in gene splicing offered experimental advantages, it also posed potential hazards. In the past few years, controversy has raged over recombinant DNA research—involving newly developed techniques that permit scientists to take segments of genetic material (DNA) from one organism and incorporate it into living cells of another, potentially creating a completely new organism. Advantages could involve new kinds of food crops, but the research has the potential danger of creating novel forms of life possibly hazardous to humans and other organisms. The controversy lies in whether such research should be continued or not; and if so, under what conditions it should be conducted to make it extremely safe. The actions of Dr. Singer and her colleagues led, among other things, to the development of the National Institutes of Health (NIH) guidelines for genetic research.

With her Ph.D. from Yale in 1957, biochemist Singer has worked at NIH since 1956. She maintains an active pace as lecturer and author; has been on the editorial board of several publications; was director of the Foundation for Advance Education in the Sciences, Inc.; and has received many honors. In 1977, for instance, she received the Association for Women in Science Award, and the Director's Award of the NIH; she also became the G. Burroughs Mider Lecturer of NIH, and received a D.Sc. from Wesleyan University.

Renaissance Woman: Interface of Science and Society

Vienna-born biologist-cum-sociologist RUTH HUBBARD has turned from pure biological research toward sociology and history of science. With a Ph.D. in biology from Radcliffe, a Guggenheim fellowship at Copenhagen's Carlsberg Laboratory in 1952, and marine biology research at Woods Hole, she became a biology professor at the Massachusetts Institute of Technology in 1972 and later joined the biology department at Harvard. She has won professional recognition and honors for her work on the synthesis of visual pigments leading toward clearer understanding of vision. She has won equal acclaim by becoming involved with broader issues of society: setting up health care activities, counseling on pregnancy and abortion, and speaking out on the problems women face in a male-oriented environment. Dr Hubbard considers sociobiologists a threat, particularly against women in their efforts to interpret women's social roles as biologically determined. In an interview in the November/December 1976 issue of the Association for Women in Science *Newsletter,* she states that she doesn't think there has been a decrease in sexism in science (or elsewhere). Rather, "There has been an increase in tokenism. . . . Women are allowed into the lower ranks of the professions and looked over. If it looks like they'll conform, maybe they pass. . . . In many ways things could get worse, rather than better, because at the beginning of our new 'era of equality,' there were people like myself who had been on the periphery so long that we had to be let into the club [of university-trained, European-American, white, economically privileged males]. . . . With the younger women . . . those who don't play by the (male) rules, simply may not make it." She is the wife of biologist Nobel laureate George Wald.

Contributor to Genetic Theory

By her extraordinary work with cells of maize, BARBARA MCCLINTOCK was able to greatly facilitate genetic studies. Among her outstanding contributions is her analysis of the control of gene action in maize and the discovery of the two-unit interacting system—a concept that was the precursor of the gene regulation theory put forward by François Jacob and Jacques Monod, who won the Nobel Prize for their work in 1965. She published a series of papers that clearly established her as the foremost investigator in cytogenetics—the study of heredity by cellular and genetic methods. Dr. McClintock holds her master's, Ph.D., and an honorary doctorate of science from the University of Rochester, and has taught at Cornell and the University of Missouri. A fellow of the National Research Council and the Guggenheim Foundation, and a researcher at Cold Spring Harbor on Long Island, she is now investigator in genetics at the Carnegie Institution of Washington, D.C. Dr. McClintock has received an achievement award from the American Association of University Women and the National Medal of Science in 1970.

First American Indian Woman Ph.D. in Botany

Instructor of biology at the New Mexico Highlands University, LORA MANGUM SHIELDS is the first American Indian woman to obtain a Ph.D. in botany, from the University of New Mexico, where she had also obtained her master's degree. Dr. Shields, a Navajo, has held research grants from the National Science Foundation, National Institutes of Health, Squibb Corporation, and Eli Lilly and Company Foundation. Her major research interests are environmental biology, the effects of nuclear testing on desert vegetation, studies on serum lipids in southwestern ethnic groups, and other studies of blood chemistry. Dr. Shields has published more than 70 articles in professional journals, and received honors, including a Scientist of the Year Award from the New Mexico Academy of Science.

In the Interest of Genetics, She Starves Algae

Hunter College professor of biology RUTH SAGER has pioneered the concept that a second set of genes exists outside the nucleus chromosomes of a living cell and is a permanent cell constituent that can replicate and segregate in a normal manner consistent with cell division. Dr. Sager, educated at Rutgers and Columbia, where she got her Ph.D. in 1948, joined the staff of the National Research Council as Merck Fellow in 1949. At the Rockefeller Institute in 1951 she began exploring ideas in genetics that differed from the generally accepted theories, and in 1955 joined the staff of Columbia University. Her outstanding reputation is largely based on her genetic research with the alga *Chlamydomonas*—nicknamed "Clammy"—minute greenish plant found in ponds and mud puddles. Because sexual mating of these plants was unpredictable, genetic studies had been limited until Dr. Sager found that mating could be induced by nitrogen starvation. With this new discovery, she has made a series of significant findings in the field of genetics, for which she was elected a member of the National Academy of Science in 1977.

Pioneer DNA Researcher

MIRIAM SCHWEBER, research associate in the biochemistry department at Harvard, has done pioneering work on the properties of DNA (deoxyribonucleic acid), a pivotal area in understanding the role of genes in cell division and the study of cancer. She received her master's degree from the University of Wisconsin, with honors in population genetics, but decided to change to another field because of her tendency to pass out from the ether applied to many thousand fruit flies in order to count their genetic characteristics. So she turned to studies of the distribution of DNA, RNA (ribonucleic acid), and proteins found only in fruit-fly larvae—the subject of her Ph.D. thesis in cytology from the University of Chicago. Since then Dr. Schweber has done research and taught at Brandeis, Wellesley, Simmons, and the American College in Jerusalem. A recipient of many grants and awards, Dr. Schweber has been an inspiration to a number of students who have continued to do their own pioneer research and to receive honors.

Unraveling the Double Helix: Her Story

In the late 1950s, British ROSALIND FRANKLIN was one of four scientists responsible for determining the molecular structure of deoxyribonucleic acid (DNA)—an extremely important contribution to the field of genetics. Working at King's College, London, under the direction of Maurice Wilkins, she provided the basic scientific evidence that gave final credence to the theories of the early double helix models. Controversy over the credit for this discovery erupted in the scientific world in 1962, when the Nobel Prize was awarded to biophysicists Wilkins, James Watson, and Francis Crick for the work—four years after the death of Rosalind Franklin from cancer at the age of 37. (The Nobel Prize committee recognizes only living scientists.)

Belgian Researcher's Breakthrough on Circadian Rhythms

Belgian researcher THERESE VANDEN DRIESSCHE, a biology professor at the Université Libre in Brussels, has been working since 1964 to determine the circadian rhythms (growth periods over a 24-hour cycle) in the unicellular alga *Acetabularia*. Perhaps the most important of her many scientific developments in this area was her demonstration that the mechanism of periodic rhythms involves principally the molecular messenger ribonucleic acid (RNA), encoded within the nucleus—a discovery that has provided other molecular biologists with evidence on which to base continued study of biological rhythms.

Founding Director of Shark Study Lab

EUGENIE CLARK, one of the world's foremost marine biologists, won a Fulbright fellowship to study poisonous fish in the Red Sea, and thus attracted the notice of marine biologists throughout the world, a number of whom followed her to carry on their own research in that sea. A careful researcher of the nature and behavior of sharks, she was able to teach them to choose between targets of different designs and colors. In 1965 she was the founding director of the Cape Haze Marine Laboratory in Florida (now the Mole Marine Lab), the world's leading institute on the study of shark behavior.

Only Indian Woman Staff Member at Los Alamos

F. AGNES N. STROUD, a member of the Tewa tribe of the Santa Clara Indian Pueblo, is the only Indian woman employed at the level of staff member at an important scientific laboratory. She is a radiobiologist at the Mammalian Biology Group of the Los Alamos Scientific Research Laboratory. With a Ph.D. in biology and zoology from the University of Chicago in 1966—probably the only Pueblo woman to date with such a degree—Dr. Stroud has held several important positions; as research associate at the Argonne National Laboratory; as director of the Department of Tissue Culture at the Pasadena Foundation for Medical Research; and as senior biologist at the Jet Propulsion Laboratory. She has also held offices with professional societies such as the American Association for Cancer Research and the Tissue Culture Association, and been honored with the A. Cressy Morrison Prize in Natural Sciences given by the New York Academy of Sciences, and the Diploma of Honor in Cytology at the First Pan American Cancer Cytology Congress.

Leader of All-Woman Underwater Team

In 1970 marine biologist SYLVIA EARLE MEAD, who has had more than 20 years of diving experience, led an all-woman, five-member team in the Tektite II program of marine research in the Great Lameshur Bay in the Virgin Islands. The team lived for two weeks in an underwater capsule, spending from 6 to 10 hours a day swimming outside the habitat observing marine plant and animal life, and turned up 153 different species of marine plants, of which 26 had never before been recorded in that area. The women received the Conservation Service Award from the U. S. Department of the Interior for their work. Dr. Mead, who holds a master's and Ph.D. (1966 from Duke University), has been a research scholar at Radcliffe, Harvard, the Marine Science Institute, the University of California at Berkeley, and the Los Angeles County Museum of Natural History, where she is at present an associate in botany (her husband is the director). She has worked as a fisheries biologist for the U. S. Fish and Wildlife Service with a Smithsonian project in the Bahamas and the International Indian Ocean Expedition, a long-term cooperative research undertaking. She also has been resident director of Cape Haze Marine Laboratory at Sarasota, Florida, and holds appointments at Harvard and the University of South Florida.

First Women Scientists to Winter-Over in Antarctica

In 1974 MARY ALICE MCWHINNIE and Sister MARY ODILE CAHOON were the first two women who spent the winter (summer in the Southern Hemisphere) in frozen Antarctica engaging in scientific research. Both Ph.D. biologists, they were there to study krill, those tiny shrimp-like animals of the ocean that provide the principal food of whales and seals, and are now being considered as a potential major source of protein for human beings and livestock. (The Russians have been harvesting them since the 1960s.) Sister Cahoon, who has her master's degree from De Paul University and Ph.D. from Toronto and served as assistant to Dr. McWhinnie on that first trip, is now teaching at the College of St. Scholastica in Duluth, Minnesota. Dr. McWhinnie, biology professor at De Paul, who received her master's and Ph.D. degrees from Northwestern University and also has taught at the University of Chicago, now heads the United States' first intensive study program—at Palmer Station—on krill and on the effects of their harvesting, under a grant from the National Science Foundation. She has suggested an international convention to help set limits to the amount that legally may be harvested in order to preserve their fragile and important ecosystem.

Discoverer of a Key to Photosynthesis

Research biologist ELIZABETH GANTT has worked for more than a decade at the Radiation Biology Laboratory of the Smithsonian Institution to isolate and comprehend, for the first time, the medium through which the visible energy of the sun (light) is transmuted into the chemical energy needed for plant life and growth. Her studies of red and blue-green algae have pointed up the existence of "phycobilisomes" (her term), which are large pigmented molecular aggregates essentially responsible for the absorption and transfer of light energy in photosynthesis. The application of this discovery could help create an energy-harvesting system that could function at low-light intensities and use most of the energy in the visible part of the electromagnetic spectrum. Dr. Gantt was born in Gakovo, Yugoslavia, in 1934, received her M.S. and Ph.D. from Northwestern University in Illinois, and went on to teach there and at Dartmouth before becoming a biologist at the Smithsonian. It was while she was a microbiologist at Dartmouth Medical School in 1965 that she made the first in-depth ultrastructural study of the red alga *Porphyridium*. This and further research enabled Dr. Gantt and her colleagues to report other important factors in the mechanisms of photosynthesis.

CHEMISTRY

First Garvan Medal Winner

Professor and research chemist EMMA PERRY CARR was the first recipient (1937) of the American Chemical Society's prestigious Francis Garvan Medal for her pioneering work on the ultraviolet spectra of simple unsaturated hydrocarbons. She is also widely recognized for her development of group research techniques, which made Mount Holyoke College's Carr Chemistry Laboratory (named for her) one of the most advanced in the country, and an inspiration to her students (many of whom followed in her footsteps to become distinguished chemists themselves). Dr. Carr died in 1972 at the age of 92.

The Garvan Medalists*

1937 Emma Perry Carr (d. 1972)
Mount Holyoke
Hydrocarbon Structure by Far
Ultraviolet

1940 Mary Engle Pennington (d. 1952)
Private Consultant
Food Chemistry

1942 Florence B. Seibert
University of Pennsylvania
Chemistry of Tuberculosis

1946 Icie Macy-Hoobler
Children's Fund of Michigan
Nutrition Chemistry

1947 Mary Lura Sherrill (d. 1968)
Mount Holyoke
Molecular Structure

1948 Gerty T. Cori (d. 1957)
Washington University School of
Medicine
Enzymatic Synthesis and Reactions

1949 Agnes Fay Morgan (d. 1968)
University of California at Berkeley
Chemistry of Vitamins

1950 Pauline Beery Mack (d. 1974)
Pennsylvania State College
Calcium Chemistry of Bone

1951 Katherine Blodgett
General Electric Research Lab
Monomolecular Films

1952 Gladys Emerson
Merck Institute for Therapeutic
Research
Chemistry of Vitamin E

1953 Leonora Neuffer Bilger
University of Hawaii
Asymmetric Nitrogen Compounds

1954 Betty Sullivan
Russell-Miller Milling Company
Cereal Chemistry

1955 Grace Medes (d. 1969)
Lankenau Hospital Research Institute
Discovery and Study of Tyrosinosis

1956 Allene R. Jeanes
United States Department of
Agriculture
Fundamental Research on Dextran

1957 Lucy W. Pickett
Mount Holyoke
Vacuum Ultraviolet Pioneer

1958 Arda A. Green (d. 1958)
Johns Hopkins
Purification of Enzymes

1959 Dorothy V. Nightingale
University of Missouri
Organic Synthetic Reactions

1960 Mary L. Caldwell (d. 1972)
Columbia
Crystalline Enzyme Preparation

1961 Sarah Ratner
Public Health Research Institute,
New York
Protein Production Controlling
Enzymes

1962 Helen M. Dyer
National Cancer Institute
Experimental Carcinogenesis
Mechanisms

1963 Mildred Cohn
Johnson Foundation, University of
Pennsylvania
Oxygen 18 Enzyme Mechanism Studies

1964 Birgit Vennesland
University of Chicago
Enzymic Hydrogen Transfer Studies

1965 Gertrude Perlmann (d. 1974)
Rockefeller Institute
Studies of Protein Structure

1966 Mary L. Petermann (d. 1976)
Sloan-Kettering Institute for Cancer
Research
Cellular Chemistry

1967 Marjorie J. Vold
University of Southern California
Theoretical Models of Colloids

* Francis P. Garvan was president until his death in 1937 of the Chemical Foundation, which facilitated U.S. manufacturers using patents, trademarks, copyrights, and contracts that had been seized by the alien property custodian following World War I. Shareholders received no dividend; the president and vice-president worked without salary. The Foundation contributed 72 per cent of its income to the support of scientific research and education. The Garvan medals were established in his memory "to honor an American woman for distinguished service in chemistry."

1968 Gertrude B. Elion
Burroughs-Wellcome and Company
Drugs for Chemotherapy
1969 Sofia Simmonds
Yale University
Bacteria Amino Acid Metabolism
1970 Ruth Benerito
United States Department of
Agriculture
Studies on Cellulose Properties
1971 Mary Fieser
Harvard
Chemical Literature
1972 Jeannine M. Shreeve
University of Idaho
Inorganic Fluorine Compounds
1973 Mary L. Good
Louisiana State University
Mossbauer Spectroscopy
1974 Joyce Kaufman
Johns Hopkins
Quantum Calculations of Drug Action
1975 Marjorie C. Caserio
University of California at Irvine
Physical Organic Chemistry
1976 Isabella L. Karle
Naval Research Laboratory,
Washington, D.C.
Crystallography
1977 Marjorie G. Horning
Baylor College of Medicine
Pharmacology

Columbia University's First Woman Chemistry Professor

MARY L. CALDWELL spent years developing precise methods of isolating enzymes so they could be individually analyzed. Now her techniques are used throughout American and European laboratories. Born in Bogotá, Colombia, of missionary parents in 1890, she received her B.A. from Western College for Women in Ohio, where she taught for four years; and her Ph.D. from Columbia University, where she became the first woman professor in chemistry. Many of the principles taken for granted today in enzymology were first applied to amylases (starch enzymes) in her laboratories. A memorable teacher, Dr. Caldwell inspired her students to strive for technical and scholastic excellence. After her retirement in 1959 to the country near Fishkill, New York, she continued working on papers for publication until her death in 1972.

First Woman Division Chairperson, the American Chemical Society

ICIE MACY-HOOBLER was the first woman to chair a division of the American Chemical Society and first to chair the Detroit section. She was also first woman member of the Detroit Engineering Society. Dr. Hoobler has published several hundred papers and books, mainly in the field of nutrition. With a Ph.D. from Yale, she became assistant biochemist at the West Pennsylvania Hospital at Pittsburgh, instructor at the University of California, and a nutrition researcher before becoming director of the research laboratory of the Children's Fund of Michigan and Children's Hospital. Her special field of research has been physiological chemistry and nutrition, mineral metabolism in human pregnancy, secretion of human milk, and chemistry of red blood cells. She was awarded the Garvan Medal for chemistry in 1946.

Discoverer of the 87th Element and First Woman Elected to the French Academy of Sciences

MARGUERITE PEREY, discoverer of a radioactive element that she named francium, died when she was 65 years old after a 15-year struggle with cancer believed to have resulted from her work with radioactive materials. The French scientist began her work as a laboratory assistant with Madame Curie at the French Radium Institute when she was 20 years old. Ten years later she isolated francium, the 87th element in the periodic table. She became professor of nuclear chemistry at Strasbourg University and director of the Strasbourg Center for

Nuclear Research—and in 1962 the first woman member in the 200-year history of the French Academy of Sciences when she was elected a correspondent of the physics section.

First to Note Vitamin/Hormone Relationships

AGNES FAY MORGAN was the first person to prove in laboratory experiments many things about interrelationships between vitamin and hormone activities and their effects on health. To name a few, she was first to produce graying of hair through vitamin deficiency, first to observe damage to the adrenal glands caused by an acid deficiency, first to record heat damage to proteins, and first to note certain supplementary effects of vitamin D. After obtaining her M.S. and Ph.D. in physical and organic chemistry at the University of Chicago, Dr. Morgan decided to find a job in some related

field where there was less prejudice against women chemists She was interested in improving health and diet, and when she was invited to teach dietetics at the University of California at Berkeley in 1915, she accepted. At that time there were only three textbooks in English on nutrition. Dr. Morgan organized the available material and started the first scientific human nutrition courses taught by a woman. She proceeded to build up a Department of Home Economics that became world-famous. During World War II, she worked for four years with the Office of Scientific Research and Development, then returned to Berkeley, where she was the first woman chosen to deliver the Faculty Research Lectures. She founded the chemistry honor society Iota Sigma Pi, was elected the first woman fellow of the American Institute of Nutrition, and remained an active, influential teacher until her death in 1968.

She Discovered Why Fireflies Glow

In 1956 ARDA A. GREEN successfully isolated and crystallized the enzymes called luciferases by which living creatures such as fireflies are able to "light up." She thus discovered the long-sought mechanism of firefly luminescence—something chemists had been working toward for decades. Dr. Green received her M.D. from Johns Hopkins University, then went to Harvard, where she did outstanding work on purifying hemoglobin and plasma proteins. At Washington University (St. Louis), she was equally successful in isolating the muscle proteins, and at Cleveland Clinic she worked on isolating proteins involved in hypertension. Here she helped isolate the substance serotonin, an important regulator of the central nervous system. In 1953 Dr. Green began her work in the field of bioluminescence, for which she received the Garvan Award, at McCollum-Pratt Institute of Johns Hopkins, where she

worked as a research biochemist until her death in 1958.

Only Woman Heart Association Career Investigator

Chemist MILDRED COHN has helped open up a whole new field in understanding the nature of enzyme substrate compounds. For her work, which has furthered the understanding of the most basic problem of catalysts in biological systems, Dr. Cohn in 1963 was awarded the Garvan Medal by the American Chemical Society, and in 1964 was named a lifetime career investigator by the American Heart Association—an honor with a stipend that enables her to devote the rest of her active career to research. She is one of 13 researchers and the only woman to receive this award. In 1971 she was elected a member of the National Academy of Sciences. She received her Ph.D. in 1938 for work in physical chemistry on isotopes under Nobel laureate Harold Urey at Columbia University. Later, at George Washington University and at Cornell University Medical College, she applied her knowledge of isotopes to a new field: tracing the metabolic processes in rats, the complex physical and chemical processes of life. At Washington University in St. Louis, she studied the processes by which energy from ingested food is stored as chemical energy within the body and then released as muscular or other energy. She now is professor of biochemistry and biophysics at the University of Pennsylvania. Dr. Cohn, who is married to Dr. Henry Primakoff, has also raised three children who are making their marks in the science field: DR. NINA ROSSOMANDO, who did her graduate work in psychology; Dr. Paul Primakoff, who did graduate studies in biochemistry; and Dr. LAURA PRIMAKOFF, who did her studies in clinical psychology.

Inventor of Nuclear Explosive Device

MARGUERITE SHUE-WEN CHANG, a research chemist and inventor in the Department of the Navy, works on materials used in making explosives, and has eight or more inventions to her credit—most of which are classified. She invented the device that triggered an underground nuclear explosive in a 1969 Atomic Energy Commission test supervised by the Los Alamos Scientific Laboratory. Emphasizing personnel safety and quality control in the manufacturing process, she has been responsible for a number of research projects seeking new missile propellants and improving the efficiency of existing ones. Dr. Chang, born in Nanking, China, earned her B.A. in organic chemistry at Wu-Han University before coming to the United States in 1946, where she earned her Ph.D. in organic chemistry at Tulane University in 1959. She has received two special awards from the Department of the Navy for her achievements, and in 1973 received the Federal Woman's Award for outstanding government service.

First Woman Division Director of Argonne Laboratory

The first, and so far only, woman division director at the Argonne National Laboratory, HOYLANDE D. YOUNG is also the first woman chairperson of the American Chemical Society. With a Ph.D. from the University of Chicago, Dr. Young was a research chemist at the Van Schaack Bros. Chemical Works, Inc. She then taught chemistry and nutrition at the College of Industrial Arts (now Texas Woman's University); worked on the survey of petroleum literature at the Pure Oil Company; and was research associate at the University of Chicago and the Metallurgical Laboratory of the Argonne National Laboratory. She was the general editor for the National Nuclear Energy Series, the Atomic Energy Commission report of wartime research on nuclear energy. She has received the Chicago Section American Institute Chemical Award and the Chicago Section of the American Chemical Society Award for distinguished service.

Innovator in Biochemistry

BIRGIT VENNESLAND, born in Norway, came to Chicago as a child during World War I and has stayed ever since. After receiving her B.S. and Ph.D. degrees in biochemistry from the University of Chicago, she began a lifetime association with that university, taking a few years out to work at the Harvard Medical School and at the Max Planck Institute for cell physiology in West Berlin. Dr. Vennesland was one of the first chemists to use radioactive carbon-11 to study carbohydrate metabolism—research that gave a clearer understanding of the role of carbon dioxide in the metabolism of animal tissues. Winner of the American Chemical Society's Garvan Medal, a biochemist "because the field encompasses both the physical and biological sciences," Dr. Vennesland also has been interested in languages and the humanities.

First Woman Member of the Sloan-Kettering Institute for Cancer Research

In 1963 MARY L. PETERMANN received the Sloan Award in cancer research and also became the first woman member of the Sloan-Kettering Institute for Cancer Research. This 1929 graduate of Smith College, with high honors in chemistry, who received her Ph.D. in physiological chemistry from Wisconsin in 1939, won her claim to fame because she decided to investigate the particulate material that kept interfering with her efforts to study deoxyribonucleic acid (DNA) and ribonucleic acid (RNA). The material was called "Petermann's particles" for a short while, but since has been named ribosomes, now known to be the sites of protein synthesis. She was the first to isolate and characterize animal ribosomes, and she went on to establish the importance of magnesium ion concentration in stabilizing the ribosome, and the degree to which the ribonucleoprotein particles became associated or contaminated with other proteins. Until her death in 1976, Dr. Petermann continued her interests in the transformations that ribosomes may undergo.

Protein Enzyme Specialist

GERTRUDE E. PERLMANN was one of the first people to realize the possible importance of the chemical phosphate in proteins. This realization led her to an important scientific understanding of the chemical breakdowns and restructurings of proteins in the stomach as acted upon by pepsin, an enzyme that speeds food digestion. Born and educated in Czechoslovakia, Dr. Perlmann acquired her D.Sc. in chemistry and physics from the German University of Prague. She then continued her research at Copenhagen, and came to the United States in 1939 to teach physical chemistry at Harvard Medical School. She became visiting in-

vestigator and then associate professor at Rockefeller University in New York, where she made many contributions in the study of protein structure, particularly in the activities of enzymes. She remained with Rockefeller for 28 years until her death from cancer in 1974.

First Woman President of American Chemical Society

ANNA J. HARRISON, who became president of the American Chemical Society in 1976, is the first woman to hold that office in the Society's 102-year history. Dr. Harrison earned her Ph.D. from the University of Missouri, and now is a professor of chemistry and researcher at Mount Holyoke College. She also holds honorary doctorate degrees from Smith College and Tulane University. Dr. Harrison sees four long-range goals for the Society: to enhance the growth of individual chemists; to increase the vitality of chemical institutions; to facilitate the extension of chemical knowledge; and to further the use of chemistry in the service of humanity.

Leading Intramolecular Researcher

MARILYN E. JACOX is one of the world's leading researchers in the field of intramolecular biology. A physical chemist for the National Bureau of Standards (NBS) in Washington, D.C., she has received awards for determining certain properties of charged radical ions and for shedding light on the structure and chemical reactivity of these ions. Dr. Jacox, born in 1929 in Utica, New York, gained her Ph.D. from Cornell in physical chemistry. In 1962 she began work with the U. S. Government and since 1974 has been chief of environmental chemical processes at NBS.

International Expert on Polymers

Italian-born GIULIANA TESORO is an internationally recognized expert on the science and technology of polymers, which are natural or synthetic chemical compounds consisting of large molecules formed of repeated, linked units of smaller, simpler molecules. After receiving her Ph.D. in organic chemistry from Yale University, she worked with American Cyanamid, then Onyx Chemical Company (now Millmaster Onyx), and then with J. P. Stevens & Co. After a year with the Textile Research Institute in Princeton, she was with Burlington Industries, until 1972, and since then has been teaching at the Massachusetts Institute of Technology. Dr. Tesoro has published extensively in technical journals, and holds more than 100 U.S. patents in fields that affect the strength, durability, and color qualities of textiles.

Co-author of Unique Chemical Dictionary

MARY FIESER, research fellow in chemistry at Harvard, was awarded the Garvan Medal in 1971. A central figure in chemical education and research references, she has written a dozen highly successful texts and reference works in collaboration with her husband, Dr. Louis F. Fieser, also of Harvard. The dual-author series began in 1944 with *Organic Chemistry* and continued with further organic texts including a style guide for chemists. In 1967 Mary Fieser and her husband co-authored *Reagents for Organic Synthesis,* a unique, dictionary-form work. For her publications, her research, and her skill in teaching students how to write about chemistry, she was recognized and honored by her colleagues with the Garvan Medal.

Pioneer in Vacuum Ultraviolet

An authority on identifying organic compounds by techniques using X rays and ultraviolet rays, LUCY W. PICKETT was one of the few researchers who pioneered in studies of vacuum ultraviolet (that part of the electromagnetic spectrum where radiation waves are very short). Vacuum ultraviolet, still a new field of research, is an important, although little studied, area because it is here that all simple organic compounds

absorb radiation to produce electronic transitions. After receiving her M.S. in chemistry from Mount Holyoke, and a Ph.D. from the University of Illinois in 1930, Dr. Pickett went on to teach at Mount Holyoke, where she became head of the Department of Chemistry. She has many publications to her credit and won the American Chemical Society's Garvan Medal in 1957 for her research on molecular structure using far ultraviolet spectroscopy.

Influential Organic Chemist

Equally productive in the classroom and the laboratory, British-born MARJORIE C. CASERIO is one of the most important educators in the field of organic chemistry. Dr. Caserio has written and co-authored several textbooks—one of which, *Basic Principles of Organic Chemistry,* has had a direct influence on changing the emphasis of undergraduate studies on organic chemistry. After receiving her B.S. from Chelsea College of the University of London, she came to the United States, where she earned her master's degree and later her Ph.D. at Bryn Mawr. She returned to England, where she was a research chemist for the Fulmer Research Institute in Stoke Poges for a time, and then became a fellow of the California Institute of Technology. Since 1965 she has been a professor at the University of California at Irvine. She is a member of the Chemical Society of London, the American Chemical Society, and a 1975 winner of the Garvan Medal.

Foremost Woman Theoretician in Structural Chemistry

JOYCE KAUFMAN became interested in the theoretical aspects of structural chemistry after receiving her Ph.D. at Johns Hopkins. Today considered the foremost woman in this field, she performs quantum chemical calculations of the action of drugs that affect the central nervous system. Her work has aroused international interest, and she has lectured in Copenhagen, Stockholm, and

Paris. She is now the principal research scientist in the department of chemistry at Johns Hopkins, associate professor in the division of anesthesiology of the School of Medicine, and serves on the editorial advisory board of a molecular pharmacology journal.

First Woman on American Chemical Society Board

As director of a particular region of the American Chemical Society, MARY L. GOOD was the first woman to become a member of the Society in its 96 years of existence. She was also the first woman to be named to the board of the Oak Ridge Associated Universities and to a chemistry advisory panel of the National Science Foundation, After getting her Ph.D. at the University of Arkansas, Dr. Good began teaching at the Louisiana State University at Baton Rouge, where she was also director of the radiation laboratory. When the university opened another section at New Orleans in 1958, Dr. Good helped to set up the chemistry curriculum, plan the science building, and design the laboratory for radiochemical research. Dr. Good is best known for her work with a specific method of spectroscopy—the study of energy emit-

ted by a radiant source. Her laboratory is one of three in the world where spectroscopy of ruthenium compounds is being done.

First Woman Senior Participant of Arthur D. Little, Inc.

First woman named a senior participant of the research and management-consulting firm of Arthur D. Little, Inc., JOAN B. BERKOWITZ received her M.S. and Ph.D. in physical chemistry from the University of Illinois, and did postdoctoral work in polyelectrolytes and the structure of ionic solutions at Yale. She joined Arthur D. Little in 1957 and has been responsible for research problems in high-temperature chemistry and environmental science, while doing her own research on chemical crystals for applications in solar cells. She is concerned with cleaning up the environment and carries on programs on effluent wastes in streams and on emissions into the air from power plant boilers. Dr. Berkowitz holds patents as co-inventor of two developments in ceramics and is the author of more than 35 technical papers and articles in high-temperature chemistry and oxidation of refractory hard metals.

Eco-Active Chemist

Chemist and environmentalist RUTH WEINER, born in Vienna, is professor of chemistry at Florida International University and also associate director of the Joint Center for Environmental and Urban Problems in Miami. With a Ph.D. in chemistry from Johns Hopkins, she attributes her profound involvement with the ecology movement to the fact that "opportunities in my chosen professional area—chemistry—were so severely curtailed by sex discrimination." The University of Denver, where her husband teaches, would not consider her application because of nepotism; the Colorado

School of Mines told her (although their policy has since changed), "We never hire women in the sciences."

She finally found a position at the University of Colorado School of Medicine as research associate and later as professor of chemistry at Temple Buell College in Colorado. She became active in the conservation movement and in 1965 helped establish the Colorado Open Space Council. In 1969 she was founder and chairwoman of the Colorado Citizens for Clean Air. She has testified on air and water resource problems before legislative committees of states and the

U. S. Congress; and has helped draft several state laws, including the Colorado Air Pollution Control Act. In 1970 Dr. Weiner, a specialist in photochemistry, chemical air pollutants, and water resources, accepted the university position in Miami, where she teaches and also channels her ecological energies on the Board of the Florida Clean Air Council. For the present, her husband, professor of chemistry, remains in Colorado; each of them has care of two children.

She reports that the life of a single married woman is very lonely.

"Our situation certainly focuses a major problem for women (or perhaps one ought to say for married couples) pursuing professional careers," she says. "Unless we initiate jobs that are filled by a married couple rather than by a single person, we cannot guarantee a husband and wife equally satisfying professional appointments in the same geographic location, because there are so few positions available."

ENVIRONMENTAL SCIENCES

Geology/Meteorology/Oceanography

First Woman to Gain B.S., M.S., and Ph.D. from Johns Hopkins and to Be U. S. Government Geologist

Education for women along with men was still a precarious phenomenon when FLORENCE BASCOM was admitted to the University of Wisconsin at the age of 15 in 1877. It was a time when women could use the library only on separate days from the men. They were not allowed to listen to lectures if there was no more room in the classroom after all the

men were seated. Nevertheless, with the encouragement of an eminent geology professor, she persisted and became the first woman to obtain her B.S., M.S., and Ph.D. from Johns Hopkins. Her research subject was the analysis of geological formations in Maryland's South Mountain. After teaching at Bryn Mawr College for a while, she was appointed assistant geologist with the U. S. Geological Society of America, and later the first woman vice-president. She died in 1945.

First Woman Member of the Canadian Geological Survey

For more than thirty years, Canadian ALICE WILSON, wearing her favorite Cossack outfit and driving a Model T Ford, explored the St. Lawrence River lowlands to study fossil remains. In 1911 she became the first woman to hold a professional rank (museum clerk) for the Canadian Geological Survey. In 1945 she broke the all-male barriers of the Survey to be made a member. In 1938 she was named the first woman fellow of the Royal Society of Canada. Dr. Wilson, who wrote *The Earth Beneath Our Feet*, died in 1964 at the age of eighty-three.

Award-Winning Danish Geodesist

Danish INGE LEHMANN, co-founder and former president of the Danish Geophysical Society, is one of the world's noted geodesists and the author of numerous papers on seismology. In 1965 she was awarded the Gold Medal of the Royal Danish Society of Science and in 1967, at the age of 79, was awarded Denmark's much prized Tagea Brandt Scholarship for the second time—she had received the same honor 29 years before in 1938. Dr. Lehmann was elected a member of the Royal Society in London in 1969 and received the American Geophysical Union's William Bowie Medal in 1971.

First American Woman Chief Scientist on Major Oceanographic Expedition

ELIZABETH T. BUNCE was the first woman to go to sea on a Woods Hole Oceanographic Institution research ship. She also was the first American woman to serve as chief scientist on a major oceanographic expedition. With a master's degree (1949) in physics from Smith College, which gave her an honorary doctorate of science in 1971, Ms. Bunce taught physics at Smith for two years before joining Woods Hole as a research associate and later senior scientist in geology and geophysics. Her first cruise on the research ship *Bear* opened a new and exciting field for other women thinking of entering oceanography/geology as a profession. She has been chief scientist on many geological/geophysical cruises— including those of the *Glomar Challenger* drilling into the floor of the oceans. She also has served several years on a major phase of the International Indian Ocean Expedition; and recently has headed a team conducting site surveys in the Indian Ocean for future drillings of the ocean bottom. A fellow of the Geological Society of America and a member of several professional societies and committees, she is the author and co-author of many papers in marine geophysics.

First to Earn Her Ph.D. in Meteorology

JOANNE SIMPSON, the first woman to receive a Ph.D. in meteorology in the United States, was director, 1965–73, of the U. S. Weather Bureau's (now National Oceanic and Atmospheric Administration) Experimental Meteorology Laboratory at Coral Gables, Florida. Here she was instrumental in studying the structure and behavior of powerful storm systems with airplanes, satellites, and computers. She was also responsible

for experiments with cloud seeding to diminish the strength of storms and modify their behavior. During World War II she took special meteorology training at the University of Chicago and then trained weather forecasters for the military services. After the war she continued her studies despite encountering some hostile reactions against a woman entering the field. When she married, she faced the problems of putting her husband's career before her own, and as a mother faced the anguish of being split between tending for her children and absorption in her work. With all, Dr. Simpson has succeeded in being generally acknowledged the foremost woman in her field. She won the Meisinger Award in 1962, the Department of Commerce Gold Medal in 1972, the University of Chicago Achievement Award in 1975. The author of more than 80 research papers and two books, she has taught at the Woods Hole Oceanographic Institution, the Illinois Institute of Technology, the University of Chicago, the University of California at Los Angeles, and became the first woman to be the William W. Corcoran Professor of Environmental Sciences at the University of Virginia. She was elected to the Council of the American Meteorological Society in 1975 and to its executive committee in 1977.

From First US. Woman Weather Forecaster to First Woman Meteorologist at Argonne Laboratory

Top-notch women meteorologists are relatively scarce, but BERNICE ACKERMAN has made many marks by her research in the fields of cloud physics, radar meteorology, and urban meteorology—the study of the effects of heat, pollution, and air currents caused by cities upon the weather of the area downwind. She got started in this business, she says, "at the bottom"—as weather observer in the U. S. Navy WAVES during World War II, when she became the first woman weather forecaster in the United States. She went on to receive her master's and Ph.D. from the University of Chicago, studying the relationship between cloud buoyancy and precipitation and the turbulence in hurricanes. As the only woman research meteorologist in the Cloud Physics Laboratory of the University of Chicago in 1952–64, she took part in programs in cloud physics and radar meteorology. As the first woman meteorologist at the Argonne National Laboratory, she became interested in urban meteorology, and designed and worked on a field program to study the effects of St. Louis on surrounding weather. She joined the Illinois State Water Survey in 1972 and continued her research, directing a major field effort as part of the five-year Metropolitan Meteorological Experiment (METROMEX).

Lunar Geologist

A month after they were married, URSULA B. MARVIN—then preparing her Ph.D. at Harvard—and her mining-geologist husband, Thomas, were on their way to Brazil to search for manganese and titanium ore deposits. It was, reported their sponsors, Union Carbide Ore Company, the first time a wife had gone on an expedition as a paid geologist employee. Their next assignment took them to Central Africa and the source of the Zambezi River, with two tents—one for themselves and the other for mapping and prospecting equipment. After six years of such field assignments in these two continents, the Marvins returned to Cambridge, Massachusetts, where Ursula joined the research staff at the Smithsonian Astrophysical Observatory to study the mineralogy of meteorites and, as a result of the Apollo mission, of samples of the moon. She also was able to complete her Ph.D. in geology from Harvard—after 23 years of interruptions.

In her student days at Tufts College, Dr. Marvin was headed toward earning her degree in history. But in her junior year she "accidentally" took geology

MIT Storm Warner

PAULINE M. AUSTIN, director of weather radar research at the Massachusetts Institute of Technology (MIT), has been concerned primarily with exploring the structure and behavior of storms by using radar. She probes different kinds of storms, adding basic data on their possible modification to benefit man in producing crops and avoiding disaster. After earning her master's degree in physics from Smith College, and a Ph.D. from MIT, Dr. Austin received an honorary doctorate in science from Wilson College. She is an associate editor of the *Journal of Applied Meteorology* and councilor of the American Meteorological Society.

while fulfilling what she thought was a disliked science requirement. This basic course in geology, combined with her inherent love of the outdoors, dramatically changed her college career and her life. In addition to publishing more than 60 papers on meteorites and the moon, she has also written a book on the history of the continental drift concept. She has taught courses in mineralogy, meteoritics, and planetary geology at Tufts, where she was elected to the Board of Trustees; and she continues to lecture in two departments, geology and astronomy, at Harvard.

Paleontologist for Conservation

ESTELLA LEOPOLD comes from a famous family of scientists and conservationists. She holds degrees from the universities of Wisconsin, California, and Yale and has worked in the areas of botany, geology, and paleontology. An active member of many conservation groups in Colorado, where her work on wildlife gained her special recognition, Dr. Leopold helped stop a proposed hydroelectric dam in the Grand Canyon—only to have her joy turn to despair when she and fellow protesters learned that the alternative energy source (massive coal-fired electric plants) created devastating amounts of air pollution. She now is director of the University of Washington's Quaternary Research Center—an interdisciplinary group dedicated to the study of the Pleistocene and the Ice ages. The Northwest is an area where she can readily pursue her studies in reconstruction of ancient environments and her interest in current environmental sciences and conservation.

A Three-Times-First Geologist

IRIS Y. BORG was the first woman to be awarded a Ph.D. in geology from the University of California at Berkeley; the first woman to become a member of the Princeton geology department (as research assistant and fellow), and first and only to date woman on the geological staff of the Lawrence Livermore Laboratory. Dr. Borg's primary interest is in the peaceful use of atomic energy. She has actively participated in programs to test nuclear devices underground at the Nevada test site and hopes to see a wide use of nuclear devices in exploring geological problems. Author and editor of many books and scientific articles and the recipient of numerous scholarships and fellowships, including a Guggenheim fellowship to pursue crystallographic studies in Switzerland, she is a fellow of the Geological Society of America and a member of the governing board of the American Geological Institute. Also concerned about the preservation of flora and fauna, she is active in the Sierra Club and the Save-the-Redwoods League.

Japan's Leading Woman Geochemist

Japanese geochemist KATSUKO SARU-HASHI graduated from Toho University in 1943. At the Meteorological Research Institute, she has done pioneering research on the world's distribution of artificial radioactivity in seawater, and been head of the Institute's geochemistry laboratory since 1973.

Founder of Women Geoscientists Committee

THERESA F. SCHWARZER, senior research specialist of the Exxon Production Research Company, as a member of the American Geological Institute founded and has been chairperson of the Women Geoscientists Committee. Here her activities have included organizing career-oriented activities for professional women geoscientists and publishing newsletters for them. Educated at Rensselaer Polytechnic Institute, she has specialized in inorganic and organic geochemistry, remote sensing techniques, multivariate statistics analysis, seismic interpretation, energy resources, and geologic manpower. She has published numerous papers and given many lectures on geoscience and the role of women in this field.

First Woman Director of American Geographical Society

In 1976 SARAH KERR MYERS, who was born in Brazil in 1940 and spent much of her childhood traveling the world with her mother and research-physician father, became the first woman director of the 124-year-old American Geographical Society. Holder of an M.A. degree from Stanford University in Hispanic-American studies and a Ph.D. from the University of Chicago in geography, Dr. Myers joined the staff of the American Geographical Society in 1972 and the next year became editor of its *Geographic Review*. She is well known for her successful combination of sociology with geography and has written widely on language shifts in migrant populations of Latin America. She lives in Teaneck, New Jersey, with her husband and two daughters.

Cloud Watcher

Meteorologist MARGARET LE MONE, research scientist with the National Center for Atmospheric Research in Boulder, Colorado, has documented relationships of cloud formation to the dynamics of air layers below the cloud base. Her research using aircraft and tall towers may one day provide a guide to modeling the behavior of the layer of air beneath clouds for large computer models used for weather forecasting. A. Ph.D. in atmospheric sciences from the University of Washington in Seattle, Dr. Le Mone worked as acting project leader of the Global Atmospheric Research Program, Atlantic Tropical Experiment in 1974–75 on the relationship of cumulus and thunderstorm clouds to the weather systems in which they are embedded.

MATHEMATICS

Most Significant Abstract Algebraist

On the death in 1935 of AMALIE NOETHER, Albert Einstein wrote in the *New York Times*, "In the judgment of the most competent living mathematicians, Fraulein Noether was the most significant creative mathematical genius thus far produced since the higher education of women began. In the realm of algebra, in which the most gifted mathematicians have been busy for centuries, she discovered methods which have proved of enormous importance in the development of the present-day younger generation of mathematicians." Emmy Noether, as she was always called, was born in a small university town in Germany and grew up in a family of strong-minded mathematicians. She was tutored by brilliant family friends from the University of Erlangen, where her father taught, and received her doctorate from that university. Occasionally she substituted as lecturer for her father when he was ill. Working with researchers at Göttingen University on the general theory of relativity, Dr. Noether's theoretical knowledge of invariants proved useful, and she became part of one of Germany's foremost circles of mathematical research. The university still strongly opposed granting "habilitation" to women, so she and Professor David Hilbert worked out a method whereby she would give lectures although they continued to be announced under his name. Eventually she was nominated to the position of professor at the University—but received no salary. By 1930 she was renowned as a vigorous focus for the traditionally strong mathematical center at Göttingen, and her considerable ability to work with abstract concepts became recognized. An exceptionally influential teacher, she maintained an unusual capacity for clarifying very difficult concepts so students could understand them. With the rise of Nazi power, she was prohibited from academic activity, and came to the United States, where she taught at Bryn Mawr and later worked (along with Einstein) at the Institute for Advanced Study in Princeton.

First Woman President of AAAS

MINA S. REES holds the honor of being the first woman president of the United States' largest scientific society, the American Association for the Advancement of Science (AAAS). Professor of mathematics and dean of the faculty of Hunter College, New York, Dr. Rees is internationally recognized as a mathematician, statistician, and teacher. She won particular renown for her farsighted guidance of postwar research programs from 1946 to 1953 with the Office of Naval Research, where she spurred mathematical research in the design and engineering of hydrofoil craft, high-speed computers, and logistic data for a society at peace. For her service during World War II, she received the United States'

President's Certificate of Merit and the United Kingdom's King's Medal for Service in the Cause of Freedom. The Mathematical Association of America gave her its first award for distinguished service to mathematics.

Originator of Mathematics Programs at Bryn Mawr

British-born CHARLOTTE ANGAS SCOTT was educated at Cambridge University, where she made an outstanding scholastic record but did not graduate because at that time women were "not allowed" to receive degrees from Cambridge. She stayed on at Cambridge as resident lecturer in mathematics while she continued her studies at the University of London, from which she received her doctorate of science in 1885. She then came to the United States, where she started the undergraduate and graduate programs in mathematics at Bryn Mawr—and spent the next 40 years teaching there. Dr. Scott kept alive her special interest in the analysis of singularities for algebraic curves and wrote some 30 papers on the subject. She is also the author of a textbook on plane analytical geometry. On retirement, she returned to England.

World-Renowned Abstract Algebraist

Mathematician HANNA NEUMANN emigrated from Nazi Germany in 1938 to England, where she continued her studies and received her doctorate at Oxford. She specialized in modern abstract algebra, centering her main interest in group theory of math, particularly in free groups. In a relatively new area of pure mathematical research, Dr. Neumann's studies, often in collaboration with her husband, are cited as basic to further investigations. A lucid and prolific writer who could make difficult mathematical theories understood by the layman, Dr. Neumann's publications continue to be read as source material. She died in 1971.

First Woman Department Head at North Carolina State University

Statistician GERTRUDE COX founded the statistics department at North Carolina State University and, as its chairperson, was the first woman to head a department there. The building that houses the department is now called Cox Hall. She did graduate work at the University of California at Berkeley and at Iowa State University, which also gave her an honorary D.Sc. in 1958. One of the key pioneers in applied statistics, Dr. Cox went to Egypt to establish the Institute of Statistics at the University of Cairo and to act as program specialist, 1964–65, and she continues to serve as an independent statistical consultant to governments and industry throughout the world. At age 75, in 1975, she became a member of the National Academy of Sciences. Other awards have come from the American Public Health Association, the American Association for the Advancement of Science, the Institute of Mathematical Statistics, the South African Statistical Association, and the Société Adolpha Quatelet of Brussels, Belgium.

Impossible Problem Solver

One of the foremost professionals in U.S. cryptology, MARY H. BUDENBACH for more than 25 years has been engaged in work involving preparations and analysis of codes and ciphers concerned with communications security of the United States. She started this work with the U. S. Navy and has been with the National Security Agency (NSA), where she now holds the position of deputy group chief, since 1953. Ms. Budenbach, who holds a B.A. in English from Smith College but has long had an interest in the highly sophisticated mathematical analysis necessary for her work, has distinguished herself by solving "impossible," highly classified problems for collaborating agencies within the U. S. Government. She has received both the NSA and the Navy Meritorious Civilian

Service Award, and a Federal Woman's Award (1969).

Prime Contributor to Mathematics

Several Italian women have turned out to be brilliant mathematicians, and MARIA PASTORI is one of the most noted. She has furthered the understanding of tensor calculus, which is of prime importance in the theoretical treatment of classical physics and extremely useful today in the pure mathematical investigation of generalized spaces. Coming from a very poor family, in her early years she and her equally brilliant sister GIUSEPPINA, who became a biologist, had to rely on their own initiative and hard work. Their elementary education ended when they were 13 years old; they took on jobs and studied together, unassisted by anyone else, early in the morning and late at night. Both took the strict Italian state examinations for baccalaureate and passed with highest honors. Maria then passed a difficult entrance exam for the Scuolo Normale Superiore of Pisa, and became an assistant at the University of Milan, at the same time holding a teaching job in the secondary schools. She kept being promoted at the university and eventually was offered a professorial chair at the university's Istitutio Matematico—one of the three honored chairs held by women in Italy at that time, the late 1950s.

Mathematical Logician

MARIAN BOYKAN POUR-EL, professor of mathematics at the University of Minnesota, claims that her career as a logician "refutes a commonly held conviction—that a woman is not logical, but acts on the basis of intuition alone." One of the first women to get her Ph.D. from Harvard's Graduate School of Mathematics, Dr. Pour-El then taught mathematics at Pennsylvania State University and at the University of Minnesota. She has been a member of the Institute for Advanced Study of Princeton and a grantee of the National Academy of Sciences. Dr.

Pour-El grew up at a time when it was assumed that a woman's role in life "was considered secondary to her husband's, her status achieved as a reflection of his status, and her success depended on his success." She was able to break out of this mold and says that she is now "completely assimilated in the mathematical community. My presence as a woman, although noticed, virtually plays no role in the professional relations between myself and my colleagues."

Only Female Full Mathematics Professor at the University of Paris

JACQUELINE LELONG-FERRAND started her successful career in mathematics early—she received the first prize in a national competition in mathematics while she was still a student at the *lycée* (high school) in Nîmes, France. Encouraged to compete again, she was among the first group of girls permitted to take the entrance examinations to the Paris École Normale Superieure; in 1939 she ranked first in the mathematical examination for a degree from this renowned school. She then taught at the Sèvres normal school for girls, and was assistant professor at the University of Bordeaux, and later at Caen. From 1948 to 1956 she held the chair of calculus and higher geometry at the University of Lille. In 1956 she and her professor husband carried on research at the Institute for Advanced Study at Princeton. Mme. Lelong-Ferrand was eventually awarded a full professorship in pure mathematics at the University of Paris.

Japan's First Woman to Get Sc.D. in Mathematics

Born in Hokkaido, YOSHI KATSURADA became Japan's first doctor of science in mathematics, in 1950. She taught at Hokkaido University, and in 1967 became the first woman full professor of that university. For a few years in the early 1960s, she studied in Italy and Switzerland doing joint research with a Swiss mathematician on the theory of numbers.

"Pencil and Paper" Mathematician

"Famous women mathematicians throughout history can be numbered on the fingers of one hand," says Polish-born EDITH H. LUCHINS, professor of mathematics at Rensselaer Polytechnic Institute. And she finds that the proportion of women receiving doctorates in mathematics is less now than it was fifty years ago, even though, she says, "There is perhaps no other career in science which lends itself as readily to being combined with marriage and children, since the work can be done at home, using mainly pencil and paper. And of course, now computer outlets can be connected to the home." A wife, mother, and grandmother, Dr. Luchins earned her B.A. degree, cum laude, at Brooklyn College, her M.S. at New York University; and her Ph.D. at the University of Oregon. In addition to holding university research and teaching posts at Brooklyn College, New York University, and at the universities of Oregon and Miami, she has been a government inspector at Sperry Gyroscope Company and a research associate for the U. S. Air Force Systems Command, and for the National Institute of Mental Health. The author and co-author of books and numerous scientific papers, she is a member of several organizations including the American Mathematical Society and the Mathematical Association of America.

She Helped Develop Early Digital Computer

The career of mathematician MARGARET BUTLER, director of the Code Center of the Argonne National Laboratory, extends back over a quarter of a century to her participation at the Laboratory in what she describes as "the excitement of the beginning of both atomic energy and the computer industry." As staff mathematician in the early 1950s, she assisted in the development of one of the first digital computers for science. She later became active in the development of computer programs for reactor physics design and engineering problems. As director of the Code Center, she runs the software exchange service, helps develop standards in the field of computer technology both in the United States and abroad, and continues to engage in computer science research. Holder of a fellow award of the American Nuclear Society, and a member of the Society's Board, she also has been active in the Association for Computing Machinery and the Midwest Computer Club. In the past few years, she has worked to improve the status of women and for ratification of the Equal Rights Amendment.

Top Statistician at NBS

JOAN RAUP ROSENBLATT, chief of the Statistical Engineering Laboratory with the National Bureau of Standards (NBS), is internationally recognized for her work in developing the application of statistics in the physical sciences. Dr. Rosenblatt, a Ph.D. in statistics from the University of North Carolina, has taken special interest in theoretical work in applications of statistical techniques and rank-order methods. A member of the editorial board of the Society for Industrial and Applied Mathematics' *Journal of Applied Mathematics,* she has served as chairwoman on the American Statistical Association's Section on Physical and Engineering Sciences, and on the Council of the Institute of Mathematical Statistics. She was presented with the Federal Woman's Award in 1971 and the Department of Commerce Gold Medal in 1975.

First Woman Scientist Awarded Research Grant by Alfred Sloan Foundation

Born in the Ukraine, Russia, CHARLOTTE FROESE FISCHER came to Canada in 1930, where she won her bachelor's degree with honors in math and chemistry, and her master's degree, at the University of British Columbia. She obtained

NOW's Housewife President

When "ELLIE" SMEAL took office as the first housewife president of the United States' 65,000-member, 700-chapter National Organization for Women (NOW) in 1977, she said: "This is a unique time for all of us and that's why I agreed to do this. I would have rather not. If they could have found anyone else—well, there were people who thought I brought something special to the job and that my background as a housewife would change some images. Otherwise I would not have wanted to spend so much time away from home." (*New York Times,* September 2, 1977) (Photo courtesy of NOW)

President of North American Indian Women's Association, Athabascan Indian MARY JANE FATE, mother of four, heads the national association of Indian women in addition to running a home and taking an active role in many community affairs in Alaska. (Photo courtesy of the Women's Bureau, Department of Labor)

Reading Is FUNdamental, an organization that encourages children to learn to read by giving them books of their own to keep, was the brainchild of MARGARET C. MCNAMARA, seen here with young readers. Projects are sponsored by colleges, clubs, and business firms in 50 states, with matching funds topping $14 million earmarked for RIF by the U. S. Office of Education. (Photo courtesy of Shirley Katzander, from the *Los Angeles Times*)

The first black woman to be elected president of the Girl Scouts of America (founded in 1912 in Savannah, Georgia) was GLORIA DEAN SCOTT, who took office in 1975 and has worked to bring more poor and minority-group children into scouting. (Photo by Bradford Bachrach)

TISH SOMMERS (left) and LAURIE SHIELDS, co-coordinators of the NOW Task Force on Older Women since 1976, in 1975 lobbied the United States' first Displaced Homemaker Act into law in California. They are also co-coordinators of the grass-roots coalition of feminists and traditional churchwomen's groups that have joined to form the national Alliance for Displaced Homemakers.

CATHY by Cathy Guisewite

HI. I'M CATHY FROM PRODUCT TESTING INC., DOING A SURVEY ON WORKING WOMEN. THIS ARTICLE SAYS YOU'RE THE PRESIDENT OF MOXEY, INC.

THAT'S RIGHT.

ACCORDING TO THIS, YOU NOT ONLY BUILT THE COMPANY FROM SCRATCH, BUT CONTINUE TO HANDLE PERSONNEL, FILING, BILLS, BUYING AND LEGAL.

THAT'S RIGHT.

WHEW! WHY DID YOU DECIDE TO GIVE UP YOUR LIFE AS A WIFE AND MOTHER FOR THIS?

I COULDN'T STAND THE PRESSURES OF HOUSEWORK.

Former sociologist and today one of the foremost U.S. potters, CAROL RIDKER teaches ceramics at American University in Washington, D.C., and works out of her home, where, she says, her craft provides her with "instant gratification (or instant failure)" and "a more harmonious life."

The chances are great that every other pillow decorated with crewel embroidery in either a British or American home has been worked according to instruction from ERICA WILSON, whose needlework empire has quadrupled in the 1970s into a million-dollar industry. (Photo courtesy of Jack Shipley)

The chances are even greater that every other dish from the French cuisine served on an American table in the past decade has been made according to JULIA CHILD, of cookbook and TV demonstration fame. (Courtesy of Paul Child)

Foremother

MARIE CURIE, the first woman in the world to win the Nobel Prize, pictured at a young age in her laboratory in France. Born in Warsaw in 1867, she was forced to leave Poland because of her participation in revolutionary student activities. She studied at the Sorbonne, married physicist Pierre Curie in 1895, and with him won her first Nobel Prize, in physics, in 1903. The Curies discovered two new elements in pitchblende: polonium, named for her native country, and radium. It was for the latter that Marie Curie, after her husband was run over by a dray and killed instantly in 1906, won the 1911 Nobel Prize in Chemistry—becoming the first woman and first person to win the coveted award twice. (Courtesy of *New Scientist Magazine*, London)

ANNIE JUMP CANNON, "census taker of the sky," classified about 400,000 stellar bodies according to their temperature. Dr. Cannon was the first woman elected an officer of the American Astronomical Society and one of the first women to hold a titled corporation appointment at Harvard (1938), as the William Cranch Bont Astronomer. (Courtesy of Harvard College Observatory)

Charivari, Honoré Daumier, September 22, 1858. "Monsieur Babinet apprised by his concierge of the comet's arrival."—It takes a woman. (Courtesy Museum of Fine Arts, Boston)

Among the many young women graduates in astronomy from Harvard University is CHRISTINE JONES-FORMAN. In 1977 she was a member of a team at the Harvard-Smithsonian Center for Astrophysics that made an important discovery of "super-clusters" of galaxies bound by a hot gas that is believed to be linked to the universe's so-called missing mass. (Courtesy of Harvard College Observatory)

her Ph.D. at Cambridge University, and then became the first woman scientist to win an Alfred P. Sloan fellowship to Harvard College Observatory, in 1955. She has been teaching math at the University of British Columbia since 1957. The author of several publications, she is editor of *Computing Reviews* and *Computer Physics Communications,* and a member of the Canadian Mathematics Congress, the Canadian Information Processing Society, the Computer Science Association (director, 1972–74), and the Association for Computing Machinery.

Chief Prober in Science of Surveys

Chief of the Research Center for Measurement Methods at the U. S. Bureau of the Census, BARBARA A. BAILAR graduated magna cum laude in mathematics from the State University of New York at Albany. She started out teaching high school math in Katonah, New York, then took a graduate fellowship at Virginia Polytechnic Institute, where she taught elementary statistics courses. While holding a job at the U. S. Census Bureau, she continued her studies in mathematical statistics and completed her master's degree in 1958 and her Ph.D. in 1972 at the American University in Washington, D.C. Dr. Bailar

worked on various projects in the 1960 U.S. population census, then contributed to the 1970 census. President of the Woman's Caucus in Statistics and of the Washington Statistical Society, she also is chairwoman of the American Statistical Association's Committee on Women in Statistics and its Subsection on Survey Research Methods.

Many Times Founder of Nuclear Information Centers

A founder and director of the Radiation Shielding Information Center of the Neutron Physics Division at Oak Ridge, and a founder and director of the Biochemical Computing Technology Information Center, BETTY F. MASKEWITZ has also founded, and is president of, the Cak Ridge National Laboratory Information Analysis Centers Forum. Ms. Maskewitz, who has a master's degree in mathematics from the University of Tennessee (1962), also has worked at the Nuclear Codes Group, Central Data Processing Facility of the Union Carbide Nuclear Division. The mother of two children, she has been presented with the National Women's League Outstanding Woman Award (1974) and the American Nuclear Society Shielding and Dosimetry Award for outstanding service (1975).

Developer of Machine for Bibliographies

Computer systems analyst HENRIETTE AVRAM, chief of the Machine Readable Cataloguing (MARC) Development Office of the Library of Congress, directs research and development projects for automation of the Library's bibliographic services. Since 1965, when she joined the Library, she has been one of the most influential people in the field of library automation, both nationally and internationally. She is best known for developing a standard format for the interchange of bibliographic records in machine readable form—the MARC, which has been

endorsed by the American Library Association and recommended by computer experts to libraries around the world. Today this format is an international standard that makes possible worldwide sharing of automated bibliographic information.

First Director of NBS's Institute for Computer Sciences and Technology

Computer scientist and mathematician RUTH M. DAVIS joined the National Bureau of Standards (NBS) in 1970 and when the Institute for Computer Sciences and Technology was established in 1972 became its first director. With her master's degree and Ph.D. from the University of Maryland, Dr. Davis started work for the Department of the Navy on nuclear reactor design in 1953, and in 1958 established and became the first director of the operations research division of the David Taylor Model Basin. She served as technical director of the Navy's shore-based Command and Control Systems activities until 1961. Now teaching at the Moore School of Engineering at the University of Pennsylvania, she has

been visiting professor at the University of Pittsburgh since 1968 and has taught mathematics at American University and the University of Maryland. From 1961 to 1967 Dr. Davis was staff assistant for intelligence and reconnaissance with the Office of the Secretary of Defense, then went to the National Library of Medicine as associate director for research and development and next became the first director of the Lister Hill National Center for Biomedical Communications in 1968.

PHYSICS

First American Woman to Receive Göttingen Ph.D.

With a bachelor of science degree from the Massachusetts Institute of Technology, MARGARET ELIZA MALTBY became a physics instructor at Wellesley, and then went on to study at the German University of Göttingen, where she was the first American woman to receive a Ph.D.—on the measurement of high electrolytic resistances. She taught at several colleges in the United States (including Wellesley and Barnard) and appeared in the first edition (1906) of American Men of Science, where she was starred as one of America's most important 150 physicists. She worked on the committee for the American Association of University Women, which, after her death in 1944, established a Margaret E. Maltby fellowship in her honor.

First Woman in General Electric Research Laboratories

KATHERINE B. BLODGETT made her mark on the world when she developed a technique for depositing successive monomolecular (one-molecule-deep) layers on glass by picking them up from the surface of water. Using her technique, General Electric was able to produce "invisible" glass. Of Maine ancestry, Dr. Blodgett received her Ph.D. in physics at Cambridge, England, studying with Sir Ernest Rutherford at the Cavendish Lab-

oratories—the first woman to receive a doctorate in physics from that institution. At a time when "a woman scientist was not considered so much a rarity as an impossibility," she was helped by the labor shortage during World War I and by the intercession of friends of her late father, the former head of General Electric's patent department, to become the first woman to work in the GE research laboratories. It was here that, together with Irving Langmuir, she pioneered in monomolecular films.

First Woman to Receive Enrico Fermi Award

In 1938 Austrian physicist and mathematician LISE MEITNER played a crucial role in one of the most important scientific achievements of this century— the splitting of the atom. Working to release the energy within the atom's nucleus, Dr. Meitner and her colleagues, Drs. Otto Hahn and Fritz Strassmann, fired slow-speed neutrons at the uranium nucleus. They were startled and puzzled to note the appearance of barium, an element that had not been present at the beginning of the experiment. Shortly thereafter, Dr. Meitner, fleeing Nazi Germany and en route to Sweden, solved this mystery mathematically. She reported that the presence of barium indicated the fission or splitting of the uranium atom, one part being barium, the other krypton. She was the first woman to be awarded the Enrico Fermi Award (1966) for this discovery. One of the leading mathematical physicists of this century, she received her doctorate at the University of Vienna, then went to Berlin to study atomic theory with the renowned physicist Max Planck. In her later years she worked at the Nobel Institute in Stockholm. Dr. Meitner died in 1968.

Builder of the First Nuclear Reactor

Between 1943 and 1947, Dr. LEONA M. LIBBY was a prominent member of the Manhattan District group of scientists who built the first nuclear reactor, the first and second Argonne reactors, the Oak Ridge reactor, and the three Hanford reactors for plutonium production. In short, Dr. Libby has been at the forefront of nuclear energy technology since the atom was split and science was plunged into the nuclear era. She has been a professor of physics at various American universities (currently at the School of Engineering of the University of California at Los Angeles), served as a senior scientist at the Brookhaven National Laboratory, and worked as a staff member of the Rand Corporation analyzing foreign nuclear explosions and diffusion of neutrons in the atmosphere. The author of numerous papers, she has many "firsts" to her name, either by herself or in collaboration with well-known physicists such as Enrico Fermi and Luis Alvaraz, including the discovery of very cold neutrons, the building of the first thermal column, and the building of the first rotating neutron spectrometer. She also discovered that historical climates can be measured from isotope ratios in tree rings.

The Nuclear Physics Community Depends on Her Data

KATHERINE WAY has been described as a "nuclear physicist whose tireless efforts have touched and informed the work of virtually every nuclear physicist in the world." As adjunct professor at Duke University, Dr. Way has used the Triangle Universities Nuclear Laboratory as a base for her work as editor of the journal *Atomic Data and Nuclear Data Tables*. After receiving her Ph.D. from the University of North Carolina, she joined the faculty of the University of Tennessee until the events in nuclear development in World War II brought her to the Manhattan Project at Oak Ridge. One of those rare scientists who can explain extremely precise and complex methods and theory in understandable prose, she was instrumental in compiling and editing the bewildering and rapidly accumulating mass information on atomic nuclei. Her publications are ones upon which the nuclear physics community has come to depend.

She Overthrew the Principle of Parity

Columbia University professor of physics CHIEN-SHIUNG WU, born and educated in China, is one of the world's foremost female experimental physicists. She gained this distinction through her significant contributions to the research of nuclear forces and structures and, in particular, for her work in overthrowing the principle of parity, regarded as a fundamental law of physics for the past 30 years. This principle held that a phenomenon of nature looks the same whether observed directly or through a mirror, with right and left reversed. With theorists Tsung-Dao Lee and Chen Ning Yang, Dr. Wu devised and conducted experiments that in 1956 proved the parity principle unacceptable when dealing with weak interactions of subatomic particles.

Lee and Yang were awarded a Nobel Prize in 1957 for their theoretical work on this; Dr. Wu was not. She has, however, received many honorary degrees from Princeton, Smith, Goucher, Rutgers, and Yale, and is an honorary Fellow of the Royal Society of Edinburgh. She was the first woman to receive the Comstock Prize from the National Academy of Sciences; the first woman to receive the Research Corporation Award; the first woman at Princeton to receive an honorary degree of doctor of science (and congratulated for proving "the unwisdom of underestimating the powers of a woman"). In 1975 she became president of the American Physical Society.

Dr. Wu obtained her B.S. from the National Central University in China in the mid-1930s and emigrated to the United States soon after. She earned her Ph.D. from the University of California at Berkeley.

Second Woman Physicist Elected to the National Academy of Sciences

GERTRUDE SCHARFF GOLDHABER, born in Mannheim, Germany, earned her Ph.D. in Munich and is now senior physicist at the Brookhaven National Laboratory. She is one of only two women physicists so far elected members of the National Academy of Sciences. Dr.

Chien-shiung Wu was elected in 1958; Dr. Goldhaber in 1972. As a research physicist at the Imperial College in London and at the University of Illinois, Dr. Goldhaber has made many contributions to physics in fields of ferromagnetism, electron diffraction, spontaneous fission neutrons, and nuclear disintegrations. One of several prominent foreign-born physicists, including Nobel Prize winner MARIA GOEPPERT MAYER, Dr. Goldhaber believes that in the United States, unlike Europe and the Orient, the notion that it is unfeminine to excel in a career usually delegated to men has held women back. This inner, self-imposed constraint, "this absurd belief," she believes, is fortunately now being swept away, and some outstanding young U.S.-born women scientists are emerging.

Outstanding Japanese Physicist Honored by French

TOSHIKO YUASA, born in Tokyo, was graduated from the Tokyo Women's Higher Normal School and in 1934 received her degree in physics from the Tokyo University of Science and Literature, now the Tokyo University of Education. She studied in France 1940–45, then returned to Japan and taught at her alma mater, the Tokyo Women's School. In 1949 she again went to France and has been in Paris ever since, engaged in research in nuclear physics and chemistry. She was honored with a French doctorate for her research on beta-disintegration of artificial radioactivity.

Founder, Committee on the Status of Women in Physics

VERA KISTIAKOWSKY founded and was the first chairperson of the Committee on the Status of Women in Physics, part of the American Physical Society. She also serves on the Society's Council. A high-energy experimentalist by profession, Dr. Kistiakowsky was the first woman full professor of physics at the Massachusetts Institute of Technology, and still teaches there. For the past 17 years, she has

been engaged in experiments carried out at Argonne National Laboratory, Stanford's Linear Accelerator, and Illinois's Fermi National Accelerator Laboratory, which has the highest energy accelerator in the world. These experiments investigate interactions of elementary particles. The daughter of George Kistiakowsky, former presidential science adviser, mother of two, and author of juvenile science books, Vera Kistiakowsky admits she had difficult times trying to combine a science career with marriage and motherhood in the years when many Americans did not accept or understand this dual role. But she strongly believes that "anyone with a strong interest in science will not and should not let obstacles stop them."

First to Discover Crystal Excitons

Russian physicist ANTONINA FYODOROVNA PKIKHOT'KO is most noted for her experimental proof of the theory that electrons of crystal atoms may move faster into an excitonic state under the influence of light. A doctor of physics and head of the Institute of Physics at the Ukrainian Academy of Sciences, she was the first scientist to discover and describe the waves of excitations—excitons, as they are called—in the atoms of crystals. In 1966 she was awarded a Lenin Prize for her research.

Discoverer of a New Method for Analyzing Crystals

Crystallographer ISABELLA KARLE, head of the X-ray analysis section of the U. S. Naval Research Laboratory since 1959, has gained worldwide recognition for her discovery in 1963 of a new method of crystal structure analysis, the "symbolic addition procedure," which has completely revised earlier, time-consuming procedures and is now used throughout the world in studies ranging from radiation damage to depressants of blood pressure. Taught at home by her Polish parents, she later found schoolwork easy and interesting, and progressed rapidly, getting her Ph.D. at the University of Michigan only 15½ years after she entered first grade.

First Woman Sloan Foundation Fellowship Winner

Physicist LAURA M. ROTH, research professor at the State University of New York (SUNY) at Albany and one of the world's leading solid state theorists, in 1963 was the first woman to be awarded a Sloan Foundation fellowship. Before joining the staff at SUNY, Dr. Roth was the Abby Rockefeller Mauze Professor at the Massachusetts Institute of Technology—a Chair established to bring to MIT distinguished women scholars who would inspire and teach women students. She also has held positions at a number of other universities and research institutes, including Harvard, Tufts, MIT's Lincoln Laboratory, General Electric Research and Development Center, and the Institute for Theoretical Physics of the University of Colorado. She received her M.S. and Ph.D. in physics from Radcliffe. Dr. Roth worked on the "Hubbard model," a mathematical model of a magnetic metal, aimed essentially at understanding why and when ferromagnetism is possible. More recently, she writes, she's become interested in liquid metals, trying to understand how electrons behave when the ions are not set in a crystal but are in some random arrangement.

Principal Woman Scientist at Xerox

Electronics, particularly semiconductors, electron scattering, acoustic and optical surface waves, and organic conductors, is the principal research interest of ESTHER M. CONWELL, manager of the electro-optics program at Xerox's Rochester Corporate Research Center. Dr. Conwell completed her master's degree in physics at the University of Rochester and her Ph.D. at the University of Chicago in 1948 and taught physics at the universities of Rochester and Chicago and at Brooklyn College. She then became a staff member of Bell Telephone Laboratories and held positions at the General Telephone and Electronics Laboratories. She has been a visiting professor at the University of Paris, and a staff member of the applied physics department of Stanford. In 1972 she was appointed the Abby Rockefeller Mauze Professor at the Massachusetts Institute of Technology (MIT). As a member of the American Physical Society's Committee on Women and chairwoman of its Committee on Professional Concerns, Dr. Conwell has worked with other women physicists in government, industry, and academia to define and diminish sex discrimination.

Inventor of the HRES

Senior scientist at Ford Scientific Laboratory, MARY BETH STEARNS is probing the atom with a contraption she made called the High Resolution Electron Spectrometer (HRES). Used to study the structure and properties of electrons and the way they behave, HRES concentrates on metals and alloys. Dr. Stearns, who holds degrees in nuclear physics from the University of Minnesota and Cornell, and has been a research fellow at the Carnegie Institute of Technology in Pittsburgh and at the University of Pittsburgh, and a research scientist at an atomic research firm in La Jolla, California, has long been interested in magnetism. Her work explores how electrons line up to form the familiar north and south poles of a magnet. The north-south polar conditions that create magnetic attraction, she explains, are caused by certain kinds of "itinerant" electrons that move independently of an atom, lining up the "local" electrons associated with a specific atom. Her theory on magnetism may eventually be applied to developing new metal alloys, electronic devices, and new magnetic research techniques.

She Helped Design the World's First Proton Synchrotron

Canadian-born M. HILDRED BLEWETT, senior physicist in the Argonne National Laboratory's Accelerator Division, remembers well the time she and her husband were alone in the control room watching the world's first accelerator of high-energy protons go over the billion-electron-volt (BeV) mark. They both had helped design, construct, and operate

this cosmotron—the first proton synchrotron—built at the Brookhaven National Laboratory. After that, she was put in charge of designing the magnet system for the next Brookhaven machine, the 33 BeV synchrotron. While that was in construction, she traveled to Europe to help assist in designing and operating some of the world's most powerful accelerators: in 1953 the synchrotron at CERN, which is the European nuclear physics center in Switzerland; and in 1957 the French Government's Saturne accelerator near Paris. In 1959 she presided at CERN's initial test to obtain maximum energy; and in the mid-1960s she came back to the Brookhaven control room to help bring that machine to top energy. With a B.A. in physics at the University of Toronto, and further studies at Rochester University and Cornell, Ms. Blewett has made renowned records in advising high-energy physicists on designing their experiments and building and using high-energy accelerators for world research.

First Woman Member of Nuclear Board of Directors

ANN W. SAVOLAINEN was the first female member of the American Nuclear Society standards committee, first female elected to their board of directors, and first woman elected chairperson of a technical committee of the International Organization for Standardization. She also is the only woman to receive the Union Carbide Incentive Award in recognition of her work on nuclear reactor concepts. With degrees in physics and mathematics, Ms. Savolainen began her career in 1948 when she was employed by the newly formed U. S. Atomic Energy Commission. She then moved to the Knolls Atomic Power Laboratory, and from 1951 to 1971 was a staff member of the director of the Reactor Division of the Oak Ridge National Laboratory. She then worked for the American Nuclear Society, and from 1971 to 1975 was director of the Nuclear Program of the American National Standards Institute, where she was responsible for the management and coordination of the United States' national nuclear standards program. Since 1975 she has been a full-time consultant to the U. S. Nuclear Regulatory Commission, where she is helping to establish the management and administrative procedures needed to produce, disseminate, store, and retrieve the massive amount of information developed in the licensing and regulation of the nuclear industry.

Chilean Specialist in Nuclear Fusion

A Chilean by birth, LUISA FERNANDEZ HANSEN, who got her bachelor of science degree from the University of Chile, Santiago, and her master's and Ph.D. (1959) from the University of California at Berkeley, is a senior physicist at the Lawrence Livermore Laboratory in California. She has held teaching positions at both of her alma maters and conducted research on cosmic rays in high-energy physics, nuclear physics, and nuclear fusion reactors. She describes the thrust of her present fusion research as follows: "The growing energy needs of the nation have focused attention on new means of generation of power. Solar and fusion energy are posed as clean alternatives to fossil fuel systems and fission reactors. Fusion energy has not yet been demonstrated as feasible, but the rewards for success are so profound that a vigorous international effort is now being pursued." Dr. Hansen is chairwoman of a non-political group that works through the U. S. Congress and State Department to attempt to stop the violation of human rights and civil liberties that has been occurring in Chile since the military coup of 1973.

Prominent Elementary Particle Physicist

NINA BYERS, professor of physics at the University of California at Los Angeles (UCLA) and a member of the American Physical Society, is a prominent re-searcher in the exciting field of elementary particles, where new discoveries in the past decade have changed man's (and woman's) understanding of the nature of the universe. She earned her Ph.D. from the University of Chicago, and was research fellow in the Department of Mathematical Physics of the University of Birmingham in England, and assistant professor at California's Stanford University before joining the UCLA faculty. The author of numerous papers, Dr. Byers has worked at the European Organization for Nuclear Research and the Centre d'Études Nucléaires, and served as consultant to the Argonne National Laboratory, the Fermi National Accelerator Laboratory, and the Lawrence Berkeley Laboratory. She has held a Guggenheim fellowship (at UCLA) and another at the Somerville College of Oxford University in England. Her current research includes studies of the decay of newly discovered elementary particles, and of possible unifications of strong, weak, and electromagnetic interactions.

Harvard's Woman Cyclotron Researcher

With degrees in physics and chemistry, KRISTEN JOHNSON pioneers as a woman research assistant at the cyclotron laboratory at Harvard University. The work she does there is primarily directed toward treating tumors, both cancerous and benign, by means of a proton particle beam. With this beam, she and her co-workers have been able to take photographs, similar to X-ray photos, of various human organs and tissues. In trying to correlate what one sees in the photographs with the density of the tissues, on which the absorption of the proton beam is largely dependent, Dr. Johnson centers much of her work around new ways to determine these density values. Dr. Johnson has felt no problems in working in a male-oriented research environment and being a successful scientist in her own right. She feels unrestrained by male

Distribution by Sex of Principal Scientific Awards and Membership in Academies of Science

Prize	Women	Men	Prize	Women	Men
Nobel prizes[1]			Literature	6	63
			Peace	3	54[2]
Physics	2	99	Economic science[3]	0	9
Chemistry	3	83			
Physiology, medicine	1	112	Fields medal[4]	0	20

Country	Members		Corresponding members		Foreign members		Engineering sciences	
	Women	Men	Women	Men	Women	Men	Women	Men
Belgium	0	60	2	27	0	92	–[5]	–
Bulgaria	1	51	0	67	0	78	–	–
Canada	–	–	–	–	–	–	–	–
Czechoslovakia	0	51	3	138	0	34	–	–
Finland	10	238	0	10	0	106	2	131
France	–	–	–	–	–	–	–	–
German Democratic Republic	4	137	0	43	1	115	–	–
German Federal Republic	–	–	–	–	–	–	–	–
Greece	0	41	1	38	0	16	–	–
Hungary	1	211	6	112	–[6]	–[6]	–	–
Iceland	1	40	–	–	–	–	5	579
India	–	–	–	–	–	–	–	–
Japan	0	206	–	–	–	–	0	30
Netherlands	6	235	1	78	3	71	–	–
New Zealand	6	108	–	–	–	–	3	4,801
Nigeria	0	35	–	–	–	–	–	–
Pakistan	–	–	–	–	–	–	–	–
Sweden	0	210	–	–	0	118	1	448
U.S.S.R.	3	247	9	441	0	65	–	–
United Kingdom	22	658	1	76	–	–	–[7]	–[7]
United States	16	1,040	–	–	2	136	2	500
Yugoslavia	3	314	5	154	3	123	–	–

[1] Data taken from the annual *Nobelstiftelsen Kalendar,* Stockholm.

[2] Plus twelve institutions.

[3] This prize was first awarded in 1969; all others were first attributed in 1901.

[4] Often referred to as the "Nobel Prize for Mathematics," first awarded in 1936. Data obtained from the International Mathematical Union.

[5] Not applicable or information not available.

[6] Women and men make a total of eighty-five foreign members of the Hungarian Academy.

[7] The Council of Engineering Institutions combines aggregate individual memberships of about 185,000 men as against less than 185 women.

Sources: the respective governments.

—from *Impact of Science on Society,* Vol. 25, No. 2, April–June 1975, p. 154.

pressure, and independent in pursuing her profession as well as her own personal interests—one of which is being a licensed amateur radio operator.

MIT's First Black Woman Theoretical Physicist

SHIRLEY JACKSON, a theoretical physicist at the Fermi Accelerator Laboratory in Illinois, is working to understand a major issue in her field: the behavior of basic constituents of matter as they interact at high energy. A graduate of the Massachusetts Institute of Technology—the only black woman in theoretical physics —Dr. Jackson has been a lecturer at Fisk University, a special instructor in physics at MIT, and a participant in the International School of Subnuclear Physics in Erice-Trapani, Sicily. Has she had a problem gaining acceptance in a white-male-oriented profession? "I hesitate to call it a real problem," she told *Ebony* magazine, "because I'm not really asking for acceptance, just respect, and that comes—grudgingly—but it comes."

ENGINEERING

First Woman Member of American Society of Mechanical Engineering

KATE GLEASON made history for women engineers when she became the first woman member of the American Society of Mechanical Engineering (ASME) in 1914. She pioneered in several other ways: She was admitted as a special student in mechanical arts at Cornell University, where she was the first woman to enroll in the Sibley College of Engineering. She did not graduate from Cornell but continued her engineering education while working for her father's Gleason Works—eventually becoming its director. By 1914 she had achieved recognition for her design of the worm gear, a screw with axles at right angles to prevent its driving in reverse. A proponent of low-cost housing construction on a large scale, she purchased a village in France in 1927 and redesigned it for improvements. She also began extensive real estate developments in California and South Carolina and worked on one of the early low-cost housing developments in the Rochester, New York, area. She was chosen several times to represent ASME at world conferences, and in 1930 she was appointed special representative of the Engineering Society at the World Power Conference in Germany. Ms. Gleason died in 1933.

First Woman Admitted to American Society of Civil Engineers

Engineer ELSIE EAVES was the first woman admitted to two engineering societies—the American Society of Civil Engineers (1927) and the American Association of Cost Engineers (AACE). Also one of the first women to be national chairperson of a technical society committee (the AACE's International Cost Index Committee), first to receive the AACE's award of merit (1967) and to be made an honorary life member (1973), and the first woman life member of the National Society of Professional Engineers, Ms. Eaves says that she and her career advanced because she had the approval and backing of top management. But she thinks that "girls coming into engineering now have a problem," because of the growing pressures put on male employers and their colleagues as their numbers increase.

In the Back Door to Bioengineering

ALICE STOLL entered the engineering field by way of "the back door" in "the days when bioengineering had not yet been invented and interdisciplinary activities scarcely existed." Head of the Biophysics Laboratory, Crew Systems Department of the Navy in Warminster, Pennsylvania, Ms. Stoll has been active in the American Society of Mechanical

Engineering's Committee on Heat Transfer in Technology as technical reviewer, occasional chairwoman of sessions, and author and symposium participant. Receiving her master's degree in physiology and biophysics from Cornell, she served in the U. S. Navy during World War II, and retired as commander from the Naval Reserve. She has worked on the cardiovascular effects of acceleration and carried out research on tissue damage and pain sensation. She is a fellow of the American Association for the Advancement of Science and associate fellow and charter member of the Biophysical Society. Alice Stoll believes that, although engineering traditionally has been considered other than "woman's work," much of the necessary pioneering by women is already done and opposition to female engineers is gradually crumbling.

First Fellow of the Canadian Aeronautical and Space Institute

Canadian ELSIE GREGORY MACGILL, the first woman in North America to become a chief aeronautical engineer of any company, and the first woman to design, build, and test her own plane, is internationally known for her work on engineering designs of both fighter and transport aircrafts. During World War II, she was in charge of engineering for Canadian production of the Hawker Hurricane fighter aircraft for England and the Curtiss Helldiver for the U. S. Navy; later she was aeronautical engineer for Fairchild Aircraft Ltd., and chief aeronautical engineer for Canadian Car and Foundry Company, Ltd. Ms. MacGill received her bachelor of applied science degree in electrical engineering at the University of Toronto in Ontario, and her master's degree in aeronautical engineering at the University of Michigan—first woman at both these universities to obtain these degrees. She studied for her doctorate at the Massachusetts Institute of Technology. She holds several other "firsts": first female corporate member of the Association of Professional Engineers of Ontario, of the Engineering Institute of Canada, and of the Association of Consulting Engineers of Canada; and first female fellow of the Canadian Aeronautical and Space Institute. She has received the Gzowski Medal from the Engineering Institute of Canada, the annual medal of the Society of Women Engineers, and she was the only woman among 50 Canadian business leaders to receive the Gevaert Gallery recognition.

Society of Women Engineers Achievement Award*

1952 Maria Telkes
      utilization of solar energy
1953 Elsie Gregory MacGill
      aeronautical engineering
1954 Edith Clarke
      stability theory and circuit analysis
1955 Margaret H. Hutchinson
      chemical engineering
1956 Elise F. Harmon
      component and circuit miniaturization
1957 Rebecca H. Sparling
      high-temperature metallurgy, non-destructive testing of metals

1958 Mabel M. Rockwell
      electrical control systems
1959 Désiree LeBleu
      rubber reclamation
1960 Esther M. Conwell
      solid state research
1961 Laurel van der Wal
      space biology
1962 Laurence D. Pellier
      metallurgy
1963 Beatrice Hicks
      theoretical study and analysis

* This award is given each year to a woman who has made a significant contribution in the field of engineering practice, research, education, or administration.

of sensing devices under extreme environmental conditions

1964 **Grace Murray Hopper**
original computer programming systems

1965 **Martha J. Thomas**
engineering, education, and combustion

1966 **Dorothy Martin Simon**
space engineering, especially in combustion

1967 **Marguerite M. Rogers**
air-delivered tactical weapons

1968 **Isabella L. Karle**
development of unique procedures for crystal structure analysis

1969 **Alice Stoll**
development of fire-resistant fibers and fabrics, based on studies of heat transfer by flame contact

1970 **Irmgard Flügge-Lotz**
fluid mechanics, particularly wing theory and boundary layer theory

1971 **Alva T. Matthews**
engineering mechanics and applied mathematics

1972 **Nancy D. Fitzroy**
heat transfer, fluid flow, properties of materials, and thermal engineering

1973 **Irene Carswell Peden**
radio wave propagation and electrical engineering education

1974 **Barbara Crawford Johnson**
manned space flight program support

1975 **Sheila E. Widnall**
research on aircraft wake turbulence and aerodynamic noise

1976 **Ida I. Pressman**
power control systems

1977 **Mildred S. Dresselhaus**
electrical engineering

First Recipient of the Society of Women Engineers Achievement Award

Hungarian-born MARIA TELKES was the first recipient, in 1952, of the Achievement Award given by the Society of Women Engineers as the highest tribute each year to a woman who has made a significant contribution to engineering. Dr. Telkes received her bachelor's degree and Ph.D. in physical chemistry from the University of Budapest. An early and consistently devoted believer in the ultimate feasibility of solar energy as the earth's major power source, she has devised numerous solar-powered appliances —among them a solar still for life rafts, a solar-powered oven, and solar heating equipment for houses. She holds many patents. Since coming to the United States in 1927, she has held research jobs with Westinghouse, the Massachusetts Institute of Technology, and the College of Engineering of New York University; and was research director of the solar energy laboratory of the Princeton division of Curtiss-Wright Company, and for the Institute for Direct Energy Conversion of the University of Pennsylvania.

First Woman Engineering Professor at Stanford

IRMGARD FLÜGGE-LOTZ, born and educated in Germany, became the first woman to attain the rank of full professor in the engineering college at Stanford University. With a doctor of engineering degree from the Technical University of Hannover, Germany, she became a department head (of theoretical aerodynamics) at Göttingen University and was a scientific adviser in fluid mechanics to German and French research institutes. She joined the Stanford faculty in 1949 and in 1960 was made professor emerita of engineering mechanics and aeronautics and astronautics. Among the world's leading authorities and major theorists of fluid mechanics, in particular the theory of aerodynamics wing and boundary layers, as well as satellite stability control, she wrote numerous papers and articles, one of which, on the computation of the lift distribution of wings, represents a major contribution to modern aircraft design. Dr. Flügge-Lotz died in 1974.

First Chairperson of MIT Department of Electrical Engineering

Electrical engineer MILDRED S. DRESSELHAUS grew up in the ghettos of New York City during the Depression. She describes her background as one "of extreme poverty and disadvantage." As a child she taught mentally retarded children to read and write; she worked three hours a day, five days a week, for 50 cents a week. During her high school years she worked in factories and sweatshops, under difficult conditions for very low wages, and came to realize that an education was imperative. With no encouragement from her teachers or friends she studied hard by herself and passed the entrance exams to Hunter College High School, where she excelled in her studies. She then was accepted at Hunter College and in 1951–52 was awarded a Fulbright fellowship to the Cavendish Laboratory in England. After further study at Radcliffe and the University of Chicago, where she earned her Ph.D., she went on to spend seven of "the most productive years of my research career" at MIT's Lincoln Laboratory. In 1972 Dr. Dresselhaus became the first woman to chair the Massachusetts Institute of Technology's prestigious Department of Electrical Engineering. There she encourages other women to pursue engineering careers, has established the Institute's Women's Forum, and has held the Abby Rockefeller Mauze Professorship. Dr. Dresselhaus became the second of five women members of the National Academy of Engineers. The others are GRACE MURRAY HOPPER (see "Women in the Military," p. 538), Drs. BETSY ANCKER-JOHNSON, RUTH DAVIS, and JEAN E. SAMMET). In 1977 Dr. Dresselhaus received the Award of the Society of Women Engineers.

First Woman Engineer from George Washington University

Electrical engineer and manager MARJORIE RHODES TOWNSEND, who was born in Washington, D.C., and became the first woman to receive an engineering degree (B.E.E.) of any kind from George Washington University, has pioneered in the use of satellites to study X rays in galactic and intergalactic space. In 1948 she joined the National Bureau of Standards as a physical science aide and successively took more important positions with the Naval Research Laboratory and then with the Goddard Space Flight Center. As director of the Small Astronomy Satellite Program, Ms. Townsend is responsible for the inception, design, construction, and testing of the satellites as well as for the launches themselves. The satellites locate and map sources of X rays and gamma rays in the earth's other galaxies, which provide information on the existence and location of pulsars and black holes. She has received several awards, including NASA's Exceptional Service Medal, and in 1973 the Knight of the Italian Republic Order from the Italians for her outstanding contribution to joint United States-Italian space exploration efforts.

Scientific Information Innovator

JACQUELINE JUILLARD, of Swiss nationality, received her early schooling in England, Germany, Spain, and Switzerland, and was graduated as a chemical engineer from the École Polytechnique Fédérale of Lausanne, Switzerland. Assistant manager of the Geneva Radium Institute after World War II, she then became scientific collaborator for information and documentation for Swiss pharmaceutical firms. While publishing scientific articles, she worked as literature scientist in the technical information division at the Battelle Geneva Research Center and was the first to head its newly established Information and Public Relations Service. After other assignments at Battelle, she left in 1976 to create her own firm in industrial documentation and scientific information. She has been active as a member of the executive bureau of the Swiss Association for Atomic Energy and of the Swiss National Commission for UNESCO and is a member of the Swiss Society of Engineers and Architects, the American Society of Women Engineers, and the Academic Council of the University of Geneva. The mother of three, and grandmother of one, Ms. Juillard is also the author of *The Atom, a Source of Energy,* published in French and German.

Her Career: Putting a Man on the Moon

BARBARA CRAWFORD JOHNSON, **in 1946 the first woman to earn a bachelor's degree in engineering from the University of Illinois, has devoted much of her career to putting an astronaut on the moon and, more specifically, getting him safely home. (In the first years of the space program, all astronauts were men. The women chosen in early 1978 appear in "Far-Out Women," p. 740.) Manager of systems requirements for the space shuttle program in Rockwell International's Space Division in California, she supervised early trajectories and was in charge of design and performance analysis for the Apollo missions, Skylab, and the Apollo-Soyez test programs. She has received numerous honors and awards, including the Achievement Award of the Society of Women Engineers, and a medallion presented by NASA in recognition of the role she played in support of the first lunar landing.**

First Woman Member of American Institute of Chemical Engineers

MARGARET HUTCHINSON, elected a member of the American Institute of Chemical Engineers, was also the first woman to earn a Ph.D. in chemical engineering from the Massachusetts Institute of Technology. After graduation from Rice University, Texas, she went to work for E. B. Badger and Sons, which later merged with Stone and Webster Engineering Corporation, where she is now a chemical engineering consultant. One of the few women in the field who have been in actual charge of designing a large chemical plant, in the early 1950s, she was personally responsible for the design of radically new equipment that significantly improved the productivity of modern chemical plants. In 1955 she was given the Achievement Award of the Society of Women Engineers.

First Woman to Serve on Board of World's Largest Engineering Society

IRENE CARSWELL PEDEN, professor of electrical engineering and associate dean of the College of Engineering at the University of Washington, Seattle, was in 1975 the first woman to serve on the Board of Directors and the executive committee of the world's largest engineering society, the Institute of Electrical and Electronics Engineers (IEEE). In 1976 she was reelected to a second term as vice-president for educational activities of the Institute. An IEEE fellow (one of six women) and a member of the Engineers Council for Professional Development, she was also the first woman to receive an engineering doctorate from Stanford University and the first American woman engineer/scientist to conduct fieldwork in the interior of the Antarctic continent. Dr. Peden has been cited by the Society of Women Engineers for outstanding achievement in two distinct areas—as a prominent radio scientist active in research on radio wave propagation, with emphasis on studies in the Antarctic region; and as a distinguished educator in the field of electrical engineering. "Engineering is a reasonable, workable, and potentially satisfying career choice for young women," she says.

First Director of DOT Office of University Research

At the U. S. Department of Transportation, SHEILA E. WIDNALL, as the first director of the Office of University Research, was responsible for a $5 million program. Dr. Widnall, who holds an M.Sc. and Sc.D. in aeronautics and astronautics from the Massachusetts Institute of Technology, and was a Ford postdoctoral fellow there, is now on the MIT faculty. Her major research activities have included experiments on aerodynamics noise, aerodynamics of wings and bodies, aeroelasticity and vibration, and prediction of unsteady air loads on launch vehicles due to turbulence, shock oscillation, and flow separation. She has served as adviser to the National Science Foundation and the U. S. Air Force, received the American Institute of Aeronautics and Astronautics Lawrence Sperry Award and in 1975 the Achievement Award of the Society of Women Engineers, including a life membership in the Society.

First Woman to Become a Certified Clinical Engineer

THELMA ESTRIN has a long list of "first woman" titles—first to be president of the 7,000-member Engineers in Medicine and Biology Group of the Institute of Electrical and Electronics Engineers (IEEE); first to become a council member of the Alliance for Engineering in Medicine and Biology; first to become a member of the board of directors of the Biomedical Engineering Society; and first to be named chairperson of the Sig-

nal Processing and Information Handling Technical Committee of IEEE. As one of six women who are IEEE fellows, out of a total of 3,600, she also chairs the organization's Committee on Professional Opportunities for Women.

First Woman Scholar of ASME

The regional industrial hygienist of Shell Oil Company's occupational safety and health program, CAROLYN F. PHILLIPS was the first woman recipient of the Woman's Auxiliary Sylvia W. Farny Scholarship given by the American Society of Mechanical Engineers (ASME). She was also the first woman named to the policy board of the 70,000-member American Society of Mechanical Engineers. With degrees from the New York Institute of Environmental Medicine and Post-Graduate Medical School, she received her Ph.D. from the Graduate School of Engineering and Science. She found her own special niche in the field of industrial hygiene, which intrigued her because of the interdisciplinary nature of the work—engineering, health, the laboratory, and the assembly line. Her jobs of identifying and preventing occupational health problems have taken her into many areas and activities of industry, from tiny electronics parts to massive turbines, from quarries to refineries, from the beginnings to the ends of production lines.

First to Develop a Cost Estimate and Schedule for Coal Plant

MARJATTA STRANDELL PAYNE, born in Finland, initiated and taught the first cost engineering course given by a woman—at Portland State University in Oregon. This sophisticated method of analyzing cost as a factor of design is very rarely taught in engineering institutions. She also was the first woman to develop a specialized analysis and schedule plan (WBS or work breakdown structure, as it is called in the trade) on how much it costs to build a coal-fired plant and operate a coal mine. With an engineering and business administration degree from the University of Helsinki, she worked as technical adviser to the Finnish Government, and also counseled the German and French governments, until she came to the United States and started working with Southern California Edison. At present employed with the Pacific Power and Light Company in Portland, this knowledgeable engineer in cost and scheduling practice was the first woman to carry out studies of labor productivity in power plant construction and to present a technical paper on that subject.

First Woman Registered Structural Engineer in California

District structural engineer in California's Office of the State Architect, RUTH VIDA GORDON is responsible for the safe construction of public schools and hospitals, particularly in line with the earthquake safety acts of that state. Earning her master's degree from Stanford University, she was the first woman recipient of the Wing and Garland scholarships given to civil engineering students. She worked for San Francisco firms on the designs of various types of buildings, power plants, and dams, and became Registered Structural Engineer No. 980, State of California (the first woman), and first woman member of the Structural Engineers' Association of Northern California. Married and the mother of three college students, Ms. Gordon believes that career guidance for young women should begin earlier than in the junior and senior high school years, before it is too late for them to take the whole sequence of math and science courses that are prerequisite to freshman college requirements, and before they have been "turned off from those subjects." She strongly urges that girls in the elementary and particularly the primary grades be taken on field trips to places where they can see professional women working not only as engineers, but as "physicians, attorneys, veterinarians."

First Woman Award Winner in Electronics Quality Control

The director of corporate strategic resources for Westinghouse Electric Corporation, NAOMI J. McAFEE, who has a B.S. in physics from Western Kentucky State College and took postgraduate courses at Johns Hopkins, is the first woman to be presented a major award of the electronics division of the American Society for Quality Control—"for outstanding services to the society, division, and profession." She is also the first woman elected to the Society's board of directors and executive committee and first woman member of the board of directors of the Engineering Joint Council. Ms. McAfee is married to an engineer with whom she shares many interests. She believes that marriage and career can mix, and advises young woman engineers, "Know your boss. Learn to talk to him on a reasonable, rational basis. Tell him . . . what your career goals are and the time schedule for accomplishing them. If you don't tell him, he will never know."

Shock Waves, Concrete, and Helicopter Blades Expert

Research engineer ALVA T. MATTHEWS, consultant and former senior research engineer with Paul Weidlinger Associates, is noted in the engineering world for fundamental research on the mechanical behavior of materials subjected to dynamic impact loads, called shock waves. Her basic work has influenced the development of models for shock-wave propagation in soil and rock and has extended to studies of the effects of nuclear explosions on structures. Dr. Matthews' other achievements include the structural design of thin shell concrete, the development of Telstar tracking antennas, and the design of helicopter blades. Consultant to the Rochester Applied Science Associates, and associate professor in the University of Rochester's Department of

Mechanical and Aerospace Science, she holds a master's degree with honors and a doctorate in engineering mechanics from Columbia University.

First Woman Faculty Member in Canadian Engineering Department

HELEN E. HOWARD-LOCK became the first woman faculty member in the Department of Engineering Physics at McMaster University, Ontario. She has been carrying out research and teaching in areas including holography, applications of lasers and spectroscopy, and the molecular dynamics and morphology of materials. She is particularly interested in applications of spectroscopy to remote sensing of the environment, and is currently coordinating a new graduate course on this topic. She also has undertaken a research study for Environment Canada on the development of remote-sensing technology, particularly for detecting and monitoring petroleum spills on water. As spectroscopy consultant for the Coderg Company in France, she does interpretive work in this area and makes recommendations on instrumentation. Dr. Howard-Lock has also been interested in the production and properties of cement for obtaining ultra-high-strength concrete and applying it to construction. Concerned over the lack of women in engineering and physics, Dr. Howard-Lock believes that positive steps should be taken to encourage women to enter these fields. "The restraining forces of tradition, women's perception of themselves, and men's perception of women must be changed," she says.

First Woman President of the Society of Engineering Illustrators in Detroit

In 1971 ANN FLETCHER, technical assistant to the chief engineer at Shatterproof Glass Corporation, was elected the first woman president of the Society of Engineering Illustrators in Detroit; she was then reelected for another term. In 1975 she was the first woman chairperson of

the Affiliate Council of the Engineering Society of Detroit—a group of 50 engineering societies representing some 7,000 engineers. In 1976 she was named to the College of Fellows of the Engineering Council of Detroit—the first woman among the 83 selected during that group's 80-year history.

First Woman Member of Policy Board of Engineering Society

NANCY D. FITZROY is the only woman member of the Policy Board of Education, one of five policy boards of the American Society of Mechanical Engineers (ASME). A graduate of Rensselaer Polytechnic Institute in 1949, she went to work as a practicing engineer at General Electric's Corporate Research and Development Division because she enjoyed it—and more than a quarter century later she still enjoys working. As advanced product planner for General Electric's gas turbine division, Ms. Fitzroy has been honored for her contributions in fields of heat transfer, fluid flow, properties of materials, and thermal engineering. She received an Achievement Award in 1972 from the Society of Women Engineers, has been elected chairperson of the Hudson-Mohawk Section of ASME—the first woman to be so honored—and was the first woman to serve as secretary of ASME's Mid-Atlantic Regional Activities Council. "Working with all male engineers seems to pose no more problems than it did when going through engineering school," she says. "Engineers in general are some of the most even-tempered, steadiest people I have met. . . . But may I add that, for a girl, it helps to be just a little bit better."

First Woman Engineer with Ford Motor Company

YVONNE CLARK, born in 1929, was the first woman in the history of Howard University, Washington, D.C., to receive a B.S. in mechanical engineering, first woman in the Vanderbilt University

Graduate School of Engineering Management, and then became the first female engineer to be employed with the Ford Motor Company glass plant, at a time when many industries weren't hiring black engineers—and certainly not black women engineers. When Ms. Clark was a little girl, she had dreams of flying airplanes and fixing everything from the home toaster to the furnace. But as a Kentucky high school student, she was not permitted to study mechanical drawing. It wasn't "proper" for girls. Today she is an associate professor in the mechanical engineering department at Tennessee State University. Lack of understanding and counseling should be blamed for the scarcity of women in technical fields, Ms. Clark believes. "Women engineers are qualified and competent, and do just as good a job as men," she said. "It's not a man's field, and there's no reason we shouldn't be equal."

First Woman Engineer at Western Electric

Electrical engineer BEATRICE HICKS, who resolved while still in high school that engineering was to be her field, in the 1960s became the only woman engineer at Western Electric. President and director of her late husband's consulting firm of Rodney D. Chipp & Associates, and consultant to Nus Corporation, an equipment-manufacturing company once owned by her father, Ms. Hicks graduated from Newark College of Engineering, and worked there while studying for a master's degree in physics at Stevens Institute. With an honorary Sc.D. from Hobart and William Smith colleges, Geneva, New York, Dr. Hicks became chief engineer in 1945 at Newark Controls Company, a firm specializing in environmental sensing devices, and in 1955 was made its president. A registered professional engineer in New York and New Jersey, Dr. Hicks is one of the founding members of the Society of Women Engineers.

At Work on the World's First Floating Nuclear Plant

As manager of radiation engineering at Offshore Power Systems, a subsidiary of Westinghouse Electric Corporation in Jacksonville, Florida, MARY ANN CAPO is helping to develop the first floating nuclear power plant in the world. She is responsible for all safety shielding of biological organisms around the plant, as well as for defining the radiation sources and determining radiation exposure inside and outside the plant. A 1952 graduate in mathematics and physics from Carlow College in Pennsylvania, Ms. Capo spent six years in methods development related to radiation analysis for the General Electric Corporation on their aircraft nuclear propulsion project. She then worked eleven years with Westinghouse Astronuclear Laboratory on design and analysis for the nuclear engine rocket vehicle application project.

First Woman Engineering Mechanics Ph.D. at University of Alabama

RUTH ANN CADE, born in 1937, associate professor of computer science and statistics at the University of Southern Mississippi, was the first woman engineer on the faculty. She is also the first woman to complete a Ph.D. degree in engineering mechanics at the University of Alabama, and the first woman engineering instructor at that university. At a time when no women members were allowed, she was recognized by the men's engineering honor society Tau Beta Pi at Mississippi State University, but had to wait for the rules to be changed before she could be initiated.

First Nuclear Power Plant Operator

In 1976, at the age of 23, nuclear engineer ROBERTA A. KANKUS became the first woman—and almost certainly the youngest person—ever licensed to be a commercial nuclear power plant operator. She had been working as an assistant mechanical engineer for the Philadelphia Electric Company when she discovered that no woman in the country held the position of operator, nor were any in training. She applied, went through 14 months of on-the-job training, and passed the rigorous operator's license test.

First Woman Graduate of Stevens Institute of Technology

In 1974 19-year-old LENORE H. SCHUPAK was the first woman to be graduated from the 104-year-old Stevens Institute of Technology. She had been among the first 18 women to be admitted to the school in 1971. By taking extra courses in the summer and during the regular academic year, she completed the four-year program in three years. She concentrated her research on waste-disposal projects, studying legal economics and the effects on public opinion of recycling garbage into useful products such as building materials. After college she continued studying, taking special seminars on environmental law and effectiveness of impact statements, and she received her master's degree in environmental engineering from Syracuse University in 1977. From 1974 to the present she has worked as a development engineer in resource recovery and solid waste management at an air-conditioner corporation in Syracuse. Ms. Schupak's home environment may have contributed to her career choice—her father is a structural engineer. Another factor was her involvement in a solid-waste disposal science project in her high school. "I was trying to find a use for refuse," she said, "and I thought the only way that I could further the study was to go to an engineering school."

5

Women in Medicine and Health Care

By Carol Eron

Dr. Jane Wright and Dr. Lawrence J. Eron,
consulting editors

"Certain women seek to rival men in manly sports . . . and even the strong-minded ape them in all things, even in dress. In doing so they may command a sort of admiration such as all monstrous productions inspire, especially when they tend towards a higher type than their own . . ."

That was the president of the American Medical Association addressing the organization in 1871. To judge by the outrage of the profession when a few determined women began in the mid-19th century to acquire medical education, one might think that the concept of woman as physician was revolutionary. It was nothing of the sort.

Since antiquity women have served as healers, doctors, nurses, and midwives. One of the earliest recorded was an Egyptian, Merit Ptah, who was described as "Chief Physician" and is pictured in the tomb of the Valley of the Kings. Among Roman physicians, Aspasia was well known. Her medical writings were lost, but her work and ideas survive in the writings of her colleagues. There were prominent women physicians throughout succeeding centuries, and in the art of midwifery women reigned.

In 1754, DOROTHEA CHRISTIANE ERXLEBEN, the daughter of a German physician, obtained a medical degree—the first woman in Germany to do so. Her father instructed her in medicine and she assisted him in his practice. Frederick the Great ordered her admitted to the University of Halle and later presented her with the medical degree.

But generally, in early modern times, women began to be pushed out of medicine. They were discouraged and then prohibited outright from studying and practicing. In England from the early 17th century, women could not be licensed to practice surgery, and pharmacology was closed to them as well, although English women continued to make important contributions to medicine. One of them, Lady MARY WORTLEY MONTAGU, living in Constantinople at the beginning of the 18th century, observed that Turkish mothers had their children inoculated by specially trained women against smallpox. She had her own son successfully inoculated and, returning to England, introduced the method of protection there—years before Edward Jenner made his discovery.

In Colonial America, there were many women healers, both general practitioners and midwives. ANNE HUTCHINSON, a founder of Rhode Island, was a general practitioner, as was HARRIET TUBMAN. But here too, as the medical profession developed, women began to be excluded.

In the mid-19th century, ELIZABETH BLACKWELL caused a scandal when she succeeded in being admitted to Geneva Medical College in New York. She completed the one-year course of study, passed the examinations, and after much debate by the faculty received a medical degree in 1849, becoming the first accredited woman doctor in the country. (Her alma mater did not admit another woman for many years.) Small numbers of women followed her example, but opposition was fierce. The profession protested that it was improper, unnatural, and wasteful, since most women would never practice anyway.

Despite such opposition, the first medical school in the world for women, the Boston Female Medical College, which trained midwives, opened in 1848. And the following year, the first coeducational medical school was founded, Central Medical College of New York. Harvard Medical School attempted coeducation in 1850; one woman was admitted (along with three blacks), but the students rioted and HARRIOT HUNT withdrew. Harvard did not venture into coeducation again until 1945.

The year 1850 also saw the opening in Philadelphia of the Female Medical College of Pennsylvania—the first medical school in the world devoted exclusively to the education of women physicians. Other women's medical colleges were soon established, and by the 1880s there were 2,400 accredited American women doctors, most of them working in obstet-

rics and gynecology, with a few in internal medicine and general practice. Their patients were reported to be primarily women and children. A study conducted by the dean of the Female Medical College showed that marriage was interfering very little with women physicians' professional work: two thirds of those surveyed were married and only 5 per cent were not practicing medicine because of marriage or family.

In Europe also, and in Asia, women were breaking down barriers. Switzerland was the first European country where women gained the right to study medicine, at the University of Zurich in 1864. Before the end of the century women had gained access to the medical examinations in Scandinavia, Holland, France, and England. Actually, the first woman doctor in Britain was Dr. JAMES MIRANDA BARRY, who successfully impersonated a man for over 50 years, from the time of her student days at the University of Edinburgh until she died in 1865 after a long career as a medical officer of the British Army and as the first Inspector-General for Hospitals in Canada. The fact that she was a woman —who had once given birth to a child— was only discovered after her death at the age of 68.

In a number of European countries, women have gone on to achieve a fair place in the profession: in Finland, 28 per cent of physicians are now women; in Denmark and Britain, 25 per cent, and in the Soviet Union, 70 per cent. In India, large numbers of women have become physicians and surgeons since the 19th century.

Progress in the United States has not been steady. The first outstanding men's medical college to accept women regularly was Johns Hopkins, in 1893; MARY E. GARRETT, a Baltimore millionaire, contributed the funds needed to open the newly completed medical school—on the condition that women be admitted on the same terms as men. Following the example of Johns Hopkins, some other schools began accepting women as medical students, but there were holdouts until 1960, when the last school to bar women, Philadelphia's Jefferson Medical College, capitulated. Once educated, women had difficulty obtaining internships, residencies, and hospital staff positions. In 1934, 28 per cent of medical schools still had no women graduates, and in 1944, 21 per cent of the hospitals in the country had never employed a woman physician.

During World War I, women doctors who volunteered to serve in the military were turned down, although during the Civil War Dr. MARY WALKER (see the chapter "Women in the Military," p. 534) had earned the Army's Medal of Honor for her service on the battlefield. By World War II, however, American attitudes had shifted sufficiently that women were inducted and allowed to serve on a temporary basis. More women began to enroll in medical schools after the war, but the proportion of women doctors rose only slightly, reaching a high of 10 per cent. Currently, 8 per cent, or about 30,000 of the United States' 400,000 doctors, are women.

The good news is that the number of women entering medical school has doubled recently. In 1975, 24 per cent of new medical students were women—an increase of 700 per cent since 1959. This means that in approximately seven years almost one fourth of doctors entering practice will be women, and knowledgeable health professionals estimate that the pattern will continue. If it does, by the end of the century up to 50 per cent of U.S. doctors will be women.

Many of the women who have led the way are scarcely known. Until recently there was little effort made to document their work. *Two Centuries of American Medicine: The Men Who Made It Great* is typical of reference works on the subject. As far as possible, I have included those women who made major contributions to medical knowledge and to nursing, and women who have set an example with their special cunning or intrepidity. To be sure, many have been left out—to write about all the women who have made or are making contributions to medicine would take volumes.

CAROL ERON, *a writer whose articles and reviews have appeared in the* Washington Post, *the international* Herald Tribune, Boston Magazine, *the* Boston Globe, Reader's Digest, *and other publications, has been an editor of the* Washington Post *and managing editor of the* Boston Phoenix. *In 1977 she did a study of rural doctors for the U. S. Department of Health, Education, and Welfare and in 1978 began work on a book about viruses. Ms. Eron lives in Washington, D.C., with her doctor husband (below) and 3-year-old son, Ethan.*

Consulting editor LAWRENCE J. ERON, M.D., *is a specialist in infectious diseases. He has been a senior research investigator at the Food and Drug Administration, where he studied slow viruses that cause the neurological disease, subacute sclerosing panencephalitis. A 1966 graduate of Princeton University, he received his medical training at Harvard and Massachusetts General Hospital.*

Consulting editor JANE WRIGHT, M.D., *is a professor of surgery at New York Medical College (see p. 215).*

PHYSICIANS

First Woman Doctor in the United States

A friend suggested that ELIZABETH BLACK-WELL become a doctor. "The very thought of dwelling on the physical structure of the body and its various ailments filled me with disgust," she said later, but she was bored with teaching school and the idea of becoming a doctor began to grow on her. She took positions as governess in the homes of physicians in order to read in their libraries and prepare for medical school. One doctor told her: "You might as well lead a revolution as try to be a physician." But another, a prominent Philadelphia physician, recommended her to a small school (later to become Hobart) in Geneva, New York, and it was because of him that she wasn't rejected out of hand by the faculty. She had applied to 11 medical schools and was rejected by all before being admitted to the Geneva school in 1848. The faculty left the question of her admittance up to the students, a rowdy group by all accounts, who voted to admit her as a joke. There was widespread shock at the idea of a woman medical student, and boardinghouses in the town refused to take her in.

Elizabeth Blackwell proved to be a fine student, and after much debate among the faculty as to whether a woman should receive an M.D., she was graduated in January 1849. The medical profession was not amused. No American hospital would admit her. She went to Paris, then England for further study, and returned to New York in 1851 to open a practice.

Dr. Blackwell had wanted to become a surgeon, but the loss of vision in one eye while she was abroad put an end to that plan. At first she was ostracized; no one would even rent her space for an office, so she purchased a house and later established a small dispensary, which in 1857 was expanded to become a hospital —the New York Infirmary for Women and Children. It was the first hospital with an all-woman staff and the first in the country where female students could get clinical experience. Her older sister, EMILY BLACKWELL, had also become a physician, and she was a partner in the hospital—said to be the first to provide home visits for poor patients and to employ a physician as a "sanitary visitor" to advise women on hygiene and nursing care. In 1868 Dr. Blackwell went on to establish the Women's Medical College of the New York Infirmary. It set high standards, requiring a longer course of study than many other schools, and entrance exams; it also was the first medical school to create a chair of hygiene, which Elizabeth Blackwell held for a year before deciding to return to her birthplace, England, where she had earlier helped found the London School of Medicine for Women. Although she was an American citizen, she remained abroad, devoting herself to the cause of women in medicine. She herself taught hundreds of women, in addition to practicing and writing.

Dr. Blackwell never married, although she adopted an orphan who was her friend and companion for the rest of her life. She authored a number of books, including an autobiography, *Pioneer Work in Opening the Medical Profession to Women,* and many pamphlets and essays on moral reform. She opposed vaccinations and animal experimentation. At the age of 89, Dr. Blackwell was injured in an accidental fall in Scotland, and she died in 1910.

"It is to be regretted that she had been induced to depart from the appropriate sphere of her sex and led to aspire to honors and duties which, by the order of nature and the common consent of the world, devolves alone upon men."—The *Boston Medical and Surgical Journal,* when Elizabeth Blackwell was awarded an M.D., the first woman in the United States to attain this distinction, in 1849.

"Dr. Webster sent for me to examine a case of a poor woman at his rooms. 'Twas a horrible exposure; indecent for any poor woman to be subjected to such a torture . . . I felt more than ever the necessity of my mission. But I went home out of spirits, I hardly know why . . . I felt alone. I must work by myself all life long."—Dr. Elizabeth Blackwell, December 4, 1847

The Second Woman Doctor in the United States and First Woman Professor in a Medical School

LYDIA FOLGER FOWLER was born in Nantucket, Massachusetts, in 1822 and received her early education there. In 1849 she was admitted to the Central Medical College of New York and graduated in 1850, the second woman in the country to receive an M.D. degree. She went on to become the first woman professor in an American medical school, at her alma mater. After the college folded, Dr. Fowler was active as a practitioner and lecturer, and she is remembered for her advocacy of women physicians. She argued that many women would rather not be treated than be examined by a man.

First Woman Intern in the United States

In 1851, SARAH ADAMSON DOLLEY, a graduate of Central Medical College in New York, became the United States' first woman intern, at Blockley Hospital, Philadelphia. The following year she married a professor of anatomy and went into a practice devoted to the care of women and children. Dr. Dolley was a Quaker who became determined to study medicine after seeing an anatomy text-

book belonging to an uncle who was a physician. Her "highest ambition" was to "help to open up to women a higher plane of thought and labor." She lived from 1829 to 1909.

The Second Dr. Blackwell

An older sister of the first American woman doctor, EMILY BLACKWELL was accepted at Rush Medical College, Chicago, in 1852. But the college was reprimanded by the state medical society for admitting a woman and she was barred after her first term. Eventually, Emily Blackwell graduated from Western Reserve University and went to work in New York with her sister. Together they turned their dispensary into the New York Infirmary for Women and Children, a sizable hospital. After her sister departed for Europe, Emily Blackwell had control of the hospital and many advances were made under her direction, particularly the setting of its high standards. It is for her insistence on excellence in women doctors that she is best remembered.

Founder of the New England Hospital for Women and Children

Daughter of a midwife and granddaughter of a veterinary surgeon, Dr. MARIE E. ZAKRZEWSKA founded the New England Hospital for Women and Children in 1862. Under her direction, it became a training center for many of the finest women physicians of the time. Dr. Zakrzewska had trained as a midwife in Berlin and was a professor of midwifery. But due to opposition and hostility from her male associates she decided to emigrate. In the United States she was befriended by Elizabeth Blackwell, who urged her to attend medical school. She was graduated in 1856 from Western Reserve. An ardent advocate of women physicians and of the highest quality training, Marie Zakrzewska has been credited with having more to do than anyone else with the success of American women in medicine. She lived from 1829 to 1902.

First U. S. Black Woman Trained in Medicine

REBECCA LEE completed the 17-week course at the New England Female Medical College in Boston and graduated in 1864, becoming the first black woman to receive medical training in the United States.

First Black Woman to Receive M.D. Degree

At the age of 23, SUSAN SMITH MCKINNEY STEWARD received her M.D. from the New York Medical College for Women, becoming the first black woman to be so honored. She was valedictorian of her class. The following year, 1871, she opened a practice in Brooklyn. Later, she did postgraduate studies at Long Island College Hospital, where she was the only woman student. In 1880, Dr. Steward helped to found a hospital for the treatment of "indisposed" shop girls. She practiced medicine and surgery among white and black patients, men, women, and children, and by the 1890s her practice had grown so large that she maintained two offices. She was married twice, had several children, and served as a church organist and choirmaster for 28 years. Dr. Steward died in 1918.

There were 65 black women physicians in the United States in 1920, according to the Census Bureau. In 1970, there were 1,051.

England's First Woman M.D.

ELIZABETH GARRETT started out as a nurse. When she finished first in a medical examination at Middlesex Hospital, the students (male) had her banned. Eventually, she gained formal recognition as an apothecary in 1865, and as a physician in Paris in 1869. Only later was she accepted in the British Medical Register. In 1866 Dr. Garrett opened a dispensary in London for women and children, staffed entirely by women, which developed into the New Hospital and London School of Medicine for Women. After World War I, the hospital was renamed for its founder. Elizabeth Garrett was inspired to become a doctor through hearing lectures by Elizabeth Blackwell and worked ceaselessly for the rights of women in medicine. She succeeded in having medical examinations opened to women candidates. Born in 1836, she died in 1917 at the age of 81.

First Woman Admitted to the École de Médecine, Paris

MARY PUTNAM JACOBI, daughter of the founder of G. P. Putnam's, publisher, had been educated in medicine in the United States but was not satisfied with the quality of her education. She became determined to study at the École de Médecine in Paris, although no woman had ever done so, and was graduated in 1871 with honors. Returning to the United States, she established herself as the leading woman physician in the country, noted for her training and her clinical abilities. She wrote on a range of topics from pathology to neurology and pediatrics, and was one of the first women to present a paper to the New York Medical Library and Journal Association. Out of concern for the quality of medical education women were receiving, she founded the Association for the Advancement of the Medical Education of Women in 1872, and by her own example is credited with doing much to raise the standards and reputation of women physicians.

First Woman Member of the AMA

SARAH HACKETT STEVENSON was educated at the State Normal University of Illinois and became a teacher in 1863. Several years later she went to Chicago to study anatomy and physiology at the Woman's Hospital Medical College. She was graduated in 1874 and, after postgraduate study abroad, opened a practice in Chicago. A year later, in 1876, Sarah Stevenson was admitted to the American Medical Association meeting in Philadelphia, having been chosen by the Illinois State Medical Society as a delegate. Dr. Stevenson is thus recognized as the first woman member of the AMA. She was also the first woman appointed to the staff of Cook County Hospital, Chicago, in 1881, and the first woman on the Illinois Board of Health, in 1893. In addition to the practice of medicine, she served as professor of physiology and histology and of obstetrics at her alma mater, helped found a school for nurses, and contributed much to the cause of medical education for women. She wrote *The Physiology of Woman, Embracing Girlhood, Maternity and Mature Age,* a popular book published in 1880. Another of her interests was the Women's Christian Temperance Union, and she was president of the National Temperance Hospital, where no medicine containing alcohol was permitted. Dr. Stevenson retired in 1903 after a cerebral hemorrhage and died six years later at the age of 68.

First Chinese Woman to Earn an M.D.

SHIH MAI-YU (Dr. MARY STONE) graduated from the Medical School of the University of Michigan in 1876, becoming the first Chinese woman to attain an M.D. She returned to China, where she founded a women's hospital in Kiukiang and served as its director for 25 years.

Founder of the San Francisco Children's Hospital

After her third child was born, CHARLOTTE BROWN left her family in California for two years to study at the Women's Medical College of Pennsylvania. She received her M.D. in 1874. Returning to California, she practiced medicine and with several other women founded a clinic for women and children. Their intent was to provide women with medical care by female doctors and to give female doctors clinical experience. In 1878 the clinic became a full-fledged hospital and later a nurses' training program was added. It eventually became known as the San Francisco Hospital for Children. Dr. Brown was one of the first four women admitted to the California Medical Society in 1876. In 1878 she was finally admitted to the San Francisco Medical Society—which had earlier rejected her—after she performed an ovariotomy, reportedly the first by a woman on the West Coast. Dr. Brown died in 1904.

First Woman to Receive a Ph.D. from the University of Pennsylvania

Dr. ALICE BENNETT (1857–1925), a graduate of the Woman's Medical College of Pennsylvania and an anatomy demonstrator there, became the first woman to receive a Ph.D. degree from the University of Pennsylvania, in 1880. The degree was in anatomy. The same year Dr. Bennett was appointed to direct the women's division of the State Hospital for the Insane in Norristown, Pennsylvania—the first woman, as far as it can be determined, to hold such a position. Dr. Bennett was widely recognized for her innovations in the care of the insane: particularly, abolishing restraints and introducing occupational therapy. Later, she had a private practice and served as an obstetrician at the New York Infirmary for Women and Children.

Canada's First Accredited Woman Doctor and Her Daughter, First Woman to Receive an M.D. in Canada

When EMILY STOWE applied to the University of Toronto to study medicine, she was told by the president: "The doors of this university are not open to women, and I trust never will be." That was in 1865. Emily Stowe reportedly replied, "I will make it the business of my life that they will be opened." After training in medicine in New York, she returned to Toronto, where she was fined for practicing illegally. The law required that doctors be members of the Ontario College of Physicians and Surgeons, which she could not join because she had not attended a Canadian medical school. Finally, her colleagues relented and Emily Stowe was permitted to attend classes at the university—although the walls had to be whitewashed four times during her year there because the other students drew pictures to shock her. In 1880 Dr. Stowe was recognized as a practitioner, and in 1883 she helped organize the Women's Medical College. She also established the first women's suffrage club in the city, camouflaged as the Women's Literary Club.

Fittingly, Emily Stowe's daughter AUGUSTA STOWE-GULLEN became the first woman to receive a medical degree in Canada; it was from the Toronto School of Medicine in 1883.

An Early Public Health Reformer

Dr. ANNIE DANIEL was graduated from the Woman's Medical College of the New York Infirmary in 1879 and specialized in obstetrics, gynecology, and pediatrics. As director of the "out-practice" service of the New York Infirmary, be-

ginning in the late 1880s, she observed the sordid, unsanitary conditions of tenement life and campaigned for legislation to improve housing standards and for an end to home manufacturing, which she believed exploited women and children and spread diseases via the manufactured items. As a physician for the Women's Prison Association of New York, Dr. Daniel instigated the employment of women matrons in police stations. But the social service of the infirmary, which she directed for sixty years, was her most valued contribution; it was a model and preceded the services of such organizations as the Henry Street Settlement and the establishment of hospital social services. Dr. Daniel died in 1944.

First Woman the AMA Listened to

In 1886 MARY HARRIS THOMPSON became a member of the American Medical Association and presented a paper before the organization. She was the first woman to do so. A graduate of the New England Female Medical College, she had come to Chicago to practice and had founded the Chicago Women and Children's Hospital, observing a great need among the poor for such an institution. In 1890 Dr. Thompson earned a second medical degree, from Chicago Medical College—the first that institution awarded to a woman.

First Hindu Woman Doctor

ANANDIBAI JOSHEE graduated from the Woman's Medical College of Pennsylvania in 1886 at the age of 21. She was the first Hindu woman, and first Indian woman, to become a medical doctor. Dr. Joshee returned to her home in Poona, India, to practice, but died the following year. Ninety years later, India has many women physicians practicing in its cities and going into its villages to attend the

sick and teach modern hygiene and birth control.

Pioneer Educator of Chinese Women Doctors

The daughter of an Ohio lawyer, MARY FULTON received her M.D. from the Woman's Medical College of Pennsylvania in 1884. She became a medical missionary to China, and in 1885 went to a remote interior area of the Kwangsi Province, where no white woman had ever been. She opened a mud-hut dispensary, but in less than a year rioting forced her to retreat to Canton. There she established and ran several dispensaries and a large general practice and taught pediatrics at the Canton Hospital. Through funds raised by Fulton and her brother many medical institutions were soon built, including a hospital for women and children, a training school for nurses and (in 1902) a medical college for women. Her goal was to train two physicians for every city and town in two provinces; by 1915 there were over sixty graduates of her medical college. Her Cantonese translations of English medical textbooks were widely used. Due to poor health she retired to California in 1918.

Founder of the First Women's Hospital in Korea

Methodist missionary Dr. META HOWARD opened the first hospital for women in Korea in 1887. Three years later, more than 3,000 patients were being treated there. It was known as "The House Where Sick Women Are Cured."

Founder of Tokyo Women's Medical College

In 1900 Dr. YAYOI YOSHIOKA, born in 1872, established Japan's first medical school for women, now known as Tokyo Women's Medical College.

First Woman M.D. of the Philippines

Dr. MARÍA PAZ MENDOZA-GUAZÓN was the first of her countrywomen to receive a high school diploma, the first to graduate from the College of Medicine, University of the Philippines, in 1912, and the first Filipina to become a certified physician. She did postgraduate work at Chicago, Harvard, and Columbia universities and went on to head the department of pathology and bacteriology at

her alma mater. She became a full professor of the University of the Philippines in 1927, organized the Philippine Association of University Women in 1928, and was first president of the Philippine Women's Medical Association.

First Woman Physician in New Zealand

Dr. FLORENCE KELLER started her career as a nurse but was advised by her professors to become a doctor. She was graduated from the American Medical Missionary College in 1900, and she and her husband, also a physician, went to Australia to practice. They next moved to New Zealand, where Florence Keller became the first woman physician. Subsequently, she was appointed physician to the Maoris and their royal family, a factor in the appointment being her ability as a horsewoman, since the job entailed much traveling through the bush.

First Woman Ophthalmologist at the Massachusetts Eye and Ear Infirmary

Daughter of a physician who so disapproved of her intention to study medicine that he withdrew financial support, MAUD CARVILL found that Harvard Medical School wasn't any help either, refusing her admission. She wound up at Tufts Medical School, studying medicine while supporting herself by simultaneously teaching in the Tufts department of physical education. After her graduation in 1905, she joined her father's practice for a time before seeking specialty training abroad. In 1914 Dr. Carvill became the first woman ophthalmologist on the staff of the estimable Massachusetts Eye and Ear Infirmary in Boston. An associate once characterized Dr. Carvill as being tough-minded but feminine—if with a touch of puritan austerity—in addition to being a first-rate physician. She was a good dressmaker and herself repaired the roof of her summer cottage in Maine. In 1933 Dr. Carvill retired from the Eye and Ear Infirmary. She died of cancer in 1944.

Industrial Medicine Pioneer and First Woman on Harvard's Medical Faculty

Early in this century, ALICE HAMILTON (1869–1970) began her crusade for worker safety. She was hired by the federal government to study and teach the prevention of factory poisons, and her work led to the introduction of worker compensation laws. She became known as the founder of the field of industrial toxicology. Appointed professor of industrial medicine at Harvard (1919) at the age of 50, Dr. Hamilton became the first woman on the Harvard medical faculty. She continued to crusade for industrial safety and health legislation well into her 80s and lived to 100.

"In dealing with manufacturers reluctant to introduce reforms," the *New York Times* once noted, "Miss Hamilton was said to rely on a disarming smile and gentle manner, but there was determination in her hazel eyes." She seemed to be willing to go to any lengths for the cause. In middle age, she inspected an Arizona copper mine by riding a flimsy elevator down 800 feet, then descending an 80-foot ladder and following a guide on her hands and knees across slippery rails above open pits. There was little in her background to augur such a career. Hamilton grew up in Fort Wayne, Indiana, one of five children in a well-to-do Irish family, attended Miss Porter's School, and earned an M.D. from the University of Michigan. In Germany she was permitted to study pathology "on condition that I make myself as inconspicuous as possible." For a time she worked at Hull House, Chicago, which inspired her to found Chicago's first baby health center, and treated many immigrants who were fatally ill from steel mill fumes as well. She quickly perceived management's technique: "to encourage a large labor turnover so that no one worker would be exposed too long."

In 1910 the state of Illinois appointed her head of its new occupational diseases commission. Shortly thereafter she was hired by the federal government, and much of her research was done as a medical consultant to the U. S. Department of Labor. Hamilton was always, as she herself put it, "on the trail of lead, mercury, nitric acid, carbon disulphide, carbon monoxide, explosives, aniline dyes, benzol, and a long list of chemicals with complicated names." She first identified silicosis in miners and wrote many important papers and several books on industrial poisons. Due largely to her early efforts, nearly every state adopted safety codes and worker compensation.

Pioneer in Therapy for Tuberculosis

In 1922 Dr. EDITH MAAS LINCOLN, a pediatrician, was appointed to start a children's chest clinic at New York's Bellevue Hospital. As head of the clinic for more than 30 years, she pioneered in using drugs to treat tuberculosis. In 1949 Dr. Lincoln reported that 12 children treated with streptomycin and promizole were recovering from two fatal forms of the disease. Later she showed that children with pulmonary tuberculosis could be treated with a drug that would prevent the development of fatal complications. A 1912 graduate of Vassar College, Dr. Lincoln attended Johns Hopkins University Medical School, and in 1917 became one of the first women interns admitted to Bellevue Hospital. On arriving at Bellevue, she once reminisced, she was urged to eat her meals with the nurses, but she insisted on eating with the other interns. In 1930 Dr. Lincoln became a member of the faculty of the New York University School of Medicine and eventually—20 years later—a clinical professor of pediatrics there. But acclaim from her colleagues came earlier: in 1939 she was appointed chairman of the pediatrics section of the New York Academy of Medicine. After retiring, Dr. Lincoln did a follow-up study on all the children she had treated, and published her findings in *Tuberculosis in Children*. She died in 1977.

First Black Woman Intern at Harlem Hospital

Dr. MAY E. CHINN was not only the first black woman to graduate from the University of Bellevue Medical Center but the first to intern, in 1926, at Harlem Hospital, then predominantly white. Until ill health forced her to retire in 1976 at the age of 80, Dr. Chinn worked as a doctor with the New York Department of Health. May Chinn's father, who had been a slave, did not approve of her going to college, but her mother scrubbed floors and cooked to help her. Reminiscing recently about the opposition to black women doctors when she was a student, Dr. Chinn said the major problem was that they were denied admission to postgraduate medical schools and hospitals. The black male doctors, she was quoted as saying in the *New York Times,* could be divided into three groups: "those who acted as if I wasn't there; another who took the attitude 'what does she think she can do that I can't do,' and the group that called themselves supporting me by sending me their night calls after midnight." In 1975, Dr. Chinn helped to found the Susan Smith McKinney Steward (see p. 202) Medical Society, one of the first organizations of black women doctors in the United States.

According to the Census Bureau, there were 65 black women doctors in the United States in 1920. By 1970, according to the Bureau, there were 1,051.

Savior of Blue Babies

The most celebrated woman doctor in the world is HELEN BROOKE TAUSSIG, who

First to Describe Kwashiorkor

Dr. CICELY WILLIAMS, who devoted her career to the health of mother and child, particularly in developing countries, was the first to describe in English a protein deficiency disease of children, kwashiorkor, prevalent in poor countries and fatal if not treated. Her observations, made while she was stationed on Africa's Gold Coast in the British Colonial Medical Service, brought the disease to wide attention. The first woman appointed to the service, Dr. Williams, who was born in Jamaica in 1893 and attended school in England, qualified in medicine at Oxford in 1923 and received the diploma in tropical medicine and hygiene from London University in 1929. Assigned to the Singapore College of Medicine, she later continued her work in mother and child health—combating malnourishment and ignorance—and made observations on other diseases common among poor children, such as malaria and pellagra. When Singapore fell to the Japanese in 1942, Dr. Williams was taken prisoner of war and subjected to harsh treatment because of her demands for the women and children of the camp. In 1948 she was appointed the first head of the World Health Organization's Maternal and Child Health division. Thereafter, she held positions at London University, the American University of Beirut, the University of Maryland, and other institutions. On her 80th birthday in 1973, she was reported to be still going strong as a full-time professor and consultant at the University School of Public Health, Tulane University. Dr. Williams once said: "We worry a great deal about the persons we want to liberate from political tyranny, and we ignore those we could and should liberate from the tyrannies of dirt, ignorance, and hunger."

originated the idea for the first successful operation for those "blue babies" born with a constricted artery between the heart and lungs that limits their oxygen. A pediatrician at Johns Hopkins for more than 30 years, Dr. Taussig said that the idea for the procedure came to her after reading about a surgeon who succeeded in tying off a vessel leading to the lungs. "Not being a surgeon," she said, "it gave me no difficulty to ask, if you can tie off a ductus, why can't you build a new one altogether?" Working with a Hopkins surgeon, Taussig developed the operation, first performed in 1945. The idea was hers, the surgical execution Dr. Alfred Blalock's. Around the world the operation was recognized as a milestone, and Blalock—a full professor at Hopkins—was elected to the National Academy of Sciences the following year.

Dr. Taussig, an assistant professor at Hopkins, was not appointed a full professor until 1959. But honors came. In 1964 she was the first woman elected president of the American Heart Association. In 1972 she was named the first woman master in the American College of Physicians and in 1973 elected to the National Academy of Sciences (see p. 223). She was made a chevalier of the French Legion of Honor and has received the Medal of Freedom, the highest civilian award a U. S. President can give, and honorary degrees from 20 universities.

The Blalock-Taussig operation has saved thousands of children's lives, but it had further implications. As a prominent surgeon explained: "By demonstrating that even the deeply cyanotic (oxygen-deprived) child could tolerate heart surgery, the Johns Hopkins team of Blalock and Taussig showed that almost any other child could, as well as adults. Their accomplishments prompted surgeons to venture where they had not dared to venture previously. The result is much of present-day cardiac surgery." Dr. Taussig also made important discoveries in the physiology of the heart and contributed to knowledge about rheumatic disease.

She was born in Cambridge, Massachusetts, in 1898 into a family of scholars. Her mother was one of the first graduates of Radcliffe College and her father an eminent Harvard economist. After attending Radcliffe and the University of California at Berkeley, where she completed her A.B. degree, Helen Taussig was determined to study medicine and was permitted to take certain courses at Harvard but not to work for a degree. She remembers a histology course in which she was not allowed to speak to any of the male students. After her graduation from Johns Hopkins Medical School in 1927, Dr. Taussig became a pediatrician and took her fellowship in cardiology. "I grew up in an atmosphere that greatly differs from that of today," she once said. "Fifty years ago, an error made by a woman was held against her, whereas any error made by a man was just a mistake!"

Since being officially retired from Hopkins, Dr. Taussig, cheerful and energetic, has continued to work an eight-hour day.

"Women are a natural in the field of medicine. Give them technique and training and you will furnish mankind with better doctors than ever before." —Bernard Baruch

Leader in the Field of Mental Retardation

One of the first clinics in the country devoted exclusively to retardation was founded by Dr. MARGARET GIANNINI in 1950. The Mental Retardation Institute of New York Medical College, directed by Dr. Giannini, is recognized as the world's largest and leading treatment center for the developmentally disabled. Dr. Giannini graduated from Hahnemann Medical College in 1945 and completed residencies in pathology and pediatrics at New York Medical College, where she later became a professor of pediatrics. As a pediatric consultant to the New York Department of Health, she has served on numerous governmental committees at state and national levels. The recipient of many awards and honors, she became president of the American Association on Mental Deficiency in 1977.

The Woman Behind the Apgar Score

The Apgar Score System is used in hospitals throughout the world to evaluate the health of newborn babies. It was devised in 1952 by anesthesiologist VIRGINIA APGAR, who observed that too little attention was being paid to newborns at the time of delivery. Often they were wrapped in a blanket and not examined in the nursery until later, when serious problems might already have developed. Dr. Apgar decided to develop a test that could be conducted by a nurse and could be done quickly, and arrived at a list of five key vital signs to be checked: heart rate, respiration, muscle tone, reflexes, and over-all color. The score could be tabulated within 60 seconds of birth; as a result of this simple test, the lives of innumerable babies have been saved. Dr. Apgar, born in 1909 in New Jersey, had intended to become a surgeon until a professor talked her out of it and encouraged her to go into anesthesiology. She took her medical training at Columbia, was graduated in 1933, and was one of five women ever to have served a surgical internship at New York's Presbyterian Hospital. In 1949 she was the first woman appointed a full professor of anesthesia at Columbia Medical School, where she taught for 10 years. Later, as director of the division of congenital malformations for the March of Dimes, Dr. Apgar became an expert in birth defects. She taught, lectured, wrote, and was responsible for allocating the foundation's research grants. This work led to her appointment as a lecturer in teratology at Cornell Medical School, the first appointment in the country in the subspecialty of birth defects. Dr. Apgar died in 1974.

First Woman Professor of Clinical Medicine

The first woman to become a professor of clinical medicine was Dr. CONNIE GUION, at New York Hospital in 1946. She was associated with the hospital for more than 50 years and maintained a busy practice as physician to many distinguished New York families until the age of 87, when her health failed. She is known for founding the Comprehensive Care Program, which has affected practice in hospitals around the world. It involves coordinating all aspects of each patient's medical care and extends the personal attention of the general practitioner into big city clinics. Dr. Guion was born on a plantation in North Carolina, was graduated from Wellesley and taught chemistry at Sweet Briar before entering Cornell Medical College. She was graduated at the top of her class in 1917 and interned at Bellevue Hospital. Among her achievements and honors, Dr. Guion was the first woman to win New York University's alumni Award of Distinction, the first woman to be an honorary member of the New York Hospital board of governors, and the first to serve on the hospital's medical board. She died in 1971 at the age of 88.

First Woman President of a State Medical Society

Dr. LESLIE SWIGART KENT was elected president of the Oregon Medical Society, becoming the first woman to be so honored—in 1948.

First Woman Doctor in the Regular United States Navy

Women had served in the reserve forces during World War II on a temporary basis. The first woman physician to be commissioned in the regular U. S. Navy was Dr. FRANCES LOIS WILLOUGHBY, in 1948. Her rank was lieutenant commander.

First Woman Doctor in the U. S. Army

A WAC reserve medical officer, Dr. FAE MARGARET ADAMS was the first woman physician to be commissioned in the regular U. S. Army, in 1953. A native of San Jose, California, Dr. Adams obtained her medical degree under the GI bill.

First Woman to Command a U. S. Army Medical Unit

Russian-born Dr. CLARA RAVEN, the first woman to command a medical unit in the United States Army, during World War II did overseas duty in Châlons-sur-Marne, Paris, and Berlin, and during the Korean War in Tokyo and Osaka. In 1961 she became the first woman to wear the eagles of a full colonel in the Medical Corps. Dr. Raven received her B.A. from the University of Michigan in 1927 and her M.D. from Northwestern University School of Medicine in 1941. She was certified in pathology. Following retirement from the military, she became deputy medical examiner in Los Angeles.

First Woman President of a Major Medical Society

Dr. EMMA SADLER MOSS of New Orleans in 1955 achieved the distinction of being the first woman to head a major medical society when she was elected president of the American Society of Clinical Pathologists.

First Woman Physician of Thailand

She ran away from home to obtain a medical education in Paris and returned ten years later to practice medicine in Thailand. Under her influence, prostitution was outlawed by the Thai Government in 1962 and homes were established for the rehabilitation and training of street women. Eventually Dr. PIERRA HOON VEIJJABU became an official in the Thai Ministry of Health's Department of Venereal Diseases. She organized and directed an orphanage and rehabilitation homes and herself adopted more than 600 children of prostitutes— keeping them until their mothers wanted them and were able to support them. She has been an ardent advocate of education for Thai women. The name Veijjabu, which means "great woman doctor," was bestowed on Dr. Hoon by the government of Thailand.

First Women Physicians at the White House

The first woman physician to a U. S. President was Dr. JANET TRAVELL, 1926 graduate of Cornell Medical School, who was the personal physician of President John Fitzgerald Kennedy. Said Robert Kennedy once: "My brother owed his very life to her medical genius." Said Dr. Travell of her appointment; "It's not I but the President who did something important . . . he put the emphasis where it belongs—on skills and training which he believes have helped him. If this has assisted others to shift their point of view about women in medicine, it will be good for all of us."

Dr. Travell was not, however, the first woman appointed to serve at the White House. Dr. ANNA EASTON LAKE was designated physician to Grover Cleveland's daughter, a cerebral palsy victim. But she suffered a stroke before she could take up the position and died in 1899. Well known in Baltimore, where she turned the ground floor of her home in a fashionable neighborhood into a free clinic and specialized in the treatment of handicapped children, she began the study of medicine while convalescing from tuberculosis and gained admittance to an all-male medical school upon one condition: that she sit behind a screen.

The Doctor Behind Dr. Kildare

After marrying, Dr. PHYLLIS WRIGHT chose to work part-time for many years. Her jobs varied from research for the Atomic Bomb Casualty Commission in Nagasaki to teaching medical students, clinic work, and medical writing. She has been medical editor of the *Ladies' Home Journal* and has served as the medical technical adviser for the "Doctor Kildare" television show. "So *many* possibilities other than practice," she has said. ". . . there was always something interesting and challenging for me to do." After her husband's death, Dr. Wright, a 1945 graduate of Cornell Medical Center, returned to work full-time to support her family. She became chief of the Crippled Children Branch for the Hawaii Department of Health.

Shared Careers

Dr. DOROTHY FEDERMAN, a 1971 graduate of the University of Pennsylvania Medical School, found a new way to be both physician and mother. She and her husband decided to share one job in a family practice in Saranac Lake, New York. The arrangement allows wife and husband to maintain separate practices and also "to live our lives without imposing on others—for example, my maternity leave means my husband fills in for me . . . providing continuity." In the tcwn of 7,000 where Dr. Dorothy Federman became the only woman physician, acceptance of her and this non-traditional arrangement by both patients and the other partners has been enthusiastic. Together the Federmans put in about 60 to 70 hours a week at work; one of them is usually at home while the other is at the office. "I never felt that my desire to be a doctor as well as a mother was unnatural," she wrote in 1977 in the Barnard alumnae magazine. "Perhaps this unselfconscious confidence in women was the important thing."

Medical Director of the International Rescue Committee

As medical director of the International Rescue Committee in Thailand, Dr. DOMINICA GARCÍA has had the impossible task of dealing with the health care needs of more than 100,000 Indochinese refugees in camps there. The refugees—from Laos, Vietnam, and Cambodia—flooded into the country at the rate of thousands each month, according to *New York Times* reports in 1977. Medical problems ranged from wounds to malaria, malnutrition, dehydration, and respiratory infections, as well as psychological problems. Mortality rates were high. Trained staff and medical supplies were in short supply. Yet Dr. García did not express despondence over her Sisyphean task but dispensed care from her house and traveled the countryside seeing as many patients as she could. Dominica García received her medical degree in 1969 in the Philippines and worked in a Cambodian clinic with the Catholic Relief Service before going to Thailand.

1977 Blackwell Medalists

Drs. EDITH P. BROWN of Benson, Arizona, and EVA F. DODGE, of Little Rock, Arkansas, were the recipients of the American Medical Women's Association (AMWA) 1977 Elizabeth Blackwell Medal, initiated in 1949 and awarded annually to persons who have made the most outstanding contribution to the cause of women in the field of medicine. Since 1949, 28 women physicians have been so honored.

SURGEONS

A Founder of Modern Obstetrics

As head of obstetrics at the Woman's Medical College in Philadelphia, Dr.

ANNA BROOMALL was noted for establishing the first of a number of medical school-affiliated clinics in surrounding neighborhoods where poor patients could receive high-quality medical care. She is credited, too, with the low mortality rate at the Maternity Hospital of the Woman's Medical College, due to her adoption of the latest knowledge from abroad and her emphasis on prenatal care, episiotomy, and Caesarean section, among other new procedures. Dr. Broomall, born 1847, of Quaker background, was encouraged in her career aspirations by her father. She attended the Woman's Medical College and in 1869 was one of the first female medical students permitted in the clinics at Pennsylvania Hospital, and in 1892 was among the first women to become members of the Philadelphia Obstetrical Society. She died in 1931.

First Woman on the Faculty at Johns Hopkins

ELIZABETH HURDON received an M.D. from the University of Toronto in 1895 and then went to the United States to study gynecological pathology with a professor at Johns Hopkins. In 1898 she was recommended by her mentor for the position of teaching assistant in gynecological pathology, and thus became the first woman on the faculty of Johns Hopkins Medical School and on the staff of Johns Hopkins Hospital. In 1913 Dr. Hurdon was among the first group of women elected to the American College of Surgeons. After World War I she returned to her native England and cofounded a hospital for the research and treatment of female cancer patients, the Marie Curie Hospital. She became its director of medical service and research and held the position until she retired at the age of 70. In 1938 she was honored for her work with the order of Commander of the British Empire. She died of cancer in 1941.

First Woman Ambulance Surgeon in New York City

EMILY DUNNING BARRINGER, a 1901 graduate of Cornell Medical School, was the first woman ambulance surgeon in New York City. After receiving her degree, Dr. Barringer entered a competition for a position at Mount Sinai Hospital and won first place, but the job was denied to her because she was a woman. The same thing happened when she applied to Gouverneur Hospital; this time the mayor heard about her plight and ratified the appointment. Thus, her ambulance job. There was considerable publicity over it, and she became known around the city as "the beautiful girl on the Bowery run." Dr. Barringer moved on to more prominent positions, including fellowship in the College of Surgeons and the New York Academy of Medicine, and directorship of gynecology at a Brooklyn hospital.

An Early Reformer of Childbirth Practices

DOROTHY REED MENDENHALL was one of the first women to attend Johns Hopkins Medical School, from which she was graduated in 1900. She and FLORENCE SABIN (p. 216) were two of the top 12 students in their graduating class. As a fellow at Johns Hopkins, she studied Hodgkin's disease and found the causative cell, later named the Dorothy Reed cell. Dr. Mendenhall lost her first and only daughter to poor obstetrics. In this, she was by no means alone among American women of her day. The fact that in Denmark, maternal and neonatal death rates were much lower than in the United States greatly interested her. She traveled to Denmark, studied their practices, and widely reported her findings. In Denmark midwives delivered most babies and childbirth was widely regarded as a natural process rather than a surgical problem. A Danish doctor told her: "You interfere—operate too much. We give nature a chance." For many years she investigated the subject and helped revolutionize childbirth practices in the United States.

First Women Members of the American College of Surgeons

Two Boston women physicians were among the 1,065 candidates admitted at the second annual meeting of the American College of Surgeons in June 1914, in Philadelphia: Dr. ALICE GERTRUDE BRYANT, an 1890 graduate of the Women's Medical College of New York, and Dr. FLORENCE WEST DUCKERING, who was graduated from Tufts Medical School in 1901.

Founder of the American Women's Medical Association

An obstetrician and surgeon, Dr. BERTHA VAN HOOSEN founded and was first president of the American Women's Medical Association in 1915. Throughout her life she was a strong supporter of women in medicine. Born on a farm in Michigan, Bertha Van Hoosen had been encouraged by her family to obtain an education, but when she announced plans to study medicine, after obtaining her college degree, the family wept. In 1919 she was appointed acting head of the Department of Obstetrics at Loyola Medical School. Later, she was the only woman among more than 300 physicians competing for the position of chief of gynecology at Cook County Hospital; she finished first. Early on, Dr. Van Hoosen was convinced of the importance of breast milk for infants and started a breast milk bank in Chicago. She was also an early advocate of good nutrition during pregnancy and opposed to drinking, smoking, or taking unnecessary medications during pregnancy—long before such ideas had been proved. Her story is told in detail in her autobiography, *Petticoat Surgeon.* Dr. Van Hoosen died in 1952.

First Female House Officer of New York Hospital

A surgical resident, Dr. MARGARET CASTEL STURGIS of North Carolina became the first woman physician on the house staff of New York Hospital. She graduated from the Woman's Medical College of Pennsylvania in 1915; her specialty was gynecology.

First Woman to Practice "Aesthetic" Surgery

SUZANNE NOEL married a dermatologist and decided to train in medicine so she could work with her husband. She received her medical degree in 1916 from the Faculty of Medicine of Paris. But she then began to operate on scars and wrinkled faces, becoming one of the earliest "aesthetic" surgeons—as they were known at the time—and the first woman to enter the field. Mme. Noel made many innovative contributions and was the first to describe in detail various techniques. Some of her colleagues were defensive about their work, but she was not. In 1926 she published *La Chirurgie Esthétique, Son Rôle Social,* discussing the importance of cosmetic surgery and the effects of physical appearance on the personality. In the 1930s she practiced in a large apartment near the Champs Élysées and operated on many celebrities. Often there were other physicians present, who came to observe her work. Mme. Noel, who practiced until the age of 74, herself had a number of face lifts in her later years. She died in 1954.

Only Woman Plastic Surgeon in the Allied Armies

Dr. GENIA SAKIN, a glamorous blond woman, was born in Lithuania before World War I and studied medicine in Berlin. She practiced there in the early 1930s, fled from the Hitler regime in 1937, and in 1943 enlisted in the U. S. Army Medical Corps, where she rose to the rank of major. She was the only woman plastic surgeon to serve in the Allied Armies during World War II. Following the war, she was chief of surgery and plastic surgery in a Berlin hospital and became famous for her operations on disfigured war veterans. In 1948 a law was enacted discharging all female medical officers, and Dr. Sakin went into private practice in New York, although she continued her work on victims of the war. It was her custom never to charge for the rehabilitative surgery she did on her extensive trips abroad. During one postwar visit to Greece, she performed an estimated 5,000 operations. Her immodest goal: rehabilitating the disfigured of the world.

First Black Woman Fellow of the American College of Surgeons

Dr. HELEN OCTAVIA DICKENS was the first black woman to be made a fellow of the American College of Surgeons (1950). Born in 1900, she earned her M.D. from the University of Illinois in 1933, was certified in obstetrics and gynecology in 1946, and set up a practice in Philadelphia. She went on to become chief of obstetrics and gynecology at Women's Hospital, Philadelphia, in 1956.

First Woman to Operate on the Heart

In 1943 Dr. MYRA LOGAN became the first woman surgeon to operate on the human heart; it was the ninth such operation. Dr. Logan took her specialty training at Harlem Hospital, where she later became an associate surgeon. In the 1940s she was a member of the New York State Committee on Discrimination and was one of the group that resigned when Governor Dewey refused to act on antidiscrimination legislation that the committee had prepared. Most recently, she served as a member of the New York State Workman's Compensation Board. Dr. Logan, born in 1908 in Tuskegee, Alabama, received her premedical education at Atlanta University and Columbia, where she earned an M.S. in psychology. The first person to win a scholarship for Afro-Americans to New York Medical School, she received her

M.D. in 1933. She was made a fellow of the American College of Surgeons in 1951. Dr. Logan died in 1977.

First U. S. Female Professor of Surgery

Dr. ALMA DEA MORANI was born in 1907, the daughter of sculptor Salvatore Morani. Her father urged her to follow his profession. Surgery is "very nice work," he said, "but art in a patient will die with the patient while a good piece of sculpture will live forever." Alma Morani became a plastic surgeon. A Girl Scout first aid training course first interested her in medicine, and she was graduated from the Women's Medical College of Pennsylvania in 1931. Following specialty training, she was appointed professor of clinical surgery at the Women's College—the first woman in the United States ever asked to teach surgery. From the beginning, Dr. Morani desired to be a plastic surgeon but could not get into a training program until after World War II, when, after 15 years as a surgeon, she went back to school. Dr. Morani has received several honorary degrees and numerous awards, including the Elizabeth Blackwell Award of the American Medical Women's Association for 1972 and the Distinguished Daughter of Pennsylvania award in 1973. A sculptor and photographer, she has had several shows of her work.

First Open-Heart Surgeon

The first woman in the United States to perform open-heart surgery was Dr. NINA STARR BRAUNWALD. She was also the first woman to be certified by the American Board of Thoracic Surgery. A 1952 graduate of New York University College of Medicine, Dr. Braunwald was a member of the surgical team that in 1960 reported the first clinical success in completely replacing a mitral valve with an artificial one. She has been a staff member of the National Heart Institute and was later appointed to the staff at Harvard Medical School and Peter Bent Brigham Hospital, where her husband is chief of medicine. "It just seemed the natural thing," she said once when asked why she went into medicine. "My father is a doctor and so is my uncle."

"Is there a significant difference in the productivity of women and men physicians? Some medical educators and physicians believe there is and have voiced concern that training women physicians may not be an effective means of meeting the nation's physician needs. . . . Our research shows that both women and men physicians work productively. Although it has been said that women physicians spend a great deal of time out of the work force, our data indicate otherwise. . . . After one adjusts for those physicians of both sexes who are ill or retired there is no question about the fact that the difference in the work ratios between men and women is the result of time taken out by women for child bearing and child rearing. Yet despite major responsibilities for the home that most female physicians have, it is apparent that they take little time out from the work force compared to men physicians who do not have these added responsibilities."
—from *A Comparison of the Productivity of Women and Men Physicians*, by Marilyn Heins, M.D., Sue Smock, Lois Martindale, Jennifer Jacobs, and Margaret Stein, *Journal of the American Medical Association*, June 1977.

Like Father, Like Daughter

In 1967 Dr. JANE C. WRIGHT was appointed a dean and professor of surgery at New York Medical College—the highest post ever held at that time by a black woman in an American medical school. Dr. Wright came from a long line of doctors; one of her grandfathers was an early graduate of Meharry Medical

College and her father was one of the first black graduates of Harvard Medical School and an eminent surgeon. Dr. Wright was graduated from Smith College in 1942 and received her M.D. in 1945 from New York Medical College. Following the death of her father, Wright succeeded him as head of the Cancer Research Foundation, which he had established at Harlem Hospital. In 1955 she joined New York University Medical School as an instructor in research surgery and later became director of cancer chemotherapy research there. She has tested and found effective a number of drugs and surgical procedures against cancer and extensively published her findings. Dr. Wright has been a member of the New York State Commission Against Discrimination, the President's Commission on Heart Disease, and in 1975 she was honored by the American Association for Cancer Research for her contributions to research in clinical cancer chemotherapy. The mother of two daughters—a physician and a clinical psychologist—she has also found time to enjoy swimming, mystery novels, and painting in watercolors.

Founder of Two Medical Associations in Sri Lanka

SIVA CHINNATAMBY, who obtained her medical degree and early hospital experience in Sri Lanka (Ceylon), went to England for postgraduate training in 1950. Since that time she has held many top posts in gynecology and family planning in her home country. A fellow of the Royal College of Obstetricians and Gynaecologists of Great Britain (1964) and a fellow of the American College of Surgeons (1966), she founded and served as secretary of the Association of Medical Women of Ceylon and of the Association of Obstetricians and Gynaecologists of Ceylon. She has presented more than 40 professional papers in Asia and Europe.

Women Doctors Storm Male Bastion

There are 6,500 accredited urologists in the United States. Of these, according to *Parade* magazine, in 1977 three were women: Dr. OCCO ELAINE GOODWIN of San Francisco and Drs. MARY GANNON and MARY CHRISTINE WEBSTER of Iowa City.

Other women have since begun their residencies in the specialty. The first woman to be admitted to Harvard's program in urological surgery at Peter Bent Brigham and Massachusetts General hospitals was Dr. LUCILLE JOYCE NORSTRAND. Dr. LARRIAN GILLESPIE was the first woman resident in urology at UCLA Hospital. According to Dr. Gillespie, "a girl who sets out to specialize in urology finds she gets more trouble from other doctors than from patients. They seem to treat us as if we were storming some male bastion, and they resent it." (She added that this was not true at UCLA, which was why she was there.) Dr. Gannon reported similar reactions from associates. "They think there's something weird about a young woman who wants to specialize in urology," she said. "The truth is we're just about as weird as the guys who want to specialize in ob-gyn."

MEDICAL RESEARCHERS

First Woman in the National Academy of Sciences

One of the first women to enter medical research, Dr. FLORENCE SABIN made her earliest major discoveries as a medical student at Johns Hopkins. After graduation in 1900, with the fourth class at Hopkins, Dr. Sabin investigated the origin of the lymphatic vessels, overthrowing accepted medical knowledge with her findings. In 1902 she joined the faculty at Johns Hopkins as an assistant in anatomy and taught in addition to continuing her research. In 1905 she became an associate professor and in 1917 a full professor of histology and head of the department. She was the first full-time woman professor at the medical school. During this period Dr. Sabin and her collaborators devoted themselves to the study of red and white corpuscles. With arduous, painstaking work, she established a technique for studying the corpuscles and by 1919 had determined the origin of red corpuscles.

In 1925 Dr. Sabin was asked to establish and head a department of cellular studies at the Rockefeller Institute for Medical Studies. Here she did important work on tuberculosis, inquiring into the reaction of the body's cells to the disease. She believed the fight against tuberculosis could be won, saying: "If I didn't believe the answer could be found, I wouldn't be working on it." The same year she was elected to the National Academy of Sciences (see p. 223), the first woman in the United States to achieve the distinction. Born in 1871, daughter of a miner and a housewife, she was seven when her mother died in childbirth. In 1893 she was graduated from Smith College, with an interest in zoology, and spent the next three years teaching in order to save for a medical education.

Recognized as one of the foremost scientists of all time, Dr. Sabin published many articles in medical journals and wrote a biography of her mentor, Franklin Pane Mall, whose suggestions had led to some of her early discoveries, a book the *New York Times* called a model of its kind. The first woman member of the Rockefeller Institute, and the first woman president of the American Association of Anatomists, she received honorary degrees from a dozen leading universities as well as the National Achievement Award, the Trudeau Medal, the M. Carey Thomas Prize, and other awards. At the age of 67, Dr. Sabin retired from the Rockefeller Institute, but she continued to work avidly on public health and preventive medicine, investigating farms, sanatoriums, sewage systems, and so on in her native Colorado. Eventually, the state passed the Sabin Health Bills, which contributed substantially to lowering Colorado death rates. She died in 1953.

The Slye Cancer Theory

MAUD SLYE became famous for her theory—based on studies of mice begun in 1908—that cancer could be eliminated by selective breeding. She had refused to accept the popular idea that cancer was not inheritable in any way, and her theory was a major advance in knowledge of the disease. Pathologist Slye was graduated from Brown University and did postgraduate work at the University of Chicago, where she became an associate professor in 1926. As a postgraduate she made the observation that led to her later work: a herd of cattle afflicted with cancer of the eye all had come from the same ranch. Her theory that certain animals had a disposition toward cancer was not readily accepted, but she held fast in the fact of opposition. One leading authority denounced her work as "pure poppycock." The American Medical Association recognized her work early on, however, and awarded her its gold medal in 1914.

First Woman President of the Society of American Bacteriologists

ALICE EVANS was best known for the discovery of an organism in raw cow's milk that causes chronic disease. She was the first woman to be elected president of the Society of American Bacteriologists, in 1928, and was also the first woman scientist to hold a permanent appointment in the U. S. Dairy Division of the Bureau of Animal Industry, 1913. Her finding of brucella in cow's milk was met with cynicism and controversy. In 1901 the eminent Robert Koch had declared that bovine tuberculosis was *not* com-

municable to man, and there was a general disinclination at the time to accept the idea that milk could be a disease carrier. Her critics, as she herself magnanimously explained later, were simply "not accustomed to considering a scientific idea proposed by a woman." Alice Evans received an M.S. degree in bacteriology from the University of Wisconsin in 1910 and many honorary degrees, among them an M.D. from the Women's Medical College and doctorates from Wilson College and the University of Wisconsin. In 1922 she was infected with one of the organisms she was studying and suffered from recurrent illness for many years, but 50 years later was still active and in reasonably good health.

Discoverer of the Cause, Prevention, and Cure for Scarlet Fever

In 1923 GLADYS HENRY DICK and her husband, George Frederick Dick, isolated the streptococcus that causes scarlet fever and went on to prepare the toxin and antitoxin that act as preventive and cure for the disease—a serious one that often results in complications. In 1924 they developed the Dick test, a skin test for susceptibility to the disease.

First to Isolate Tuberculin Agent

FLORENCE SEIBERT, born 1897, in Easton, Pennsylvania, went off to Goucher College intending to become a physician, but she fell in love with chemistry. Her graduate work was done at Yale, and she received her Ph.D. in 1923. While there, she discovered the cause of the fever in patients who had received triple-distilled water intravenously, and she developed a method of producing bacteria-free distilled water in a single process. Her celebrated work on chemistry and immunology of tuberculosis was begun at the Sprague Institute in Chicago and continued at the University of Pennsylvania. Dr. Seibert isolated the active agent in tuberculin, a discovery ·that greatly helped improve diagnosis in patients and made possible accurate skin tests. In honor of this work, she received the Trudeau Gold Medal in 1938 and the Garvan Medal in 1942. Her main hobby was her work, although she also liked to play the violin in her free time.

First Report on Tularemia

CORA DOWNS once said it was the search for a research project that wouldn't require much money that led her to investigate tularemia, a deadly infectious disease transmitted by insect bites or handling infected animals. Dr. Downs was on the faculty at the University of Kansas during the Depression, when many people had resorted to hunting for food. The first case that came to her attention was of a rabbit hunter who was suffering from aches and pains and had a persistent sore on a finger. He was one of the cases described in her first report on tularemia, published in 1930. Dr. Downs went on to contribute much to understanding the nature of the disease, its immunology and epidemiology, and the causative organism. Some of this work was done at Camp Detrick during World War II. In the 1950s and 1960s Downs turned to the study of rickets and then, with others, to perfecting the technique of fluorescent antibody staining that became a useful diagnostic and research tool. The daughter of a Kansas City physician, Cora Downs obtained her training in bacteriology at the University of Kansas and was made a full professor there in 1936. In 1972 she was named Summerfield distinguished professor of bacteriology, an honor she particularly relished—reportedly because the founder of the chair had said no woman would ever receive the appointment because none would ever deserve it.

Mother of Perinatal Pathology

In the mid-1930s when Dr. EDITH POTTER was appointed a research associate in fetal pathology at the University of Chicago the field was new. Causes of fetal and neonatal mortality were mostly unknown, and death certificates often gave "intrauterine asphyxia" or "malformation" as the cause of death. Dr. Potter and her boss, Dr. Fred Adair, persuaded the head of the Chicago health department to require autopsies of all fetuses and infants; the results were revealing. Interest was attracted to the problem by this, as well as by Dr. Potter's book *The Pathology of the Fetus and Newborn,* and the Chicago Lying-In Hospital became a center for the study of perinatal pathology. Edith Potter received her education, including M.D. and Ph.D. degrees, at the University of Minnesota. After internship she went into private practice, but at the urging of the chief pathologist at the University of Minnesota took specialty training in pathology. "I have never felt myself handicapped by being a woman and have felt accepted on an equal basis with men," she wrote several years ago. "What I did is a result of several happy accidents."

First to Find a Treatment for Cyanide and Carbon Monoxide Poisoning

Discovery of a treatment for victims of cyanide and carbon monoxide poisoning was made by Dr. MATILDA MOLDENHAUER BROOKS, a research associate in biology at the University of California. Her findings that methylene blue was an effective antidote to two of the quickest and most deadly poisons was published in 1932. The theory was not new at that time, but she was the first to realize its application to human cases. Of German-American ancestry, Dr. Brooks was educated at the University of Pittsburgh and at Harvard University, where she received a Ph.D. in 1920. Dr. Brooks worked as a biologist for the United States Public Health Service prior to her appointment at the University of California. Since her husband was on the faculty at the university and there was a rule forbidding a husband and wife both to hold salaried positions, Dr. Brooks's work was done gratis.

First Honorary Female Fellow in Microscopy

Lady MARY BRUCE was the first woman to be made an honorary female fellow of the Royal Microscopical Society, in 1936. She was recognized for her work, with her husband, in culturing the organism that causes Malta fever.

Penicillium Detector

For 40 years at the University of Wisconsin, Dr. ELIZABETH McCOY conducted research ranging from studies of bacteria that causes fermentation to the effects of pollution on spawning fish. She also studied and reported on the growth of staphylococci in dairy barns, manure, and soil and the presence of staphylococci in dried milk. But one of her most important accomplishments was detecting a high-yielding strain of Penicillium, which allowed the release of penicillin to civilians during World War II. Dr. McCoy received a Ph.D. in 1929 from the University of Wisconsin and became an assistant professor of bacteriology there the following year. In 1943 she was promoted to full professor—only the second woman at the university to attain the rank, outside of the departments of home economics and nursing.

Discoverer of a Cure for Bacterial Meningitis

As an intern at Johns Hopkins Hospital, Dr. HATTIE ALEXANDER began searching for a cure for a common and 100 per cent fatal disease of babies, *Hemophilas influenza* meningitis. For several years she tried one thing then another, including a horse antiserum that proved unsuccessful. Then, using techniques she had learned as a bacteriologist and a recently discovered principle—that antibody produced in rabbits is more effective than that of horses—Dr. Alexander developed a new antiserum. Working with another scientist, she injected rabbits with masses of the baccilli from the spinal fluid of stricken children and measured the concentration of antibody in the resulting antiserum. It worked. A critically ill infant injected with the new antiserum recovered. Word of the treatment spread quickly and it became a standard procedure. Within two years fatalities from the disease had dropped by 80 per cent, and Dr. Alexander was world renowned. Eventually she perfected antibiotic therapy and fatalities diminished to 10 per cent.

Hattie Alexander grew up in Baltimore, in a family of eight children, and won a scholarship to Goucher College. After graduation she worked for three years in order to put herself through medical school. She obtained an M.D. from Johns Hopkins in 1930 and took specialty training in pediatrics at Babies Hospital. Her work on meningitis led to studies of the mechanism of bacterial resistance to antibiotics and to research in bacterial genetics. She and her assistant first demonstrated the transformation of *Hemophilas influenza* and showed that its activity is due to desoxyribonucleic acid. In 1961 she became the first woman to receive the Oscar B. Hunter Memorial Award, and she was one of few women to head a major medical society, as president of the American Pediatric Society in 1964. Prior to her death in 1968 of cancer, Dr. Alexander was professor of pediatrics at the College of Physicians and Surgeons of Columbia University.

First Woman Doctor to Win a Nobel Prize

In 1947 Dr. GERTY CORI and her husband, Dr. Carl Cori, were awarded the Nobel Prize in Physiology and Medicine (see "Women in Science," p. 144). She was the first woman physician to receive the prize. The Coris' early work was in carbohydrate metabolism, including that of tumors. They went on to isolate several new enzymes and explain the mechanisms by which glucose is stored in the liver and used in the muscles. Their work made possible the first synthesis of a biological macromolecule in a test tube. Gerty Cori subsequently did research into a group of heritable diseases of children, which, she showed, were due to single enzyme deficiencies. Her work demonstrated the importance of isolating and understanding individual enzymes in order to understand complex metabolic processes that occur in normal and diseased tissues. Gerty Cori was born in Prague in 1896. With the encouragement and example of an uncle who was a professor of pediatrics, she entered medical school and received her M.D. in 1920. She married a fellow student from the German University of Prague, and had one son. The Coris came to the United States in the 1920s, because political conditions in their homeland made pursuing scientific careers difficult. She worked first at a routine pathologist's job, which gave her free time to collaborate with her husband. In 1931 she became a research associate at Washington University School of Medicine and, after World War II, professor of biochemistry. She died in 1957.

Pioneer in Polio Research

The presence of the poliovirus in the bloodstream of victims at very early stages of the disease was discovered by Dr. DOROTHY HORSTMANN in 1952. The finding was a milestone in the search for a vaccine. Dr. Horstmann's career has been devoted to studies of epidemiol-

ogy and pathogenesis of viral infections, particularly polio and rubella. She established many important characteristics of polio—including its high communicability. And she studied the effect of a live vaccine on various populations, establishing its effectiveness. She also has studied enteroviruses, the effects of rubella on pregnant women, and rubella vaccines. Dr. Horstmann was appointed an instructor at Yale University Medical School in 1943. Twenty years later, she became the first woman to hold two full professorships at the university as professor of epidemiology and pediatrics.

Early Inquirer into Causes of Cancer

Most of the work done by Dr. HELEN DYER centered on the mechanisms of carcinogenesis, although she also made major discoveries in the fields of metabolism and nutrition. A graduate of Goucher College in 1917, Dr. Dyer studied and taught at Mount Holyoke College and took her Ph.D. degree at George Washington University in 1935. She taught biochemistry for a dozen years at George Washington University before joining the Cancer Institute in 1942. She studied vitamin B_6 and its antimetabolite, which itself causes cancer in certain animals. Her investigations of amino acid analogues had impact on the development of sulpha drugs, the first antibiotics discovered. In 1949 Dr. Dyer prepared the first comprehensive index of tumor chemotherapy, which was used by the Institute to begin its chemotherapy program. Among other honors, she received the Garvan Medal of the American Chemical Society.

Collaborators in Cancer Research

After receiving her Ph.D. from the University of Chicago in 1939, Dr. SARAH STEWART went to work as a microbiologist at the National Institutes of Health. Her true goal was cancer research, but the field was apparently closed to her.

So she became an instructor at Georgetown University Medical School, which did not accept women students, in order to take the medical courses she needed on the side. When women were admitted in 1947, Stewart enrolled and two years later became Georgetown's first woman graduate. She went on to do research that is recognized as a cornerstone of viral oncology.

Working at the Cancer Institute of the National Institutes of Health, Dr. Stewart, in collaboration with Dr. BERNICE EDDY of the Department of Biological Standards, first characterized the polyoma virus and demonstrated that it causes many types of tumors in mice, rats, hamsters, rabbits, and guinea pigs. They also showed that tumors could be spread from one animal to another. Stewart and Eddy's important work, which was begun in the mid-1950s, led the way to much later research.

The two women had been good friends for years prior to their collaboration, and it was Dr. Eddy who developed the early tissue culture techniques for tumor viruses that made their work possible. Bernice Eddy received her Ph.D. from the University of Cincinnati in 1927 and joined the Public Health Service in 1931. She retired in 1973. Dr. Stewart—the first woman to be featured in the "Medical Men of Georgetown" column of Georgetown University's *Medical Bulletin*—was born in Mexico of an American father and Mexican mother, and moved to the United States at the age of five. She died in 1976 of cancer. Dr. Eddy since retiring has lived in Maryland.

First to Determine Accurate Mortality Rates for Cancer in the United States

For over forty years, ELEANOR MACDONALD has pioneered in cancer epidemiology. Shortly after graduating from Radcliffe (1928) with a degree in statistics, she began the first of a series of studies proving that complete records aid in the control of cancer. For five years she checked all cancer death records in Massachusetts by a house-to-house investigation, and she examined twenty years of autopsy records at a major Boston hospital. When Ms. Macdonald presented the results of her work in 1937, it was immediately acclaimed as the first accurate calibration of cancer mortality in the country. She didn't stop there but urged communities to set up cancer awareness centers, and for several years presented a weekly radio show on public health. Among many other accomplishments, she discovered the association between the intensity of the sun and skin cancer by showing that melanoma increased with proximity to the equator. Although her only degree was a B.A., she went on to become a full professor of epidemiology at the University of Texas. Now retired, she has recently sent to press two books on cancer and its relation to environmental and genetic factors.

First Woman President of the American Physiological Society

In 1975 Dr. BODIL SCHMIDT-NIELSEN became the first woman president of the American Physiological Society in its history. The daughter of Nobel Prize-winning physiologist August Krogh, Dr. Schmidt-Nielsen started out with a degree in dentistry, but she turned to physiology, studying books she found at home. Most of her research has been on the kidneys, of invertebrates, mammals, even camels—whose specialized organs allow them to survive in deserts. Dr. Schmidt-Nielsen held the position of associate professor in the department of zoology and physiology at Duke University before becoming a researcher at the Mount Desert Island Biological Laboratory in Maine in 1971. She has published extensively and more than 150 of her articles have appeared in the *American Journal of Physiology*.

Pioneer in Neonatal Toxicology

A professor of biochemistry at Baylor College of Medicine, Dr. MARJORIE HORNING pioneered in the field of neonatal toxicology. Her studies revealed vital information about the effects of medicines on newborn babies, for instance, that the placental barrier is not effective against drugs, that human infants are able at birth to metabolize drugs and other foreign substances. Dr. Horning received her Ph.D. from the University of Michigan in 1943 and conducted research at Michigan, the University of Pennsylvania, and the National Heart Institute before going to Baylor in 1961. She is a member of the American Chemical Society and in 1977 she received the society's Garvan Medal for her contributions to the development of safer drugs.

A Leader in Chemotherapy Research

One of few scientists without a Ph.D. degree and one of few women to attain a high position in a drug firm, GERTRUDE ELION won recognition as a leader in the field of anticancer agents. She also synthesized and studied drugs to treat gout, organ transplant recipients and leukemia. In 1968, Ms. Elion received the Garvan Medal in recognition of her chemotherapy work. After graduation from Hunter College in 1937, *summa cum laude,* Gertrude Elion was unable to obtain a graduate assistantship, so she worked at menial laboratory jobs, taught high school, and attended New York University part time. In 1941 she received her master's degree and shortly went to work for Burroughs Wellcome pharmaceutical firm, where she advanced to become director of experimental therapy. She has received several honorary degrees and been named adjunct professor of pharmacology at Duke University and the University of North Carolina.

Discoverer of the Radioimmunoassay

The first woman, and first nuclear physicist, to win the prestigious Albert Lasker Medical Research Award was Dr. ROSALYN S. YALOW (see "Women in Science and Technology," p. 144) in 1976. She received the $10,000 prize for her role in the discovery of the radioimmunoassay, a method of measuring minute concentrations of hundreds of substances in body tissues. This technique, by which radioactive isotopes are usd to measure hormons, viruses, vitamins, enzymes, and drugs, is invaluable in determining the difference between diseased and normal states. It was first employed in 1959 to measure insulin and led to the discovery of high levels of insulin in adult diabetics. The assay is widely used to detect hepatitis virus in potential blood donors, and has been put to such varied tasks as determining whether hormone therapy can help dwarfs and detecting curare in the bodies of New Jersey doctor Mario Jascalevich's patients.

In 1977 Dr. Yalow, 56 and the mother of two children, also won a Nobel Prize for the development of the radioimmunoassay—the second woman ever to win a Nobel Prize in medicine and the first in 30 years. A senior medical investigator at the Veterans Administration Hospital in the Bronx, she was elected to the National Academy of Sciences in 1975.

"You Just Get Up and Fight"

As a professor of medicine at George Washington Medical Center in Washington and director of the Laboratory for Virus and Cancer Research there, Dr. ARIEL HOLLINSHEAD has conducted basic and clinical research into many different types of cancer and worked to develop immunotherapy for breast, lung, and gastric cancers and melanoma. Named Medical Woman of the Year by the Board of American Medical Colleges and Distinguished Cancer Scientist in the United States by the American Association for the Advancement of Science, in 1977 Dr. Hollinshead also became the first woman appointed to chair the review board in oncology for the Veterans Administration. She obtained her Ph.D. in 1957 from George Washington University, and her undergraduate degree from Swarthmore College. "I love my research," she says, explaining that her career was chosen at the age of 15 after she read Paul De Kruif's *The Microbe Hunters* (1926). As a woman in a highly competitive field, she reports: "You get knocked plenty, but you just get up and fight."

Women in the National Academy of Sciences Who Have Contributed to Medicine

Of the 1,200 members in the august National Academy of Sciences, 32 are women. The first was FLORENCE SABIN (see p. 216), elected in 1925. HELEN TAUSSIG (see p. 207) was elected in 1973 and ROSALYN YALOW (see p. 222) in 1975. Others honored with membership specifically for their contributions to medical science have been:

1967

BERTA VOGEL SCHARRER, an anatomist, together with her husband, Ernst Scharrer, conducted cytological studies which showed that certain nerve cells synthesize and secrete hormones. Theirs was the first coherent statement of the theory of neurosecretion. Another of their major findings, reported in 1940: that the hypothalamus exerts control over the pituitary gland by neurohormones. A milestone, the Scharrers' theory of neurosecretion is now a central concept of physiology, providing a crucial link between the nervous and endocrine systems.

1968

RITA LEVI-MONTALCINI, neurobiologist, has made highly influential contributions to neurogenesis, or the development of the nerve connections in the brain. Her detection of the complex way the neuroblasts migrate within the central nervous system contributed to understanding the embryonic development of the brain. She is best known for her co-discovery in 1954 of the Nerve Growth Factor, isolated in collaboration with Stanley Cohen. NGF, a new type of control mechanism that enhances growth of young nerve cells, was previously completely unknown. Dr. Levi-Montalcini showed NGF to be necessary for the development of the sympathetic ganglion cells—the backbone of the sympathetic nervous system—of the mouse, responsible for many of the creature's physiologic responses.

One of Italy's top scientists and director of the Laboratory of Cell Biology, Dr. Levi-Montalcini is the only woman ever elected to the Papal Academy of Rome.

1970

REBECCA LANCEFIELD is famed for her work on streptococci and their relation to rheumatic fever. A bacteriologist, she was the first to categorize accurately the organism responsible for rheumatic fever and was largely responsible for most of the conceptual schemes, methodology, and detailed experimental analysis that form the basis for understanding this important group of disease-causing organisms. Most of her work was done at Rockefeller University. In 1943 Dr. Lancefield became the second woman president of the Society of American Bacteriologists and in 1961 she was the first woman to be president of the American Association of Immunologists.

1972

Dr. ELIZABETH RUSSELL pioneered in mouse genetics. She discovered the cause of several types of anemia in mice as a tool to understand the orderly process of red blood cell production, and discovery of a mutant gene in the mouse became a model for the study of human muscular dystrophy.

1973

BEATRICE MINTZ, a medical geneticist, began her research career with important contributions to the understanding of how hormones regulated development in amphibians. Dr. Mintz then turned to experimentation with mice to illumine developmental genetics, including the question of inherited susceptibility to certain tumors; and how the development of skin and pigmentary systems, the skeletal system, the retina of the eye, sexual systems, brain, liver, and other organs takes place.

A hemoglobin biologist, Dr. HELEN RANNEY is noted for her work in the genetics and structure-function relationships of hemoglobin. A protein in the red blood cells, hemoglobin is responsible for the transport of oxygen from the lungs to the body's tissues. Dr. Ranney's research was central to the development of understanding how hemoglobin carries oxygen. Professor of medicine and chairwoman of the department at the University of California in San Diego, Dr. Ranney was elected president of the American Society of Hematology in 1972 and the same year received the Martin Luther King Medical Achievement Award for outstanding contribution in the field of sickle cell anemia.

1974

Biochemist SARAH RATNER did classic studies of the biochemistry of amino acids and protein metabolism. Her work led to understanding of the chemistry of several diseases and the detection and treatment of metabolic abnormalities in human infants. Earlier in her career, Dr. Ratner made the first observation of a compound in human semen that could produce uterine contractions. The compound, which was later shown to belong to a new class of hormonal compounds, prostaglandins, was widely used to induce labor. Ratner also contributed to the elucidation of the structure of penicillin through her work with a closely related compound. Prior to becoming a member of the Public Health Research Institute of New York, she held positions at the College of Physicians and Surgeons, Columbia and New York University College of Medicine. Dr. Ratner has received the Carl Neuberg and Garvan medals.

Oncologist CHARLOTTE FRIEND is credited with being one of those who laid the foundations of viral oncology, or virally caused cancer. She discovered what came to be called the Friend leukemia viruses of mice and produced evidence that forced acceptance of the controversial notion that leukemia in mice could be caused by viruses. Another of her key findings concerned the ability of certain cells to synthesize hemoglobin, which was useful in understanding the regulation of hemoglobin synthesis. Dr. Friend obtained her Ph.D. at Yale University in 1950 and went on to become professor and director of the Center for Experimental Cell Biology at Mount Sinai School of Medicine as well as a member of the Sloan-Kettering Institute.

A leading international authority on human genetic diseases, biochemist ELIZABETH FONDAL NEUFELD made major discoveries into disorders of sugar metabolism in humans. Her research revolutionized the conceptual and experimental approaches to inherited disorders such as Hurler's syndrome, in which defective sugar accumulates within the cells of a fetus. The disease causes stunting of mental and physical growth and is often fatal. Her work opened the way for successful prenatal diagnosis of the disease, genetic counseling, and new possibilities for enzyme replacement therapy. Dr. Neufeld, born in Paris, earned her Ph.D. at the University of California. In 1975 she became chief of the section on Intermediary Metabolism at the National Institutes of Health, Institute of Arthritis and Metabolism Diseases. She is the recipient of many awards, including the Department of HEW Superior Service Honor Award of 1972.

DENTISTS

First Woman Dentist in the United States

Dr. LUCY B. HOBBS was not the first woman to practice dentistry in the country, but she was the first to obtain a D.D.S. degree. Hobbs was rated "second to none" in her class at Ohio College of Dental Surgery and graduated in 1866, a year after she became the first woman member of a dental society in Iowa. At first she found the practice of dentistry tough going, but once she relocated in Iowa she was quite successful. She died in 1910.

First British Woman Licensed in Dental Surgery

The Royal College of Surgeons licensed FANNY HARWOOD in dental surgery in 1912. The same year she was hired to direct what is thought to be the first dental clinic in a school in Britain. Her father was a doctor and her husband, who did much to encourage her career, was a dental surgeon.

First Woman Dentist in the U. S. Army

In 1951 Dr. HELEN E. MEYERS became the first woman dentist in the U. S. Army Dental Corps. She was commissioned as a first lieutenant and served two years before entering private practice.

VETERINARIANS

In 1974 there were 1,110 women veterinarians in the United States. In 1969 there were only 650. With the increase, women still represent only a small proportion of the country's 30,000 veterinarians.

First Woman Veterinarian at the U. S. A.'s National Zoo

Since becoming the first woman veterinarian at the National Zoological Park in Washington, D.C., in 1976, SUZANNE KENNEDY has worked 10–11 hours each weekday, and about 5 or 6 hours on Saturdays and Sundays. Sometimes when an animal is sick enough, she has spent the night. A graduate of veterinary medicine from Michigan State University, 24-year-old Dr. Kennedy has worked with animals from serpent eagles to tigers to elephants to the tiny meercats, one of her favorites, making cage calls every morning, and giving hospital treatment when necessary. In the afternoons she works on her special research project, fungal diseases of birds. In recent years there has been a big shift toward accepting more women in the once male-dominated veterinarian colleges, she points out. "It's expected that, soon in fact, more women than men will be accepted—a situation that exists in Europe and Russia today." There still is a much smaller percentage of women veterinarians than men in zoos. The Philadelphia and San Diego zoos each have hired a woman vet, and the Metro Toronto Zoo in Canada has had a woman vet for quite some time. At the National Zoo there were no women until 1971, when Brenda Hall, who, working with reptiles, was accepted as the first woman keeper.

HEALTH SERVICE OFFICIALS AND FOUNDERS AND HOSPITAL DIRECTORS

Only Woman Commissioned Officer in the Confederate States of America

SALLY LOUISA TOMPKINS (1833–1916) didn't like taking orders, so Jefferson Davis commissioned her as a captain in the Confederate States of America. This enabled her to run the hospital that she had established at her own expense in Richmond, Virginia, during the Civil War as she pleased. The most critical injured cases were sent to her, yet her hospital had the lowest mortality rate of any soldiers' hospital in the South.

First Woman Physician to be Board of Health Director

Dr. ESTHER POHL LOVEJOY served as head of the Board of Health in Portland, Oregon—the first woman doctor in the United States to hold such a post—from 1907 to 1909. She drew wide attention with her campaign against rats, which were carriers of bubonic plague. At the time there was no protective antiserum against the disease. In 1917 Dr. Lovejoy served with the American Red Cross in France, investigating the wartime needs of women and children. For her work in Europe during and after the First World War, she received the French Cross of the Legion of Honor and decorations from other countries. She was also a founder and first president of the Medical Women's International Association, 1919–24. Esther Lovejoy's decision to study medicine followed tragic events in her personal life. In 1897, her first husband and her brother joined the gold rush to Alaska and lost their lives there. She remarried and had a son, who died at the age of seven. Following his death, she became the second woman graduate of the Medical School of the University of Oregon (working her way through by clerking in Portland department stores) and the first woman physician to practice

in the state. Among Esther Lovejoy's other achievements is a book of lasting value she published in 1957, *Women Doctors of the World.*

Founder of First Public Child Health Agency

The first public agency devoted entirely to child health was founded in 1908 by Dr. SARA JOSEPHINE BAKER, who received her M.D. from the Women's Medical College of the New York Infirmary for Women and Children in 1898. She had been working as a medical inspector for the New York City Health Department and was assigned to locate sick babies among the immigrants of the city. Struck by their extremely high mortality rate, she developed a program to try to reduce it. With a team of nurses she visited homes and taught basic hygiene: proper ventilation, bathing, clothing, and breast feeding to avoid the dangers of bottled milk. In the district where she worked, infant deaths dropped sharply in one year, while in other districts they did not. This led to the establishment of the Bureau of Child Hygiene in the City Health Department, with Dr. Baker as director. Throughout her career she lectured and wrote on the subject of child hygiene. Author of a number of books, among them *Healthy Babies, Healthy Mothers, Healthy Children* and her autobiography *Fighting for Life,* in 1901 she co-founded the American Child Hygiene Association, in 1911 organized and was the first president of the Children's Welfare Federation of New York, and in 1917 became the first woman to receive a doctorate in public health—from New York University. "It's six times safer to be a soldier in the trenches of France than to be born a baby in the United States," she said during World War I. But by the time of her retirement from the health department, infant mortality rates had dropped dramatically in New York City, from among the highest to the lowest of any major American city.

Maternity/Child Care Specialist the First Woman President of the American Public Health Association

A woman who devoted her life to problems of maternity and child care, Dr. MARTHA MAY ELIOT died at 86 in early 1978. For more than 30 years she served as an official of the United States Children's Bureau while also teaching at Yale (1921–46) and at Harvard after leaving the Bureau in 1956. Assistant director general of the World Health Organization, 1949–51, Dr. Eliot in 1947 was the first woman to be elected president of the American Public Health Association. In 1964 the association honored her by establishing an annual award in her name to recognize achievement in maternal and child health. Three years ago, Dr. Eliot completed taping 20 hours of interview recounting her experiences that have been placed on file at the Schlesinger Library at Radcliffe College, from which she was graduated in 1918. She received her medical degree from Johns Hopkins School of Medicine in 1918. With Dr. Edward Park of Yale, Dr. Eliot was credited with developing a cure (plenty of sunshine and cod liver oil) for rickets.

Director of the Mississippi Health Project

In the 1930s, Dr. DOROTHY FEREBEE directed the Mississippi Health Project, through which mobile medical clinics were taken into neglected rural areas. Under her leadership, the project was acclaimed as one of the "finest pieces of volunteer medical service" of the time. Dorothy Ferebee graduated from Tufts Medical School in 1927. In 1935 she became an instructor in obstetrics at Howard University, where she remained on the faculty for over 30 years.

Founder of the First Cancer Detection Clinics

The first clinic in the United States for the detection of cancer was established by Dr. ELIZE L'ESPERANCE at the New York Infirmary for Women and Children in 1932. She went on to found others. Dr. L'Esperance was graduated from Cornell Medical School in 1899 and entered private practice in pediatrics before specializing in pathology. She was on the faculty at Cornell Medical School for 40 years, and the first woman—with her appointment in 1950—to hold a full professorship there, in preventive medicine. The first of her clinics was founded in memory of her mother, who had died of cancer. Dr. L'Esperance "thought it made more sense than a stained-glass window."

Architect of Rehabilitation Services for the Handicapped

As director of the U. S. Office of Vocational Rehabilitation, MARY SWITZER was responsible for the growth of federal and state programs for the handicapped. Soon after taking office, she commissioned a study that resulted in the Vocational Rehabilitation Act of 1954 and the expansion of the very limited rehabilitation program to 250,000 people a year. During her tenure, the number of persons returning to work annually rose from 56,000 in 1950 to 88,275 in 1960. Self-described as a "dedicated bureaucrat," Mary Switzer was born in Massachusetts and educated at Radcliffe College. In 1960 she was the first woman to win one of medicine's highest honors, the Albert Lasker Award, for her role as "the prime architect of a workable rehabilitation service for the nations's physically handicapped."

First Woman Commissioner of Health of New York

In 1954 Dr. LEONA BAUMGARTNER became the Health Commissioner of New York City, the first woman to hold the position. Later, she became a high official of the Agency for International Development under President Kennedy, with responsibility for $400 million in AID expenditures. Dr. Baumgartner received her Ph.D. and M.D. degrees from Yale University. One of her firm beliefs: "Before a country can achieve economic and political health, it needs a healthy people."

She Said No to Thalidomide

As a medical officer with the United States Food and Drug Administration, Dr. FRANCES OLDHAM KELSEY was instrumental in preventing a thalidomide disaster in this country. A month after Dr. Kelsey, a Canadian-born physician and pharmacologist, joined the F.D.A., she received an application for the licensing of thalidomide, in September 1960. Studying the data from the drug company, on animal and human testing of thalidomide, she was perturbed by the fact that the tranquilizer didn't put animals to sleep, which suggested to her that the drug might affect animals and humans in quite different ways. She rejected the application. Several months later another application was submitted. This time there was pressure—phone calls, letters, and personal visits to her superiors. Dr. Kelsey told *Newsweek* later that there were suggestions that she was being "stupid." Meanwhile in Germany, where it was introduced in 1958, thalidomide had become a best-selling pill. In February 1961, Dr. Kelsey saw a report on inflammation of nerves in longtime thalidomide users and called attention to it. Due to her, and her superiors, the drug remained off the market in the United States. In November of that year, the first announcements came from Germany that the drug might be responsible for the hideous birth defects that had been increasing in that country. A few months later, testing of the drug stopped altogether.

First Woman Director of the Danish National Health Service

Dr. ESTHER AMMUNDSEN was appointed to the post of Director General of the Danish National Health Service by King Frederik IX in 1962. For ten years prior to the promotion she had been chief medical officer of the health service.

First Lady of Sex Education

Ten years later, her goal sounds modest: "to establish human sexuality as a health entity." Yet in the mid-1960s, Dr. MARY CALDERONE, a founder and first director of the Sex Information and Education Council of the United States (SIECUS) was widely denounced and vilified. Believing that sexuality was distorted by bigotry, fear, and "just plain ignorance," she persevered in her crusade to bring sex out in the open, to dignify it, and to increase understanding that sex might be freed from exploitation. One outcome of this pioneering work was sex education in the schools. Born in 1904, the daughter of photographer Edward Steichen and the niece of Carl Sandburg, Mary Calderone graduated from Vassar with a major in chemistry, then studied drama. Following the death of a daughter, she enrolled in medical school at the University of Rochester. As a physician she went to work for Planned Parenthood but was frustrated at not being able to help the many people she saw who suffered from sexual problems. As a result, she and five associates formed the Sex Education Council.

Specialist in Dying

ELISABETH KÜBLER-ROSS, psychiatrist, has devoted her career to helping people deal with death. Her best-selling study *On Death and Dying* was first published in 1969. Since then she has continued to work zealously, lecturing, writing, consulting, seeing patients, and directing a center for the terminally ill in California. Her mission is to help people understand what she calls the "final stages of growth," and she has defined four stages dying people pass through—denial, anger, bargaining, and depression—before reaching the last stage, which is acceptance. She is also concerned with overcoming survivors' guilt. Swiss-born Dr. Kübler-Ross, 51 and the mother of two children, received her M.D. from the University of Zurich in 1957 and then came to the United States to complete her training at Manhattan State Hospital.

Spokeswoman for Childhood's "Magic Years"

SELMA FRAIBERG's life work has been understanding the minds and needs of children. Author of the widely read work *The Magic Years* (1959), which deals with the patterns of thought of earliest childhood, she also has published *Every Child's Birthright* (1977). In it, she makes a convincing case that contradicts prevailing ideas about child-rearing: she argues that all further development depends on the child's first attachments, that children need the continuity that

comes from being with familiar, loving people, and that this is not the situation at many day care centers. She urges careful reconsideration before we go ahead and construct many more such centers. Dr. Fraiberg is a professor of child psychoanalysis at the University of Michigan Medical School and directs a Child Development Project in Michigan that aids children with emotional difficulties.

Deputy Medical Director, American Psychiatric Association

After obtaining her M.D. from Howard University School of Medicine, Dr. JEANNE SPURLOCK interned at Chicago's Provident Hospital and served her residency in psychiatry at Cook County Psychopathic Hospital. From 1953 to 1959 she directed the Children's Psychosomatic Unit at the University of Illinois and from 1968 to 1973 was professor and chairman, Department of Psychiatry, Meharry Medical College. In 1974 she became deputy medical director of the American Psychiatric Association.

Hospices

In England there are over 25 hospices for the dying in operation. One of the best known is St. Christopher's, founded by Dr. CICELY SAUNDERS 10 years ago. In the United States there are only a few in existence, but many groups are actively organizing and planning to open hospices to provide comforts and care to the dying and their families that cannot easily be offered in a large hospital.

The U.S. movement has been bogged down partly due to technical obstacles, including questions about whether Blue Cross and Medicaid will cover hospice care and licensing regulations. There are also philosophical questions involved. Hospices are based on doctors and patients admitting the truth about an illness, and it is debated whether either group is truly willing to do so. One ardent hospice advocate who thinks they should is Dr. JOSEPHINE MAGNO, a cancer

specialist at Georgetown Medical Center.

"When you stop treating, you are admitting failure," she points out. "It is easier to go on treating than to admit failure. But that is why the hospice concept is such a great thing, because it allows the physician to say, 'Okay, we cannot cure you any more, but we can start caring for you.'"

Doctor, Lawyer, Hospital Chief

ROWINE HAYES BROWN was the first woman to become medical director of Cook County Hospital, in 1973, and the first woman in the country to be given directorship of a hospital of that size. Dr. Brown, a pediatrician, pioneered in the cause of child abuse and labeled the battered child syndrome as an identifiable childhood disease. She graduated from the University of Illinois Medical School in 1938. After her husband died, she attended school at night for ten years to obtain a law degree. Reason: so that she could better testify in battered child cases.

First Woman to Head Children's Hospital of Boston

The first woman to be physician-in-chief at the Children's Hospital Medical Center of Boston and the first woman to head a major clinical department at Harvard Medical School was Dr. MARY ELLEN AVERY. Dr. Avery was born in Camden, New Jersey, in 1927. She was graduated from Wheaton College and in 1952 from Johns Hopkins Medical School. Following completion of pediatric specialty training, she became an assistant professor at Johns Hopkins in 1960. In 1961 she was the first woman to be selected a Markle Scholar in medical science. In 1969 she was appointed professor of pediatrics at McGill University

—the first woman to chair a clinical department in Canada—and at the same time became physician-in-chief of Montreal Children's Hospital. At McGill, Dr. Avery was responsible for the pediatric care of the Eskimos in the eastern Arctic, and Arctic medicine continues to be an interest of hers. In 1974 she was appointed head of Children's Hospital in Boston and also became the Thomas Morgan Rotch Professor of Pediatrics at Harvard Medical School. Her major research, begun in 1958, has been to work out the pathogenesis of hyaline membrane disease—a respiratory affliction that is the leading cause of death in premature infants. The author of a classic reference, *The Lung and Its Disorders in the Newborn Infant* (1964), and co-author of *Diseases of the Newborn* (1960), she has received "five or six" honorary degrees. Dr. Avery once described herself as an avid golfer and fisher, but added with a laugh: "I've won no trophies in either—ever."

NURSES

Founder of Modern Nursing

Early in the 19th century, nursing was a menial job filled by unskilled women. The daughter of wealthy English people, FLORENCE NIGHTINGALE shocked society in 1850 by studying nursing at the Institute of Protestant Deaconesses in Germany. Soon she became superintendent of an Establishment for Gentlewomen During Illness in England. But it was during the Crimean War, in 1854, that she began her famous work. No plans had been made to care for the wounded, and more soldiers were dying of disease than of battle wounds. Patients lay on dirt floors in the blood-covered uniforms, there was no food for the very ill, and poor food for the others. Arriving at the huge hospital in Scutari, Turkey, Nightingale began to institute sane nursing methods. Prior to her appearance, the

hospital had a mortality rate of 42 per cent; under her direction it dropped to 2 per cent. After the war Florence Nightingale was idolized in England and a fund was raised to establish the Florence Nightingale Training School at St. Thomas's Hospital, London. Here, scientific nursing was first taught, and from here her pupils spread her ideas through the world.

Florence Nightingale first put forth the basic principles of modern nursing in her *Notes on Nursing*—ideas such as the importance of ventilation, warmth, and cleanliness in the sick room and the general comfort of the patient. These notions seem no more than common sense, but were then far from prevalent. One of her monumental works was *Notes Affecting the Health, Efficiency, and*

Hospital Administration of the British Army, which became a bible for hospital reform, and helped to make her a great world authority on hospital management and construction.

All this is not to say that Florence Nightingale was perfect. She believed strongly in cleanliness, but did not subscribe to the germ theory of disease. Nonetheless, she managed to revolutionize medical care and in the process to raise the art of nursing from a menial job to a respected profession. She "taught nurses to be ladies, and she brought ladies out of idleness to be nurses."

In 1907 Florence Nightingale was the first woman to receive England's Order of Merit. She died in 1910, aged 90.

The United States' First Trained Nurse

LINDA RICHARDS (1852–1912) graduated from the New England Hospital for Women and Children in 1873. She became superintendent of nurses at Massachusetts General Hospital, where she developed the program which established that trained nurses give better care than those without formal training. She introduced the idea of keeping patient records and the practice of uniforms for nurses, and was a pioneer in industrial and psychiatric nursing.

Angel of the Battlefield

She started out teaching school, became dissatisfied and founded her own school, then went to work in the Patent Office in Washington and quite by accident began to aid wounded soldiers. Observing the lack of first-aid supplies of any sort at an early Civil War battle, she advertised in a small, local newspaper for provisions, which she proceeded to distribute via mule team to camps, hospitals, and battlefields. The rest is legend. CLARA BARTON became known as "the Angel of the Battlefield" and a war heroine for her aid to the wounded and her ceaseless work on their behalf.

She worked so hard that she had a breakdown. While recovering in Europe, she heard about the International Committee of the Red Cross and she launched a five-year campaign to organize the American Red Cross and to persuade the United States to accept the Geneva Treaty providing for neutrality for war wounded and medical personnel. The American Red Cross was formed in 1881 and a treaty was signed the following year.

For the next 20 years, Clara Barton worked with the Red Cross, developing their programs and providing relief for disasters of every type, from yellow fever in Florida to famine in Russia. She lived to the age of 91 and died in 1912, one of the most acclaimed women of all time.

The United States' First Black Nurse

A graduate in 1879 of the New England Hospital for Women and Children, MARY MAHONEY became the country's first black professional nurse. She was among only three people in her class to complete the 16-month program. In recognition of her, the Mary Mahoney Award was established in 1936.

Nurse's Nurse

Aware of the difficulties that nursing students had in studying drugs, LAVINIA DOCK wrote one of the first nursing textbooks, *Materia Medica for Nurses*. She also co-authored with ADELAIDE NUTTING (p. 232) the famous four-volume *History of Nursing*. Ms. Dock graduated from Bellevue Training School for Nurses in 1886 and went on to become night supervisor at Bellevue Hospital. During her long career she also worked at Henry Street Settlement and at Johns Hopkins School for Nursing. Secretary of the International Council of Nurses for over 20 years, she was also a devoted suffragette and political activist who advocated legislation to control nursing practice. She lived from 1858 to 1956.

Heroic Yellow Fever Volunteer

CLARA MAASS (1876–1901) worked as an army nurse in Florida, Cuba, and the Philippines during the Spanish-American War. In 1900 she was asked to return to Cuba, where she became involved in a dispute over the cause of yellow fever. The question was whether the disease resulted from filth or the bite of a mosquito. Seven volunteers, among them Clara Maass, agreed to be bitten by the mosquitoes. Two of the men died, but Maass survived. The second time she volunteered to be bitten a year later, she suffered from severe pain and fever and died at the age of 25. Her death, having proved the point, ended the experiments. The *New York Times* wrote: "No soldier in the late war placed his life in peril for better reasons than those which prompted this faithful nurse to risk hers." The Newark German Hospital Training School for Nurses, from which Clara Maass was graduated in 1895, was renamed in her honor, the U. S. Postal Service has issued a stamp commemorating her, and she is a member of the Hall of Fame of the American Nurses' Association.

Crusaders for Equal Opportunity

One of the first black nurses to campaign for equality in the profession was MARTHA FRANKLIN, who organized the National Association of Colored Graduate Nurses in 1908. Another who worked for the acceptance of black nurses was ADAH THOMS—for 18 years assistant superintendent of the Lincoln School for Nurses in New York, at a time when blacks rarely held high positions. She campaigned for black nurses in the U. S. Army Nurse Corps and in the American Red Cross, wrote a history of black graduate nurses, and in 1936 was the first nurse to receive the Mary Mahoney Medal.

First Nurse to Become a University Professor

MARY ADELAIDE NUTTING is best known for her advocacy of university education for nurses, and she was instrumental in developing the first programs. In 1899 she persuaded the Dean of Teachers College, Columbia University, to establish a nursing education program which she directed. In 1906 she was appointed professor of household administration at Teachers College, becoming the first nurse to hold a university professorship. In 1910 her program was made a separate department and she was made Professor of Nursing Education. The era was important in the history of nursing; her work at Columbia and her writings made major contributions to the advancement of the profession. She wrote *A Sound Economic Basis for Nursing* and co-authored with LAVINIA DOCK (p. 231) the four-volume *History of Nursing*. Born in 1858 in Quebec, Mary Adelaide Nutting graduated from Johns Hopkins Training School for Nurses and later became principal of the school, instituting such revolutionary reforms as abolishing the 12-hour work day and replacing it with a three-year course of training and study. She also instituted tuition fees, so that the school was not dependent on free lectures from the doctors and the school in turn was not obligated to provide free labor for the hospital.

Dean of the First Graduate School of Nursing

ANNIE WARBURTON GOODRICH (1866–1954) was appalled that nursing schools demanded, at best, a grade school education from applicants. As Director of nurse training at St. Luke's and Bellevue hospitals in New York, she insisted on a high school diploma for admission. During World War I she helped found and was a dean of the Army School of Nursing. In 1923 Annie Goodrich and a small committee established the Yale University School of Nursing. She became its first dean. Ten years later she was responsible for developing the program into the Yale Graduate School of Nursing. Among nurses she was known as a crusader and diplomat. An 1890 graduate of the New York Hospital Training School for Nurses, she held many prominent positions during her career: president of the American Nurses Association, a director of nursing service at the Henry Street Settlement, New York State Inspector for Training Schools, and a professor of nursing at Teachers College, Columbia University.

First U. S. Public Health Service Nurse

In 1933 PEARL MCIVER became the first public health nurse in the U. S. Public Health Service. She served for a time as chief of the nursing division, also as vice-president of the American Public Health Association.

First Woman to Win the Rockefeller Public Service Award

In 1965 the $10,000 Rockefeller Public Service Award first went to a woman, MARGARET ARNSTEIN, who was dean of the Yale University School of Nursing, and a former chief nurse of the United States Public Health Service. During her career, Ms. Arnstein also served as chief nurse of the Balkan mission of the United Nations Relief and Rehabilitation Administration, as the first nursing adviser for international health in the Office of the Surgeon General, and as a professor of public health at the University of Michigan. She died in 1972 of cancer.

The New Nurse-Practitioners

They work in hospital clinics, in private practices with physicians, and, in some remote areas where there are doctor shortages, they staff clinics single-handedly. They handle many duties once the sole domain of the physician, such as physical examinations, medical histories, follow-up of chronic-disease patients, and preliminary diagnoses. They may also—with a physician's approval—prescribe drugs.

The concept was developed about 10 years ago by a doctor and a nurse, LORETTA FORD, at the University of Colorado. There are now 12,000 nurse-practitioners in the United States, many of whom are specialists in family practice, pediatrics, psychiatry, or other areas. They earn more than an average nurse, although much less than an average physician.

It's an idea that seems to be meeting with approval all around. Nurses like the added responsibility; patients, once they get used to the idea, appreciate the personal attention nurse-practitioners are known for; and doctors like the assistance, which means that, relieved of many routine duties, they are freer to give their attention to sicker patients. A nurse-practitioner is what is called "cost effective," too.

6

Women in Fashions and Home Furnishings

By Molly G. Schuchat and Louise Edie Kerrigan

Frances Dalessandro, consulting editor

Design is as old as Eve, who fashioned fig-leaf aprons for herself and Adam. In North America decorative objects are documented back at least 11,000 years, the date assigned to a necklace of thong and shell worn by a young woman who apparently drowned in a glacial lake in Minnesota. Creativity has marked clothes and home decoration and furnishings since the beginning. Blankets have always been woven not army plain but in a variety of designs, in a rainbow of colors made from dye stuffs available not only locally but through trade. Pottery has always been more than functional; firing color, glaze, and decoration as well as handles, spouts, lips, and lids have distinct local and time styles. The items found in both simple burials and the most elaborate tombs attest to humanity's constant preoccupation with the manufacture of pleasing, as well as useful, articles for household and personal use.

But it is one thing to knit oneself a gorgeous sweater from purchased wool and quite another to keep a household in clothing, bedding, and towels completely manufactured (spun, woven, dyed, cut, and sewn) by a housewife simultaneously engaged in agriculture, bearing and raising children, working the garden, cleaning, and cooking—from scratch—as well as doctoring the physical and emotional ills that befall a family. These methods of production did not change much from the inventions of pottery and the loom until the Age of Discovery combined with the Industrial Revolution at the end of the 19th century. Then one side of the coin of progress showed terrible human conditions at mills and the colonial exploitation of new lands and peoples. But the other side offered the possibility of making attractive clothes and home furnishings easily available for all people.

Modern fashion apparel can be said to have begun with Rosa Bertin, dressmaker to Queen Marie Antoinette, who was given the title "Minister of Fashion" before the French Revolution. She originated the practice of dressing "fashion babies" in her latest designs and sending them to customers at other European courts. The use of fashion babies continued until Charles Worth, the Britisher who became the father of French couture, introduced live models in his Paris showroom in the 1860s. Although women's ready-to-wear was reported in the U.S. census of 1860, American fashion was then largely a matter of traditional embroideries for linens and lingerie or emulating what was decreed in Paris by home sewing or the hiring of a local seamstress to copy the creations of French couturiers in locally purchased materials.

Change followed fast as ready-made fashions and housewares became more widely available. And part of the change was that women were in the workforce in other capacities than as individual dressmakers. Elias Howe perfected the sewing machine in the United States in 1849, and men's work clothing was the initial product made in America's earliest machine-powered factories (Mr. Levi first produced his quintessential American fashion in 1850 for California goldminers). Then the Civil War created an unprecedented demand for ready-made clothes and marked the real turn from homemade, hand-sewn garments. War also brought about the beginning of size standardization, first developed for military uniforms.

The great increase in production of both men's and women's ready-to-wear came, however, with the labor pool made available by the mass immigrations of the late 19th and early 20th centuries. A veritable army of skilled seamstresses and tailors came to the major manufacturing cities of North America. The garments they made were turned out not in the tradition of the couturiers of Paris with meticulous stitching and fitting and restitching, but as piecework hurriedly produced on rented or dearly bought sewing machines.

The sweatshop conditions of the Triangle Shirtwaist Factory Fire days are for-tunately long gone. But most sewing in the United States is still done by production line piecework in small shops that fill orders for manufacturers via members of the International Ladies' Garment Workers' Union. (See "Women in the Labor Movement and Organizations, p. 284.) Following the pattern of migration to the East Coast from Europe and the South, the union members have been progressively, Italian, Jewish, Negro, Spanish-speaking, and now increasingly Asian in origin. And so have the designers.

U.S. fashion and design for the home really came into its own after World War I. The great couturiers of the 1920s were still the French, but Americans were learning. Mostly they were learning for the mass market, not the individual customer. The majority of American clothes today are designed for off-the-rack sales. At the upper end of the price range they carry designers' names. These designers may have spent their whole careers in wholesale work. Or they may have shifted from couture (individually fitted and sewn garments copied from the designer's model from a collection). Or they may have made their names in their own boutiques, those now ubiquitous small shops where a designer, with the help of a few seamstresses, makes up a limited quantity of ready-to-wear items of clothing—and, increasingly, furnishings for the home—sold interspersed with other things of beauty carefully collected by the owner-designer. Sometimes a boutique line is bought by a major manufacturer or store (Neiman Marcus and Henri Bendel pioneered in this practice).

One exciting thing about fashion design and production is that it continues to be an individual business to a much greater extent than other industries of like importance (astonishingly, out of every eight persons in manufacturing, one is in textile and apparel manufacture). Today's boutique designer may become tomorrow's big name with her concepts turned into large-scale business. The few lucky stars, no matter how they start, explode into giant galaxies, lighting both fashion and home, like VERA, or ARMI RATIA, or DIANE VON FURSTENBERG.

Textiles play a key role in all this. In Europe, couturiers have always commissioned small-production runs of fabric designs. But not until the 1930s did the development of screen printing finally allow manufacturers to try short runs of experimental designs without the heavy expense of engraved rollers or the laborious process of hand-block printing. And American manufacturers really began to listen to designers only in the 1950s—then principally in order to spread the use of new man-made fabrics. As designers began to influence textile innovations, they in their turn exerted more influence on fashions. New dyes, new knitting patterns, and new finishes have all had important effects on style for the home and for clothing.

Always, of course, what royalty, first ladies, and actresses wear or use has excited attention. Prizes also affect the national and world fashion parade. The Museum of Modern Art awards in contemporary design, and the Neiman-Marcus and Coty awards in fashion have been major forces in both recognizing and creating high style. Objects and textiles themselves have more often been admitted to museum collections than have the results of draping, sewing, and fitting cloth. But with the tide of costume shows mounted at the Metropolitan, the Smithsonian, and other major museums in the last decade, women's clothing, as well as knights' shining armor, has arrived at the status of art.

In the 20th century, still and cinema photography, television and Telstar have created an instant worldwide audience for new and old styles that move from place to place at the speed of sound and light. The world of design is truly an international world, with the people of the developing countries turning toward modern Western clothing and household furnishings as designers jet around the world seeking new/old ideas from traditional societies for dress and the home. Middle-Eastern women are fast emerging from behind their voluminous overgarments and veils; Western women have recently taken the caftan to their hearts and wardrobes. Asians turn to plastic buckets as Westerners collect one-of-a-kind ceramic and brass pots.

Fashion looks everywhere for inspiration. Following MARY QUANT's revolutionary move to dress the young and the not-rich, designers turned to the '60s counterculture and to the cities' street people for new ideas. And in 1977 and '78 "the latest" focus in Parisian couture and American ready-to-wear was on tunics worn with wide pants pulled in at the ankle—the very costume AMELIA BLOOMER invented to free the New American Woman 125 years ago.

MOLLY SCHUCHAT is an anthropologist interested in ethnicity, food habits, and leisure-time activities who has done fieldwork in Eastern Europe and in the United States. She has twice visited the People's Republic of China (the first time with the National Delegation of American Women Professional Leaders). Director of evaluation for Behavior Service Consultants, Inc., Greenbelt, Maryland, she previously taught anthropology at several universities and coordinated a community mental health program at one of them. She has a B.A. from Vassar College, a Ph.D. from Catholic University, and is married to an attorney. They have five children.

LOUISE EDIE KERRIGAN, who contributed the material on home furnishings to this chapter, is also the author of "Women in the Home and Community" (pp. 98–140).

Consulting editor FRANCES DALESSANDRO started her career in fashion the same year she was graduated from

Georgian Court College in Lakewood New Jersey, when she went to work for *Mademoiselle* magazine. In 1966 she joined the May Merchandising Corporation in the fashion office and eventually moved into merchandising with responsibility for ready-to-wear and menswear. In 1976 Ms. Dalessandro, who is married to a stockbroker, was named vice-president and director of Creative Merchandising.

PERSONAL FASHION, STARTING WITH THE TOP

Most Influential Fashion Figure of the Decade 1910–20

IRENE CASTLE, the most famous ballroom dancer of her time, made and set style with her appearance. To balance her above-the-ankle dancing skirts, in 1915 she cut her hair short, establishing the 20th-century head. Fashion designers followed suit for their models. Milliners rushed to design new styles in hats to wear with the new headshapes. And designers also shortened skirts to balance the new small heads.

First American-Born Hat Designer

SALLY VICTOR (1894–1977), born in Scranton, Pennsylvania, started as a stock girl in millinery at Macy's and was an assistant buyer well before she turned 20. By the 1930s Sally Victor's label was in all the best retail stores in New York and points West. The *New Yorker* described her as "a sculptress of straws and felts." During World War II this designer of expensive hats for the most fashionable women turned to the ordinary working woman. She designed a work hat of denim with an adjustable fabric snood for General Electric's production line workers. The snood, previously a fashion item only, served to confine long hair and so prevent accidents. Ms. Victor said that she liked "designing hats that made pretty women look prettier." Her most famous styles were the baby bonnet, the Flemish sailor, and the Greek pillbox. MAMIE EISENHOWER's bangs were topped by Sally Victor pillboxes throughout her eight years as First Lady of the United States.

First French Milliner to Make Her Fame in America

LILLY DACHÉ was born in France, where she was apprenticed to a milliner at 14. She went to Paris to work for Reboux, who introduced the cloche—one of the new hat shapes to go with women's newly short hair—in 1923. Immediately thereafter, Lilly Daché came to the United States and opened her first shop, where she introduced hats made-in-America that were molded to the head in the latest fashion. Her name became synonymous with elegant, beautiful hats, but she also made gloves, hosiery, lingerie, loungewear, and, eventually, dresses to go with her headgear. After that she branched out into men's ties and wrote two books that added to her fame as a celebrity as well as a designer. Her daughter, Suzanne, has followed in her designing footsteps.

Sister Wigmakers

MARIA and ROSITA CARITA, two Parisian hair stylists of Spanish birth, were responsible for the rebirth of the wig for fashionable use. The Carita sisters insisted that a well-groomed woman needs two coiffures, her own hair and a wig ready for quick changes. In 1958 they created a wig with strands of hair woven into a cap of lightweight and airy elasticized net held securely and simply by a snug elastic band. Givenchy put them on his mannequins that season, and the huge chrysanthemum heads created a sensation. A craze for wigs to match costumes saw them dyed in such shades as light green and shocking pink. Shortly thereafter, wigs became available in synthetic materials, with permanent styling built in at incredibly reasonable prices by any standards.

Top Model Who Introduced Wigs for Black Women

NAOMI SIMS, born in 1949 in Oxford, Mississippi, was the first famous black model. After high school and fashion school in Pittsburgh she stormed the Big Apple, where, after her stunning success as a top model, she has moved on to design wigs and hairpieces for black women. More recently, Ms. Sims has branched out into cosmetics and written a fashion guide entitled *All About Health and Beauty for the Black Woman* (1976).

Other Designers Who Began as Models

Models may work in showrooms to display clothes to buyers and in fashion shows for the general public as well as for photographers. Although she never was employed as one, CLAIRE MCCARDELL (p. 244) designed with herself in mind and frequently was photographed for high fashion magazines. *Time* wrote that she was her own best model. More than that, she taught her models to walk the way she did, drooping at the neck and slumped at the waist, and this stance and gait were copied widely.

Below are the names of some other women fashion designers (in addition to Naomi Sims, above) who have modeled professionally. Some of them were the leading models of their day and turned to design after that; others used a brief modeling stint as a wedge to get designing jobs:

> Britta
> Anne Fogarty
> Emmanuelle Khanh
> Beth Levine
> Vera Maxwell
> Pat McDonagh
> Efi Melas
> Elsa Peretti

Dress and Personal Ornament

Fashion is of utmost importance not only to modern Western city-dwellers, but also to people like the villagers of Aritama in the tropical mountain country of northern Colombia. Their way of life—and fashion—in the 1950s was described by anthropologists Gerardo and Alicia Reichel-Dolmatoff: ". . . dress and ornament are the most important exterior manifestations of a person's status and are thus the center of constant preoccupation, discussion, and gossip. Any commodities are willingly sacrificed in order to save money for clothes, and some people will go to the limit of physical starvation only to be able to appear in public in new suits and dresses.

"But those who can afford to buy new clothes at least once a year—and they form the majority, as much of their total economic production is spent in this way—also have difficulties. Their choice of fabric, style, cut, color, or print is certain to be discussed by neighbors who will doubt the person's 'right' to use a certain kind of suit, a certain quantity of dresses, or who will criticize the occasion upon which they are worn . . . On the other hand, the complexities of modern dress have not been fully mastered yet by many people, and the correct use of certain items has led, not to reinterpretation, but to outright confusion. Women can be seen stumbling along with new shoes put on the wrong foot, while others wear their dresses backward. Men are unable to knot a tie but insist on wearing one on certain occasions, inventing their own version of knots. Felt hats that have a broad hatband often are worn with the bow in front, and some men can be seen carrying women's handbags of plastic or leather when traveling. Belts, kerchiefs, umbrellas, fountain-pens, and other details also cause confusion and are sometimes affected out of place and in a manner which hardly corresponds to their basic functions.

"We have seen people break out in tears or run away frantically when surprised in their working clothes. Doors are bolted and windows are closed as soon as a visitor arrives, and people will show themselves only after they have changed into new, or at least clean and mended, clothes.

"The high-prestige value of clothes is very characteristic for most of Colombia, but in Aritama it reaches a point where it becomes a preoccupation . . . charged with anxieties."

From *The People of Aritama* by Gerardo and Alicia Reichel-Dolmatoff, the University of Chicago Press, 1961. © The University of Chicago.

COUTURIERS TO BEGIN WITH

First to Cut Clothes on the Bias

MADELEINE VIONNET (1877–1975) revolutionized women's dressing by cutting fabrics on the bias and eliminating fastenings to free the silhouette. The daughter of a plumber, she began her fashion career in London and first opened her own shop in Paris, briefly, before World War I. In 1919 she reopened her House of Vionnet and immediately became a dominant fashion influence. Her bias cut and her skirts of pointy, handkerchief draperies were famous. Her innovations extended beyond fashion itself. She provided advanced social services for her workers, along with medical clinics and a gymnasium. She closed her shop with the beginning of World War II.

Inventor of Contemporary Dress

GABRIELLE "Coco" CHANEL (1883–1971) set her stamp on fashion over a period of fifty years. Her revolutionary simple short skirts, low waistlines, and loose jackets were "The Look" of the 1920s. *Vogue* said that she designed out of "understanding of the times" and the "unusual necessities of present-day life." Chanel was born in the Auvergne region of France and as a child developed a passion for riding and for horses. Her design career began in Deauville with a millinery shop to which she shortly added simple little dresses. By 1914 she felt ready to move to Paris, where she was an immediate success. She shortened skirts to match the new vogue in short hair, introduced the use of jersey as a fashionable fabric, and packaged her famous perfume, Chanel Number 5. (She believed the number 5 was good luck, and so it proved to be for both perfume sellers and buyers.) Chanel liked, wore, and made high fashion fake pearls, elaborate costume jewelry, and sweaters. When she wore a man's trench coat to the races, the passionate affair of women and trench coats, lasting to this day, began. With the advent of World War II, she closed her house of fashion. During the German occupation, she remained in Paris. Thought by some French critics to have been too friendly with the Germans, she was in eclipse for a time but at age 71, in 1954, she reopened her couture house. Once again the open jacket suit and loose overblouse became high fashion. Chanel herself was always high fashion. She has been the subject of many biographies and figured prominently in those of the famous men with whom she was involved. In 1969 KATHARINE HEPBURN (see "Women in the Arts and Entertainment," p. 657) played her in the musical *Coco*. Gabrielle Chanel died in her home in the Ritz Hotel in Paris in 1971. Her styles and her scents live on—still major 20th-century fashion.

Founder of American Couture

HATTIE CARNEGIE (1889–1956) was born in Vienna but spent her adult life in America. Out of admiration for American success stories, she changed her last name from Kanengeiser to Carnegie. She began at the bottom of the ladder as a messenger girl at Macy's, but she was even then a person of enormous style. In 1909, with a seamstress friend, Rose Roy, she opened a shop called "Carnegie —Ladies' Hatter." She designed the hats. Ten years later she bought out her partner and began the expansion that made hers a multimillion-dollar business, covering not only custom clothing but wholesale, resort shops, and an assortment of accessories. Hattie Carnegie brought Paris design to American couture. Famous for her ability to discover fashion talent, she made her workrooms the training ground for some of the great American designers of the 20th century, including Norman Norell and CLAIRE MCCARDELL (p. 244), PAULINE TRIGÈRE (p. 242), and NETTIE ROSENSTEIN (p. 243). In 1948 Ms. Carnegie won the Coty Award for "consistent contributions to American elegance."

She Introduced Abstract Designs for Fashions

SONIA DELAUNAY, born 1885, an artist of increasingly appreciated note, was the daughter of Russian Jews. She went to Paris to study in 1904 and there married another artist, with whom she shared the ferment of the exciting developments in modern art. After the Russian Revolution she had to work for a living as well as painting for art's sake. Ms. Delaunay began by designing costumes for Sergei Diaghilev's productions and then for Dadaist theatrical productions. In 1922 she introduced simultaneous or multiple scarves for women's accessories and in 1924 set up her own workshop to produce women's clothes, including woven tapestry coats. In 1925 she and Jacques Heim, the couturier, had a boutique at the famous Art Deco Show. For the balance of the 1920s she created imaginative, vividly colored clothes for international celebrities. After World War II Ms. Delaunay returned to painting. The Musée National d'Art Moderne held a one-woman retrospective in honor of her 90th birthday in 1975 and in 1977 a New York Gallery held a large ret-

rospective of her fabrics, gouaches, and oils timed to coincide with a boutique showing of 900 shawls, scarves, tablecloths, and plates of Delaunay design, signed by the still-active artist.

The Unconventional Inventor of Shocking Pink

ELSA SCHIAPARELLI (1890–1973) introduced flamboyance to fashion between the Depression and World War II. She invented the term "Shocking Pink," which became her trademark. Born in Rome, raised in Europe, married in the United States, she returned to Paris when her marriage ended, in 1920. There she began her career by promoting the first dressy sweater, a black silk pullover. She was a close friend of Salvador Dali, Jean Cocteau, and other artists, several of whom worked for her in designing the extravagant prints for which her clothes were known. She introduced accessory novelties, such as handbags that lit up and glowing phosphorescent brooches, and designed knickers for ski wear as early as 1937. After the war, "Schiap" retired from fashion to write her autobiography, *Shocking Life,* while living on the proceeds of her perfume business. Her granddaughters, model-actress MARISA BERENSON and fashion photographer BERRY BERENSON, continue her traditions.

First Black Couture Designer

ANN LOWE has created original designs for Hattie Carnegie, Henri Bendel, Neiman Marcus, I. Magnin, and Saks Fifth Avenue as well as through her own workroom, Ann Lowe Originals. The daughter and granddaughter of seamstresses, she was born in 1898 in Montgomery, Alabama, where she went to school to study design. In order to study and receive a diploma, she was forced to learn in isolation, in a room by herself at the school. By the age of 21 she had the leading dress shop in Tampa, Florida, and seven years later made the switch to New York City. There she began designing gowns for debutantes and social register brides. Ms. Lowe made JACQUELINE BOUVIER's (see "Far-Out Women," p. 751) wedding dress for her marriage to John F. Kennedy. In later years, her vision severely limited by glaucoma, she developed a technique of dictating sketches to an illustrator, correcting the draft herself, and then turning it back to the artist for completion.

First American Designer Honored by Both French and Americans

PAULINE TRIGÈRE, daughter of Russian immigrants to France and herself an American immigrant, was elevated to the Coty Hall of Fame in 1959 and received the Medal of the City of Paris in 1972. A highly individual designer, a master of the French tradition, and an able American businesswoman, she provided made-to-order couture for the wholesale market. Trigère's work is sought after for the draped dresses that look so deceptively simple and for dramatic capes. She is the acknowledged master in cutting and draping. Ms. Trigère's parents had made military uniforms for the Russian aristocracy and in Paris they were, respectively, a wholesale clothing contractor and a dressmaker. At 15 the daughter was apprenticed to a famous tailoring establishment in the Place Vendôme where she mastered, effortlessly, the difficult bias cut and other advanced dressmaking techniques. ADELE SIMPSON (p. 243) met her in Paris and helped her to settle in New York when the Trigère family—mother, brother, herself, her two children, and husband—arrived there in 1937. Ms. Trigère was working for HATTIE CARNEGIE (p. 240) until that designer closed down many of her workrooms immediately after Pearl Harbor. Undaunted, Pauline Trigère and her brother, Robert, went into business in January 1942. As she later said, "I had to make a living to support my children." (Her marriage had ended.) Her first collection was an immediate success and her life has gone on that way ever since, built on skill and meticulous perfectionism, and her creative ability with fabrics and fit. Ms. Trigère leads the kind of life for which she designs her clothes. She entertains in the city and in her country home, is a regular theatergoer and an art collector. The turtle is her favorite symbol, reflected in gold jewelry, a large art collection depicting turtles in every medium, and in her trademark tortoise-rimmed spectacles. Since 1973 Pauline Trigère has also been a formal teacher, involved with the Design Studio Classes at the Fashion Institute of Technology.

Lone Couturier for Eastern Europe

KLARA ROTSCHILD (1903–76) designed for all of the important women throughout Communist Eastern Europe. The daughter and granddaughter of court dressmakers, Ms. Rotschild opened her studio in 1937 on fashionable Vaci Street in Budapest, with her husband. During World War II her husband was killed by the Nazis and she had to go into hiding. After the war she reopened her business alone. In 1950 it was turned over to the state, but she continued to serve as the artistic director and designer until her death. Her clients included not only the wife of Andrei Gromyko of the Soviet Union and Communist Party members' wives from Yugoslavia and Mongolia but other visitors as well, including Queen FARAH DIBA of Iran.

Russian-Born American Couturier and Costume Designer

VALENTINA, Russian-born (1904) and European-trained, began by designing clothes for herself. People always talked as much about the costumes she wore to Broadway openings as the First Night itself. She opened her couture establishment in New York in 1928 and shortly thereafter began to design for Broadway shows as well. Her designs for the theater, if not the plays they graced, were always received with raves. Brooks Atkinson of the New York Times once wrote that "Valentina has designed clothes that act before a line is spoken." Always her own best advertiser, not only wearing the clothes but making quotable statements that have passed into fashion history, she is credited with saying: "Mink is for football, ermine is for bathrobes" and "In choosing clothes what women want is nearly always wrong."

Ireland's Number One Designer

SYBIL CONNOLLY was born in Wales and raised in southern Ireland but first worked in London. After two years with a designer there she moved on to Dublin as a buyer for an exclusive store. In 1950 Ms. Connolly showed her own first collection at the store and her work was seen, shortly thereafter, by a visiting American Fashion group. In 1953 she came to New York for the first time. Her one-of-a-kind designs of natural Irish fabrics—Donegal tweeds, homespun, fine linen—became high fashion immediately. Ms. Connolly opened her own couture establishment in Dublin in 1957 and also added a boutique for ready-to-wear.

First Ladies' Gowns

The hall of the First Ladies is one of the most popular at the Smithsonian Institution in Washington. In it the gowns worn by the wives of American Presidents for their husbands' inauguration festivities are displayed on mannequins in period settings. Since the inauguration of President Dwight D. Eisenhower, designers' names have been attached. Four of them are women.

For ·Mamie Eisenhower: Nettie Rosenstein

For Jacqueline Kennedy: Ethel Frankau of Bergdorf Goodman

For Pat Nixon: Karen Stark of Harvey Berin

For Betty Ford: Frankie Welch of Alexandria (Virginia)

DESIGNERS FOR THE TRADE

First Young High-Salaried Woman Designer in New York

ADELE SIMPSON, who has had her own firm under her own name since 1949, began her career as a success. At 21, graduated from Pratt Institute of Design with top honors, she became one of the youngest and highest-salaried designers in New York. Innovative as well as meticulous, she was one of the first to introduce clothes that could be stepped into rather than pulled over the head, cotton for evening wear, day and evening boots (before Courrèges), and she was the first American designer to use Indian sari cloth in high fashion. Adele Simpson has always been known for pretty, very wearable clothes. She was the favorite designer of Pat Nixon when she was First Lady. Ms. Simpson is the winner of many awards, including both the Neiman-Marcus and the Coty awards.

She Called It "Spinach"

ELIZABETH HAWES (1903–71) was one of the first young American designers to receive public acknowledgment for her work. In 1933 *Vogue* credited her in its pages and Lord & Taylor ran a newspaper ad doing the same. She studied in Paris in 1925 and opened her own private business in New York in 1928 and quickly became known as one of the young designers who made it fashionable to wear New York-conceived clothes. By 1932 she was designing for manufacturers, but it was a discouraging experience for her. At the height of her designing fame, she quit the business to write

Fashion Is Spinach (1938). The allusion was to E. B. White's caption for a *New Yorker* cartoon wherein a mother urged her little girl to eat: "It's broccoli, dear," The reply was: "I say it's spinach, and I say the hell with it."

Inventor of the "American Look"

In 1938 a tent dress cut on the bias with no waistline was designed by CLAIRE McCARDELL (1905–58). When belted it markedly but casually defined a good figure. McCardell had designed it originally for herself from an Algerian costume and then adapted it in street length for the fall collection of Townley Sportswear. No buyer wanted it and the dress hung limply on a hanger in her office while she went off on a vacation. Best and Co.'s buyer, looking for an exclusive, saw it and ordered a hundred. His advertising staff named the dress "The Monastic" and featured it in a full-page Sunday ad. On Monday afternoon the buyer ordered two hundred more, and then more. The dress was copied up and down Seventh Avenue and put Claire McCardell on the fashion map as the designer of the "American Look."

Claire McCardell was born in Frederick, Maryland. After one unhappy year at local Hood College she went to New York to study at the Parsons School of Design (then called the New York School of Fine and Applied Arts), which also had a branch in Paris where she spent a year. When she went to work in the late 1920s, Ms. McCardell quickly developed a reputation for being difficult to work with although she designed excellent sports clothes of all kinds for several manufacturers. She settled down with Townley Sportswear and stayed till it went out of business the year after the success of her tent dress.

Next she worked for HATTIE CARNEGIE (p. 240), whose customers found her clothes too plain for the money and their mature, frequently plump, figures. Hattie Carnegie believed in and promoted her new protégé anyway. She gave GERTRUDE LAWRENCE (see "Women in the Arts and Entertainment") a very plain McCardell design for a glamorous 1939 stage role in *Skylark*. The actress did not like it at all, and another Carnegie designer (Norell) made it over with beads. But DIANA VREELAND (p. 262), who got a one-piece McCardell design instead of the two-piece Chanel-like dress she had ordered from Carnegie, liked what she saw and became one of Claire McCardell's most powerful admirers.

Even so, the designer left the Carnegie establishment and although she incorporated custom details she had learned there, she returned to her life work of making attractive and practical clothes for all American women, not just for those who could afford custom-made designs. By now World War II had begun in Europe, and American designers no longer had French fashion on which to lean. In 1941 Claire McCardell took her wear-anytime-anywhere clothes that were casual and easy-fitting but elegant back to a rebuilt Townley Company. She stayed with the firm with her name on the label and from 1951 on as a partner until her death.

Among the innovations that sold under the Townley-McCardell label and were her inspiration and design were diaper bathing suits and dirndl skirts. When leather for shoes was rationed, she covered ballet slippers in fabrics to match the dresses. Another McCardell first was the "Popover," designed to be worn by servantless wartime ladies. She used double stitching (top or blue-jean stitching) and fasteners that showed, including metal zippers that were part of the design. She preferred the functional appearance of rivets, grommets, and dime-sized brass snaps and gilt hooks and eyes. Most famous and repeated touch of all were the thin bias cords, "spaghetti ties," that could crisscross down a natural waistline or wrap the high Empire Style, tie a halter neckline or keep a bolero together.

From the mid-1940s on, Claire McCardell clothes appeared in art shows, including a one-person show of dress designs exhibited like any other works of art. She was on the cover of *Time* magazine in 1956. In the middle 1950s, Claire McCardell also became one of the first franchised designers. Jewelry, sweaters, raincoats, head- and foot-gear and "sunspecs" (tinted granny glasses) were so marketed. There were future plans, too, for a set of McCardell-dressed paper dolls, but the designer died of cancer before this and other of her endless ideas were realized.

She Pioneered Junior Clothes for Elegant Women

ANNE KLEIN (1921–74) transformed junior clothes from sprightly little things with buttons and bows to sleek, sophisticated clothing for worldly women with still-youthful figures. Through 1978 she remained the only designer to win the Neiman-Marcus Award twice (1959 and 1969). She was elected to the Coty American Fashion Hall of Fame in 1971. Ms. Klein began life as Hannah Golofski in Brooklyn and was doing free-lance sketching on Seventh Avenue at age 15. A year later she joined Varden Petites. It was there that she pioneered the transformation of junior clothes. In 1948 she and her first husband, Ben Klein, formed Junior Sophisticates, for which she created the skimmer dress-plus-jacket and then the A-line dress and long, pleated plaid skirts with blazers. Gradually she moved into more expensive and high-style fashion. In 1968, with her second husband, she formed Anne Klein and Company, for which she continued to design. She also franchised the name. Anne Klein died March 20, 1974,

but her name has been carried on in many facets of the fashion world, as well as in the sportswear itself.

First American Woman to Win Transatlantic Fashion Awards

BONNIE CASHIN is probably the winner of more awards than any other American designer. She has won all of the top American ones and is a member of the Coty Hall of Fame (1972). She also, in 1966, won the *Sunday Times* of London's Fashion Award. Her clothes were the first American fashions to be carried in a British store, Liberty of London. The daughter of a California dressmaker and an inventor, Ms. Cashin studied at the Art Students League of New York and then returned to her native state. Her first designing was not of the sportswear for which she is so famous, but for the movie industry. Ms. Cashin designed clothes for sixty major films, including *Anna and the King of Siam* and *Laura*. She came to New York to design stage shows and was, at the time, the youngest designer ever to hit Broadway. When she also began designing outdoor clothing, her first collection was staged at the Roxy Theatre. Famous for the layered look, featuring natural materials including wool, canvas, and leather, she coordinates her functional layers of clothing with her own designs of hoods, bags, boots, and belts.

Anglo-American Winner

JEAN MUIR has always been involved in large operations. She began as a sketcher-salesgirl at Liberty of London and moved from there to Jaeger, where she quickly became responsible for the design of major dress and knitwear collections. In 1961 she was asked to start a new company, called Jane and Jane. In 1966 she left to work independently under her own name, with her husband as financial manager. From the start she sold throughout Britain and to Henri Bendel in New York. Her clothes are always recognizable as Jean Muirs and, despite their fashionable variations, are always gentle, pretty clothes. A winner of many major awards in England and America since she was with Jane and Jane, in 1973 she was elected a fellow of The Royal Society of Arts and also received the Neiman-Marcus Award. In 1974 she opened an office in New York.

Israel's Promoters of Ethnic Fashions

FINI LEITHERSDORF, godmother of the Israeli fashion image, born 1906, learned her trade in her native Hungary. She came to Jerusalem as a refugee in 1939 and her first work utilized native handwoven crafts as well as the embroideries of the people in the refugee camps. Still spreading the word in 1968, she founded Ulpana, a studio-school modeled on the Bauhaus idea.

ROJY (HANANEL) BEN JOSEPH, a Bulgarian-born Israeli, first designed modern adaptations of traditional costumes of the Jews of North Africa and Yeman. Since 1968 she has used native crafts in garments produced by factory methods, primarily for beach and at-home wear. To her ethnic styling, Hananel has added traditional Arabic designs, including Hebron glass, olive-wood belts, and embroidery and braidwork.

Couture Look at Moderate Prices

ELEANOR BRENNER describes herself as a camouflage designer who realizes the imperfections of the average woman's figure and feels a responsibility to make this woman prettier and more elegant. She uses couture touches such as expensive buckles, antique buttons, unpressed hems, but the dresses themselves are bared down to their essentials. A Phi Beta Kappa from New York University who began her career as a TV fashion commentator but dropped out of the work world when she became pregnant, Ms. Brenner attended design school to keep busy and continued on after the birth of her eldest son. Her first attempts at designing met no success with com-

mercial manufacturers. Briefly, then, Ms. Brenner did interior decorating and, although she was an immediate success in this field, soon returned to dress designing, selling directly to Henri Bendel and other exclusive stores, rather than trying to have her clothes wholesaled. In 1969 she and her husband became manufacturers of her designs under the name Brenner Couture. In 1973 a sweater-knit division was added and in 1975 her designs were cited by the Knitted Textile Association. In addition to designing, Ms. Brenner has worked with the Costume Institute of the Metropolitan Museum in New York.

Pioneer in Soft Sportswear

ADRI (STECKLING) started her fashion career as an editor of *Mademoiselle*'s College Issue while a student in her native Missouri. She switched to the Parsons School of Design, where she was a student of CLAIRE MCCARDELL. Adri shared the spotlight with her late great teacher in a Smithsonian Institution two-woman show on the theme of innovative contemporary fashion in 1971. Following this exposure, she began her own business and by 1975 was establishing herself in the international market. In 1977 she was again designing for major sportswear manufacturers. She has designed fabrics as well as clothing, on at least one occasion stitching together abstract shapes in bold colors to make a mosaic.

First Named Dress Designers in the Soviet Union

In 1973 the Soviet Union broke with socialist precedent regarding anonymity in the design of clothing. For the first time a series of photographs of fashion identified the designer of each dress. The styles came from the Riga, Latvia, House of Fashion and five of the six designers named were women: GUNTA ZILE, RITA PETERSON, ARIYA PUPENOVA, RASMAR BAITMAN, and MARA NEZUDULKINA.

First to Westernize the Sari

ARDASH and SURJIT GILL are a sister act from Delhi, India, known as Saz. Their first westernized sari had a zipper and a simplified wrap-shawl for the American woman who did not know the traditional wrapping method but greatly admired both the sari drape and the fabrics. The Gill sisters came to New York in 1967 to study fashion. In 1970 they founded SAZ. They design their fabrics and their samples in the United States and have the clothes made in India. Alternating three-month stints supervising their work in the two countries, they also design and sell intricate jewelry to go with their luxuriously embroidered silk dresses.

Japan's Tri-Directional Clothing Designer

SUMAKO ITO heads the fashion departments of all branches of Takashimaya, the leading department store that has branches in as far-flung places as New York City, has her own design company as well, and runs a fashion school for over 150 students. She has devised an innovative cutting technique, "Ito," a method of speed garment-cutting that is now widely used in Japan. In addition, Ms. Ito is the dressmaker to Princess Michiko and members of the Imperial Family.

Coty Fashion Award Women

Fashion is a woman's world, *but*. In 35 years of New York fashion world's coveted Coty Awards, fewer than one third of the winners in all categories have been women. Their names:
1943
Special Award: Lilly Daché (millinery)
1944
Winnie: Claire McCardell
Special Award: Sally Victor (millinery)
1945
Winnies: Tina Leser (at-home clothes); Emily Wilkins (teenage clothes)
1946
Winnie: Clare Potter
1947
Winnies: Nettie Rosenstein; Adele Simpson
1948
Winnie: Hattie Carnegie
1949
Winnie: Pauline Trigère
1950
Winnie: Bonnie Cashin
Special Awards: Mabel (and Charles) Julianelli (shoes)
1951
Winnie: Jane Derby
Return Award: Pauline Trigère
Special Awards: Vera Maxwell (sports-

wear); Anne Fogarty (prettiest dresses); Sylvia Pedlar (lingerie)
1952
Special Award: Karen Stark (of Harvey Berin) (for her concept of dressing)
1953
Special Award: Helen Lee (children's designer)
1955
Winnies: Jeanne Campbell; Anne Klein
1956
Winnie: Sally Victor
1958
Hall of Fame Award: Claire McCardell (posthumous)
1959
Hall of Fame Award: Pauline Trigère
1960
Special Award: Roxanne (of Samuel Winston) (beaded evening clothes)
1961
Special Award: Bonnie Cashin (deep-country clothes)
1963
Special Awards: Theodora (with Arthur Edelman) (leather design)
1964
Return Special Award: Sylvia Pedlar
1965
Special Awards: Anna Potok (of Max-

imilian, furs); Gertrude Seperak (foundation garments)

Joint Special Award to Designers of Young Fashions: Sylvia de Gay; Gayle Kirkpatrick; Edie Gladstone; Deanna Little

1967
Special Award: Beth (and Herbert) Levine (shoes)

1968
Return Award: Bonnie Cashin

1969
Return Award: Anne Klein

1970
Special Award: Eileen (and Will) Richardson (tie-dyed fabrics)

1971
Hall of Fame Award: Anne Klein
Winnie: Betsey Johnson (of Alley Cat)
Special Awards: Nancy Knox (men's shoes); Elsa Peretti (jewelry)

1972
Hall of Fame Award: Bonnie Cashin

Special Award: Dorothy Weatherford (for Mountain Artisans) (patchwork and quality)

Special Men's Wear Award: Pinky Wolman and Dianne Beaudry

1973
Joint Special Awards for Accessory Design: Beth (and Herbert) Levine (shoes) Judith Leiber (handbags); Celia Sebiri (jewelry)

1975
Winnie: Carol Horn
Special Award: Monika Tilley (for Ellon) (swimsuits)
Special Men's Wear Award: Nancy Knox (leather design)

1976
Winnie: Mary McFadden
Special Awards: Barbara Dulien (work clothes); Vicki Davis (menswear: ties)

1977
Marsha Adkins (Special award: menswear, hats)

BOUTIQUE DESIGNERS

Originator of Play Clothes

TINA LESER (Christine Shillard-Smith), born 1911, studied at the Philadelphia Academy of Arts and the Sorbonne, married and moved to Honolulu. Impressed with the materials of the Orient she found there, she opened a boutique in 1935 and went on to design her own clothes, not infrequently influenced by the Eastern fabrics and designs with which she had become acquainted. After Pearl Harbor she returned to the States where she has been designing sportswear ever since. She is credited with originating play clothes as distinct from active sportswear. Ms. Leser holds a Doctor of Fine Arts degree from Moore Institute.

First Western-Style Japanese Designer

As the first designer to incorporate Japanese fabrics and styles in Western dress,

HANAE MORI has a discerning clientele in Japan, the United States, and Europe. She came to fashion from the textile business and opened a boutique in Tokyo at the same time as the post-war boom in the Japanese film industry began. Her work attracted film people and she designed for over 1,000 movies. In 1955 Ms. Mori opened her first shop on the Ginza, Tokyo's major fashion street. She designed in one way for the more conservative Japanese women who think the West is exotic and in another way for bolder Westerners who wear larger sizes and think the East is exotic. Today Hanae Mori designs haute couture and extensive lines of ready-to-wear. In 1972, in connection with the winter Olympic games at Sapporo, she introduced a line of ski-wear. More recently she has spread out to luxury bath towels and sheets. She is married to a textile manufacturer and has two sons, one of whom manages her New York business.

She Changed the Shape of Knitwear

Six months after CLARA MARA was graduated from the Fashion Institute of Technology in 1946, she began designing sportswear for Puritan—and she has been with that firm ever since. In 1961 they developed a knitwear division and she started designing exclusively for it. Her innovations have helped the spectacular growth of the knitwear field, and she has received many awards for her contributions, including honors from the Dupont Chemical Company.

Young Mother of the Miniskirt

Most successful among designers of fashions for the anti-Establishment youth wave on both sides of the Atlantic, MARY QUANT, born 1934, created the "Mod Look" and the first miniskirts. In 1953 she and her future husband opened Bazaar, a Chelsea shop. At first they bought from other manufacturers but shortly Ms. Quant decided to learn to design and cut what she wanted to sell.

She had one or two seamstresses sew up the next day's items each night. The young flocked to her shop. In fact, shopping became an entertainment itself. Having set the style, Mary Quant next studied mass production methods because that was the only way to achieve the price that made her goods more generally available. She had her first show in the United States in 1965 and her first Paris show as well. In 1966 she was presented with the Order of the British Empire for her services to British export —and wore a miniskirt, of course, to the Buckingham Palace presentation ceremony. Since 1970 Mary Quant no longer produces 28 collections a year, but designs and presents more along Establishment lines. Nor does she design specifically for the young. She now feels that fashion is no longer an age matter, but a life-style. And with this in mind, she has moved into cosmetics franchises, household textiles, and interior decorating, as well as continuing to produce clothes, boots, and tights.

Other Fashion Franchisers

Designing of clothes has led a number of women into franchising their style and name for many other products. Although this is a comparatively recent phenomenon in fashion, leading women designers began to be involved more than twenty years ago. Some of them and of the more recent female fashion makers, in addition to Mary Quant (above) who have lent their names and their talent to the design of bath and bed sheets, umbrellas, sunglasses, and a staggering array of other accessories for the body and the abode include:

> **Bonnie Cashin**
> **Kathy Hardwick**
> **Carol Horn**
> **Anne Klein**
> **Claire McCardell**
> **Mary Quant**
> **Gloria Vanderbilt**
> **Vera**

Her Dress Fad Swept the Country

Wealthy (in her own right) socialite LILLY PULITZER was the wife of a socially prominent Florida citrus grower and grandson of the prize-awarding publisher when she came up with a prize herself: a bright pastel flower-printed cotton shift with lace trim to wear in the Sunny South amid all those oranges. Her Palm Beach friends and neighbors asked for copies of the dress so she hired seamstresses to make up her "Lillys." This was the start of what became a nationwide fashion in the 1960s. Ms. Pulitzer, now Ms. Rousseau, is still active in her business, with a series of Lilly Shops in fashionable American resorts. Her Lilly line, expanded to include men's print slacks, children's clothes, and home furnishing fabrics, also is sold in department stores throughout the country.

Other Socialites in Fashion

A number of wealthy women in the United States and abroad who have become familiar with high style by wearing it have not been content to be consumers of fashion Like Lilly Pulitzer (opposite page), they have gone into the design business for themselves. The first, Lucille, dates back to World War I, but their ranks have increased in recent years as it has become ever more fashionable to have a career no matter the source or extent of one's income. Below are a few of the most successful wealthy (and often titled) women who have become designers:

Lucille (Lady Duff Gordon)
Mirsa (Marchesa Olga di Gresy)
Simonetta (Countess Simonetta Colonna di Cesaro)
Mila Schoen
Diane Von Furstenberg
Gloria Vanderbilt
Mary McFadden
Charlotte Ford
Ava Bergmann
Betsy Bloomingdale

She Put Dresses Back on Women

DIANE VON FURSTENBERG began her spectacularly successful career in 1969. After a brief apprenticeship with an Italian textile manufacturer, she married another young member of the international set, wearing a gown of her own design, and then they came to New York to set up business. She realized that women had a need for a dress that was neither for an old lady nor too expensive and she put one together: a simple, body-skimming jersey. She showed it to Diana Vreeland who encouraged her and called it "the little bourgeois dress." For the first few years Ms. von Furstenberg made the same basic pattern with only slight variations in fabric and cut, but in 1972 she also showed a striped sweater dress named "Angela" for the young black philosopher-militant Angela Davis (see "Women Activists, Heroes, and Heroines," p. 715). Shortly thereafter she brought out her most sensational success, a wraparound, one-piece, low-necked, torso-hugging jersey tied at the waist. Since then, Diane von Furstenberg has had two children, divorced her husband, and expanded and franchised her design skills to costume jewelry, furs, handbags, scarves, shoes, sunglasses, cosmetics, and bed and bathroom accessories.

"Poor Little Rich Girl" Now Multifaceted Designer

GLORIA VANDERBILT COOPER, multimillionaire heiress who at the age of 10 became known as "the poor little rich girl" during a bitter custody battle today is a highly successful, multitalented artist and designer of interiors, home fashions, and women's clothes. She spent the first eight years of her life "growing up in hotel rooms in Europe," later studied at the Mary C. Wheeler School in Providence, Rhode Island, but left school at 17 to marry actor's agent Pat DiCicco; the marriage lasted three years. At 21 she eloped with symphony conductor Leopold Stokowski, 40 years her senior (he died in 1977 at 95) and had two sons, now grown. She was then married briefly to television producer Sidney Lumet. In 1963 she married writer Wyatt Cooper, who died in early 1978. They also had two sons. During her 10-year marriage to Stokowski, Gloria Vanderbilt launched her career—acting, writing and painting. Completely self-taught, she is known for her bright, clear colors and innovative collages. Ms. Vanderbilt had 25 art exhibits and three museum retrospectives, has written four books, including *Designs for Your Home* (1977) and has written a new book, *Woman to Woman,* on "how I became my own person" and encouraging others to do so—

EUGENIE CLARK is a woman who gets along with sharks. At least, as one of the world's foremost marine biologists, and a researcher of the nature and behavior of sharks, she has been able to teach them to choose between targets of different designs and colors. She is seen here under water. Right, Eugenie Clark posing for her own version of *Jaws*. (Courtesy of University of Maryland)

The first woman on the geological staff at the Lawrence Livermore Laboratory, where she is pictured at work (above), geologist IRIS Y. BORG was also the first woman to earn a Ph.D. in geology at the University of California at Berkeley and the first to become a member of the Princeton geology department. (Courtesy of Lawrence Livermore Laboratory)

Nuclear engineer ROBERTA A. KANKUS was the first woman and almost certainly the youngest person to be licensed as a commercial nuclear power plant operator. (Courtesy of the Philadelphia Electric Company)

MARION STIRLING is seen here perched on a massive stone head from the Olmec period in Mexican culture, now generally recognized as the earliest civilization in the New World. Ms. Stirling, who has been a member of many archaeological expeditions, has received the gold medal of the Society of Woman Geographers for her achievements. (The National Geographic Society/The National Science Foundation)

Foremothers

ELIZABETH BLACKWELL, first woman doctor in the United States. When she received her M.D. in 1849, the medical profession was dismayed and no American hospital would admit her. Elizabeth Blackwell persisted, however, and in 1851 set up her own practice and eventually established the New York Infirmary for Women and Children. (The Bettman Archives)

ADAH BELLE THOMS, pioneer black nurse. As assistant superintendent of New York City's Lincoln School for Nurses in a period when few blacks, especially black women, were permitted to hold administrative positions of such responsibility, Adah Belle Thoms worked hard to open new opportunities for her race and sex. (United Press International)

CLARA MAASS, who gave her life in a yellow fever experiment. In 1900 Clara Maass, a nurse in the U. S. Army, volunteered to be bitten by mosquitoes in an experiment to determine whether yellow fever was so transmitted. Nurse Maass survived, only to die a year later in a repeat of the experiment.

Not all of the heroes of medicine hold medical degrees—ROSALYN S. YALOW, the 1977 winner of the Nobel Prize in Medicine, is a nuclear physicist. Her discovery of the radioimmunoassay is a contribution of immeasurable value to medical research. A radiant Dr. Yalow is seen here just after accepting her Nobel Prize. (United Press International)

And not all doctors treat human patients—photographed with a bear she has just injected is SUZANNE KENNEDY, the first woman veterinarian at the National Zoo in Washington, D.C.

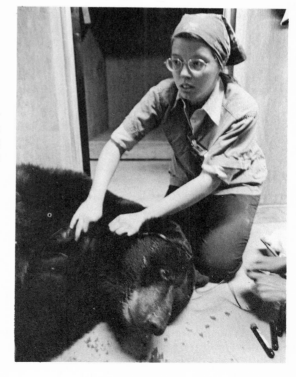

The Flapper

Fashion changes that swept Europe and the United States in the years immediately preceding and following World War I were based on new freedom in attitudes and manners.
Bobbed hair was part of it, but probably nothing epitomized the 1920s better than the
loose-fitting clothes and unbuckled galoshes of the American flapper, so called because
of her flapping footgear. (Photo courtesy of Library of Congress)

COCO CHANEL, dressed for evening in one of her timeless creations. Chanel introduced short, pleated skirts, fitted her dresses and "easy" suits loosely, with low waistlines, and established fake pearls, elaborate costume jewelry, sweaters, knitted jerseys, and trench coats for women as high-fashion items. She closed her business at the beginning of World War II but remained in Paris during the German occupation. At the age of 71, in 1954, she reopened her couture house and was again immediately acclaimed for her open-jacket, soft tweed suits with silk overblouses. Chanel died in 1971 but her styles and her scents—notably Chanel No. 5—live on. (Photo courtesy of Library of Congress)

The structured fashions of the '50s: (left) an ADELE SIMPSON suit and (right) a CEIL CHAPMAN party dress. (Photos courtesy of Library of Congress)

scheduled for 1979. When her collages appeared on the "Tonight Show," Hallmark called her and she spent two years designing greeting cards, stationery, puzzles, and candles. Fabric firms then asked her to design materials, and she created pillows, sheets, towels, china, wallpaper, stemware, tableware, linens, eyeglasses, watches, and needlecraft kits. Herself named to the Best Dressed Hall of Fame, in 1977 she did a moderate-price blouse collection for Murjani USA, designing the soft prints (and including blouses with her "signature," the Pierrot collar) and has designed skirts and a novel version of jeans. She enjoys wearing her designs and finds meeting people who own them to be "life-enhancing . . . the most marvelous feedback." Basic to her accomplishments is discipline—she rises at 5 A.M., works 7-hour days at design office or painting studio, with family dinner at 6 and bed at 9:30.

French Designer Who Began with Maternity Clothes

SONIA RYKIEL first worked from her home, making maternity dresses for herself and then for her friends. She quickly began to design other clothes as well, which were manufactured by her husband's firm. In 1968 she opened her own boutique in the Galeries Lafayette, a Paris department store. Ms. Rykiel has been known for her sweaters in all lengths and for all purposes but has branched out in both men's and women's wear as well as household accessories. She now has boutiques throughout Europe, Japan, and the United States. Today her seasonal collections are reported along with the more traditional couture designers in the Paris Collections.

Korean-American Success

CATHY HARDWICK (Kashina Shura) began dressmaking in the sixth grade in Korea. The daughter of one of that country's aristocratic families, she was programmed to study music and was sent first to Japan and then to San Francisco. She managed to squeeze in a dressmaking course in Japan and she married and had a son in San Francisco. Next she opened a small boutique, "Cathy's." She shortly began designing for a junior knitwear manufacturer, Alvin Duskin, and eventually closed her shop to work for him full time. By the late 1960s, Cathy Hardwick, now divorced, was ready to move to New York. There she worked for five sportswear houses in five years. In 1972 she opened her own design studio and then her own manufacturing firm, Cathy Hardwick and Friends. Having her own factory assures her of the finer workmanship that she missed when she worked for other New York firms. Her designing has spread from sportswear to prints and colors on the one hand and to a franchising operations as well.

She Revived Patchwork for Fashion

DOROTHY WEATHERFORD, a long-time artist and craftswoman, revived the use of patchwork for clothing and in 1968 combined forces with Mountain Artisans, one of the burgeoning Appalachian crafts group. (For others, see "Women in the Home and Community," pp. 98–140.) In 1972 she was the recipient of a special Coty Award, for her use of patchwork in skirts and other articles of apparel.

Appliqué Designer: Pillows to Robes

Married at 18 to a New York film producer, socialite AVA BERGMANN left behind a life of charity balls and world travel when her marriage dissolved and she plunged into unaccustomed hard work to earn a living. She turned her Victorian farmhouse into a design studio where she singlehandedly turned out Irish linen pillows appliquéd with Dutch batiks, osnaburg, and bright cottons. A Bloomingdale buyer ordered 60 pillows, and soon her work was displayed in major stores throughout the country. The

Dallas-born designer learned the difficulty of manufacturing, shipping, and selling in the competitive market—the "hardest thing I ever did," she says. Frequently working 14 hours a day, seven days a week, she found the work hard and tedious but also enjoyable and absorbing. Recently Bloomcraft, Inc., ordered the Ava Bergmann Gallery Collection of bedspreads, osnaburg, showcase fabrics and linens; and Swirl, Inc., asked her to design leisurewear. Her Swirl designs for home, beach, and club wear carry the appliqués that are her unofficial trademark—colorful tropical birds, exotic water lilies, hummingbirds, a monkey in an orange tree.

Total Wardrobe Designer

CAROL HORN, born 1938, opened her own company, Carol Horn's Habitat, only months before she received the Coty "Winnie" Award as the most innovative designer of 1975. However, she had been designing for other firms for 12 years. Before that she studied art history at Columbia and worked at several fashion-fringe jobs, including dressing windows for Macy's. It was in that position that she realized that she wanted to make clothes herself. So she talked herself into a job designing with a friend in the business. In creating her total wardrobes, she uses such unconventional things as woolly hopsacking, Guatemalan blankets, and old-fashioned snuggies in new ways. Dyeing the snuggies to coordinate with dyed thermal underwear and heavy mercerized cotton stockings, she turned layered warmth into high fashion. Ms. Horn has joined the franchisers of fashion.

First to Dye Hair to Match Costumes

For several years England's most romantic boutique designer, ZANDRA RHODES launched the return to crinoline and tulle in British fashion. She has since dramatized her designs with bizarre eye makeup and many-colored hair tints. Ms. Rhodes began her career as a designer of individualistic textiles and turned to fashion only in 1969. She was immediately discovered by American *Vogue* and has been featured on both sides of the Atlantic ever since. She received the Designer of the Year Award of the British Clothing Institute in 1972.

Famed for Whimsy

BETSEY JOHNSON, a Phi Beta Kappa graduate of Syracuse University, worked at *Mademoiselle* in 1964 and spent her spare time sewing up outfits for the editors. Shortly after that she became a designer for the trendy 1960s boutique Paraphernalia. TWIGGY, BRIGITTE BARDOT, and ANOUK AIMÉE wore her whimsical, delightful clothes. Her safari jacket was worn by JACQUELINE KENNEDY (see "Far-Out Women," p. 751) when as First Lady she was pictured on the cover of *Life* riding an elephant on her trip to India. In 1971 Betsey Johnson won the Coty "Winnie" Award for her work with Alley Cat. She is now a free-lancer, with projects that include designer patterns for Butterick—complete with instructions for embroidering the fantastic drawings and decorations that characterize all her work.

Designer Who Started with Her Own Show

When RABEA BENNANI needed some clothes to wear on her own Moroccan television news show, her designing career began. The things she designed for herself were widely commented upon, and she launched a second career in her boutique Samia, in Rabat. There she features richly embroidered caftans and gonduras that nicely blend Paris and Morocco.

Originator of the Eight-Ounce Knit Dress

MADY GERRARD learned to knit at the age of five in Budapest. Educated in England, she opened a boutique and bought her first knitting machine in

Cardiff, Wales. Following its success she opened others in London and in Canada, and then moved to New York in 1969. She designs elegant crochet and knit clothes for day and evenings and accessories as well, most recently men's sweaters. In New York she discovered a special machine that can knit a dress that weighs only eight ounces and is so bulkless it can fold into a handbag. For the handmade look she brought to American machine knit and crochet Ms. Gerrard received the 1974 Woolknit Design Award for creative achievement.

She Introduced Eastern Opulence to Western International Set

Born in Damascus, brought up in the Middle East, married to an Englishman and living in London, THEA PORTER was a painter at the time her marriage dissolved in 1963. She opened a shop on Greek Street in London for which she imported caftans. When they became the rage, she began to design them herself to satisfy the demand for couture Orientalia. Ms. Porter is known for her fantasy long clothes—timeless, in unusual fabrics, easy to slip into. Currently she claims to be influenced by Chekhov, but there are still echoes of Eastern opulence, medieval high bodices, as well as Art Deco in her overwhelmingly romantic costumes. Although her business center is still Greek Street, her clothes are sold in her own shop in Paris and in elegant stores in America, Caracas, Riyadh, Cairo, and Switzerland.

First to Make Her Name from a Mail Order Dress

Fashion artist BARBARA HULANIKI originally sold her designs by mail for the equivalent of $6.00 or less. In 1964 she submitted a design to a newspaper contest and received 12,500 orders. Shortly after, she opened a boutique, Biba, to sell directly to the public. It was one of the trendiest of the new London boutiques and by 1971 there was a Biba in Bergdorf Goodman in New York. In 1973 Ms. Hulaniki opened a department store in London full of Art Deco objects as well as Art Deco clothes. Her theme throughout her career has been that fashion is a total look and that it need not be expensive.

She Changed the Way That Women Look at Night

Since MARY MCFADDEN was graduated from the exclusive Foxcroft School in Middleburg, Virginia, in 1956, her career has been extremely various, including several jobs in fashion publicity in New York, Paris, South Africa, and Rhodesia. She also ran a sculpture workshop where African artists were given opportunities to develop their artistic skills. All the time she was designing clothes, but her first sale, of three, was to Henri Bendel in 1973. The dresses, which Ms. McFadden had designed during her travels and while living in Africa and Hong Kong, were made up in a tiny East 80s basement in New York. Today she has a factory on West 35th Street from which she produces her individualistic, expensive, floating gowns and frequently quilted jackets. Most recently she has designed accessories to go with each dress. *Vogue* credits her with changing the way women look at night, moving 1970s style from offbeat chic to soft, shimmering elegance. Ms. McFadden won the 1976 Coty Winnie Award for her beautiful clothes.

For Her, Nostalgia Paid off

When HOLLY HARP put a harp and a collection of genuine 1930s fabrics along with a collection of new clothes starry-eyed with the past into a boutique in Los Angeles in 1968, she hit a rich and enriching vein of nostalgia. In no time at all, Ms. Harp was running a fashion factory with 45 employees. Over the years her romantic dresses have become ever more classical. Like many Californians, Holly Harp came from back East. She was raised in Buffalo and started college at Radcliffe, then switched to North Texas State University, where she majored in art and costume design, and went on to Los Angeles for further study. Within three months of their arrival, she and her husband had opened the boutique. Soft colors in handpainted or airbrushed designs on floating skirts made of ultra-soft fabrics distinguished Holly Harp clothes. Wrapped, tied, twisted, and draped, they float on the body and off the floor.

Anne Klein's Successful Protegé

At age 25, DONNA KARAN was ANNE KLEIN's personal choice as successor. But when Ms. Klein died in 1974, the industry was not so sure that this comparatively untried designer could begin to produce on her own for a major firm. Ms. Karan's first collection ended their doubts. The buyers, the press, and the public loved her well-cut blazers, pants, and skirts. The company's retail sales kept right on growing. Ms. Karan was raised on the edges of the fashion industry. Her father made custom-tailored suits and blazers for theater people. ("I can remember going to his shop and seeing rows of the bright-colored gabardine blazers he specialized in—I still love blazers," she says.) Her mother had been a model. She herself sold clothes at a Long Island store from the age of 14 and, after high school, went to Parsons School of Design. At 19 she was permanently employed at Anne Klein and Co.

Ms. Karan works with an associate designer and 12 assistants to shop the fabric market, drape her sketches, and cut samples. She also directs the 15 designers at the Anne Klein Studio as they plan the perfume, household, and other accessories for the company's franchise business. Married and a mother, Donna Karan made the best-dressed list in 1976.

Western-Style Korean Designer

NORAH NOH, who staged the first Western-style fashion show in Korea, began her career when her own wardrobe was noticed by her employer's wife. Subsequently she went to the United States to study fashion design and then returned to Korea. Her collection of ready-to-wear fashions using Korean fabrics and Western design is world-famous.

First American-Afro Designer in Togo

BEVERLY MAJORS, born 1951, first lived in Africa when she was 14 and her family worked in Ghana. She went to college in Quincy, Illinois, and while there began working with a local seamstress. When her father later opened a trucking business in Lomé, the capital of Togo, she returned to Africa and began making fashions for the resident diplomatic corps. Ms. Majors uses African printed and tie-dyed cottons and camel's-hair blankets purchased from desert tribes in styles inspired by American and Paris designers and sells them from a boutique, Akuya, in a hotel in Lomé.

DESIGNERS FOR STAGE AND SCREEN

Costume Designer Who Married a Screen Idol

NATASHA RAMBOVA married the screen idol of the 1920s, Rudolph Valentino. She was well known in her own right, particularly for Nazimova's costumes for *Salome* (1923).

First Costume Designer to Win the Capezio Dance Award

Born in 1886 in Russia, BARBARA KARINSKA moved to Paris and in 1938 arrived in the United States, where she has worked ever since. She was associated with George Balanchine both in

Paris and at the New York City Ballet. He has described her in superlatives: "There is Shakespeare for literature and Madame Karinska for costumes." Her costumes have been considered an integral part of the dance and she was for this reason awarded the Capezio Dance Award for her contribution to the field. In 1948 she also won an Oscar for the costumes she designed for the movie *Joan of Arc.*

Hollywood's First Female Head of Design

EDITH HEAD studied at Stanford and while working on her M.A. in languages began sketching at Paramount. She stayed on and in 1938 became the first female design head. Her first great success was with Barbara Stanwyck in 1941, when the star said that Edith Head made her feel glamorous for the first time. Nominated for the award 31 times, Ms. Head has won seven Oscars for her costumes. She has dressed male stars—including Paul Newman and Robert Redford—as well as female. She de-signed the costumes for the first joint American-Russian movie venture, *The Bluebird,* starring ELIZABETH TAYLOR (see "Far-Out Women," p. 751). She has also designed new uniforms for the 40 guides from 22 countries who show people around the United Nations headquarters in New York. For them in 1977 she created "a classic silhouette that would not be thought of as any particular country's fashion attitude."

She Designed First American Princess's Wedding Gown

HELEN ROSE sketched dress designs, fitted them on plywood dolls and sold them in a local music store when she was 13. The following year she started studying at the Chicago Academy of Arts and subsequently was hired by a theatrical costumer. In the late 1930s she went to Hollywood where she began to design for the stars on the screen and in their private lives. GRACE KELLY (see "Far-Out Women," p. 751) chose Helen Rose to fashion her wedding dress for her marriage to Prince Rainier of Monaco.

JEWELRY DESIGNERS

Cartier's Directrice-Artistique

JEANNE TOUISSANT first designed women's handbags in Paris after World War I. Her work attracted the attention of Cartier's, who invited her to design jewelry for them. As Directrice-Artistique for Cartier's, Ms. Touissant has provided the resettings for the gems of royalty around the world. For her leadership in the field of jewelry design, she was made a chevalier of the Legion of Honor.

Originator of Use of Natural Shells as High Fashion Jewelry

MARGUERITE STIX (1907–75) was born and educated as an artist and sculptor in Vienna. In 1941 she moved to the United States where her successful career continued. She developed a great interest in sea shells both for themselves and as natural design. She began to combine her interest and her profession and designed jewelry, treating natural shells as precious jewels, which she set in gold and other metals. She also wrote, with her husband, Hugh, the popular book *The Shell: 500 Million Years of Inspired Design,* published in 1972.

She Created New Style in Women's Spectacles

ALTINA SANDERS, an American, designed the Harlequin frame for eyeglasses in 1944. The creation of a frame with an upward tilt, made of 20th-century plastic, turned glasses into an accessory as well as an aid to vision. The new frames were flattering to many faces and immediately became fashionable for general and sports use with plain or tinted frames.

Jeweler Who Treats Silver as a Precious Metal

CELIA SEBIRI studied art history at Hunter College. She knew the fashion world from her parents, well-known millinery designers. But Ms. Sebiri did not follow in their footsteps. Her first work was free-lancing for some of Henri Bendel's shops—the picture shop, paper shop, and cosmetics. One of the jewelry buyers thought her designs would make imaginative jewelry. And so they have. She received a special Coty Award in 1973. Silver is her favorite substance. She combines it with semiprecious stones and natural raw materials. First the materials are cut and fashioned in shapes—natural sea creatures and objects of the night sky are among her favorites. Then they are mounted in silver. Ms. Sebiri has combined silver with ivory, as well as with more colorful substances. She also designs compacts, boxes, and sundry items for Revlon.

Model Launched by a Dress Designer as a Jeweler

ELSA PERETTI, born in 1940, came to the United States as a fashion model from Rome. Her avocation was always jewelry and she spent weekends working on it at home. Halston appreciated her work and incorporated it into his shows in 1970 and launched her jewelry as a high-fashion craze. Her gold "tear drop" pendant and miniature flower vase on a chain became important accessories, as did a large silver loop belt buckle. In 1974 she began to work through Tiffany's and her designs branched to include such accessories as gold mesh scarves. She now spends much of her time in Spain, where she finds she works best, and is remodeling a number of houses she has bought in a village to which she hopes her friends will move.

FUR AND LEATHER DESIGNERS

The Female House of Fendi

The House of Fendi consists of five sisters who, with their mother, run one of the two most successful leather and fur businesses in Italy. The House was begun when mother ADELE FENDI opened a shop in Rome in 1918 when she was about 20 years old. In 1954 when their father died the daughters, ranging from 14 to 24 years of age, began to help. First they told the manufacturers how they wanted their bags made and then they evolved the distinctive soft, light leather handbags for which they became famous. Next they began using canvas and then, in 1966, introduced plastic for evening clutches. Since 1962 Karl Lagerfeld has designed their furs, using new skins including mole and unshaved beaver. The House of Fendi was the first to color fur.

Youngest Woman to Have a Custom Fur House

Born in Russia and raised in Boston, ESTHER DOROTHY opened her own custom fur house in 1940, when she was not quite 20 years old. She met with immediate success and shortly had stores elsewhere. She moved to New York where she continued to design high-style and award-winning fur coats, wraps, and other items. She launched the fashion for furs dyed in bright colors in the United States, immediately after World War II. She was the recipient of a special Coty Award in 1948.

First Woman Apprentice and Master in Hungarian Leather Guild

JUDITH LIEBER became the first woman apprentice in the Hungarian handbag guild system, at the outset of World War

II. By the time she had married an American soldier and was ready to move to the United States in 1947 she had advanced through journeyman to the rank of master in the system. Once in America she immediately found work in the handbag industry as a designer and sample maker—another first for a woman. In 1963 she founded her own firm so that she could be freer to design and meticulously manufacture the high-fashion, high-priced handbags she has become famous for. Ms. Lieber has broadened her designing and manufacture to include belts and jewelry.

Coty Award to Her for Furs

ANNA MAXIMILLIAN POTOK's brother founded the House of Maximilian in Warsaw in the 1930s. She studied art. With the advent of World War II they fled Europe and relocated in New York, where their first customer was Helena Rubinstein. Ms. Potok took over the entire business when her brother died in 1952. The firm has won two Coty Awards, the most recent a special award to Anna Potok herself in 1965.

Innovative Israeli Leather Worker

An Israeli designer of leather sportswear, LILY TOPOREK has her own firm, Jadoli, for which she puts together unusual combinations of leather textures and strong colors.

LINGERIE, LOUNGEWEAR, AND INTIMATE APPAREL DESIGNERS

Founder of Maidenform Bras

IDA ROSENTHAL, founder of Maidenform, Inc., escalated the switch from home sewing to ready-to-wear dresses after World War I by her home manufacture of brassieres that helped clothes fit. Born in 1889, she became a dressmaker in Hoboken, New Jersey, and moved to Washington Heights, New York, where her seamstresses stitched away in her living room. By the early '20s she was able to afford a fashionable shop on 57th Street, Manhattan, and started to make two-cup breast containers and give them to her customers to wear under their short, flat-chested, flapper dresses. In 1924 her husband William, a ready-to-wear dress manufacturer, quit his job. A designer (and later a sculptor), he established standardized brassiere sizes and worked out a system of mass production, while his 4'11" wife managed sales and finance. By the time she died in 1973, her daughter BEATRICE ROSENTHAL, who graduated from Barnard (1938), had worked her way up from the family sewing machine to become manager of the family business.

She Introduced the Baby Doll Nightgown

SYLVIA PEDLAR (1901–72) introduced the baby doll gown and the sleep toga to American women, thus covering both the long and the short of it, and integrated modern easy-care fabrics with her elegant, contemporary night fashions. Born in New York City, she studied at Cooper Union and the Art Students League but never designed anything but lingerie. Her sumptuous fashions earned her a Coty Award in 1951.

She Began the Body Shirt Fad

PAULA CARBONE played a vital role in transforming the lingerie industry, which today is a vigorous, glamorous part of the fashion world whose products can just as easily be worn on the outside as next to the skin. She was graduated from the Fashion Institute of Technology and has worked for a range of manufacturers in the field. In 1967, the year she joined

Van Raalte, she began the body shirt fad. She has worked with American Enka on the development of crepeset fabric, now used in almost all lingerie manufacturing. Married to a fashion photographer, Ms. Carbone has one daughter.

Outstanding Intimate and Nighttime Apparel Patent Holder

OLGA (Erteszek) was born in Krakov where her mother was famed as a corsetiere. After a dramatic escape from Nazi-occupied Poland, the family came to the United States. There, to help keep them going, Olga, trading on family knowledge, designed and sewed her first foundation garments. Today, she holds 28 patents and has 1,500 people working for her producing the girdles, pants slips, divided slips, and figure-supporting nightwear for which she is well known.

Founding Member of Association of Canadian Fashion Designers

CLAIRE HADDAD is a member of a large clan of designer-manufacturers. Her father produced heavy, utilitarian, cold-weather bathrobes. Ms. Haddad works at the other end of the spectrum, making filmy lingerie and seductive loungewear. Her line is wholesaled both in Toronto and New York. She received a Canadian Coty Award in 1967.

LEGWEAR AND SHOE DESIGN

First to Dye Leotards

RIKKI (Kilsdonk) introduced leotards dyed to match shirts, using red, blue, green, and black, at Haymaker Sports (David Crystal). *Vogue* named them "Glamor Gams." Leotards were originally only in white and came from "le bas Sebel" in France. In the United States they had been used primarily by dancers and nurses. Rikki was born in Holland, studied and worked in Paris, moved on to the Orient and Australia and finally settled in New York where she worked for several sportsmakers, including her own firm. In 1973 she moved to Florida and retirement. But she actually is still working there, for a Miami firm, as well as enjoying the sun.

First Shoe Designer to Receive a Grant to Design a Foreign Shoe Industry

MABEL JULIANELLI, born 1919, since 1940 has been designing high-fashion shoes. In 1950, together with her late husband, she was recognized with a special Coty Award. More recently she received a grant to help design a shoe industry for India.

Creator of the Stretch Boot and the Vinyl Shoe

The designing half of the firm of Herbert and BETH LEVINE since 1949, Ms. Levine's first job in shoes was as a secretary at Palter DeLiso. She spoke up about her ideas and her creative effort was encouraged. After she and Herbert Levine married, they set up their own business, where her creative talents and his brilliant merchandising methods brought them almost immediate recognition. They made use of stretch materials to create the stretch boot and introduced the vinyl shoe. They have also changed heel shapes, heights, and materials and added jewels and other decorations to them. They have designed shoes for a variety of theatrical productions and received the Neiman-Marcus Award in 1954 and special Coty Award in both 1967 and 1973.

She Launched New Casual Shoe Styles

EVE SONNINO, born and raised in Milan, walked casual shoes off the beachfront into the urban world of fashion. She and her husband bought the Bernardo footwear firm in 1950. Since that time she has expanded the range of styles and their uses and moved into the American market. In 1963 she won the American Shoe Designer Award of the leather industry. Both Ms. Sonnino and her husband commute between their factories in Italy and Ohio.

Designer of the Earth Shoe

ANNA KALSØ began her career in Denmark as a teacher of yoga, learned in her world travels. She had always admired the straight carriage of barefoot members of the primitive tribes she encountered and their easy breathing as they walked many miles. She wanted to develop a shoe that would allow the same healthy movement on Western civilization's concrete sidewalks. In the 1950s Ms. Kalsø designed a shoe with several orthopedic arch supports, a lowered heel, and a sole that helped to ensure a gently rolling gait. All of these features contributed to a shoe in which the wearer would move erectly and breathe more easily and naturally. Her original store was in Copenhagen but branches quickly were opened throughout Western Europe. The shoes made their U.S. debut as the counterculture was celebrating Earth Day in 1970. The Day gave the shoes their American name. Ms. Kalsø, now in her 70s, divides her time between Arizona and Denmark. Officially retired from the manufacture of Earth Shoes, she has turned to making other "healthy" apparel.

SPECIALTY DESIGNERS

First to Make Maternity Clothes for the Active American Woman

In the early days of the 20th century, pregnant women were not supposed to be seen outside their homes. But one fashionable New Yorker wanted to continue the active life even though she was expecting. She went to her clever dressmaker, a young immigrant widow, and requested something stylish. LANE BRYANT complied, and her very satisfied customer sent a stream of other women for the same kind of clothes. By 1909 the fame of the Lane Bryant maternity gown with an elasticized waist had spread by word of mouth around New York, and Ms. Bryant had opened a store. But it took a few more years to talk newspapers into advertising such an unmentionable. At last, in 1911, the *New York Herald* was induced to sell the store an advertisement. Lane Bryant's complete stock was sold out by the next day. By 1917 the firm had done a million dollars' worth of business in maternity clothes. Some years later the store was so famous that a letter from Poland addressed simply "Maternity Dress, size 32, Amerika" was quickly delivered to its Fifth Avenue location. Ms. Bryant died in 1951, by which time her designing included clothes for non-pregnant fuller-figured women, the line for which the company is now best known.

First to Design Fitted Daytime Dresses

At a time when garment manufacturers concentrated on high-priced copies of imports or on cheap, shapeless "housedresses," NELL QUINLAN DONNELLY REED designed and put into production the first attractive "day aprons." Born on a farm in Kansas in 1889, youngest of 12, she attended business school, became a stenographer, and at 17 married a stenographer, Paul Donnelly. Her husband recognized her intelligence and drive and with some help from both sets of parents sent her to Lindenwood College; she was graduated in 1909. Next she took up sewing, making brightly colored dresses for her sisters. In 1916 she persuaded a Kansas City store to display her clothes; they sold before noon the first day, and the buyer ordered more. Her husband then put up $1,270 and, with two hired girls and two power machines in the attic of their house, Nell began making 24 "day aprons" a day. After World War I Paul left his job to be president of the Donnelly Garment Company; Nell became secretary-treasurer. Using the label "Nelly Don" they grossed up to $3.5 million annually in the 1920s, and sales continued high during the Depression, when Nell added wool and silk dresses, also well-fitted, fadeproof, and reasonable. In 1931 Nell and her chauffeur were kidnapped for $75,000 ransom. Missouri Senator James A. Reed managed her release. At age 43 she was divorced and married the 72-year-old senator. Now president of her company, she sold her stock for more than $1 million, and retired 10 years later, in 1954. She remains active in Republican Party politics, and is an inveterate world traveler.

Friend of the Bride

PRISCILLA KIDDER, born in Quincy, Massachusetts, has made Boston the headquarters of the bridal world. After high school she worked in several department stores and, despite the Depression of the early 1930s, was an assistant buyer at age 22. She also studied Fashion Design at the New England Art School. In 1945, just as World War II was over and the boys were coming home to get married, Ms. Kidder opened a bridal shop with a custom operation attached. In 1950, riding the crest, she created a wholesale bridal business, Priscilla of Boston. The firm not only designs wedding gowns but clothes for the entire bridal party. Ms. Kidder has done thousands of weddings for people of all backgrounds, including one in which President Lyndon Johnson was Father of the Bride.

She Designs for Sand and Snow

MONIKA TILLEY, born in land-locked Austria, emigrated to two-ocean America, where she made her name designing swimsuits. She worked for several sportswear firms and in 1970 formed her own company, Monika for Elon. Her collections include not only swimwear, but also ski clothes for women and children. In 1975 she was the recipient of a special Coty Award.

SPORTS DRESSERS

Active sport clothes began to take on style even before GUSSIE MORAN wore lace-edged panties at Wimbledon in the 1950s. But the boom in fashion has gotten bigger and bigger in recent years, and women of all ages are wearing tennis dresses and golf skirts and shirts whether they play or not. Some of the best have been designed by starring sportswomen:

Jane Regny (golf and tennis in the 1920s and 30s)
Louise Suggs (golf in the 1930s)
Billie Jean King
Chris Evert
Lillo Zandelin (designer-player for John Mayer of Norwich)
Doli Cole (under the name Love Stitch designed a do-it-yourself kit of a precut tennis dress to sew up at home in 1971)

Fashion for the Handicapped

In Osaka, Japan, in the middle 1960s, a local clothes designer, NAMIKO MORI, was invited by a young friend to speak to what she thought would be a school full of handicapped teenagers on the subject of women's fashions. However, the school allowed her to speak only to the one girl she knew. The designer decided then that she would have to do something to change the climate for the handicapped. In 1977 she opened a boutique especially designed, equipped, and tailored for the physically handicapped and their clothing needs. The store features low display cases designed to be examined from wheelchairs. It is located in a central part of Osaka, in a hotel with good-sized elevators, to make it easier for her special shoppers to get there.

Items included at the boutique, called Helpers, which may be the only one of its kind in the world, include raincoat ponchos that cover wheelchairs as well as their riders. Pajamas and shirts have expanded arms and legs so that they are easy to put on. Ms. Mori also has designed shirts and blouses with buttoned cuffs that are linked by elastic strands so that persons with arthritic hands, or the one-handed, have no trouble with the fashionable clothes. Some of the articles are for men and children, but most are designed to make life both more fashionable and more convenient for women.

WOMEN DESIGNERS FOR CHILDREN AND MEN

First Children's Designer to Receive Neiman-Marcus Award

FLORENCE EISEMAN, born 1899, sewed organdy pinafores for her children and her friends' children in Milwaukee until Marshall Field and Co. decided that they were very salable. Starting with her husband as manager, herself as designer, one seamstress, and one sewing machine, she went into business in 1945. The American baby boom took off, and Ms. Eiseman led the field in designing simple, uncluttered clothes for children. Over the years she has made dresses, jumpers, skirts, blouses, boys' suits, swimwear, playclothes, and sleepwear for small customers as well as mother-and-daughter fashions. In 1955 she became the first children's wear designer to receive the Neiman-Marcus Award.

She Made Good Children's Clothes Grow

An Iowa housewife who went to work for FLORENCE EISEMAN (above) as a designer when Ms. Eiseman expanded her business, GLORIA NELSON designed and patented the "add-a-hem," a clever way of making fine clothes last a child another year. By simply pulling a thread, the hem is lowered four inches.

First Coty Award Winner for Children's Clothes

A 1953 Coty-award winning children's designer, HELEN LEE joined Sears, Roebuck in 1963 to design its better priced children's wear and brought color coordination and style to its operation. In this manner, she extended her own ideas of children's fashion to a new, moderate-priced market with 800 stores and a worldwide mail order business. Previously and since, Ms. Lee has designed for most of the better children's clothing manufacturers as well as for her own firm. Most recently, with a partner in Athens, she has been having her designs manufactured in Greece of American fabrics.

Women Designers of Men's Ties

IVONNE FINELLI was born in Italy and lived in Buenos Aires before coming to the United States. She always wanted to design men's ties and worked for Sulka for many years. In 1967, as SIVONE, she opened her own business.

VICKI DAVIS, winner of the 1976 Coty Award for her men's tie designs, began her career in the basement of her suburban Michigan home in 1970. Nowadays she commutes to New York where she has an apartment-showroom on Park Avenue. In the beginning she bought her fabrics retail in Hudson's basement in Detroit. More recently she has been shopping in Europe, buying directly from textile manufacturers only enough fabric for a few ties of each design. Her ties are sold, by her, to Saks Fifth Avenue, Neiman Marcus, and Bergdorf Goodman, as well as other fine stores throughout the country.

From Doll Clothes to Menswear

MARION HOLMES actually began designing with the Negro Ensemble Company while she was a scholarship student at the Fashion Institute of Technology. But her first full-time job was designing doll clothes for the Ideal Toy Company. For the past several years Ms. Holmes has been designing menswear with the aim of producing a mass product at moderate prices. She begins with textile design itself and works on through production, packaging, marketing, and sales.

LEGENDARY TASTE-MAKERS

The Elegant Editors

Long-time arbiter of personal elegance, DIANA DALCIEL VREELAND was born in Paris of English parents. She had a childhood straight out of an international fairy tale, came to the United States when World War I broke out, married in 1922, spent the next four years in Albany, New York, and the following nine in Paris, France. Again she lived a rich international life from which, again, she returned as war clouds gathered. In 1938 she went to work and stayed for 25 years, creating a legend. She "wound women's hair with leopard chiffon scarves, sheathed them with jungle print underwear and handed them great pouches of fur to wear as handbags." At the *Bazaar* she wrote a "Why don't you?" column leaning heavily on fantasy, because fantasy, she felt, was needed in the world at that time. She left the magazine, after being inexplicably passed over for its editorship when CARMEL SNOW retired, and went to *Vogue* where she became editor-in-chief and stayed until 1971.

For forty years Ms. Vreeland has encouraged designers, decided what is in and what is out, and presented exciting new fashion-photography and artists. She has been described as "a woman who can make high fashion as emotional as religion." She is supposed to be the one who first said, "No woman can ever be too rich or too thin." She heralded the bikini as the greatest thing since the atom bomb. Ever the enthusiast and statement maker, Ms. Vreeland since her retirement from the *Bazaar* has continued to influence the fashion world through the extraordinary shows she has mounted (six to date) at the Metropolitan Museum's Costume Institute. Her most recent exhibit, "Vanity Fair," culled 500 fashion treasures from the Museum's 30,000-item collection. It included every kind of wearing apparel from ballgowns to tiny Chinese shoes to the Worth-designed riding habit worn by Czar Nicholas' wife, ALEXANDRA.

Today's single most influential woman in home interior design and decoration is PAIGE RENSE, editor-in-chief of *Architectural Digest*. Ms. Rense, born in Des Moines, Iowa, moved to Hollywood, California as a child, received her degree in English from California State, Los Angeles, and embarked on a career in advertising, public relations, writing, and editing. She had never studied interior design when she joined Knapp Communications Corporation in 1970 as writer and associate editor of *Architectural Digest*, then an architectural trade journal with a circulation of 50,000. By 1977 she had increased the magazine's circulation to more than 275,000 (at $2.95 an issue) and made it one of the most prestigious interior design publications in the world. Ms. Rense, now in her mid-forties, and editor-in-chief of *AD, Bon Appétit* (purchased in 1975), and Knapp Press, a book-publishing subsidiary, concentrated from the first on outstanding international designers to counteract *AD*'s low "respect factor." She attended scores of parties to "snare just one or two top designers," landed several young San

Franciscans, then well-known New York designer Angelo Donghia, and in January 1973 published a spread of COCO CHANEL's (p. 240) Paris apartment. Now homeowners and designers line up to appear in her pages; she has refused bribes ranging from thousands of dollars to a marriage proposal and resisted the blandishments of total strangers who gave black-tie dinners in her honor for 300 guests. She considers 700 interiors a year, visiting 250 and studying photographs of others; about one in ten is selected. Her criterion is "magic" (*"style,* with an authoritative touch") displayed throughout the house (*AD* won't show just one room). Money is not important—Ms. Rense turns down many million-dollar homes and has shown one $1,500 apartment. The average income of *AD* readers is $59,000; the average house shown costs $250,000 (the interiors, one third of that). Among the many celebrities whose homes have appeared in *AD* are Gore Vidal, INGRID BERGMAN (see "Women in the Arts and Entertainment," p. 659), BARBARA WALTERS (see "Women in Communications," p. 504), and Robert Redford. In 1977 Ms. Rense increased bimonthly publication to nine times annually, and began to include architectural features; her goal is a publication like a European art book, or *Connaissance des Arts.* For her dynamic editorial policies Paige Rense was named Woman of the Year in 1976 by the *Los Angeles Times.*

She Revolutionized Fashion Writing

Syndicated Columnist EUGENIA SHEPPARD introduced a breezy style of writing unknown to fashion commentary in U.S. newspapers, where reverent descriptions of socialites and designers were *de rigueur.* Her first "Inside Fashion" column, launched in 1956, went beyond the other accounts of Princess GRACE's trousseau with its report on her yellow lingerie; Ms. Sheppard quickly became known for her sharp tongue and knowledgeable eye, both of which she delights in employing in her descriptions of people, fashions, and fads. A native of Columbus, Ohio, and a graduate of Bryn Mawr, she worked briefly on the *Columbus Dispatch* before moving to New York in 1939. Next came a temporary reporting job at *Women's Wear Daily.* In 1940 she went to work on the *Herald Tribune*'s women's section, rising to fashion editor in 1947 and women's feature editor in 1949. After the *Trib* folded, she accepted a job as editor of the ill-fated *World Journal Tribune;* after it went out of business Eugenia Sheppard joined a syndicate.

First Famous Woman Fashion Photographer

LOUISE DAHL-WOLF, who retired in 1962, first appeared in *Vanity Fair* in November 1933 and was hired by *Harper's Bazaar* in 1937. Within five years she was the sole woman on the top rungs of fashion photography. She introduced sophisticated ways to the breezy, outdoor American girl; never did anyone appear with an uncombed head or a chipped fingernail in her elegant picnic or fantastic beach scenes. Ms. Dahl-Wolf was one of the first photographers to travel to exotic places to find settings for fashion stories.

World Crafts Editors

ROSE SLIVKA, editor since 1955 of *Craft Horizons,* only magazine covering crafts internationally, is generally considered the world's foremost writer on modern crafts. Ms. Slivka lectures and acts as juror at museums, conferences, and universities throughout the United States and has received a number of invitations from foreign countries to do research abroad. Fascinated with the paradox of the handicrafts revival in today's industrial world, she edited and was a writer for *The Crafts of the Modern World* (1968), the first complete work on world crafts, including anonymous folk crafts as well as signed objects.

Craft Horizons, which has won many awards and citations for editorial content and graphic design, began as a mimeographed newsletter edited by AILEEN O. WEBB (see "Women in the Home and Community," p. 124), founder of American House and of the American and World Craft Councils.

MARY LYON (1890–1977) became the first professional editor of *Craft Horizons* in 1947 after three years as a reporter for the *New York Herald Tribune.* She became crafts editor for *House Beautiful* in 1955. Ms. Lyon published *Elements of Weaving* in 1967, and was one of the first craftswomen elected a fellow of the American Crafts Council.

TEXTILES AND FURNISHINGS FOR THE HOME

Her Designs Opened New Fields for Woman

CANDACE THURBER WHEELER (1827–1923) was born in Delhi, New York, and learned spinning, weaving, and needlework as a child. At 17 she married Thomas M. Wheeler, by whom she had four children. They moved to Brooklyn, where artist and painter friends encouraged Ms. Wheeler's artistic interests. The Wheelers toured Europe's art galleries in 1865, and the following year attended the Philadelphia Centennial, where the work of a group of English needlewomen inspired her to establish the Society of Decorative Art to exhibit and sell handwork and teach embroidery and china painting. In 1878 she helped found the Women's Exchange, an outlet for women's work of all kinds. Louis Tiffany asked her to help form As-

sociated Artists, an interior decorating firm, in 1879; she created textiles and embroideries for the Union League Club and the White House, then left to found her own all-woman Associated Artists. She designed many new fabrics, and was especially interested in creating needlewoven American tapestries including large murals embroidered in silk for such clients as Cornelius Vanderbilt. Candace Wheeler directed the women's applied art exhibit and decorated the Women's Building at the Columbian Exposition of 1893, Chicago (see "Women in the Arts and Entertainment"). As a result of her prize-winning work, American designs for carpets, wallpaper, and textiles began to replace the French and English then used almost exclusively. Candace Wheeler continued writing extensively on applied and decorative arts until she was 96.

The Cranbrook Influence

Early Architectonic Fabric Designer

LOJA SAARINEN, Finnish-born wife of architect Eliel Saarinen, was an important influence on textile art both in Finland and the United States. A weaver from 1900 of rugs and wall hangings in the long knotted pile of Finnish rya (see also pp. 274–75), she created a new tapestry style for his architecture. Flat and architectonic, the tapestry emphasized the expressive qualities of materials

variously woven, with some in discontinuous brocade over linen gauze. She used subtle, light colors and an open weave, with contrasting yarns. She and her husband were noted as teachers and admirers of crafts—he was commissioned to work on a series of buildings in Bloomfield Hills, Michigan, in 1925, which became the Cranbrook Boys Academy. The Cranbrook Academy of Art was founded there in 1926 and many commissions offered to weavers, potters, and sculptors who came with the architect from Sweden and Finland. From 1929 Loja Saarinen directed weaving at the Academy, one of the most influential arts and crafts centers in the country. Her department produced both fabrics and carpets. In 1937 MARIANNE STRENGEL succeeded Ms. Saarinen as studio director.

Head of Cranbrook's Ceramics Department

Another early émigrée from Finland was MAIJA GROTELL, born 1889, who studied at the Central School of Industrial Art in Helsinki. The dynamic craftswoman went to New York City in 1927 and taught at the Henry Street Craft School for several years, then became head of the ceramics department at the Cranbrook Academy of Art, where she taught for 28 years before her death in 1973. In 1977 a court at Cranbrook was dedicated in her name and an oak tree planted in memory of Maija Grotell and her powerful, classic pottery.

Co-Designer of World's Most Famous Modern Chairs

RAY KAISER EAMES, co-designer with her husband Charles of the molded chairs that placed the United States in the forefront of modern design, met her future husband in 1936 at the Cranbrook Academy of Art, Bloomfield, Michigan, where he was teaching at the invitation of architect Eliel Saarinen. Ray, a sculptor and painter who also studied dance with MARTHA GRAHAM (see the chapter "Women in the Arts and Entertainment," p. 647), worked with Charles and with Eero Saarinen (1910–61), son of Eliel and weaver Loja Saarinen (above), to develop the revolutionary molded plywood chair that won Eames and Saarinen the organic design competition of the Museum of Modern Art (MOMA) in 1941. The same year,

Charles Eames divorced his first wife and married Ray; they went to California to work on devices for wounded Navy veterans—work that helped them develop their techniques. He spent considerable time designing movie sets, while she worked in their small apartment on molding problems, curing rubber shock mounts for the wood in their oven. Both labored with a bicycle pump as a compressor—the result was their shock-mounted "potato chip" chair with separate pads of molded plywood as back and seat on a steel tubing frame. In 1946 Herman Miller Company hired them and began to produce and market their furniture. There followed the Eames molded chair of plastic impregnated with fiberglass (a MOMA prizewinner in 1950), their wire basket chair, stacking chair, the 1956 molded rosewood and black leather lounge chair with ottoman, 1958 aluminum furniture, 1960 *Time* and *Life* lobby chairs, tandem seating at Dulles and O'Hare airports, and variations grossing an estimated $1 million a year.

The Eameses live in a cliffside home overlooking the ocean at Santa Monica, California, and spend seven days a week, some 12 hours a day, at their workshop in a converted garage 10 miles away. Besides furniture, they are known for their toys, films, exhibitions, and educational work. They began making movies in the late '50s, producing *Toccata for Toy Train* in 1957; *Powers of Ten,* probably their best-known film on the powers of ten and *The Relative Size of Things in the Universe,* shown daily at the Smithsonian's Air and Space Museum; and *The World of Franklin and Jefferson,* film and exhibition shown around the world for the United States Bicentennial. In 1975 they produced *A Metropolitan Overview*—a proposed central guide to the collection of the Metropolitan Museum of Art—and with architect/designer George Nelson pioneered in using multiscreen slide projections to accelerate the transfer of information. In 1975

Minneapolis' Walker Art Center showed "Nelson/Eames/Girard/Propst: The Design Process at Herman Miller" and PBS/TV featured "An Eames Celebration: Several Worlds of Charles and Ray Eames"; the University of California showed "Connections: The Work of Charles and Ray Eames" in 1977.

Fiber Artist and Educator

DOROTHY L. MEREDITH, born in 1906 in Milwaukee, Wisconsin, trained as a painter. She studied at the Layton School of Art in Milwaukee and received her bachelor's degree in education at Wisconsin State Teacher's College and an M.A. from the Cranbrook Academy of Art (Michigan). She taught herself weaving and studied in New Zealand and at the University of Wisconsin-Milwaukee, where she became professor of weaving 1953–75 and professor emeritus in 1975. She traveled widely to study the ikat technique, in which yarns are tie-dyed before weaving, and wove space-hangings and three-dimensional constructions, emphasizing color. A trustee of the American Craft Council from 1958–61 and state representative 1962–63, Dorothy Meredith was named an ACC fellow in 1975.

Total Design Award Winner

FLORENCE (SCHUST) KNOLL BASSETT, who fully shared the leadership of Knoll International with her partner/husband, Hans Knoll, studied at Kingswood School and at the Cranbrook Academy of Art, where she was a protégée of the Saarinens (above). From Cranbrook, Florence Schust went to London to study at the Architectural Association, and several years later completed her architectural studies under Ludwig Mies van der Rohe at the Illinois Institute of Technology. She and Hans Knoll founded Knoll Associates in 1946; as head of the Knoll Planning Unit and company president for ten years, she designed complete interiors and developed the Unit into an experimental laboratory for new furniture. Knoll designers have included Franco Albini (Italy), Hans Bellman (Switzerland), Pierre Janneret (France), Ilmari Tapiovaara (Finland), van der Rohe, Saarinen, and Isamu Noguchi.

In a 1977 speech accepting the Total Design Award of the American Society of Interior Designers, Florence Knoll recalled the early days of her 35-year career when as "the only lady architect in a New York office, I was called upon to design the few interiors that were requested [and] . . . discovered that suitable furniture, textiles and lighting fixtures for commercial interiors did not exist . . . We started in a modest way using available materials of a wartime economy—non-priority solid wood, reject parachute belting . . . Not only were materials scarce—so were clients willing to trust upstarts in the contemporary field. We found the only way to get new ideas accepted was to do them for ourselves." After Saarinen and Eames won the Museum of Modern Art Furniture Competition, professionals and public became interested. The designer's parallel bar and rivet construction, used in the 1976 2500 series, has changed only slightly since she used it in her 1950s 1200 series, incorporating the then unique combination of cushions with Dacron fill around a foam rubber core; she has retained a tailored look, adding tufting and stitching for softness. Ms. Knoll's many awards include the Museum of Modern Art Good Design Award, annually from 1950 to 1957 for furniture designs; American Institute of Decorators First Award (1954) for table with parallel bar and rivet construction; American Institute of Architects Gold Medal Award (1961) for developing contemporary design here and abroad.

British Master Ceramists

Famed British potter LUCY RIE, born in 1902 in Austria, studied at the Kunstgewerbeschule in Vienna, where she established her own kiln in 1926. Ms. Rie left Austria in 1938 for London and started her own studio there the following year. A master of porcelain and stoneware, she can deftly shape her material by hand on the wheel. Her work, which includes delicate coffee cups and small porcelain pieces as well as heavier pots, is always thrown on the wheel. Influenced as a child by finds at Roman excavations on the Austro-Hungarian border, and later by the work of Bernard Leach, she is especially noted for her light bowls. Her glaze and decoration appear to grow from the clay. Ms. Rie often gives her porcelain a partial glaze and paints it with dark brown manganese oxide; her stoneware sports a variety of glazes, including strong yellows, rosegray, and blues. Lucy Rie lives over her studio, and since 1960 has taught at the Camberwell Art School.

RUTH DUCKWORTH, born in 1919 to a Jewish family in Hamburg, Germany, met Lucy Rie in England in 1953 and became interested in ceramics, studying at the Hammersmith School of Art (1955) and the Central School, London. She made tableware on the wheel, including cylindrical coffee sets considered the best made in England, and small utilitarian pieces such as a well-known cruet set (1958). Before World War II she had left Germany to stay with her sister in Liverpool, and studied sculpture and painting at the Liverpool School of Art 1936–40. With a friend she organized a traveling puppet show in 1940, did war work, in 1944 went to London to sculpt in wood and stone, and in 1949 married Aidron Duckworth. During the 1960s she turned to sculptural ceramics, taught briefly at the University of Chicago (1964), but soon went back to England. Her asymmetrical sculptures show uncanny balance, often with coil-built, heavy organic shapes curving up from tiny bases. She also began work on more delicate porcelain pieces in 1962, usually with white glaze, and has done commissions for architects such as the four-room ceramic mural environment for the entrance to Chicago's Department of Geophysics (1967).

The Bauhaus International Style

Lübeck's Great Woman Weaver

ALEN MUELLER-HELWIG, who first attracted attention with her soft off-white, natural-wool rugs—a sensation in the early modern interiors of Ludwig Mies van der Rohe/Lilly Reich in the '20s and '30s—celebrated the 50th anniversary of her workshop in 1977. Now 75 and white-haired, Ms. Mueller-Helwig grew up in Lübeck, Germany, where her mother's best friend, MARIA BRINKMAN, had started the first weaving school of the century. At the Kunstgewerbeschule in Hamburg, headed by Brinkman, Alen was considered too frail to weave, so she studied embroidery, taught herself to dress a loom, and went to work. Far ahead of the faculty at her next school, in Munich, she set up her own workshop in her home town in 1926. The monochromatic rugs she wove from handspun wool depended for interest on texture rather than color. "People were not prepared for the variation this makes possible," she explains today. They had enormous impact. Reich first saw her weaving at the Leipzig Fair in 1926, asked her to teach weaving to an old people's group, then gave her many commissions. Forbidden to weave in the Bauhaus (later called the International) Style during World War II, Ms. Mueller-Helwig raised two small children in Ger many while her husband was a soldier-prisoner in Russia. There were almost no commissions then, and she was able to weave her own designs, with stylized forms, and flowers of medieval simplicity. In the early 1960s she began using metallic threads, and her later hangings are lighter, softer, transparent, with frequent open spaces. In 1977 she still had her school and workshop in the city wall of Lübeck, with seven workers and a few apprentices.

Textile Master at Black Mountain College

Weaver ANNI ALBERS was born in Berlin, Germany, in 1899 and studied at the Bauhaus (Weimar and Dessau, 1922–30), becoming assistant (1931), then interim director of textiles. In 1933 she and her husband, painter Josef Albers, went to the United States, where Ms. Albers taught weaving (1933–49) at Black Mountain College, North Carolina, initiating and leading workshops, lecturing, and developing concepts for production fabrics. A master of handloom and machine work, she emphasized the importance of structure in weaving both utilitarian fabrics and pictorial textiles woven on the loom by established methods. In 1961 Anni Albers won a Gold Medal from the American Institute of Architects, and in 1965 received the Decorative Arts Book Award Citation for *Anni Albers: On Weaving*. A fervent admirer of the sixteenth-century textiles found in Peru, she commented that "playful invention" can be coupled with the inherent discipline of a craft. "Form . . . is our salvation," the innovative weaver wrote. "Acceptance of limitations, as a framework rather than as a hindrance, is always proof of a productive mind." Ms. Albers maintained a studio in New Haven, Connecticut, until her husband left Yale University. They continued their work in Orange, Connecticut, where Josef Albers died in 1976.

Pond Farm Potters

MARGUERITE WILDENHAIN, who with her husband Franz founded Pond Farm Pottery on a mountaintop in redwood country north of San Francisco, was born in Lyon, France, in 1896 and educated at the School of Fine and Applied Arts, Berlin. She designed porcelain for a factory in Thüringen, then trained seven years at the Bauhaus, and next taught at the Municipal School for Arts and Crafts, Halle-Saale, also making models for Royal Berlin Porcelain. When Hitler came to power in 1933 she moved to Holland and in 1940 to the United States. She taught at the College of Arts and Sciences in Oakland, California, 1940–42, then settled at Guerneville, where she and her husband themselves built their renowned school of ceramics and conducted workshops for hundreds of students. Ms. Wildenhain brought her own strong values to pottery, which, she wrote, "is not based on success and money, but on human independence and dignity . . . the person making the pots is the key to the quality of the pot, not any technique."

Honored International Textile Artist

TRUDE GUERMONPREZ (1910–76) was born in Austria, studied textiles at colleges in Cologne and Halle, Germany, and the Textile Engineering School, Berlin, apprenticed in Czechoslovakia, and also studied in Finland and Sweden. When her parents left Germany in 1939 and became teachers at Black Mountain College, North Carolina, Trude remained in Europe, designing for the weaving studio Het Paapje in the Netherlands. She married photographer Paul Guermonprez, who was shot and killed by the Gestapo on D-Day. In 1947 Trude Guermonprez came to the States and taught weaving at Black Mountain, then at Pond Farm in Guerneville, California, at the San Francisco College of Fine Arts, and after 1952 at the California

College of Arts and Crafts, Oakland, where she was head of crafts. She married cabinetmaker John Elsesser and designed for architects and for Owens Corning Fiberglas and Dupont Nylon Carpet. Her European concern for structure and dignity and her exquisite use of color and texture characterized her modern fabric designs. Trude Guermonprez was one of the first fellows of the American Crafts Council and won the American Institute of Architects' 1970 National Craftsmanship Medal of the Year.

First Woman Student at N. Y. School of Textile Technology

Versatile textile artist LILI BLUMENAU (1912–76) studied painting in Germany in 1932 at the Berlin Academy of Fine Arts and for two years at the Académie Scandinave, where she also first became interested in weaving. In 1938 she emigrated to the United States, enrolled as the first woman student at the New York School of Textile Technology and then went to Black Mountain College, North Carolina. Ms. Blumenau became curator of woven and printed textiles at the then Cooper Union Museum, New York (1944–50), taught industrial arts weaving at New York University (1948–50), and weaving and technical design at Columbia Teachers College (1948–52). Beginning in 1950, she wove samples and commissions for the textile industry in her own workshop and taught weaving there. Lili Blumenau was among the first group of fellows elected by the American Crafts Council. She wrote for *Craft Horizons* and *Handweaver and Crafts-*

man, served on *Craft Horizon*'s editorial board for 20 years, and in 1966 published *Creative Design in Wall Hangings*.

She Opened Canada's First Professional Weaving Studio

Quebec fabric designer and weaver KAREN BULOW was born in Denmark and came to Canada in 1929. Two years later, after learning English, she opened a business in the hall of a Montreal flower store, selling small items like scarves and bags. In two more years she moved to a larger place on Sherbrooke Street, where she attracted attention by weaving at a loom in her studio window. Neckties were her best seller—she sold 50,000 a year in stores across Canada—but Ms. Bulow wanted to specialize in textured upholstery and draperies. At the Canadian National Exposition she displayed ties, scarves, bags and belts, decorated her booth with fabrics, and added a weaver working at a loom. Buyers including decorators from Eatons and Simpsons soon placed orders; the company that is now Air Canada ordered upholstery for a fleet of planes. The Trade Commissioner to the Caribbean asked to include Bulow wares with other Canadian products for sale there. Karen Bulow's shop, first professional weaving studio in Canada, employed as many as 20 weavers of fabrics, with 70 women weaving smaller items at home. Karen Bulow took to weaving naturally; she took only one course in the subject. Now retired, she lives in Caledon, near Toronto. In 1976 she was one of the first group awarded honorary membership in the Canadian Crafts Council.

The Scandinavian Influence

Denmark's Democratic Pioneers

In the late 1920s a decline in domestic demand and an increase in foreign competition impelled the Cabinetmakers'

Guild of Copenhagen to start annual competitions to arouse public interest in craftsmanship. Socially oriented designers, and architects who could not find furniture for small apartments, promoted development away from prestige furniture toward smaller pieces with simple lines.

The revolution in furniture affected other applied arts, and ceramist NATHALIE KREBS and textile artist MARIE GUDME LETH (both born in 1895) became outstanding pioneers in their fields. At a time when Danish manufacturers of stoneware were making collector's items, Ms. Krebs with Swede Gunnar Nylund established Nylund and Krebs, a workshop where they planned to make stoneware in sufficient quantity for sale at moderate prices. The following year (1930), Nylund left and Ms. Krebs, who had trained as a civil engineer at the Danish College of Technology, continued under the firm name "Saxbo." Her stoneware soon had an important place in the Danish market. In 1932 EVA STAEHR-NIELSEN (born 1911) joined the company and helped develop a "classic Saxbo style"—generally undecorated, of one color and simple shape, with semi-matte glazes by Ms. Krebs, whose staff actually formed the stoneware.

Ms. Leth, who trained at the Copenhagen Industrial Art School for Women and Academy of Art, and the Kunstgewerbeschule in Frankfurt-am-Main, Germany, was in charge of fabric-printing instruction at the Copenhagen Kunsthaandvaerkerskolen 1931–48. She was an expert in block printing but sought a faster, more precise method, and one for fabrics to be used in ordinary homes. In 1934 she went to Germany and for the first time saw screen-printing, which she introduced to Denmark. Co-founder of the Danish Calico-printing Works in 1935, and its director until 1940, she found she could print quantities of material perfectly. Non-wealthy Danes had always used imported materials in their homes; now for the first time they could use Danish prints.

Prewar Danish weavers worked at handlooms, and manufacturers imported fabrics. In the 1950s, however, the manufacturers became interested in producing for export. One of the most important weavers to adapt to expanding production was LIS AHLMANN, born in 1894. Ms. Ahlmann opened her own workshop in 1933 and worked closely with architect/designer KAARE KLINT, drawing inspiration from textiles around the world. She emphasized simple weaves, fabric structure, and restrained color, often limited to natural wool tones. She began to work with furniture designer Borge Mogensen, learning to use machinery and adapt craft qualities to mass production, and using increasingly strong colors and large patterns to bring new life to fabrics. In 1953 she became art consultant to C. Oleson Ltd.; her work for the company's Cotil collection set an example for the industry in technique and artistic consistency.

PAULA TROCK, born 1889, learned her craft in Denmark, Sweden, and Finland and on trips to Germany, Italy, and England. She established the Askovhus weaving school in 1928, directing it until 1943. In 1949 she began making special yarns in her own factory in Askov, "Spindegaarden," to curtain large window areas in modern houses. She saw light as an independent element in design. Her curtains of loosely spun wool allowed light to enter and at the same time be refracted and softened. At first only Spindegaarden produced the coarse-spun yarns for her curtains; later they were made industrially.

FRANKA RASMUSSEN, born 1909, dean of Danish weavers and an instructor at the Copenhagen School of Arts and Crafts, studied at the Kunstgewerbeschule, Frankfurt-am-Main, Germany, where she began lecturing in 1949. She has designed for a number of theaters in Copenhagen. She combines different techniques and a variety of yarns in her hangings, which are influenced by her impressions of nature.

Sweden's Textile Designers

Handarbetets Vänner (Friends of Handicraft), founded 1874, is the center of Sweden's monumental fabric art and its important pictorial tapestries. Leader of HV since 1951, textile artist EDNA MARTIN is an expert in coordinating artists, and HV's 15 weavers. Ms. Martin, born 1908, trained at Göteborg's Crafts Association School and designed for Molnlycke Textiles Ltd., Oskarström linen works, and the Swedish Domestic Crafts Association (where she was artistic director 1945–51). She also became head instructor at the Konstfackskolan, Stockholm, inspiring her students to independent expression and experimentation.

MÄRTA MÅÅS FJETTERSTRÖM (1873–1941), for many years Sweden's most significant textile artist, made her debut around 1900 and remains an important influence. She founded Märta Måås-Fjetterström AB (MMF) in Båstad in 1919 and created a modern rug influenced by peasant textiles and Persian carpets but primarily Nordic. When she died her workshop continued under BARBRO NILSSON, known for monumental tapestries and vibrant colors that are considered to be classics. Born in 1899, she trained at Johanna Brunsson's school in Stockholm and at the Konstfackskolan. She taught at Brunsson's 1918–20, at Göteborg's Nordenfeldt School 1925–27, and at the Konstfackskolan 1931–57, becoming director of the textile department in 1974. In 1971 KAISA MELANTON followed Barbro Nilsson as artistic leader at MMF. Born in 1920 in Stockholm, Ms. Melanton was graduated from the Konstfackskolan there in 1943 and became a teacher of composition at the Friends of Handicraft in 1952, doing secular and ecclesiastical weaving. She has also organized industrial manufacture of linen and floor coverings. Ms. Melanton has been influential as chief teacher of textile arts at the Konstfackskolan since 1970, has long had her own workshop at Viggbyholm, and has exhibited around the world.

In addition to the weaving done in Sweden's large workshops or by independent young artists is that done by smaller workshop owners. Weaver ALICE LUND, whose tapestries, rugs, and curtains decorate many public buildings, was born in 1900, attended the Stockholm Konstfackskolan, and opened her own workshop in 1936. Her work is characterized by quiet colors, strong feeling for materials, great skill, and simple geometric designs. Ms. Lund makes carpets and upholstery fabrics and plans designs for industrial production.

During the 1950s Alice Lund worked with textile artist SOFIA WIDÉN, who was born in 1900 and studied at the Konstfackskolan, started work with the Licium fabric studios in 1923, and headed the firm from 1930 to 1951 (it became part of Friends of Handicraft). She also had her own shop in Hytting, Borlänge. Sofia Widén specialized in textiles for churches—her fabrics are said to decorate some 1,000 churches in Sweden—as well as churches in the rest of Scandinavia, Paris, and London. Ms. Widén died unexpectedly at age 60.

INGRID DESSAU first worked for home industries, then became a leading weaver of rugs, both privately and for industry, for which she developed geometric and linear figures and supervised their manufacture. Born in 1923 and a student of the Konstfackskolan, she worked for Malmöhus and Kristianstad Domestic Crafts. Her patterns for the Kasthall carpet factory were important to the renewal of industrial rugs, especially rya and rolakan (a kelim type).

ULLA SCHUMACHER-PERCY, born 1918, studied at Otte Sköld's school of painting, 1936–37, and at the Konstfackskolan, 1938–41, became an artistic assistant for Swedish Domestic Crafts in the mid-1940s and has her own workshop in Stockholm. In the 1960s Ulla Schumacher-Percy developed into one of Sweden's outstanding free textile artists, exhibiting rya rugs with color variations based on a common pattern theme (1960) and a few years later, textiles including large embroidered works inspired by the buildings of Spanish architect Gaudí.

ELSA GULLBERG, leader in developing Sweden's textile industry, was born in 1886 and learned to weave at her home in the province of Skåne. She also took up metal work, carpentry, and printing, and attended the Stockholm Konstfackskolan. An expert artist and administrator, she became director early in the century of Svensk Hemslöjd, government-subsidized organization for the improvement of textiles on the basis of old weaving techniques, sending designs to peasant women at branches throughout the country, then worked for Svenska Slöjdföreningen, advising artists and manufacturers in producing fabrics deriving from Swedish culture. She placed young artists (many later well known) in industry and helped them find commissions. In 1927 she opened her own company, and in the mid-1930s introduced film printing, soon a thriving business. Her commissions included textiles for the Göteborg Town Hall, the Stockholm Concert Hall, and the Malmö City Theater. Elsa Gullberg retired in 1955, passing her business on to her children; her daughter ELSA-MARIE GULLBERG became director.

ASTRID SAMPE, born 1909, head of the Nordiska Kompaniet Textile Studio, 1937–40, studied at Stockholm Konstfackskolan and the Royal College of Art, London. She has made an outstanding contribution to the development of furnishings and industrial textiles in Sweden. In 1937 she organized NK's textile-manufacturing section at the Paris Exhibition; in 1946 she brought glass cloth to Sweden, and in the early 1950s worked with the Kasthall carpet works for the revival of Wilton industrial carpets (then developed by Ingrid Dessau, above). In 1955 she worked with artist MARIANNE NILSON and the Almedahl factory to improve linen closets. An ingenious and expert designer, ASTRID SAMPE is also outstanding as a coordinator of production and of sales collections, and as a color planner; besides the companies mentioned she has worked also for Donald Brothers Dundee, Knoll International, Svängsta Klädesfabrik (floor coverings), and has furnished a number of Swedish embassies. In 1948 she published *Textiles Illustrated* with Vera Diurson.

Born 1910 in Finland, VIOLA GRÅSTEN trained at the Helsinki College of Industrial Art and worked for the Friends of Finnish Handicraft from 1938 to 1944. She was already known for her colorful knotted rya rugs in Finland when she came to Sweden, joining Elsa Gullberg Ltd. in 1945 and NORDISKA KOMPANIET, 1945–46. A Swedish citizen since 1949, in 1950 she began to design printed fabrics ranging over an extraordinarily wide spectrum. Her patterns, both geometric and figurative, include classics such as "Hazel" and "Ulmus" and are of surprising colors and color combinations. She also has designed bedspreads and prints for clothing and curtains and been internationally recognized in awards and exhibits.

Sweden's Glass Makers

Kosta, Sweden's oldest glass company, established in the mid-1700s, is known for the work of such artists as MONA MORALES-SCHILDT (formerly with Arabia and Nordiska), famed for multicolor polished glass cubes. In the mid-1960s it combined with Åfors and Boda. Three women designers today work for the Åfors group:

MONICA BACKSTRÖM uses glass with metal—creating patterns by placing paper clips and pins in the bottoms of her bowls and plates; ANNE WARFF, who with Göran Warff won the Lunning Prize in 1968, enjoys allowing molten glass to run down into a hollowed form to make plates in swirls of color; SIGNE PERSSON-MELIN, ceramist who began glass design a few years ago, has produced a collection for Boda Nova including flameproof cooking and baking ware and warming tiles. She practices first by making her products for her own experimental use. She began making pottery in Malmö in 1951 in her own shop. Her work has included wall decoration for the Malmö Simhall baths and Stockholm's underground, People's House, and Forestry headquarters. At Orrefors glassworks, INGEBORG LUNDIN, born 1921 and educated at Stockholm Konstfackskolan, makes light pieces such as shimmering bubbles with abstract designs. She has been with Orrefors since 1947.

ÅSA BRANDT is an independent craftswoman who unlike most Swedish glass artists makes glass in her own shop, completing all the processes herself. Ms. Brandt prefers to allow each step its own time, and to be able to change her ideas as she proceeds, letting them evolve from her original sketch. She is interested in the tactile qualities of glass as a living material.

Sweden's Industrial Ceramists

Rörstrand (founded 1726) and Gustavsberg (1827), Sweden's most important ceramics works, employ many women artists to design tableware for mass production. HERTHA BENGTSON, born 1917, and trained at Hackefors porcelain works, joined Rörstrand in 1941 and specializes in tableware of simple form and decoration.

MARIANNE WESTMAN, born in 1928, and both artist and pattern designer, was trained at Stockholm Konstfackskolan and became a designer at Rörstrand in 1950 and pattern designer and part owner of Westmans Textilateljé, Falun (founded 1958 to make hand-printed fabrics). She is known for the fresh folk style decoration of her tableware.

KARIN BJÖRQUIST, born in 1927, and trained at Stockholm Konstfackskolan, started work for Gustavsberg Studio in 1950 and a few years later designed a set of tableware known as "Vardag" (Everyday). During the 1960s she worked primarily with architects; she made one decoration for one of Stockholm's new subway stations and is interested in ceramics in public buildings and in common plastic objects.

Norwegian Designers

ELSE HALLING, weaver of modern Norwegian pictorial tapestries, was born in 1899 and educated at the State School of Crafts and Industrial Art and at Frk. Stoltenberg's school of weaving. She worked in the United States for three years, then returned to Norway to teach at schools, including the State Industrial School for Women. In 1951 she became head of the weaving studio connected with the Oslo Industrial Art Museum and is credited with bringing about a renaissance in tapestry art. With others at Norwegian Tapestries Ltd. she produced a number of monumental works for the Oslo Town Hall and other public buildings. She uses fiber made from the outer wool of the "Old Norwegian" sheep, producing a soft, glossy surface of rich, deep color. Else Halling's research in old Norwegian fabrics and techniques resulted in substantial improvements in the country's textiles.

SIGRUN BERG, distinctive Norwegian textile artist born in 1901 and educated at the State School of Crafts and Industrial Art and the State Academy of Art, went to work for Teletweed Weaving Company in 1936 and opened her own workshop in 1947, weaving at Trysil on contract. She became a dyeing instructor at the State S.C.I.A. in 1956. Using color schemes derived from old Norwegian traditions, she adapted her artistry to machine work, winning a number of important international awards. Her commissions have included fabrics for Bodø Cathedral and for the royal yacht *Norge*.

Woodworker HANNA CHRISTIE ABRAHAMSEN, born in 1907, studied at Bergen's arts and crafts school, at École Nationale Supérieure des Beaux Arts in Paris, and with sculptor Despiau at the

Oslo Academy of Art. A teacher and designer in several fields, she began working with wood in her workshop on a Vestland island. Her skill and sensitivity to her material as she turns and carves handsome wooden bowls, some almost paper-thin, produce objects representing a new development in woodworking art.

An expert in enamel work, often considered a Norwegian specialty because the pure colors of the enamel applied to gold metal suggest the amazing fjord landscape, is silversmith GRETE PRYTZ KORSMO. Born in 1917, Ms. Korsmo attended the State College of Industrial Art and the Chicago Institute of Design before joining the Norwegian firm of J. Tostrup. A frequent prizewinner, Grete Korsmo began applying an enamel overlay to stainless steel and to copper, producing simple dishes and bowls at much lower cost than those of silver and gold. (The more precious metals are visible through the enamel, whereas steel and copper are not.)

Finnish Designers

During the 1920s Finland witnessed renewed interest in weaving, with women designers leading in textile arts. Encouraged by the Friends of Finnish Handicraft and by several competitions, the ancient rya rug and Finn (double) weave underwent a revival.

EVA ANTTILA, born in 1894, became known for her vivid imagination in producing tapestries as colorful and carefully shaded as oil paintings. Ms. Anttila trained at the Helsinki College of Industrial Art and University, and opened her own workshop in Helsinki. She wove many delicate small sketches and also monumental hangings. LAILA KARTTUNEN, born in 1895, an expert in double weave and a teacher of textile design, also opened her own workshop. She based most of her patterns on folklore, using subdued colors such as shades of gray. EVA BRUMMER, rug artist known for her rich colors, and a painter, was born in 1901 and studied at the Helsinki College

of Industrial Art. She began working on her own in 1929 and was one of the craftswomen who helped revive the old folk-weave techniques in fine rugs.

DORA JUNG, long Finland's outstanding textile artist, was born in 1906 and trained at the Helsinki College of Industrial Art. She established a workshop in 1932 and has designed fabrics for the Tampella linen works, Tammerfors. Her work is noted for its restraint and quality of calm refinement; adhering to the precepts of functionalism, it stresses construction and the use of natural colors in designs carefully patterned according to the texture of the cloth. Dora Jung is an important weaver of damask, having created technical aids with which to produce a remarkable range of pattern in Finn (double) weave. Her larger works include a tapestry made for Turku Castle's restored Renaissance wing, and she has woven fine church vestments of rare intricacy.

UHRA BEATA SIMBERG-EHRSTRÖM, outstanding colorist among Finnish textile artists, born in 1914, trained at the Helsinki College of Industrial Art, and became a rug designer for Friends of Finnish Handicraft in 1935. An industrial designer for Inhemsk Ull (1938) and for Finlayson-Forssa (1958), she was an art consultant for Norna Domestic Crafts from 1950 to 1958. Her quiet color schemes use brown, gray, lilac, and green not only for rugs but also in manufactured woolens and shawls. She also produces ecclesiastical fabrics.

KIRSTI ILVESSALO, born in 1920 and trained at the Helsinki College of Industrial Art, headed the Friends of Finnish Handicraft from 1947 to 1952, and established her own workshop in 1947. In 1958 she became art assistant at Barker-Littoinen Ltd. A frequent prizewinner for rugs, fabrics, and silver, she is best known for her rugs, in which she uses patterns from ancient Finnish folk art and deep shades, as in her rya series in red and black. She produces upholstery fabrics for industry and for her workshop, and has worked with Alvar Aalto on interiors of such structures as the Hall of Culture in Helsinki. She has also made silver jewelry for Kalevala Koru.

ELSA ELENIUS, one of Finland's rare studio potters, was born in 1897 and studied under Anglo-Belgian potter A. Willy Finch (1854–1930), who founded the short-lived Irish factory at Borgå, Finland, with Swedish furniture designer Louis Sparre. Elsa Elenius, one of Finland's foremost ceramists in the '20s and '30s, became a ceramics teacher, transmitting the classic Finch pottery methods to later generations of students.

FRIEDL HOLZER-KJELLBERG, born in 1905 in Austria, began work at Arabia, Finland's major producer of ceramics, in the mid-'20s, making bowls and coffee sets in rice porcelain and fine plain sets in bone china. She also has produced stoneware with intense glazes, including sang de boeuf and celadon.

Other women ceramists, all trained at Helsinki's College of Industrial Art, joined Arabia over the years. TOINI MUONA, born in 1904, studied under potter A. Willy Finch and began work for Arabia in 1931. Highly intuitive, she has produced fine, classic work that is both powerful and refined. AUNE SIIMES, born in 1909, joined Arabia in 1932 and favors porcelain, although she has also worked in glazed stoneware and chamotte. Her principal work has been thin vases and bowls with transparent patterns in delicate colors. RUT BRYK, born in 1916, started work at Arabia in 1942, painting brilliant glazes in two dimensions in faïence and chamotte surfaces. Her trays, tiles, and plaques reflect her romantic outlook; an example of her monumental work is the ceramic wall surface created for the Rosenthal works in 1960. KYLLIKKI SALMENHAARA, born in 1915, joined Arabia in 1947. Inspired by nature, her glazes often suggest birchbark, mountains, and leaves. The objects became more robust after a 1956 trip to the United States to study Indian art.

RAIJA TUUMI, born in 1923, came to Arabia in 1950, and throws rough shapes in stoneware and chamotte, with uneven glazes, often browns, adding to the charm of her simple forms.

GUNNEL NYMAN (1909–48) was an important representative of Finnish craftsmanship in the war-shadowed 1940s. She began as a furniture designer, winning several prizes for her chairs, then became increasingly interested in glass, making simple objects of great character. Often inspired by nature, she produced highly varied work. Gunnel Nyman made both art glass and functional objects and worked for three leading Finnish glassworks before her untimely death.

LISA JOHANSSON-PAPE, born in 1907 and trained at Helsinki's College of Industrial Art (C.I.A.), became one of Scandinavia's leading lamp designers. She worked for Kylmäkoski Ltd., 1928–30, and for Stockmann Ltd., 1937–42, as a furniture designer, designed textiles for Friends of Finnish Handicraft in 1932 and 1935–37, and in 1942 began to design light fixtures. She has planned lighting for medieval Finnish churches and for a number of public buildings, always emphasizing simplicity of form.

HELLIN HELENA TYNELL, born in 1918 and educated at C.I.A., made light fittings for Taito Ltd., 1943–55, and worked as a potter for Wärtsila/Arabia. She joined Riihimäki glassworks in 1945 and in 1957 started assisting at Nord in New York. NANNY STILL, born in 1926 and also trained at C.I.A., became a well-known glass artist and has created important work in wood.

Founder of Marimekko

Scandinavia's most famous textile designer, ARMI RATIA, was one of 400,000 Finns who abandoned home and possessions when the Russians annexed one tenth of the country in 1944. Her husband, army officer Viljo Ratia, bought an oilcloth factory in Helsinki when he returned to civilian life; in 1951 they founded Marimekko. Using quality white Finnish wools and cottons as basecloth, Ms. Ratia designed cheerful, easy-care moderate-price dresses (the company name means Mary's dress) and boldly printed drapery and upholstery fabrics. She abandoned conventional textile design to produce fabrics that are considered graphic art, with an unusual sense of color quality and juxtaposition—some colors brilliant and sunny, others somber and offbeat—all used in unique combinations (such as red and hot pink on bittersweet), and in highly original patterns such as her now-classic "Bricks." The Ratias were divorced in 1969. He runs a rug-weaving factory using Marimekko materials. She sells both dresses and decorated fabrics for the home in more than 20 countries and says that "money comes back through the door after you have thrown it out of the window" (in 1971 her firm's after-tax profit was $250,000 on sales of $5 million—half exports). Armi Ratia, now in her mid-60s, has been awarded the highest Finnish honor, the Order of the White Rose, First Class.

She Set New Horizons in Textile Design

DOROTHY WRIGHT LIEBES MORIN, outstanding American designer of handwoven and industrial textiles, was born in 1899 in Santa Rosa, California. She attended San Jose State Teachers College and the University of California, and obtained her master's degree at Columbia. She turned from painting to textile design, studied weaving at Hull House, Chicago, and in France, taught four years at Horace Mann, and then returned to San Francisco in 1928 to resume weaving on the two looms she had set up in her parents' attic. She established Dorothy Liebes Designs, Inc., in 1934. Her innovative use of colors, textures, and materials drew international admiration when in 1939 she organized the Decorative Arts Exhibit at San Francisco's Golden Gate Exposition and her fabrics were featured at the New York World's Fair Terrace Club. Ms. Liebes realized her handwoven fabrics could be afforded only by the wealthy, and described the day she began working with DuPont synthetic fibers as one of "the most thrilling moments of my life." Drawing inspiration from her travels (the "staff of life" to a designer), she loved the vibrant colors, beading, and glitter of Chinatown, combined the blue and green of nature, contrasting textures, and an extraordinary variety of materials including bamboo strips, lucite, jute, leather, lace, ticker tape, and tape measures. She established a Red Cross crafts program for World War II veterans involving renowned artists, served on the boards of many museums, and planned and judged many exhibits. Dorothy Liebes died in 1972, but the unexpected horizons she opened in the textile arts continue to expand.

The Scalamandrè Family

Textile designers FLORA ADRIANA SCALAMANDRÈ and ADRIANA SCALAMANDRÈ BITTER are the talented mother and daughter of the noted family firm of Scalamandrè Silks, Inc., Long Island City, New York. Flora Baranzelli, born in 1907 in Greenwich Village, won a scholarship to study in France at age 16, and received her B.A. at the Parsons School of Design in 1926. She became industrial stone estimator for her father's cast stone business, the only woman in the field at the time (1926–29), and in 1929 married Franco Scalamandrè, becoming his business partner. Both did all their own design, and she helped her husband organize production. They have cooperated in redecorating the White House for a series of Presidents beginning with Calvin Coolidge, and Flora Scalamandrè has designed reproduction fabrics and wallpapers for Monticello, Mount Vernon, and some 50 other historic American mansions. She won the American Institute of Interior Designers award in 1967 for her Hancock House wallpaper reproduction, the first use of silk-screen to achieve the hand-brushed look of an authentic rainbow paper. She has served on the board of directors of the Italian Welfare League, is still active in design, and manages traveling museum exhibitions.

One of her two children, Adriana (born 1934) is among the rare women today who are executives of interiors firms founded by their fathers. Always interested in drawing ("I was born into something that I loved"), she drew a design of deer jumping through trees at age eight and was thrilled to see it woven into fabric at Scalamandrè Silks; soon she became interested in fabric reproduction at the mills and started designing. She studied at Marymount Academy, with weekends at Parsons School of Design, and on graduation began working at the mill, attending Parsons in the mornings. At 20 she married Edwin Ward Bitter, whom she had met at 12; he is now president of the firm, while she is vice-president, in charge of all design, styling, and importing for Scalamandrè and business manager for the Scalamandrè corporations. She has worked on restorations of the White House; Blair House; Monticello; Andrew Jackson's home, The Hermitage; Colonial Williamsburg; Deerfield Village; Sturbridge Village; Manoire du Fresne, Canada; and Historic Savannah (Georgia).

Leading Influence on Home Furnishings Consumer

FREDA DIAMOND, home furnishings consultant and coordinator and a designer of interiors and home products, works professionally for both retailers and manufacturers and only in home products. According to the *New York Times,* she "probably exerts more influence on the taste of the average home furnishings consumer than any other individual in the United States." The daughter of dress designer IDA DIAMOND, she believes that "one of the strengths of America lies in

its beautiful homes" of every price range. She landed her first job as a furniture designer at an elegant Fifth Avenue store when she was studying to become a mural painter; after three years in its "rarefied atmosphere," she left for Stern Brothers department store. She also worked for manufacturers, pioneering the principle that "taste and style have no price tag," and reaching distributors that ranged from fine specialty shops to mail order houses, supermarkets, and premium users. After World War II, Ms. Diamond was one of the first civilians to arrive in Italy (on V.J. Day) to advise Italian manufacturers on production for the U.S. market. On two occasions the Japanese Government hired her to advise "small makers" on adapting Japanese designs for Americans, and she has served as consultant in countries including Israel, India, the Dominican Republic, and Czechoslovakia. Her clients have included stores like the Maison Blanche (New Orleans), Hess's (Allentown, Pennsylvania), the Associated Merchandising Corporation and the May Company, Greatermans Stores, Ltd. (Johannesburg, South Africa), and such manufacturers as Libbey Glass, Continental Can, General Electric, Lightolier, Yale and Towne, Regina Corporation, Tomlinson Furniture, and Pennsylvania House. The author of *The Story of Glass* (1953), Ms. Diamond received Museum of Modern Art citations in three successive years for her glassware designs for the mass market, which have been exhibited internationally. She has served on the Advisory Board of the Smithsonian's Cooper-Hewitt Museum of Decorative Arts and chaired the Consumer Affairs Committee of the Industrial Designers Society of America.

Her Signature Prints Linked Scarves to Sheets

VERA SALAFF NEUMANN, whose bold, colorful prints in scarves, blouses, dresses, tablecloths, sheets, and many other products are known the world over, grew up in Stamford, Connecticut, where her father paid her 50 cents a page to fill her art book with sketches and her teachers encouraged her to draw the "flower of the month" on the blackboard in each classroom. The family moved to New York City after the market crash in 1929, and Vera worked as a designer while attending Cooper Union Art School and later the Traphagen School of Fashion Design. Soon after graduation she met George Neumann, in her words a "very attractive and sophisticated" Viennese whose family had been in indigo printing and knew fabric and color. They started Printex in 1946 in a "lucky" studio apartment (Henry Luce started *Life* magazine there) at 17th Street and Irving Place, printing her designs on linen placemats with a single silk-screen set up on the kitchen table. Joined by another European, F. Werner Hamm, who was their first salesman and is now chairman of the board, they changed to parachute silk (linen was scarce) and produced the first signature scarves, the first monochromatic designs with shadow effects, to sell for $3.00 to $5.00. With little collateral, "just on our faces," they borrowed $80,000 for a silk-screening machine capable of speed and precision—quality even in quantity. They also bought an old mansion overlooking the Hudson in Ossining, New York, where Printex now prints textiles while Vera paints designs in a top-floor studio—her two tiny dachshunds watching politely from a dilapidated plum-colored Peruvian hat. In 1967 Vera, by then printing all kinds of household linens and fashion fabrics, needlepoint, and stoneware, reached sales of $12 million and became a subsidiary of Manhattan Industries, of which Ms. Neumann is a director. (She is also president of Vera Industries.) Just as she early adopted the Japanese "sumi" calligraphy or brushstroke technique, she starts each collection by choosing a country to visit, sketch, and photograph, buys its artifacts and observes the life of the people until

she has a feeling, such as a "temple feeling" or a "teepee feeling," to translate into graphic design. "You have to be a believer," she says. "You must be able to trust the freshness of the first inspiration or idea." Vera paints some 600 new designs every year. She knows both the mechanical and the aesthetic sides of her business ("we are the only ones who start with the original sketch and supervise the operation through to the final hem"). A widow since 1960, with two adopted children, now grown, Ms. Neumann sponsors work-study programs at Printex for American and foreign students and has established a scholarship fund; she often donates work to school benefits. In 1971 the Emile Walter Galleries presented a traveling exhibit tracing 25 years of her original design paintings; in 1972 the Smithsonian paid tribute to "Vera: The Renaissance Woman"; in 1974 she became an honorary member of the Philadelphia Textile Museum and visited China as a guest of the government; and in 1975 the Fashion Institute of Technology opened a new wing with a 30-year retrospective called "Vera: The Artist in Industry."

First Textile Designer to Organize Courses at Art Students League

KAY LEWIS, textile designer, stylist, and consultant, pioneered the first attempt to use wallpaper printing machines modified with rubber rollers for fabrics; this became the best method (1950 on) for printing Fiberglas. In 1959 she organized a two-year course in Textile Design at the Art Students League of New York, where she continues to teach and is head of the Textile Design Department. Ms. Lewis, born in 1921 in Greenbackville, Virginia, grew up in Williamsport, Pennsylvania, received her bachelor's degree from Pennsylvania State University in 1942, joined Macy's Junior Executive Squad, 1942–44, then worked as a designer for a number of firms before establishing her own New York studio, Kay Lewis, Inc., in 1961. The studio specializes in designing, printing, and serving as consultant for a series of curtain, bedspread, and drapery lines. A charter member of the National Home Fashions League, who served four times on the National Screening Committee for the Fulbright-Hays Graduate Study awards, Ms. Lewis also served on the Friends Committee for the Department of Textiles for New York's Cooper-Hewitt Museum of Decorative Arts and Design (1972–73) and on several juries, including those for the Pennsylvania Scholastic Art Award and the Tiffany Foundation Fellowship awards. In 1978 she was named a Distinguished Alumna by Pennsylvania State University.

INTERIOR DECORATORS

First to Be Called "Interior Decorator"

ELSIE DE WOLFE (Lady Mendl), who made interior decorating a woman's field and was first to be called "interior decorator" (a title conceived for her in the early 1910s), was born in New York City on December 20, 1865. She attended private schools in New York and completed her education in Edinburgh, Scotland. When she returned to New York she discovered an aptitude for amateur theatricals, then a popular way to raise money for charity. After her father died in 1890, leaving little money, she became a competent professional actress, mainly in secondary roles. She next turned to a career in interior decorating, a field in which she had achieved some fame in the 1890s when she redecorated her own home on Irving Place—painting the exterior bright yellow with deep-green shutters, and replacing the heavy Victorian velvets and potted palms with light colors and materials and an emphasis on simplicity and convenience. In 1905 she received a major commission—to decorate the Colony Club. This commission established Elsie de Wolfe, Inc. Ms. de Wolfe paid careful attention to detail in each room. She removed objects, painted with light colors such as gray and ivory, used chintz and toile de Jouy for slipcovers, substituted fine muslin curtains for lace. Her innovations included the liberal use of mirrors, wall brackets, chandeliers, and table lamps rather than hanging lamps, and the concealment of electric cords inside walls. Her ideas appeared in 1912 and 1913 in *Delineator* and *Good Housekeeping* and were collected in her very successful book, *The House in Good Taste*. Ms. de Wolfe flew with Wilbur Wright in 1908, becoming one of the first women to fly; she also was one of the first to dance the fox trot. She received the Croix de Guerre and ribbon of the Legion of Honor for her hospital work with soldiers during World War I in France. After the war she became a member of "the International Set" and in 1926 married Sir Charles Mendl, an attaché at the British Embassy, Paris. A woman who took pride in her youthful looks, Ms. de Wolfe at 69 was named best-dressed woman in the world. A Hollywood hostess during World War II, she returned to France and died at her famous home, Villa Trianon in Versailles, in 1950 at 84.

Interior Designer and Antiquary Won Legion of Honor

NANCY MCCLELLAND, who in 1913 founded Wanamaker's "Au Quatrième," said to be the first antique and decorating department in a department store, was born in Poughkeepsie, New York, and graduated Phi Beta Kappa from Vassar College there in 1897. She worked for the *Philadelphia Press*, 1897–1901, on the advertising staff of Wanamaker's Philadelphia store, 1901–7, lived in Paris, 1907–13, then joined Wanamaker's in New York City. She established her own business, Nancy

McClelland, Inc., in 1922, specializing in wallpaper, antiques, and interior design and decorations. In 1924 she published *Historic Wallpapers* (first complete history on the subject), for which she was named a chevalier of the French Legion of Honor. Ms. McClelland's major interest lay in restoring the interiors of American historic buildings and museums, and she did restoration work on the interiors of Mount Vernon, General Lee's headquarters in Fredericksburg, Virginia, the Henry Wadsworth Longfellow House, Portland, Maine, and the House of History, Kinderhook, New York. Nancy McClelland was made a fellow of the Royal Society of the Arts in London in 1944, and in 1948 received the Michael Friedsam Medal from the Architectural League of New York for service to industrial art. She was president of the American Institute of Decorators for three years and author of a number of books on interior decoration. She died in 1959 at the age of 82.

She Started the Vogue for All-White Rooms

SYRIE MAUGHAM, interior decorator often considered the inventor of all-white rooms, did her own music room in London's Chelsea with white walls, white satin curtains and slipcovers, white lilies, white velvet lampshades, and two four-foot white porcelain camellia trees—"the joy of the owner's heart and the envy of her friends," *Harper's Bazaar* commented in 1929. The vogue for white reached a peak in 1932, popularized by Hollywood's clinging white satin gowns, platinum blond hair, and lavishly furnished all-white sets, but was out of style by 1934. Ms. Maugham next became identified with French provincial-type furniture painted in colors such as ivory with pale pink moldings and given a "crackle" finish, and with triangular corner tables, bedside tables with raised lamp shelf, and the use of long fringe in place of braid or gimp. Syrie Maugham married novelist Somerset Maugham in

1916; they had one daughter and were divorced in 1928. Ms. Maugham died in London in 1955.

Decorator Who Founded Residential Firm at Home

ELEANOR MCMILLEN BROWN, who founded McMillen, Inc., New York decorating firm, more than 50 years ago, entered her profession on impulse. As a young Missouri bride new to New York City and looking for ways to fill her days, she ran into a school friend who raved about her courses at the Parsons School of Design. Ms. McMillen enrolled, worked for two years with ELSIE COBB WILSON after graduation, then in 1924 set up shop in her brownstone house at 148 East 55th Street, its location today. Known mainly for her residential work, she began to include contract design in the '30s, when she designed New York's Cosmopolitan Club and the Steuben Glass store. Over the years her residential clients have included the Bliss, Choate, Busch, Lambert, Duke, Post, Ford, Vanderbilt, Mellon, Dillon, Revson, and other famous families. Known for the timeless aspect of her work, the decorator (she divorced engineer Drury McMillen in the late 1920s and later married architect Archibald Brown) says that "quality . . . is not datable."

In the prosperous 1950s, Ms. Brown decided that because so many new ideas were coming from France, McMillen should exhibit contemporary French furniture, pictures, and art objects in the brownstone rooms. For this exhibit, "Paris 1952," which launched the trend to French contemporary design, she was made a chevalier of the Legion of Honor, and moved to the forefront of her profession.

France's Antiquarian Designer

Noted French antiquarian designer MADELEINE CASTAING has furnished her Left Bank house in Paris as combination shop/home done in the *style anglais* for which she is known. Mme. Castaing recalls as a favorite memory her grandfather's rather "Proustian" country house and garden at St. Pré, near Chartres. She bought her first home four kilometers away when she married Marcellin Castaing, herself designed the garden and found furnishing and decorating "instinctive" for her; the Castaings enjoyed entertaining friends, including Picasso, Modigliani, Vuillard, and the Expressionist Chaim Soutine, who sometimes used her as a model. The house was taken over during World War II and Mme. Castaing began creating showrooms, ultimately acquiring her present house. Here the ground-floor rooms are arranged as though lived in; the second floor comprises high-ceilinged rooms furnished as an apartment, with fine Victorian pieces throughout. Mme. Castaing actually resides in the *entresol* between the floors. The decorator, who stresses the importance of knowing and liking her clients, then waiting for "inspiration," designed the home of Jean Cocteau at Milly, and has been working on small European houses with gardens, townhouses, and apartments.

Woman Decorator Famed for Her Home and Hotel Work

DOROTHY TUCKERMAN DRAPER (1889–1969), born in New York City, a member of a family long in the Social Register, married Dr. George Draper in 1912. Her success in decorating their homes and those of friends became known in the profession, and she was asked to decorate the Hotel Carlyle. Ms. Draper also designed and furnished the Hampshire House in New York City, the biggest decorating project that had ever been awarded to a woman; the Terrace Club at the World's Fair; the Mayflower Hotel in Washington, D.C.; the Greenbrier in West Virginia; the Quintadinha in Brazil; San Francisco's Mark Hopkins and many other hotels, as well as restaurants, theaters, and airplane interiors. She "Draperized" the apartments of society leaders, and developed Sutton Place in Manhattan from tenements. A pioneer in vivid colors and "total coordination" of decor, she emphasized intelligent economy and cheerful effects, such as the cabbage rose design she used everywhere. She was named to the Hall of Fame in 1933 for decorating the River Club and for her tenement work. The National Federation of Business and Professional Women's Clubs selected her as sole representative in decoration in 1934. She became editor in charge of Architecture and Building for *Good Housekeeping* in 1941 and conducted an extension course, "Learn to Live." She wrote a syndicated newspaper column from 1959 to 1967, and published three books for laymen on decorating. Mother of three children, Ms. Draper considered talk about the difficulty of combining home and career to be nonsense—women should just "combine the two . . . not dramatize them." She died in 1969.

Major Corporate Designer

ELLEN LEHMAN MCCLUSKEY, president of one of the United States' largest decorating firms, has a high-powered roster of corporate clients, including McGraw-Hill, Inc., the Allied Chemical Corporation, and Washington's Watergate complex. Ms. McCluskey was born in New York City, was graduated from Vassar College and from Columbia University, and studied at the New York School of Interior Design. She was interior decorator for many celebrities before turning increasingly to design for institutions and commercial buildings, in close cooperation with architects. Among her work are interiors for the Regency Hotel and the New York Infirmary, New York City; the Paradise Island and Brittania hotels, Nassau; and United Airlines' Red Carpet Room at O'Hare International Airport in Chicago. An advocate of state legislation to register interior designers in a field that can be capricious in its fee structures, she says that people are unaware of the sophistication a designer must bring to the job. "An interior designer must understand blueprints, design, lighting, and elevations," she told a reporter for *Women's Wear Daily.* "You must know your design periods, know construction materials, and know how to coordinate, say, six subcontractors working with you. You must know . . . air conditioning, heating, and wiring. Interior design sounds as if it's simply adding a ball to a Christmas tree. It isn't." Ellen McCluskey was co-founder with her brother Orin Lehman of Just One Break (JOB), a charity providing vocational training and placement for the physically handicapped; she designs the annual JOB ball.

Innovative Interior Designer

MELANIE KAHANE, internationally known for her innovations in interior decoration, was born in 1910 in New York City, the daughter of an architect and a millinery designer. As a child she enjoyed painting and architecture, and made all her dolls' clothing and furniture. She attended grammar school in Sioux Falls, South Dakota, and high school in Hackettstown, New Jersey. She then studied at Parsons School of Design, New York City, and in Paris, considering the "regional diversity" of her education its most important aspect. The president and owner of Melanie Kahane Associates, Inc., New York City, her innovations include the use of colored light bulbs, hard-surface floorings such as vinyl tile, and unusual colors, materials, and textures. She has designed airplane interiors, buildings, banks, the Ziegfeld Theatre, Playbill Restaurant, Billy Rose's mansion, the home of then Princeton president Robert Goheen. Named decorator of the year in 1953, Ms. Kahane has won many other awards, produced a film on contemporary Scandinavian design, and toured Russian housing developments to record her impressions. She is the widow of commentator Ben Grauer, with whom she co-hosted the radio program "Decorating Wavelength," and has one daughter.

White House Decorator

"SISTER" PARISH, the White House Fine Arts Committee interior decorator who redecorated the presidential mansion in 1961 for the John F. Kennedys, attended Miss Chapin's School and Foxcroft, married in 1929 and lived well in a Manhattan apartment provided by her parents along with a parlor maid. She had a small baby and no career training when her husband announced a severe salary cut on Christmas Eve, 1932. The day after Christmas she found a shack suitable for a shop at their country farmhouse, then persuaded a New York firm to give her samples of papers and materials, moved furniture from house to shack, and within the week put up her sign, "Mrs. Henry Parish II, Decorator." Friends who had seen how she decorated her own home immediately hired her, and were followed by clients including Rockefellers, Percys, Whitneys, Paleys, Coolidges, and Astors. After World War II, she opened an office on East 69th Street, also working at her 150-year-old island home at Dark Harbor, Maine, with the frequent company of seven grandchildren. When the Kennedys asked for a White House with space for family living, she put in an upstairs kitchen, dining room, and nursery, redesigned all private and entertaining space, and decorated the yellow and white Oval Drawing Room. More recently, "Sister" (so called as the only girl in a family with three brothers) and her partner for 15 years at Parish-Hadley, Arthur Hadley, have been developing homecraft cottage industries, including quilting projects for impoverished rural and mountain homemakers in West Virginia. Research turned up old skills and patterns used extensively by Ms. Parish in such items as afghans in hot pastels, multicolor sofa pillows in woven grosgrain, patchwork quilting for upholstery and curtains, basketry. Herself a weaver and needlewoman, she says that real luxury comes from crafts—warm, human, of unique design.

One of America's Ten Most Influential Designers

EMILY MALINO, recognized by *Interiors* magazine as one of the ten most influential American designers, is a native New Yorker who now lives in Washington, D.C., and is the mother of four children and the wife of Congressman James H. Scheuer (D., N.Y.). Ms. Malino received her bachelor of arts from Vassar and attended Columbia University's School of Architecture. She is a former vice-president of the Architectural League and former treasurer and program chairman of the National Home Fashions League, winner of the *Institutions* magazine award for interior design for seven consecutive years, and in 1976 won the Burlington award for hospital design. Her decorating projects include Georgetown University Law Center, the New York Hospital Pediatric Division and many other hospitals, the Smithsonian, the American Film Institute, and a project familiar to many citizens—the red, white, and blue quarters of the American Revolution Bicentennial Commission. Emily Malino has decorated homes across the country, including model homes and room settings for the media. She is a design consultant to Sears, Roebuck, Time-Life Books, and many other organizations, a member of the President's Federal Design Task Force, and author of *Super Living Rooms* (1976). Perhaps most important to Emily Malino's influence as a designer, however, is her syndicated news column, "Design for People," based on the "Malino philosophy," urging her readers to save what is good from the past. American ingenuity with hammer, saw, and a can of paint is imaginatively fostered in Emily Malino's highly practical decorating advice—the sort that enabled her to decorate a three-room Model Cities Program apartment in New York's Bedford-Stuyvesant for $600.

7

Women in the Labor Movement and Organizations

By Grace E. Moreman

Pearl G. Spindler, consulting editor

In most nations of the world, the degree of labor organization for both men and women bears a direct relation to the political circumstances of those nations. Yet even where the climate is favorable toward labor, women's participation and leadership tend to be far less than men's. In the United States, active participation in unions began early, but it was not until the 1970s that American labor saw numbers of women begin to assume leadership roles. And although women became a vital force in the labor movement (and in successive Labour Party governments) in Britain with the founding of the Women's League, in 1874, it was nearly 50 years before the British Trade Union Congress elected its first woman chairperson, MARGARET BOND-FIELD, in 1923.

There are bright spots. Canada's largest union, the Canadian Union of Public Employees, with 210,000 members, is headed by GRACE HARTMAN. In Denmark the huge, 300,000-member Joint Council of Danish Civil Servant and Functionary Organizations has KIRSTEN STALLKNECHT as its deputy chairperson. Israel's GOLDA MEIR was a labor leader before she became her nation's Prime Minister (see "Women in Politics and Government," p. 46).

In the United States, two organizations played significant roles in helping turn-of-the-century working women: the National Consumers League (NCL) and the Women's Trade Union League (WTUL). The WTUL, which is no longer in existence, was made up of educated middle-class and some wealthy women joining to help its third group of members: working women. Names such as MARGARET DREIER ROBINS and of settlement founders JANE ADDAMS, LILLIAN WALD, and MARY McDOWELL (the latter appear in the chapter "Women Activists, Heroes, and Humanitarians") are part of WTUL history. Its fourth president, MAUD SWARTZ, was the first working woman to serve in this capacity. The organization is remembered for its efforts to organize working women, its strike assistance, and its leadership in getting Congress to finance a comprehensive study of the working conditions of women and children (1908–11).

The National Consumers League, founded in 1899 (the New York League dates from 1891), from the start brought consumer pressure to bear to fight economic injustice. It still does and is still going strong. In its early years, the NCL also was in the vanguard of the struggle to aid working women and was particularly active in pushing for minimum wages and for what is a bugaboo to today's feminist: "protective labor laws."

Since 1920, U.S. working women have had a powerful ally in the Women's Bureau, the only federal agency concerned solely with the interests of women. Established by an act of Congress on June 5, 1920, the Bureau was preceded by the Women's Branch of the Ordnance Department, renamed the Women in Industry Service and shifted to the Department of Labor in 1918. MARY VAN KLEECK was the director of the original Branch and of the Service until 1919. A former shoe worker, MARY ANDERSON succeeded Ms. Van Kleeck and also became the first head of the Bureau. Under the leadership of ALEXIS M. HERMAN, appointed in 1977, the Bureau continues to work for the 39 million women in the labor force and the women and girls who are potential workers. It reaches the organized and the unorganized—in particular, those of low income (including private-household workers), black, Hispanic, American Indian, and Asian-American women, rural women, teenagers, older women, and women offenders. The Bureau focuses on improving the employability of and increasing employment opportunities for women and minorities, and reducing discrimination in employment based on sex and race. To combat sex discrimination in hiring and on the job, the Bureau in 1970 and 1971 held a conference and series of consultations with business, industry, and union representatives in vari-

ous cities across the country. In the mid-1970s, it was working with union women and men to expand non-traditional job opportunities for women.

Today, many women in the U.S. labor movement—mediators like ANNA WEINSTOCK, lobbyists like EVELYN DUBROW and JANE O'GRADY, and lawyers like RUTH WEYAND (see also "Women in Law and the Justice System," p. 349) have helped working women to gain higher wages, better working conditions and, some day, full equality with working men. The founding of the Coalition of Labor Union Women (CLUW), in March 1974, by 3,200 women and men, marked the first time that U.S. union women coalesced on a nationwide scale. Basically CLUW's aims are to encourage millions of non-union working women to join unions; to increase women's participation within unions; to seek "affirmative action" on the part of unions against employers' discriminatory practices; and to press for legislative action to further women's interests. By the end of 1976, CLUW's membership, with chapters across the country, came from approximately 60 unions. CLUW is making itself heard; unionists such as OLGA MADAR and ADDIE WYATT have taken their places in today's top labor leadership, and there is now more than a pious hope that many women will do what is still "non-traditional": take leadership roles in their unions.

U.S. women have never joined unions in great numbers. Today, they make up a little more than one fifth of union membership. However, less than 15 per cent of the women in the labor force are union members and few are union leaders. None serve on the executive board of the AFL-CIO, which is only open to union presidents. But as CLUW grows, more union women are becoming activists in fighting remaining employment discrimination—for example, in job classifications and in inequitable practices against women in health insurance (pregnancy benefits, in particular)—and in testifying on legislation and involving themselves in politics. An area of concern shared by women workers in all nations is the necessity of quality child care. In May 1977 a group of 24 CLUW members from the United States visited child-care centers in Israel, Sweden, and France.

All the nations involved in World Wars I and II saw an increase in women's participation in the labor force, and women participated from the beginning in the International Labor Organization (ILO). Britain sent MARY MACARTHUR ANDERSON as a delegate to the first ILO conference, in 1920. In 1945 the ILO came under the aegis of the United Nations. During the International Women's Year (IWY), the nations participating in the 1975 ILO conference in Geneva sent a high proportion of women representatives, who debated in committee the Declaration on Equality of Opportunity and Treatment for Women Workers. Their resolutions directed the ILO to collect statistical data on women and men from both developed and developing countries relating to the status of women workers, and to study the need for new international standards concerning equal opportunities and treatment in employment. The Declaration and resolutions were forwarded to the United Nations' IWY Conference, meeting in Mexico City, and to the Tribune, which was a non-governmental group meeting at the same time. The Tribune strongly endorsed the benefits of unionism for all women and saw these as crucial to the economic development of each nation. (To the regret of many U.S. women, in 1977 the United States withdrew from the ILO.)

In an address to the United Nations, HELVI SIPILA, of Finland, Secretary General for IWY and UN Assistant Secretary General (see "Women in Politics and Government," p. 65), pointed out that the world can no longer afford to underutilize women (who make up 51 per cent of the world's population) and still expect to solve the world's growing economic and social problems or improve the quality of life.

The declarations of the ILO and IWY cannot effect any immediate improvements in women's employment; they do establish guidelines for the future on ways of ensuring equality on an international scale.

GRACE E. MOREMAN, *a free-lance writer who has contributed to* Parade *magazine,* Woman's Day, Working Woman, *and the* Wilson Quarterly, *is also the author of two children's books published in 1973 and 1976. A graduate of Pomona College, in California (1952), she holds an M.A. in religion and art from the University of Chicago Divinity School (1956), has taught school in California and worked at the National Gallery of Art, in Washington. In 1977 she joined the staff of the Alban Institute, in Washington. Married, with three children, she lives in Arlington, Virginia.*

Consulting editor PEARL G. SPINDLER *retired from the Women's Bureau of the U. S. Department of Labor in 1976 after 33 years as a federal employee, 26 in the Labor Department. A graduate of Hunter College (1940) and of George Washington University Law School (J.D., 1945), she is a member (inactive) of the Washington, D.C., bar and of the Federal Bar Association, the Industrial Relations Research Association, the National Organization for Women, Women's Equity Action League, National Women's Political Caucus, and Women's Legal Defense Fund. She is married, has three children and six grandchildren, and lives in Bethesda, Maryland.*

HISTORIC FOUNDERS AND PIONEERS, WORLD-WIDE

First to Document Abuse of Women and Children in U.S. Industry

LEONORA MARIE KEARNEY BARRY (1849–1930) was born in Cork, Ireland, and came to upstate New York as a child. At 16 she was certified as a teacher and taught in a rural school. She married William E. Barry in 1871, bore three children, and was widowed in 1881. To support her children, she went to work as a machine operator in a hosiery mill in Amsterdam, New York. She earned 11¢ her first day, and a total of 65¢ for the first week. She joined the Knights of Labor, the first group to attempt the creation of a national labor organization in the United States, and quickly rose to leadership. She was elected Master Workman of nearly 1,000 women and in 1886 was a delegate to the Knights' general assembly, held in Richmond, Virginia. This date marked the peak of progress for the Knights of Labor and a new step for working women: Leonora Barry was elected by the convention of 660 delegates, 16 of whom were women, to be general investigator in the organization's new Department of Women's Work. For three and a half years she traveled, investigated, spoke, and organized. Her inspections were hampered by the fact that many employers would not admit her to their workplaces and women workers were afraid to talk freely. However, her reports stand as the first systematic documentation of the industrial abuse of women and children in the United States.

Co-Founders of the New York Consumers League, First in the United States

JOSEPHINE SHAW LOWELL (1843–1905), a Civil War widow in her early 30s, was the first woman appointed (1876) to the New York State Board of Charities, on which she served for 13 years. Her book *Public Relief and Private Charity* (1884) and other writings provided a basis for state-administered philanthropy. But Josephine Lowell resigned from the Board after concluding that treating the symptoms was not the answer to poverty. Poor working conditions and low wages were the root cause. Conceiving the idea that buyers could put pressure on factory owners and retailers by refusing to purchase their products unless the conditions under which they were manufactured or sold met reasonable standards of health, safety, and pay for the workers, she envisioned the New York Consumers League as an organization to arouse the buying public, a thitherto untapped source of support for labor.

With a friend, MAUD NATHAN (1862–1946), she founded the New York Consumers League (1891) with the aim of improving the conditions under which women and girls had to work in New York shops and factories. Maud Nathan later became president of the New York League and held the post for 20 years, working tirelessly to get across the purpose of the League's "white lists" of stores that sold only goods manufactured in accord with minimally decent working conditions and standards of pay. Other state leagues aimed at fighting the sweatshop were soon formed in Massachusetts, Pennsylvania, and Illinois, and in 1899 the state leagues banded together to form the National Consumers League. Members inspected workplaces, certifying manufacturers who met their standards with a "Consumers Label," and eventually moved into working for labor legislation.

Women Leaders of the National Consumers League

General Secretaries

Florence Kelley	1899–1932
Mary W. Dewson (Molly)	deputized for Florence Kelley, 1919–32
Lucy Randolph Mason	1932–38
Mary Dublin Keyserling	1938–41
Ms. Warwick Hobart	1942–43
Elizabeth Magee	1943–59
Vera Waltman Mayer	1959–62
Sarah H. Newman	1962–72
Alice Shabecoff	1972–74
Sue Byrnes	1975–76
Sandra L. Willett	1976–

Chairwomen of the Board

Ms. J. Borden (Daisy) Harriman	1926–32
Dorothy McAllister	1947–54
Susana Zwener	1958–61
Louise Stitt	1961–

Presidents

Josephine Roche	1938–44
Dr. Alice Hamilton	1944–49
Margaret Ackroyd	1968–73
Esther Peterson	1973–76
Mary Gardiner Jones	1976–77
Erma Augevine	1977–

First General Secretary of the National Consumers League

FLORENCE KELLEY (1859–1932), known as "the impatient crusader," fought to abolish child labor and helped to shape such basic American social legislation as minimum wage and workmen's compensation by inspiring others to lobby for labor laws and to argue test cases in the courts. She died before all of her ideas were widely accepted. But, after 1933, many were adopted by the federal government on a national scale. Born in Philadelphia to a congressman father and a Quaker mother, she received a B.A. from Cornell (1882) but was refused admission to law school at the University of Pennsylvania on grounds of her sex. Her father took her on a walking tour of the industrial counties in England, where the deplorable living and working conditions of factory workers awoke in her the desire to become a social reformer. In 1884 she married Lazare Wischnewetzky, a Russian medical student. They had three children. She divorced him in 1891 for nonsupport and resumed her maiden name. Miss Kelley lived at Hull House, in Chicago, from 1891 to 1899. From 1892 to 1897 she served as the first female factory inspector in Illinois, earned a law degree from Northwestern University, and was admitted to the Illinois bar. In 1899 she was hired as the first general secretary of the newly formed National Consumers League and moved to New

York City with her children, where they lived at the Henry Street Settlement. She held this position for 33 years, until her death.

First President of the National Women's Trade Union League (NWTUL)

MARY MORTON KIMBALL KEHEW (1851–1918), daughter of a Boston merchant banker, granddaughter of a governor of Massachusetts, and wife of a Boston manufacturer, used her private fortune to further the cause of labor and education. When she was elected the first president of the National Women's Trade Union League (NWTUL), in 1903, she already had behind her a long voluntary career in support of organized labor, and had seen the need to organize women in industry. As president of the Women's Educational and Industrial Union (1892–1918), she organized a research department to gather industrial data that furnished the basis for the establishment of the Massachusetts Department of Labor and Industry. She enlisted the talents of MARY KENNEY O'SULLIVAN (p. 294) to draw working girls into informal gatherings where trade unionism could be encouraged, was active in the Massachusetts branch of the Association for Labor Legislation, Denison Settlement House (of which she was a founder), the State Commission for Industrial Education, and the Massachusetts Child Labor Commission, and also encouraged the establishment of day nurseries and a number of projects for the blind, including founding Woolson House, a settlement for blind women. Most of these were pioneering ventures —but none more remarkable than her support for trade unionism in a day when it was considered economic and political heresy.

Longest Term as President of the NWTUL

MARGARET DREIER ROBINS (1869–1945) for 38 years was an influential force behind the National Women's Trade Union League (NWTUL). Born into a prosperous Brooklyn family, she first encountered the conditions of poor people at age 19 while working as a hospital volunteer. In 1905 she married Raymond Robins (a settlement worker and millionaire from the Klondike gold rush) and moved to Chicago, where she came in contact with some of the great social reformers: JANE ADDAMS, of Hull House (p. 699), AGNES MCEWEN NESTOR, of the glovemakers union (p. 295), MARY ANDERSON, of the boot and shoe workers (p. 330), and MARGARET ANGELA HALEY of the Chicago Teachers Federation (p. 297). She joined the NWTUL, was elected president in 1907, and succeeded in making it an effective force for organizing women into unions and striving for laws to better women's working conditions, wages, and hours. With ROSE SCHNEIDERMAN, of New York, she aided strikers during the garment workers' strikes of 1909–11 by raising money for relief, obtaining legal counsel, and gaining influential support. She founded a training program to prepare women for local union leadership, for a time edited *Life and Labor,* the NWTUL official publication, and won acceptance from Samuel Gompers, president of the American Federation of Labor. Though she resigned in 1922 as president, she was reelected to the NWTUL executive board in 1934 and remained interested and active in the organization until the end of her life.

Only Woman Appointed to New York State's 1911 Factory Investigation Commission

MARY ELIZABETH DREIER (1875–1963), younger sister of MARGARET DREIER ROBINS, was arrested, on November 4, 1909, for picketing with shutout working girls from the Triangle Shirtwaist Company, in New York City. Because of her social prominence this event drew press attention to the conditions under which women were employed and gained public support for sweatshop workers and for the New York Women's Trade Union League, of which Margaret Dreier was president. In March 1911 occurred the Triangle Shirtwaist Company fire, in which 146 persons, most of them young women, lost their lives. Public outcry over this tragedy led to New York State's establishment of the Factory Investigation Commission. Mary Dreier became its only woman member. The Commission, which existed from 1911 to 1915, was responsible for New York State's first industrial reform laws, including the 54-hour week. Mary Dreier was president of the New York Women's Trade Union League from 1906 to 1915 and later head of the New York Women's Suffrage Party Industrial Section, worked for the Child Labor Amendment, and in 1942 was chairperson of the War Labor Standards Committee.

Youngest Woman Factory Worker to Rise to National Leadership

The daughter of a widowed Irish immigrant mother, LEONORA O'REILLY (1870–1927) was only 11 years old when she went to work in a New York collar factory. In 1886, at the age of 16, she joined the Knights of Labor and helped to organize the Working Women's Society. This effort brought her into contact with JOSEPHINE SHAW LOWELL, MARY and MARGARET DREIER (ROBINS), and LILLIAN WALD, upon whom the young factory girl made a tremendous impact. These women, of widely differing social and economic backgrounds, became lifelong friends and, with others like themselves, led the women's labor movement through its turbulent and productive early years, in the first part of the 20th century. Leonora O'Reilly was a founding member of the National Women's Trade Union League, in 1903, and devoted full time to it as a gifted speaker and organizer (1909–15). She helped to found unions in the garment trades that still exist today.

First Working Woman to Serve as President of Women's Trade Union League

MAUD O'FARRELL SWARTZ (1879–1937) was born in Ireland and educated at convent schools in France and Germany. She worked as a governess in Italy before emigrating to the United States, in 1901. Her linguistic ability helped her find work in New York as a proofreader in a foreign-language printing firm. Active in the suffrage movement, she often spoke to Italian audiences. In 1905 she married a printer, Lee Swartz, from whom she soon separated. Trade unionism became her career. In 1913 she joined Typographical Union No. 6, of New York City. She also joined the Women's Trade Union League, becoming its full-time secretary in 1916. Her language ability again was useful in helping foreign women workers who were seeking compensation for industrial accidents but because of the language barrier were ignorant of the laws. She was elected the League's fourth president in 1922. In 1931, she was appointed the first woman to be secretary of labor for the state of New York, serving under FRANCES PERKINS (p. 331) who was industrial commissioner. She was the first trade-union member to hold either the League's presidency or the state's secretary-of-labor post.

First Editor of *Life and Labor*

ALICE HENRY, born in 1857 in Australia, for nearly 20 years was a journalist for the *Melbourne Argus*. She emigrated to the United States in 1906. Having already developed an interest in women's suffrage and the labor movement, she was drawn to Hull House, in Chicago, where she met MARGARET DREIER ROBINS, of the Women's Trade Union League. Enlisted to edit the WTUL section of the *Chicago Union Labor Advocate*, she later (1911–15) served as first editor of the WTUL's new publication *Life and Labor*. Her highly readable and lively style did much to enhance the effectiveness of the League. Her book *Women and the Labor Movement* was published in 1923. In 1933 she retired to Australia, where she died in 1943.

Founder of Boston's Trade Union College

As executive secretary of the Boston Women's Trade Union League for more than 20 years, MABEL EDNA GILLESPIE (1877–1923) effected close cooperation between the women's labor movement and such older, more powerful organizations as the Boston Central Labor Union. By 1911, she had brought five established unions into affiliation and doubled the membership of the Boston WTUL. She helped provide support for the Lawrence, Massachusetts, strike in 1912, helped the effort to get a state minimum-wage law for women—the first such law passed in the United States (1912)—and was appointed the employees' representative on the three-member Minimum Wage Commission, set up to administer the law. With the support of several strong men's unions, the Boston WTUL organized newsstand and periodical workers (1915) and added necktie workers, hatmakers, and jewelry workers (1917). She herself organized and became the first president of a stenographers' union and in 1918 was named the first woman on the Board of the Massachusetts State Federation of Labor. After World War I, during which she served on the Women's Committee on Industry, she became active in labor education at Bryn Mawr and also founded Boston's Trade Union College (1919).

First Person to Research Labor Reform Laws in the United States

At a time when there was very little labor legislation and the relevance of social conditions to production was not understood, JOSEPHINE CLARA GOLDMARK (1877–1950) researched the briefs for Louis Brandeis and Felix Frankfurter (both later Supreme Court justices) used in cases to test new labor laws, e.g. *Muller* v. *Oregon* (1908). She is generally credited with being the first person to present scientific evidence that efficiency decreases with fatigue—a concept that became an important weapon in the fight for shorter working hours. As research director for the National Consumers League, she produced many influential publications, including *Child Labor Legislation Handbook* (1907) and *Fatigue and Efficiency* (1912).

Young Woman Who Touched Off First General Strike in Garment Industry

CLARA LEMLICH was a girl in her teens when she first went out on strike against her employer, the shirtwaist factory of Leiserson & Company, in New York, and suffered broken ribs from a police beating while on the picket line. On November 22, 1909, she attended a mass meeting of garment workers at Cooper Union called to decide what to do about further strikes. After listening to hours of speechmaking and no action, Clara Lemlich asked for the floor. She identified herself as a working girl out on strike against intolerable conditions, said she was tired of hearing generalities, and offered a resolution "that a general strike be declared—now!" The jam-packed crowd reacted with wild enthusiasm, touching off the first general strike in the New York garment industry. It lasted from November 1909 to February 1910 and involved between 20,000 and 30,000 workers, 75 per cent of whom were women.

Oldest Active Labor Radical

MARY HARRIS "MOTHER" JONES (1830–1930), born in Ireland, with her family emigrated to the United States in 1853. At the age of 100 years, though bedridden, she actively campaigned to oust John L. Lewis as president of the United Mine Workers. Married to a labor organizer, she lost her husband and four young children in a single week in a yellow-fever epidemic in Memphis, Tennessee. The experience left her unafraid of death and utterly committed to the cause of workers against monied interests. For more than 50 years she traveled the United States aiding strikers, especially miners, and holding rallies. No compromiser, and gifted with a sense of the dramatic, she could move an entire community to go out on strike and maintain the strikers' loyalty over long periods. When she died, seven months after her 100th birthday, she was given a high requiem mass in Washington, D.C., and was buried in the union miners' cemetery, Mt. Olive, Illinois.

Britain's Industrial Poverty Pioneer

BEATRICE POTTER WEBB (1858–1943) is perhaps best known for her collaboration with her husband, Sidney Webb, on a number of books including *The History of Trade Unionism* (1894) and as a moving spirit in the Fabian Society, in Britain, before World War I. Born into a well-to-do family with Radical sympathies, she was the eighth of nine daughters. A prime concern all her life was the linkage of the industrial system of free enterprise to wage slavery and poverty, and she was instrumental in the setting up of trade boards to regulate wages and conditions in the unorganized industries where many women were employed. Before she married Webb, in 1892 at the age of 34, she also had already been active in the Charity Organisation Society and had made a distinctive contribution to a major study, *Life and Labour of the People in London*, by Charles Booth. In 1905 she was appointed to the Royal Commission on the Poor Law, and in 1909 was the founder of the National Committee for the Break-Up of the Poor Law. In 1932, Beatrice and Sidney Webb visited the U.S.S.R. and became nonparty converts to Soviet communism.

Founder of the National Federation of Women Workers in Britain

MARY MACARTHUR ANDERSON, born in 1880 in Glasgow, Scotland, the eldest daughter of a drygoods-shop proprietor, in 1901 joined the shop assistants' union, became active in the labor movement, and in 1903 was appointed general secretary to the Women's Trade Union League (of Britain). She created a large number of women's local unions, and in order to stabilize these unions, in 1906 she established the National Federation of Women Workers, of which she became secretary. That same year, she also assisted in the founding of the National Anti-Sweating League, which worked for a minimum wage and against "sweated" labor. A dramatic and effective advocate, she impressed a parliamentary committee with her evidence in favor of a minimum wage, and in 1909, as a representative of the women chainmakers to the chainmaking trade board, she was able to influence a fixed legal minimum wage rate. In 1910 she led a strike to compel employers to pay that rate without delay. She served throughout the First World War as honorary secretary of the Central Committee on Women's Employment and helped write the Wages Act of 1918, which stabilized wages after the Armistice. In 1920 Mary MacArthur Anderson went to the United States to attend the first labor conference convened under the League of Nations. She returned to Britain to arouse enthusiasm for the labor charter that she had helped to create but soon after became ill, and died in 1921.

A Lone Voice for Equal Pay in Australia

The struggle for equal pay and economic independence for women has had an uphill struggle in Australia—as in many other countries—even though the nation pioneered in setting a minimum wage for unskilled workers in 1907. Historically, Australian women received only about

54 per cent of the median male wage until World War II (when their portion was raised to about 66 per cent). It was against this early background that MURIEL HEAGNEY in 1927 was appointed to a committee to investigate the employment of women at the H. V. McKay iron and steel works. In 1930 she organized the Unemployed Girls' Relief Movement (UGRM) under the Ministry of Sustenance. As secretary, she handled all claims and saw her work as the first effort in building up a women's cooperative movement in Australia. In 1932 a change in government ended these services. Muriel Heagney then published a book entitled *Are Women Taking Men's Jobs?* which argued that if men were being laid off instead of women, it was because women were paid only half of what men got. She challenged the government to take responsibility for women workers, but not until 1941 was a Council for Action for Equal Pay set up, with her as its secretary. By 1950, Australian women's wages had been raised to 75 per cent of men's. By 1969, limited acceptance was given to the principle of equal pay for equal work, and in 1973, a new Labour Party government moved to fully implement this policy.

Leader and Editor in Austria's Labor Movement

Although women were excluded from membership in trade unions in Austria until about 1892, they had their own newspaper, *Working Women*, edited by ADELHEID POPP (1869–1939), a leader of the movement for women's political equality, who also, in 1893, founded a reading and debating club called "Libertas" to provide a forum for women to prepare for activity in politics. In May 1893, for the first time in Austrian history, 600 women went out on strike in four men's clothing factories near Vienna in order to get better wages and working conditions. On the first International Women's Day, in March 1911, Austrian

women passed a resolution emphasizing the demand of all working women for political equality, their right to vote and to be elected to office.

Co-Founder of Women Workers' Council in Israel

RACHEL SHAZAR-KATZNELSON, born in 1888 in Bobruisk, White Russia, was educated at the University of Petersburg, and emigrated to Israel in 1912. She lived in the Kinnereth Kibbutz from 1914 to 1917. Co-founder and member of the Women Workers' Council and founder and editor of the weekly *Davar Hapoelet*, she worked at various positions in the Histadrut (women's labor union organization), traveled on behalf of women workers to the U.S.A., Poland, and Germany, and became a member of the Educational Advisory Commission of the Ministry of Education and Culture. In 1958, she was awarded the Israel Prize. Her husband, Zalman Shazar, was President of Israel from 1963 to 1973.

Organizer of India's First Major Strike

Born into a multimillionaire family in Ahmedabadin in 1885, ANUSUYABEN SARABHAI became an orphan at 10 and was married at 12 to a boy little older than herself. Later she was able to have the marriage annulled. In 1911 she traveled to England, where she studied at the London School of Economics and was influenced by the Fabian socialism of BEATRICE and Sidney WEBB (p. 292) and by the woman suffrage movement. Back in India, with the encouragement of her brother, a textile-mill owner, she became a social worker among desperately poor millworkers in Ahmedabad. In 1914 she rented two rooms and started classes for workers' children, something that had never been done in India. In 1917 the mill workers asked her to preside over their meeting, which turned out to be a historic event—as Anusuyaben Sarabhai gave the millowners 48 hours' notice before calling a strike on December 4, 1917, the first major strike in the history of India's trade unions. That same year, she founded the Warpers' Union, which was followed by the establishment of several other craft unions and the Drivers' and Firemen's Union, and in 1920 she founded the Textile Labour Association, a merger of the individual unions. A follower of Gandhi, Anusuyaben Sarabhai, who died in 1972, furthered the principles of conciliation and arbitration, and the Textile Labour Association (TLA) has not had a major strike since 1923.

Trade Unionist—First Indian to Receive a Diploma in Social Work in Britain

MANIBEN KARA, like ANUSUYABEN SARABHAI born into a wealthy, millowning family, did social service work in the slums of Bombay while still a high school student, then studied at the University of Birmingham, in England, becoming the first Indian to receive a degree in social work in Britain. She worked in London, Manchester, and Birmingham before returning home to Bombay, where in 1925 she set up a social service center. Realizing that she was only touching on the fringes of poverty, she turned to the trade unions as a way of getting to some of the root causes. She joined the All India Trade Union Congress (AITUC) and helped to reactivate it. Following India's independence, she was active in promoting the growth of the Bombay Municipal Workers' Union, the Indian Railwaymen's Federation, the Cashewnut Workers' Union, and the Merchant Navy Officers' Union. In 1946 she occupied one of three seats reserved for trade unionists in the central legislative assembly. In 1949 she was elected to the executive board of the International Confederation of Free Trade Unions; in 1952 was invited by the AF of L to lecture in the United States; in 1968 represented India at the 100th anniversary celebration of the British Trades Union Congress and received a gold medal from the International Transport Federation on behalf of trade unions in general and transport workers in particular; in 1970 received India's highest civilian award, the Padma Shree; and in 1971 was named to the Commission on the Status of Women in India.

UNION OFFICERS AND RANK AND FILE, U.S.A.

Organizer of First Women's Typographical Union

AUGUSTA LEWIS TROUP (c. 1848–1920), reporter and printer for the New York Sun and later typesetter for the New York World, became a skilled typesetter in the days when women were not admitted to typographers' unions. She organized the first Women's Typographical Union, becoming its president in 1868. So skilled was she as a compositor that she set Washington Irving's "Rip Van Winkle," 24,993 ems of solid agate type, in 6½ hours, and was chosen to test the Alden, one of the first typesetting machines. After marrying Alexander Troup, she moved to New Haven, Connecticut, had seven children, and continued to write for the New Haven Union, a daily paper published by her husband.

First Woman General Organizer for AF of L

The daughter of Irish immigrants and organizer of Chicago women bookbinders, MARY KENNEY O'SULLIVAN (1864–1943), so impressed Samuel Gompers that he hired her in 1892 to be the AF of L's first woman general organizer. In five months she organized garment workers in New York City and Troy, New York, and printers, binders, shoe workers, and carpet weavers in Massachusetts. But in September 1893 the AF of L's executive council, which had no interest in the organization of women, did not renew her appointment. She returned to Chicago, lobbied at the Illinois state capitol for the state's first factory law, which regulated women's and children's employment, and inaugurated Illinois's first factory-inspection department—in which she served as deputy to Chief Inspector FLORENCE KELLEY (p. 288). In 1894 she married Jack O'Sullivan and they settled in Boston, where, between 1894 and 1902 four children were born to them. She kept up her work, organizing the rubber workers, shoe workers, and garment workers. In 1902 her husband was killed, and she began supporting herself and her children by managing property, including a model tenement where she ran a school in the basement to teach English and housekeeping to the tenants. In 1903, during the AF of L's annual convention, in Boston, she and New York settlement worker William E. Walling were the two principal founders of the National Women's Trade Union League, and Mary O'Sullivan was elected its first secretary (and later vice-president). From 1914 to 1934, her 70th year, she worked as a factory inspector for the state of Massachusetts.

Organizer and First President of the American Nurses Association

ISABEL ADAMS HAMPTON ROBB (1860–1910), a graduate of the Bellevue Hospital Training School for Nurses (which she entered in 1881), was the prime mover in establishing, in 1896, the group that became the American Nurses Association, the recognized bargaining agent for registered nurses in the United States. Isabel Robb also founded, in 1893, the Society of Superintendents of Training School for Nurses, which became the National League of Nursing Education in 1912, and she was one of the original members of the committee to found the *American Journal of Nursing*.

Co-Founder of Hebrew Trades Council

REBECCA BECK AUGUST worked for 53 years in the needle trades, primarily as a buttonhole maker. Born in 1883 in Latvia, she emigrated to London with her father in 1890. After attending school for three years, at age 12 she went to work in a tailor's shop. In 1904 she came to Chicago. While an employee of Hart, Schaffner & Marx, she protested a wage cut and was fired. She helped to found the Hebrew Trades Council and a women's branch of The Workmen's Circle. In 1910 she moved to Seattle and was active in the Industrial Workers of the World, striving for the eight-hour day. She continued to work after her marriage (1912) and following the birth of her two sons. A member of the Amalgamated Clothing Workers of America until she retired, in 1948, she helped establish a Retired Members Club, and even after she moved to the Jewish Home for the Aged in Los Angeles, in 1973, continued her organizing activities, advocating the rights of senior citizens.

First U.S. Woman to Be Elected President of an International Union

AGNES MCEWEN NESTOR (1880–1948) went to work in a factory when she was 14 and worked ten hours a day, six days a week. As an employee of the Eisendrath Glove Factory, in Chicago, at the age of 18 she led her fellow workers out on strike. Their success spurred her on to a lifetime of organizing women workers. She was a delegate to the organizational meeting of the International Glove Workers Union in 1902, and, with ELIZABETH CHRISTMAN, (p. 332), founded Operators Local No. 1 of the IGWU in 1902. A member of the executive board of the Women's Trade Union League for 41 years and president of the Chicago chapter from 1913 to 1948, she was largely responsible for the passage, in 1937, of the 8-hour law in Illinois. Among the few women ever elected to top union office in the United States, she served on the executive board of the IGWU from 1906 to 1948, and as its president from 1913 to 1915—the first woman ever to be elected president of an international union.

Longest Career with the International Ladies' Garment Workers

PAULINE M. NEWMAN, born in Russia c. 1891, emigrated to New York City as a child and was sent to work in 1902 in a shirtwaist factory. She remembers being hidden by supervisors when inspectors came because she and other 8-to-10-year-olds were too young to be working, even under the laws of the time. During the general strike of 20,000 garment workers, in 1909–10, already a convinced and a convincing advocate as a very young woman, she was sent to the Labor Council in Buffalo, New York, to raise money for the strikers. She raised $6,000 and remained a union organizer for four years. From 1913 to 1918 she was an inspector for the Joint Board of Sanitary Control in the ladies' garment industry and established the first health clinic for the New York ILGWU, in 1918, where she has remained for 59 years (as of 1977, she was still walking to work there every day). A member of the Women's Trade Union League from 1905 until it disbanded, in 1951, she organized the Philadelphia Branch and chaired it from 1918 to 1923. She served on the advisory committee of the Women's Bureau, U. S. Department of Labor, from 1943 to 1953, and during her long career has been a member of countless delegations and committees and a frequent contributor to the WTUL's *Life and Labor,* the *Cleveland Federationist, Justice,* and other labor-oriented journals.

First Full-Time Woman Organizer and Vice-President for Amalgamated Clothing Workers

DOROTHY JACOBS BELLANCA (1894–1946), an immigrant from Russian Lat-via, went to work at 13 as a hand but-onhole sewer in a men's overcoat factory in Baltimore. From that work, she was to have a misshapen index finger all her life and a dedication to the organization of women workers. In 1909 she joined with other immigrant girls from Europe in their teens to found a garment workers' local, becoming its president in 1914, at the age of 20. Following a split in the parent union (the United Garment Workers of America) she led her local into the newly formed Amalgamated Clothing Workers of America (ACWA) and, not quite 22, was elected to the ACWA's general executive board. In 1917 she was appointed the union's first full-time woman organizer. She married fellow ACWA member August Bellanca, a Sicilian immigrant, in 1918. They had no children. She devoted her life to organizing unions and supporting strikers. Her major work was among the non-union cotton-garment workers, mostly women and girls earning substandard wages. From 1934 until her death, she served as the ACWA's only woman vice-president.

Teen-age Co-Founder of the United States' First Industrial Union

BESSIE ABRAMOWITZ HILLMAN (1889–1970) came to Chicago in 1910 as a Russian immigrant girl of 15 and found work at Hart, Schaffner & Marx as a button sewer. One month later, when her piece rate was lowered from 4¢ to 3¾¢, she led seven of her fellow button sewers out on strike. Immediately fired and blacklisted, Bessie was nevertheless able to encourage others to strike, and eventually some 30,000 Chicago garment workers walked out. It was a brutal experience, lasting five months. Most of the strikers returned to work with nothing changed. However, at Hart, Schaffner & Marx the workers won the right to have three representatives—Bessie Abramowitz was one of them—on an arbitration committee, which resulted in the signing of the first collective-bargaining agreement in American industry. In 1914, Bessie, at age 19, and Sidney Hillman, whom she later married, established the Amalgamated Clothing Workers of America, which organized an entire industry (in contrast to an individual craft union). It was the first union to demand a 40-hour week and to establish unemployment insurance and child-care and health centers for its members.

UMW Woman Organizer Shot and Killed

FANNIE MOONEY SELLINS (1872–1919), a widow and mother of four children, went to work in a St. Louis garment factory and later became the secretary of a garment workers' local in Chicago. Her union concerns led to organizing for the United Mine Workers (UMW) in West Virginia, where she was arrested and charged with inciting to riot. After serving six months in prison, she was pardoned by President Woodrow Wilson and went to Allegheny County, Pennsylvania, where she organized for the UMW and served as secretary to the Allegheny Trades Council. When miners struck against the Allegheny Coal & Coke Company in July 1919, the company brought in private guards and strikebreakers. On August 26, 1919, Fannie Sellins led a group of protesting miners to the Brackenridge mine, where, witnesses reported, she was shot and killed by company guards while trying to protect miners' children on the scene.

Early Activist in the Teachers Union

MARGARET ANGELA "MAGGIE" HALEY (1861–1939) was the first woman and first elementary-school teacher ever to speak from the floor at the general convention of the National Education Association (1901). A district vice-president of the newly formed Chicago Federation of Teachers (CFT), in 1900 she organized a court action to hold the Chicago

School Board to its promised salary increase and became full-time business agent for the CFT, a job she held all her life. In 1902 she brought the CFT into the Chicago Federation of Labor. Her teachers' pension plan became state law in 1907, and she won the state tenure law for teachers in 1917. For a short time she was a national organizer for the American Federation of Teachers (its first one), and was elected a national vice-president of the Women's Trade Union League. Throughout her career, she agitated for the right of teachers to unionize.

First Woman Elected to the Executive Board of the Cloth Hat and Cap Makers Union, 1904

ROSE SCHNEIDERMAN (1882–1972) emigrated from Russian Poland to New York as a child and went to work at 17 as a lining maker in the hat and cap industry. While she was still in her teens she persuaded the United Cloth Hat and Cap Makers (UCHCM) to take women into their union. In 1903 she helped organize Local 23, UCHCM, and was a delegate to the Central Federated Union of New York City. In 1904 she was the first woman elected to the general executive board of the UCHCM. She joined the Women's Trade Union League in New York in 1905 and became a full-time organizer for the national League in 1910. A witness to the Triangle Shirtwaist Company fire, in 1911, she spoke as a representative of the Shirtwaist Makers Union at a mass meeting held after the fire at the Metropolitan Opera House. Her long career spanned almost 50 years in the labor movement. President of the National WTUL from 1928 to 1947, she also served on the Labor Advisory Board of the National Recovery Administration from 1933 to 1934 and was secretary of the New York State Department of Labor from 1933 to 1944.

First Female Vice-President of Hotel & Restaurant Employees International Union

ELIZABETH MALONEY, of Chicago, a leader in the National Women's Trade Union League (active from 1911 to 1921), was elected the first woman international vice-president of the Hotel & Restaurant Employees International Union in 1911 and served on its executive board until 1921—one of only a handful of women who have risen to top union leadership in the United States.

General Organizer for Ladies' Garment Workers Is Consultant to African Labor History Center

MAIDA SPRINGER KEMP, born in 1910 in Panama City, Panama, attended Wellesley College and the Rand School of Social Science, in New York, joined Local 22 of the Dressmakers Union in 1933, and was a member of the executive board from 1938 to 1942. From 1959 to 1965 she was an international representative for the AFL-CIO, and a general organizer for the ILGWU from 1965 to 1968. Since 1973 she has been on leave from the ILGWU as a consultant to the African Labor History Center. Ms. Kemp is a vice-president of the National Council of Negro Women and a life member of the NAACP.

Former Executive of Mining Company Becomes First Director of United Mine Workers Welfare and Retirement Fund

JOSEPHINE ASPINWALL ROCHE (1886–1976), the daughter of a Colorado coal mine operator, was six years old when her father told her she couldn't visit his mine because it was dangerous. Josephine then asked why it was safe for the miners if it wasn't safe for her? A graduate of Vassar College (B.A., 1908) and Columbia University (M.A., 1910), she did settlement work for the New York Probation Society and for a short while was Denver, Colorado's first policewoman. In 1927 she inherited her father's holdings in the Rocky Mountain Fuel Company (the second-largest coal mining company in Colorado). She defended the strikers at one of the mines and proposed that the United Mine Workers be asked to organize the Rocky Mountain employees. Josephine Roche helped form the Bituminous Coal Code during NRA days, in the 1930s, and ran for governor of Colorado in 1934, touring the state in her old Buick under the banner "Roosevelt, Roche, & Recovery." She lost but was appointed Assistant Secretary of the Treasury in charge of the U. S. Health Service, serving from 1934 to 1937. From 1939 to 1944 she was president of the National Consumers League and from 1947 to 1971 was the first director of the United Mine Workers Welfare & Retirement Fund.

Organizer of U.S. Grand Opera Artists

ELIZABETH HOEPPEL, an opera singer, organized and became first president of the Grand Opera Artists Association, in 1934. In 1936 she aided in the establishment of the American Guild of Musical Artists and served on the executive board.

Highest-Level Woman Staff Member in Early Days of CIO

While union presidents John L. Lewis and Sidney Hillman and others decided how to organize steel, autos, and other industries, KATHERINE POLLAK ELLICKSON, the only woman present, as assistant to the director of the CIO, took the minutes of CIO board meetings from 1935 to 1937. From 1942 to 1955, as secretary of the CIO Social Security Committee, she organized meetings of national-union social security directors to discuss collective bargaining and legislative problems, was a liaison between union research directors and government research agencies, and represented the CIO to government advisory committees on social security, manpower, and women. After the merger of the CIO with the AFL, she served, from 1955 to 1961, as assistant director of the Social Insurance Department, cooperating closely with legislators in the first determined push for a limited program of national health insurance. From 1961 to 1963, Katherine Ellickson was executive secretary of President John F. Kennedy's Commission on the Status of Women, and the top staff person under ESTHER PETERSON (see "Women Activists, Heroes, and Humanitarians," p. 724) for the original planning and functioning of the Commission.

International Union Vice-President Began Career with Sitdown Strike

In a career that was to take her to one of the highest executive positions in the Hotel & Restaurant Employees & Bartenders International Union (HREBIU), MYRA KOMAROFF WOLFGANG (1914– 76) achieved notoriety as a young employee of a downtown Woolworth's store in Detroit by organizing a 1937 eight-day sitdown strike among 120 fellow employees and negotiating their contract. It was the first of many organizing battles over a 40-year period by this Canadian-born woman who entered the United States and was naturalized at the age of two. Secretary-treasurer of Detroit's HREBIU Local 24, and elected secretary of the Detroit Local Joint Executive Board in 1936, during the '50s and '60s she was active not only in her union but also on a variety of state commissions related to labor. A founder member of the Michigan Committee on Employment Problems of Working Women, in 1964 she became co-director of the Detroit Waiter-Waitress Training School.

She Introduced the Concept of Collective Bargaining to the American Nurses Association

EDNA BEHRENS, R.N., pioneered the concept of collective bargaining in the California Nurses Association (of which she was president) in 1943, after convincing members of the futility of gentleman's agreements and the necessity of joining together. She then persevered in helping nurses nationally to get salary increases and to develop written documents describing working conditions— often against strong opposition from employers and resistance from nurses against being unionized. In 1946 the collective bargaining concept was endorsed by the national association, which negotiated its first contract, and Edna Behrens signed it as national president. In 1976 she received the Shirley Titus Award from the ANA recognizing her contribution to the Association's Economic and General Welfare Program.

First Woman Legislative Director for the International Ladies' Garment Workers' Union (ILGWU)

EVELYN DUBROW, "dean of the labor lobbyists," came to her present position as legislative director and executive secretary of the Political Department of the International Ladies' Garment Workers' Union (ILGWU) by way of 30 years of lobbying experience. A graduate of New York University School of Journalism, she first worked in editing and reporting and later served as education director for the New Jersey Textile Workers Union of America. In 1947 the New Jersey CIO president assigned her to the state legislature to lobby for the interests of labor. After two years in Washington with the Americans for Democratic Action, she joined the ILGWU staff, in 1949, as assistant political director. Today, dividing her time between Washington and New York, she serves as chairperson of the AFL-CIO Committee on Consumer Legislation, besides representing the ILGWU in several national organizations. The recipient of numerous awards, in 1975 she was a fellow at Harvard University, Institute of Politics. Ever an effective advocate for labor and for American union-made clothing, soon after the inauguration of President Carter she personally introduced ROSALYNN CARTER (see "Women in the Home and Community,"

p. 129) to New York's Seventh Avenue garment showrooms.

Organizer of the First Women's Local in a Coat Factory Becomes First Woman Elected to Executive Board in the ILGWU

At 17, ANGELA BAMBACE, born in 1898 in Brazil (her family lived for a short while in Italy before emigrating to the United States in 1904), joined the International Ladies' Garment Workers' Union in New York. In 1936 she began organizing for the union in Baltimore, where she formed the first women's local in a coat factory. The only woman to be elected to the ILGWU's international executive board, as a vice-president (1956), she continued to be the only woman on the board until she retired, in 1972. Angela Bambace was co-chairperson of the American Trade Union Council for Histadrut and a member of the executive boards of the American Civil Liberties Union, the Italian-American Labor Council, and the Histadrut Council of Greater Baltimore. She died in 1975 in Baltimore.

Selected Union and Association Offices Held by Women, 1952, 1962, 1970, 1972[1]

Position	Unions				Associations[2]	
	1952	1962	1970	1972	1970	1972
Total positions held by women	31	28	37	37	31	44
Total women	30	24	34	33	30	41
Elective Offices						
President	2	0	1	2	2	6
Secretary-treasurer	9	7	10	13	18	17
Appointive Positions						
Director, organizing activities	(*)	1	1	0	0	2
Research director	10	3	7	3	0	2
Research and education director	1	3	7	3	0	3
Education director	2	2	2	3	0	0
Director, social insurance	(*)	5	7	6	0	1
Editor	6	6	4	3	5	5
Legal activities	(*)	1	1	1	0	1
Legislative activities	(*)	(*)	2	3	0	0
Public-relations activities	(*)	(*)	2	3	1	1
Other	1	0	0	0	5	8

[1] In 1952, 215 unions were surveyed; in 1962, 181; in 1970, 185; and in 1972, 177. In 1970, 23 associations were surveyed; in 1972, 35.
[2] Associations were first surveyed in 1970.
(*) Not surveyed.
Appointive positions surveyed for unions and associations varied somewhat. Appointive positions included in the category "other" for associations are executive director, collective-bargaining director, and government-relations director. In 1952, the union position "other" is executive secretary.
Figures taken from "Women's Participation in Labor Organizations," by Virginia Birquist, *Monthly Labor Review*, October 1974, p. 8.

First Woman to Work on Teamsters Arbitration Case

In 1958 the Eastern Conference of Teamsters (ECT) assigned ELIZABETH C. NORWOOD to work on an arbitration case between two New York locals in the International Brotherhood of Teamsters (IBT) and a bakery union. It was the first time a woman had worked on an ECT arbitration case, and the case was settled in favor of the Teamsters. A staff member of the ECT since 1957 and assistant research director from 1961 until she retired, in 1975, Ms. Norwood was the first woman to serve on a subcommittee covering clerical workers under the IBT National Freight Agreement. She attended the first class for the Teamsters Labor Institute, held in Florida in 1969—one of two women attending— and was the first woman to represent the Teamsters on a federal government advisory council. A consultant to the Department of Labor on discrimination in the employment of women (1970–71) and a member of the Advisory Council on Social Security for the Department of Health, Education, and Welfare (1974–75), she was sent by the Teamsters to the founding convention of the Coalition of Labor Union Women (CLUW) in 1974 to represent the IBT. Ms. Norwood, born in North Carolina, was graduated from Georgetown University, in Washington, D.C.

First Black Woman to Serve as Vice-President of the Retail, Wholesale and Department Store Union (RWDSU)

DORIS TURNER is the second woman and first black woman to serve as a vice-president on the RWDSU board. Active as a rank-and-file leader in 1959, she led a 46-day strike at Lenox Hill Hospital, New York City, which launched the National Union of Hospital & Health Care Employees, now affiliated with the RWDSU, AFL-CIO. As executive vice-president of the union's District 1199, she heads the District's 40,000-member Hospital Division and supervises a staff of 40 in administering contracts with some 200 health-care institutions, including most of New York City's major hospitals. She is president of 1199 Plaza Housing Corporation, which sponsors 1,600 units of cooperative apartments in East Harlem, is a commissioner of the New York City Human Rights Commis-

sion, and is on the board of directors of the Martin Luther King Center for Social Change.

First Woman Lobbyist Hired by the AFL-CIO

JANE O'GRADY, who holds a master's degree in political sociology from the University of California and has studied labor relations and statistics at New York University and the City College of New York, was hired in 1963 by the Amalgamated Clothing Workers of America to be their lobbyist (legislative representative) in Washington. In 1968, she became the lobbyist for the Committee for Community Affairs, and in April 1977 she became the first woman legislative representative for the AFL-CIO, working out of its headquarters in Washington.

Longest Fight to Get Her Job Back

MAUREEN HEDGEPETH, a woman in her 40s and worker for 17 years in cotton mills owned by J. P. Stevens in Roanoke Rapids, North Carolina, was fired for union organizing in 1965 during an unsuccessful campaign by the Amalgamated Clothing & Textile Workers Union (ACTWU). Because the right to organize unions is guaranteed by the Labor Relations Act of 1935, the National Labor Relations Board (NLRB) went to her defense. After a series of hearings, court appearances, and legal briefs, the union and the NLRB got Ms. Hedgepeth's job restored—and $21,114 in back pay. The effort had taken four years and twenty-one days. Advised to take the money and leave, she went back to the mill.

Union Leader Elected Chairperson of First Permanent State Advisory Commission on the Status of Women

RUTH MILLER, national representative of the Amalgamated Clothing and Textile Workers Union (ACTWU) in Los Angeles, was appointed by the governor of

California in 1965 to the first permanent state commission on the status of women in the country. The 15-member group elected her its chairperson. ACTWU's membership is 75 per cent female, and the union is concerned about specific issues women face in the workplace, such as the wide differential between men's and women's wages. In 1968, Ruth Miller led a small group of union women in drawing up a policy statement on "Women in the Workforce," which they presented to the Los Angeles County Federation of Labor, AFL-CIO; it was later adopted by the Federation. The statement focuses on goals that today, a decade later, have not yet been fully realized: (1) All jobs must be evaluated as *work* with a rate of pay based on job content; (2) promotions should be granted on the basis of competence and qualifications; (3) equal pay for equal work should be enforced; (4) protective legislation should be extended to men; (5) disability insurance benefits for women employees should be provided for a limited time before and after childbirth through state disability insurance funds and union-negotiated plans; (6) women workers hospitalized for reasons of pregnancy should be entitled to coverage for hospital costs; (7) child-care services must be expanded and improved. A graduate of Hunter College, Ruth

Miller in 1974 was a founding member of CLUW.

First Woman Vice-President of United Auto Workers and First National President of CLUW

OLGA M. MADAR broke new ground in 1966 when she was the first woman elected to the International Executive Board of the United Auto Workers. In 1970 and 1972 she was elected vice-president. In a union career going back to 1941, Ms. Madar has scored many firsts: as head of the UAW's Department of Recreation, she eliminated racial discrimination in organized bowling in the mid-1950s and established the first UAW retiree center; as the first head of the union's new Department of Consumer Affairs, in 1968, she became an outspoken advocate of the Consumer Protection Act, was the first labor official to testify in support of federal legislation on "Truth in Housing," and has been a leader in eliminating discrimination against women in obtaining credit; and in 1971 she appeared before a House Judiciary subcommittee to plead the case for the Equal Rights Amendment (the UAW was the first union to support the ERA). In 1974 Olga Madar spearheaded the formation of the Coalition of Labor Union Women (CLUW), and at the founding convention was elected its first national president.

Coalition of Labor Union Women, 1974: Founding Officers and Steering Committee Members, and Their Union Affiliations

Officers

President—OLGA M. MADAR, **United Auto Workers**
National vice-president—ADDIE WYATT, **Amalgamated Meatcutters & Butcher Workmen**
East Coast vice-President—JOYCE MILLER, **Amalgamated Clothing & Textile Workers of America**

Midwest vice-president—CLARA DAY, **International Brotherhood of Teamsters**
Southern vice-president—DANA DUNHAM, **Communications Workers of America**
West Coast vice-president—ELINOR GLENN, **Service Employees International Union**
Secretary—LINDA TARR-WHELAN, **American Federation of State, County, & Municipal Employees**

Treasurer—GLORIA JOHNSON, International Union of Electrical, Radio, and Machine Workers

Steering Committee

RITA SKLAR, International Brotherhood of Electrical Workers

OLA KENNEDY, United Steelworkers of America

CAROL L. BUSH, Transport Workers Union of America

KELLY RUECK, Association of Flight Attendants

TRUDI SOUTHERN, United Electrical, Radio & Machines Workers of America

JUDITH BEREK, Retail, Wholesale, & Department Store Union

DIANE S. CURRY, Brotherhood of Railway, Airline & Steamship Clerks

DEBBY LEONARD, Oil, Chemical and Atomic Workers International Union

VELMA WOODS, Union of Carpenters & Joiners of America

LOIS FELDER, Retail Clerks International

LUELLA HANBERRY, Office & Professional Employees International Union

CINDA HARGRAVE, National Association of Letter Carriers

MARJORIE STERN, American Federation of Teachers

KATHERINE HUNNINEN, United Association of Plumbing & Pipe Fitting Industry of the United States and Canada

KATHERINE DORSEY, Union of Transport Workers

ANNE GALLOWAY, Bakery & Confectionary Workers International Union

YETTA RIESEL, the Newspaper Guild

Organizer of the Nation's First Statewide Conference of Union Women

JEANE LAMBIE, born in 1922 in Alicia, Arkansas, now of Little Rock, a member of the American Federation of State, County & Municipal Employees (AFSCME) since 1954, organized and presided over the nation's first statewide conference of women members of AFL-CIO-affiliated unions and independent unions, in April 1972. Since 1966 she has consistently been reelected to her present position as president/director of Arkansas State Council 38 of AFSCME, AFL-CIO—the only woman in Arkansas to head the state body of an international union. She served on the coordinating committee that founded the Coalition of Labor Union Women (CLUW), in 1974, was elected president of the Central Arkansas CLUW Chapter in '74, '75, and '76, and serves on the national CLUW executive board. The first woman appointed to the Arkansas Governmental Efficiency Commission (1967), she also has been appointed by three governors to serve on the state commission on the status of women and chairs Arkansas's employment task force. Ms. Lambie is the only woman to receive AFSCME's national award as Political Action Chairperson of the Year (1972).

First Woman Elected to the Board of the Service Employees International Union

ELINOR MARSHALL GLENN organized Los Angeles County hospital workers for the United Public Workers from 1946 to 1953. In 1966 she participated in the historic strike of the Los Angeles Hospital workers, resulting in the first collective-bargaining law for public employees. She also negotiated the first child-care provision in a union contract with Los Angeles County. She was the first woman elected to the International Executive Board of the Service Employees International Union (SEIU). In 1974 she became West Coast vice-president (the first) of the Coalition of Labor Union Women (CLUW). Ms. Glenn, born in 1915, graduated from New York University in 1934 and was a teacher of remedial reading in New York City for the federal Works Progress Administration (WPA), and organizer for the American Federation of Teachers.

Trade Union Leader One of Founders of NOW

The small group that met with BETTY FRIEDAN (see "Women Activists, Heroes, and Humanitarians," p. 703) in 1966 to found the National Organization for Women (NOW) included UAW international representative DOROTHY HAENER. Born in 1917 in Detroit, Ms. Haener attended the University of Detroit, Detroit Institute of Technology, and the Ford Trade School, and first joined the United Auto Workers in 1941. In 1942 she entered defense work at the Ford Motor Company Bomber Plant, where she was in turn assembler, sewing-machine operator, receiving inspector, final inspector, department clerk, and statistical controller, and became active in UAW Local 50, later joining Local 769. She joined the UAW staff in 1952, serving for nine years in the Office and Technical Department, and in 1961 was appointed international representative of the UAW Women's Department. A founding member of the national Women's Political Caucus and Michigan delegate to the National Steering Committee, and a founding member of the Coalition of Labor Union Women, she attended the 1975 IWY Conference in Mexico City and was a speaker and delegate at the Tribune, and was appointed by President Carter to the IWY Commission in 1977.

Founder of National Domestics, Inc.

In 1968, DOROTHY BOLDEN founded National Domestics, Inc., in Atlanta, one of the pioneer groups attempting to organize household workers. Born in Atlanta in 1920, Ms. Bolden is a member of the board of directors of the NAACP and of the Black Women's Coalition of Atlanta, and in 1975 was appointed adviser to the Secretary of Health, Education, and Welfare. She is the recipient of numerous awards including the Black Women's International Award of 1975.

Organizer of 10,000 Household Workers

As a field officer for the National Committee on Household Employment, a non-profit service organization dedicated to the problems of domestic workers,

JOSEPHINE HULETT between 1969 and 1976 participated in the organization of over 40 NCHE affiliates. Household workers (97 per cent women) were not protected under the Federal Wage and Hour Law until 1974; they are still not covered by much of the labor legislation that workers in most other areas take for granted. The median annual wage for U.S. domestic workers (in 1972, $2,072) is far lower than the national median; two thirds of household workers are black women with an average age of 46, six years older than the average for other female workers. NCHE has some male members—chauffeurs, housemen, gardeners, etc.—but the vast majority of its 10,000-strong membership is female. A former household worker herself, Ms. Hulett served as president of the Youngstown (Ohio) Household Technicians from 1969 to 1970. A member of the Afro-American Labor Council, she was the first woman to receive the Council's Special Recognition Award in 1971. In 1972 she set up the Ohio Coalition of Household Employees, the first step toward a national organization. She was presented with the key to the city of Dayton, Ohio, in 1971 and the key to the city of New Orleans in 1974. Ms. Hulett, born in 1927 in Portland, Arkansas, is a graduate of the Philadelphia School of Practical Nursing (1957) and has attended Temple Business School, Montgomery College, and Catholic University.

United Farm Workers Vice-President

DOLORES HUERTA was elected vice-president of the United Farm Workers (UFW) in 1970 after 15 years of organizing agricultural workers. Born in 1930 in Dawson, New Mexico, she moved to Stockton, California, as a child, and it was in Stockton in 1955 that she became involved in voter-registration drives and political education within the Mexican-American community for the Community Service Organization (CSO). In this work she met Cesar Chavez and, in 1962, assisted him in organizing for the

Farm Workers of America in Delano, California. She also succeeded in organizing migrant workers in Stockton and Modesto, and in 1970, as a member of the United Farm Workers Organizing Committee, she negotiated a contract with Delano grape growers, which was among the UFW's first contracts. After years of her lobbying efforts in Sacramento and Washington, migrants were granted disability insurance, old-age pensions, and unemployment insurance—all previously unavailable to them. Nearly half of the UFW organizers are women, and women run many of the UFW's credit unions and clinics. Ms. Huerta, who considers herself a feminist and a part of the women's movement (although she is opposed to abortion and the use of contraceptives), believes that unless an organizer can involve the woman of a family, that family will not come into the union.

Founder of Veterans Administration Independent Service Employees Union

MARY MATTIE SMITH organized the Veterans Administration Independent Service Employees Union in Chicago in the early 1970s. An ex-officio member and past president of the union, she believes that the Veterans Administration service employees have inspired other federal employees to challenge unacceptable practices and procedures. Ms. Smith, a member of the Illinois Black Political Caucus, was honored for her union leadership by Chicago's Black Labor Leaders in 1973.

Founder of Boston's Nine-to-Five

KAREN NUSSBAUM in 1973 originated Boston's Nine-to-Five, the first city-wide and currently largest organization for women office workers in Boston. It was also one of the first such organizations in the country; there are others now in Chicago, Cleveland, Dayton, and New York City. What makes the Boston group unique is that in 1975 it became an autonomous local (925) within the Service Employees International Union (SEIU), AFL-CIO; Karen Nussbaum is its founder and president. At Brandeis University Library, Local 925 organized private university professional librarians for the first time in the United States and has also been the first to organize publishing houses in Boston. In 1977 Ms. Nussbaum became the eastern-area organizer for the women office workers' movement sponsored by Nine-to-Five and Cleveland Women Working. The objective is to establish working women's organizations in cities throughout the eastern United States, the first time such an effort has been made in today's working women's movement. Karen Nussbaum, born in 1950, was a clerk-typist working for a Boston college when she began attempting to change things. At a YWCA-sponsored conference she met other women who shared her concern over low pay and undervalued, dead-end jobs. They decided to put out a newsletter, distributing it before work at subway stops. Soon they had a long mailing list and the nucleus of an organization for women office workers. Today they hold workshops to inform women of their rights as employees and recourse to legal action.

First Top Officers of Association of Flight Attendants

KELLY RUECK and PAT ROBERTSON were president and vice-president, respectively, when the Association of Flight Attendants became a separate entity from the Air Line Pilots Association (ALPA), in 1973. Since 1970, Ms. Rueck, born in Louisiana and a holder of both B.A. and B.S. degrees in English and journalism from Louisiana State University, had been chief executive of the Steward/Stewardess Division of the ALPA. As an employee with United Airlines, she served as master chairperson of United's flight-attendant group. She is a founding member of the Steering Committee of the Coalition of Labor Union Women

(CLUW). PAT ROBERTSON, who succeeded Ms. Rueck as president in 1976, brought to the position 16 years of airline experience, including nine years as a flight attendant with Piedmont Airlines. She was master executive council chairperson for Piedmont's flight-attendant group. She served on the negotiations committee for two contracts, helped coordinate the 1969 Air Safety Forum, and participated in the Flight Attendant Jumpseat Survey and the Radioactive Material Survey. As president, she is responsible for the management of national and local services provided for 18,000 flight attendants from 19 U.S. airlines represented by the Association of Flight Attendants.

First Director of Safety for New Association of Flight Attendants (AFA)

When the Association of Flight Attendants (AFA) was established as a separate body from the Air Line Pilots Association, in December 1973, DEL R. MOTT became the AFA's first director of safety. She had been with the Flight Attendants in this capacity, under the old structure, since 1970. A stewardess with Western Airlines from 1961 to 1970, currently on official leave of absence in order to devote full time to AFA's Safety Department, Ms. Mott for eight months in 1966 conducted research and recommended safety revisions for all Western Airlines manuals. Since 1969 she has participated in approximately 25 National Transportation Safety Board investigations of aircraft accidents. She works directly with all accident-debriefing and coordination-of-safety problems with suggestions for AFA member airlines, including contact with federal agencies, manufacturers, and individuals. She received the Air Line Pilots Association Steward/Stewardess Air Safety Award for 1968, SAFE Woman of the Year 1973, and Flight Safety Foundation Certificate of Appreciation in 1976.

First Woman International Organizer for Service Employees

ROSEMARY TRUMP born in 1944 in Smithfield, Pennsylvania, received a B.A. from American University, in Washington, D.C., in 1966 and entered the work force as a social worker in 1967. She joined the Social Workers' Guild, an affiliate of the Service Employees International Union (SEIU), AFL-CIO, and was elected recording secretary of her local in 1969. From 1970 to 1973 she served as the first woman international organizer on the staff of the SEIU. In 1973 she was elected president of SEIU Local 585, the first woman to be president of an SEIU local of over 5,000 members. Also since 1973 she has served on the International Executive Board of the SEIU and holds several other regional positions. She was a founding member of the Coalition of Labor Union Women (CLUW) in 1974. Her union activities have included testifying before the Senate Labor Relations Committee in 1974 on legislation to put public employees under the National Labor Relations Act and leading a demonstration in April 1976 of Allegheny County (Pennsylvania) employees to communicate wage demands to the county commissioners to avoid a strike (it worked).

Three-Times Elected At-Large Vice-President of the Newspaper Guild

Although DOROTHY M. SAIN has several firsts to her credit, the one in which she takes the most pride is running three times for vice-president-at-large of the international Newspaper Guild and coming in first each time. Over 16 years, she has held every unpaid office in her local union with the exception of treasurer, and in 1970 was a member of the Guild's planning committee for a conference on sex discrimination and women's rights. Co-founder of the Cleveland Council of Union Women (forerunner of what became the Cleveland chapter of the Coalition of Labor Union Women) and a member of the planning committee of CLUW, Ms. Sain now serves on the national executive board as the Newspaper Guild's representative.

Originator of First All-Indian Union for Ceremonial Performers

In the spring of 1970, a group of American Indian ceremonial performers in Wisconsin Dells formed a union. Its originator was DELLA LOWE, who for 20 years had been a dancer at the Stand Rock Ceremonial. The advantages of a union were not new to Ms. Lowe, who had been president of her local (International Ladies' Garment Workers' Union) when she worked at a nearby garment factory, in Baraboo, Wisconsin. The performers, most of whom were Winnebagos, had grown increasingly angry at their lack of a voice regarding conditions of their employment with the American Legion post that managed the ceremonial. Ms. Lowe was on a committee of five, three men and two women, who rallied support from the performers to stop the show if they were not given the right to organize and hold an election. Among their demands were better wages and overtime pay; information as to box-office income (on which pay was based); compensation for rehearsals and rain-interrupted performances; job security; compensation for cost of costumes; adequate dressing and sanitary facilities; and a first-aid station. The union was recognized, and Della Lowe was on the negotiating committee that drew up the first contract between the American Legion post and the Realistic Professional Indian Performers of America (AFL-CIO), Local No. 1, with Lyle Greendeer as its first president. The union remains active.

President of New York State Coalition of Household Workers

An organizer and secretary-treasurer for the Household Technicians of America (HTA), an affiliate of the National Committee on Household Employment, and president of the New York State Coalition of Household Workers, CAROLYN COULTER REED, born in 1939, has been a full-time household worker since the age of 16. She has testified before the New York State legislature on behalf of a bill that would place household workers in New York under the National Labor Relations Board and open the way for the formation of their own union, with bargaining powers. Most household workers at present have no health benefits, are not covered by workmen's compensation laws or unemployment insurance, and are further handicapped by working in isolated and scattered places. With the encouragement of the Women's Political Caucus and the Women's Action Alliance, Ms. Reed organized a National Workshop for the HTA, where household workers could listen to each other and, among other things, learn how to talk to an employer. She is working toward the goal of a self-run household-workers' union hiring hall, which would set daily, weekly, and monthly rates of pay and keep records for employees of health, welfare, pension, and Social Security benefits.

Originator and First Head of Women's Rights Committee of the American Federation of Teachers (AFT)

MARJORIE HEFTER STERN created the American Federation of Teachers' first national Women's Rights Committee and chaired it from 1971 to 1974. She organized and led the AFT's first national conference on Women in Education (1972) and its first conference on Women in Higher Education (1973), and while chairwoman, wrote a column, "Women's Rights Report," for the *American Teacher,* and numerous articles and pamphlets. She was instrumental in drawing up the "Women's Rights Policy Resolutions," which were adopted by the Annual Convention of the AFT in 1973; from 1973 to 1975 headed NOW's Labor Union Task Force; and in 1974 served on the program staff of the George

Meany Center for Labor Studies, Washington, D.C. As a consultant on leadership, collective bargaining, contracts, and women's rights, Ms. Stern has led workshops in many states and is a charter member and founder of CLUW. Ms. Stern was born in 1918 in Chicago, Illinois, earned her B.A. and M.A. from San Francisco State University, and since 1959 has taught in the San Francisco Unified School District Secondary Division and, concurrently, since 1974 in the San Francisco Community College District, where she is an instructor in labor studies.

First Woman Lobbyist for the United Mine Workers of America

Assistant director and legislative representative for the United Mine Workers of America (UMWA) since 1971, SYDNEE M. SCHWARTZ got her training to be an effective lobbyist while working for a Washington law firm whose resident partner was the legal counsel to the House Ways and Means Committee. Ms. Schwartz, born in 1941, was graduated from American University with both a B.A. and an M.A., and was appointed to her present position in 1971. Her department closely monitors all federal issues supporting coal miners and their families. This involves coordination, research, and analysis of pertinent legislation, recommending courses of action to the UMWA's officers, and identifying federal candidates for public office who are supportive of the views and actions of the UMWA and its membership.

Drafter of ERA Resolution Adopted by the AFL-CIO Convention, 1973

YETTA RIESEL, a 25-year member of the Newspaper Guild, drafted the Guild's Equal Rights Amendment resolution, introduced to the AFL-CIO convention and adopted in 1973. Ms. Riesel was born into the trade union movement. Her father held the number one card in his local of the International Ladies' Garment Workers' Union. Active in the Young People's Socialist League in the 1930s, she attended City College and the New School for Social Research, in New York. As a staff member of the Newspaper Guild, she has worked in its collective-bargaining department, in establishing its human rights program, and as a Guild representative to groups of trade union leaders from other countries, and to consumers and community affairs groups. A member of the Steering Committee of the Coalition of Labor Union Women, she became CLUW's public relations director at its inception.

Second Woman UAW Vice-President Concerned for Promotion of Assembly Line Workers into Less Repetitive Jobs

ODESSA KOMER, born in 1925, the second woman to be elected an international vice-president of the United Auto Workers (June 1974), worked before her children were born and joined the UAW in 1944. Reentering the work force as an assembler at Ford in 1953, she joined Local 228 and in the 1960s played a key role in achieving a national contract concerning promotion of assembly line workers into better, less repetitive jobs. She held many elected positions in her 7,000-member local, and in each instance was the first woman elected to the job. A rank-and-file member who made it to the top over a 19-year period, she heads the international union's consumer affairs and women's departments, and as of June 1977 was in charge of the Bendix Corporation section and several auto-supply divisions.

Founding Officer of CLUW and Member of Executive Board of International Union of Electrical, Radio, and Machine Workers (IUE)

GLORIA TAPSCOTT JOHNSON, a graduate magna cum laude in business administration (B.A.) and economics and statistics (M.A.) from Howard University, and former economist in the Bureau of Labor Statistics, has been on the national staff of the International Union of Electrical, Radio, and Machine Workers (IUE) since 1954. As director of education and women's activities for the union, she was a member of the 24-person delegation sponsored by CLUW to visit child-care centers in Israel, Sweden, and France in May 1977. In June 1977 she was appointed to the executive board of the international union. A founding officer of the Coalition of Labor Union Women (CLUW), Ms. Johnson was elected treasurer by the first national conference, in March 1974.

First Editor of CLUW News

Elected to the 25-member steering committee of the Coalition of Labor Union Women at its first national conference, in March 1974, DIANE SUTHERLAND CURRY is also the first editor of the organization's quarterly newsletter, *CLUW News*. Born in 1939 in New Jersey, she attended St. Petersburg Junior College and the University of Maryland and was administrative assistant to the executive secretary of the Railway Labor Executives Association in Washington, D.C., from 1961 to 1967; was assistant to the editor for the Brotherhood of Railway, Airline and Steamship Clerks, AFL-CIO, from 1967 to 1969; and has been director of publications at the union's Chicago headquarters since 1969. She is vice-president of the International Labor Press Association and a member of the Newspaper Guild, the National Organization for Women, and the NAACP. In 1976 she visited Israel on a Histadrut-sponsored tour as a member of a group of ten labor editors. Ms. Curry writes a column entitled "Among Other Things," in which she discusses issues of special interest to working women.

First Coordinator of Women's Activities in the AFL-CIO

Following the AFL-CIO convention in 1975, President George Meany ap-

pointed CYNTHIA MCCAUGHAN as the federation's first coordinator of women's activities. Prior to her appointment, she was community services representative of the Los Angeles AFL-CIO, had been labor coordinator with the United Way there since 1953, and for 20 years was president of Local 30, Office & Professional Employees International Union (OPEIU). Very active in labor affairs in Los Angeles, she served on a number of public-service-agency boards. Born in 1928, she attended the University of Southern California, took labor courses at Los Angeles State College and UCLA, has been a member of OPEIU since 1949, and is a past president and board member of the Western Labor Press Association, and a member of the Newspaper Guild, the NAACP, the Jewish Labor Committee, and the Coalition of Labor Union Women (CLUW).

Newspaper Guild's First National Human Rights Coordinator

HANNAH JO RAYL was named the first national human rights coordinator of the Newspaper Guild, in June 1975. Born in Bloomingdale, Ohio, Ms. Rayl received a B.S. degree from Marion College, in Indiana, in 1950. From 1948 to 1972 she held a variety of jobs with several Ohio and Indiana newspapers, from proofreader to assistant city editor. In 1968 she joined the Newspaper Guild, was chairperson of her unit in Canton, Ohio, from 1972 to 1973, and for five and a half months in 1972 led her unit in a successful strike against the *Canton Repository*. In 1974 she became a full-time organizer for the Guild, before coming to her present post.

First Woman Elected President of the Screen Actors Guild in its 43-Year History

In November 1975, KATHEEN NOLAN was elected president of the Screen Actors Guild, AFL-CIO, along with three other women among seven other officers. (On the Guild's national board, of 70

FROM DOMESTIC SERVANTS TO SECRETARIES

THE 10 LEADING OCCUPATIONS OF U.S. WOMEN WORKERS 1870-1970
In order of size, and as reported in each census regardless of changes in definition

	1870	1880	1890	1900	1910
1	Domestic Servants	Domestic Servants	Servants	Servants	Other Servants
2	Agricultural Laborers	Agricultural Laborers	Agricultural Laborers	Farm Laborers (members of family)	Farm Laborers (home farm)
3	Tailoresses and Seamstresses	Milliners, Dressmakers and Seamstresses	Dressmakers	Dressmakers	Laundresses (not in laundry)
4	Milliners, Dress and Mantua Makers	Teachers and Scientific Persons	Teachers	Teachers	Teachers (school)
5	Teachers (not specified)	Laundresses	Farmers, Planters and Overseers	Laundry Work (hand)	Dressmakers and Seamstresses (not in factory)
6	Cotton-mill Operatives	Cotton-mill Operatives	Laundresses	Farmers and Planters	Farm Laborers (working out)
7	Laundresses	Farmers and Planters	Seamstresses	Farm and Plantation Laborers	Cooks
8	Woolen-mill Operatives	Tailoresses	Cotton-mill Operatives	Saleswomen	Stenographers and Typists
9	Farmers and Planters	Woolen-mill Operatives	Housekeepers and Stewards	Housekeepers and Stewards	Farmers
10	Nurses	Employees of Hotels and Restaurants (not clerks)	Clerks and Copyists	Seamstresses	Saleswomen (stores)

SOURCES: Decennial Census, 1870-1940; Janet M. Hooks, *Women's Occupations Through Seven Decades* (Women's Bureau Bulletin #218, U.S. Department of Labor); U.S. Dept. of Commerce, Bureau of the Census: Census of Population. 1960. Detailed Characteristics, U.S. Summary, Table 202; U.S. Dept. of Commerce, Bureau of the Census: Census of Population,

IN ONE HUNDRED YEARS

1920	1930	1940	1950	1960	1970
Other Servants	Other Servants, Other Domestic and Personal Service	Servants (private family)	Stenographers, Typists and Secretaries	Stenographers, Typists and Secretaries	Secretaries
Teachers (school)	Teachers (school)	Stenographers, Typists and Secretaries	Other Clerical Workers	Other Clerical Workers	Sales Clerks (retail trade)
Farm Laborers (home farm)	Stenographers and Typists	Teachers (not elsewhere classified)	Saleswomen	Private Household Workers	Bookkeepers
Stenographers and Typists	Other Clerks (except clerks in stores)	Clerical and Kindred Workers (not elsewhere classified)	Private Household Workers	Saleswomen	Teachers (elementary school)
Other Clerks (except clerks in stores)	Saleswomen	Saleswomen (not elsewhere classified)	Teachers (elementary school)	Teachers (elementary school)	Typists
Laundresses (not in laundry)	Farm Laborers (unpaid family workers)	Operatives and Kindred Workers, Apparel and Accessories	Waitresses	Bookkeepers	Waitresses
Saleswomen (stores)	Bookkeepers and Cashiers	Bookkeepers, Accountants and Cashiers	Bookkeepers	Waitresses	Sewers and Stitchers
Bookkeepers and Cashiers	Laundresses (not in laundry)	Waitresses (except private family)	Sewers and Stitchers, Manufacturing	Miscellaneous and Not Specified Operatives	Nurses, Registered
Cooks	Trained Nurses	Housekeepers (private family)	Nurses, Registered	Nurses, Registered	Cashiers
Farmers (general farms)	Other Cooks	Trained Nurses and Student Nurses	Telephone Operators	Other Service Workers (except private household)	Private Household Cleaners and Servants

1970, Detailed Characteristics, U.S. Summary, PC (1) D 1; U.S. Women's Bureau, "Occupations of Women, 1950, 1960 and 1970, Tables Reprinted from the Economic Report of the President 1973," 1973.

members, 12 are women.) Ms. Nolan, who had served 12 years on the board as vice-president and director, was not the choice of the nominating committee (they favored a man). She came onto the ballot as an independent petition candidate and won with a tally of 5,887 votes, over her nearest competitor's 2,367. Born into a theatrical family, Kathleen Nolan started acting at the age of 13 months on the showboat operated by her parents. She has acted on and off Broadway, played Wendy in *Peter Pan* with Mary Martin, starred in the TV series "The Real McCoys," made more than 800 guest appearances on major network shows, and appeared in NBC's bicentennial special "Our Foremothers." The Screen Actors Guild was founded in 1933, when actors had no regular hours or methods for arbitrating disputes. It took four years to win union recognition and their first contract, in 1937. By then the Guild had mobilized 98 per cent of the "stars" in support of a threatened strike. Their first contracts set minimum rates, continuous employment and grievance procedures, and also a limitation on the number of hours an actor was required to work.

First Woman Up Through the Ranks to Be Appointed Assistant to the President of Communications Workers of America

PATSY LOU FRYMAN, born in 1934, began her union career in the Communications Workers of America after she went to work for the Michigan Bell Telephone Company in Battle Creek in 1953. She rose through the ranks from local steward to CWA representative in New York and then Michigan, and was the first woman appointed to be Ohio director of the union. In 1975 she became the first up-through-the-ranks woman to be appointed assistant to the national CWA president, in Washington, D.C. She is the first national recording secretary of CLUW and was a member of the

International Women's Year World Tribune in Mexico City in 1975. She serves on the President's Task Force for Older Americans and several national committees in the field of alternative work patterns.

First American Indian Appointed to Staff of Communications Workers

BURLDENE LEININGER is the CWA representative (organizer) for eastern Oklahoma. An American Indian, born in 1933 at Council Hill, Oklahoma, Ms. Leininger has been a CWA union member and active in the labor movement for 25 years. She has held various positions in Local 6012, Tulsa, Oklahoma, and has served as a delegate to the Tulsa Labor Council, Oklahoma State AFL-CIO conferences, and the annual CWA convention.

Founder of Union-Sponsored Day Care Center Leads Study Tour

JOYCE D. MILLER established the first day care center for the Chicago Joint Board of the Amalgamated Clothing Workers of America while she was on the Chicago staff as administrative assistant and director of social services. During this time she also initiated a legal aid program, scholarship fund, and full-time center for retired workers. After being transferred to New York, in 1972, she initiated a national social services program to help workers with personal off-the-job problems through information and referrals. In 1976, she was elected a national vice-president of the newly merged Amalgamated Clothing and Textile Workers Union (ACTWU). Because both she and her union are recognized leaders in the field of day care, she was chosen to head a delegation of 24 women trade unionists on a study tour of day care facilities in Israel, Sweden, and France in May 1977, sponsored by the Coalition of Labor Union Women (CLUW). A graduate of the University of Chicago (B.A. and M.A.) and the mother of three children, Ms. Miller also serves as the East Coast vice-president of CLUW, of which she was a founder.

First Paid President of the American Nurses Association

ANNE ZIMMERMAN, who in 1976 became the first person to serve in the American Nurses Association presidency as a subsidized office, began her career as a pediatric nurse in Montana, after earning her diploma at the Sisters of Charity of Leavenworth School of Nursing, in Helena. She spent seven years in pediatrics and then became executive director of the Montana Nurses' Association and served as associate director of the California Nurses' Association before becoming executive administrator of the Illinois Nurses' Association, a post in which she served for 22 years, developing the first program of continuing education in Illinois to be accredited by the American Nurses Association. An activist, Ms. Zimmerman wants to see the ANA increase its efforts to influence such issues as national health insurance, Medicare, nursing education, and third-party reimbursement for nurses.

First Woman Elected International Vice-President of Amalgamated Meat Cutters and Butcher Workmen (AMCBW)

Unanimously elected in June 1976 by the union's general convention, ADDIE L. WYATT became the first woman international vice-president of the 550,000-member Amalgamated Meat Cutters and Butcher Workmen (AMCBW) in its 79-year history. In January 1976, her picture appeared on the cover of *Time* magazine as one of the 12 "Women of the Year," the first union leader ever thus honored. Born in 1924 in Brookhaven, Mississippi, she came to Chicago at an early age. At 17 she went to work at Armour & Company putting lids on cans of stew, and discovered that the cannery workers earned more than the

clerical workers because they were unionized. In 1942, she joined Local 56 of the United Packinghouse, Food & Allied Workers (which merged with the Amalgamated Meat Cutters in 1968) and became the first woman president of a packinghouse local in 1953. From 1954 to 1974, she served as one of five international union representatives. In February 1974 she was appointed director of AMCBW's new Women's Affairs Department (the union's membership is 20 per cent women) and in March was elected vice-president of the newly formed Coalition of Labor Union Women (CLUW), which she helped to found. Mrs. Wyatt has eliminated wage differentials between men and women workers in her union and persuaded AMCBW to promote women to more demanding, previously all-male jobs.

First Woman Manager of New York City Local of Garment Workers

In June 1977 the International Ladies' Garment Workers' Union announced the appointment of BELLE HORENSON to head the 6,500-member Children's Dressmakers Union Local 91. Ms. Horenson, whose career with the union goes back to the 1930s, is the first woman to be manager of a New York City local in the ILGWU.

First Woman President of Engineers Local

A laboratory technician since 1966 at Hooker Chemicals and Plastics Corporation and member of Local 57, International Federation of Professional and Technical Engineers, JEANNE LENNOX REILLY is president of her local, one of the few women ever to hold the office in her union. Born in 1942 the daughter of a long-time shop steward in the Oil, Chemical and Atomic Workers International Union, she has studied at the Institute for Labor Affairs (University of Massachusetts), the George Meany Center for Labor Studies (Washington D.C.), and Cornell University's School for Industrial and Labor Relations. She considers her greatest accomplishment to be the successful negotiation of a contractual agreement. ("There are so many unwritten rules governing . . . negotiations. Men know them, women can learn them.")

First Woman Elected to Executive Board of 30,000-Member Teamsters Local

Starting as an information clerk at Montgomery Ward & Company in Chicago in 1947, CLARA BELLE TAYLOR DAY joined Warehouse & Mail Order Employees Union Local 743 in 1955, the largest local in the International Brotherhood of Teamsters and in the state of Illinois. Today she is the local's first woman executive-board member and its first woman business representative. Chosen to represent the local in the historic March on Washington led by Dr. Martin Luther King, Jr., in 1963, in 1974 she was elected Midwest vice-president by the Coalition of Labor Union Women (CLUW). She is a commissioner on both the Chicago commission on human relations and the Illinois commission, and vice-chairperson of the Illinois commission on the status of women, has been named Woman of Distinction by the Chicago Citizens Scholarship Committee, and has received many other honors, including the Beautiful People Award from the Chicago Urban League. Clara Day was born in Northport, Alabama, and attended Roosevelt University's labor institute leadership program and the University of Illinois Institute of Labor and Industrial Relations.

Labor Woman Member of First Official U.S. Delegation to Visit Cuba Since 1961

JOAN M. GOODIN, former assistant director of the International Affairs Department of the Brotherhood of Railway, and Airline, and Steamship Clerks, AFL-CIO, in June 1977 was a member of the first official United States delegation to visit Cuba since diplomatic relations were broken off, in January 1961. Born in 1934 in St. Petersburg, Florida, she studied at George Washington University and joined the union in 1960 as an employee of the Railway Labor Executives Association. From 1966 to 1970 she was an administrative assistant in the Lima, Peru, regional office of the International Transport Workers' Federation, and from 1970 to 1976 she was assistant director of her union's International Affairs Department. Since December 1976, she has served as a consultant in the State Department. A participant in many national and international organizations concerned with the status of women, Ms. Goodin is a frequent speaker on the role of the trade union movement in national development, the international labor movement, labor union women, and the impact of the International Women's Year. Since September 1, 1977, she has been executive director of the National Commission on Working Women of the National Manpower Institute, a private, non-profit organization in Washington.

First Woman Lawyer for the United Mine Workers of America

SUZANNE RICHARDS was the first woman lawyer hired by the United Mine Workers of America and the first woman executive assistant to the UMWA president. In June 1977, Ms. Richards was elected president of the D.C. Women's Bar Association.

Assistant Treasurer of World's Largest Local

The largest union local in the world is Local 2 of the American Federation of Teachers AFL-CIO, representing 70,000 members. Its assistant treasurer and an executive board member is PONSIE BARCLAY HILLMAN, who serves on many committees within the union. Holder of a

B.S. (*magna cum laude*) from Morgan State College and an M.A. from Columbia, both in mathematics, she has had many years as a teacher, is a charter member of the Black Trade Unionists Committee of the Central Labor Council and a member of the NAACP (from which she received a Distinguished Service Award in 1961), has served on the Secretary of Labor's Advisory Committee on Women, and has served or assisted as an organizer in collective-bargaining campaigns in Philadelphia and in St. Paul, Minnesota.

Top Women in American Unions or Other Recognized Bargaining Agencies, July 1977

Amalgamated Clothing & Textile Workers
vice-presidents: JOYCE MILLER, DOROTHY CONGOS, EMMA DAMERON, DIANA NUNES, OMA BARTON

Amalgamated Meat Cutters & Butcher Workmen
vice-president: ADDIE WYATT

American Federation of Government Employees
women's activities director: LOUISE SMOTHERS

American Federation of Teachers
vice-presidents: ANTONIA CORTESE, SANDRA FELDMAN, VELMA HILL, SANDRA IRONS, MARY ELLEN RIORDAN, FLORA ROGGE, JACQUELINE VAUGHN
asst. to the president: EUGENIA KEMBLE
director, Department of Human Rights: BARBARA VAN BLAKE

American Guild of Variety Artists
executive president: PENNY SINGLETON
secretary-treasurer: SUZANNE BERRY

American Nurses Association
president: ANNE ZIMMERMAN
executive director: MYRTLE AYDELOTTE

Association of Flight Attendants
president: PAT ROBERTSON

Communications Workers of America
vice-president: DINA BEAUMONT
asst. to the president: PATSY FRYMAN
asst. to the secretary-treasurer: GLORIA SHEPARDSON
women's activities director: LELA FOREMAN

Distributive Workers of America
vice-presidents: ESTHER LEVITT, RENEE MENDEZ

Graphic Arts International Union
vice-president: FELICIA BONELLI

International Ladies' Garment Workers' Union
vice-president: MATTIE JACKSON

International Union of Electrical Workers
vice-president, Canadian District: EVELYN MCGARR
director, education and women's activities: GLORIA JOHNSON

National Union of Hospital & Health Care Employees
secretary: DORIS TURNER

The Newspaper Guild
regional vice-presidents: SHIRLEY CALDWELL, DIANE WOODSTOCK, BETSY WADE
vice-president at large: DOROTHY SAIN
human rights coordinator: HANNAH JO RAYL

Office and Professional Employees International Union
vice-presidents: GWYN NEWTON, KATHLEEN KINNICK, LYDIA RONCHEZ

Retail, Wholesale & Dept. Store Union
vice-president: DORIS TURNER

Screen Actors Guild
president: KATHLEEN NOLAN

Service Employees International Union
executive board members: ELINOR GLENN, GLORIA MARIGNY, ROSEMARY TRUMP

United Automobile Workers
vice-president: ODESSA KOMER

United Farm Workers
vice-president: DOLORES HUERTA

United Garment Workers
secretary-treasurer: CATHERINE PETERS

United Rubber Workers
international executive board members: SHELBY J. McLAUGHLIN, IRENE L. TANTILLO
Source: Washington Women Union Leaders, July 1977

What Ever Became of "Rosie the Riveter"?

In 1942, during World War II, EDITH VAN HORN, born in 1923, went to work on an assembly line as a riveter in an Ohio Goodyear plant and joined Local 856 of the United Auto Workers. When the war ended, her job and wages disappeared. But unlike most of the thousands of other women in that position, she neither quit working nor went into a clerical job. Instead she moved to Detroit and UAW Local 3, and started building cars in a Dodge plant. She became chief steward in the automobile wire room and held the job for 16 years. Today she is on the community action staff of the UAW and is a believer that women have to fight for equal rights.

Are There Any Women Miners? Yes!

Why would women want to go into a coal mine to work? Because the pay is high and they have families to support and because the union provides them with benefits such as the miner's health card. Other advantages are the variety of duties, the challenge, and the lack of emotional energy drain (in contrast to most service jobs, for example), according to Virginian JEAN MILLER, who runs a heavy piece of machinery called a continuous miner at Island Creek's Pocahontas No. 2 mine. Before going to work digging coal, Ms. Miller was a beautician with her own shop. It took her 15–17 hours to make what she can make now in one shift, and there were no paid holidays or insurance benefits; the only other job available in her area was as a waitress at $40 plus tips for a 6-day week. As of March 1976, it was reported that over 200 women belonged to the United Mine Workers of America—although not all go down into the mines.

Six Firsts for the International Association of Machinists (IAM)

May 1973 DELORIS YOUNG was the first woman to become an IAM machinist's apprentice in Baltimore, at the Coppers Company.

May 1973 ELLEN JOHNS was the first woman to be enrolled as an apprentice at the Lockheed Aircraft Corporation, in Burbank, California, since the corporation was formed, in 1939. She enrolled as an electronic technician's apprentice to train as a "journeyman" (job description since officially changed to "craftsworker") over a four-year period.

Dec. 1973 PAMELA HONEYCUTT was the first woman machinist's apprentice at the Naval Ordnance Laboratory, Silver Spring, Maryland, since it opened, in 1946. A member of IAM Local 174, Washington, D.C., she supplemented her work by classroom attendance and college credits at Montgomery Community College.

Aug. 1974 JOYCE HOLDEN, a member for ten years of IAM Local 2113, Scarborough, Ontario, Canada, was the first woman to be elected to a provincial or state council of Machinists, thereby representing some 15,000 IAM members.

Sept. 1975 MARGARET BUTLER, a member of IAM Local 802, an all-around machinist at the Brown & Williamson Tobacco Corporation, Petersburg, Virinia, under the new title for journeyman of "craftsworker," was the first woman to complete apprenticeship training in the history of the local.

Dec. 1975 KAREN CASEBEER became the first female parts worker in the history of Walnut Creek, California, Datsun dealership. As one of two women in a class of 50 men, she attended an apprentice school for parts workers required by the state, finding nothing unusual in this since her family is in the parts business and she has been around people working with automotive parts all her life. She is a member of IAM Local 1173.

First Woman Union Gaffer

An "insatiable curiosity regarding light placement and its effects on film" led CELESTE GAINEY, a free-lance lighting technician, to become the first (and so far only) woman "gaffer" in Local 52 of the IASTE (International Alliance of Theatrical Stage Employees, the oldest, largest, and most powerful union in the film industry). Ms. Gainey, who works regularly for several network news and documentary features, lists two film experiences as her most memorable: as lighting consultant and chief gaffer on the first feature film ever made with an all-woman crew, *The Waiting Room,* and an ABC "Close-Up" documentary entitled *Women in Prison.*

First Emmy-Award-Winning Cinematographer

Whether perched on top of a 100-foot water tower or dangling from the end of a 40-foot crane, JULIANA WANG will take her 20-pound camera anywhere to get the best creative shot. Free-lancing Ms. Wang, a member of the International Photographers of the Motion Picture Industries, is an entirely self-taught camerawoman, and has reached the heights of her profession with her work on television feature documentaries, live news, and independent film features. In 1974, she became the first union woman to receive an Emmy Award for cinematography for the NBC "NewsCenter 4" report on Lesbianism.

First Network Field Sound Technician

In March 1972, CABELL SMITH became the first woman field film technician

hired by any network. She went to work as a sound technician for news and documentary programs with NBC-TV in New York City. After two years on staff, in a position usually governed by the union, IASTE Local 52, Ms. Smith was still being denied membership. Like other women in her trade, she was forced to file a sex-discrimination suit before the barriers were broken. In 1973, Ms. Smith went to China with SHIRLEY MACLAINE (see "Women in the Arts and Entertainment," p. 661) and her all-woman crew to produce *The Other Half of the Sky,* a documentary film that was nominated for an Academy Award in 1975. She left NBC in 1974 to form her own company.

She Sued Cinematographers for Sex Discrimination

After successful free-lancing for *Life, Look, Fortune,* and *Time,* and a political coverage award from *Newsweek* for pictures of the 1972 Republican convention, photojournalist HOLLY BOWER was offered a job shooting publicity stills at Paramount Pictures in New York. Credentials in order and job in hand, all Ms. Bower needed was a union card from Local 644 of the International Photographers of the Motion Picture Industries to get on the set, but the union refused to issue her one. Ms. Bowers charged the union, which represents some 600 East Coast movie cameramen, assistant cameramen, and still photographers, with sex discrimination under Title VII of the Civil Rights Act. The New York State Attorney General's Office agreed. *Bower v. Local 644* marked the first time the attorney-general's office filed a sex-discrimination complaint against a labor union. After two years of research, hearings, interviews, and changes of attorneys, Ms. Bower obtained her card, in 1974. Since joining the union, she has produced stills, movies, advertising campaigns, magazine covers, and TV specials.

First Black Woman in Cinematographers Union

In 1975, 23-year-old JESSIE MAPLE PATTON, an independent film producer and film editor, became the first black woman to be admitted to Local 644 of the International Photographers of the Motion Picture Industries. Ms. Patton, who earned full camerawoman status, has been active in promoting minorities in apprentice positions with the motion picture trade unions. She is vice-president of L. J. Film Productions, which she established with her husband, also a documentary cinematographer.

First Woman Carpenter Apprentice to Compete in Local and International Contests

Upon completing her carpentry apprenticeship training in 1976, ELIZABETH HOWARD became the first female "journeyman" (craftsworker) carpenter in the Washington, D.C. area. In May 1976 she was the first-place winner and the first woman contestant in Washington's annual Carpenter Apprentice Contest and in December 1976 the first woman to be a contestant in the annual International Carpentry Apprenticeship Contest, Las Vegas, Nevada—both events sponsored by the International Brotherhood of Carpenters and Joiners of America, of which she is a member (Local 132). In 1975, Ms. Howard, with ANI DURST (carpenter apprentice) and MARTHA TABOR (pile driver), founded Women Working in Construction (WWIC). Its purpose is to provide mutual support and job availability information for construction working women in the Capital area and to push for implementation of existing affirmative-action regulations; with several similar groups, WWIC through the League of Women Voters filed suit against the U. S. Department of Labor for its failure to enforce affirmative action in hiring women on federally funded construction sites.

Where to Learn a Trade

Do American women really want to break into skilled construction trades? The Labor Department contends that they do and cites as proof the growing number of grass-roots organizations, such as Women Working in Construction, in Washington (above), Women's Enterprises, in Boston, Better Jobs for Women, in Denver, and San Francisco's Women in Apprenticeship Program, as examples. The San Francisco program has helped double the ranks of female apprentices in the building trades. In Seattle, home of a group called Mechanica, women are said to be working on almost every construction site in the city. Recently, 600 Seattle women turned out for 30 job openings.

The largest of these organizations, Recruitment and Training Programs, Inc., operates 56 offices in 23 states. Its headquarters is in New York City. Also active in New York is the All-Craft Foundation, which offers basic training in carpentry, cabinetmaking, electrical work, and plumbing. Its graduates are either placed in jobs or hired by its affiliate Mothers and Daughters Construction Company. Still another New York City group is Women in the Trades, an organization of skilled craftswomen that serves as a resource and information center.

Typically, these programs and others like them are run by blue collar working women and funded at least in part under the Comprehensive Employment Training Act (CETA) of 1973.

UNION WOMEN, OTHER NATIONS

Chairperson of the Trades Union Congress, in Britain, 1974–75

CONSTANCE MARIE PATTERSON, a graduate of the University of London, was elected chairperson of Britain's Trades Union Congress (TUC) in 1974. There have been other women chairpersons of the TUC, the first of whom was MARGARET BONDFIELD (p. 343) in 1923, the second being ANNE LOUGHLIN in 1943. A staff member of the Transport & General Workers Union since 1957, Ms. Patterson has served on various negotiating committees and has been its women's officer since 1963. She is a member of the Industrial Injuries Advisory Council, the Central Arbitration Commission, and the Equal Opportunities Commission. Miss Patterson was on the Queen's Honours List of 1973, receiving the Order of the British Empire (OBE).

Co-Founder of Canadian Textile and Chemical Union

MADELEINE PARENT, a graduate of McGill University, in Montreal, and her husband, Kent Rowley, were organizers for the United Textile Workers of America (AFL) at a time when children worked for 18¢ an hour in Quebec textile mills and adults worked 65 hours a week, with no job security or seniority benefits. They led a 100-day strike against Dominion Textile cotton mills when the company refused to recognize the union. Ms. Parent was the target of Quebec premier Maurice Duplessis between 1944 and 1959 and had to carry her birth certificate at all times to disprove the rumor that she was a foreign-born spy. She was jailed many times. In 1947, during a strike, she was charged with seditious conspiracy but was acquitted after two trials. In 1967, she and her husband moved to Brantford, Ontario, where they organized the Canadian Textile and Chemical Union, and Madeleine Parent became secretary-treasurer. They led strikes in 1971 in Brantford and in 1973 in Toronto. She feels that most unions have not done a proper job for women in the work force and that government and business have not acted on their goals of affirmative action (for example, equal pay for equal work).

Canadian Becomes First North American Woman to Head Major Union

In 1975, GRACE HARTMAN, at the age of 56, was elected president of Canada's largest (210,000-member) union, the Canadian Union of Public Employees (CUPE), the first woman in North America to hold the top office in a major national union. Beginning her career in 1954 as a clerk in North York township and eventually elected president of her local, Ms. Hartman moved up through the ranks to become one of four women on CUPE's 17-member executive board and secretary-treasurer for eight years before becoming president. The percentage of women in CUPE has been increasing. Between 1974 and 1975, women delegates attending the annual convention increased from 20 to 34 per cent.

Participants in Canada's First Conference for Women Trade Unionists

Canada's first Conference of Women Trade Unionists was held from March 5 through March 7, 1976, in Ottawa. SHIRLEY CARR, executive vice-president of the Canadian Labour Congress, sponsor of the conference, welcomed the 400 delegates. The opening speaker was LAURA SABIA, who chairs the Ontario Status of Women Council. Also participating as leaders at the conference were GRACE HARTMAN, national president of the Canadian Union of Public Employees, VIVIAN ZACHON, a Montreal representative of the Office and Professional Employees' International Union, MARY EADY, director of the Women's Bureau in Manitoba, and JOY LANGAN, who chairs the Women's Rights Committee of the British Columbia Federation of Labour. The conference recommended to the Canadian Labour Congress Executive Council that a women's department and annual conferences of women unionists be established and that priority be given to elimination of wage differentials and discrimination against women in seniority, fringe benefits, and job evaluation, as well as to the negotiation of 24-hour child-care service.

Danish Union Heads

First Woman Deputy Chairperson of 300,000-member Labor Organization

KIRSTEN STALLKNECHT, born in 1937 the daughter of a shipmaster, attended the Danish Nursing High School and served as a trained nurse at the Rigshospitalet. She was elected chairperson of the Danish Nurses Council in 1968. In 1969 she became a member of the Joint Council of Danish Civil Servant and Functionary Organizations (FTF), which has almost 300,000 members, and was named deputy chairperson, the first woman to hold this position, in 1972.

Chairperson of the Danish Bank Functionaries National Association

BIRTE ROLL HOLM became shop steward in Denmark's Handelsbank in 1968, and in 1972 a member of the Board of its personnel association. In 1974 she became a member of the Board of the Danish Bank Functionaries National Association, and in 1975, at age 34, was elected chairperson of the association. She is also a member of the executive board of the Joint Council of Danish Civil Servant and Functionary Organizations (FTF).

First Woman Chairperson of a Mixed Labor Union

As chairperson of the Tobacco Worker Union (1963–75), ELLA JENSEN became the first woman to be chairperson of a mixed labor union (one made up of both men and women) in Denmark. Its membership is about 5,000. Ms. Jensen, who was born in 1907 in Copenhagen and graduated from public school in 1921, worked as a shop assistant until 1929 and a tobacco worker until 1958. She is married and was secretary of the Tobacco Worker Union from 1958 to 1963 and a member of the Danish Trade Union Federation executive board from 1955 to 1976.

Pioneer in Danish Women Workers Union

FANNY JENSEN (1890–1969), former chairperson of the Danish Women Workers Union and a pioneer in Danish labor women's affairs, was also a member of the Folketing from 1947 to 1953 and Minister Without Portfolio in the Social Democratic Hedtoft government from 1947 to 1950. In Denmark the labor movement is defined by many as the Social Democratic Party, the trade unions, and the cooperative movement. The Danish Women Workers Union has a membership today of about 70,000. Its present chairperson is TONI GRON, the daughter of a German-born mother and an Italian father.

Chairperson of Domestic Workers Union

Chairperson of Denmark's Domestic Workers Union RUTH KRISTENSEN is also a member of the executive board of the Danish Trade Union Federation (LO).

Chairperson of 20,000-member Garment Worker Union

ANNY BENGTSSON, born in 1918, was elected chairperson of the large, mixed

Danish Garment Worker Union at the National Congress in 1973. She had been acting chairperson since 1972.

Chairperson of Swedish Primary School Teachers Association

HANNA WANNGÅRD, born in 1892 the daughter of missionaries, taught in Stockholm from 1913 to 1955, became a member of the Board of the Swedish Association of Primary School Teachers in 1926 and served as its secretary from 1928 to 1947 and as chairperson from 1948 to 1955. She also was a member of the Board of the Swedish General Association of Primary School Teachers from 1941 to 1955 and is a member of the Swedish Central Organization of Salaried Employees.

Member of Central Board of the Swedish Association of Infant-School Teachers

EDIT V. RYDELIUS, a kindergarten teacher in Stockholm, born in 1903 in Gothenburg, completed secondary school in 1920, began teaching in Gothenburg in 1923, and became a member of the Central Board of the Swedish Association of Infant-School Teachers in 1948 and its chairwoman in 1952. She was a member of the Board of the Swedish Central Organization of Salaried Employees from 1955 to 1961 and vice-chairperson of the section for state employees.

Two Book Workers Prominent in the Finnish Cooperative Movement

MARTTA SALMELA-JARVINEN, born in 1892 and a book worker from 1906 to 1910, became active in Finland's Social Democratic Women's League in 1921 and was secretary from 1937 to 1953. She was a member of Parliament from 1939 to 1966, active in Helsinki city government from the 1920s into the 1960s, a member of the Board of the cooperative movement "Elanto" from 1934 to 1960, and a member of the breakaway

left wing of the Social Democratic Party in the 1960s (the Social Democratic Union of Workers and Small Farmers). TYYNE PAASIVUORI, born in 1907, a book worker from 1924 to 1952, has held many posts in Finland's cooperative movement. Active in the Social Democratic Women's League and on the Helsinki city council, she was a member of Parliament from 1954 to 1958 and from 1962 to 1975, and a presidential elector in 1956 and 1962.

President for 21 Years of the International Confederation of Working Women of Christian Unions (CISC)

SIMONE TROISGROS, born in 1904 in Paris and an employee of a metal-working plant from 1921 to 1945 and assistant secretary of her union (CFDT), served as president of the International Confederation of Working Women of Christian Unions for 21 years (1948–69). Since 1969 she has been the organization's delegate to UNESCO. She has also served as president of the French Federation of Popular Tourism (1945–69) and as president of the International Office of Social Tourism since 1974. She is the recipient of the Companion of the Legion of Honor award and is an officer of the Order of National Merit.

Union Activist First Clerk-Typist to Run for French Presidency

ARLETTE LAGUILLER, 37-year-old French Marxist, won almost 600,000 votes in her 1974 campaign for the French presidency, coming in just behind the four major candidates in a field of 12 (the winner: Valéry Giscard d'Estaing). That she did so well was interpreted as proof of a growing French women's movement. With two invalid parents and no money, Arlette Laguiller went to work at 16 as a clerk-typist for Crédit Lyonnais, the nation's third-largest bank. There she saw thousands of other clerks working 10 hours a day for the equivalent of $50 a week. She became an active union organizer and leftist, and during the riots and strikes of May 1968 she was largely responsible for calling a massive walkout at Crédit Lyonnais. In 1973 she ran for the National Assembly. In 1974 she headed a nationwide bank strike that threatened to cripple France's economy, and in April, when Georges Pompidou died, launched her unsuccessful bid for President. After the election, she returned to work as a clerk-typist.

Equal Pay and Opportunity Worker President of the New Zealand National Organization of Women

Social and travel officer for the Auckland, New Zealand, branch of the Clerical Workers' Union, CONNIE PURDUE in addition to her union work has been secretary of the Equal Pay Council, president of New Zealand's National Organization of Women, secretary of the Birkenhead Labor Party, and delegate to the Auckland Trades Council. Reviewing the history of equal pay in New Zealand, Ms. Purdue cites 1957 as an important year; it was then that the Equal Pay and Opportunity Council of 22 trade unions and eight major women's organizations was formed. New Zealand's Equal Pay Act came into force in 1973. It states that no subsequent law shall contain "classifications or work that differentiate, on the basis of the sex of the employee, in the work which male employees or female employees may perform." Female wages in New Zealand in 1973 were 70 per cent of the male rate (in the United States in 1977 female wages were only 57 per cent of the male). New Zealand women are not yet reaching the higher pay brackets, however, and are asking, "After equal pay, what?" according to Ms. Purdue.

Trade Union Leaders in Japan

Among the first women leaders at the first stage of Japan's trade union move-

ment in the years after World War II were MAKIKO YAMAMOTO and TOYOKO TAKA. Both concentrated their work on protecting women's rights and were active representing women workers of Japan in many international conferences. Ms. Yamamoto, born in 1920, was director of the Women's Division of the General Council of Trade Unions of Japan 1958 to 1976. Ms. Taka, born in 1925, is director of the Women's Division of the Japan Federation of Textile Workers' Unions.

First and Only Woman to Head a Union in Jamaica, First Jamaican Woman to Represent Her Country at the ILO

EDITH NELSON joined the trade union movement in 1938 when the first recognized and registered trade union, the Bustamante Industrial Trade Union, was formed in Jamaica. In the early days, her union persuaded some churches to baptize children born out of wedlock and also set up social centers to teach union members cooking, sewing, and other skills. Ms. Nelson was named assistant general secretary in 1939, and in 1962 general secretary, becoming the first and so far only woman to hold this post in Jamaica and the only Jamaican woman to take part in negotiations to settle disputes, arbitration, and decision-making. One of her most significant "firsts" was winning a claim for strike pay taken to arbitration; never before had such a claim been accepted by an employer in Jamaica. Another "first" for Ms. Nelson was convincing the United Nations and the International Labor Organization of the necessity of a Workers' Population Education Project in Jamaica; this program is now being operated successfully and is the only one of its kind in the Western Hemisphere. In 1975 Ms. Nelson represented Jamaica at the ILO conference, in Geneva—the first time that any Jamaican woman had ever attended the Conference as a representative.

Today's Young Designers

CAROL HORN was a window dresser at Macy's when she decided to start designing clothes herself. After 12 years of working for other firms, she opened her own company, Carol Horn's Habitat.

DONNA KARAN, star of the house founded by the late ANNE KLEIN, was Ms. Klein's personal choice as her successor. She is best known for her well-cut blazers, pants, and skirts, but has branched out as the creative force behind the Anne Klein Studio's 15 designers.

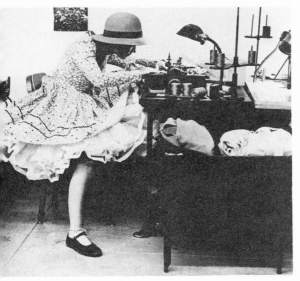

BETSEY JOHNSON, famed for her whimsical approach to dress design, often sews on, as well as for, herself. She began designing for the trendy 1960s boutique Paraphernalia, and in 1971 won a Winnie for her work with Alley Cat. (Photo by Deborah Tuberville, courtesy of Betsy Johnson)

Designers, manufacturers, and restorers of fine fabrics and wallpaper, Scalamandre Silks, Inc. is a family business in which two of the principal talents are mother FLORA ADRIANA SCALAMANDRE, seen above at work on the Hannock House restoration, and her daughter ADRIANA SCALAMANDRE BITTER.

The down-to-earth, modern decorating advice proffered to her private and Model Cities government clients plus the bright charm of the rooms she has decorated for young homemakers with more taste than money have won for EMILY MALINO recognition as one of America's 10 most influential designers.

Named assistant general secretary of Jamaica's Bustamente Industrial Trade Union in 1939 and general secretary in 1962, EDITH NELSON, above with union members on the job, was the first woman to hold such a post in Jamaica. (Photo courtesy of Fraser's Studios)

Meeting of the Canadian Conference for Women Trade Unionists—first of its kind —in March 1976. SHIRLEY CARR, executive vice-president of the sponsoring Canadian Labour Congress, is at left. (Photo courtesy of the Canadian Conference for Women Trade Unionists)

KELLY RUECK and members of the Association of Flight Attendants at the Coalition of Labor Union Women convention, 1975. In 1976 PAT ROBERTSON succeeded Ms. Rueck as head of the 18,000-member organization of flight attendants from 19 U.S. airlines. (Photo courtesy of Coalition of Labor Union Women)

KATHLEEN NOLAN, first woman president of the Screen Actors Guild, AFL-CIO.

ADDIE L. WYATT, first woman international vice-president of the Amalgamated Meat Cutters and Butcher Workmen.

They Sued Their Unions

The first field technician hired by a TV network, CABELL SMITH was denied membership by the union governing the position, IASTE Local No. 52, and was forced to file a sex discrimination suit before the barriers were broken.

It was Local 64 of the International Photographers of the Motion Picture Industries that gave HOLLY BOWER trouble when she was offered a job shooting stills at Paramount Pictures in New York. Her sex discrimination complaint was the first filed by the New York State attorney general's office against a labor union. Both Ms. Bower and Ms. Smith were admitted to their unions in 1974. (Photo courtesy of Holly Bower)

ALEXIS M. HERMAN, director of the Women's Bureau in the U. S. Department of Labor. The youngest director in the Bureau's 57-year history, Ms. Herman was 29 when she was sworn in on March 23, 1977. (Photo courtesy of the Women's Bureau, Department of Labor)

ANA FIGUEROA, first woman to hold the post of assistant director-general of the International Labor Organization (ILO), from 1960 to 1967. (Courtesy of International Labor Office)

NOBUKO TAKAHASHI, assistant director-general of the ILO since 1976. Ms. Takahashi has been active in Japanese and international labor politics since 1945. (Courtesy of International Labor Office)

HARRIET FLEISCHL PILPEL, attorney. Forty years a fighter in the battle for women to control conception, Ms. Pilpel also is internationally recognized for her expertise in the field of copyright, authors' royalties, and contracts in the arts and entertainment fields.

PRISCILLA RUTH MACDOUGALL, activist counsel. "For Women Who Wish to Determine Their Own Names After Marriage," the basic guide to the women's names issue, was co-authored by lawyer MacDougall. She has participated in virtually every major case involving this matter since 1972. (Photo by Bruce M. Fritz, *The Capital Times*)

FAITH SEIDENBERG, civil rights and civil liberties lawyer. Among the many legal battles she has fought and won, none brought Ms. Seidenberg more attention than the one against bars for restricting the admittance of women: *Seidenberg* v. *McSorley's* ended the men-only rule at this renowned New York City alehouse.

Watergate prosecutor JILL WINE-VOLNER. The Justice Department trial attorney who earned a national reputation during the Watergate hearings, Ms. Wine-Volner in 1977 was named by President Carter general counsel for the U. S. Army, overseeing 2,000 attorneys at the Pentagon.

LABOR EDUCATORS AND SUPPORTERS

Director of the First Summer School for Women Workers

HILDA WORTHINGTON SMITH was born in 1888 in New York City to a businessman father and a teacher mother. The "firsts" in her life centered around worker education. After she was graduated from Bryn Mawr College, in 1910, she was appointed director of the first community center set up in the town of Bryn Mawr, Pennsylvania, and later named dean of the college. In 1921, the president of Bryn Mawr, M. CAREY THOMAS, returned from a trip to England, where she had seen worker education classes in settlement houses, eager to start a summer school for women workers at the college; she appointed Hilda Smith the school's first director. It was the first time a women's college had opened its doors to women industrial workers and offered them the opportunity of intellectual enrichment and political direction. The idea spread. Classes were set up on other campuses and at the American Museum of Natural History, in New York. The Bryn Mawr school later was moved to the site of her family's estate on the Hudson River. Eventually Rutgers University took over the program, which is now carried out on some 50 campuses around the country. In 1934, Hilda Smith went to Washington, D.C., with a one-page memo to Harry Hopkins, adviser to President Franklin D. Roosevelt and later head of the Works Progress Administration. In a 20-minute interview, she persuaded Hopkins to establish a federal labor education project. As a result, the federal government hired about 2,000 unemployed teachers, who were trained under her direction and placed back in their own communities, if possible, to teach workers. Ms. Smith, who retired in 1972 and still lives in Washington, D.C., reports that Harry Hopkins was a very cas-

ual boss. He met her in the hall one day and told her the administration wanted her to do something about unemployed women. With ELEANOR ROOSEVELT'S co-operation, she set up pioneering women's camps and schools that taught English, science, labor economics, and most popular of all, music appreciation, until the end of the 1930s depression.

Co-Founder of Brookwood Labor College

FANNIA MARY COHN (1888–1962), a Russian immigrant, joined the International Ladies' Garment Workers' Union (ILGWU) in her early 20s, in 1909, and quickly moved into leadership in Kimona Wrappers & Housedress Workers Local 41. In 1915 she organized garment workers on strike to form Local 51 and served as its president. Moving to Chicago, Fannia Cohn organized for the ILGWU and in 1916 was elected vice-president, which she remained until 1925. In 1921 she helped to found Brookwood Labor College and was on its board of directors until 1937; she also founded the Workers' Education Bureau of America, of which she was executive secretary until retiring, in 1961, edited *Workers' Education*, the quarterly journal of the Workers' Education Bureau of America, and established the Manumit School for Worker's Children, directing it until 1933.

First Director of American Labor Education Service

ELEANOR GWINNELL COIT, born in 1894, became director of the new American Labor Education Service in 1934, when it emerged out of the old Affiliated Schools for Workers. A pioneer in the establishment of resident schools for workers, labor education for white collar workers, worker exchange programs with foreign countries, anti-discrimination education, and study of farmer-labor relationships, she was still the director of The Service when it closed, in 1962, at the end of an era in which trade unions had made an effort to improve the educational level of their members. When Ms. Coit retired, in 1962, the workers' education movement had grown to 75 labor colleges, almost all at universities offering degree credit and diploma and certificate courses, many financed by state governments. She died in New York City in 1976.

Leader of Grassroots Organization to Aid Coal Miners

Coal miners' wives over countless years have carried the burden of hardship caused by such hazards as cave-ins or explosions in the mines, strike violence (even jail), poverty, black lung disease. In the late 1950s and early '60s, grassroots organizations began to emerge in the coal fields, working alongside the unions for better conditions and prevention of and compensation for black lung disease. FRANCIE "GRANNY" HAGER, widow of a miner killed by black lung, helped to organize one of these groups, called the Appalachian Committee for Full Employment, and became a leader in the Kentucky Black Lung Association. Together with other widows and disabled miners, she put together a caravan that became a traveling picket line going from mine to mine asking the men to come out on strike until better conditions were achieved. Recently, in the spirit of Granny Hager, wives and widows of United Mine Workers played a major role in achieving passage in the U. S. House of Representatives of the black lung bill in September 1975 by organizing a march on Washington in its support.

First President of the National Committee on Household Employment

When ETHLYN CHRISTENSEN became the first president, in 1964, of the National Committee on Household Employment, a federally funded pilot project, the appointment capped a professional interest extending back to the 1930s, when, as director of the Industrial Department of the YWCA in Buffalo, New York, she organized the Household Employees Club and set up discussions and informal bargaining between workers and employers. In 1935, she became a charter member of the Buffalo Teachers' Union, the only union then available to social agency employees. Her YWCA staff eventually negotiated the first contract in the social agency field, and in 1948 she was hired as the first paid organizer for the Community and Social Agency Employees Union-CIO, Local 1707. Ms. Christensen, born in 1901 the daughter of Danish immigrant parents, grew up in Laramie, Wyoming, and holds an M.A. in political economy from the University of Wyoming. Since retiring, in 1967, she has lived in Denver, Colorado, where she is a member of the Governor's Advisory Committee on Employment, a member and past chairperson of the Denver Commission on Aging, and chairperson of the Advisory Committee on Transportation for the Elderly and the Handicapped. In 1971 she helped secure a grant from the U. S. Department of Labor for a pilot project, "Better Jobs for Women," now in its seventh year.

Founder of Trade Union Women of African Heritage

THELMA DAILEY is the founder and president of Trade Union Women of African Heritage (1967), which seeks affirmative action for black women within unions. She also founded the Minority Institute for Education in Governmental Sciences, Inc., whose purpose is to inform Third World women, through seminars, about government, and to develop contacts with women in Africa in the trades and crafts. Ms. Dailey, born in Baltimore, Maryland, studied at the Fashion Institute of Technology (A.A.S. degree) and

Empire State College, in New York (B.A.). From 1948 to 1976, she held various union administrative positions with the Distributive Workers of America, serving as vice-president from 1969 to 1976. From 1951 to 1956 she was associate director of the Development & Training Center for District 65 of the union, developing educational programs for school dropouts and adults in dead-end jobs. As director of the White Collar Division of the union, from 1969 to 1975, she placed approximately 7,000 persons yearly with some 2,000 employers. Ms. Dailey also has taught women's studies at the Fashion Institute of Technology and New Rochelle College.

Organizer to Educator-Writer-Ombudsman

ALICE H. COOK, born in 1903, in the 1930s worked for several unions either as organizer, business agent, or education director. In 1952 she joined the faculty of Cornell University's School of Industrial and Labor Relations, where she taught the history, structure, and function of American trade unions, and at one point directed a degree program for trade unionists in New York City. From 1969 to 1971 she served as Cornell's first ombudsman and is now on the Board of the University's Women's Studies Program. Ms. Cook has written extensively on labor problems in Japan and the United States; she was the recipient of a Ford Foundation grant, for 1972 to 1974, for her study *The Working Mother in Nine Countries,* and of a German Marshall Fund of the United States grant, for 1976–77, for a report, *Women in Trade Unions in Five Countries.*

First Chairperson of Labor Committee for Equal Rights Amendment

MARJORIE B. RACHLIN, a charter member and first chairperson of the Labor Committee for the Equal Rights Amendment, since 1970 has been senior staff associate at the George Meany Center for Labor Studies, Silver Spring, Maryland (near Washington, D.C.), where she sets up and runs training programs for union staff including many for women on their role in unions. A graduate of Wells College (Phi Beta Kappa) and a junior Fulbright Scholar at the University of London from 1952 to 1953, she joined the staff of the International Association of Machinists, AFL-CIO, in 1956 as an associate in its Education Department, where she conducted some of the first union-sponsored programs for women in the work force. From 1967 to 1968, she was assistant director of the Labor Education Study, National Institute of Labor Education, at American University, Washington, D.C., which published a report entitled *Labor Education in the United States.*

Founders of Union WAGE

JEAN MADDOX, an office worker and member of Local 29 of the Office and Professional Employees International Union, in March 1971 with JOYCE MAUPIN founded the Union of Women's Alliance to Gain Equality (WAGE)—an organization of women workers dedicated to achieving equal rights, equal pay, and equal opportunities.

Ms. Maddox, born in 1915 in Idaho, grew up in the mountains with her father, a forest ranger of Native American ancestry, and her schoolteacher mother. She graduated from high school in Ventura, California, worked for a time waiting on tables, and in 1941 took a job driving a milk truck. Later, in a soap factory, she was an inside organizer for the West Coast Congress of the CIO, became a steward, participated in grievance negotiations, and was active in the union's steward council. In 1975 Ms. Maddox was named California Woman of the Year by the California Commission on the Status of Women.

Joyce Maupin, born in 1914 the daughter of a farmer and a teacher-mother who was also a journalist and suffragist, left school at 17 to become self-supporting, also by waiting on tables, and later was employed as a textile worker, machinist, and office worker. She was an active participant in a five-month strike against Boeing Aircraft and a shop steward of her local. In 1975 she also received the California Woman of the Year award.

Organizer of First AFL-CIO-Sponsored National Institute on Day Care

BOBBIE LITTLE CREQUÉ, a member of the Office and Professional Employees International Union (OPEIU) since 1967, was a community services intern (AFL-CIO) from 1970 to 1971 and has been a national AFL-CIO community services liaison representative since 1972. Her job is to work with the labor movement (specifically the AFL-CIO) and the United Way of America to develop quality child care and related services through conferences, workshops, and institutes. In 1970 she organized and led the first National Institute on Day Care, sponsored by the Community Services Department of the AFL-CIO, at which twelve international unions were represented. That same year, she became the first woman to attend a staff development seminar at the George Meany Center for Labor Studies, in Washington. Ms. Crequé, born in 1936 in East St. Louis, Illinois and the mother of two children, is the author of "Labor and Child Care," which appeared in *Educational Comment 1976*, published by the University of Toledo College of Education.

Chairperson of Canada's Advisory Council on the Status of Women

In 1971 the Royal Commission on the Status of Women in Canada presented 167 recommendations addressed to government, crown corporations, and chartered banks, for changes in law and prac-

tices affecting women. Out of the 167, at least 75 were directly or indirectly related to women's employment or income. A quantitative summary of the degree of implementation prepared by the 30-member Advisory Council on the Status of Women, chaired by KATIE COOKE, who has for many years been involved with the role of women in rural development and economic expansion, was released in 1976. It showed that out of the total number of recommendations, 50 had been implemented, 53 had been partially implemented, and 19 had not been implemented.

Author of First Book Written for Workers on Health Hazards in the Workplace

JEANNE M. STELLMAN, co-author (with SUSAN DAUM) of *Work Is Dangerous to Your Health* (1973), the first practical handbook of its kind written for workers, as assistant to the president for health and safety of the Oil, Chemical and Atomic Workers International Union (1972–75), was the first woman to be in charge of a nationwide health and safety program for an international union. At Rutgers Labor Education Center from 1970 to 1972 she developed and taught the first course in the United States for workers and laymen on occupational health and safety. Ms. Stellman, born in 1947, received a B.S. in chemistry in 1968 and a Ph.D. in physical chemistry in 1972 from the City University of New York, and has taught at the City College of New York, Rutgers Labor Education Center, Cornell University (N. Y. State School for Labor and Industrial Relations), and the University of Pennsylvania School of Medicine. She serves as scientific consultant to the Coalition of Labor Union Women (CLUW) and is the author of numerous articles and a second book, *Women's Work, Woman's Health: Myth and Realities* (1978).

Leader of Only International Women's Labor Seminar Held During IWY

ANNE NELSON chaired the plenary sessions and was a lecturer at the international labor women's seminar held in Tel Aviv, Israel, in 1975, attended by women from 15 countries, representing most of the continents of the world, and a wide variety of unions. It was the only such seminar held during the International Women's Year. Ms. Nelson, born in 1925, is the associate director of the Institute of Research & Education on Women & Work, of Cornell University, the first and only university program that offers a year-long college credit sequence in labor relations. Co-author with BARBARA WERTHEIMER (p. 328 of *Trade Union Women: A Study of Their Participation in New York City Locals* (1975), Ms. Nelson is a founding member of the Coalition of Labor Union Women and has achieved many firsts in labor education, including initiating the first New York Trade Union Women's Conference, in January 1974.

Director of One-Year Oral History Project of 20th-Century Trade Union Women

JOYCE KORNBLUH has been involved in workers' education since 1947. She has written materials for workers' classes in Pennsylvania and California. With a B.A. from the University of Pennsylvania (1948) and an M.A. from UCLA (1950), she worked for the Amalgamated Clothing Workers of America as assistant education director (1953–59), as labor consultant to the Fund for the Republic (1956), and as editor of the newspaper of Detroit Local 876, Retail Clerks International Union (1959–61). She began her association with the University of Michigan in 1969 as an editor with the Center for Research on Utilization of Scientific Knowledge and in 1974 established the summer school for women workers. From 1975 to 1976 she was director of the University of Michigan's One-Year Oral History Project of 20th-Century Trade Union Women.

Author of First Nationally Funded Survey of Chinese American Manpower and Employment

BETTY LEE SUNG is the author of several books about Chinese-Americans, including the first *Survey of Chinese American Manpower and Employment,* which was named an outstanding book of 1976 by *Choice* magazine. Professor Sung, a member of the Department of Asian Studies at City College of the City University of New York, taught the first courses on Asian Americans offered on the East Coast. Born in Baltimore, Professor Sung graduated from the University of Illinois in 1948 and received a Master of Library Science degree from Queens College in 1968. She lectures widely on the subject of Chinese Americans, and, under a government grant, is currently doing research on Chinese immigrant families. In private life she is Mrs. Charles Chung and mother to eight children.

Only Woman Member of Board of Inquiry During 1978 Coal Strike

In March 1978 EVA ROBINS, a member of the American Arbitration Association, was asked by President Jimmy Carter to serve on the three-member Presidential Board of Inquiry during the coal miners' strike. Ms. Robins, in her 60s, is an attorney who has worked as a mediator in strikes in New York City. The Board heard 50 witnesses during one day, concluding in its report to the President that a national emergency existed. Labor women members of the American Arbitration Association listed in Who's Who in Labor, 1976, in addition to Ms. Robins, were: EVELYN S. BRAND, Brooklyn, New York; ALICE HANSON COOK, Ithaca, New York; BARBARA W. DOER-

ING, Indianapolis, Indiana; and ALICE BACON GRANT, Rochester, New York.

Women Active on Committee on Political Education, AFL-CIO

COPE, the branch of the AFL-CIO that gets out the vote for candidates for public office who support labor programs, has had a number of women active in its behind-the-scenes political work: Eastern Director of Volunteers in Politics (VIP) RUTH COLOMBO, Washington, D.C.; Western VIP Director MARGARET THORNBURGH, Oklahoma; Research Director MARGARET CRONIN, Washington, D.C.; FANNIE NEAL (Alabama); and ESTHER MURRAY and MARY ZON, both now retired.

Only Woman Director of a United Labor Agency

SUSAN ELLEN HOLLERAN in October 1976 became the first executive director of the United Labor Agency of Greater Washington and the only woman director among twelve such agencies around the United States. Ms. Holleran, born in 1941 in Philadelphia, has studied at George Washington University and at Catholic University, in Washington, D.C. From 1974 to 1975 she was assistant to the director of the Labor Studies Center at Federal City College, where she initiated and administered the first training programs for trade union women. She is a member of the Office and Professional Employees International Union (OPEIU), a member of the American Federation of Teachers (AFT), and a founding member and vice-president for the mid-Atlantic region of the Coalition of Labor Union Women (CLUW).

Three "Union Maids" Star in Film

KATE HYNDMAN, SYLVIA WOODS, and STELLA NOWICKI, rank-and-file union activists in the 1930s, were interviewed separately in the 55-minute documentary feature *Union Maids* (1977), based on the 1973 book *Rank and File*, by ALICE and Staughton LYND. In the film, Ms. Hyndman (garment trades), Ms. Woods (laundryworkers), and Ms. Nowicki (packinghouse) recall their early days as unskilled laborers in Chicago. Sylvia Woods, the only black of the three, speaks of her father's advice when she went out to work, saying if there was a union, join it, if there wasn't, organize one, because any union was better than none. Interwoven with their stories and union songs of the '30s is some remarkable film footage of events as they occurred. Of the three film makers behind the production, one is a woman, JULIA REICHERT, who is also the unseen interviewer.

First Director of Institute on Women and Work at Cornell University

In May 1977 the faculty of Cornell University's School of Industrial and Labor Relations voted unanimously to establish the Institute for Education and Research on Women and Work. Director of the Institute is BARBARA MAYER WERTHEIMER, who previously had been directing, at Cornell, the first Trade Union Women's Studies program in the United States, an accredited program designed especially for union women. In 1975 Ms. Wertheimer and her associate ANNE H. NELSON (p. 327) published *Trade Union Women,* and in 1977 Ms. Wertheimer published *We Were There: The Story of Working Women in America.* Ms. Wertheimer received her B.A. from Oberlin College in 1946 and an M.A. from New York University in 1960. From 1946 to 1958 she was on the staff of the Amalgamated Clothing Workers of America as an organizer, and then as associate national education director. She joined the Cornell faculty in 1966 as an associate of the School of Industrial and Labor Relations, in New York City. Ms. Wertheimer is a founding member of CLUW.

GOVERNMENT LABOR OFFICIALS, U.S.A.

The First and Second Directors of the Children's (Labor) Bureau

Daughter of an Illinois congressman and a suffragette, JULIA CLIFFORD LATHROP (1858–1932) was appointed the first director of the U.S. Children's Bureau by President William Howard Taft, in 1912, and held the post until 1921. She was the first woman to head an important government bureau in the United States. Originally established in the Commerce Department, the Children's Bureau moved to the Labor Department in 1913; its purpose was to investigate and report on the welfare of children. From 1916 to 1918, Julia Lathrop and the Bureau took on the enforcement of a federal child labor law, that was later declared unconstitutional. Another project was a study of infant mortality and maternal deaths. An early resident of Hull House, she was the first woman appointed to the Illinois state board of charities, in 1893, and helped to establish the state's first juvenile court. After retiring from the Children's Bureau, she served on the Child Welfare Committee of the League of Nations.

In 1921, Julia Lathrop was succeeded as Children's Bureau director by GRACE ABBOTT (1878–1939), who also had been a resident of Hull House. Ms. Abbott, who held an M.A. in political science from the University of Chicago (1909), participated in the Chicago garment workers strike of 1910. From 1908 to 1917 she served as head of the Immigrants Protective League. While director of the Children's Bureau, from 1921 to 1934, she helped FRANCES PERKINS (p. 331) draft the Social Security Act. (A movement during President Herbert Hoover's term urging him to appoint Grace Abbott as Secretary of Labor failed but paved the way for Franklin D. Roosevelt's appointment of Frances Perkins.

First Head of Pioneer Women's Industrial Organization in U. S. Government

MARY VAN KLEECK (1883–1972) was appointed head of the Women's Section of the Industrial Service Section of the Ordnance Department, in Washington, in 1918. It was her responsibility to oversee the placement and care of thousands of women in the war industries during World War I, a task that had never before been attempted on such a national scale. Ms. Van Kleeck appointed a field assistant with a talent for getting down to essentials and settling shop disputes. Her name was MARY ANDERSON (p. 330). Together they investigated industrial sites all over the country, including 156 sites in the Midwest employing over 16,000 black women, where they found standards even lower than the already substandard level for white women in industry. On the day of the Armistice, November 11, 1918, Mary Van Kleeck sent a note to the chairman of the War Policies Board strongly recommending that women be recognized as in industry to stay. Soon thereafter the Women's Section, now under the Department of Labor, issued a compact pamphlet entitled *Standards for the Employment of Women in Industry,* recommending wages, hours, and working conditions for women, including equal pay for equal work, and the same proportionate increases that men received (the latter remained unfulfilled goals for decades). In August 1919, Mary Van Kleeck retired and Mary Anderson became her successor and eventually head of the new Women's Bureau the following year.

Directors of the Women's Bureau

Mary Anderson
1920–44
Frieda S. Miller
1944–53
Alice K. Leopold
1953–61
Esther Peterson
1961–64

Mary D. Keyserling
1964–69
Elizabeth Duncan Koontz
1970–73
Carmen Rosa Maymi
1973–77
Alexis M. Herman
1977–

Top Women in the U. S. Department of Labor as of June 1977

Carin Clauss, solicitor
Alexis Herman, director of the Women's Bureau
Janet Norwood, deputy commissioner, Bureau of Labor Statistics
Eula Bingham, assistant secretary for Occupational Health & Safety

First Director of the Women's Bureau

MARY ANDERSON (1872–1964), the first "up through the ranks" union woman to head an executive department of the U.S. federal government, was born in Linköping, Sweden and at the age of 16 emigrated with a sister to the United States. After washing dishes for $1.50 a week in a lumberjack's boarding house in Michigan, she found a job as a shoe worker in Illinois, eventually earning $14 a week. At the age of 22 she joined the International Boot and Shoe Workers' Union and served as president of Local 94 for 15 years and as the only woman on the union's executive board for 11 years. She joined the Chicago branch of the Women's Trade Union League (WTUL) soon after it was founded, in 1903, quit factory work seven years later to become the WTUL's representative to the United Garment Workers Union, and served as an investigator to monitor the agreement ending the Hart, Schaffner & Marx strike of 1910. She continued to organize and to investigate strikes for the national WTUL, from 1913 to 1920. During World War I she began her gov-

ernment career (p. 329), and in 1920, when Congress established the permanent Women's Bureau in the Labor Department, Mary Anderson was appointed its first director. Under her, the Bureau published findings to provide back-up data needed to reform labor laws, and she was largely responsible for the inclusion of women in the federal minimum wage and hour law. After 25 years as director, Mary Anderson retired, in 1944, thereafter devoting her energies to lecturing, writing, and testifying before Congress on behalf of better working conditions for women. At the age of 90 she was given the Labor Department's Award of Merit for her contribution to the "welfare of the wage earners in the United States."

First Woman Federal Mediator

At about the time when most young women are finishing college, Boston-born ANNA WEINSTOCK was beginning a career as a labor mediator. At 14 she joined a textile workers local, and from 1918 to 1920 was business agent for the Neckwear Workers Union in Boston and an organizer for the Massachusetts Suffrage Association. President of the Boston Branch of the Women's Trade Union League from 1919 to 1922, in 1920 she got involved in a strike and served on the negotiating committee. The *Boston American* termed her "the girl Gompers" (the reference was to Samuel

Gompers, then president of the AF of L). In 1922 she became the first woman appointed to the U. S. Conciliation Service, and for some years was the only woman in the Service. Anna Weinstock married Dr. Jesse Schneider in 1929 but continued to work all over the country; 95 per cent of her cases involved textile workers and 99 per cent of the settlements were accepted. In 1947 she was appointed commissioner for New England under the new Federal Mediation and Conciliation Service (FMCS), now an independent federal agency, and held the post until 1965. Since then she has fulfilled fact-finding assignments, notably during the 1967 police strike in Boston. A member of the American Arbitration Association, she received the Distinguished Service Award from the FMCS in 1957 and a citation from Cornell University for her 40 years as a federal mediator.

First Woman to Be U. S. Secretary of Labor

The first woman ever named to the President's Cabinet in the United States was Franklin D. Roosevelt's Secretary of Labor, FRANCES PERKINS (1880–1965). Her swearing in, on March 4, 1933, was the culmination of more than 20 years already spent in the field of labor reform.

Frances Perkins, born in Boston and raised in Worcester, Massachusetts, and Newcastle, Maine, was graduated from Mt. Holyoke College (1902), taught school, became involved in settlement work, and attended classes at the Pennsylvania Graduate School of Arts and Sciences. There she was influenced by the ideas of Professor Simon N. Patten, who believed that a society of great industrial wealth could aid masses of citizens through programs based on taxation. After receiving an M.A. from Columbia University in 1910, she was hired as head of the New York Chapter of the Consumers League, becoming closely associated with Florence Kelley (p. 288).

On March 25, 1911, in New York City, she was a witness to the disastrous fire in the Triangle Shirtwaist factory, in which 146 persons died, mostly young women, many of whom jumped or fell to their deaths. This "never-to-be-forgotten reminder of why I had to spend my life fighting conditions that would permit such a tragedy" led her to serve as an investigator on the New York State Factory Commission from 1912 to 1913 and as executive secretary of the Committee on Safety in New York from 1912 to 1917.

In 1913, Frances Perkins married Paul Wilson, retaining her maiden name. Their only child, Susanna, was born in 1916. In 1919, Governor Alfred E. Smith appointed her the first woman member of the New York State Industrial Commission, and in 1926 she became chairperson. Her annual salary, $8,000, was said to be the highest paid to any woman in state government at that time. In 1929 Governor Franklin D. Roosevelt appointed her industrial commissioner—the first woman to serve in a governor's cabinet. Under her influence, New York became the first state to establish a committee to stabilize employment and to recommend state-supported unemployment insurance.

"Ma" Perkins's appointment as U. S. Secretary of Labor was unpopular with organized labor, because she was not a union member. To show the new administration's concern for workers and unemployment, a few days after the inauguration she called the first conference ever held at the Department of Labor for leaders of organized labor. Included were the AF of L, independent unions, and the National Women's Trade Union League. In two days this group drew up a 10-point program and presented it to President Roosevelt. She was also the first Secretary of Labor to take an active interest in the state departments of labor, and in July 1933 presided over the first of many national conferences designed to encourage the states to pass progressive labor laws. Her greatest contribution, however, was a body of social legislation passed between 1933 and 1941, that included federal aid to the states for unemployment relief, public works, a law to prohibit child labor and laws on maximum hours and minimum wages (Fair Labor Standards Act, 1938), encouraging the states to adopt workmen's compensation, and unemployment and old age insurance (Social Security Act, 1935). Shy of publicity, preferring a role behind the scenes, she suffered from an unsympathetic, often sexist, reaction from the press and was charged with being un-American by some congressmen. She resigned after Roosevelt's death, in 1945, and with Howard Taubman, wrote *The Roosevelt I Knew* (1946). From 1946 to 1952 she served on the Civil Service Commission. After her husband's death, in 1952, she lectured at Cornell University as a visiting professor in the School of Industrial and Labor Relations; from 1960 to 1965 she was a resident of Telluride House, on the campus, the first woman ever invited to live there.

First Woman Appointed to the Code Authority of FDR's National Recovery Administration

ELIZABETH CHRISTMAN was appointed by President Franklin D. Roosevelt to represent the glove industry on the Code Authority of the NRA in 1934. The first woman to serve on the Code Authority, she was at the time vice-president of the International Glove Workers Union, a post she held from 1931 to 1937. Her years of experience went back to 1902, when she and AGNES NESTOR (p. 295) co-founded Operators Local 1 of the International Glove Workers Union, in Chicago. An active supporter of leadership training for women in the labor movement, she achieved the executive committee of the Labor Education Service, which maintained the Bryn Mawr and Wisconsin summer schools for women workers, and was secretary-treasurer of the National Women's Trade Union League for 30 years, from 1921 until it was dissolved, in 1951. During World War II she was on the advisory committee of the Women's Bureau, concerned with women's employment in war industries. She intervened personally in controversies, in one case convincing male union members that equal pay for women workers was to the men's advantage also. In 1951 she became legislative representative in Washington, D.C., for the Amalgamated Clothing Workers of America.

First Woman to Be Deputy Director of Bureau of Labor Standards

CLARA MORTENSON BEYER set up the Labor Department's new Bureau of Labor Standards in 1934 and served as its associate director and then deputy director until 1958. During this time she was for 15 years (1938–53) a technical adviser to the annual conference of the International Labor Organization. Prior to joining the Labor Department, she had served as director of the Children's Bureau, Industrial Division. Born in 1892 in Middletown, California, Ms. Beyer was trained as an economist at the University of California at Berkeley, where she received a B.A. in 1915 and an M.S. in 1916. She taught economics at Berkeley and then at Bryn Mawr College. She served on the War Labor Policies Board from 1918 to 1919 and the Minimum Wage Board of the District of Columbia from 1920 to 1921. She married Otto Beyer in 1920 and had three sons. Following her career in the Labor Department, she was a consultant for several years to the State Department and in her mid-80s remained active in the Overseas Education Fund, in the League of Women Voters, and on the National Democratic Committee.

National Labor Relations Board Women in Top Positions

Besides chairperson BETTY SOUTHARD MURPHY (p. 340) the National Labor Relations Board has had five other women in top positions, dating back to the NLRB's beginning in 1935.

Named as the first directors of two of the new NLRB regional offices were ELINORE MOREHOUSE HERRICK in the East (New Jersey, eastern New York, and Connecticut) and ALICE M. ROS-SETER in the West (San Francisco). Ms. Herrick, a graduate of Antioch College, held the post until 1942 and settled more than 7,000 cases involving more than 1 million workers. Ms. Rosseter remained as director for seven years in the San Francisco office.

It was 40 years (1975) before another woman, NATALIE PANNES ALLEN, was named to head the San Francisco office, which processes the greatest number of cases among the NLRB's 31 regional offices. Ms. Allen, a Phi Beta Kappa graduate in economics from the University of Chicago, was the only current woman regional NLRB director until 1976, when WINIFRED "PEGGY" MORIO was appointed to direct the New York City office. Ms. Morio, a native New Yorker, received her LL.B. from Fordham University Law School.

In 1975 chairperson Murphy announced the appointment of ENID W. WEBER as an associate executive secretary of the NLRB. Ms. Weber has substantial responsibility for managing the flow of cases through the Board's decision-making process—from receipt to final decision. Ms. Weber holds both a B.A. and an M.A. in economics from the University of California and San Francisco State College, respectively. She grew up in Cuba but fled with her family to Miami, Florida, at the time of the Castro takeover. Ms. Weber became the NLRB's highest-ranking employee of Spanish heritage.

Organizer of Administration of Child Labor Organization, 1938–47

BEATRICE MCCONNELL was chosen in 1938 by Secretary of Labor FRANCES PERKINS (p. 331) to implement the long-hoped-for laws regulating child labor. The Fair Labor Standards Act of 1938 set a minimum age of 16 for employment in factories producing goods for interstate or foreign commerce and limited employment of children in other occupations to 14- and 15-year olds, outside of school hours; a minimum of 18 years was set for persons in work found especially hazardous. As chief of the Industrial Division of the Children's Bureau from 1935, Ms. McConnell was overseer of these laws from 1938 to 1946. From 1946 to 1958 she was chief of the Division of State Services in the Bureau of Labor Standards and from 1958 to 1962 the Bureau's assistant director. She then became deputy director of the Women's Bureau until 1964. Ms. McConnell, born in 1894 in Sherrard, West Virginia, received her B.A. (Phi Beta Kappa) from the University of Wisconsin in 1921 and an M.A. in labor economics from Simmons College in 1922. She was executive secretary of the Pennsylvania Consumers League from 1923 to 1925, joined the Pennsylvania department of labor in 1925, where she served in the women and children's division until 1935, and served as technical adviser to several ILO conferences in the 1930s and '40s. A member of the National Committee for Children and Youth, she helped plan both the 1950 and the 1960 White House Conferences on Children and Youth.

Only Woman Regional Director of War Manpower Commission and Assistant Secretary of Defense for Manpower

ANNA ROSENBERG HOFFMAN, in 1942 an experienced mediator in New York City and State labor disputes, was appointed by President Franklin D. Roosevelt to be one (and the only woman) of the 11 regional defense coordinators, a post she held until 1945. She devised a system of labor priorities in industry that have since been applied elsewhere, and recruited wartime workers—in one case refusing to fill a large West Coast order for workers until the company assured her it did not discriminate against blacks. Born in 1902 in Hungary, she emigrated to New York at the age of 10. At Wadleigh High School, in Manhattan, when the students went on strike against compulsory military training, she organized a political club and took part in arbitrating the strike. In 1924 she opened an office as a consultant in public relations and labor mediation. By the '30s she was known as a successful mediator often called upon by Mayor Fiorello La Guardia and Governor Roosevelt and respected by both labor and management. From 1936 to 1942 she was regional director of the Social Security Board, with a preponderance of women employees working with her. After World War II, President Harry S. Truman appointed her Assistant Secretary of Defense with the task of coordinating manpower activities in the Pentagon. She served in this post, the highest held up to that time by a woman in the national military establishment, from 1950 to 1952. After that assignment she returned to her private consulting work in New York City. Divorced from her first husband, she married Paul G. Hoffman in 1962. She received the Medal of Freedom in 1945 and in 1947 became the first woman to be decorated with the U. S. Medal for Merit.

First Woman Attorney to Argue Before the Supreme Court for the National Labor Relations Board

Labor lawyer RUTH WEYAND (see also "Women in Law and the Justice System," p. 349) went before the Supreme

Court in 1944 to argue for the National Labor Relations Board (NLRB) in a case that would prevent an employer from offering a wage increase to employees if they would abandon the union. She won. It was the first case presented for the NLRB before the Supreme Court by a woman attorney. Since then, Ms. Weyand has argued 10 cases before the Supreme Court and 40 cases before the U. S. Court of Appeals, the majority of them labor cases. She was born in 1912 in Grinnell, Iowa, where her parents were teachers. Her career began in 1932, when she graduated *cum laude* from the University of Chicago Law School at 20. As a member of a Chicago law firm, she provided legal counsel to those investigating violence that occurred during a Chicago steel strike in 1937. From 1938 to 1950 she was an attorney for the National Labor Relations Board, from 1950 to 1965 was in private practice, and since 1965 has been associate general counsel for the International Union of Electrical, Radio, and Machine Workers, AFL-CIO. Perhaps her most important case involving women workers was *Gilbert* v. *General Electric* (Fort Wayne, Indiana)—a case filed in 1972 under Title VII of the Civil Rights Act on behalf of *all* U.S. women employees, challenging discriminatory denial of sickness and accident benefits during absence because of pregnancy. In December 1976 the Supreme Court ruled in this pivotal case for all private employers in the nation, 6–3. Ruth Weyand sees it as the most disastrous court decision affecting women in 50 years. To fight it by means of new legislation, she has formed the Coalition to End Discrimination Against Pregnant Workers. Ms. Weyand is also representing plaintiffs in a number of other Title VII cases and equal-pay cases pending in the federal courts, and serves with the American Civil Liberties Union Women's Rights Project (see also "Women in Law and the Justice System," p. 357).

**Second Director of Women's Bureau
First U.S. Woman on ILO Governing
Body**

FRIEDA SEGELKE MILLER, the second
director of the Women's Bureau
(1944–53), attended four conferences
of the International Labor Organization,
in Geneva, Switzerland, and in 1946 became the first woman to represent the
United States on the governing body of
the ILO and a member of the committee
that carried out negotiations for bringing
the ILO into the United Nations. Ms.
Miller, born in 1890 in LaCrosse, Wisconsin, grew up in her grandparents'
home and received her B.A. from Mil-
waukee-Downer College, followed by
four years of graduate work as a fellow
in economics at the University of Chicago. From 1916 to 1917 she taught social economics at Bryn Mawr College.
Her involvement in labor began in 1918,
when she became the executive secretary
of the Philadelphia branch of the
Women's Trade Union League, a position she held until 1923, when she went
to the International Conference of Working Women, held in Vienna, and spent a
year in Europe studying labor conditions.
From 1924 to 1926 she was a factory inspector for the New York City Joint
Board of Sanitary Control of the ladies'
garment industry, from 1929–39 director of the Division of Women in Industry
in New York State's labor department,
and until 1942 industrial commissioner
for the state. During her tenure in the
Women's Bureau, she was particularly
concerned with the readjustment of
women workers after World War II. She
has opposed the Equal Rights Amendment (as did FRANCES PERKINS, p. 331),
because in her view it would take away
all the hard-won industrial gains for
women.

**Connecticut Assemblywoman Third
Director of Women's Bureau**

ALICE KOLLER LEOPOLD, in 1949 the
first woman from her district elected to
the Connecticut Assembly, wrote the
state's equal pay and minimum wage
bills, both of which were passed. In 1950
she was elected Connecticut secretary of
state and served on a federal commission
to study a means of achieving a sounder
relationship between federal and state
governments. President Eisenhower appointed her director of the Women's Bureau in November 1953, and, concurrent
with that position, in 1954 appointed her
assistant to the Secretary of Labor to
plan and carry out a program, for the
benefit of women workers. During her
tenure, she discussed the Equal Rights
Amendment at conferences and came
out in favor of protective legislation.
Born in 1909 in Scranton, Pennsylvania,
Alice Koller entered the personnel field
after graduation from Goucher College,
in 1927, and married Joseph Leopold in
1931. The mother of two sons, she established her own toy manufacturing
business in 1946.

Co-Authors of the Equal Pay Act

The Equal Pay Act, passed by the U. S.
Congress on June 10, 1963, prohibited
"discrimination, on account of sex, in the
payment of wages by employers engaged
in commerce or in the production of
goods for commerce" and provided for
"the restitution of wages lost by employees by reason of any such discrimination." Although its terms were applicable to both men and women employees, it was intended to aid the
woman worker and resulted from almost
100 years of effort to establish a federal
standard of equal pay for equal work.
Seen as a milestone in women's progress
toward full economic opportunity, it was

amended in 1970 to prohibit discrimination against women in federally assisted programs and in administrative, professional, and executive employment, and "to extend the jurisdiction of the U. S. Commission on Civil Rights to include sex."

Its co-authors were BESSIE MARGOLIN, then associate solicitor in the U. S. Department of Labor, and MORAG McLEOD SIMCHAK, then chief of the Equal Pay–Age Discrimination Branch of the Women's Bureau.

Bessie Margolin was graduated from Yale Law School in 1933 and was an attorney with the Tennessee Valley Authority from 1933 to 1939. She joined the staff of the solicitor, U. S. Department of Labor, in 1939, as assistant solicitor in charge of Supreme Court and appellate legislation—the first woman to attain this post, which she held for 20 years. From 1962 to 1970 she was associate solicitor in charge of litigation, and it was during the early part of this period that she shared with Morag Simchak the major responsibility for the writing and passage of the landmark legislation. The recipient of several awards, including the Federal Women's Award in 1963, Ms. Margolin now teaches on the faculty of George Washington University.

Prior to becoming chief of the Equal Pay–Age Discrimination Branch of the Women's Bureau, Department of Labor, a job she held from 1963 to 1971, Morag McLeod Simchak was special assistant to the director of the Women's Bureau (1961–63). Born in 1914 in England, Ms. Simchak worked for the Agency for International Development (AID) of the U. S. State Department after leaving the Department of Labor in 1974. She also has worked with the United Nations Relief and Rehabilitation Administration (UNRRA) and as chief of the Women's Division of the UN Information Office.

First Woman Named Assistant Administrator of Wage and Hour and Public Contracts Division, Department of Labor

CLARA F. SCHLOSS, a specialist on the minimum wage, gained her expertise in 20 years of continuous research for the Department of Labor, beginning in 1950. Following her appointment as the first woman to be assistant administrator of the Wage and Hour Division, in June 1963, she prepared statistical data on the then newly passed Equal Pay Act of 1963. This assignment culminated in the adoption by the U. S. Congress of the 1966 Fair Labor Standards Act amendments that provided minimum-wage protection for millions of men and women workers; for many months of congressional proceedings the integrity of Clara Schloss's division data was of key importance. In 1970 Ms. Schloss became an economic consultant on minimum-wage legislation to the AFL-CIO. She also worked with the labor committees of both the Senate and the House on the 1974 amendments to the Fair Labor Standards Act, which brought minimum-wage protection to some of the lowest-paid workers in the country, including domestics, and in 1977 gathered the facts necessary for updating the minimum wage law, including recommendations for raising the minimum wage and including an automatic adjustment provision to ensure that low-wage workers will receive an above-poverty wage.

One Woman's Firsts in the Federal Mediation and Conciliation Service

A native of Gloucester, Massachusetts, SORINE A. PRELI began work with the FMCS in 1952 as a secretary with a GS-5 rating. She proceeded to move up through the ranks over the next 25 years and became the first woman to reach a top executive position within the FMCS, as associate director of the Office of Administration and assistant director for budget and financial management (a GS-15 rating). Ms. Preli is also the Federal Women's Program coordinator and the Spanish-Speaking Program coordinator for the FMCS. Married and the mother of two sons, she was the first woman to receive an award for Outstanding Performance from the FMCS and also its first nominee for the Federal Women's Award.

First Black Named to Be Assistant to Director of Women's Bureau

Having served as secretary of the New York State department of labor from 1956 to 1958, DOLLIE LOWTHER ROBINSON in March 1961 was appointed special assistant to the fourth director of the Women's Bureau, ESTHER PETERSON (see "Women Activists, Heroes, and Humanitarians" p. 724). Ms. Robinson was the first black to hold the position. Ms. Robinson, who received her LL.B. from New York Law School, from 1941 to 1951 was an organizer for the Amalgamated Clothing Workers of America and educational director of the Laundry Workers' Joint Board. She served on the New York State Laundry Minimum Wage Board, on many other state and city boards, as director (1968–70) of the Department of Educational Affairs of the A. Philip Randolph Educational Fund, and as director of Political Education and Voter Registration for Minorities for the New York State COPE, AFL-CIO. A member of the executive board of the NAACP and of the American Labor Education Service, she teaches at Brooklyn College and is a recipient of the Sojourner Truth Award of the Association of Business and Professional Women.

First Economic Analyst to Become Director of the Women's Bureau

MARY DUBLIN KEYSERLING, associate director of the Conference on Economic Progress, a national research organization, and a consulting economist in private practice with her husband, Leon H. Keyserling (chairman of the Council of Economic Advisers in the Truman administration), was appointed director of the Women's Bureau, U. S. Department of Labor, by President Lyndon B. Johnson in 1964. She held the post until 1969. Ms. Keyserling received her B.A. from Barnard College and studied at the London School of Economics and Columbia University. From 1933 to 1938 she taught economics and statistics at Sarah Lawrence College (Bronxville, New York) and from 1938 to 1941 was general secretary of the National Consumers League. A leading authority on child care, she has more recently directed a project for the National Council of Jewish Women on day care needs and services, resulting in the widely quoted report *Windows on Day Care,* published by the Council in 1972. Her contribution led the 1977 U. S. Congress Joint Economic Committee's compendium of papers entitled *American Women Workers in a Full Employment Economy.*

First U.S. Woman Labor Attaché

The first woman appointed a U.S. labor attaché, MARGARET L. PLUNKETT served in The Hague from 1962 to 1967, and in Israel from 1967 to 1971. A long-time federal employee, she had been on the staffs of the Women's Bureau and the Bureau of Labor Statistics of the Department of Labor and had served as labor adviser in the U.S. technical assistance mission to Israel in 1953 and 1954. Ms. Plunkett holds a doctorate from Cornell University.

Federal Mediation and Conciliation Service Women Mediators as of June 1977 and Their Duty Stations

Nancy Fibish, national representative, Washington, D.C.

Ruth Carpenter, San Francisco, Calif.

Magdalena Jacobsen, San Francisco, Calif.

Bonnie Graczyk, Santa Ana, Calif.

Phyllis Schectman, St. Louis, Mo.

Rosemary LeBoef, Chicago, Ill.

Julia Greer, Detroit, Mich.

Christina Sickles, Philadelphia, Pa.

Sally Swerbilov, East Orange, N.J.

Eileen Hoffman, New York, N.Y.

Carol Holter, New York, N.Y.

Recipient of Two Fulbright Scholarship Grants Becomes Federal Mediator

NANCY CONNOLLY FIBISH has been a mediator with the Federal Mediation and Conciliation Service (FMCS) since 1968. Prior to her appointment, she did graduate work in labor relations at the University of Chicago. Awarded a Fulbright scholarship to study at the University of Strasbourg (France) Institute of Labor and a second Fulbright to teach American studies at the University of Strasbourg's School of Foreign Studies, while in France she also studied working and living conditions of Algerian migrants employed in the mining industry of eastern France, working with the University's Institute of Labor and the French Department of Health. In 1974 to 1975 she was a congressional fellow, assigned first to the Senate Labor and Public Welfare Committee and subsequently to that of Congressman Joseph L. Fisher (D., Va.). The author of *A Mediator's View of Federal-Sector Labor Relations* (1974) and numerous articles on the subject of mediation, Ms. Fibish continues to work in the Washington, D.C., office of the FMCS.

First Black Woman Director of the Women's Bureau

ELIZABETH DUNCAN "LIBBY" KOONTZ, director of the Women's Bureau from 1969 to 1973, was the first black woman to hold the position. On January 30, 1969, she was appointed U.S. delegate to the United Nations Commission on the Status of Women, also the first black woman to serve in that capacity. In 1972 she became deputy Assistant Secretary of Labor and special counselor to the Secretary for women's affairs. A former president of the National Education Association (its first black president), she initiated its conference on Critical Issues in Education, seeking to eliminate discrimination against women, minorities, and the handicapped. Ms. Koontz, born in 1919, received a B.A. from Livingstone College (North Carolina) in 1938 and an M.A. in elementary education from Atlanta University in 1941, did graduate work at Columbia and Indiana universities, and received training in special education for the mentally retarded at North Carolina College. Dr. Koontz is assistant superintendent of public instruction for North Carolina and chairs the National Commission on Working Women.

First Woman to Head Wage and Hour Division of U. S. Department of Labor

LUZ M. VILLARIÑO, named director of the Caribbean Office of the Wage and Hour Division of the U. S. Department of Labor in 1970, is stationed in Puerto Rico and is responsible for enforcing the Fair Labor Standards Act and other laws concerning payment of wages in a geographical area covering Puerto Rico, the U.S. Virgin Islands, and the Canal Zone. She has been able to develop and maintain a close working relationship with both labor and government officials, and her office has ranked high in the amount of back-wage monies collected for employees per case hour of time utilized. Prior to 1970 Ms. Villariño on a six-month assignment to Guatemala for the Organization of American States prepared a minimum wage-setting system, which was put into effect and has since been operating successfully; on a two-month assignment to Honduras took a leading part in drafting a minimum wage bill that became law and has proved effective; participated in a labor administration seminar in Santiago, Chile; and was an instructor on wage and hour programs with the Pan American Union, in Washington, D.C.

Seventh Director of the Women's Bureau the Highest-Ranking Hispanic Woman in the U. S. Government

During her term as director of the Women's Bureau, June 1973 to March 1977, CARMEN ROSA MAYMI was the highest-ranking Hispanic woman in the federal government. Born in 1938 in Santurce, Puerto Rico, she received a B.A. in Spanish and an M.A. in Education from De Paul University, and began her career as an employment counselor with the Migration Division of the Commonwealth of Puerto Rico in Chicago. In 1965 she went to work for the Chicago Committee on Urban Opportunity as assistant director of the Montrose Urban Progress Center; from 1966 to 1968 served as a community services specialist directing programs for Indians and migrants in the Office of Economic Opportunity, Great Lakes Region; and later worked on OEO-funded projects related to model housing and service to Indian reservations and migrant programs. As director of the Women's Bureau, Ms. Maymi traveled extensively to provide linkages with unions, women's groups, and minority organizations, and served as a liaison with government agencies regarding the status of women, particularly

with the U. S. Department of Labor on the International Women's Year.

Senior Labor Economist Influential in Uniting Women Union Leaders

LUCRETIA DEWEY TANNER, senior labor economist with the Federal Mediation and Conciliation Service (FMCS) since 1974, in a 1971 article, "Women in Labor Unions," in the *Monthly Labor Review* attempted to quantify the number of leadership positions of women in unions, using the Bureau of Labor Statistics listing of elected and appointed positions, to show the relative change over a 10-year period. The article, widely circulated among trade union women, assisted in the formation of the Coalition of Labor Union Women (CLUW). It was followed by a second article, using similar methods, published in 1974. Ms. Tanner received her B.A. from the University of Connecticut in 1962, and an M.A. in industrial relations from the University of Wisconsin in 1964, and was a research assistant with the Service Employees International Union (SEIU) from 1965 to 1968, an analyst for the Industrial Union Department, AFL-CIO, from 1966 to 1968, and assistant director, Economic Security Program, for the American Nurses Association from 1968 to 1969. Since 1969 she has worked for the federal government, first with the Bureau of Labor Statistics, then with the Pay Board, and since 1974 with the FMCS.

First Black Woman to Be a Federal Mediator

JULIA L. GREER, born in 1936 in Madison, Georgia, received her higher education at Wayne State Labor and Industrial School and Wayne State University, in Detroit, Michigan. After a career as a grievance processor with the Communications Workers of America and as president of Local 4010, Michigan Bell Telephone Company, she was hired by the Federal Mediation and Conciliation

Service (FMCS) in January 1975 as a mediator trainee. After training periods in Washington, D.C., Philadelphia, and Cleveland, she was promoted to FMCS commissioner in April 1976, becoming the first black woman to achieve that position. She is currently stationed in Detroit, Michigan.

Top Women in the U. S. Department of Labor as of June 1977

Carin Clauss, solicitor

Alexis Herman, director of the Women's Bureau

Janet Norwood, deputy commissioner, Bureau of Labor Statistics

Eula Bingham, assistant secretary for Occupational Health & Safety

First Woman to Be Named Solicitor in Department of Labor

At 38, CARIN A. CLAUSS became the first woman to hold the U. S. Department of Labor's top legal post. She was appointed by President Carter in February 1977. As associate solicitor for fair labor standards in the Department since 1971, she supervised all litigation under federal minimum-wage, overtime-pay, equal-pay, and age-discrimination laws, and advised the Secretary of Labor on related legislative and policy matters. As solicitor, she directs all of the Labor Department's legal activities, including litigation, rule-making, and advisory-opinion services, under more than 130 federal labor laws and executive orders. Ms. Clauss won recognition for her successful arguments in precedent-setting court suits under the Equal Pay Act of 1963 and the Age Discrimination in Employment Act of 1967. Born in Knoxville, Tennessee, she won a four-year scholarship to Vassar College and in 1960 received her B.A., followed by an LL.B. from Columbia University Law School in 1963. She first joined the Labor Department as an attorney in 1963. Her many awards include the Young Federal Lawyer Award in 1970, the Labor Department's Distinguished Career Service Award in 1976, and the Federal Women's Award, also in 1976.

First Woman to Head the Occupational Safety and Health Administration, U. S. Department of Labor

EULA BINGHAM, nominated by President Carter in March 1977 to be Assistant Secretary of Labor for Occupational Safety and Health, became the first woman to hold the position. She is responsible for setting and enforcing workplace safety and health standards under the Occupational Safety and Health Act of 1970. Prior to her appointment as Assistant Secretary of Labor, Ms. Bingham served from 1972 as associate director of the Department of Environmental Health, University of Cincinnati School of Medicine, having taught in the Department since 1961 (among her courses were physiology for engineers and the biological effects of air pollutants and chemical carcinogens). She has been a member of numerous federal and national advisory groups, including the Food and Drug Advisory Committee and the Labor Department Advisory Committee on Carcinogens, and was chairperson of the Labor Department Standards Advisory Committee on Coke Oven Emissions. Among her affiliations is the Society for Occupational and Environmental Health, of which she has been vice-president since 1975. Ms. Bingham was born in Covington, Kentucky, and received a B.S. degree from Eastern University, Richmond, Kentucky, in 1951 and M.S. and Ph.D. degrees in zoology from the University of Cincinnati in 1954 and 1958. She has three daughters.

First Woman Appointed Chairman of the National Labor Relations Board

BETTY SOUTHARD MURPHY (p. 333), a graduate of American University's College of Law in 1958, became an attorney for the NLRB writing briefs and presenting arguments to obtain enforcement by the Court of Appeals. (The National Labor Relations Board was set up in 1935 as the regulatory agency to enforce the Wagner Labor Relations Act, which guarantees the right to unionization and collective bargaining.) Following this job, she was a partner in a Washington, D.C., law firm specializing in labor, corporate, and administrative law and gained experience representing both international unions and employers. She served as wage-hour administrator in the Department of Labor directing enforcement of the Fair Labor Standards Act, the Equal Pay Act, and other legislation affecting 73 million workers. In 1975, President Gerald Ford appointed her chairwoman of the five-member National Labor Relations Board, the first woman to sit on the Board or to be chairperson.

Youngest Director of the Women's Bureau

The success ALEXIS M. HERMAN has had in helping minority women enter professional white-collar jobs in Atlanta and Houston resulted in her nomination as head of the Women's Bureau of the Department of Labor at age 29. She was sworn in on March 23, 1977, becoming the youngest director in the Bureau's 57-year history. As director, she is responsible for policies and standards to promote and advance the welfare of working women. Her particular concerns are teen-age women's unemployment, the older woman's reentry into the job market, apprenticeship and skilled blue-collar jobs, and women's needs for flexible working hours. Ms. Herman earned her B.A. in sociology from Xavier University, in New Orleans, and did graduate work in counseling and guidance at the University of South Alabama, before venturing to her home town of Mobile, Alabama, where she was a social worker until hired in 1972 for a pilot program, being set up in Atlanta by the Southern

Regional Council, aimed at finding professional jobs in the private sector for minority women. Her group placed the first black woman in the Bell System's management training program and put minority women into retail management training and into banking. In 1974, Ms. Herman was appointed national director of the Minority Women Employment Program, a 10-city effort. She received the Outstanding Young Person in Atlanta Award (1974) and Atlanta's First Woman Award from the Negro Business and Professional Women's Club (1976).

Early Labor Activist in California

KATHERINE PHILIPS EDSON (1870–1933), whose father, a surgeon and a member of the Ohio Constitutional Convention in 1873, was a proponent of women's rights. She moved from Ohio to California in 1890, living first on a ranch and then in Los Angeles. In 1912 she was elected to the L. A. Charter Revision Committee and was the first woman member of the National Municipal League. Also in 1912, Governor Hiram Johnson appointed her to study California labor problems. She received student nurses' complaints of 12-hour days and successfully lobbied the state legislature to correct the situation. Her greatest contribution, however, was in minimum-wage legislation for women. She analyzed the pioneering statutes of Massachusetts and of Victoria state in Australia, and adapted them to California conditions. Her bill established an Industrial Welfare Commission of five members with the authority to investigate working conditions of women and children, to set minimum wages, maximum hours, and working standards. Ms. Edson was nominated to the Commission and served on it for 18 years. During World War I she was a federal mediator for California, helping to enforce proper labor conditions for workers on navy contracts. In 1927 she became chief of the state Division of Industrial Welfare.

First Woman to Be Commissioner of Labor and Industry in Maine

For 25 years MARION E. MARTIN was the state of Maine's first woman commissioner of labor and industry, from 1947 to 1972. Born in 1900, in Kingman, Maine, she studied at Wellesley College, was graduated from the University of Maine, and did graduate work in law at Yale University and Northwestern. From 1931 to 1935 she served as a state representative and from 1935 to 1939 as a state senator, was a member of the Republican National Committee from 1936 to 1947 and assistant chairwoman from 1937 to 1947. During the time she was commissioner of labor and industry she also served as a member of the Industrial Accident Commission and was chairperson of the Board of Elevator Rules and Regulations, of the Board of Boiler Rules and Regulations, and of the Construction Safety Board. She was an adviser to the ILO conference in 1958 and 1959, and from 1971 to 1972 was a member of the National Commission on State Workmen's Compensation Laws. In 1974 she was appointed to the advisory committee of the Maine Apprenticeship Council, has served since 1952 on the National Safety Council, becoming its vice-chairperson in 1974, and has been on the American Arbitration Association panel since 1972.

First Woman to Hold the Highest-Ranking Labor Post in the District of Columbia

SARAH HERMAN NEWMAN served as chairwoman of the Minimum Wage & Industrial Safety Board of the District of Columbia from January 1967 to May 1976, the first woman to hold this highest-ranking labor position in the government of the U.S. federal capital; executive secretary of the National Consumers League from 1962 to 1972, and since 1972 its vice-chairwoman. Ms. Newman, born in 1907 in Austria, emigrated to the United States in 1912, became a U.S. citizen in 1923, and in 1926 received a B.A. from Goucher College. Married to Simon Newman, she is the mother of three children.

First Asian-American Appointed to California Apprenticeship Council

In 1976, VIRGINIA GEE became the first Asian-American appointed to the California Apprenticeship Council, on which she is a commissioner and chairs both the Equal Opportunities in Apprenticeship Committee and the Appeals Hearing Board. In 1977 she was appointed by Secretary of Labor Ray Marshall to the Federal Committee on Apprenticeship, the first Asian-American on this committee also. A native San Franciscan, third-generation Chinese-American, and 37-year-old wife and mother, Ms. McGee works for Stanford University as an employment service coordinator in the Personnel Office. She was instrumental in the hiring of the first women maintenance trainees in the university's steam plant, and is a staunch advocate of women's right to seek non-traditional jobs. In 1974 she was the first Chinese-American woman appointed to be a chief line assigner with Pacific Telephone Company and in 1976 was the first woman keynote speaker at the Los Angeles Joint Training Committee completion ceremonies. She is affiliated with the International Brotherhood of Electrical Workers.

Top State Labor Posts (Appointed) Held by Women, 1977

Colorado: JURITA SMITH, member of State Industrial Commission

District of Columbia: PAULA L. JEWELL, chairwoman, Minimum Wage and Industrial Safety Board

Ohio: HELEN W. EVANS, director, Department of Industrial Relations

Wisconsin: VIRGINIA B. HART, chairwoman, Department of Industry, Labor, and Human Relations

GOVERNMENT LABOR OFFICIALS, OTHER NATIONS

First Woman to Be Labour Minister in Britain

MARGARET GRACE BONDFIELD (1873–1953) became Britain's first woman cabinet member in 1929 as Minister of Labour, and also the first woman member of the Privy Council. She had already achieved several other firsts: In 1923 she became the first woman chairperson of the Trades Union Congress (TUC). After she was elected Labour MP for Northampton, also in 1923, her speech to the House of Commons was described as the "first intellectual speech" ever given by a woman in the House of Commons. Born in Furnham, Somerset, to parents with strong radical interests, she was apprenticed at 14 to a draper and at 19 went to London, where she found a job as shop assistant. Shocked by the 74-hour work week for below-subsistence wages offered to women, she joined the National Union of Shop Assistants and did a two-year survey of working conditions for the Women's Industrial Council while continuing to work. She joined the Independent Labour Party and was the only woman delegate to the Trades Union Congress in 1898. She was a cofounder in 1906 with MARY MAC-ARTHUR (p. 292) of the National Federation of Women Workers and became its chief woman officer in 1921. In the meantime, she had been elected to the Parliamentary Committee of the Trades Union Congress. She continued her trade union work through all the years in government and after retiring in 1938. Her autobiography, *A Life's Work,* appeared in 1949.

Youngest Member of the House of Commons in Britain's 1929–31 Labour Government

Daughter of a Fifeshire miner and granddaughter of a pioneer member of the Fife Miners' Association, JENNIE LEE was born in 1904 in Lochgelly, Fifeshire, Scotland. With the aid of scholarships, she put herself through the University of Edinburgh, receiving an M.A. in education in 1926 and an LL.B. in 1927. While still a student, she took part in Britain's general strike in 1926, working at strike headquarters in Edinburgh and raising funds in the summer in Ireland. For two and a half years she taught school in an impoverished mining village. However, seeing no hope of eliminating the causes of her students' poverty by teaching, she eagerly accepted the opportunity to be an Independent Labour Party candidate for North Lanark in a by-election in 1929, and won a seat in Parliament at the age of 24, becoming the youngest member of the House of Commons in the 1929–31 Labour Government. In 1929 she studied the Austrian socialist youth movement in Vienna, and in 1930 she visited industrial and mining centers in the Soviet Union. In October 1931 a coalition government was elected, and Jennie Lee lost her seat. In 1934 she married Aneurin Bevan, also a Labour M.P., who later became Minister of Health in Prime Minister Clement Attlee's government (1945). She spent her years out of office making frequent lecture tours of the United States, Europe, and Russia, often ignoring the official itinerary. For example, she addressed cotton workers in the southern United States who were trying to form an integrated union, and miners in Kentucky. During World War II it was her responsibility to keep production lines moving in the Ministry of Aircraft Production. She was reelected in 1945 (from Crannock) and served in several ministries until 1970, when she was created a life peeress, Baroness Lee of Asheridge.

Labour MP Most Responsible for British Equal Pay Act

BARBARA ANNE CASTLE, in 1937 one of the youngest members ever elected to the St. Pancras Borough Council, in London, in 1945 became a Labour Member of Parliament. She carried through the British Parliament the legislation giving women the right to equal treatment with men in pay and other terms and conditions of employment. Passed in 1970, the Act came fully into effect at the end of 1975. Ms. Castle has held several cabinet positions: Minister of Overseas Development (a new department), 1964; Minister of Transport, 1965–68 (she was the first woman to hold this post and was responsible for the most comprehensive Transport Act in British history); Secretary of State for Employment and Productivity, 1968–70; and Secretary of State for Social Services, since 1974. Born in 1911 in Bradford, England, she campaigned, as a member of the Independent Labour Party Guild of Youth, in the general election of 1929. She received a scholarship to and was graduated from St. Hugh's College, Oxford. A journalist in London in the 1930s, she became active in local government and held a post in the Ministry of Food during the early years of World War II. As an active member of the Fabian Society, she helped prepare its recommendations on social insurance, many of which were embodied in the Beveridge Report. She is co-author of *Social Security*, published in 1943. She is married to Lord Castle of Islington.

Early Finnish Female Cabinet Minister an Active Trade Unionist

MIINA SILLANPAA (1866–1952) was one of the first women elected to the Finnish Parliament, serving four terms between 1907 and 1947, and became Finland's Assistant Minister for Social Affairs in 1927. She was the chief editor of women's trade unionist papers at various periods, beginning in 1905 and continuing into the 1920s. She was twice elected a member of the Helsinki city council, 1919–25 and 1930–36, was chairwoman of the Social Democratic Women's League, in 1931 made a study trip to the United States, and at the end of her career was chairwoman of the Board of the cooperative movement "Elanto."

Ombudsman in Sweden's Central Organization for Salaried Employees

MAY-BRITT CARLSSON, ombudsman (hearer of grievances) for Sweden's Central Organization for Salaried Employees, 1966–76, and a member of the Advisory Council to the Prime Minister on Equality between Men and Women, 1972–76, studied sociology, political science, law, and journalism. Her specialties are labor market policy, social and family policy, and health and welfare questions. In 1976, she was appointed Labor Attaché for a three-year tour of duty at the Swedish Embassy in Ottawa, Canada. Attending a conference in Canada, Ms. Carlsson spoke of what equality of opportunity has meant so far in Sweden: parenthood insurance has replaced maternity insurance; it is required that half the jobs resulting from government grants to depressed regions be allocated to women; and educational leave is a right for any employee with six months continuous service or a total of 12 months with the same employer in the previous two years.

Specialist on Women Worker Questions Is Head of Committee on Equality Between Men and Women

Sweden's ANNA-GRETA LEIJON was elected chairperson in 1974 of the Advisory Council to the Prime Minister on Equality Between Men and Women. Born in 1939 in Stockholm, she studied at that city's university, and in 1964 started to work for the Labor Market Board. In 1970, she became head of section there, dealing with female labor questions, legislation on older workers, and employment adaptation for certain groups of workers. Always active in the Social Democratic Party in local politics, she was county councilor from 1970 to 1973, was elected to the Riksdag (Parliament) in 1974, and was appointed Minister Without Portfolio with a special responsibility for labor questions, in the Cabinet. In 1976, the Social Democratic Party lost the election and Ms. Leijon resigned her cabinet post but remains a member of the Riksdag.

From Union Clerk to Swedish Cabinet in Twenty-four Years

Sweden's GERTRUDE SIGURDSEN became Minister for International Development Cooperation in 1973—a post she held until 1976. Born in 1923 in Tuanberg, in the county of Sörmland, in 1949 she moved to Stockholm and took a job as a clerk at the Confederation of Swedish Trade Unions. She was active in the Swedish Commercial Employees Union, and from 1964 to 1973 was secretary for family policy in the information department of the Confederation of Swedish Trade Unions. In 1969 she was elected to the Riksdag (Parliament) as a member of the Social Democratic Party and is a member of the party's Executive Committee. Since 1976, she has been the political adviser to the president of the Confederation of Swedish Trade Unions.

Three Major Firsts for Puerto Rican

On January 3, 1969, the governor of Puerto Rico appointed the first woman ever named to a cabinet post: JULIA RIVERA DE VINCENTI, the first woman Secretary of Labor of the Commonwealth of Puerto Rico. The appointment was widely publicized, for it was felt that the labor post was the most sensitive and difficult in the cabinet. Her second "first" was becoming the first Puerto Rican, man or woman, to be appointed as a member of the U. S. Mission to the United Nations, in September 1972. On

October 11, 1972, she took the podium in the General Assembly to counter statements made by Cuba's representative, that Puerto Rico was a subjugated colony of Yankee imperialism, by pointing out that island government itself, not Washington, had raised agricultural wages and stimulated the ailing sugar industry. Ms. de Vincenti, holder of a Ph.D. from Cornell University in management and collective bargaining, who was then still secretary of labor for Puerto Rico, also defended herself against the Cuban representative's charge that she was a puppet with no knowledge of her job. When she spoke, she was wearing a bright red pants suit; it was the first time, U.N. officials believed, that a woman had addressed the General Assembly while wearing pants (another first).

First Woman to Be Minister of Labor in Colombia

MARÍA ELENA JIMÉNEZ DE CROVO, born in Medellín, Colombia, in 1935, after following a career as a journalist was elected to the Colombian State Assembly and then the Senate, where she served as vice-president, and she went to London as General Consul of Colombia before serving as Minister of Labor and Social Security, the first woman to hold the position. Her book *Hacia la Reforma Social*, published in 1976, describes her work as Minister of Labor. She was very active in promoting producers cooperatives and seeking other ways of alleviating poverty. In 1976 she was appointed Ambassador to Mexico, the third woman in Colombia to achieve ambassadorial rank, and also represented Colombia as a government delegate to the International Labor Organization Conference, in Geneva, Switzerland.

Prominent Leader in the German Labor Movement

ANKE FUCHS, a member of the German Metal Workers Union, in the Federal

Republic of Germany, in 1977 became Parliamentary Secretary of State in the Federal Ministry of Labor and Social Affairs. It is thought by many that she could someday become Germany's first woman chancellor.

Many "Firsts" for Leaders in the Women's Bureau of Japan

The Director-General of the Women's and Minors' Bureau in the Japanese Labor Ministry (appointed in 1974) is MAYUMI MORIYAMA, born in 1927 in Tokyo. Ms. Moriyama became the first woman to hold a responsible post in a prefectural bureau when she was appointed, in 1962, as head of the Labor Inspection Section of the Labor Standards Bureau. She was also the first woman to head the Employment Statistics Division (1967–70) and the first woman to head the Labor Policy Division in the Labor Policy Bureau. Another first for the Women's and Minors' Bureau belongs to HISAKO TAKAHASHI, born in 1927, who became the first woman to head the Industrial Home Work Division of the Labor Standards Bureau (1970–74) before taking up her present position in the Women's and Minors' Bureau as head of the Women Workers Division, in 1975.

Head of Canadian Women's Bureau Is Deputy Chief of Delegation to International Women's Year Conference in Mexico City, 1975

SYLVIA M. GELBER, a graduate of the University of Toronto and Columbia University, and Director of Canada's Women's Bureau, Department of Labour, from 1968 to 1975, served as deputy head of the Canadian delegation to the IWY Conference. One of Canada's major contributions to the conference, widely supported by other countries, was the proposal to retain the U.N. Commission on the Status of Women, which was on the verge of being dissolved. Also in 1975, Ms. Gelber challenged Canadian insurance companies for their frequently unequal treatment of women policyholders, who are often charged higher premiums and receive inequitable pensions and benefits; she pointed out that their data are based on U.S. rather than Canadian figures. The third director of the Women's Bureau, founded in 1967 (the first two directors stayed only a short time), Ms. Gelber, born in 1910, retired in December 1975 but has continued to serve as a consultant to the Department of Labour during a reorganization of its operations affecting women.

THE INTERNATIONAL LABOR ORGANIZATION OF THE UNITED NATIONS

Chilean Achieves Three Firsts on the International Front

In February 1960, ANA FIGUEROA, of Chile, became the first woman to hold the position of Assistant Director-General of the International Labor Organization (ILO) in its 41-year history. Ms. Figueroa had already achieved other notable firsts: In 1951, as Chile's envoy extraordinary and minister plenipotentiary to the United Nations, she was the first woman chosen to head a main committee of the General Assembly (the Social, Humanitarian, and Cultural Com-

mittee). In 1952, when she was named Chile's alternate delegate, she was the first woman ever to sit on the U.N. Security Council. Born in Santiago, Chile, in 1908, she graduated from the University of Chile in 1928 and became a high school teacher and principal. Following World War II, she studied in the United States at Columbia University and at Colorado State College. From 1947 to 1949 she was general supervisor for the high school system of Chile. A member of several teachers organizations, including the Union of Chilean Teachers, Ms. Figueroa was also an advocate of women's rights, a member of the board of the YWCA, and president of the national committee that obtained women's suffrage in Chile. From 1949 to 1950 she administered the Women's Bureau in the Ministry of Foreign Affairs. She retired from her ILO post in 1967, and died in April 1970.

Highest-Ranking Woman International Labor Official

NOBUKO TAKAHASHI, of the Japanese Labor Insurance Appeals Board, in January 1976 was named Assistant Director-General of the International Labor Organization, becoming the ILO's highest-ranking woman. Ms. Takahashi, born in 1916 in China, was graduated from Tokyo Woman's University with a de-

gree in liberal arts and from Wareda University in sociology. Active in labor politics since 1945, she has held many posts in the Women's and Minor's Bureau of the Ministry of Labor in Japan. She attained the rank of director-general of the bureau in 1955, and in 1974 joined the Labor Appeals Board. A participant in several U.N. and other international conferences and seminars, in her present post she is responsible for programs concerning women workers and advises the ILO's director-general both in this field and an ILO activities in Asia. The author of numerous articles, including "Women's Wages in Japan and the Question of Equal Pay," in the *International Labor Review*, 1975, she is married and the mother of four children.

74 Countries That Sent Women Participants to the International Labor Conference, Sixtieth Session, Geneva, Switzerland, in 1975, the International Women's Year

*Algeria
Argentina
Austria
*Belgium
*Byelorussian SSR
Bolivia
*Bulgaria
Cameroon, United Republic
Canada
Cyprus
*Colombia
Costa Rica
*Cuba
*Czechoslovakia
Denmark
Egypt
**Finland
*France
*Germany, Federal Republic
German Democratic Republic
Greece
Guyana
*Hungary
*India
Indonesia
Iraq
*Iran

*Israel
Italy
Jamaica
Japan
Kenya
Kuwait
Lebanon
*Liberia
Libyan Arab Republic
Malaysia
**Malta
*Mauritania
Mauritius
Mexico
*Mongolia
*Netherlands
*New Zealand
Nicaragua
Niger
Nigeria
Norway
Pakistan
Peru
*Philippines
Poland
Portugal
*Romania

Senegal
Sierra Leone
Spain
**Sri Lanka
**Sweden
Switzerland
Syrian Arab Republic
*Trinidad & Tobago
Uganda
*Ukrainian SSR
United Kingdom
United States

U.S.S.R.
*Uruguay
Venezuela
*Yugoslavia
Zambia

Women participants on observer delegations:

Angola (transitional government)
Papua, New Guinea
Surinam

(*) indicates a woman (or women) were delegates or substitute delegates.
(**) indicates a woman was a cabinet minister.
In all other cases, the women participants were advisers.

74 Countries That Sent Women Participants to the International Labor Conference, Sixtieth Session, Geneva, Switzerland, in 1975, the International Women's Year

Israel	*Algeria
Italy	Argentina
Jamaica	Austria
Japan	**Belgium
Kenya	**Byelorussian SSR
Kuwait	Bolivia
Lebanon	*Bulgaria
Liberia	Cameroon, United Republic
Libyan Arab Republic	Canada
Malaysia	*Cyprus
*Malta	**Colombia
**Mauritania	Costa Rica
Mauritius	*Cuba
Mexico	**Czechoslovakia
Mongolia	Denmark
**Netherlands	Egypt
*New Zealand	**Finland
Nicaragua	*France
Niger	*German Federal Republic
Nigeria	German Democratic Republic
Norway	Greece
Pakistan	Guyana
Peru	*Hungary
*Philippines	*India
Poland	Indonesia
Portugal	Iraq
*Romania	Iran

8

Women in Law and the Justice System

By Janice M. Horowitz

Brenda Feigen Fasteau, consulting editor

At an early age I observed that lawyers as individuals exercised far greater influence over the course of history in recent times than persons identified with any other occupation. Those who shaped the American states, Thomas Jefferson, James Madison, James Monroe, Abraham Lincoln, Franklin Roosevelt; the father of communism, Karl Marx, and Nicolai Lenin; the architect of Indian independence and non-violence, Mahatma Gandhi, were all lawyers. The majority of those who have run all three branches of our government, executive, judicial, and legislative, have been lawyers. In big business, the majority of the presidents of Fortune's list of 50 largest corporations and 500 largest corporations are lawyers.

These are the words of RUTH WEYAND, associate general counsel of the International Union of Electrical, Radio, and Machine Workers, AFL-CIO (see "Women in the Labor Movement and Organizations," p. 334). In 1945 she argued the first decision by the Supreme Court that employees could lawfully solicit union membership on company property. Her sentiments reflect the motivation of many women around the world, who have gone to law school or read for the law in the offices of established legal practitioners over the past century. Some of them have sought the opportunity to influence politics and government by running for office or taking appointive positions in councils and bureaus of nations, states, and cities. Others have gone the business route—working for major corporations, using their legal skills to set up businesses for themselves, or building their own lucrative private law practices. Still others have used their knowledge of the law in the cause of women's rights, civil rights, or on behalf of ethnic minorities or society's displaced and abused.

Many noted women lawyers appear elsewhere in this book. Their records and achievements are described in accounts of women in government in activist movements (including the Women's Movement), in business and industry, even in religion. Thus, Dr. PAULI MURRAY, civil rights lawyer who in 1977 became an Episcopalian priest, can be found in the chapter "Women in Religion" (p. 385). And BETTY SOUTHARD MURPHY, an attorney who was appointed the first chairwoman of the National Labor Relations Board in 1975, like Ruth Weyand, appears in "Women in the Labor Movement and Organizations" (p. 340).

In general, however, women who have concentrated on law as a career are recognized in this chapter even though their achievements may also be linked to such realms as housing (CARLA ANDERSON HILLS, PATRICIA ROBERTS HARRIS), equal opportunity (ELEANOR HOLMES NORTON), or birth control and copyright (HARRIET FLEISCHL PILPEL).

Today, more and more young women enter law school every year. The opposition and discrimination they still face is nothing to what it was in the 19th and early 20th centuries. Nonetheless, as attorney and author HELENE SCHWARTZ writes in *Lawyering* (1976), sex discrimination against women law students persisted through the 1960s. Once out of school most women still had to fight to avoid being channeled into areas considered "proper"—especially family and child law—and they were paid on a lower scale relative to their male coworkers. Ms. Schwartz credits the growth of the Women's Movement for awakening her to "what she might hope to accomplish as a lawyer"; one of her accomplishments was to represent the Chicago Eight in their successful appeal against their conviction following the protests at the Democratic Convention in 1968 during the Vietnam War.

In addition to describing the accomplishments of U.S women attorneys, law professors, judges, and so on, this chapter notes such outstanding women lawyers as West Germany's highest-ranking judge, GERDA KUGER NIELAND, and Dr. SAMIA SADEEK RASHED of Cairo University, who is using her knowledge to help change the laws affecting women in Egypt.

In a final section, we take a brief look at women working in the realm of law enforcement—with special emphasis on the United States, where, in 1972, Title VII of the Civil Rights Act was extended to state and local government employers and women in city after city began moving onto the streets as active police officers.

"Life Faces Portia" *Ms.* magazine editors headlined a 1974 article on how feminists are changing the law. More and more, these feminists are themselves part of the justice system.

JANICE M. HOROWITZ *was graduated cum laude from Barnard College, Columbia University, in 1975 with a major in political science, and earned her M.Sc. in 1976 from the London School of Economics. She is now a researcher, freelance writer, and aspiring journalist. Her interest in the law was sparked when she worked as a paralegal aide on welfare-related problems in the Community Law Office of East Harlem, New York.*

Consulting editor BRENDA FEIGEN FASTEAU, *a widely recognized feminist lawyer, co-founded the Women's Rights Project of the American Civil Liberties Union* (see also p. 356).

SOME WHO LED THE WAY

First Woman Admitted to the Bar in the United States

ARABELLA "BELLE" MANSFIELD in 1869 at Mount Pleasant, Iowa, became the first woman admitted to the bar in the United States. Born Arabella Aurelia Babb in Iowa on August 23, 1846, she attended public schools and in 1863 entered Iowa Wesleyan University with her brother, who was two years her junior. They received their degrees three years later in a graduating class of three; Belle Babb was the valedictorian and her brother the salutatorian. Later he apprenticed in a law office and encouraged her to do the same. She did, and continued to study there after her marriage to John Mansfield, an Iowa Wesleyan faculty member, who subsequently joined her in her pursuit of a legal education. The couple applied together for admission to the bar.

The examiners noted that Ms. Mansfield had passed the examination with high honors, giving "the very best rebuke possible to the imputation that ladies cannot qualify for the practice of law." Belle Mansfield was not automatically admitted to the Iowa bar along with her husband and other male candidates, however, since the Iowa Code provided only that "any white male person" was admissible. But later that same day Judge Francis Springer, known for his liberal views, cleared the way through statutory interpretation of this language to mean that "the affirmative declaration [for male persons] is not a denial of the right of females."

Belle Mansfield later received a master of arts and a bachelor of laws degree from Iowa Wesleyan and became an educational leader. In 1872–73 she studied more law in London and Paris, including courses on Hindu and Mohammedan law, equity, and "the science of jurisprudence." Essentially scholars, both Mansfields taught at Iowa Wesleyan and later at Indiana Asbury University, which became DePauw University. Neither ever practiced law. Ms. Mansfield died on August 1, 1911. —Adapted from an article by Aleta Wallach, *Women's Rights Law Reporter*, April 1974

First Woman Admitted to Israeli Bar

ROSA GINOSSAR (GINZBERG), born in 1890 in Russia and trained in the law in Paris, settled in Palestine determined to practice law there. She was responsible for the removal of the ban against women's admission to the bar of Israel and was the first woman attorney to practice in the country. During World War II, Ms. Ginossar became actively engaged in promoting the immigration and adoption of orphaned children.

First Female Member of the Bar, New South Wales

The Honourable MARY GAUDRON has been deputy president of the Australian Conciliation and Arbitration Commission since 1974. Born in 1943, she was the first woman member of the Bar, Council of New South Wales.

"Personhood" Winners

In the United States

In 1920 ADA LEWIS SAWYER had to fight her way to become the first woman in Rhode Island admitted to the bar. Although she had been a senior partner in the Providence firm of Gardener, Saw-

yer, Cottam, Gates, Day, and Sloan, Ms. Sawyer had nonetheless been denied entry to the bar because only the word "person," not the specific pronoun "she," was mentioned in the rules on admission. Due to Ms. Sawyer's perseverance, the

Rhode Island Supreme Court in June 1920 finally ruled that a woman was, in fact, considered a person. The statement handed down said that "the word 'person' contained in the rules regulating the admission of attorneys and counsellors should be construed to include a woman as well as a man."

In Canada

Judge EMILY MURPHY heard her first case in an Alberta courtroom and, on July 1, 1916, found the prisoner at the bar guilty. The prisoner's attorney promptly challenged her authority to pass sentence. "You are not even a person," he said, and when Judge Murphy urged him to develop his argument, he noted that under a British common law decision of 1876, women were "persons in matters of pains and penalties but not in matters of rights and privileges." The Provincial Supreme Court denied the attorney's appeal. But the principle had not been established anywhere else in Canada. Judge Murphy decided that she would try. She discovered Section 60 of Canada's Supreme Court Act, which said that if five interested persons petitioned the government for a ruling on a constitutional point, the government would have to respond. She lined up the five—herself, NELLIE McCLUNG, LOUISE McKINNEY, HENRIETTA MUIR EDWARDS, and Dr. IRENE PARLBY. In March 1928, the Supreme Court took the question under consideration. Five weeks later, the Court ruled that "women, children, criminals and idiots" were not legally "persons." The five appealed to the British Privy Council, then Canada's court of last resort. Nineteen months later, on October 18, 1929, they won. "The word 'persons' includes members of the male and female sex," the Council pronounced.

Blind Woman Receives Law Degree

Blind and partially deaf as a result of having been given excessive oxygen when

One of the First Women to Represent Defendant in a Murder Case

When ELIZABETH BLUME-SILVERSTEIN, born in 1892 in New Jersey, initially ventured into the field of law, she had to work for nothing. She later became the first woman lawyer in Essex County to practice law on the same basis as men attorneys—opening a law office, employing help, trying cases before juries—all considered freakish for a woman. In 1917 she was the first woman to represent a defendant in a murder case in New Jersey. In 1932 she was the first woman in the 12th Congressional District to serve as a delegate to a national presidential convention. Her more than 60 years of law experience have culminated in a successful Newark, New Jersey, chancery and general practice. "I had to fight my way up the ladder all the way," she says. "I couldn't even earn a dollar a week in those [first] days because I was a girl."

A "First" 50 Years Ago and Still Practicing

There may be scores of women lawyers around the country who were "firsts" in their areas, but it is doubtful that there are more than a few who equal VIVIAN SIMPSON, the first woman admitted to the bar of Montgomery County, Maryland. That was in 1927. AT 74, in 1978 Ms. Simpson was still in active practice in the county seat of Rockville, a country town when she graduated from George Washington University Law School, but now the center of one of the richest suburban counties in the United States. Ms. Simpson has other "firsts" to her credit: first woman member of the State Workmen's Compensation Board; first woman head of the Montgomery County Bar Association; and first woman secretary of state for Maryland.

born prematurely, LINDA SNYDER, despite all obstacles to her education, in May

1977 was graduated from Georgetown University Law School, Washington, D.C. Ms. Snyder credits her father with providing her with vital support; he frequently accompanied her to classes and served as "part reader, part book finder, part law professor." When she started law school, she says, people asked her how she was "going to do this or that." Now she would "like those people never to have the excuse to say that to anybody else again," she told a reporter for the *Washington Star.*

PRACTICING ATTORNEYS—PRIVATE, CORPORATE, PRO BONO

Top Copyright Lawyer and Birth Control Champion

HARRIET FLEISCHL PILPEL is a highly respected practitioner in two diverse fields of the law: the right of women to control conception, and the rights of authors, actors, and actresses to get full rewards for their talents.

Her activities in the first category spanning forty years have won her the gratitude of millions of women, for whom she fought and won most of the important legal battles over birth control. She continues to fight today for women's rights to abortion. In 1973 she received the SIECUS Award for "an enduring contribution to the advancement of knowledge about human sexuality," and in 1974 the Margaret Sanger Award for distinguished service to Planned Parenthood; as a young lawyer, she worked with MARGARET SANGER (see "Women Activists, Heroes, and Humanitarians," p. 720).

Her other legal expertise in the fields of copyright, authors' royalties, and acting contracts has protected hundreds of people in the arts and entertainment fields. Although she does not talk much about her clients, among them have been Erich Maria Remarque, James Thurber, and Edna Ferber, for whose estate she is trustee and sole executor. Ms. Pilpel is a member of the firm of Greenbaum, Wolff & Ernst. She joined the firm in 1936 after being graduated from Columbia Law School, where she was second in a class of 269.

Ms. Pilpel, Vassar '32, is now past the qualifying age for Social Security. However, she has not curtailed her activities, only "ameliorating the conditions" of her daily tasks by taking the time to walk more than two miles daily from her apartment to her midtown office instead of riding to work. Weekends she spends with her husband, Robert, on their farm in Connecticut, where their four children and grandchildren visit.

First and Second Woman Partners, Major National Capital Law Firm

Washington, D.C.'s first woman law partner in a major firm, CAROLYN AGGER, brilliant, cigar-smoking wife of former Supreme Court Justice Abe Fortas, is senior partner at Arnold & Porter, one of the most powerful and prestigious law firms in the capital and in the nation.

BROKSLEY ELIZABETH LANDAU, born in 1940 in California, a first-rank graduate of Stanford University Law School in 1964, and editor-in chief of the *Stanford Law Review,* is the second woman to become a partner in any of the top Washington firms. She too became associated, in 1968, with Arnold & Porter.

She Shattered Protective Clauses

SYLVIA ROBERTS, in her various capacities as president of NOW Legal Defense and Education Fund, chairperson of the Committee of Rights for Women of the American Bar Association, and a member of the Equal Employment Opportunity Law Committee, has litigated precedent-setting cases in sex discrimination in employment. In 1969 Ms. Roberts appeared as counsel in the first Title VII case of the Federal Equal Rights Amendment to reach federal courts; she acted against the Southern Bell Telephone and Telegraph Company, which allegedly had denied employment to a woman because of her sex. In this case, Ms. Roberts was successful in establishing that an employer could not lawfully refuse to consider a woman for a certain position by classifying the position as a "man's job" through protective clauses, unless there were a reasonable basis to support a claim that all, or substantially all, women could not perform that job safely and efficiently. Ms. Roberts won for the plaintiff $30,781, which included the overtime the woman would have earned had she been hired for the job for which she had applied. Ms. Roberts defended the same principle at the University of Pittsburgh when she served the first preliminary injunction to protect an academic woman's job in *Dr. Sharon Johnson* v. *University of Pittsburgh*. A scholarship student at Tulane College of Law, Ms. Roberts got her LL.B. in 1956. She is in private practice in Baton Rouge, Louisiana.

Activist Lawyer in Case That Legalized Abortion

SARAH RAGLE WEDDINGTON, born in 1945 in Abilene, Texas, was graduated from Vernon (Texas) High School two years early and, at the age of 16, entered McMurry College in Abilene. A magna cum laude graduate in 1965, she began her studies the same year at the University of Texas Law School. Even though working to pay all expenses, she was graduated in the top fourth of her class only 27 months later. Ms. Weddington served for three years as assistant reporter to the American Bar Association Special Project to Reevaluate Ethical Standards and practiced for a year as assistant city attorney for Fort Worth, before resigning to start her private law practice and to prepare for oral arguments before the United States Supreme

Court in *Roe* v. *Wade*. This landmark case, which Ms. Weddington won in 1972, allowed women the right to choose whether or not to have an abortion. In 1972 Weddington was elected the first woman to represent Travis County in the Texas house of representatives. She is now serving her third term and is dean of the Travis County delegation to the legislature. The *Texas Monthly* magazine named her one of the ten best legislators in Texas in 1975.

Pro Bono Clearinghouse Founder

In 1969 DEBORAH SEIDEL, University of Chicago Law School graduate and the executive director of the Council of New York Law Associates, embarked on one of the most intensive efforts attempted to that date to involve the organized bar and private firms with public interest law. The 1,600-member Council initiated a Public Interest Resource Center to serve as a clearinghouse for young lawyers who wanted to do pro bono work. The plan called for major firms to commit 250–500 hours each year to handle major public interest suits. Deborah Seidel hoped the Center might counteract young lawyers' fears about doing public work "too quickly" because it could "interfere with their careers in private law firms." Happily, Ms. Seidel today can claim that the response to this public/private admixture has been "uniformly positive."

International Family Lawyer

German HELGA STOEDTER, a specialist in family law and former president of the International Federation of Women Lawyers, has devoted her legal career to initiating and supporting legislation to aid women to achieve job equality and to remove the stigma against children born out of wedlock. She has traveled and spoken throughout the world comparing women's legal and social status to help spread advances in women's equality from one country to another.

She Won at McSorley's and in the Classifieds

FAITH SEIDENBERG, a past vice-president of the National Organization for Women, a director of the National Board of the American Civil Liberties Union (ACLU), and legal counsel for the Congress of Racial Equality (CORE) in the critical years 1965–66, was victorious in one of the most publicized early cases brought against bars for restricting women, *Seidenberg* v. *McSorley's* (the renowned New York City alehouse). Ms. Seidenberg was also one of three lawyers who brought suit requiring the U. S. Equal Employment Opportunity Commission to outlaw separate "male" and "female" jobs in newspaper job listings. A graduate of Syracuse University College of Law in 1954, she is a partner in Seidenberg & Strunk, Syracuse, New York.

Egyptian Law Professor/Activist

Dr. SAMIA SADEEK RASHED, a professor in the Private International Law Department, Cairo University, is an active supporter of legislation governing the status of women and family life in Egypt. Married, with two children she holds a B.A. (honors) in law and a Ph.D. (honors) in international law from Cairo University and spent one year on a research scholarship at Yale University.

Housing Lawyer, First Woman to Head Legal Service Program in New York City

For 15 years NANCY E. LEBLANC, a Yale Law School graduate (LL.B., 1957), has been the director of Mobilization for Youth Legal Services, making her the first woman to head a legal service program in New York City. Although her involvement in legal services is very broad, her area of special concern is housing problems of the poor. She successfully directed and developed the MFY's role in designing cooperative housing on the Lower East Side of New York. Ms. LeBlanc says that "the development of decent low-cost housing for poor people, under their own control, is something I have worked on for many years."

First Woman President of Arlington County Bar Association

Engaged in her own private practice in northern Virginia since 1959, BETTY A. THOMPSON was the first woman president of the Northern Virginia Trial Association from 1970 to 1971. She also was the first woman president of the Arlington County Bar Association from 1971 to 1972, even though at that time membership at Arlington County was 99 per cent male.

Leading Advocate for a Woman's Right to Determine Own Name

PRISCILLA RUTH MACDOUGALL, former assistant attorney general, Wisconsin, now staff counsel for the Wisconsin Education Association Council in Wisconsin, has participated in virtually every major case since 1972 regarding determination of married women's names. Her article for the *Women's Rights Law Reporter,* "Married Women's Rights to Their Own Surname," spearheaded the names movement. The booklet that she co-authored, "For Women Who Wish to Determine Their Own Names After Marriage" serves as the basic guide to the names issue. Ms. Macdougall claims that the United States law on names follows the common law of England, and under common law, a woman can retain her own name in marriage and change her name at will. In changing one's name back to the premarriage name, or to any other name, Ms. MacDougall advises filing a change of name with federal and state agencies, creditors, banks, and employers. Ms. Macdougall, regularly called upon for consultation, continues to develop the movement in many states and on many fronts, including the names of our children irrespective of the parents' marital status.

Co-Founder of the ACLU Women's Rights Project and of National Women's Political Caucus

BRENDA FEIGEN FASTEAU, born in 1944, is a cum laude graduate in mathematics from Vassar College who earned her law degree at Harvard and has become one of the leading activist women lawyers in the United States. She also has done graduate work in political science at Columbia University, where she was Honorary President's Fellow, 1977–78. Since 1974 she has been a partner in Fasteau and Feigen, attorneys at law, in New York City, and has served as a consultant, the U. S. Department of Justice, Civil Rights Division. In 1972 with RUTH BADER GINSBURG (p. 362) she co-founded the American Civil Liberties Union Women's Rights Project and served for over two years as its coordinator and its first director, preceding KATHLEEN WILLERT PERATIS (below). Widely known for her commitment to the Women's Movement, she also co-founded the National Women's Political Caucus and has been active in NOW (1971 national vice-president, legislation, and member of the Board and the executive committee), and in the Women's Action Alliance, Inc., and Working Women United. She has made numerous radio broadcasts and TV appearances and has published widely; her diverse publications include a report of the Columbia University Law School Equal Rights Advocacy Project, "The Legal Status of Women under Federal Law," co-authored with Ruth Bader Ginsburg, and articles in *Ms.* magazine and the *Village Voice*.

Director of the ACLU Women's Rights Project

KATHLEEN WILLERT PERATIS, 33, became director of the Women's Rights Project of the American Civil Liberties Union in 1974. The Women's Rights Project of the ACLU is the largest women's litigation unit in the country, with a staff of six and an annual budget of $300,000. A graduate of the University of Southern California (1966) and the USC Law School (1969), Ms. Peratis has written briefs in many sex discrimination cases, including four cases before the Supreme Court involving issues of pregnancy discrimination and Social Security discrimination. She is former counsel for the Los Angeles Chapter of the National Organization for Women, incorporator of the legal defense program of the L.A. Women's Center, and has been coordinating counsel for Stewardesses for Women's Rights from 1974 to the present. Married and the mother of two young children, Ms. Peratis combined career and family responsibilities by bringing both of her children to work with her until they were four months old. The children slept in a cradle in her office.

Attorney Instrumental in Privacy Act

HOPE EASTMAN, cum laude graduate of Harvard Law School (1967), as associate director of the American Civil Liberties Union's Washington office, was a prime mover in the ACLU's representation of the victims of the Watergate bugging—the Association of State Democratic Party chairmen, a number of individual chairmen, and two employees of the Association whose telephone was tapped inside the headquarters of the Democratic National Committee. This notorious bugging case led to the ACLU's initial plunge into the movement to impeach Richard Nixon. The enactment of the 1974 Federal Privacy Act occurred largely because of Ms. Eastman's efforts. To her, "privacy is the 20th-century equivalent of freedom." Overall, Ms. Eastman tries to impede government snooping into private action. Ms. Eastman was a co-founder of the Women's Legal Defense Fund, an early organization established to provide free legal services specifically for women.

Women's Rights Project Clinical Director

SUSAN DELLER ROSS joined the other prominent women at the American Civil Liberties Union Women's Rights Project as the clinical director in 1975. She has published extensively; her book *The Rights of Women* appeared in 1973. Prior to her ACLU involvement, Ms. Ross, in 1973–74, was a founding partner of the women's law firm Bellamy, Blank, Goodman, Kelly, Ross, and Stanley in New York; this firm, one of the first of its kind, is now defunct. Ms. Ross has been a guest speaker on women's rights and employment discrimination before many law associations and has testified in numerous congressional hearings.

General Counsel, Washington's Legal Services Corporation

A summa cum laude graduate of Columbia Law School in 1963, ALICE DANIEL is general counsel for the Legal Services Corporation, Washington, D.C. Active in civil rights and prisoners' rights in 1975 she was deputy legal affairs adviser to Governor Edmund G. ("Jerry") Brown, Jr., in California, where she specialized in civil liberties and criminal law aspects of policy and planning; served briefly as interim director of the ACLU of Northern California; and was western regional director, Prisoners' Rights Project, the NAACP Legal Defense Fund, 1970–72. She has also taught contracts and criminal law and is a member of the California and New York bars, admitted to practice before the United States Supreme Court.

Consumer Affairs Specialist

Unlike any woman before her, MARY GARDINER JONES in 1975 became the vice-president of Western Union Telegraph Company in the consumer affairs department. She has galvanized the department by using consumer complaints as the basis for change in company policy. Ms. Gardiner began this job at 55 years of age, after attaining a distinctive reputation in law and public affairs. She worked as the first woman attorney with Donovan, Leisure, Newton, and Irvine right after graduation from Yale Law School in 1948. She went on to practice for the Department of Justice's antitrust division, and then worked in a private firm where she engaged exclusively in trial and antitrust work for 14 years. In the 1960s, national recognition was bestowed on Ms. Jones as a consumer specialist when President Johnson appointed her the first woman member of the Federal Trade Commission.

Only Woman Wall Street Partner Without a Law Degree

On New Year's Day, 1971, CHRISTINE BESHAR became the first woman partner in a top Wall Street firm, Cravath, Swaine & Moore—without a law degree. Ms. Beshar, now a specialist in estates and trusts, started as a trial assistant in 1955 when she was asked to travel around the country as a litigator for her husband's New York City law firm. The following year she became the managing clerk and librarian for a New York City law firm and was exposed to various law tools and research methods. "The deeper I became involved," she says, "the more determined I became to become (a lawyer) myself." Many apprentices are admitted to the bar, as was Ms. Beshar, and become top lawyers. Rarely, however, do they become partners in a large firm.

Environmental Lawyer

KARIN SHELDON, born in the Pacific Northwest, is a young woman lawyer active in the U.S. alternative energy movement. Ms. Sheldon entered the University of Washington Law School at Seattle in 1967. She participated in what many environmentalists consider the most serious national challenge to the Atomic Energy Commission: the Bethesda hearings, an eight-month series of hearings on the safety of nuclear reactors. Ms. Sheldon states that she has "more than a professional interest in ecology." She believes that "the environment, in all its forms and relations, sustains us," and "the fundamental principles of ecology govern our lives, wherever we live, and that we must wake up to this fact or be lost."

Founder of San Francisco Public Interest Firm

Before becoming a lawyer, NANCY L. DAVIS was active in the civil rights movement (she organized and registered voters for the Mississippi Freedom Democratic Party in 1965). Now she is concentrating on remedying sex-based discrimination. Toward this end, she jointly founded the public interest firm Equal Rights Advocates Inc. in San Francisco, California. The firm concentrates on education and litigation and offers help to clients in need, without charge. At law school (Boalt Hall, University of California at Berkeley, LL.B., 1972), Ms. Davis was the first president of the Women's Association. She demanded the hiring of more women law professors and educated employers about discriminatory practices in order to press them to hire women graduates.

Attorney for POWER

SHERIBEL ROTHENBERG, a Chicagoan, graduate of Northwestern University School of Law (J.D., 1967), and senior trial attorney for the U. S. Equal Opportunity Commission in the Chicago regional office, is also a founder of Professional Women for Equal Rights (POWER). Ms. Rothenberg in 1974 tried a case against a major downtown club in Chicago, which allegedly acted in violation of the state constitution in denying females membership. An adverse decision was reached in this case, but four of the seven major Chicago clubs have admitted women to full member-

ship. Ms. Rothenberg is a frequent speaker on legal issues with special pertinence for women and the author of several publications, including "The Legal Status of Homemakers in Illinois," a part of the International Women's Year (IWY) study of all states in the nation, with MARIAN BARNES, Center for Women Policy Studies, Washington, D.C., 1977.

First Woman President of Chicago Council of Lawyers

The first woman president of the Chicago Council of Lawyers (1973–74), SHELI ROSENBERG is a junior partner specializing in real estate law at the large Chicago corporate firm of Schiff, Hardin & White. Ms. Rosenberg successfully juggled her work for the Council, her practice, and motherhood, staying home in suburbia with her children two days out of what she called her "nine-day week."

Head of Washington Women's Rights Project

MARCIA D. GREENBERGER heads the Women's Rights Project of the Center for Law and Social Policy, Washington, D.C. Her work in the areas of health care, law, and educational practices related to women extends beyond the scope of the Project itself. She was also the co-convener of the National Health Task Force of the Women's Agenda, is a member of the Joint Commission on Prescription Drug Use, and has been instrumental in the attempt to rectify problems in the distribution of birth control contraceptives—contending, with others, that warnings concerning the adverse side effects and contraindications of "the pill" should be clearly presented to its users to ameliorate its misuse. Ms. Greenberger was born in Philadelphia in 1946 and is a graduate of the University of Pennsylvania Law School.

Counsel to Vital ERA Commission

ELLEN LUFF, one of the few female attorneys in Annapolis, Maryland, has been on the Counsel to the Commission to Study Implementation of the Equal Rights Amendment in Maryland since 1974. Maryland, which had embraced the cause of the ERA three years prior to other states, was the showcase for states vacillating between the pros and cons of the ERA. As counsel to the Commission, Ms. Luff had to answer to anti-ERA groups who were disseminating false information that Maryland's ERA law forced women and men to sleep together in mental institutions, required women to be drafted into the National Guard, and held women criminally liable for support of their husbands. The Commission has been instrumental in researching, formulating, and pushing detailed bills through the state assembly, and making them known to nationwide ERA supporters and opponents alike. More than 50 of these measures have been passed since 1972. "If anyone can claim credit for that record, it is Ellen Luff" (*Juris Doctor*, 1976).

Co-Founder of Women's Law Center

EMILY JANE GOODMAN with ROBIN MORGAN co-founded New York City's Women's Law Center, staffed by volunteers, in order to get fundamental legal information to women. Ms. Goodman, attorney, and former *New York Times* editorial assistant, has turned her talents to breaking down the intricacies of the law into understandable language for the lay person. One of her first publications is *The Tenant Survival Book* (1972). Since Ms. Goodman's involvement with the Women's Law Center, she has focused her legal advice particularly on women's needs. In 1976 she published *Women, Money and Power*.

Founder of Equal Rights Advisors, Inc.

Working in San Diego, California, 32-year-old LYNN A. SCHENK is the founder and first vice-president of Equal Rights Advisors, Inc. The group handles sex discrimination cases for low-income women. Ms. Schenk, adjunct professor of law at the University of San Diego and an attorney for San Diego Gas & Electric Co., was also an originator and director of the Women's Bank. Influential in the Women's Movement, Ms. Schenk also serves on the state attorney general's Women's Rights Task in California.

Founder of Center for Women Policy Studies

MARGARET GATES, a founder and co-director of the Center for Women Policy Studies in Washington, D.C., is an attorney and adjunct professor at the Georgetown University Law Center. She has repeatedly been called to testify before Congress concerning women's issues and consumer affairs. In 1973 she and one other woman were called to make a statement to the Joint Economic Committee on Economic Problems of Women. She gave testimony before the House Subcommittee on Consumer Affairs in 1973, and again in 1974. Furthermore, her prolific pen attests to her industrious work for women's rights. Her recent publications include "Credit Discrimination Against Women: Courses and Solutions," *Vanderbilt Law Review* (April 1974); "Women and Policing: A Legal Analysis," *Rape and Its Victims: A Report for Citizens, Health Facilities and Criminal Justice Agencies,* Law Enforcement Assistance Administration (1975); and "Occupation Segregation and the Law," *Women and the Workplace,* University of Chicago Press, Chicago (1976).

She Speaks to the Offender

New York lawyer PAULINE FEINGOLD is the author of two publications on prisoners' rights—one a directory of services for former prisoners in New York State. Speaking directly to ex-offenders, and not merely about them, Ms. Feingold engages in her unique work in prison and post-prison reform as director of the New York State Coalition for Justice and Women in Criminal Justice. Previously, she was the first woman to chair the New York State Legislation Committee Citizens' Union.

Women Lawyers Breaking Ground for Housewives

In 1975 New York University's SYLVIA LAW and Rutgers' NADINE TAUB, researching and analyzing the subject of payment to housewives for work done in the home, got into the explosive area of examining the parallels between housework and involuntary servitude. Quick to disclaim any conclusions that might be drawn from these parallels, and pointing to the "voluntary" nature of the marital contract, the two law professors explained that the law as it now stands is archaic. Because it is based on the expectancy of an equal division of labor between the man as breadwinner and the woman as houseworker, no protection is provided the woman to ensure that she is adequately "supported" for her share of the work in the bargain. All solutions thus far proposed, ranging from a suggestion that men be required to pay a fixed percentage of their incomes to their wives to the idea that government stipends be paid to women for the care of children, have proved unfeasible. Professors Law and Taub are working to legislate basic changes in marital law that would, first of all, validate any contracts made between husband and wife relating to their income and division of labor and, second, require both husband and wife to contribute financially to the running of the household.

First Woman President of the Lawyers' Club of San Francisco

In November 1975 RUTH CHURCH GUPTA was named the first woman president in the 30-year history of the Lawyers' Club of San Francisco. She is especially sought after as a political educator in the field of women in financial and estate planning. Since 1955 she has served as the legislative advocate for the Cali-fornia Federation of Business and Professional Women. An advocate of environmental issues, she was in 1959 appointed by Governor Edmund G. Brown, Sr. to the Bay Area Water Pollution Control Board, and later to the State Water Quality Control Board. She is currently vice-chairperson of the Advisory Council of the Bay Area Air Pollution Control District, and chairperson of the Citizens for Clean and Quiet Transit.

Georgia Civil Liberties Lawyer

A practicing lawyer since 1961, MARJIE PITTS HAMES is engaged in full-time practice in civil rights in Atlanta, Georgia. Her involvement began when she was a volunteer attorney with the Georgia Civil Liberties Union abortion case, which set a Supreme Court precedent, *Doe* v. *Bolton* (1973). As lead counsel, she twice argued the case before the Supreme Court on behalf of the Civil Liberties Union. Out of this decision, which Ms. Hames considers her most important work, she and sympathizers in the medical community were instrumental in avoiding the passage of a "right-to-life statute."

First Lawyer to Head Consumers Union

A graduate of Yale Law School (J.D., 1953), RHODA HENDRICK KARPATKIN is the first lawyer to be executive director of the Consumers Union. Appointed in 1974, after serving 16 years as the Union's general counsel, she also has been a member of the Consumer Advisory Council of the City of New York and chairperson of the Special Committee on Consumer Affairs of the city bar association. Aspiring to move the Consumers Union "beyond the lab and into the legal battlefield," she hopes to get effective legal representation against fraud and misrepresentation of products sold to the public. She envisions having a large impact on "complaints processing and the general commercial conduct in a community, because every person who has a complaint would also be a potential litigant."

Full Partner in Black South African Law Firm

A full partner in a Durban, South Africa, law firm and secretary of the Durban Women's Federation (Black), ZUBEDA KASSIM SEEDAT has also been a lecturer in Bantu law at the University of Natal, where she got her B.A. and M.A. in anthropology and her LL.B.

First Black Chairwoman of the NAACP

MARGARET BUSH WILSON, a prominent St. Louis lawyer who has won numerous professional and civic awards for her work in aiding the black population of that city, was elected chairperson of the National Association for the Advancement of Colored People in 1975. Ms. Wilson comes from a long line of NAACP lawyers and administrators and her election to this position is the culmination of 10 years of work in the organization.

Californian Recipient of International Women's Year Award

In 1975, on behalf of the Queen's Bench, MILDRED W. LEVIN was awarded a certificate for Significant Contributions to International Women's Year 1975 Goals of Eliminating Discrimination Against Women and Improving the Status of Women. The award was for her work against rape and toward equal rights for women. Ms. Levin, as vice-president and director of the Queen's Bench Foundation, had prepared a study, "Victims of Rape," which culminated in beneficial changes in the treatment of victims by police and hospital personnel.

First Woman, First Black General Counsel for Motion Picture Association

The first woman, and the first black, general counsel for the Motion Picture Association of America is BARBARA SCOTT PRIESKEL. The Yale Law School graduate (LL.B., 1947) is in charge of censorship matters. She has been instrumental in initiating such landmark cases as *Freedman* v. *Maryland*, which limited the power of motion picture censor boards. A member of the President's Commission on Pornography and Obscenity, she is also among the founding members of the Media Coalition, organized in 1976 against the onslaught of obscenity legislation resulting from a Supreme Court ruling.

Associate General Counsel at Ford Foundation—the Youngest Officer

When SHEILA AVRIN McLEAN was named associate general counsel of the Ford Foundation in 1975, she became the only woman officer and the youngest officer at the Foundation. She was consultant for the publication *Reproduction and Human Welfare,* and a member of a consultant panel of the ethical, legal, and social implications of advances in biomedical and behavioral research and technology. Ms. McLean, born in Philadelphia, Pennsylvania, has an LL.B. from Yale Law School (1966).

Only Attorney Admitted to Practice in Both Japan and the United States

Japanese-born MICHIKO ITO CRAMPE, the only attorney admitted to practice both in Japan and the United States, began her career in international corporate law in 1972 when she was admitted to the Tokyo Daini Dengoshikai (Bar Association) and joined the law offices of Logan, Okamoto, and Takashima as an associate. In February 1976, while working for Whitman & Ransom, a New York firm, she was admitted to practice before the district courts for the southern and eastern districts of New York. Ms.

FEMALE LAW PROFESSORS

First Tenured Woman on Columbia Law Faculty

RUTH BADER GINSBURG, after being the first mother to attend Harvard Law School (she has two children), went on to become the first tenured woman professor at Columbia Law School. Recently she has also taught at Stanford. Her expertise as an academic and an activist, especially in the women's rights movement, is continually sought by her legal peers. Ms. Ginsburg was born in Brooklyn, New York, and attended Columbia University and Columbia Law School (LL.B., 1959), as well as Harvard. She has been involved in women's projects throughout the country and was the co-founder, with BRENDA FEIGEN FASTEAU (p. 356) of the American Civil Liberties Union Women's Rights Project, which she continues to serve as general counsel. In addition to arguing the landmark sex-discrimination cases, *Reed* v. *Reed* and *Frontiero* v. *Richardson et al.*, she co-authored a major sex-discrimination text with HERMA HILL KAY (below). "Ruth will make it to the Supreme Court" says Brenda Feigen Fasteau.

Youngest to Become Tenured Woman Law Professor at Berkeley

Immediately following her graduation in 1959 from the University of Chicago Law School, HERMA HILL KAY, born in 1934 in Orangeburg, South Carolina, was asked by the prestigious Boalt Hall Law School at the University of California at Berkeley to eventually succeed its long-time head BARBARA ARMSTRONG. Three years and voluminous publications later, Ms. Kay became the youngest woman to that time awarded tenure at Boalt Hall. She has also been a visiting professor at Harvard Law School (fall 1976),

Crampe was born in Tokyo in 1947 and received her education at the University of Tokyo.

and has co-authored a major 1974 work entitled *Text, Cases and Materials on Sex-Based Discrimination*, with Kenneth Davidson and RUTH BADER GINSBURG (above).

First Full-Time Woman Faculty Member at University of Alabama Law School

MARJORIE FINE KNOWLES, first tenured woman faculty member at the University of Alabama Law School, also serves as a program associate in the office of the university's president. A graduate of Smith College, she earned her Ph.D. in government from Radcliffe in 1962 and her law degree from Harvard in 1965. In 1978 she took a year's leave of absence from Alabama to serve as assistant general counsel, Office of the Secretary, the Department of Health, Education, and Welfare. Ms. Knowles, who was chosen one of the 10 Outstanding Young Women in America in 1976, says, "I do appreciate the efforts of those who are the first, the leaders, the only." She believes, however, that "women working together on boards, committees, or informally is a more significant achievement in many ways." To this end, she has served on the executive committee of the Southern Regional Council, the steering committee of the National Conference of Women and the Law, as chairwoman of the advisory committee of the ACLU Women's Rights Project, and has been an active participant in the National Women's Political Caucus, the Women's Action Alliance, and the Equal Rights for Women in Education Task Force. Among her many other activities, she is also a member of the editorial board of SIGNS: *Women in Culture and Society* (see "Women in Education, Social Sciences, and the Humanities," p. 424).

First Woman To Hold Endowed Chair on Yale Law School Faculty

At 26 years of age, in the mid-1950s, ELLEN ASH PETERS became Yale Law School's youngest faculty member and only woman member. The then dean, Eugene Rostow, said of her, "She has more than fulfilled our hopes." In 1963 Ms. Peters became the first woman to receive tenure at this esteemed law institution. Her legal writing and teaching focus on various aspects of the law of contracts, especially on the commercial law under the Uniform Commercial Code. Over a decade ago, Ms. Peters devised a legal writing on Article 2 of the Uniform Commercial Code that is still the starting point for serious study of method and pathology of modern sales codification. In 1975 Ms. Peters was appointed Southmayd professor, and became the first woman to be named an endowed chair.

Academic with Tenure

Professor VIVIAN BERGER was the first woman to have received tenure by "coming up through the ranks" at Columbia University Law School. After being graduated first in her law school class at Columbia University in 1973, and first from her college class at Radcliffe in 1966, she has consistently excelled in academia.

High-Ranking Academic and Public Interest Contender

Assistant dean HARRIET RABB is a public interest lawyer as well as a prominent lecturer and co-director of the Employment Rights Project at Columbia University. From 1969 to 1970 she was the special counsel to BESS MYERSON, then the commissioner of consumer affairs for New York City. Ms. Rabb has written numerous articles on fair employment, and has conducted employment litigation through her clinical seminar at Columbia University.

Activist Law Professor at Cleveland (Ohio) State University

A Phi Beta Kappa graduate of Swarthmore College in 1957, with an LL.B. from Yale in 1960, JANE MOODY PICKER was an associate in a general-practice law firm in Bangkok, Thailand, then joined the RAND Corporation in California as a member of the social science department, then was a Russian-speaking legal-medical guide in Moscow and Kiev for the United States Information Agency's "Medicine U.S.A." exhibit (1962). In 1964 she joined the Communications Satellite Corporation's international staff and later was a guest lecturer at the law schools of numerous foreign universities, speaking on "Legal Aspects of Outer Space." She practiced law with a Cleveland firm before becoming a lecturer at the Case Western Reserve University School of Law and later an associate professor and in 1975 a full professor at Cleveland (Ohio) State University College of Law. She is a member of many professional associations and has published widely in specialized journals.

First in International Law: Cairo

One of Egypt's foremost academics in the field of law, AISHA RATEB in 1970 became the first professor of international law at Cairo University. In 1971 she was named Egypt's second woman Minister of Social Affairs.

Dean of University of Miami Law School

In 1974 SOIA MENTSCHIKOFF was named dean of the University of Miami Law School. Her deanship was the culmination of over 25 years of university work. She was a post-war visiting professor at Harvard University (1946–47), and a professor of law at the University of Chicago from 1951 to 1974. A Columbia University graduate in 1937, Ms. Mentschikoff engaged in private practice in the late '30s and '40s, and she has worked on national legislation.

WOMEN LAWYERS IN GOVERNMENT, WORLDWIDE

Legal Adviser, Kuwait's Ministry of Foreign Affairs

A senior official in the Legal Department, the Ministry of Foreign Affairs, for the government of Kuwait, KAWTHAR AL-JOUA'N holds her B.A. and 1st Diploma for postgraduate work in law from Cairo University. She is also secretary-general of Kuwait's Women's Social and Cultural Society and first secretary-general of the Kuwaiti Women's Union.

Legal Adviser, National Bank of Greece

MARIA MIHOPOULOU, legal adviser to the National Bank of Greece in Athens, also serves as head of the community development project sponsored by the Greek alumni of American universities. She holds her M.Sc. in sociology from the University of Michigan, earned her law degree at the University of Athens, and is a member of the Athens bar.

Israel's Citizens' Rights Advocate

Born in Tel Aviv, Israel, and graduate of the Faculty of Law of the Hebrew University, Jerusalem, SHULAMIT ALONI was in 1974 a member of the eighth Knesset as head of the Movement for Citizens' Rights. In Israel, Ms. Aloni acts as an outspoken information source on matters concerning the citizen's rights in the state, social rights, and problems of church and state. She was formerly an editor of radio programs concerning law and civil rights. She has published three books and hundreds of articles on these subjects and she is a columnist for a daily and weekly newspaper, the *Yediot Aharonot* and *La'Isha* respectively.

Activist Mexican Government Lawyer

MARÍA PATRICIA KURCZYN VILLALOBOS, the divorced mother of one child, is legal adviser to the Federal Power Commission, Mexico, D.F. Also a professor of labor law at the National University Law

School, and ex-director of the Women's Federal Prison, Mexico City (1971–74), she has written extensively about women's prisons and about labor problems.

First Puerto Rican Woman to Pass Bar in New York

IRMA SANTAELLA began her career by being the first Puerto Rican woman in New York to pass the bar. Ms. Santaella went on to be chosen by Governor Carey as the chairperson for the New York State Human Rights Appeal Board. This appointment followed her work as founder of the Legion of Voters, Inc., in which Ms. Santaella had played an instrumental role in advising the late Senator Robert Kennedy and Senator Jacob Javits on the need to include Puerto Ricans in the provisions of the Voting Rights Act of 1965. By 1970 all literacy tests were abolished. In 1972 Governor Rockefeller said of her: "As leader of the Puerto Rican and Hispanic community of New York, she has been a strong force for advocating human and voting rights for members of her community."

Nation's First Black Woman Prosecutor

A graduate of Howard University College of Law in 1964, ANNE THOMPSON in 1970 became the first black woman prosecutor in the United States. From 1970 to 1972 she was a prosecutor in the township of Lawrence, New Jersey, and then became the prosecutor of Mercer County, New Jersey.

Prominent in International Law

Becoming the only woman member of the Commission on U.S.-Latin American Relations (1974) is one of RITA HAUSER's distinctions in the international political arena. Appointed by President Nixon in 1972 to a three-year vice-chairpersonship of the U. S. Advisory Commission in International Educational and Cultural Affairs, Ms. Hauser was also the U.S. representative on human rights, the United Nations, 1969–72 and a member of the advisory panel on international law of the Department of State, and became the only woman trustee of the International Legal Center. She is a partner at Stroock, Stroock & Lavan, New York.

First Woman on the FCC

The first female commissioner on the U. S. Federal Communications Commission, FRIEDA B. HENNOCK was sworn in July 6, 1948. Prior to assuming that position, she had been a partner in the New York law firm of Choate, Mitchell & Ely—the first woman partner in that prestigious firm, third oldest in the nation. Ms. Hennock, born in 1904 in Poland, immigrated to the United States with her family at the age of six. On completing her education in New York City public schools, she became interested in law and studied at night while working during the day to earn her living and gain legal experience. The youngest woman lawyer in New York when she was admitted to the bar in 1926, Ms. Hennock attracted attention for her skillful handling of spectacular criminal cases.

Highest-Ranking Woman, Board of Governors of the Federal Reserve System

The highest-ranking woman with the Board of Governors of the Federal Reserve System, JANET HART is an attorney who joined the Federal Reserve in 1958 as an assistant counsel in the Legal Division. She developed a rare expertise in understanding and implementing security credit regulations, one of the most socially and economically important of the Board's responsibilities and the most complex and difficult area of regulatory law. Prior to her appointment as director of the Division of Consumer Affairs on September 1, 1976, Ms. Hart was assistant director, Division of Supervision and Regulation, an appointment she received in 1968. Her work in the improvement of these regulations, and in the development of new ones, has assured that both borrowers and lenders in the area of security credit meet their responsibilities and that the public interest is protected. She received an LL.B. degree from Duke University Law School, where she was first in her class.

Highest-Ranking Career Employee Woman Lawyer in the Department of Justice

MARY CECILIA LAWTON was named deputy assistant attorney general in the Office of Legal Counsel of the Department of Justice on February 17, 1972, becoming the highest-ranking career employee woman lawyer in the Justice Department. Ms. Lawton, 36 when she was named to the job, joined the Justice Department after receiving her law degree from Georgetown University in 1960. She was first in her law class of 118 and the only woman.

Attorney to Justice Department to Cabinet: First Woman Secretary of Housing and Urban Development

CARLA ANDERSON HILLS, who chose the profession of law at the age of 12 and later earned her way through Yale Law School, became a prominent trial attorney in Los Angeles with her own firm by the age of 28, and acceded to two of the highest positions ever held by women in government before she was 50. In 1974 she was appointed assistant attorney general in the Justice Department's Civil Division, in charge of over 250 Justice Department lawyers in Washington, D.C., and 94 U.S. attorneys across the country. On March 10, 1975, the 41-year-old Californian became Secretary of Housing and Development in the Cabinet of President Ford—the third woman to hold a cabinet position in American history—and proceeded to confound critics and please her admirers with her tough, no-nonsense take-over of the agency.

Ms. Hills and her husband, Roderick, who also served in the Ford administration as head of the Securities and Exchange Commission, have four children. They have always made two careers a life-style but find that balancing them isn't easy. "Sometimes I feel like a long piece of salami with a slice here for one and a slice here for another, and there is not enough to go around," Ms. Hills told a reporter. She was succeeded at HUD in 1976 by another woman lawyer, PATRICIA ROBERTS HARRIS (p. 368).

Watergate Prosecutor, First Woman General Counsel, U. S. Army

During the heated legal confrontations of the Watergate proceedings, JILL WINE-VOLNER, the sole woman on the Watergate special prosecutor's staff, investigated the Nixon tapes and Watergate cover-up conspiracy, and cross-examined such witnesses as Rose Mary Woods. Immediately after being graduated from Columbia Law School, Ms. Wine-Volner joined the Justice Department as a trial attorney. In 1973 she was appointed assistant special prosecutor in the Watergate case by Archibald Cox. She served under Cox and later under Leon Jaworski and Hank Ruth until the termination of the trial in 1975, when she became a consultant to the Watergate Special Prosecutor's Office. Since March 1977 Ms. Wine-Volner, as general counsel for the U. S. Army, has been overseeing 2,000 attorneys at the Pentagon. President

Carter chose her as the first and only woman in her position in the Army's 200-year history.

General Counsel for the U. S. Department of Transportation

LINDA HELLER KAMM became one of the highest-ranking woman appointees in the Department of Transportation on February 18, 1977, when she was sworn in as DOT's general counsel. Ms. Kamm was general counsel to the House Budget Committee from October 1975 until she resigned to take her Transportation Department position. She has held a variety of positions on Capitol Hill and with the Department of Housing and Urban Development. She received her law degree from Boston College Law School in 1967.

First Woman to Chair the Equal Employment Opportunities Commission

When ELEANOR HOLMES NORTON, a 39-year-old black lawyer who was New York City's Human Rights commissioner, was named to head the embattled Equal Employment Opportunities Commission in March 1977, the National Women's Political Caucus credited President Jimmy Carter with "seeking out and finding the most qualified person in the country for this job." Ms. Norton, born in 1937, grew up in Washington, D.C. One of the few black women law students of the 1960s (she was graduated from Yale), she took an active part in the civil rights movement. Later, as an attorney with the ACLU, she specialized for five years in freedom of speech cases. As the first woman head of the New York Human Rights Commission, she attacked housing bills that were "segregationist in intent and effect," opposed sex discrimination in jobs, cited advertising agencies for poor hiring practices of minorities, and set guidelines on the use of arrest and conviction records as job criteria. She ruled that the Biltmore Hotel could no longer bar women from the

Men's Bar. In 1968 she defended George Wallace's right to free speech, when he was barred from New York's Shea Stadium, saying, "If a person such as George Wallace is denied his rights, then it sets a dangerous precedent and others can be denied this same right."

Three Firsts—and an Important Second as U.S. Assistant Attorney General

Supervisor for 262 lawyers who prosecute for and defend the U. S. Government in a wide range of cases, BARBARA ELLEN BABCOCK was named assistant attorney general in charge of the Civil Division, Department of Justice, in 1977. The second woman to hold the job (CARLA ANDERSON HILLS [p. 365] was the first), she is a 1963 graduate of Yale Law School. Ms. Babcock was the first woman appointed to the position of director of the District of Columbia's Public Defender Service, 1968–72, and prior to that was the first woman appointed to the Stanford Law School faculty and the first woman granted tenure there.

First Woman Securities and Exchange Commissioner

ROBERTA S. KARMEL, 40, was appointed by President Carter to the Securities and Exchange Commission, the federal agency that regulates the stock market, and is the only new commissioner whose most recent background was in private industry. She was a member of the New York securities law firm of Rogers & Wells, among whose clients was Merrill Lynch. However, she has signed what is described as the broadest "recusal" statement ever agreed to by a commissioner, disqualifying herself in all ways in any proceeding before the SEC in which she or her law firm has or had any connection to the parties concerned. She says of her new job, "The perspective of a commissioner is really quite different from that of an attorney. Now *I* have to make

the decisions." Ms. Karmel attended Radcliffe, got a law degree from New York University, and worked in the SEC's New York regional office from 1962 to 1968. She is married to a professor of engineering at New York's City College and has four children, ages 7 to 14.

Deputy Counsel to the President, U.S.A.

At 31 years of age, MARGARET McKENNA, a graduate of Emmanuel College and Southern Methodist University Law School, was named deputy counsel to President Jimmy Carter. Ms. McKenna joined a special program for honors law graduates in the Justice Department and was a trial lawyer for three years in the civil rights division of the Department before being named to her post with the President in 1977.

First Woman Assistant Attorney General for the Office of Legislative Affairs, the Justice Department

When in February 1977 President Carter nominated PATRICIA M. WALD of Maryland to the post of assistant attorney general for the Office of Legislative Affairs, the Department of Justice, she became, at 48, the first woman ever selected for that position. It entails maintaining liaison between the Department of Justice and the U. S. Congress and working on proposed legislation. Prior to assuming her powerful post in the Carter administration, Ms. Wald had been the director of litigation of the public interest group, the Mental Health Law Project, which represents the mentally ill and juveniles. Earlier in her career she wrestled with public health issues at the Center for Law and Social Policy in Washington, D.C. Her casework at the time resulted in expanding the authority of the Food and Drug Administration. Ms. Wald, who received her law degree from Yale in 1951, is the mother of five children.

Highest-Ranking Woman Lawyer in U. S. Government

The first black woman appointed to a President's Cabinet and the first to be named an American ambassador, PATRICIA ROBERTS HARRIS as of 1977 was the highest-ranking woman lawyer in the U. S. Government. The daughter of a Pullman waiter and a schoolteacher, she was graduated first in her class at George Washington University Law School.

Patricia Harris was appointed Secretary of Housing and Urban Development on December 21, 1976, by President Jimmy Carter. The Senate confirmation hearing drew attention because of the acerbic questioning of Ms. Harris by Senator William Proxmire (D., Wis.). "Will you really make an effort to get the views of those who are less articulate and less represented and certainly less likely to be knocking on your door with outstanding credentials?" he asked. Ms. Harris angrily shot back: "Senator, I am one of them. You do not seem to understand who I am. I am a black woman, the daughter of a dining car waiter. I am a black woman who even eight years ago could not buy a house in some parts of the District of Columbia. If my life has any meaning at all, it is that those who start as outcasts may end up being part of the system. I assure you that while there may be those who forget what it meant to be excluded from the dining rooms of this very building, I shall not forget."

On July 9, 1965, Patricia Harris was sworn in as ambassador to Luxembourg, an appointment she received from President Lyndon Johnson. A staunch Democrat, she had seconded President Johnson's nomination in 1964. She served as Howard University Law School's dean for one month in 1969 but quit rather than submit to students' demands for a more important role in running the school. She has been a partner in a Washington law firm and is a specialist in litigation.

In 1943 Ms. Harris was one of a group of Howard University students who tried to force the desegregation of a Washington white-only cafeteria through a sit-in. In 1969, as a member of the National Commission on the Causes and Prevention of Violence, Ms. Harris filed a minority report endorsing the concept of non-violent civil disobedience, including acceptance of the penalty as a technique that "may well prevent, rather than cause violence."

WOMEN ON THE BENCH, WORLDWIDE

First Woman Judge, European Court of Human Rights

With experience behind her as Denmark's Minister of Justice, 1950–53, Member of Parliament, 1953–64, Supreme Court judge, 1964–71, and member or chairperson of several delegations to international conferences and commissions (including the United Nations' Commission on the Status of Women), Danish HELGA PEDERSEN was eminently qualified to become the first woman judge at the European Court of Human Rights in 1971. Ms. Pedersen is internationally recognized for her efforts in prison and penal code reform and the general advancement of women in society.

First and Second Women Judges, England's High Court

In 1965 Dame ELIZABETH LANE became the first woman judge of the High Court, Family Division, in Great Britain. Her appointment topped a long career as judge and lawyer specializing in the areas of mental health, abortion, and the deposition of criminal cases. In 1974 the Honourable ROSE HEILBRON became the second woman High Court judge, with authority over 300 barristers in the Northern Circuit in the Family Division. Earlier, in 1956, Judge Heilbron was the first woman in England to become a recorder (a civil and criminal magistrate or judge in a city or borough).

Highest-Ranking Judge in West Germany Is a Woman

President of the Civil Senate of the Federal Court in Karlsruhe, Dr. GERDA KÜGER NIELAND is the first woman in the history of West Germany to have gained such a high position. The Civil Senate is the First Division of the Federal Court, and the Federal Court at Karlsruhe claims the final authority in legal matters in West Germany.

Argentinian Judge Holds Many Legal Firsts

MARGARITA ARGUAS started her career as a specialist and teacher in international law in 1926. Over the next 40 years she became one of the most noted authorities in the field, but was not awarded her full professorship until 1966. By that time, however, she had already claimed numerous "firsts" in the legal world, which include first woman judge of Argentina's National Civil Court of Appeals; first woman member of the Academy of Law and Social Sciences; first woman president of the International Law Association; and first woman member of the Argentine Supreme Court.

First Woman Lawyer and Judge: Korea

LEE TAI-YOUNG earned a law degree from Seoul National University at the age of 38. As an attorney, Ms. Lee has participated in a modernization movement in Korea that has been going on in the past three decades. Women have been accumulating various rights: No longer are girls given away during child-

hood in arranged marriages; widows now can remarry; and property rights, divorces, and schooling have become more available to women. Judge Lee has been in the forefront of this struggle. Since 1956 she has operated a private nonprofit Legal Aid Center providing free legal counsel to illiterate and poor women. In 1963 she was instrumental in the enactment of the Law Concerning Judgment of Family Affairs and the establishment of the Seoul Family Court. In honor of her sustained commitment, Judge Lee in 1975 received the Ramón Magsaysay Award for Community Leadership.

Outstanding Judge in Madagascar

GEORGETTE RABENO, judge of the Court of the First Instance of Tananarive, Madagascar, is committed to the betterment of humanity through working with the United Nations. She was the assistant secretary-general of the Central Committee of the Red Cross Society of Madagascar in 1965. She had also been judge of the Juvenile Court of Tananarive.

First Woman Judge: Ghana

ANNIE JIAGGE was admitted to the bar of the Gold Coast in 1950, became a magistrate in 1955, a senior magistrate of the Ghana Court in 1957, judge of the High Court in 1961 and of the Court of Appeals in 1969. In addition to this swift career rise, she became Ghana's representative to the United Nations' Commission on the Status of Women in 1961 and its first African chairperson in 1968.

Tradition-Breaking U. S. Tax Court Judge

At the time of her appointment in 1960 by President Dwight D. Eisenhower to the 16-member U. S. Tax Court, the Honorable IRENE F. SCOTT was the only woman federal tax judge in the country. She was reappointed in 1972 for 15 years, but this time with a sister appointee. U. S. Tax Court judges travel to various cities to hold temporary sessions.

In the course of her work, Ms. Scott, an Alabama native, continually broke tradition by appearing in cities that had never before received women jurists: St. Louis in 1960, Portland in 1961, Cleveland in 1965.

First Black Woman Appointed a Federal Judge

CONSTANCE BAKER MOTLEY was known as a formidable civil rights attorney for 20 years before her appointment as the first black woman to sit as a federal judge. The first black woman elected to the New York State senate and the first woman borough president of Manhattan, in 1966 she was appointed U.S. district judge, Southern District of New York, by President Lyndon Johnson, acting on the recommendation of the late Senator Robert F. Kennedy of New York. After a delay caused by Senator James O. Eastland of Mississippi, she was confirmed on August 30, 1966. When she donned the judicial robe and descended to the bench, Ms. Motley did not abandon her role as pioneer, nor shed her interest in the rights of minorities—ruling on behalf of welfare recipients, low-income Medicaid patients, and a prisoner who claimed to have been unconstitutionally punished by 372 days of solitary confinement. She awarded the prisoner damages.

Best-known for her battles as an attorney in striking down state-enforced segregation laws in the South, she worked on all the major school segregation cases supported by the Legal Defense Fund and argued and won nine civil rights cases before the U. S. Supreme Court. James Meredith entered the University of Mississippi and CHARLAYNE HUNTER (see "Women in Communications," p. 462) and Hamilton Holmes entered the University of Georgia as a result of her legal successes. She also persuaded the Supreme Court to order the desegregation of buses in Jackson, Mississippi, as well as the airport restaurant in Memphis, and dime-store lunch counters in Birmingham. She was firm and forceful in her arguments, and a persistent questioner. But she was also respectful to-

ward the judges and her adversaries. A reporter once wrote that she had "demanded" an action by the court. The next day she asked the reporter: "What do you mean, I 'demanded'? You don't demand in court, you pray for relief for some action."

Judge Motley was born in New Haven on September 14, 1921, the ninth of 12 children who were emigrants from the British West Indies. Her father was a cook.

Highest-Ranking Woman Jurist

In 1968 SHIRLEY HUFSTEDLER was appointed justice on the U. S. Court of Appeals—one step below the Supreme Court—the first and (to date) only woman among its 97 justices. Ms. Hufstedler, born in 1925 in Denver, Colorado, and educated at Stanford University, was a lawyer in private practice for 11 years until 1961, when she was appointed to the Superior Court of Los Angeles County. Of her present position, she says: "It's a constant intellectual challenge, in quantity and complexity. We deal with deep, sensitive socioeconomic problems, like ecology and integration."

Michigan's Sister Judges

The 1970 appointment of CORNELIA KENNEDY as judge of the U. S. District Court was the first instance of a woman from Michigan chosen to be a federal judge. Earlier, Ms. Kennedy had been elected judge of the Third Judicial Circuit of Michigan. Her sister, MARGARET G. SCHAEFFER, the first woman appointed to Michigan's Workmen's Compensation Board (1973) also is a judge —of the State District Court.

First Woman Associate Justice of the Rhode Island Supreme Court

For more than 20 years, the Honorable FLORENCE K. MURRAY has served as Rhode Island's first woman associate justice of the state's Supreme Court. She was appointed in 1956, more than 10 years after completing wartime service in the U. S. Army as a lieutenant colonel. In the years prior to 1956, she and her husband practiced as Rhode Island's only husband-and-wife law firm, and she also served in the Rhode Island senate.

First Woman Elected Chief Justice of a State Supreme Court

The first woman elected chief justice of a state Supreme Court, SUSIE M. SHARP of North Carolina assumed office on January 2, 1975. When she is forced to retire from the Court on July 31, 1979, because she will have reached the mandatory retirement age of 72, Ms. Sharp will have served the state as a trial and appellate judge for 30 years, a record that few men in North Carolina's judicial system have equaled. She had already been the state's first female city attorney, first woman appointed to the Superior Court bench, and first woman appointed to the Supreme Court as an associate justice, when in 1972, as the senior member of the Supreme Court, and by tradition first in line for the post of chief justice, her six male colleagues urged her to run. She was already past 65 and had hoped to retire to her home in Reidsville, where she was born on July 7, 1907. But she knew that her father, James M. Sharp, an attorney who had made her career possible, were he still alive would have said to her, "Don't quit now." She won easily.

According to the magazine *North Carolina* (February 1975) at the time Governor Kerr Scott made history by appointing her to the Superior Court bench in 1949, a male journalist asked in his newspaper column: "What if she were faced with trying a case of rape? Wouldn't that be too much for her delicate sensibilities?" She responded in a letter that read: "In the first place, there could have been no rape had not a woman been present, and I consider it eminently fitting that one be in on the 'pay-off.'"

Only Woman Federal Lawyer of the Year, 1966, Now a Judge

As assistant U.S. attorney for ten years, MERNA MARSHALL, a former schoolteacher, was honored by the Southeastern District of the Federal Bar Association as Federal Lawyer of the Year in 1966, the only woman so honored. In 1971 she was appointed judge of the Consumers Pleas Court of Philadelphia and then elected to a 10-year term in 1973. Among other legal interests, Ms. Marshall is working for rehabilitation, education, and better facilities for women in the prison system.

First Woman to Break 120-Year Tradition in Court of Claims

In 1973 CHARLOTTE P. MURPHY became the first woman appointed to be trial judge in the U. S. Court of Claims in the court's 120-year history. The appointment came as no surprise. As youngest lawyer and second woman elected director of the Bar Association of Washington, D.C. (1956–57), editor of the American Bar Association's publication for young lawyers, widely recognized for her work in the Chief Counsel's Office of the Internal Revenue Service in the litigation division (1960–71 and again in 1973), she had early acquired a sterling reputation.

First Louisiana Judge

JOAN ARMSTRONG in 1974 was named to the Orleans Parish Juvenile Court bench in Louisiana. At 32 she became the youngest member of the state's judiciary and Louisiana's only female judge. Previously Ms. Armstrong was an attorney for the U. S. Housing and Urban Development Corporation and president of the Community Relations Council of Greater New Orleans.

Mississippi's First Woman and First Black Special Judge

In 1975 CONSTANCE IONA SLAUGHTER was selected to serve as the special chancellor for the second Judicial District of Mississippi, making her the first black and first female special judge in Mississippi. The first black woman to enter and graduate from the University of Mississippi School of Law (1967–70), the Jackson-born Judge Slaughter was also the first black attorney to establish private practice in south central Mississippi.

First Woman Superior Court Judge in Connecticut

Yale Law School graduate ELLEN B. BURNS at 52 years of age was sworn in as Connecticut's first woman Superior Court judge in April 1976. Prior to this appointment, Ms. Burns had been appointed by Governor Thomas Meskill to the Circuit Court, in 1973.

Award-Winning Judge

In 1976 Judge JOYCE HENS GREEN, associate judge of the Superior Court of the District of Columbia, was awarded the Women's Legal Defense Fund First Annual Award for Outstanding Contribution to Equal Rights.

D.C. Woman Lawyer Appointed by President Carter as Judge

In 1977 President Jimmy Carter appointed GLADYS KESSLER, Harvard Law School graduate, to serve on the Washington Superior Court. She was a partner in her law firm in the District of Columbia, and was an appellate attorney for the National Labor Relations Board. In the women's rights arena, Ms. Kessler was the first president of the Women's Legal Defense Fund, and one of its founders.

First Woman Chief Justice of California

California's ROSE ELIZABETH BIRD was named chief justice of the California Supreme Court by Governor Edmund G. Brown, Jr., on February 12, 1977, the first woman to hold the post. She was also the state's first woman secretary of agriculture and services. Ms. Bird, who was 40 at the date of her appointment to the court, had no judicial experience but was known for her legal acumen and administrative ability, which included drafting the state's historic Agricultural Labor Relations Act. She is a graduate of the University of California, where she first met Governor Brown. She taught law at Stanford University, was the first female deputy defender in San Jose, California, and, on her first job, in 1965, was the Nevada Supreme Court's only female law clerk.

WOMEN LAW ENFORCEMENT OFFICERS

New York's Finest

New York City has added nine women to the police department's Homicide Squad, until recently an elite all-male unit. In announcing the move, John I. Keenan, the city's chief of detectives, said that women also would be added to other all-male detective units, including the robbery and burglary squads. "One of the problems we are facing," he said, "is that there are not enough women investigators available to fill the demand." There were 68 women detectives in the New York Police Department at the beginning of 1978 out of a total detective force of about 1,000.

First New York Police Precinct Captain

In December 1976 Captain VITTORIA RENZULLO, 44, became the first woman to command a New York City police precinct, the 1st, a largely business and commercial downtown area that includes part of Greenwich Village. Captain Renzullo joined the force in 1959, was the top graduate in her class at the Police Academy, and the first woman to attend the FBI Academy. Before her transfer to the 1st Precinct, she was executive officer in an uptown area. The official department announcement of her new position said, "She has performed in an excellent capacity and deserves the command." A former colleague put it, "She's got more guts than most guys on the job."

Highest-Ranking New York City Policewoman: Her Many Firsts

Deputy Chief GERTRUDE D. T. SCHIMMEL, a 38-year veteran of the force, is the highest-ranking regular woman cop in New York City. The first woman promoted, successively, to sergeant (1965), lieutenant (1967), captain (1971), deputy inspector (1972), inspector (1974), and deputy chief, she assumed her latest rank when she was designated commanding officer of the Office of the Deputy Commissioner, Community Affairs, on March 31, 1978. Ms. Schimmel, who was born and resides in the Bronx and is the mother of two sons, also is the author of a novel for young adults, *Joan Palmer, Policewoman*, published in 1960; it illustrates the real-life experiences of a woman police officer in an urban precinct.

First Woman Deputy Commissioner of Public Information, New York City Police

As deputy commissioner of public information, ELLEN FLEYSHER acts for the New York City police commissioner with the media and in public policy matters. Born in Buffalo, New York, in 1944, Ms. Fleysher holds a B.A. from the State University of New York at Buffalo and an M.A. from the Annenberg School of Communications, University of Pennsylvania. She had extensive experience as a reporter for the *New York Daily News* and as a correspondent with WCBS-TV News before being appointed to the police department in 1978.

Radio-Car Duty Women

In Indianapolis, Indiana, in September 1968, BETTY BLANKENSHIP and ELIZABETH COFFAL became the first policewomen assigned to radio-car duty. Indianapolis Police Chief Winston Churchill granted them the assignment, with one day's notice, after the women had been demanding the position for a year. In time, their "Car 47" built up a successful record of dealing with wide-ranging day or night calls. Their example led other reluctant departments in Detroit, Miami, Washington, Los Angeles to name a few, to follow suit. Ms. Blankenship and Ms. Coffal are presently both administrative aides to separate sector commanders.

Undercover Detective

Since 1969 New Yorker KATHY BURKE, in her 30s, has engaged in what some call the "most dangerous job in the police department" (*Parade*, 1976). She was an undercover agent, representative of dozens of other such women throughout the country, who might pose as junkies in order to track down dope dealers or to close in on syndicate leaders. Ms. Burke's work was rewarded with promotion to the rank of detective in 1971, after she had narrowly escaped death at the hands of dealers whom she was pursuing.

Seattle's Top Cop

Lieutenant MARY F. STOWE achieved the rank of lieutenant in 1971 after getting the top score out of 115 applicants on the Seattle Civil Service promotional examination. Ms. Stowe, who has been with the Seattle Police Department for 25 years, was the first woman to compete in the exam after being refused the option to take it on two occasions (1967 and 1969); she scored 95.3. Ms. Stowe was in 1972 the only woman to be a precinct patrol watch commander in the history of the department.

Woman State Trooper

REGINA ROBBINS, a Syracuse University graduate, achieved the highest academic record in her state trooper academy. At 26 years of age in 1976, she was assigned to the New York State Thruway patrol out of Albany.

Kansas City Policewomen

MARILYN BRAUNINGER is the first policewoman sergeant in the Kansas City Police Department. Detective ROSIE MASON is the city's first black woman police officer.

Woman Detective's Landmark Decision

Her promotion to the rank of detective signaled a turnabout for the Honolulu Police Department and was a personal triumph for Hawaiian-Scottish-Portuguese-Filipino LUCILLE ABREU. Prior to her promotion, women were relegated to the ranks below sergeant. In 1972 she filed a sex discrimination charge against the Honolulu Police Department pointing out her credentials: only woman class valedictorian in police training school, 22 years of service on the Honolulu police force, high marks on promotion examinations. Ms. Abreu won her case, and received her deserved promotion in May 1975.

She Foiled Hijackers

Former landscaping and architecture draftsperson, officer MARTY GREEN, at 35 years of age, foiled an armed hijacker at a Louisville airport in January 1973. A 170-pound hijacker had been holding a hostage in a plane and demanding to be flown to Africa. Ms. Green disguised herself as an off-duty stewardess and made five trips up the boarding ramp to negotiate for the hostage's release. On her fourth trip, the hijacker agreed to surrender the hostage, and on the fifth, his gun—on the condition that he first be allowed to hold Ms. Green's hand. At that point, Ms. Green took control and successfully overpowered the hijacker.

First U.S. Policewoman to Die in Line of Duty

Policewoman GAIL A. COBB, at 24 years of age, was the first United States policewoman to die in the line of duty. The fatal shooting occurred in September 1974 in an underground garage in midtown Washington, D.C. The funeral was one of the most impressive ever seen in the District of Columbia, with a large number of police officials from all over the country attending.

California Governor's Bodyguard

PENELOPE CRAVENS, former airline stewardess and State Department clerk, was appointed by California Governor Edmund Brown, Jr., to serve as one of his bodyguards. She was the first woman to join the all-male police security staff. At 27 years of age, Ms. Cravens had already acquired a string of firsts in the police profession: She was the first woman ever hired by the state police, and a member of the first group of women to join the California Highway Patrol.

Policewoman on Rape Squad

Thirteen years on the police force, JULIA TUCKER, lieutenant of the 88th Precinct in New York City, is most noted for helping to revolutionize the Rape Squad. She was instrumental in creating specialized units to investigate sex crimes in Brooklyn, and in training officers in the sensitive handling of a sex crime and its victims. Ms. Tucker testified as an expert witness before the Senate Crime Committee, investigating the inadequacies of laws in this area.

She Aids Women Offenders

MARGERY L. VELIMESIS co-founded the Pennsylvania Program for Women and Girl Offenders, and is now the executive director of the program, engaged in trailblazing efforts to meet the needs of women offenders. She graduated in psychology in 1945 from Ohio State University, and was the first woman to receive a graduate degree in the Continuing Education Program for Women at the University of Pennsylvania (1965). In 1968 Ms. Velimesis designed and directed the first statewide survey in the United States of county jail services and conditions for female defendants in the United States. She also assembled and staffed the Citizen Task Force Community Treatment Center for Women in Pennsylvania, which was used as the model for all state community centers for men as well as women. In 1975 Ms. Velimesis received the governor's commendation for work with the Pennsylvania Commission on the Status of Women, regarding health problems as they relate to women in prison.

Britain's Highest-Ranking Policewoman

Among many changes made by Scotland Yard in the summer of 1977 was the assignment of Commander DAPHNE SKILLERN, 49, the country's highest-ranking woman officer, as chief of a department that includes the "Porn Squad." Commander Skillern has been on the force since 1949. Having been a detective in Soho for many years, she is no prude. "I don't want to go back to Victorian prudery and ridiculousness," she said, "but perhaps it is time to stand back and take a look at some of the objectionable things which are being openly paraded." Commander Skillern sees no reason why a woman police officer cannot aspire to and become commissioner, the system's highest-ranking officer.

9

Women in Religion

By Catherine O'Neill

The Reverend Alison M. Cheek, consulting editor

Until recent times women's history—including that of women in the church—has been largely ignored and sometimes deliberately suppressed. And so we have been robbed of the full inheritance of our foremothers, and our knowledge of their achievements has been limited. How many of us in the 20th century know, for example, what Quaker women, extended equality by their religion from the beginning, were doing from the 1640s onward in England and later in the New World for free speech, in prison reform, against slavery, racism, and war?

Only a few years ago the phrase "women in religion" might have summoned up the image of a contemplative nun deep in prayer behind a convent wall, of a missionary teaching in Africa or China, of a kindly minister's wife putting flowers on the altar at her husband's country church. And, of course, none of these visions is a false one. But today the words "women in religion" also summon up other figures—the newly ordained woman minister in her pulpit, the nun in

modern dress doing research at an urban institute while sharing a communal home with sisters of other orders, the female rabbi and cantor in the previously all-male sanctum of the synagogue, the woman theologian at the traditional all-male seminary, the politician in the modern, short-skirted habit of a nun, the woman serving as co-pastor with her husband, the diverse group of women from many denominations coming together to share ideas and energy and faith.

The list runs on. In religion, as in so many other realms, women are going public. The work of the teaching sister continues, the prayers still sound in the convent, the missionary still brings the messages of her faith to remote parts of the world, but these women are being joined in increasing numbers by others who express their religion in newly recognized ways.

What is a woman's ministry? It appears to be something that tends to break down the barriers of hierarchical structure in traditionally male church leadership, that brings a re-created freshness to many rites and creeds. Perhaps women, because they have been denied a part in the formal structure, have developed a more holistic and truly human vision of religion than their male counterparts. Certainly many practices among women clergy, religious, and lay persons are widely ecumenical, openly expressive of humanity, and represent a breaking down of barriers among the various sorts of religious people. Perhaps women's work in religion is more fluid, more responsive to the differences in people, because it has had to operate for so long in quiet, behind-the-scenes ways.

Many women in the following pages demonstrate a remarkable capacity for being more than one thing at a time— they are writers *and* ministers, administrators *and* teachers, theologians *and* mothers. They also bring the warmth of traditionally female roles to the practice of their ministry, as in the beautiful service of baptism, cradling the new child, comforting it with a maternal as well as a sacramental presence. Many women in this chapter have achieved remarkable things within the boundaries of their orders and denominations. Others, dispossessed by the structure and meeting whatever comes realistically and creatively, have forged new forms. Whatever their religion, all these women share generosity, daring, faith, and joy in their work.

CATHERINE O'NEILL *taught English and religion at the National Cathedral School, 1972–76. She holds a B.A. from Middlebury College and an M.A. from Georgetown University, both in English literature. In 1977 she joined the staff of the* New Republic *magazine and in 1978 was named a staff writer on the* Chronicle of Higher Education.

Consulting editor the Reverend ALISON M. CHEEK *was one of 11 women ordained in the Episcopal Church in Philadelphia in 1974. The first woman to celebrate the Eucharist in the U. S. Episcopal Church, she was named by* Time *magazine as one of the 12 women of the year in 1976. Described by* Time *as both a leader and a symbol of the women's drive for an active role in the clergy, Ms. Cheek earned her master of divinity degree from Virginia Theological Seminary in 1969. Since then she has become a pastoral psychotherapist with her own practice in Washington, D.C., has been a priest on the staff of the parish of St. Stephen and the Incarnation, and is a pastoral counselor on the staff of St. Alban's Episcopal Church, Annandale, Virginia. A native of Australia, she is the widow of Bruce Cheek and the mother of four children.*

STUDENTS OF THEOLOGY

Seminarians, Yesterday and Today

The first U.S. woman to register at Boston University School of Theology did so under an assumed name so as not to embarrass her family. ANNA OLIVER, who lived and preached until 1893, was graduated in 1876 and was chosen by her class to give the closing oration. She went on to work in a Methodist church in Passaic, New Jersey, where she hired a black evangelist as her assistant. According to a contemporary report, "Passaic is having a lively time . . . what with two women in the pulpit, one of them black, the buzzing grows apace!"

A hundred years later, women are flocking to the seminaries in unprecedented numbers. Enrollment in U.S. theological schools has gone from 3 to 30 per cent of the total in the last 10 years. According to EFTHALIA WALSH, who is working toward her master's degree in religion at American University and has written on women in religion for the *New York Times,* the *Washington Star,* and *Face to Face,* an international religion bulletin published by B'nai B'rith's Anti-Defamation League: "Women are finally in. They've broken the barriers that have kept them out of seminaries and out of the ministry. . . . But many problems remain for women seminarians —often inner ones. These women, who have a strong sense of mission and claim that they are being swept along by something greater than themselves, are often unsettled by people, not always men, who say to them accusingly, 'What are you—some kind of a women's libber?'"

For white women, the biggest hurdle seems to be fear of preaching in the pulpit. The didactic tone of most Protestant preaching does not come easily to them. For black women, the free-flowing, charismatic style of preaching used in black churches presents fewer difficulties; in any case, within their cultural group,

they say, women have always been and can be more aggressive.

First Married Woman to Complete Academic Requirements for Priesthood

ROSALIE MUSCHAL-REINHARDT, as a 43-year-old mother of four, became the first married woman to have completed all the academic requirements for admission to the Roman Catholic priesthood. The Reverend William G. Guindon, president of Chicago's Jesuit School of Theology, which awarded Ms. Muschal-Reinhardt her master of divinity degree in 1977, said she represents ". . . the first of a courageous group of women . . . who have completed all the requirements for ordination." Ms. Muschal-Reinhardt began her studies about 10 years ago, and hopes that the Catholic Church will open its priesthood to women like her sometime in the next 10 or 15 years. "The fact that I'm a woman has been a great help to my pastoral ministries. . . . I understand family life. I long for the Church, the institution, to understand that," she says.

First Lay Woman on Catholic Seminary Board

JANE TOTAH DAVIS, a married Catholic woman, mother of four, and campus minister at Montclair State College in New Jersey, entered Drew University's theological school in 1970, 20 years after graduation from Swarthmore College. She planned to be a religious education coordinator, but a priest suggested that she apply for the campus position. She works with students and faculty, and is on the payroll of the Archdiocese of Newark, just as a priest would be. Her work at Montclair State has led to an interest in pastoral counseling, which she is pursuing at Drew in a three-year marriage-and-family-counseling program. Ms. Davis says that things are changing in the Catholic Church as far as women are concerned, although ordination of women may not come soon. "Our Catholic Diocese of Newark now accepts lay students, men *and* women, and will give them a master's degree or an M.Div. This was not so in 1970 when I applied.

At that time the Catholic seminary was not open to anyone except male students studying for the priesthood. For two years now, however, I've been a member of the board of trustees of the seminary. Another woman, a sister, and I are on the board—the only women ever to be named to it."

MEMBERS OF THE CLERGY

First U.S. Woman to Be Ordained a Minister

On September 15, 1853, ANTOINETTE L. BROWN was ordained in the Congregational church in South Butler, New York, making her the first woman minister in the United States. She was a member, with Lucy Stone, the woman suffrage leader, of Oberlin College's class of 1847, and then went on to become its first woman theology student. For many years Oberlin did not list her name among its 1850 theology graduates, but in 1909 finally added her to its alumni rolls and awarded her with an honorary doctor of divinity degree. Horace Greeley, founder of the *New York Tribune,* was one of her champions and tried to convince her to take up a pulpit in New York City. She declined the offer because of her inexperience, settling instead on the smaller South Butler parish. She and Lucy Stone were related by marriage as well as being classmates, for they married brothers in 1855. Their sisters-in-law were Elizabeth Blackwell, the first woman doctor in the United States, and Emily Blackwell, who founded the New York Infirmary for Women and Children, the first hospital for women in the United States (see "Women in Medicine and Health Care," p. 200). Reverend Brown was the mother of six daughters, and wrote ten books. While in her 70s she traveled to the Holy Land to get water from the Jordan to baptize her grandchildren and later went on a missionary trip to Alaska. She died in 1921 at the age of 96. A contemporary account estimated that at the time of her death there were 3,000 female ministers in the United States.

Founder of Christian Science

MARY BAKER EDDY (1821–1910) founded the Church of Christ, Scientist in 1879. In 1866 she had fallen on ice in Lynn, Massachusetts. According to the official church history she went to bed and turned to the Scriptures for healing. On the third day she arose, her pain gone, and began spreading the doctrine that pain could be healed through mental processes. Her church grew quickly, adding a publishing concern in 1898; a newspaper, *The Christian Science Monitor,* began publication in 1908. When Ms. Eddy died she left an estate of more than $2 million, 22,000 practitioners, and 420 churches behind her.

Co-Founder of Seventh-Day Adventists

ELLEN G. WHITE (1827–1915) and her husband James worked together to found the Seventh-Day Adventists, a Christian group based on the achievement of spiritual and bodily health through correct eating and temperance. The Whites also started a publishing business, and encouraged the early career of the man who went on to develop Kellogg's Corn Flakes. Ms. White, who thought of herself as shy, began to preach in her 40s, speaking to crowds of up to 2,000 people. When she died in

1915, the Adventists had 140,000 members, 2,500 clergy, 6 medical centers, and more than 40 publishing centers across the country.

First Ordained Woman Presbyterian

A professor emerita of Christian education at Austin Theological Seminary in Texas, the Reverend RACHEL HENDERLITE was the first woman ever ordained to the ministry of the Presbyterian Church in the United States. Born in Henderson, North Carolina, in 1905, Reverend Henderlite received her B.A. from Agnes Scott College, her M.A. from the Biblical Seminary at NYU, and her Ph.D. from the Yale Divinity School. She taught English for a few years, and then became the first woman professor at a seminary when she joined the staff at Austin Theological. Reverend Henderlite, also an author, in 1945 published the widely used *Exploring the old Testament* and *Exploring the New Testament,* both still in print. In November 1976 she was named the first woman president of the Presbyterian Council of Church Union, a group studying the possible merger of the various branches of the Presbyterian Church that were separated at the time of the Civil War.

Minister of Church of Christ in Japan

In 1946 the Reverend Ms. TAMAKI UEMURA, an ordained minister of the Church of Christ in Japan, became the first civilian permitted to leave Japan and enter the United States following the Second World War. She came on the invitation of United Presbyterian Women to speak at their national meeting. Because she was a day late, the embarrassing question of whether or not she could serve as officiating clergy in a communion service (the Presbyterians did not ordain women at that time) did not come up, but she later heard of the controversy. She is reported to have said, "Oh, I think I will go around creating more commotion. God, give me wisdom."

From Circuit Rider to City Preacher

The Reverend ABIGAIL EVANS, associate pastor at Broadway Presbyterian Church in New York, and chaplain at Columbia University, made her decision to go into the church after attending a Billy Graham revival. She entered Princeton Seminary in 1958, where she met and married her husband Bob, also a minister. They went to Brazil for several years to do evangelical work. Later Reverend Evans studied in Switzerland with Karl Barth, returning to the U.S.A to become a circuit-riding minister in rural Kentucky for two years. When interviewed for her post at Broadway Presbyterian she was asked whether being a woman would be an asset to her ministry. She asserted that it would, saying, "First of all, the majority of church members are women. Secondly, I think there's an innate feminine ability to care and be concerned and open to people—an ability that isn't necessarily true of a man."

Pastor of Seven Steeples

In her book *Seven Steeples,* published in 1953, MARGARET HENRICHSEN tells how, feeling restless after her husband's death, she offered her services to the Methodist Church in Maine. What began as the pastorship of one small church in a tiny seacoast town quickly blossomed into a ministry to seven churches on the Maine coast. After two years serving the people of these churches, Reverend Henrichsen was ordained, but she was so busy that a special Friday afternoon service had to be arranged for her. A Mother's Day service was coming up, and she could not miss seeing a young parishioner return to the church as a gift to his mother. Reverend Henrichsen spent her few vacation days visiting lectures at Union Seminary in New York.

President of Church Women United

The Reverend MARY LOUISE ROWAND, elected president of Church Women

United in the U.S.A., for the 1978–80 term, previously served as the organization's deputy vice-president. An ordained minister in the Disciples of Christ Church, she has received many awards, among them selection by the *Dallas Times Herald* as one of the top 10 news shapers in the Dallas, Texas, area. She was named one of the 10 most valuable women in civic affairs by the YWCA. June 23 is Mary Louise Rowand Day in Dallas, an honor extended to her in 1974 by Mayor Wes Wise, who said, "Her enthusiasm for life is contagious. Her genuine love for all those about her, her matchless contribution cannot be measured. . . ." Ms. Rowand also serves on the regional staff of the American Bible Society, which dedicated the 31st millionth copy of the *Good News for Modern Man* paperback Bible to her.

Literacy Movement Founder

LUISA GONZALEZ, an ordained minister in the Methodist Church, founded the Alfalit movement in 1961 with her husband, Justo. Their program, designed to promote literacy, is now carried on in 12 Latin American countries. Originally from Cuba, Dr. Gonzalez was a professor of Spanish literature, and the author of 11 children's books. She also served as president of the Woman's Society for Christian Service in Cuba. Now retired, Dr. Gonzalez served as Alfalit's director of education for 11 years, writing books on subjects ranging from cooking to Bible studies. Her sons are professors of religion in the United States.

Human Liberation Theologian

LETTY MANDEVILLE RUSSELL, a minister in the Presbyterian Church in the U.S.A. and a 1951 Wellesley graduate, worked in East Harlem before beginning her studies at Harvard Divinity School. She graduated cum laude, and was ordained by the Presbytery of New York in 1958 to serve the Church of the Ascension in East Harlem. During the 10 years she

was pastor there she published the quarterly *Bible Study Guide* for inner-city churches, and co-authored two books on inner-city church work. In 1965 she became coordinator of the various parts of the East Harlem Protestant parish, and began to work toward higher degrees in theology at Union Seminary. Upon receiving her doctorate in 1969, she taught at Manhattan College, Bronx, New York. The year 1970 saw her marriage to Johannes C. Hoekendijk, professor of World Christianity at Union. During 1970–71 she served as a consultant to the Religious Board of the YWCA, and began writing on women's role in the church. During the 1970s she has taught in India, at Yale, at Princeton, and published *Human Liberation in a Feminist Perspective—A Theology* (1974). Letty Russell, a Presbyterian delegate to the World Assembly of the World Council of Churches, has contributed frequently to theological and church journals. She serves as a consultant to the U. S. Working Group on Participation of Women in the World Council of Churches, and teaches at Yale Divinity School and the New York Theological Seminary.

World's First Women Anglican Priests

In 1971 the Anglican Consultative Council at the World Anglican Conference in England decided by a one-vote margin that "it will be acceptable" for bishops to ordain women priests with the approval of their provinces. Accordingly, in November 1971 the Right Reverend Gilbert Baker, Bishop of Hong Kong, ordained the Reverend JANE HWANG HSIEN YUEN and the Reverend JOYCE BENNETT, making them the first women priests in the entire Anglican Communion. Both had previously been ordained deacons. Reverend Hwang, born near Canton, and Reverend Bennett, from England, are both school principals, Reverend Hwang heads Yuek Wing Primary School, Reverend Bennett St. Catherine's Girls' School.

World's First Woman Rabbi

SALLY PREISAND, the first woman rabbi in the United States and the world, was ordained in 1972. Assistant rabbi at the Stephen Wise Free Synagogue in Manhattan, she has received numerous honors for her outstanding work with Jewish youth, and for championing the rights of women. Among these are life memberships in Hadassah and the Women's League for Israel, Woman of the Year awards from various Jewish organizations, Ohio's Outstanding Young Woman of the Year (1972), and Man of the Year from Temple Israel in Columbus, Ohio (1973).

First in Episcopal Church in the United States

In July 1974, 11 female deacons were ordained to the Episcopal priesthood in Philadelphia's Church of the Advocate. At the front of the church hung a banner reading: "In Christ There Is Neither Male Nor Female." Four bishops officiated at the ceremony. A little more than a year later four other women were ordained in Washington, D.C., at St. Stephen and the Incarnation Church. These two services forced clarification of the issue of women's ordination before the Church's general convention in Minneapolis in 1976. The meeting voted to clarify the canon on ordination as inclusive of women as well as men, and since then many women deacons have been ordained. The way was then opened for the 15 women previously ordained in Philadelphia and Washington to be officially recognized in their own dioceses.

Ordained in Philadelphia
July 29, 1974

Rev. Merrill Bittner
Rev. Alla Bozarth Campbell
Rev. Alison Cheek
Rev. Emily Hewitt
Rev. Carter Heyward
Rev. Suzanne Hiatt
Rev. Marie Moorefield

First Woman Rabbi Outside the United States

In July 1975 JACQUELINE TABICK became, at the age of 26, the first woman ordained a rabbi outside the United States. The ceremony took place in London, where Mrs. Rabbi Tabick, as she said she liked to be addressed, serves as education officer at the West London Synagogue. It is customary for persons about to be ordained to wear a prayer shawl, but Jacqueline Tabick chose not to, explaining "it is traditionally for the men."

Rev. Dr. Jeannette Piccard
Rev. Betty Scheiss
Rev. Katrina Swanson
Rev. Nancy Wittig

Ordained in Washington
September 1975

Rev. Lee McGee
Rev. Alison Palmer
Rev. Dr. Betty Rosenberg
Rev. Diane Tickell

First Ordained by Husband

The Reverend CAROL OLSON, the seventh woman to be ordained a minister in the American Lutheran Church, was the first woman in the U.S.A. ever ordained by her husband. The ceremony conducted by the Reverend Steve Olson took place in May 1975 after her graduation from Wartburg Theological Seminary. She then joined him as co-pastor of two Iowa churches: Salem Lutheran Church in Spragueville, and Ascension Lutheran Church in Goose Lake. As a rule, the Olsons have shared their pastoral duties by each preaching in both churches on alternate Sundays, with whoever is not on duty as pastor caring for the three Olson children.

Canada's First Lutheran Pastor

On May 7, 1976, PAMELA JO MCGEE was ordained as Canada's first woman Lutheran pastor. The ordination, while a first for Canada, was not unprecedented in the denomination, which has about 30 women ministers in the U.S.A. Reverend McGee's ordination took place in the oldest Protestant church in Upper Canada, St. John's, organized in 1784. Born in Alaska in 1947, Reverend McGee became a landed immigrant in Canada in 1971. There she attended Waterloo Lutheran Seminary, originally entering only to pursue her own spiritual growth. Later, ordination became her goal as women were accepted into pastorates in the U.S.A. Reverend McGee, who hopes eventually to do chaplaincy work, believes the Lutheran Church, with an estimated 70 million members worldwide, making it the largest Protestant denomination in the world, must become more involved in social action. "A church has no choice but to be involved in social concerns . . . because it lives and its mission is in the world," she says.

First Black Ordained United Presbyterian Minister

The Reverend JOAN MARTIN, the first black woman student at Princeton Theological Seminary, was the first black woman to be ordained to the United Presbyterian Church ministry. The ceremony took place in October 1976. A representative to the National Council of Churches Commission on Women in Ministry, she chairs its Task Force on Ethnic Women in Ministry.

First Female Bishops in Black Church

On Sunday, October 31, 1976, the Shrines of the Black Madonna, Black Christian Nationalist Church, which is headquartered in Detroit, Michigan, consecrated two female bishops. They are: the Reverend DIANA STEWART and the Reverend BARBARA MARTIN. Bishop Stewart will act as the national coordinator of office management, while Bishop Martin will be the national coordinator of all cultural centers. Both bishops will serve as administrative assistants to the presiding bishop, the Reverend Albert Cleage. The Church was incorporated in 1970 in Detroit, and has expanded to include shrines in Michigan, Georgia, and Texas. The first women in the denomination were ordained in 1972.

COMMITted Minister

The Reverend GRACE MOORE, an ordained minister in the United Church of Christ, is administrator of COMMIT (Center of Metropolitan Ministries In-Service Training) and the convenor of Women Committed to Women, an interdenominational group engaged in creating a "sisterhood" within Christian church structures. Reverend Moore has written on women in the church for numerous publications, her subjects ranging from history to theology. She is also associate pastor of the Cross Roads Community Church in Lakewood, California.

First Anglican Communion Priests in Canada

Canada was a leader in beginning the switch from all-male to all-person priesthood in the North American Anglican Communion, ordaining six women in ceremonies across the country in November 1976.

Ordained in Canada on November 29, 1976, were:

Mary Lucas, in St. Catharines, Ontario.

Beverly Shanley, in St. Catharines, Ontario.

Mary Lake Mills, in London, Ontario.

Pat Reed, in the Diocese of Caribou, British Columbia.

Virginia Briant, in Vancouver, British Columbia.

Elspeth Alley, in Vancouver, British Columbia.

First Woman Officially Acclaimed U. S. Episcopal Priest

On January 1, 1977, the Reverend JACQUELINE MEANS, wife of an Indiana truck driver and mother of four, became the first woman to be ordained with the official sanction of the Episcopal Church in the U.S.A. Ms. Means is modest about her position: "I'd probably be the last person you'd expect to be ordained," she says. Born in Peoria, Illinois, to a traveling salesman and his wife, her childhood was unsettled both by her father's work and by her parents' alcoholism. She dropped out of school at 16 to marry. Settled in Indianapolis, and raising a family, Ms. Means earned her high school equivalency diploma, and then became a practical nurse. Eventually she turned her sights on the priesthood, studying at Catholic and Disciples of Christ seminaries in Indianapolis, and later pursuing private courses. After her ordination as a deacon in 1974, she was assigned to All Saints, a racially mixed inner-city parish. She also serves as a prison chaplain at the Indianapolis Women's Prison. Asked her feelings on the eve of her ordination, Ms. Means replied: "I feel a great heaviness, knowing that I have a lot of responsibility for how I act. The Church is being tested through people like me."

National Coalition for Women's Ordination Leader

PAT PARK, the second woman ordained to the Episcopal priesthood in 1977, was chairperson of the National Coalition for Women's Ordination, an organization devoted to persuading delegates to the national convention in 1976 to vote formal approval of women priests. Reverend Park's ordination took place in President Ford's church in Alexandria, Virginia, Immanuel Church on the Hill. Her husband Stephen was one of her sponsors, and assisting at communion were two of the women Episcopal priests ordained in 1974, ALISON CHEEK (p. 377) and LEE McGEE in 1975 (p. 382). The service took place on January 2, 1977.

Called to the Priesthood as a Child

The Reverend CARTER HEYWARD'S path to recognition as an Episcopal priest in 1977 was a long one. As a child she felt a call to the priesthood, later decided to become an Episcopal nun, and then majored in religion at Randolph-Macon College. After college, she entered seminary at Union in New York, but soon left to do parish work in North Carolina. Returning to Union in 1970, she finished her degree and succeeded in being ordained to the diaconate of the Episcopal Church, the first step toward official ordination. A tumultuous few years followed, during which she was active and vocal in promoting ordination of women. Once she was clawed and cursed by a young priest to whom she was serving the communion chalice in Riverside Church in New York. In 1974 she was ordained in a Philadelphia service with 10 other women, later celebrating the Eucharist with two of their number, ALISON CHEEK (p. 377) and JEANNETTE PICCARD (below), in a controversial New York Service. Reverend Heyward, now an assistant professor at Episcopal Divinity School in Cambridge, Massachusetts, was officially recognized by the church in January of 1977.

Balloonist to Priest

The Reverend Dr. JEANNETTE PICCARD, the first of the 11 women ordained in Philadelphia in 1974, turned 82 and was officially recognized as a priest "in good standing" in January 1977. She was recognized, along with another of the original 11, the Reverend Dr. ALLA BOZARTH CAMPBELL (p. 382) at a communion service conducted by the Episcopal Bishop of Minnesota. Dr. Piccard and her late husband Jean were pioneer balloonists. In 1934 she got her pilot's license and made six trips into the upper atmosphere, where her husband studied cosmic rays. Dr. Piccard is a member of a mostly black congregation in St. Paul, Minnesota, where she plans to exercise her right to preside at communion. "I will be much more useful now that I can celebrate the Eucharist," she said.

First Negro Woman Ordained by Episcopal Church

At 66 Dr. PAULI MURRAY, civil rights pioneer, lawyer, and former law professor, became the first Negro woman priest in the history of the Episcopal Church. She was ordained in January 1977 with two other women and three men. It was the first time that men and women were ordained together. Dr. Murray has been active in civil rights since 1938, when she tried unsuccessfully to be the first Negro (the racial description she prefers) to enter the University of North Carolina graduate school. In 1940 she was jailed for trying to sit with whites on a Petersburg, Virginia, bus. In 1944 she was turned away from Harvard Law School, which did not admit women. Instead she studied at Howard University, and while there participated in sit-ins that in 1953 led to a Supreme Court decision banning segregation in public places in the District of Columbia. After receiving a doctorate in law from Yale University, she began teaching, eventually holding the Stuhlberg Professor of Law chair at Brandeis University. She resigned in 1973 to study theology—a decision that led her to Washington Cathedral for ordination in 1977.

First Woman Rector

The Reverend BEVERLY MESSENGER-HARRIS, another of the first women to be ordained to the priesthood in the Episcopal Church in the U.S.A., became that Church's first rector on June 1, 1977 and took up her duties at Gethsemane Episcopal Church in Oneida, New York. The 100-member church's vestry chose Reverend Messenger-Harris with a unanimous vote, after initial doubts about having a woman serve in the position.

Born in April 1949, she studied at William Smith College, receiving a B.A. in religion, and went on to Bexley-Hall Seminary in Rochester, New York. There she met and married James Messenger-Harris, a Presbyterian minister.

First Woman to Celebrate Communion in Britain

The Reverend ALISON PALMER, a U. S. Foreign Service officer and one of the Episcopal priests ordained in Washington in 1975, became the first woman to celebrate the sacrament of Holy Communion in Britain. The service was performed in a Unitarian church. "Tally" Palmer has a long history of fighting discrimination against women; she filed the first ever discrimination suit involving the State Department (and won), helped form the American Federation of Government Employees, and was the first Foreign Service officer in the world to qualify as a union shop steward in the AFL-CIO. In 1977 she was active in the drive to "rescue" one of the priests ordained in Philadelphia in 1974, the Reverend KATRINA SWANSON, from the Missouri diocese where she had been summarily denied recognition by Bishop Arthur Vogel. Swanson and her husband, also an Episcopal priest, had been searching fruitlessly for a new church in which to work, until Reverend Palmer and other sister priests raised enough money to subsidize their work at the Church of the Ascension in Jersey City, New Jersey. It was there on July 29, 1977, that Reverends Palmer and Swanson were finally formally recognized by the Episcopal Church. Reverend Palmer could have joined in the recognition service earlier, but had refused to do so until Katrina Swanson was also recognized.

First Elected Executive Presbyter

In May 1977 the Reverend MARGARETHE B. J. BROWN became the first woman ever to serve as an executive presbyter for the United Presbyterian Church. The position involves the administration of 75 churches in five upstate counties in New York. A graduate of Union Theological Seminary, Reverend Brown also studied in Denmark, Scotland, England, and Switzerland. She is married to another Presbyterian minister, William E. Brown, and the mother of two children. She has had experience in many positions—with the United Presbyterian Commission on Ecumenical Mission and Relations, as a professor at the Methodist Theological Seminary and the Lutheran School of Theology in Columbus, Ohio, as an adviser at the fifth assembly of the World Council of Churches, and as an active member of the National Council of Churches.

First Woman Canon Residentiary, First to Preach in Westminster Abbey

In 1977 Canon MARY MICHAEL SIMPSON became the first Episcopal nun to be ordained to the priesthood, and then the first woman installed as a canon residentiary at the Cathedral of St. John the Divine in New York City. (Canons residentiary are part of the Cathedral Chapter, which runs the church.) In April 1978 she became the first woman ever to preach in England's Westminster Abbey. Canon Simpson, born in 1926 in Texas City, Texas, was converted to the Episcopal faith in college. She went on to the New York Training School for Deaconesses and Other Church Workers, and went to Liberia as a missionary. She joined the Order of St. Helena, and took the vows of poverty, chastity, and obedience. As a religious, she spent several years as head of a convent in Liberia, as the academic head of Margaret Hall, a girl's school in Kentucky, and as director of novices at her mother house in Vails Gate, New York. She became involved in the move toward the priesthood for women in 1973, and was ordained in January 1977 after three years as a deacon. The appointment as canon came soon after, in October 1977. Asked

about being called "Canon Simpson," she said: "None of us know what the equivalent of Father is. None of us want to be called Mother. Canon solves it."

Cathedral Staff Assistant, Now Priest

The Reverend ELIZABETH WIESNER, a staff assistant at Washington's Episcopal Cathedral, also was ordained there in 1977 in the historic service involving both men and women. Reverend Wiesner, a mother of four, worked without pay in the National Cathedral during her two-year wait for ordination. She became eligible in 1975, but opted to delay until the approval of the general convention, rather than to take part in one of the earlier ordinations. Before study for the ministry Reverend Wiesner worked with the Family Welfare Society of Boston, with the American Red Cross in Europe and Africa, and in pastoral and mental health care programs in universities and hospitals. She likes to serve without pay, seeing this as the wave of the future. "There's so much work that can be done, but not enough money to do it," she says. In August 1978, Reverend Wiesner became the second woman ever to preach in Westminster Abbey, following Canon MARY MICHAEL SIMPSON (above).

First Married Couple Ordained Together in U. S. Episcopal Church

On December 17, 1977, the Right Reverend John B. Coburn, Episcopal Bishop of Massachusetts, in St. James Episcopal Church, Danbury, Connecticut, where his father, the Reverend Aaron Coburn, had been rector, 1913–28, administered ordination vows to his son and daughter-in-law. Michael and ANN STRUTHERS COBURN are the first married couple in the United States to be ordained together to the priesthood. After graduation from the Church Divinity School of the Pacific, Berkeley, California, the Coburns shared the job of deacon at St. James Church and they continue to work as assistant rectors there. St. James is the second largest Episcopal church in New England, with almost 3,000 members. The Coburns met at a religious conference when both were 16. They married at 21 and attended divinity school together. Each now works part-time in their shared rector's position, with Ann Coburn concentrating on counseling, her husband on preaching. The Reverend Ann Coburn was the 90th woman to be ordained to the Episcopal priesthood in 1977, and the first in the state of Connecticut.

FOREMOTHERS

Friendly Women—Some Historical Notes

Quakerism has extended equal opportunities to its women members since its beginnings in the 1640s. Founder George Fox's central notion of "Inner Light" includes the spiritual equality of all people. Inspired by their participation in the Society of Friends, many women took their Inner Light into the world. They included:

MARY FISHER, one of the first Quakers to come to Massachusetts in 1656. Sent back to England by Puritan authorities, she embarked on a missionary visit to Turkey, walking partway through 600 miles of rough country. Received by the Sultan as an ambassador, she was able to preach her Quaker word as she had been unable to do in the New World.

MARY DYER, one of four Quakers hanged on Boston Common in 1659, and part of the reason England forced the Puritans to modify their harsh anti-Quaker laws. Her statue now stands near the Massachusetts State House in Boston.

ELIZABETH HADDON, one of the few women ever to found a town, who came to the New World as a very young woman in about 1700. For many years she lived alone among Indians, offering a haven to traveling Friends. Eventually her settlement became Haddonfield, New Jersey.

ELIZABETH FRY, one of the most renowned women of her time, a great Quaker prison reformer in England. She made the improvement of the women's prison at Newgate her life's work, founding an organization to that end in 1817. Her methods were adopted throughout England, and on the Continent. She was probably the first woman whose advice was sought by a committee of the House of Commons. She also founded a girls' orphanage, and the first institute for nurses' training, later used by Florence Nightingale. A contemporary wrote of seeing her that it was one of the great experiences available in London—the other being St. Paul's Cathedral.

LAURA HAVILAND, known as "President of the Underground" for her work in the cause of escaping slaves. A Michigan native, she and her husband founded the Raisin Institute in 1837, probably the second school in the U.S.A. (after Oberlin, also a Quaker institution) to have both black and white students.

LUCRETIA MOTT, involved in both the anti-slavery and the women's rights movements, a Friends' minister and leader within Quakerism. She helped to found Swarthmore College, worked with the Underground Railroad, founded the Philadelphia Female Anti-Slavery Society, and called, with ELIZABETH CADY STANTON, the Seneca Falls Convention of 1848. The Convention, where a Declaration of the Rights of Women (based on the Declaration of Independence) was drawn up, marked the beginning of the women's rights movement.

MEMBERS OF RELIGIOUS ORDERS

First U.S. Citizen to Be Canonized

In 1889 Mother FRANCES XAVIER CA-BRINI sailed to New York City to work among its impoverished Italian immigrants. Mother Cabrini, now St. Frances Xavier Cabrini, had been sent by Pope Pius XIII. She had requested an assignment as a missionary to China, but he, recognizing the American immigrants' great need for help and sure of Mother Cabrini's abilities, sent her to the United States with six other sisters under her direction. The Italian-born foundress of the Missionary Sisters of Charity and her followers went on to build an international network of institutions, among them Chicago's Columbus Hospital, numerous schools, and orphanages. Her labors necessitated 30 crossings of the Atlantic between Italy and the United States. She became an American citizen in 1909, and but for a period during World War I spent working among Italy's wounded, she devoted the rest of her life to the immigrants in America's cities. She died in 1917 of malaria, and was buried in New York. Cardinal George Mundelein of Chicago launched the process for her eventual canonization, and on July 7, 1946, she became the first U.S. citizen to be a saint. She is remembered as "the saint of the immigrants."

President of Nun's Coalition

Sister DOROTHY DONNELLY, author and professor at the Jesuit School of Theology at Berkeley, is president of the National Coalition of American Nuns, as well as a frequent contributor to *Commonweal* and *New Catholic World*. The Coalition's cause is the right of nuns to run their own congregations without interference from male clergy.

First Woman President of the Religious Education Society

Immediate and radical change marked the start, in 1957, of Sister ANN IDA GANNON's 18-year term as president of Mundelein College in Chicago. She diversified the faculty to provide commuter students with an opportunity to obtain a full liberal arts education while pursuing studies geared toward non-academic careers. She established the first continuing education program in the Midwest for mature women, a program in early childhood education, and, perhaps most revolutionary of all, she set up a weekend college for working men and women. The first woman president of the Religious Education Society and president of both the Association of American Colleges and the American Council on Education, in 1975 she was awarded the Laetare Medal—the first nun ever to receive this highest honor given by Notre Dame. Sister Ann Ida retired from her administrative duties at Mundelein in 1975, but after a year of graduate study at Notre Dame, went back as a professor of philosophy.

First to Found an Alternative Community

In 1970 the Immaculate Heart Sisters of Los Angeles, wishing to use their own names, wear contemporary clothes, handle money, and do work other than the teaching traditionally associated with their order, broke away from their mother congregation. The split came after some years of conflict with the male hierarchy of the Church both in California and finally in Rome. Under the leadership of Sister ANITA CASPARY, who had been their superior, 400 became an independent order of lay women. One of these, Sister ANNA, who made her original vows in 1905, was 99 when she signed the mimeographed document indicating her commitment to the new order.

From Nursing Nun to Political Activist

Sister MARY ROSE CHRISTY, a Mercy sister, spent 21 years as a nurse in Phoenix, Arizona. Wishing to understand better some of the problems she saw in the hospital, she began to study social work, later turning to political science, feeling that she had to be more aggressive to become an advocate for the oppressed. She worked as an intern in the state legislature from 1970 to 1972, concentrating on civil rights bills. Later she became active in the Arizona United Farm Workers struggle, becoming a key speaker for the movement. She also has worked on a study of corruption in the welfare department in Arizona, and has continued her formal education in political science.

Medievalist for Renewal

Sister ELIZABETH CARROLL, a member for more than forty years of the Religious Sisters of Mercy, is one of the leaders of the movement for reform and renewal among American nuns. Formerly known as Mother M. Thomas Aquinas, she was superior-general of the order in Pittsburgh until 1974. In wide demand as a speaker, Sister Elizabeth

Mother Teresa

Mother TERESA of Calcutta, born AGNES BOJOXHIU of Albanian parents in Yugoslavia in 1910, is the first female recipient of the $80,000 Templeton Prize for Religion, an award given to "stimulate the knowledge and love of God on the part of mankind everywhere." The award was presented to Mother Teresa in recognition of the work that her order, the Missionary Sisters of Charity, does among the hungry, dying, and impoverished people of the world.

Mother Teresa first felt the stirrings of a religious vocation when she read some letters from Jesuits working in the

brings to the topic of women a sound historical view. A Ph.D. in medieval history, she is also well versed in the theology of women and has had wide experience in the Leadership Conference of Women Religious on topics relating to women, especially the question of ordination. She is a staff member of the Jesuit-founded Center of Concern in Washington, where she does research on women and other human rights and social service issues.

First Executive Director of Network

CAROL COSTON, a Dominican sister born in September 1935, began her religious career as a parochial school teacher and community organizer. In December 1971 she and a group of women religious founded Network, a Washington lobby of women religious for social justice. Coston travels throughout the U.S.A. running workshops on the legislative and political process to help nuns learn to lobby effectively on human rights issues with local legislators. These issues— chosen by vote among Network members —include national health care, international peace and justice, welfare, penal reform, full employment, women's rights, congressional reform, and demilitarization of the national budget.

Bengal Mission in Calcutta. She volunteered for the Mission, and in 1928 entered the convent at Loreto Abbey, Rathfarnham, in Ireland. The nuns there sent her directly to India to start her novitiate training. She was to remain in India. For some years she taught at a girls' high school in Calcutta, but soon requested permission to live alone, outside the cloister, working among the poor in Calcutta's slums.

In 1950 her own order—the Missionary Sisters of Charity—was approved. Joined by the Brothers of Charity in

1963, the orders gained pontifical recognition in 1965, a remarkable feat for such a young religious organization. In the late 1960s Mother Teresa traveled throughout the world opening branches of her order in Venezuela, Ceylon, Tanzania, Rome, Australia, Jordan, and London.

In 1971 she received the Pope John XXIII Peace Prize from Pope Paul VI. After all the travel and prizes, however, she always returns to her Home for the Dying in Calcutta, where she and the other sisters tend the sick and destitute, work among lepers, and give shelter to those incurables whom no one else will help. A few years ago, Mother Teresa told Malcolm Muggeridge, who had come to India to write a book about her, that she and her order exist to "do something beautiful for God."

Revitalizer of Swedish Medieval Order

MARIA ELISABETH HESSELBLAD, born in Sweden, came to the United States as a young woman in an effort to help her family. She found her first vocation as a nurse in New York City's Roosevelt Hospital, where she stayed for 18 years. Becoming ill herself, she wished to travel to Rome to die in the House of Birgitta, a Swedish saint. She traveled there, to recover and become a nun under the direction of the Carmelite sisters. She took her vows as a sister of the medieval Order of St. Birgitta, and under her leadership the Order was revitalized and brought back to Sweden after an absence of 300 years. Seventeen new convents joined the nine surviving from earlier times, and the Order came to extend as far as India and America. Mother Elisabeth died in 1957, fulfilling her wish by dying in the House of Birgitta, which the Carmelites had returned to the Order, and which remains its mother house today.

Mobile Medical Sisters

Sister DOROTHY PETERSON, with five other Sisters of Nazareth, established a Home Health Agency serving four counties in central rural Kentucky. This agency was one of the first to be funded by the Campaign for Human Development. The six sisters' work involves service with over 70,000 people.

First Nun President of Western U.S. Hospitals

Sister VIRGINIA SCHWAGER joined the Sisters of Providence in 1946. After studying hospital administration at St. Louis University she worked in Pennsylvania, Oregon, and Washington medical facilities before being named administrator of Seattle's Providence Hospital in 1961. She spent 11 years there, acting as supervisor for the more than 1,100 employees of the establishment known familiarly in Seattle as "the hospital with a heart." In 1972 Sister Virginia moved to Washington to become director of the Division of Health Affairs for the United States Catholic Conference. She is the recipient of numerous awards, among them Phi Khi Theta's Woman of the Year in 1970, and was the first nun ever elected president of the Association of Western Hospitals (1968–69).

Hospital Expander

Sister M. INNOCENT HUGHES, a Sister of Mercy, runs a multimillion-dollar business. She is executive vice-president of Holy Cross Hospital in Ft. Lauderdale, Florida. As chief operating officer of the only non-profit hospital in Broward County, Florida, Sister Innocent presides over 50 departments in the large building that is now Holy Cross. When Sister Innocent, formerly administrator of Mercy Hospital in Pittsburgh, came to Holy Cross in 1959 it was a small, four-year-old hospital of 125 beds, and was in deep financial trouble. Since her arrival, Sister Innocent has been the guiding spirit of the hospital's expansion into a 596-bed, ultramodern, and nationally respected medical center. A native of Philadelphia,

Sister Innocent joined the Mercy sisters at age 21. A long-time member of the American College of Hospital Administrators, on the Board of the American Red Cross, she is also active in civic affairs and helped write the new Broward County charter in 1975.

First to Head Catholic Office of Education

In 1972 Sister ELINOR RITA FORD, a Dominican nun, was named superintendent of the New York Archdiocese's Office of Education—the first nun and first woman to hold such an office in any major U.S. city. The job entails responsibility for 314 elementary and secondary schools that serve 184,000 students in Manhattan, the Bronx, Staten Island, and seven upstate counties. Sister Elinor is a Bronx native, born in 1931, and a graduate of Dominican-run St. Nicholas of Tolentine High School. She thinks her experience there led to her decision to join the Dominican Order in 1949. She holds a B.A. and two M.A.s from Fordham University, and is working toward her Ph.D. from Teachers College of Columbia University. A veteran of 14 years as an elementary school teacher, she sees herself as an innovator, and is interested in the open-school system developed in England. Sister Elinor is continuing her fight for a long-held belief in more public money for non-public education.

First to Head Major School System

Sister MARYELLEN HARMON is the first woman to head a major Roman Catholic school system in the U.S.A. She remains head of the Convent of the Sacred Heart School while presiding over the 91,000 students in 211 schools in the Detroit parochial system. As an elementary school teacher for 23 years in Albany, New York, Sister Maryellen was an active member of the Urban League and United Black Parents. In Detroit she continues her devotion to creating and bettering cooperation between school administrators and parents of children in inner-city areas.

Religious Agri-Woman

Sister THOMAS MORE BERTELS, a member of the Franciscan Sisters of Christian Charity and a professor of history at Silver Lake College in Wisconsin, speaks around the United States and in Canada on the subject of agriculture. A nationally known authority on farm organizations, Sister Thomas More won the American Agri-Woman Award in 1976 for "her courageous involvement in promoting justice in agriculture." She is the recipient of many other honors, including Outstanding Educator of 1975 and "Spokesman" of the Year Award from Chevron Chemical in 1974.

A Conservative Voice

Mother M. CLAUDIA, mother superior of the Sisters/Servants of the Immaculate Heart of Mary, who staff 180 schools in North and South America, also serves as an officer of Chicago's Institute for Religious Life, which promotes a conservative interpretation of the Vatican II decrees allowing the relaxation of rules governing religious life. "Women religious should be in the classroom, where they're needed," she writes.

Ministering to Brazil's Poor

In 1965, after leaving her position at New York City's Sacred Heart High School, Sister MARY ELIZABETH KREAMER joined three other sisters in a rural area near Rio de Janeiro to minister to the spiritual, social and medical needs of 15,000 poor families. Her energy and mercy missions have become local legends. At 65, Sister Elizabeth is not considering a return to the United States. "When I'm older and can't run around like a crazy person, I'll go to a house they have over in Tijuca where the older sisters live," she told the *Washington Post*. "There's a slum down below where I can work."

Sister Named Pittsburgh's "Man of the Year" in Education

In 1975 Sister JANE SCULLY, a member of the Sisters of Mercy of Allegheny County and president of Pittsburgh's Carlow College, became the first woman director of the Gulf Oil Corporation. Sister Jane, well known in Pittsburgh because of her numerous civic activities, was nominated after feminist shareholders' resolutions at the 1974 annual meeting had resulted in a promise that a woman would be named to the Board. A native of Pittsburgh, Sister Jane received a bachelor of arts degree from Mount Mercy College in 1939. Mount Mercy would later be renamed Carlow College, due to Sister Jane's efforts to have the institution bear the name of Carlow, Ireland, the birthplace of the Sisters of Mercy Order. Sister Jane has taught every grade from first through college, and has library science degrees from Carnegie-Mellon and the University of Michigan. At Carlow she served as college librarian, then as director of development, raising $3 million for a new library. Following this success she was named mother-general of the Order and president of the college in 1969. In 1970 she was appointed as the first woman director of the Port Authority in Pittsburgh, and in 1972 was named Pittsburgh's Man of the Year in Education.

Founder of the Southern Mutual Help Association

In 1972 Sister ANNE CATHERINE BIZALION, a Dominican rural missionary from France, started the Southern Mutual Help Association in Abbeville, Louisiana. Dedicated to helping the poor, especially Louisiana's sugar-cane workers, improve their standard of living, SMHA concentrates on housing needs and uses a grassroots, self-help strategy. A former medical social worker, Sister Anne Catherine, 52, hopes that her organization "sparks a newfound and newly developed sense of community that will allow residents to improve their world, and not only in material ways."

Marian Scholar

Sister ANGELITA MYERSCOUGH, a Marian scholar at St. Louis University, researches and teaches on Jesus and woman, St. Paul and woman, woman in the history of the church, woman and ordination—and most recently the question of the Virgin Mary, in terms of Mary as new woman, Mary and women's liberation, and similar topics.

Floating Minister

Sister JEREMY DAIGLER, a Sister of Mercy, received a master's degree in classics as a Woodrow Wilson fellow at the Johns Hopkins University. Following that accomplishment, she worked for nine years in teaching and administrative posts at Catholic institutions before becoming assistant coordinator of campus ministries at Loyola College of Baltimore. There she became a full-time member of Loyola's first campus-ministry team, involved in dorm counseling, overseeing liturgical programs, teaching, and functioning as a "floating minister." Added administrative responsibility has led her to become, she says, "In effect, the pastor of the church on campus, drawing heavily on the cooperation of very supportive Jesuit faculty members."

Searcher for Roots

Sister FRANCIS BORGIA, president of the School Sisters of St. Francis, also has been president of the Leadership Conference of Women Religious (1973–74) as well as a member of the theology faculty of the Institute of Women Today, a church-related women's coalition organized to search for the religious roots of women's liberation.

First Native-Born U.S. Saint

ELIZABETH ANN SETON, the first native-born U.S. citizen to become a saint (1975), was born Elizabeth Ann Bayly to a well-to-do doctor and his wife in New York in 1774. Her father was a health inspector of incoming ships at Staten Island, and there he contracted a disease from which he died in 1801. His daughter's comfortable life was saddened but not drastically changed, for in her 20th year she had married an Episcopalian merchant, William Seton. She had five children, and lived a busy social life in New York City. Her husband became consumptive, and she took him on a trip to Italy for a cure, but he died there, leaving her a widow at 29. The family with whom she stayed, who were later to become her benefactors, began the process of her conversion to Catholicism. Upon returning to the United States she did convert, and moved with her children to Emmitsburg, Maryland. There she became a nun, opened the first free parochial school in the United States, and founded the American branch of the Sisters of Charity. Mother Seton's good works, her reputation for saintliness, and miracles later attributed to her intercession, led first to her beatification and finally to her canonization.

THE LAITY

First President of the National Council of Churches

When she was elected president of the National Council of Churches in 1969, CYNTHIA WEDEL became the first woman to hold the highest ecumenical post in the U.S.A. Dr. Wedel also has served as president of Church Women United, as head of the Church Executive Development Board, as associate director of the Center for a Voluntary Society, and was one of three Protestant women to attend Vatican II. A psychologist, she also holds an M.A. in history, and has received a doctor of humane letters degree from Fordham University. While remaining active in both Episcopal Church work and the ecumenical movement, Dr. Wedel recently became the director of volunteers for the National Red Cross.

First Black Woman Moderator of the Presbyterian Church

In 1976 THELMA DAVIDSON ADAIR, a professor of elementary and preschool education, became the first black woman ever elected moderator of the 2.7-million-member United Presbyterian Church. A former schoolteacher, and director of the Mount Morris Children's Center, which she and her husband founded in the 1940s, Dr. Adair received her master's and Ph.D. degrees from Columbia Teachers College. Since then she has lectured at both New York University and Princeton theological seminaries and been a consultant in several African countries, including Liberia, where she worked with Operation Crossroads Africa.

First Woman General Secretary of National Council of Churches

CLAIRE RANDALL, general secretary of the National Council of Churches, first took office in 1974, and was reelected in 1975 for the next triennium. Dr. Randall is the first woman to be chief administrative officer of the Council, a cooperative agency of Protestant, Anglican, and Orthodox churches. She has helped coordinate the churches' world hunger concerns, and has been active in promoting strengthened associations with Jews and Roman Catholics. Dr. Randall was also associate executive director of Church Women United, an ecumenical women's movement. Her early career in the church included work as a Christian educator on a local level, and on the missionary board and as director of art of the United Presbyterian Church in the U.S.A., in which she is an ordained elder. She has been the recipient of many honors, among them an honorary doctor of divinity from Yale Divinity School.

Ecumenical Executive

As executive director of the study department of the World Council of Churches for many years, Swiss Dr. MADELEINE BAROT helped provide an ecumenical forum for the discussion of women's position in the churches. The department has issued a report, *Cooperation of Men and Women in Church, Family, and Society,* which provides a comprehensive survey of the position of women in terms of ordination in the various denominations, and provides an opportunity for exchange among women of many nations on the issues of parenthood, family planning, and world population.

First Woman Elected a Presbyter

The first woman to become a presbyter in the United Presbyterian Church was JOREEN JARRELL of Paoli, Pennsylvania. Presbyters are the ruling elders in particular regions of the church, and serve in an essentially administrative capacity. She will serve as general presbyter of the Presbytery of San Fernando, Synod of Southern California. Ms. Jarrell is associate for educational planning and support in the denomination's program agency. While the first woman elected to such a post, she is not the first to so serve: MARGUERITE BOWDEN serves as a non-elected executive in the Presbytery de Cristo, in the Synod of the Southwest.

First Moderator of the Presbyterian Church

LOIS H. STAIR, ordained a ruling elder of the Presbyterian Church in the U.S.A. in 1957, was elected the first woman moderator of its General Assembly in 1971. Ms. Stair had previously served the church as secretary to its Standing Committee on Theological Education, and as moderator of the Presbytery of Milwaukee, which elected her to two successive terms, making her the first person so honored. She has also served on the United Presbyterian Church in the U.S.A.'s Task Force on Women, which asked in its 1971 report that "women take on the responsibilities of freedom, to give strength and courage to each other, and to trust the movement and power of God's spirit in the world. The Task Force calls men to think on these things and to seek their own liberation from the idols of our time."

Church Women United President, 1974–77

MARGARET L. SONNENDAY was national president of Church Women United in the U.S.A. for the 1974–77 triennium. Her successor is MARY LOUISE ROWAND (p. 380). Ms. Sonnenday, a member of the United Methodist Church, has had 20 years' experience with Church Women United, an ecumenical movement open to Protestant, Orthodox, and Roman Catholic women across the country. She served for seven years as vice-president, with special responsibility for the national priority program to strengthen the organization at the grassroots level. From 1970 to 1974, she represented the U.S.A. on the International Committee for the World Day of Prayer and traveled widely under the auspices of Christian Causeway, an organization of international women dedicated to peace. She was chosen Ecumenical Woman of the Year in 1967 by a church federation in St. Louis for her involvement in the life of the church on the local, national, and worldwide levels.

National Council of Negro Women President and YWCA Activist

DOROTHY HEIGHT, president of the National Council of Negro Women, has

Judge SUSIE M. SHARPE. A trial and appellate judge in North Carolina for 30 years, Susie M. Sharpe was elected chief justice of her state's Supreme Court in 1975—the first woman in the nation to reach that level.

BARBARA FRITZ, detective. One of the few women detectives among New York's finest, Barbara Fritz was serving with the Investigations Unit, 23rd Precinct, New York City, even before the ranks were more widely opened to women in early 1978. (Photo by Neal Boenzi, the *New York Times*)

ELLEN FLEYSHER, appointed deputy commissioner of Public Information of the New York City Police Department in 1978, is the first woman in the history of the department to serve as deputy commissioner in that post, in which she advises the police commissioner on policy matters. (Photo by Doug Malin: courtesy of the Manhattan Police Department)

PATRICIA ROBERTS HARRIS, cabinet member. As secretary of the Department of Housing and Urban Development, Ms. Roberts is the highest-ranking woman lawyer in the U. S. Government. (Her sister in the Cabinet, JUANITA M. KREPS, Secretary of Commerce, is an economist.) Ms. Roberts is also the first black woman in the President's Cabinet and the first to have been named a U.S. ambassador.

Women as Episcopalian Priests

The Reverend Dr. PAULI MURRAY, only Negro (the designation she prefers) among the women priests who were the first to be ordained in the Episcopal Church in the United States in 1977, is seen above (center, facing camera, smiling) receiving congratulations immediately following her ordination. Murray is a civil rights pioneer, lawyer, and former law professor. (Michael Glennon)

JOAN MAYER, one of several young women enrolled in Wesleyan Theological Seminary, Washington, D.C., wears jeans and boots under her alb as she crosses the campus. (Rosemary Martufi, the *Washington Star*)

MOTHER TERESA, Yugoslavian nun who for many years has ministered to the dying in Calcutta, India, photographed in 1962, was the first female recipient of the Templeton Prize for Religion. Mother Teresa won the award in recognition of the work done by the order she founded, the Missionary Sisters of Charity among the hungry and impoverished people of the world. (Photo courtesy of the Ramón Magsaysay Award for International Understanding)

MOTHER SETON, only U.S. citizen to be canonized, in a miniature portrait painted when she was 19-year-old ELIZABETH BAYLEY and presented to her on her wedding day, January 25, 1794, by her husband. (Photo courtesy of the Sisters of Charity by Chris Sheridan)

This painting shows her at a much older age. The Setons had five children before her husband died of consumption, leaving her a widow at 29. She later converted to Catholicism, became a nun, opened the first free parochial school in the United States, and founded the American branch of the Sisters of Charity. Miracles later attributed to her intercession led to her beatification and, in 1975, to her canonization. (Photo courtesy of the Sisters of Charity)

Its founders, clockwise from the bottom left, were MARY ALLEN (STAFFORD), ELLA STEWART, ALICE BIRD (BABB), HATTIE BRIGGS (BOUSQUET), FRANC ROADS (ELLIOTT), ALICE VIRGINIA COFFIN, and SUELA PEARSON (PENFIELD). They met while students at Iowa Wesleyan College and formed a secret society as a protest when some of them were asked to join a campus sorority and others were not. Out of this grew the Philanthropic Educational Organization (PEO), still flourishing, with 231,207 members in every state of the United States, Canada, and abroad; an educational loan fund that since 1907 has lent about $12.3 million to some 19,200 women; and its own two-year women's college in Nevada, Cottey College. (Photographs courtesy of the Philanthropic Educational Organization)

Yanks at Oxford

Three of the 14 U.S. women who were among the first female Rhodes scholars selected in 1977 under new rules, which eliminated "qualities of manhood" from the specifications, stop to chat in the High Street, Oxford, England. Left to right, they are SUE HALPERN, DARYL KOEHN, and LISSA MUSCATINE. (Susan Semple, the *New York Times*)

Among the Presidents

PAULINE THOMPKINS, president of Cedar Crest College. Dr. Thompkins, a former research associate in international relations at MIT, is seen above with students on Cedar Crest's Pennsylvania campus. (Courtesy of William J. Keller)

HANNA HOLBURN GRAY was named to president of the University of Chic while she, as provost of Yale Univer was also acting as Yale's president du the search for a successor to King Brewster. After the Yale Corpora chose its new president, a man, it nounced that he would be the 19th p dent and Dr. Gray would officially known as the 18th — and thus the woman president of Yale or of any League college.

Editor of *SIGNS: a Journal of Women in Culture and Society*, CATHERINE R. STIMPSON is an associate professor of English at Barnard College in New York.

spent most of her life in the church and related activities. After a conference in Europe representing the Christian youth of the U.S.A., Ms. Height joined the Harlem branch of the YWCA, and rose rapidly in the executive ranks. She has served extensively in the U. S. Government and was a consultant on African affairs, using her influence to help win American aid for new black African nations. Since 1963, Ms. Height has led an intensive integration drive within the YWCA, and has contributed time, money, and womanpower, through the National Council, to the cause of civil rights. During the 1970 convention of the YWCA, Ms. Height rejected any women's liberation that did not relate directly and specifically to the problem of racism, and forcefully launched the Y on a campaign that went beyond tokenism to "a bold assault on racial injustice." A member of many presidential committees, and the recipient of awards and honorary degrees, Dorothy Height has lived in Harlem for over 30 years.

First Woman Commander of the Salvation Army

EVANGELINE BOOTH, commander of the U.S. Salvation Army from 1904 to 1934, and then general of the International Salvation Army to 1939, was the daughter of CATHERINE BOOTH and General William Booth, co-founders of the militant Christian charitable organization in England in 1865. Partly because of the influence of Catherine Booth, women have shared equally in the Army since its beginnings. ("Some of my best men are women," General Booth said.) In the case of marriage between officers, one or the other must be promoted to the higher rank held between them, so they can work as partners on the same level.

Order of Canada Winner

Brigadier ELIZABETH PEACOCKE of the Salvation Army superintends The Homestead, Toronto, Canada's only rehabilitation center for women with drug or alcohol problems. Brigadier Peacocke joined the Army in 1943, and worked in the wilder sections of Canada and in Bermuda before coming to The Homestead. In January 1973 she was awarded the Order of Canada for her outstanding work with addicts.

Salvation Army Educator

Lieutenant Colonel ANNA BEEK of the Salvation Army was appointed principal of the European Training College in Johannesburg while retaining her office as secretary for education and literary affairs for the Salvation Army in all of South Africa. Lieutenant Colonel Beek joined the Army in her native Netherlands, and spent her early career as headmistress of the Fred Clark Institute, a training college situated in the middle of an area where thousands of detribalized Bantu live. After a period of teaching in Zaire, she returned to South Africa to continue her work with the Bantu and other tribal people.

First Synagogue President

FAYVELLE MERMEY, born in 1916, was the first woman to serve as a president of a synagogue. She headed the Larchmont, New York, Temple for two terms, from 1960 to 1962 and from 1972 to 1974. Her election in 1960 was hailed as evidence of Reform Judaism's efforts to make women equal with men in temple administration. During her presidency Ms. Mermey founded the Women's Interfaith Seminar. A graduate of New Jersey State College, she attended Georgian Court College and the Columbia Graduate School of Journalism. In addition to her duties at Larchmont Temple, Ms. Mermey was a journalist, a career she pursued until her death in March 1977.

Highest-Level Executive in Church's History

PATRICIA ANN MCCLURG was elected administrative director of the General Assembly Mission Board of the Presbyterian Church in the United States, a position she will hold for four years, in 1977. She is the first woman to hold an executive position of this level in the church's history. The Reverend Ms. McClurg is a native of Bay City, Texas, and a graduate of Austin's Presbyterian Theological Seminary. As a minister, she served as assistant pastor of Westminster Church in Beaumont, Texas, and as associate pastor of First Church in Pasadena, Texas. She has held presbytery offices, was vice-chairperson of the Austin Seminary's board of trustees, and, before election to her current office, directed the Mission Board's Division of Court Partnership Services.

First to Head American Baptists

CORA SPARROWK was elected head of the American Baptist Churches in the U.S.A. in July 1977. The first woman to hold the position, she was national secretary of Church Women United (CWU) at the time of her election. Ms. Sparrowk has been active in her church at the local, regional, and national levels for many years, and has also been a member of many interdenominational organizations. Berkeley Baptist Divinity School awarded her a Layman's Citation in 1959. At the time of her election to her present position, she was president of the American Baptist International Ministries, and chairwoman of its Commission on Institutional Support. She served as a delegate to the U.S. Conference of the World Council of Churches, was the American Baptist delegate to the Baptist World Alliance Congress in Stockholm, Sweden, and delegate to the General Assembly of the National Council of the Churches of Christ in the U.S.A. She participated in the Christian Causeway to Asia, sponsored by CWU, and in connec-

tion with that experience traveled to a peace consultation in Japan. She has made three trips around the world visiting American Baptist overseas missions, the most recent in 1977. Ms. Sparrowk has a son, a daughter, and four grandchildren.

Ministry to Women Secretary

ROSE CATCHINGS, secretary for the Ministry to Women, Board of Global Missions in the United Methodist Church, sees her role as one of "advocacy for women in developing countries on behalf of women in this country." Under her direction the Ministry has become involved in such issues as nuclear proliferation. Due to a visit to her from women from the Mariana Islands in the South Pacific, the Nuclear Free Pacific Conference was held in 1976. The Ministry works with women in 52 countries, mostly in Africa, Asia, and the Caribbean. Prior to joining the Methodist organization in 1969, Ms. Catchings and her husband spent eight years in Singapore, where he worked for the International YMCA and she taught at the American School. Born on the campus of Bennett College in Greensboro, North Carolina, in 1925, she later graduated from Bennett and now sits on its board of trustees. After her graduation she earned an M.A. in social work and religious education at Atlanta University, and then went to work for the National YWCA. She has a son, and two Ethiopian foster daughters. Ms. Catchings maintains that being one of only a few blacks in the Methodist Board of Global Missions has been no problem, because "the constituency for whom I work have common grounds simply because they are women."

Historian of Presbyterian Women

ELIZABETH HOWELL VERDESI, a graduate of Elmira College and Union Theological Seminary, has served the Presbyterian Church in the U.S.A. all her life, and has written a historical study of Presbyterian women entitled *In But Still Out: Women in the Church* (1976). Ms. Verdesi began her career as a "traveling fellow," recruiting young people for church vocations. She then served the Presbyterian Board of National Missions as secretary for youth work, and later as a consultant. Married to a Presbyterian minister and mother of two sons, Ms. Verdesi is a ruling elder and a member of the professional staff of Church Women United.

Head of Christian Feminists

SONIA QUITSLAND, professor of religion at George Washington University in Washington, D.C., heads Christian Feminists, an organization committed to expanding the role and status of women in the Catholic Church. In 1976 the group sponsored the incorporation of the Catholic Women's Seminarian Fund to help pay for the priestly education of qualified women in Catholic seminaries. Catholic law forbids the ordination of women to the priesthood, but Ms. Quitsland asserts that one objective of the organizations in which she is involved is to "give public testimony to a new phenomenon in the Catholic Church, to our recognition of the seriousness of the call to the priesthood which many women have experienced."

Feminist Jewish Scholar

A prominent scholar, JUDITH HAUPTMAN specializes in the Halacha, the body of

Jewish law supplementing the scriptural and forming the legal part of the Talmud. She concerns herself with how to change Jewish law to accommodate feminist ideas. She is instructor of the Talmud in the Teachers Institute of the Jewish Theological Seminary in New York City, one of the first women in Conservative Judaism to teach in this field.

International Christian Educator

EMILY GIBBES, associate general secretary of the National Council of the Churches of Christ in the U.S.A., spent 19 years in Christian education in Kenya, Cameron, and seven other African countries, India, Pakistan, Thailand, and Mexico, as well as working with church women in South America. A Presbyterian, Ms. Gibbes was educated at Hunter College and New York University, and now works in her native New York City administering programs for the Council's Division of Education and Ministry, where she concerns herself with developing resources that reflect the diversity of Christian perspective in cultures throughout the world. She is also chairperson of the executive committee of the Religious Education Association, a member of the NAACP and the National Council of Negro Women, and serves on the Board of the New York Theological Seminary.

Founder: the "Catholic Worker"

DOROTHY DAY, born in 1897, converted to Catholicism after an early career as a socialist reporter for the *Call* and the *Masses,* an IWW supporter, a suffragette sympathizer, and a novelist. Her autobiography, *The Long Loneliness* (1954), tells the story of her conversion. In 1933 she and Peter Maurin founded the *Catholic Worker,* a monthly newspaper to promote the idea of social reconstruction that was based primarily on communal farming and the establishment of hospitality houses for the urban poor. The first

of these, St. Joseph's House in New York City's Bowery, still feeds, clothes, and shelters many. Within three years the paper's circulation grew to 150,000 and "houses" were established in major cities throughout the country. Eventually the *Worker,* under Dorothy Day's direction, took vocal and radical stands on pacifism in support of Catholic conscientious objectors during World War II and agitated vehemently against nuclear weaponry. She continues to contribute a regular column to the *Catholic Worker,* which has maintained its penny price and bold layout illustrated with woodcuts since the first issue appeared on May 1, 1933.

First Woman Faculty Member at a Jesuit Institution

NANCY KEHOE, a former high school teacher with a Ph.D. in counseling psychology, did retreat work and geriatric counseling before coming to the Weston School of Theology. After a year's training, she became the Jesuit institution's first woman faculty member. She hopes that the Roman Catholic Church will soon open the diaconate, and eventually the priesthood, to women, and works to support this cause.

Feminist Theologian

MARY DALY, radical feminist and theologian, is author of The Church and the Second Sex (1973) and Beyond God the Father (1974) as well as a contributor to such feminist anthologies as Sisterhood Is Powerful (1970). She was born in Schenectady, New York, earned her B.A. from the College of St. Rose, and received doctorates in both philosophy and theology from the University of Fribourg in Switzerland in 1965. She has been on the faculty of Boston College, a Jesuit institution, since 1969. Dr. Daly's writings explore the anti-female bias and patriarchal language she sees in the Roman Catholic Church and society at large, and call on women to form a sisterhood "beyond God the father."

Catholic Scholar and Women's Studies Expert

ROSEMARY RADFORD REUTHER of Howard University's School of Religion in Washington holds a Ph.D. in classics and patristics from the Claremont Graduate School in California. She has taught at both Harvard and Yale universities as well as at Howard in the fields of historical theology, Roman Catholic theological studies, and women's studies. In addition, Dr. Reuther is the author of several

books, among them The Church Against Itself (1967) and The Radical Kingdom (1970). She was editor of the 1974 book Religion and Sexism, is a member of the editorial board of the Journal of Religious Thought, and a contributing editor to Christianity and Crisis and the Ecumenist.

Co-Founder of Ecumenical Journal

ARLENE ANDERSON SWIDLER, author and translator, was co-founder of the Journal of Ecumenical Studies, and served as its managing editor for many years before becoming education editor. She has been a research fellow at the Institute for Ecumenical and Cultural Research in Collegeville, Minnesota, and an editor for Word, the monthly magazine of the National Council of Catholic Women. Ms. Swidler, an enthusiastic worker for the advancement of women in the Catholic Church, has examined their position in her book Woman in a Man's Church (1972). She is also the author of Sistercelebrations: Nine Worship Experiences (1974), a collection of services designed especially for women.

Jailed Black Churchwoman

CLARIE COLLINS HARVEY, past president of Church Women United, and Churchwoman of the Year 1974, earned a B.A. from Spelman College in Atlanta, Georgia, and was graduated from Union Theological Seminary in 1950. Founder of Womanpower Unlimited, she and her organization sheltered freedom riders in Jackson, Mississippi, during the early days of the civil rights movement, an activity which earned her a jail sentence. Ms. Harvey also attended the Paris peace talks during the war in Vietnam. A native of Mississippi, she is an executive in the mortuary firm belonging to her family.

Walker for the Hungry

Working from the First Baptist Church in Abington, Massachusetts, KAY DOHERTY founded Sharing, Inc., an organization dedicated to supporting farm co-operatives. She has walked many miles each Good Friday since 1972 to raise money for farm co-ops. Since then about 2,000 people have walked approximately 60,000 miles, raising more than $100,000. Ms. Doherty is also involved with Bread for the World, a Christian citizens' lobby group working on Capitol Hill for legislation on "the right to food."

Guatemalan Adult Educator

ESPERANZA DE LOPEZ, daughter of the governor of a Guatemalan province, has devoted much of her life to visiting rugged rural areas of her country as a teacher and Christian missionary. As Guatemalan national promoter for Alfalit, a literacy movement, she has traveled throughout the country, often to areas that can be reached only on foot through jungle trails. A mother of five, and a grandmother, Ms. de Lopez also leads courses in nutrition in addition to her adult education classes. She says, "In my country, illiteracy and malnutrition are our greatest social problems. It is just impossible, as Christians and as countrymen, to remain mere spectators of the bitter reality in which we live."

Missionary Artist

MARJORIE MURRAY, a Canadian missionary sponsored by the United Methodist Church, gave up a successful career as an artist in New York City to go to Africa in the early 1960s. There she created the Art Studio of the African Literature Centre in Zambia, where she trains artists from all over Africa, India, and Pakistan. Their work includes illustrations for Christian publications, Sun-day school books, and stained-glass windows.

Volunteer Against Hunger

PATRICIA YOUNG, a ruling elder in the United Presbyterian Church, has served as a voluntary consultant on the world food problems for both church organizations and the U. S. Government. Among Ms. Young's many positions have been chairperson of the National Council of Churches Crusade Against Hunger, national vice-president of the American Freedom from Hunger Foundation, a White House consultant for the Task Force on Food, Nutrition, and Health, U.S. representative to the Hague World Food Conference in 1970, and appointee to the Rome Conference on Hunger in 1976.

Child Rescuer in Chinatown

Called "Lo Mo," "Beloved Mother," by the girls she protected, and "Fahn Quai," "White Devil," by the underworld of San Francisco's Chinatown, DONALDINA CAMERON served for more than 40 years as director of the Presbyterian Mission Home for girls. Between 1895 and her death in 1968 at age 99, often at great danger to herself, she rescued hundreds of the young girls of Chinatown from child slavery and prostitution. Two thousand girls were saved this way and given housing and education at the Home. Once the "yellow slave trade" was banished from California and her girls were grown up, she transformed the Home into a social service center. Still at 920 Sacramento Street in the heart of Chinatown, it now bears her name.

1977 Templeton Prize Winner

CHIARA LUBICH, an Italian Roman Catholic, received the 1977 $80,000 Templeton Foundation Prize for Progress in Religion for her work with the Focolare Movement. Founded by her in Trent, Italy, in 1943, Focolare, which means "heart of the home" in Italian, is a spiritual association with members in 150 countries. Called *focolarini*, the movement's adherents work at normal jobs, but live together in spiritual communities. The Templeton Foundation cited Lubich's fostering of unity among Christians of all denominations as "one of the most outstanding achievements in interchurch and interfaith relations today." Chiara Lubich, born in Trent in 1920, is a university graduate, leader in the Italian Catholic Action Movement, and member of the Franciscan Third Order. She founded Focolare to "introduce the gospel into modern life."

Four American Evangelists

AMANDA SMITH was born in Long Green, Maryland, in 1837, the fifth child of a slave who was later to buy his family's freedom. Unable to attend school due to mounting family pressures—her siblings eventually numbered 12—she taught herself to read and write. Her first husband disappeared during the Civil War while fighting for the North, and her second, a Philadelphia minister, died soon after their marriage. Ms. Smith embarked on her own evangelical career in 1865, supplementing her income by taking in laundry. She preached all over the East and as far south as Texas. She traveled alone, carrying an old carpetbag and wearing a plain Quaker-style bonnet. Her ministry was successful enough to raise funds for a trip to Great Britain in 1876, where she preached throughout the island, including Scotland. From there she set off for Egypt and India, where she spent 19 months preaching and making converts. On her return she published her autobiography, *The Lord's Dealings with Mrs. Amanda Smith*. Later travels included Africa, where she adopted two children. Until her death in 1915 she ran the Amanda Smith Orphans' Home in Chicago. When she died Bishop J. M. Thoburn, the Anglican Bishop of India, said that only a few women of her type "would suffice to revolutionize an empire."

AIMEE SEMPLE McPHERSON, founder of the International Church of the Foursquare Gospel, was the most visible—and most successful—evangelist of her time. Known by her detractors as "the P. T. Barnum of religion," she was among the first preachers to put modern technology to work in the service of religion. Born in Canada in 1890, she grew up in the Bible-thumping atmosphere of the Salvation Army, encouraged by her mother Minnie Kennedy, who later was to manage her business affairs. Her first husband, a Pentecostal preacher, took her to China to do missionary work, but died there. She returned to the U.S.A., and soon married Harold McPherson, but left him to embark on a barnstorming trip across the country as an itinerant preacher, riding in "the Gospel Car." She settled in Los Angeles and began her services in the Angelus Temple, using various kinds of publicity stunts to gain a congregation. She traveled about by car, in airplanes, dressed in costumes, and got as much press coverage as she could muster. In 1924 she acquired her own radio station, KFSG (Kall Foursquare Gospel), and eventually ran off with its engineer in a bizarre false kidnapping episode that had all Los Angeles out searching for her. Although her life was checkered with nervous breakdowns, public court battles, and scandals of all kinds, the church she founded was an enormous success. When she died in 1944 from an overdose of sleeping pills, it claimed 22,000 members, and by the 1960s claimed as many as 80,000 around the world.

KATHRYN KUHLMAN, charismatic Christian faith healer, died in 1976 in the middle of a spectacular career. Ms. Kuhlman, born about 1910 in Concordia, Missouri, began preaching at 16 and for almost 20 years worked as an itinerant minister in the Midwest. She had no formal theological training. Nominally a Baptist, who attributed her power to the Holy Spirit, she conducted interdenominational services and had an especially large following among Catholics.

In 1947 she settled in Pittsburgh, beginning her extraordinary healing ministry. During the 1960s she began to carry her work into other parts of the country, drawing huge crowds in major cities across the nation. Ms. Kuhlman claimed that her staff did follow-up research on the cases she "healed," but *Time* magazine reported that little was actually done except in the most dramatic cases. She was president of the Kathryn Kuhlman Foundation, a multimillion-dollar enterprise that paid her $25,000 salary, and operates a number of charities. Her weekly television broadcasts were seen on 65 stations, and her daily radio message was heard over 50. She was the author of four books and also produced a record—all best sellers.

RUTH CARTER STAPLETON, wife of a Fayetteville, North Carolina, veterinarian and sister of President Jimmy Carter, has been an evangelist since the late 1950s, but has only gained national and international attention since her brother's political success. Ms. Stapleton, who has studied psychology, has her largest following among charismatic Christians, who believe in the healing power of the Holy Spirit, the gift of tongues, and a personal relationship with Christ. Her following at the beginning of her preaching career was largely among Southern Baptists, but since the publication of her book *The Gift of Inner Healing* in 1976, and the increased publicity surrounding her role in President Carter's rededication to Christianity, she has acquired followers all over the United States and in the Orient and Latin America. Ms. Stapleton does not see herself as a "faith healer," but rather as a "spiritual counselor" who can help people get in touch with the inner gifts of the Holy Spirit.

10

Women in Education, Social Sciences, and the Humanities

By Nicole Fermon
Bernice Sandler, consulting editor

The questions that we have to ask and to answer about that [academic] procession . . . are so important that they may well change the lives of all men and all women forever. For we have to ask ourselves, here and now, do we wish to join that procession, or don't we? On what terms shall we join that procession? Above all, where is it leading us, the procession of educated men? . . . Let us never cease from thinking— what is this "civilization" in which we find ourselves? What are its ceremonies and why should we take part in them? What are these professions and why should we make money out of them? Where in short is it leading us, the procession of the sons of educated men?— Virginia Woolf,* *Three Guineas* (1938)

Since the day in 1882 when ELIZABETH CABOT CARY AGASSIZ became the first president of a corporation called "The Society for the College Instruction of Women," better known as Radcliffe Col-

* See also "Women in the Arts and Entertainment," p. 674.

lege, women appear on the surface at least to have made great gains in the academic world. President Agassiz's duties included fund raising and establishing relations with Harvard—then the most feasible step toward giving women access to university resources. Ninety-five years later the arrival at Oxford University in autumn 1977 of the world's first 24 female Rhodes scholars capped two decades of tumbling barriers as educational places and privileges once labeled "For Men Only" became available to women.

Yet women who finish college and enter graduate or professional schools to pursue careers in education, the social sciences, and the humanities are still faced with obstacles similar to those of their predecessors in the 19th century. Equal education does not mean equal opportunities in future academic employment. Even at its most liberal, the university today remains a place where women can buy but not work as equals. Paradoxically, the very women who have long been indispensable to children's earliest education have historically been and continue to be excluded from secure and adequately paid positions in the university's hierarchy. According to *Sex Bias in the Schools,* edited by JANICE POTTKER and Andrew Fishel (1976), women nationally are 20 per cent of the faculty of four-year universities and 10 per cent of "elite" universities, yet they are only 1 or 2 per cent of tenured faculty; U.S. women on campus make $150 to $200 million dollars less per year than men in comparable faculty positions, and individually during 1975–76 earned on the average $3,096 less than men as opposed to a differential of $2,820 in 1974–75. The *Chronicle of Higher Education* noted a slight raise in women's employment, from 369,442 in 1974–75 to 377,157 in 1975–76, but women also continue to be paid less for comparable work than their male colleagues, in spite of a 6.6 over-all increase in faculty salaries, 1975–76. As public awareness of existing inequalities has increased, the inequalities have in fact become even greater.

In 1859 and 1865 ELIZABETH AGASSIZ published introductory guides to marine zoology. She joined her husband, renowned Swiss-born naturalist Louis Agassiz, on various expeditions, collaborated with him on an account of a trip to Brazil, and as the scribe with the Hassler Expedition through the Strait of Magel-

lan, 1871–72, wrote and published the only account of his discoveries concerning glaciation. But Radcliffe's first president was not typical of her times. Nor are the women portrayed here. This chapter documents the achievements of 20th-century women in many nations, but particularly in the United States, who have attained professional and sometimes even popular recognition in their chosen academic fields. A small yet significant minority, their careers provide valid paradigms for continued struggle within and outside the established educational structures.

NICOLE FERMON, *a graduate student in political theory at Columbia University, took as the subject of her thesis "The Bourgeois Family and Its Impact on Political Order," a treatment of major changes in family structures in 18th-century France. She also has done research on the relationship between social stratification and political socialization in the early grades of elementary school. Ms. Fermon taught the first course on Women's Social History at the University of Hawaii in 1971.*

Contributing editor BERNICE SANDLER is director of the Project on the Status and Education of Women, the Association of American Colleges (see p. 432).

UNIVERSITY AND COLLEGE ADMINISTRATORS

First Woman President of Wellesley

At the time ALICE FREEMAN PALMER (1855–1902) was born in Colesville, New York, higher education for women was considered useless by many and freakish by some ("They'll be educating the cows next"). Troubled by lack of money and ill health, she nevertheless finished with the 11 other women of her graduating class at the University of Michigan. After teaching at Saginaw, Michigan, for several years, Ms. Palmer accepted the chair of Wellesley's Department of History. Much loved and very successful as a teacher, in 1880 she was asked to become vice-president of the college and acting president for that year. Her administration at Wellesley transformed the college into a respected institution of higher learning through innovative changes in organization, curriculum, and finances. She instituted the borrowing of faculty from Harvard and met her husband, George Herbert Palmer, when he was "on loan" in 1886. When Ms. Palmer retired from Wellesley in 1887 she was approached by the president of the University of Chicago and was hired to work as Chicago's first dean of women 12 weeks out of the year—any 12 she chose.

First Woman President of Bryn Mawr

At the age of 14 MARTHA CAREY THOMAS (1857–1935) wrote: "If I ever live and grow up, my one aim and concentrated purpose shall be and is to show that women can learn, can reason, can compete with men in the grand fields of literature and science and conjecture that open before the 19th century, that a woman can be a woman and a true one without having all her time engrossed by dress and society." At 20, overcoming her parents' objections, Ms. Thomas went to study at Cornell University, then in 1879 took herself to Leipzig, Germany, later on to transfer to Zurich,

Switzerland, where she received a doctorate summa cum laude. Bryn Mawr College opened in 1875, resolved to employ only Ph.D. scholars. She was appointed dean and professor of English in 1883. Her years as dean proved to be an apprenticeship for the presidency, which she attained in 1894.

Early Women's College and Human Rights Champion

Because of her great determination and financial independence, New York City-born VIRGINIA CROCHERON GILDERSLEEVE (1887–1965), was able in 1908 to earn a Ph.D. in philosophy and proceeded to teach English at Barnard College. She became dean of the college and served in that capacity for 36 years, 1911–47. A strong advocate of the women's college, Dr. Gildersleeve at a convention of the American Association of University Women in 1937 advised women to steer clear of coed institutions and their "lordly male complex" and denounced male professors and presidents of women's colleges as "softies" whose decisions "are more often swayed by emotions than women's." She strongly influenced the expansion and development of both Barnard and Columbia University, in particular the modernization of curriculum in government and international affairs. In addition to her academic career, Dr. Gildersleeve became a distinguished figure in international affairs. In 1945 she was the only woman appointed by President Franklin D. Roosevelt to the seven-member delegation representing the United States at the San Francisco Conference that drew the Charter of the United Nations, and she is credited with the leading role in implementing a special provision in the UN charter to safeguard human rights. Dr. Gildersleeve was one of the founders of UNESCO and of the International Federal of University Women and the recipient of nine honorary degrees.

Founder and First President of College for Black Girls

MARY MCLEOD BETHUNE (1875–1955), born the 15th child of freed slaves on a cotton plantation near Mayesville, South Carolina, was educated by the Presbyterian Board of Missions for Freedmen, then at Scotia Seminary (now Barber-Scotia College) in Concord, North Carolina, and the Moody Bible Institute in Chicago. After serving as a teacher for several years in mission schools administered by the Presbyterian Church, she moved to Daytona Beach, Florida, and founded the Daytona Literary and Industrial School for Training Negro Girls. This school was kept open only by her personal appeal for funds from both impoverished blacks and wealthy northern families in the area. In 1923 her school was merged with the Cookman Institute of Jacksonville and the Methodist Church assumed financial support for the new college, which Ms. Bethune served as president until her retirement in 1947. Well known for her work both in black organizations and in national educational and government agencies, she was invited to attend a child welfare conference at the White House by President Calvin Coolidge in 1928 and became the only black woman adviser to President Franklin D. Roosevelt in the 1930s. As director of the Division of Negro Affairs at the National Youth Administration, she helped thousands of black youths acquire jobs in work projects and scholarships to college during the Depression. Her lifelong dedication to young people won her worldwide recognition and acclaim.

She Persuaded Harvard Men to Share Classrooms

In 1943 ADA COMSTOCK NOTESTEIN, Radcliffe's first full-time president, persuaded Harvard to accept classroom coeducation. Cited as the "chief architect of Radcliffe's greatness," she is also remembered as the only woman named by President Herbert Hoover to the 11-person commission to study problems of law enforcement with particular reference to the 18th (Prohibition) Amendment. She was not among the four favoring continued enforcement but with the five advocating modification. Many years later, as chairman of the international relations department of the American Association of Universities, she leaned to the interventionist side of the isolation-versus-intervention debate before the United States entered World War II. Ada Notestein died in 1973.

Cornell's First Woman Dean of Students

Education research specialist Dr. PATRICIA CROSS, who in 1960 was named the first woman dean of students at Cornell University, is one of America's foremost proponents of educational reform. A former president of the American Association for Higher Education, now at the Center for Research and Development in Higher Education at Berkeley and a research scientist for the Educational Testing Service, Dr. Cross envisions a future with "a 180° turnaround, from selecting students to fit colleges we happen to have, to creating colleges to fit the needs of the students who are walking through the open doors." She is an advocate of education "for everyone as a broad, lifelong process," and believes that universities will eventually accept and encourage various modes of education.

College President Twice

ROSEMARY PARK, born in 1907 in Andover, Massachusetts, on April 22, 1963, was the first person to be inaugurated as president of Barnard College, where the head administrator was previously called "dean." Dr. Park is also the first American woman to have twice become a college president. Prior to her Barnard appointment, she served as president of Connecticut College, in New London, Connecticut. During her presidency, Connecticut College underwent dramatic academic growth: undergraduate enrollment grew from 700 in 1947 to 1,150 in 1961. Dr. Park's father and brother also have been college presidents, at Wheaton College in Norton, Massachusetts, and Simmons College in Boston.

First Woman President of a Major Coed College

Dr. MARY L. GAMBRELL in 1967 became the first woman president of a major coeducational college when she was appointed to administer Hunter College of the City University of New York. In her three decades at Hunter College Dr. Gambrell served as professor, chairperson of the history department, dean of faculties, and president. She was 76 years old when she died in August 1974.

From Religious to Secular Presidencies

In 1967 JACQUELINE WEXLER, at that time a nun and president of the Roman Catholic Webster College, left the sisterhood with the words: "The notion of cloister . . . is not valid for some of us who must live our lives as dedicated women in the public forum." More dramatic still, she requested and received ecclesiastical permission to guide Webster to its present status as a secular institution. During her 10 years as vice-president and president of Webster, before her later appointment as president of Hunter College in New York, Ms. Webster turned its educational department into a pioneering teacher-training and curriculum-research center with national influence; built a $2 million arts complex dedicated to drama, ballet, and opera; set up an experimental elementary school; and established the Webster Institutes of Mathematics, Science, and the Arts, as well as a laboratory school.

Princeton's First Woman Dean

HALCYONE H. BOHEN, in 1969 appointed the first woman dean in the history of Princeton's undergraduate college, created the Resident Adviser Program, which trains and places older, more experienced students in contact with younger ones to serve as counselors, has been active in career programing, and organized the annual "Lifestyle Colloquia" on dual-career families. Ms. Bohen is completing a Ph.D. in counseling psychology from N.Y.U. and in 1977 was awarded a presidential fellowship by the Aspen Institute for Humanistic Studies.

Highest Woman Administrator at Columbia

SUSAN RITNER, a political scientist at Columbia University appointed assistant vice-president for Academic Affairs in February 1972, assumed the highest administrative post to which a woman had up to that time been appointed at Columbia at age 32. Her work has emphasized academic planning, organization, and development. Susan Ritner's Ph.D. dissertation was entitled "Salvation through Separation—the Role of the Dutch Reformed Church in South Africa in the Formulation of Afrikaner Race Ideology."

Youngest President of Radcliffe

In 1972, at the age of 32, MATINA HORNER was elected the youngest president in the history of Radcliffe College. Professor Horner, an experimental psychologist, conducted a pioneering study entitled "Sex Differences in Achievement Motivation in Competitive and Non-Competitive Situations" and concluded that many gifted women are deterred from fulfilling their potential, especially in male-dominated fields, by "fear of success"—a phenomenon present in 88 per cent of Radcliffe women tested. The search committee that spent a year examining 400 candidates before selecting Professor Horner for the presidency found that her study on achievement motivation among women qualified her particularly well for the post. In 1978 she was one of two women elected to the Board of Directors of Time-Life, Inc.—along with JOAN MANLEY of Time-Life

Books (see "Women in Communications," p. 487).

Columbia's First Woman Trustee

MARTHA TWITCHEL MUSE, president and executive director of the Tinker Foundation, the only private foundation in the country that concentrates on projects to foster friendship among the people of the Americas, in 1973 became the first woman to be appointed to Columbia University's Board of Trustees. Ms. Muse is also a member of the Council on Foreign Relations and of the Center for Inter-American Relations and the Spanish Institute.

Canada's First Woman College President

Dr. PAULINE JEWETT was named president of Simon Fraser in 1974, becoming the first woman college president in Canada. A former Member of Parliament who holds a Ph.D. from Harvard University, she commanded a salary of $50,000 a year—thus becoming the highest-paid woman in Canada at the time. "I was a woman going into this position for the first time, and I really felt I would be sort of letting down the side if I didn't go in at roughly the same level as a man," Dr. Jewett commented. In November 1977 Dr. Jewett was awarded the Ceres Medal by the Food and Agriculture Organization of the United Nations in recognition of her work and support of the FAO's goals of freedom from hunger and want (see "Women in Agriculture and the World Food Movement," p. 38).

First Cambridge Woman Vice-Chancellor

In 1975 ROSEMARY MURRAY, a professor of chemistry who had been president of New Hall at Cambridge University in England, assumed the position of vice-chancellor of the university. She is the first woman to hold the post (the equivalent of the presidency at an American college), first established at Cambridge in 1412.

Wheaton's First Woman President

ALICE FREY EMERSON in 1975 was named first woman president in the 141-year history of Wheaton College (Massachusetts). A political scientist with a formidable list of credentials, she served as the first dean of students at the University of Pennsylvania in 1960 when the separate posts of dean of women and dean of men were abolished, is the first woman director of Philadelphia's third largest bank, and was a founder of HERS, the middle Atlantic Office of Higher Education Services, which refers women to jobs in higher education. Long a proponent of what she calls "single-sex education," Ms. Emerson said of her new job: "Women's colleges may be the only place where we can fill in the gap about women in history . . . after all, how can women know what their future is when we know nothing about their past."

Smith's First Woman President

In 1975, JILL KER CONWAY, a historian whose doctoral dissertation at Harvard was on "Women Reformers and American Culture," became the first woman president at Smith College in its 100-year history. In her inaugural address, President Conway said that the college must prepare women to deal with a culture that "has seen female generativity as incompatible with intellectual life and . . . the exercise of power by women as anomalous and dangerous."

First Black Woman Dean of Douglas College

Former professor of zoology JEWELL PLUMMER COBB, member of the National Science Board and noted cancer researcher in cell biology, in 1976 was the first black woman appointed dean of Douglas College (the all-woman school of Rutgers University). Dean Cobb recognizes no problems in combining seemingly disparate careers, although she acknowledged that researching might have to wait as she learned to "be a good dean" and said that she intended to draw on her personal experience as a working woman "to ensure that we prepare women students in the best way we can for new opportunities in both professional and business world."

President and Legislator

In 1976 FRANCES (SISSY) FARENTHOLD became the first woman president of Wells College, a women's liberal arts college founded in 1868. This appointment is only the most recent of a long list of outstanding achievements in Ms. Farenthold's career as educator, lawyer, and legislator. In academia she serves as a member of the Board of Trustees of Vassar College and adviser to Radcliffe's Schlesinger Library on the History of American Women. As lawyer and politician, she has taught at the University of Houston and Texas Southern Law School, served two terms as the only woman in the Texas House of Representatives (1968–72), and was the first woman to have her name placed in nomination—in a spontaneous draft—for the vice-presidency of the United States. She finished second in the balloting, receiving over 400 delegate votes. In 1973 she was elected chairwoman of the National Women's Political Caucus. In 1976 she was recipient of the Yale Women's Forum Medal, an award established to honor the career excellence of women who have succeeded in their chosen professions and who have promoted the welfare of women in general. Ms. Farenthold is a native of Corpus Christi, Texas, where she was born October 2, 1926.

First Woman and Youngest Dean at NYU

ANN LEE MARCUS, named dean of New York University's School of Continuing Education in 1976, is the first woman and the youngest among the university's 14 deans. At the time of her appointment, Dean Marcus said she planned to accomplish "interesting work" in the field of adult education, for which NYU's program is the largest at any private school in the United States.

Barnard President an Advocate of Liberal Education

President of Barnard College JACQUELINE MATTFELD is devoted to the ideal of liberal education "because it remains the best means yet found by which scholars, artists, and teachers can contribute to the solution of the critical condition that threatens to engulf the human race." A professor of music and dean of faculty and academic affairs at Brown University, from 1974 to 1976, Dr. Mattfeld proved her ability to juggle budgets, faculty, and board members to achieve a vital, creative atmosphere of learning, and fellow educators credited her with bolstering the "spirit of the new curriculum" at Brown, which eliminated course requirements and provided students with a pass/fail grading option.

First Woman President at the Sorbonne

The first woman president of the Sorbonne in its 700-year history, HÉLÈNE AHRWEILLER, appointed to the post in 1976, is an expert on Byzantine civilization, with doctorates in history and letters. Her studies of Byzantium's social and administrative structures make her uniquely suited for her Paris post as organizer and administrator of academic life at the Sorbonne, where she is responsible for 30,000 students, 700 professors, and as many as 2,000 guest lecturers. Dr. Ahrweiller, born in 1916 in Athens, Greece, studied Middle East medieval archaeology and history before moving to France in 1950. In 1967 she took over as head of the Sorbonne's Department of History—the first woman to be made head of a department—and in 1970 became one of the Sorbonne's vice-presidents and a prime mover in the sweeping reorganization that split the ancient university into two schools.

"Comparative University" Specialist-President

Dr. PAULINE THOMPKINS, president of Cedar Crest College in Pennsylvania, is internationally recognized for her studies of "comparative" university administrations. A former research associate in international relations at MIT, Dr. Thompkins has served on the faculty of Tunghai University, Taiwan, and at several American universities. She spent a year in Australia and New Zealand under a Carnegie Corporation Grant to study university administration and, in 1964, was appointed to the U. S. Advisory Commission on International Education and Cultural Affairs.

First Woman Dean of Princeton's Graduate School

NINA G. GARSOIAN, professor of history and a pioneer in Armenian studies, in 1977 was named the first woman dean of the Graduate School of Princeton University, where she is also a professor in the Department of Near Eastern Studies. Professor Garsoian was instrumental in developing the study of Armenian Civilization at Columbia University, where she served as chairman of the Department of Middle East Languages and Culture, making it into an interdisciplinary program.

Princeton's First Woman Dean of the College

Dr. JOAN GIRGUS, a psychologist and former dean of social sciences at City College, New York, in 1977 was appointed the first woman dean of the college of Princeton University. Her responsibilities include oversight of the undergraduate program and the student's academic standing and general responsibility for admission and financial aid. Dr. Girgus is well known as an experimental psychologist specializing in perceptual-cognitive development.

First Chicano Academic Administrator in Social Work

Chicano MARTA SOTOMAYOR, assistant dean of the Graduate School of Social Work at the University of Houston, was the first Chicano to get a doctorate degree in social work in the United States and the first to achieve university administrative position in that field. Dr. Sotomayor believes that "different cultural and linguistic groups in any country provide a richness and depth that homogeneous, segregated communities do not have." In an effort to preserve ethnic distinctions in American "populations at risk," she chose higher education as the vehicle by which she could help train "a different breed of social workers . . . able to respond to the devastating poverty conditions faced specifically by Mexican-American populations."

Duke's First Woman Vice-President Now the United States' First Woman Secretary of Commerce

Economist JUANITA M. KREPS, the nation's first woman Secretary of Commerce, was sworn in on January 23, 1977, becoming one of five women in the nation's history to hold a cabinet position. (See also "Women in Politics and Government," p. 82.) Former Duke University vice-president, and also the first woman to hold that position, she has been described by a colleague as "a bright, sensitive humanist, aggressively looking for a place in the sun for women." She is not reticent. On the eve of her appointment Dr. Kreps informed President Jimmy Carter on national television that "it would be hard to defend the proposition that there are not a great many qualified women" for cabinet positions and that "we have to do a better job of looking." The President swallowed and said, "I think she said she disagrees with me."

As board member of several major corporations, Dr. Kreps frequently raised the question of the manner in which racial minorities are dealt with in those companies. "It is our responsibilities to make a fuss. Equal employment is the law of the land." She has worked in the fields of labor, manpower, the problems of the aging, and in both the academic community and the business world (she was the first woman public director of the New York Stock Exchange). Juanita Kreps, born in 1921 in a coal mining town in Harlan County, Kentucky, discovered her vocation in her first economic class: "I was interested in social problems and there was massive unemployment. I thought economics would give me more insight into what was going on." In 1942 she went to Duke University's graduate school, where she met and married fellow economist Clifton H. Kreps. Asked how she has managed career and family, Dr. Kreps, who has three children, answered, "Badly."

First Black Woman Chancellor of the University of Colorado Now Highest-Ranking Educator in Carter Administration

As assistant secretary for education in the Department of Health, Education, and Welfare, MARY BERRY, the Carter Administration's top education official, has suggested that the federal government develop national tests in reading, writing, and math to enable schools to judge students' performance and try to improve it. Dr. Berry told a Senate subcommittee that she opposes a national standard of minimum competency—a logical result of her suggestion—but would like to see instead a national yardstick. She would make these tests optional, to be administered at the discretion of local school districts. "There may come a time when we [in the federal government] can make a judgment of what a nationally imposed standard should be, but at this time we don't know." Dr. Berry was formerly Chancellor of the University of Colorado at Boulder—the first black woman to hold that title at an institution with a predominantly white student body.

First Woman President of Hampshire College

In 1977 ADELE SIMMONS, dean of students at Princeton University, became the first woman president of New England's Hampshire College. Before moving to Princeton in 1972, she was a dean at Jackson College, Tufts University, and also the third woman (and, at the time of her election, youngest person ever) to be named to the Harvard Board of Overseers. In an article on Princeton's women (*Change* magazine, December 1977) Adele Simmons, whose own academic specialties are African history and women in the 19th century, noted that Princeton admitted its first women stu-

dents in 1969. (Yale and Wesleyan did so a year earlier; Brown, Williams, Dartmouth, Amherst, and Haverford followed in the first half of the 1970s.)

Reviewing some of the problems female students had adjusting in these once all-male schools, she wrote:

". . . the majority adapt to their setting, assuming the characteristics that are associated with highly competitive white men. The route is easy and the immediate rewards are often considerable. Successful women feel little need to challenge current expectations about professional school admissions or the organization of work. After all, most have not experienced overt sex discrimination. . . . Male faculty by and large take them seriously and may even buy more cups of coffee for them than for male students. The possibility that they, like other women, will one day experience sex discrimination seems improbable.

"Women faculty could tell them otherwise. They could explain that being the colleague of a male professor poses far more problems than being his student, that one day they may be viewed as threatening competitors rather than as intellectual comrades. But because the number of women faculty has been small, these faculty-student discussions have not taken place often enough. In 1969–70 Princeton had two women assistant professors and one tenured (woman) professor out of a faculty of 709. By fall 1977 the faculty of 697 included 43 women assistant professors and 11 female tenured professors.

". . . At Princeton and on other campuses where most adult authority figures are still male, broad counseling efforts for women should be provided. In the decade to come, these women and their male partners will be facing extremely complicated decisions regarding careers and lifestyles. They need to learn through discussions with faculty and advisers that there are no easy, clean-cut solutions. . . ."

Black Historian Now Vice-President for Academic Affairs, Howard University

History professor LORRAINE A. WILLIAMS in 1977 became vice-president for Academic Affairs at Washington, D.C.'s predominantly black Howard University. From 1970 to 1974 she was chairwoman of Howard's Department of History, a job in which she showed herself to be a creative and innovative force, introducing new courses, instituting a faculty-student

research exchange program with the University of Idaban, Nigeria, and setting up contacts with public schools and various community services. Professor Williams also edited the *Journal of Negro History*, 1974–76, and has written numerous books and articles. "Because there are a lot of misnomers, misconceptions, and distortions concerning the history of blacks in America, it is the responsibility of the black historian to reinterpret and reassess history," she says.

First Woman President of the University of Chicago (and of Yale)

HANNA HOLBORN GRAY, who in late 1977 was named to what *Newsweek* magazine described as the "most prestigious academic post ever held by a woman," the presidency of the University of Chicago, has had many firsts in addition to this one. First woman dean at Northwestern University, she was appointed provost of Yale University in 1974—the first woman to hold this post, and the first provost without a degree from Yale. After Kingman Brewster announced his retirement as Yale's president, Dr. Gray filled in for him and was one of nine candidates on the search committee's final list of possible replacements before she took her name off by accepting the Chicago job. When the Yale Corporation first announced the name of the new president they designated him the 18th since the university's founding. Later, this was changed to the 19th and Hanna Gray, after the fact, was listed as the 18th president of Yale and "first woman president of an Ivy League College." Hanna Gray, born in 1930 in Germany, fled as a child with her family to escape the Nazi regime. She was graduated from Bryn Mawr and earned her doctorate in European history from Harvard. She taught at the University of Chicago for 12 years before being named dean of the College of Arts and Sciences at Northwestern.

NOTED SCHOLARS AND PROFESSORS

First and Second Women Presidents of the American Psychological Association

The first woman to be elected president of the American Psychological Association (1905) was MARY WHITON CALKIN, chairwoman of the Department of Mental Philosophy at Wellesley College until 1930. At Harvard, where she had completed all doctorate requirements in 1895, Mary Calkin was refused the Ph.D. after being told by the noted philosopher William James that her "oral exam ranked above any he had ever heard." Mental philosophy, a discipline that combined metaphysics and psychology, provided an ideal niche for a woman who was essentially a philosopher with a strong involvement in psychology. Ms. Calkin established the first psychological laboratory in a woman's college at Wellesley, incorporating elements of behaviorism, Gestalt psychology, and psychoanalysis.

MARGARET FLOY WASHBURN (1871–1939), who was elected president of the American Psychological Association in 1921 (the second woman to be so honored and the last for another half century), received her Ph.D. in 1894. Her thesis on the influence of visual imagery on judgments of distance and direction became the first foreign study published in the famous Wundt's *Philosophische Studien*. Animal psychology was a special interest of hers and her book *Animal Mind* was published in 1908. She also developed a motor theory of consciousness, elaborated in *Movement and Mental Imagery* (1916).

Firsts at Cambridge and in the House of Lords

Baroness BARBARA WOOTEN of Abinger in 1920 became the first woman director of studies and lecturer in economics at Girton College (Cambridge). She later became director of Morley College for working people in London (1926–27), and was active as an economist, sociologist, and in politics. On October 21, 1958, she took her seat in the British House of Lords as one of two newly created baronesses admitted that day— the first women to have the right to sit, speak, or vote in the Upper Chambers of Parliament since that body came into existence.

First Woman President of American Geographers

ELLEN CHURCHILL SEMPLE (1863–1932) helped to establish geography as a respected university discipline. She classified the various kinds of geographic influences and described how each affected man at every stage of his development; her belief that certain factors of the physical environment have determined man's choice of places to live, as well as his activities and general viewpoints, evoked much controversy within the profession. Professor Semple taught at Oxford University (1912), Wellesley (1914–15), Columbia (1915), and in 1921 was the first woman to be elected president of the Association of American Geographers.

Austria's First Woman Professor

After brilliant studies in the demanding discipline of philosophy at a time when few European women were permitted in universities, ELISE RICHTER became the first woman to teach at an Austrian university. She qualified to teach in 1907 and in 1922 became the first woman professor in Austria. Elise Richter died a victim of Germany's Third Reich in the concentration camp of Theresienstadt in 1942.

Pioneer Freudian and Neo-Freudian Analysts

The youngest of Sigmund Freud's six children, ANNA FREUD, born in 1895 in Vienna, in 1938 emigrated to London with her famous father. She organized a residential nursery for war-orphaned or homeless children. After World War II ended, she observed and wrote about children who had survived Nazi concentration camps, finding that they had developed cooperative and protective familial behavior toward one another. Over the years Ms. Freud has written numerous works dealing with the psychological development of children, including *Introduction to Psychoanalysis: Lectures for Child Analysts and Teachers* (1931), *Ego and the Mechanisms of Defense* (1937), *War and Children* (with DOROTHY T. BURLINGHAM, 1934), and many others, still in print. In 1952 she became director of the Hampstead Child Therapy Course and Clinic, a position she has held since that date. The University of Chicago, Clark, and Yale are among the institutions that have awarded her honorary doctorates, and in 1975 the Austrian Government gave her its Grand Decoration of Honor in Gold.

HELENE DEUTSCH, born in 1884 in Przemysl, Poland, was graduated from the University of Vienna Medical School in 1912. She was analyzed for a year by Freud in 1918 and during that year became the second woman admitted as a full member of the Vienna Psychoanalytic Society. In 1925 she helped found the Vienna Psychoanalytic Training Institute and became its first director. She worked with Freud for 20 years, and accepted his views of female sexuality, but later appeared to have modified her views on penis envy, saying: "Yes, there is penis envy, but in a society open to women, with accepting parents, the impact will be very different than it used to be." A prolific writer about women, she published her famous two-volume *Psychology of Women* in 1944.

MARIE BONAPARTE (1882–1962), born near Paris, a descendant of Napoleon Bonaparte, became a lay analyst after her psychoanalysis with Freud and eventually turned her attention to the study of female sexuality. She founded the Paris Psychoanalytic Society in 1926 and was extremely influential in the psychoanalytic movement in Europe. With her mentor, Marie Bonaparte believed that physical differences between the sexes account for personality traits associated with women. Femininity is seen as a product of the traumatic realization of anatomic difference, and viewed as an inadequacy.

KAREN HORNEY (1885–1952), born in Hamburg, Germany, and an émigrée to New York, was responsible for decisively influencing the development of psychoanalysis through her contributions to feminine psychology and her identification of cultural and social determinants as agents of individual psychological makeup. In 1939 she published a thorough critique of the inadequacy of Freudian doctrine entitled *New Ways in Psychoanalysis* that placed her at the vanguard of the Neo-Freudian movement. Dr. Horney believed that Freud's libido theory reduced most adult behavior to mere repetition of the experiences of childhood. She also disagreed with the view that the "death instinct" doomed man to destructive impulses. These radical differences with the tenets of psychoanalysis led to her expulsion from the New York Psychoanalytic Society and to her founding the Association for the Advancement of Psychoanalysis (1941). Dr. Horney's greatest contributions were made in the field of female psychology. She argued that feminine psychology was neither a by-product of genital differences between men and women, nor as devoid of cultural implication as Freud had presented it to be. If women were allowed to lead independent lives, with the distorting pressures of culture alleviated, they would be on better terms with themselves and the world. Feminine masochism, she wrote, is not an inevitable consequence of female anatomy but "must be considered as importantly conditioned by the culture-complex or social organization in which the particular masochistic women have developed."

MELANIE KLEIN (1882–1960), born in Vienna as Melanie Reizes, decided at 14 to study medicine. However, she became engaged at 17 and gave up her plans to become a doctor. Later, while in analysis herself, she began to think about the application of psychoanalysis to young children. She read her first paper, "The Development of a Child," in 1921 before the Hungarian Psychoanalytic Society and thereafter worked on techniques for analyzing children using a psychoanalytic setting similar to that created by Freud for adults, and providing a simply furnished room containing a box of toys on the assumption that a child expresses himself/herself more in play than in words. Ms. Klein also found that children have a strong superego much earlier than Freud had postulated and were capable of complicated parental relationships, whereas Freud believed that Oedipal conflict did not arise until a child was three or four years old. Her discoveries culminated in the publication of *The Psychoanalysis of Children* (1932). Ms. Klein also worked with the concept of envy as it affects the therapeutic process—a concept that became one of the major controversial aspects of her pioneering work.

Pioneer Feminist Historian of Culture

HELEN DINER was the pseudonym of BERTHA ECKSTEIN-DIENER, a sociologist who published extensively in Germany between 1929 and 1940 and was the author of the first popular feminine history of culture. This work's central thesis is that primitive social organizations were matriarchies and that the patriarchal family is a comparatively recent development. Her partisanship was clearly stated: "This history of cultures, time and again, thoroughly describes phases in which man coined his image of the world, while the feminine element could not achieve its realization at all, or at best, could do so only indirectly through him. Consciously or unconsciously, the male stage remains the darling object of historical contemplation." Sociologist Eckstein-Diener also wrote some early literary work under the name Sir Galahad.

Classical Scholar the First Woman Admitted to the University of Munich

EDITH HAMILTON, born in 1867 in Dresden, Germany, died in 1963, a world-renowned classicist. *The Greek Way* (1930), in which she sought to clarify and revive the Greek ideal by comparing it to modern realities, is her most popular book. She also wrote *The German Way* (1932), *Prophets of Israel* (1936), and *The Echo of Greece* (1957). Edith Hamilton, who learned Latin at seven, in 1895 was the first woman admitted to the University of Munich. She was not allowed to sit with her male colleagues but instead had a little desk all by herself on the teacher's platform. Later she taught at the Bryn Mawr School, which prepared young girls for Bryn Mawr College. In 1922 she left the school and began writing. The editor with H. Cairns of the *Collected Dialogues of Plato* (1961), Ms. Hamilton in 1957 was made an honorary citizen of the city and demos of Athens and decorated with the Greek Government's Golden Cross of the Order of the Benefaction. She was the recipient of several honorary doctorates in literature, most notably from Yale and the University of Pennsylvania.

First Full Graduate Professor at Columbia

One of America's foremost women scholars, MARJORIE HOPE NICOLSON was the first woman to be appointed to a full professorship in the Graduate Faculties of Columbia University. At the time of her retirement in 1961, she held the position of William Peterfield Trent Professor of English and chairperson of the Department of English and Comparative Literature at Columbia, after having taught at the university for 20 years. Earlier, Dr. Nicolson had been dean of Smith College for 12 years and also had served two terms as president of the United Chapters of Phi Beta Kappa—the first and to date only woman elected president, and the only person, male or female, ever asked to serve a second term. A graduate of the University of Michigan, Dr. Nicolson received her Ph.D. from Yale in 1920, holds honorary degrees from a dozen universities and colleges, and has received the Crawshay Prize for English Literature, presented by the British Academy in 1947, for *Newton Demands the Muse* (one of many books she has published) and the 1954 Achievement Award of the American Association of University Women as the outstanding woman scholar of the year.

First Woman and First American to Receive the Sonning Prize

Political philosopher HANNAH ARENDT (1906–75) in the last year of her life became the first woman and the first American to receive Denmark's Sonning Prize for her contribution to European Civilization. Described in her *New York Times* obituary as "absolutely fearless intellectually," Dr. Arendt at the time of her death was university professor of political philosophy at New York City's New School for Social Research and was writing a three-volume study, *The Life of the Mind* (*Thinking, Willing,* and *Judging*). The first two volumes were published in 1978, and the third, for which she left only notes, will be covered as an appendix by her friend and literary executor, novelist MARY MCCARTHY (see "Women in the Arts and Entertainment," p. 686).

The author of eight other major books, Hannah Arendt established her international reputation with the publication of *The Origins of Totalitarianism* (1951). This highly controversial study of the rise of Nazism and Communism in the 20th century linked their origins to the development of anti-Semitism and imperialism in the 19th century. Her coverage of the 1963 trial of Adolf Eichmann for the *New Yorker* magazine drew attention to what she termed the "banality of evil." Hannah Arendt escaped Nazi Germany in 1933, fleeing to Paris, where she worked for Youth Aliya, a relief agency that placed Jewish orphans in Palestine. In 1940 she was forced to leave France as well, and came to New York where she served as research director of the Conference on Jewish Relations. Although she had received her doctorate at the age of 22, under the supervision of Karl Jaspers at Heidelberg, she encountered great difficulties in finding a permanent academic position. She taught at the University of Chicago, Berkeley, and Columbia before joining the New School. In 1959 Dr. Arendt was a visiting professor of politics at Princeton, at the time the only woman there to hold the rank of full professor.

Critic of French Literature the First Woman to Head NYU Romance Language Department

GERMAINE BRÉE, one of the most prominent contemporary critics of French literature, is the author of works dealing with Marcel Proust, André Gide, Albert Camus, and Jean-Paul Sartre. She has also contributed to women's historiography, notably with her book entitled *Women Writers in France: Variations on a Theme* (1973). Of Franco-British origin, Germaine Brée was educated in France and England, and came to the United States as a foreign fellow at Bryn Mawr in 1931. She was called back to lecture at the college in 1936, and eventually became a full professor there. During World War II she served with the French Army as an ambulance driver in North Africa, and later as an intelligence officer for U.S. forces in France was awarded a Bronze Star. Professor Brée became the head of New York University's Romance Language Department, the first woman in that post, 1954–60. She has also taught in Algeria, Egypt, Australia, England, and became Kenan Professor of Humanities at Wake Forest University in North Carolina in 1973 and president of the Modern Language Association of America in 1975. Professor Brée was named Chevalier of the Legion of Honor in 1958 and is the recipient of 18 honorary degrees.

First Woman to Head Hebrew University Institute of Languages and Literatures

ALICE SHALVI, of the Hebrew University of Jerusalem's English Department, was the first woman elected to serve as head of the Institute of Languages and Literatures at the university (1963). Professor Shalvi was born in 1926 in Essen, Germany, and went to England in 1934. After studies in English literature at Cambridge University (1947) and the London School of Economics (1949), she emigrated to Israel, where she has taught literature at the Hebrew University of Jerusalem since 1950. Between 1969 and 1973 Professor Shalvi was instrumental in establishing the Department of English at the newly founded University of the Negev. In 1977 she was serving in a voluntary capacity as principal of Pelech, which she calls "a very exciting experimental high school for religious girls," while continuing to teach at the Hebrew University.

She Recorded One Hundred Indian Languages

In 1964–65, MARY R. HAAS, professor emeritus of linguistics at the University of California at Berkeley, in recognition of her standing as one of the nation's top linguists was named faculty research lecturer by the Academic Senate—the highest honor the faculty can confer on one of its members. Dr. Haas headed a long-term project to record the 100 or more California Indian languages. (California, she says, is linguistically one of the three most complex areas in the world, ranking with New Guinea and Southern Asia in this respect.) Her research has given new clues to the origin and migration of American Indians. Also an expert in Thai, Professor Haas in 1976 headed a group that developed a Thai-English dictionary, believed to be the first of its kind.

First Woman Named William F. Russell Professor at Columbia

MAXINE GREENE, professor of philosophy and education, Teachers College, Columbia University, in June 1965 was appointed the William F. Russell Professor in the Foundations of Education—the first woman to hold this position. President of the Philosophy of Education Society in 1966, and of the American Educational Studies Association in 1972, Professor Greene is the author of *Existential Encounters For Teachers* (1967), *Teacher as Stranger* (1972), for which she was awarded the Kappa Delta Gamma Educator's Award for Best Educational Book of the Year, and *Landscapes of Learning: Notes on Choice, Autonomy, and Freedom* (1977).

Political Scientist the First NOW Chairwoman

KATHRYN CLARENBACK, who says she came in with the 19th Amendment (Women's Suffrage) in 1920, is an educator whose career has been devoted to writing, teaching, and lobbying to further the cause of women's rights. A founding member and the first chairwoman of the National Organization for Women in 1965, she has headed the Governor's Commission on the Status of Women in Wisconsin since 1964. One of her main concerns is the legal status of women in marriage: "Without the equal rights amendment we just don't know what protection of economic support a woman has a right to . . ." In addition to her position as associate professor of political science at the University of Wisconsin, she also holds the department's chair for Women's Educational Resources and is the author of numerous papers on sexism in academia, notably "American Sports: For Men Only," "Can Continuing Education Adapt?," "Sexism in the Schools," and "People's Jobs Should Be Our Vocabulary—Women's Police."

Thirty-Five Years a Family Watcher

Prolific writer, editor, professor of sociology, and a leading U.S. authority on personal and community relationships, JESSIE BERNARD published *American Family Behavior* in 1942 and has since written numerous books on subjects ranging from the sociology of remarriage through discussions of the roles and behavior patterns of women as wives and mothers and the black family in the United States. In a study conducted in the early 1960s, she sought clues to the manner in which "sex influences the development of science" and predicted a change in the status of academic women. In a later work she noted that "the major sociological paradigms are defective and deficient because of their male bias." Jessie Bernard has been recipient of many awards, has edited several professional journals, and was a delegate to the White House Conference on Youth in 1971.

She Won the Pulitzer Prize for History Twice

MARGARET LEECH (1894–1974), who twice was awarded the Pulitzer Prize in history, won her first award in 1942 for *Reveille in Washington,* an account of the national capital during the Civil War, published on the eve of World War II. In 1959 she won again for *In the Days of McKinley*—a portrait of an epoch rather than a personality—and was praised for having written "a first-rate study of a second-rate President."

Other Women Winners of Pulitzers in U. S. History and Biography

1917 Laura E. Richards and Maude Howe Elliott, assisted by Florence Howe Hall, for *Julia Ward Howe* (biography)

1941 Ola Elizabeth Winslow, for *Jonathan Edwards* (biography)

1943 Esther Forbes, for *Paul Revere and the World He Lived In* (history)

1948 Margaret Clapp, for *Forgotten First Citizen: John Bigelow* (biography)

1951 Margaret Louise Coit, for *John C. Calhoun: American Portrait* (biography)

1959 Leonard D. White and Jean Schneider, for *The Republican Era, 1869–1901* (history)

1963 Constance McLaughlin Green, for *Washington: Village and Capital, 1800–1878* (history)

Official Historian of International Woman's Year

A graduate of Vassar in 1934, with an M.A. from the University of Toledo and further study at the University of Wisconsin, CAROLINE BIRD became a researcher at *Newsweek* in 1942–43, went on to *Fortune* magazine, 1944–46, and later became a popular historian of the women's movement. She is the author of *The Invisible Scar* (1966), *Born Female* (1970), *Everything a Woman Needs to Know to Get Paid What She's Worth* (1973), *The Case Against College* (1975), and *Enterprising Women* (1976). Ms. Bird was Froman Distinguished Professor at Russell Sage College, 1972–73. In 1977 it was announced that she was writing the official account of the United Nation's International Woman's Year.

Revisionist Historian of the Crimean War

CECIL WOODHAM-SMITH, a British historian and biographer best known for her work on the Crimean War, was educated at Oxford University. In *The Lady and the Lamp* (1950), she wrote of Florence Nightingale's aid to English troops in the Crimea, 1854–56, and in *The Reason Why* (1953) devastatingly revised the Tennysonian view of the famous Charge of the Light Brigade. Ms. Woodham-Smith also wrote of the Irish Famine of the 1840s in *The Great Hunger* (1962) and had published the first volume of a work on Queen Victoria's life and times when she died at the age of 80 on March 19, 1977.

Two-Time Pulitzer Historian

Her 1963 Pulitzer Prize in general nonfiction for her 1962 Book-of-the-Month-Club selection, *The Guns of August,* and her second, 1972 Pulitzer in the same category for her 1971 work, *Stilwell and the American Experience in China, 1911–1945,* gratified but did not surprise admirers of historian BARBARA WERTHEIM TUCHMAN. Since 1938 she has been publishing books that clarify in cool prose charged historical situations. Other titles include: *Bible and Sword* (1956), *The Zimmerman Telegram* (1958), *The Proud Tower* (1966), and *Notes from China* (1972). New York-born (1912) and Radcliffe-educated, Ms.

Tuchman married in 1940 and is the mother of three children; daughter Jessica works in Jimmy Carter's White House (see "Women in Politics and Government," p. 81). After her graduation from college Ms. Tuchman went to work for the *Nation* as an editorial assistant, later covered the war in Spain and was a correspondent in London for the *Nation* in 1939, as well as American correspondent for the *New Statesman.* She holds honorary doctorates in literature from Yale, Columbia, New York University, Williams, and other institutions.

Britain's Historian of Women and Revolution

SHEILA ROWBOTHAM is the author of a narrative history of feminism, *Women: Resistance and Revolution* (1972), an exploration of the relationship between feminism and social revolution. In it she chronicles the varied historical forms that the attempt to change the position of women in society has taken in the West, and in revolutionary countries like China, the U.S.S.R., Cuba, Algeria, and Vietnam. Ms. Rowbotham was educated at Oxford, where, she says, "little social and economic history seemed to have reached even by 1961," and where she realized the extent to which historical scholarship had been neglectful of women. "We were always led to believe that women were not around because they had done so little. But the more I read the more I discovered how much women had in fact done." Ms. Rowbotham, who lives, and lectures in history, in England, has also published *Hidden from History* (1976), a rediscovery of women from the 17th century to the present.

Yale Logician First Woman Named Reuben Post Halleck Professor of Philosophy

One of America's most distinguished philosophers, RUTH BARCAN MARCUS, was the first woman to receive the Reuben Post Halleck Professorship of Philosophy (1973) at Yale University. Dr. Barcan Marcus is also the first woman named chairperson of the National Board of Officers of the American Philosophical Association (1977), as well as the first woman elected to the American Academy of Arts and Sciences (1977). Her major contributions have been made in the highly specialized field of modal logic. While head of the Department of Philosophy at the University of Illinois (1964–70), she solicited and administered a large grant for the development of a quality graduate program in philosophy and guided the growth of the department from 2 to 20 members by 1968.

Social Anthropologist the First Woman Chairperson at Princeton

HILDRED GEERTZ, a distinguished social anthropologist who received her doctorate from Radcliffe College's Department of Social Relations in 1956, was the first faculty woman at Princeton ever to be appointed chairperson of a department. Ms. Geertz's research has taken her from Indonesia, where she studied kinship and socialization patterns, to Roxbury, Massachusetts, where she observed juvenile delinquent groups. She has also written on kinship relationships among older middle-class Americans and in Java and Bali. Hildred Geertz is at work with her husband Clifford Geertz on a computerized statistical study of the entire population of a single town in Morocco.

She Revived Oldest Known Tune

ANNE D. KILMER, a professor of Assyriology at Berkeley whose specialty is Akkadian cuneiform—the clay tablet writing of ancient Mesopotamia— worked for 15 years to decipher the oldest known tune in the world. It was performed in 1974, the first such performance in 3,400 years, on an 11-string lyre built as a replica of an ancient in-

Sociologist of the World of Work

MIRRA KOMAROVSKY, born in Russia and a naturalized citizen of the United States, has studied the effects of social stratification on men and their families, the problems and uses of leisure time in the suburban environment, the unemployed breadwinner, blue collar marriage, and the entry of women into the world of work. In her long and distinguished career, Barnard Professor Komarovsky has been the recipient of numerous honors, and in 1977 the Eastern Sociological Society recognized her outstanding contribution to the development of sociology. Her book *Blue-Collar Marriage* (1964) is a classic in the field. Her latest work is *Dilemmas of Masculinity: A Study of College Youth* (1976). She was recently holder of a fellowship from the Midwest Council of Social Research on Aging.

Poet-Scholar Berkeley "University Professor"

Poet-scholar and professor of English at Berkeley, whose work has received international acclaim, JOSEPHINE MILES was honored for her far-reaching contributions by her appointment as university professor in 1972. At that time Professor Miles was described as having provided "unparalleled inspiration by the clarity of her thinking, her imagination, will, integrity, and humanity." She has published over half a dozen volumes of poetry and is the author of *Eras and Modes in English Poetry* (1976) and other scholarly works.

strument. Professor Kilmer, a former chairperson of the Department of Near Eastern Studies and dean of humanities at the University of California at Berkeley, began her research into Mesopotamian music in 1959 with the cooperation of other authorities on cuneiform and several musicologists. Their findings "revolutionized our thinking about the age of Western music," according to Dr. Kilmer. "We now see that the basic musical system of today dates back at least 1800 B.C. . . . some 14 centuries older than ever imagined."

Major Scholar of Jewish History

LUCY S. DAWIDOWICZ, an American who has taught modern Jewish history at Yeshiva University in Israel, is best known for her 1976 work *The War Against the Jews, 1933–1945,* in which she argues that the Final Solution, far from being an accidental by-product of Hitler's policies, was a primary objective. In her latest work, *The Jewish Presence: Essays on Identity and History* (1977), Ms. Dawidowicz observes that "Jews have always, for better or worse, lived in the vortex of history."

Orientalist with a Special Interest in Female Poets

BARBARA STOLLER MILLER, a professor of oriental studies at Barnard College, Columbia University, has lectured on translation and Sanskrit poetry throughout India. The author of *The Split Tongue of a Poetess: Bengali, Spanish, and English Poems and Translations* (1967), in which she discusses the problems of translations and the relation between language and cultural roles for the female poet, has recently edited and translated *Love Song of the Dark Lord: Gitagovinda of Jayadeva* (1977), making the text accessible for the first time to Western fans of Indian poetry. Dr. Miller has been the recipient of several grants, including a Guggenheim Fellowship, a Smithsonian Grant for Senior Research in India (1974–75), and the Mellon Fellowship (1976).

Economist Who Studies Women's Role

CYNTHIA B. LLOYD, an economist and the acting chairperson of Barnard College's economics department, has written extensively on women's role in modern economic life and since 1972 has taught courses on the role of women in economic life. Her studies elucidating sex differentials in earnings and in unemployment rates and the impact of government subsidies on fertility have included "The Effect of Economic and Demographic Change on Sex Differentials in Labor Supply Elasticity," co-authored with BETH NIEMI.

First Black Woman Faculty Member at Duke

JACQUELYNE JOHNSON JACKSON was the first black woman faculty member at Duke University, where she is a medical sociologist in the Department of Psychiatry. Among the first to focus significant attention on the need for adequate gerontological studies of aging blacks, with special attention directed to black women, she is also the first black woman member of the Board of Trustees of the Carver Research Foundation of Tuskegee Institute and of the Aging Review Committee of the National Institutes of Health. Since 1975 she has been the editor of *Black Aging.* Sociologist Jackson has advised black women to seek work that will free them to "do things" and says that "we must make black movements serve black women as well as black men."

Author of First Nationally Funded Survey of Chinese-American Manpower and Employment

BETTY LEE SUNG, a member of the Department of Asian Studies at City College of the City University of New York, who taught the first courses on Asian-Americans offered on the East Coast, is the author of several books about Chinese-Americans, including the first such federally funded work. It is *Survey of Chinese-American Manpower and Employment,* named an outstanding book of 1976 by *Choice* magazine. Professor Sung, born in Baltimore, was graduated from the University of Illinois in 1948 and received a Master of Library Science degree from Queens College in 1968. She has lectured widely on the subject of Chinese-Americans and engaged in research on Chinese immigrant families. In private life she is married to Charles Chung and the mother of eight children.

International Economist-Teacher First Female Member of the CEA

MARINA VON NEUMANN WHITMAN, born in 1935, an international economist who has taught and practiced economics since 1962, was appointed senior staff economist for the Council of Economic Advisers in 1972 and was its first female member. She was instrumental in drafting the proposals presented by the U.S. representatives to the international monetary negotiation held in Paris in March 1973 and was considered by her male colleagues an expert on international monetary trade agreements, foreign investments, currency exchange rates, and government risk sharing. Marina Whitman is a member of the Board of Overseers, Harvard University, and a member of the editorial boards of the *American Economic Review* (since 1973) and *Foreign Policy* (since 1974).

Practicing Scholar-Economist, First Director of the Congressional Budget Office

ALICE MITCHELL RIVLIN, first director of the Congressional Budget Office, is an economist educated at Swarthmore and Radcliffe, who has worked primarily at Washington's prestigious Brookings Institution and produced a large body of research, especially in the creation of government policy in the social sphere. The Congressional Budget Office, created in 1976, has given the U. S. Congress its first effective control of the federal budget in decades.

She Chairs Committee on the Status of Women in Economics

BARBARA B. REAGAN, national chairperson of the American Economic Associa-

tion Committee on the Status of Women in Economics, and a professor of economics at Southern Methodist University, Dallas, Texas, conducts research and publishes in the fields of human resources, minority problems, urban rural adjustments, levels of living, wage studies, occupational patterns, and segmented labor markets. Professor Reagan has been on numerous national, regional, state, and local committees, was leader for the Southwestern Assembly on the Role of Women in the Economy, and was co-editor of studies on *Women in the Workplace: Implications of Occupational Segregation,* published in book form in 1976. She has also written on "De Facto Job Segregation" in *American Women Workers in a Full Employment Economy: A Compendium,* issued by the Joint Economic Committee, U. S. Congress.

American Historian of Revolutionary China

ROXANE WITKE is visiting research associate at the East Asian Institute of Columbia University, on leave from the history department of the State University of New York at Binghamton. The assistant editor for China of *The Journal of Asian Studies,* she has lectured extensively on various aspects of modern and revolutionary China and has been a frequent guest on TV and radio in the United States and abroad. A research grant from the National Endowment for the Humanities enabled her to complete *Comrade Chiang Ch'ing,* a book based on interviews with the late Mao Tsetung's wife in China not long before the controversial woman leader's political downfall. *Time* magazine excerpted it in March 1977 and it was subsequently translated into 15 languages. Dr. Witke has two more books, a generational study of revolutionary women leaders in China, and a cultural portrait of Shanghai in the 1930s, in progress.

Director, Treasurer, and Only Woman in New York's Municipal Assistance Corporation

DONNA SHALALA is an assistant secretary at the Department of Housing and Urban Development (HUD) and professor of politics and education at Teachers College in New York. As director, treasurer, and the only woman member of the Municipal Assistance Corporation (Big Mac) for the city of New York, she participated in the attempt to restructure the city's budget. In 1975 Ms. Shalala and her graduate students designed Connecticut's new school finance equalization program. She is also an economic consultant in numerous states on school finance and is the author of several articles on school finance, state politics, and decentralization.

Major Housing Field Scholar

FRANCINE FISHER RABINOVITZ, professor of public administration, urban and regional planning, and political science at the University of Southern California, is a major scholar in the housing field and one of the very few women in the mostly honorary National Academy of Public Administration. She has also served on numerous domestic policy boards and task forces, and is the author of several planning studies.

Innovator in Children's Counseling

JUDITH WALLERSTEIN, head of the nation's only research and counseling group specializing in the study of normal children during divorce of their parents, teaches at the University of California, Berkeley, School of Social Welfare, where she is responsible for all clinical courses dealing with children and adolescents as well as their families. She was the recipient of the prestigious Koshland Award from the San Francisco Foundation for designing and helping direct Marin County's unusual Children of Divorce Project and has engaged in re-

search and written numerous articles in a number of areas, including the psychology and psychotherapy of borderline children and the impact of therapeutic abortion in young unmarried women.

Authority in Gifted Underachievers

MIRIAM GOLDBERG, a former nursery school teacher and counselor in a residential school for the emotionally disturbed children, is a professor of psychology and education at Teachers College in New York. Widely regarded as one of America's foremost authorities on the childhood education of gifted underachievers, she has researched and published numerous studies concerning the motivation of exceptional children; the teaching characteristics of primary school teachers who are successful in teaching reading to disadvantaged pupils; achievement patterns as they relate to sex, socio-economic status, and ethnic group membership; and the processes by which beginning readers develop decoding strategies.

Director of Toddler Development

A psychology professor at Barnard College, FRANCES SCHACTER directs a center for toddler development that attempts to correct personality imbalances as early as 15 months. Professor Schacter has her class in developmental psychology—and other advanced students—use the nursery as a workshop, observing the toddlers through one-way mirrors. The teaching function is just one of the center's purposes: "Top priority is the baby's development," she says. "We feel that every aspect of development is interrelated with the others—the educational, the social, the emotional."

Director of Reading Research

JEANNE S. CHALL, professor of education and director of the Reading Laboratory, Graduate School of Education, Harvard University, has made many contributions in the field of reading research and teacher education. The author of *Reading 1967–77: A Decade of Change and Promise* (1977), as well as other books and numerous journal articles, Dr. Chall has also been involved in testing and has published, with Florence G. Roswell, the *Roswell-Chall Diagnostic Reading Test* and the *Roswell-Chall Auditory Blending Test*. She is a past president of the National Conference on Research in English, and a member of the Board of the National Society for the Study of Education.

Major Researcher on Women and Higher Education

Dr. HELEN ASTIN, a professor of higher education at UCLA and vice-president of the Higher Education Research Institute, states that her "primary research interests are in the field of educational and career development, and of higher education with an emphasis on women." She has published many books and articles on this subject and in 1976 received the Award for Outstanding Contributions to Research and Literature from the National Association of Student Personnel Administrators.

Sociologist with a Specialty in Women's Careers

CYNTHIA FUCHS EPSTEIN, professor of sociology at the University of California at Berkeley, specializes in the problems and behavior of women in professional careers. In various papers and magazine articles she has considered this topic from the viewpoint of limitations that a professional career places on a woman vis-à-vis her traditional role in society, the strains and problems of marriage when both partners are actively involved in separate professional careers, and the effect and influence of women in largely or all-male fields. Dr. Epstein served as consultant to the White House Conference on Children (1970) and was a

White House Appointee to the Advisory Committee on the Economic Role of Women (1972). "Given the taste and experience of success," Dr. Epstein thinks women not only "will fear it no longer but will actively seek and enjoy it." She also believes that "the inclusion of women in the elite sphere will do much to raise the general level of talent and discovery in the society."

Psychologist Who Advises Law Enforcement Agencies

KATHERINE WHITE ELLISON, a psychologist who teaches at the State University of New York at Stony Brook, from 1973 to 1975 worked for the New York City Police Department, Sex Crime Unit, as well as being on the Advisory Board of the Mayor's Task Force on Rape. She has served as consultant and lecturer to various law enforcement agencies, police academies, and prosecutor's offices and has published various sex crime studies, including "Crisis Intervention and Investigation of Forcible Rape" (May '74 *Police Chief*), "Training Police to Handle Cases of Forcible Rape" in *Issues in Law Enforcement* (1975).

Classic Scholar of Women in Antiquity

SARAH B. POMEROY began her scholarly career with the publication of her work on papyri documenting the financial transaction of women in Roman Egypt and has since written numerous articles exploring the public and private lives of women in antiquity. She has also written on Plato, on the relationship of the married woman to her blood relatives in Rome, and on Andromache as a misunderstood example of matriarchy. In her work entitled *Goddesses, Whores, Wives, and Slaves: Women in Classical Antiquity* (1975), Professor Pomeroy, who teaches at Hunter College of the City University of New York, traces the Western origins of misogyny and explores the impact of various Greek and Roman legal codes on the status and rights of women and their emancipation from husband and father.

Classicist Using Psychoanalytic Theory

MARY L. LEFKOWITZ, professor of Greek and Latin and chairwoman of the classics department at Wellesley College, is collaborating with a small group of psychiatrists and other classicists in the use of psychoanalytic theory for the interpretation of ancient texts. Dr. Lefkowitz's field of specialization is Greek lyric poetry. Her latest (co-edited) publication is *Women in Greece and Rome* (1977), a source book of historical documents in English translation. The recipient of several fellowships and an active member of the American Philological Association, she is a consultant of the National Endowment for the Humanities and a member of the Managing Committee of the American School of Classical Studies in Athens, Greece.

SIGNS Editor

CATHARINE R. STIMPSON, an associate professor of English at Barnard College in New York, and former head of its Women's Center, sums up her career in the following statement: "Among other things, I have tried to help develop the new scholarship about women, the amassing of evidence and the constructing of theories that give us fresh, accurate representations of women in particular and of sex and gender in general. To that end, I have written articles; taught, lectured, and served as the first editor of *SIGNS: a Journal of Women in Culture and Society.* I have wanted the new scholarship to be, not simply another academic specialty, but a force that would alter the existing body of knowledge, academic institutions, and people's lives. To have such an ambition is to experience a passionate commitment to an idea."

She Teaches Humanities, Women's Studies, and Is President of the Feminist Press

Known in the publishing world as the president (since 1970) of the Feminist Press, a publishing house specializing in books on women and women's history, FLORENCE HOWE is even more widely known in academic circles for her career as a teacher of English (since 1971 professor of humanities, SUNY/College, Old Westbury, New York) and her very active role in promoting women's studies (as writer and as coordinator of the Clearinghouse on Women's Studies, 1969 to the present). Professor Howe holds a B.A. from Hunter College, 1946, and an M.A. from Smith, 1954. In addition to her professorship at Old Westbury, she has taught at the University of Wisconsin, Hofstra, Queens, and Goucher, and was visiting professor of women's studies at the University of Washington, summer 1974. She also taught in the Mississippi Freedom Schools, summer 1964. First woman president of the Modern languages Association (1973), and the recipient of numerous grants and awards, she has been a consultant to the Ford Foundation, the National Endowment for the Humanities, and a number of school districts and colleges and universities. She also is the author of a long list of articles, chapters in books, and editor of the anthologies of syllabi and bibliographies *Female Studies II* and *III* (1970 and 1971), which followed the first of these landmark monographs edited by SHEILA TOBIAS (p. 425). Her other books include *The Conspiracy of the Young* (with Paul Lauter, 1970), *No More Masks! An Anthology of Poems by Women* (with ELLEN BASS, 1973), and *Women and the Power to Change* (1975). In 1976 she did a study commissioned by the National Advisory Council on Women's Educational Programs, a body established by the U. S. Congress in

1974 as part of the Women's Educational Equity Act. Among her findings: "more than 270 programs have been organized and some 15,000 different courses developed by 8,500 teachers of 1,500 different institutions."

She Organized the Pioneering Cornell Conference on Women

SHEILA TOBIAS, one of the most active feminist scholars in the United States, in 1969 while she was assistant to the vice-president of Academic Affairs at Cornell University organized the Cornell Conference on Women, which put many scholars concerned with the feminine consciousness and the emerging field of women's studies into touch with one another for the first time. A graduate of Radcliffe in 1957, with an M.A. (1961) and a M.Phil. (1974) from Columbia, Ms. Tobias lectured in history at the College of the City of New York 1965–67, and more recently has been an associate professor at Wesleyan University. She has written widely on affirmative action, women's studies, and the subject of "math anxiety" in women, and edited *Cornell Conference on Women* (1969) and *Female Studies I* (1970). In 1976 Ms. Tobias lectured in Eastern Europe for the Department of State and delivered the eulogy at the memorial service for ESTHER MANNING WESTERVELT (p. 432).

Writer on Women in Academe

PATRICIA ALBJERG GRAHAM, former dean of Radcliffe Institute and vice-president of Radcliffe College, is now head of the National Institute for Education. She also is known for her writings on women in education and teaches at Harvard University's Graduate School of Education. She was co-editor of *Women in Higher Education,* published in 1974.

Unearthing American Women's Past

LINDA GRANT DE PAUW has written extensively on women in New York and in America generally in the Revolutionary era and on the founding mothers. In 1976 she published *Remember the Ladies: Women in America 1750–1815.* Her doctoral dissertation on New York State and the Federal Constitution won the Beveridge Award of the American Historical Association in 1964. A professor of American history at George Washington University, since 1965 she has been the editor of *The Documentary History of the First Federal Congress,* an enterprise supported by grants from the National Historical Publications and Records Commission.

Founders of Women's History M.A. Program

Chairperson of the Committee on Women Historians of the American Historical Association, JOAN KELLY-GADOL in that capacity helped develop the Summer Institute for High School Teachers of Women's History held at Sarah Lawrence the summer of 1976. The American Historical Association is seeking to set up four such institutes throughout the country modeled on this pilot. Her publications include "Notes on Women in the Renaissance and Renaissance Historiography" in *Conceptual*

Frameworks for Studying Women's History (1976) and "Did Women Have a Renaissance?" in *Becoming Visible* (1977). Professor Kelly-Gadol teaches history at City College, New York, focusing particularly on Renaissance history and the history of women.

In 1972 she collaborated with GERDA LERNER (below) in setting up the first M.A. program in women's history at Sarah Lawrence. Austrian-born Gerda Lerner, who came to the United States in 1939, was educated at the New School and Columbia University. A well-known American historian, she is the author of *Rebels Against Slavery* (1967), *The Woman in American History* (1971), and *Black Women in White America: A Documentary History* (1972).

Swedish Feminist Investigating the History of Literature

In response to requests by women and women's organizations from all parts of Sweden, the Swedish Government has created a personal research appointment for KARIN WESTMAN BERG as assistant professor at Uppsala University to develop new approaches in the study of the history of literature. As a result of her work, Professor Berg writes that she has been involved in "disclosing the patriarchal biases of universities and supporting research on women in all disciplines." Karin Berg, born in 1914 in Uppsala, learned about racial discrimination in the 1930s when she and her husband worked to rescue young German-Jewish students fleeing from the Nazis. More recently she has been a member of the first Women's Rights Organization in Sweden.

First Incumbent of Barnard's Ochs Chair in History

ANNETTE K. BAXTER, professor of history and chairperson of the department, as well as of the American Studies Program of Barnard College, is also the first incumbent of the Ochs Chair in History (1975). (Out of an existing 550 endowed chairs at American universities only 65 were held by women in the spring of 1975.) Professor Baxter has published several studies on Henry Miller, was co-editor of the 44-volume *American Women: Images and Realities* (1972) and the 59-volume *Women in America: From Colonial Times to the 20th Century* (1974), and has contributed several biographical articles to *Notable American Women*. She was chosen

by the American Association of University Women to write its Centennial history.

First Woman Harmsworth Professor

The first woman to be appointed to the Harold Vyvyan Harmsworth professorship by Oxford University, 1977–78, WILLIE LEE ROSE teaches American history at the Johns Hopkins University, in Baltimore, Maryland, where she specializes in the mid-19th century. The Harmsworth professorship is exclusively for Americans who teach U.S. history. Professor Rose writes about slavery, Reconstruction, and the relationships of blacks and whites. Her 1964 book, *Rehearsal for Reconstruction,* was an investigation of the effects of slavery and Reconstruction in the island microcosm of Port Royal, South Carolina; her most recent study is a compendium of records of slave dealers and owners, statutes that reinforced slavery, prescriptions for punishment of slaves, stories of revolts, and black folklore. She is at work on an analysis of the novel (and film) *Gone With the Wind.*

Sociologist of the Future Makes History

SUZANNE KELLER, professor of sociology, in January 1977 became the first woman to receive tenured faculty rank at Princeton University. One of her central professional concerns is environmental design (she holds a part-time appointment at Princeton's School of Architecture and Urban Planning and for three years directed a multidisciplinary research project on planned communities, funded by the National Science Foundation). Social stratification, the family, and sociology of the future are other particular interests. She has worked in Paris, Munich, and Athens as a research analyst, collecting and analyzing data about children's intelligence, doing public opinion and market research, and analyzing European and American elites. In 1972 Professor Keller was the first woman at Princeton ever to receive a Guggenheim Fellowship; she studied the effects of space on human behavior. A contributor to numerous professional journals, she is also the author of *Beyond the Ruling Class* (1963), *The Urban Neighborhood* (1968), and co-author of a widely used textbook, *Sociology* (1975).

Princeton's (Second) Guggenheim Philosopher

A 1977 Guggenheim fellow and a professor of philosophy at Princeton, MARGARET D. WILSON was awarded the coveted fellowship for a projected study of Locke's position on the knowledge of matter and mind. Professor Wilson, who studied at Vassar, Harvard, and Oxford, was chairperson of the subcommittee on the Status of Women in the Profession of the American Philosophical Association, 1969–71.

An Old Girls' Women's Education Network Founded in the 1860s and Still Thriving

"Everybody knows about old boys' networks. But not infrequently in these days of intense focus on the forces that determine the destinies of women, the complaint can be heard that there is no female counterpart to these groups of men who—sharing some common background of school or war—help one another through life.

"Yet there is such an organization—an organization created not in response to the resurgent feminism of the 1960s but in response to the ideals of seven young women of the 1860s.

"Today, 108 years after it started, this old girls' network spreads across international boundaries and numbers 231,207 women—in every state, in the six provinces of Canada, and abroad.

"Its assistance to women is measured monetarily in the millions of dollars. Its impact on lives is immeasurable." (The *New York Times,* December 21, 1977)

Leader of this group, the Philanthropic Educational Organization (PEO), today is IRENE SNELL, of Hendersonville, North Carolina, elected president in September 1977. Its founders were ALICE BIRD, ALICE COFFIN, ELLA STEWART, FRANC ROADS, HATTIE BRIGGS, MARY ALLEN, and SUELA PEARSON. They met while students at Iowa Wesleyan College. Their original secret society was started as a protest when some of them were asked to join a campus sorority, others were not.

The PEO has provided more than 21,600 women with some $15 million in educational opportunities through its three educational fund programs, which are maintained by gifts from members and friends. The educational loan fund, started in 1907, has lent about $12.3 million to some 19,200 women. The International Peace Scholarship Fund, begun in 1949, has dispensed $2.42 million in scholarships to about 1,400 foreign students from 93 countries for enrollment at 300 schools. The program for continuing educations, launched in 1973, has made 1,066 grants valued at a total of $259,722.

They also own and operate Cottey College, a two-year women's college in Nevada, Missouri, given to PEO 50 years ago by one of its members, VIRGINIA ALICE COTTEY STOCKARD, and maintained through annual dues of $4.00 paid by PEO members.

ELEMENTARY AND SPECIAL EDUCATION TEACHERS AND ADMINISTRATORS

She Established Philadelphia's Free Kindergartens

ANNA HALLOWELL (1831–1905) was one of the many American women who, at the end of the 19th century, worked to help the nation's industrial cities absorb immigrants from all parts of the world. Cramped living and working conditions were taking a heavy toll on the newcomers' children, and Ms. Hallowell in Philadelphia in 1879 established free kindergartens in slum neighborhoods. The city began partial financing in 1882 and took over the kindergartens completely in 1887—the same year Ms. Hallowell became the first woman member of the Board of Public Education.

Founder of the Montessori Method

Perhaps the most significant, the most revolutionary, and certainly the most famous among modern women educators is MARIA MONTESSORI. Her teaching methods, which she developed in the early 1900s while working with mentally handicapped children at the Psychiatric Clinic at the University of Rome, are based on the principle that children have a natural desire and aptitude for learning. She allowed her students freedom to work, to play, and to discover for themselves their natural interests. She also designed teaching aids to stimulate and direct their development. When these children, first the retarded and then the poor, began to read, write, and count before the age of six, their success gained the startled attention of the world. A staunch feminist and enthusiast, Maria Montessori also was the first Italian woman to qualify as a doctor under modern rules. She died in 1952 at the age of 81. Her work is continued at Montessori schools throughout the world.

Educator of Mentally Retarded Children

SARA ELLEN FISK (1886–1976), a leader in the education of mentally retarded children, in 1913 took charge of one of three demonstration classes in an innovative program pioneered by a close friend for the New York Board of Education. Responsible for many new methods of teaching retarded children, which had wide-ranging effects on curriculums around the United States, in 1916 she became director of a laboratory school founded by the Neurological Institute and Bureau of Education. When the nation entered World War I, realizing the contribution that the handicapped could make, she spent a year working in plant and factories to discover what type of jobs handicapped young girls were best able to perform. In 1946 she donated her library of more than 1,000 volumes on teaching retarded children to the Board of Education; a Sarah Fisk Library Fund has been started to update the much needed reference materials. After her retirement in 1954, she strove to set up at the United Nations an international exchange of information and resources to serve handicapped children throughout the world.

Pioneer Teacher of the Dyslexic

At the age of 42, in 1951, ALICE HAWES GARSIDE embarked on a new, challenging life-style with training at Massachusetts General Language Clinic to teach children with reading disabilities. Ms. Garside practices a technique developed by Samuel Oriton and ANNA GILLINGHAM in the 1930s that uses visual, auditory, and kinesthetic senses to help the dyslexic to read. Ms. Garside became supervisor at the Cambridge School in Weston in 1959. Her work at Massachusetts General had emphasized the neurological and physiological origins of reading disabilities, and under her guidance the evolution of Weston's language clinic generated a parallel growth in public awareness.

Champion of Delinquent Children

Teacher and consultant EDNA L. GOODRICH has devoted a lifetime to improving conditions and prospects for young people in correctional institutions. She began her career as a teacher at the Maple Lane School (a Washington state school for delinquent girls) in 1951. Named principal in 1954, she established and organized the nation's first coeducational program within an institutional setting. In 1964 she received the National Outstanding Principal's Award, and the Maple Lane School was named the outstanding institution serving delinquent children. Since that time, as director of Juvenile Services, King County Juvenile Court, Seattle, she has been adviser and consultant on juvenile delinquency and coeducation for institutions in several states.

Founder of Instructional Strategy Council

In 1975 RUTH B. LOVE was appointed superintendent of Oakland (California) schools. Ms. Love also established the 150-member Instructional Strategy Council to determine the specific curriculum of children's education, year by year. The dynamic and dedicated educator is the great-granddaughter of a slave who ran away when he was 12 years old, subsequently to found a school for blacks in Lawton, Oklahoma. Her grandmother was also a slave in Tennessee.

Toddler Care Advocate

MARIE T. DIAS, executive director of Children's World Educational Centers, Inc., who has been working toward her Ed.D. at Boston University School of Education, was a member of the Infant and Toddler Day Care Task Force and helped to draw up rules and regulations dealing with day care centers. She has lectured at universities and to businesses and appears on television and talk shows highlighting the problems of infant care. The recipient of several fellowships and awards, Ms. Dias was chosen an Outstanding Young Woman of the Year in 1975 and appointed to a White House fellowship, 1975–76.

Chippewa Speakers and Teachers

One of the first speakers (Indian elders who are being trained as teachers) chosen by the Great Lakes Tribal Council because of her history as a progressive force among her people was HANNAH MAULSON, who became the first teacher of Wisconsin Indian languages to be certified by the state of Wisconsin. There are a great variety of methods of teaching Indian languages, from sophisticated and intricate show-and-tell to more conventional teaching techniques developed by linguists. Speaker Maulson says that

she is reaffirmed in her belief that children are interested in learning their ancestral language when she meets them and they greet her in Chippewa phrases she has taught them.

ANDREA PETERSEN teaches a combined class of first, second, and third graders in a two-room log cabin that serves as an elementary school on a Chippewa reservation in Grand Portage, Minnesota. Until she arrived 15 years ago, prejudice, lack of skills, and pervasive alienation were the norm for the children now in her care. She has attempted to instill self-confidence and pride in their Indian heritage. Ms. Petersen believes that "Education should begin in delightful discovery and end in wonder." When the

community bestowed its highest honor—a tribal eagle feather—upon Andrea Petersen she said, "The spirit of the Chippewa has touched my soul."

WOMEN IN ELEMENTARY AND SPECIAL EDUCATION

"Each One Teach One": She Erected India's Literary House

WELTHY HONSINGER FISHER took her friend Gandhi's teaching to heart. His plea to "go to the villages and help them, India is the villages" led Ms. Fisher, widow of an American missionary, to create Saksharta Niketan (Literacy House) in Allahabad in 1953. This school, which moved to Lucknow in 1957, has trained over 7,000 teachers. Following Ms. Fisher's motto, "Each one teach one," they in turn have spread the basic skills of elementary reading and writing to over a half million Indian villagers and city laborers. These lessons are followed with instructions on hygiene, on local government for elected village councilmen and for their constituency, and programs that teach women to become community development workers. In 1964 Ms. Fisher, then 84 years old, received the Ramón Magsaysay Award for International Understanding in recognition of her unstinting personal commitment to the cause of lit-

eracy in India and other Asian countries and was lecturing around the world to raise money for her beloved school. Fourteen years later she remained active as she neared 100.

World Curriculum Surveyor

Since 1942, when ALICE MIEL began a career as an elementary school teacher in Michigan, she has been actively aware of modern curriculum problems. She has traveled the world to study, compare, and consult the instruction methods at school systems both inside and outside the United States. Following 30 years with numerous leaves and sabbaticals to Japan, Denmark, Puerto Rico, and Australia, Ms. Miel, in 1970, organized a world conference on education from more than 350 educators from 60 nations. Out of that meeting grew the World Council for Curriculum and Instruction; as its executive secretary, Ms. Miel helps to prepare studies, fund research, and compile data on curriculum development around the world.

LIBRARY SPECIALISTS

Founder of the International Association of School Libraries

JEAN LOWRIE, former president of the American Library Association (1973–74) and founder of the International Association of School Librarians in 1971, is a specialist in the function and development of school libraries. She has been extremely outspoken in her attack on government efforts to curtail spending for both public and school libraries

and has received numerous awards for her work in this area.

She Pushed Library Services for Out-of-School Adults

ALLIE BETH MARTIN (1914–76), president until her death of the 30,000-member American Library Association, believed that libraries should be informal learning centers for all and provide educational opportunities not available elsewhere. Much of her career was devoted to establishing special reading rooms and setting up lecture series and other educational programs designed to help out-of-school adults continue to expand their horizons.

The ALA's First Black President

In 1976 CLARA STANTON JONES became the first black president of the American Library Association (and as the 92nd person to hold office, only the 19th woman). The first woman and the first black to head the Detroit Public Library (1970), she was the recipient of the first award for Distinguished Service Librarianship from the Black Caucus of the ALA and over the past 30 years has been given many other awards—including two honorary doctorates—in tribute to her outstanding work toward the revitalization and cultural development of the city of Detroit. Clara Jones also is an active supporter of the Afro-American Museum, a member of the ACLU and NAACP, and has traveled extensively in the cause of international peace—most recently to Mainland China, Germany, and eight West African countries.

Director of the Largest Library on Women in the United States

PATRICIA MILLER KING, director of the Arthur and Elizabeth Schlesinger Library on the History of Women in America at Radcliffe, has observed a major shift in historical scholarship: Historians are focusing less on military and political leaders and more on the "less prominent and less visible in society, which means that they are looking at women," she says. She describes her work as "identifying, acquiring, and preserving materials illuminating the roles of women in the history of the United States; making such materials available to researchers . . . and creating new resources through techniques such as oral history."

EDUCATION LEADERS OUTSIDE SCHOOLS AND LEARNING CENTERS

First Woman and First Black Commissioner at HEW

In 1965 REGINA GOFF, specialist in childhood education, was named assistant federal commissioner of education for the Department of Health, Education, and Welfare. She was the first woman, and the first black to be named to this post, with responsibility to coordinate "all the programs related to disadvantaged children." Dr. Goff, who retired from HEW in 1971, had had extensive experience in this field, from her studies at Columbia University to her teaching in nursery schools and kindergartens and as supervisor of Negro Elementary Schools in Florida. An active supporter of Head Start and other programs to help deprived preschool children, she believes that there is a great need for expanding these programs in order to further aid children's development, with special emphasis on high school graduates who are ill prepared to attend college and therefore programmed to fail.

Educational Legislator

Until her retirement in 1975, EDITH GREEN was one of the most influential representatives in the U. S. Congress on education legislation. The outspoken congresswoman from Oregon wrote, among other bills, the Higher Education Acts of 1965, 1967, and 1972, the Higher Education Facilities Act, and an amendment to end sex discrimination in education and health "manpower" training. For many years she chaired the Special Subcommittee on Education and later moved to the House Appropriations Committee.

First Congressional Staffer to Work in the Area of Women's Rights

Education specialist with a particular interest and wide experience in sex discrimination cases, BERNICE SANDLER as a staff member of the U. S. House of Representatives' Special Subcommittee on Education was the first person ever assigned to work specifically in the area of women's rights. Her major assignment was the preparation of the two-volume set of hearings conducted by Congresswoman Edith Green (above), entitled *Discrimination Against Women* (1970). These hearings laid the groundwork for the passage of several laws that prohibit sex discrimination against students and employees. Now director of the Project on the Status and Education of Women of the Association of American Colleges, Dr. Sandler earlier was deputy director of the Women's Action Program at HEW and former head of the Action Committee for Federal Contract Compliance of the Women's Equity Action League (WEAL); in the latter capacity she filed formal charges of sex discrimination against more than 250 universities and colleges and was the first person to testify before Congress concerning discrimination against women in education. She has been a teacher, research assistant, employment counselor, psychologist, and secretary, holds three honorary doctorates, and in 1976 was the co-winner of the Rockefeller Public Service Award.

Bibliographer of Women's Continuing Education

Dr. ESTHER MANNING WESTERVELT, who died in 1975, was a scholar and advocate for women's education. Among her accomplishments was one of the first comprehensive bibliographies on women, *Women's Higher and Continuing Education: An Annotated Bibliography with Selected References on Related Aspects of Women's Lives*. At the time of her death she was a member of the Association of American Colleges' Project on the Status and Education of Women.

She had been co-director of the National Coalition on Women's Education and Development from 1970 to 1972, alumnae professor at Simmons College from 1972 to 1974, and the director of the Mid-Hudson Continuing Education Project at the State University at New Paltz, New York. She was the author of a review of research, *Barriers to Women's Participation in Post-Secondary Education*, published by HEW, shortly before her death.

SHEILA TOBIAS (p. 425) eulogized Dr. Westervelt at a memorial service in 1976: "It was she among all her colleagues in the field of Continuing Education who saw the promise in Women's Studies first. It was she who taught us activists . . . that if our work is to endure it must be evaluated systematically and not merely uncritically promoted. . . . There is a missing generation of women in American life. . . . I have been trying to trace that group who but for the Depression, World War II, and the Feminine Mystique of the 1950s would have been in positions of leadership and authority now. . . . Esther belonged to that generation, but unlike most, she survived the pressures not to succeed."

PEER Monitor

As director since 1974 of the Project on Equal Education Rights (PEER), sponsored by the NOW Legal Defense and Education Fund, HOLLY KNOX has been responsible for monitoring enforcement progress under federal laws forbidding discrimination against girls and women in education. Formerly a legislative aide at the U. S. Office of Education at HEW, Ms. Knox was appointed in 1972 by the U. S. Commissioner of Education to chair the Task Force on the Impact of the Office of Education Programs on

Women. She headed a six-month effort to identify sex bias in the agency's $5 billion education aid program and was the principal author of "A Look at Women in Education: Issues and Answers for HEW," a report credited with changing policies and procedures within HEW to bring about educational equity for women. In May 1975 Ms. Knox was appointed by President Gerald Ford to the National Advisory Council on Women's Educational Programs.

Director of U.S. Fund for the Improvement of Postsecondary Education Now President of Vassar

VIRGINIA SMITH, economist, lawyer, and former director of the U. S. Government's Fund for the Improvement of Postsecondary Education, and a long-time activist in the college world, in 1977 was named president of Vassar College. President Smith has extensive experience as an administrator; she has worked at the University of California at Berkeley and served with the Carnegie Commission on Higher Education as an associate director for many years.

She Monitors Women's Progress in Psychology

NANCY FELIPE RUSSO, formerly a health scientist administrator with the National Institute for Child Health and Human Development, is the administrative officer for Women's Programs of the American Psychological Association. This program has been set up to monitor women's status in the field of psychology and government actions, as well as to compile information from psychologists regarding public policy issues that particularly affect women. Dr. Russo, who has published various articles dealing with personal space, population, and the psychology of women, is also president of the American Psychological Association's Division of Population and Environmental Psychology. This organization, founded in 1892, is the major psycho-logical organization in the United States; women make up 27 per cent of its 45,000 members.

Educational Testing Service Chairperson

Interested and experienced in several levels of education, from teaching in grade schools to the administration of a reading clinic at university level, Dr. BETTY J. HUMPHRY, senior examiner and chairperson of Text Development, Higher Education, and Career Program Division, at the renowned Educational Testing Service in Princeton, New Jersey, has primary responsibility for the development of test specifications and for the assembly of tests in a variety of fields. Dr. Humphry is a prolific contributor to professional journals and keeps abreast of developments and innovations in curriculum advancement and teaching methods by conducting workshops around the country.

President of the AAUW

Dr. MARJORIE BELL CHAMBERS, a political activist and contemporary historian, was elected president of the American Association of University Women in June 1975 for a four-year term. Dr. Chambers, formerly president of Colorado Women's College, taught American and European history, including the history of women, at the University of New Mexico's Northern Branch College. Earlier a project historian for the U. S. Atomic Energy Commission's Los Alamos Area office, she has been a strong and active advocate of the Equal Rights Amendment, and had hoped to see it pass by the 200th anniversary of the Declaration of Independence so that all women could indeed say, "All in the United States are equal."

Director of International Center for Research on Women

MAYRA BUVINIC, research associate at the Office of International Science of the American Association for the Advancement of Science, and director of the International Center for Research on Women for a two-year term beginning in 1977, was born and spent her childhood in Punta Arenas, Chile (the southernmost city of the world, facing the Strait of Magellan). She obtained her Ph.D. in Social Psychology in 1975 from the University of Wisconsin with a dissertation on sex differences in aggressive behavior. Dr. Buvinic has done several cross-cultural studies on violence, attitude change, and the psychological impact of mass media and has extended her work on sex differences and the social psychology of women to cross-national and interdisciplinary research on the roles, status, and behaviors of women, with special emphasis on women in Latin America.

The World's First Women Rhodes Scholars

When Cecil Rhodes, British Empire builder and diamond king (who gave his name to Rhodesia), died in 1902, he left a will that established the Rhodes scholarships at Oxford University, England, for college graduates from the onetime British colonies (including the Americas) who displayed outstanding capacities for scholarship and leadership—and the "qualities of manhood." Rhodes's will was later embodied in an Act of Parliament. When large numbers of young women, especially Americans, began inquiring about their eligibility for these prestigious scholarships, new legislation was required. The Sex Discrimination Act of 1975 (see "Women Activists, Heroes, and Humanitarians") among its other provisions gave the Rhodes trustees, an international body, the right to modify the will. In 1976, they did.

The result: in 1977, of the 72 new Rhodes scholars arriving to take up graduate work at Oxford 24 were women. Thirteen were from the United States, four were from Canada, and three were from Australia, and other former British colonial nations that sent one woman apiece were New Zealand, South Africa, and India. Under additional changes in the Rhodes Trust, one young woman also came from West Germany.

These young women were under a special pressure, according to R. W. Apple, in a story to the New York Times from Oxford in November 1977. One of those he interviewed said, "I don't like the thought of somebody saying, 'She was one of the first women to get a Rhodes scholarship, and she hasn't done a thing with it.'" But for the most part, Apple reported, "they were taking Oxford in their stride, marveling at its beauty, rebelling slightly at its teaching methods" (in her first week, one young woman scholar read nine chapters of a 17-chapter textbook on microeconomics, wrote two eight-page essays, and conferred with her tutor six times) and "beginning to learn a bit about the Britain that lies beyond its gates."

First Female Yanks at Oxford

LAURA GARWIN, Massachusetts
   Radcliffe College of Harvard University
DIANE L. COUTU, Rhode Island
   Yale University (also Providence College)
SUE M. HALPERN, Connecticut
   Yale University (also Smith College)
MAURA J. ABELN, New York
   Vassar College
CATHERINE LYNN BURKE, Virginia
   University of Virginia
CAROLINE E. ALEXANDER, Florida
   Florida State University
SARAH JANE DEUTSCH, Illinois
   Yale University
MARY CARGILL NORTON, Indiana
   Michigan State University

DENISE THAL, **Michigan**
  Radcliffe College of Harvard University

DARYL KOEHN, **Kansas**
  University of Chicago

NANCY LEE COINER, **Oklahoma**
  St. John's College

ALLISON MUSCATINE, **California**
  Radcliffe College of Harvard University

SUZANNE PERLES, **Alaska**
  Princeton University (also Harvard University Business School)

Firsts from Other Nations

MELANIE DOBSON, **Canada**
  University of Dalhousie

MARY SHEPPARD, **Canada**
  University of Newfoundland

EILEEN GILLESE, **Canada**
  University of Alberta

JESSIE SLOAN, **Canada**
  Queen's, Kingston

CAROL A. JAY, **Western Australia**
  University of Western Australia

LYNNE PRESSLEY, **Victoria, Australia**
  University of Monash

ELIZABETH J. WOODS, **Queensland, Australia**
  University of Queensland

STEPHANIE KINGSLEY, **New Zealand**
  Auckland University

SHEILA NIVEN, **South Africa**
  University of Natal

SHALINI RANDERIA, **India**
  Delhi University

ERIKA KRESS, **West Germany**
  Fredericiana, Karlsruhe

11

Women in Communications

By Avis Berman and Frances Peter

Rollene Saal, consulting editor

Communications—the exchange of thoughts and messages by speech, signals, or writing—has no sex, and the field has been accessible to women for several hundred years.* Women are known to have had a hand in relaying the events of their times as printers and broadside writers in Elizabethan England and in colonial America. Could there have been an unsung woman working beside Gutenberg himself?

But the fact that women have had a place in the history of communications does not mean that conditions for them have been ideal or opportunities equal. The tendency—documented as far back as the 1890s—to place men in charge of important departments and to relegate women to writing or researching for them has not gone the way of the Model A. On 20th-century newspapers and magazines, in radio and television, most women have worked at the bottom of the pyramid as researchers, reporters, production assistants, and in other jobs that

have little or no influence on policy-making. (Temporary gains made during World War II often were rescinded when the men returned from battle and successfully demanded their jobs back.) Some women on newspapers and magazines have advanced to middle-level management positions as editors and directors. In book publishing, long an industry heavily dependent on women, the record has been better. Yet even there only a few have been promoted to the highest echelons. And there are still few managing or executive editors or publishers in the print media; comparatively few producers, highly visible anchorwomen, or network executives in the electronic media.

Washington Post publisher KATHARINE GRAHAM, like some other newspaper owners and publishers covered in the pages that follow, inherited her property. What she has done with it financially, however, is so spectacular that she does not even appear in this chapter, but in

"Women in Business, Industry, and Finance," (p. 514) as the only woman president of a Fortune 500 company.

In *Up from the Footnote* (1977), her welcome and thoughtful history of women journalists, MARION MARZOLF reports that of the 26,000 women in newsrooms in 1975, an estimated 226 were in the executive positions of news and political editors, managing editors, and publishers. A 1970 survey of 1,340 journalists showed that women were being paid about $4,500 a year less than men for doing the same job. *Newsweek,* with its practice of hiring men as writers (receiving bylines) and women as researchers (receiving legwork), did not promote a woman to a senior editorship until 1975.

With a few brilliant exceptions like HELEN SIOUSSAT, CBS's powerful director of talks, and ANNE O'HARE MCCORMICK, first woman to sit on the editorial board of the *New York Times,* it is an all-too-recent phenomenon, in all areas of communications, that women have reached positions of substantial responsibility. Newspaperwomen in the first half of this century achieved distinction as correspondents and columnists. Only with the feminist activism of the late 1960s have influential editorships come to a wider range of women, including CHARLOTTE CURTIS, MEG GREENFIELD, CAROL SUTTON, and BARBARA COHEN. In early radio, several women, notably MARY MARGARET MCBRIDE, emerged as "personalities" but few had any power to make decisions. PAULINE FREDERICK was not allowed to appear on television until she turned in an exclusive, whereas the early male broadcasters only had to rewrite copy to get on the air. Even today, successful TV correspondents have told us that although they've overcome the useful (for men) myth that the female voice carries insufficient authority for effective newscasting, few have any executive control in the TV news business. They place the blame more on subconscious male attitudes than on intentional repression on the part of male network executives with the power to mold the policy-making superstructure. In magazines, women are still writing and publishing primarily for women (arts excepted), perhaps because the subject matter for each periodical is so well defined. And in all these areas, although opportunities have expanded, there is still room for great improvement because equal practices in hiring, delegating assignments, determining salaries, and promoting are not yet a reality.

Small wonder that chance has figured almost as largely as hard work and talent in some of the success stories this chapter recounts. Nevertheless, we found ourselves with a delightful and solid array of talents to be recognized and the dismaying inevitability of having to omit many women deserving of recognition. We include only those women with demonstrable firsts in their professions or those whose achievements have placed them at the top of the communications industry. The length of the entries does not always reflect relative importance. Some women asked not to be included, and we respected their wishes. Others were too busy (e.g., those covering elections, floods, the Sadat visit to Israel) to give us more than a brief account of their careers.

We salute the gumption and resilience of these women—some famous, some unpublicized—who have made it; we are proud, if angry, that they have had to prove themselves by being at least twice as good at their work as any man. We accord them deep respect for their sense of responsibility and acute cognizance that what they write, say, or decide can influence the thinking of the world.

AVIS BERMAN, *a Washington-based writer and editor, has contributed to* Museum News, *the* Wilson Quarterly, *the* Feminist Art Journal, *and the* Baltimore Sun. *She is at work on a biography of* JULIANA RIESER FORCE, *the first director of the Whitney Museum of American*

Art. She received B.A. and M.A. degrees in English from Bucknell and Rutgers universities and formerly worked for the National Academy of Sciences and the Smithsonian Institution.

FRANCES PETER, *an editor in the medical and biological sciences at the National Academy of Sciences, Washington, D.C., has been managing editor of the scientific journal* BioScience, *author and editor of several newsletters, and has*

worked in various communications positions in Europe, Southeast Asia, and Africa, and in production of the Metropolitan Opera broadcasts. She was an English honors student at Syracuse University, where she received her B.A., and did graduate work at New York University and the University of Maryland.

Consulting editor ROLLENE SAAL *is editorial director of the Literary Guild (see also p. 488).*

NEWSPAPERWOMEN

The U.S.A.'s First Famous Girl Reporter

Although other daring and capable women reporters preceded her, ELIZA-BETH COCHRANE SEAMAN (1865?–1922), better known as "NELLY BLY," was one of the earliest to achieve notoriety and fortune in the smoke-filled city rooms of American newspapers. One of her most celebrated exploits came in 1890 when, traveling alone, she circled the globe for Joseph Pulitzer's *New York World*, beating the fictional record of Philéas Fogg, hero of Jules Verne's *Around the World in 80 Days*. Her penchant for reporting on social inequities rather than "ladylike subjects" was typified by her first articles on the conditions of working girls in Pittsburgh. Through the device of disguise, which became her trademark investigative technique, Ms. Bly would infiltrate an institution or unobtrusively observe a social or political evil, unmask herself, and then expose the perpetrators of injustice in print. In 1888, on one of her first assignments for the *World*— which she cooked up—Ms. Bly had herself committed for 10 days to New York's Blackwells (now Welfare) Island. Her narratives resulted in a grand-jury investigation of the asylum's neglect of its patients and subsequent improvements in their care. Her vivid but brief career (she married in 1895 and her attempt at a comeback in 1919 was unsuccessful) helped pave the way for the more solid and scrupulous efforts of the muckrakers and their heirs in investigative journalism.

First Woman Drama Critic of the *Chicago Daily News*

In 1889, grief-stricken by the death of her young son, light-opera singer AMY LESLIE (1855–1939), born LILLIE WEST, quit the stage, settled in Chicago, and turned to journalism. In 1890 she sold a play review to the *Chicago Daily News* and soon after was taken on as its drama critic, a job she held for the next 40 years. Ms. Leslie was one of the few female drama critics of her time and for years the only one in Chicago; her explanations of dramatic technique and her personal acquaintance with most of the great stage players, reflected in her detailed reporting of their personalities, gained her a large following.

"The Greatest Sob Sister of Them All"

WINIFRED SWEET BLACK BONFILS (1863–1936), the *San Francisco Examiner* reporter who wrote under the name "ANNIE LAURIE," was dubbed "the greatest sob sister of them all" for her vivid, often heart-rending prose. As William Randolph Hearst's answer to Joseph Pulitzer's NELLY BLY (above), Ms. Bonfils participated in her share of tricks, exposés, and other "girl reporter stunts" typical of the period. She joined the *Examiner* in 1890, and from 1895 to 1900 traveled across the country as a Hearst feature writer, turning up at political conventions, sporting events (she is believed to be the first woman to have covered a prize fight), and the 1900 tidal wave disaster in Galveston, Texas (disguised as a boy, she slipped through police lines). On orders from Hearst, she returned to San Francisco to chronicle the earthquake, and in 1907 she had a front-row seat at the trial of Harry Thaw for the murder of Stanford White. It was for their descriptions of Evelyn Nesbit Thaw that she and three other women reporters were dubbed "sob sisters." Ms. Bonfils reported from Europe during World War I, became a columnist after the war was over, and groomed ADELA

ROGERS ST. JOHNS (p. 441) as her successor. When she died, her body lay in state in the rotunda of San Francisco's city hall.

Pioneer Black Woman Activist-Journalist

In 1891, writing under the pseudonym "Iola," Memphis schoolteacher IDA BELL WELLS-BARNETT (1862–1931) wrote several articles for the Negro Press Association, criticizing the inadequate schooling given to black children, and was fired as a result. Switching to journalism, she bought an interest in the *Memphis Free Speech* in 1892. In the spring of that year, three black men she knew were lynched and Ms. Wells-Barnett condemned the hangings on the pages of the *Free Speech*. Next she published the findings of her investigations of other lynchings in the South. When her offices were destroyed while she was visiting in the North, she gave up any idea of returning to Memphis and carrying on her activities there. Marrying and moving to Chicago in 1895, Ms. Wells-Barnett immersed herself in cultural and social welfare activities in the black community. A distinguished life as an activist, suffragist, and clubwoman followed. Present at the founding meeting of the National Association for the Advancement of Colored People, she refrained from participating in it because it was not militant enough for her. She founded a suffrage club for black women and marched in the 1913 parade for women's rights in Washington and the 1916 demonstration staged in Chicago during the Republican National Convention.

First Editor of the *Suffragist*

War correspondent, writer, and editor for more than 30 years, RHETA CHILDE DORR (1866–1948) was a steady and ardent campaigner for women's rights. During her tenure as women's editor for the *New York Evening Post* from 1902 to 1906, she collected material for her book on suffrage called *What Eight Million Women Want*. Thereafter, as the first editor of the *Suffragist* (later *Equal Rights*), a paper of the National Women's Party, she fought for the passage of the Nineteenth Amendment. In 1928 her *Life of Susan B. Anthony, The Woman Who Changed the Mind of a Nation* was published. Yet Ms. Dorr never completely gave up her work as a European correspondent. Her first assignment, to cover the coronation of King Haakon of Norway, came in 1906. Her experiences as a reporter covering the Russian Revolution included battle training as well as interviewing the Czarina's sister and other followers of Rasputin. Ms. Dorr was a foreign correspondent for 21 papers during the final year of World War I.

First Important Woman Art Critic/Editor in the United States

As art critic for the *Washington Evening and Sunday Star* from 1900 to 1945, LEILA MECHLIN (1874–1949) was a force to be reckoned with on the Washington and national art scene. Conservative in her tastes, she deplored in many articles what she believed to be the ugliness and ephemerality of modern art. In 1909 Ms. Mechlin helped to found the American Federation of Art and served as its secretary, 1912–33. From its inauguration in 1909 until January 1931, she edited the Federation's periodical, the *American Magazine of Art* (called *Progress in Art* before 1915). Through this organ's editorial pages she lobbied for the establishment of the National Gallery of Art, a long-time personal cause of hers.

The *New York Times*'s First Full-Time Art Critic

In March 1908 Adolph Ochs, publisher of the *New York Times*, was introduced to the *Scrip*, a monthly that was designed, written, and produced by translator and art critic ELISABETH LUTHER

CARY (1867–1936). On the strength of one issue of the journal, he invited its author to join the *Times* staff as the first person to report exclusively on the art world. Ms. Cary accepted the offer and contributed features and reviews of openings, exhibits, galleries, and museums for the rest of her life.

Sixty Years a Reporter

In a career spanning more than 60 years, ADELA ROGERS ST. JOHNS since 1913 has reported, sensationalized, and created news events for various Hearst publications. Born in Los Angeles on May 20, 1894, she wrote and sold her first story to the *Los Angeles Times* when she was nine. Novelist, screen writer, lecturer, and author of hundreds of short stories for popular magazines, she also became known as "Mother Confessor of Hollywood" for *Photoplay* magazine. In the muckraking days of the 1920s, she uncovered and exposed political corruption at the highest levels of Los Angeles government. Wearing an outfit borrowed from the M-G-M wardrobe, she posed as a "poor girl" looking for work to write about the city's neglect of its poor, covered such news events as the Lindbergh kidnapping trial and the abdication of Edward VIII, and as a political reporter in Washington, D.C., got an exclusive interview with Senator Huey Long. In 1969 she chronicled her memories of people, events, and scoops in her autobiography, *The Honeycomb*. In 1970 President Nixon presented her with the Medal of Freedom in recognition of her dedication to "the ideal that a democracy cannot survive without a free press." In 1976 she came out of retirement to cover the bank robbery and conspiracy trial of PATRICIA HEARST.

President of the *Herald Tribune*

The life of HELEN ROGERS REID (1882–1970), who began her career as a secretary and ultimately became president of the legendary *Herald Tribune,* is an archetypal success story. The eleventh child in an Appleton, Wisconsin, family of modest means, Helen Rogers became accustomed to hard work early in life. She was able to attend Barnard College by working her way at a variety of jobs and was graduated in 1903. Instead of becoming a teacher of Greek, as she had originally planned, Ms. Rogers chose to become social secretary to ELIZABETH REID, wife of the publisher of the *New York Tribune.*

In 1911, with the blessings of her employer, who had grown to admire her intelligence and crisp efficiency, she married the Reids' only son, Ogden Mills Reid, who took over the editorship of the *Tribune* upon the death of his father in 1912. Ms. Reid immersed herself in the suffrage cause; as treasurer of the New York State Women's Suffrage Party in 1917 she raised $500,000. In 1918 her husband asked her to join him at the newspaper. Beginning as an advertising solicitor, she assumed the directorship of the department within three months. One year after her arrival linage had doubled; within five years it was raised from 4 million to 11 million lines.

In 1922 Ms. Reid was made vice-president of the paper, a position she retained after the *Tribune* bought and merged with the *New York Herald* in 1924. It is said that all departments came under her scrutiny and it is known that she made or influenced major editorial and production decisions. Through her offices, women were appointed as book and Sunday magazine editors, and women's achievements were copiously reported. Ms. Reid sponsored the Fresh Air Fund for underprivileged children, engaged Walter Lippmann as a columnist, and improved the readability of the paper's type faces. On the death of her husband in 1947, Helen Rogers Reid became the president of the *Herald Trib-une* and later (1953–55) chaired the Board of the "Old Lady of Park Row."

First Editor of *This Week* Magazine Supplement

Magazine editor and close friend and associate of HELEN ROGERS REID (p. 441), MARIE MATTINGLY MELONEY (1878–1943) became editor of the *Herald Tribune*'s Sunday magazine supplement in 1926. In 1935 the section was expanded into the nationally distributed Sunday section, *This Week*, and she remained in charge of it until her death. Working with Ms. Reid, Ms. Meloney was also responsible for organizing the *Herald Tribune* Forum on Current Problems, an annual affair for clubwomen that evolved into a prestigious conference with international participations. Marie Meloney's newspaper career began at age 16 with a short-lived job with the *Washington Post*. By age 18 she was Washington bureau chief of the *Denver Post*, a job she held for three years. Reporting jobs for *Washington Post*, the *New York World*, and the *New York Herald* followed; in 1904 she married and retired from journalism for 10 years. She returned as the editor of the *Woman's Magazine*, and upon its demise, she moved to another woman's journal, the *Delineator*, which she edited until 1926. Ms. Meloney was decorated by the French and Belgian governments for her work with war relief. She also raised $100,000 to buy MARIE CURIE (see "Women in Science and Technology," p. 144) a gram of radium for her cancer research, and in 1921 brought the Nobel Prize winner to the United States to receive it.

First Woman to be Appointed Chief Central European Correspondent for the *Chicago Tribune*

Caught in Germany with her parents in 1914 and with them declared an alien in 1917 when the United States entered World War I, SIGRID SCHULTZ, born in 1893 in Chicago, was a firsthand observer of the German defeat and its aftermath. Her journalism career was launched in 1919 when she got a job with the *Chicago Tribune*'s Berlin bureau, the first American woman to get the No. 2 spot on the staff of its chief correspondent, Richard Henry Little. Ms. Schultz risked her life several times to cover civil disorders in the strife-torn Weimar Republic. In 1926 she was named chief Central European correspondent for the *Chicago Tribune*, a job she held until 1941. Sigrid Schultz grasped before many others the dangers that German militarism and Hitler represented. By the early 1930s, convinced that Germany was preparing for war, she began cabling home long, incriminating interviews with leading Nazis, including Hitler and Göring, and warning of the imminent menace. She witnessed Hermann Göring charm Charles Lindbergh and heard Hitler state that his will would be done. In 1938 Ms. Schultz began making weekly broadcasts as correspondent for the Mutual Broadcasting Company; her voice announced the outbreak of World War II in Europe at almost the same time as William L. Shirer's did for CBS. In 1977 Ms. Schultz was at work on two books on international affairs and an oral history of anti-Semitism, commissioned by the library of the American Jewish Committee. Of her collection of front-page stories in the 1920s and '30s, she says, "I hope and believe they helped encourage editors to risk entrusting important posts to females of the species."

Founder of the First Illustrated Press Service in Europe

War photographer THERESE (born MABEL) BONNEY, who called herself "dean of the American press corps in Paris," took up residence in France in 1919. After earning a doctorate of letters at the Sorbonne, she decided to immerse herself in the pageantry of the times by taking pictures of those she believed to be the vital people of the age—the statesmen, nightclub singers, dress designers, and artists of Paris—and founded the first American illustrated press service in Europe. During World War II, she took the devastating pictures of European children uprooted by Nazi invasions that moved Churchill to lift the Atlantic blockade so that Red Cross ships could reach them with $4 million in aid. She was one of the first foreign correspondents to sense the coming of the Russo-Finnish War and was known primarily as a chronicler of war, although she was more concerned with its aftermath—"its effects on people, their lives, their homes, their possessions, their hope, and their despair" (Museum of Modern Art press release, 1940). At the time of her death at 83 in January 1978, Ms. Bonny was working on her autobiography, pursuing another doctorate (in gerontology), and considering presenting her thesis to the Sorbonne in pictures showing the predicament of the old.

First American Woman to Head a News Bureau in Europe; First American Correspondent to Be Expelled from Europe

DOROTHY THOMPSON (1894–1961), one of the best-known newspaperwomen of her day and one of the few who never wrote "women's items," got the *Philadelphia Public Ledger* to assign her to Austria as its foreign correspondent in 1921. Her reports from Vienna and Berlin were admired for their color and political insight, and by 1925 she was bureau chief in Berlin for the *Ledger* and the *New York Evening Post.* After an early interview with Hitler, she characterized him as too insignificant to ever amount to much, but once she realized how totally she had underestimated him, she spent most of her time trying to warn the world of the Nazi terror. Ms. Thompson in 1928 married novelist Sinclair Lewis (they were divorced in 1942). In 1934 she was expelled from Germany

as soon as the Führer came into full power. In 1936 the *Herald Tribune* hired her to write a thrice-weekly political column, "On the Record," in which she continued her campaign against Hitler. Dorothy Thompson's strongly worded opinions and analyses made her *persona non grata* in many quarters. Once an opponent of the New Deal, she threw her support to Roosevelt in 1940, for fear that presidential contender Wendell Willkie would be an isolationist. In 1941 she moved her column to the *Post,* but it was dropped in 1947 when she opposed the creation of the state of Israel. Her byline appeared in other papers until 1958.

First Woman Foreign Correspondent for the *Chicago Daily News*

In 1939 top-notch correspondent HELEN KIRKPATRICK (now Helen Kirkpatrick Milbank) became the first woman to be hired by the *Chicago Daily News* Foreign Service. ("If they wanted me," she recalls, "they had to change their policy since I wouldn't change my sex!") A 1931 honors graduate of Smith College, Ms. Kirkpatrick moved to Geneva to do foreign policy research for the League of Nations and to write about her activities and impressions of Europe. By 1937 she had advanced from stringer to regular correspondent for the *London Daily Telegraph* and the *New York Herald Tribune,* and soon her work was appearing in the *Manchester Guardian* and *London Daily Chronicle* as well. She and Victor Gordon-Lennox, a colleague at the *Telegraph,* also found time to establish and edit the *Whitehall Newsletter,* an uncensored news digest of foreign affairs that counted Winston Churchill, Anthony Eden, and the King of Sweden among its readers. To get stories for this bulletin, Ms. Kirkpatrick followed the breaking news through Europe—she was in Prague when Hitler annexed the Sudetenland and observed events of similar portent in the Balkans, Italy, Poland, and France. In 1938 her first book (*This Terrible Peace*) was published, and 1939 brought scoops that excited the envy of her male competitors. Although she became an accredited correspondent to the U. S. Army and Free French forces in Europe, Ms. Kirkpatrick had to battle to be accepted by the military. "However," she notes, "they unbent enough to name me as one of the [press] planners—with Ed Murrow, Bob Bunnell of AP, and Joe Evans of *Newsweek*—for the Normandy invasion." Awarded the French Medal of the Resistance and the U. S. Medal of Freedom for her war work, in civilian life Ms. Kirkpatrick went on to hold executive positions in the State Department (where in 1953 she became the first woman to receive the Rockefeller Public Service Award), RCA, and Smith College.

First Woman to Win a Major Pulitzer Prize in Journalism; First Woman on the Editorial Board of the *New York Times*

Called by the *New York Times* "the expert the experts looked up to," ANNE O'HARE MCCORMICK (1882–1954) of the *Times* won the 1937 Pulitzer Prize for distinguished correspondence, becoming the first woman to be awarded a major Pulitzer Prize in journalism (see also p. 452). A roving correspondent for the paper since 1921, when she timidly offered to submit articles on a young newspaper editor named Benito Mussolini who was being ignored by the rest of the press (prophesied Ms. McCormick: "Italy is hearing its master's voice"), she became an authority on international affairs and at home in the mountains, foothills, and marketplaces of Europe as well as in its chanceries.

The *Times* had not allowed women into its city room until 1934, but in 1936 Ms. McCormick was asked to become a member of the editorial board. Upon issuing the invitation, publisher Arthur Hays Sulzberger told her: "You are to be the 'freedom editor.' It will be your job to stand up on your hind legs and shout whenever freedom is interfered with in any part of the world." Thus American-European and American-Asian relationships became her beats. She delineated the character and philosophy of De Valera, Hitler, Stalin, Dollfuss, Roosevelt, Truman, Eisenhower, and other world leaders and showed her keen grasp of crises and revolutions in her thrice-weekly column "Abroad" and in her frequent editorials.

Numerous journalistic and academic honors came to Ms. McCormick, and she was decorated by the French Government. She was a contributor to the *Times* until her death. In tribute, Sulzberger summarized her achievements: "Those who read her writing relied upon her."

Political Reporter Who Helped to Found the American Newspaper Guild

New York Daily News columnist DORIS FLEESON (1901–70), known for political analyses that pulled no punches, was taught aggressive reporting in the city room of the *News:* "There we learned to hit 'em in the eye," she said. After a reporting job with the *Pittsburg* (Kansas) *Sun,* and stints as society editor of the *Evanston* (Illinois) *News-Index* and city editor of the *Great Neck* (Long Island) *News,* Ms. Fleeson came to the *Daily News* in 1927 and moved to its Washington bureau in 1933. During this year she also worked with Heywood Broun to establish the American Newspaper Guild and was a delegate to the founding convention and was elected a member of its executive committee. An enthusiastic supporter of the New Deal, she was at one time the only permanent woman member of the press corps to accompany Franklin Roosevelt on his campaign tours. In 1943 Ms. Fleeson resigned from the *News* and became a war correspondent for the *Woman's Home Companion,* reporting from the French and Italian fronts. Back in Washington after the war, she began writing a political column for the *Washington Star*. Her revelations of feuds between Supreme Court Justices Robert H. Jackson and Hugo Black and continued hostilities between President Harry S. Truman and General Douglas MacArthur made headlines across the country and led *Newsweek* to observe, "There is, in fact, almost no Washington figure, Republican or Democrat, who has not felt the sharp edge of her typewriter." A winner of numerous honors, including the first award given by the New York Newspaper Women's Club for outstanding reporting and two honorary doctorates in humane letters, Ms. Fleeson was an avid and outspoken champion of women's rights, a member of the Women's National Press Club, and a gadfly to the all-male National Press Club. At the time of her retirement in 1967, her twice-weekly column was being distributed to 90 papers.

Maine's Only Full-Time Washington Correspondent for 40 Years

The journalistic career of ELISABETH MAY CRAIG (1889–1975) spanned seven presidential administrations, from Calvin Coolidge to Lyndon Johnson. The only full-time Washington correspondent for Maine newspapers from 1924 until her retirement in 1965, she was celebrated for her unflagging feminism, her merciless questions designed to skewer equivocating politicians, her lobster-like tenacity, and her flowery hats (which made it easier for Presidents at press conferences to pick her out of a crowd of reporters). Long an activist, Ms. Craig marched in the suffragist parade staged during Woodrow Wilson's inauguration, but she did not contemplate a newspaper career until 1923 when she began helping her husband with a column he wrote for the *Portland* (Maine) *Press Herald;* by 1924 the by-line was hers alone. Eventually she became correspondent for all of the Guy Gannett newspapers in the state. May Craig excelled at the quick re-

tort, and sparring with Presidents became her specialty. When Franklin D. Roosevelt labeled newspaper columnists "an unnecessary excrescence on our civilization," Ms. Craig pointed out that he had a columnist in his own family—his wife, the writer of "My Day," (see "Women Activists, Heroes, and Humanitarians," p. 738). As one of the correspondents present at ELEANOR ROOSEVELT's first press conference, Ms. Craig was a founder of the First Lady's Press Conference Association. In 1947 she was the only woman correspondent covering President Harry S. Truman's trip to the Inter-American Defense Conference in Brazil. Denied a berth for the trip home on the battleship *Missouri* (BESS and MARGARET TRUMAN *were* allowed aboard), she made headlines with her objections that as an accredited White House correspondent she had the right to stay with the President throughout his visit. She was flown home under protest but in 1949 she did get her way and became the first woman allowed on the battleship *Midway;* she was promptly dubbed "Admiral Craig." She was also the first woman to be accredited by the U. S. Navy, first to fly the Berlin airlift, first to fly over the North Pole (in 1952), first to cover the Korean truce talks, and was responsible for getting women's washrooms installed in the House and Senate press galleries. During the 1950s she became a regular on "Meet the Press," where her trademark hats made her instantly recognizable to all television viewers. Her status as a Washington institution was captured by a *New Yorker* cartoon depicting a senator sitting at his desk while a clerk dumped thousands of letters in front of him and admonished, "Well, there you are, Senator. You would snap at May Craig!"

First Female "Voice of Broadway"

In 1938 DOROTHY KILGALLEN (1913–65) nailed the plum job of Broadway columnist for the *New York Journal-American,* invading a preserve that had been exclusively male. "The Voice of Broadway," her mixture of gossip about show business, politics, and cafe society, was soon a success (appearing in 24 additional papers), and even Walter Winchell, king of the gossip beat, praised it. In 1941 Ms. Kilgallen began broadcasting a "Voice of Broadway" radio show once a week; in 1947 it was expanded to a daily program of news and interviews. By 1950, 45 papers were taking her column. Only 25 when she landed the Broadway assignment, Ms. Kilgallen was already an experienced newspaperwoman. At the end of her freshman year in college she took what was supposed to be a summer job as a cub reporter at the *New York Evening Journal.* The sight of her own by-line changed her mind about returning to school and her name was soon familiar to *Journal* readers. International recognition came in 1936 when the paper sent her on a round-the-world race in competition with other reporters. Her 24½-day time was second to a Scripps-Howard reporter, but she finished first in publicity and front-page copy. In 1937 the *Journal-American* (the *Journal* and the *American* had merged that year) assigned her to Hollywood for a stint as a movie correspondent. In addition to her columns and radio shows, Dorothy Kilgallen covered many big news events, including the coronation of George VI, the Lindbergh kidnapping, FDR's first campaign, and the 1948 Democratic convention. From 1945 to 1963, with her husband, actor Dick Kollmar, she broadcast a daily radio program, and in 1949 agreed to be a panelist on a TV guessing game called "What's My Line?" which made her a national TV celebrity. Credited with coining the quintessential "What's My Line?" question, "Is it bigger than a breadbox?" she appeared regularly every Sunday night, including the night of her death, for 16 years.

First Woman Elected to the National Press Club

ESTHER VAN WAGONER TUFTY, affectionately known as "the Duchess" to the Washington press corps, was the first woman elected to the National Press Club when it lifted its 40-year ban against women members (in 1971). A tenant of the National Press Building longer than any other Washington correspondent, in 1978 she was still, at 82, working every day as president and editor/writer for the Tufty News Service, covering Washington for Michigan newspapers. Since FDR's second term, her by-line has appeared in more than 300 papers across the country and her news service has employed and trained, among others, Edwin Newman of NBC News and LIZ CARPENTER, former press secretary to LADY BIRD JOHNSON (see "Women in Agriculture and the World Food Movement," p. 18). In addition to writing about the news, Ms. Tufty has frequently made it—as she did when she flew the Berlin airlift atop 10 tons of coal, when she was injured in the wreck of Dewey's 1944 campaign train, and when her impersonation of Roosevelt at a Gridiron Club party at the White House brought Secret Service men running to her side. Ms. Tufty was a war correspondent during World War II, the Korean War, and in Vietnam. She made her TV debut in 1952, covering the political convention for NBC. The only woman to have been elected president of three top newspaperwomen's organizations—American Women in Radio and Television, the American Newspaper Women's Club, and the Women's National Press Club (now the Washington Press Club)—in June 1976 she became the second woman to be inducted into Sigma Delta Chi's Hall of Fame for journalists. (The first was MAY CRAIG; p. 445.) In the early 1930s she was the managing editor of the *Evanston* (Illinois) *News Index,* one of the first women to hold that job on a daily paper. When she came to Washington in 1935, the Duchess told an interviewer for *Matrix* magazine, women reporters found a powerful ally in ELEANOR ROOSEVELT (see p. 445 and "Women Activists, Heroes, and Humanitarians," p. 738). According to Ms. Tufty, the President's wife "held so many press conferences for women only that editors were forced to hire women to cover her" and "caused more to be written by women, for women, about women than any other First Lady or maybe any other American woman, as far as I know."

First Female *Life* Photographer

MARGARET BOURKE-WHITE, born in 1904, began her career in photojournalism at the age of 19, using a $20 secondhand camera with a cracked lens. Her work as an industrial photographer attracted the attention of Henry R. Luce, who asked her to prepare the first cover of his new business magazine, *Fortune*. In the 1930s, as a staff photographer for *Fortune*, she traveled through the South to capture the plight of the sharecroppers and tenant farmers in photographs later published as a book (with Erskine Caldwell) entitled *You Have Seen Their Faces*. One of the four original photographers for *Life*, Ms. Bourke-White contributed the cover and several pictures to its first issue (November 23, 1936). During World War II, as the first woman photographer accredited to the Army Air Forces, she was torpedoed off North Africa, rode with an artillery spotter in Italy, and was the only American photographer in the Soviet Union in 1941 while the battle for Moscow was being fought. At a meeting with Stalin in the Kremlin that same year, she determined to make him smile and got her picture by getting down on the floor and trying out "crazy postures searching for a good camera angle." Ms. Bourke-White's most unforgettable series of photographs was taken in 1945 when, attached to General George C. Patton's Third Army, she marched into Buchenwald concentration camp and saw the carnage. Her photos of stacks of naked dead bodies filled the world with revulsion. In 1952, after a stint at the Korean front, Ms. Bourke-White began to be plagued by aches in her left arm and leg, the first symptoms of Parkinson's disease, which caused her to quit *Life* in 1957 and begin a battle against Parkinson's disease which she fought until her death in 1971.

The Unholy Trio

Feared, hated, and indispensable to the movie industry, LOUELLA O. PARSONS (1893–1972), HEDDA HOPPER (1890–1966), and SHEILAH GRAHAM were the first reporters to realize the news potential of Hollywood and its stars. Their stinging or treacly commentary could destroy or establish an actor's career. All three learned to barter their silence about unsavory activities for exclusives and to shower "good" publicity on favorites that put recipients and studios in their debt. Their life-and-death power earned them a place akin to the Three Fates in movie mythology and played a major part in shaping Hollywood in its heyday.

Louella Parsons is credited with writing the first movie column in this country, in the *Chicago Herald* in 1914. It ran until 1918, when William Randolph Hearst bought the paper. Out of a job because of the new management, Ms. Parsons moved to Manhattan and went to work as the *New York Morning Telegraph*'s gossip columnist. Soon after, Hearst rehired Ms. Parsons as his syndicate's gossip columnist, which she remained for the rest of her career. In

1925 she moved to California. Ms. Parsons tried her hand at a radio program as early as 1928 but was not successful in that medium until 1934, when she hit upon an interview show called "Hollywood Hotel." To gain Ms. Parsons' favor and publicity for their latest picture, stars would appear on the program for free. Few guests refused her invitations. In the 1930s and '40s, her daily column appeared in some 400 newspapers in the United States and abroad. Despite her frequent inaccuracies, she was accepted as a moral and cinematic policeman, judge, and executioner. Her influence declined after World War II, but she continued to write her column until 1965.

Ms. Parsons' arch-rival Hedda Hopper (born ELDA FURRY) began broadcasting Hollywood gossip in 1936. She turned what had been a lackluster career as a bit player to advantage as a reporter by drawing upon her knowledge of movie personalities' habits and private affairs to get exclusives and gain entry into many inner circles. In 1938 she began a syndicated column with *Esquire,* moving in 1942 to the *Chicago Tribune-New York Daily News* syndicate. Ms. Hopper pioneered the wearing of outrageous hats as a trademark well before BELLA ABZUG (see "Women in Politics and Government," p. 71) or MAY CRAIG (p. 445) and saw the value of escalating the feud between Ms. Parsons and herself.

By 1964 Sheilah Graham (born LILY SHEIL), who had been in Hollywood since 1935, had usurped Ms. Parsons' and Hopper's popularity. Her column was carried by 178 papers, well ahead of Ms. Hopper's 100 and Ms. Parsons' 69. Accepting the decline of the Hollywood movie industry after World War II, Ms. Graham added television interviews to her enterprises and in 1969 announced that she would no longer depend on Hollywood as her sole source for material, preferring to report on newsworthy people wherever she found them. Ms. Graham has the distinction of being the only gossip columnist ever praised by literary critic Edmund Wilson—for *Beloved Infidel,* her portrait of her close friend F. Scott Fitzgerald.

First Woman Publisher of a Washington Daily Paper

In 1930, at age 48, ELEANOR "CISSY" MEDILL PATTERSON (1884–1948) abandoned her life as a professional socialite to become a newspaperwoman. She had no experience in journalism yet started at the top—instantly becoming the only woman editor-publisher of a large metropolitan daily in the U.S.A.—by pulling strings. Ms. Patterson simply badgered her friend William Randolph Hearst into letting her edit his floundering morning paper the *Washington Herald.* The newspaper business was in her blood. Her grandfather, Joseph Medill, founded and edited the *Chicago Tribune;* her father and cousin were its subsequent publishers and editors. Ms. Patterson's brother was the publisher of the New York *Daily News* and her niece ALICIA (p. 449) would eventually found *Newsday.* Ms. Patterson soon showed her good business sense. She raised the *Herald*'s weekly circulation from 60,000 to 115,000 within a few years. She also went out on stories, often disguising herself à la NELLY BLY (p. 439) to expose injustice or social evils. One of the most famous of these exploits was her masquerade as a destitute woman needing food, shelter, and a job; she spent three nights in the Salvation Army quarters and days in employment agencies and later reported her experiences and impressions. By 1937 Ms. Patterson was so committed to the newspaper profession that she took over the Hearst evening paper, the *Washington Times,* and in 1939, when Eugene Meyer, her competitor as publisher of the *Washington Post* tried to buy the *Herald* from Hearst, Ms. Patterson beat him by purchasing the *Herald* and the *Times* herself and merging them into the *Washington Times-Herald*. (Six years after her death, the *Times-Herald* was bought and absorbed by the *Post*.)

Founder of *Newsday*

In 1940, with her husband Harry Guggenheim, ALICIA PATTERSON (1906–63) of the Medill-Patterson-McCormick publishing dynasty founded and became editor and publisher of *Newsday*, Long Island's largest daily paper and one of the most successful suburban dailies in the nation. After her debut in 1925, Ms. Patterson went to New York City to be with her father, who was busy supervising his young publication, the *Daily News*. She learned the reporter's trade by working as a cub reporter on the *News* and *Liberty* magazine, another family property. In 1931 she took a year off to become a transport pilot and set several records as a woman flyer, but returned to the *News* as a literary critic, a job she kept until 1943. *Newsday* was distinctly Alicia Patterson's creation. It went against her father's instructions—"Don't try a tabloid"—and against the family tradition of implacable opposition to the Democratic Party. Under her leadership,

the paper won several design awards and, in 1954, a Pulitzer Prize for public service in exposing graft in harness racing.

New York City's First Woman Newspaper Publisher

From 1939 to 1976, as owner, editor in chief, president, and treasurer, DOROTHY SCHIFF published the *New York Post*, since 1801 the nation's oldest newspaper with a direct line of daily publication. Ms. Schiff became the major stockholder of her family's paper in 1939 and in 1943 assumed the title of publisher and owner. A friend of Franklin Roosevelt's and a firm supporter of the New Deal, under her direction the *Post* maintained a consistently progressive liberal-Democratic stance on the issues of the day. (Walter Winchell once called it the "New York *Pravda*" and was promptly and successfully sued.) In *Men, Money and Magic* (1976), her account of her life, Ms. Schiff wrote, "When I took on the *Post*, I didn't have much faith in myself or the paper, and I didn't really think I could pull it out. Now it's part of me— we are part of each other."

Dean of American Financial Writers

SYLVIA PORTER, author of the syndicated column "Your Money's Worth," has been advising Americans on how to spend their money for more than 40 years. Preeminent in the field of financial writing—with readers numbering Presidents, government officials, and the business world—her path to obtaining a job and recognition was not easy. Ms. Porter's fascination with finance began in October 1929. Her mother, heretofore a successful businesswoman, was nearly wiped out by the stock market crash. Resolving to find out what had happened, Ms. Porter switched her major at Hunter College from English to economics and was graduated at age 18 with a magna

cum laude degree. However, in 1932, the demand for a woman financial writer was not overwhelming. She worked in a series of Wall Street firms, did some graduate work, and eventually advanced to partner in an investment counseling firm. Armed with a sheaf of her articles from commerce journals, Ms. Porter got a job as financial writer for the *New York Post*, where she was made to use the by-line "S. F. Porter" because her editors said that no one would read a female money adviser seriously. It took seven years for the *Post* to let her "publicly become a woman." In addition to her newspaper columns, Ms. Porter has published *Sylvia Porter's Money Book*

(1976), writes a monthly question-and-answer column for the *Ladies' Home Journal,* and prepares an annual paperback guide to income taxes. In 1965 Lyndon Johnson offered her the presidency of the Export-Import Bank (she refused), and 1974 she was the only journalist invited to President Gerald Ford's economic summit conference.

First Lady of White House Reporting

HELEN THOMAS, White House bureau chief for United Press International, has achieved many firsts for women in the newspaper profession: first to head the presidential coverage of a major news service; in 1975, first to be elected president of the White House Correspondents Association, as well as the first to be elected to the prestigious Gridiron Club, which had limited its membership to men since it was formed in 1885; first to close a presidential press conference, an honor she assumed during the Kennedy administration in the absence of Merriman Smith, then dean of White House correspondents. (She has since opened and closed press conferences under all succeeding administrations.) In addition to traveling extensively with Presidents Kennedy and Johnson, Ms. Thomas covered Richard Nixon's trips to China and the Soviet Union in 1972, Henry Kissinger's 1973 missions to the Middle East and China, and Gerald Ford's visit to Peking. Following her graduation from Wayne State University, Ms. Thomas was hired by the *Washington Daily News* in 1942 when men were leaving for service in World War II. She advanced to cub reporter before moving to UPI's Washington bureau, where she got a job in the city room and thus avoided the women's features pigeonhole. In 1956 she transferred to the wire service's national staff and was assigned to the Justice Department, then to the Department of Health, Education, and Welfare, and finally, following JFK's inauguration, to the White House beat.

First Black Woman Accredited to the White House

ALICE DUNNIGAN, retired Washington bureau chief of the defunct Associated Negro Press, made history in the process of reporting it through her embattled efforts to get her stories out to the black newspapers. In 1948 she became the first black woman White House correspondent and was one of 60 reporters accompanying Harry S. Truman on his whistle-stop election campaign. At the Cheyenne, Wyoming, stop, Ms. Dunnigan, although wearing prominent identification, was grabbed by a military officer, removed from the group of correspondents walking behind the presidential motorcade, and shoved into the crowd. She was not allowed to proceed until another reporter verified her credentials. "Later in the trip," Ms. Dunnigan recalled in an interview with the *Washington Post,* "Truman poked his head into my compartment and said, very quietly, 'I heard you had a little trouble. Well, if anything else happens, let me know.'" During the Eisenhower years, Ms. Dunnigan was consistently ignored at press conferences because of her questions about racial discrimination. "I always felt," she told the *Post,* "that a journalist should be a crusader. I went to every press conference with a loaded question. And [no matter] if I got an answer or a no comment or nothing, I had a story." Among Ms. Dunnigan's other firsts as a black woman journalist are memberships in the Senate and House press galleries, the State Department Correspondents Association, and the First Lady's Press Association.

Terror of the White House Press Conferences

Famous for her blunt and unrepentant interrogations of Presidents at their televised press briefings, correspondent SARAH MCCLENDON over the years since 1946 has operated her own news bureau reaching a string of newspapers in New England and Texas. According to WIN-ZOLA MCLENDON and SCOTTIE FITZ-GERALD SMITH in *Don't Quote Me* (1971), Ike's angry answer to her query about which policy decisions Vice-President Richard Nixon had helped to make —that if given a week, he might think of some—may have cost Nixon the 1960 election. The first to turn up the Bobby Baker story during the Johnson administration, Ms. McClendon had to fight for national coverage of the breaking scandal despite her reputation for accuracy because no one wanted to print it. When she asked President Kennedy why "two well-known security risks" were allowed to reorganize the State Department, JFK asked her for names, she told him, "lawsuits were threatened, and Sarah was barred from using a State Department telephone." Unabashed, Ms. McClendon noted that being a reporter was a "public trust" she intended to uphold and that forceful, if ugly, questions were what made press conferences useful. A native of Tyler, Texas, and a 1931 graduate of the Missouri School of Journalism, Sarah McClendon began her career reporting for Texas newspapers. She joined the WACs during World War II, and afterward moved to Washington, where she has been firing journalistic salvos ever since.

First Woman City Editor of a Major Daily Newspaper

After 12 years as a police reporter specializing in murder stories, AGNESS M. UNDERWOOD became the city editor of the *Los Angeles Evening Herald-Express* (now the *Herald-Examiner*). The first woman city editor of a major daily paper, Ms. Underwood, who occasionally fired a jesting, but nevertheless impressive, blank from her desk-drawer pistol, earned the respect of reporters for her knowledge of the city's business, political, and criminal worlds. She was named the National Federation of Press Women's Outstanding Woman in Journalism in 1962.

First Woman to Win Sigma Delta Chi Award

In 1950, for a series on Minnesota mental hospitals, GERI JOSEPH became the first woman to win the Sigma Delta Chi Award. During her career as staff writer for the *Minneapolis Tribune* (1945–53), Ms. Joseph developed expertise in health, education, and welfare reporting and racked up five American Newspaper Guild awards. Since retiring from journalism in 1953, she has been nationally prominent as an organizer for the Democratic National Committee—she was the only chairwoman of a major committee at the 1964 convention—and has continued her work in health and education as a member of several presidential councils and commissions. Since 1970 she has concentrated on the problems of delinquency and crime in Minnesota and has served as an adviser to the Rutgers University Center for American Women and Politics.

First Woman to Win a Pulitzer Prize for International Reporting

MARGUERITE HIGGINS' lifelong ambition was to be a war correspondent; she never deviated from that goal. Born in 1921, she received a master's degree in journalism from Columbia in 1942, joined the *New York Herald Tribune,* and in 1944 persuaded the paper to send her to Germany to cover the war. She arrived in time to be one of the first to report on the liberation of Dachau concentration camp, covered the Nuremberg trials, and became the *Tribune*'s Berlin bureau chief in 1947. Assigned to Tokyo as bureau chief in 1950, Ms. Higgins was the only woman correspondent in Korea during the "police action." She refused to leave the front when military personnel informed her there would be trouble; trouble, she averred, was news. The Army, like the *Tribune,* gave in and "Maggie"

Higgins received the 1951 Pulitzer Prize for international reporting for her accounts of events in Korea. In Vietnam to cover the early days of that war, she contracted a tropical disease, which ended her life in 1966 at age 45.

Pulitzer Prizes in Journalism

Local Reporting

1955 Caro Brown, *Alice* (Texas) *Daily Echo*
1959 Mary Lou Werner, *Washington Evening Star*
1960 Miriam Ottenberg, *Washington Evening Star*
1972 Anne De Santis, *Boston Globe*
1977 Margo Huston, *Milwaukee Journal*

National Reporting

1971 Lucinda Franks, United Press International

International Reporting

1951 Marguerite Higgins, *New York Herald Tribune*

Correspondence

1937 Anne O'Hare McCormick, *New York Times*

Editorial Writing

1964 Hazel Brannon Smith, *Lexington (Mississippi) Advertiser*

Criticism or Commentary

1970 Ada Louise Huxtable, *New York Times*
1974 Emily Genauer, *Newsday*
1975 Mary McGrory, *Washington Star*

First Woman to Win a Pulitzer Prize for Local Reporting

CARO BROWN's first job at the *Alice* (Texas) *Daily Echo* was as a proofreader. She inherited a column, and in her second year as a columnist, won a statewide contest conducted by the Texas Press Association. After a stint as a society editor, in 1955 she won the Pulitzer Prize for local reporting (edition time) for her exposure of corruption and illegal practices in Duval County, Texas. The second woman to win a major Pulitzer Prize in journalism, she was the first to win the award for reporting. In a letter of commendation, the attorney general of Texas wrote in part: "I'm sure few people outside Duval County realize that what you have done was at the risk of your life, and that even your young daughter has lived under threats of physical mistreatment and violence." The county for years had been ruled by one family's pistols and political chicanery. When Ms. Brown made up her mind to expose the rampant terrorism and dishonesty, she risked the retaliation of George B. Parr, the political boss credited with turning up a crucial number of tardy votes and giving "Landslide Lyndon" Johnson a Senate seat in 1948. One reporter had died trying to trace the influence of Parr on the election and, Ms. Brown recalls, "most of the reporters were terrified to come to Duval County." Yet a quirk of fate caused her to save Parr's life: In the wake of a political slaying, an incensed Texas Ranger pulled a gun on Parr; an eyewitness, she persuaded the Ranger not to shoot. Caro Brown now lives and works in Corpus Christi, Texas.

The Most Widely Read Columnists in the World

They are syndicated to more than 1,500 newspapers. Between the two of them they reach over 100 million readers, and each claims to be the world's most widely followed columnist. Both receive thousands of letters a day. ESTHER "EPPIE" LEDERER and PAULINE "POPO" PHILLIPS, the Sioux City, Iowa, twin sisters better known as ANN LANDERS and ABIGAIL VAN BUREN, dispense pungent advice on every topic from marital instability and adolescent growing pains to diagnoses of medical and behavioral problems to the ins and outs of being buried in a 1939 Dodge (buy three adjoining plots or have yourself cremated, then stored in the ashtray was Ann's reply). Their columns are often read before the headlines by an audience of unparalleled size and scope. An inaccurate or misleading comment, no matter how picayune, unleashes torrents of reader response; a *New York Times Magazine* article reported that 7,000 lawyers wrote in to protest some gratuitous legal advice and 20,000 letters were received on various ramifications of a misprinted meatloaf recipe.

Esther Pauline (Eppie/Ann Landers) and Pauline Esther (Popo/Abigail Van Buren) Friedman, born in 1918, were identical twins who did everything together, culminating in a double wedding ceremony two days before their twenty-first birthday. Both settled down as housewives and mothers until 1955, when Eppie, who had never held a job or written a line for publication, showed up at the *Chicago Sun-Times* and took over the three-year-old "Ann Landers" column. Six months later (January 1956) Popo offered the name "Abigail Van Buren" and an identical column to the *San Francisco Chronicle,* and blithely displaced the paper's reigning advice columnist. Their sassy, irreverent but basically conservative answers were immediately successful and syndication quickly

followed for both, triggering a feud between them over newspaper space and supremacy. However, the rivalry has allegedly cooled and the sisters are said to be at peace again.

First Woman Journalist Jailed for First Amendment

MARIE TORRE, a TV-radio columnist for the *New York Herald Tribune,* spent 10 days in the Hudson County, New Jersey, women's prison in 1959 for refusing to divulge a news source. Called the "Joan of Arc of her profession" by the judge who sentenced her, she was the first newspaperwoman to serve a contempt-of-court sentence for citing the guarantees of the First Amendment as her defense. In her column of January 10, 1957, Ms. Torre quoted an unidentified CBS network executive as making derogatory remarks ("doesn't want to work," "has an inferiority complex," "won't make up her mind about anything," "is fat") about Judy Garland. The singer responded by filing a $1,393,000 breach-of-contract and libel suit against CBS; neither the reporter nor the paper was named as a defendant, but the statements in the column were the basis of the suit. Rather than violate a confidence, Ms. Torre held out against the pre-trial requests of the judge and Ms. Garland's lawyer to disclose the identity of her source, saying, "There's too much at stake, not only for me, but for all members of our profession." The suit was settled out of court after Ms. Torre served her time.

One Paper's Pulitzer-Winning Women

With MARY LOU WERNER FORBES, MIRIAM OTTENBERG, and MARY MC-GRORY, the *Washington Star* holds the record for the greatest number of women Pulitzer Prize winners on staff. Until 1975, when Ms. Ottenberg retired, all three were working continuously and si-

multaneously at the paper; in 1978 Ms. Forbes and Ms. McGrory are still there.

Mary Lou Werner Forbes, deputy "Portfolio" editor of the *Washington Star,* was the fourth woman to win the Pulitzer Prize in journalism. She earned the prize (for local reporting) for her coverage of the school integration crisis in Virginia. During 1958 Ms. Forbes (then Mary Lou Werner) carried the burden of the deadline coverage of public school integration as the *Star*'s chief correspondent in Virginia. Often she would have to dictate major news breaks in the continuing story within minutes of going to press. Because of her knowledge of sources and of the issues involved she was able to get exclusives for her paper and whenever necessary wrote interpretative material to explain the background of the crisis. Ms. Forbes's initial foray into journalism was something of an accident. She applied for work at the *Star* in 1944 at age 17, after one and a half years of studying mathematics at the University of Maryland, as an accountant. That opening had been filled, however, and the *Star* offered to make her a copygirl instead. She had no idea what such activity entailed, but accepted the job and fell in love with journalism. In 1947 Ms. Forbes was made a staff writer for Virginia and was named assistant state editor in January 1959. She became director of the *Star*'s news coverage of Maryland and Virginia. On her way to her current position, to which she was appointed in 1975, Ms. Forbes served as principal assistant metropolitan editor and as metropolitan editor. She is particularly proud to be the *Star*'s first woman editor outside of the traditional women's section.

With a 40-year career of exposing crime, corruption, and fraud, Miriam Ottenberg may well be the first woman to break into modern investigative reporting. She won a Pulitzer for a 1960 series revealing the used-car racket in the Washington, D.C., area. A 1935 graduate of the University of Wisconsin, she joined the *Washington Evening Star* in 1937 as a police reporter, the first woman on that paper to specialize in straight news, particularly murder stories, and not women's features. She broke a story on police corruption that led to a major administrative shake-up and a new police chief and was the first to disclose publicly that the Mafia still thrived in America as the Cosa Nostra. When she moved into consumer fraud and white-collar crime, Ms. Ottenberg took on far more than the shoddy used-car swindle. Pretending to be an adoptive mother, she exposed the baby broker racket; posing as a frustrated, suicidal wife, she unmasked a ring of phony marriage counselors. Impersonating a variety of other "marks," she investigated and exposed a wig racket, fake charities, and pyramid schemes. Ms. Ottenberg even discovered that the same group of crooks she had driven out of the used-car business were the ones selling low-grade wigs. Marine authorities credited her series on the inadequacy of safety measures on many "pleasure" cruises with spurring "safety at sea" legislation. In an unprecedented tribute to a newspaper reporter, the law-enforcement community and civic leaders of Washington in 1958 gave a reception in her honor at which she was presented with a plaque signed by the U.S. Attorney General, congressional leaders, judges, prosecutors, and the District of Columbia chief of police. Retired from the *Star* since 1975, Ms. Ottenberg has been working on a book on multiple sclerosis.

Washington Star syndicated columnist Mary McGrory, winner of the 1975 Pulitzer Prize for commentary, made the White House enemies list (with two asterisks and a check mark) for her scathing reports of the Watergate hearings. Her Pulitzer recognized 20 years of shrewd insights and crystalline writing on the national political scene. Ms. McGrory illuminates her 850-word columns, essays of passionate moral intensity, with historical and literary allusions and sharp phrases: Gerald R. Ford was "a blind date who has been proposed to"; the Watergate defendants "came on like

Chinese wrestlers bellowing and making hideous faces as if to frighten the prosecutors to death"; on the thirtieth day of his trial, Nixon's former chief of staff, H. R. Haldeman, had eyes "like two burnt holes in a blanket"; in the Nixon pardon "sabotage of equal justice was billed as an act of conscience." Ms. McGrory, born in 1918 in Boston, received a B.A. in English from Emmanuel College in 1939 and went to work at Houghton Mifflin book publishers cropping pictures at $16.50 a week. Within three years she left to become a secretary at the *Boston Herald;* soon she was reviewing books and writing features. In 1947 she moved to Washington as a book reviewer for the *Star.* Her break came in 1954 at the Army-McCarthy hearings when her editor, Newbold Noyes, Jr., assigned her to cover them and told her: "Write it like a letter to your favorite aunt." She wrote 16 stories and that same year joined the national staff of the *Star,* although on the basis of her coverage of the hearings, James Reston had offered her a job at the Washington bureau of the *New York Times*—writing in the afternoons and running the switchboard in the mornings. By 1960 her regular columns were syndicated to 40 papers; today "Point of View" appears four times a week in the *Star* and 50 other subscribing newspapers.

Fighting Editor of Illinois Town's First Newspaper

BESSIE STAGG wanted to know what went on at closed school board meetings and got angry when information that was supposed to be part of the public record was denied to her. One day in 1959, she set a borrowed typewriter on her kitchen table and the weekly *Bartonville* (Illinois) *News* was born. She had no previous experience in journalism, but Bartonville had never had a newspaper. Local officials were accustomed to looking on

their jobs and agencies as private fiefdoms. Ms. Stagg fought alone until she received access to public records, had a corrupt mayor removed from office, got the town to install a park and a public library, investigated a dump operator who was polluting the local creek, and helped to enforce zoning ordinances. Some citizens responded by tapping her telephone, bringing libel suits, bullying her children, and attempting to bulldoze her car while she was in it; others cooperated in her crusades or offered her money to help stay in business. Before it was crushed by an advertising boycott in 1974, the *News* had 3,000 subscribers in the 5,000-member community. In 1972 Ms. Stagg won the Elijah Parish Lovejoy Award for Courage in Journalism, named in honor of a 19th-century newspaper editor who died defending his presses. Even without a paper of her own, at 59 the indomitable Ms. Stagg was still leading the fight to bring irregularities in county financial records to light. She has finally been able to enlist state and federal officials on behalf of her cause and in 1978 expected to prove that tax monies were not being returned to the citizens through public works projects. Ms. Stagg's credo: "A journalist can't have any friends. If you're going to do something, I'll squeal."

First Woman to Receive a Full-Time White House Beat

White House correspondent for the Hearst newspapers MARIANNE MEANS has been reporting on Washington politics and national events since 1959. She has covered every national party convention and every presidential and congressional campaign since then, and in 1966 became the first woman ever assigned full-time to cover all presidential activities. In May 1977 Ms. Means earned a law degree from the George Washington University Law Center.

Advice and Comfort for the Homemaker

Public Housekeeper No. 1

Housekeeping whiz HELOISE BOWLES until her death at age 58 in 1977 wrote one of the most popular columns in the history of syndicated women's features. Her daughter, PONCE CRUSE, now carries on "Hints from Heloise," which runs in more than 600 papers. Heloise, who never allowed her last name to be disclosed while she was alive and writing, walked into the *Honolulu Advertiser* in 1959 and asked for a chance to do a column on household tips; it was credited with increasing the paper's circulation by more than 25,000 in three years. In 1961, her first year of syndication, by King Features, her column was picked up by more than 200 newspapers; shortly after King Features started syndicating it, Heloise offered her readers a free leaflet on how to wash clothes whiter that drew 100,000 responses in five days—"the largest single delivery of mail in Hawaii's history," according to the postmaster. Heloise's books, all on aspects of housekeeping, have been best sellers. The first, *Heloise's Household Hints* (published in 1963), sold more than 500,000 copies in hardback and then became the fastest-selling paperback in the history to that time of Pocket Books. Heloise, whose column kept her from doing all her own housework (she had a part-time maid three times a week), had been married several times but was single when she died of pneumonia and heart failure.

Troubadour of the Suburbs

"At Wit's End," the column written thrice weekly by ERMA BOMBECK, whose specialty is satirizing life in suburbia, particularly the excesses of compulsive, Heloise-style housekeeping, is syndicated in some 800 newspapers (more than male humorist Art Buchwald can boast). In the Bombeck universe, waxy yellow buildup and "a dog that giggles when I come out of the shower" are the milder occupational hazards of existence as a professional denizen of life's split-level septic tank. Ms. Bombeck began her journalistic career as a copygirl at the *Dayton Journal-Herald*. She moved up to cub reporter and spent five years in the women's department until she left to raise children. When she returned to the *Journal-Herald,* her column ran on the editorial page. Within three weeks of its introduction, the editor had called "At Wit's End" to the attention of a syndicate; it now reaches more than 40 million readers. In 1973, Ms. Bombeck received the Mark Twain Award, presented annually to the top humorist in the nation. Each of her books has been more successful than the last. When the paperback rights for *If Life Is a Bowl of Cherries—What Am I Doing in the Pits?* sold before its 1978 hardcover release for $1 million, Ms. Bombeck, wife of a high school principal and mother of three grown children, who writes from nine to three every day in the garage of her home outside Phoenix, Arizona, celebrated by not doing her laundry for three days.

Specialist in National Economic Policy

From 1962 until 1977, when she was designated as the assistant secretary for public affairs at the Department of Health, Education, and Welfare, EILEEN SHANAHAN covered taxes, antitrust and business regulation, and other areas of finance and government policy for the *New York Times.* Ms. Shanahan also has been on the faculty of the University of California at Berkeley, and a member of Harvard's Nieman Foundation Advisory Committee and the Pulitzer Prize jury in 1973. Named Newspaperwoman of the Year in 1972 by New York Women in Communications, she also has worked for the United Press, the *New York Journal of Commerce,* and Walter Cronkite and has been the U. S. Treasury Department's official spokesperson for tax affairs.

Founder-Publisher of *Encore*

As a young girl growing up in Morton, Pennsylvania, IDA LEWIS, founder in 1972 and publisher of *Encore* magazine, "always wanted to write, to be a journalist." After graduating from Boston University, where she majored in communication and economics, she wrote financial columns for two black newspapers and then became a free-lancer, spending a lot of time at the United Nations where she met all of the black heads of state of the new African nations. *Life* magazine sent her to Paris in

1964 and from there she filed her first big story on John Okello, the self-styled field marshal who had led a left-wing revolt in Zanzibar (now part of Tanzania). Later she left *Life* to spend five years in Paris working on assignments for magazines and news organizations including *L'Express,* the British Broadcasting Corporation, the *Washington Post, Jeune Afrique.* She started *Essence* with $40,000 of her own money. After five pilot issues, she was able to obtain a bank loan of $300,000 to meet her payroll and keep going. Since then the semimonthly has grown to a circulation of 150,000. Its multi-racial staff identifies with "that two thirds of the non-white world out there," Ms. Lewis has said. "It's an interpretation that's lacking in the general press."

In Russia, Alone

Between 1959 and 1962 UPI correspondent ALINE MOSBY was the only American woman reporter permanently based in Moscow. She interviewed Lee Harvey Oswald when he first arrived in Russia, and that interview was incorporated into the transcript of the Warren Commission's report on President Kennedy's death. Ms. Mosby joined UPI's Seattle bureau in 1943. She has also worked in Hollywood (where she wrote more than 1,800 stories about the movie colony in six years), Vienna, and since 1970 has been assigned to the wire service's Paris bureau.

AP reporter LYNNE OLSON was the only American woman journalist in Russia from February 1974 to March 1976. Hired by the AP's Salt Lake City bureau, she was the first woman to integrate the University of Utah press box. After this and other triumphs, she was transferred to San Francisco and then New York, where she wrote feature stories. After her stint in Moscow, Ms. Olson was assigned to AP Washington. She then became a general news reporter for the *Baltimore Sun*'s Washington bureau.

First Woman Senior Editor at the *Christian Science Monitor*

CHARLOTTE SAIKOWSKI, the first woman to edit the *Christian Science Monitor*'s editorial page, has several other firsts to her credit. After five years on staff, she was sent to Tokyo, making her the paper's first woman correspondent there. Transferred to Moscow in 1969, she became the *Monitor*'s first woman correspondent and eventual bureau chief for that location. Since 1972 Ms. Saikowski has been based in Washington as the *Monitor*'s diplomatic correspondent. Her five-part Soviet series, "Letters to President Nixon," won the 1975 Overseas Press Club Award for best daily newspaper reporting from abroad.

No. 1 Journalist in the Oil World

Out of a job in 1961, commerce reporter and editor WANDA JABLONSKI founded *Petroleum Intelligence Weekly,* now considered to be indispensable reading in the top echelons of the oil industry. On the strength of her 8 to 12 pages of inside stories and judgments on the geopolitics of oil, leading energy economists have cited Ms. Jablonski as a journalist "of unmatched knowledge in oil analysis." Ms. Jablonski attributes her expertise and clout to more than 30 years of diligent journalistic attention to Arab affairs. "I got there first," she told the *New York Times,* because no one else was interested in the Mideast when she started. As a young reporter at the *Journal of Commerce,* she realized in the late 1940s that the Persian Gulf countries, with their vast oil reserves, would one day be able to dictate economic policy to the world. Fascinated by the potential of the Arab nations, she began making long visits to the Middle East, once spending six months "locked up in King Saud's harem." However, the Arabs eventually accepted her as a professional woman and they remembered her long-standing interest in their future. The nomadic chieftains with whom Ms. Jablonski formed friendships 25 years ago now rule the Arab world and its international oil cartel, OPEC.

She Brought the *Chicago Daily News* Its First Pulitzer

In 1963 LOIS WILLE, a 6-year veteran city reporter for the *Chicago Daily News,* won the paper its first Pulitzer Prize for public service with her series on birth control. Made a national correspondent in 1975, she has since written stories about Chicago-area survivors of Nazi death camps, returning Vietnam veterans, blue-collar workers, the Joan Little murder trial, the Carter campaign from the early days when he was "Jimmy Who," and dwindling funds for urban education. Her exposés on building decay and her 1969 documentary on child abuse led to several local and federal investigations; her reports on lead poisoning from paint on slum walls helped to institute an emergency repair program in Chicago.

Nationally known Movie Critic

Film and drama critic JUDITH CRIST gained a national audience during her 10

years (from 1963 to 1973) as a reviewer on NBC's "Today Show," but she has been a commentator on movies and plays since 1945. As critic for the *Herald Tribune, World-Journal-Tribune, New York Post, Ladies' Home Journal, New York, Saturday Review, Texas Monthly, TV Guide,* and numerous other magazines, she is one of the most widely read film reviewers in the nation.

In an interview with *American Way,* Ms. Crist explained her feelings about films and about film criticism as follows: "I'm bound to the movie industry by the fact that I love movies—I'm a movie freak. If it's on the screen and it moves, I care. . . . I don't like everything I see . . . but I don't see any point in building a career on the broken bones and blood of people who don't have the platform I have. . . . Critics are not the voices of God, not apostles, not the elect. They are individuals putting up an individual opinion, nothing more and nothing less. . . ."

"Through Hazel Eyes"—1964 Pulitzer for Editorial Writing

In 1964 HAZEL BRANNON SMITH, owner of four weekly newspapers in rural Mississippi, became the first woman ever awarded the Pulitzer Prize for editorial writing. Her editorial column, "Through Hazel Eyes," has never slackened in its attacks on local political and social injustices. After receiving a B.A. in 1935, Ms. Smith bought the weekly *Durant News,* serving Holmes County, Mississippi. Her paper supplied the requisite social annals but also introduced crusades against graft and corruption; when Ms. Smith used it to call for the establishment of a clinic to treat venereal disease, many of her readers were disturbed, considering the subject unsuitable for public discussion and in particular not one that a woman should have broached. In 1943 Hazel Smith acquired the *Lexington Advertiser,* put it in the black within three years, and purchased two other weeklies in 1955 and 1956. The *Advertiser,* featuring "Through Hazel Eyes," became her most influential and controversial paper. In 1953 Ms. Smith declared war on racism in Mississippi when she branded a white sheriff's shooting of a black youth as unprovoked, abusive, and unjust. The sheriff filed a libel suit; the local jury upheld it. Although the Mississippi Supreme Court reversed the decision, thus freeing Ms. Smith of the obligations to pay damages, the *Advertiser* nonetheless was boycotted by advertisers and subscribers. Her enemies later burned a cross on her lawn and struck again in 1964 while she was away working as a commentator at the Democratic convention by firebombing the *Advertiser*'s editorial offices. The Pulitzer Prize was awarded to her in this same year and the committee also established a separate fund for the sole purpose of keeping Ms. Smith in business.

Editor of the *Washington Afro-American Newspaper*

LILLIAN WIGGINS, an editor of the *Washington Afro-American Newspaper* since 1964, is one of two female journalists who covered the civil war in Nigeria (1967) and two inaugurations in Liberia. Her investigative reporting brought her a commission from a Washington radio station to produce a special documentary on Ghana. A graduate of Howard University, Ms. Wiggins served as press and information officer for the Ghanaian Government for more than five years and organized the 1968 Democratic campaign called "Dollars for Humphrey-Muskie." She traveled extensively on the campaign trail as the troubleshooter for Humphrey and Muskie with women's organizations.

Front-Line Battle Photographer and Journalist

Combat photographer and correspondent GEORGETTE "DICKEY" MEYER CHAPPELLE (1920–65) covered 20 years of wars and revolutions without flinching, without asking for favors, and without

regard for risks. In 1939 her future husband, Tony Chappelle, taught her to take pictures. Her first big break came in 1945 when Fawcett Publications sent her to Iwo Jima, where she photographed the wounded being brought aboard a hospital ship and followed them into the operating room. According to Stanley P. Friedman's *Ms.* profile of her, "In an operating room where arms and legs were amputated every 30 minutes, she had herself and her camera tied to overhead pipes. If she fainted while taking pictures, she would not fall on the surgeons." Covering the Hungarian Revolution for *Life* and the International Rescue Committee, Ms. Chappelle typically would go to the front 15 or 20 times a day. One night in December 1956 she was captured by the Russians and turned over to the Hungarian secret police. Isolated, interrogated, starved, and threatened with rape and torture, she was falsely sentenced to 50 days in prison. Upon her release, she set off to cover the French-Algerian War in North Africa. There she was smuggled through French lines to the rebels. She sneaked into Cuba to photograph Castro, took combat assignments in Korea, Okinawa, Kashmir, the Dominican Republic, and in 1961 found time to write her autobiography, *What's a Woman Doing Here?* In Vietnam for the *National Observer,* she jumped into battle zones with paratroopers and sent dispatches reporting that the war was not being won. In November 1965 a Marine walking in front of Dickey Chappelle tripped a land mine that ended her life.

One Woman's Detroit

Award-winning columnist for the *Detroit News,* JUNE BROWN is one of the few black women in the United States writing a regular column for a major daily newspaper. "June Brown's Detroit," begun as a column about businesses and products, was quickly expanded into a general-interest column. Today Ms. Brown covers newsworthy but generally offbeat events throughout Detroit. She is the recipient of the Best Original Column Award for 1967 and 1968 from the National Newspaper Publishers Association, and in 1971 and 1973 received the Distinguished Expression of Editorial Opinion Award from the Detroit Press Club Foundation.

International Symbol of Integrity

HELEN VLACHOS, born in 1911 in Athens, inherited the management of *Kathimerini,* an independent Greek daily, from her father, a renowned journalist and patriot. No one believed she would be able to live up to the reputation of George Vlachos, who had defied Hitler on his editorial pages: "We have sent you the Olympic torch of enlightenment, and the olive branch, symbolic of peace, and you are returning to us destruction and obliteration. No matter what you do to this small nation, it will survive. It is the invaders who will perish." Parliament member and staunch Democrat, Helen Vlachos did more than live up to her heritage; she burnished it. Her actions have become landmarks in the history of journalistic integrity. When Greece was taken over in 1967 by a military junta, Ms. Vlachos, editor in chief and publisher of *Kathimerini,* refused to submit to government censorship. Rather than cooperate, she chose to suspend all publishing operations. Such uncompromising adherence to the principle of free speech raised a public outcry that embarrassed and endangered the regime. Its leaders responded by placing her under house arrest. The army may have prevented Ms. Vlachos from communicating with the outside world, but it did not subdue her. One morning she applied black shoe polish to her blond hair, slipped through her guards, and made her way to London on a forged passport. There, for the next seven years, she worked for the restoration of democracy to Greece. After the colonels were ousted she returned to Greece a hero, resumed publication of *Kathimerini,* and was made a deputy in the new ruling party.

Foreign Correspondent with a String of Firsts

When foreign correspondent GEORGIE ANN GEYER arrived in Guatemala in 1967 in search of guerrilla leader César Montes, she knew that two other Americans had lost their lives on the trail of that story. Ms. Geyer persisted until she was taken to the insurgents' mountain stronghold and obtained an exclusive interview with Montes and his followers. That same year, Ms. Geyer toured Cuba for six weeks and got exclusive interviews with Fidel Castro. For these exploits, she was honored with an Overseas Press Club Award for the best reporting on Latin America in any media. In 1967 she also made a visit to Beirut, where Arab commandos accused her of spying for the Israelis and held her at gunpoint for three hours. A 1956 graduate of the Medill School of Journalism and a former Fulbright scholar, she joined the *Chicago Daily News* in 1959 as a society reporter. In 1962 she won a Chicago Newspaper Guild Award for her account of her masquerade as waitress at a party given by the local crime syndicate. Ms. Geyer has had an impressive list of firsts and exclusives. In addition to her conversations with Montes and Castro, she has had exclusive interviews with a former Nazi leader hiding in South America, with King Hussein of Jordan, the BEGUM AGA KHAN, and Muammar el-Qaddafi of Libya. Ms. Geyer was the first Western journalist to be granted an exclusive interview with JIHAN SADAT (see "Women Activists, Heroes, and Humanitarians," p. 708), activist wife of the President of Egypt, and the only American correspondent to have an exclusive interview with Argentine President Juan Perón and his eventual successor, MARÍA ESTELA DE PERÓN (see "Women in Politics and Government," p. 48).

First Woman Editor of Magnum

After working for the RAF during World War II LEE JONES decided to take up journalism. She got a job as a copygirl with United Press and advanced to radio newswriter. In 1948, after several years as a feature writer for UP (during which she gave English lessons to Jean-Paul Sartre), Ms. Jones returned to the United States. She went to work for the Sunday magazine supplement *This Week* as an assistant picture editor. A year later she was made picture editor. In 1958 she joined Magnum as an assistant editor, was made bureau chief in 1962, and in 1967 became the international photography cooperative's first woman editor.

Publisher of *L'Aurore*

FRANCINE LAZURICK became chief editor-publisher of the French daily *L'Aurore* in 1968, succeeding to the position after the death of her husband Robert. Born in Paris in 1909, Ms. Lazurick studied law and was a practicing attorney and journalist from 1934 to 1968. Decorated for her work in the Resistance, she is active in various French press associations and institutes.

Authority on Science and Public Policy

JUDITH RANDAL, science correspondent for the *New York News,* is a journalistic expert on science and public policy. Her work as a syndicated columnist and reporter for the *Washington Star,* Newhouse National News Service, *Change, Science Year, BioScience,* and many other technical and popular publications has earned awards for investigative and public-service reporting, for excellence in medical reporting, for outstanding coverage of the swine flu epidemic and its aftermath, and for stories on molecular biology and cancer. A graduate of Wellesley College and the Columbia School of Journalism, Ms. Randal was president of the National Association of Science Writers from 1974 to 1975 and occasionally appears on "Meet the Press" and "Washington Week in Review."

Top Maritime Reporter's Unusual Firsts

HELEN DELICH BENTLEY became one of the United States' leading authorities on foreign and domestic maritime affairs during her 25 years as maritime reporter and editor at the *Baltimore Sun.* She joined the paper as a general assignment reporter but in 1948 was directed to "go down and look at the port; we've had nobody there since before the war." One of her earliest stories was about a group of allegedly Communist sailors who had mutinied and gone up the mast. "I wanted to talk to them," Ms. Bentley said, "so I scooted up the mast. I didn't have any better sense." Between 1950 and 1964 she created and produced a weekly TV series—"The Port That Built a City and State"—while simultaneously serving as the *Sun*'s maritime editor (promoted in 1952) and writing a nationally syndicated magazine column. In 1969 Ms. Bentley was the only woman aboard the tanker S.S. *Manhattan* when it made its landmark voyage through the Arctic waters of the Northwest Passage, thus becoming the first woman in history to transit that hazardous waterway. That same year she also became chairwoman of the Federal Maritime Commission, the first woman to hold a presidential appointment as chairperson of a U.S. regulatory agency, and the first woman to serve in a key government post in the maritime field. Ms. Bentley is the first woman to be named to the board of managers of the American Bureau of Shipping, the first non-Briton to address the prestigious 98-year-old Chamber of Shipping of the United Kingdom, and the first woman to receive the Society of Naval Architects and Marine Engineers Award for outstanding accomplishments in the maritime field (1974). Since leaving the government, Ms. Bentley has been an international consultant and president of an export-import corporation she established. Despite her many breakthroughs and achievements, "It's still a tough world out there," she says. "Just the other day (October 6, 1977) in this day and age I became the first woman to address the Chamber of Commerce of Metropolitan Baltimore after 147 years of existence. Imagine."

History-Making Black Woman News Reporter

One of the first two black students to enroll at the University of Georgia, CHARLAYNE HUNTER GAULT majored in journalism, and nine years later, while working as a "Talk of the Town" reporter for the *New Yorker,* contributed an article to the *New York Times Sunday Magazine* in which she reflected on her history-making experience. In 1969 she joined the *Times* metropolitan staff. Ms. Hunter has received three *New York Times*'s Publishers awards for her reporting: in 1970, a shared award with a colleague at the *Times* for a story on a 12-year-old who died of a drug overdose; in 1974, for "writing under deadline pressure" about the mayor's selection of the city's first black deputy mayor; and in 1976, for "outstanding performance on a beat," citing her front-page stories on black crime and the renaming of Harlem's Muslim Mosque for Malcolm X. In 1978 she joined the MacNeil-Lehrer Report on public television, broadcasting a half hour daily. She sees her TV job as a "chance to expand to a broader range of interests." "When you look around the media," she says, "There are no blacks where I am. I've still got enough of the pioneer left in me to see that as a challenge."

First and Only Woman Editor on the Editorial Board of the *Washington Post*

As deputy editor of the *Washington Post*'s editorial page, MEG GREENFIELD's name is on its masthead. The only other woman whose name has appeared there is publisher KATHARINE GRAHAM (see "Women in Business, Industry, and Finance," p. 514). In addition to her duties as editor, Ms. Greenfield also writes editorials on such subjects as strategic arms limitation, politics, and civil rights, and since 1974 has been a chronicler of the Washington scene for *Newsweek* as a columnist and contributing editor. Before joining the *Post* in 1968, she was Washington bureau chief for the now defunct *Reporter* magazine, a publication she had worked for since 1957. Born in Seattle, Ms. Greenfield was graduated summa cum laude from Smith College in 1952 and studied at Cambridge University for a year as a Fulbright scholar.

First Black Woman Editor of *Washington Post*'s "Style"

DOROTHY GILLIAM, the first black woman to be appointed an editor of the *Washington Post*'s "Style" section, entered journalism in the late 1950s as an associate editor of *Jet* magazine. In 1961 she received the Anne O'Hare McCormick Award from the New York Newspaper Women's Club; in 1967 she was named Journalist of the Year by the Capital Press Club, which also awarded her the 1969 Achievement in Journalism Prize. Ms. Gilliam, who holds a master's degree from the Columbia School of Journalism, lectures on the history and evolution of the black press in America. In 1976 she published her first book, *Paul Robeson, All-American.*

First Woman Hired by Reuters North America's General News Division

In 1969 MARCIA DUBROW became the first woman to report general news for the North American division of Reuters Ltd., the international wire service. She has covered Mafia shoot-outs, prison riots, space shots, the Watergate trials, and had exclusive interviews with Duke Ellington, Joe Frazier, James Brown, and Tom Jones. Insisting that the women's movement deserved full-scale news coverage, she also has worked to secure space and front-page play for women's issues. A 1965 graduate of Adelphi University, Ms. Dubrow since 1975 has been a duty editor, selecting and editing news files for North American and world wires, managing a newsroom of up to 20 reporters, and delegating assignments and articles for coverage, editing, and rewriting. Before being hired by Reuters, Ms. Dubrow worked for UPI and *Mademoiselle* and contributed articles to *New York, Harper's Bazaar, Viva,* the *Village Voice,* and other magazines and newspapers.

Winning Women Sportswriters

Her Triple Firsts

A reporter for the *Detroit News* since 1970, CYNDI MEAGHER was the first woman to join the Detroit Sports Broadcasters Association, the first woman to become a sports columnist for a major metropolitan newspaper, and the first woman to be seated on the dais of a National Football Foundation and Hall of Fame Awards Program.

First Woman Sportswriter for AP New York

After six years with the Associated Press wire service, KAROL STONGER was made the first and only woman sportswriter on the AP's New York staff in 1970. She was the first woman to cover the Indianapolis 500 from the pits and was one of the few reporters to slip inside the Olympic Village in Munich during the 1972 Arab raid on Israeli quarters. Ms. Stonger pulled off that coup by borrowing a U.S. team jacket and posing as a swimmer. Once inside, she kept watch on the guerrillas from a vantage point in the Puerto Rican headquarters. Ms. Stonger had an excellent view of the Arabs—and they had a good view of her while she eyed them with a rifle scope borrowed from a member of the Puerto Rican team.

First Woman Sportswriter at the *Washington Post*

NANCY SCANNELL, the *Washington Post*'s first woman sportswriter, took first prize for sports reporting from the Baltimore-Washington Newspaper Guild for her series on the federal Title IX law that bars education programs and activities—including sports and physical education—that discriminate on the basis of sex from receiving federal aid. After receiving an M.S. from the Columbia University Journalism School in 1969, Ms. Scannell joined the *Post* as a reporter on the metropolitan Virginia desk.

First Woman Sportswriter Columnist Syndicated by the *Washington Post*

JOAN RYAN, whose weekly column is syndicated nationally by the *Washington Post,* has been a sportswriter for 14 years. A sports reporter for the *Post* from 1975 until 1977, she had a sports column in the *Washington Star* from 1972 to 1975 and in the *Cleveland Plain Dealer* from 1964 to 1968. Ms. Ryan was graduated from Rice University in 1968 and is married to Frank Ryan, a professional football quarterback, later athletic director at Yale University.

First Woman Sportswriter on the *New York Times* Staff

In 1975 traveling sports reporter ROBIN HERMAN became the first woman on the *New York Times* sports staff of 52. A Phi Beta Kappa graduate of Princeton and managing editor of the school's daily paper, she joined the *Times* in June 1973 and worked her way up to reporter-trainee by February 1974. Ms. Herman specializes in professional hockey, but covers other sports as well. Dissatisfied with some of the limitations of her job, Ms. Herman began a campaign for access to hockey players' dressing rooms to provide equal opportunity for reporters to obtain postgame interviews and has managed to infiltrate the locker rooms of the New York Rangers.

First to Write About Homosexuals in Sports

LYNN ROSELLINI of the *Washington Star* hit a raw nerve in December 1975 with a four-part series about the agonizing secret lives gay professional athletes lead, the pressure they have to withstand, and the hostility of the official sports world toward admitting that homosexuality exists in what one official termed "an area of total manhood." In answer to the more than 600 overwhelmingly negative phone calls and letters received, the *Star*'s ombudsman, George Beveridge, defended her articles as being part of an honest journalist's obligation: to report on the human condition, to depict life as it is, and when a useful purpose is served, to expose the phony myths that surround legitimate news subjects even when that involves attacks on sensitive social perceptions or institutions that are deeply rooted in tradition. A member of the *Star*'s sports staff from July 1975, in early 1976 Ms. Rosellini moved to the paper's "Portfolio" section.

First Winner of the Pulitzer Prize for Criticism

In 1970 ADA LOUISE HUXTABLE, architecture critic and member of the *New York Times* editorial board, won the first Pulitzer Prize to be given for distinguished criticism. Her direct, barbed prose, her attacks on mindless buildings and misguided urban renewal efforts, her eloquent, impassioned defense of quality, graciousness, and suitability of purpose in past and present architectural design —all have earned her a large and appreciative audience. She draws upon sociology, economics, art and architectural history, and residential and commercial planning theory in her work. Ms. Huxtable is credited with bringing about the establishment of the New York City Landmarks Preservation Commission and with saving the New York Customs House and the St. Louis Post Office. At a testimonial dinner held in the Customs House in honor of her appointment to the *Times* editorial board (in 1973), her colleague John B. Oakes described her as "unerring in her aim; undeviating in her standards; unshaken in her principles; undaunted in her courage; and, I might add, unflinching in her attack on the editor who dares to tamper with her copy." Ms. Huxtable, born Ada Louise Landman, has been a New York City resident all her life and was graduated from Hunter College. As assistant curator of architecture at the Museum of Modern Art, she quit her job to accept a Fulbright scholarship for the study of design and architecture in Italy. The years that followed brought a Guggenheim fellowship and numerous contributions to *Progressive Architecture, Art in America, Saturday Review,* and the *New York Times Magazine* before the *Times* created the post of architecture critic and offered it to Ms. Huxtable. She is the author of *Classic New York; Georgian Gentility to Greek Elegance* (1964), *Will They Ever Finish Bruckner Boulevard?* (1970), and *Kicked a Building Lately?* (1976).

First Black Investigative Reporter on the *Miami Herald*

BEA HINES, a widow and mother of two small sons, in 1970 became the first black investigative reporter for the *Miami Herald.* Four years earlier she had been supporting both her sons and her mother on wages earned as a cleaning woman. When her main source of income was unexpectedly terminated, she realized, "I wanted a future. I was convinced it was not too late to make a change." After some searching, Ms. Hines landed a job as a library clerk at the *Herald.* At the same time she signed up for writing courses at the local junior college and obtained loans to continue her studies at night. She wrote a story about two boys, one black and one

Communications 465

white, growing up in Georgia. The story, published in the college paper, was circulated among *Herald* editors; two days later, Ms. Hines was on her way to the city room as a reporter.

First Woman to Chair the International Press Institute

Chairwoman of the executive Board of the International Press Institute (an organization of 1,500 editors from more than 50 countries) from 1970 to 1971, SALLY AW SIAN is the publisher of Hong Kong's Sing Tao (Singapore) Newspapers. She is also the founder and chairwoman of the Chinese Language Press Institute. Born in 1931 in Rangoon, Burma, Ms. Aw Sian was educated at French Covent School in Hong Kong and at Northwestern University in Chicago. She is the managing director of Singapore Amalgamated, Hong Kong Ltd.; publisher of the *Singapore Daily News*, the *Singapore Evening News*, the *Singapore Weekly*, and the *Hong Kong Tiger Standard*; and director of several other newspapers and presses in Hong Kong, Singapore, and Bangkok.

Publisher of *Die Zeit*

Countess MARION GRÄFIN DÖNHOFF, publisher and former editor in chief of the political weekly *Die Zeit,* is one of the most influential women in German journalism. Born in 1909 in East Prussia, she was educated in several German universities and ran the family's agricultural estates from 1936 to 1945. She joined *Die Zeit* in 1946, was made its political editor in 1955, its chief editor in 1968, and took over as publisher in 1972. Awarded an honorary doctorate in humane letters from Smith College in 1962, the countess was cited for her "fearless discussions of tabooed subjects in German politics and her constant reaffirmation of spiritual values in the face of material success." She has also won the Theodore Heuss Prize and the Peace Prize of the German book trade.

First Woman to Win a Pulitzer Prize for National Reporting

LUCINDA FRANKS got her start as a reporter in 1968 on a six-month tryout basis at UPI's London bureau. Two years later she collaborated with colleague Thomas Powers on a five-part series on DIANA OUGHTON, the society girl turned radical who died in an explosion on West 11th Street in New York City, and their stories won the 1971 Pulitzer Prize for national reporting. Ms. Franks is now a reporter for the *New York Times*.

First Woman to Head a Copy Desk at the *New York Times*

BETSY WADE, the first woman copy editor hired by the *New York Times,* in 1957, since 1972 has been head of the foreign copy desk—the first woman to be head of a copy desk on that newspaper. In 1977 she received the Columbia Journalism Alumni Award for distinguished service to journalism. Born in 1929 in New York City, a graduate of Barnard College in 1951 and the Columbia School of Journalism in 1952, Ms. Wade has lectured at Columbia, Syracuse, the University of Kansas, and other schools. Co-author of *The New York Times Book of Antiques* (1972), she is a member of the *Times* Women's Caucus, the Women's Media Group, the steering committee of the Coalition of Labor Union Women, and in 1975 was elected a regional vice-president for New York of the Newspaper Guild, becoming one of its five women vice-presidents. Ms. Wade was named a plaintiff in a Title VII (of the Civil Rights Act) class action in 1974 charging discrimination based on sex.

Paris Bureau Chief and European Diplomatic Correspondent for the *New York Times*

FLORA LEWIS, appointed head of the *New York Times*'s Paris bureau in 1972, has covered the news worldwide since 1942, when she worked as an AP reporter assigned to the Navy and State departments. From 1946 to 1956 she was a free-lance foreign correspondent, contributing articles to *Time,* the *London Observer, France-Soir,* the Sunday *New York Times,* and many other magazines and papers. In 1956 Ms. Lewis became the *Washington Post*'s correspondent in Eastern Europe. After being posted in London, she opened the *Post*'s New York bureau in 1965. Based in Paris since 1967, she was given the additional title of European diplomatic correspondent in 1976.

Largest Women-Owned and -Operated News Service in the United States

In 1973 journalist GAIL COLLINS founded and still directs the largest news service in the United States that is wholly owned and operated by women—the Connecticut State News Bureau. To compete with bigger, more established wire services and the evening news, both of which concentrated on big political events, Ms. Collins decided to emphasize what local legislators had or had not been doing at the state capitol and how their actions would directly affect the lives of their constituents. Result: More than 30 Connecticut newspapers purchase the service because of its specific orientation toward local concerns.

Head of the Copley Newspaper Chain

In October 1973, when HELEN COPLEY took over as chairwoman and chief executive officer of the family business, the multimillion-dollar Copley Newspapers, she began reorganizing the corporation's management, holdings, and personnel. By 1975 she had raised company profits almost 10 per cent by selling 14 of the chain's weakest papers and by cutting more than 6 per cent of the staff. Also publisher of the *San Diego Union* and the (San Diego) *Evening Tribune,* Ms. Copley oversees 9 daily and 24 weekly newspapers. She was the first woman elected to the board of trustees of the California chamber of commerce and is a director of the American Newspaper Publishers Association. A founding director and first vice-chairperson of the Women's Crusade for a Common Sense Economy, and trustee of the Scripps Clinic and Research Foundation and the University of California at San Diego, Ms. Copley attended Hunter College and holds an honorary doctorate in humane letters from Coe College.

Winner of the 1974 Pulitzer Prize for Criticism

EMILY GENAUER, winner of the 1974 Pulitzer Prize for criticism, was for 17 years the chief art critic of the *New York Herald Tribune* and its successor, the *World-Journal-Tribune,* which closed in 1969. A critic for the *Newsday* syndicate since 1967 and a commentator on the arts for commercial and public television, Ms. Genauer has lectured at museums, colleges, and civic organizations throughout the United States. She joined the *New York World-Telegram* as art critic and editor in 1932 and moved to the *Tribune* in 1949. Born in New York in 1911, she attended Hunter College and Columbia University Graduate School of Journalism.

First Woman Ever Listed on the Masthead of the *New York Times*

CHARLOTTE CURTIS, editor of the *New York Times* "Family/Style" section, 1966–74, became an associate editor of the paper and editor of its Op-Ed (opposite the editorials) page in 1974. The first woman ever listed on the masthead of the *Times,* Ms. Curtis, who joined the paper as a reporter in 1961, decides what subjects will be discussed on this influential part of one of the world's most influential newspapers. As women's editor of the *Times,* Charlotte Curtis refused to let her section be the dumping ground for blandly reported throwaway stories. Under her direction, "society" was redefined as cultural anthropology and reports on abortion clinics and plastic surgery coexisted with accounts of

Widely respected economist JUANITA M. KREPS in 1977 was named Secretary of Commerce by President Carter. Dr. Kreps, who is married to fellow economist Clifton H. Kreps and has three children, was once asked how she managed career and family. Her reply: "Badly." (Courtesy, U. S. Department of Commerce)

FRANCES (SISSY) FARENTHOLD, president of Wells College. Educator, lawyer, legislator, Ms. Farenthold was the first woman to have her name placed in nomination for the vice-presidency of the United States at a national convention. In 1976 she became president of Wells, a women's liberal arts college. (Courtesy of Wells College)

NELLIE BLY (1867–1922), star reporter, had circumnavigated the globe in the fashion of Jules Verne's hero Phileas Fogg, taking only 72 days, 6 hours, and 11 minutes to his 80 days, and reporting all her adventures to the *New York World*. (The Bettman Archives)

Foreign correspondent HELEN KIRK-PATRICK, first woman hired for its overseas service by the *Chicago Daily News*, is pictured above in her World War II correspondent's uniform. (Courtesy of Mrs. Robbins Milbank)

HELEN SIOUSSAT, TV pioneer who succeeded Edward R. Murrow at CBS as director of talks in 1937, with Wendell Willkie when he came direct to her studio immediately upon his return from his famous One World trip in 1942. (Courtesy of Ms. Helen Sioussat)

One of the few and undoubtedly the best-known of female maritime reporters and editors, the *Baltimore Sun's* HELEN DELICH BENTLEY in 1969 became the first woman to hold a presidential appointment as chairwoman of a U.S. regulatory agency when she was named by President Nixon to head the Federal Maritime Commission.

TAD BARTIMUS, head of the Associated Press office in Anchorage, Alaska, filled her first staff opening with another woman to make the outpost the wire service's only all-female bureau.

White House reporters HELEN THOMAS of United Press International (left) and BONNIE ANGELO (right), who was *Time* magazine's woman in Washington for 20 years before she took over as chief of its London bureau January 1, 1978. Ms. Thomas remained very much on the job in which she has scored many firsts for women in the news business— including her election as first woman president of the White House Correspondents Association and admission to the formerly all-male Gridiron Club. (Photos courtesy of United Press International and David Hume Kennelly)

The Dean of Women Broadcasters

PAULINE FREDERICK, seen here at work in the booth at one of the many national political conventions she covered for TV, started reporting via radio with her first overseas broadcast from Chungking, in 1945. Now an international affairs analyst for National Public Radio, she co-produces her own weekly program. (Photo courtesy of Camera One)

ERMA BOMBECK. Her housewife's column, "At Wit's End," and a few best-selling books about the hazards of suburban life have earned her 40 million regular readers, a tidy income, and, in 1973, the Mark Twain Award, presented annually to the top humorist in the United States.

PERRY ADATO MILLER. Her first TV documentary in 1968, "Dylan Thomas: The World I Breathe," captured an Emmy. She has gone on to produce and direct many other stunning TV shows. (Photo by Bert Andrews)

MARGO HUSTON. Her "general local reporting" on the neglected elderly of the Milwaukee area brought a 1977 Pulitzer to Ms. Huston and her paper, the *Milwaukee Journal.* (Photo courtesy of the *Milwaukee Journal*)

GRACE MIRABELLA, editor in chief of *Vogue* since 1973, worked for the magazine for two decades before being named to the top job. Her credo for today's *Vogue* is "to give a woman a full menu—fashion, beauty, and health as well as interesting things to read."

HELEN GURLEY BROWN, "that *Cosmo* girl," became editor in chief of *Cosmopolitan* in 1965. Under Ms. Brown's editorial direction, the magazine assumed a personality and grew spectacularly.

weddings and turtle soup, and women's editors all over the country soon followed her lead. As a reporter and editor she covered Europe, the Middle East, Asia, national political conventions, and presidential campaigns, as well as the manners and mores of the rich. The uproar from her 1970 story on the Leonard Bernsteins' radical-chic party for the Black Panthers reverberated to the *Times*'s editorial page and her observations on Princess Margaret's shopping spree in Arizona—when royalty departed without paying its bills—incensed the British Embassy. She still takes time to cover the jet set—but never quite as they like. Her fourth book, published in 1976, is titled *The Rich and Other Atrocities*. Ms. Curtis was born in Chicago and grew up in Columbus, Ohio. A graduate of Vassar College, she began her newspaper career working summers at the *Columbus Citizen*. She is the recipient of dozens of reporting and news-writing awards. Her mother, LUCILE ATCHERSON CURTIS (see "Women in Politics and Government," p. 90), was the first woman in the U. S. Foreign Service.

Food Page Reformers

Originally the food pages of newspapers were designed as catch-alls for recipes and supermarket and food industry advertising. Their nearly sole purpose was to bring in revenues. Within the last five years, food editors and writers have begun to rebel against the lack of substance in their sections and press for more consumer and investigative features. An important step was taken in October 1973 when 97 food journalists banded together in a Newspaper Food Editors and Writers Association and approved a code of ethics emphasizing the separation of editorial and advertising responsibilities. Three who were instrumental in the fight to elevate the food sections to the professional standards required of political and general news re-

Specialist in the Dynamics of Social Change

Humorous feminist ELLEN GOODMAN, whose *Boston Globe* column is broadly syndicated, specializes in commentary on attempts to cope with the pressures of social change. Ms. Goodman was graduated from Radcliffe in 1963, worked for *Newsweek* and the *Detroit Free Press*, and became a staff writer for the *Globe* in 1967. Her work has been published in *McCall's, Ms.*, the *Village Voice, Family Circle*, and *Harper's Bazaar*. Winner of several media awards, Ms. Goodman in 1973 received a Nieman fellowship from Harvard and in 1974 began her twice-weekly "At Large" column. She is proudest of the fact that her presentation of subjects often relegated to the back pages of feature sections—women, children, personal relationships, psychology, and the pace of social change—is topical enough and hard enough to appear on the Op-Ed pages of many newspapers.

porting were MARIAN BURROS, PEGGY DAUM, and CAMILLE STAGG.

Specialist in the Politics of Food

Marian Burros, food editor of the *Washington Post* since 1974, was one of the first journalists to focus on the consumer aspects (economics, health, safety) of food and eating. In her own words, her job has changed from being a "recipe lady" to "pioneering work in investigative and consumer food journalism on the food pages of a newspaper with stories on sodium nitrites, saccharin, Red ⅜2 food coloring, and sugar content of breakfast cereals." Her favorite "first" story, she says, had to do with the "powdered cellulose" in ITT Continental's Fresh Horizons bread. "I may have been the first to report in the lay press that the substance is derived from wood pulp, or as Senator George McGovern called it during Senate hearings, 'sawdust.' " Ms. Burros is distrustful of products loaded with food additives, saying, "It isn't just the crackpots any more who are worried about the chemical inclusion in our food." One of the earliest TV consumer reporters dealing exclusively with stories on cosmetics, food additives, food composition, drugs, and other public health subjects as they related to eating and nutrition, Ms. Burros has combined three careers—as a newspaper journalist, television commentator, and cookbook author—all in service of informing the public of what it needs to know about food. Since 1960 she has been a food editor and writer for various Washington-area newspapers; worked on the consumer news staff of NBC Radio network news in 1975; prepared a food commentary, "Eater's Digest," for NBC in 1973; and written six cookbooks, the latest of which combines recipes with discussions of food and food safety. Her consumer affairs reporting earned her an Emmy (in 1974) as well as awards from the Association of Federal Investigators and the American Association of University Women in Mass Media.

First President of the Newspaper Food Editors and Writers Association

Peggy Daum, food editor of the *Milwaukee Journal* since 1968 and the first president of the Newspaper Food Editors and Writers Association, contends that food pages should include controversy even when a story attacks a supermarket or product that contributes advertising to the paper. Under her direction, the *Journal* began a weekly comparison of food prices in Milwaukee-area supermarkets in July 1973. An advocate of investigative reporting, Ms. Daum names names of food stores and food products. Shoppers check close to 100 prices every week at the five supermarket chains that nearly 90 per cent of the *Journal's*

readers patronize. The result, a chart and accompanying analysis, is considered by consumer experts to be the most comprehensive local treatment of food economics in the country.

Crusading Food Editor of the *Chicago Sun-Times*

Appointed food editor of the *Chicago Sun-Times* in October 1965 at age 23, Camille Stagg believes herself to be the youngest person ever made a food editor of a metropolitan paper. Since fall 1977 she has been food editor of *Sphere Magazine.* When, as food editor of the *Sun-Times,* she and reporter BEVERLY BENNETT tried to run their first consumer exposé, they were blocked at several turns. When their story, on unsanitary conditions in city food stores, did appear, an Illinois congressman read excerpts from it on suspect supermarket practices into the *Congressional Record.* Ms. Stagg has hit hard on the ills of sugar ("The truth is, no one needs sugar") and was characterized as a "rebel" and a "food radical" when she first opposed preservatives, processed foods, and cured meats and stated that consumption of health foods was not a passing fad. In 1974 Field Enterprises reported that, under Ms. Stagg's direction, the "Good Food" section had gained the highest readership in the history of the *Sun-Times*—attracting 80 per cent of the total daily circulation of 600,000.

First Woman to Manage a Major Metropolitan Daily in the U.S.A.

After nine years editing the women's pages of the *Louisville Courier-Journal,* CAROL SUTTON was made its managing editor in 1974, becoming the first woman in the country to manage a major metropolitan daily. During her term as women's editor, Ms. Sutton changed the name and scope of the section—in place of the usual mélange of recipes and society reporting, subjects such as birth control and no-fault divorce were introduced. Upon her promotion to managing editor, Ms. Sutton appointed a man as editor of the section called "Today's Living," formerly known as "Women's World."

First Woman to Be a National Editor, then World Editor, then Managing Editor of a U.S. Newspaper

BARBARA COHEN, national editor since 1974 of the *Washington Star,* joined that paper as a copy desk trainee in 1968 after being graduated from Swarthmore College and earning a master's degree at the Columbia School of Journalism. She is particularly respected in Washington for her direction of the Watergate and House Judiciary Committee impeachment coverage and for the reporting of the Carter political campaign. Wife of *Washington Post* writer Richard Cohen and mother of one son, Ms. Cohen says that for women combining careers and home life, the newspaper business is "tough for reporters, not so bad for editors." In 1977 Ms. Cohen was named world editor for the *Star* and in 1978 again promoted—this time to the position of managing editor for news.

First Female Board Member of the AP Managing Editors Association and Founder of the Women's Network

Remembering a 40-year newspaper career as a token woman, DOROTHY MISENER JURNEY determined to help other women break into top-level positions in journalism. After retiring as assistant managing editor for features from the *Philadelphia Inquirer* in 1975, she founded the Women's Network, an executive placement agency for women journalists with management potential. The service, operated out of her home in Wayne, Pennsylvania, is free for women and is the nation's only executive search firm in the newspaper profession that recruits women. Ms. Jurney, born in 1909, was the first woman assistant city editor and later acting city editor at the *Wash-*

ington Daily News. She worked for the *Miami Herald* for 10 years as women's editor. In 1959 she joined the *Detroit Free Press* as women's editor and was made assistant managing editor in 1972. Ms. Jurney was the first woman named to this position on a paper with a circulation of more than 100,000—no women managed papers of that size then (cf. CAROL SUTTON, p. 468). She left for the *Inquirer* in 1973. Ms. Jurney was the first female board member of the Associated Press Managing Editors Association. Because she was the 1974–75 chairwoman of the nominations committee of the American Society of Newspaper Editors, she was the first woman chosen to accompany its delegation to the People's Republic of China in 1975.

UPI's First and Only Woman Senior Editor

New York-based GAY PAULEY became UPI's first and to date only woman senior editor in December 1975. She joined the wire service in the early 1940s and in 1953 was made supervisor of all women's coverage. UPI has a total of eight senior editors.

First Woman on the Editorial Board of the *Chicago Tribune*

JOAN BECK is a trailblazer at the *Chicago Tribune.* The sole female member of the paper's editorial board as of 1977, she is also the first woman to write an editorial page column for the *Tribune.* Ms. Beck was appointed to the Board in November 1975; previously she was the first editor of the "Tempo" section, the successor to the traditional women's pages. She has written a nationally syndicated column, "You and Your Child," twice a week since 1961. Her first book, *How to Raise a Brighter Child,* was a Literary Guild selection in 1967. A second, dealing with prenatal development and birth defects, was co-authored with Dr. VIRGINIA APGAR (see "Women in Medicine and Health Care," p. 209).

Namesake Award Created by Colleagues

CAROLYN ANSPACHER, whose by-line has run in the *San Francisco Chronicle* since 1933, in 1976 covered every day of the PATRICIA HEARST trial (see also p. 441). Three of her articles were incorporated into the public transcript of the trial and the *Chronicle* nominated her reports for a Pulitzer Prize. These honors were still considered insufficient recognition by her colleagues in the newsroom, who created a special award commemorating her "consistently superb reporting of the Hearst trial." The first Carolyn Anspacher Award went to Ms. Anspacher herself and cited her "accuracy, literacy, and fairness under incredible daily deadline pressure." In 1972 Ms. Anspacher received a press award from the American Bar Association of San Francisco for the 56 articles she wrote on the ANGELA DAVIS (see "Women Activists, Heroes, and Humanitarians," p. 715) murder-kidnap-conspiracy trial.

First Woman Bureau Chief for AP's Domestic Operations

TAD BARTIMUS, appointed head of the Associated Press's newly created Anchorage, Alaska, office in 1975, is the first woman bureau chief in the AP's domestic service. She filled her first staff opening with another woman, making the Anchorage outpost the AP's only all-female bureau.

First Woman Named State Bureau Chief of the *New York Times*

In 1976 LINDA GREENHOUSE was named chief of the Albany (capital) bureau of the *New York Times* after two years of covering New York State's legislature and administration. Ms. Greenhouse, a magna cum laude graduate of Radcliffe, was hired by the paper in 1968 as a news clerk. She worked her way up to general assignment reporter in 1969, to Westchester County correspondent in 1970, and handled rewrite in 1973 before switching to the Albany assignment.

First Woman Bureau Chief in North America for a British Newspaper

At 34, ANTHEA DISNEY is the first female bureau chief in North America for a British newspaper and believes she may be the first woman to head a foreign bureau for any British paper. She was made head of the *London Daily Mail*'s New York office in November 1976 after two years as the paper's first woman editor of the political features section (akin to the American Op-Ed page), following earlier assignments as a reporter and features writer. In Britain in the late 1960s, Ms. Disney filed a series of sensational inside accounts of what it was like to be an Asian immigrant in England. Like John Howard Griffin for his 1961 book *Black Like Me*, Ms. Disney took massive doses of pigmentation-altering drugs to make her skin turn dark enough to pass as an East Indian and worked in factories and lived in the worst slums of Birmingham for a month.

First Woman President of the New York Financial Writers' Association

MARGARET KLEIN, financial services editor of Reuters North America, became the first woman president of the New York Financial Writers' Association in January 1977. Ms. Klein, who supervises the production of all of Reuters' financial and business news services in the United States and Canada, believes she is the first woman financial editor for a wire service. After receiving a B.A. in journalism and history from the University of California at Berkeley in 1961, she was hired by the Associated Press, where she remained until 1968. She then joined Reuters' financial desk in New York and in April 1973 was appointed financial services editor for North America.

Winner of the 1977 Pulitzer for General Local Reporting

MARGO HUSTON spent many months of 1977 interviewing the neglected elderly of the Milwaukee area—those who won't live in nursing homes or can't afford to, yet are unable to take adequate care of themselves. She found their condition miserable. She also discovered that the authorities were not enforcing the licensing law regulating profit-making home health care agencies. She told this story in the *Milwaukee Journal* in a week-long series of articles titled "I'll Never Leave My Home. Would You?" Her work won the 1977 Pulitzer Prize for general local reporting. The *Journal* published her lists of nursing care agencies and retirement communities with full details on staff, costs, and licensing or accreditation. A week after the series ended, Wisconsin's lieutenant governor and the State Board on Aging recommended a study of home health care and an effort to expand Medicaid to allow the subsidizing of personal care services outside institutions. Ms. Huston, born in 1943 in Waukesha, Wisconsin, was graduated from Marquette University. After working as magazine editor and teacher, she became a women's food section reporter at the *Journal* in 1972 and thereafter a staff member for the family and consumer section. In the years 1976–78, in addition to the Pulitzer, she won two Penney-Missouri $1,000 Paul Myhre awards for excellence in reporting (series), the Clarion Award from National Women in Communications, and a number of other prizes and citations.

MAGAZINE WRITERS, EDITORS, AND PUBLISHERS

Founders of *Poet Lore*

CHARLOTTE ENDYMION PORTER (1857–1942) first met HELEN ARCHIBALD CLARKE (1860–1926) when she published one of Ms. Clarke's poems in *Shakespeariana,* a periodical she edited for the Shakespeare Society of New York from 1883 to 1887. A close friendship developed between these two devotees of Shakespeare, who were also both founding members of the Browning Society of Philadelphia. In January 1889 the two women launched *Poet Lore,* a monthly magazine "devoted to Shakespeare, Browning, and the Comparative Study of Literature." Moving to Boston and changing their publication to a quarterly, the two women eventually broadened their magazine's content to cover emerging talents in Europe, Asia, and the Middle East (Maurice Maeterlinck, Anatole France, Gerhart Hauptmann, and others). They became charter members of JULIA WARD HOWE's Boston Authors Club and, to encourage artistic development in America, they founded the American Music Society and the American Drama Society (later, the Drama League of America). In 1903 they sold *Poet Lore* and entered a variety of publishing ventures—together and individually. Ms. Porter's most ambitious project was a 40-volume First Folio edition of Shakespeare, which appeared between 1903 and 1913. Ms. Clarke published music, dramatized poetry, and wrote a number of works.

First Female Muckraker

From 1894 to 1906, hard-hitting journalist IDA MINERVA TARBELL (1857–1944) edited the United States' pioneer muckraking journal, *McClure's Magazine,* whose articles and editorials exposed political and industrial corruption and emphasized the need for reforms. Her articles attacking the Rockefeller oil interests resulted in the dissolution of the Standard Oil Company of New Jersey in 1911 under the Sherman Anti-Trust Act. In 1906 she, with others, purchased the *American* magazine and was associate editor there until 1915. A biographer and early feminist, Ms. Tarbell wrote numerous portraits of business and political leaders as well as *The Business of Being a Woman* (1912) and *The Ways of Women* (1915).

She Led the *Companion* to the Top

In 1903 at the age of 29 GERTRUDE BATTLES LANE (1874–1941) spent her last $10 for a Boston-to-New York train ticket to assume an editorial post on the *Woman's Home Companion*. With only slim editorial experience in Boston, Ms. Lane's blossoming talents came to fruition and won her a promotion to managing editor in 1909, and three years later, to editor in chief—a post she held for 29 years. Under her lead the *Companion* rose from fourth place among women's magazines to first, with a circulation of 3 million in 1937, and took positions against child labor, encouraged the development of home economics (then in its infant stages), advocated business training for women, and provided the first counsel on psychological problems within the family. Presidents Taft, Wilson, Coolidge, and Hoover all wrote for the *Companion,* and in the 1930s a feature by ELEANOR ROOSEVELT (see "Women Activists, Heroes, and Humanitarians," p. 738) appeared regularly on its pages. Ms. Lane also attracted notable fiction writers to her magazine—WILLA CATHER, EDNA FERBER, PEARL BUCK (see "Women in the Arts and Entertainment," p. 678), Sherwood Anderson, Booth Tarkington, and Sinclair Lewis, among them. She served on the board of directors of the Crowell publishing company for several years and in 1929 became a vice-president—the only woman on the executive staff.

Founder of Poets' Showcase

In 1912 HARRIET MONROE (1860–1936) created her place in literary history by founding *Poetry: A Magazine of Verse,* which was published under her direction for 24 years. Her magazine became the preeminent showcase for major contemporary poets including Ezra Pound (*Poetry*'s London editor for its first six years), W. B. Yeats, T. S. Eliot, Wallace Stevens, Vachel Lindsay, Carl Sandburg, and many others who first came to public attention through its pages. Although she and Ezra Pound championed the Imagists, the magazine did not confine itself to any school. Its policy of innovation shattered convention and drew a steady stream of bright young writers. In 1917 Ms. Monroe with ALICE HENDERSON (the magazine's assistant editor) published the influential *The New Poetry: An Anthology of Twentieth-Century Verse in English.* Through the years Harriet Monroe continued writing and publishing her own verse, but her success as an editor overshadowed her accomplishments as a poet. An inveterate traveler, she died at the age of 76 while visiting Incan ruins high in the Andes on her return from a literary conference in Argentina.

First to Publish *Ulysses* Excerpts in the United States

Between 1914 and 1929, in Chicago, MARGARET ANDERSON founded, edited, and published the *Little Review,* the most avant-garde arts and literature magazine of its day. In it she publicized and published the works of some of the greatest artists and writers of this century—Ezra Pound, T. S. Eliot, Sherwood Anderson, William Carlos Williams, Pablo Picasso, Paul Klee, William Butler Yeats, GERTRUDE STEIN, James Joyce, and others. The appearance of excerpts from Joyce's *Ulysses* the first time they appeared in the United States led to Margaret Anderson's prosecution on obscenity charges. The case came to trial in 1921. She and her partner were fined $50 each and prohibited from publishing any more of the book in the *Little Review.* Margaret Anderson died at the age of 82 in 1975.

Long-Time *Nation* Crusader

When FREDA KIRCHWEY began a journalistic career in 1919 as a cub reporter for the *Nation,* she embarked on a series of crusades that led to her ultimate purchase of the magazine and alteration of its content to serve as a platform for the support of liberal causes. Referred to by *Time* as a "pulp-paper pinko weekly" in 1943 and banned in 1948 from the official periodical list of the New York public schools, the *Nation* under Ms. Kirchwey's direction never stopped fighting for political, economic, and social reform. As editor and publisher until 1955, she used the magazine to speak out against oppression of minorities, oppose McCarthyism, and promote the cause of world disarmament. Ms. Kirchwey died at the age of 82 in 1974.

Co-founder of the *Reader's Digest*

In 1922 LILA ACHESON WALLACE, with her husband DeWitt Wallace, founded the *Reader's Digest*. They served as co-chairpersons of the Reader's Digest Association, Inc., from then until 1973, and today are still active as directors of the company. Together they built the *Reader's Digest* into the world's most widely circulated periodical. Its 1976 average U.S. circulation was 17.75 million, and its worldwide circulation, more than 30 million monthly copies in 13 languages. The company also publishes books, records, educational publications, and general reference works. Canadian-born Ms. Wallace is well known for her philanthropy. Among the recipients of her generosity are the YWCA and the Bronx Zoo, which used her $4 million gift for its World of Birds—a cluster of buildings in which birds from around the world fly free in natural surroundings. Ms. Wallace has received numerous honorary doctorates and awards including the Order of Civil Merit from the government of the Republic of Korea, a gold medal from the Architectural League of New York, and, in 1970, the American Council for Nationalities Service's Golden Door Award—the first woman to be so honored. In January 1972 President Nixon presented Ms. Wallace and her husband with the Medal of Freedom, the highest honor that can be given to an American citizen.

First Full-Time Editor of the *Journal of Home Economics*

In 1923 HELEN WOODWARD ATWATER (1876–1947) became the first full-time editor of the *Journal of Home Economics,* a position she held until her retirement at age 65. After being graduated from Smith College in 1897, she assisted her father, a professor at Wesleyan College, with his papers on colorimetry until he died in 1907. In 1909 she joined the scientific staff of the Bureau of Home Economics, U. S. Department of Agriculture, spending the next 14 years interpreting to rural women the new knowledge of food values and the best methods of food preparation. She also served as an active member of the Women's Joint Congressional Committee, formed in 1920 as a clearinghouse for organizations promoting federal measures of interest to women, was a member of the committee for the White House Conference on Child Health and Protection in 1930, participated in the President's Conference on Home Building and Home Ownership in 1931, and was a member of the American Public Health Association and chairwoman of its committee on the hygiene of housing in 1942. After her death in 1947, the American Home Economics Association established an International Fellowship Award in her name.

The *New Yorker***'s First Fiction Editor**

Six months after its founding, she joined the staff of the *New Yorker* as a manuscript editor in 1925. Steeping herself in all aspects of the fledgling publication, KATHARINE WHITE exerted a profound influence that eventually transformed it from a satirical weekly to a vehicle for some of the best short-story writers in the country. As the magazine's first fiction editor, she is credited with discovering writers John O'Hara and Vladimir Nabokov, and she sponsored MARY MCCARTHY (see "Women in the Arts and Entertainment," p. 686), John Cheever, John Updike, Irwin Shaw, Ogden Nash, and Theodore Roethke, among others. Devoted to her authors, she spent much time encouraging, counseling, and reassuring them. On her death in 1977, at the age of 84, the *New Yorker* published a tribute to her that read in part: "No one can estimate how much good writing might have been less good if it had not been for Katharine White, or how much writing would have been done at all if she had not been waiting, at her desk, to receive it. For many writers, she was the only muse they needed."

The *New Yorker*'s American in Paris

As "Genêt," JANET FLANNER wrote her first "Letter from Paris" for the October 10, 1925, issue of the fledgling *New Yorker* magazine. The feature appeared regularly up to the first rumblings of World War II, then less frequently after the war until as recently as 1975. The "Letters," noted for their sophisticated wit and polished style, won her a faithful following. Born to an Indiana Quaker family in 1892, Ms. Flanner first settled in Paris at the end of a trip through Turkey, Greece, and Austria. Armed with brief experience in Indianapolis as probably "the first cinema critic ever invented" in 1916 and 1917, and an unsuccessful novel written in Paris, "Genêt" began to write about French life and politics. Through the years she penned letters from other cities as well—Brussels, Beirut, Rome, London, Berlin, to name a few—but her contributions to the *New Yorker* were not confined to her letters. She also provided several Reporter-at-Large articles and a series of brilliant profiles. Her personal favorites were those of Hitler, EDITH WHARTON (see "Women in the Arts and Entertainment," p. 673), Thomas Mann, and ELSA MAXWELL, of whom she said: "She was built for crowds. She has never come any closer to life than the dinner table." These profiles, combined with other material, comprised her book, *An American in Paris*, published in 1940.

The Women Behind That *Mademoiselle* Look

When *Mademoiselle* magazine was launched in 1935 by Street & Smith, publishers, BETSY TALBOT BLACKWELL joined the staff as fashion editor. In 1937 she became editor in chief. The success of her innovations was reflected in the circulation figures, which rose to 178,000 in 1939, and in 1953 tallied over 539,000. Her introduction of the special college issue, written and edited by college girls during their summer vacation, was one of her spectacular successes. Her "theme" issues were also innovative and enormously popular. Ms. Blackwell won the Neiman-Marcus Fashion Award for distinguished service in the field of fashion (1942), was named a Key Woman of the Year (1947) by the Federation of Jewish Philanthropies, and received the Junior Achievement Award for Inspiration to Youth (1953). Before joining *Mademoiselle,* she was fashion reporter for the *Breath of the Avenue* and served on the editorial staff of *Charm* magazine for nine years.

EDITH RAYMOND LOCKE, editor in chief of *Mademoiselle,* has worked for that magazine for over 25 years She began as dress and millinery editor in 1948. In 1971 she took over every aspect of the "*Mademoiselle* look"—from the physical appearance of its fashion and beauty pages to the editorial content of its columns. Ms. Locke was born in Vienna, Austria, and came to the United States at the age of 15. After graduating from New York University, her early fashion career included stints as associate merchandising editor with *Junior Bazaar* and in fashion advertising. An active member (and past president) of the Fashion Group in New York, she is on the American Fashion Critics (Coty) Award Jury.

Mademoiselle's fashion editor NONNIE MOORE is responsible for 28 to 60 fashion pages a month—from concept to finished layout. In 1969 she was a co-founder of the Fashion Coalition—an organization formed to assist and advise black men and women seeking careers in the fashion industry—and has served on the board of directors of the Fashion Institute. Ms. Moore is a 1943 graduate of Barnard College and an alumna of the Art Students League.

Founder of *Seventeen*

Founder and from 1944 to 1950 editor in chief of *Seventeen* magazine, HELEN VALENTINE was one of the first in the beauty magazine industry to combine fashion with fiction, and fiction with "mind-improving" articles to appeal to the intelligent teen-age market. Her philosophy as a journalist centered on her belief that fashion promoters have the responsibility of offering their ready-made market a broader exposure to the arts, politics, and career possibilities. After receiving her B.A. at Barnard College in 1915, Ms. Valentine's career progressed from advertising copywriter to the promotion and editorial departments at Condé Nast Publications. She was promotional director of *Mademoiselle* from 1939 to 1944, editor in chief of *Charm* from 1950 to 1958, and became contributing editor to *Good Housekeeping* in 1960. She was president of the Fashion Group from 1948 to 1950.

From *America* to *Atlas*

MARION K. SANDERS, managing editor of *Atlas* magazine when she died in 1977 at the age of 72, received her B.A. from Wellesley College in 1925, worked with the federal government during the '40s and '50s first as a Washington news writer for the U. S. Office of War Infor-

mation, then as editor in chief of *America* magazine and chief of the magazine branch of overseas publications for the State Department. In 1958 she joined the staff of *Harper's Magazine*, retiring in 1970 as senior editor. Ms. Sanders, a native New Yorker, also contributed to *Harper's*, *Columbia Journalism Review*, the *New York Times Magazine*, and wrote books ranging from a detective story to politics topics to the biography *Dorothy Thompson: A Legend in Her Time* (1973).

Founder of *Elle*

Born September 21, 1909, at Rostov-sur-le-Don in Russia, HÉLÈNE GORDON-LAZAREFF became a leader of the fashion world in the capital of haute couture, Paris. She founded the weekly magazine *Elle*, becoming its director and editor in chief in 1945. In 1965 she was awarded the Neiman-Marcus Fashion Award for services rendered to the cause of fashion.

Publisher and Editor of *Satri Sarn*

NILAWAN PINTONG, publishing manager and editor of *Satri Sarn*, a Bangkok weekly woman's magazine, has worked in women's groups and social, cultural, and literary organizations since her graduation from Chulalongkorn University in 1937. A former consultant to the Thai Prime Minister's office, she has been decorated by the King of Thailand for her contributions to public service.

Pakistani Editor-Publisher

Publisher and editor since 1951 of *Mirror*, a popular magazine in Pakistan, ZEB-UN-NIRSA HAMIDULLAH has furthered the cause of Pakistani women. Begum Hamidullah is also a well-known author and poet.

Cosmo's Chief

A long way from the Ozarks, where she was born in 1922, HELEN GURLEY BROWN in 1962 topped the best-seller list with her revolutionary advice book, *Sex and the Single Girl*. Three years later she became editor in chief of *Cosmopolitan* magazine. Under her direction, the magazine has grown spectacularly to become one of the five largest-selling magazines on U.S. newsstands. Ms. Brown has used *Cosmo* to continue her counsel on matters of love, sex, and life-style for the modern woman. Married for the first time at the age of 37, she offers herself as proof of her wisdom. After so long a time as a single, she says, "I got the man I wanted."

Modern Photography Editor

In addition to her duties as editor of *Modern Photography*, JULIA SCULLY writes a monthly column on photographic trends and many of the magazine's feature articles. Before joining *Modern Photography* over 10 years ago, Ms. Scully was editor of *Camera 35* magazine. After her graduation from high school in Nome, Alaska, Ms. Scully received her B.A. from Stanford University and her M.A. from New York University.

Hybrid Scientist/Science Writer/Editor

Senior editor of *Physics Today*, published by the American Institute of Physics, and the only physicist on the staff when she joined the magazine, GLORIA B. LUBKIN developed "Search and Discovery," a section reporting recent discoveries in physics, research in the United States and abroad, and conferences. Although she began her professional life as a physicist, Dr. Lubkin considers herself "something of a hybrid, a cross between a scientist and a science writer." The recipient of a Nieman Fellowship at Harvard, she is a fellow of the American Physical Society and a member of the New York Academy of Sciences and of the Forum on Physics and Society.

Prix de Paris Winner Now Chief of *House & Garden*

The 1946 winner of *Vogue*'s Prix de Paris competition, MARY JANE POOL, has seen her journalism career culminate in her position as editor in chief of *House & Garden* magazine. Beginning in 1948, Ms. Pool was merchandising editor, promotion director, then in 1968 executive editor of *Vogue*. In 1968 she became editor of *House & Garden* and in 1970 was named editor in chief. Ms. Pool has edited two books for *House & Garden* and has received the Distinguished Alumnae Award from Drury College and a special award from the National Society of Interior Designers.

Editor in Chief of the World's Largest-Selling Fashion Magazine

Editor in chief of *Glamour* magazine, which is aimed at women between 18 and 35 and is the world's largest-selling fashion magazine, RUTH WHITNEY has complete responsibility for the supervision and coordination of the editorial department. Since 1968, when she took over *Glamour* after 11 years as executive editor of *Seventeen* magazine, she has created the "How to Do Anything Better Guide," the Top Ten College Women Contest, strengthened the feature section to include new topics of interest to young women, and added monthly columns on money, jobs, sex, movies, books, and cooking. In addition to keeping her readers apprised of the latest fashion trends, Ms. Whitney in her magazine emphasizes the transition from college to career—one she says she remembers very well herself. In 1976 she was president of the American Society of Magazine Editors.

Her Magazine Has Over 8 Million Readers

Woman's Day vice-president and editor GERALDINE RHOADS is one of the few women to edit a magazine with a multimillion circulation (averaging over 8 million). Before joining Fawcett Publications as *Woman's Day* editor in 1966, Ms. Rhoads, born in 1914 in Philadelphia and a Bryn Mawr graduate, was executive editor of *McCall's* and, before that, managing editor of the *Ladies' Home Journal*, editor of the *Reader's Digest* "First Person" series, an editor of *Today's Woman*, producer of NBC's "Weekday" featuring Margaret Truman and Mike Wallace, and a lecturer at Columbia University. In 1975 she was awarded the New York Women in Communications Matrix Award, and she is past chairwoman and current member of the executive committee of the American Society of Magazine Editors and a member of the board of trustees of the Consumer Research Institute.

VP and Chief at *Parents' Magazine*

Editor in chief and vice-president of *Parents' Magazine*, GENEVIEVE MILLET LANDAU is also well known as an author. She has written many articles on medicine, education, and community affairs, and two books on children. Ms. Landau, born in Dallas, Texas, is a Phi Beta Kappa summa cum laude graduate of William Smith College in Geneva, New York, and received her M.A. in English literature at Columbia University.

First at *Life* and *McCall's*

SHANA ALEXANDER began her career in journalism with New York's experimental newspaper *PM*, for which, at the age of 16, she interviewed a pregnant stripper, GYPSY ROSE LEE. Her terror at conducting her first interview was compounded by the fact that she had "never seen a stripper before." She went on to a distinguished career, and her comments on current news and life-styles have been featured in radio, television, and magazines for over 25 years. She joined *Life* magazine in 1951, soon became its first woman staff writer, and in 1964 launched her well-known column "The Feminine Eye" in its pages. In 1969, after *Life* folded, Ms. Alexander became editor of *McCall's*—its first woman editor in over 50 years. Fired from *McCall's* in 1971, she explained that she "wanted to write a magazine for and about women" while "they wanted to sell advertisements." She has been a CBS commentator on the popular-opinion radio program "Spectrum" and a regular on CBS-TV's "60 Minutes." An active advocate of women's rights, she was a founder of the National Women's Political Caucus and author of the *State-by-State Guide to Women's Legal Rights* (1975). She has also been a director of the American Film Institute and a contributing editor at *Newsweek*.

The *New Yorker*'s Half-and-Half Film Critics

She Won It at the Movies

Regarded by many as one of America's most perceptive film critics, PAULINE KAEL claims a lifelong passion for "the movies" a term she prefers to "films." She began reviewing movies in the 1950s while managing two art film houses in Berkeley, California. Reviewing her 1965 book *I Lost It at the Movies*, a best seller, for the *New York Times*, Richard Shickel said: "Her collected essays confirm what those of us who have encountered them separately over the last few years . . . have suspected—that she is the sanest, saltiest, most resourceful, and least attitudinizing movie critic currently in practice in the United States." She often differs with her peers and was in a distinct minority when she panned *The Sound of Music* and championed *Last Tango in Paris*. A free-lance reviewer for numerous magazines, Ms. Kael goes to the movies for the *New Yorker* six months of each year, covering the choice winter releases.

She Shares the Bench

PENELOPE GILLIATT provides the *New Yorker* with film reviews for the six months covering the summer season. Ms. Gilliatt, born in London and educated in England and America, and previously film critic for the London *Observer*,

1961–67, began as guest critic at the *New Yorker* in 1967 and assumed regular assignments in 1968. Well acquainted with the film industry, Ms. Gilliatt has herself written an award-winning screenplay: *Sunday, Bloody Sunday* won the 1971 Best Original Screenplay award from the New York Film Critics, the National Society of Film Critics, and the Writers Guild of America, and was nominated for an Academy Award. In 1972 the American Academy—National Institute of Arts cited her for her creative work in literature. Multitalented Ms. Gilliatt has also written two collections of short stories, several novels, and an anthology of film criticism.

Award-winning Writer of *Passages*

An award-winning feature writer since 1964 and, more recently, contributing editor of *New York Magazine*, GAIL SHEEHY has tackled such subjects as prostitution, black interrelationships, single mothers, and identity crises. For "Cleaning Up Hell's Bedroom," a two-part *New York Magazine* series on prostitution, she was cited in 1972 by the mayor of New York City for journalistic excellence, and in 1973 was presented the New York Front Page Award and the National Magazine Award. She also received a 1970 fellowship in interracial reporting under MARGARET MEAD (see "Women in Science and Technology" p. 145) at the Columbia University School of Journalism, the 1973 ALICIA PATTERSON (p. 449) Award for the study of adult development, and the 1975 Penney-Missouri Journalism Award for her *New York Magazine* articles "Catch-30 and Other Predictable Crises of Growing Up Adult," which were later incorporated in a best-selling book, *Passages: Predictable Crises of Adult Life* (1976). A 1958 graduate of the University of Vermont, Ms. Sheehy won a Front Page Award while feature writer for the *New York Herald Tribune* (1963–66).

Best-Selling Poet a Contributing Editor to *Redbook*

"It really comforts a woman to know that other women have sagging kneecaps, too," says writer JUDITH VIORST, housewife's and mother's friend. Ms. Viorst, born in Newark, New Jersey, was a Phi Beta Kappa at Rutgers University, married Washington, D.C., political writer Milton Viorst, and became a housewife with three "fierce" sons. She has written seven children's books, adult fiction, and non-fiction, but it is her wry poems, in such collections as the best-selling *It's Hard to Be Hip over Thirty and Other Tragedies of Married Life* (1968) and *How Did I Get to be 40 & Other Atrocities* (1973), that have won her a permanent place in women's hearts. Ms. Viorst confronts daily life head on. "Does Golda Meir feel diminished because of dry skin?" she asks. And "This morning I was seventeen/I had barely begun the beguine and it's/Good-night ladies/Already," she laments, having reached the age when "peace of mind is o.k., but trust funds help." A columnist and a contributing editor for *Redbook* since 1972, Judith Viorst has won an Emmy (1970) for poems used on TV's Anne Bancroft show; the Silver Pencil Award (Holland, 1973) for her children's book *The Tenth Good Thing About Barney;* and the Georgia Children's Storybook Award (1977) for *Alexander and the Terrible Horrible No Good Very Bad Day*.

The Scribblers' Scribbler

A Hollywood child who grew up to be New York's brightest writer on the media, NORA EPHRON has written for various magazines and for two years contributed a column on writing, magazines, newspapers, and the profession of journalism in general to *Esquire* magazine. In a review of her 1978 book *Scribble, Scrabble: Notes on the Media,* the most recent collection of her articles, *New York Times* reviewer John Leonard said that she "writes better than anybody."

Many readers of her earlier books, *Wallflower at the Orgy* (1970) and *Crazy Salad: Some Things About Women* (1975) agree. Ms. Ephron is married to journalist Carl Bernstein, of Watergate renown.

Essence Editor in Chief

A 1966 graduate of Lake Forest College, superachiever MARCIA GILLESPIE first worked for Time-Life books, then in 1971 joined *Essence* magazine, the arbiter of elegance for black women, as editor in chief. Ms. Gillespie is on the board of directors of the Hollingsworth Group/*Essence* magazine, and is a member of the National Council of Negro Women. In 1973 she was presented with the Outstanding Alumni Award of Lake Forest College.

L'Europeo's Prizewinning Interviewer

Florence-born ORIANA FALLACI, international correspondent for the Italian weekly *L'Europeo,* noted for her demanding interviews, has twice received the St. Vincent Award for Journalism (Italy's equivalent of the Pulitzer Prize) and a special citation from the Overseas Press Club. Denying her critics' attributes of ruthlessness, she calls herself, rather, a historian who is interested only in what is correct and honest. She has lured Henry Kissinger into describing himself as a "lone gunslinger on a horse," flown on a bombing run in Vietnam, and been wounded by gunfire in Mexico. Her articles and reviews appear in magazines and newspapers around the world, and her books have been translated into thirteen languages. In her 1976 book *Interview with History,* she stated her credo: "I have always looked on disobedience toward the oppressive as the only way to use the miracle of having been born."

They Started *Ms.*

In 1972, GLORIA STEINEM, a free-lance writer who emerged in the 1960s as a leader in the Women's Movement, co-founded *Ms.* magazine with PATRICIA CARBINE as publisher and editor in chief (see also p. 484). The new publication won an instant readership with its first appearance as a supplement to *New York Magazine* at the end of 1971. Its first solo issue the following July sold out quickly. By 1973 its circulation was 350,000, with an estimated readership of 1.4 million for its reporting on the status of the Equal Rights Amendment, alimony, abortion, child care, day care, and other issues confronting women.

Ms. Steinem, born in Toledo, Ohio, "to a mother who had been a journalist and a father who ran a resort in the summer and sold antiques in the winter," was a 1956 Phi Beta Kappa, magna cum laude graduate of Smith College. She studied in India for a year on a Chester Bowles Asian Fellowship and spent an additional year there writing for Indian publications. Immediately prior to founding *Ms.,* she was a contributing editor and political columnist for *New York* magazine. Named *McCall's* Woman of the Year in 1971, she was the first recipient of Simmons College's doctor of human justice degree, received the 1974 National Fellowship Award, and was honored by the American Civil Liberties Union of Southern California with the 1975 Bill of Rights Award. In 1971 Ms. Steinem was one of the conveners of the National Women's Political Caucus. She serves on its advisory committee and is chairperson of the Women's Action Alliance, a non-profit organization set up to help women help themselves. In 1977-78 she spent a year as a fellow at the Woodrow Wilson International Center for Scholars at the Smithsonian in Washington, D.C., working on a book exploring the impact of feminism on the premises and goals of current political theory.

Patricia Carbine brought to *Ms.* 20 years of experience in publishing. Beginning at *Look* magazine in 1953, she rose through the ranks to executive editor in 1969, the highest position held to date by a woman in a general-interest magazine. She left *Look* to become editor of *McCall's* and, eventually, vice-president of the McCall Publishing Company. Among other outside professional activities, Ms. Carbine is a member of the executive committee of the American Society of Publishers and vice-chairwoman of the board of directors of the Magazine Publishers' Association.

Prominent Ghanaian Publisher

Since 1971 KATE ABBAM has been publisher and editor of *Ideal Woman* (*Obaa Sima*), whose offices are located in Ghana's capital, Accra. Ms. Abbam, born in 1934 in Cape Coast, studied at Queen Elizabeth College, University of London (1957–58) and the University of Ghana (1962–64). She started her journalism career as assistant editor at *Junior Graphic* and was also a free-lance journalist before assuming the direction of *Obaa Sima*.

Egyptian Editor's Several Firsts

Editor, journalist, and writer AMINA EL SAID is editor of Egypt's *Hawa* and *Elle* magazines. *Hawa* was the first and after two decades remains the most widely read woman's publication in the Arab world. Ms. Said, one of Egypt's first full-time women journalists and the first to be an editor in chief of a magazine, was also the first woman elected to the Board of the Journalists Syndicate in Cairo and, later, the first woman vice-president and acting president of the board. She has contributed to *Dar Al-Hilal* and *Al-Moussawar* and is the author of a number of books.

First Woman Editor in Chief of the *Texas Observer*

KAYE NORTHCOTT, first female editor in chief of the *Texas Observer,* had no problem breaking into journalism because of her sex, noting that "journalism is a profession easily accessible to women —if for no other reason than that it pays so little." What discrimination the 5-foot, 95-pound Ms. Northcott has encountered has been based on size rather than on sex, she says. "I compared notes on this subject with my co-editor on the *Observer,* MOLLY IVINS, who is 6 feet tall and strong enough to hold her own on the Capitol Press Corps basketball team. We agree that sheer bulk has a certain natural advantage. When I was running for editor of the student newspaper at the University of Texas, some beef brain asked me if a 'girl' my size could command the respect of the staff. Well, I won that election, and [in 1970] after college [and two years at the *Observer*] I became the only female editor in chief in the magazine's history." Since 1977 Ms. Northcott has been a free-lance journalist.

Bazaar Bosses

Successor to DIANA VREELAND (see "Women in Fashions and Home Furnishings," p. 262), long the editor in chief of *Harper's Bazaar,* JANE OGLE took over the top job in 1972. Ms. Ogle worked her way up in the fashion journalism industry, starting soon after her graduation from Smith College. In 1944 she was fashion editor at *Vogue.* She joined *Flair* in 1949, then in 1951 left for the *Harper's Bazaar* staff as a fashion copywriter, and from 1958 to 1964 worked on Elizabeth Arden advertising.

Vogue's Editor in Chief

GRACE MIRABELLA, editor in chief of *Vogue* since 1973, has worked with the magazine continuously for over 23 years except for one year spent in Rome where she handled public relations for Fabiani and Simonetta, the famous fashion team. Originally a member of *Vogue*'s merchandising department, she later transferred to the editorial staff, where she edited the shopping column and covered the sportswear market. Before joining *Vogue*, Ms. Mirabella worked in New York with Saks Fifth Avenue and Macy's. Her editorial credo: "to give a woman a full menu—fashion, beauty, and health—as well as interesting things to read."

One Woman's World

As co-editor of the *Ladies' Home Journal* from 1935 to 1962, BEATRICE GOULD was instrumental in making it the most profitable of all the Curtis magazines, and in 1940, the magazine with the largest paid circulation in the entire world. A talented and noted writer, Ms. Gould began her career reporting for newspapers and magazines. Her husband, Bruce, also a noted writer, followed the same career pattern, joining the staff of the *Saturday Evening Post* when their first child was born in 1928. In 1935, they were offered the co-editorship of the *Journal*, a position which they held until retiring in 1962. *American Story*, their dual autobiography published in 1968, is the story of those sometimes rocky but successful years.

Editor Voted One of Most Influential Women in America

Editor of *Ladies' Home Journal* since 1973, LEONORE HERSHEY has earned distinction as a writer, editor, businesswoman, and community leader. She is well known as creator of the *Journal*'s annual feature, "Women of the Year," and as executive producer of the four NBC special "Women of the Year" broadcasts. Ms. Hershey created and conducted seminars on the role of women in the economy which led in 1972 to the creation of the Presidential Advisory Committee on the Economic

Role of Women. In 1975 Ms. Hershey was named "one of the 50 most influential women in America" by the Newspaper Enterprise Association.

Editor of Israel's Unique Magazine for Working Women

ZIVIA COHEN has been editor of *Na'amat* magazine since 1973. *Na'amat*, established in 1934, was the first magazine of its kind in Israel. A publication of the movement of working women and volunteers, the largest women's organization in Israel, it is also a women's magazine "with all the usual ingredients." In journalism since 1960, Ms. Cohen was formerly editor of the Women's Page in the daily newspaper *Lamerhav*. In 1966 she was awarded a best-interview prize for "The Woman in the Palmach" and in 1970 one for best reporting ("The Wayward Girl"). She was the first woman member of the committee of the Association of Newspapermen in Israel. Ms. Cohen received her B.S. from New York University and her M.A. in journalism from Temple University in Philadelphia.

Book-Award-Winning Magazine Writer

In 1973 FRANCES FITZGERALD won the National Book Award in contemporary affairs for her best seller *Fire in the Lake*, an in-depth study of Vietnam based on her own experiences and observations. While in Vietnam as a free-lancer in 1966, she wrote on the politics, social problems, and economic situation in the war-ravaged country for the *Atlantic*, the *New York Times Magazine*, the *Village Voice*, and *Vogue*. She was twice given the Overseas Press Club Award: in 1967 for "best interpretation of foreign affairs" and in 1975 for "best magazine reporting from abroad" for a *Harper's* article on the Shah of Iran. Ms. Fitzgerald has traveled extensively since graduating from Radcliffe in 1962. She worked for two years with the Paris-based Congress for Cultural Freedom—a job that took her through Europe, the

Middle East, and Africa. More recently, she has gone to North Vietnam for the *New Yorker* and to Northern Ireland for *Redbook.*

First Female Senior Editor at the *New York Times Magazine*

Former free-lance writer, assistant editor of *Interiors* magazine, book reviewer for the *Saturday Review,* associate editor and European correspondent for *Look* magazine, and founding editor (1973) of *Homelife* magazine, MARY SULLIVAN SIMONS in 1974 became the first woman senior editor on the *New York Times Sunday Magazine.* She is responsible for fashion and design supplements and articles dealing with architecture, design, fashion, food, parents, and children. While with *Look,* Ms. Simons produced award-winning pieces on architecture, design, and major news stories in Europe, including the legal heroin program in England. Pendleton scholar at Wellesley, she was graduated in political science and at the start of her career taught school in Indonesia. Ms. Simons calls herself a "feminine feminist with a great belief in the equal rights of women and a hard-core interest in the affairs of the home."

First Woman Senior Editor at *Newsweek*

In 1975 LYNN YOUNG was the first woman to be named a senior editor of *Newsweek,* with over-all responsibility for the news media, TV, entertainment, Ideas, religion, "Life/Style," and "Periscope" sections of the magazine. Ms. Young, who received her B.S. from Vassar College in 1965, started with *Newsweek* in 1969. She was editorial assistant, girl Friday in the Paris bureau, and in 1974 was named general editor in charge of the popular "Life/Style" section. She has written such major stories as "Halston," "Exploring America's Past," and "The POWs a Year Later."

Leading Photography Editor

CAROLINE KISMARIC, managing editor of *Aperture* since 1975 and contributor to several European photographic and art magazines, has won acclaim as both a photography editor and a writer. After receiving her B.A. from Pennsylvania State University in 1964, Ms. Kismaric joined Time-Life Books, where she was picture editor from 1964 to 1975. Her publications include: *Duel of the Iron-clads* (1969), *The Boy Who Tried to Cheat Death* (1971), and *On Leadership* (1974).

Chief of Israel's Only Monthly Magazine

As chief editor of *AT,* Israel's only monthly magazine, in a country of 3 million, SARAH RIPPIN takes her responsibility to the Israeli woman seriously. *AT,* which translates as the feminine "you," contains little on fashion and food; through its concentration on reportage, literature, and regular columns, Ms. Rippin hopes "to propagate feminist views and ideas in a way that will not antagonize the Israeli woman" by addressing the reader as "an intelligent person," interviewing women of achievement (not wives of celebrities), and supporting feminist causes. Ms. Rippin received her B.A. from the Hebrew University in Jerusalem in 1959 and spent two years in Boston while her husband was a research fellow at Harvard Medical School. Back in Israel, she joined *AT* in 1968, was promoted to her present position in 1974. She hopes that "the magazine is contributing something to the liberalization and improvement of the life of the Israeli woman."

Top Travel Editor

PAMELA FIORI, long involved in various phases of editorial work in the travel industry, was named editor in chief of *Travel & Leisure* magazine in 1975. Outlining her intentions for the magazine at that time, Ms. Fiori stated, "I want the pieces to be a lot more timely. There will be no attention to nostalgia. Instead of just observing the travel scene, we believe we can shape attitudes." Ms. Fiori finds expression for her views in the monthly editorial column, "Window Seat." Prior to joining *Travel & Leisure* in 1971 as senior editor, Ms. Fiori worked as associate editor of *Holiday* magazine.

L'Egale: New and Different Canadian Journal for Women

In 1977 the first issue of *L'Egale* (a play on the words "equal" and "legal") received wide acclaim for its innovative offerings to Canadian women. Under the editorship of CHRISTINE MITCHELL, the magazine deals with law as it affects women. The 42-page pilot issue contained book reviews and articles covering a variety of problems affecting Canadian women in the 1970s. Future publication of *L'Egale* will depend on financing according to Ms. Mitchell. She hopes it will be incorporated as a non-profit organization.

First Woman to Head Foreign Bureau for *Time*

On January 1, 1978, when BONNIE ANGELO assumed the responsibilities of *Time* magazine's London bureau chief, she became *Time*'s first woman to head a foreign bureau. She had been a Washington correspondent for *Time* since 1966, assigned principally to the White House and national politics. In 20 years as a Washington correspondent, she had reported on major stories from all 50 states and more than 50 foreign countries on six continents, and covered summit conferences, political conventions, manned

space shots, and presidential campaigns, as well as the inaugurations of six U. S. Presidents (Eisenhower to Carter), the assassination of one, and the resignation of another. In addition to her work for *Time,* Ms. Angelo was a weekly participant on the television program "Panorama (1967–78), Channel 5, Washington, and appeared often on a number of other television programs, including "Meet the Press," "National Town Meeting," and other public affairs programs. As a past president (1961–62) of the Women's National Press Club (now the Washington Press Club), Ms. Angelo was a leader in removing professional barriers and discrimination against women journalists. In 1976 the *Ladies' Home Journal* nominated her as one of the nation's outstanding women in communications. In 1977 she chaired the Robert F. Kennedy Journalism Awards. The Paul Tobenkin National Award was presented to her in 1961 for best news writing in the field of civil rights. In 1977 she served on the board of governors of the White House Correspondents Association. Before joining *Time,* Ms. Angelo was a national correspondent for the Newhouse newspaper chain (1963–66), author of a syndicated column, and a Washington correspondent for *Newsday* (1957–63), the Long Island newspaper. Her journalism career began at her hometown paper, the *Winston-Salem* (N.C.) *Journal and Sentinel.* Her alma mater, the University of North Carolina at Greensboro, named her an outstanding alumna, and in 1975 she was the first alumna ever to deliver the commencement address at that institution.

Feminist Publishing Ventures, U.S.A.

Feminist publishing in the United States has its roots in the rise of radical feminism and suffrage after the Civil War. In 1868 SUSAN B. ANTHONY and ELIZABETH CADY STANTON established

Revolution, **the first important women's rights paper to appear after abolition, although** AMANDA BLOOMER'S *Lily* **flourished earlier during the 1850s.** LUCY STONE **introduced the** *Woman's Journal* in 1870; this influential suffrage organ did not cease publishing until 1917. With the passage of the Nineteenth Amendment, many feminists disbanded their papers and periodicals, believing their work was done (cf. Rheta Childe Dorr).

The tradition of women-oriented, -owned, and -operated media ventures was revived in the late 1960s as a natural and essential requirement of the women's movement for articulating and publicizing grievances. In the November 1977 issue of *Ms.*, LINDSY VAN GELDER observed of the feminist press: "It [was] a cutting edge, a conscience . . . particularly around 1969 and 1970, when the printed word *was* feminism. . . . it's no accident that our first 'leaders'— were writers; there was a *hunger* for information. . . ."

Not only were women starving for news of their peers and issues they couldn't glean from the apathetic or scornful establishment media, but some strategists and activists in the movement realized that the power of the press came easiest to those who owned the press. Accordingly, Susan Davis in Chicago inaugurated a monthly newsletter called the *Spokeswoman* and Donna Allen in Washington, D.C., put out *Media Report to Women.* Both reported on legislation, legal challenges to women's rights, meetings, opinions, and ran discussions on such topics as health care and job discrimination. *Women: A Journal of Liberation,* a scholarly periodical, and *Aphra,* a literary journal, were founded in 1969. Soon after, *Rat* came out of New York City, *Lilith* (for Jewish feminists) out of Seattle, and *No More Fun and Games* out of Boston. *Off Our Backs,* a Washington-based news report, amassed a circulation of 10,000. *The Ladder* and *Lavender Woman* were vanguard Lesbian publications, and *Prime Time,* designed for older women, made its debut, as did *Up and Under* for working women. The Feminist Press, a publishing house specializing in non-

sexist textbooks and juvenile literature, was established in 1970 by Florence Howe, who continues to be its president while also pursuing an active career as a teacher and writer (see "Women in Education, Social Sciences, and the Humanities," p. 424). In 1973 Daughters, Inc., a radical feminist house for fiction, was founded.

Despite this information explosion and the recognition of the potential for a network of women's media, mainstream publishing, journalism, and television executives continued largely to ignore the possibility of alternative communication as a response to their inadequate or grudging reporting of issues of interest to women. Thus they watched in astonishment when Gloria Steinem and Patricia Carbine (see pp. 479–80) brought out the first issue of *Ms.,* a magazine attempting to speak to and for women's liberation on a national scale, which hit the stands in 1972 and was pronounced a financial success by September 1973. Combining the delivery of facts, features, fancy, and unstereotyped advertising with the slick graphics and design made famous by *New York Magazine, Ms.* not only prospered but made magazine publishing history with its editorial innovations.

Today feminist presses, periodicals, pamphlets, and newspapers flourish, although many, started on a shoestring and a dream, are still in the category of profit-seeking ventures. In a survey of feminist book publishers released in 1978, POLLY JOAN and ANDREA CHESSMAN reported that 82 presses in the United States and Canada are currently publishing books covering Women's Movement ideologies from "strict feminist separatism to cooperative non-sexism." Some presses specialize in poetry or novels, some in "non-sexist children's stories." Some have men as partners. The names of the houses include: Out & Out Books, Shameless Hussy Press, Vanilla Press, Times Change Press, Vanity Press.

Among the specialists in children's books are New Seed Press, Lollipop Power, All of Us, Over the Rainbow Press, Joyful World Press, and Dustbooks of Paradise,

WOMEN IN THE BOOK WORLD

Co-Founder, Director, and Publisher of Alfred A. Knopf, Inc.

When Alfred Knopf announced his decision to publish books rather than study law at Harvard, the interest of the young girl he had known as a friend quickened and the two, in his words, "began to keep company." In 1916 they were married and a partnership unique in the annals of publishing was sealed between Alfred and BLANCHE WOLF KNOPF (1894–1966). Their love of fine books and each other resulted in what Alistair Cooke called the "most civilized and elegant" of American publishing houses. The Knopfs founded their firm in 1915 and Blanche Knopf was made director and vice-president in 1921. Their Borzoi Books included belles-lettres, philosophy, and the humanities, and the house wooed foreign as well as domestic authors. Every year between World Wars I and II Ms. Knopf went to Europe as a roving scout in quest of authors; every year she returned with contracts with many distinguished names. To a trade list headed by the Americans H. L. Mencken and WILLA CATHER (see "Women in the Arts and Entertainment," p. 674), she added Thomas Mann, Sigmund Freud, André Gide, Albert Camus, Jean-Paul Sartre, SIMONE DE BEAUVOIR (see "Women Activists, Heroes, and Humanitarians," p. 703), and numerous others. In fulfilling their dream of presenting great European writing to the American public, the Knopfs managed to publish more Nobel Prize winners than any other U.S. publisher. During World War II, Ms. Knopf turned her sights toward South and Central America and was responsible for bringing much Latin American literature to the attention of American readers. In

California—the publisher of the Joan-Chessman survey (above), *Guide to Women's Publishing.*

1957 she assumed the presidency of the firm and her husband became chairman of the Board. She remained active until her death. Despite her stature in the book world, Ms. Knopf was denied membership in prestigious publishing clubs (to which her husband belonged) because of her sex and once (in 1957) declined an invitation to lecture at a women's college on the future of women in publishing on the grounds that "there was no future worth mentioning." The tribute Thomas Mann paid to her sums up her contribution to the history of publishing: "Far be it from me to minimize or to underestimate the share of my friend Alfred in building up the famous institute. After all he is the spirit, the spiritus rector of it. But Blanche is its soul. And where spirit and soul are working together, there is creation."

Dell's Former Chairwoman of the Board

HELEN MEYER, retired chairwoman of the Board of Dell Publishing Co. Inc., for many years as its president was the only woman to be operating head of a major publishing house. Ms. Meyer started with Dell in 1923 as the first assistant to George T. Delacorte. From her various viewpoints in every one of Dell's departments, she watched the company grow from five employees and two pulp magazines to over 900 employees and an annual volume exceeding 100 million books. Dell publications, now owned by Doubleday & Company, range from a line of children's paperbacks, Purse-books, to mass-market paperbacks, higher-priced paperbacks, hardcover books, and many magazines. Ms. Meyer has been director of the American Association of Publishers and chairwoman of the Department of State Government Advisory Committee on International Book and Library Programs. In defense of her company's early attention-grabbing paperback covers, which drew some criticism, she told *Publishers Weekly* in 1972 that "today they would be child's play as far as sex is concerned. [But] what it did do was to bring people to the newsstand, and it made readers out of them. To me, that's the important thing —read anything, but read." Ms. Meyer now acts as Editorial Consultant at Doubleday.

Governing Director of Victor Gollancz, Ltd.

"I couldn't publish an author I didn't like," British book publisher LIVIA GOLLANCZ told the *London Times*. Her personal response to writers and their work is an attitude which her father, Victor Gollancz, publisher, humanitarian, author, pamphleteer, and founder of Victor Gollancz, Ltd., a publishing house with a decided political, philosophical, and moral stance, would have approved. Director of the firm since 1967, Ms. Gollancz was a professional musician for many years with the London Symphony Orchestra and the Hallé, Scottish, and Covent Garden orchestras, but during a period of disgruntlement with her chosen career in 1953, her father put her to work as filing clerk typing review labels. She learned typography and graduated to being an editor. Music is now her relaxation.

Owner and President of Peter Pauper Press

Publisher, printer, editor, and designer EDNA BEILENSON assumed responsibility for the daily administration of Peter Pauper Press after the death of her husband in 1963. Known for its inexpensive editions of literature, proverbs, and wit and whimsy, the Press was established in 1929 and Ms. Beilenson has been active in the business since 1930. With more

than 200 titles to her list, she believes herself to be the only woman printer-publisher operating on this scale. To promote awareness of women's roles in graphic arts, in 1937 she helped to found an informal organization called the Distaff Side, a club for women directly concerned with fine printing. (The group is no longer active but during its lifetime it published a series of collector's volumes, with the proceeds donated to worthy causes.) A 1928 graduate of Hunter College, Ms. Beilenson was named to its alumnae Hall of Fame in 1973. She was the first president of the American Institute of Graphic Arts (from 1958 to 1960) and has been a director and president of the Goudy Society, a non-profit organization devoted to educational, literary, scientific, and philanthrophic activities in the field of graphic arts.

Book Director and Editor of Johnson Publishing Company

The book division director and editor of the Chicago-based Johnson Publishing Company, Inc., DORIS EVANS SAUNDERS is one of the highest-ranking black women in publishing. The company, which publishes non-fiction, children's books, and scholarly books primarily by and about black people, was founded in 1942. Ms. Saunders, born in 1928 in Chicago, earned her B.A. at Roosevelt University. She began her career as a reference librarian at the Chicago Public Library, and joined the Johnson Publishing Company as librarian in 1949, remaining in that position until 1966. She has been a newspaper columnist, a radio program host, and the writer and producer of a television show called "Our People." She is active in numerous organizations in Chicago and nationwide including the NAACP, Media Women, Inc., and the Black Academy of Arts and Letters. While working at Johnson she has also served as editor for *Negro Digest* magazine. Among the books she has compiled and edited are *The Day They Marched*

(1963), *The Kennedy Years and the Negro* (1964), *The Negro Handbook* (1966), and *The Ebony Handbook* (1974). Ms. Saunders also teaches and contributes frequently to various professional and scholarly publications.

Founder-Publisher of Lisbon's Dom Quixote

SNU ABECASSIS, born into the famous publishing family of Bonnier, dreamed of newspaper work before marrying and settling into Portugal. Under the regime of dictator Salazar, such a career was not open to her. Instead, she founded the now well-known Lisbon firm Dom Quixote, moving strongly into reference books, dictionaries, and university level texts. The firm gradually expanded to include titles on cinema, psychology, semantics, sociology, and literature, as well as fiction and poetry. Since few Portuguese writers could publish, most of the books on Dom Quixote's list have been by internationally recognized authors. When Salazar was overthrown, "We thought that everything would be wonderful . . . that all the good books would come out now," Ms. Abecassis told *Publishers Weekly*. "But with so many years of dictatorship, there were no manuscripts in drawers."

Successful Publisher and Champion of England's Press Freedom

In 1968 MARION BOYARS won, on last appeal, one of the most widely publicized court cases involving freedom of the press in England. The case centered on her firm, then Calder and Boyars (since 1975 Marion Boyars Publishers), which in 1966 had published an American novel, *Last Exit to Brooklyn*, that the prosecutors claimed was pornography. As a result of this case and the efforts of publishers, a bill in Parliament limiting press freedom was defeated. Ms. Boyars, an American citizen, was born in Hamburg and went to the United States at 16. After completing high school in New York and beginning her studies at New York University, she married and moved to England, obtained a degree at Keele University in 1954, had two children, and in 1960 took over half interest in a one-man publishing firm. As financial officer and co-editor, she put the firm on a paying basis and drew numerous avant-garde literary and intellectual talents to its lists. Now on her own, Ms. Boyars publishes novelists (including Ingmar Bergman, Robert Creeley, Hubert Selby, and many European writers in translation) and poets (Yevtushenko, among others), as well as belles-lettres, criticism, cinema, travel, drama, and music. Ivan Illich is a contributor to her "Open Forum/Ideas in Progress," working papers on pressing contemporary problems.

First Group Vice-President of Time Inc.; Chairwoman of the Board of Time-Life Books

As group vice-president of Time Inc. and chairman of the Board and chief executive officer of its subsidiary, Time-Life Books, JOAN MANLEY runs one of the nation's largest publishing empires. Time Inc.'s interests—and Ms. Manley's supervisory responsibilities—encompass not only Time-Life Books but also Little, Brown & Co., the New York Graphic Society Ltd., and several foreign houses. Ms. Manley was appointed to the position of publisher of Time-Life Books in July 1970, became Time Inc.'s first woman vice-president in July 1971 and its first woman group vice-president in October 1975. In January 1978, she and MATINA HORNER, president of Radcliffe (see Women in Education, Social Sciences, and the Humanities," p. 406), became the first two women named to the Board of Time-Life, Inc., the parent corporation. A member of the Nominating Committee of the New York Stock Exchange, a trustee of Bennington College, and a former chairwoman of the Association of American Publishers, Ms Manley holds an honorary doctorate in business administration from the University of New Haven and received a B.A. in English and history from the University of California at Berkeley in 1954. She joined Time-Life enterprises in 1960.

Popular Library's First Woman VP

In 1971, when CBS acquired Popular Library, CAROL KLAPPER had been vice-president and editorial director of the magazines and special book projects department for five years and the only woman vice-president in Popular Library's history to that time. She was appointed publisher of the Popular Magazine Group in 1974.

President of the Times-Mirror's Book Division

President of the book division at Times-Mirror Magazines, New York, and the company's only woman corporate vice-president, ADELE BOWERS oversees two of the largest special-interest book clubs in the country, the Outdoor Life and Popular Science book clubs. Together they total 500,000 members and gross millions of dollars annually. In 1947 Ms. Bowers took a job as a junior copywriter in the circulation department of the Los Angeles division of Times-Mirror, Inc. In 1953, still under the auspices of circulation, she was given $25,000 to start the Outdoor Life Book Club. Its success led to the establishment of the Popular Science Book Club in 1963. In 1971 she was made head of the book division (in name as well as in fact) and the only woman corporate vice-president.

President and General Manager of U.S. Publishing's Largest Marketing Group

Since 1974, ROBIN B. SMITH has been president and general manager of the Book Clubs Division of Doubleday & Company. The division, Doubleday's largest, has sales of over $100 million and employs about 700 people, and as such is the largest marketing operation of general books in the U.S. industry. Included in the division are the Doubleday Book Club and the Literary Guild, plus 10 special-interest clubs. Ms. Smith was, among other positions with the company, group marketing director and director of marketing before becoming president of the division. She came to Doubleday in 1965, after two years at the Carnation Company in Los Angeles. Ms. Smith holds a B.A. from Wellesley (1961) and an M.B.A. from Harvard (1963).

Editorial Director of the Literary Guild

Doubleday divisional vice-president and editorial director of the Literary Guild, ROLLENE SAAL decides the fate of manuscripts for the largest book club (1.5 million members) in the world. She makes the final decision on the fourteen major selections offered to the Guild's members each year, thereby catapulting some authors to success and sustaining the prominence of others. Denying that the Guild caters to "low-brow tastes," Ms. Saal points out that Saul Bellow, LILLIAN HELLMAN (see "Women in the Arts and Entertainment," p. 671), Jerzy Kosinski, and Robert Penn Warren have numbered among their authors. Aware of her career goal since age 10, Ms. Saal left her home in Massachusetts for New York soon after graduating from Wellesley College with a major in English. Feeling her way through the publishing world in a series of jobs, including one as a book reviewer for the *Saturday Review*, she eventually became a reader for the Literary Guild and progressed to director.

Editor of Canada's *Scholarly Publishing*

Associate director of the University of Toronto Press since 1970, ELEANOR HARMAN is also the original editor of *Scholarly Publishing*, a journal for authors and editors published by the Press. After receiving an M.A. from the University of Toronto in 1930, Ms. Harman entered the book world and worked in various editorial, promotional, and business capacities for Clarke, Irwin, & Company and Oxford University Press before joining the University of Toronto Press in 1946. She is also the author of several books on Canadian history.

Bantam's First Publicity Director

ESTHER MARGOLIS' first brush with publishing, while on a temporary secretarial job at Dell Publishing in 1961, lured her permanently to New York in 1962, fresh from earning her M.A. in English at the University of Michigan. After only four months as a secretary at Dell, she became assistant to the promotion director at *Ingenue* magazine, a Dell publication. In November of 1962, she moved to Bantam Books as assistant director and in 1965 was appointed Bantam's first publicity director. Elected vice-president of Bantam in 1971, Ms. Margolis' purview expanded to encompass the restructuring and over-all direction and administration of all Bantam's promotion-related departments including sales promotion, advertising, educational promotion, publicity, and public relations. She has worked closely with such authors as William F. Buckley, Gore Vidal, Leon Uris, and JACQUELINE SUSANN. She has been actively involved in the publishing and promoting of Bantam's "instant books," which began in 1964 with *The Warren Commission Report* and have since included *The Pentagon Papers* (1971) and others of timely significance.

First Women Editors in Chief at Sister Companies

PATRICIA SOLIMAN began her career as an editorial assistant at Harper & Row. She joined Coward, McCann & Geoghegan in 1965 as associate editor, became executive editor in 1971, and in 1972 was made vice-president and editor in chief. A 1959 graduate of Tufts University, she completed her M.A. at Stanford in 1962.

PHYLLIS GRANN became vice-president

and editor-in-chief of Putnam's in June 1976. Previously she was vice-president and editor-in-chief of paperback editions at Simon & Schuster. Ms. Grann is a graduate of Barnard College of Columbia University.

Co-Founder and Executive Vice-President of Rawson Associates

ELEANOR S. RAWSON, editor and publisher, is executive vice-president of Rawson Associates, publishers of America, social science, medical, science fiction, and sports and hobbie books. Ms. Rawson has been a reporter, a free-lance writer, the fiction editor of *Today's Woman* and *Collier's* magazines, and a teacher and lecturer in journalism. Before founding Rawson Associates with her husband, Kennett L. Rawson, in 1975, she was a vice-president and executive editor at David McKay Company, where her husband was president. In addition to her work in publications, Ms. Rawson has taught at Columbia, the New School, and NYU, and serves on the Boards of several hospitals and museums.

Associate Publisher, Simon & Schuster

Former book and fiction editor JONI EVANS was named associate publisher of Simon & Schuster in January 1977. She began her publishing career as a fiction editor for *McCall's* and *Ladies' Home Journal* in 1963, but in 1966 moved into book publishing when she joined William Morrow & Co. as an associate editor. Leaving Morrow as a senior editor, Ms. Evans went to Simon & Schuster in 1974 as vice-president and director of rights.

First Woman Division Head at Fawcett Publications

In 1977 LEONA NEVLER was named a vice-president of CBS Publications. She is publisher of the Fawcett Books Group, which includes Crest, Gold Medal, and Popular Library. She previously was publisher of Fawcett World Library. She joined the book department of Fawcett

Publications in 1955 as an associate editor, was named managing editor in 1957, editor-in-chief in 1965, one of the first two women vice-presidents of Fawcett in 1972, and a division head in 1974. As division head, she was the first woman at Fawcett to serve in that position. A Phi Beta Kappa graduate of Boston University, Ms. Nevler lives in Manhattan with her teen-age daughter and son.

Only Female Head of a Washington Book-Publishing Operation

At 27, in late 1974, JOAN TAPPER opened up shop for New Republic Books in Washington, D.C. She remains head of the sister company of the long-established weekly journal, the *New Republic,* acquiring and editing trade books and directing the staff. Ms. Tapper holds a B.A. in linguistics from the University of Chicago and an M.A. from Harvard in comparative literature. She began her editorial career at *Boston Magazine.* In 1969 she joined Chelsea House in New York City, then worked for Scribner's and as a free-lancer. Soon after she and her husband moved to Annapolis, Maryland, she became an associate editor in the Washington office of Praeger Publishers, where, with its then director, LOIS DECKER O'NEILL (see "Introduction," p. xiii), she developed general and public affairs books.

National Geographic Society's First Woman Book Author Now a Publisher on Her Own

TEE LOFTIN was the first woman author of a book in the National Geographic Society's Special Publications Division, *The Wild Shores: America's Beginnings,* published in 1974. A late starter, Ms. Loftin began her career in 1966 at the age of 45. Her child-rearing days were far from intellectually deprived, however; she obtained an M.A. in journalism at American University and undertook a number of free-lance, contract, and part-time jobs with newspapers, radio and television, and in public service and politics. In 1978 she founded her own publishing house, Tee Loftin, Publisher, in Washington, D.C.

Vice-President, Public Relations and Subsidiary Rights at Morrow

SHERRY W. ARDEN came to publishing in 1968. She says, "When I was getting divorced and needed a job for all the obvious reasons, plus having two children to support, I really thought long and hard about what I'd like to do most. I came up with publishing. After wearing down a lot of shoe leather during one whole year, I got a series of jobs as assistant publicity director at Putnam's, Coward-McCann, John Day." She went on to work for the renamed Coward, McCann & Geoghegan as publicity director, then took a year off to co-produce, co-write, co-direct, and co-edit a television show investigating the phenomenon of JACQUELINE SUSANN and *Valley of the Dolls.* When Ms. Arden returned to publishing, "my first love," as publicity director of Morrow, she took Ms. Susann along as a new Morrow author. Ms. Arden was publicity director for six years, during which time she became a vice-president of the company handling subsidiary rights and public relations.

First Subsidiary Rights Manager to Negotiate a Million-Dollar Paperback Sale

Although her record has since been broken—by others and by herself—MILDRED MARMUR, then head of the rights department at Simon and Schuster, on April 15, 1974, became the first person to sell paperback rights to a book (*All the President's Men* by Carl Bernstein and Bob Woodward) for $1 million. The next day she announced her resignation to become vice-president and director of subsidiary rights for Random

House. Later that same year she handled the sale of paperback rights to *Ragtime* by E. L. Doctorow for $1,850,000. Ms. Marmur, born and raised in Brooklyn, New York, was graduated at 20 from Brooklyn College and went on to earn her M.A. in French literature from the University of Minnesota. Her first job was as a switchboard operator for the Jewish Labor Committee. She later became secretary to the manager of subsidiary rights at Simon and Schuster, where, after six years, she was given the foreign rights job and eventually made head of the entire rights department.

Co-Founder of Persea Books

In 1975, KAREN BRAZILLER and her husband, Michael, co-founded Persea Books, Inc., a small independent publishing house, which, in her words, "is the only full-service house of its size or kind." Drawing upon their joint editorial experience, they decided to handle their own promotion and distribution of titles in order to maintain complete editorial authority about who and what get published. Persea Books, Ms. Braziller explains, "was the most exciting thing we could do." Their first titles—mostly poetry and literary biographies—were released in January 1976.

RADIO AND TELEVISION PROFESSIONALS

First Station Master of One of the United States' First and Largest Radio Stations

In 1922, when JUDITH CARY WALLER was asked to run a radio station, she confessed that she had never heard of one. Her only experience had been in advertising. Learning that her prospective associates also were unfamiliar with radio, she accepted and became station master of the *Chicago Daily News* station WGU in February 1922. Its first program was broadcast in April. As WMAQ, the call letters assumed in the fall of 1922, the station under Ms. Waller's guidance was innovative and grew to be one of the nation's largest. The first broadcast featured opera star SOPHIE BRASLAU backed by a piano and violin, thereby setting the trend for fine music that became associated with WMAQ. Beset with technical problems, Ms. Waller nonetheless enthusiastically developed a variety of programs. In 1925 WMAQ was the first station to broadcast a play-by-play baseball game from a home team ballpark. That same year the station broadcast a prearranged telephone conversation from the *Daily News* London correspondent dispelling rumors concerning the health of King George V. Not having obtained permission to do this, it was fined $75. WMAQ featured "Amos 'n' Andy" in 1928 and soon aired the program six nights a week—the first time that had been tried in radio. The show eventually went on network with NBC and enjoyed a 20-year success.

A pioneer in educational radio, Ms. Waller provided Chicago schools with a program series on music, geography, and kindergarten fare, and at CBS president William S. Paley's request helped the network organize "The American School of the Air." Her lectures were broadcast from Northwestern University and the University of Chicago; the latter developed into "The University of Chicago Round Table," which NBC moved to its network. She also headed the "airborne" TV workshops at Purdue University—an experiment in which courses were transmitted from an airplane to effect wider coverage—and served on the Federal Radio Education Committee, the National Association of Broadcasters Education Standards Committee, and the

Board of the University Association for Professional Radio Education. In 1942 she helped develop the first radio institute for careers in broadcasting and in 1946 wrote a college text, *Radio, the Fifth Estate*. Her "Ding Dong School," the first successful preschool TV program, won a Peabody Award. In 1950 Ms. Waller was U.S. representative at a Paris UNESCO conference on school broadcasting. She died in 1973, leaving a decided mark on broadcasting in the United States.

Early Radio Exec and Peabody Winner

In 1925 jobs at radio stations were not yet structured. So when MARGARET CUTHBERT, born in 1887 in Saskatchewan, Canada, joined the staff of New York's WEAF (now WNBC) as director of speakers, she performed any work that needed doing. When WEAF became the NBC radio network's key station in 1926, she became director of women's activities. Sixteen years later, she was named director of women's and children's programs. Always interested in children's programming, she was active in developing codes to keep violence off the airwaves. John Galsworthy was the first of many prominent figures that Ms. Cuthbert brought before the mike. Among the programs she developed and produced were "Gallant American Women," "Echoes of History," and the long-running "NBC Theater," which earned a Peabody Award for excellence in drama. When Ms. Cuthbert retired from NBC in 1952, she was supervisor of public affairs for NBC radio. She was cited by the New York League of Business and Professional Women (1936) and the General Federation of Women's Clubs (1941), was entitled to wear the King Haakin Liberation Medal for her aid to Norway's fight for freedom in World War II, and in 1946 was named to the Women's National Press Club list of 10 women "Promoters of Progress." Ms. Cuthbert died in 1968 on Cape Cod.

First "Musical Clock Girl": She Went on to Many Broadcasting Achievements

EDYTH J. MESERAND joined NBC's Press Department when WJZ and WEAF joined to form the National Broadcasting Company in 1927. She held a succession of positions: with Hearst Radio as their first "Musical Clock Girl," as publicity director for WINS New York, then as executive officer handling promotion for Hearst Radio's 10 stations. At WOR for 15 years, she was assistant director for news and special features for radio, then television. On V-E Day she was the first to air a background documentary and her subsequent documentaries captured many awards: Peabody, Ohio State, Freedom Foundation, and countless others. Ms. Meserand was the first woman executive to receive *McCall's* Golden Mike Award. She was organizing convention chairwoman (1950) and first national president of American Women in Radio and Television (1951–52). Not content with a well-earned retirement, Ms. Meserand opened her own advertising agency in New York State.

Pioneer Talk Show Hostess

The University of Missouri journalism school prepared MARY MARGARET MCBRIDE for the "sob sister" journalism of the 1920s. With other newspaperwomen of that era, she reported on stories involving murder, tragic fires, and other heart-rending events. She came into her own in 1934 when she was hired by New York's WOR to play homely, grandmotherly "Martha Deane" (see also p. 494). Soon confessing on the air that the character was a fake and that she was really an unmarried reporter, Ms. McBride thereafter pursued subjects of interest to her. Her mixture of interviews with colorful personalities and tidbits of miscellaneous human interest won her a loyal and ever increasing audience. A skillful interviewer and facile ad-libber, she was eventually hired by CBS, then by ABC for network spots. When her

"Mary Margaret McBride Show" closed in 1954, she had marked 20 years in radio and uncounted interviews with guests ranging from Harry Truman to fan dancer SALLY RAND. She retired to her farm in the Catskills but remained active writing her autobiography and a newspaper column, and doing interviews three times a week on local WGHO radio until shortly before her death in 1976 at the age of 76.

A Leader in the Establishment of Radio Standards

Soon after JANET MACRORIE joined NBC in 1934, she was made head of the newly formed continuity acceptance department. As such, she was responsible for the establishment of standards that determined the on-air acceptability of scripts. Ms. MacRorie also developed formulas for comedians to prevent their telling jokes that would be offensive in different parts of the United States. Although born in New York, Ms. MacRorie spent the better part of her childhood in Scotland. Returning to New York, she studied at Columbia University and the Wheatuck School of Dramatic Art before launching her 40-year career in journalism, publicity, advertising, and the theater. At one time, she was director and vice-president of Advertising

Women of New York. Her last job was as editor and writer for W. H. Freeman technical book publishers in San Francisco. She died on February 4, 1950, at the age of 60.

First Woman Coast-to-Coast Commentator

In 1936 news commentator KATHRYN CRAVENS marked a first for women when her voice was carried coast-to-coast by CBS. The following year the Texan, a former film actress, was tagged "The Flying Reporter." Logging over 100,000 air miles annually in her quest for stories, she was a guest of Mexico's President Ávila Camacho in 1941 and during World War II traversed Europe, Asia, and the Middle East. She was the first woman to broadcast from Berlin following the Allied victory, and she covered elections in the Balkans and riots in Palestine. Her stories have appeared in national magazines, the *St. Louis Dispatch,* and the *Dallas Morning News.* Ms. Cravens was the first woman to be elected vice-president of the Overseas Press Club, was twice honored with citations by the National League of American Penwomen, and was voted Best-Dressed Woman in Radio and one of the Best-Dressed Women in the United States during the years 1938 to 1954.

Top Woman Network Exec in 1930s

Eschewing women's programs, HELEN SIOUSSAT brought the world's famous before CBS's mikes for over 26 years. Succeeding Edward R. Murrow, whose assistant she had been, as director of talks for CBS in 1937, Ms. Sioussat decided on all participants for any CBS talk, debate, or discussion program. When she took over the talks department, it was slightly over a year old. As it grew with the radio industry, she carefully formulated policy that would withstand the test of time.

An acknowledged expert in politics and government who could count many

of the world's leaders as personal friends, Ms. Sioussat attracted such guests as the Roosevelts, Harold Stassen, Alf Landon, Clement Attlee, the Trumans, the Nixons, Herbert Hoover, and Bernard Baruch. She drew eminent speakers from other fields as well: education, labor, industry, religion, patriotism, civil rights, culture, international affairs. Her broadcasts originated from around the world. In 1936 she broadcast King Edward's abdication speech, and in 1942 Wendell Willkie came to her studio immediately upon his return from his famous One World trip.

In 1941 she brought the talks department into television by planning, producing, and chairing the first "Round Table" discussion on television ("Table Talk with Helen Sioussat"). In 1945 she led the CBS delegation in San Francisco at the birth of the United Nations. In 1954 her "Man's Right to Knowledge" program won a Peabody Award as the best education program, was named as one of the outstanding broadcasts by the *Radio-Television Daily*, and in 1955 took the General Federation of Women's Clubs Awards. Ms. Sioussat was also honored by the American Medical Association for "Frontiers in Medicine," the American Heritage Foundation for her "distinguished aid to the crusade for freedom—1954," and the New York chapter of the American Red Cross "for meritorious service." In 1958 Ms. Sioussat became assistant vice-president of CBS in Washington. Her expanded executive responsibilities prevented her from continuing her programing and found her concentrating on policy until her retirement in 1962. Throughout her years with CBS, she was that network's liaison with Congress.

Thirty Years as Martha Deane

Following MARY MARGARET MCBRIDE (see p. 492) as WOR Radio's Martha Deane, MARIAN TAYLOR logged well over 10,000 interviews with famous figures in politics, literature, the theater, academe, and science. Among her favorite guests were Dwight D. Eisenhower, Robert Graves, Averell Harriman, the Duke and DUCHESS OF WINDSOR (see "Far Out Women," p. 751), and ELEANOR ROOSEVELT (see "Women Activists, Heroes, and Humanitarians," p. 738). Her votes for funniest went to Buddy Hackett and Zero Mostel. In 1968 she won the Broadcast Pioneer's Distinguished Service Award. But awards were not new to her. She won several during her 11 years with the Scripps-Howard syndicate before she

became Martha Deane. Two of her most outstanding achievements were an exclusive interview with MAGDA GOEBBELS, wife of the Nazi propaganda minister, and her reports from within the Reichstag when Hitler announced his invasion of the Rhineland. Attributing her success as an interviewer to her attitude toward interviews as "good conversation," Ms. Taylor in 1971, during her 30th year as Martha, told Ben Gross of the *New York Sunday News:* "There is nothing to equal an exchange of ideas or information between two, or more, well-informed, civilized persons."

Woman's Voice from War-Embroiled Europe

One of only a few women correspondents covering the World War II years in Europe, 26-year-old BETTY WASON set out for the Continent as a free-lance correspondent for Transradio Press Service in 1938 with $300, a one-way ticket, and no reporting experience. She quickly found herself covering the Nazis' march through Europe. Her broadcasts from Stockholm describing the Norwegian royal family's daring escape earned her a full-time assignment from CBS, but letters objecting to a woman broadcasting war news led CBS to drop her eventually, then rehire her. Her last European assignment was in Athens, where she reported the German invasion and takeover of Greece. Back in the United States, Ms. Wason used her home economics degree from Purdue University in the writing of 16 books dealing with food, cookery, and wine.

One Woman Broadcaster's Firsts

Her unquenchable thirst for adventure took IRENE CORBALLY KUHN far from Greenwich Village, where she was born on January 15, 1900. Traveling and working throughout the world, she has been a columnist, broadcaster, war correspondent, Hollywood scenarist, novelist, and radio executive. Her first job (1920) was as a reporter on the *Syracuse* (New York) *Herald* for $18 a week. While covering a state fair she became one of the first women reporters to fly for a story. In 1921 she left for Europe and the Paris office of the *Chicago Tribune*. In 1922 she left France for Shanghai without a job and with little money. The American newspaper, The *Evening Star* hired her soon after her arrival. Except for a brief interlude in Hawaii, Ms. Kuhn stayed in Shanghai until 1926 working as a foreign correspondent for International News Service, a reporter for China Press, and as one of the first women to broadcast in the Orient, from a radio station built with bootlegged parts and located in a sheet-draped room in the China Press offices. She interviewed Chiang Kai-shek and MME. CHIANG, among others. Back in the United States, in 1926 she joined the *New York Mirror*, for which she covered the Lindbergh flight, moved on to the *News,* where she covered scandals and murder, and then to *Liberty* magazine. After a short stint in Hollywood as scenarist for 20th Century-Fox, M-G-M, and Paramount, she joined New York's *World-Telegram,* left to become managing editor of the *New York Woman* in 1936, then in 1940 moved to NBC as special writer and assistant to the vice-president in charge of the press. She became NBC's assistant director of information in 1944. In 1945 she was an accredited war correspondent for NBC in the CBI (China-Burma-India) Theater, logging over 24,000 miles in Air Transport Command planes. She was the first woman to broadcast from a U. S. Navy vessel (Admiral Thomas C. Kinkaid's flagship *Rocky Mount,* anchored in China's Whangpoo River), the only civilian to write for the *Stars and Stripes* in 1945, the first woman to broadcast from liberated Manila, and in September 1945, 20 years after her first broadcast from Shanghai, the first person to broadcast from that liberated city. Ms. Kuhn was twice elected as the only woman vice-president of the Overseas Press Club.

Radio-TV's Peter Pan

As moderator of the *"New York Times Youth Forum,"* 1943–60, DOROTHY GORDON (1889–1970) brought high school and college students together with adult guests to discuss a variety of topical questions. Over the years, her guests included FANNIE HURST, William O. Douglas, and Ralph J. Bunche, and GOLDA MEIR (see "Women in Politics and Government," p. 46). First broadcast over WQXR, the program went on television in 1952, and in 1960 continued over WNBC-TV as "Dorothy Gordon's Youth Forum." In 1951 it won *McCall's* award for outstanding service, and in 1952, a Peabody "for outstanding service to the teen-age listening audience." Born in Odessa, Russia, to American diplomatic corps parents, Ms. Gordon traveled extensively as a child, and picked up her love of languages and folk music. After studying at Hunter College and the Sorbonne, Ms. Gordon entered children's programing by singing folk songs and directing radio programs. In 1924 she was in charge of the first program for children over WEAF and later directed, produced, and wrote many other children's programs for the CBS, NBC, and Mutual networks as well as for the Office of War Information and the State Department. Her seven books were also written for children. In 1953 she was honored by the Town Hall Club of New York "as a builder of good citizens and champion of the free exchange of ideas," and in 1954 received the Columbia Scholastic Press Gold Key Award. The woman Sir James Barrie once called "the Peter Pan of America . . . (who) will *never* grow old" died on May 11, 1970, at the age of 81. Until the month before her death, Ms. Gordon was moderator of the *Times* In-Service Courses for New York high school teachers.

Pioneer Film Editor

In 1951 the debut of "See It Now" with Edward R. Murrow and Fred W. Friendly marked the beginning of MILI BONSIGNORI's career in film editing. Seventeen years at CBS editing that series and the first "CBS Reports," 22 documentaries, 12 major journalism awards, and much critical acclaim in the United States and abroad highlight the career since then of this pioneer in a technical area of electronic media largely inaccessible to women—even today. A freelance film editor since 1968, Ms. Bonsignori has been recognized for her work on such well-known documentaries as "FDR: The Man Who Changed America," for CBS, 1975; "Anatomy of a News Story," for CBS, 1973; "The Culture Thieves," for ABC, 1974; and "Hunger in America" for CBS, 1968—the latter remembered as one of the most powerful films ever produced for television.

First Woman VP at NBC

From budget clerk in the NBC advertising department in 1944 to the first woman vice-president in the history of NBC and its parent company, RCA, in 1962, and later general manager of the NBC radio network, MARION STEPHENSON also has been the first woman member of the Northwestern Mutual Life Insurance Company Policyholders Examining Committee (1970–71), a member of the State Department's Inter-American Advisory Council, a visiting professor for the Woodrow Wilson National Fellowship Foundation, and a member of the Manufacturing Division Council of the American Management Association. During her early years with NBC, Ms. Stephenson attended the New York University Graduate School of Business at night, earning her M.A. degree in 1948. In the same year she was awarded the first Marcus Nadler Key for "Excellence in finance" and was named business manager of NBC's advertising and promotion department.

An Emmy for Her First Documentary

The first documentary produced and directed by PERRY MILLER ADATO, "Dylan Thomas: The World I Breathe," in 1968 captured an Emmy for "outstanding achievement in cultural documentaries." Ms. Adato brought Jacques Cousteau's films to U.S. audiences for the first time and with Robert Flaherty created New York's Film Advisory Center. Early in her career she also traveled the world for the United Nations, reviewing social welfare films for an international catalogue. CBS hired her in 1954 to supply film for such shows as "Adventure" and "Odyssey." In 1964 she became involved in production with National Educational Television. More recently, "An Eames Celebration" (see RAY EAMES in "Women in Fashions and Home Furnishings," p. 265) won for Ms. Adato the silver Hugo in the 11th annual Chicago International Film Festival (1975) and a red ribbon in the American Film Festival (1977). "Gertrude Stein: When You See This, Remember Me" (see GERTRUDE STEIN in "Women in the Arts and Entertainment," p. 678) received two Emmy nominations. In late 1977 Ms. Adato's hour-long film portrait of GEORGIA O'KEEFFE (see "Women in the Arts and Entertainment," p. 600) was aired on WNET as the first in a seven-part series called "The Originals: Women in Art." Ms. Adato has been named a Poynter fellow at Yale, and in 1977 won the Christopher Award for Best Directorial Achievement for a Documentary.

TV News Anchorwoman with Most Years of Continuous Service

At 84, DOROTHY FULDHEIM in 1977 continued to anchor the evening news at WEWS-TV in Cleveland 30 years after becoming television's possibly first and certainly longest-serving anchorwoman. The fiery, redheaded octogenarian also tapes two daily TV commentaries and hosts a daily live interview program. During her career, Ms. Fuldheim has interviewed notables from Hitler to President Jimmy Carter. In 1947, when a transit strike appeared imminent, she brought representatives of both labor and management onto her TV show to discuss their differences; this unprecedented encounter averted a strike. In 1955, on assignment in Hong Kong, she obtained the only recorded interview with two reportedly brainwashed American prisoners released by the Chinese Communists. Dorothy Fuldheim progressed through a series of careers—actress, lecturer, radio commentator—before landing in front of the TV camera, where, she told *Ms.* in December 1976, she intended to stay rather than take an "early" retirement. In this "youth-oriented society," she said, "anyone over 40 has a hell of a time trying to get a job, and if you're over 60, you're over the hill. Well, the fact that I'm 83 and retaining this dominant position is a satisfaction to me."

First Woman Network Correspondent at a National Political Convention, 1948; First to Moderate a Presidential Debate, 1976

In 1948 PAULINE FREDERICK was the first woman network correspondent to cover a national political convention for television. She not only interviewed officials and delegates but also served as "makeup expert" for BESS TRUMAN and FRANCES DEWEY. From that assignment, Ms. Frederick went on to many triumphs in a distinguished career that earned her the respect and admiration of everyone in the TV industry. For 12 years thereafter, she was the only woman broadcasting hard news on network radio and television.

Armed with a master's degree in international law, Pauline Frederick made her entrance into the world of journalism by interviewing diplomat's wives and selling her stories to the *Washington Star* and *U.S. News*. In 1945 she made her first overseas broadcast from Chungking. Undaunted and more determined than ever after being rejected by Edward R. Murrow in 1946 for a full-time radio news position (said Murrow, "I would not call her material or manner particularly distinguished"), she continued writing features for the North American Newspaper Alliance and stringing for ABC News. In 1948 several weeks of reporting a foreign ministers' conference earned her a full-time position on the ABC News staff. In her first regular assignment with ABC she covered the United Nations, did an early morning radio show, and often appeared before the camera on the evening news. At the advent of the Korean War in 1950, for six weeks she provided continuous news coverage of the UN Security Council meetings, which brought her into the spotlight. Moving to NBC in 1953, she soon became that network's only UN correspondent. She covered all major world crises—Suez, the Congo, Hungary, Cuba, Cyprus, the Dominican Republic, Laos, Vietnam, the Middle East. She reported the resignation of Trygve Lie, the troubled months following the death of Dag Hammarskjöld, and U Thant's decision to accept a new term. She was the first woman president of the UN Correspondents' Association.

The first woman to win the DuPont Commentator's Award (1954), she also won the George Foster Peabody Award in 1955 for her contribution to international understanding and in 1960 scored another "first" by being the first woman to anchor network radio's convention coverage. For two consecutive years, she was the only reporter in a

Gallup poll of the world's "10 most admired women." She was elected to the New York Professional Journalists' Society Hall of Fame, was named by the New York Deadline Club as one of the top 10 journalists in the last 50 years, and has been awarded 22 honorary doctorates.

During the second Carter-Ford debate on October 6, 1976, Ms. Frederick was the first woman to moderate a presidential campaign debate. As international affairs analyst for National Public Radio, with emphasis on the United Nations, she co-produces NPR's weekly program "Pauline Frederick and Colleagues," on which she discusses world affairs with a panel of distinguished experts in the area of foreign relations.

First for CBS, First for NBC, and First for Convention Coverage

In 1960 NANCY DICKERSON became the first woman TV correspondent at CBS. For its new Washington correspondent, the network had looked for a man with Washington savvy and the ability to produce political programs—but Ms. Dickerson was selected because of her successful production of CBS's "The Leading Question" and "Face the Nation." Among her envied scoops were her reporting of Senator Eugene McCarthy's plans to challenge President Lyndon Johnson's Vietnam policy and her revelation of the details surrounding LBJ's selection of Hubert H. Humphrey as his running mate. As the sole correspondent at an Atlantic City Reception for Lady Bird Johnson to observe that Ms. Muriel Humphrey was the only senator's wife in attendance, Ms. Dickerson confronted LBJ and was rewarded with the story hours before he announced his decision. In 1963 she moved to NBC, where she became the first—and for a while the only—woman to have a daily network TV news program, "Nancy Dickerson with the News." Many of her interviews also appeared on "Today," "The Hunt-

ley-Brinkley Report," and dozens of specials. Ms. Dickerson also was the first woman in television to report from the floor of a national political convention and to work in the anchor booth of Edward R. Murrow and Walter Cronkite. Selected by *Harper's Bazaar* as one of the 100 American Women of Accomplishment and in 1964 voted Woman of the Year for her reporting of President Kennedy's assassination in the Annual All-American Awards poll by *Radio-TV Daily,* Nancy Dickerson, in spite of all her success, bemoans the fact that women still have a way to go in the TV news business. They "will not really have arrived," she says, "until [they] are allowed to share in the top decision-making and to do regular political commentary."

Lone Woman on CBS Network News Staff in the 1960s

Successful as associate producer of CBS's election unit, MARYA McLAUGHLIN was moved to the New York news desk in 1966 as CBS's only woman network reporter. Prior to the 1964 presidential campaign, Ms. McLaughlin had done editorial research in Washington, D.C. She returned to the national capital as a general assignment reporter for CBS, concentrating on Senate activities. It was a Cabinet member's wife, however, who gave her one of the most memorable interviews of the early 1970s. In MARTHA MITCHELL's Watergate apartment, Ms. McLaughlin recorded the late Ms. Mitchell's comments about sending all the demonstrators to Russia.

First NBC News Exec

In June 1967 HELEN MARMOR was the first woman named to an executive position in the NBC News Division when she was appointed as an NBC news manager. In 1970 Ms. Marmor became manager, NBC News Program Service, feeding about 15 stories a day to 41 stations in 31 states over closed-circuit TV. She headed a staff of 50, including technicians and cameramen in NBC-owned stations in New York, Chicago, Washington, Cleveland, and Los Angeles. Between 1972 and 1974 Ms. Marmor produced a number of news specials. In 1973 her widely acclaimed coverage of Watergate won the 1973 Silver Gavel Award from the American Bar Association and her special on Vietnam, "Peace Begins," earned the Overseas Press Club Award. In 1973 her study of returning POWs was also nominated. Two other memorable specials were those covering the deaths of former Presidents Harry S. Truman and Lyndon B. Johnson. A native of New Jersey, and a 33-year veteran of the news business, who began as a reporter for the *Bergen Evening Record* in Hackensack, New Jersey, Ms. Marmor in 1944 became a writer and regional editor for the Associated Press. She joined NBC News in 1955 and in 1975 was named manager of the NBC network's "Weekend News," a rigorous assignment she continues to hold.

TV Producer with Some Unusual Firsts

First to gain film access to the interior of the Kremlin, first to be allowed the use of lights inside the Louvre for a TV documentary, and first American to receive an invitation from the People's Republic of China to produce film news documentaries, LUCY JARVIS is one of network television's most accomplished producers. A long list of important television programs has resulted in her impressive collection of awards and honors, including six Emmys, a Peabody, and the honor of being knighted by the late French President Charles de Gaulle and André Malraux as a *chevalière* in the Order of Arts and Letters. In 1964 Ms. Jarvis was named Producer of the Year and in 1967 received the Golden Mike Award from American Women in Radio and Television. Among her non-television pursuits, Ms. Jarvis is founder and a member of the board of directors of the First Women's Bank of America and a member of the board of governors of the National Association of Television Arts and Sciences.

TV's Gift to Preschoolers

JOAN GANZ COONEY, founder and executive director of the Children's Television Workshop, is the mastermind behind the highly successful "Sesame Street" and "The Electric Company." In 1966 Ms. Cooney began to develop the theory that the television medium could be adapted to stimulate the education of preschool children. She and her associates designed a format that combined fast-paced entertainment with the teaching of cognitive skills. Aired for the first time in 1969, "Sesame Street" quickly became the first educational TV program to have ratings equaling those of commercial network offerings. In 1970 "Sesame Street" received an Emmy, a Peabody Award, and the *Saturday Review*'s TV award for children's programing. Ever changing to meet the needs of the times, the programing concepts have expanded from teaching basic skills to introducing awareness of societal interaction, health, and different cultures. Ms. Cooney, born in 1929, the daughter of an Arizona banker, was graduated cum laude from the University of Arizona in 1951. She progressed from a short stint as a newspaper reporter in Arizona through several TV writing jobs to producer of public affairs documentaries for WNET in New York. In 1966 her three-hour documentary "Poverty, Anti-Poverty, and the Poor" won her her first Emmy.

NPR's Telephone Interviewer

SUSAN STAMBERG, co-anchor of National Public Radio's hour-and-a-half nightly news and feature program "All Things Considered," makes it her policy to "keep in touch with our listeners" by telephoning them and airing those conversations. Her interviews with "non-official" persons on matters of national and world importance have given average citizens a forum in which to make their opinions known. The program has won Peabody and Headliner awards for its solid in-depth reporting of major news stories. "All Things Considered" is broadcast nationally over most of NPR's member stations, providing a 90-minute mix of news, investigative reports, commentaries, features, and interviews. Ms. Stamberg was the first radio network news anchor in 1972. Prior to joining NPR, she earned the 1968 Major Armstrong Award for excellence in educational broadcasting while producer and host of "Kaleidoscope," a nightly magazine-format radio program on WAMU-FM, Washington, D.C. This program became the model for "All Things Considered."

Director of NPR's Specialized Audience Department

In March 1976 JANET DEWART became the director of National Public Radio's newly created Department of Specialized Audience Programs. Her goal, and that of the department's, has been to stimulate the input of minorities and women into NPR's programing and to assure that the programing needs and interests of those groups are met by NPR on a daily basis. Ms. Dewart's sensitivity to the programing needs and wants of minorities and women developed during her experiences as an executive assistant for a member of the Washington, D.C., city council, communications officer for the National Committee on Household Employment, community relations specialist for Freedmen's Hospital in Washington, D.C., and associate producer for WTOP-TV. In 1978 she was the first vice-president of the Washington Urban League. In 1974 she was listed in *Outstanding Young Women of America* and was

similarly cited in 1971 by *Ebony* magazine. She has also been selected for *Who's Who Among Outstanding Black Americans*. For her work as co-producer of the Washington television show "Harambee," she was awarded a D.C. Chapter Emmy. Ms. Dewart was born in Erie, Pennsylvania, on September 9, 1946. She holds a B.A. degree from Antioch College.

CBS News Deputy

SYLVIA WESTERMAN earned her position as deputy director of news, CBS News, New York, after many years' outstanding work as producer at the network's Washington bureau. There she served as co-producer of "Face the Nation," a weekly interview series, coordinated CBS coverage of the House Judiciary Committee Hearings on Impeachment, the Senate Select Committee Hearings on Watergate, the civil rights filibuster in 1964, the networks' pool for the 1969 presidential inauguration, and the international broadcast pool for the flights of Apollo 11 (humankind's first landing on the moon) and Apollo 13.

Her White House Scoops Earned Her Hometown and National Fame

CONNIE CHUNG began her career at WTTG-TV, a Metromedia station in her hometown, Washington, D.C., shortly after graduation from the University of Maryland in 1969. As co-anchor of CBS's 5 and 11 o'clock news, reporting on-the-scene from the capital some of America's most important political events in the 1970s, she earned many honors, including one for Outstanding Excellence in News and Public Service from the Chinese-American Citizens Alliance. Ms. Chung collared a White House aide who "just about confirmed" Nixon's impending resignation and went on the air with the story. Nixon resigned that night. While at CBS, she followed Senator George McGovern's presidential campaign and the House Judiciary Committee's impeachment hearings from

1971 to 1974. Then, until she left for KNXT in July 1976, she was permanently assigned to cover Vice-President Nelson Rockefeller and followed him wherever he went. On *Air Force 2* she elicited from him a long-awaited admission that he would not run for President in 1980.

A First at 1972 Convention

In 1972 CATHERINE MACKIN attracted widespread attention as the first woman TV news floor reporter assigned to cover both the Democratic and Republican national conventions. Floor reporter for NBC then and again in 1976, she also co-anchored the NBC News national election night returns both years. In the intervening years, she was NBC network correspondent covering the U. S. Senate and anchored the "NBC Sunday Night News." Ms. Mackin joined ABC in September 1977 as Washington-based correspondent, contributes to ABC documentaries, and undertakes assignments with the newly established investigative teams headed by ABC vice-president Sander Vanocur. Prior to joining NBC in 1971, Baltimore-born Ms. Mackin worked in Washington for the Hearst newspaper chain and WRC-TV. She is an English honors graduate of the University of Maryland and was a Nieman fellow at Harvard in 1967–68.

First Network Camerawoman

In 1972 at the age of 27, ALICIA WEBER became the first camerawoman ever put on staff by a television network. NBC hired her on the heels of a successful class action suit against the networks charging sex discrimination. Ms. Weber says that "the pressure of being the first was unbelievable," and she had to battle for camera responsibility on stories. She adds that she doesn't mind shooting woman-related issues ("I care and I want them done right") but thinks that her male counterparts should "learn to handle these issues, too."

Only Camerawoman for CBS News

As the only camerawoman (to 1978) for CBS News, RISA KORRIS and her crew—a soundman, an electrician, and an assistant cameraman—have traveled extensively throughout the United States filming assignments for "60 Minutes," "Who's Who," "CBS Reports," "Lamp Unto My Feet," and special hour-long film documentaries. "Each week brings new challenges, new environments. We contend with all sorts of weather. When the story breaks in Maine or Alaska," she says, "we go!" Prior to joining the CBS documentary division, Ms. Korris was one of five staff camerapersons in the Northeast bureau who filmed for the "CBS Evening News" with Walter Cronkite and the "CBS Morning News" with Hughes Rudd. Her 1973 classification as CBS camerawoman came only four years after she began her first professional assignment.

Award-Winning Foreign Correspondent

NBC News investigative reporter LIZ TROTTA has earned distinction for her coverage of the Indochina war, the 1973 Israeli-Arab conflict, and the 1974 Sahara famine. In 1965 Trotta left *Newsday* to join WNBC-TV's "Sixth Hour News" as the first woman on the local news staff. She covered New York politics and followed Eugene McCarthy during his presidential primary campaign, but within six months she embarked on a career as a foreign correspondent. Trotta covered the fighting in Vietnam from August 1968 through February 1969, work that earned her a citation from the Overseas Press Club for "best television reporting from abroad." She was reassigned to cover the India-Pakistan war of 1971 and later developments in India and Bangladesh. Subsequently she was based for a year in Singapore, where she was responsible for news reporting in 20 nations. That tour included martial law in the Philippines, political and military situations throughout Indochina, the arrival at Clark Air Force Base of the first American POWs, and a trip to Hanoi to cover the departure of the final group of POWs. Reporting on the 1974 Sahara famine, Ms. Trotta was a member of the "NBC Nightly News" team that won an Overseas Press Club award for "Best TV interpretation of foreign affairs" for special reports on the world food shortage. Her other honors have included a Woman Behind the News Award (1971) from the Los Angeles chapter of Theta Sigma Phi, and a Spirit of Achievement Award (1972) from the National Women's Division of Albert Einstein College of Medicine.

First Woman Unit Manager

Following an extensive free-lance career as associate producer on such telecasts as the Miss America pageant, the Emmy awards, and "The Bell Telephone Hour," MADELINE DAVID in 1970 joined NBC as a unit manager—the first woman to hold this position at any network. In that capacity she handled NBC-TV coverage of several major news events, including the signing of the Vietnam peace treaty in Paris. Ms. David left NBC in 1974 to join Metromedia as an associate producer on "How to Survive a Marriage" but returned in 1976 to become vice-president, daytime programs.

First to Hold Full Producership in Network Sports

The first woman to hold a full producership in network sports, ELEANOR RIGER (see also "Women in Sports and Games," p. 557) from 1965 to 1969 was manager of client relations for ABC Sports. Later she produced promotional films for ABC Sports, and also (1968) the nightly 15-minute Winter Olympics recaps from Grenoble and the Summer Olympics preview from Mexico City. After a period as a writer-producer and executive assistant in new program development at Tomorrow Entertainment,

Inc., she rejoined ABC Sports in 1973. In addition to her responsibilities as staff producer, she is in charge of production and development of sports programing for women. Her outstanding work on the Winter and Summer Olympics of 1976 won her two Emmys. Ms. Riger, who was born in Hong Kong and had her early education in British schools, was graduated magna cum laude from Smith College and was a scholarship student at the Russian Institute at Columbia University before going into television.

The *Post*'s Star: She Went Back to Print

After a four-year stint as a society reporter for the *Washington Post*, SALLY QUINN accepted in 1973, amid much publicity, a job as co-anchor of "CBS Morning News." She was to be CBS's answer to BARBARA WALTERS (p. 504). Ms. Quinn had worked for the television network previously, covering the 1968 presidential campaigns, but she found day-to-day electronic journalism intolerable and left after six months to return to the *Post*. In *We're Going to Make You a Star* (1975), her account of the fiasco, Ms. Quinn bared the foibles of network news personalities and practices. More recently she has been following the progress of the Carter administration's relationship with social Washington and in 1977 reported at length on a visit she made to Cuba.

First Regional Anchor Woman for CBS Election Coverage

As the first woman regional anchor for CBS News, LESLEY STAHL reported on the issues and results of the 1974 political campaign for the western United States. After covering Scoop Jackson's campaign for President in 1976, Ms. Stahl appeared on "Election Night '76" as the only woman onstage with Walter Cronkite to report and comment on the results of the all-important California vote. Ms. Stahl has also gained recognition for her coverage of Watergate and, more recently, for her stories on malpractice insurance, birth control pills, Red Dye ⩰2, and the U. S. Army's LSD experiments. Originally interested in a career in medicine, Ms. Stahl switched to politics in 1966 when she assisted New York mayor John Lindsay's speech writer.

First in News Directing at NBC

In 1974, when ENID ROTH was appointed director of WNBC-TV's "NewsCenter 4" in New York, she became the only woman director of a news program on a major TV station and was the lone woman member of the National Board of the Directors Guild of America. In 1976 she was the first and only woman network director of election news coverage beginning with the New Hampshire primary through the Democratic and Republican conventions to election night. Her 15 years as associate news and drama director for NBC equipped her well for the minute-by-minute directing required for a live news operation. Ms. Roth, a Brooklyn native, earned tuition money by reading radio commercials, and was graduated from Syracuse University with a degree in communications. She rose to prominence through the ranks, her first job in the TV industry having been as a secretary at CBS.

Britain's Broadcasting Women

In March 1974 there were nearly 9,000 women out of some 26,000 full-time and part-time staff of the British Broadcasting Corporation (BBC), including the manual, catering, clerical, and secretarial staff, producers, news reporters, script writers, studio managers, monitors, education officers, and research workers. There were three women governors and women were represented on the general advisory council of the BBC and on the other BBC advisory councils—for example, those for the regional, religious, and educational broadcasting, and local radio.

Women are also employed in varying capacities on the staff of the Independent Broadcasting Authority (IBA) and the commercial television and radio program companies. The advent of Independent Local Radio has provided more opportunities for women. The Independent Local Radio stations have between them 24 women on their boards. Senior staff appointments held by women include those of program controller of Radio City, general secretary of the Association of Independent Radio Companies, and sales manager of Radio Forth.

Executive Producer of CBS Weekend News

One of the few women decision makers in network news is JOAN RICHMAN. As executive producer of CBS News since September 1976, Ms. Richman guides the Saturday and Sunday editions of the "CBS Evening News" and the "CBS Sunday Night News." Before her present assignment, she was executive producer of "CBS Sports Spectacular" for the CBS television network (from July 1975) and senior producer of ABC's "The Reasoner Report" (October 1972–July 1975). Ms. Richman's career with CSB first began in 1961, when she was hired as a newspaper clipper in the company's research library. By 1968 she had risen to producer of special events. In 1971 she received an Emmy for CBS News coverage of the space flights of Apollo 13 and 14, and in 1972 she received another Emmy for coverage of Apollo 15. She has been manager of research for the 1968 national conventions, producer of the Congressional Issues Desk for "Election Night '70," and producer of CBS News's "Campaign '72." A native of St.

Louis, Ms. Richman was graduated from Wellesley College in 1961.

Highest-Level TV News Executive

In 1976 MARLENE SANDERS was named ABC's vice-president and director of television documentaries—the highest position held to that time by a woman in television news programing. Ms. Sanders joined ABC in 1964, where she had her own daily newscast, "Marlene Sanders with the Woman's Touch," and became the first woman to anchor a network evening newscast on the "ABC Evening News," substituting for an ailing anchorman. Reflecting on that and a subsequent substitution in 1972, Ms. Sanders in 1976 observed that "on local stations, management began to see that it was safe to take such a drastic step. . . . Now women reporters on television are taken for granted." In 1974 she wrote and produced "The Right to Die," which explored the ethical and legal issues surrounding the rights of the terminally ill. For this she was awarded the Ohio State Award, the Front Page Award, and the Writers Guild of America Award. Assembling an all-woman crew, she produced "Women's Health: A Question of Survival," a documentary for ABC's Closeup series, which dealt with breast cancer, birth control devices, and the Pill. This program, aired in January 1976, won for her the 1976 Clarion Award and led to her promotion to ABC vice-president. Ms. Sanders' other documentaries have examined the changing role of women in today's society, population growth, child abuse, and the legal profession. They have won for her the *McCall's* Golden Mike Award in 1964, a Brotherhood Award in 1972, and the Women in Communications Award in 1973.

First Woman to Co-Host Super Bowl

Miss America 1970 PHYLLIS GEORGE's success as a sportscaster won her a spot as a principal CBS-TV commentator for the 1976–77 National Football League season and the distinction of being the first woman to co-host a Super Bowl. On her first sports assignment, the 1974 Fiesta Bowl in Phoenix, Texas-born Ms. George discovered that her only responsibilities were to "stand around and look terrific." Complaining got her a successful interview with Boston Celtics star Dave Cowans and successive well-received interviews with O. J. Simpson, Muhammad Ali, and Jimmy Connors.

First Woman to Record the Sounds of War for a Major TV Network

When NAN SEGERMAN landed in Phnom Penh on April 2, 1975, she was the first female technician assigned to a war zone by a major network. She worked as "sound woman" with the NBC crew until they were evacuated shortly before the fall of the Cambodian capital. Back in New York, she believes that she is now the first sound technician to move into documentary production for a network. Born in New York City in 1949, Ms. Segerman received her B.F.A. from New York University's Institute of Film and Television.

First Woman Evening Network News Co-Anchor

Hailed as "Today's Woman" in a 1974 *Newsweek* cover story and named by *Time* magazine as one of the 100 most influential leaders in the United States, BARBARA WALTERS is among television's most honored journalists and the first woman in the history of network news to co-anchor an evening program. In 1975, after 12 years on NBC's popular "Today Show," she was named Broadcaster of the Year by the International Radio and Television Society and awarded an Emmy by the National Academy of Television Arts and Sciences. In 1976 she moved over to ABC to co-anchor the network's evening news program, participate in 12 "Issues and Answers" programs a year, and do a series of specials on topics of her own choosing.

Early in her career, Ms. Walters was a writer for CBS Television network news broadcasts and later became the youngest woman producer at WNBC-TV. Joining the "Today Show" in 1961 as a writer, she became a reporter-at-large within a year, co-host in 1974, and in addition, hosted her own syndicated program, "Not for Women Only" for five years. Ms. Walters scored a major coup in arranging the only TV interview with H. R. Haldeman just prior to the Nixon China trip. Her incisive questioning of Secretary of State Henry A. Kissinger, Egypt's President Anwar el-Sadat and his wife, the Shah of Iran and his wife, and Prince Philip of Great Britain made headline news, as did her 1975 trip to Cuba with Senator George McGovern, during which she interviewed Premier Fidel Castro.

In 1976 Barbara Walters was named Woman of the Year by a poll of the broadcast clients of UPI, and in 1977 presented with the Lowell Thomas award as the "outstanding electronic journalist of the year."

ABC's Only Woman Anchor Before Barbara Walters

ABC News Washington correspondent MARGARET OSMER has a distinguished record as both reporter and producer. With ABC's "Good Morning, America" she was the network's only woman anchor before BARBARA WALTERS (above). She has also appeared as interviewer on ABC's "Issues and Answers" and traveled with Rosalynn Carter to South and Central America. Her 1976 hour-long documentary for ABC's Closeup series, "Divorce: For Better or for Worse," won the National Council on Family Relations Award of 1977. As producer/correspondent for "The Reasoner Report," she obtained the first interview with the fugitive financier Robert Vesco and pro-

duced several documentaries. One, "Come Fly a Kite," won the National Press Photographers Award in 1974. She has also reported for "ABC News with Harry Reasoner" and has conducted the Saturday Closeup feature on "ABC News with Ted Koppel." Previously with CBS, Ms. Osmer covered the United Nations during the 1962 Cuban missile crisis and the 1967 war in the Middle East. In 1969, for CBS's "60 Minutes" she obtained the first U.S. interview with Libya's Qaddafi and produced the first film piece on Henry Kissinger. In 1970 she shared a Peabody Award with the "60 Minutes" crew and in 1972 produced one of the first serious documentaries on rape ("No Tears for Rachel") for Public Broadcasting's "Bill Moyers' Journal." Originally headed for a career in law, Ms. Osmer joined CBS in 1961 as a researcher in the legal department soon after graduating from Cornell University.

Youthful "Today Show" Regular

In October 1976, after less than four years of TV reporting at local Midwest stations, 26-year-old JANE PAULEY took over veteran BARBARA WALTERS' (above) spot, though not her co-host title, on NBC's "Today Show." NBC News president Richard C. Wald said that viewer response to the guest appearances of Ms. Pauley and others during the preceding summer indicated that she was "the clear favorite . . . for the assignment." She shares with host Tom Brokaw the food and other features traditionally reserved for women (and readily admits, "I can't cook to save my life"). Ms. Pauley's early rise to prominence in this highly competitive field began at WMAQ-TV, the NBC television station in Chicago, where she was that city's first woman co-anchor on a nightly news program.

Superior Achiever

Two-time recipient of RKO's Superior Achiever Award (1976 and 1977), JUNE CARTER PERRY produced and hosted three programs for WGMS Radio: "Heritage," an award-winning weekly series aired nationally by RKO and featuring such guests as Alex Haley, Andrew Young, and Senator Edward Brooke; "Soul of the Classics," a weekly one-hour black cultural presentation; and "Dialogue," a Washington-area public affairs program. Ms. Perry, well known for her work in radio within metropolitan Washington, created, wrote, produced, and hosted a special series in science, the arts, and black history for D.C. public school children. These programs were aired over WGTS-FM National Public Radio. She has held positions as a national teaching fellow and national Woodrow Wilson intern, and is a recipient of many awards (Black Achievers in Industry, 1975; American Association of University Women Media Award, 1975; D.C. Youth Orchestra Award for Community Service, 1974) and citations. As first vice-president of the Women's Institute at Washington's American University, she has "promoted the goal of 'partnership' with men in the professional world." She says, "I also strongly subscribe to that in the home as well"—

and practices it with her husband. In 1977 Ms. Perry was named special assistant for Public Affairs with the Community Services Administration.

Station Manager of Network-Owned TV Station

In January 1977 ANN BERK became station manager of NBC's flagship station, WNBC-TV in New York City. It is believed that she is the first woman station manager at any network-owned television station. Ms. Berk joined WNBC-TV in 1971 as manager of advertising and promotion. Later she advanced to director of station operations and program director. From 1966 to 1969 she had been advertising manager for the NBC radio network and the NBC radio stations. While she was advertising and promotion manager, her on-the-air campaign for WNBC-TV's "NewsCenter 4" won an award "for outstanding creativity" from the U. S. Television Commercial Festival. Another promotion and advertising campaign, for a WNBC-TV month-long program series focusing on the economy, won the Broadcasters Promotion Association On-Air Award.

From "Cookie Correspondent" to Network News

On November 6, 1977, only two months after she joined NBC News in Washington, JESSICA SAVITCH became anchor woman of the Sunday edition of "NBC Nightly News." Before then, she worked at KYW-TV in Philadelphia, starting as a general assignment reporter in November 1972 and quickly rising to anchor slots. Ms. Savitch involves herself thoroughly in her work. For one of her two series on rape, she served as a decoy while the police followed in a battered bread truck. "Rape—the Ultimate Violation" received the Clarion Award from the National Chapter of Women in Communications (1974).

She also received the Special Award for Outstanding Achievement in newscasting from the Sales and Marketing

Executives of Philadelphia (1975), the Broadcast Media Conference Award (1977), the Philadelphia Press Association Award for best news feature (1977), and the Women in Communications Award for her documentary "Lady Law," which focused on a class action suit against the Philadelphia police department for discriminating against women police officers. To do "Lady Law," Ms. Savitch went on night patrol with police in Florida and the District of Columbia, and passed a six-week course at Philadelphia's Police Academy.

She believes that her NBC job is 'the first time [her] being hired wasn't a first' —that she was hired for herself, not for her gender. In 1962, while in high school in Atlantic City, New Jersey, she was one of the first female radio disc jockeys in the country. Her first journalism jobs were covering women's news—from teas to girl scouts—a "cookie correspondent," she called herself. Later she became the first newswoman at KHOU in Houston and was promoted to anchorwoman there—was one of only three or four in the country. Moving to Philadelphia, she became the first prime-time woman anchor, then the first woman late evening anchor. Ms. Savitch, born in Kennett Square, Pennsylvania, was graduated from Ithaca College and attended graduate school at New York University.

12

Women in Business, Industry, and Finance

By Mayanne Karmin and Donna Orem

Gigi Mahon, consulting editor

As every schoolgirl doesn't know, MARY KATHERINE GODDARD published the Declaration of Independence. And MARGARET GAFFNEY, "the Breadwoman of New Orleans," founded a baked goods business in 1858 that's still bringing in the dough. For the most part, historians have ignored these and other enterprising females, possibly out of deference to the idea that a woman belonged at home and any achievements elsewhere were better overlooked. Until the 1960s, the world of business, industry, and finance was a lonely place for a woman. Moreover, many of the women at the top were those who had founded their own companies, sometimes beginning in their own homes, like MARGARET RUDKIN of Pepperidge Farm (see "Women in the Home and Community," p. 135). Or they were co-founders with their husbands of companies like Beech Aircraft Corporation, which OLIVE ANN BEECH has run masterfully for many years since her husband's death.

When *Redbook* magazine tried to draw up a list of 10 companies that offered the best employment opportunities to women in 1977, the magazine found not one worth noting. Despite the many "firsts" and breakthroughs of the past 10 years, there has been a scarcity of women at upper corporate levels and "in the pipelines" heading that way. Efforts to remedy this situation sometimes have been purposely shielded from public notice. Many a captain of industry, revising policies on hiring and promoting women, has preferred to keep a low profile lest he attract adverse attention to past discriminatory practices. And it also could be that his perception of who has, and who does not have, top management "potential" is skewed by a lack of knowledge of women's past and current managerial achievements.

For the woman with a similar perspective, this represents a serious net loss, for without knowing her own history she cannot draw strength from it to assuage the inevitable self-doubts that accompany a corporate climb. It's essential for women to know that they have a *tradition* for business success. The young, determined businesswoman can find inspiration from ELIZABETH EATON BOIT, founder of the Harvard Knitting Mill, fifth in size of the giant New England textile mills. The fact that MARGARET GETCHELL LAFORGE improved management systems and served on the executive committee during Macy's earliest years certainly says something about female "potential." The woman of today cannot draw from her enterprising forerunners if she is not aware of their existence.

Schoolboys read the same textbooks the girls do. Those incomplete records, in combination with other societal mores, have in the recent past, and even in the present, led many men and women to regard an aspiring businesswoman as something separate, almost unnatural. Some able women have actually feared success, lest their achievements be regarded as "unfeminine" or, if not that, unattractive to potential mates who resist women more successful than they.

But all things are subject to change. Although women now hold less than 1 per cent of top management jobs, the potential "pipeliners" are increasing. Almost one quarter of the current M.B.A. students are female. This may be one of the most significant achievements of the past 10 years. There are more.

In 1974 the National Association of Women Business Owners (p. 516) was founded to provide access to customers, technical assistance, an "old girls' network," a policy voice in government practices, and other forms of mutual assistance. The book *The Managerial Woman* (1977) by MARGARET HENNIG and ANNE JARDIM highlighted reasons why women may not know the rules of the corporate game. Not all women will agree with everything these remarkably popular authors set forth, but their point that the successful executive constantly assesses her situation to uncover any obstacles in her path is well taken. How a woman plays the game can determine whether she wins or loses.

In business, industry, and finance, women continue to face different, and perhaps greater, problems than their male counterparts. Generally, the dividing line between middling success and outstanding achievement is how these problems are handled. Female executives and entrepreneurs can look to the past to draw strength to cope with their challenges. In the late 1970s, they can view their present with increasing pride. And they can undoubtedly look to a future with a better "bottom line."

MAYANNE SHERMAN KARMIN *is director of communications for the National Training & Development Service, Washington, D.C., which provides management training to government officials throughout the country. Before that she was a consultant with John Adams Associates, Inc., a Washington, D.C., public affairs concern. She served on the board of directors of a suburban Maryland bank that initiated the area's first "women's headquarters," and in 1973 won an award for feature writing. Ms. Karmin, daughter of the noted vaudevillian* MARIE WHITE *of "Marie White and the Blue Slickers," is a graduate of Russell Sage College, where she majored in business.*

DONNA MARIE OREM, *an editorial assistant at the National Training & Development Service, has been working toward her master's degree in journalism at the University of Maryland. She has a B.A. in English literature from St. Joseph's College, Philadelphia.*

Consulting editor GIGI MAHON *is an associate editor and feature writer with* Barron's Financial Weekly. *A 1971 graduate of Boston University's School of Public Communications, Ms. Mahon started out as an assistant editor of* Mademoiselle *magazine and later worked in research on Wall Street. She writes a monthly column on personal finance for* Mademoiselle *and free-lances on nonfinancial subjects.*

FOUNDERS AND OWNERS

She Helped to Found the International Harvester Company

NETTIE FOWLER MCCORMICK (1835–1923), an astute businesswoman, married in 1857 to Cyrus Hall McCormick, inventor and manufacturer of the McCormick mechanical reaper, was a moving force in consolidating her husband's farm machine industry into what eventually would be known as the International Harvester Company. She was his right-hand woman, serving alternately as private secretary and business counsel, and eventually became president of the firm after his death in 1884. Known also for her extensive philanthropy, Ms. McCormick contributed to more than 40 schools and colleges throughout the United States and was the leading American benefactor of the Presbyterian Church.

Anna Bissell's 60 million Carpet Sweepers

An invention bearing the name of one of the first female American corporation presidents celebrated its 100th birthday and the "60 million sold" mark in 1976.

The Bissell carpet sweeper, conceived and patented in 1876 by Melville R Bissell, a Grand Rapids shopkeeper and part-time inventor, was nurtured to financial maturity by his enterprising wife ANNA BISSELL—first sharing in and later directing the company.

Early production of carpet sweepers relied heavily on women working in their homes, where they wound tufts of hog bristles with string, dipped them in hot pitch, inserted them in brush rollers, and trimmed them with scissors.

Each day Ms. Bissell collected the brush parts in clothes baskets and hauled them by horse and buggy to a loft above the Bissells' crockery shop. There they were fitted into solid walnut cases supplied by a local cabinetmaker.

Then the Bissells took to the road, traveling from city to city in the Midwest and East, to sell their sweeper to merchants and housewives, often demonstrating by picking up a handful of dirt and throwing it on the floor before prospective customers, who watched popeyed as dirt dramatically "disappeared" into the sweeper. The price was a dirt-cheap $1.50.

With Bissell's death in 1888, his widow Anna took over as president of the 12-year-old company, steering Bissell through its formative years, and establishing national distribution. Ms. Bissell remained active in management until the 1920s, and held the position of chairman of the Board until her death in 1934.

First to Found Major U.S. Cosmetics Company

HARRIET HUBBARD AYER (1849–1903) in 1886 became the first U.S. woman to found a major cosmetics company. She started with a line of facial cream that she discovered in Paris, which she claimed had been used by Madame Récamier, a famous beauty of Napoleon's day. Packaging it with her name along with Madame Récamier's on the label, Ms. Ayer, a pioneer in modern merchandising methods, used extensive newspaper advertising to sell her product. She eventually lost control of the company and in 1896 began a new career as a beauty columnist for the *New York World,* remaining on the staff until her death in 1903.

First to Introduce Gelatin as a Dessert Food

ROSE MARKWARD KNOX (1857–1950), with her husband, Charles, established a business in 1890 that introduced gelatin, originally considered a food for invalids, as a dessert. The Knoxes instituted an extensive promotional campaign to sell their product to the general public. With the death of her husband in 1908, Ms. Knox focused her advertising campaign on women, setting up experimental kitchens and fellowships at the Mellon Institute to discover new uses for gelatin. Long a member of the American Grocery Manufacturers' Association, she became the first woman elected to its board of directors in 1929.

They Founded the First All-Women Secretarial Schools in the United States

A 33-year-old schoolteacher, MARY SEYMOUR, opened the Union School of Stenography and Typewriting in New York City in 1879. This was not the first business college to offer typewriting instruction, but it was the first whose entire student body was made up of women.

Ms. Seymour knew the importance of a woman getting her foot in the office door, as did KATHARINE GIBBS (1865–1934), who established the first school for secretaries 32 years later. A 46-year-old widow with two sons and no experience, Ms. Gibbs opened the school with proceeds from the sale of her jewelry. She felt that no existing school offered adequate education for women who wanted to be secretaries, and therefore developed a curriculum of business law and liberal arts as well as secretarial subjects to meet the market need she had correctly identified. With the increase in demand for trained women brought on by World War I, Ms. Gibbs's school flourished. "Kate Gibbs" has long been the most prestigious secretarial school in the United States.

Forerunner of the Management Consultant

A brilliant intellectual who always worked as a volunteer, MARY PARKER FOLLETT developed revoluntionary solutions for business and industrial problems of her time that form the basis of management training to this day. Ms. Follett, born 1868 in Quincy, Massachusetts, never married and was able to pursue her interest in group psychology and industrial management without concern for income because of a private inheritance. She attended the Women's College at Harvard (later Radcliffe) for two years, studied philosophy at Newnham College, Cambridge, 1890–91, and returned to Radcliffe in 1891–92 and 1894–97, taking time out to write *The Speaker of the House of Representatives* (1896), the first work on that office and an important contribution to constitutional law.

She received her B.A. summa cum laude in 1898 at age 29, and began a volunteer career in social work. This activity convinced her that neighborhood groups, not big political parties, were the key to democratic social development, and on the basis of it she wrote *The New State* (1918), widely reviewed in the United States and Britain. Her vocational guidance work and her membership on minimum wage-setting boards introduced her to businessmen and turned her interest to industrial relations. In 1924 she published *Creative Experience,* in which she wrote that "majority rule" and the use of experts would not solve social problems and advocated "integration" (or "interpenetration of minds"), in which real interests are discussed and identified, then solved by consensus. She believed that labor relations should be a creative encounter between worker and employer.

A friendly, soft-spoken woman and a good listener with provocative ideas, she liked businessmen and their tendency to talk more from experience than in generalities, and to be more open to fresh concepts. In 1925 she presented four papers before the Bureau of Personnel Administration in New York City and began a lecture career in industrial management. Some of her practical suggestions: Give orders about the work to be done, not according to status; pay attention to semantics ("Adjustments" is better than "Complaints Department"). She urged that management be viewed as a profession like medicine and law, with its own professional education, ethical code, and responsibility for public welfare. From 1928 on Ms. Follett lived in London, where she delivered her final lectures at the London School of Economics in February 1933. She died later that year.

She Made Cosmetics Respectable

ELIZABETH ARDEN (1884–1966), originally FLORENCE NIGHTINGALE GRAHAM, founded a cosmetics corporation that still operates under her adopted name. She was perhaps the most influential among a group of women including HARRIET HUBBARD AYER (p. 510) and HELENA RUBINSTEIN (p. 518) who raised the use of beauty aids from their onetime connection with "low women" to their present status as an acceptable (even essential) part of all women's (and, increasingly, men's) lives. Ms. Arden also founded "Maine Chance"—the first of the health-and-beauty spas that are now so numerous in the United States—and bred and raised racehorses. She cofounded her corporation with another woman in 1910. The partnership eventually split up. At the time of her death, there were more than 100 Elizabeth Arden beauty salons in principal cities throughout the world, and the corporation was manufacturing and marketing some 300 products.

The BPW

"Equal pay for equal work . . ." was included in the call sent forth by Kentucky lawyer LENA MADESON PHILLIPS in 1919 when she founded the first organization for women of varying professional and

First Black Millionaire Businesswoman

SARAH BREEDLOVE (Madame C. J.) WALKER (1867–1919) is generally credited with being the first black woman millionaire. She earned her fortune through development of "the Walker method," hair-straightening process for Negro women. Her company, the Madame C. J. Walker Manufacturing Company, of which she was founder-president and sole owner, gave employment to over 3,000 persons, principally women. Many of them, known as "Walker agents," made house calls throughout the United States and the Caribbean selling and delivering Walker products. In 1913 she organized her carriers into "Walker Clubs," giving cash prizes to the ones who did the greatest amount of community philanthropic work. She also instituted a hygienic regimen for her employees that later was incorporated into state cosmetology laws.

Her Business Was Music

In 1915 ADELLA PRENTISS HUGHES (1869–1950) formed an organization of Cleveland businessmen that would later underwrite the founding of the Cleveland Orchestra in 1918. Ms. Hughes served as the orchestra's business manager for 15 years and raised most of the money necessary for its support. She also played a significant role in planning and fund raising for a new concert auditorium, Severance Hall, completed in 1931. Upon her death in 1950, the Cleveland Plain Dealer noted two of her most outstanding qualities: "business acumen of the highest order coupled with an exceptional talent for social diplomacy."

business backgrounds, the National Federation of Business and Professional Women's Clubs, Inc., informally referred to as BPW. The stage had been set for Ms. Phillips' action by the federal government's funding of the National Businesswomen's Commission when it was realized that no women's organization drawing members from various fields existed and such a group could help the nation's 1917–18 war effort.

Ms. Phillips' group would help the nation and more, it would help women too. Her call did not go unheeded. BPW now has 165,000 members in more than 3,700 clubs in 50 countries (the International Federation was founded in Geneva in 1930).

The organization itself was a first. So were many of its activities. In 1919 BPW undertook the first national survey of working women, and in 1922 called for uniform marriage and divorce laws. In 1924 BPW endorsed the proposed Equal Rights Amendment and has been a staunch supporter ever since, voting to raise $250,000 in a year in 1973 to help the drive for ERA ratification. (Subsequently, membership dues were raised to provide the same amount of money every year.) As early as 1928 the organization established National Businesswomen's Week, which is held each year in October—a useful reminder to all women that Ms. Phillips' call for "equal pay for equal work" has been only partially achieved.

Co-Founder of Billion-Dollar Hotel, Restaurant Chain

In 1927 ALICE S. MARRIOTT and her husband John opened a small restaurant in Washington, D.C. Today that restaurant has grown into the billion-dollar Marriott Corporation. Originally called Hot Shoppes, Inc., the large chain includes hotels, restaurants, fast-food shops, and a cruise line. Ms. Marriott serves as vice-president and director of the corporation.

First Woman to Run a Large Shipping Company

Becoming co-owner of the Indian Scindia Steam Navigation Company in 1929, SUMATI MORARJEE, together with her husband, who inherited the company from his father, expanded the business to include over 50 ships. In 1957 she negotiated an exemption for Indian shipping from the wealth tax on companies, and has continued to be a vital force in her nation's maritime industry.

Co-Founder of Large Aircraft Corporation

In 1932 OLIVE ANN BEECH and her husband, Walter, founded Beech Aircraft Corporation, a small commercial enterprise that she eventually converted into a huge defense company. The firm supplied the planes on which 90 per cent of all American bombardiers and navigators were trained in World War II. Assuming various duties with the corporation, she took full control of the firm after the death of her husband in 1950. With stern hand and keen mind, she successfully boosted sales, increasing them to well over $200 million today. She is active in many organizations and serves on the advisory board of the National Air and Space Museum of the Smithsonian Institution.

First to Introduce Italian Tomato Industry in the United States

Determination and ingenuity are the key words behind the success of TILLIE LEWIS (born MYRTLE ERLICH), the entrepreneur who introduced the Italian tomato industry to the United States. Ms. Lewis began her business career at age 12 folding kimonos at $2.50 a week for a Brooklyn garment manufacturer. That was in 1913; by 1932 she was making $12,000 a year selling securities on commission. In 1934, under the direction of Florindo del Gaizo, a Naples canner who was the leading exporter of Italian tomatoes, Ms. Lewis founded Flothill Products, Inc., to produce, can, and market these tomatoes in the United States. Although there was a certain amount of hesitation on the part of the farmers who were to grow the tomatoes, her business was a success within a year. Ms. Lewis sold her company to the Ogden Corporation in 1966 for $9 million and became the first woman director of this billion-dollar company.

Founder of Gasoline Marketing Company

MARY HUDSON VANDEGRIFT has remained tops in her field since founding Hudson Oil Company, Kansas City, Kansas, in the 1930s. An independent gasoline marketer, Ms. Vandegrift has managed to keep her firm afloat and prosperous despite tremendous odds during the Depression era and more recently the Arab oil embargo. Hudson Oil today has more than 300 stations in 35 states and revenues in excess of $175 million.

Ghanaian Founder of Large Fruit Drink and Bottling Industry

In 1943 ESTHER OCLOO made her mark on a male-dominated business by founding her own fruit drink and bottling industry in Ghana. She studied various preserving processes in England, and eventually extended her business to the canning of soup. The founder of many women's associations in Ghana, Ms. Ocloo has been active in encouraging village women to raise their standard of living by learning trades.

Chairman/Co-Founder of the 1970s' Leading Cosmetics Company

Few entrepreneurs of either sex can match the panache of ESTÉE LAUDER, who pioneered the giveaway sample as a marketing technique and is considered today's reigning beauty queen. In 1946 she co-founded, with her husband Joseph, the cosmetics company that bears her name and of which she is chairwoman. Fourteen years later the company reached the million-dollar sales mark. By 1974 Estée Lauder, Inc., was coolly looking toward 200 million in sales and was still entirely family-owned. "The first million is the hardest," Ms. Lauder has said. Prestigious department and specialty stores throughout the United States and in 70 foreign countries sell the Lauder products.

President/Founder, Large Scientific Supply Firm

With keen insight into a growth industry, NAN WOOD almost thirty years ago founded N. Wood Counter Laboratory, Inc., for the purpose of supplying radiation detectors to scientists and to the nuclear industry. While developing her own career, she also devoted time to advancing the interests of women throughout the United States and served as national secretary for the National Organization for Women from 1968 to 1975.

Chairperson and Founder of Largest Textile Company in Taiwan

In 1951 VIVIAN YEN set up and has since managed a textile-manufacturing company, eventually turning it into the top company in the major industry of Taiwan. Since then the Tai Yuen Textile Company has won many awards, including the quality prize from the Chinese Society of Quality Control and the export award from the Board of Foreign Trade. In addition Ms. Yen is also managing director and executive vice-president of Yue Loong Motor Company, one of Taiwan's largest automotive businesses. Astute but unassuming, she attributes her success to "a case of fortune knocking at my door."

Only Female Head of Fortune 500 Company

KATHARINE GRAHAM, president of the Washington Post Company, is principal owner and working boss of the most powerful news publishing syndicate in the United States. She took over the media empire, founded by her father, on her husband's death in 1963. In addition to the *Washington Post,* her company owns *Newsweek* magazine, paper mills, and other newspaper and TV properties. Colleagues and competitors alike pay tribute to her business acumen and unfailing journalistic professionalism—the latter demonstrated in allowing maximum responsibility to editors, paying top salaries to attract top reporting talent, and in her courageous support of the *Post*'s 1973–74 investigation of Watergate.

She Started World's Largest Secretarial Service

MARGERY HURST, founder and managing director of the Brook Street Bureau of Mayfair, Ltd., and one of the first women members of Lloyd's of London, elected in 1970, established schools and colleges for administrative and secretarial studies, and the Society for International Secretaries (London, 1960). The Society now has non-profit social clubs in New York, San Francisco, Boston, and Sydney. She is joint chairperson of the Bureau and a spokeswoman for women's equality. Margery Hurst was awarded the Pimm's Cup for Anglo-American business friendship (1962), served on the American Committee of the British National Economic Commission (1967–70) and on the executive committee of the Mental Health Research Fund (1967–72), and was awarded the Order of the British Empire (1976). Her autobiography, *No Glass Slipper,* was published in 1967.

Co-Founder/Manager of Top German Insurance Company

Manager of an insurance company that she founded with her husband, MARGOT HAMBURGER is responsible for moving her company into the top position in the German insurance world, and for establishing contacts around the world.

First Female Member, National Association of Minority Contractors

GILDA BOJORQUEZ GJURICH, founder and president of Amigos Construction Company, is the first female member of both the National Association of Minor-

ity Contractors and the California Association of Mexican-American Contractors. A native Californian of Mexican descent, she has worked for over 20 years in the construction industry. In 1974 Ms. Gjurich received the Outstanding Woman of the Year Award from the Mexican-American Opportunity Foundation and in 1977 was appointed to the National Commission for the Observance of International Women's Year.

Chairwoman and Co-Founder of Large Cosmetics Company

In 1963 MARY KAY ASH co-founded with her son a cosmetics company that goes under the name of Mary Kay Cosmetics, Inc. As chairwoman of a relatively new company in a tight market, Ms. Ash has managed to boost revenues from $200,000 in its first year of operations to over $35 million in annual sales today. According to *Business Week,* Ms. Ash began her own business because she found male refusal to give women a chance too forbidding.

Co-Founder of Merchandising Company

Judging from PATRICIA SCHOENBERG, the ladder to the top is not all that steep; for her it was just a short climb from temporary secretary in 1963 to executive vice-president in 1969. As co-founder and executive vice-president of International Merchandising Associates, Inc., Ms. Schoenberg represents a growing field of consumer electronic products. Of her success, Ms. Schoenberg quotes a favorite saying of her grandmother's, "You can't keep a good man down, and you cannot pull a bad man up."

Chief Executives of Only Top 20 Public Relations Agency Owned by Women

In 1970 two sisters, JEAN WAY SCHOONOVER and BARBARA HUNTER, bought the controlling interest in the public relations firm Dudley-Anderson-Yutzy, making it the only PR agency in the Top 20 to be owned by women. Ms. Schoonover began her employment at D-A-Y, the oldest PR counseling firm in the nation, in 1950 as a food field reporter, with Ms. Hunter entering the firm six years later and moving into her sister's spot. After 20 years of experience as account executive of every major account in the agency, Ms. Schoonover assumed the presidency. The same year, Ms. Hunter became executive vice-president in charge of coordinating consumer education programs as well as specializing in food and other consumer-product publicity. Both women have earned the respect of the public relations industry, with Ms. Schoonover recently being elected first woman president of the New York Public Relations Society. Ms. Hunter was elected a trustee of the Foundation for Public Relations Research and Education in 1977.

Chief Executive/Founder of Major Advertising Agency May Be Highest-Paid U.S. Businesswoman

MARY WELLS LAWRENCE, chairwoman of the Board and chief executive officer since 1971 of Wells, Rich, Greene, Inc., is one of the most powerful advertising executives in the country and the most influential woman in the industry. In 1966 Ms. Lawrence and two colleagues at another agency founded the firm she now heads. Within seven years it had soared to thirteenth in billings in a ranking of 689 agencies compiled by *Advertising Age.* Believed to be the highest-paid woman executive in the United States for several years running, Ms. Lawrence has a base salary (until 1981) of $225,000 plus deferred compensation of $30,000 a year, plus incentive awards. Those figures do not include any stock earnings (of record in 1975 she owned about one fourth of the agency's shares) or income from sales of stock. Ms. Lawrence began her advertising career with a year's stint (1951–52) at McKel-vey's Department Store in her hometown of Youngstown, Ohio. She worked for several outstanding New York advertising agencies, progressively bettering her position and pay. She turned down a 10-year million-dollar-contract offer to found her own business.

First Washington Black Woman to Establish Commercial Design Firm

INEZ AUSTIN, president of Jumanne Design, Inc., is the first black woman to establish and incorporate a commercial design firm in Washington, D.C. In 1973 Ms. Austin's firm won its first major contract, for all of the design aspects of the new Harambee House Hotel, the first black-owned luxury hotel in the nation's capital. Immediately prior to founding her own company, Ms. Austin was senior contract designer for Sears, Roebuck and Company, where she designed an innovative showroom for contract interiors.

They Founded the Organization for Women Business Owners

In 1972 U.S. women entrepreneurs did not have an organization to which they could turn for assistance with business problems, or through which they could exercise their collective influence to broaden business opportunities for women. Thirteen women in Washington, D.C., changed all that. ANNE BANVILLE, ANN BARKER, KATHLEEN BOWERS, DENISE CAVANAUGH, DOROTHY COOK, SUSAN EISENBERG, DAISY FIELDS, JOSEPHINE GIBSON, SUSAN HAGAR, MARY KING, KATHY KRAEMER, JINX MELIA and GILLIAN NIXON founded the Association of Women Business Owners. National interest was immediate and by 1974 the AWBO had expanded to become the National Association of Women Business Owners.

Generally NAWBO members are more oriented to the "bottom line" than to the

Women's Movement. While they encourage and assist themselves and others in the economic arena, business decisions are usually based upon careful consideration of hard financial and other data. The new organization has attracted corporate funding for various projects, including the publication of a directory of women business owners throughout the nation. They have brought the interests of women in business to the attention of Congress, federal departments, and the White House.

In 1977 NAWBO appointed its first executive director, HELENE C. BLOOM. That same year President Jimmy Carter established a new Interagency Task Force on Women Business Owners to identify obstacles that discourage women from entering business, including federal discriminatory practices. CHARLOTTE TAYLOR, a former management consultant, was appointed executive director of the new federal task force.

EXECUTIVES AT, OR NEAR, THE TOP

Business Promotion Pioneer

As secretary-treasurer for her father's company, KATE GLEASON (1865–1933) instituted a business promotion campaign that turned a small machine tool factory into the leading American producer of gear-cutting machinery. Ms. Gleason began her career as a bookkeeper in the family-held company and plotted her advancement with the encouragement of her mother, a staunch suffragist. She served as the family company's chief sales representative, traveling widely in the United States and Europe between 1890 and 1913. In 1913 Ms. Gleason ventured out on her own, nursing another machine tool factory, which had been ailing, back to financial health. Later she served as the president of the First National Bank of East Rochester, New York, helping to launch eight new businesses in the East Rochester area. She experimented with the construction of low-cost housing attached to various recreational facilities, activities that foreshadowed the national trend toward suburban development.

Her Every Word Was Worth its Weight in Gold

BERNICE FITZ-GIBBONS, famous in the advertising industry for over 40 years, is probably best known for coining the Macy's slogan, "It's smart to be thrifty,"

and the Gimbels retort, "Nobody, but nobody, undersells Gimbels." She was long one of the highest-paid women in advertising; Gimbels gave her $90,000 per year to "play ball on their side." Ms. Fitz-Gibbons, who believed that advertising agencies were "overmanned and undergirled," also is remembered for the slogan, "If you want more legal tender, hire more of the female gender."

Famous Retail Executive

In 1946, when DOROTHY SHAVER (1897–1959) became president of Lord & Taylor, she also became the first woman to assume the presidency of a major department store. Reportedly, Ms. Shaver earned $110,000 per year for her efforts. She joined Lord & Taylor in 1927, 10 years later was appointed first vice-president, and served as president from 1946 until her death in 1959. Under her leadership, both the store and its president became famous. Ms. Shaver also raised the status of American designers and the Seventh Avenue fashion industry by according recognition to the achievements of these groups long before others realized their import. She was elected director or trustee of numerous philanthropic and cultural organizations, received many honorary degrees, and was made a chevalier of the Legion of Honor by France in 1950.

First to Develop Cosmetic Techniques for Television

As executive vice-president of the Helena Rubinstein Corporation, MALA RUBINSTEIN, daughter of the founder, Madame HELENA RUBINSTEIN, in the 1950s developed makeup shades and techniques for television, promoting the company's cosmetics to a new, much wider audience. Perhaps even more notable were the services she provided for the handicapped, creating camouflage makeup for disfigured veterans and developing a program of skin care for the blind. She has received numerous honors for her many philanthropic endeavors.

President of New York City Specialty Store

GERALDINE STUTZ was a well-versed professional woman in the fashion field before being named president of Henri Bendel, a New York City specialty store, in 1957. She began her career as an associate fashion editor for *Glamour* magazine in 1947 and became the fashion and promotion director for I. Miller & Sons, New York City, in 1953, assuming that company's vice-presidency a year later. Since taking charge of Henri Bendel, Ms. Stutz has been instrumental in making the store one of Manhattan's most innovative.

Only Woman Executive to Deal Regularly with a Major Union

GERTRUDE G. MICHELSON, vice-president for consumer and employee relations at Macy's, New York, in a tough job with a unique distinction has been the only woman in the United States to deal regularly with a major union. Hired by Macy's in 1947 as a member of the executive training squad, Ms. Michelson achieved her vice-presidency in 1963.

RCA's First Female Vice-President

As vice-president and general manager of NBC's radio network, MARION STEPHENSON became the RCA Corporation's first female vice-president and No. 2 executive at the network. Ms. Stephenson began her career with NBC in 1944 and was director of business affairs and vice-president of administration for the radio network before assuming the vice-presidency in 1966. She is in charge of sales, programs, and the operations of affiliates.

From Junior Chemist to Executive VP

JULIETTE M. MORAN began her work with the GAF Corporation in New York City as a junior chemist and 24 years later, in 1967, attained the position of executive vice-president for communications services. As director of all communications ventures for the billion-dollar company, Ms. Moran gained a salary and bonuses package of more than $120,000 per year, helping to close the rewards gap between women and their equally qualified male counterparts.

President and Chairwoman, World's Largest Hobby Company

ROYLE G. LASKY, president and chairwoman of Revell, Inc., Los Angeles, heads the world's largest model and hobby company, with subsidiaries and licensees in eight foreign countries. She began her career in 1957, served as vice-president, product development (1962–69), and as executive vice-president before becoming president of Revell in 1970. In 1972, she became chairwoman of the Board. Under her direction, sales of the multimillion-dollar company have doubled, and profits have increased tenfold. In 1971 and 1972 Ms. Lasky was named Industrialist of the Year by the Los Angeles Chapter of the Society of Manufacturing Engineers.

Senior VP for Corporate Information at McGraw-Hill

As senior vice-president for corporate management information services at

McGraw-Hill, Inc., BERYL ROBICHAUD directs the computerization of one of the nation's largest publishing houses. Beginning her career at McGraw-Hill in 1946 as the accounting systems manager, Ms. Robichaud moved up the data-processing ladder to her vice-presidency, which she assumed in 1971.

Avon Ladies

Avon Products, Inc., the world's largest cosmetics company, began in 1886 as the California Perfume Company. Shortly thereafter, Ms. P. F. E. ALBEE sallied forth calling on housewives to sell them the company's wares. She was the first of approximately 450,000 Avon ladies who have gone "calling" in the United States, Canada, and 15 foreign countries.

Today the billion-dollar corporation is an industry leader, in no small measure due to the efforts of this incredible sales force. Nonetheless, corporate policy at Avon Products, Inc., historically has been to let other companies go first in testing and developing the market for new products. A similar hesitation can be detected in the company's personnel decisions. Most major cosmetics companies have long had (or been founded by) female executives. Not until 1972 were women brought into the previously all-male officer ranks at Avon. That year PHYLLIS DAVIS was named vice-president for advertising, PATRICIA NEIGHBORS vice-president for district management field operations, and CECILY CANNAN SELBY became the first woman ever to be elected to the Avon board of directors. In 1974 ERNESTA G. PROCOPE, president of E. G. Bowan, the nation's largest black-owned insurance brokerage firm, joined Ms. Selby as an Avon Board member.

Influential Record Company Executive

ESTHER G. EDWARDS became an administrator of Motown when the firm was founded, and grew along with it to her present status of senior vice-president. For the first years of the record company's existence, few outsiders knew that Ms. Edwards was the sister of the firm's founder, Berry Gordy. "It just seemed like we'd be more effective if people thought they were talking to a vice-president," she said. The company is now the largest independent record manufacturer in the world, and Ms. Edwards is considered to be one of the nation's most influential black businesswomen. She is a trustee of the School of Management, University of Michigan-Dearborn and in 1973 became the first woman in its 79-year history to be elected to the board of directors of the Greater Detroit chamber of commerce.

Avco's High-Paid Research VP

Physical chemist DOROTHY M. SIMON has distinguished herself as both a researcher and an administrator in a predominantly male field. She has an international reputation in combustion and has been vice-president of research at the Avco Corporation, Greenwich, Connecticut, since 1972. There she conducts and oversees most of the research for the $1.3 billion conglomerate. Dr. Simon earns more than $100,000 per year. She began her career in 1941 as a graduate teaching assistant at the University of Illinois.

She's Been to the Top of Many Mountains

In 1966 JANE CAHILL PFEIFFER took a year's leave of absence from IBM and headed for Washington, D.C., as the first woman ever appointed a White House fellow. Lyndon B. Johnson was then President. At the end of her fellowship, Ms. Pfeiffer returned to IBM, where she had begun her career as a systems engineer and had headed the company's Bermuda installation, which tracks missiles from Cape Canaveral. She entered the

IBM executive suite as administrative assistant to the chairman of the Board. Promotions came quickly and within a few years she was appointed vice-president and director of corporate communications. In 1976 another U.S. President, Jimmy Carter, offered Ms. Pfeiffer the post of Secretary of Commerce. She was the first woman in history to be so honored, but she was unable to accept the position, filled by JUANITA KREPS (see "Women in Education, Social Sciences, and the Humanities," p. 409). Ms. Pfeiffer, a graduate of the University of Maryland who began her career as a fifth-grade teacher, is at present a management consultant.

Key Executive of Largest Black-Owned Manufacturing Company in the World

DOROTHY MCCONNER, vice-president for administration and corporate secretary since 1973 of Johnson Products Company, has played the key role in shaping the business and public affairs policies of the largest manufacturing company controlled by blacks in the world. Joining Johnson Products, which manufactures hair care and facial cosmetics, in 1960 as a clerk-typist, Ms. McConner quickly moved up the ranks to senior management. In 1974 she was named to the board of directors of the Chicago Economic Development Corporation; in 1975 she was named Urban Leaguer of the Year by the Chicago Urban League, and Businesswoman of the Year by the *Blackbook*.

High-Level Executive in Auto Industry

The first top female executive at the Ford Motor Company, MARY BETH STEARNS was a senior research scientist in 1973 when she acquired this title. Now, as principal scientist, she sets the direction of research at Ford. A 17-year employee of the large auto company, Dr. Stearns has her Ph.D. in physics from Cornell.

First Woman VP/General Manager in Broadcasting

Vice-president/general manager of WVON radio station in Chicago, BERNADINE C. WASHINGTON was the first female in the broadcast media to hold this high a post. In 1973 she was chosen Woman of the Year by the National Association of Radio and Television Announcers and had the honor of having a day named after her by the mayor of Chicago in 1971. She is also one of the first two women accepted for membership in the Chicago Economic Club.

Economist Vice-President of Trade Association Position

A powerful woman in a demanding position, economist NORMA PACE commands industry respect as senior vice-president for the American Paper Institute, the national trade association for pulp, paper, and paperboard companies. Joining the Institute as vice-president in 1973, she moved to the position of senior vice-president in less than one year. Formerly a consultant to such corporations as General Motors, General Electric, and Sears, Roebuck, she now serves on a variety of corporate boards including Sperry-Rand, Sears, and Milton Bradley.

First High-Ranking Executive in Public Utilities Industry

VIRGINIA SMITH claimed the title of the first top-ranking woman in the public utilities industry with her appointment as vice-president and corporate secretary of Intermountain Gas Company, Boise, Idaho, in 1974. In her role as vice-president of the over $60 million utility company, Ms. Smith supervises the personnel and communications departments, while as corporate secretary she serves as a liaison between Intermountain's directors and executives. Ms. Smith has been with the company for more than 30 years.

First Management-Level Woman in Top Furniture Company

Determining markets, selecting designs or products, and then promoting the actual sale of a successful line of contract furniture is the responsibility of JOAN M. BURGASSER, vice-president of marketing services and design at Thonet, in York, Pennsylvania. Ms. Burgasser joined Thonet in 1957 as a designer, was director of design for three years, and became the first woman to be elevated to the management level when she assumed her present position in 1974. The line that Ms. Burgasser represents accounts for over $20 million in sales for this independent affiliate of Simmons Corporation.

Outstanding Public Relations Executive

Considered by many to be the top-ranking woman in public relations, MURIEL Fox commands a powerful position in the industry as group vice-president, senior consultant and member of the executive committee of Carl Byoir & Associates. The company, located in New York City, presently ranks as the third largest public relations firm in the United States. Ms. Fox joined Byoir in 1950 as a TV-radio writer and was appointed to her present post in 1974. She has served in various capacities in professional and civic organizations and was a founder of the National Organization for Women (NOW) in 1967 and vice-president of NOW until 1970. Ms. Fox began her career as an art critic and bridal editor with the *Miami* (Florida) *News*.

First Female Officer in Large Forest Products Company

As vice-president and corporate secretary of the Boise-Cascade Corporation, ALICE E. HENNESSEY in 1974 became the first woman among 24 high-level officials of this $1.5 billion forest products company. In a field where women are virtually unrepresented, Ms. Hennessey oversees the many facets of the company's relations with the Board, investors, shareholders, and the public at large. She began working at Boise-Cascade in 1958 as secretary to the president and advanced to her present position in 1974.

Executive VP and One of the Most Influential Women in Advertising

REVA KORDA, executive vice-president of Ogilvy & Mather, Inc., New York City, one of the top 10 advertising agencies, is probably the second-ranking advertising woman in the United States. A competitive woman in a creative field, she began her career as a copywriter for Gimbels, New York City, in 1949 but quickly switched to Macy's in the same position just one year later. Hired as a writer by Ogilvy & Mather in 1953, she moved up the ranks to become senior vice-president in 1962 and attained her present position in 1974.

From Assistant Shoe Buyer to President of Butterick in Nine Years

JANE ROSSER EVANS, who was born in Hannibal, Missouri, became president of the Butterick Fashion Marketing Company in 1974, just nine years after beginning her career. Ms. Evans received a B.A. from Vanderbilt University, attended the Fashion Institute of Technology, signed on as an executive trainee at Genesco, Inc., Nashville, and became assistant shoe buyer for that corporation's I. Miller division—all in 1965. By 1970 she had attained the presidency of the I. Miller division. From 1973 to 1974 Ms. Evans was a member of the advisory board, Genesco, Inc., and vice-president, international marketing, Genesco's International Group. Among other professional affiliations, she is a member of the Young Presidents Organization.

First Officer in Bell System

GRACE FIPPINGER became the first woman executive in the Bell System when she assumed the position of vice-president and secretary-treasurer of the New York Telephone Company in 1974. She supervises the general services department, handles corporate financing and banking policy, and administers a $1 billion pension fund. Ms. Fippinger began her career with the company in 1948 fresh out of St. Lawrence University, and earned successively more responsible positions leading to her present post. She is a member of the board of directors of several other major corporations and has been honored as Woman of the Year by chapters of the Business and Professional Women and Soroptimist.

Top Insurance Industry Executive

PHYLLIS A. CELLA, the first woman to become a full vice-president with the John Hancock Mutual Life Insurance Company, was promoted to that position in 1975, and the same year was appointed president and chief executive officer of Hanesco Insurance Company, a Hancock subsidiary. Ms. Cella has been with the firm since shortly after her graduation from Boston University, where she trained as a teacher. Instead, she became a statistician. She moved to a management position in 1943, continued her climb through the corporate structure, and is now one of the most important women in the insurance industry. Ms. Cella serves on the advisory committee to the M.B.A. program for women at Simmons College, Boston.

Vice-Chairwoman, Amtrak

Railroad executive MARY JOHNSTON HEAD successfully transferred management experience and knowledge of transportation issues gained through service on various advisory committees to an appointment to the Board of Amtrak in 1974. The following year she became vice-chairwoman. She serves as a liaison between Amtrak and the nation's railroads, is instrumental in developing new routes for the Amtrak network, and represents the rail network on Capitol Hill.

Toy and Game Company Executive Who Decides What Will Sell

In her capacity since 1974 as vice-president for market research at Milton Bradley Company, Springfield, Massachusetts, DOROTHY F. WORCESTER virtually directs what toys and games will be placed on the American market each year. The first woman to attain such high status with the company, she has veto power over the 50 new toys and games the company produces each year and is responsible for more than half of the company's over $174 million in sales. In 1976 Ms. Worcester took on the added responsibility of director of creative services for the company's newly formed subsidiary, MB Communications, Inc. For the first time that year and again in 1977 the company won U. S. Television Commercial Festival awards for the creativity of their advertising. A cum laude graduate of Radcliffe in 1950, Ms. Worcester was appointed to the Citizens Stamp Advisory Committee in 1975.

Executive in Largest U.S. Packaged Grocery Company

Named vice-president for consumer affairs at General Foods Corporation, White Plains, New York, in 1974, MARGUERITE C. KOHL is an integral part of an operation that produces the largest line of packaged groceries in the United States. With a staff of 80 persons, Ms. Kohl supervises numerous company affairs, working with a budget of over $2 million. She has been with General Foods since being hired as a publicist in the consumer services department in 1955.

World's Most Powerful Female Shipping Executive

With the death of her father in March 1975, CHRISTINA ONASSIS assumed control of Olympic Maritime, possibly the most powerful shipping company in the world. The wide-ranging multinational, of which she became the head began with the acquisition of six old freighters during the Depression era, but by the mid-1970s included 15 supertankers and 26 conventional tankers. At age 18, Ms. Onassis went to work in her father's business as a secretary in his Manhattan office. By 1974 she had begun a serious apprenticeship in the shipping industry under Constantine Gratos, head of Victory Carriers in New York. Determined to continue the operation with the same success as her father, she told the *New York Times* the day after his death, "I'm going to run the business and give my life to it."

First Woman Officer of Major Oil Company

An oil industry rarity, CAMERON COOPER is the first (and to 1978 only) woman officer at Atlantic Richfield Company, Los Angeles. Attaining the position as investment officer in 1975, Ms. Cooper started her career with ARCO in 1974 as manager of investor relations. She is responsible for managing over $700 million in company benefit funds.

Executive at Nation's Fifth-Largest Oil Company

JAYNE BAKER SPAIN, senior vice-president for public affairs at Gulf Oil Corporation, Pittsburgh, has directed public, financial, and government relations for the nation's fifth-largest domestic oil company since 1975. No stranger on the executive scene, Ms. Spain also has served as vice-chairwoman of the U. S. Civil Service Commission and as president of the Alvey-Ferguson Company. Noted for her humanitarian activities, she is vice-chairwoman of the President's Commission on Employment for the Handicapped and serves on a host of other committees devoted to improving conditions for the physically disabled.

Pizza-Maker First to Achieve Post of Corporate Vice-President at Pillsbury

ROSE TOTINO became the first woman corporate vice-president in the 106-year history of the Pillsbury Company when Pillsbury purchased Totino's Finer Foods in 1975. With her husband, Ms. Totino in 1951 introduced pizza to the University of Minnesota campus. It was an instant hit, and in the next 20 years the Totinos' Italian Kitchen was forced to expand three times to meet the Minneapolis public's demand, going from 25 pizzas a week to 200,000 daily. The Totinos sold their business to Pillsbury to achieve national distribution. In her new role as corporate vice-president, Ms. Totino works with the Research and Development Department as a consultant on new product ideas and ethnic recipes.

Communications VP First Woman Officer at Celanese Corporation

As corporate vice-president of communications since 1975 at Celanese Corporation, the giant chemical and fiber company, Dr. DOROTHY GREGG coordinates and supervises public relations in all five of the company's divisions. Dr. Gregg received a Ph.D. in economics from Columbia University and was the first woman to become an officer at Celanese, which she joined in 1974 after 16 years with U. S. Steel. In 1968 she was awarded the Top Hat Award for doing most to advance the status of employed women by the National Federation of Business and Professional Women's Clubs, Inc.

First to Head Crown Corporation in Canada

As president and general manager of the Crown Assets Disposal Corporation, responsible for disposing of items unwanted by federal departments, CLAUDETTE NADEAU became the first woman to head a Crown corporation in Canada. The Montreal-born woman assumed her position in 1975. Claudette Nadeau has a varied background—auditing to administration. She doesn't believe that being a woman hampered her career but remarks, "If I were a man it would have been faster."

Legal Executive for Forest Products Company

Combining her legal background with business acumen, FRANCES DAVIS became vice-president and general counsel for the Potlatch Corporation, San Francisco, in 1975. A graduate of the University of California at Berkeley Law School, Ms. Davis is one of the 12 top executives at this multimillion-dollar forest-products corporation.

Top Women Executives in Largest Food Services Company in the United States

A registered dietitian, MARILYN A. RAYMOND was appointed president of ARA Hospital Food Management in 1976, a division of ARA Food Services Company, Philadelphia, Pennsylvania. Ms. Raymond represents the largest food services company in the United States. In addition, she is vice-president for health care services, in charge of contract food and dietetic services for hospitals and nursing homes.

MARY BETH CRIMMINS also holds a powerful position in a growing industry as vice-president for school services at ARA Food Services Company, the industry leader. Ms. Crimmins, appointed in 1972, oversees contract food and dietetic services to schools for this billion-dollar corporation. Joining ARA in 1968, Ms. Crimmins began as an operations analyst for the business and industry division. Previously she had been a dietitian for the Hospital of the University of Pennsylvania.

Women Executives in High-Level Network Financial Posts

In 1973 ANN MAYNARD GRAY, a young woman with "M.B.A. just in hand," joined the American Broadcasting Company, New York City. By 1976 she had been elected treasurer. Ms. Gray is responsible for the treasury operations of the youngest network in television. In her role, she directs cash control, credit and collections, and short-term portfolio management.

A rising star in a large network, KATHRYN PELGRIFT became vice-president for corporate planning at CBS, Inc., New York, in 1976. Joining the company as an assistant to the president in 1972, Ms. Pelgrift has moved quickly up the corporate ladder. She is responsible for making recommendations on corporate objectives for growth and profitability.

Coca-Cola Consumer VP

Appointed vice-president for consumer affairs at Coca-Cola Company, Atlanta, in 1976, DIANNE MCKAIG directs the company's domestic soft-drink and foods division. In addition, she is the main force behind the formation of consumer policies for Coca-Cola Export Corporation, the company's foreign subsidiary that brings in more than half of Coca-Cola's multimillion-dollar earnings.

She Runs Betty Crocker

Food industry pioneer MERCEDES A. BATES, vice-president and director of the Betty Crocker Food & Nutrition Center, General Mills, Inc., since 1976 has supervised three areas: the Betty Crocker Kitchen, the Nutrition Department, and Publications and Publicity. An employee of General Mills since 1964, she has served in various capacities, all focused on food and nutrition. Ms. Bates began her career in cafeteria work. She also hosted her own cooking show on television and owned and operated a food consulting agency for 12 years. Before beginning work for General Mills, she was the food editor for *McCall's* magazine.

First High-Ranking Advertising Woman in Auto Industry

In 1976 CHRISTINE MEYERS became a first in the auto industry when she was made advertising manager of the Pontiac division of General Motors. Of her appointment, Ms. Meyers told *Advertising Age,* "Somebody had to be first. If it was me, that's fine." Formerly the director of publicity for the J. L. Hudson Company, a department store chain in the Detroit area, and named the 1976 Advertising Woman of the Year by the Women's Advertising Club of Detroit, Ms. Meyers admits she has found the transition from clothes to cars somewhat difficult.

First to Win Hotel Sales Executive Award

In 1976 NITA LLOYD, director of sales-corporate accounts, southern division, Hilton Hotels Corporation, became the first woman in the 50-year history of the Hotel Sales Managers Association to win the coveted CHSE (Certified Hotel Sales Executive) Award. The CHSE Award is "an industry acknowledgment of professional sales ability and performance." Ms. Lloyd was also the first woman to be named to the Association's executive committee.

Top Corporate Planner

In 1977 ALETA STYERS was appointed supervisor of corporate planning by the $48 billion communications giant American Telephone & Telegraph. Her earlier experience as a planner was with an equipment and machine manufacturer,

and the U. S. Department of State. Ms. Styers was among the few women to work on the expansion of the European Economic Community in the late 1950s. In 1962 and 1963 she wrote public messages for President John F. Kennedy. Ms. Styers has graduate degrees from both Yale and Northwestern universities.

One of the First Women Chartered Property and Casualty Underwriters

Assistant vice-president and casualty specialist at Marsh & McLennan, international insurance brokers, PATRICIA A. ELLIS is among the first women chartered property and casualty underwriters. In earlier years, Ms. Ellis was also one of the first women to enter the insurance teaching field, as an instructor for the Chicago Board of Underwriters.

Brazil's Only Woman Chief Executive of Major Enterprise

Industrious Reunidas F. Matarazzo, Brazil's 10th largest private company, is the country's only major enterprise with a woman chief executive. MARIA PIA ESMERALDA MATARAZZO inherited the family business, having been named over her brothers in her father's will, in 1977 at the age of 35. The company has 76 factories, employing 21,000 workers, and interests in cement, chemicals, mining, textiles, food products, paper, and real estate. "My grandfather's passion was marketing," this Brazilian businesswoman has said. "My father's was technology. What I am interested in is profit."

BANKERS, BROKERS, AND OTHER MONEYWOMEN

The Frugal Financier

One of the shrewdest financiers ever, HETTY GREEN (1834–1916), considered "the richest woman in the world" at the time of her death, parlayed inheritances of $10 million into a fortune of $100 million. An astute but cheerless

investor, Ms. Green was often referred to as "the witch of Wall Street." She wore old clothes despite her wealth, denied herself and her family basic comforts, and was the object of much adverse publicity and gossip for such actions—particularly when she was said to have taken her ailing son to a free clinic rather than pay a doctor to treat his injured leg, reportedly resulting in an unnecessary amputation.

First Woman Bank President in the United States

MAGGIE LENA WALKER (1867–1934) became simultaneously the first female and the first black female bank president when she assumed the presidency of the St. Luke Penny Savings Bank in Richmond, Virginia, in 1903. As a young girl she had joined the Grand United Order of St. Luke, a Negro fraternal organization founded in 1867 by an ex-slave to assure proper health care and burial arrangements for members. She moved up through the ranks to become the organization's secretary-treasurer in 1899 and in 1902 became the publisher of the *St. Luke Herald,* the group's newsletter. The following year she became president and founder of the order's newly established bank. Ms. Walker served as the president of the bank until 1929, when it was absorbed by the other Negro banks of Richmond and became the Consolidated Bank and Trust Company, of which she was chairwoman of the board of directors until her death in 1934.

First Woman Bank Officer in New York City and First President of the National Association of Bank Women

VIRGINIA FURMAN, the first woman bank officer in New York City, was hired in 1919, at age 54, to organize a women's department at the Columbia Trust Company. Her appointment set off a wave of such departments at other New York banks, and the idea soon spread to the rest of the country. The first few women who entered the New York banking world, recognizing that they needed to band together for education and mutual support, founded the National Association of Bank Women (p. 527). Ms. Furman was instrumental in bringing these women together, and served as the Association's first president from 1921 until 1923.

Bank of America Firsts

In 1921 the first women's department at a bank on the West Coast was organized in the San Francisco office of the Bank of Italy, forerunner of the giant Bank of America, by HELEN M. KNIGHT. Two years later GRACE R. STOERMER organized the bank's Los Angeles women's department. When the bank changed its name in 1930, the women's departments were merged with general departments, and both women were named assistant vice-presidents. In 1949 CLAIRE GIANNINI HOFFMAN, daughter of the founder, became the first female to be elected to the Bank of America's board of directors.

Role Model for United States Women Bankers

HALLIE SOUCHE, president of what is probably the oldest bank in the country to be continuously operated by a woman, began her career with the West Point (Kentucky) Bank in 1924 as a part-time helper for $1 a day. When the bank's manager died in 1941, the male members of the Board asked her to take charge. She did but was not officially named president until 1951. At first she thought the president's job should "go to a man." She soon changed her mind, however. Now she owns most of the bank's stock. Women in West Point don't receive any special treatment at Ms. Souche's bank. They don't need it. Years before the federal government passed equal credit laws, women could take out loans from the West Point Bank without their spouse's signature. (The same was true for men.) A native of West Point, Ms. Souche has been interviewed on her banking career by newspapers and television stations throughout the country. "Next summer (1978) it'll be 54 years I've been here," she told one interviewer.

They Set the Course for Women in Banking

When the National Association of Bank Women was founded in 1921 by VIRGINIA FURMAN, NATHALIE LAIMBEER, KEY CAMMACK, MINA M. BRUÉRE, and JEAN ARNOT REID, it was an act of pragmatism and foresight. Ms. Furman had been hired in 1919 to organize a "women's department" in a major New York City bank for the purpose of attracting new business. Soon other banks hired women officers for the same reason.

"The men executives of the banks had no clear conception of the program they wished the women they were inviting into their organizations to enter upon," Ms. Bruére later told an interviewer from the *New York Commercial* (April 28, 1926). "The women themselves had none either, because they had no precedent to follow, nothing to guide them in the new work they were taking up. They were starting out in an entirely new direction and had to chart their own course by experience."

The new employees had access to women of wealth and social position in the city but no formal training in banking. Realizing their need for professionalism, they formed the new Association to establish standards for themselves and others to come, and to provide financial education and training.

"Such a grouping will impress upon people the fact that women in banking are no longer a casual experience but an increasingly growing body," it was said at one of the founding meetings of NABW. "By organizing, we women in banks will bring more efficiency to the position of each woman in the group."

In 1949 a national office was set up by SARAH ARTHUR, and the organization's first permanent secretary, LULA DUTY MAZE, was engaged. During the intervening years the Association had organized divisions in each section of the country, established an award for outstanding accomplishment, provided numerous opportunities for professional contacts and education, and reached out to college women to make them aware of the careers available to women in banking.

First President of a Federally Chartered Savings and Loan Company

When LORNA MILLS joined the Laguna Beach (California) Federal Savings & Loan in 1936, she was one of three employees of a bank with assets of about $300,000. In 1957 she assumed the presidency and has been instrumental in increasing assets to well over the $200 million mark. Ms. Mills was the first woman to become president of a federally chartered savings and loan company.

She Sold *Gone With the Wind* to the Movies

One of the first female literary agents to successfully negotiate large subsidiary rights contracts with the film industry was ANNIE L. WILLIAMS, who died in May 1977. She sold the film rights to MARGARET MITCHELL's *Gone With the Wind* (see "Women in the Arts and Entertainment," p. 681) to David O. Selznick in 1936; she had originally asked for $100,000, but settled for half of that from the Depression-plagued movie industry. She handled sales of numerous other books to Hollywood, including John Steinbeck's *The Grapes of Wrath* and *Of Mice and Men* and Patrick Dennis' *Auntie Mame*. She also sold the Broadway rights to *Stalag 17*, and until her death continued to handle several authors.

First Female Governor of the American Stock Exchange

The first woman governor of the American Stock Exchange (1958) and one of the first U.S. women bank presidents, MARY G. ROEBLING is a woman of many achievements. Ms. Roebling served as the president of the Trenton (New Jersey) Trust Company, 1937–72, and when it merged with the National State Bank, Elizabeth, New Jersey, in 1972, was elected chairwoman of the enlarged organization. She is also a member of the New Jersey Investment Council (a state advisory group) and numerous other state and national committees.

Vice-Chairwoman of Second-Largest Savings and Loan Branch Network in the Nation

In 1963 MARION O. SANDLER, with her husband, Herbert, formed the holding company that acquired Golden West Savings & Loan. Quickly building its assets from $35 million to over $1.8 billion, they merged with Trans-World Financial Corporation in 1975 to become Golden West Financial Corporation, the second-largest savings and loan branch network in the United States. As vice-chairwoman of Golden West, Ms. Sandler oversees its 107 offices spread throughout California and Colorado. Since the merger, annual earnings have exceeded $100 million.

First to Own Seat on New York Stock Exchange

In 1967 MURIEL SIEBERT put up a reported $445,000 and became the first woman ever to own a seat on the New York Stock Exchange. Ms. Siebert began her career as a research trainee on Wall Street in 1954. Within a few years, she had earned a reputation as one of the country's most astute airlines stock analysts and was paid a salary reported to top $500,000 a year. As head of her own brokerage firm, Muriel Siebert & Company, she deals strictly with corporate or institutional clients but recalls her earlier years when she was active as a consultant for women investors. In 1974 Governor Carey appointed her New York State banking commissioner. A strong feminist, she faults educational institutions for not providing women with even a rudimentary understanding of financial management.

First Belgian Bank Director

In 1968 Belgian-born ELIZABETH MALAISE became the first woman to be appointed a director of the Belgian National Bank. Ms. Malaise credits her position to the rising pressure throughout the international world of finance to place women in executive posts.

First to Manage Branch for Major New York Stock Exchange Company

A managing partner in the L. F. Rothschild Company's San Francisco office since 1968, PATRICIA M. HOWE is the first woman to manage a branch for any major New York Stock Exchange company. An institutional sales assistant at Blyth & Company, 1954–55, Ms. Howe joined Rothschild in 1957, rising to the position of San Francisco branch manager in 1965. She is also the only woman among 40 partners in this prestigious investment house.

She Learned All the Way Up

SALLY A. STOWE was appointed director and corporate secretary at the founding in 1962 of Keefe, Bruyette & Woods, Inc., a major Wall Street firm that specializes in banking industry research and trading of bank securities. In 1968 Ms. Stowe was appointed treasurer of the firm and achieved her present rank of senior vice-president and chief financial officer in 1972. She is also a trustee of the company's profit-sharing plan. Ms. Stowe began her career in 1942. Early on she was a bank security analyst and cites on-the-job experience and learning as an important factor in her rise to her present position.

First President of Major Bank She Did Not Inherit

CATHERINE B. CLEARY, president and chief executive officer of the First Wisconsin Trust Company, rose through the administrative ranks of this $1.25 billion bank to assume her present position in 1970. She is also a member of the Board of General Motors, Kraftco, Northwestern Mutual Life Insurance Company, and American Telephone & Telegraph, as well as a member of the bar of the state of Wisconsin.

Vice-President of Second-Largest Investment Counseling Firm in the United States

An employee since 1943 of Loomis, Sayles & Co., Inc., the nation's second-largest investment counseling firm, GLORIA LUDWIG MUIR achieved executive status in 1971 as vice-president and managing partner. Among Ms. Muir's responsibilities are the operation of a department for accounts of $100,000 to $400,000, which she established.

First Woman Broker, Lloyd's of London

In addition to being the first woman broker at Lloyd's of London, LILLIANNA ARCHIBALD is a specialist in 18th-century Russian history, and a university lecturer in the subject.

Women Investment Trust Partners First Admitted to French Association of Financial Analysts

In 1970 MICHELINE COURTY and MONIQUE KAPLAN started an investment trust company that in 1972 and 1973 achieved the top performance of all French investment funds. They became the first women admitted to the French Association of Financial Analysts.

One of First to Become Partner in Big Eight Accounting Firm

A partner at Price, Waterhouse & Company, New York, since 1973, MARIANNE BURGE is one of the few women in the nation to reach such heights in a largely male-dominated industry. In her position at this Big Eight accounting firm, Ms. Burge is an integral part of the many operations of this successful organization.

First President of First Women's Bank (New York)

When she was named president of the First Women's Bank in New York City in 1974, MADELINE H. McWHINNEY assumed the top position in the nation's first commercial bank to begin operations with totally non-discriminatory hiring, promotion, and credit policies. Previously she had served as a financial analyst with the Federal Reserve Bank of New York as its first woman officer. Unhappily, the bank had some problems getting started. In 1976 Ms. McWhinney accepted a post at New York University and was replaced by LYNN SAVAGE.

Vice-President of Nation's Second-Largest Bank

Joining Citibank, New York City, in 1973 as vice-president, MARILYN LA-MARCHE presides over the business development and personal financial management divisions of the nation's second-largest bank. She is an allied member of both the New York and American Stock Exchange and was previously a general partner in the investment banking firm of Ladenburg, Thalmann & Company.

Senior VP of the Largest and Oldest U.S. Mutual Savings Bank

Forty-five years ago FREDA I. MILLAR was hired as a stenographer at the Philadelphia Saving Fund Society, the largest and oldest mutual savings bank in the country; in 1973 she made it to the top as senior vice-president. Ms. Millar, who was employed by the Society right out of high school, held numerous jobs ranging from security analyst to assistant accountant before being named a top corporate officer.

First Woman Among GE's Corporate Officers

In 1974 MARION KELLOGG became the General Electric Company's first woman among 22 corporate officers. An employee of the company for more than 30 years, Ms. Kellogg is an internationally known management expert. In her position at this multibillion-dollar U.S. company, she supervises more than 400 employees working with a budget of more than $19 million.

Top Executives in Second-Largest Minority-Owned Savings and Loan Company in the Nation

As president and chief executive officer of the Illinois/Service Federal Savings and Loan Association of Chicago since 1975, LOUISE Q. LAWSON heads the second-largest minority-owned savings and loan company in the nation. Starting with the bank in 1946 as a general clerical worker, she moved up quickly to become the first woman elected to the board of directors in 1963. Her second-in-command, THELMA J. SMITH, assumed the position of vice-president and corporate secretary in 1975. Pursuing much the same path as Ms. Lawson, Ms. Smith joined the company in 1951 as a clerical worker.

Mellon Bank Vice-President

Vice-president for retail services at the Mellon Bank, Pittsburgh, since 1975, SANDRA J. McLAUGHLIN heads three divisions of the country's 15th-largest bank. A consumer adviser to the American Bankers Association, Ms. McLaughlin started with the bank as a teller in 1958.

First Full-Time Woman Broker on the Floor of the New York Stock Exchange

ALICE JARCHO, a floor broker for Oppenheimer & Company, in 1976 became the first woman on Wall Street to spend all of her working time on the floor of the New York Stock Exchange. A graduate of Queens College, Ms. Jarcho began her career as a receptionist for another Wall Street firm, Hirsch & Company, in 1965, and held other jobs in the city's financial center before joining Oppenheimer & Company in 1969 as an order clerk.

Youngest Brokerage Firm Partner

In 1977 at age 22, JO ANN HUME was named a general partner by the prestigious Wall Street brokerage firm of Spear, Leeds & Kellogg. The firm's first woman partner, she heads its Chicago office, where she supervises four other employees and is also the firm's major broker on the floor of the Chicago Board Options Exchange. Little in her background would have forecast such rapid achievement save her propensity for movement. She started college at one university and soon transferred to the University of Oregon, where she majored in finance and made A-minus grades. But Ms. Hume didn't stay to graduate. She moved to Chicago, worked for several months as a production assistant on a play, and then took a job as a "runner" at the brokerage house of Bear, Stearns & Company. Gradually she was given more responsibility, but when the firm

refused a raise she felt she deserved, Ms. Hume quit. "They didn't realize my potential," she said. A colleague on the exchange recommended her to Spear, Leeds & Kellogg, which was then opening a Chicago office. She began as a clerk and moved up with astonishing rapidity. When the New York partner who had come to Chicago to establish the branch office left the area, Jo Ann Hume ascended to her present position. "I was definitely in the right place at the right time," the New York Times quoted her.

Top Washington Woman Broker

The first woman to be accepted in and graduated from the advanced management program at the Harvard Graduate School of Business, and one of the first women to hold a seat on the American Stock Exchange, JULIA WALSH represents the combination of talent and perseverance that makes the successful businesswoman. Ms. Walsh began her career in the U. S. Foreign Service in 1945, and served in various consulates, including those in Germany and Turkey. She ended what she thought was destined to be her life career because of what she terms "a crazy rule that a married woman was automatically kicked out of the Foreign Service." (The rule is no longer in effect.) After joining Ferris & Company, a Washington, D.C., brokerage house, in 1955 she scaled the corporate ladder to eventually become vice-chairwoman. Then, after 22 years of service, Ms. Walsh in 1977 branched out to found Julia M. Walsh & Sons, Inc., Washington, D.C. She is chairwoman of the Board of her own investment company, one of only three women in the United States to head an investment firm, and the only one east of the Mississippi.

13

Women in the Military

By Dody W. Smith

Major General Jeanne M. Holm (USAF, ret.),
consulting editor

In one way or another, in all parts of the world, women have always played a part in warfare. All major wars since remote antiquity have had a certain number of women involved. Traditionally, however, bearing arms has been a man's calling; until the 20th century, women's participation in military activity in the United States, and elsewhere in the world, was limited and unorganized.

World War I, and to a much greater extent World War II, required the utilization of women's talents and skills in a wide range of environments and duties. In countless tasks previously considered men's jobs only, women performed with competence, efficiency, and determination. During World War II, approximately 1 million women, of a total military strength of 12 million, served in the Soviet Armed Forces. Most of them were in non-combat jobs, but many served with active combat units in tank crews, machine gun detachments, and as snipers. The need for women as an integral part of the U.S., British, and Ca-

nadian armed forces also was firmly established during this period. Over 300,000 served in the U.S. forces alone, some at home to release men for fighting jobs but many in non-combat roles in combat theaters all over the world.

The postwar (1948) passage of the Women's Armed Services Integration Act marked a giant step forward for U.S. women. It provided both Regular and Reserve status. Today more than 100,000 skilled women in the U. S. Armed Forces are performing hundreds of important jobs at home and abroad, on land, at sea, and in the air—demonstrating on a daily basis that military manpower has truly become man-and-womanpower.

Clearly, military women in the United States have emerged from the tokenism that marked their status for many years. Full equality is still an elusive goal for them—as it is for women in the armed services of other countries for which current information is available. (Some nations that are known to have many women in service classify most information about their numbers, ranks, and duties.) But significant advances for American women in the 1970s included increased promotion and assignment opportunities. Virtually all U.S. armed services jobs are now open to women except those categorized as direct combat or close combat support.

In 1977, according to news stories in the *Washington Post* and the *New York Times,* the U. S. Navy in "a major break from tradition" was "quietly seeking to assign more women to duty on ships." Proposed changes in the law would permit women to serve aboard a wide variety of non-combat support ships and to go aboard combat ships on a temporary basis. Also in 1977, the U. S. Coast Guard sent its first women to sea. The announcement of this break with precedent was made on May 25 at the Coast Guard Academy, New London, Connecticut.

In June 1978 eight women became the nation's first graduates of a service academy, receiving commissions in the U. S. Merchant Marine, along with commissions in the Navy or Coast Guard Reserve. The first of the eight to receive her diploma, by virtue of alphabetical position in the graduating class at the Merchant Marine Academy at Kings Point, Long Island, New York, was 24-year-old Third Mate IVY BARTON.

The U. S. Army, Navy, Air Force, and Coast Guard academies all admitted women cadets and midshipmen for the first time in the autumn of 1976. West Point officials at the end of the first year announced that the drop-out rate for women was 5 per cent higher than for men but that adjustment had been "less difficult than administrators had anticipated." Assuming near-normal attrition rates at all of the academies, there will be more than 200 women firsts receiving active (Regular rather than Reserve) commissions on graduation in 1980.

DODY W. SMITH *served as communications watch officer in the U. S. Navy's Women Accepted for Volunteer Emergency Service (WAVES), 1943–46. Married to a retired U. S. Navy captain, and the mother of one son, Ms. Smith lives in Arlington, Virginia. She writes occasionally for the* Washington Post, *the* Baltimore Sun, *and* Naval Institute Proceedings *and contributed to* The People's Almanac *(Doubleday, 1975). Ms. Smith was born Dody Wilson in Georgia and was graduated from Valdosta (Georgia) State College in 1939.*

Major General JEANNE M. HOLM *retired from active duty with the U. S. Air Force in 1977 (see also p. 539).*

U. S. WOMEN IN SERVICE

Only Medal of Honor Holder

For her services to the Union Army as a medical officer during the Civil War, Dr. MARY WALKER in 1865 was awarded the Medal of Honor—the only woman ever to receive this highest award for valor. It was presented to her by President Andrew Johnson. The citation read in part: "she has devoted herself with much patriotic zeal to the sick and wounded soldiers . . . and also endured hardships as a prisoner of war for four months." Following her release from prison in Richmond, exchanged "man for man," as she said, Dr. Walker continued to serve on the battlefield until the war was over. Her usual costume consisted of pants, vest, and long tunic. ("Why don't you wear proper clothing? That toggery is neither one thing nor the other!" General William Tecumseh Sherman chided her.)

Off the battlefield, Dr. Walker continued her fight in other areas, among them the women's rights movement. A militant advocate for dress reform, she regularly wore striped trousers, a silk hat, and frock coat by day, changing to full male evening dress for lectures and social events.

Her name was among 911 removed from the Medal of Honor rolls in 1917, when the awards up to that time were reviewed to determine whether or not they met new and stringent criteria. In her case, the question was whether she had been an actual member of the Ohio infantry regiment with which she served or a contract doctor. Asked to return her original medal and one of later design given her in 1907, Dr. Walker replied, "Over my dead body." She continued to wear one or the other until her death in 1919 at age 87. In 1977 the U. S. Army officially reinstated Dr. Mary Walker's Medal of Honor.

First Woman Assistant Surgeon in the U. S. Army and Founder of the Army Nurse Corps

At the start of the Spanish-American War in 1898, ANITA NEWCOMB MCGEE was appointed an assistant surgeon, the first woman to hold the title in the history of the Army. As director of the Daughters of the American Revolution Hospital Corps, McGee was responsible for the screening and training of nurses for the Army and Navy. After the war Anita McGee drafted the section of the 1901 Army Organization Bill that established the Nurse Corps as a permanent part of the Army. In this respect she could also be called a founder of the Army Nurse Corps. Anita McGee was born in 1864 and died in 1940.

First Superintendent of Navy Nurses

ESTHER VORHEES HASSON, of Baltimore, Maryland, was appointed first superintendent of the Navy Nurse Corps on August 18, 1908. She was 41 years of age. The so-called First Lady of the Navy was a graduate of the Connecticut Training School for Nurses, New Haven. She resigned January 16, 1911, and died March 8, 1942.

First Director of the WAAC

OVETA CULP HOBBY was a lawyer and a politician in her native state of Texas when she married William Pettus Hobby, who, in 1931, was governor of Texas and publisher of the *Houston Post*. They had two children, but Ms. Hobby continued an active public life in addition to her role as wife and mother; a special interest was handling the women's news section of the *Houston Post*. In July 1941 Ms. Hobby went to Washington, D.C., as War Department public relations executive, and was asked by Chief of Staff George Catlett Marshall to map out plans for the new women's Army Corps. The day after President Franklin D. Roosevelt signed the bill creating the Women's Army Auxiliary Corps (WAAC), Ms. Hobby was sworn in as its director. Under her dedicated leadership and direction, the organization developed and expanded. Changed from its auxiliary status in 1943, the Women's Army Corps (WAC) reached a peak strength by April 1945 of more than 99,000 women serving in the United States and overseas. Ill health forced her resignation in mid-1945, but she later was able to return to public service (1953–55) as the first Secretary of Health, Education, and Welfare (see also "Women in Politics and Government," p. 82) in the Cabinet of President Dwight D. Eisenhower.

First Director of the WAVES

Immediately after President Franklin D. Roosevelt signed the bill creating the Women's Reserve of the Navy, MILDRED HELEN MCAFEE was sworn in as lieutenant commander (August 3, 1942) and placed in charge of the Women Accepted for Volunteer Emergency Service. She was promoted to the rank of captain in 1943. Captain McAfee, who came from a long line of "educators, writers, and church people," had, since 1936, been president of Wellesley College (where the trustees, in an exhaustive search for their seventh president, had weighed "100 candidates, quizzed 1,000 alumnae to find a woman who combined intellectual honesty, leadership, tolerance, savoir faire, sympathetic understanding of youth, vision, and sense of humor"). While she was on leave from Wellesley to serve in the Navy, an executive body of three women jointly shared her duties until her release to inactive duty in 1946. In August 1945 Captain McAfee married the Reverend Dr. Douglas Horton, internationally known author and clergyman, now deceased. Ms. Mildred McAfee Horton lives in New Hampshire.

First Director of U. S. Marine Corps Women's Reserve

Prior to public announcement of the new Marine Corps Women's Reserve, RUTH CHENEY STREETER was commissioned a major, USMCWR, and sworn in on January 29, 1943. Ms. Streeter, age 47, had the combination of personal characteristics and organizational abilities required for her job as first director of the women Marines. She had been president of her class at Bryn Mawr College and was the mother of four grown children, including two sons in the Navy and one in the Army. She held both private and commercial pilot's licenses, and for more than 20 years had been active in New Jersey health and welfare work. Upon completion of her tour as director, in December 1945, Colonel Streeter received a commendation letter from General A. A. Vandegrift, then commandant of the Marine Corps, expressing appreciation for her outstanding service from the inception of the Women's Reserve to its strength of 831 officers and 17,714 enlisted. Of her performance of duty he said, "It set a standard of excellence which, in my opinion, could not have been excelled and would be difficult to equal." Since 1945 Colonel Streeter has lived in Morristown, New Jersey.

First Commissioned Officer in Marine Corps Women's Reserve

As a civilian, Ms. ANNE A. LENZ, a clothing expert, helped outfit the WAACs. In December 1942 she was on a 30-day assignment at Marine Corps Headquarters to design the uniform for women Marines. Public announcement of the new Women's Reserve had not yet been made, and the director had not yet been commissioned when Ms. Lenz was sworn in with the rank of captain.

Second Director of Women Marines First to Serve a Second Time

KATHERINE A. TOWLE originally came to the Marine Corps in February 1943, from the campus of the University of California at Berkeley. The following month Captain Towle was ordered to the Marine Detachment Naval Training School (Women's Reserve) at Hunter College, New York City, as senior woman officer. Later she was assigned to the Women's Reserve Training Center at Camp Lejeune, North Carolina. Following other assignments and other promotions, she became the second director of the Marine Corps Women's Reserve when Colonel Ruth Cheney Streeter resigned in December 1945.

Colonel Towle served as director until the Women's Reserve was demobilized, at which time she returned to the Berke-

ley campus as assistant dean of women. But not for long. After Congress authorized the acceptance of women into the Regular armed services, the Marine Corps called Colonel Towle back to active duty as director. She served in that capacity from November 1948 until her retirement in April 1953. She was awarded a letter of commendation, for "meritorious service during the entire period of the growth and development of the United States Marine Corps Women's Reserve."

After her Navy retirement, Colonel Towle served in various capacities at the University of California at Berkeley, including dean of students, 1965–66, and became dean of students, emeritus, in 1966.

World War II's Women Pilots

The Women's Air Force Service Pilots (WASPs) in World War II went through officers' training, lived in military barracks, were subject to military discipline, and wore men's GI uniforms (which they called "zoot suits"). They had been promised military commissions but were disbanded after the war without having attained military status and veterans' benefits.

Between September 1942 and December 1944 more than 1,000 women were accepted into the WASPs—one of whose creators was famed flyer JACQUELINE COCHRAN (see "Women in Sports and Games," p. 590). Enthusiastically supported by Commanding General of the Army Air Forces, H. H. "Hap" Arnold, the women pilots ferried fighter and bomber planes to points of embarkation in the United States and Canada, towed targets for combat pilots' practice shooting, and performed other duties to free male pilots for combat. According to former WASP Margaret Boylan (three

decades later a branch chief for the Federal Aviation Administration), they "worked seven days a week, sunup to sundown."

Approximately 850 surviving members of the group in 1977 successfully lobbied Congress for veterans' benefits. In the past, several attempts to pass legislation in their behalf had failed, despite efforts by Senator Barry Goldwater (R., Ariz.), their sponsor on Capitol Hill, who flew with WASP ferry pilots during the war and said that their performance was equal to or better than that of their male counterparts. In November 1977, however, President Carter signed into law a bill giving these women the legal status of other World War II veterans.

First Director of WAF

In 1948 Colonel GERALDINE P. MAY, at age 53, became first director of the newly organized Women in the Air Force (WAF). Prior to her enlistment in the Army in 1942, Colonel May had been graduated from the University of California at Berkeley, had done social work in San Francisco, was married, and had lived in Tulsa, Oklahoma, about 10 years. After her husband died, she went into the Army and was graduated with the first WAC officer candidate class at Des Moines, Iowa. She was one of the first 18 WAC officers to be assigned to the Air Force when it became a separate service. Colonel May left active duty in 1952.

From Yeoman (F), World War I, to Director of WAVES, World War II

The long and distinguished career of JOY BRIGHT HANCOCK began in 1918 when she enlisted as a yeoman (F) in the U. S. Naval Reserve. Between World War I and World War II, she was a civilian employee in the Navy's Bureau of Aeronautics, and the years of experience there helped prepare her for demanding duty during World War II as special assistant for the Women's Reserve to the deputy chief of Naval Operations (Air). She was commissioned a lieutenant in the Women's Reserve in 1942; promoted to lieutenant commander in 1943; to commander in 1945; and to captain on July 26, 1946, at which time she became director of the WAVES and served as a key figure in the preparation and promotion of what became the Women's Armed Services Integration Act, signed by President Harry S. Truman in 1948. She served as assistant chief of naval personnel for women from 1948 until her retirement in 1953.

Captain Hancock has written many magazine articles on aviation and related subjects and a book, *Lady in the Navy, A Personal Reminiscence* (1972). The first director of the WAVES, Captain MILDRED MCAFEE HORTON (p. 535), wrote in the introduction for the book, "No WAVE of the Navy knows more about the experience of women in the service than Joy Hancock. . . . This is a memorable story, told by a woman memorable in naval history." Captain Hancock was born in Wildwood, New Jersey, and spent her early years there. The widow of three naval aviators, she has lived for some time in the Washington area. Her first husband, Lieutenant Charles G. Little, was killed in a dirigible crash in England in 1921; the second, Lieutenant Lewis Hancock, Jr., died in the crash of the airship U.S.S. *Shenandoah* in 1925. Her last husband, Vice-Admiral Ralph A. Ofstie, USN, whom she married after she retired, died in 1956.

"Once a Marine, Always a Marine"

Two women who served in the Marines in World War I came back to the Corps to serve as officers in the Marine Corps Women's Reserve in World War II. MARTRESE THEK FERGUSON was graduated at the top of the first officer's class in the Marine Corps Women's Reserve, rose to the rank of lieutenant colonel, and commanded more than 2,000 women at Henderson Hall in Arlington, Virginia. LILLIAN O'MALLEY DALY also wore the Marine green uniform in both wars. She was one of the eight women who came into the new Women's Reserve directly from civilian life in 1943. She was immediately sent to Camp Pendleton, California, where she served as West Coast liaison officer for the new women's organization.

Marine Corps Woman Unveils a First Statue

On November 10, 1943, in New Orleans, Louisiana, a statue, "Molly Marine," dedicated to the U. S. Marine Corps Women's Reserve (and donated by the citizens of New Orleans), was unveiled by Admiral A. C. Bennett, commandant 8th Naval District, together with Captain HELEN G. O'NEILL, USMCWR, one of the Marine Corps's first women officers. As far as can be ascertained, this is the first statue dedicated to a woman in uniform of the armed forces of the United States. Captain O'Neill was a chief yeoman (F) in World War I and continued her affiliation with the Navy after the war in a civilian capacity. She served as private secretary to three assistant secretaries of the Navy. In 1940 Joseph W. Powell, special assistant to Secretary of the Navy Frank Knox, made a special request for Miss O'Neill as his administrative assistant. After Mr. Powell and Secretary Knox returned from an inspection of Pearl Harbor, December 15, 1941, it was she to whom they entrusted their notes for typing; notes containing information that became a part of the Pearl Harbor Report. In 1943 Captain O'Neill was commissioned in the Marine Corps Women's Reserve direct from civilian life. She retired as a lieutenant colonel in 1958 and remains active in the American Legion, the Reserve Officers Association, and the Marine Corps Retired Officers Association.

Oldest Officer on Active Duty

Captain GRACE MURRAY HOPPER, USNR, at 71 years of age in 1978, was still on active duty with the U. S. Navy as head of the Training and Technology Directorate, Naval Data Automation Command, Washington, D.C. Captain Hopper, a math major, earned her B.A. and was elected to Phi Beta Kappa at Vassar (1928). She holds an M.A. (1930) and Ph.D. (1934) from Yale. Dr. Hopper first joined the Navy in 1943, completed Officer Training School at Northampton, Massachusetts, and was ordered to the Bureau of Ordnance Computation Project at Harvard, where she worked on the Mark I digital computer during World War II. In 1946 she joined the Harvard faculty as a research fellow in the computation laboratories and continued work on the Mark II and Mark III computers for the Navy.

Youngest to Serve as Director of Marine Corps Women's Reserve

JULIA E. HAMBLET served as director of the Marine Corps Women's Reserve from 1946 (when she was 30 years old) to 1948 and as director of women Marines from 1953 to 1959. Commissioned a first lieutenant upon completion of officer training in May 1943, she was selected as adjunct to Captain KATHERINE A. TOWLE (p. 536) at the Women's Recruit Training Center at Hunter College in New York. After distinguished service in this and subsequent tours during World War II, she was released to inactive duty in July 1946, but after two months was recalled to active duty as a major, to succeed Colonel Towle as director. Other outstanding performances of duty in diversified assignments followed until again, in 1953, she was named director of women Marines with the rank of colonel.

Over the years Dr. Hopper retained her status in the Naval Reserve and was retired with the rank of commander in 1966. Recalled to active duty in 1967, she was promoted to captain on the retired list in 1973, marking the first time an officer in the Naval Reserve was promoted to captain while on the retired list. Scientist, researcher, writer, educator, and lecturer, Captain Hopper has served on the staffs of five universities, lectured in Europe, Japan, Canada, and elsewhere, attained international stature, and received numerous honorary degrees and major awards (see "Women in Science and Technology," p. 189). The Navy's "computer pioneer" says that her highest award is "the privilege and the responsibility of wearing this uniform and very proudly serving the United States Navy." Other Navy women regard

HELEN MEYER, who recently retired as chairperson of the Board of Dell Publishing Company, was for many years as president of Dell the only woman operating head of a major publishing house. She now serves as editorial consultant at Doubleday, Dell's parent company. (Photo by George Janoff)

ESTHER MARGOLIS, like Helen Meyer, started at Dell. She moved to Bantam Books as assistant promotion director, in 1965 was appointed the company's first publicity director, and in 1971 was elected vice-president. (Photo by Sue Marx)

The women on this and the following page represent areas of business, industry, and finance in which the female sex has been able to display its acumen to best effect. Below, with the late President Lyndon B. Johnson when he visited the *Washington Post* offices after he had decided not to seek office again and to return to Texas, is publisher and president of the Washington Post Company, KATHARINE (KAY) GRAHAM. She runs the only Fortune 500 company headed by a woman.

Overleaf are women who have made their mark in the cosmetics, advertising, and banking industries—all, like publishing, fields into which women moved comparatively early. (Photo courtesy of the *Washington Post*)

MALA RUBINSTEIN, daughter of the founder, is executive vice-president of the Helena Rubinstein Company. In the 1950s she developed new makeup shades and techniques for television use.

MARY WELLS LAWRENCE, whom many believe to be the highest-paid woman executive in the United States, is chairwoman of the Board and chief executive officer of Wells, Rich, Greene, Inc., one of the nation's leading advertising agencies.

MADELINE H. McWHINNEY was the first president (1974–76) of the first women's bank established in New York City.

Dr. MARY WALKER, photographed in 1912 in her habitual dress for evening, wearing the U. S. Army's highest award, the Medal of Honor, bestowed on her by President Andrew Johnson for medical services on the battlefield during the Civil War. The medal was later officially recalled (though she refused to return it) on the grounds that she was not a regular member of the armed services but a contract surgeon. In 1977, 60 years after her death, the U. S. Army restored Mary Walker's name to the list of Medal of Honor holders. (Photo courtesy of the Library of Congress)

U. S. Navy women on review in World War I. A young woman who served with a unit like this, few in number and generally assigned to office details, was called a "yeoman (F)" (for female)—not, as is erroneously supposed, a yeomanette. (Photo courtesy of the Library of Congress)

May 1953. WAVEs of ship's company, Bainbridge (Maryland) Naval Training Center, salute reviewing officer Captain JOY BRIGHT HANCOCK, USN, the assistant chief of naval personnel for women, on the occasion of her last official appearance before she retired in June. (Photo courtesy of the U. S. Navy)

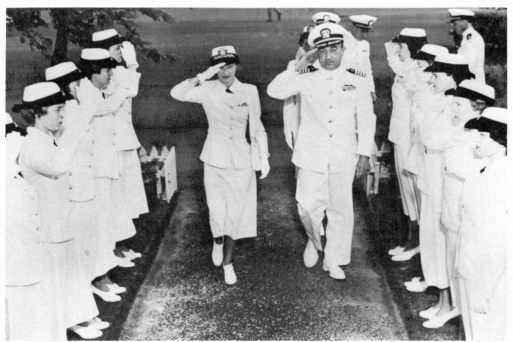

The highest-ranking woman officer in the U.S. armed services, Major General JEANNE M. HOLM, USAF (ret.), has her second set of stars pinned on.

Commander GRACE M. HOPPER, USNR (retired, but back on active duty in her 70s), is nationally and internationally known for her work in computer programming.

Ensign ANNA MARIE FUQUA at the controls of an SH-3A Sea King helicopter. Ensign Fuqua was assigned as a pilot with Helicopter Combat Support Squadron Six stationed at Norfolk, Virginia, in 1975. (Photo courtesy of the Department of Defense)

Personnelman Seaman NANCY K. GARNER became the first woman graduate of a Navy diving school in 1973. (Photo courtesy of the Department of Defense)

"The Babe"

MILDRED ELLA "BABE" DIDRIKSON ZAHARIAS (1914-56), one of the greatest U.S. athletes, male or female, of all time, was a basketball, track and field, and golf champion. In the 1932 Summer Olympics, with many awards and records already to her credit, she won 3 gold medals and set 3 records—for javelin throw, 80-meter hurdles, and high jump. She turned professional in the mid-1930s, giving exhibitions throughout the United States, and in 1935 took up golf, soon becoming a champion in this sport, too. In 1947 she won 17 straight golfing titles, including the British Women's Amateur, of which she was the first U.S. winner.

her as their answer to Admiral Hyman Rickover (still on active duty in 1978 at 78).

Commander of First WAAC Unit to Go to Europe in World War II

Colonel MARY A. HALLAREN, affectionately known to the Army as the "Little Colonel," was director of the Women's Army Corps from May 1947 to January 1953. Her military career began before the Corps became a permanent part of the Regular Army and Reserve, with her graduation from the first officer candidate class at Fort Des Moines in August 1942. Two months later she was appointed commanding officer of the 1st

WAAC Separate Battalion, which arrived in Scotland in July 1943—the first WAAC unit in the European Theater of Operations in World War II. After her return from Europe, Colonel Hallaren became deputy director of the WAC and served in that capacity until her appointment as director in May 1947. She has been considered the WAC most responsible for the 1948 legislation that put women in the Regular Army and Reserve. Colonel Hallaren retired from the Army in 1960. Since March 1965 she has served as executive director, Women in Community Service (WICS), Department of Labor.

Highest-Ranking Woman in the U. S. Armed Forces

"I never really planned anything far ahead. . . . I was not sure [in 1948] that I wanted to make a career of this, but the Air Force kept sending me to interesting places and giving me good jobs. I never asked for an assignment, though, I just took what came." "What came" for Major General JEANNE M. HOLM turned out to be challenging assignments of increasing responsibility; promotions to match the assignments; and a distinguished career with an outstanding record of honors and awards, capped by attainment of the highest rank to date of any woman in the U. S. Armed Forces.

General Holm, a native of Portland, Oregon, first enlisted in the Women's Army Auxiliary Corps in 1942, received her commission as second lieutenant in 1943, and by the end of World War II was a captain commanding a women's training regiment. After the war she returned to civilian life and to college, but was recalled to active duty in 1948 and transferred to the Air Force. General Holm retired in 1975, but it was not long before she was back at work—this time at the White House, where she served as special assistant for women until President Gerald Ford left office. General

Holm is perhaps best-known for the work she did as director, Women in the Air Force, from 1965 to 1972. During that time, she is credited with effecting major changes in the utilization, assignments, and career opportunities for Air Force women. She also fought for revisions to policies and laws that discriminated against women in all of the armed forces.

Although military women have made enormous strides in the United States in recent years, General Holm believes that there is much yet to be done to ensure women the opportunity to contribute as co-partners in the nation's defense. She remains active—speaking, writing, and consulting—in the areas of women's rights, national defense, and manpower issues. In 1977 she was invited by the Secretary of Defense to serve for three years as a member of the Defense Advisory Committee on Women in the Services (DACOWITS).

First Marine Corps Woman Officer to Command a Predominantly Male Battalion

Commissioned as a second lieutenant in 1952, Colonel MARY E. BANE has served in diversified assignments including administrative officer on the staff at Headquarters, U. S. European Command; commanding officer, Woman Recruit Training Battalion, Marine Corps Recruit Depot, Parris Island, South Carolina; and assistant plans and policy officer on the staff at Headquarters, Fleet Marine Force, Pacific. She has also served as the commanding officer, Headquarters and Service Battalion, Marine Corps Base, Camp Pendleton, California. As the commanding officer, she was the first woman officer in the Marine Corps to command a predominantly male battalion. She has also attended the Armed Forces Staff College. Colonel Bane is currently head, Separation and Retirement Branch, Personnel Management Division, Headquarters, United States Marine Corps, Washington, D.C.

First American Women to Reach Star Rank

Brigadier General ANNA MAE HAYS entered active duty as an operating-room nurse in 1942 and progressed through the ranks to become chief of the Army Nurse Corps in 1967. On June 11, 1970, (then) Colonel Hays was promoted to the rank of brigadier general. This was the first time in the 196-year history of the U. S. Army that any woman had been promoted to the rank of general officer. General Hays, a native of Buffalo, New York, attended nurses' training in Allentown, Pennsylvania, received her nursing education at Columbia University and her master's degree from Catholic University, Washington, D.C. She was a nurse for President Eisenhower during his hospitalization at Walter Reed Hospital in 1956. General Hays retired in 1971 after more than 29 years of active service. In 1977 she was named an outstanding alumna of Catholic University.

ELIZABETH P. HOISINGTON, the first Women's Army Corps officer to be promoted to brigadier general, attained that rank on the same day as Brigadier General Anna Mae Hays, June 11, 1970. General Hoisington was born in Newton, Kansas, but was graduated from high school (1936) and college (1940) in Maryland. She enlisted in 1942 and was commissioned a third officer (second lieutenant) in the WAAC in 1943. During World War II she served in the European Theater of Operations. Her outstanding performance of duty in progressively more responsible and challenging assignments both overseas and in the United States earned for her an imposing record of citations and decorations. She served as director of the Women's Army Corps from August 1966 until her retirement in 1971.

First Air Force Nurse to Achieve Star Status

On July 1, 1972, E. ANN HOEFLY, chief of the Air Force Nurse Corps, Headquarters U. S. Air Force, Washington, D.C., became the second Air Force woman, but the first Air Force nurse, to be promoted to general officer status. (The first Air Force woman general officer was Major General JEANNE M. HOLM, p. 539.) During World War II, Brigadier General Hoefly entered the U. S. Army Nurse Corps and served in the European Theater of Operations. She returned to the United States in 1946 and continued serving in the Army until 1949, at which time she transferred to the newly established U. S. Air Force Nurse Corps. During her career she completed the flight nurse course at the USAF School of Aviation Medicine and obtained her B.S. and M.A. degrees, the latter from Columbia University. In 1967 she served as chief nurse of the AF Systems Command at Andrews AFB, Maryland and attended the Air War College. She assumed duties as chief of the U. S. Air Force Nurse Corps in August 1968, and in 1971 attended the Industrial War College. Brigadier General Hoefly retired in 1974.

First Female Admiral

Captain ARLENE B. DUERK, head of the Navy Nurse Corps, in April 1972 became the first woman admiral in the history of the U. S. Navy. The importance of her nomination to other women, she said at the time, was that "They can see that the sky's the limit now." A native of Defiance, Ohio, Admiral Duerk was commissioned in the U. S. Navy Nurse Corps in 1943 when she was 22 years old. Her assignments have included the hospital ship *Benevolence* during World War II, various naval hospitals from Virginia to California, and overseas tours in Japan and the Philippines.

First Woman Line Admiral

Rear Admiral FRAN MCKEE, U. S. Navy, in 1976 became the first woman line officer selected for flag rank. (Two previously promoted to rear admiral were in the Navy Nurse Corps.) Rear Admiral McKee's early duty assignments were, in her words, "fairly typical of the assignments given to women officers" at the time she was commissioned an ensign in 1950 after earning her degree in chemistry from the University of Alabama. She also has a master's degree in international affairs from George Washington University. In 1978, Rear Admiral McKee serves as director of Navy Education on the staff of the chief, Navy Education and Training Division, Pensacola, Florida.

First Indian in the Women Marines

Private MINNIE SPOTTED-WOLF, of Heart Butte, Montana, enlisted in the Marine Corps Women's Reserve in July 1943. She was the first full-blooded Indian recruit. The slight, 114-pound, 20-year-old girl had worked on her father's ranch doing such chores as cutting fence posts, driving a two-ton truck, and breaking horses. Her comment on boot camp training: "Hard but not too hard."

First WAC Master Sergeant and Sergeant Major

CAROLYN H. JAMES was the first enlisted WAC to be promoted to the grade of master sergeant (E-8), in April 1959, and the first enlisted WAC to be promoted to sergeant major, in June 1960. She retired in April 1965.

First Woman to Head Navy's Food Service Program

A 21-year Navy veteran, Supply Corps Captain RUTH TOMSUDEN, now retired, took over as commanding officer of the Navy Food Service Systems Office when a male officer was reassigned from that post. Captain Tomsuden's responsibilities as head of NFSSO included the technical direction and financial control of the Navy's 1,000 general messes, and the training of more than 23,000 Navy personnel employed in food supply programs.

Triple Firsts

Captain LINDA BURCH was the first WAC officer assigned as assistant professor of military science at the University of Wisconsin; the first WAC officer to be instructor at the Fort Riley, Kansas, ROTC Advanced Camp; and the first WAC officer to be adviser for a Pershing rifle company, another position she held at the university.

Spar/WAC/WAVE: A Three-Service Career

Personnelman First Class DOLORES GENEVIEVE KENNEDY retired from the U. S. Navy in 1967 after having previously served in the U. S. Coast Guard from 1943 to 1946 and the U. S. Army from 1949 to 1952. In 1952 she enlisted in the Navy, where she remained on active duty until retirement.

Pioneer Engineer in the Air Force

ARMINTA J. HARNESS, an engineering graduate from the University of Southern California, was the first woman engineer to join the United States Air Force. During the 24 years of her military career, her assignments included duty in a variety of engineering projects as well as research and development. She was the first woman on orders as a test engineer during flight testing of experimental equipment, the first woman to receive the specialty rating of staff development engineer, and the first woman to be awarded both the Senior and Master Missileman badges. After her retirement (as a lieutenant colonel) from the Air Force in 1974, she joined the Westinghouse Company and became manager of laboratory planning, Hanford Engineering Development Laboratory, Richland, Washington.

Highest-Scoring Surveyor

WAF Staff Sergeant GRETE M. BOHANNON, a native of Austria, graduated in survey engineering from the Technical University of Vienna, and worked as an illustrator for the U. S. Air Force in that city before emigrating to the United States. She joined the Air Force Reserve in 1957 and became an American citizen five years later. In civilian life, she was the only woman (as of 1973) registered by the Massachusetts Board of Registration of Civil Engineers and Land Surveyors. In her Air Force job as site development specialist with the 901st Tactical Airlift Groups at Hanscom Field, Massachusetts, she was the only female member of the 901st Civil Engineering Flight and got the highest score possible on her level-three career development surveyor's course.

First Woman Veterinarian in Air Force Reserve

In 1967 Dr. ALEXANDRA C. BAKARICH was graduated from Washington State University as a doctor of veterinary medicine. She spent the next few years gaining professional experience with a research facility associated with the University of Illinois, then accepted a commission in the Veterinary Corps, Air Force Reserve, in 1971, and became its first woman veterinarian. She entered active Air Force service as a Reserve officer in 1973. By 1975 Captain (Dr.) Bakarich was a graduate patrol-dog handler, having completed a patrol-dog handler course conducted by the School of Applied Aerospace Sciences at Lackland Air Force Base. With more than 400 military dogs at Lackland, Dr. Bakarich has her hands full. However, treating sick or injured animals is not the only thing that Air Force vets do. They also work with food hygiene and sanitation programs as well as with maintaining control over diseases that are transmitted from animals to people.

First Two Women Assigned to Duty in Vietnam

At the request of the Republic of Vietnam, two members of the United States Women's Army Corps were sent to Saigon in January 1965 to act as advisers to Vietnam's then newly formed Women's Armed Forces Corps. Major KATHLEEN I. WILKES, of Cobbtown, Georgia, was designated to assist Major Tran Cam Huong, director of the WAFC, with the development of organization and policy. Master Sergeant BETTY ADAMS, of Woodside, Long Island, New York, was selected to assist the deputy director, Captain Ho Thi Ve, in the establishment of a training program.

Air Force's First Woman Flight Medical Officer

Captain PATRICIA A. NELL was the first woman to complete the primary course in aerospace medicine, Brooks AFB, Texas, graduating on April 15, 1966. As the Air Force's first woman flight medical officer, she served on active duty from June to December 1966 and April to June 1967 with the 820th Medical Group at Plattsburgh AFB, New York. Since separation from active duty, Dr. Nell maintains Reserve status as a rated flight surgeon with the 440th Tactical Airlift Wing at Billy Mitchell Field, Milwaukee, Wisconsin.

First Female Orbital Analyst in the Air Defense Command

Lieutenant DEBORAH G. JOHNSON, who holds a B.S. degree in chemistry from Texas Tech and was graduated with distinction from Officer's Training School, in 1967 was assigned to the Space Defense Center in Colorado, where data is received from Air Defense Command spacetracking sensors throughout the world. When a satellite is located, it is given a code number and the radar sites maintain a watch on its orbiting characteristics. Lieutenant Johnson's job was to study the orbital data and predict when and where satellites would reenter the earth's atmosphere and burn up.

First Woman to Receive Commission Through ROTC

LESLIE HOLLEY attended Auburn University and participated in the Air Force ROTC program. When she graduated in 1971 and was commissioned a second lieutenant in the Air Force, she became the first woman to receive a commission through the Reserve Officer Training Program.

First Woman to Command OpCon Unit

Commander KATHERINE JOAN HINMAN in 1973, became the first woman officer to command an Operational Control Unit in the Naval Air Reserve Command. The 25-member OpCon Unit 5-W3, which drills at Naval Air Station, Willow Grove, Pennsylvania, directs the search and tracking operations for Reserve antisubmarine warfare aircraft. Commander Hinman was well qualified for the commanding officer's job. A graduate of Vassar with a degree in mathematics and later a masters in business adminis-

tration from American University, she also had extensive active duty training in antisubmarine warfare work.

First Woman Hurricane Hunter

In 1973 JUDITH ANN NEUFFER was the first of eight women to be selected for the Navy Flight Training Program. As a pilot-trainee, she underwent rigorous physical conditioning and intensive in-flight instruction in various aircraft. Her first assignment upon successful completion of the program was with the Navy's Hurricane Hunters Squadron in Jacksonville, and her first taste of hurricane hunting was piloting the four-engine P-3 Orion straight through the eye of hurricane Carmen, with winds of 150 mph. Her performance won the approval of her fellow officers—all male.

Female Whirlybird Pilot

Following her graduation from Officer Candidate School in 1973, Ensign ANNA MARIE FUQUA reported directly to Pensacola, Florida, for flight training. She earned her wings of gold in May 1974, and with further training learned to fly the H-3 helicopter. As of 1975, Ensign Fuqua was assigned to Helicopter Combat Support Squadron 6 at Norfolk, Virginia.

First Navy Woman Scuba Diver

On November 30, 1973, Personnelman Seaman NANCY K. GARNER became the first woman to graduate from a Navy diving school. Prior to her admission into the Scuba School at the Naval Station, San Diego, California, only males had been selected for such training. Garner said, "I'm planning on a Navy career. I want to make a substantial contribution, and I can do that as a diver."

First Female Flight Surgeons in the Navy

In December 1973 two women physicians were awarded their wings of gold after graduating in the top half of their class at Pensacola, Florida. As flight surgeons, Lieutenants JANE O. McWILLIAMS of Nags Head, North Carolina, and VICTORIA M. VOGE of Austin, Texas, are responsible for keeping air crews flying safely and effectively. (Flight surgeons do not have actual control of aircraft.) At the graduation ceremony, Rear Admiral Oscar Gray, Jr., head of the Naval Aerospace and Regional Medical Institute at Pensacola, commented: "The women participated in every aspect of the training program with a capability equal to that of their male counterparts. They have vividly shown that women doctors represent a strong and qualified source of Navy flight surgeons. We consider the Navy fortunate to have our first two female flight surgeons in our 51-year history."

First Woman Optometrist in Air Force

When Captain ALLISON SMITH went on active duty in January 1973, she was the only female optometrist in the U. S. Air Force. She is a graduate of the University of California at Berkeley, School of Optometry, and was in private practice for two years before joining the Air Force. At Sheppard AFB, Texas, she attended the medical service officer orientation course before being assigned to Altus AFB, Oklahoma.

First Women Crew Members of the Pacific Fleet P-3 Orion

At Moffet Field, California, in 1973 two Navy enlisted women qualified as observers in P-3 Orion antisubmarine warfare patrol planes at the Naval Air Station. Aviation Maintenance Administrationman Third Class LEE RUTH ALVERSON and Training Devicesman Third Class CAROL L. KOKES were certified after passing a rigorous written exam and a four-and-a-half-hour in-flight test, which required the two women to carry out routine observer duties as well as to participate in emergency drills ranging from ditching and bailout procedures to emergency decompression and fire.

Navy Woman Dons a Hard Hat

Among the new assignments women began taking on circa 1973 was that of

Lieutenant (junior grade) ISABEL M. DEVINE, who wore her hard hat to monitor repairs aboard the guided missile destroyer *Lynde McCormick* in her duties as assistant ship's superintendent. She is a civil engineering graduate of Mississippi State University and worked at the Charleston Naval Shipyard before entering the Navy.

First Woman Quartermaster to "Crew" at Sea

Seaman RACHEL WORLEY (later Rainey) believes she was the first woman to go to sea in preparation for her training as quartermaster. In 1974 she was serving on the Staff, Air-Surface Coordinating Office Mediterranean, Naples, Italy, where her duties included the plotting of passenger and cargo ships' movements in the Mediterranean. As part of her training, Worley was permitted to "crew" with the destroyer escort U.S.S. *Courtney* during a one-day daylight maneuver. Although women are currently prohibited by law from serving on combat ships, Worley's day on the *Courtney* enabled her to fulfill the "practical skills" requirements for advancement in grade.

First Woman Combat Targeting Officer

Air Force Lieutenant CARLA ORNDOFF was in 1974 hailed as the first woman combat targeting officer at Malmstrom Air Force Base, Omaha. She and her husband, Lieutenant David Orndoff, were both serving as CTT officers at the time and looking forward to full careers in the Air Force. Because there are only six bases that use Combat Targeting Teams, they anticipate few problems with separations. Ms. Orndoff was graduated from Washington State University in 1969 and was commissioned in the Air Force. For her specialty, she received technical training at Chanute AFB, and completed the School of Military Sciences, Officer, at Lackland AFB. She says of her work, "Anyone properly trained can do the job. The fact that I'm a woman neither adds to nor detracts from my ability to function as a targeting officer."

First Female Aviator in the U. S. Navy

In 1974 Lieutenant (Junior Grade) BARBARA ALLEN (now Barbara Allen Rainey) completed a year of flight training and became the first woman to wear the U. S. Navy's Wings of Gold. Lieutenant (jg) Allen completed all her flights as scheduled and required no extra instruction. She attended Long Beach Lakewood High School and Long Beach City College before entering Whittier College, where she received a bachelor's degree in physical education. She is now stationed with a Pacific Fleet Squadron in California. Because women by law are restricted from combat roles, Ms. Rainey and other women aviators will be limited to flying aircraft or fleet-type helicopters.

First U. S. Air Force Woman to Attend National War College

Brigadier General CHRIS C. MANN had the distinction of being the first Air Force woman to attend the National War College at Fort McNair, Washington, D.C. After graduation from there in 1974, she assumed command of the 3504th USAF Recruiting Group at Lackland Air Force Base, Texas. General Mann entered the Air Force with a direct commission in 1953 and attended officer basic military training at Lack-

land. After various administrative and personnel assignments in the United States and overseas, General Mann, who is the wife of a retired Air Force officer, in August 1971 became chief of the Classification and Evaluation Standards Branch at Air Force Headquarters in Washington, D.C. She was promoted to the grade of brigadier general with date of rank August 19, 1975.

First Woman to Command a Wing in the Air Force

On December 1, 1974, Colonel NORMA E. BROWN assumed command of the 6940th Security Wing at Fort Meade, Maryland, becoming the first woman to be assigned to command a wing in the Air Force. Colonel Brown entered the Air Force through the Officer Candidate School commissioning program, and received her second lieutenant's bars in 1951. Her first assignment was with Headquarters Flight Service, Washington, D.C., where she was chief of military personnel. After other assignments, including a tour in Newfoundland, she was selected in 1961 for an exchange tour with the Royal Air Force. She served as personnel staff officer with the RAF Technical Training Command Headquarters, Brampton, England. Later Colonel Brown attended the Professsional Personnel Management Course at Maxwell AFB, Alabama. In 1977 Colonel Brown was selected for promotion to brigadier general.

Army Times Firsts

In January 1975 the *Army Times* newspaper reported a number of firsts achieved by Army women in installations and schools around the world. Among them:

At Fort Amador, Canal Zone, Private First Class CATHY NEWBY and Privates BARBARA RIMIL, TERRY BAKER, and SANDRA HARRIS—the first WACs serving as MPs. Pfc. Newby in addition is one of the first female dog handlers in the Army.

In Bremerhaven, Germany, Private LESLIE ANN HURFF, the first policewoman with 1st Platoon, Company C, 94th MP Battalion.

At Fort Lewis, Washington, Private First Class SHELLEY BADHAM, the first woman member of the 9th Infantry Division Band.

At the Army Communications Electronics School, Fort Dix, New Jersey, Specialist Fourth Class MARY POLLARD, the first woman honor graduate of the camera equipment repair course.

Specialist Fifth Class JENNIFER M. TUCKER, the first woman to receive distinguished graduate honors at the Fort Riley, Kansas, Noncommissioned Officer Academy (1975). She also received the Commandant's Inspection Award.

In the Primary NCO Academy class's combat support service at Fort Carson, Colorado, Specialist Fifth Class JAN SCHREINER, first woman distinguished graduate and winner of the Commandant's Award.

At Fort Sill, Oklahoma, Private First Class NICOLE CRUFT, distinguished graduate in the meteorological observation class. Three of the four honor graduates in this class also were women: Specialists Fourth Class VALERIE SEDLAK and SUSAN A. SMITH, and Private ELLEN PANCEREV.

In addition, at Schofield Barracks, Hawaii, 27 WACs from the 25th Infantry Division qualified with the M-16 rifle. All but one achieved scores meriting the expert rating. The women were on the range as a result of a policy change in the Army that made weapons qualification mandatory for WAC reenlistment and requires that all women enlisting in the active Army or reserves must take defensive weapons training as part of basic training. One of the group at Schofield Barracks, Specialist Fourth Class FLORA MCLEAN, commented, "I have to admit that I was kinda scared at first, but after the instructors explained things to us and we shot a couple of times it was really no big thing."

First Female Skipper of Yard Patrol Craft

Lieutenant BONNIE LATSCH in April 1975 was assigned to duty as officer-in-charge of yard patrol craft at the Newport Training Center. The YP Division provides "at sea" training for students as well as refresher training for Destroyer 28 ship personnel and submariners from New London, Connecticut. Lieutenant Latsch joined the Navy in 1971 after graduation from the University of California at Berkeley with a degree in history and attended Officer Candidate School at Newport, Rhode Island, then went on to become one of the first women to complete the surface warfare officers course at Newport's Naval Education and Training Center.

First Women Instructors for Air Force Male Recruits

In early 1975 the Air Force began a test program at Lackland Air Force Base, Texas, using six female instructors to teach male recruits the rudiments of Air Force life, including close order drill, discipline, and the care and folding of uniforms. The women were Staff Sergeants JUDITH L. BABSON, GINGER K. JONES, DONNA S. BUCKLEY and Sergeants JEAN C. SIELOFF, MURLENE B. ANCAR, and PATRICIA M. ALLAN. The Air Force reported a favorable initial reaction: Recruits obeyed the female instructors just as they did the males.

Flight Test Engineer Marks a First

The Air Force's Test Pilot School at Edwards AFB, California, graduated its first female officer, Captain JANE HOLLEY, in 1975. Although not a pilot, she logged more than 100 hours in the air to complete the 44-week course. She entered the Air Force in 1971 with an AFROTC commission and an aerospace engineering degree from Auburn University.

First Woman to Receive Cheney Award

The Cheney Award for 1975 went to Captain (then First Lieutenant) REGINA C. AUNE, who "distinguished herself by conspicuous acts of valor" at Saigon, while serving as medical crew director in an aircraft bringing Vietnamese orphans and civilians to the United States. The

Air Force C-5A crashed shortly after takeoff, killing all but 176 of the 330 passengers aboard. It was only after most of the survivors had been evacuated that Captain Aune lost consciousness and it was discovered that she had been seriously injured. The Cheney Award is given annually to a selected member of the U. S. Air Force or its Reserve Components as a memorial to First Lieutenant William A. Cheney, brother of RUTH CHENEY STREETER, first director of the women Marines (p. 535). Lieutenant Cheney was killed in action in Italy in 1918. Captain Aune, who is married and a mother, began activity with the Air Force in 1973.

First WAF Member of Capital's Armed Forces Police

When Airman First Class ALTHERIA WATKINS, at age 26, joined the Armed Forces Police Detachment in Washington, D.C., in 1975, she had to become accustomed to startled stares and the inevitable question, "What are *you* doing wearing a gun?" The first Women's Air Force (WAF) policewoman in that assignment came to it with impressive qualifications. Prior to completion of the Security Police School at Lackland Air Force Base, Texas, she had worked with a deputy sheriff's office in her native Oregon and completed three years of corrections education study. Her assignment with the Armed Forces Police was not considered as dangerous as that of a civilian policewoman, for, despite the large concentration of service members in the Washington, D.C., metropolitan area, the serious-incident crime rate is relatively low.

Four Air Force Women Serve at Sea

Sergeant JO A. BEALE, Airmen First Class BETTY L. BAKER and JOANN GIBSON, and Airman LORNA JOHNSON were part of the instrumentation team running test equipment aboard the advanced range instrumentation ship *General H. H. Arnold* (1975). Although the ship, which receives and records radar and telemetry data of the missile reentry system, is operated by the Military Sealift Command at the Air Force Eastern Test Range at Patrick AFB, Florida, the Air Force controls the technical operations and equipment aboard.

First Flag Secretary and Aide

Lieutenant Commander KATHLEEN BYERLY, flag secretary and aide (the first woman to hold that position) to Rear Admiral Allen E. Hill, Commander, Training Command, U. S. Pacific Fleet, was chosen one of *Time* magazine's 12 Women of the Year for 1975. *Time* described her as "one of the fast-rising women in the armed forces." Lieutenant Commander Byerly's job at COMTRAPAC included management of the admiral's staff of about 55 officers, enlisted, and civilian men and women. She also served as liaison between other commands as well as with offices in Washington, D.C.

First Female Officer to Head Naval Officer Candidate School

In July 1975 Commander LUCILLE R. KUHN took over as head of the Navy's coeducational Officer Candidate School at the Naval Education and Training Center, Newport, Rhode Island—the first woman to become director of the school in its 24-year history. While serving in this assignment, she was promoted to the rank of captain. Captain Kuhn, who enlisted in the Navy as a radioman, was the first woman to participate in the Navy's "five-term" college program in 1958, and earned an A.B. in psychology from George Washington University in 1960. Among her various assignments were those of recruiting in Washington, D.C.: military personnel director for the Twelfth Naval District, San Francisco; and deputy director for research and administration in the Office of Legislative Affairs, Washington, D.C. She had been serving as assistant director of the Officer Candidate School prior to becoming director.

Army's First Female Tank Driver

Specialist Fourth Class DEBRA HOUGHTON first enlisted in the Army Medical Corps but could find no assignment there to suit her. Since Army tests showed that she had mechanical and electronic aptitudes, she was transferred to the Ordnance Corps and sent to a tank turret class. After finishing the course, ranking second in her class, Houghton was certified in 1975 as the first woman tank driver at the Tank-Automotive Command, Warren, Michigan. She compensates for her 5′3½″ height by using a booster seat to give her the proper field of view. But locking the parking brake and raising the engine grill door require muscle, and, she said, "are the toughest things for me to do."

First to Direct Helicopter Small-Deck Landing

It is believed that Aviation Machinist's Mate (J) Airman CHERYL L. HARGIS, of Helicopter Antisubmarine Squadron Light 30, was the first woman in the Navy to direct a helicopter aboard a ship with a small deck. In 1976 she directed a Seasprite helicopter aboard the Military Sealift Command surveying ship *Harkness,* which was berthed at Little Creek (near Norfolk), Virginia.

First Woman Midshipman to Receive Varsity Letter

U. S. Naval Academy Midshipman Fourth Class PEGGY FELDMAN, of San Antonio, Texas, was the first woman midshipman to receive a gold "N" varsity letter. In March 1977 she swam five events in the Eastern Intercollegiate Women's Swimming Championships at the University of Delaware. She piled up 68 points for the Naval Academy, which finished 13th in a field of 48 teams. Midshipman Feldman broke meet records in the 200- and 400-yard individual medleys; took second place in the 500-yard freestyle, third in the 200-yard freestyle, and eighth in the 100-yard freestyle. The only Naval Academy woman swimming at the intercollegiate level, she practiced with the varsity men's team, putting in 10,000 to 15,000 yards a day in workouts before breakfast and after classes.

Half of the Only Husband-Wife Flight Surgeon Team

In addition to being half of the only husband-wife flight surgeon team in the military service, Captain (Dr.) FIONA CLEMENTS is the only female USAF flight surgeon on active duty (as of March 1977). Dr. Clements, a native of England, met her husband, Dennis Clements, while he was studying in London on an elective from the University of Rochester. They were married in England and returned to the United States to complete their medical training. Commissioned in the Air Force and certified as rated flight surgeons, they were assigned to the 63rd Military Airlift Wing at Norton AFB.

First Woman Company Officer at the U. S. Naval Academy

Lieutenant SUE STEPHENS not only was instrumental in the Naval Academy's planning for the admission of women, but she was the first woman in the Academy's 131-year history to be named a company officer. In 1977 she was the only woman of the 36 Navy and Marine Corps officers who were company officers for the 4,200 midshipmen. Company officers deal with the usual Navy paperwork and inspections, but they also have a lot of personal contact with midshipmen, counseling them in everything from academics to professional matters. Being a company officer is no 9-to-5 job. Stephens' office hours often started at 7:30 A.M., then she was on the sports field in the late afternoon cheering her company on in intramurals, and back in the office after dinner clearing up paperwork. The daughter of a minister, Lieutenant Stephens majored in math at Mary Baldwin College and joined the Navy after her graduation in 1970. She reported to the Naval Academy as conduct officer before becoming a company officer.

The Coast Guard's First Woman Pilot

On March 4, 1977, Ensign JANNA LAMBINE graduated from naval aviation training at Naval Air Station, Whiting Field in Milton, Florida, to go on record as a first for the Coast Guard—its first woman aviator. Ensign Lambine completed four weeks of aviation indoctrination training at NAS Pensacola, Florida, and learned to fly fixed-wing aircraft before specializing as a helicopter pilot. She had no flight experience before joining the Coast Guard. Her college studies led to a B.S. degree in geology, with oceanographic subjects her main interest. Ensign Lambine's first duty assignment at Coast Guard Air Station, Astoria, Oregon, was flying search-and-rescue missions, as well as air surveillance of pollution and of fisheries.

First Female Marine Officer to Attend Naval War College

In 1977 Colonel ROBERTA N. PATRICK was a student at the Naval War College, Newport, Rhode Island, the first woman Marine officer selected for this assignment. Her previous service was as officer on the staff at Headquarters, Fleet Marine Force, Pacific; administrative officer on the staff at Headquarters, U. S. European Command; commanding officer Woman Recruit Training Battalion, Marine Corps Recruit Depot, Parris Island, South Carolina; and director Marine Corps Extension School. She has also attended the Marine Corps Command and Staff College.

First Woman Physician Army War College Graduate

Dr. CHRISTINE E. HAYCOCK, director of surgical trauma services at Martland Hospital and an associate professor of surgery at the New Jersey College of Medicine, is the first woman physician to be graduated from the Army War College (1977). Dr. Haycock, then a colonel in the Army Medical Corps, was president of her class at the War College.

First Women Assigned to Sea Duty with Coast Guard

DEBRA GAIL SNELSON, 23, of Frostburg, Maryland, and TERRY BURTON, 26, of La Habra, California, were the first females assigned as permanent shipboard crew members aboard U.S. ships. On June 2, 1977, the two women officers graduated from the Officers' Candidate School at the Coast Guard Reserve Training Center, Yorktown, Virginia. They volunteered for assignment aboard 378-foot cutters after Secretary of Transportation Brock Adams announced (on May 25, 1977) the history-making decision that Coast Guard women would be eligible for sea duty.

First Woman Marine General

In May 1978 Colonel MARGARET A. BREWER became the first woman brigadier general in the history of the U. S. Marine Corps. Her assignment upon promotion also made her the first woman to serve as director of information at Marine Corps Headquarters in Washington, D.C. During her 26-year career, General Brewer held many positions, including that of seventh and final director of Women Marines (an office disbanded in 1977). She entered the service as a second lieutenant in 1952, having attended officer candidate training between college years at the University of Michigan. After serving for the duration of the Korean conflict, General Brewer had planned to return to inactive duty, but challenging and enjoyable assignments prompted her to make the Marine Corps her career. Although women in 1978 were still not eligible for combat-related assignments, General Brewer's promotion reflects the expanding opportunities for women in the Marine Corps, whose 190,-000 members in 1978 included 4,400 women. Over the next decade the Marines hope to increase the number of women to about 10,000.

First Woman AFROTC Commander

Major MARY N. ABBOTT, the first woman ROTC unit commander in the U. S. Air Force, reported for duty in July 1978 at Valdosta State College, Valdosta, Georgia. A native of Texas, she was graduated from Mississippi State College for Women in 1962 and commissioned in the Air Force through Officers Training School the same year. Major Abbott had served in training, recruiting, and administration assignments in the United States, Thailand, and Taiwan before being selected to attend Florida State University, where she earned an M.B.A. in 1974. Her strong background as a personnel officer contributed to her qualifications for the ROTC commander's job, in which counseling cadets and managing cadet personnel actions are key parts of the assignment.

MILITARY WOMEN, OTHER NATIONS

Some Soviet Women Firsts

In World War II Russian women pilots were assigned to combat units, and in 1941 three aviation regiments formed were "manned" solely by female personnel. One of these, the 586th Women's Fighter Regiment, defended its combat route so effectively that no enemy bombers reached the Soviet Union's protected industrial centers and railway junctions. The entire personnel of the regiment was awarded orders and medals of the U.S.S.R.

Here, according to the *Soviet Military Review* (March 1977), are some of them: VALERIA IVANOVNA KHOMYAKOVA was credited as being the first woman pilot in the history of aviation to shoot down an enemy bomber. In September 1942, over Saratov on the Volga, she destroyed a German Junkers-88.

OLGA YAMSHCHIKOVA, squadron leader, instructor, and test pilot, made 93 sorties and took part in many air combats. In 1947 she became the first Russian woman to fly a jet aircraft.

RAYA SURNACHEVSKAYA and TAMARA PAMYATNYKH engaged 42 enemy bombers in a battle over a big railway junction and a bridge over the River Don. Fighting against terrific odds, they shot down four bombers and broke up the attack with not a single bomb hitting the objective they were covering.

LILYA LITVYAK and KATYA BUDANOVA attained such high levels of skill that they were members of ace teams carrying out "lone-wolf" operations. Litvyak destroyed 12 enemy planes and Budanova 10. Both were awarded the Order of the Red Banner and the Order of the Patriotic War.

KATHERINE I. ZELENKO, on a reconnaissance flight, encountered seven Messerschmitt Me-109s. It was her 13th dogfight, and with the odds against her, she shot down one of the fighters and was attacking a second when her plane was hit and nose-dived to the ground. Her heart was pierced by a cannon splinter.

Director of Women's Royal Canadian Naval Service in World War II

Ms. D. B. (ADELAIDE) SINCLAIR, distinguished lecturer in economics and political science, holder of five college degrees and two orders of merit, served as director, Women's Royal Canadian Naval

Service, 1943–46. She retired with the rank of captain and was awarded the Order of the British Empire (Military). Ms. Sinclair received her B.A. (1922), M.A. (1925), and LL.D. (1946) degrees from the University of Toronto. Laval University awarded her a D.Sc.Soc. in 1952, and in 1956 she was awarded an L.H.D. by the University of Rochester. After World War II, she became executive assistant to the Deputy Minister of National Welfare, Ottawa, Ontario, until 1957. From 1957 to 1967 she served as deputy executive director, UNICEF. Ms. and children's societies. In 1967 she was Sinclair was active in numerous welfare awarded the Order of Canada.

First Canadian Woman to Go to Sea in a Wartime Ship

As a young girl, FERN BLODGETT, of Cobourg, Ontario, loved to go down to the shores of Lake Ontario and watch the lake boats pass. She yearned to be a sailor, and the lure of the sea remained a stronger fascination for her than the stenographer's job she went to in Toronto. When World War II loomed, she enrolled in night classes and became a trained wireless operator. Her dream of sailing the high seas became a reality in June 1941, when the Norwegian cargo ship *Mosdale* needed a wireless operator and she was the only one available. The *Mosdale* was later to hold the record for more wartime crossings (98) of the Atlantic than any other Allied ship, and Fern Blodgett was aboard for most of them (78). From July 1942 she sailed as Ms. Gerner Sunde, wife of the 31-year-old captain. After the war she went ashore to stay and since that time has made her home in Norway. Although she has met other women who went to sea in wartime ships, she believes that she was the first.

First Woman Doctor to Enter Canadian Armed Forces

For her work in the Royal Canadian Air Force, JEAN DAVEY was awarded the Order of the British Empire. A graduate of the University of Toronto, she was the first woman doctor to enter the Canadian Armed Forces, and the first Canadian woman to become a fellow of the Royal College of Physicians by examination (1945). Dr. Davey has also been awarded the Order of Canada and elected a fellow of the American College of Physicians. Former chief of the Department of Medicine, Women's College Hospital, Toronto, Ontario, she was associate professor of medicine, University of Toronto, 1961–68, and in 1968 was appointed professor in the Department of Medicine, University of Toronto, Ontario.

Canada's Only Woman Fighter-Pilot Trainer

In 1976 MARGARET LITTLEWOOD, age 60, of Edmonton, Canada's only woman fighter-pilot trainer during World War II, was awarded the Amelia Earhart Medallion for her pioneering contributions.

First WRAC in U.S.-England Exchange Program

In 1975 the Women's Army Corps participated in an exchange program whereby two WAC officers went to England and Lieutenant PRUNELLA J. SAMSON, of the Women's Royal Army Corps, came to the United States. Samson's first assignment involved training WAC recruits at Fort McClellan, Alabama. The following year she worked as assistant plans and policies officer for the U. S. Army's 7th Infantry Division. She "enjoyed the field training the most."

NATO Conference of Women Officers

The military women listed below were representatives of their country at the latest NATO Senior Service Women Officers Conference in Brussels on May

3–5, 1977. The North Atlantic Treaty Organization and Supreme Headquarters Allied Powers Europe (NATO/SHAPE) sponsor such meetings every two years. Briefings and discussions include NATO political and military matters as well as the role of women in the alliance. Delegates work together toward an understanding of problems, goals, and objectives in their joint effort to resist armed attack and settle disputes by peaceful means.

Canada

Lieutenant Colonel MARION GAY, Director, Women Personnel
Colonel JESSIE LAWSON, Director of Nursing Services

Denmark

Lieutenant Colonel BODIL WESTERHOLM, Director, Women's Army Corps
Commander GURLI VIDO, Acting Head of Service, Women's Naval Corps
Colonel ELSE MARTENSEN-LARSEN, Director, Women's Air Force
First Lieutenant INGE HANSEN, Platoon Officer, Women's Army Corps

France

Lieutenant Commander French Navy ANDRÉE RAMBERZ, Recruiting Office, HQ Mediterranean Zone
Major JEANNINE CLEMENT, Assistant to the CO of the Armed Forces School for Female Military Personnel, Caen, France
Lieutenant LARYSE DUMONT, Tactical Air Force, HQ, Metz, France

Germany

Dr. (Major) WALTRAUD THOMAS, Representing Women in the German Armed Forces

Netherlands

Lieutenant Colonel CATHARINA ADANK, Commanding Officer, Royal Netherlands Army Women's Corps
First Officer CAROLINE POMÉS, Personnel

Officer, Royal Netherlands Navy Women's Corps
Lieutenant Colonel JOSINA VAN DER WERF, Director, Royal Netherlands Air Force Women's Corps
Lieutenant Colonel WILHELMINA VLASMAN, Chief Officer, Royal Netherlands Army Nursing Corps

Norway

Major ELISABETH SVERI, Women Inspector, Norwegian Army
Major EVA BERG, Chief of Joint Norwegian Military Nursing Services

Turkey

Dr. (Lieutenant Colonel) AFET AKYOL, doctor at Mevki Hospital, Ankara, Turkey
Major GULER TIRYAKIOĞLU, Chief of Adjutant General Staff, Turkish General Staff, Ankara
Major YUKSEL GÜLER, English Instructor at Military High School, Isiklar, Turkey
Major SEREFNUR KOR, Air Supply Command, Izmit
Lieutenant Commander SERPIL ERDEMLI, Ordnance, Main Jet Base Commander, Izmit

United Kingdom

Commandant VONLA MCBRIDE, Director, Women's Royal Naval Service
Brigadier EILEEN NOLAN, Director, Women's Royal Army Corps
Air Commander JOY TAMBLIN, Director, Women's Royal Air Force
Miss PATRICIA GOULD, Matron in Chief, Queen Alexandra's Royal Naval Nursing Service
Brigadier JOAN MORIARTY, Matron in Chief (Army) and Director of Army Nursing Services
Air Commandant BARBARA DUCAT-AMOS, Matron in Chief, Princess Mary's Royal Air Force Nursing Service

United States

Brigadier General MARY CLARKE, Director, Women's Army Corps

Colonel MARGARET BREWER, Director of Women Marines

Rear Admiral FRAN MCKEE, Director of Naval Educational Development

Brigadier General CHRIS MANN, Deputy Director, Personnel Plans for Human Resources Development, DCS/Personnel Air Force

Brigadier General MADELYN PARKS, Chief, Army Nurse Corps

Rear Admiral MAXINE CONDER, Director, Navy Nurse Corps

Brigadier General CLAIRE GARRECHT, Director, Air Force Nurse Corps

Observers

Colonel VIRGINIA BROWN, U.S. Chief of Nursing, Europe

Major MARY MACKENZIE, Officer Commanding 29th Company, WRAC Administrative Officer (United Kingdom)

First Woman Regular Officer in the Norwegian Army

Major ELISABETH SVERI participated in the Norwegian resistance movement in 1945. She served on the Army Signal Staff as signal and personnel officer from 1946 to 1949, and became inspector of the Norwegian Army Women's Service in 1959. The first woman appointed a regular officer in the Norwegian Army, Major Sveri holds the top rank for women in Norway. She was a member of the committee planning women's service in the armed forces, 1970–73, and is a member of the joint working group concerning women in armed forces. Major Sveri was a Norwegian delegate to the NATO Conference of senior women officers in Brussels, Belgium, on May 3–5, 1977 (p. 552).

Director of Joint Norwegian Military Nursing Services

Major EVA BERG's nursing education included special training in hospital lab work and in the nursing of cardiac patients. She attended the Norwegian School of Advanced Nursing Education, worked in civilian hospitals as well as in university medical labs, and became matron of Medical Department B in the University Clinic of the State Hospital in Oslo. In 1976 Major Berg was appointed chief of the Joint Norwegian Military Nursing Services. She also has been a member of the joint working group concerning women in the armed forces and was a Norwegian delegate at the 1977 NATO conference of senior women officers in Brussels, Belgium.

Israeli Women Firsts

According to *Military Review* and *Army Reserve Magazine,* Israel is the world's only country with a full-scale peacetime conscription of young women. Drafted at age 18, as are the young men, Israeli women since 1949 have shared the same rights and obligations and serve in all branches of the military forces. Policy dictates that women will not be assigned fighting roles unless it is a matter of national survival. During the Sinai-Suez campaign (1956), women pilots flew troop transports, medical evacuation planes, and reconnaissance aircraft.

RENA LEVINSON is said to be the first woman jet pilot in Israel. In 1975 Colonel RUTH MUSCAL was director of the Israeli Defense Force and the Cheil Nashim ("Women's Army"), familiarly known as Chen, which means "charm" in Hebrew.

In Greece, a New Generation of Lysistratas

In most modern nations, women are seeking equal opportunity in the armed services. Not in Greece. The Greek Defense Ministry in 1977 shelved a controversial bill to draft women for military service when the proposed legislation brought a storm of protest from modern-day Lysistratas ranging from militant feminists to conservative housewives. Aristophanes' heroine Lysistrata persuaded the women of Athens to stay away from their husbands until the men gave up fighting the Peloponnesian War; her spiritual descendants are not so much against war as against the proposed draft that anticipated an initial peacetime in-duction of 12,000 women, who would have been mainly volunteers. (During general mobilization, all women between the ages of 20 and 32, plus others up to the age of 50 who had needed special-ized training and skills, would have been drafted.)

Reasons for the opposition were diverse. According to MARY ANNE WEAVER, writing from Athens for the *Washington*

Women in the Military, Selected Countries, 1976

Country	Military strength[a]		Women as a percentage of total strength
	Total	Women	
Australia	69,350	3,500	5.0
Belgium	88,300	600	c
Canada	77,900	3,450	4.4
China, Republic of (Taiwan)	470,000	12,500	2.7
Denmark	34,700	550	1.6
France	512,900	8,550	1.7
Germany, Federal Republic of	495,000	b	c
Greece	199,500	0	0
Israel	158,500	8,000	5.0
Italy	352,000	0	0
Japan	235,000	2,300	1.0
Netherlands	112,200	1,900	1.7
New Zealand	12,600	750	5.8
Norway	39,000	1,250	3.2
Philippines	78,000	450	c
Portugal	59,800	0	0
Soviet Union	4,410,000	10,000	c
Turkey	480,000	100	c
United Kingdom	344,150	14,700	4.3
United States	2,086,700	108,800	5.2
Yugoslavia	250,000	2,600	1.0

Sources: Total military strength, except Soviet Union, International Institute for Strategic Studies, *The Military Balance 1976–1977* (London: IISS, 1976); Soviet Union, David Smith, "Soviet Military Manpower," *Air Force,* vol. 60 (March 1977), p. 78. Figures on women's participation based largely on authors' correspondence with appropriate embassies in Washington, D.C.; supplementary data in *The Military Balance 1976–1977;* Verna J. Dickerson, "The Role of Women in the Defense Force of Israel" (U. S. Army War College, May 1974; processed); and U. S. Defense Intelligence Agency, "Women in the Soviet Armed Forces," DDI-1100-109-76 (DIA, March 1976; processed), p. 5.

a. Rounded to nearest 50 people; includes active strength only; reserves, paramilitary forces, and the like are excluded.

b. Less than 50.

c. Less than 1 per cent.

Adapted from Women and the Military *by Martin Binkin and Shirley J. Bach. Copyright 1977, the Brookings Institution, Washington, D.C.*

Post in June 1977, LINA KOUTIFARI, a member of Parliament and Deputy Minister of Education, who was not consulted by the government in the writing of the legislation, was "delighted that it was abolished. A woman's first responsibility is to her children," she said. "Drafted into the Army? Living in a barracks? It couldn't happen. A woman must remain at home." Many Greek women agreed with her and with the antidraft conservative members of the armed forces who protested that there was a danger of young girls' losing their virginity and prostitutes' taking advantage of the situation if the legislation passed. But other women were outraged because the defense legislative committee had relegated them to auxiliary positions, stating that they were "generally incompetent to carry arms."

"That's pure nonsense," said ASPASIA PAPATHANOSSIOU, one of Greece's most prominent tragic actresses, who at 23 in the 1940s commanded a brigade in the resistance army fighting during the Nazi occupation. "We don't like war," she was quoted as saying, "but when it's needed we know how to fight, and certainly not in auxiliary positions." Another woman who refused to be identified because her husband is on the Defense Ministry staff said, "They're asking us to walk behind a soldier, carrying his equipment in the army, just as we've always walked behind a man on a donkey, as we've gone to plow the fields."

One of the few proponents of the legislation was member of Parliament and prominent newspaper publisher ELENI VLACHOS. Holding that Greek men must be relieved of their heavy family and military duties, she said that she did not see "why this bill has created such an uproar, since it was concerned primarily with volunteers." The 66-year-old woman added that she was sorry she was too old for induction. "I would have loved to join the air force."

14

Women in Sports and Games

By Elaine Romanelli

Eleanor Riger, consulting editor

Nowhere has the current movement for equal rights for women had a more dramatic effect on women's opportunities and achievements than in sports, especially in the United States. The National Association for Girls and Women in Sports estimates that in 1974 more than 60,000 women entered official collegiate competitions, double the 1972 figure and more than four times the entries for 1967. The revolution in life-styles, a developing taste for the informal outdoor life, and a change in women's over-all outlook—all three help to account for women's new-found confidence and importance in the world of athletic competition.

During the 1920s, a brief surge in women's athletics took place. Tennis, basketball, ice hockey, and many other team and individual sports for women enjoyed a popularity in high schools and colleges around the country. Unfortunately, opposing forces—such as the Na-

tional Amateur Athletic Federation, a coalition of church and social groups led by the wife of Herbert (later President) Hoover—lobbied so successfully against women's sports that by 1930 the percentage of colleges sponsoring varsity competitions for women students had dropped to 12 per cent. By the 1960s the only "acceptable" sports for women were the individual sports like swimming, diving, figure skating, golf, and tennis. The financial rewards on the professional level were far below those for men.

But the 1970s have seen a dramatic change. BILLIE JEAN KING's defeat of Bobby Riggs in a much-publicized tennis match on September 20, 1973, and her dynamic, all-out effort to create a rightful place for women in the professional sports world spurred a movement for equality in media attention and money, and for social acceptance of all sports for women. The movement will not soon be slowed. In recent years Ms. King has been responsible for the founding and development of World Team Tennis (for men and women) and the Women's Professional Softball League, which has drawn outstanding amateurs into professional play. And she has continued to provide proof that women are attractive, exciting athletes and, most important, can win.

Other factors—both cultural and legal—have contributed to the change. In 1972, Title IX of the Education Amendment Act established basic and revolutionary guidelines to provide adequate funding and facilities for women's sports in federally aided high schools and colleges. The Little League was forced to franchise teams for girls in baseball in January 1974, thus allowing young girls to experience the pleasure of perfecting their athletic skills and contributing to the effort of a team.

Before Title IX, women swimmers generally did not compete after the age of 16—not because they had peaked physically, but because there was no competition, no scholarships, and because "older" women in their 20s were not encouraged to compete in sports. Now, with the aid of scholarships, coaching, and facilities, women swimmers and many other kinds of women athletes are continuing their competitive lives into college and on a level comparable to that found in world competition. Women skiers are in a similar situation, with professional skiing leagues only recently founded. No official championships yet exist, but the competitions are growing more numerous and rules for judging and competing are slowly being established.

The increasing admission of women's events to the Olympic Games is another positive gauge of the tremendous international expansion of women's sports. This increase aids the development of sport on the local level. In the United States, the media attention accorded the Olympics attracts participants, funding, and good coaching. In Eastern European and other countries where sport is state-supported, the prestige of the Olympics dictates an all-out effort to produce winners, as demonstrated by the fabulous record-breaking and medal-winning success of the East German women in swimming and in track and field at the 1976 games.

The gains made by professional women athletes have included increasing monetary rewards. World tennis champion CHRIS EVERT earned $300,000 in 1975—more than any male player that year. In golf, in the older of the two major professional sports for women, a record total purse of $2.6 million was offered in 1976 (doubling the $1.2 million figure of 1975) and that year for the first time in golf history, a woman, JUDY RANKIN passed the $100,000 mark with total earnings of $150,734.

But women athletes have gained more than money, more than recognition. As they break ground in new sports and extend their capabilities in old sports, the impetus to further excellence is enjoyment. The fun and the thrill of competition adds the crowning touch to women's participation in the sports arena, where they have finally won virtually unlimited admittance.

ELAINE ROMANELLI *has been a freelance writer and editor in New York City since her graduation from the University of California, Berkeley, in 1973, where she received her B.A. degree in English Literature, magna cum laude, and was elected to Phi Beta Kappa. In 1978 she entered the Columbia University Graduate School of Business in pursuit of an advanced degree in marketing.*

ELEANOR RIGER, *staff producer for ABC Sports Television, is the first woman to hold this position at any of the major networks.* (*See "Women in Communication," p. 502.*)

INDIVIDUAL SPORTS

ARCHERY

World Record Champion

RUSTAMOWA ZEBINISSO of the Soviet Union at the 1977 tournaments in Belgium scored 1,285 points (possible 1,440), which stands as the women's world record for a FITA (Fédération Internationale de Tir à l'Arc, founded in 1931) single round.

World Double Round, Olympic Champion

U.S. archer LUANN RYAN scored 2,499 points (possible 2,880) at the 1976 Summer Olympics in Montreal to win a gold medal and achieve the highest score ever recorded by a woman for this event. In 1978 Ms. Ryan confirmed her national standing by winning her third consecutive National Archery Association Championship title.

Most Titled

Polish JANINA SPYCHAJOWA-KURKOWSKA won seven world titles between 1931 and 1947, the most any archer has ever won. (The male record is four.)

U.S.A.'s First World Champion

In 1973 LINDA MEYERS became the United States' first archer to win the World Championship. She has been shooting since she was 12 and competed in her first World Championship in 1970.

U.S. Freestyle Champion

In 1977 JANET BOATMAN won her second straight Women's Open Freestyle, Outdoor Field Archery Championship with a record 2,617 points out of a total 2,800. (This is a national tournament recognized under rules accepted only in the United States.)

BOWLING

World Record Champion

In 1975 West German ANNEDORE HAEFKER bowled down a women's record of 4,615 pins in 24 games at a tournament in England sponsored by the Fédération Internationale des Quilleurs (instituted in 1963). It is the only international women's bowling tournament.

Highest U.S. League Scorer

BEV ORTNER holds the record number of 818 points for individual women's scoring, achieved in 1968 during a standard three-game tournament.

U.S.A.'s First World Cup Champion

College student LUCY GIOVINCO, who won the all-events title at the 1976 Women's National Intercollegiate Championships, became the first U.S. bowler to win the Women's Bowling World Cup competition in 1977. Ms. Giovinco averages 178 points per game and bowled an outstanding 620 in a three-game round to beat her opponent by 116 points.

Most Titled

PATTY COSTELLO, of the United States, won the 1976 Professional Women's Bowlers Association championship to set two PWBA records: most national championships (3); and most career victories (16). That year she was also named Woman Bowler of the Year by the PWBA.

All-Time Highest Earner

Leading money winner in women's professional bowling, JUDY SOUTAR, has earned $90,640 (through 1977) in a much-titled career extending back to 1963 when she won the Women's International Bowling Congress "Star of Tomorrow" award. One of the most consistent competitors in bowling history, Ms. Soutar holds the WIBC record for 5- and 10-year highest averages. Her 5-year average score (through 1976) was 196, which, when computed with 10-year figures, dropped only to 192.

Highest Earner in a Single Year

In 1976 BETTY MORRIS, of the United States, set a new world record for highest earnings in one year: $35,375 for 15 tournament wins. She has held this record, which was not broken in 1977, since 1974 when she earned $26,547 in 33 tournaments. Ms. Morris also holds the women's world record points total of 1,564 for a tournament 6-game block. She scored this victory at the Tulsa Championships of the 1974 PWBA (Professional Women's Bowling Association founded in 1959, the first professional league for women in the United States), opening and closing the set with perfect 300 games.

Most Titled Amateur

The United States' DOROTHY MILLER holds the record for most Women's International Bowling Congress championship titles—10 between 1928 and 1948. (The WIBC is an international organization, established originally as an amateur league, that now oversees the tournaments, rules, and records of all leagues. It does, however, still hold its own amateur championships.) Ms. Miller also holds the WIBC record for most championships in a team event, six, and most in doubles events, three.

BOXING

First to Fight in the Golden Gloves

MARION BERMUDEZ, at age 23, became the first U.S. woman to compete in the formerly all-male Golden Gloves boxing tournament held in Mexico City in 1975. She won her first match against a man after only seven practice rounds the week before. Ms. Bermudez is also a national karate champion and has competed successfully against men in that sport.

First Boxing Judge

In 1974 CAROL POLLS became the United States' first licensed woman boxing judge. She officiates mainly in New York.

CYCLING

Most Titled

Though she slipped to second place in the 1976 World Bicycling Championships behind Sheila Young, all-around athlete/cyclist SUE NOVARA of the United States has dominated women's cycling tournaments since 1972 when she took her first national title. She won the national championship in 1974, in 1975 when she won the world title as well, and in 1977. Like Sheila Young, she also is a world class speed skater and has several times broken world and national records. Ms. Novara intends to remain a serious contender in bicycling at least until 1980 when it is hoped that women's cycling will be admitted to Olympic competition.

Fastest Ice Skater on Wheels

Gold medalist and world champion speed skater SHEILA YOUNG, of the United States, defeated 28 rivals at the National Bicycle Track Championship in

1976 before facing National and World Champion Sue Novara to win in a best two-out-of-three series on a 1,000-meter course. Ms. Young, who won the 1975 World Sprint Championship in speed skating and holds the women's world record of 37 seconds for skating 500 meters, is the only athlete ever to become world champion in two different sports. (Many skating and cycling champions train and compete in both sports because muscle development is similar.)

FENCING

Most Titled

Hungarian ILONA SCHACHERER-ELEK, winner of two Olympic gold medals and three world championship titles between 1939 and 1951 for women's individual foil events, ranks first among woman fencers for the greatest number of victories. (She shares the record of three world championship titles with German HELENE MAYER and Austrian ELLEN MÜLLER-PREISS.

Most Medaled

Hungarian ILDIKO REJTO-SAGINE won six Olympic medals (two gold, three silver, one bronze) between 1960 and 1972.

Four Out of Five Team Golds

In 1976, led by ELENA BELOVA, the Soviet Union's Women's Foil Fencing team won a gold medal—their fourth in five Olympic competitions. (The women's team foil event was admitted in 1960.)

Champion Coach

JULIA JONES PUGLIESE, one of the founding members of the U.S. Intercollegiate Women's Fencing Association (IWFA) in 1929, has paralleled the growth of the organization (from 4 teams in 1929 to 52 teams in 1976) with her own distinguished career as champion and coach. After four years as reigning intercollegiate champion at New York University, she turned coach and led her team to four titles—most in the league—in 1931, 1932, 1933, 1938. Over three decades later, as coach at Hunter College in New York in 1970, she led that team to victory and became the third person and only woman ever to win the IWFA championship at two different schools. Back at NYU as coach, in 1976 she was inducted into her alma mater's Women's Sports Hall of Fame.

GOLF

Most Titled and Lowest Scorer Ever

MICKEY WRIGHT of the United States, an international golf champion since the early 1960s, has won more than 80 professional victories in her career and holds the record for the most titles gained in one season—13 in 1963. In 1964, the same year Ms. Wright achieved the lowest recorded score for women—62 on an 18-hole course (over 6,000 yards) in Midland, Texas—she also tied BETSY RAWLS as a record 4-time winner of the U. S. Women's Open Championship.

Japanese European Women's Golf Champion

Seven-time Japanese national golf champion CHAKO HIGUCHI won the 1976 European Women's Championship title, and $13,500, with a 72-hole total score of 284. It was her first LPGA (Ladies Professional Golf Association) win, and she beat her closest competitor by an amazing six strokes.

First Women's "Master"

South African SALLY LITTLE, in 1976, won golfing's first Women's International tournament (the "Masters" for women), $10,000, and her first tournament victory in six years of professional playing.

Youngest in the LPGA

In May 1977, when she qualified for the Coca-Cola Classic at the age of 14, the United States' LISE ANN RUSSELL became the youngest amateur ever to compete in an LPGA event.

Lowest-Scoring Average

CAROL MANN, of the United States, holds the LPGA record for lowest scoring average in a single year—72.04 strokes per round, which she accomplished in 1968. The record is so far unbeaten.

First to Top a Half Million

KATHY WHITWORTH, of the United States, who held the highest earnings record until 1977, was the first woman on the professional golf circuit to exceed $500,000 in total earnings. This feat added impetus to the fast-growing status and acceptance of women as professional golfers. A top contender since the early 1960s, Ms. Whitworth had won every major LPGA title except the Open by 1971, and by 1973 had been named LPGA Player of the Year seven times, the AP's Woman Athlete of the Year twice, been the recipient of the Vare Trophy for lowest scoring average seven times, and the leader in LPGA earnings

for one year eight times. Her career total for golf earnings stands at $678,016.37.

All-Time Highest Earner

In 1976, when she was named LPGA Player of the Year, JUDY RANKIN, of the United States, became the first woman golfer to pass the $100,000 mark when she earned $150,734. Her winnings for 1977, again topping the $100,000 mark, have placed her well on her way toward earning her first million—and the first for a woman golfer—as she approaches the $800,000 level.

All-Time Rookie Winner, Male or Female

In a feat unprecedented in the LPGA's 20-year history, 21-year-old NANCY LOPEZ of the United States by midseason 1978 had captured five consecutive tournament wins. In so doing, she became the all-time rookie money winner in professional golf. Her earnings totaled $153,336, $233.10 more than previous record-holder Jerry Pate had won on the entire men's tour in 1976.

In 1900, U.S. golfer MARGARET ABBOT won the first *official* gold medal for the United States. It is probable, since the 1900 Paris Olympics were held at the same time as another international exhibition and since no mention of golf as an Olympic sport had been made before this time, that Ms. Abbot never actually competed in the Olympics. Early Olympic history is so confused (in some cases, nonexistent) that no record or account can be considered entirely official until 1912, when Sweden put on the first well-organized Games.

GYMNASTICS

Russia's "Absolute Champion"

At the 1972 Olympic Games, Russian OLGA KORBUT became the first person, male or female, to do a backward somer-

sault on the uneven parallel bars. Her routines, more intricate and more daring than any before performed by women in official competitions, changed the face of women's gymnastics and vaulted these events to the top in popularity and spectator interest. Ms. Korbut was named the AP's Female Athlete of the Year in 1973 and the Absolute Champion of the U.S.S.R. in 1975.

Highest Olympic Scorer

Romanian NADIA COMANECI, the 19-year-old "darling" of the 1976 Summer Olympics in Montreal, astounded spectators and judges alike by performing seven perfect 10.0 routines (four times on the uneven bars and three times on the beam). She is the first athlete in Olympic history ever to achieve a 10.0 score in any event. It had been considered unattainable. But not by Nadia, who said of her achievement, "I've done it 20 times now." And indeed, she had achieved the 10.0 score 16 times in the Olympic qualifying events alone. In 1977 the Associated Press named Nadia Comaneci 1976 Athlete of the Year.

First World Cup Champion

In 1975 Russian LUDMILLA TOURISHEVA, a many-medaled champion of the Olympic Games, took all five individual and the all-around gold medals at the first World Cup Competition, held in London. She is the only woman ever to hold all the gold medals in both the European and world championships at one time.

World's Most Titled

The women's record for the greatest number of world gymnastics championships is held by Russian LARISSA SEMYONOVNA LATYNINA. Between 1956 and 1964 she achieved 10 individual and 5 team titles.

Most Medaled

VERA CASLAVSKA-OKLOZIL, of Czechoslovakia, holds a record seven individual gold medals for Olympic gymnastics events—three won at the 1964 games and four in 1968. (The male record for gold medals in this event is six.)

United States' Most Titled

ROXANNE PIERCE is the United States' top-ranked woman gymnast. She has held this position since 1971 when she took the All-Around title at the Pan American games in Cali, Colombia, and has placed consistently at or near the top of all gymnastic competitions—except in the Olympics, where the Russians and Eastern Europeans hold sway.

First to Sweep the AAU

In June of 1977, 12-year-old sensation STEPHANIE WILLIM of the United States swept the All-Around title as well as every individual event for the first such scoring in AAU history at the Elite Gymnastics Championships.

Frist U.S. Medalist

In 1970 KATHY RIGBY, of the United States, became the first U.S. gymnast, male or female, to win a medal—a silver for the balance beam—at the World Gymnastics Championships. No other U.S. gymnast has earned one since. In other international competitions she scored numerous victories and achieved a bronze medal in 1967—that one a first for any U.S. gymnast in 32 years.

Three-Time U.S. Trampoline Champ

SHELLY GRANT, of the United States, who was told at the age of seven by her coach that she "couldn't make a career out of trampoline," won the National Trampoline Championship in 1977 for the third consecutive time. Her routine includes some of the most difficult routines performed by a woman, including a double front somersault with one and one half twists in the second flip and a two-and-three-quarter front somersault.

ICE SKATING

Figure Skating

World's Most Titled and Medaled

Norwegian SONJA HENIE (1912–69) holds the women's record number of 10 world figure-skating titles, earned between 1927 and 1936. She also holds the greatest number of Olympic gold medals —three.

Most Titled in the United States

In the 1930s, MARABELL VINSON OWEN won the women's U.S. National Figure Skating Championship nine consecutive times—a record for men and women. In world competition she consistently placed second to Norwegian Sonja Henie. Upon retirement, Ms. Owen was hired by the *New York Times* as the paper's first woman sports columnist.

Most Titled Canadian

Between 1968 and 1973, KAREN MAGNUSSEN won the Canadian Women's Figure Skating Championship five times—the most ever won by a Canadian woman.

Highest Earner

In 1977, DOROTHY HAMILL, of the United States, retired from amateur competition and signed contracts with ABC and the Ice Capades that will earn her over $2 million. In an unprecedented sweep of titles in a single year, Ms. Hamill in 1976 won first place in the U.S. National, World, and Olympic figure skating championships. She views figure skating as a sport rather than an art, as does her early tutor, world-famous coach Carlo Fassi, and is noted for her flawless execution of athletic spins and jumps, which dramatically break tradition with the "graceful" style so long associated with women figure skaters.

Pair Skating

Most Titled Pair Skater

IRINA RODNINA, of the U.S.S.R., has won a total of 10 World Championship pairs titles—four with Alexei Ulanov (1967–72) and six with her husband, Alexander Zaitsev (1973–76)—and two gold medals. In 1976 Ms. Rodnina and her partner won the double-title World and European championships for the fourth consecutive time.

Ice Dancing

First Gold Medal Ice Dancers

The undisputed champions of world ice dancing competitions since 1970, LUDMILLA PAKHOMOVA and Alexander Gorshkov confirmed their position in 1976 when they won the first Olympic ice dancing gold medal.

Speed Skating

World Record Champion

The U.S.S.R.'s TATIANA AVERINA, one of the fastest speed skaters in the world, holds the women's world record in both the 1,000-meter race (1:23.46) and the 1,500-meter. Her world record of

2:09.90 in the 1,500 would have won the 1973 World Championship—for men. In 1975 Ms. Averina set six world records in 18 days, twice lowering the 500 record and three times the 1,000.

Most Titled

Russian INGA VORONINA and Dutch ATJE KEULEN-DEELSTRA share the women's record for the most speed skating titles ever won—four.

Most Medaled

The most Olympic gold medals in speed skating have been won by Russian LIDIA SKOBLIKOVA—two in 1960 and four in 1964. (The male record is four.)

First Skating "Superstar"

At the 1972 Winter Olympic Games, the United States' ANNE HENNING won a gold medal for the 500-meter race and a bronze for the 1,000-meter. In 1976, going back on her decision to leave competitive sports behind, Ms. Henning won five of the seven Superstars events (at the second annual Women's Superstars Competition) to capture first place and $35,300.

Women's World Speed Skating Records

500 meters	37.00	Sheila Young (U.S.A.)	Inzell, West Germany	3-13-76
1,000 meters	1:23.46	Tatiana Averina (U.S.S.R.)	Medeo, U.S.S.R.	3-29-75
1,500 meters	2:09.90	Tatiana Averina (U.S.S.R.)	Medeo, U.S.S.R.	3-11-75
3,000 meters	4:31.00	Galina Stepanskaya (U.S.S.R.)	Medeo, U.S.S.R.	3-23-76

JUDO

Most Titled Heavyweight

Heavyweight "Grand Champion" of the 1976 Senior AAU championship matches was MAUREEN BRAZIEL, one of the USA's top-ranked women judo experts and an international title-winner. The year 1976 marked her third straight Senior AAU win (she has lost only six matches in 10 years of tournament play). In international competition Ms. Braziel took a gold medal in the fourth Women's European Championships in Switzerland in 1974 and a silver medal in the heavyweight class and a bronze in the open class at the British Women's Open in 1972.

Most Titled Lightweight

The United States national lightweight judo champion, DIANE PIERCE, has racked up more national titles than any other woman judo expert. In over 10 years' play she has won the National YMCA Championship four times, the USJA Women's Championship four times, and the Senior AAU Championship four times, the latter most recently in 1976.

LUGE

Most Titled

Two East German women, OTRUM ENDERLEIN and MARGIT SCHUMANN, share the women's record for the most number of luge titles held by women— four. Ms. Enderlein held the championship from 1964 through 1967 and Ms. Schumann equaled the achievement when she gained her fourth consecutive title (Olympic) in 1976. (Luge is an ama-teur sport, and the Olympic gold medal is considered the equivalent of a world title.)

ROLLER SKATING

First American World Champion

NATALIE DUNN, at the age of 20 in 1976, became the first U.S. woman to win the world title in figure roller skating and the gold medal that goes with it. Ms. Dunn won her first event at the age of 7 and at 16 took the national women's singles title. She bristles at any comparison of her sport with "roller derby roughs" and hopes to see it qualify as an Olympic event in 1980.

Fastest in an Hour

The greatest distance skated in one hour on a rink by a woman is 21.995 miles. This was achieved by West German MARISA DANISI in 1968.

SHOOTING

Best Shot and First Gold

According to the National Rifle Association, "no other woman in the world comes close" to matching the United States' MARGARET MURDOCK in "all-around shooting excellence." At the 1975 Pan American Games, Ms. Murdock outgunned all of her male competitors to become the first woman ever to win a gold medal in the over-all events. At the 1976 Olympic Games, she tied for first place in the small-bore rifle three-position event, but placed second on the judges' decision in favor of Lanny Bassham for his higher score in the final round. He refused to place the gold medal around his neck on the victory stand. Instead, they held it jointly while the national anthem was played.

SKIING

Downhill

Five-Time World Cup Champion

The Women's World Cup (instituted in 1967) has been won five times by Austrian downhill skier ANNEMARIE PROELL MOSER—1971 through 1975. In 1973 she completed a record sequence of 11 consecutive downhill victories. Ms. Proell Moser is also a former world cup giant slalom champion and the only skier—male or female—to win three times in this event.

Most Titled

German CHRISTEL CRANZ holds the greatest number of world titles—12 (4 slalom, 3 downhill, 5 combined). The male record is 7.

Most Titled Slalom Champion

French BRITT LAFFORGUE, World Slalom Cup winner of 1971 and 1972, is the only skier to win the women's cup twice.

Only Double Gold-Medaled U. S. Skier

In 1952 ANDREA MEAD LAWRENCE took a gold medal for the women's giant slalom skiing event—the first year it was admitted to Olympic Competition—and a gold for slalom, becoming the first U.S. skier—male or female—ever to win two gold medals for skiing. (No male skier from the United States has ever taken a gold medal for skiing.)

Most Titled Canadian Skier

Between 1959 and 1968, alpine skier NANCY GREENE won more world skiing championships than any other Canadian. She was a member of Canada's Olympic Team in 1960, 1964, and 1968, when she won a gold medal for the Giant Slalom and a silver medal for Slalom. She was the Women's World Cup winner in 1967 and 1968, and was named Canada's Woman Athlete of the Year in 1967.

Cross Country

Most Titled

Russian GALINA KULAKOVA is the most decorated cross country skier in history, with nine gold, one silver, and two bronze medals to her credit in Olympic Games and World Competitions. In 1972 she swept the Olympic women's cross country competition, taking golds in the 5- and 10-km. races and the 4×5-km. relay. She repeated this feat in the 1974 World championships.

The United States' Most Titled

Nordic skier MARTHA ROCKWELL, the most successful and until recently, virtually only woman cross country racer in the United States, has won 15 national titles since she began competition in 1969. (No U.S. woman has placed in this event in World or Olympic competition.)

Freestyle

First Ski Ballet Champion

In 1974, at the first Women's International Ballet and Freestyle Competition, 19-year-old MARION LEE POST became the first women's champion when she skied a nearly perfect run in the 60-second routine (done to music), which requires the utmost control, fluidity, and skillful use of the terrain while doing stunts and tricks.

First Freestyle Champion

JULIE MEISSNER, a ski instructor and racing coach from Idaho, won the All-Around Freestyle event at the first Women's International Ballet and Freestyle Competition in 1974.

Jumping

Longest Jumper

Norwegian ANITA WOLD jumped 321 feet 5 inches at Okura Sapporo, Japan, in 1975 to achieve the longest jump ever recorded in women's skiing.

TEAM GAMES

BASEBALL

First General Manager of a Minor League Team

In 1974 LANNY MOSS took over the Portland Mavericks, a minor league team. She is the first woman to manage any league team.

First Little League No-Hitter

In 1974, 11-year-old BUNNY TAYLOR, of the United States turned in the first no-hit game ever pitched by a female in Little League. (Girls were admitted to official Little League play in 1974.)

Three-Time All-Star Little Leaguer

In 1976, 11-year-old pitcher and short-stop AMY DICKINSON, of the United States, was selected for the American Little League All-Star team for the third consecutive time. In 1974, in a history-making debut, Amy and 26 other New Jersey girls earned front-page copy on the *New York Times* and the *New York Daily News* as the first girls ever to play on a team sponsored by the 38-year-old Little League, founded in 1939.

BASKETBALL

First Gold Medal Team

In 1976, the first year that women's basketball was admitted to Olympic play, ULIANA SEMENOVA, the 7'2" Soviet center, led her Russian teammates through the round robin tournament virtually unchallenged to collect the first Olympic gold medal in women's basketball. The Soviet women's team, foremost in the world, has not been beaten in international competition since 1971. In 1976 they won the Women's World Championship for the sixth consecutive time.

First AIAW Title Team

In 1974 Pennsylvania's Immaculata College (enrollment 700) won its third straight AIAW (Association for Intercollegiate Athletics for Women) basketball championship. They were the first champions of the first official AIAW match in 1972 and in 1975 beat Queens College in the first women's basketball game ever played in Madison Square Garden.

Champion Coach

LIDIA ELEKSEEVA, of the U.S.S.R., was a member of the Soviet women's basketball team for 10 years before she took over coaching duties in 1958, which was the last time the Soviet team lost a European championship. She says, "My philosophy of basketball is simple . . . for women, the game must be played in all ways like the men."

Star Amateur Center

Averaging 31 points per game, LUCY HARRIS is the United States' star amateur center. In 1976 she led the Delta State University "Lady Statesmen" to their third straight national championship victory and the U.S. Olympic teams silver medal. Opponents double- and triple-team her and still she averages a 62 per cent field goal success.

The United States' Top-Ranked Professional

KAREN LOGAN, who was a major contender in 1976 for the Superstar title, is considered by many to be the best woman basketball player in the United States. She averaged 23 points per game during her three years' tour on the only pro women's team in the United States—

they played against men—and gave dribbling exhibitions during half time.

Twenty-one years ago *Parade* magazine presented the first annual all-American high school boys basketball team. In 1977 the magazine chose the first all-America high school girls basketball squad.

Polling hundreds of college and high school coaches, college recruiters (usually male faculty members), and scores of writers, *Parade* compiled a squad of 40 who will most likely be hailed as tomorrow's college stars and representatives for the United States in the 1980 and 1984 Olympic Games.

There are two types of female basketball played in high schools today. The majority play the five-woman type akin to the masculine brand of the game. But there are still participants in the six-woman style of basketball, which places a heavy accent on the three forward positions. The three front-court players are the scorers, and the other three players are basically defenders. Iowa has traditionally excelled in the six-woman game and is—along with a few diehard adjoining states and some Southern areas—adamant about continuing with the "old-fashioned" style of ball, which is not played internationally.

Twenty-six states were represented on the first *Parade* All-America High School Girls Basketball Team. The players were chosen solely on ability, not by position. One of the first-squad members, KIM PETERS of Andrew, Iowa, was born without a right hand but overcame her handicap and is acknowledged to be the finest defensive player in her state.

In most cases, those selected to the basketball squad are also topflight competitors in other sports. For example, Ms. Peters is a high-jump qualifier in state meets. Several of the others are all-state stars in volleyball. Thus far, it seems, most female basketball stars have not become specialists in the one sport, as have their male counterparts.

FIELD HOCKEY

First Touring Team Captain

ANNE TOWNSEND was a champion field hockey player in the United States from 1923 to 1947. (The U.S. Field Hockey Association, which sponsors teams and tournaments, was instituted in 1923.) She was team captain every year except 1933 and a member of the first touring team to Europe in 1924.

Yale All-American

ANNE KEATING, playing field hockey for Yale University's women's team, has received three letters and All-American recognition.

Undefeated U.S. Champs

The United States' Golden Rams, of West Chester (Pennsylvania) State College, won their second straight national championship title in 1977, completing a sensational, 2-year, 50-game streak of undefeated matches. (Field hockey in the United States exists only on the college level.)

HANDBALL

First Gold Medal Team

In 1976 the U.S.S.R.'s women's handball team took the first gold medal ever awarded to women for this event. The Russian team, with East Germany and Romania, dominates the international women's team handball championships.

Top-Ranked in the United States

Voted the United States' top female college athlete in 1974 and twice winner of all-State honors in basketball, volleyball, and softball, REITA CLANTON

turned to handball in 1976 and qualified as a backcourt player on the United States' first Olympic women's handball team.

ICE HOCKEY

Most Titled Team

Ice Hockey champions Assibet Valley Girls Club won the U.S. National title in 1975 and 1976. They are the only team to win this title twice.

First Major League Coach

LAURA STAMM is the first woman coach in major league hockey. She coaches for

the San Diego Mariners. She says that skaters get "lots of instruction on stick-handling, shooting, and defense," but "they don't always skate right." Originally a figure skater herself, Ms. Stamm conducts power-skating clinics.

LACROSSE

First U.S. International Title

Co-captains MERYL WERLEY and CONNIE LANZEL led the U.S. women's

lacrosse team in 1975 to England where they beat the British for the first time in lacrosse history.

SOFTBALL

Most Strike-Outs in a Single Game

In 1953, "Blazin'" BERTHA TICKEY pitched 20 strike-outs in seven innings—the all-time record for most strike-outs in a single game. She pitched for 23 years on various Amateur Softball Association (ASA) teams and is the only player to compete with 11 National Championship teams. Ms. Tickey, who pitched in the first international World Championship in 1965 at Melbourne, Australia, was named to the National All-Star team and chosen most valuable player of the tournament eight times.

Highest Batting Average

Third basewoman MARGARET DOBSON holds the ASA record for an all-time batting average of .615.

Most "All American"

Catcher DOT WILKINSON, during a 25-year career with the PBSW Ramblers

of Phoenix, Arizona, was named to the All-American team 19 times.

First World Series Champions

In 1976, after a grueling first season as professional softball players, the Connecticut Falcons beat the San Jose Sunbirds for the first women's World Series championship title. The Women's Professional Softball League was founded in 1975 by BILLIE JEAN KING (p. 582).

Most Titled Amateurs

In 1977, at the Women's National Fast-Pitch Tournament, the Raybestos Brakettes captured their seventh consecutive national title. They have been the top-ranked amateur softball team in the United States for several years and remained the champions in 1977 despite losing, in 1975, several of their best players to the Women's Professional Softball League.

VOLLEYBALL

Most Titled

The U.S.S.R. won the women's championship in 1952, 1956, 1960, 1968, 1970, and 1973 for a total of six titles—the most ever won by any team. In 1976 the Russian team took its third consecutive Olympic gold medal for this sport—also a record.

Most Olympic-Medaled

Russian INNA RYSKAL received a silver medal in 1964 and golds in 1968, 1972, and 1976. She is the only woman to receive four Olympic medals for volleyball.

First Superstars Winner

MARY JO PEPPLER, of the United States, winner of the first women's Superstars competition in 1975, voted outstanding volleyball player in the world at the 1970 International Games in Bulgaria, a member of the 1968 U.S. Olympic volleyball team, and named the International Volleyball Association's (IVA) 1975 Coach of the Year, has devoted her career to the promotion of women's competitive sports, specifically volleyball, as well as to athletic excellence. Admired as one of the few women in the world who can compete successfully against men, off a men's net, she has switched her goal from expanding women's volleyball on the pro level to developing talent on the college level. "The sooner we have volleyball all over the country," she says, "the sooner the sport will be played at its top level."

"Rookie of the Year" to "Most Valuable Player"

In 1963 NANCY OWEN FORTNER, playing in her first USVBA (U. S. Volleyball Association) tournament for the Long Beach Shamrocks, was named "Rookie of the Year." Over the next 11 years, playing for the L.A. Renegades as well as the Shamrocks, Ms. Fortner was a member of a winning team at the USVBA Nationals seven times, selected to play on three Pan American Games teams, two Olympic teams, and two World Game teams. She was named Most Valuable Player at the 1966 U.S. National tournament.

Women in the Olympics

In 1976, at the Summer Olympic Games held in Montreal, women's basketball, rowing, and team handball were admitted to Olympic competition, raising the total number of women's sports to 17 and events to 65. (The totals for men's sports and events are 28 and 136.)

Since 1896, the first year of the modern Olympic Games, when a woman named MELPOMENE was refused entry in the marathon race, women have fought for admission against such Victorian notions as those expressed by Baron Pierre de Coubertin, founder of the modern Olympics, when he said: "It is indecent that the spectators should be exposed to the risk of seeing the body of a woman being smashed before their very eyes. Besides, no matter how toughened a sportswoman may be, her organism is not cut out to sustain certain shocks."

The heavy financial burden of sponsoring an Olympics, and philosophical concerns about elevating the status of amateur athletic competition to an international honor for which athletes will train above all else, have also served to hinder the admission of women's events even to the present day.

Interestingly, serious opposition has

come from women as well as men. In 1929 the Section on Women's Athletics within the American Physical Education Association "disapproved" competition for women on the grounds that the games "entail the specialized training of a few and offer opportunity for the exploitation of girls and women." As late as 1966 the Chairwoman of the Women's Board of the United States Olympic Development Committee wrote: "To most of the women in the United States and to many women of other nations, the shot put and discus throw are forms of competition that are generally unacceptable to the feminine image. They are men's sports, requiring tremendous, explosive strength and a large physique for superior performance . . . It is a known fact that chiefly the hefty, masculine woman gains sufficient satisfaction from performance of these two athletic activities."

Luckily, all of these objections were overruled. Since 1912, when the International Olympic Committee (IOC) finally began to regularize the games and women were allowed to compete in the swimming events, women athletes have proven themselves to be worthy competitors and, perhaps more importantly, crowd pleasers. In swimming, gymnastics, track and field, and now basketball, the women's events equal, and in some cases surpass, the men's events in spectator popularity.

Today, although the IOC is still dominated by men and the suitability of women for certain kinds of athletic endeavor is still questioned, the main barrier is financial support. For every new event added, the athletic housing facilities must be increased by at least 100 units. Olympic stadiums, already overcrowded, become unmanageable and the resources necessary to support them more scarce. Because of the great difficulty in cutting an Olympic event from the program once it has gained entrance, pressure is brought to bear to limit the number of new events. The women's events carry the weight of this problem.

The argument about the nature of amateur sports being altered to the status of professional continues, but the increasingly political overtones of the Games have lessened its consideration.

One iron-clad rule prohibiting the admission of certain sports for women still exists. The official Olympic rule book, echoing the sentiments of Coubertin, states that no woman shall be allowed to compete, with men or with each other, in a contact sport. So far no serious challenge has been raised concerning this ruling. Women's competition in contact sports on the non-Olympic level is still underdeveloped.

Numerous non-contact sports, however, are the cause of much controversy. Women are fighting for entrance in the cycling and long-distance running events, competitions that require a strength and endurance not yet recognized for women by the IOC. Again political interests of major Olympic countries are a factor.

Until 25 countries on two continents establish organized women's competitions in these sports, the events will not be considered to have international status and thus will not be admitted to the Olympics. However, in marathon running, women have demonstrated their abilities in official track and field meets, by gaining entrance in the formerly all-male Boston Marathon and by staging their own marathon runs to prove their long-distance endurance and speed capabilities. International women's competitions do exist for cycling, but until all the major track and field nations (the U.S.S.R., East and West Germany, and the United States) express interest and petition strongly, women's cycling will not be made part of the Olympics.

In any case, for women's cycling and long-distance running, the push is on. The year 1980 may well see women's Olympic competitions in both these sports.

Summer Sports

Sport	Date Admitted	First Gold Medalist	Location
Archery	1972	D. Wilbur (U.S.A.)	Munich
Basketball	1976	U.S.S.R.	Montreal
Canoeing	1948	Karen Koff (Denmark)	London
Diving			
Springboard	1920	Aileen Riggin (U.S.A.)	Antwerp
Platform	1912	Greta Johansson (Sweden)	Stockholm
Equestrian*			
Fencing			
Individual Foil	1924	Ellen Osiier (Denmark)	Paris
Team Foil	1960	U.S.S.R.	Rome
Golf**	1900	Margaret Abbot (U.S.A.)	Paris
Gymnastics			
Team All-Around	1928	Netherlands	Amsterdam
Individual	1952	Maria Gorokhovskaya (U.S.S.R.)	Helsinki
Vault	1952	Yekaterina Kalintschuk (U.S.S.R.)	Helsinki
Uneven Parallel Bars	1952	Margit Korondi (Hungary)	Helsinki
Balance Beam	1952	Nina Botscharova (U.S.S.R.)	Helsinki
Free Exercise	1952	Agnes Keleti (Hungary)	Helsinki
Handball	1976	U.S.S.R.	Montreal
Rowing			
Single Sculls	1976	Christine Scheiblich (East Germany)	Montreal
Double Sculls	1976	Bulgaria	Montreal
Coxed Fours	1976	East Germany	Montreal
Coxswainless Pairs	1976	Bulgaria	Montreal
Eights	1976	East Germany	Montreal
Coxed Quad Sculls	1976	East Germany	Montreal
Shooting*			
Swimming			
100 m. Freestyle	1912	Fanny Durak, (Australia)	Stockholm
200 m. Freestyle	1968	Debbie Myer (U.S.A.)	Mexico City
400 m. Freestyle	1924	Martha Norelius (U.S.A.)	Paris
800 m. Freestyle	1968	Debbie Myer (U.S.A.)	Mexico City
100 m. Backstroke	1924	Sybil Baver (U.S.A.)	Paris
200 m. Backstroke	1968	Pokey Watson (U.S.A.)	Mexico City
100 m. Breaststroke	1968	Djurdjica Bjedov (Yugoslavia)	Mexico City

Sport	Date Admitted	First Gold Medalist	Location
200 m. Breaststroke	1924	Lucy Morton (Great Britain)	Paris
100 m. Butterfly	1956	Shelley Mann (U.S.A.)	Melbourne
200 m. Butterfly	1968	Ada Kok (Holland)	Mexico City
400 m. Individual Medley	1964	Donna de Varona (U.S.A.)	Tokyo
4×100m. Medley Relay	1960	U.S.A.	Rome
4×100 m. Freestyle Relay	1912	Great Britain	Stockholm
Tennis**			
Track and Field			
100 m.	1928	Elizabeth Robinson (U.S.A.)	Amsterdam
200 m.	1948	Francina Blankers-Koen (Netherlands)	London
400 m.	1964	Betty Cuthbert (Australia)	Tokyo
800 m.***	1928	Lina Radke (Germany)	Amsterdam
	1960	Lyudmila Schevtsova (U.S.S.R.)	Rome
1500 m.	1972	Lyudmila Bragina (U.S.S.R.)	Munich
100 m. hurdles	1932	Mildred Didrikson (U.S.A.)	Los Angeles
High Jump	1928	Ethel Catherwood (Canada)	Amsterdam
Long Jump	1948	Olga Gyarmati (Hungary)	London
Shot Put	1948	Micheline Ostermyer (France)	London
Discus	1928	Halina Konopacka (Poland)	Amsterdam
Javelin	1932	Mildred Didrikson (U.S.A.)	Los Angeles
Pentathlon	1964	Irena Press (U.S.S.R.)	Tokyo
4×100 m. Relay	1928	Canada	Amsterdam
4×400 m. Relay	1972	East Germany	Munich
Volleyball	1976	U.S.S.R.	Montreal
Yachting*			

* No ruling has ever barred women from competition in Equestrian, Shooting, and Yachting sports. No information exists to disclose the first date that a woman actually competed, but it is certain that a woman did not win the first gold medals.

** Official Olympic history lists Golf and Tennis as competitions of the early Olympics. It is likely, given the confusion of the early Games, that these sports were included accidentally, and the Olympic committee dropped them shortly thereafter.

*** The 800-meter race was run once in 1928, but discontinued until 1960.

Winter Sports

Sport	Date Admitted	First Gold Medalist	Location
Alpine Skiing			
Downhill	1948	Hedy Schlunegger (Switzerland)	St. Moritz
Giant Slalom	1952	Andrea Mead Lawrence (U.S.A.)	Oslo
Slalom	1948	Gretchen Frazer (U.S.A.)	St. Moritz
Figure Skating			
Individual Competition	1908	Madge Sayers (Great Britain)	London
Pairs	1908	Anna Hubler, with H. Burger (Germany)	London
Ice Dancing	1976	Ludmilla Pakhomova, with A. Gorschkov (U.S.S.R.)	Innsbruck
Luge	1964	Ortrun Enderlein (Germany)	Innsbruck
Nordic Skiing (Cross Country)			
5 km.	1964	Klaudia Boyerskikh (U.S.S.R.)	Innsbruck
10 km.	1952	Lydia Wideman (Finland)	Oslo
4×5 km. relay	1956	Finland	Cortina d'Ampezzo
Speedskating			
500 m.	1960	Helga Haase (Germany)	Squaw Valley
1,000 m.	1960	Klara Guseva (U.S.S.R.)	Squaw Valley
1,500 m.	1960	Lidia Skoblikova (U.S.S.R.)	Squaw Valley
3,000 m.	1960	Lidia Skoblikova (U.S.S.R.)	Squaw Valley

TRACK AND FIELD

RUNNING

Short-Distance Runners

Fastest Sprinter

Taiwanese CHI CHENG, in 1970, became the first and so far only woman ever to run the 100-yard dash in 10 seconds flat. That year, at the Women's National AAU championship track and field meet in Los Angeles, Ms. Cheng set another world record of 22.6 seconds in the 220-yard heat. Both records stand unequaled and unbroken.

Fastest Miler

Romanian NATALIA MARACESCU, in 1977, ran the fastest mile, at 4:23.8, ever run by a woman. That same year she set a new women's world record of 15:41.4 for the 5,000-meter race. Her "mile time" settles the long-standing dispute among officials as to whether the indoor or outdoor record, when the indoor is faster, is the truest time. Ms. Maracescu beat them both by a long shot.

World 3,000-Meter Champion

In 1976, a Soviet distance runner, LYUDMILLA BRAGINA, lopped 18 seconds off the world 3,000-meter mark to set a new women's record of 8:27.1. She managed this feat at the 14th U.S.A.-U.S.S.R. track meet. Over-all the Soviet team set one other world record (running the mile relay in 3:29.1 seconds) and eight meet records, beating the Americans 104–42.

Most Gold-Medaled

The most gold medals won by women runners is four. This record is shared by FRANCINA BLANKERS-KOEN, of the Netherlands, for the 100-meter, 200-meter, and 80-meter hurdles and the 4×100-meter relay in 1948, and Australian BETTY CUTHBERT, who earned golds in the 100-meter, 200-meter, and 4×100-meter relay in 1956 and the 400-meter in 1964.

Most Medaled

With the words "These, I think, are the last Olympics for me," Polish IRENA SZEWINSKA closed out a remarkable track and field career in 1976. Leaving Montreal with a gold medal and women's world record (49.29) for the 400-meter run, she brought her total of Olympic medals to seven, including a complete set in the 200, in five different events. Ms. Szewinska also left an indelible mark on the record books, scoring twice in the 100, four times in the 200, three times in the 400, and twice in the 400-meter relay.

The United States' Most Medaled

At the 1960 Olympic games in Rome, the United States' WILMA RUDOLPH took gold medals for the 100- and 200-meter races and anchored the 400-meter to another. Her three golds are the most ever won by a U.S. woman in track and field events.

Breaker of 18-Year Record

In 1978 at the European Track and Field Championships held in Milan, Italy, East German MARLIES OELSNER broke a women's world record of 18 years standing for the 60-meter dash. She finished with a time of 7.12 seconds, .88 seconds under the previous record set in 1960 by Australian runner BETTY CUTHBERT. In the intervening years, four other women had managed to tie that old record but never to break it.

Marathon Runners

First to Run the Boston Marathon

In 1967, world-class long-distance runner KATHRINE SWITZER became the first woman ever to run in the United States' famed Boston Marathon. Unable to gain official entrance as a woman to the formerly all-male race, she registered as K. Switzer and ran alongside for the entire route after officials attempted to tear her number from her back and in other ways hinder her starting. Her run created such a stir that the AAU—then the only official organization that allowed women to run long-distance even competing among themselves—barred women from all competition with men in these events on pain of losing all rights to compete. In 1972, after a long and hard five-year battle, Kathrine Switzer became the first woman to run officially and legally in the Boston Marathon. Today women are admitted as competitors to most world long-distance competitions and are scored and ranked only among themselves.

World's Fastest Marathoner

French CHANTAL LANGLACE took more than 3 minutes off the old women's world marathon record when, in 1977, she ran the 26-mile race in San Sebastian, Spain in 2:35.15. Until 1976, French women were not allowed to complete in long-distance events and her victory came after long years of solitary and unsupported training.

Fastest in the World's Largest Foot Race

Ten thousand meters is a distance not included in official track and field competitions, but it is a distance run more and more often on the more and more popular marathon circuit. In 1978 MARTHA WHITE of the United States, a 5-foot, 90-lb. high school senior from State College, Pennsylvania, set a new women's world record of 33:29.7 at the Bonne-Bell Mini-Marathon in Central Park, New York City. The event itself set a record for the largest women's distance event ever held with 4,310 entrants from 36 states.

Women's Track and Field Records

Running

* 100 yards	10.0	Chi Cheng (Republic of China)	Portland, Ore.	6/13/70
* 220 yards (turn)	22.6	Chi Cheng (Republic of China)	Los Angeles, Ca.	7/03/70
* 440 yards	52.2	Kathy Hammond (U.S.A.)	Urbana, Ill.	8/12/72
	52.2	Debra Sapenter (U.S.A.)	Bakersfield, Ca.	6/29/74
* 880 yards	2:02.0	Judith Florence Pollock (Australia)	Helsinki, Finland	6/28/67
	2:02.0	Dixie Willis (Australia)	Perth, Australia	3/03/62
60 meters	7.12	Marlies Oelsner (East Gemany)	Milan, Italy	3/78
100 meters	10.88	Marlies Oelsner (East Germany)	Dresden, East Germany	1977

200 meters (turn)	22.21	Irena Szewinska (Poland)	Potsdam, Poland	6/13/74
400 meters	49.29	Irena Szewinska (Poland)	Montreal, Canada	6/29/76
800 meters	1:54.9	Tatyana Kazankina (U.S.S.R.)	Montreal, Canada	6/26/76
1,000 meters	2:32.7	Ulrike Bruns (East Germany)	Formia, Italy	6/78
1,500 meters	3:56.0	Tatyana Kazankina (U.S.S.R.)	Podolsk, U.S.S.R.	6/28/76
3,000 meters	8:27.1	Lyudmilla Bragina (U.S.S.R.)	College Park, Md.	8/07/76

Hurdles

100 meters	12.48	Grazyna Rabsztyn (Poland)	Fürth, West Germany	4/78
400 meters	55.63	Karin Rossley (East Germany)	Helsinki, Finland	1977

Field Events

High Jump	6'6¾"	Rosemarie Ackermann (East Germany)	Helsinki, Finland	1977
Long Jump	22'11¼"	Sigrun Siegl (East Germany)	Dresden, East Germany	5/20/76
Shot Put	73'2¾"	Helena Fibingerova (Czechoslovakia)	Nitra, Czechoslovakia	1977
Discus Throw	231'3"	Faina Myelnic (U.S.S.R.)	Sochl, U.S.S.R.	4/24/76
Javelin Throw	227'5"	Kate Schmidt (U.S.A.)		1977

Pentathlon

	4,932	Burglinde Pollak (East Germany)	Bonn, West Germany	9/22/73

Relays

* 4×110 yards	44.07	West Germany	Durham, N.C.	7/18/75
* 4×220 yards	1:35.8	Australia	Brisbane, Australia	11/09/69
* 4×440 yards	3:30.3	West Germany	Durham, N.C.	7/19/75
4×100 meters	42.5	East Germany	Karl Marx Stadt, East Germany	5/29/76
4×200 meters	1:33.8	Great Britain	London, England	8/24/68
4×400 meters	3:19.12	East Germany	Montreal, Canada,	7/31/76
4×800 meters	7:52.3	U.S.S.R.	Podolsk, U.S.S.R.	1977

* These distances, measured in yards, are no longer recognized in either national or international competitions. Meters are now the official, standard measurement for all track and field competitions, though for the throwing events distances are still often listed in feet.

Record-breaking U.S. Amateur

ROSALYN BRYANT, team captain of the United States' number 1 ranked track and field team, the Mercurettes, set a total of four world, indoor marks in the 220-, 440-, 500-yard and 500-meter distances in 1977. Ms. Bryant has an assured place, with several of her teammates, on the U.S. track and field team to the 1980 Olympics. The Mercurettes, also in 1977, set a new world record of 1:43.7 in the 880-yard medley.

In 1928 sportswriter John R. Tunis witnessed the first women's 800-meter race ever run and reported: "Below us on the cinder path were 11 wretched women, 5 of whom dropped out before the finish, while 5 collapsed after reaching the tape. I was informed later that the remaining starter fainted in the dressing rooms shortly afterward." The race was dropped from future Olympics, considered too strenuous for the obviously weaker sex, and was not readmitted until 1960 when modern women athletes had proved themselves able. The 1928 race, however, was significant in establishing Olympic qualifying standards for all athletes, by requiring that every competition be well established in several countries and that proved champions exist for each event.

HIGH JUMP

Highest Jumper

The greatest height cleared by a woman above her own head is 9½" by East German ROSEMARIE ACKERMANN, who jumped 6'6¾"—the women's world record—at West Berlin in 1977. It was her fourth consecutive European title. In 1976, she took an Olympic gold medal for this event.

Youngest Champion

West German ULRIKE MEYFARTH (b. May 4, 1956) equaled the then world record for the women's high jump at 6'3½" and earned a gold medal at the 1972 Olympics, at the age of 16 years 4 months.

Most Gold-Medaled

Romanian IOLANDA BALAS is the only high jumper—male or female—ever to win two gold medals for the high jump. She took the golds in 1960 and 1964, both times breaking Olympic records with heights of 6'1⅞" and 6'2¾" respectively.

LONG JUMP

Longest Jumper

East German SIGRUN SIEGL, who took a gold medal for women's pentathlon at the 1976 Olympic games with 4,745 points, is best in the long jump event; she holds the women's world record of 22'11¼".

Olympic Record Holder

Romanian VIORICA VISCOPOLEANU holds the Olympic women's record of 22'4½" in this event, which was set at the 1968 Summer Olympics. It is seven inches shorter than pentathlon star Sigrun Siegl's best, but still one and one half inches longer than the closest Olympic jumper.

SHOT PUT

First Gold for Bulgaria

Bulgarian IVANKA KHRISTOVA, who has held the women's world record at 71'9¾" since 1976, forged ahead of 12 of the greatest women shot putters in history, including Russian NADYEZHDA CHIZOVA, the former Olympic record holder, to earn Bulgaria its first track and field gold medal.

Only U.S. Champion

With virtually no competition in the United States or Western Europe and far superior competition in Eastern Europe and the U.S.S.R., the United States' MAREN SEIDLER's record shot puts of 56'11" indoors and 56'7" outdoors are important milestones in track and field history. The 26-year-old Ms. Seidler has been competing in national and Olympic championships since the age of 14 when she broke her first record at her first meet. Her efforts, and the recognition she receives for them, are lending strength to the slow-growing movement among Western women to consider the shot put as proper competition for women.

DISCUS THROW

Record Thrower

Olympic and World Champion discus thrower FAINA MYELNIC of the U.S.S.R. threw the discus 231'3" in April 1976, establishing a new women's world record. Since 1971 she has raised the world record for this event 11 times and increased her distance over 15 feet.

JAVELIN THROW

World Record Champion

The United States' KATE SCHMIDT holds the current world record javelin throw of 227'5", set in 1977. Ms. Schmidt, two-time AAU National Javelin Champion in 1975 and 1976, is admired as one of the world's greatest natural athletes. At the age of 15, because of her outstanding talent, she was invited to go to Finland for a four-year training program. She declined the offer, but has since been told by East German and Soviet coaches that with Eastern training she'd be throwing 240'. She may get there yet, anyway.

Olympic Record Holder

East German RUTH FUCHS, the 1976 world record javelin champion and KATE SCHMIDT's only real challenger, in 1976 set an Olympic record and earned a gold medal with a throw of only 216'4". Far below her world best of 226'9", Ms. Fuchs has been the first woman ever to break the 65-, 66-, 67-, 68-, and 69-meter marks.

PENTATHLON

(In 1977 scoring rules were changed to include longer running distances and a new format for throwing events. Thus, two sets of records exist for this competition. The new competition is distinguished from the old by being termed Modern Pentathlon.)

Final Record Champions under the "Old" Rules

In 1973 East German BURGLINDE POLLAK scored 4,932 points for the world title and her score has never been broken. In 1975 hurdler JANE FREDERICK set the U.S. record for the "old" pentathlon with 4,676 points. Ms. Frederick has also twice won the AAU championships, in 1975 and 1976, for pentathlon and the 100-meter hurdles. Ms. Pollak retired from competition shortly after her record score in 1973, but Ms. Frederick is expected to be a strong competitor in the new Modern Pentathlon.

First World Modern Pentathlete

In June 1977 West German EVA WILMS became the first world champion in the modern pentathlon with a point total of 4,823. She accomplished this feat in Bernhausen, West Germany.

U. S. Record Modern Pentathlete

Even under the new rules, the United States' GINA SWIFT amazed officials with an outstanding score of 4,708.20 points to win the first Women's National Championship in the Modern Pentathlon in 1977. (The new rules have generally produced scores below the old records.) Ms. Swift's nearest competitor was 354.9 points behind.

All-Time Champ

BABE DIDRIKSON ZAHARIAS, born 1914, over four decades earned more medals, set more records, and swept more tournaments, in more sports, than any other athlete, male or female, of the 20th century.

First honored while she was still in high school, she was twice named All-American forward for her performance with the Golden Cyclone squad, one of the best girls' basketball teams in the country. In a fast rise to fame and prominence as captain of women's track and field team, she set 8 track and field records for the South, 3 for the nation, won 17 loving cups and 19 medals, and took prizes for life-saving and figure skating. She also won first place for her designs of sport dresses at the Texas Fair.

By the early 1930s she held the Southern AAU record for every track and field event she had ever entered and in the 1932 summer Olympics took three gold medals and simultaneously set three world records (breaking her own) for the javelin throw, 80-meter hurdles, and high jump. Later that year, she singlehandedly won the National Women's Track and Field Championship with an over-all total of 30 points. The 22-member Illinois track team came in second.

After a few more years on the amateur sports circuit, Babe Didrikson turned pro. She toured the country as the only woman on the Babe Didrikson All-American Basketball team, which she established, did some vaudeville, and saved enough money—while supporting her parents and putting her nieces and nephews through school—to live on for three years. She devoted those years to becoming a golf champion. "I'd done everything else," she said.

From 1940 to 1950 she won every available golf title, including the World and National Opens. She had only one tournament defeat in seven years and in 1945 was named Woman Athlete of the Year by a unanimous poll of Associated Press sportswriters. In 1956 she became the first winner of the American pro-golf title. Only eight male golfers could outdrive her. In 1953, after a major cancer operation, she came back to again win the Women's National Open.

Throughout these years, in addition to setting her records and winning her titles, Babe Didrikson toured as a member of the National Exhibition Billiards Team, became recognized as one of the nation's best field place kickers, and proved her ability to throw a baseball over 300 feet (as far as many outfielders). She was also an expert diver and lacrosse player.

Babe Didrikson was married to George Zaharias, a wrestler. Their devotion to one another and his care of her when she developed cancer, from which she died in 1956, were considered remarkable in the sports world.

RACQUET GAMES

BADMINTON

Most Uber Cups

The Ladies International Championship or Uber Cup (instituted in 1956) has been most often won by Japan (1966, 1969, 1972) and the United States (1957, 1960, 1963).

RACQUET BALL

The United States' Most Titled

In 1977, at the U.S. Ladies' Professional Racquetball Championships, PEGGY STEDING played a spectacular final match to win her fourth national title. She established her dominance in the sport in early 1976 when, at the Pro-Am Tournament of Champions, "she never allowed an opponent to score more than 10 points in any given game." Previously Ms. Steding had taken the national title in 1973, 1975, and 1976.

Most Titled and First Pro Champion

Australian HEATHER McKAY, world squash racquets champion, has dominated the sport for over 15 years. There are no records that she does not hold. In

TENNIS

Grand Slammers

Australian MARGARET SMITH COURT, in 1970 won all four major tennis titles—Australian, French, Wimbledon, and the U.S. Open (Forest Hills)—becoming the second woman in history to achieve the "grand slam." Her sweep of these four national championships duplicated the feat of the United States' MAUREEN CONNOLLY in 1953.

Biggest-Time Wimbledon Winner

BILLIE JEAN KING of the United States holds her place in the record books as

All England Champion

JUDY DEVLIN of the United States between 1954 and 1967 won 10 singles titles—the women's record for the most world singles victories—at the All England Championship tournaments. She has a total of 17 titles, including doubles.

1977 Ms. McKay, who hasn't lost a squash match since 1960, kept her winning streak alive with a victory in the $6,500-purse Bancroft Open, the first women's professional tournament in the United States. That title was added to her already formidable string, which includes the 1976 Women's World Open Championship, the British Women's Open, 1962–76 inclusive, the Australian Women's Open, 1960–73 inclusive, and the New South Wales and Victorian Women's Championships, 1961–73, for a grand total of 54 titles. In 1967 Ms. McKay was given the Australian Broadcasting Company's Sportswoman of the Year award and in 1969 was made a member of the Order of the British Empire.

the woman to win the most Wimbledon titles ever: 19 (6 singles, 9 doubles, and 4 mixed doubles from 1961 through 1975). She is also the first athlete to earn $100,000 in a single year. In the greater world of women's sports, however, Ms. King will be remembered as the champion who almost singlehandedly put women into the mainstream of tennis and had an immeasurable effect in raising the pay and recognition of women athletes in virtually every sport. Her activities off the court include starting a professional women's softball league, launching a professional mixed doubles tennis circuit, and establishing the World Team Tennis league. Her team, the New York Sets, won the first league championship in 1976.

Japan's First, First and Only

KAZUKO SAWAMATSU, who in 1974 became the first Japanese tennis player in 41 years to win a major title at the prestigious All-England Lawn Tennis Championships held at Wimbledon, also, in entering this competition, became the first woman tennis player in Japan to turn professional. She is the only known winner, in international play, of 192 consecutive (Japanese) tournaments—a record no player, male or female, has ever come close to breaking.

Most Wimbledon Singles Victories

HELEN WILLS MOODY, of the United States, won the Wimbledon Women's Singles title eight times between 1927 and 1938. This stands as the record for the most singles titles ever won by any player. (The men's record is seven.)

First Black Singles Champion

In 1924 ORA WASHINGTON became the first black woman to win the American Tennis Association singles title. She held it for 12 years—longer than any other woman for any tournament in tennis history. In 1976 she was inducted into the Black Athletes Hall of Fame, but could not be located to accept her award.

First on a Male Varsity Squad

In 1971 PHYLLIS GRABER made history by becoming New York City's first officially sanctioned female member of a previously all-male high school varsity tennis team. As a sophomore at Jamaica High School in Queens, she tried out for the boys' varsity tennis team because there was no team for girls. Having been thwarted once before in her sporting ambitions—she was the softball team star in junior high, but was cut from the team because of her sex—she was this time determined to play. She took her complaint to the New York Civil Liberties Union and the Human Rights Commission. Result: Girls can now compete with boys in non-contact sports in New York.

Highest Earner

In 1974 CHRIS EVERT, of the United States, won her first Wimbledon singles title. She became the undisputed best woman tennis player in the world. Her unparalleled record of straight victories on a clay court by 1978 totaled 118 matches. The winner of two Wimbledon singles titles, Ms. Evert has logged more wins than losses against every major contender in the tennis world and her overall earnings mount into the millions. In 1976, because she "dominated her game as no other man or woman did in any sport," she was named "Sportsman of the Year" by *Sports Illustrated* magazine—the first woman to be so honored.

Youngest at Wimbledon

In 1977, at Wimbledon's prestigious All-England Lawn Tennis Championships, 14-year-old TRACY AUSTIN, of the United States, became the youngest competitor, male or female, ever admitted to this century-old tournament. A few weeks later, at the 1977 U.S. Open Championships, she justified her billing as the "future Evert" when she made the quarter finals by defeating Number 4 seed, Sue Barker. In 1978, at the age of 15, she was the youngest player to attain the finals competition in a Virginia Slims contest.

Jubilee Champion

In 1977, after winning every major tennis title but the Wimbledon over a long career, Great Britain's VIRGINIA WADE capped Queen Elizabeth II's Silver Jubilee Celebrations with England's first women's Wimbledon title in eight years.

WATER SPORTS

DIVING

Highest Scoring Diver

JENNY CHANDLER, 17-year-old U.S. diver at the 1976 Summer Olympics, racked up 506.19 points—the most ever accumulated by a woman for the 10 required competition dives—and a gold medal. Ms. Chandler has been a world champion since 1973 when she was the youngest U.S. athlete at the World Games in Belgrade. In 1974 she became the youngest AAU diving champion in 42 years when she won the 1-meter indoor springboard event; in 1975 she took a gold medal for springboard at the Pan American Games.

Most Gold-Medaled

PATRICIA MCCORMICK of the United States won four gold medals—the women's record for individual golds in all water events—for the high and springboard diving double in 1952 and 1956.

Youngest Gold-Medalist

MARJORIE GESTRING, of the United States, the youngest person ever to receive a gold medal in any Olympic event, at age 13 years 9 months, took a gold medal for the women's springboard event in the 1936 Olympic games.

First to Execute a Three-and-One-Half Somersault off a 3-Meter Board

At the 1977 AAU Indoor Nationals, CYNTHIA POTTER MCINGVALE became the first woman diver ever to successfully execute a three-and-one-half somersault off the 3-meter board and racked up two wins to raise her national title total to 26, which ties gold-medalist Pat McCormick for the women's record for most national wins. Ms. McIngvale, herself a bronze medalist at Montreal in 1976, has been twice nominated for the Sullivan Award (given each year to the United States' top amateur athlete), been selected for the All American diving team nine times, and was twice-picked World Diver of the Year for the 3-meter springboard event.

ROWING AND SCULLING

World Champion—First Gold Medalist

In 1976 East German CHRISTINE SCHEIBLICH, who has held the women's world record of 3:46.52 in single sculling on a 1,000-meter course since 1974, collected the first Olympic gold medal ever awarded in the women's category for this event. (In 1976 women's rowing, in all categories—single sculls, double sculls, coxswainless pairs, coxed fours, eights, and coxed quad sculls—was admitted to Olympic competition for the first time.)

First U.S. Olympic Single Sculler

JOAN LIND, an international sculling competitor since 1972, has helped spearhead a rapid improvement in U.S. women's rowing in recent years. In 1973 she won the national title and became the first U.S. woman to make the finals in the World Rowing Championships at Moscow. She held her title through 1974, didn't compete in 1975, and regained it in 1976, the same year she competed and won an Olympic silver medal as the first U.S. Olympic woman single sculler. In 1977 she again took the national title. In 1978 she declined to compete.

Most Medaled in a Single Tournament

Competing in the 13th annual U. S. Women's National Rowing Cham-

pionship in 1978, LISA HANSEN took four out of five gold medals available—a feat billed as "the grand slam" of women's rowing. In addition to becoming the new national singles champion, Ms. Hansen won golds for competition in the Open Quad, Open Doubles, and Open Dash events.

Women's Place in the National Gallery of Canada: First and Second

Saltwater Fish

Jewfish	680 lbs.	7'1½"	66"	Fernandina Beach, Fla. 5/20/61	Lynn Joyner
Shark, Blue	410 lbs.	11'2"	52½"	Rockport, Mass. 8/17/67	Martha Webster
Snook	521 lbs. 6 oz.	4'1½"	26"	La Paz, Mexico 1/09/63	Jane Haywood
Tuna Blackfin	381 lbs.	3'5"	28"	Islamorada, Fla. 5/21/73	Elizabeth Wade

Freshwater Fish

Char, Arctic	291 lbs.	39¼"	26"	Arctic River, N.W.T. 8/21/68	Jeanne Branson
Grayling, American	51 lbs. 15 oz.	29⅞"	15⅛"	Katseyedie River, N.W.T. 8/16/67	Jeanne Branson
Perch, White	41 lbs. 12 oz.	19½"	13"	Messalonskee Lake, Me. 6/04/49	Mrs. Earl Small
Salmon, Silver	31 lbs.			Cowichan Bay, B.C. 11/11/47	Mrs. Lee Halberg

* As of December 1976.

SURFING

Most Titled World Champion

In 1966 JOYCE HOFFMAN, of the United States, won her second straight World Surfing Championship, inaugurated in 1964 at Sydney, Australia. She won her first title in 1965 and is so far the only woman to have won this title twice.

First "Hang Ten" Champion

MARGO OBERG, of the United States, 1976 world champion surfer, won her first surfing title at the age of 12 when

she entered her first contest (The Menehune at La Jolla, California) and wiped out all 50 boys in her division. By the age of 15 she was a member of the U.S. surfing team and today holds the women's world record for most surfing titles—five—though she's only won the World Championship once. In 1975 she won the landmark Hang Ten International at Malibu Beach—the first professional surfing contest ever held for women.

SWIMMING

East Germany's First Gold

Led by star swimmer KORNELIA ENDER, the East German women's swimming team achieved an amazing and absolute dominance in the swimming events at the 1976 Olympic Games. Coming into the games, they held the world record in every Olympic event except the 800-meter freestyle and proceeded to break their own world and others' Olympic records in nearly every event. The East Germans had never before won an Olympic gold medal for swimming: in 1976 they took 11 of the 13 golds available in the swimming complex.

Most Gold-Medaled

In 1976 East German KORNELIA ENDER dominated the Olympic swimming competitions to rack up four gold medals (100- and 200-meter freestyle, 100-meter butterfly, and 4×100-meter relay)—the women's record for most gold medals won in a single year for swimming events. In world competitions during the two years prior to the Olympics, Ms. Ender had been the first woman to break 58, 57, and 56 seconds for the 100-meter freestyle and in 1976 set yet another record of 55.65 seconds for this event. Ms. Ender shares the record of four golds with Australian DAWN FRAZER, who was awarded hers for the 100-meter freestyle in 1956, 1960, and 1964 and the 4×100-meter freestyle relay in 1956.

Most Medaled

Australian DAWN FRAZER, who in addition to her four gold medals (see above) won four silvers for the 400-meter freestyle in 1956, the 4×100 freestyle relay in 1960 and 1964, and the 4×100 medley relay in 1960, shares the women's over-all record for most Olympic medals with SHIRLEY BABASHOFF, of the United States, who won two golds for the 4×100-meter freestyle relay in 1972 and 1976, and six silvers for the 100-meter freestyle in 1952, the 200-meter freestyle in 1972 and 1976, 400-meter and 800-meter freestyles in 1976, and the 400-meter medley in 1976.

Most Titled

Danish RAGNHILD HVEGER won 42 world titles for swimming between 1936 and 1942. The record number won by a man is 32.

First Channel Swimmer

GERTRUDE EDERLE, of the United States, in 1926 became the first woman ever to swim the English Channel. She swam the 21 miles of cold, choppy water in 14 hours, 31 minutes—a time two hours better than any man had ever done.

Fastest Channel Swimmer

In 1973 LYNN COX, of the United States, swam from England to France in nine hours, 36 minutes—the fastest time ever recorded for a woman.

Youngest Channel Swimmer

Egyptian ABLA KHAIRI, at the age of 13 in 1974, swam the English Channel in 12 hours, 36 minutes.

First to Swim Lake Ontario

In 1975 DIANA NYAD, of the United States, became the first person to swim across Lake Ontario. It was a 32-mile, 20-hour, non-stop journey. Later that same year she broke another record, set in 1927, for swimming around the island of Manhattan. She swam it in 7 hours, 57 minutes, taking a full hour off the old record. One of the world's greatest modern marathon swimmers, Ms. Nyad has swum in shark cages in the Caribbean and off the shores of Australia, across the bays and lakes of Canada and Europe, and down the great rivers of Latin America and Africa.

Boston Harbor Marathon Champion

In 1977 marathon runner RO ANN COSTIN, of the United States, completed a surf-'n'-turf double by winning the second annual Boston Harbor Marathon Swim covering the 12-mile course in record time of 5 hours, 21 minutes. Earlier Ms. Costin, a former Radcliffe All-American, had run the Boston Marathon in 3:40.

Women's World Swimming Records

Freestyle

100 meters	0:55.65	Kornelia Ender	E. Germany	Montreal	1976
200 meters	1:59.26	Kornelia Ender	E. Germany	Montreal	1976
400 meters	4:08.91	Petra Thurmer	E. Germany	Sweden	1977
800 meters	8:30.53	Tracey Wickham	Australia	Brisbane	1978
1500 meters	16:24.60	Alice Browne	U.S.A.	Mission Viejo	1977

Breaststroke

100 meters	1:10.86	Hannelore Anke	E. Germany	Montreal	1976
200 meters	2:33.35	Marina Koshevala	U.S.S.R.	Montreal	1976

Backstroke

100 meters	1:01.51	Ulrike Richter	E. Germany	E. Berlin	1976
200 meters	2:12.47	Brigit Treiber	E. Germany	E. Berlin	1976

Butterfly

100 meters	59.78	Christiane Knacke	E. Germany	E. Berlin	1977
200 meters	2:11.22	Rosemarie Gabriel	E. Germany	E. Berlin	1976

Individual Medley

200 meters	2:15.85	Ulrike Tauber	E. Germany	E. Berlin	1977
400 meters	4:42.77	Ulrike Tauber	E. Germany	Montreal	1976

Freestyle Relays

4×100 meter	4:07.95	U.S.A.	Montreal	1976

Medley Relays

4×100 meter	4:07.95	E. Germany	Montreal	1976

WATER SKIING

Fastest Water Skier

SALLY YOUNGER of the United States, at the age of 17, set a women's world record for the fastest speed on water skis—105.14 mph—at Perris, California, in 1970.

Most Titled

WILLA MCGUIRE and ELIZABETH ALLAN-SHETTER, both of the United States, share the record number of three women's world championship titles. Ms. McGuire won in 1949, 1950, and 1955; Ms. Allan-Shetter in 1965, 1969, and 1975. Ms. Allan-Shetter also holds the women's world record for the longest jump on water skis—125 feet—which she achieved on August 25, 1974.

EQUESTRIAN SPORTS

Grand Prix Individual Champion

CHRISTINE STUECKELBERGER, of Switzerland, took a gold medal in the Grand Prix Dressage Individual event with 1,486 points. She was the only woman medalist at the 1976 Olympic equestrian competition and won Switzerland its only gold.

Most Titled

French JANOU TISSOT, riding Rocket, has won the women's world championship for equestrian sports (instituted in 1965) twice—in 1970 and 1974.

Trials Champion

LUCINDA PRIOR-PALMERS, a member of the British equestrian team at the 1976 Olympics, is one of the world's great champions of the three-day event. Riding her 13-year-old horse, Be Fair, she won the 1975 European Championship and in 1976, returned to win the Badminton Horse Trials—Britain's premier equestrian event.

Youngest Licensed Trainer

Groom, hot-walker, and exercise rider since she was a child, LAURE CONNELLY, of the United States, became the youngest licensed trainer in thoroughbred racing at the age of 19 in 1976. She saddled her first winner—a two-year-old filly named Jen de Clar—who crossed the tape at Belmont Park in New York by four lengths her first time out in 1976.

The United States' Top Jockey, Male or Female, 1972

ROBYN SMITH, of the United States, began a career as a jockey in thoroughbred racing in 1969. In 1972 she finished 7th in international jockey standings with 98 mounts and a 20 per cent winning percentage that could be bettered by only one other jockey. Since the first six jockeys were all European, the best U.S. jockey in 1972 (and up to 1978) was therefore a woman.

First Licensed in the United States

In 1968 KATHY KUSNER, of the United States, became the first licensed female jockey in the country. It was an important step denoting a slow but growing acceptance of women jockeys as important competitors in the world of horse racing.

DRIVERS AND FLYERS

CAR DRIVERS

First Woman to Qualify at "Indy"

In 1976 JANET GUTHRIE of the United States became the first woman driver to qualify for the Indianapolis 500. After three years of competing in every auto race she could get to, Ms. Guthrie was unable to make the "Indy" starting lineup because her sponsor took back his car. Lack of money and equipment has plagued Ms. Guthrie throughout her brief driving career, but she has earned the respect of many of her male competitors. In 1977 she went 27 laps but had to quit because of mechanical problems. In 1978 she finished the race, placing ninth in 190 laps.

All-Around Rallyer

PAT MOSS of the United States, world-famous among drivers of the early 1960s, has successfully competed against and beaten men in such international rally competitions as the Liège–Rome–Liège Rally in 1960, the Tulip and German Rally in 1962, the Sestriere Rally, and many others.

Most Titled "Ladies' Champion"

French CLAUDINE TRAUTMANN has won the Ladies' Championship (among many other events) nine times and has been appointed the first woman works driver by Citroën.

First Soap Box Derby Winner

LAURA CROSS of the United States, in 1974 at the age of 12, became the first girl ever to win the 37-year-old Detroit Soap Box Derby. One of five girls in the 33-car field, she dedicated her victory to "womanhood."

Fastest on Land

KITTY O'NEIL, of the United States, holds the women's world land-speed record of 612 m.p.h., a feat achieved in 1976 that broke the former women's record by close to 300 m.p.h. She has unfortunately not been allowed to attempt to break this record since the men's record is only 627.287 m.p.h. and her backers insist that she was engaged only to top the women's record, not to compete with the men. Ms. O'Neil, deaf since birth and once consigned by doctors to lifelong paralysis after a bout with spinal meningitis, once also held the title of fastest woman water skier and was the first woman ever admitted to Stunts, Unlimited.

Drag Race Champion

In 1975 SHIRLEY "CHA CHA" MULDOWNEY, at the age of 35, became the first woman driver in the 21-year history of the U. S. National Hot Rod Association (NHRA) to qualify for the supercharged, nitro-burning, unlimited AA-Fuel dragster category—that's the top in drag racing. Record-breaking history has been hers ever since. She survived four days of elimination meets to compete against past champion "Big Daddy" Garlits in the finals of the 1975 Fall Nationals. She placed second there, but at the 1976 NHRA Spring Nationals, she emerged with the lowest time (5.964 seconds), the fastest speed (243.90 m.p.h.), and the first victory ever for a woman in this top competition. Ms. Muldowney repeated her victory at the Spring Nationals of 1977 and that summer broke the world record with an elapsed time of 5.78 seconds, well under the 1976 record of 5.94 seconds, set by a man.

MOTORCYCLE RIDERS

Grand National Motocross Champion

At the United States' 1976 National Women's Motocross Championships the person to beat was 17-year-old SUE "FLYING FISH" FISH of California. No one did. Ms. Fish is the undisputed champion of women's motocross, having taken most of the available U.S. titles in the 125cc and 250cc Expert class categories in races around the country since then.

"First" in Off-Road Racing

Off-road racer MARY McGEE of the United States drives motorcycles, cars, trucks, anything on off-road courses as tough as the Baja 1000 and the Mexico Wild Desert Peninsula. She is unique among women—and almost among men —racers of this kind. Ms. McGee was the first woman to race in the treacherous many-hour motorcycle race on the Mexican desert and one of the few riders to actually finish the race. She was the first woman to race in the International Motocross Series and the first to race in Grand Prix motorcycle tournaments— executing 90 m.p.h. turns on asphalt and up and over rocky hillsides in motocross. In 1976, driving a Toyota pickup truck with car racer JANET GUTHRIE (p. 589) as co-driver mechanic, she became the first woman—and again one of the few drivers to finish—in the Baja 1000 off-road competition.

AIRPLANE PILOTS

Farthest Flyer

British SHEILA SCOTT completed the longest consecutive solo flight ever when she flew 31,000 miles around the world in 1965. She has broken over 100 world flying records and won over 50 racing trophies. Since her flight in 1965, Ms. Scott has flown around the world twice more by herself and completed the first solo light aircraft flight over the North Pole in 1971.

World Aerobatics Champion

In 1970 SVETLANA SAVITSKAYA, a Russian engineer, became the first woman to win the World Aerobatics Championship, a competition noted for demanding both outstanding precision in flying and raw nerve.

Farewell "Powder Puff" Champion

The 1976 Powder Puff Derby (officially the All-Woman Transcontinental Air Race, instituted in the United States in 1947) was won for the second year in a row by TRINA JARISH of California. Due to lack of funding, the 1976 Derby, covering a grueling 2,930-mile course from coast to coast, was the last of these competitions.

First to Break the Sound Barrier

In 1948, flying a Sabre jet F-86, JACQUELINE COCHRAN (see "Women in the Military," p. 536) of the United States became the first woman to exceed the speed of sound. Ms. Cochran was an international air race competitor for over 30 years (circa 1930–65) and has held more air speed records than any other woman. She was the first woman to fly in the famous Bendix transcontinental race in 1934, and the first woman to win in in 1934, and the first woman to win it in 1937—the year she became the first woman ever awarded the Clifford Burke Harmon Trophy for her contributions to world aviation. She won the Harmon Trophy again in 1938, '39, '46, '50, and '53 and in 1971 was elected to the United States' Aviation Hall of Fame.

GLIDERS AND SAILPLANERS

First Gliding Champion

In 1966 British ANNE BURNS became the first woman to win the British Gliding Championship. Ms. Burns has competed in gliding championships around the world and holds four women's records in South African competitions. Ms. Burns received the Queen's Commendation for valuable services in the air in 1955 and 1963.

Most Accurate Parachutist

In 1977 MARIE LEDBETTER became the first woman to win the World Accuracy Title at the 12th Annual Parachuting Championship in Rome. In eight jumps from 2,500 feet, Ms. Ledbetter's total accumulate distance from the target was 3⅓".

BOARD AND CARD GAMES

BACKGAMMON

Most Often Victorious Backgammoner

MARY JACOBY, of the United States, is a former tennis champion who has been winning world bridge championships since 1935 and has won more unofficial (there are no official) backgammon tournaments than any other woman.

BRIDGE

First Grandmaster

British RIKA "RIXI" MARKUS, the first woman to attain the rank of World Bridge Federation "Grandmaster," won the first two European Women's Championships in 1935 and 1936. She went on to win 10 more international championships—a record for women—by 1974. Ms. Markus, with her partner FRITZI GORDON, is probably the greatest woman bridge player competing on an international level.

Most Titled

HELEN MARTIN SMITH, of the United States, has won over 30 national bridge championships—more than any other woman—since her first tournament in 1937. She also holds the greatest number of master points for women, first calculated in 1964. No woman has yet caught up.

Most Pairs Titled

MARGARET WAGAR and KAY RHODES, both of the United States, share the women's record number of four pairs titles.

CHECKERS

First and Only Champion

Schoolteacher GERTRUDE HUNTLEY, of the United States, has so far been the only woman player to enter any national checkers tournament, which she did for the first time in 1939. She has been listed as the unofficial U. S. Women's Champion since that time and no challenger has yet come forth.

15

Women in the Arts and Entertainment

By Judith B. Prowda

Lois Craig, consulting editor

Not all arts entertain, and not all entertainers are artists. Yet many of the serious women artists in this chapter are also superb entertainers—BEVERLY SILLS, EUDORA WELTY, several of the prima ballerinas and choreographers, even, in some of their works, certain painters and sculptors. And all of the entertainers we have chosen to include are artists—LILY TOMLIN, MABEL MERCER, DOROTHY SAYERS, among others.

The happy fact is that many 20th-century women have been able to move confidently back and forth between high and popular art—singing opera *and* the blues, playing Greek tragedy *and* Hollywood comedy, dancing classical ballet *and* modern jazz routines, writing detective stories *and* philosophical treatises or poetry.

Their own creative flexibility, combined with the burgeoning opportunities opened to them by film and TV and the interest many communities today show in supporting art galleries, museums,

dance performances, and concert series, have made the past few decades generally exciting ones for women in the arts and entertainment fields. Nowhere has this been more evident than in the United States, which has given an enthusiastic welcome to all the arts and to women artists from all countries of the world. London, of course, competes as always. So does Paris. And Vienna. Oslo. Rio de Janeiro. Moscow. But the greatest excitement has been generated in the United States, where, particularly in very recent years, artists and entertainers— live, on film, on records, on TV, in "little" magazines and paperback books— have enjoyed a level of audience interest and a measure of government support never before accorded them in modern history. It is generally agreed that the impetus for the governmental side of this heartening situation arose with the New Deal's Works Progress Administration (WPA) programs that employed artists, writers, and theater people and was kept strong by the use of thousands of artists and entertainers in the propaganda and morale activities of World War II (from the OSS to the USO).

Official American commitment to the arts has been spurred by a succession of Presidents' wives, beginning with ELEANOR ROOSEVELT (see "Women Activists, Heroes, and Humanitarians," p. 738). JACQUELINE KENNEDY ONASSIS (see "Far-Out Women," p. 751) gave the tradition a new boost, greatly broadening the kinds and numbers of artists and entertainers invited to perform at the White House. BETTY FORD, herself once a student of MARTHA GRAHAM, did much to promote dance. ROSALYNN CARTER has been especially interested in presenting the work of U.S. craftswomen on various occasions in the White House (see "Women in the Home and Community," p. 129) and in attending musical and theatrical performances and art exhibitions with the President in a capital city much better equipped for the encouragement and display of culture than it was only a decade or so past. And with the Carter Administration, for the first time, a Vice-President's wife, JOAN MONDALE, herself an aspiring potter (see "Women in the Home and Community," p. 128) has been given a heavy schedule of duties as a semi-official "arts advocate."

Far and away the most important woman involved in U.S. government support of the arts to date, however, has been NANCY HANKS. From 1969 to late 1977 Ms. Hanks chaired the National Endowment for the Arts and its predecessor agency, the National Council for the Arts. Prior to becoming the first woman to chair the first official over-all U.S. arts agency in the nation's history, Ms. Hanks had been an adviser on cultural resources and special assistant to the White House, coordinator of two projects on the performing arts for the Rockefeller Brothers Fund, and president of the Associated Councils of the Arts. Under her direction, the Arts En-

dowment has given grants and assistance of many kinds to individual women and men in the theater, dance, music, literature, every visual art including photography and architecture, and to museums, magazines, orchestras, ballet companies, drama groups, schools, colleges, and communities.

Does all this mean that no prejudice or problems exist today for women in the arts and entertainment fields? Unfortunately, no. In most countries in the West, women have long been able to work on relatively even terms with men in the performing arts. (It has, after all, been some time since Shakespeare's women were played by boys.) Yet it was not until 1971 that Ringling Brothers Circus hired its first female clown (see "Far-Out Women," p. 749), and women have only begun to escape being cast in what increasingly are seen as sexist roles on stage and screen.

In the visual arts, the record has been quite dismal. JOAN SUTHERLAND HARRIS, who with LINDA NOCHLIN organized the "Women Artists: 1550–1950" exhibition, notes that very little was documented on women artists before the mid-16th century. Ms. Nochlin in her catalog article "Why Have There Been No Great Women Artists?" answers that loaded question by maintaining that it was "indeed *institutionally* made impossible for women to achieve excellence on the same footing as men, no matter what the potency of their so-called talent or genius." Prior to the 20th century, women painters were almost without exception the daughters of painters, with whom they trained, or at the least the unusually indulged offspring of privilege, who could hire private instruction.

Women sculptors and architects, like painters, have had to wait until recent years for equal opportunities to train and practice. The new fiber artists are, it is true, predominantly women, but this (usually monumental) art is one that has evolved from weaving, traditionally a home craft more practiced by women than by men, at least in the Western world. And women as directors of museums or conductors of orchestras are almost entirely a mid-20th-century phenomenon, and a distinct minority.

Nevertheless, except for those areas noted just above, so many women have been prominent in the arts and entertainment for so many years that to cite important "firsts" among them has proved difficult. Rather than neglect women whose achievements and distinction are remarkable if not necessarily pioneering, this chapter includes a number in various fields nominated by advisers whose names are listed below. Not all the women we have included are their recommendations, though the majority are. Not all of whom they said, "But you can't leave *her* out!" are here.

For the omissions we apologize, to our advisers and our readers. Many marvelous women artists and entertainers had to be dropped, for reasons of space . . . and still it's a very long chapter.

JUDITH B. PROWDA, *a graduate of the Baldwin School in Bryn Mawr, Pennsylvania, received her bachelor's degree from Sarah Lawrence College and master's degrees from Middlebury College, in French literature, and from the Johns Hopkins School of Advanced International Studies, Bologna, Italy, and Washington, D.C. She also has studied art history, film, music, and literature in Paris, and received a Certificat d'Études Politiques from the Institut d'Études Politiques. She has worked as art and photography editor at* Newsweek *magazine in Paris and on* Horizon *magazine. In January 1978 she visited the People's Republic of China with a group from the Johns Hopkins University. Ms. Prowda works as an interpreter for the Department of State.*

Consulting editor LOIS CRAIG *was the director through 1977 of the Federal Architecture Project, sponsored by the National Endowment for the Arts, Wash-* ington, D.C. In 1975 she was awarded a Loeb Fellowship in Advanced Environmental Studies at the Harvard Graduate School of Design. Ms. Craig, a graduate of New York University with a major in political science and a minor in art history, did graduate work in painting and art history at American University. The mother of three, she has been a senior editor of City magazine and staff member of Urban America and has published numerous magazine articles. Ms. Craig edited The Federal Presence, a book about the history of U.S. government buildings, published in 1978. Now resident in Boston, she is working under an NEA Design Project Fellowship on public design and public life.*

Grateful acknowledgment for special assistance on this chapter is made to:
ADELYN D. BREESKIN, *consultant on 20th-century painting and sculpture, National Collection of Fine Arts (see p. 614)*
Dr. STEPHEN PROKOPOFF, *director, Institute of Contemporary Art, Boston*
Dr. ELLIOTT GALKIN, *director of the Peabody Conservatory*
Dr. MICHAEL HARRISON, *professor, The Johns Hopkins School of Advanced International Studies*
FRANÇOIS-BERNARD MÂCHE, *composer, Prix d'Italia, 1977, Paris, France*
WAYNE SHIRLEY, *Library of Congress, and chairman, Capital Chapter, the American Musicological Society*
SALI ANN KRIEGSMAN, *Washington-based writer on dance*
GARY ARNOLD, *movie critic, the* Washington Post
RICHARD HENSHAW, *author with a special interest in films*
JEAN MITRY, *film historian and professor of cinema, the Sorbonne, Paris, France*
DAVID PARKER, *Motion Picture Section, the Library of Congress*
WINSTON SHARPLES, *Archives, the American Film Institute*
CATHERINE O'NEILL *(see* "Women in Religion," *p. 377)*

PAINTERS AND PRINTMAKERS

The Chosen Thirty-Four

In 1976, a major event in the art world was the first international exhibition of paintings by women, assembled by the Los Angeles (California) County Museum of Art from private and public collections throughout the world. Art historians ANN SUTHERLAND HARRIS and LINDA NOCHLIN prepared the catalogue for the show, which spanned the years 1500–1950.

Eighty-four women painters were represented, including the following 20th-century artists:

Mary Cassatt (1844–1926)
Lilla Cabot Perry (1848–1933)
Lady Elizabeth Butler (1850–1933)
Cecilia Beaux (c. 1855–1942)
Edith Hayllar (1860–1948)
Suzanne Valadon (1865–1938)
Käthe Kollwitz (1867–1945)
Florine Stettheimer (1871–1944)
Romaine Brooks (1874–1970)
Gwen John (1876–1939)
Paula Modersohn-Becker (1876–1907)
Gabriele Munter (1877–1962)
Vanessa Bell (1879–1961)
Nataliia Sergeevna Goncharova (1881–1962)
Alexandra Exter (1882–1949)
Sonia Delaunay (1885–   ) (See "Women in Fashions and Home Furnishings, p. 241.)
Marie Laurencin (1885–1956)
Nadezhda Andreevna Udaltsova (1885–1961)
Olga Vladimirovna Rozanova (1886–1918)
Georgia O'Keeffe (1887–   )
Hannah Höch (1889–1971)
Liubov Serbeevna Popova (1889–1924)
Sophie Taeuber-Arp (1889–1943)
Marlow Moss (1890–1958)
Agnes Tait (1879–   )
Kay Sage (1898–1963)
Franciska Clausen (1899–   )
Isabel Bishop (1902–   )

Alice Trumbull Mason (1904–1971)
Leonor Fini (1908–   )
Lee Krasner (1908–   )
Loren MacIver (1909–   )
Frida Kahlo (1910–1954)
Dorothea Tanning (1910–   )

First U.S. Impressionist a Woman

MARY CASSATT, born in 1844, spent most of her childhood in her birthplace, Pittsburgh, Pennsylvania, and in Philadelphia. Like many American artists during the second half of the 19th century, she pursued her studies in Europe, where she remained to play a significant part in the Impressionist movement. Her work shown at the Philadelphia Academy of the Fine Arts show in 1876 introduced Impressionist paintings to the United States. Closely associated with Edgar Degas, she was a great artist in her own right, who, like Degas, drew much inspiration from Japanese art. Mary Cassatt's "maternity" paintings gained popularity in the period before World War I. The last years of her life were frustrating, for failing eyesight forced her to give up painting some years before her death in 1926.

French Individualist

While studying drawing at the Académie Humbert, MARIE LAURENCIN, born in 1885 in Paris, made the acquaintance of Georges Braque. Together they sought a new artistic direction away from Impressionism and Neo-Impressionism. Picasso introduced them both to Apollinaire, with whom Marie Laurencin had a passionate love affair for many years. Both were illegitimate, but her bastard birth prevented their marriage. She was the inspiration of many of his love poems, including "Le Pont Mirabeau," and he was her introduction to the

Cubist circle of painters and a strong supporter of her work. Gertrude Stein was one of the first to buy a painting from her. Marie Laurencin married a German aristocrat painter named Otto von Waltjen, and when World War I broke out both fled to Spain. Her poems written while in exile reflect her depression and longing for Paris during this time. She divorced her husband and returned to Paris two years after the end of the war to pursue a career as a book illustrator, doing drawings for André Gide's *La Tentative Amoureuse* (1921) and Lewis Carroll's *Alice in Wonderland* (1930). She also designed costumes and sets for the Ballets Russes and Art Deco wallpaper and textile patterns. Her portraits of women often have narrow faces, slanting eyes, full lips, and curly hair— very much her own physical traits. She died in 1956. Marie Laurencin did not belong to an artistic group, nor did she establish a school. Her work reflects an independent vision.

First American Woman Asked to Present Self-Portrait to the Medici Gallery

When CECILIA BEAUX's mother died shortly after her birth, circa 1855, she and her sister were raised by their maternal grandmother and aunts in Philadelphia. As a young girl, she developed an interest in Europe culture (her father was French) and at the age of 16 began drawing lessons, studying with a distant relative, Katherine Drinker, and later with Dutch artist Adolf van der Whelan and William Sartrain in Philadelphia. By the turn of the century she was established in New York as a prominent portraitist, commissioned to paint Ms. Theodore Roosevelt and Ms. Andrew Carnegie, among others, and was an important member of artistic circles. After her first one-woman show in Boston's St. Botolph's Club in 1897, she had 14 more in Philadelphia, New York, and Paris before 1933, and won innumerable awards from the Philadelphia Academy of Fine Arts, the Carnegie Institute, and the Paris Exposition. She was presented an honorary degree from the University of Pennsylvania, and elected to the Academy of Arts and Letters, the Society of American Artists, and the National Academy of Design. In 1925 she was the first American woman asked to present a self-portrait to the Medici Gallery. She died in 1942, and her work was revived by a retrospective at the Philadelphia Museum of Art in 1974.

First Woman to Be Elected to the Prussian Academy of Art

One of the greatest graphic artists of the first part of the 20th century, KÄTHE KOLLWITZ (1867–1945), was born in Konigsberg, East Prussia. She portrayed the poverty and suffering she witnessed and lived through during the Franco-Prussian War, both World Wars, and the interwar Depression. While her husband, Dr. Karl Kollwitz, practiced medicine in Berlin, she worked to improve her etching techniques. A series of her prints based on Gerhart Hauptmann's *The Weavers,* which affected her strongly, was called "gutter art" by Kaiser Wilhelm II, and vetoed as a nominee for the Gold Medal in 1898 at the Berlin Art Exhibition. However, it was awarded a gold medal by the King of Saxony. Her second print cycle, "The Peasants' War," representing revolts in 16th-century Germany, won her the Max Klinger Villa Romana Prize and a year in Florence. In 1910 she started working on sculpture and did a life-size statue of grieving parents for the soldiers' cemetery of Roggeveld, after her son was killed at Flanders. Her art was declared "degenerate" by Hitler and the Third Reich, and galleries were not allowed to show or handle her work. Nevertheless, she continued to work in her studio until the last months of the war when she was forced to go to Moritzburg, near Dresden. The first woman elected a full member of the Prussian Academy of the Arts (1919), she became professor and director of graphic arts of the Academy, but resigned with the advent of the Nazi regime. The last cycle she completed, "Death" (1935), consisted of a stark and powerful series of eight lithographs on the theme, the final one portraying the artist herself.

Germany's First Experimental Post-Impressionist Painter

PAULA MODERSOHN-BECKER's short life as an artist began in Dresden. Born in 1876, the daughter of an aristocratic family, she studied in Bremen, where her family lived after leaving Dresden, then in an art school in England, and attended the School for Women Artists in Berlin (as did KÄTHE KOLLWITZ, above). Although she respected the lyric representations of landscapes that prevailed in Germany at the time, she grew weary of working in this style and left for Paris where she experimented with many styles, including Impressionism and Post-Impressionism, Primitivism, and Cubism, ending the German isolation in painting. Though this trip resulted in a great evolution in her style, it also caused a separation from her painter husband, Otto Modersohn. She returned to him when she discovered she was pregnant, and died in 1907 at the age of 31, after the birth of her daughter. Among her greatest works are still-lifes inspired by Cézanne's "color harmony and dynamic pictorial organization," portraits of peasants, nude maternal figures, and a nude self-portrait.

"Symboliste" Portrait Painter

Expatriate American painter ROMAINE BROOKS, born in 1874, was a "Symboliste" whose view of the art world was less cheerful though not remote from that of GERTRUDE STEIN (p. 678). After studies in Rome, Ms. Brooks inherited a family fortune, traveled to England to paint, and finally established herself in Paris as a popular portraitist whose Whistlerian black, white, and gray palette dramatized the inner life of her sophisticated subjects. Her sitters included poet Gabriele D'Annunzio, avant-garde writer Jean Cocteau, and writer and salonnière NATALIE CLIFFORD BARNEY (her companion for more than 40 years). Ms. Brooks was in the United States for the exhibition of her drawings at the Arts Club of Chicago in 1935–36, but returned to Europe, where she continued to paint into her late 80s. She died at the age of 96 in 1970. The National Portrait Collection in Washington, D.C., which owns a large number of her works, held a retrospective exhibition in 1971.

Parisienne Acrobat and Artist

Though her themes derive from Degas, Gaugin, Toulouse-Lautrec, Van Gogh, and Matisse, SUZANNE VALADON's paintings are unique in their robust imagery and bold use of color. Her well-known nudes, sitting or reclining, dominate colorful, decorative backgrounds, and her still-lifes in rich energetic settings won her attention from critics and collectors in France and abroad. Ms. Valadon lived outside the conventional standards of late 19th-century France. Born in 1865, the illegitimate daughter of a laundress, she began her career by frequenting the artistic circles of Montmartre, and took various jobs, among them performing acrobatics in a circus. In 1883 her illegitimate son, painter Maurice Utrillo, was born. She posed for and observed many artists, including Toulouse-Lautrec and Renoir, and eventually met Degas, who admired her work and nicknamed her "Terrible Maria." Her early paintings include portraits of Eric Satie, her lover. In 1911 she held the first of many one-woman shows at the Clovis Sagot Gallery. The Salon d'Automne, where she also was shown regularly, elected her *sociétaire* in 1920, and from 1933 until her death in 1938 she participated in the Salon des Femmes Artistes Modernes.

Russian Co-Founder of Rayonism

Leader, with Mikhail Larionov, of the Rayonist movement, NATALIIA SERGEEVNA GONCHAROVA (1881–1962) was one of the major figures of modern art in Russia during the early part of the 20th century. She combined elements from the Russian folk art tradition with brilliant Fauvist colors and Primitivist style, eventually evolving toward Cubism and Futurism. She and Larionov collaborated to develop this style, and published a Rayonist Manifesto in 1913, the year she gave her first one-woman show in Moscow (it included her famous Rayonist painting "Cats"). Her interest in Futurism led to her illustrating Futurist publications, which were spotted by Diaghilev, who was then organizing the Ballets Russes in Paris. In 1915 she and Larionov left Russia to travel with the Ballets Russes in Italy and Spain, working on theatrical decor and costumes, and settled permanently in Paris in 1917. Ms. Goncharova continued to paint and to design for the Ballet Russe and exhibit until her death in 1962.

Only Female Member of Berlin Dada Group

The only female member of Berlin's Club Dada, HANNAH HÖCH, born in 1889, was a major participant in the post-World War I anti-establishment art movement. Her greatest contribution was photomontage, which she is thought to have invented with artist Raoul Hauseman. Her forceful, satirical imagery, achieved by cutting up photographs, magazines, newspapers, and postcards, and juxtaposing them in provocative arrangements, attacked corruption in Germany. During the '20s, she broke with the Dadaists, but with the exception of two trips to Paris in 1924 and 1925, and three years in Holland, 1926–29, she spent her life in Berlin until her death in 1971. She experimented with other media including collage, watercolor, and oil, but she remained primarily concerned with satirizing the human experience.

U.S. Caricaturist, Landscape Painter, and Award-Winning Mystery Writer

The work of PEGGY BACON, admired as a caricaturist in the 1920s and '30s, is "a witty and revealing record of a whole society," according to the catalogue of the major retrospective of Ms. Bacon's work at the National Collection of Fine Arts in 1976. Ms. Bacon, born in 1895, has worked in various media: pastel, drypoint and etching, oil, gouache, and ink. Her early concentration on social satire has given way to an interest in color and composition—and now, in her 80s, Ms. Bacon is doing landscape painting. A writer and illustrator of books and magazines, she received the Edgar Allan Poe special award for her first mystery novel, *The Inward Eye,* from the Mystery Writers of America (1953). She has taught at several colleges and universities.

Grand Old Lady of American Primitive Painting

Primitive painter ANNA MARY (better known as GRANDMA) MOSES, began her career as an artist in her late 70s, after farming and household work became too strenuous for her. As a child she had experimented in painting when her father brought home blank sheets of newspaper for his children to draw on. She liked to draw pictures and color them in with berry juice, "the gayer the better." In 1887 she married and moved to a farm in Eagle Bridge, New York, which she continued to run with the help of her youngest son after her husband's death in 1927. When arthritis made it difficult for her to embroider, her sister suggested she paint. Thresher cloth served as her first canvas. She copied postcards and Currier and Ives prints, but soon turned to her own ideas, giving away her paintings or selling them "according to size," until an art collector discovered them at the Woman's Exchange in Thomas's Drugstore in Hoopsick Falls, New York. Later her work was shown at the "Contemporary Unknown American Painters" show at the Museum of Modern Art and in a one-woman show at the Galerie St. Étienne (1940). Gimbels department store arranged a Thanksgiving show for her, and in 1941 she won the New York State Prize in Syracuse, New York, followed by the Woman's National Press Club Award in Art in 1949. After World War II she gained recognition in Europe, and her designs for tiles and Christmas cards were known to all. Grandma Moses has been compared to Pieter Breughel in her "understanding of the eternal importance of small things," according to author Louis Bromfield. Nelson A. Rockefeller declared September 7 "Grandma Moses Day" in New York State in honor of her 100th birthday. At the time of her death in 1961, President John F. Kennedy said that "the directness and vividness of her paintings restored a primitive freshness to our perception of the American scene."

Winner of Brazilian and French Awards

MARIA HELENA VIEIRA DA SILVA, Portuguese-born painter, is a major figure in the post-World War II School of Paris. Encouraged by her family to pursue her studies in art in Lisbon, where she was born in 1908, Vieira da Silva, in order to better understand human anatomy, also took courses at medical school. Before World War II she had three exhibitions. She went to Brazil when the war broke out and there had several one-woman shows and painted murals for the University of Agriculture. Her first postwar exhibition took place in New York in 1946, followed by exhibitions in Paris and Hanover, where she held her first retrospective. In 1959 she made 25 engravings for a book of poems by René Char. She and her Hungarian husband, painter Arpad Szenes, became French citizens in 1956. Her awards include

first prize at the São Paulo Biennale in 1961 and the Grand Prix des Arts from the French Government.

Winner of the National Institute of Arts and Letters Gold Medal for Painting

"Finally, a woman on paper!" Alfred Stieglitz is said to have exclaimed when he first saw an abstract charcoal drawing by GEORGIA O'KEEFFE. Then a New York gallery owner as well as a photographer, he included her work in his next show. A romance and a career were thus begun. Ms. O'Keeffe's first major exhibition in 1923 was followed by successive and numerous one-woman shows and major retrospectives, and she and Stieglitz were married in 1924. Over the years he did a "composite portrait" of her in some 500 photographs. Since his death in 1945, she has made her home in New Mexico in an adobe house filled with a collection of desert objects—bones, skulls, small rocks—that reflect her love of nature and her sensitivity to the texture and color of the Southwest. Her style, which ranges from representational to abstract, emphasizes rhythmic forms in nature and often the female body. Her paintings on board and canvas, variously called "Spartan," "austere," "lurid," and "epic," have earned her innumerable awards, including membership in the American Academy of Arts and Letters in 1963, and the Gold Medal of the National Institute of Arts and Letters, 1970. In 1977 Georgia O'Keeffe celebrated her 90th birthday, published an autobiographical book of her work with her own comments on it, and was busy experimenting with an art form new to her—pottery.

Master Calligrapher

Internationally known Japanese artist TOKO SHINODA, now in her 60s, has developed her own style of calligraphy and abstract India ink painting, or *saiboko*. Rather than follow the custom of using poems from the Chinese T'ang Dynasty or Waka poems of the Japanese Heian Period as sources of inspiration, Ms.

Shinoda works with the modern verses of Tatsaji Miyoski (1900–64). But while she uses her ink sticks, some dating from China's Ming Dynasty, and her specially ordered resilient brushes to explore and to reflect the day-to-day "color of her life," Ms. Shinoda remains a traditional Japanese artist, honored in her own country, as well as in the United States and Europe.

Artists' Portraitist

Now in her 70s, ALICE NEEL is best known for portraits that reflect the sitter's inner reality. A fellow artist commented after seeing her own portrait, "I recognize myself, my father, my brother, and my sister in it all at once." Though born and raised in Merion, Pennsylvania (she completed her studies at the Philadelphia School of Design for Women, now Moore College of Art), Ms. Neel is perhaps best characterized as a New York City painter who portrays obscure habitués of Greenwich Village and other Manhattan neighborhoods, as well as prominent New Yorkers like Andy Warhol and Virgil Thompson—always aiming for "the complete person, inside and outside." Ms. Neel in 1971 was awarded the Benjamin Altman Figure Prize of the National Academy of Design, and in 1976 the Endowment for the Arts Award. The Moore College of Art gave her an honorary doctorate in 1971, and she was elected a member of the National Institute of Arts and Letters in 1976. A major retrospective exhibition was held at the Whitney Museum of American Art in 1974.

Surrealist Painter

Surrealist painter LEONOR FINI, born 1908 in Buenos Aires of German, Slovak, and Venetian stock, spent most of her childhood in Trieste. Later she lived for many years in Italy and France, and has shown her work worldwide. Her fascination with death and her memories of visiting morgues as a young girl in Trieste are translated onto canvas as skeletons, bones, and decomposition. To paint, she says, is almost the equivalent of exorcism. Close to Max Ernst, Salvador Dali, Man Ray, and other surrealists during the 1940s and '50s, Ms. Fini illustrated books (including an edition of Baudelaire's Les Fleurs du Mal) as well as designing decor and costumes for ballet and theater. Her androgynous figures in dreamlike settings, with eyes peering out of eerie backgrounds, often include Ms. Fini's own features.

Inventor of Soak-Stain Technique

The paintings of HELEN FRANKENTHALER, born in 1928, are not merely conceptual in expression, as noted critic BARBARA ROSE writes. One does not just look at her painting, Ms. Rose explains, one enters it, and becomes aware of the participation of the artist's body— her physical immersion—in creating the work. Following the example of Jackson Pollock, Ms. Frankenthaler since the 1950s has been pouring paint on canvases placed on the floor. Her forms are often loose, irregular, and amorphous, creating a complex relationship between "flatness and illusion of depth." And her aqueous use of radiant colors is in effect a translation of watercolor into oil painting, with the ambiguity of space accentuated even more by her use of the soak-stain technique, which she invented. She has earned many prizes, including First Prize at the first Biennale in Paris in 1959, been honored with doctorates from several colleges and universities, and has taught art at Yale.

Abstract Expressionist

Born in a large Russian Jewish family in Brooklyn in 1908, LEE KRASNER was a member of the group who called themselves the American Abstract Artists. During the early '30s her work was greatly influenced by Impressionism and Post-Impressionism. Later she was affected by Picasso, Mondrian, and especially Matisse, the favorite of her teacher Hans Hofmann. Her style evolved toward Abstract Expressionism, the use of Fauvist color, and Cubist composition, as she grew interested in surrealist theories and Jungian concepts of the unconscious. Lee Krasner married Jackson Pollock in 1945, and for a time her own talents were obscured by her duties as an "art widow" after he was killed in a car accident in 1956. She admits that he influenced her painting, although she never lost her artistic independence. Lee Krasner has been represented in many group exhibitions, as well as in a retrospective exhibit at the Whitney Museum of American Art.

First British Woman Painter to Win Venice Biennale International Prize for Painting

The work of BRIDGET RILEY, a British artist in her 40s, who has endeavored to extend light functions of Impressionism and Pointillism, is considered one of the best painters to have come out of the short-lived Optical (Op) Art movement. Her work was represented at the Museum of Modern Art in New York in the 1965 exhibition, "The Responsive Eye," and at the Musée d'Art Moderne fourth "Biennale des Jeunes Artistes." She represented England at the XXXIV Venice Biennale in 1968, and won the International Prize for Painting—the first British woman to receive this honor.

Innovative Collage Artist

During the six years before her death in 1954, ANNE RYAN produced intimate and delicate collages that put her in the ranks of important 20th-century artists. Inspired by German Kurt Schwitters' first one-man show of collage in the United States in 1948, Ms. Ryan, who had been encouraged as a painter by Hans Hofmann, juxtaposed materials and paper of different colors and textures in abstract compositions. In her "white" collages, considered her most dramatic, Ms. Ryan explored "shades" of white (sand, eggshell, silver, and gray) as well as the effects of texture and pattern.

American (Expressionist) in Paris

Although she has lived in France since 1959 and her most recent work has taken on some of the characteristics of the School of Paris, Chicago-born JOAN MITCHELL is identified most often with the New York School. She has been influenced by de Kooning, Gorky, and Kline and has moved from figure painting to abstraction to "remembered landscapes." Her canvases are large (often polytychs). She has shifted her emphasis on shape created by multi-colored nervous lines to large areas of "color and form," unified by quick brush strokes. Ms. Mitchell, born in 1926, attended Smith College, received her B.F.A. from the Art Institute of Chicago, and won a two-year Fulbright to paint in Europe. Upon returning to the United States in 1949, she continued her studies at Columbia and at New York University, where she received her M.F.A. Her work has been included in exhibitions in the United States and abroad, and she is represented in the Phillips Collection in Washington, D.C., the Art Institute of Chicago, the Museum of Modern Art and the Whitney Museum of American Art in New York, and museums in many other cities.

Influential Black Women Painters

Her exhibit of Impressionist scenes of Paris at the Vose Gallery in Boston in 1938 was a major breakthrough for LOIS MAILOU JONES—and for black American artists, male or female. Her work remained mainly in the Impressionist mode until the 1940s, when she began to paint in a more realistic manner that explicitly deals with her own background as a black American. A professor of fine arts for 45 years at Howard University in Washington, D.C., she trained several generations of young artists.

ALMA W. THOMAS, Howard University's first fine-arts graduate, who also earned a master's degree in fine arts from Columbia University, taught in a Washington, D.C., junior high school for 35 years. Over the years she continued to paint and to study art, sometimes in Europe. Following her retirement in 1960 she became an abstract color painter. In 1972 she had a one-woman show at the Whitney Museum that amazed critics (she was then 81 years of age). Later that same year she had a retrospective exhibition at the Corcoran Gallery of Art. In 1977 her painting, "Flowers at Jefferson Memorial," was used as the poster for the exhibition "Two Centuries of Black American Art," which was mounted at the Brooklyn Museum as well as other museums throughout the country. Ms. Thomas died early in 1978.

SCULPTORS AND FIBER ARTISTS

She Won the Largest Ever Commission

Perhaps best remembered for her 100 life-size bronze studies for Chicago's Field Museum of Natural History exhibition, "Races of Mankind," MALVINA HOFFMAN in 1930 was chosen from among 3,000 artists to receive this commission, the largest known ever given to a woman sculptor. For five years she traveled to remote parts of the world in search of racial types. Her bronze sculptures are considered anthropologically perfect. Replicas have been shown at the National Geographic Society in Washington and at the Trocadero Museum in Paris, where she was the first foreigner to exhibit. Born 1887 in New York, Ms. Hoffman studied painting for six years before turning to sculpture, a medium which she selected for a portrait of her father, pianist Richard Hoffman, who had first come to the United States as JENNY LIND's accompanist. Malvina Hoffman later studied with Auguste Rodin and in 1915 won international recognition for her bronze of Russian dancers Pavlova and Mordkin. In 1917 she was awarded the Shaw Memorial Prize at the National Academy of Design, and in 1920 the Widener Gold Medal and the Palmes Académiques. In 1924 she won the ELIZABETH WATROUS Gold Medal. Her "International Dance Fountain," judged as one of the finest pieces at the New York World's Fair, remained on permanent exhibition. Other works are included in collections at the Metropolitan Museum of Art, the American Museum of Natural History, the Field Museum of Natural History, the Memorial Chapel of Harvard, the Carnegie Institute, and the Corcoran Gallery of Art. Her many awards included a doctorate of Literature from Mount Holyoke College, and a doctorate of Fine Arts from the University of Rochester.

Award-Winning British Sculptor

"All my early memories are of forms and shapes and textures," writes BARBARA HEPWORTH in her autobiography. "Above all, there was the sensation of moving physically over the contours of fullnesses and concavities, through hollows and over peaks—feeling, touching, seeing, through mind and hand and eye. This sensation has never left me. I, the sculptor, *am* the landscape. I am the form and I am the hollow, the thrust, and the contours." Like her contemporary, Henry Moore, Ms. Hepworth began her career at Leeds and the Royal College of Art as a sculptor emphasizing the underlying forms of the human body by ovals and cylindrical carving. By 1934, as her work became increasingly abstract, she began to introduce geometrical shapes, and her sculpture grew progressively more geometric after she and her husband, Ben Nicholson, and their children moved to Cornwall, where the rugged coastline and imposing cliffs and boulders were an inspiration. Ms. Hepworth has been awarded honorary degrees from numerous universities, including Birmingham, Oxford, London, and Manchester. Her awards include the Hoffman Wood Trust Leeds Gold Medal (1951), the Grand Prix at the 5th São Paulo Biennale, Brazil, and the Grand Prix as Woman Artist of the Year (1970) from the Prefect of the Alpes Maritimes (she was the first woman ever to receive this honor). One of her best-known works is the monument to her friend Dag Hammarskjöld, which stands outside the United Nations building in New York.

"Scavenger Artist"

LOUISE NEVELSON, now in her late 70s, and an established figure in the New York art community, is known internationally for her personal style. She has been called a "scavenger artist" because she uses such variegated materials as furniture parts, spindles, barreltops, and wheels in boxes (she paints them one color, black or white or gold, to obscure the original identity of these objects and create a sense of architectural unity. Born in Kiev, Russia (1900), she was five when her family moved to Rockland, Maine, where her father ran a lumberyard. In 1932 she became an assistant to Diego Rivera, working on a mural for the New Workers School. Early in her career as a sculptor, she explored various media, including bronze, stone, terra cotta, wood, and fabric. During what she calls the "unfolding" of her style she let herself be influenced by Cubism, Expressionism, Surrealism, Picasso, African art, and the ritualistic art of the Mayas and Aztecs, who "created a sense of mystery by geometric forms." Ms. Nevelson began exhibiting in 1933 in New York and had her first one-woman show seven years later. She has shown extensively and regularly since then, in the United States and abroad. From 1962 to 1964 she served as president of the National Artists Equity and she was the first vice-president of the Federation of Modern Painters and Sculptors. A member of the National Association of Women Artists and Sculptors' League, she also heads the advisory council of the National Historic Sites Foundation and is a member of the Art Students League of New York and the National Association of Women Artists. Among her recent works is the chapel in St. Peter's Lutheran Church, New York City.

Contemporary Abstractionist

LOUISE BOURGEOIS, born in 1911 in Paris, is best known for her portrayal of what William S. Rubin, chief curator of painting and sculpture at the Museum of Modern Art, describes as the "robust sexuality of things under and upon the earth." She herself says that the principal theme running through her sculpture is helplessness. Aggression and adversity are represented by truncated cylindrical forms slanted toward opposite poles. Her small feminine shapes created in the 1950s and more recent explicit phallic sculptures appear in collections at the Museum of Modern Art in New York, the Whitney Museum of American Art, New York University, and the Birla Academy in Calcutta, India, to name a few.

Major Pop Sculptor

Born in Paris of Venezuelan parentage in 1930, MARISOL (ESCOBAR) has made New York her home since 1950. A major figure in the Pop Art movement, she takes her inspiration from ordinary people, animals, and things around her, and re-creates them in mixed-media sculptures whose origins lie in Pre-Columbian ritual art, Mexican masks, and early American folk art. Objects cease to have meaning in real life when they become part of her assemblages of painted, satirical representations of real people. She puts herself into her work by contributing positive casts of her face. Her "heads of state" series, including caricatures of the British Royal Family, Mao Tse-tung, and Charles de Gaulle, and her fish series, in which she integrates her own facial features with the body of the fish, are well known.

She Sculpts with Canvas, Wire, and Steel

Since the early 1960s LEE BONTECOU, born in 1931 in Providence, Rhode Island, has attracted the attention of the art world with her canvas constructions based on wire and welded steel. Though the materials utilized are industrial, the concept of the works is organic. The fabric stretched over wire and metal armatures gives the impression of skin and membranes, with earth-brown convolutions centered around a deep opening, giving a feeling of mystery and menace. Prior to her work of the '60s Ms. Bontecou produced more naturalistic bronze forms such as birds and other animals, which later gave way to large rare flowers and exotic predatory fish, some over seven feet in height. The themes of her highly finished drawings evolved with her sculpture; the earlier ones contain natural materials such as charcoal and soot on muslin, while the later drawings in ink and silver paint create a world of eerie flora and fauna. She has exhibited widely since her first one-woman show in 1959; her first retrospective exhibition was at the Museum of Contemporary Art in Chicago in 1972.

"Eccentric Abstractionist"

EVA HESSE, who died of a brain tumor in 1970 at the age of 34, was esteemed as a major artist in the '60s. Her work, generally regarded as a cross between painting and sculpture, incorporated the notion of serialism, often within a repetitive framework ("If something is meaningful, maybe it's more meaningful said 10 times"). Utilizing a wide variety of materials, hard and soft, natural and processed—fiberglass, latex, rope, string, wood, metal, papier-mâché—she produced a series of shapes, organizations, or environments, on the floor, hanging from the ceiling, quite different from traditional ideas of sculpture, and quite out of the realm of the conventional esthetic. They are described by her friend, critic LUCY LIPPARD as "Eccentric Abstraction." Ms. Hesse, born in 1936 in Hamburg, left Nazi Germany with her Jewish parents to live in Washington Heights, New York, in 1939, remaining marked by this experience as well as by her mother's suicide. The Guggenheim Museum of Art held a memorial exhibition in 1972–73. The catalogue noted her "desire to create sculpture that did not function as isolated objects placed on bases," an "additive process" rather than the traditional chiseling or carving away of form.

Creator of First Women's Art Program and "The Dinner Party"

JUDY CHICAGO, born JUDY GEROWITZ in Chicago in 1939, pioneered the first women's art program in the country. The UCLA-educated painter, sculptor, and process artist has been instrumental in introducing the idea of female imagery into the art community and in developing a new environment for women artists, a commitment she describes in her autobiography, *Through the Flower* (1975). Since 1974 she has been at work on an exhibit called "The Dinner Party," a room-sized sculpture intended as "a reinterpretation of The Last Supper from the point of view of women who have prepared the meals and set the table throughout history." Ms. Chicago and her staff of painters, potters, and needlepoint artists are completing 39 porcelain place settings consisting of plate, chalice, and flatware atop a cloth runner. Each plate and runner has been decorated to represent women who have held particularly important positions in their cultures—from an early mother goddess, through an Egyptian pharaoh, through QUEEN ELIZABETH I, EMILY DICKINSON, VIRGINIA WOOLF, and GEORGIA O'KEEFFE (see p. 600). "The Dinner Party," opens January 1979 and is scheduled to travel throughout the United States.

First in the United States to Present Nonfunctional Weaving

Not until the 1950s and '60s did weaving leave its traditional forms to break into three-dimensional objects described in terms of the fine arts. First, or one of the first, among weavers to create such hangings, free of functional necessities, was LENORE TAWNEY, born in 1925 in Lorain, Ohio. Ms. Tawney attended the University of Illinois in Champaign-Urbana (1943–44) and, with her first interest in sculpture, the Institute of Design, Chicago (1945–47). In 1948 she bought a loom and began to weave, studying with MARIA TAIPALE of Finland and becoming deeply involved in her new craft. In 1953 she moved to New York City, studied Peruvian gauze weave, and invented a new reed with which she could control the shape of her weaving, spreading the warp or choosing a narrower width. Her new techniques for shaped weaving made possible a hitherto unknown range of expression.

Spatial Environment Artist

ELSI GIAUQUE, born 1900 in Switzerland, worked as a young woman with marionettes in Zurich; her theatrical experience strongly influenced her spatial environments. Movement and light dominate such works as her "Pure Spatial Element 1968–69," in which metal frames are wrapped vertically and diagonally with colored yarns, tapestry-woven and suspended in three-dimensional arrangement. The spectator can move into the environment and around the overlapping transparent planes. In some of her environments the layers themselves may move or vibrate or movement may be in the eye of the viewer moving through the spaces. Elsi Giauque taught weaving at the arts and crafts school in Zurich from 1944 to 1970, then devoted herself entirely to her own artistic work. Her tapestries have been widely exhibited and have won gold and silver medals at several Milan Triennales.

Polish Weaver Who Opened New Perspective with Fabric Environments

MAGDALENA ABAKANOWICZ, born in 1930 in Poland, studied at the Fine Arts Academy in Warsaw (1950–55) and became a teacher there in 1965. Ms. Abakanowicz early introduced thick ropes and cords into her rectangular woven work, producing strong surface contrasts; she soon expanded her weaving beyond the loom, constructing gargantuan three-dimensional forms. Fascinated with the relation of form to space, she built extraordinary shapes whose power she reinforced by using monochromatic colors, varied by materials of differing receptivity to light. Ms. Abakanowicz was one of the first to move her wall hangings off the wall to the middle of a room, involving and enveloping the spectator from all sides. Her works reach enormous scale; the Pasadena Art Museum used a narrow space a city block long for a three-part environment of massive forms and ropes that she composed on site. Her extraordinary imagination and powerful artistic gifts have won her many Polish government prizes and the gold medal of the Biennale in São Paulo (1966), and her work has been exhibited in important shows around the world.

Pioneer Textile Artist Assists Weavers Around the World

An outstanding weaver whose hangings have been commissioned by architects of many countries, American-born SHEILA HICKS, who later moved to France, continues to study the origins of her art and has assisted the artisans of countries including India, Chile, and Morocco in adapting age-old techniques and skills to contemporary fabric.

Ms. Hicks, born in 1934 in Hastings, Nebraska, first wanted to be a painter and went to Syracuse University in 1952, later transferring to Yale University, where she received her B.F.A. in 1957. She began weaving in 1955, went to South America (Peru, Bolivia, Ecuador, Chile) on a Fulbright scholarship in 1957, in 1958 returned to Yale for her M.F.A., and then became the first woman to obtain a grant to study at the Fribourg School of Art in France.

In Europe in 1964, she established a studio in Paris and founded a pilot workshop at the Wuppertal factory in Germany where she used an electric machine-gun tool to make thick rugs of braided and wrapped piling. In 1966 she went to India to help the weavers of Calicut, Kerala, plan textiles for Western countries, and in 1968 organized a workshop in Huaquen, Chile. There she taught artisans to weave local wool and, in time of drought, linen and alpaca from the north; this workshop supports 25 families and its products have been exhibited internationally. Finally, in 1970–72 Sheila Hicks went to Morocco to help revitalize that country's traditional rug industry—and found herself as an artisan, trying new ideas in design and texture for a series of prayer rugs using the Moslem arch as a central theme but sculptured in dense pile of varying height, with the wool tied in knots and sheared with scissors. Her prayer rugs were displayed in 1971 in Bab Rouah, "gatehouse of the sunset," on the ramparts of Rabat.

Sheila Hicks's many architectural commissions have included a prayer rug for a granite wall in New York's CBS building and hangings for the Ford Foundation, the Georg Jensen Center for Advanced Design, the Conference Center (Mecca), the Rothschild Bank (Paris), and the TWA terminal at Kennedy airport.

Yugoslav Weaver of Monumental Constructions

JAGODA BUIC, born in 1930 in Yugoslavia, studied at the Academy of Applied Arts, Zagreb. Inspired by her native surroundings—the Mediterranean, the Dalmatian Coast, the rugged soil of the Balkans, and the architecture of medieval cities—Ms. Buic creates monumental works described by one critic at the 1970 Biennale in Venice as "exquisitely crafted gigantic knitted wool constructions . . . (like) sagging cones and fragments of a medieval parapet." Associated for years with the Dubrovnik Theater Festival, Ms. Buic views modern art fabrics as "a synthesis of architecture with other branches of plastic creation." Her large constructions and two-dimensional forms, often involving crenellations and chevron motifs, have won international prizes including a Silver Medal at the 1955 Triennale, Milan.

Prize-Winning South American Weaver

Fabric artist OLGA DE AMARAL, born in 1932 in Colombia, studied architectural design at the Colegio Mayor de Cundinamarca, Bogotá (1951–52), became director of architectural design there (1953), studied weaving and design at the Cranbrook Academy of Art in Michigan (1954–55), and founded and directed the weaving department at the Universidad de los Andes, Bogotá (1966–67). From 1968 to 1972 she was Columbia representative to the World Crafts Council, and she has been WCC Latin American director since 1970. Her work brought her world acclaim in her one-woman show at the Museum of Contemporary Crafts, New York (1970), and at the 1971 Lausanne Biennale. She was the first woman to win first prize at the Twenty-second Salon de Artistas Nacionales, Bogotá, and first prize at the Third Bienal de Arte de Coltejer 1972, Medellín, Colombia. As director of a large handweaving establishment in Bogotá, Olga de Amaral is in daily contact with upholstery and carpet production. Her thick spiral wrappings and prewoven tapes enable her to realize the dramatic proportions of her architectonic structures. A pair of tapestries she created for the main hall of the Peachtree Plaza Hotel, Atlanta, Georgia, each measured 83′6″ high by 14′ wide.

"Rose Path" Tapestry Artist

While other weavers break new ground in three-dimensional tapestry, HELENA BARYNINA HERNMARCK continues two-dimensional pictorial weaving, using an adaptation of the traditional Swedish "rose path" technique she has developed. In 1965, two years after she left design school in Stockholm, Ms. Hernmarck moved to Montreal, Canada, where several of her early, abstract works were hung in the Place des Arts and in Expo '67's Habitat. One of her best-known works is "The Launching of the Q.E. 2," done for the Cunard Line.

ARCHITECTS

A Backward Look

Women were actively involved in architecture (especially home design) even before its organization as a profession in the last part of the 19th century. But not until the exhibit "Women in American Architecture: An Historical and Contemporary Perspective" opened at the Brooklyn Museum in 1977 (with a book of the same name serving as the show's catalogue) was their history explored and their achievements broadly recorded.

The exhibit's curator (and book editor) SUSANA TORRE, who also organized the Archive for Women in Architecture under the auspices of the Architectural League of New York, was assisted by designers CYNTHIA ROCK, NAOMI LEFF, and JANE MCGROATY.

One of the show's revelations: The first woman graduate of an American architectural school was MARGARET HICKS, (1858–83). Even before she was awarded her degree by Cornell University in 1880, she became in 1878, with a student project, "The Workman's Cottage," the first U.S. woman to achieve architectural publication.

First to Earn MIT Degree in Architecture, Designer of the Women's Building at Columbia Exposition

The first woman to receive a degree in architecture from the Massachusetts Institute of Technology, SOPHIA HAYDEN (1869–1953) at age 22 was also the winner of the competition for a "simple light-colored classic" Women's Building for the Columbian Exposition in Chicago, 1892–93, commemorating the 400th anniversary of the discovery of America. Her Italian Renaissance design included a huge exhibit hall well lit from a skylight and clerestory windows. Unfortunately, the pressures of supervising construction and dealing with criticism resulted in Hayden's suffering a nervous breakdown.

First Woman Member of American Association of Architects

The American Association of Architects elected LOUISE BETHUNE (1856–1913) an associate in 1888, making her the first woman elected to that body. Prior to her marriage to architect R. A. Bethune, she had already practiced for 10 years, and was the most widely recognized of female architects when she declined the invitation to compete in the Chicago exhibition (above) on the grounds that she was not offered a fair honorarium. Her work included 18 schools in New York State, as well as factories, housing developments, and banks. Her Denton, Cottier, and Daniels music store in Buffalo, New York, was one of the first structures with a steel frame and poured concrete slabs in the United States.

"America's (and Perhaps the World's) First Woman Architect Who Needed No Apology in a World of Men"

MARION MAHONY GRIFFIN completed MIT's four-year architectural program in 1894 (the second woman to do so) and in 1895 entered the office of master builder Frank Lloyd Wright, becoming one of his first assistants. The first woman licensed to practice architecture in Illinois, she was largely responsible for the success of the 1910 "Wasmuth Portfolio," which introduced Wright to the world. Her drafting style was superb and she became responsible for more and more of Wright's interiors. Following her marriage to Walter Burley Griffin, she lived in Australia and India, but after his death in 1934, she returned to Chicago and worked for more than two decades on her own. Among her projects were the World's Fellowship Center in New Hampshire and a plan for redeveloping South Chicago. Much of her work remains to be discovered, but Reyner Benham, the British architecture critic, has written that Ms. Griffin was "America's (and perhaps the world's) first woman architect who needed no apology in a world of men."

First Woman to Study Architecture at the École des Beaux Arts

JULIA MORGAN (1872–1957) sailed to Paris with her degree in civil engineering from the University of California to become the first woman ever to study architecture at the École des Beaux Arts. Already laden with numerous awards when she obtained her certificate in 1902, she returned to her home state of California where she worked with John Galen Howard, who was designing the Berkeley campus. Two years later she began her own practice and designed the Mills College Library (1906), the Fairmont Hotel in San Francisco, and the home of William Randolph Hearst, San Simeon, in 1919. She also designed several YWCAs and the Berkeley Women's Club in 1929. Her designs incorporate a wide range of architectural concepts—including the practical (e.g., reinforced concrete as protection against earthquakes, San Simeon) and the decorative (e.g., exposed truss construction, St. John's Presbyterian Church in Berkeley).

Solar Pioneer

ELEANOR RAYMOND, born in 1887, was credited in a 1933 article in *Architectural Forum* with having designed the "first modern house in Massachusetts." In 1940 she built an all-plywood house; in 1944, one that featured masonite inside and out for walls, ceilings, floors, kitchen cupboards, and counter tops; and in 1948 she designed her vanguard Solar House. Ms. Raymond served as the head of the radar school at MIT during World War II.

Founders (with Husbands and Colleagues) of The Architects Collaborative

SARAH PILLSBURY HARKNESS, her partner-husband John Harkness, with JEAN FLETCHER (1915–65), her husband Norman Fletcher, and other colleagues, including the famed Walter Gropius, founded The Architects Collaborative in Cambridge, Massachusetts. The Collaborative was established in accordance with Bauhaus principles, and its influence on American architecture has been profound. Sarah Harkness has also exerted her personal influence in other ways, principally through the American Institute of Architects, for which she has chaired important commissions, and has been involved in several design-for-the-handicapped projects. Ms. Harkness is the mother of seven children.

Important Corporate Designer

A fellow of the AIA and an important figure in the postwar building boom in America, NATHALIE DE BLOIS worked for three decades with Skidmore, Owings, and Merrill. Though not visible up front in the corporate architectural firm, she worked on such major projects as the Lever House (1952), Pepsi-Cola Building (1960), the Union Carbide Building (1960), the Connecticut General Life Insurance Company Building (1962), Equibank Building, Pittsburgh (1976), the Boots Head Offices in Nottingham, England (1968), and many others. She had held the position of senior designer for 20 years when she was named an associate in the firm. Since 1975 she has been a senior project designer at 3D International in Houston, Texas.

Noted U. S. Woman Architect in Private Practice

Since she started her own practice in 1963, CHLOETHIEL WOODWARD SMITH has become one of the most noted women architects of the postwar period in the United States. She executed the master plan of the Capitol Park Apartments and Harbour Square townhouses in the Southwest Renewal area of Washington, D.C. Other commissions include Laclede Town in St. Louis and townhouses in Reston, Virginia, examples of her continuous preoccupation with architecture appealing to contemporary public taste.

Investigator of the Vernacular

DENISE SCOTT BROWN considers popular public taste and American social concerns in conceiving architectural ideas. Since she joined Venturi and Rauch in 1967, she has worked with her husband, Robert Venturi, to create architectural forms that respond to the needs and likes of contemporary Americans. She has been outspoken on the subject of discrimination against women in the profession.

International Architect-Planner

RAQUEL RAMATI, head of the New York City Urban Design Group, has achieved world prominence as an architect, urban designer, and authority on the restructuring of modern cities. She is a registered architect in Israel, has been the chief architect of municipal and corporate buildings in several countries, and in New York was project director of the Second Avenue Subway Study and served on the Mayor's Art Commission. Her numerous papers and articles on humanizing and making sense of urban layouts have resulted in her involvement in several zoning legislation projects. Ms. Ramati also has held a Loeb Fellowship at Harvard's Graduate School of Design.

Writers on Architecture and City Design

A number of women have won prominence as critics of architecture and the urban environment. Pulitzer prize winning ADA LOUISE HUXTABLE of the *New York Times* editorial staff (see "Women in Communications," p. 464) is a notable example. In 1934 CATHERINE BAUER (1905–64) published a book, *Modern Housing,* that was extremely important. Others who have been influential have included JANE BUTZNER JACOBS, best known for her *Death and Life of Great American Cities,* 1961, and *The Economy of Cities,* 1969; SIBYL MOHOLY-NAGY, architectural historian who in the 1950s attacked glass and steel hi-rises for

their lack of privacy; and ELLEN PERRY BERKELEY, who wrote for *Forum* and *Plus* for many years and also originated an annual summer educational program for women architects and planners. MILDRED FRIEDMAN is editor of *Design Quarterly;* JANE HOLTZ KAY is architecture critic for the *Nation;* and KATHERINE KUH writes on architecture and design for the *Saturday Review.* In 1978 SUZANNAH LESSARD, better known for her articles on other subjects (including politics and publishing), attracted much attention with her *New Yorker* "A Reporter at Large" essay on Manhattan's glass-walled buildings.

K. SWITZER, as she registered in order to enter Boston's famed all-male marathon, became the first woman to run in this race in 1967—even though officials attempted to tear her number from her back and she had to run alongside the designated track. She is seen above at the finish line in 1967.

DOROTHY HAMILL, Ice Capades star, retired from amateur competition in 1977 after her unprecedented sweep of titles in 1976—first place in the U. S. National, World, and Olympic figure skating championships. (Photo courtesy of the Ice Capades)

Russia's OLGA KORBUT, the first person, male or female, to do a backward somersault on the uneven parallel bars. She is pictured here on the balancing beam. (Photo courtesy of *Womensports* magazine by Tony Duffy)

Romania's NADIA COMANECI, 14-year-old "darling" of the 1976 Summer Olympics. The first athlete in Olympic history ever to achieve a perfect 10.0 score in any event, she did it not once but seven times.

Wimbledon Winners

Great Britain's VIRGINIA WADE had won every major tennis title except Wimbledon. In 1977 she delighted herself, the crowd, and Queen Elizabeth II, whose Silver Jubilee was being celebrated and who was in the audience, by finally taking the women's title—England's first win in this event in eight years. (Photo courtesy of *New York Apples*)

BILLIE JEAN KING, the woman who won the most Wimbledon titles ever—19, including 6 singles, 9 doubles, and 4 mixed doubles, 1961–75. The champion who almost single-handedly changed amateur and professional tennis for women through her crusade for women's rights at all levels of competition (and compensation) has also formed a professional woman's softball league, launched a professional mixed doubles tennis circuit, and established the World Team Tennis League.

The Women's Building, which housed the exhibit of women's applied art, was designed and built for the Columbian Exposition in Chicago, 1892–93, commemorating the 400th anniversary of Columbus' discovery of America. The architect was 22-year-old SOPHIA HAYDEN, first female architecture graduate of the Massachusetts Institute of Technology. (Photo courtesy of The Bettman Archives)

Primitive artist "GRANDMA" MOSES, with one of her paintings, popular in the United States in the 1940s and '50s. She took up painting when she was in her late 70s. (Photo courtesy of The Bettman Archives)

ELYN BREESKIN put together her first RY CASSATT exhibition more than 40 rs ago at the Baltimore Museum of ., where she was director for 15 years he days when female museum directors e a rare species. At 81 she is the con-ing curator of 20th-century art at the tional Collection of Fine Arts in Wash-ton. (Photo by Paul Schmick, the shington Star)

From the time she made her American debut with the Chicago Opera in 1916 through a decade of singing at the Metropolitan in New York before a throat operation forced her to retire, Milan-born self-trained coloratura soprano AMELITA GALLI-CURCI was a favorite among divas. (Photo courtesy of RCA Records)

Soprano LEONTYNE PRICE was the first black singer to have a leading role in a Metropolitan Opera premiere. Ms. Price was considered the finest Aida of her day (the '60s and '70s) in Europe and the United States. (Photo by J. Heffernan, Metropolitan Opera)

JOSEPHINE BAKER (1906–75), toast of Paris in the 1920s, starred in revues at the Casino de Paris and the Folies Bergère. She later appeared in London, the United States, and Latin America. (Photo courtesy of The Bettman Archives)

JUDITH JAMISON, 5-foot, 10-inch dancer who combines classical ballet with modern techniques, has appeared widely in the United States and abroad with Alvin Ailey's company. In 1972 she was elected to the Board of the National Endowment for the Arts—the first dancer and the first black chosen. (Photo by Donald Moss)

ashington, D.C.'s Arena Stage is syn- omous with the name ZELDA FICH- NDER. Producer, director, and co- under, she has taken her company on ir in Russia and has premiered dozens American plays and introduced the rk of many noted European playwrights the United States.

AGATHA MILLER CHRISTIE, at age 16 in Paris, when she was writing poetry but had not yet plotted the first of her mystery stories. The whodunits were to make her the most translated writer in the world. (Photo from *An Autobiography* by Agatha Christie, courtesy of Dodd, Mead)

One of the first explorers of the feminine consciousness, writer VIRGINIA WOOLF also ran the Hogarth Press with her husband Leonard Woolf; together they published the work of many unknown, but later noted, authors. (Photo courtesy of Harcourt Brace Jovanovich)

Diarist and novelist ANAÏS NIN. Her friends, including Henry Miller, pushed for her nomination for the Nobel Prize in 1976. She died in 1977. (Photo courtesy of Harcourt Brace Jovanovich, by John Pearson)

Architect of Women-in-Architecture Movement

A partner, along with her husband Harold Edelman, in the firm of Edelman and Salzman, JUDITH EDELMAN was in the forefront of the women-in-architecture movement that began to gain strength in the early 1970s. In 1971 she became the first woman member of the executive board of the New York Chapter of the American Institute of Archi- tects. The following year she helped organize the New York City Alliance of Women in Architecture, then co-authored a "status of women" resolution adopted at the AIA national convention, and accepted the leadership of the AIA Task Force on the Status of Women in Architecture that resulted from her resolution (see below). Her firm specializes in innovative plans for public and private housing developments.

What's Happening in American Architecture Today

In the suffragette years and again during the Depression women in the United States and abroad were actively engaged in architecture. Nevertheless, according to GWENDOLYN WRIGHT in an essay in *The Architect* (1977), the percentage of female practicing professionals dropped in each decade from the teens to the 1960s.

The 1975 report issued by the AIA's Task Force on Women in Architecture found that women now compose only 1.2 percent of all registered architects, and 3.7 percent of the entire architectural community. The problems women encounter on the job include little contact with clients, little responsibility for contract administration and site supervision. In other words, the report underscores the role-stereotyping that goes on in offices: women stay at the drafting table, the fabric sample files, and even the telephone and typewriter. The report also found that the average income of a male architect is 61.2 percent higher than that of a woman with the same experience and education.

Yet many women are actively practicing. They may be working on their own, or with male partners, and in rarer cases with female partners. The usual drawbacks in working on one's own or with another female will probably continue to discourage women architects from doing so until the public is persuaded to overlook prejudices from sex stereotyping. Organizations such as the Alliance of Women in Architecture (AWA) in New York, Women Architects, Landscape Architects, and Planners (WALAP) in Cambridge, and the Organization of Women Architects (OWA) in San Francisco have been actively attacking this problem for several years. The Women's School of Planning and Architecture in Vermont and the Archives of Women in Architecture in New York (above) also offer support.

Capping its review of the Brooklyn exhibition on Women in American Architecture, *Progressive Architecture* in March 1977 called attention to the work the following women architects are now doing:

GERTRUDE KERBIS maintains her own practice in Chicago, where her Green House condominium apartments provide individual greenhouses for each of 11 dwelling units in a four-story brick and concrete block structure.

MERRILL ELAM, associate vice-president and senior design project architect for Heery and Heery in Atlanta, Georgia, won the Georgia state AIA award for the Martin Luther King, Jr. Middle School, a poured concrete construction.

SHERRIE STEPHENS CUTLER is a principal with Lawrence Cutler in the firm of Ecodesign, Inc., which created the commercial center and condominium units for the Sugarloaf Mountain Corporation's ski village in Kingfield,

612   The Women's Book of World Records and Achievements

Maine, as well as the new fire/police headquarters for another small New England colonial town.

CYNTHIA PETERSON, adjunct professor of architectural design at City University of New York, also practices on her own in New York City.

JOAN GOODY, a partner in the firm of Goody, Clancy & Associates, of Boston, has designed a three-story wood-frame community center plus 100 units of housing for the elderly in Winthrop, Massachusetts.

MIMI LOBELL, who practices in New York City and teaches at Pratt Institute, is exploring symbolism and mythology in architecture for a book and designing meditation retreats.

BARBARA NESKI, with her New York partner-husband Julian, recently designed an admired wood-frame structure, the Simon House, on a wooded site on Long Island.

ETEL THEA KRAMER, another New Yorker with her own firm, has done a loft renovation for a sculptor and potter, and a house in Palo Alto, California.

ANDREA BROWNING, a partner in the firm of A & H Browning Architects, of Arlington, Massachusetts, also teaches at Harvard University's Graduate School of Design. The firm has done a residential hall renovation for Wellesley College and a renovation of the library at Hebrew College, Brookline, Massachusetts.

FRANCES HALSBAND, partner in the firm of R. M. Kliment, New York, has collaborated on the design for an extension of the Kingston (New York) YWCA, situated in an 1880s frame house, and another brick structure on the same ground. The firm's scheme calls for a new wing that links the two old buildings harmoniously.

PHOTOGRAPHERS

Hers Was the Longest Career in American Photography

IMOGEN CUNNINGHAM's work spans the period from *fin de siècle* aestheticism to the contemporary world of the 1970s. Born in 1883 in Portland, Oregon, she made her first photograph in Seattle in 1901; her last book, *After Ninety*, published in 1977, presented a remarkable collection of portraits of the old—in their homes, on the streets of her beloved San Francisco, and in hospitals. Ms. Cunningham early abandoned the romantic, contrived photograph for the uncompromising, unmanipulated purism of the famous West Coast group known as F/64. This purist bent, obvious in her work since the 1920s, did not prevent Ms. Cunningham from continuing to experiment, and in the '60s and '70s she produced photographs using such "manipulative" techniques as partial or fogged development and the sandwiched

negative. Much honored for her work, Ms. Cunningham was elected a fellow of the American Academy of Arts and Sciences and received a Guggenheim fellowship when she was 87.

The United States' Greatest Documentary Photographer

DOROTHEA LANGE (1895–1965), hailed by Edward Steichen as "our greatest documentary photographer," during the Depression made the American public and the federal government take notice of its citizens who had fallen by the wayside of the American dream. (See photograph accompanying "Women in Agriculture and the World Food Movement.") A successful photographer of San Francisco society in the 1920s, Ms. Lange turned away from a profitable living when she could no longer reconcile her work with seeing the 1930s' unemployed wandering in the street below her studio. In 1934 she began photographing the breadlines and soup kitchens of the city, and from 1935 to 1942 was one of a dozen photographers who took thousands of pictures of the Oklahoma dust bowl on behalf of the Federal Resettlement Administration. She photographed pea pickers, hitchhiking families, migrant workers asleep in the fields to hold their places for the next day, barren landscapes, empty schools, tent villages, and malnourished children. Her most famous photograph, "The Migrant Mother," of a gaunt woman with two ragged children at her shoulders and a mud-splotched baby in her lap, was published in hundreds of periodicals around the world and helped spur the U. S. Government to establish camps with medical facilities for impoverished farm workers. Ms. Lange went on to photograph Japanese-Americans interned during World War II, the UN conference in San Francisco, the vanishing Shaker communities. She remained active through the early 1960s and died of cancer on the eve of the opening of a one-woman retrospective show that she had finished assembling for the Museum of Modern Art.

She Portrayed the Famous in the 1920s

BERENICE ABBOTT left her native state of Ohio in 1918 at the age of 22 to study sculpture in New York on her own but soon left America to go to Berlin and Paris to seek "esthetic integration." She grew interested in photography while in Paris, where she worked as Man Ray's assistant from 1923 to 1925. Her portraits at this time include many luminaries of the epoch: James Joyce, Gide, Cocteau, MARIE LAURENCIN (p. 596), MARGARET ANDERSON (see "Women in Communications," p. 472), and Jules Romains, to name a few. She returned to the United States in 1929 and began a series of photos of New York City that was both an architectural documentary and a sociological reflection of American city life. For her the photograph is a document, but not merely a document,

and the photographer "prob . . . to reveal and celebrate r

Only Person to Receive a Pl Grant from the Museum of

In 1946 HELEN LEVITT received a grant from the Museum of Modern Art in New York and to date remains the only person to have been awarded a grant for photography from the Museum. Since then she has received numerous other distinctions, including a 1977 grant from the National Endowment for the Arts. The Museum has included her photographs of New York City street scenes in four exhibits, and her film *The Quiet One,* about a child's life in Harlem, has become a classic.

First U.S. Photographer to Be Represented at the Venice Biennale

"What I'm trying to describe is that it's impossible to get out of your skin into somebody's else's. And that's what all this is a little bit about. That somebody else's tragedy is not the same as your own," said photographer DIANE ARBUS, whose important work, done mostly between 1963 and 1971, included social and biological oddities—giants, midgets, transvestites, circus freaks, retarded women, drag queens—as well as ordinary middle-class people depicted with disturbing starkness. Ms. Arbus did not grow up in the sort of environment she photographed but as a member of the Jewish bourgeoisie of New York's Central Park West. At the age of 18, she married Allan Arbus and together they became established fashion photographers. But what she really wanted to shoot was not fashion. She won her first Guggenheim in 1963, a second in 1966, and eventually succeeded in photographing the socially taboo by wandering in nudist colonies, associating with prostitutes and others who made her feel a "mixture of awe and shame." Ms. Arbus taught at the Parson School of Design and Cooper Union from the mid-to-late

>60s. Her work was included in a group photo show at the Museum of Modern Art (MOMA) in 1967, and exhibited at the Baltimore Museum of Art, the National Gallery of Canada, the Chicago Museum of Contemporary Art, and others. In 1972, the year after her death by suicide, she was the first American photographer to be represented in the Venice Biennale.

MUSEUM PEOPLE, ART GALLERY OWNERS, AND PATRONESSES

First and Second U. S. Women Art Museum Directors

CORNELIA BENTLEY SAGE QUINTON, who assumed the directorship of the Albright Art Gallery in Buffalo, New York, in 1910 was the United States' first woman to head an art museum. The second was GRACE MCCANN MORLEY, who directed the San Francisco Museum of Art from 1935 to 1960.

Women's Place in the National Gallery of Canada: First and Second Female Directors

First woman director of the National Gallery of Canada, 1966–76, and former president of the Association of Art Museum Directors, JEAN SUTHERLAND BOGGS, born in 1922 in Peru, has become professor of 19th- and 20th-century art at Harvard University. At the age of 20, Ms. Boggs worked at the Art Association of Montreal (now the Montreal Museum of Fine Arts). For a period of two years she was, she says, "given every chance—organizing didactic exhibitions, lecturing, giving guided tours, writing exhibition catalogues, hiring models for the art school, acting as registrar for children's classes." She obtained her Ph.D. in Fine Arts from Radcliffe, and is the recipient of eight honorary degrees. She has held teaching positions at Skidmore, Mount Holyoke, the University of California at Riverside, was a Steinberg professor at Washington University in St. Louis, and as curator of the Art Gallery of Toronto (now Art Gallery of Ontario) mounted three important exhibits on Delacroix, Canaletto, and Picasso, followed by a series of radio broadcasts, "Listening to Pictures." A fellow of the Royal Society of Canada (FRSC) and an officer of the Order of Canada (O.C.), she is credited with having improved the caliber of the exhibitions and catalogues while director of the National Gallery of Canada, as well as enlarging the curatorial staff and creating a bilingual publicity department—setting high standards for her successor, also a woman, HSIO-YEN SHIH, who was formerly curator of the Royal Ontario Museum's Far Eastern Department.

First Woman Director of the Baltimore Museum

Former director (and first woman director) of the Baltimore Museum ADELYN BREESKIN, or "Mrs. B" as she is affectionately called by her co-workers at the National Collection of Fine Arts in Washington, D.C., is consultant to the NCFA on 20th-century painting and sculpture. In 1960 she headed the American Pavilion at the Venice Biennale, where she brought Franz Kline and Hans Hofmann to the forefront in Europe. Adelyn Breeskin transformed the museum in Baltimore from a local museum of little significance to one internationally recognized. Named director in 1947, after five years as acting director, she was responsible for securing the Baltimore Museum's Cone Collection of 20th-century masterpieces at a time when most board members were disinterested in modern art. The author of *Graphic Works of Mary Cassatt: A Catalogue Raisonné* (1948) and *Mary Cassatt: A Catalogue Raisonné of the Oils, Pastels, Watercolors, and Drawings* (1970) considered the most authoritative study of the artist (p. 596), Ms. Breeskin received her education at Bryn Mawr, Radcliffe, and the School of Fine Arts, Crafts, and Decorative Design, Boston. She is the recipient of honorary doctorates from Goucher, Washington, Wheaton, Hood, and Morgan State College. Now an honorary member of the Association of Art Museum Directors, she was its president, 1965–67. Her previous positions include that of assistant, Print Department of the Metropolitan Museum of Art, 1918–20, and general curator of prints and drawings at the Baltimore Museum before being named acting director. From 1968 to 1974 she was curator of Contemporary Painting and Sculpture at the National Collection of Fine Arts. At 81 in 1977 Ms. Breeskin told an interviewer, "I enjoy my work, love it. I don't want to stop." She added that despite her career she was able to devote much time to her three children, thanks to having had a wonderful housekeeper. None of the children followed in her footsteps. "They got all the art they needed from me."

Curator of Prints and Drawings and Director of Expo '67 Fine Arts Gallery

KATHLEEN FENWICK became museum director of the Fine Arts Gallery at Expo '67 in Montreal, where she was responsible for masterpieces, after 40 years as curator of prints and drawings of the National Gallery of Canada. Jean Boggs described her in an article for *ARTnews* (September 1974) entitled "In Canada, a Place for Women," as an "energetic, imaginative, and understanding woman" who symbolized "the competence of women working in art museums." Ms. Fenwick participated in establishing the first Canadian art magazine in 1943. From 1958 to 1973 she was chairwoman of the Canadian Film Awards. Active in the Eskimo Arts Center, she has made expeditions to the Arctic.

Harvard Art Museum Head

Director of the Fogg, Harvard University's Art Museum, 1969–75, AGNES MONGAN served the museum for more than 45 years. Former pupil and colleague of Harvard Professor Paul J. Sachs, who taught a famous museum course that inspired a generation of art museum directors, Ms. Mongan has gained international recognition for her research and travel to many parts of the world. She has also taught the museum course at Harvard. In 1975 a graduate fellowship was endowed in Ms. Mongan's honor, to be awarded to one fine arts student each year whose interest, like hers, is in drawing. In 1977 she won the St. Botolph Club Award for distinction in the arts (Edward Hopper, Alexander Calder, Walter Piston, and ELIZABETH BISHOP, p. 688, are among previous recipients). Ms. Mongan received her B.A. from Bryn Mawr and her M.A. from Smith College.

Women in Museums: What Other Jobs?

Although none of the major U.S. museums in 1978 had women directors, a growing number of small and medium-sized museums did, with SUZANNE DELEHANTY at the Philadelphia Institute of Contemporary Art, LISA TAYLOR at the Cooper-Hewitt Museum in New York, SUSAN STITT at the Museums at Stony Brook, Long Island, and JOY UNGERELEIDER at the Jewish Museum.

In addition, more women hold top curatorial positions than ever before. No specific survey has been taken, but figures gleaned from the most recent survey on museum personnel taken by the National Endowment for the Arts in 1973 show that approximately 325 art museum curators are women. For years the unspoken rule was that men would curate sculpture and major paintings, while women got drawings and prints. But even that hiring custom is in eclipse as women including OLGA RAGGIO, curator of Western European art at the Metropolitan, CHRISTINE LILYQUIST, curator of the Metropolitan's Egyptian department, JANE LIVINGSTON, head curator at the Corcoran Gallery of Art in Washington, D.C., DIANE WALDMAN, curator at the Guggenheim Museum, LINDA CATHCART, curator at the Albright Knox Art Gallery in Buffalo, BARBARA HASKELL, curator at the Whitney Museum, and BRENDA RICHARDSON, curator of painting and sculpture at the Baltimore Museum of Art, filter into these once all-male strongholds.

The proportion of women in top positions drops sharply from 46 percent in museums with budgets under $50,000 to 2 percent in museums with budgets of $250,000 to $499,999, 4 percent with $500,000 to $999,999, and 2 percent with 1 million and over. The Association of Art Museum Directors, an invitational organization that extends membership to art museums it considers "major" —those with budgets of $250,000 or more—has 125 members. Five of them are U.S. women—MURIEL CHRISTISON at the Krannert Art Museum, Champaign, Illinois; CATHLEEN GALLENDER at the Art Museum of South Texas, Corpus Christi, Texas; KATHRYN GAMBLE at the Montclair Art Museum, Montclair, New Jersey; KATHERINE HANNA at the Taft Museum, Cincinnati, Ohio; and JAN MUHLERT at the University of Iowa Museum of Art, Iowa City, Iowa.

No one enters museum work to "put Queen Anne chairs in the dining room or food on the table," one curator told *ARTnews* (February 1977). "It was kind of accepted that men would make more than women since they had to support their families," another curator noted. "We never really questioned it."

Salary differences are no problem at a place like the Museum of Modern Art, which is unionized, but in university museums the pay is usually low and "they can't afford to hire a man," observed CONSTANCE GLENN, director of the Art Museum of California State University at Long Beach. For Glenn the university atmosphere is ideal. "I like being around young talent," she said.

The 1973 survey by the National Endowment for the Arts showed that a male director of an art museum averaged $19,000 annually, while a woman averaged $8,000. Part of the difference, obviously, was due to the fact that most of the large museums with the large salaries were directed by men. But even at small museums, there was a consistent $2,000 to $3,000 difference.

"Art Goes On" at Her Gallery

For a little over 30 years, BETTY PARSONS has run one of the most innovative and important art galleries in the field of contemporary art in the United States. It has been described by critic Clement Greenberg as "a place where art goes on and is not just shown and sold." Among the artists given their first important shows at the Parsons gallery are Jackson Pollock, Mark Rothko, Saul Steinberg, and LEE KRASNER (p. 601). Betty Parsons has done more than any other dealer to promote women artists and is herself a painter-sculptor who has enjoyed more than 20 one-woman shows. Her work has evolved from realist landscapes to nonrepresentational compositions emphasizing bold form and startling color shifts.

The 20th Century's Principal Patroness

Twentieth-century patroness PEGGY GUG-GENHEIM's multimillion-dollar art collection is preserved in her 18th-century Venetian palazzo, Venier dei Leoni, on the Grand Canal. She acquired her collection of modern art over a 20-year period when she encouraged and patronized the modern art movement and individual talents, notably Jackson Pollock.

The niece of Solomon R. Guggenheim, whose museum in New York has made his name synonymous with modern art, she had a lonely childhood despite her father's and mother's inherited wealth. When she finished school she went to Paris, where she married and led a bohemian life. When the marriage broke up, she went to London, and with the help of her friend Marcel Duchamp opened an avant-garde gallery, which she called Guggenheim Jeune. There she exhibited Jean Cocteau (at the opening), English abstract painter John Tunnard, French surrealist Jean Tanguy, Russian abstract expressionist Vasily Kandinsky, Picasso, Braque, Miró, and many well-known sculptors.

Since the gallery was not always successful in selling work from the exhibitions, Ms. Guggenheim bought a piece each time to encourage the artist until it closed in 1938. In 1939 she decided to establish a museum of modern art, under the guidance of Herbert Read, but the project fell through when World War II broke out. She stored her collection until she was able to send it to the United States as "household items." She arrived in 1941 in New York with Max Ernst, who became her husband, and opened a gallery called Art of This Century. Many well-known European artists were exhibited there, and she also showed Motherwell, Baziotes, Hans Hofmann, Rothko, Gottlieb, and Pollock, whom she sponsored for four years.

She was given her own pavilion to show her collection at the 24th Biennale in Venice, and finally, in 1951, found a home for her collection (open to the public) in Venice. Art critic and commentator ALINE B. SAARINEN says in *The Proud Possessors* (1968) "her collection has become not only one of the sights of Venice, but also one of the sights of Europe. Nowhere else is there a similar historic survey of modern art, nor one that exhibits the Americans . . . who are major figures in the international world of art."

VOCAL ARTISTS: OPERA

Her Repertoire Included 150 Roles

ERNESTINE SCHUMANN-HEINK, one of the great contralto singers during the earlier part of the century, made her concert debut in Beethoven's Ninth Symphony at the age of 15 in Graz, and her opera debut as Azucena in *Trovatore* at the Dresden Court Opera in 1878. She also appeared with the Hamburg City Opera and at Covent Garden and the Bayreuth Festival. In 1898 joined the Berlin Royal Opera and in that year made her American debut in Chicago as Ortrude. The following year she sang in New York at the Metropolitan Opera, and, breaking a contract with the Berlin company, she remained with the Met until 1904. She then returned to Germany but continued to appear periodically at the Met until 1926. In Dresden in 1909 she created the role Klytemnestra in Richard Strauss's opera *Elektra*. Her voice was full, expressive, and of superb quality in all registers, and she possessed a powerful dramatic presence. Though she was highly acclaimed for her Wagnerian roles, her repertoire contained more than 150 operatic parts.

First Opera Singer to Have a Dessert Named After Her

One of the most famous coloratura sopranos of her generation, whose flexibility and evenness of voice embraced two and a half octaves, NELLIE MELBA, named Dame of the British Empire in 1918, was so wildly popular that an ice cream dessert, Pêche Melba, was named after her. This prima donna of the golden era of opera was born near Melbourne (the reason for her name) in 1861, made her debut in Sydney in 1885, singing in Handel's *Messiah,* and followed with a concert debut the following year in London, and her operatic debut as Gilda in Brussels in 1887. Her autobiography, *Melodies and Memories,* was published in 1925, and she was the subject of a biographical film, *Melba,* starring opera singer PATRICE MUNSEL in 1953, 22 years after her death.

Great Coloratura Whose Name Also Lives in Cuisine

Great pre-World War I Italian coloratura soprano LUISA TETRAZZINI studied in Florence before making her debut as Inez in Meyerbeer's *L'Africaine* in 1895. She has successful performances in Rome and other cities in Italy, and established a reputation in Europe and in Russia, Mexico, and South America. She made her debut at Covent Garden as Violetta in *La Traviata,* followed by Gilda and Lucia in 1907, and again debuted as Violetta at the Manhattan Opera House in 1908. She remained there until its closing in 1910, then sang with the Met, 1911–12, and with the Chicago Opera Company, 1913–14. After the war she returned to the United States for performances until 1931. Chicken Tetrazzini was named in her honor.

First Woman to Direct a Major Opera Company

Scottish soprano MARY GARDEN, born in 1877 in Aberdeen, one of the most glamorous divas of this century, as a child studied in the United States and played the violin in Gilbert and Sullivan operettas. After further studies in Paris, she became a member of the Opéra-Comique and sang her first major title role in Charpentier's *Louise* in 1900. In 1902 she was selected by Carré and Debussy for the role of Mélisande (despite the strong objections of *Pelléas et Mélisande* author Maeterlinck, who wanted it for his common-law wife, GEORGETTE LEBLANC). She became indentified with this role, and it was considered her best, though she also sang many others. In 1921 Ms. Garden replaced Campanini as general manager of the Chicago Opera, a post which she held for one season, becoming the first woman in the world to direct a major opera company. After her retirement she became vocal advisor to MGM in Hollywood, and devoted her time to lecturing and teaching. In 1951 she published her autobiography, *Mary Garden's Story.*

She Created the Role of the Goose Girl

Daughter of a professional baseball player, GERALDINE FARRAR became one of the most celebrated personalities in the history of the Metropolitan Opera House. During her 16 years at the Met she created the title role of *Suor Angelica,* and the Goose Girl in *Königskinder,* and sang roles in numerous American premieres including *Ariane et Barbe-bleu* (Dukas), *Madame Sans-Gêne* (Giordano), and *The Damnation of Faust* (Berlioz). Born in 1882 in Melrose, Massachusetts, to parents who encouraged her to study music, she made her first public appearances at 14, first in her hometown, then in Boston. After studies with Trabadello in Paris and Graziani in Berlin, she made her debut as Marguerite at the Berlin Opera in 1901. At the end of three seasons with the Monte Carlo Opera (1903–6) she had established her reputation in Europe, and in 1906 she made her Met debut as Juliette. Geraldine Farrar also became a glamorous figure in silent films between 1915 and 1919, for which she did *Carmen, Joan the Woman, Shadows, Flames of the Desert*. She gave her farewell performance in *Zaza* in 1922 but after her retirement reappeared in song recitals and served as commentator for the Met broadcasts for one season. She published her autobiography, *Such Sweet Compulsion*, in 1938.

Award-winning Singer of Lieder and Opera

Exemplary singer of lieder and opera LOTTE LEHMANN, born in 1888 in Perleberg, Germany, began her studies at the Berlin Royal Academy of Music. She made her debut singing the role of Freia in *Das Rheingold* in Hamburg in 1910. She remained with the Vienna Opera following her guest appearance in 1914, where she was selected by Richard Strauss for the role of the Young Composer in *Ariadne auf Naxos,* and a principal role as Barak's wife in *Die Frau ohne Schatten*. One of her most famous roles was the Marschallin in Strauss's *Der Rosenkavalier*. In 1927 she became the first German invited to sing in France since World War I. Having renounced Nazi Germany, she applied for U.S. citizenship in 1934, four years after her American debut as Sieglinde in Chicago, and joined the Met, where she became known chiefly for her roles in Wagnerian opera. Ms. Lehmann retired from the concert stage in 1951, becoming head of the voice department at the Music Academy of the West in Santa Barbara, California, until 1962. She received the honorary title of Kammersängerin from the Austrian Government and in 1962 the Cross of Honor, First Class, from the city of Vienna. In 1969 on her 80th birthday a building at the Music Academy was named in her honor. Other awards include the Legion of Honor and Golden Palm of France, the Golden Medal of Austria, the Golden Medal of Stockholm, and the Ring of Honor of the Viennese Philharmonic Orchestra.

She Learned to Sing by Listening to Her Own Recorded Voice

Self-taught coloratura soprano AMELITA GALLI-CURCI studied piano at the conservatory in Milan where she was born in 1882. Encouraged by Mascagni and William Thorner, she learned to sing by listening to recordings of her voice, and made her debut as Gilda in *Rigoletto* at the Teatro Costanzi in Rome in 1909, followed by appearances in Europe and South America. In 1916 she made her American debut as Gilda with the Chicago Opera, where she remained for five years. She made her Met debut in 1921 as Violetta in *La Traviata* and remained with the Met until 1930, when she was force to retire at the peak of her career after an operation for goiter. She made several appearances five years later, and though her voice had lost much of its former luster, she was applauded for her courage.

The 20th Century's Great Wagnerian Soprano

The great Wagnerian soprano of the mid-20th century, KIRSTEN FLAGSTAD made her debut in her native city of Oslo in 1913 singing a minor role in *Tiefland*. Until 1933, when she sang in minor roles at the Bayreuth Festival, she was unknown outside Scandinavia. She won international acclaim overnight in 1935 after her debut at the Metropolitan Opera in New York as Sieglinde, followed by Isolde, Brünnhilde, Elsa, and Kundry. Her reputation was affirmed with triumphant appearances in London, Vienna, Zurich, Paris, and Prague. During World War II she remained in Norway, and her husband was accused of being a Quisling. Somewhat discredited in the eyes of the world, Ms. Flagstad slowly regained recognition and continued to sing leading roles in *Tristan and Isolde, The Ring, Parsifal, Fidelio, Alceste, Dido and Aeneas,* as well as Bach cantatas and lieder. She retired in 1953, ending a career of 40 years, and became the first director of the Norwegian State Opera until ill health forced her to resign in 1960, two years before her death.

American Soprano Who Began in Vaudeville

American soprano of Neapolitan background, ROSA PONSELLE, born in 1897, began her musical career in vaudeville. She made her debut at the Metropolitan Opera in 1918 at the age of 21, singing opposite Caruso in Verdi's *La Forza del Destino*. She remained at the Met for 19 years. Her famous title roles included Norma, considered her greatest triumph, Aida, La Gioconda, Violetta in *La Traviata*, Elizabeth in *Don Carlos*, Donna Anna in *Don Giovanni*, Santuzza in *Cavalleria Rusticana*, Rachel in *La Juive*, Giulia in *La Vestale*, and Leonora in *Il Trovatore*. She met with great success for three seasons at Covent Garden (debut in 1929) and for one season at the Florence Festival (1933). In 1937 Ms. Ponselle made her final appearance as Carmen and retired from the stage at the peak of her career. Since 1954 she has been artistic director of the Baltimore Civic Opera Company.

First Black Soloist of the Metropolitan Opera

Philadelphia-born contralto MARIAN ANDERSON, whose voice was remarkable at an early age, sang in a Baptist church choir as a child. As a young woman she won a vocal competition allowing her to sing the aria "O Mio Fernando" from Donizetti's opera *La Favorita* at Lewisohn Stadium. Her 1930 success in Berlin was followed by appearances all over Europe and the United States. Toscanini, who heard her in Salzburg in 1935, commented that "such a voice occurs once in a hundred years." When she was barred from Constitution Hall in Washington, D.C., in 1939 Eleanor Roosevelt (see "Women Activists, Heroes, and Humanitarians," p.

738) sponsored a concert by her at Lincoln Memorial. In 1955 she made her debut at the Met as Ulrica in *Un Ballo in Maschera,* becoming the first black soloist in that company. The recipient of many honors, Ms. Anderson won the Bok Award of Philadelphia for a deserving citizen in 1949; she donated the cash gift as a fund for young singers. She has served as a UN delegate and has participated in State Department-sponsored tours to the Far East and elsewhere. Sibelius was so enamored of Marian Anderson when she visited Finland that he dedicated his song "Solitude" to her. She retired from the stage in 1965.

Australian Star Who Sang from a Wheelchair

Soprano MARJORIE LAWRENCE, born in 1909 in Australia, began her studies with Ivor Boustead in Melbourne, and continued with CÉCILE GILLY in Paris. After her debut as Elisabeth in *Tannhäuser* in Monte Carlo in 1932, she joined the Paris Opera and appeared in major opera houses in Europe, South America, and the United States. In 1935 she made her Met debut appearance as Brünnhilde in *Die Walküre* and joined the company. She was interrupted at the peak of her career when she was stricken with infantile paralysis in 1941, but she courageously returned to the stage for several years, singing from a camouflaged wheelchair. Her autobiography, *Interrupted Melody, The Story of My Life* (1949), was made into a film in 1955.

Flagstad's Successor

A Swedish farmgirl born in 1918 rose to succeed KIRSTEN FLAGSTAD (p. 619) as the most significant Wagnerian soprano of her time. BIRGIT NILSSON began her musical training at the Royal Music Academy in Stockholm in 1946, making her debut as Agathe in *Der Freischütz* at the Royal Opera. Her first performances were in Verdi operas, but gradually she started appearing in Wagnerian roles, eventually becoming the leading performer of Wagnerian opera. She also has triumphed in Puccini's *Turandot*, Richard Strauss's *Salome*, and Beethoven's *Fidelio*. In 1959 she made her debut as Isolde at the Met, where she remained for many years. In 1968 she was made an honorary member of the Vienna State Opera.

Supreme in Bel Canto

Australian diva JOAN SUTHERLAND, who took music lessons with her mother as a young girl, and pursued her studies at the Sydney Conservatory, made her debut in Sydney in 1947 as Dido in Purcell's *Dido and Aeneas*. Gradually she established herself in Australia, winning two prizes that permitted her to travel to London. She joined Covent Garden in 1952, taking roles in operas by Verdi and Mozart, and made a brilliant debut as Lucia in *Lucia di Lammermoor*. She appeared at the Paris Opera, La Scala, and made her American debut in Dallas in 1960 in Handel's *Alcina* and her Met debut as Lucia in 1961. She is recognized not only for her virtuosity in traditional opera, but in more obscure pieces by Handel, Rossini, Bellini, and Donizetti, and her bel canto singing has rarely been equaled.

She Sang the Leads in World Premieres of *Trionfi* and *The Rake's Progress*

ELISABETH SCHWARZKOPF won her world reputation as an outstanding singer of lieder with her debut in Vienna in 1942. Prior to that she had sung minor roles in Berlin. She remained with the Vienna State Opera until 1948 as a coloratura soprano, singing lead roles such as Verdi's Gilda, and Rossini's Rosina. In 1947 she began to sing lyric soprano roles, making her debut at Covent Garden with the Vienna State Opera company as Donna Elvira in *Don Giovanni*. In 1951 she became the first Anne Trulove in Stravinsky's *The Rake's Progress* in Venice, and in 1953 she sang the lead

role in the world premiere of Orff's *Trionfi* at La Scala. She was received with great enthusiasm at her American debut singing lieder in Town Hall in 1953. (Had she not been associated with Nazi leaders in World War II, it was said, she would have been invited to the United States much earlier.) One of her most celebrated roles, the Marschallin in *Der Rosenkavalier*, was the one in which she made her first appearances at the San Francisco Opera and the Met in 1964.

Legend in Her Time

Prima donna assoluta of the 19th-century bel canto tradition, MARIA CALLAS revived the operas of Bellini, Donizetti, and Rossini, many unheard since the time they were written. Born in 1923 in New York of Greek parentage (her real name was CECILIA SOPHIA ANNA MARIA KALOGEROPOULOU), she made her debut in Athens in 1940, in *Boccaccio*, and her first appearance in Italy in 1947, when she sang the lead in *La Gioconda*. She was soon admired throughout Italy as a leading soprano whose repertoire included all the heavy roles but whose versatility permitted her to sing Wagner and Bellini in the same week. She made her American debut in Chicago in 1954 as Norma—a sensation repeated on her opening night at the Met in 1956. Glamour surrounded Maria Callas, not only because of her theatrical image and fiery temperament, with scandals circulating about her involving everything from pasta factories to opera management, but also because of her personal life and long association with Aristotle Onassis. She set an operatic style followed by many others and, though her career lasted only 20 years, was one of the most influential figures in opera in the 20th century.

First Black Woman Singer to Have Leading Role in Metropolitan Opera World Premiere

American soprano LEONTYNE PRICE made her first major performance in

Porgy and Bess in 1952. Prior to this, while attending Juilliard, she sang the role of Mistress Ford in Verdi's *Falstaff*, followed by the leading role in Virgil Thomson's *Four Saints in Three Acts* at the International Art Festival in Paris. Her two years as Bess were so successful that they led to concert performances in 1954, and televised performances of Puccini's *Tosca* in 1955, Mozart's *The Magic Flute* in 1956, and Francis Poulenc's *Les Dialogues des Carmélites* in 1957. An invitation to sing *Aida* at the Vienna State Opera in 1958 and La Scala in 1960 brought her praise as the finest Aida of her day in the United States and Europe. In 1966 she became the first black woman singer to have the lead role in a world premiere (Samuel Barber's *Antony and Cleopatra*) at the new Metropolitan Opera House at Lincoln Center.

Brooklyn's "Bubbles" an Opera Star in the Grand Tradition.

Brooklyn-born BEVERLY SILLS (Belle Silverman) made her debut at the age of three on Bob Emery's radio program "Rainbow House." She continued radio performances and made some film appearances as "Bubbles Silverman." At the age of 17 she made her debut as Micaëla in *Carmen* with the Civic Opera. She then joined the Charles Wagner Opera Company, and for two seasons traveled coast-to-coast singing Micaëla, and Violetta in *La Traviata*. After one year with the San Francisco Opera, she joined the New York City Opera in 1955. She sang three leading principal roles in *The Tales of Hoffmann* in 1965, and in 1967 three leading roles in Puccini's *Il Trittico*. She also sang leading roles in the world premieres of *The Wings of the Dove* and Weisgall's *Six Characters in Search of an Author* and in the New York premiere of Douglas Moore's *The Ballad of Baby Doe* and the

American premiere in Boston of Nono's *Intolleranza*. Particularly remarkable have been her roles in Massenet's *Manon* and as Queen Elizabeth in Donizetti's *Roberto Devereux*. She has made guest appearances at major opera houses in South America and Europe, including Teatro Colón, Vienna State Opera, Covent Garden, and La Scala. In his book *The Grand Tradition* (1974) J. B. Steane commented, "The interesting thing, finally, is that she is so satisfying, not as a sweet sounding, highly trained nightingale, but as a singer of remarkable intellectual and emotional strength."

Winner of Spain's Highest Honor for Singing

When soprano MONTSERRAT CABALLÉ, born in 1933 in Barcelona, captivated her audience in her American debut in an American Opera Society performance of Donizetti's *Lucrezia Borgia* in 1965, she was already well established in Europe. At the time of her American debut at Carnegie Hall, her repertoire included almost 50 roles in French, Italian, and German opera. In 1954, at the age of 21, she won the Liceo Conservatory Gold Medal, the highest singing honor in Spain. Three years later she made her operatic debut in Basel, Switzerland, as Mimi in *La Bohème*. She remained with the Basel Opera for three years, while appearing in numerous opera houses in Europe. This was followed by a two-year contract as principal soprano of the Bremen Opera, her most notable role being in Dvořák's *Armida*, especially revived for her. Since 1965 Ms. Caballé has been heard extensively in the United States, singing roles in Donizetti's *Roberto Devereux*, Gounod's *Faust*, Bellini's *Norma* and *Il Pirata*, Handel's *Giulio Cesare*, Verdi's *Il Trovatore, Otello, La Traviata, I Vespri Siciliani*, Puccini's *La Bohème*, and Ciléa's *Adriana Lecouvreur*.

VOCAL ARTISTS: POPULAR MUSIC

Mother of the Blues

GERTRUDE "MA" RAINEY, a legendary blues singer and forerunner of a generation to follow, was born in 1886 in Columbus, Georgia. She started singing in cabarets when she was 14, later married Will "Pa" Rainey, who headed the Rabbit Foot Minstrels, and for several years sang with him on the road. It was not until 1923 that she began to record, accompanied by Lovie Austin's Serenaders, Tommy Lanier, Joe Smith, and Louis Armstrong. By 1929 she had made about 100 recordings, including "Bad Luck Blues," "Walking Blues," "Ma Rainey's Mystery Record," "See See Rider," "Jelly Bean Blues," "Countin' the Blues" (accompanied by Louis Armstrong, in 1925), "Slave to the Blues," "My Babe Blues," "Yonder Comes the Blues" (accompanied by Joe Smith, in 1926), "New Bo'weevil Blues," "Moonshine Blues," "Deep Moanin' Blues," and "Runaway Blues" (1927–29). Ma Rainey retired in 1933 and died in 1939.

Ma's First, Great Successor

Born and raised in the Deep South, BESSIE SMITH became famous overnight with her first recording in 1923. She had been traveling with "Pa" and "MA" RAINEY's Rabbit Foot Minstrels when she was discovered in Selma, Alabama, by Frank Walker, director of recording for Columbia Records. The most popular black entertainer in America during the mid-20s, Bessie Smith made some 160 recordings accompanied by Louis Armstrong, Joe Smith, Don Redman, James P. Johnson, Charlie Green, and Fletcher Henderson—the last in 1933. In 1929 she starred in her own vaudeville show, *Midnight Steppers,* and appeared in a Warner Brothers short, *St. Louis Blues.* "The Empress of the Blues," as she was often billed, died in 1937, having been refused admission to a hospital

after a car accident. A play by Edward Albee, *The Death of Bessie Smith,* is based on this. Some of her greatest recordings are: "Downhearted Blues," "Mama's Got the Blues," "St. Louis Gal" (1923), "St. Louis Blues," "Nobody's Blues but Mine" (1925), "Young Woman's Blues," "After You've Gone," "Mean Old Bed Bug Blues," "A Good Man Is Hard to Find" (1927).

Early Writer and Recorder of the Blues

One of the earliest recorders of blues music, ALBERTA HUNTER, was also an important song writer. She wrote and recorded "Downhearted Blues," later made famous by BESSIE SMITH (above), and during the '20s she made many recordings with Louis Armstrong, Fletcher Henderson, Fats Waller, and others. She introduced blues to European audiences, according to some, and replaced JOSEPHINE BAKER (p. 625) at the Casino de Paris and appeared at the Dorchester in London. By the end of World War II she had made six trips around the world and had made 25 concert tours for USO troops. She had several Broadway roles, co-starring with ETHEL WATERS (p. 624) in *Mamba's Daughters.* In 1954 she disappeared from the music world to enroll in nursing school. She was gone until 1977, when Hubert Saal of *Newsweek* wrote of her return at 82 to singing: "If Alberta Hunter nursed anything like the way she sings, those statues of Florence Nightingale must have quivered on their pedestals."

"Lady Day"

BILLIE HOLIDAY, born in 1915 in Baltimore, sang in Jerry Preston's Log Cabin and the Yeah Man in New York in the early '30s. Discovered by John Hammond and Benny Goodman in 1933, she made her first recording with Goodman that year, and gained international fame through a series of recordings with Teddy Wilson's orchestra in 1935. Later she sang with Count Basie (1937), and Artie Shaw (1938), and made concert tours in the United States and Europe as a soloist and with Jazz Club U.S.A. In 1946 she made a feature film, *New Orleans,* with Louis Armstrong, who was a great influence on her early music, as was Lester Young on her later music, when she incorporated strings. "Lady Day," as she was called, won the Esquire Gold Award in 1944 and 1947, the Silver Award, 1944, 1945, the Met Poll 1945–46. Some of her recordings include "Night and Day," "The Man I Love," "Strange Fruit," Fine and Mellow" (1939), "Lover Man" (1944), "Don't Explain" (1945).

Scat Artist

Discovered in an amateur show in Harlem in 1934, ELLA FITZGERALD joined Chick Webb's band and made her first recording, "Are You Here to Stay," later that same year, gaining wide recognition. Her song "A-Tisket, A-Tasket" was among her biggest hits. Others included: "I Want to Be Happy" (1938); "Dark Town Strutter's Ball" and "Strictly from Dixie" (1939); Scat: "Cow Cow Boogie" (1944); "Flying Home" (1945); and "Lady Be Good" (1946). A number of reissues of Ella Fitzgerald singing are now on the market. She assumed the leadership of Webb's band when he died in 1939, and from 1946 she appeared frequently with Norman Granz. Though she recorded many inferior ballads for purely economic reasons, she was a remarkable scat singer and one of the most highly respected jazz musicians of her era. She tied for the Esquire Gold Award in 1946, won the Silver Award in 1947, the Met poll in 1954, the *Down Beat* Critics Poll in 1937–39, and 1953–54.

Blues Singer and Actress

Blues singer and actress (on Broadway and film) ETHEL WATERS in her second autobiography, *To Me It's Wonderful* (1973), described herself as a real "Dead End Kid." In her early years in Chester, Pennsylvania, where she was born in 1900, she survived by stealing food and working as a chambermaid. She started her singing career in Baltimore and Philadelphia billed as "Sweet Mama Stringbean" and went to New York in 1917 to perform in Lincoln Theatre in Harlem. She gained popularity during the '20s singing at the Cotton Club, and in 1927 she appeared in *Africana,* the first of her long list of Broadway musical appearances, including memorable performances in *As Thousands Cheer* (1933), *At Home Abroad* (1935), and *Cabin in the Sky* (1940, later made into a film). She starred in several Broadway dramas, including *Member of the Wedding* (1950), later made into a film for which she won Academy Award nominations. Other films and TV followed. Her first autobiography, *His Eye Is on the Sparrow,* was a best seller in 1951. Until her death in 1977 she was very active with Billy Graham crusades.

Greatest Gospel Singer

"Gospel Queen" MAHALIA JACKSON began to sing in her clergyman father's choir in New Orleans at age five. At 16, when she went to Chicago to work as a chambermaid, she led a quartet that performed in neighborhood Baptist churches. She made her first recording of gospel songs in 1935, and in the next decade attracted wide attention. Following the success of "Move Over a Little Higher" in 1949 and "Silent Night" in 1952, she made her first European tour, appeared in concerts at Carnegie Hall, and at the Newport Jazz Festival. Her full alto voice is heard in her popular, enriching sacred music, "Amazing Grace" (1949), "I'm Glad Salvation Is Free" (1950), "Go Tell It on the Mountain" (1952), and other recordings. Ms. Jackson sang at the inauguration of John F. Kennedy and at the funeral of Martin Luther King, Jr.

First of the World-Famous French Cafe Singers

Partner for many years of Maurice Chevalier, JEANNE BOURGEOIS (1873–1956), better known by her stage name MISTINGUETT, began by singing in Paris restaurants while selling flowers. Before long she was popular in the Folies-Bergère, Moulin Rouge, and other music halls as a singer, dancer, and mistress of ceremonies. She sang such songs as "Moi, J'en Ai Marre," "Valencia," "I'm looking for a Millionaire," "Ça C'est Paris," and "Mon Homme." Her sensational Apache dance, which she performed with Max Dearly at the Moulin Rouge at the beginning of the century, is still in vogue in revues. She usually appeared in elaborate costumes with bird-of-paradise feather hats, chiffon, fur, and diamonds, setting a new style, and she insured her legs for a million dollars. "MEES," as her fans called her, toured in Europe, England, Canada, and the United States, and acted in several films.

"Last of the Red-Hot Mamas"

SOPHIE TUCKER, born in 1884 in Russia came to the United States as a child. By 1906 she was a vaudeville star billed as the "Last of the Red-Hot Mamas." Her theme song, which she wrote and first sang in 1911, was "Some of These Days." She organized her own jazz combo, performing in the United States and England, appeared in several films, including *Broadway Melody of 1938*, and in the late '30s had her own radio show, and performed on Broadway. She was popular for her TV appearances during the '50s and '60s, especially on the "Ed Sullivan Show." The Broadway musical *Sophie* (1963) was based on her life. She died in 1966.

First Black Star in Paris

JOSEPHINE BAKER, born in 1906 in St. Louis of mixed African, American Indian, and Spanish blood, got her start in walk-on parts in vaudeville at the age of 12, and at the age of 19 she became part of the Revue Nègre in Paris. A major attraction at the Casino de Paris and Folies Bergère, she often appeared with bananas around her waist or snakes around her neck. Her show *Paris Qui Remue* became famous on both sides of the Atlantic and introduced one of her memorable songs, "J'ai Deux Amours." She appeared in London for the first time in 1933 and in New York with the Ziegfeld Follies in 1936 and toured in Latin America in the early '50s. In 1961 she was made a Chevalier of the Legion of Honor for her work in the French Resistance. She later adopted 12 war orphans, her "rainbow tribe," and lived with them in a château in southeastern France. Her final appearance in 1968 in Paris renewed her popularity and won her a whole new generation of devotees. Josephine Baker died in 1975.

Fifty Years a Club Favorite

English-born singer MABEL MERCER toured English vaudeville in her early years and sang in Parisian cabarets during the '20s and '30s, becoming a favorite of F. Scott Fitzgerald, Ernest Hemingway, and the Prince of Wales. With the outbreak of World War II, she left Paris, never to return, settled in New York, and acquired American citizenship in 1952. She became a well-loved singer in intimate clubs, including the Cafe Carlyle, Downstairs at the Upstairs, and the St. Regis Room. Usually accompanied by piano, Ms. Mercer revived many old show tunes. Her repertoire includes such songs as "Lucky to Be Me," "Lazy Afternoon," "In Other Words," and some of her LP's are "Mabel Mercer and Bobby Short at Town Hall," "Midnight at Mabel Mercer's," and "Mabel Mercer Sings Cole Porter."

Foremost Singer of French Popular Songs

As a child, EDITH GIOVANNA CASSION traveled all over France with her father, a circus acrobat. At the age of 15 she was on her own, singing in the streets of Paris. Discovered by a night club director who brought her onto the stage, she was an instant success and by the end of the '30s, as EDITH PIAF, nicknamed "Piaf" or "Sparrow" because of her delicate appearance and simple attire, was a leading figure both as a singer and a songwriter. She introduced "Mon Légionnaire," "Un Monsieur M'a Suivi dans la Rue," "Les Trois Cloches," sang verse by Prévert, appeared in *Le Bel Indifférent*, a play written for her by Cocteau, and had roles in a number of films including Renoir's *French Cancan*. Internationally known by the '40s, she made several tours in Europe and the United States. Her most famous records were "La Vie en Rose" and "Au Bal de la Chance." Edith Piaf died in 1963.

The Original Jenny in *The Threepenny Opera*

LOTTE LENYA, born in 1900 in Vienna, became identified with the music of pre-Hitler Berlin. She married composer Kurt Weill in 1926 and was given the principal role in *The Little Mahagonny*, his first work in collaboration with Bertolt Brecht. In 1928 she took the lead role of Jenny in *The Threepenny Opera*, also jointly done by her husband and Brecht, and an enormous success. She and Weill fled to Paris in 1933, and for two years she performed her husband's work there until the couple moved to the United States. After Weill's death in 1950 she appeared in numerous productions of *The Threepenny Opera*, and received a Tony Award in 1956. She also toured in the revue *Brecht on Brecht* and has recorded extensively, including *The Threepenny Opera* (Theater de Lys version and complete original German version) and "Lotte Lenya Sings Berlin Theatre Songs of Kurt Weill" (1955). An occasional film actress since 1930, she has had parts in *The Roman Spring of Mrs. Stone* (1961), *From Russia*

with Love (1964), *Cabaret* (1972), *Semi-Tough* (1977), and has made TV appearances in the United States and Germany.

Jazz Singer to Film Star

Beautiful jazz and popular singing star LENA HORNE took her first job at Harlem's Cotton Club at 16, and later sang at Cafe Society Uptown and other New York clubs. She became a movie personality after several months with Charlie Barnet's orchestra in 1940–41, appearing in *Harlem on Parade* and *Panama Hattie* (1942), *Stormy Weather* and *As Thousands Cheer* (1943), *Cabin in the Sky* (1944), and *Words and Music* (1948). She made several successful European tours, and starred in the Broadway musical *Jamaica*, and many supper club and TV appearances in the '50s and '60s.

She Got Rhythm

Dynamic singer-actress ETHEL MERMAN won instant success in her first Broadway show, *Girl Crazy* (1930), with the song "I Got Rhythm" by George and Ira Gershwin. Among the most memorable of her 13 Broadway shows, some by Cole Porter and Irving Berlin, were *Anything Goes, Red, Hot, and Blue, Stars in Your Eyes, Dubarry Was a Lady, Panama Hattie, Annie Get Your Gun,* her longest-running musical *Call Me Madam,* and *Gypsy.* She played *Hello, Dolly!* in 1971, and has made numerous starring TV appearances. Her records, both original-cast albums and collections of show tunes, are perennial best-sellers.

Radio's "Hello, Everybody" Songstress

KATE SMITH, born in 1909 in Virginia, became one of America's great singing personalities of radio and TV. She began her radio broadcasts in 1931, opening her 15-minute program several times a week with a cheerful "Hello, everybody" and closing with "Thanks for listenin'." Her theme song, "When the Moon

Comes Over the Mountain," was popular throughout the 1930s and '40s. Kate Smith made several appearances on stage as well as in films, *The Big Broadcast of 1932* and *Hello, Everybody*. In the 1950s and 1960s she had her own popular afternoon TV show and, during the 1970s, made several stage appearances.

Most Popular U.S. Singer of the '40s and '50s?

American popular singer and comedienne DINAH SHORE, born in 1917 in Tennessee, was especially successful during the '40s and '50s. Her early radio show, "The Chamber Music Society of Lower Basin Street," was followed by appearances on Ben Bernie's and Eddie Cantor's shows and "Your Hit Parade," and by 1941 she had her own radio program and was a top singer. During World War II she entertained troops overseas and made more than 300 radio broadcasts. "The Dinah Shore Show" became an instant TV success in 1951 and remained one until the mid-'60s. Since then she has appeared mainly in night clubs and hosted TV "specials." In the early '70s 'Dinah's Place' was a successful morning talk show; a later version, called "Dinah!" has been moved to an afternoon slot.

Most Popular U.S. Singer of the '60s and '70s?

Singer and actress BARBRA STREISAND, born in 1942, became a star with her triumphant performance on Broadway in *Funny Girl*, about the life of the famous Ziegfeld star FANNY BRICE. By 1966 she had won seven awards for her first seven Columbia LP's. While her records were best-sellers, she was exploring other forms of expression as well, appearing on television specials of her own in the '60s, and performing before 150,000 people in Central Park in 1967. Her 1968 movie version of *Funny Girl* won her an Oscar (p. 654). It was followed by her first non-musical role in *The Owl and the Pussycat* (1970–71)

and the musical *Hello, Dolly!* in 1971. In the '70s, with new songs composed by LAURA NYRO, Randy Newman, and others, she produced a number of gold records including "Stoney End," her first million-copy single.

Tragic Rock Singer of the '60s

JANIS JOPLIN, whose name to many is synonymous with the 1960s, was born in 1943 in Port Arthur, Texas. Gifted with a throaty voice ranging three octaves, she started singing country western music in Texas at the age of 17, then left for California where she performed in small clubs. Later she returned to Texas and joined Big Brother and the Holding Company, a rock group organized in 1965. Her first recording, "Cheap Thrills," released in 1968, grossed over a million dollars in its first several months. Eventually Janis Joplin formed her own band, the Full Tilt Boogie, and became one of the most successful pop artists in the United States and throughout the world. She did not just sing, one critic wrote, "She became a vibrating, explosive part of her songs." Her song "Me and Bobbie McGee," written by Kris Kristofferson, was number one on the charts in 1971 and was included in her gold record, "Pearl," released posthumously. She died, reportedly from an overdose of drugs, in 1970.

From Gospel to Blues and Soul Singer

ARETHA FRANKLIN started performing at the age of 12 when she joined her father on gospel tours. During the first half of the 1960s she appeared in night clubs and concert halls, and in 1966 she changed record labels (from Columbia to Atlantic) and style, turning to blues and soul. By 1973 she had 6 gold albums and 14 gold singles. A frequent stage performer throughout the '60s and '70s, she made a European tour in 1968, sang in Australia in 1975, and gave a concert in her hometown of Detroit on "Aretha Franklin Day," as it was officially proclaimed by the mayor. Considered by

BARBARA GARDNER of *Down Beat* magazine to be the "most important female vocalist in years," Ms. Franklin has appeared on various television specials with Duke Ellington, Flip Wilson, Dinah Shore, and Bob Hope. She won the Down Beat Critics Poll in 1968, and was awarded an Honorary Doctor of Laws degree from Bethune College in 1975. Some of her great LP's include "With Everything I Feel in Me," "The Girl's in Love with You," and "Aretha in Paris."

Mother and Daughter Oscar-Winning Singer-Actresses

Introduced to the stage at the age of three by her vaudevillian parents, JUDY GARLAND made her screen debut as one of the Gumm Sisters in 1936 at 13. She played some of her most memorable roles during her teenage years (often with Mickey Rooney) including *Thoroughbreds Don't Cry* (1937) and *Everybody Sings* (1938). With the never-to-be-forgotten classic *The Wizard of Oz,* (1939), she became forever associated with the Arlen-Harburg song "Over the Rainbow." In the 1940s she starred in *For Me and My Gal* (1943) and in several films directed by her husband Vincent Minnelli, father of her talented daughter LIZA MINNELLI. Often in delicate mental health, Judy Garland was recovering when she appeared in 1954 in *A Star Is Born,* for which she was nominated for her role in *Judgment at Nuremberg* (1961) before her death in 1969.

Liza Minnelli won the Academy Award for Best Actress of the Year for her performance in *Cabaret* in 1972 (p. 654). Since then she has also appeared in the films *That's Entertainment* (1974)—in which she told viewers about her mother and father and her childhood visits to their Hollywood sets—*Lucky Lady* (1975), *Silent Movie* and *A Matter of Time* (1976), and *New York, New York*

(1977). Earlier, in 1962, Ms. Minnelli won a Tony Award for her performance in the Broadway musical *Flora, the Red Menace.*

Benny Goodman's Jazz Singer

Prominent jazz singer for 30 years, PEGGY LEE was discovered by Benny Goodman in 1941 while singing with a group in Chicago. Her first big hit with his band, "Why Don't You Do Right?" was followed by compositions of numerous popular jazz songs, which she sang accompanied by her husband, guitarist Dave Barbour. She appeared in several films, including *Mr. Music* (1950, with Bing Crosby) and *The Jazz Singer* (1953), and is an important night club and TV performer. She was the recipient of the Down Beat award in 1946.

Jazz Musician Who Has Sung with Symphony Orchestras

Jazz singer SARAH VAUGHAN during the 1940s worked with bop musicians Billy Eckstine and Earl Hines and received great support from Charlie Parker and Dizzy Gillespie, who recognized her unique talent and vocal range. A performer in intimate night clubs and large concert halls, she has appeared widely—touring more than 60 countries in the 1960s and '70s, and performing with small jazz vocal groups and combos as well as symphony orchestras, including the Boston Pops, Cleveland Symphony, Los Angeles Philharmonic, and San Francisco Symphony. She has made numerous television appearances and in 1974 flew from the Jazz Festival Showboat 2 on board the S.S. *Rotterdam* to a banquet for President Ford and President Giscard d'Estaing of France in Martinique. She was awarded the Esquire New Star in 1947, and won the Down Beat Poll in 1947–52, and the Met poll from 1948 to 1952.

"St. Louis Woman" to the UN

Jazz singer and comedienne especially prominent in the 1950s and '60s, PEARL

BAILEY began her career as a dancer and sang in night clubs in vaudeville in New York during the '40s. In 1943 she toured with Cootie Williams, and made her Broadway debut in 1946 in *St. Louis Woman*. She appeared in numerous films, including *Carmen Jones* (1954), *St. Louis Blues* (1958), and *Porgy and Bess* (1959), and was highly acclaimed for her performance in the all-black cast of *Hello, Dolly!* (1967–69). She has ap-

peared on TV and on stage, at the Concord Jazz Festival in 1974, and has made many recordings of songs including "Pearl's Pearls" and "Some Days There Just Ain't No Fish." In 1975 she was appointed by President Ford to the U.S. delegation to the United Nations. In 1977, having been awarded an honorary doctorate of humane letters from Georgetown University, she joined the freshman class there as a regular student.

Women in Country Western Music

PATSY CLINE achieved fame with her debut on "Arthur Godfrey's Talent Scouts" television program in 1957. Her country western rendition of "Walkin' After Midnight," a big hit in the late '50s, was the beginning of an outstanding career cut short when she was killed in a plane crash in 1963 at the age of 31. During the early '60s she appeared frequently on "The Grand Ole Opry," and was among the top recording artists with seven hit tunes in three years, including "Crazy," "Faded Love," and "Leavin' on Your Mind."

Born SARAH OPHELIA COLLEY in Centerville, Tennessee, in 1912, MINNIE PEARL, the "Queen of Country Comedy," has performed in many television shows. After graduation from Ward-Belmont College in Nashville, she tried her hand at dance and theater, eventually winning an audience for her country song and comedy routines. She joined the "Grand Ole Opry" in 1940, touring the country with her flower-decked hats and cotton dresses, and appeared in the 1950s and '60s in theaters and concert halls. Nashville Woman of the Year in 1965, in 1968 she was elected to the Country Music Hall of Fame. Some of her recordings include "Monologue," "How

to Catch a Man," and "Giddyup Go-Answer," a single hit in 1966.

MAYBELLE ADDINGTON CARTER's musical career spans almost three generations. She is one of the cornerstones of American music, a member of the original Carter family, country music's first and only royal family, and the mother of June Carter Cash. She created a guitar playing style which transformed the guitar from a rhythm to a lead instrument in popular music. Her daughter JUNE CARTER CASH is one of the leading women in country music today. LORETTA LYNN, probably the most interesting and complex personality among the women in country music and certainly the most beloved by her fans, was a mother at 14, a grandmother at 27, and was nearly 30 when she began performing professionally. Today she is one of country music's modern generation of superstars. DOLLY PARTON, another superstar, has been awarded the Country Music Association Female Vocalist of the Year Award, nominated for the Entertainer of the Year Award. She is perhaps the best female songwriter in America, and is the first country western singer to attempt to bridge the gap between pop and country music.

MUSIC: INSTRUMENTALISTS

First Woman Solo Pianist to Perform with Toscanini

ANIA DORFMAN, born 1899 in Odessa, made her concert debut there when she

was nine. She became a pupil of Isidor Philipp in Paris, performed in Russia at the request of the revolutionary government, and made her official debut in

Liège, followed by concerts all over Europe. She was first heard in the United States in 1936 where she appeared with the NBC Symphony directed by Toscanini—the first woman solo pianist to perform with him.

"The Valkyrie of the Piano"

Venezuelan pianist TERESA CARREÑO (1853–1917) had a long career, lasting from her first public recital at Irving Hall in New York at the age of eight in 1862 to her final appearance in Havana in 1917. A student of Anton Rubinstein's, she became particularly successful in Germany, where she taught for 30 years. During the last quarter of the 19th century she sang in opera and conducted an opera company, managed by baritone Giovanni Tagliapietra, her second husband (she was married four times). Reappearing as a pianist in 1889, she made her German debut, followed by a tour in Australia, Europe, and the United States. She was described as a performer of great feeling and intensity, "the Valkyrie of the piano." Teresa Carreño also composed several pieces for piano, a string quartet, and a festival hymn for the centenary celebration of Simón Bolívar, and one of the first to perform the music of her pupil Edward MacDowell.

Royal Philharmonic Gold Medalist for Piano

Distinguished English pianist MYRA HESS (1890–1965), whose repertory embraced works by Bach, Scarlatti, Mozart, Beethoven, Brahms, Grieg, and Schumann, as well as contemporary British composers, was one of the most noted of all English artists. She made her debut in 1907 in London, following studies at the Guildhall School of Music and the Royal Academy of Music. She appeared in England, continental Europe, and the United States with leading orchestras. In 1936 she was named Commander of the British Empire, and in 1941 Dame of the British Empire. During World War II she directed a series of noon concerts at the National Gallery, in Washington, D.C., and after the war she made solo appearances until her retirement in 1961. Described as a pianist of great intuition, she was most celebrated for her interpretations of such classics as Bach's chorale "Jesu, Joy of Man's Desiring," though she was equally praised for her virtuosity in romantic music. She received honorary doctorates from Durham, London, Cambridge, Manchester, Leeds, St. Andres, and Reading, and a Gold Medal from the Royal Philharmonic Society.

Foremost Brazilian Pianist

GUIOMAR NOVAËS, born in 1895 in Brazil, was a child prodigy whose talent was recognized early. When she began studying in São Paulo at the age of seven, she had already been playing piano for three years, and she made her first public appearance at the age of nine. Her musical promise brought her to Paris, where she won a competition against almost 400 contestants for first honors. Her playing was so extraordinary that the jury, which included Debussy, Fauré, and Moszkowski, asked her to repeat it. Two years later she was awarded the Premier Prix du Conservatoire. In 1911 at the age of 16 she made her triumphant professional debut in Paris, followed by a concert tour in Europe and her native Brazil. She appeared for the first time in the United States in 1915. Considered one of the world's greatest pianists, she continued to appear in recitals and with major orchestras in the United States, South America, and Europe into the 1970s. In 1956 she was awarded the Order of Merit from the Brazilian Government as "an ambassadress of culture and good will," and her husband, composer and architect Octavio Pinto, set up the Guiomar Novaës Prize, providing an exchange scholarship and concert tour to leading pianists. Her performances in small towns all over Brazil resulted in the "Culturas Artisticas" movement, which she headed.

First Pianist to Record Bartók

A student of Zoltán Kodály and Béla Bartók at the Royal Academy of Music in Budapest, LILI KRAUS, born in 1905 in Hungary, at the age of 20, following studies with Edward Steuermann and Artur Schnabel in Vienna, became full professor at the Vienna Academy for several years. She made a world concert tour during the 1930s. During World War II she was taken into detention by the Japanese in the Dutch East Indies. Afterward, she performed in Australia, South Africa, and England, becoming a British citizen in 1948. She has also toured the United States and made recordings of Mozart and Haydn. She made the first recordings of Bartók at his request, even before he did. Known primarily as a Mozart specialist, she attracts teachers and advanced students from all over the world to her master class at Texas Christian University, where she is artist in residence.

Spain's Award-Winning Pianist

Spanish pianist ALICIA DE LARROCHA, born in 1923 in Barcelona, made her first public appearance at the age of five, and was already known throughout Europe when she first appeared in the United States in 1954. Considered one of the finest performers of Spanish composers, she has also been widely acclaimed for her interpretations of Bach, Mozart, Beethoven, Chopin, and others, and was called the "queen of virtuosos" by the *New Yorker* in 1967. She has performed in major festivals, including the Hollywood Bowl, the Ravinia Festival, the Caramoor Festival, and the Mostly Mozart Festival and has been awarded the Paderewski Memorial Medal (London, 1961), the Grand Prix du Disque Académie Charles Cros, and the Edison Award (Amsterdam) for her superb re-cordings. One of the most recorded musicians in the world, she has won two Grammies, in 1974 for Best Classical Performance for Soloist Without Orchestra (for *Iberia*), and in 1975 for Best Classical Performance as Soloist with Orchestra (two Ravel concertos and Fauré's *Fantaisie*). Alicia de Larrocha is an honorary member of Los Lazos de Dama of the Spanish Order of Civil Merit and Isabel la Católica.

First Successful Woman Jazz Instrumentalist

Jazz pianist and arranger MARY LOU WILLIAMS is considered by some to be the first successful woman jazz instrumentalist. (Others believe LIL HARDEN ARMSTRONG was the first.) Ms. Williams, born in 1910 in Pittsburgh, Pennsylvania, started out with alto saxman John Williams, whom she later married, and became associated with Andy Kirk's Orchestra in Kansas City from 1928, first as arranger, and from 1931 as pianist. When the band came to the East she arranged several pieces for Benny Goodman and when she left Kirk in 1942 she formed a band with her second husband, trumpeter Harold Baker, and performed at Cafe Society (both Uptown and Downtown). Some of her arrangements were performed by Duke Ellington ("Trumpets No End") and her "Zodiac Suite" was premiered at Town Hall in 1946. Her style, influenced by Earl Hines and boogie-woogie, evolved during the bop revolution with her association with Bud Powell and Thelonious Monk. Some of her most famous hits of that period include "In the Land of Oo-Bla-Dee" and "Pretty-Eyed Baby." In the 1950s Ms. Williams retired and spent some time in a convent. Encouraged by a priest who became her mentor and agent, she made a successful comeback in the '60s with her own new blend of liturgical and traditional jazz. More recently she has performed at the Embers and the Hickory House in New York, appeared on a CBS

TV Christmas Eve special with her students performing, and been artist-in-residence at Duke University.

She Revived the Harpsichord

Internationally renowned harpsichordist and authority on ancient music WANDA LANDOWSKA (1877–1959) is considered responsible for reviving the harpsichord. Ms. Landowska began her studies of piano in her birthplace, Warsaw, at the age of four. She studied composition in Berlin, and went to Paris in 1900, where she married writer Henry Lew. She toured Europe as a pianist and in 1909 interested Tolstoy in her ideas of music. Three years later Pleyel built her the first of several instruments, and from 1912 to 1919 she headed a harpsichord class at the Hochschule für Musik in Berlin. In 1919, following the death of her husband, she went to Basel to direct master classes and finally established herself in St.-Leu-la-Forêt outside of Paris, where she founded l'École de Musique Ancienne, which attracted students from all over the world interested in old music. Wanda Landowska collected harpsichords, taught at the Conservatory at Fontainebleu, and gave concerts in Paris, and in her private concert hall constructed in 1927 in St.-Leu-la-Forêt, until the German occupation forced her to flee in 1940, leaving everything behind. The first modern compositions for harpsichord were written especially for her: Manuel de Falla's "Concerto," which she performed in Barcelona in 1926, and Francis Poulenc's "Concert Champêtre," which she performed in Paris in 1929. She lived in New York from 1941 to 1947, giving concerts but devoting most of her time to teaching, and later moved to Lakeville, Connecticut, where she made numerous recordings. A composer in her own right, she wrote cadenzas for Mozart concertos and many pieces for strings and voice, and she also published extensively in French and German periodicals.

Bach Specialist, Winner of First Town Hall Award

A specialist in Bach, ROSALYN TURECK (1914) founded and directed the International Bach Society and the Institute for Bach Studies. A performer on the harpsichord, clavichord, and organ, as well as piano, she is widely noted for her interpretation of the "Goldberg Variations." She had her first success in 1928 in Chicago, when she won first prize at a children's piano tournament. She made her debut at the age of 11 in 1923, and studied with SOPHIA BRILLIANT-LIVEN and at Juilliard with OLGA SAMAROFF. Early in her career, at the first of her 40 Bach marathons, she was presented with the first Town Hall Award for the most distinguished performance of the season. She joined the faculty at Juilliard in 1943. Ms. Tureck has devoted 40 years of her life to the study of Bach and is the author of the 3-volume *An Introduction to the Performance of Bach* (1960).

First Violinist to Make Recordings in the United States

American violinist MAUD POWELL (1868–1920), having studied in Chicago for four years, became a pupil in Leipzig, where she was awarded her diploma in 1881 after one year, and competed with 80 students for one of the six places in Dancla's class in Paris. While in London playing before the Royal Family in 1883 she met Joachim, who invited her to study with him in Berlin. In 1885 she made her German debut at a Philharmonic concert, playing Max Bruch's "Concerto in G minor," and later that year she made her American debut at a concert given by the Philharmonic Society in New York. She traveled in Germany with a group as a representative American violinist during the quadricentennial celebration of the discovery of America in 1892. The following year she performed at the Chicago Columbian Exposition (p. 608), and in 1894 formed the Maud Powell String Quartet, touring the United States. Later she traveled extensively in Europe and South Africa and did a brief tour with John Philip Sousa. During World War I she performed in army camps throughout America. Considered the leading woman violinist of her time, she introduced many concertos to American audiences, made numerous transcriptions and arrangements for violin, and was the first violinist to record in the United States (for the Victor Talking Machine).

Violinist Who Has Soloed with the World's Leading Orchestras

Daughter of the head of the Conservatory in Vienna, ERICA MORINI, born in 1904, studied violin with her father before becoming a pupil of Otakar Ševčik. Upon completing her courses at the Conservatory in 1916, she made her concert debut that year, followed by appearances in Germany, Poland, Romania, and Hungary. In 1920 she was the only soloist to perform with the Vienna Philharmonic for the music festival week. She made her American debut in 1921 as a soloist with the New York Philharmonic Orchestra under Artur Bodanzky, and has performed with every important American orchestra. She became an American citizen. Ms. Morini has toured South America, Australia, Europe, the Soviet Union, Egypt, India, and the Orient—everywhere confirming her reputation as one of the leading violinists of her time.

Britain's Renowned Cellist

Celebrated English cellist JACQUELINE DU PRÉ, who has been compared to leading 20th century cellists Pablo Casals, Mstislav Rostropovich, and GUILHERMINA SUGGIA, made her first appearance when she was seven. Her successful concert debut at age 16 was followed by engagements in Britain and on the continent, in recitals and with major orchestras as well as studies with Rostropovich in Moscow. In 1960 she was awarded the Guildhall

School Gold Medal and the Queen's Prize for British instrumentalists under 30. Her American debut at Carnegie Hall in 1965, playing the Elgar cello concerto with the BBC Symphony Orchestra won her praise for her "dazzling" technique and stage presence. She has received cellos from two anonymous sources—a Stradivarius dating from 1673, and another Stradivarius, the Davidov, dating from 1712 and valued at $90,000. In 1967 she married pianist and conductor Daniel Barenboim, with whom she had often performed, and was the subject of a BBC feature film. She appeared with all the major orchestras, toured the Soviet Union, Europe, the United States, Canada, and the British Isles. In 1971 Ms. du Pré was stricken with multiple sclerosis. Suddenly, "my hands no longer worked," she says. "I simply couldn't feel the strings." Since then she has become a teacher of young cellists and has struggled to live as normal a life as possible. In 1976 she received the Order of the British Empire and in 1978 went in her wheelchair to Buckingham Palace to receive an honorary degree from Salford University in what was believed to be the first ceremony of its kind.

First Woman to Hold Principal Chair in Major Orchestra

The first woman ever appointed to first chair in a major orchestra, DORIOT ANTHONY DWYER became principal flutist of the Boston Symphony Orchestra in 1952. Since then she has appeared as a soloist with the Boston Symphony and has performed with chamber groups and in solo recitals in the United States and abroad. Introduced to the instrument at the age of eight by her mother, also a professional flutist, Ms. Dwyer was engaged as second flutist of the National Symphony in 1943 upon graduation from the Eastman School of Music in Rochester, New York. Later she went to the Los Angeles Philharmonic as second flutist, a position she held for six years until 1952. In California, she became first flutist of the Hollywood Bowl Orchestra for three summers. With the Boston Symphony she has performed widely in major music halls and festivals. She has also performed with several chamber groups, including the Boston Chamber Players, with whom she has given master classes, taught at the New England Conservatory of Music, and is adjunct professor at Boston University. Highly acclaimed for her interpretations of Bach, Mozart, and Haydn, she also includes contemporary works in her repertoire and in 1972 performed the premiere of Walter Piston's flute concerto, a piece written especially for her. In 1974 Ms. Dwyer was nominated to the Women's Hall of Fame at Seneca Falls Historical Society, where she also accepted the Women of Achievement Award on behalf of her great-grandaunt SUSAN B. ANTHONY, founder of the National Council for Women.

She Revived the Lute

Lutanist SUZANNE BLOCH, born in 1907, the daughter of composer Ernest Bloch, studied music with her father and with Roger Sessions and Nadia Boulanger (below), winning first prize in a contest for women composers at the age of 19. She grew interested in early polyphonic music, asked Arnold Dolmetsch to restore a 17th-century lute, and became one of the few players of this early instrument. As a member of the American Musicological Society, she has conducted research in early music, and has learned how to read lute tablature, enabling her to revive forgotten works. She made her debut as a lutanist in 1935 at Carnegie Hall, followed by successful appearances and lecture recitals in the United States and abroad—one a recital with DIANA POULTON presenting for the first time lute duets from the British Museum manuscripts at the Haslemere Festival of Old Music. She also plays the virginal, the recorder, and the harpsichord.

Young Harpist Winner of Avery Fisher Prize

A cellist in the Seattle Symphony loved chamber music, but there were no harpists in Seattle. So when her 7-year-old daughter, HEIDI LEHWALDER, 28 in 1978, had a birthday, she gave her a harp. "And that," says Lehwalder, "was that." She went on to study harp throughout her school years, and ended up at Rudolf Serkin's respected Marlboro, Vermont, summer music school. There she encountered a certain amount of prejudice against harpists: "You get comments from mothers who want their daughters to study harp because 'they look so pretty behind a harp.' It's the sort of thing that gives harpists a bad name." But she overcame the attitude, going on to play in a touring chamber music ensemble that eventually spawned the Orpheus Trio—a flutist, a violinist, and Lehwalder as harpist. The trio is in its seventh season. She also won the Avery Fisher Prize in 1977, testimony to her virtuosity as a harpist and her musicianship. Ms. Lehwalder lives in New York City.

(Other women winners of the Avery Fisher Prize in 1977 were ANNI KAVATIAN, violinist, and URSULA OPPENS, pianist, making the score three women to one man.)

MUSIC: TEACHERS, COMPOSERS, CONDUCTORS

"The Greatest Music Teacher in the World"

NADIA BOULANGER, born in 1887 in France, was without question the most influential woman in music in the 20th century. Although she accomplished numerous breakthroughs in the male-dominated world of classical music—she was the first woman to conduct the London Royal Philharmonic Orchestra in 1937, and in 1938 she conducted the Boston, New York Philharmonic, and the Philadelphia orchestras—her fame rests on her teaching. To be a serious composer or performer today means to have studied with Boulanger. Among her pupils have been Aaron Copland, Roy Harris, Walter Piston, Elliott Carter, Marc Blitzstein, Elliott Galkin (director of the Peabody Institute), and Virgil Thomson, who has called her "the greatest music teacher in the world." Jay S. Harrison, in the *New York Herald Tribune,* wrote of Boulanger: "She is a woman of profound and enlightened spirit whose dedication to art, and the explanation of it, is unmatched in our time."

Piano Teacher at Curtis from Its Founding

Distinguished piano teacher ISABELLE VENGEROVA became professor at the Curtis Institute of Music in Philadelphia when it was established in 1924. Among her pupils were Samuel Barber, Leonard Bernstein, and Lukas Foss. Prior to teaching at Curtis, she had been a member of the faculty of St. Petersburg Conservatory from 1906 and full professor from 1910. She also performed as a concert pianist in Russia and made her performing debut in the United States in 1923. She died in 1956.

"The Last Musical Link to Imperial Russia of the 19th Century"

Juilliard teacher of noted musicians including Van Cliburn, John Browning, Misha Dichter, and many others, ROSINA LHEVINNE (1880–1976) heard pianist Anton Rubinstein play toward the end of the 19th century in Russia, where she was born in 1880. Married to one of the great piano virtuosos of this century, Josef Lhevinne, she began her own remarkable career in teaching in 1944 at Juilliard, where, on her 96th birthday in

1976, she was made honorary chairman of the piano faculty. Referred to as the "tiny Empress" by her students, she lived every romance with them into her 90s. Also a notable concert pianist, who performed until the 1960s, she was described in the *New York Times* at her death as the "last musical link to Imperial Russia of the 19th century," for whom "beauty" was the most essential element of piano playing.

First Woman to Receive the American String Teachers Association's Artist Teacher Award

DOROTHY DELAY began her very distinguished career as a violin teacher at the Juilliard School, where she was the first woman member of the Juilliard string faculty. She has taught outstanding young violinists from all over the world, who have gone on to win national and international competitions, performed with every major orchestra in North and South America, Europe, the Near East, and the Orient, and have given recitals and appeared as soloists in principal cities around the world. Others have become professors themselves in colleges and conservatories, and still others have become first violinists in prominent chamber groups. Itzhak Perlman is one of her best-known former students. Ms. Delay also teaches at the Aspen Summer School and is on the music faculty at Sarah Lawrence College. She is the first woman Starling Visiting Professor at the University of Cincinnati and was also the first woman to receive the American String Teachers Association's Artist Teacher award (previously awarded to Casals, Szigeti, Isaac Stern, Menuhin, and Piatigorsky).

First American Woman to Compose a Symphonic Work

American composer AMY MARCY CHENEY, known throughout her career as Mrs. H. H. A. BEACH, made her debut as a concert pianist in 1883 in Boston, but from 1885 devoted herself primarily to composing and toured Europe performing her own concertos. Best known for her songs "Ah, Love, but a Day," "The Year's at the Spring," and "Ecstasy," she also composed orchestral and choral works and chamber music. Her *Gaelic Symphony* (Boston Symphony Orchestra, 1896) was the first symphonic piece by an American woman. Her first important work, a Mass in E flat, was performed by the Handel and Haydn Society in 1892. Commissioned to compose a piece for the dedication of the Woman's Building at the Columbian Exposition (see p. 608) she wrote "Festival Jubilate" in 1892. In 1898 she wrote "Song of Welcome" for the Omaha Trans-Mississippi Exposition, and in 1915 "Panama Hymn" for the San Francisco Panama-Pacific Exposition.

Britain's Famed Suffragist-Composer

Regarded as one of the foremost British composers after the presentation of her Mass in D in 1893, ETHEL SMYTH (1858–1944) gained further recognition for her one-act opera, *Der Wald,* performed in Dresden in 1901, and her opera in three acts, *Les Naufrageurs,* produced in Liepzig as *Strandrecht* in 1906 and later known as *The Wreckers.* A leader of the women's suffrage movement in England, she wrote "The March of the Women," the battle song of the Women's Social and Political Union, and was held for two months as a militant suffragette in one of His Majesty's jails in 1911. A woman of considerable literary talent, she wrote some of her own librettos as well as many works for orchestra, string ensembles, violin and piano sonatas, and songs. She was made a Dame of the British Empire in 1922.

First Woman to Be Awarded the Grand Prix de Rome in Music

French composer LILI BOULANGER during her very brief life (1893–1918) wrote two symphonic poems, numerous choral and orchestral works, violin and flute pieces, psalms with orchestra, songs, and music to Maeterlinck's *La Princesse Maleine.* In 1913, at the age of 21, she was the first woman awarded the Grand Prix de Rome with her cantata, *Faust et Hélène.* Paris-born, she studied with Vidal and Caussade at the conservatory, and with her elder sister NADIA BOULANGER (p. 634), who has helped to keep her music alive.

First Woman Composer to Win a Guggenheim

Best known for her collections and arrangements of American folk songs and as the stepmother of Pete Seeger, RUTH CRAWFORD SEEGER (1910–53) was in her own right an avant-garde composer and the first woman to win a Guggenheim Fellowship for composition. Among her important works are a string quartet, works for piano and voice entitled "Sacco-Vanzetti" and "Chinaman, Laundryman," and a chamber piece, "Suite for Wind Quintet," completed just before her death. She was born in East Liverpool, Ohio, and studied in Florida, New York, and Paris. In Berlin she met Béla Bartók and incorporated such modern techniques as tone clustering, serialism, metric independence, and separation of performing sections into her work. During the 1930s, she lived in Washington, D.C., where her husband Charles Seeger was involved in the Federal Music Project of the WPA and she became interested in American folk music. She edited eight volumes of folk songs, including *American Ballads and Folk Songs* by John and Alan Lomax, made thousands of transcriptions of recordings of American folk music at the Library of Congress, and wrote piano accompaniments for about 300. She also devised methods for teaching children from folk songs. Her compositions, some based on political themes, include "Rissolty Rossolty" for 10 wind instruments, drums, strings (1941), "four Diaphonic Suites" for two cellos, two clarinets, oboe, and flute (1930), "Two Chants for Women's Chorus" (1930), "Nine Preludes" for piano (1926), "Sonata for Violin and Piano" (1927), "String Quartet" (1931). Ms. Seeger has also taught at the School of Musical Art in Jacksonville, Florida, the American Conservatory in Chicago, and at Elmhurst College of Music in Illinois.

On the Town Songwriter

With her partner Adolph Green, BETTY COMDEN has created some of the most memorable lyrics in film and Broadway theater. Ms. Comden, born in 1919 in Brooklyn, was educated at New York University and began her career as one of a night club act called "The Revuers," which performed mostly in Greenwich Village clubs, 1939–44. Green and JUDY HOLLIDAY, later to star in the Comden-Green stage and screen versions of Bells Are Ringing, (1956 and 1960) were also members of the act. In 1944, in collaboration with Green, Ms. Comden wrote and performed in On the Town, which made them famous. They went on to write Billion Dollar Baby (book and lyrics, 1945), Two on the Aisle (sketches and lyrics, 1951), Wonderful Town (lyrics, 1953), and many other stage productions. Together they also wrote a number of screenplays including Auntie Mame (Warner Brothers, 1958) and the script and lyrics for such hits as Singin' in the Rain (MGM, 1952) and many more. Betty Comden's numerous prizes include the Donaldson Award (1953), the Screen Writers Branch of the WGA Award (1949, 1952, 1955), the Off-Broadway (Obie) Award (1959), and the Antoinette Perry (Tony) Award (1953, 1968, and 1970).

Scottish Composer of Electronic Opera

Widely acclaimed Scottish composer THEA MUSGRAVE, born in 1928 in Edinburgh, has written numerous operas and ballet music. Her growing interest in electronic tape to produce new sound effects was the starting point for her opera Voice of Ariadne. Other works include The Decision (an opera performed by the New Opera Company at Sadler's Wells in 1967), Beauty and the Beast (a ballet, 1968), several chamber concertos, solo pieces for piano, "Colloquy" for violin and piano, "Music for Horn and Piano," and "Space Play" (a "dramatic abstract" piece). "I have gradually evolved toward a style where at times certain instruments take on the character of a dramatic personage," she says, "and my concern is then directed toward the working out of a dramatic confrontation." The Donald Francis Tovey Prize was awarded to Ms. Musgrave while she was still a pupil of NADIA BOULANGER. She is also the recipient of the LILI BOULANGER Memorial Prize. She and her husband, artistic director of the Virginia Opera Association in Norfolk, Peter Mack, are on the music faculty at the University of California in Santa Barbara.

Founder of the Women's Symphony Orchestra

Founder of the New York Women's Symphony Orchestra in 1935, ANTONIA BRICO began her musical career as a concert pianist. She made her debut as a conductor in 1920 with the Berlin Philharmonic Orchestra, followed by her American debut with the Los Angeles Philharmonic in 1930. The Women's Symphony Orchestra, which gave concerts at Carnegie Hall during the mid-'30s, developed into the Brico Symphony Orchestra in 1938, admitting men. In the summer of 1938 Antonia Brico conducted the New York Philharmonic Symphony Orchestra at Lewisohn Stadium, and organized the Treble Clef Choral Society in White Plains. A distinguished choral director, she has conducted various other choral groups in New York, and for almost 30 years has been head of the Denver Symphony, and has conducted in Boise and Boulder.

First Woman to Conduct at a Major European Opera House

Musical director and founder of the Opera Orchestra of New York, and assistant conductor of the New York City Opera since 1965, EVE QUELER was also the first woman to conduct in a major European opera house. Her magnificent debut at Teatro del Liceo in Barcelona featured MONTSERRAT CABALLÉ, (p. 622), Placido Domingo, Franco Bordmo, and Justino Díaz in Verdi's *I Vespri Siciliani.* She has revived pieces not usually heard at Carnegie Hall, has conducted the Mozart Festival at Lincoln Center, and holds the position of assistant conductor of the Fort Wayne Philharmonic.

Founder and Director of the American Choral Foundation

Distinguished U.S. choral director MARGARET HILLIS, born in 1921, has conducted numerous choral groups in a wide repertoire from very early to contemporary music and opera in concert form. Originally from Indiana, she went to New York after graduation from Indiana University to work with Robert Shaw. She became director and conductor of the American Concert Choir in 1950, assistant conductor of the Collegiate Chorale, 1952–53, and founder and director of the American Choral Foundation in 1954. She was also choral director of the American Opera Society, the Chicago Symphony Orchestra, the Cleveland Orchestra Chorus, and she has directed and conducted the Santa Fe Opera, and was named resident conductor of the Chicago Symphony Orchestra in 1967. She has taught at Union Theological Seminary (1950–60), Juilliard (1951–53), and Northwestern (1969–   ).

First Woman to Conduct the Metropolitan Opera

When SARAH CALDWELL, born in 1928 in Missouri, stepped onto the podium of the Metropolitan Opera on January 13, 1976, she made a major breakthrough for women not just in music, but in all male-dominated professions. Founder and artistic director of the Opera Company of Boston, which under her guidance has produced almost 50 operas, including Schoenberg's *Moses and Aaron,* Stravinsky's *The Rake's Progress,* Mussorgsky's *Boris Godounov,* and Berlioz's *The Trojans.* Ms. Caldwell is also former director of the National Opera Company and creator of a department of music theater at Boston University and has conducted the New York Philharmonic. Upon completing her studies at the New England Conservatory, Ms. Caldwell was offered positions as a violinist with two symphonies. Instead she opted for the chance to be Boris Goldovsky's assistant at the New England Opera Company, and after 11 years of hard work had her first opportunity to conduct Mozart's *La Finta Giardiniera.* Deciding to conduct rather than be a violinist was her "moment of truth," she says. "All my life I've loved both the theater and music."

First Woman to Conduct the New York City Opera

Brooklyn-born JUDITH SOMOGI at 33 became the first woman to conduct the New York City Opera (*The Mikado,* 1974). It was not until her senior year in high school that she decided to be a musician. Following completion of B.S. and M.S. degrees at Juilliard as a piano major, Ms. Somogi became one of three assistants to Stokowski at the American Symphony, which she conducted in 33 public school concerts. In 1966 she went to the City Opera as a pianist and also got experience coaching singers, rehearsing the chorus, and conducting backstage ensembles. Since 1974 she has conducted five other works for The City Opera company, including the live telecast of Douglas Moore's *The Ballad of Baby Doe* in the fall of 1976. The summer of 1977 marked her third season at the Hollywood Bowl, conducting such large-scale works as the Beethoven symphonies and Bartók's Concerto for Orchestra. Of her experiences with Julius Rudel at the New York City Opera as well as with Thomas Schippers in Spoleto and Ernest Fleischman in Los Angeles and chamber music at Tanglewood, she has said, "I was encouraged by them because I am a good musician, I like to think, not because I am a woman."

DANCERS AND CHOREOGRAPHERS

Ballerina with the "Most Beautiful Foot in History" First to Dance Outside Russia

ANNA PAVLOVA, born in 1881 the daughter of a Russian laundress, is remembered for her graceful and poetic style in dance, which she brought to countries all over the world. In 1905 she became the first ballerina to dance outside of Russia in major European cities, and by 1909 she was Diaghilev's prima ballerina in Paris. The following year she made her debut in New York and London partnered by Mikhail Mordkin, left Diaghilev, and eventually formed her own company in London. Though the repertoire of the company was considered not terribly distinguished, and the music and costumes mediocre, Ms. Pavlova excelled in a classic repertoire of small solos and pas de deux in *La Cygne* and *Autumn Bacchanale*, as well as major roles in *Giselle*, *Swan Lake*, and *Les Sylphides*. Fokine said she gave the impression of "flying through the air." AGNES DE MILLE (p. 649) wrote, "With her long-limbed and racing body, she was the supreme exponent of a new style. She had the most beautiful foot in history, superb hands, and a deeply moving face." Anna Pavlova died in 1931.

Founder of the Théâtre de Danse in Paris

With her brother Vaslav, BRONISLAVA NIJINSKA (1891–1972) was one of the original dancers of Diaghilev's Ballets Russes in 1909. She created roles in the early Fokine works such as *Carnaval* and *Petrouchka* (1911) and was equally as talented as her famous brother, according to the composer Stravinsky. In addition, she was an imaginative and influential choreographer of the 20th century, who experimented in jazz and created a new style of classical dance. Some of her best-known pieces for Diaghilev were *Les Biches* (1924) and *Le Train Bleu* (1924). She became ballet mistress of the Russian Opera in Paris, 1930–34, and in 1932 established her own Théâtre de Danse, for which she choreographed new pieces and revived old ones. In 1934 she choreographed *A Midsummer Night's Dream* for Max Reinhardt, with whom she had worked on *Tales of Hoffmann* in 1931. After 1945 she worked primarily as ballet mistress of the Grand Ballet (later Ballet Internationale) du Marquis de Cuevas, and revived *Les Biches* and *Les Noces* in the 1960s.

Founder of British Ballet

MARIE RAMBERT, born in 1888 in Poland, went to Paris to study medicine but became interested in ballet. She met and danced with Nijinsky and Diaghilev, but her accomplishments as a dancer were modest. Her great forte lay in discovering and nurturing talent in others. In 1926 she founded the Ballet Rambert, Britain's oldest ballet company, from which have come such brilliant figures as Sir Frederick Ashton and Antony Tudor. She has been credited with moving English dancers from the back of the *corps de ballet* to their premier position in the world of dance.

The Bolshoi's Principal Ballet Mistress

Considered one of the greatest dancers in Russian ballet and in all ballet history, GALINA ULANOVA has been principal ballet mistress and teacher of the Bolshoi

Ballet since 1964, two years after her retirement from the stage. She was born in 1910 in St. Petersburg, studied with her dancer mother MARIA ROMANOVNA for four years, then with Vaganova at the Petrograd State Ballet School until 1928, when she graduated into the Leningrad Company. Ms. Ulanova appeared in the Soviet ballet repertoire, and in 1935 started to dance with the Bolshoi Ballet, which she joined in 1944. She made her debut in the West in Vienna in 1949, appeared in Florence and Venice (1951), and won international recognition when the Bolshoi danced at Covent Garden in 1956. She was said to have been so moving as a dancer that her audience could not hold back their tears. Ms. Ulanova is the author of many articles on ballet and the recipient of many distinctions, including the Stalin Prize (1941, 1946, 1947, and 1950), the People's Artist of the R.S.F.S.R. (1951), the Lenin Prize (1957), and Hero of Socialist Work and Lenin Order (1974). Since 1964 she has been chairman of the Varna Competition and other juries and committees. *Trio Ballet* (excerpts from *Swan Lake* and *Fountain of Bakhchisaray*, 1953), *Romeo and Juliet* (1954), and *Giselle* (1957) preserve her radiance on film.

Founder of the Sadler's Wells Ballet

Irishwoman NINETTE DE VALOIS, founder and director of the Sadler's Wells Ballet (later the Royal Ballet), debuted as a dancer in 1914 in London and made solo appearances with the Diaghilev Ballet from 1923 to 1926. She was appointed one of the choreographers of the Carmargo Society, which was formed in 1929 under the sponsorship of many Diaghilev ballet enthusiasts, and opened the Academy of Choreographic Art in South Kensington. In 1931 she became associated with LILIAN BAYLIS, director of the Old Vic Theatre, and started a ballet troupe for which she was the principal choreographer. Her *Job* (music by Vaughan Williams) was per-

formed that same year and she accepted an invitation to choreograph from the Sadler's Wells Theatre. Eventually her repertory company became known as the Vic-Wells Ballet and was acknowledged as one of the outstanding companies of Europe. After World War II it became known as the Sadler's Wells Ballet, its connection with the Old Vic was broken, and in 1954 it was granted a Royal Charter becoming officially the Royal Ballet Company. Ms. De Valois was succeeded by Frederick Ashton as director in 1963. Ms. De Valois was awarded honorary degrees from London (1947), Reading (1951), Oxford (1955), Aberdeen (1958). She was made a Chevalier of the Legion of Honor in 1950 and received the Erasmus Prize in 1974. She is Life Governor of the Royal Ballet.

First Prima Ballerina of the Vic-Wells and Founder of the Festival Ballet

The first prima ballerina of the Vic-Wells Ballet (later Sadler's Wells and now the Royal), Dame ALICIA MARKOVA was also the first English ballerina to dance the principal roles in *Giselle* and *Swan Lake*. Earlier in her career (from the age of 14) she had danced with Diaghilev until his death in 1929, and with the Ballet Rambert and the Carmargo Society, creating title roles in several ballets before joining the Vic-Wells in 1931. She left in 1935 to found the Markova-Dolin Company with Anton Dolin and as principal dancer toured widely with her company until 1938, when she joined the René Blum-Léonide Massine Ballet Russe de Monte Carlo, gaining great acclaim in the United States as Giselle. In 1949 she returned to London to reform the Markova-Dolin Company, which became known as the London Festival Ballet, and was its prima ballerina until 1952. She made guest appearances with many companies until her retirement in 1962, directed the Metropolitan Opera ballet from 1963 to 1969, and since 1971 has been visiting professor at the University of Cincinnati. She was named Governor of the Royal Ballet in 1973. Her many distinctions include the *Dance Magazine* Award of 1957, a CBE in 1958, DBE in 1963, and a D.M. from Leicester University, 1966.

Forty Years a Prima Ballerina

Since the 1930s, Dame MARGOT FONTEYN has been a seemingly ageless star of classical ballet. Prima ballerina of Britain's Vic-Wells Ballet in the 1930s, most famous for her roles in *The Sleeping Beauty, Swan Lake,* and *Giselle,* in 1972 she told a *New York Times* interviewer, "I suspect I'll go on dancing until I can't any more." When she married Panamanian Ambassador Roberto Arias in 1955, it appeared for a time that she might retire, but her partnership with the young Russian dancer Rudolf Nureyev revived her career. Encouraged by her half-English, half-Brazilian mother as a child, Ms. Fonteyn studied ballet in Shanghai when her father was working in China as consultant engineer to the British American Tobacco Company and made her debut with Dame NINETTE DE VALOIS (p. 640) as a Snowflake in a Vic-Wells production of *The Nutcracker.* When Alicia Markova left the Vic-Wells in 1935 to start her own troupe, Ms. Fonteyn became its star. She gave her best performances in parts created for her, though she also danced the 19th-century classics with true grace and technical skill. Nureyev and Fonteyn received 23 curtain calls when they first danced together in *Giselle* with the Royal Ballet at Covent Garden in 1962. Three years later, the pair received almost twice that many curtain calls for their performance in Kenneth MacMillan's version of *Romeo and Juliet,* and they continued to generate international acclaim, dancing with the Stuttgart Ballet, the National Ballet of Washington, the MARTHA GRAHAM Dance Company, (p. 647), and other companies. Named a Dame Commander of the British Empire in 1951, Ms. Fonteyn also received the Order of the Finnish Lion in 1960, and several honorary degrees. She has been credited with giving her husband the courage and will to live and continue his work after he was partially paralyzed as a result of being shot by a political rival in 1964.

Managing Director of the American Ballet Theatre

Only after the death of her husband in 1933 did 26-year-old American LUCIA CHASE begin serious pursuit of ballet. She studied with Mikhail Mordkin, one of Pavlova's most brilliant partners, and became a principal dancer in the company he founded. When the Mordkin Ballet became the American Ballet Theatre, Ms. Chase was a charter member and major financial backer of the new company, which numbered among its original choreographers Fokine, Antony Tudor, and Agnes de Mille (below). She appeared in all but two of Tudor's works and created the Eldest Sister in one of his masterpieces, *Pillar of Fire.* Unable to develop a great classic technique because of her late beginning, she became instead a fine character dancer. In 1945, Lucia Chase was named the managing director of the American Ballet Theatre and introduced a more natively American spirit to the company, which had been largely dominated by Russian styles. Among the ballets she introduced are Balanchine's *Theme and Variations* and Tudor's *Shadow of the Wind;* the roster of her company has included NORA KAYE, CYNTHIA GREGORY, NATALIA MAKAROVA, GELSEY KIRKLAND (all below), Erik Bruhn, and Mikhail Baryshnikov. Ms. Chase was awarded New York City's Handel Medal in 1975.

American Indian Prima Ballerinas

MARIA TALLCHIEF, the first American dancer to be honored as a prima ballerina in 20th-century international ballet, made her debut in 1942 in Canada where she danced with the Ballet Russe de Monte Carlo under Serge Denham.

By 1945 her repertoire included roles in *Scheherazade, Etude,* and *Dance Indienne.* In 1946 she married George Balanchine and became prima ballerina of the New York City Ballet, of which Balanchine became artistic director. He choreographed what was perhaps her most notable role as the lead in *Firebird.* Ms. Tallchief continued her career as a dancer when their marriage broke up in 1952. She is part Scots-Irish and part American Indian, and her father, Alexander Tall Chief, was an Osage chief in Oklahoma. She was named by the Osage tribe MARIA PRINCESS WA-XTHE-THONBE, meaning "Woman of Two Standards," that is, in the Osage world and the world at large. Though she has not danced since 1966, she remains active in social and civic affairs, and has received various awards for her service, including the Indian Achievement Award in 1967. Maria Tallchief's sister, MARJORIE TALLCHIEF, also a distinguished ballerina, danced with the Grand Ballet du Marquis de Cuervas, becoming the first American Étoile of the Paris Opera Ballet as well as the first American to dance with the Paris Opera Ballet at the Bolshoi Theatre in Moscow. She has appeared before many heads of state, including John F. Kennedy and Charles de Gaulle, and has been honored by the Tunisian Government.

First Woman Director of the Paris Opera Ballet

NELLY GUILLERM, as she was born in 1933 in Brittany, or VIOLETTE VERDY as she became known in 1949 with the filming of Ludwig Berger's *Ballerina,* has been dancing with the New York City Ballet since 1958. She has long impressed critics with her sense of musicality and precise technique. Ms. Verdy made her debut at the age of 12 with Roland Petit's Ballets des Champs-Élysées. During the 1950s she danced with prominent European ballet companies and in 1957 was invited by Lucia Chase to join the American Ballet Theatre on tour in the United States and Europe, starring in *Miss Julie* and partnered by Erik Bruhn. She has created many leading roles in ballets from *Le Loup* (1953) through many by Balanchine, including *Episodes* (1959) and *A Midsummer Night's Dream* (1962), and Balanchine and Robbins' *Pulcinella* (1972). She is the recipient of the *Dance Magazine* Award of 1967, the Chevalier dans l'Ordre des Arts et Lettres in 1973, and in 1977 was named director of the Paris Opera Ballet —the first woman ever to hold that position.

Founder of the Chicago Ballet

Best known for her choreography of operas and operettas, Indianapolis-born RUTH PAGE founded the Chicago Ballet in 1955. Earlier, she was the prima ballerina and ballet mistress at the Chicago Summer Opera (1929–33) and of the Opera of Chicago (1934–37), and had toured in South America with ANNA PAVLOVA (p. 639) in 1918, joined Bolm's Ballet Intime for its guest season in London (1920) and Buenos Aires (1925), appeared as the prima ballerina of the Music Box Revue in Berlin and New York (1923–24), danced with Diaghilev's Ballets Russes in 1925, the Metropolitan Opera Ballet in 1926–28, and with Kreutzberg in 1932 and 1934. Though her ballet company went under various names (Chicago Opera Ballet, Chicago Ballet, Ruth Page Ballet), it was always headed by Ruth Page, who choreographed her own work for the company. Her themes derived especially from opera; among the best known of these are *The Merry Widow* (starring Alicia Markova, 1955) and *Die Fledermaus* (1958). Others include *The Bells* (based on Poe, music by Milhaud, 1946) and *Mephistophela* (after Heine's *Doktor Faust,* music by Berlioz, Boito, and Gounod, 1966). Her Chicago group shocked Europe in 1950 and proved very successful. The company was disbanded in 1969 but reorganized again in 1974.

Co-Founder and Director of the Ballet Nacional de Cuba

ALICIA ALONSO, born in 1921, was the founder of her own ballet company in Havana in 1948. Since Fidel Castro's accession in 1959 she has been director and prima ballerina of the Ballet Nacional de Cuba. Undisputedly one of the greatest ballerinas of the classical style, Ms. Alonso is particularly known for her interpretation of Giselle, a role that she danced alternately with ALICIA MARKOVA (p. 640) during the beginning and throughout her career with the Ballet Theatre of New York. While she was dancing with the Ballet Russe de Monte Carlo, she became the first dancer from the West invited to perform in the Soviet Union, in 1957, and was given the *Dance Magazine* Award in 1958. Since the 1960s she has toured widely with the Ballet Nacional de Cuba, which she and her husband jointly established. At 55, she danced the role of Giselle to plaudits at the Met in New York City and a year later, in 1978, again triumphed in the role at the Kennedy Center in Washington. Her daughter also dances with the Ballet Nacional de Cuba and has children of her own. Alicia Alonso is the recipient of many awards, including the Grand Prix de la Ville de Paris, the ANNA PAVLOVA Prize, the Golden Medal of the Gran Teatro Liceo de Barcelona, and the National Order, ANA BETANCOURT, the highest honor of the Cuban Woman's Federation. She is vice-president of the National Union of Cuban Writers and Artists. Her entire repertoire is recorded on film by Cuba's government-supported motion picture institute.

Prima Ballerina Assoluta of the Bolshoi Ballet

Brilliant dancer as well as actress, MAYA PLISETSKAYA has been recognized as one of the leading ballerinas of both classical and contemporary dance, and since the retirement of GALINA ULANOVA (p. 639) in 1962, has been the prima ballerina assoluta of the Bolshoi Ballet. Best known for her interpretations of Odette-Odile in *Swan Lake,* she has also given stunning performances in the leading roles of *Raymonda, The Sleeping Beauty,* and *Don Quixote,* as well as in more modern ballets. Sometimes called the world's greatest living ballerina, Ms. Plisetskaya appeared at the Paris Opera in 1961 and has made guest performances in London (1963) and New York (1966). Her many ballet films include *Master of the Russian Ballet* (1954) and *Vernal Floods* (1975). She acted in *Anna Karenina* in 1968 and in 1972 she created her own choreography for the play, with music by her husband Rodion Shchedrin, and made a film version of it in 1974. Ms. Plisetskaya is of Russian-Jewish background, born in 1925 in Moscow. She studied at the Moscow Bolshoi Ballet School, made her debut at the age of 11, and joined the Bolshoi Ballet in 1943 upon her graduation from the school. She was quickly noted for her exceptional fluidity and precision and expressive style. Her awards are many. She was made an Honored Artist of the Russian Federation in 1951; a People's Artist of the Russian Federation in 1956; named People's Artist of the U.S.S.R., the highest of all Soviet artistic titles, in 1960; awarded the Lenin Prize in 1964; and won the *Dance Magazine* Award in 1965.

Russian-Born "Beautiful Maiden"

Soviet ballerina NATALIA MAKAROVA, who danced before European and American audiences throughout the 1960s and was greatly admired for her lyricism, grace, and purity of style, in 1970 defected to the West and joined the American Ballet Theatre. Two years later she moved to London and performed with compatriot Rudolf Nureyev throughout Europe. That year she made her first guest appearance with the Royal Ballet. Ms. Makarova, who has been married two (some say three) times, lived with her mother and jazz-musician stepfather and brother in Leningrad. At age 12 she joined the "pioneers" ballet school and is reported to have cried during her first performance as a child when she threw the other dancers out of step. Known as "the Giraffe," because of her long and slender form, she became the prize pupil of former Kirov ballerina NATALIA DUDINSKAYA. Considered by many the best Giselle of her time, Ms. Makarova was the recipient of the Varna Gold Medal in 1965. In 1967 she created the role of the Beautiful Maiden in Jacobsen's *Country of Wonder*.

First U.S. Ballerina to Appear with the Ballet Nacional de Cuba since the Cuban Revolution

CYNTHIA GREGORY, who began dance training at the age of five to "acquire poise," rose to stardom when she became principal dancer of the American Ballet Theatre in 1965, only two years after she joined the company. The American prima ballerina assoluta, as she is called by Rudolf Nureyev, is best known for her virtuoso interpretation of leading roles in classic ballet, particularly *Swan Lake*, though her command of highly dramatic and abstract work is equally prodigious, dance critics agree. To avoid being typecast, Ms. Gregory has increased her repertoire by taking roles in contemporary ballets including José Limón's *The Moor's Pavane*, Tudor's *Undertow, Lilac Garden*, and all four leads in Peter Darrell's *Tales of Hoffmann*. Her partners include Erik Bruhn, Rudolf Nureyev, Jonas Kåge, Bruce Marks, Michaël Denard, Fernando Bujones, Ivan Nagy, John Meehan, and Ted Kivitt, with whom she has appeared in *Grand Pas Classique, Swan Lake*, and *Coppélia*. She danced with Cuban Jorge Esquivel at the Nacional Ballet de Cuba—the first U.S. dancer since the Cuban Revolution to appear in Havana since Castro assumed power. In 1975 she was chosen by Nureyev for the lead in his *Raymonda* and was the recipi-

ent of the *Dance Magazine* Award. After a self-imposed absence of 10 months she returned to the American Ballet Theatre in December 1976, revived in spirit, and with a "new perspective." Her performance as Kitri in Baryshnikov's *Don Quixote* in 1978 won her new plaudits.

Youngest Dancer to Have Roles Choreographed for Her by the New York City Ballet

A principal ballerina of the American Ballet Theatre since 1974, GELSEY KIRKLAND, born in 1952, was a member of the New York City corps de ballet at age 15, a soloist at 17, and a principal at 19. She has been called the first "totally credible American-born Giselle," and her ever-growing repertoire includes leading roles in many contemporary ballets. In 1970 George Balanchine selected Ms. Kirkland to dance in his new production of *Firebird*, making her at 17 the youngest ballerina to have a role choreographed for her by the New York City Ballet; he also revived *Tchaikovsky Suite No. 3* (*Theme and Variations*) for her. As Kitri in Mikhail Baryshnikov's *Don Quixote*, a role she alternated with CYNTHIA GREGORY (above) and MARTINE VAN HAMEL in 1978, she danced with "an earthy oomph . . . a winning new aspect of her stage personality," wrote one critic.

Italy's Pavlova-Prize Ballerina

CARLA FRACCI's home base is La Scala, but she is known in the United States through her regular guest appearances with the American Ballet Theatre. Her ABT partnership with Erik Bruhn, which originated in a telecast in the United States of *La Sylphide* on the Bell Telephone Hour in 1962, lasted until his retirement in 1972 and rivaled the Fonteyn-Nureyev partnership in popularity. In Italy she has appeared as Titania in *A Midsummer Night's Dream*, Ariel in *The Tempest*, the title character in Goldoni's *Turandot*, and the Moon in García

Lorca's *Blood Wedding*. She was named Woman of the Year by *Mademoiselle* in 1961 and received the ANNA PAVLOVA Prize from the Paris University of Dance in 1962.

Young American Prima Ballerina

SUZANNE FARRELL, born in 1945 in Cincinnati, Ohio, was one of the youngest ballerinas in the New York City Ballet when she joined that company in 1961. She danced her first solo in *Serenade* in 1962 and was made a principal dancer in 1965 after her superb performance as Dulcinea in Balanchine's *Don Quixote,* a role created especially for her. She left the New York City Ballet in 1969 and joined the Béjart Ballet du XXe Siècle. Since 1975 she has returned to the New York City Ballet, dancing in Balanchine's *Tzigane* (1975) and *Union Jack* (1976), and Robbins' *Piano Concerto in G* (1975). An honorary lecturer and teacher of master classes at the University of Cincinnati, Ms. Farrell received a Special Award of

Merit in Creative and Performing Arts in 1965 from the University as well as the key to the city. During the same year she won *Mademoiselle* Magazine's Merit Award, and in 1976 the *Dance Magazine* Award.

Director of the Stuttgart Ballet

Ballerina and artistic director of the Stuttgart Ballet since 1976, MARCIA HAYDÉE, born in 1939 in Brazil, became its prima ballerina in 1962 and is considered one of the greatest dancers of the last 20 years. She has created many principal roles and is remembered especially for her performance of *Giselle* in 1966. She has made guest appearances with the National Ballet of Canada (1964), the Royal Ballet (1966), and in Berlin (1964 and 1968). She also danced with the Municipal Theatre in Rio de Janeiro and the Grand Ballet du Marquis de Cuervas in 1957 before joining the Stuttgart. Ms. Haydée is the recipient of the Étoile d'Or (Paris, 1967) and the Deutscher Kritikerpreis.

Neo-Classical Spanish Dancers

ANTONIA MERCÉ, **popularly known as** LA ARGENTINA, **after her birthplace, is considered the pioneer and creator of the Spanish neo-classic dance. Her parents were both dancers, and her father, Manuel Mercé, was first dancer at the Córdoba Theatre and taught and danced at the Royal Theatre of Madrid. At the age of nine she made her debut at the Opera of Madrid, and two years later was made première danseuse. She grew interested in Spanish dance, and at the end of several years' study began performing in cafes and music halls. Pianist Artur Rubinstein admired her dancing in Buenos Aires where she was a** *tonadillera* **in a cafe. She was finally "discovered" in Paris at the end of the '20s, and soon became internationally known. Her success at the Paris Opera was followed by concerts in North and South America, and she was the first Spanish dancer to**

perform in the Far East. When she died in 1936, she was recognized as the greatest exponent of Spanish dance of the period.

ENCARNACIÓN LÓPEZ JULVES, **known as** LA ARGENTINITA, **more loved in Spain than her predecessor La Argentina, because of her Spanish nationality, in 1932 founded the Ballet de Madrid, with García Lorca, and in 1933 organized Las Calles de Cádiz, with the four gypsy dancers,** LA MACARONA, LA SORDITA, LA MALENA, **and** FERNANDA ATUNEZ. **She is said to have been one of the most eclectic of Spanish dancers, interpreting with great skill Andalusian folk dance and flamenco. Her choreography of Ravel's** *Bolero* **is still performed by the José Greco company. Though her troupe was small, it was the first all-Spanish ballet español to be seen in the United States.**

CARMEN AMAYA, described as "one of the most inspired, fiery, and passionate gypsy dancers that ever lived," performed largely in North and South America and Europe with her two sisters and father, who was a guitarist. The Amaya Theatre in Buenos Aires was built for and named after her. One man on seeing her commented that she "vibrates with the earth." She was awarded the Medal of ISABELA LA CATÓLICA in 1963.

Egyptian "People's Artist"

OUM KOULSOUM, born in the small Egyptian village of Tamai Al Zahayra, began her singing career by performing in village feasts and eventually sang with well-known singer Al Sheikh ahou El Alaa. Greatly influenced by the poet Ahmad Rami, she sang more than 250 of his songs and made numerous successful recordings during a long career. Oum Koulsoum was admired throughout the Arab world and received many official titles, the most important being "The People's Artist." She died in her 70s in 1976.

"The Divine Isadora"

Around the turn of the century ISADORA DUNCAN kicked off her ballet slippers and replaced the traditional tutu with loose, long, flowing, often transparent garments (she was the first dancer to appear sans tights) to develop a new style and philosophy of dance. Her style had no systematic base but emphasized emotion. Her basic theory was that pure movement is derived from inner impulse and simple ordinary movement, such as walking, running, reclining, and rising. Ms. Duncan appeared at a moment when women were beginning to demand the right to vote and other freedoms. She quickly found an audience receptive to her revolt against traditional form. After an initial failure in Chicago in 1899, she toured Europe gaining success and followers of her system of free dance. In 1904 she opened a school in Berlin. In 1905 she visited Russia, where, it is believed, she might have influenced Fokine in his re-evaluation of ballet. In 1921 she was invited back and founded a school in Moscow. She also founded schools in France and the United States, but none survived after her death. She is remembered for her personal style and tragic love affairs as much as her contribution to dance. Her life ended in southern France in 1928 when a long scarf she was wearing became entangled in the wheel of her convertible roadster and strangled her.

German Expressionist, Founder of Modern Dance in Europe

German dancer, choreographer, and teacher MARY WIGMAN, whose name is synonymous with modern dance, developed a style of dancing that she called "New German Dance." A reaction against the rigidity of classical ballet as well as a reaffirmation of ancient dance principles, this expressionist style evolved from her interest in eurythmics—a system of musical instruction by which rhythm is developed as the body moves in response to music. In her early dances, however, there was no music except such percussion instruments as Oriental gongs or African drums. To emphasize dance for its own sake, she appeared barefoot or in sandals, and her costumes and decor were simple. Her influence on dance in Europe is comparable to that of MARTHA GRAHAM (p. 647) in the United States. But though they explored the same problems and developed similar points of view, their techniques differed greatly. Ms. Wigman's school in Dresden, the training ground for many major dancers and choreographers, was forced to close by the Nazis, but she reemerged after World War II as a central figure in dance. Her most important choreographic works after 1947 include *Orpheus and Eurydice, Catulli Carmina, Carmina Burana,* and *Le Sacre du Printemps.* Her many distinctions include the Schiller Prize (Mannheim, 1954) and the German Critics Prize (1961). An honorary member of the Deutsche Oper in Berlin and the National Theatre in Mannheim, she became a member of the Academy of Arts (Akademie der Kunste) in Berlin and received an honorary professorship from the University of Leipzig. Mary Wigman died an octogenarian in 1973, leaving a lasting influence on modern dance.

Creator of America's First Serious School of Dance

American dancer and choreographer RUTH ST. DENIS, who brought an Eastern style of dancing to the West, in 1920 with her husband, Ted Shawn, created the Denishawn School in Los Angeles. It has been called "the first serious school of dance [in America] with a curriculum and standard of achievement." She and her husband toured the country with the Denishawn troupe until it disbanded in 1931. The troupe became the training ground for leading 20th-century choreographers, including MARTHA GRAHAM and DORIS HUMPHREY (below). Ms. St. Denis later established the Society of Spiritual Arts in New York and Los Angeles. This developed into the Church of the Divine Dance in Hollywood "to bring about a vital understanding between the church and the arts." She died in 1968 at the age of 91.

First Dancer to Receive Guggenheim Fellowship

Ideas for dance are derived from emotion, or a "stirring," according to American dancer/choreographer MARTHA GRAHAM, followed by a period of "festering" before the feeling can be translated into movement. Ms. Graham began dancing in 1916 with Denishawn School and became a student/teacher there in 1920. She left in 1923 to appear with the Greenwich Village Follies, made her debut in New York in 1926, and the following year started her own dance company, the Martha Graham School of Contemporary Dance, for which she was director and choreographer. Gradually her work became better known and her choreography more creative, finally establishing her as a major pioneering exponent of modern dance in the United States, who created "dance plays," and introduced a whole new vocabulary and concept of dance. In 1932 she was awarded a Guggenheim Fellowship to study in Mexico for a summer—the first dancer ever to receive a Guggenheim. Two years later she choreographed *Romeo and Juliet* and in 1935 helped create the school of modern dance at Bennington College. Some critics believe her most ambitious piece to be the full-length *Clytemnestra,* seen for the first time in New York in 1958. Composers who have written especially for her are Aaron Copland (*Appalachian Spring,* 1943), Norman Dello Joio, Samuel Barber, and Gian Carlo Menotti. Her long list of awards includes the *Dance Magazine* Award (1956), Capezio Award (1960), Aspen Award (1965), the Henry Hadley Medal for distinguished service to American music, and honorary doctorates from Harvard and Bard. She received the Award of Merit in 1970. Much of her work has been filmed; *A Dancer's World* won the Peabody and Ohio State awards, as well as awards from several European film festivals.

Founder of the Juilliard Dance Theatre

Modern dance theorist DORIS HUMPHREY (1895–1958), a pupil of the Denishawn company from 1917 to 1928 with Martha Graham, was one of the most influential figures in the new dance movement. Her most famous disciple was José Limón. In 1928 she formed a school and performing company in New York City with Charles Weidman, an accomplished mime artist. It lasted for two decades. She also was the founder of the Juilliard Dance Theatre in 1935 and was noted for her role in the Bennington College Summer School of Dance (1934–42). Ms. Humphrey's famous earlier pieces (on balance and fall) include *Water Study* (1928) and *The Life of a Bee* (1929). Later she developed the theme of the individual in society and choreographed pieces such as *New Dance* (1935) and *With My Red Fires* (1936). Arthritis forced her to stop dancing in 1945, but she continued to teach and choreograph, and became artistic director of José Limón's company. She codified her dance technique in her book *The Art of Making Dances* in 1959.

Choreographer of Broadway Musicals

After three seasons in the early 1920s HELEN TAMIRIS, born in 1905, decided that the Metropolitan Opera Ballet was not for her, toured South America with the Bracale Opera Ballet, returned to New York to the Music Box Revue, and made her debut in 1927. Setting out to develop a repertoire on the American theme, she was the first to tour European festivals. In 1930 she joined the Dance Repertory Theatre in which she kept her individual program, sharing only theater publicity and costs with other companies. During the 1930s she participated in the Works Project Administration's Dance Project, New York, and taught body movement to actors. She established and taught at her School of Dance until 1945, when she began choreographing for Broadway. Among her best-known musicials are *Up in Central Park, Show Boat, Annie Get Your Gun,* and the Tony Award-winning *Touch and Go.*

They Danced Their Way to Movie Fame

Fred Astaire's earliest partner was his older sister, ADELE ASTAIRE, who appeared with him from the age of six in vaudeville performances. For years they remained at the top as the darlings of Broadway and London, in shows especially written for them, including *Lady Be Good* (1922), *Funny Face* (1927), and *The Band Wagon* (1931). In 1931 they made a Vitaphone short subject as a screen test for *The Band Wagon.* The film never materialized, and this remained Adele's only screen appearance. She ended her career in 1932 when she married Lord Charles Cavendish, the second son of the Duke of Devonshire, leaving her brother to GINGER ROGERS. Adele and Fred Astaire received the *Dance Magazine* Award in the late 1960s.

"Cigarette me, big boy" was the first line uttered by Ginger Rogers in her dancing/acting career. That was in *Young Man of Manhattan* in 1930. Three years later she was dancing the "Carioca" with Fred Astaire in *Flying Down to Rio,* the film that introduced to the public the most memorable of all dance teams ever to appear on screen. They appeared together in 11 musicals—among the best being *The Gay Divorcee* (1934) and *Top Hat* (1935). As a tribute to their great predecessors they did *The Story of Vernon and Irene Castle** (1939), followed 10 years later by *The Barkleys of Broadway* (1949). Ms. Rogers won an Oscar for her performance in *Kitty Foyle* in 1940 (p. 653), and her acting repertoire expanded to include comedy and melodrama roles. She has made television appearances since the '50s, and starred in the Broadway musical *Hello, Dolly!* In 1960 she took the lead role in *Mame* in London. Since 1972 Ms. Rogers has been a fashion consultant for J. C. Penney, and has been seen on stage in Europe

* See IRENE CASTLE in "Women in Fashions and Home Furnishings," p. 238.

and the United States still dancing "like an angel."

Though ANN MILLER tapped her way through 20 years of musical films, she never quite made it as a big star. She made her screen debut in *The Devil on Horseback* in 1936 and in 1937 appeared in her first RKO picture, entitled *New Faces of 1937*. She next danced on Broadway in *George White's Scandals*, and then returned to Hollywood to star in mostly B musicals and waited for something better. Finally, in 1948 she danced with Fred Astaire in *Easter Parade*, a great MGM hit. She ended her film career in 1956, made guest appearances on television's "Laugh-In" in the late '60s, and in 1969 made a smashing return to Broadway as *Mame*. Later she received standing ovations for her tapdancing routine in *That's How Young I Feel*. Her autobiography, *Miller's High Life*, was published in 1972.

Choreographer of Afro-American Dance

Dancer and choreographer KATHERINE DUNHAM used her Ph.D. in anthropology to research dance in the West Indies and she became one of the most original choreographers of Afro-American dance. During the 1930s she was involved in the Chicago dance program of the Works Project Administration. In 1940 the first of her many Broadway musicals, and still the most famous, *Cabin in the Sky*, opened. Later she appeared in or choreographed many Hollywood films, including *Carnival of Rhythm*. Her husband John Pratt designed sets for her black revues, which met with great success in Europe. Ms. Dunham's work in the field of anthropology has also received deserved recognition from the Scientific Fraternity of the University of Chicago, her alma mater, and from the Royal Society of Anthropologists in London. Other awards include the Honorary Citizen of Port-au-Prince, Laureate of Lincoln Academy, Professional Achievement Award of the University of Chicago Alumni Association, *Dance Magazine* Award (1968). She continues to work as director of the Center for the Development of Black Studies and Culture, and the Performing Arts Training Center, at Southern Illinois University in St. Louis.

"Theater Brat" Who Brought Us *Oklahoma*

In her *Book of the Dance* (1963) AGNES DE MILLE, niece of Hollywood producer Cecil B. De Mille, includes herself among the "theater brats" who, by not being restricted by the classic style, added vitality to dance—"cross-breeding ballet with mongrel experiences and heritage." Modifying rather than eliminating popular American forms of theater, she incorporated them into what evolved as part of the American musical comedy tradition. Tap dancing was introduced into ballet, as well as cowboy riding and roping movements in her *Rodeo*, with Ms. de Mille herself playing the part of the "tomboy of the ranch outfit." The show, with Aaron Copland's score, won 20 curtain calls on opening night in 1942, and the critics' praise as the "most original and interesting innovation in ballet in modern times." In 1943 Ms. de Mille had her first financial success with *Oklahoma!* In it, for the first time, she used dancing for "character development, dramatic atmosphere, and plot reinforcement." *Oklahoma!* was eventually made into a film in 1954. Ms. de Mille went on to create the choreography for *Carousel*, *Brigadoon*, and *Paint Your Wagon*, as well as to write nine books and form the Heritage Dance Theater, which is dedicated to the "presentation and expression of American dance and song."

Director of Nigeria's Art Center of Black African Culture

Dancer PEARL PRIMUS, born in 1919 in Trinidad, like Katherine Dunham used her background in anthropology (she too holds a Ph.D.) for her research into black dance in Africa and the Caribbean. Her choreography is based on the ritualistic dances of the people she has studied. Ms. Primus made her debut as a dancer in 1941, followed by her first solo recital two years later. In 1944 she made her first appearance with her own group in her piece *African Ceremonial*. Beginning in 1949, Ms. Primus made research expeditions and performed in Africa for a period of 15 years, and created a company with her husband, Percival Borde. Now director of the Art Center of Black African Culture in Nigeria, she devotes her time to teaching and choreographing for many groups, notably for the Alvin Ailey American Dance Theater, and also teaches at Hunter College in New York. *Fanja* (1949) brought her the Order of Star of Africa, presented by the President of the Republic of Liberia, the late William V. S. Tubman.

Swedish Choreographer

BIRGIT CULLBERG, Swedish dancer/choreographer and co-founder of the Svenska Dansteater in 1946, has since 1967 been director of Cullbergbaletten at the Stockholm City Theater, subsidized by the state through the Swedish State Theater. Prior to this she was choreographer for the Royal Swedish Ballet, 1952–57, and has choreographed for the American Ballet Theatre and other ballet companies. Her ballet for television, *The Evil Queen*, won the Prix d'Italia in 1961. Among her best-known pieces is *Miss Julie*, which is based on the Strindberg play and has since its first performance in 1950 been danced by many companies. Ms. Cullberg, born in 1908 in Sweden, studied in Scandinavia and with MARTHA GRAHAM (p. 647). Combining a career in literature and dance, she has directed plays and is a lecturer and writer as well as a choreographer. Primarily concerned with psychological problems and dramatic content, she has found her best expression in modern dance.

Co-Founder of the Azuma-Kabuki Theatre

Daughter of the actor and dancer Uzaemon XV, dynastic head of the Ichimura family, which is steeped in over 350 years of Kabuki tradition, Tokyo-born AZUMA IV TOKUHO is one of the principal dancers of her own company. Kabuki, which synthesizes music, dance, and drama to symbolize emotions, is said to be the oldest classical theater in the world. Ms. Azuma, whose mother, MAASYA FUJIMA, was herself a great Kabuki-style dancer, inherited the family troupe at the death of her father in 1945. She formed several of her own groups, including the Shunto-kai (Spring Wistera Dancing Group) and the Azuma Tokuho Fufu-kai (Husband-Wife Company), in which women play both ancient and contemporary roles.

Founder of the Inbal Company of Israel

The Inbal Company of Israel, founded by SARA LEVI-TANAI in 1949, builds upon Yemenite folklore and biblical tradition to create a style of its own. Rather than formalizing movements or dance steps, Ms. Levi-Tanai allows her group to improvise within the framework of a theme or idea she would like to express. Since there is no exact choreography, she relies upon her group's memory to recreate the "intent, not the steps," and says she could detect a mistake. Ms. Levi-Tanai composes much of the music for her pieces and is the recipient of the Elkoni Prize for folk songs awarded by Tel Aviv in 1957. She also won the Histadrut Prize for Cultural Achievement that year, the Choreography Prize of the Theatre of Nations, Paris, 1962, and the Israel Prize in 1973.

Founder of the Ballet Folklorico de Mexico

Mexican dancer, choreographer, and teacher AMALIA HERNÁNDEZ founded her own folklore company, Ballet Folklorico de Mexico, in 1952. The group, which is state subsidized, gained considerable prestige in Mexico and abroad, and won the international prize for companies in Paris in 1961. Ms. Hernández, who studied ballet with Sybine of the Pavlova company, modern dance with Waldseen, and Spanish dancing with LA ARGENTINITA (p. 645), has created an original style. The dancers perform to authentic Mexican music provided by orchestras and singers from each province.

Founder of India's Best-Known School of Dance, Music, and Painting

One of India's first Bharat Natyam dancers to tour in Europe, the United States, and in other Asian countries, SUNDARI SHRIDHARANI in the 1950s retired from dancing herself to found New Delhi's Triveni Kala Sangam, a school where famous masters of the several classic types of Indian dancing teach beginner and advanced students the intricate hand, arm, foot, and facial movements of this art. Traditional Indian music and modern painting are also taught at the school, which Shrimati Shridharani, widow of an Indian journalist well known in the United States before his death in 1960, continues to direct.

First Woman Dancer, First Black to Be Elected to the National Endowment for the Arts

Principal dancer of the Alvin Ailey American Dance Theater, JUDITH JAMISON, born in 1944 in Philadelphia, Pennsylvania, has impressed critics and balletomanes with her striking appearance (she is 5'10") and exceptional talent. Combining classical ballet with training in modern dance, Ms. Jamison has created a style of her own. At the end of 1964, Agnes de Mille, who has an eye for talent, invited her student Ms. Jamison to dance the role of Mary Seaton in her new ballet, *The Four Marys.* Later in 1965 Ms. Jamison made her debut with Alvin Ailey's largely black

but integrated company in *Congo Tango Palace,* in Chicago, followed by tours to New York, Europe, and to the first World Festival of Negro Arts in Dakar, Senegal. Judith Jamison also danced briefly with the Harkness Ballet, 1966–67. Since 1967 she has traveled widely at home and abroad with Alvin Ailey. Ms. Jamison's many honors include the *Dance Magazine* Award for 1972, which she shared with Royal Ballet's Anthony Dowell. That same year she was elected to the Board of the National Endowment for the Arts—the first woman dancer as well as the first black member. In an interview with *Dance Magazine,* Judith Jamison has said, "I am a dancer who happens to be a woman, who happens to be black. I guess the three things, dancing, femininity, and blackness make up who and what I am. I have never tried to separate them because if I did I would be fragmented, maybe shattered. I have always tried to learn, not only *how* to dance, but what it is for *me* to dance. I cannot separate the personal from the abstract, the particular from the general, because dance is so very important to me."

First Choreographer to Copyright her Work in Washington

Choreographer of musicals, including *Kiss Me, Kate* (1948), *My Fair Lady* (1956), and *Camelot* (1960), HANYA HOLM has been one of the leading exponents of modern dance. In 1952 she made history by being the first choreographer to register her work, *Kiss Me, Kate,* with the Copyright Office in Washington, D.C. Ms. Holm, born in 1898 in Germany, joined Mary Wigman in 1919. In 1931 she opened the Mary Wigman School in New York, and remained its head until she opened her own school, the Hanya Holm Studio, in 1936. She choreographed her most famous work, *Trend,* to the music of Varèse in 1937 while in charge of a workshop group at the Bennington College Summer School of the Dance. For many years she returned to teach summer courses at the Center of the Dance of the West in Colorado, which she founded in 1941. One of the founder-directors of the New York City Dance Company, Ms. Holm was appointed head of the dance department of the New York Musical Theatre Academy in 1961. Her interest in theatrical dance has led her to work on operas and film, and she has written many articles and lectured widely on dance.

Pop Ballet Choreographer

One of the most inventive figures of contemporary dance is TWYLA THARP, who combines the traditional and the modern. While still at Barnard, Ms. Tharp joined the Paul Taylor Dance Company, where she remained until she founded her own troupe about a year later in 1965, at the age of 23. Most of her early works were performed on a bare stage, with very simple costumes, and no music, to "ex-plore the possibilities of pure movement." Her style was greatly influenced by Merce Cunningham, under whom she studied for several years, as well as by Paul Taylor. Ms. Tharp has succeeded in reaching the non-dance community with her "pop ballets," including *Eight Jelly Rolls, The Bix Pieces,* and *The Raggedy Dance.* The latter joined Scott Joplin rag music to Mozart variations. Her *Deuce Coupe,* which she choreographed for the Joffrey, marked, according to one dance critic, the emergence of Ms. Tharp from avant-garde cultism into an artist who could bridge the seemingly contradictory worlds of modern dance experimentation, pop, and ballet." She continues to combine pop music, ballet, and popular dances such as the jerk and the frug and bugaloo in unique compositions and to choreograph new pieces, comparing old ones to chewing gum, which "loses its flavor in a minute and a half."

STARS OF STAGE AND SCREEN

Academy Award Winners

1927/28
Best Actress: JANET GAYNOR (*Seventh Heaven, Street Angel, Sunrise*)
1928/29
Best Actress: MARY PICKFORD (*Coquette*)
1929/30
Best Actress: NORMA SHEARER (*The Divorcee*)
1930/31
Best Actress: MARIE DRESSLER (*Min and Bill*)
1931/32
Best Actress: HELEN HAYES (*The Sin of Madelon Claudet*)
1932/33
Best Actress: KATHARINE HEPBURN (*Morning Glory*)
1934
Best Actress: CLAUDETTE COLBERT (*It Happened One Night*)

1935
Best Actress, BETTE DAVIS (*Dangerous*)
1936
Best Actress: LUISE RAINER (*The Great Ziegfeld*)
Best Supporting Actress:* GALE SONDERGAARD (*Anthony Adverse*)
1937
Best Actress: LUISE RAINER (*The Good Earth*)
Best Supporting Actress: ALICE BRADY (*In Old Chicago*)
1938
Best Actress: BETTE DAVIS (*Jezebel*)
Best Supporting Actress: FAY BAINTER (*Jezebel*)
1939
Best Actress: VIVIEN LEIGH (*Gone With the Wind*)

* Not given until 1936.

Best Supporting Actress: HATTIE McDANIEL (*Gone With the Wind*)

1940

Best Actress: GINGER ROGERS (*Kitty Foyle*)

Best Supporting Actress: JANE DARWELL (*The Grapes of Wrath*)

1941

Best Actress: JOAN FONTAINE (*Suspicion*)

Best Supporting Actress: MARY ASTOR (*The Great Lie*)

1942

Best Actress: GREER GARSON (*Mrs. Miniver*)

Best Supporting Actress: TERESA WRIGHT (*Mrs. Miniver*)

1943

Best Actress: JENNIFER JONES (*The Song of Bernadette*)

Best Supporting Actress: KATINA PAXINOU (*For Whom the Bell Tolls*)

1944

Best Actress: INGRID BERGMAN (*Gaslight*)

Best Supporting Actress: ETHEL BARRYMORE (*None but the Lonely Heart*)

1945

Best Actress: JOAN CRAWFORD (*Mildred Pierce*)

Best Supporting Actress: ANNE REVERE (*National Velvet*)

1946

Best Actress: OLIVIA DE HAVILLAND (*To Each His Own*)

Best Supporting Actress: ANNE BAXTER (*The Razor's Edge*)

1947

Best Actress: LORETTA YOUNG (*The Farmer's Daughter*)

Best Supporting Actress: CELESTE HOLM (*Gentleman's Agreement*)

1948

Best Actress: JANE WYMAN (*Johnny Belinda*)

Best Supporting Actress: CLAIRE TREVOR (*Key Largo*)

1949

Best Actress: OLIVIA DE HAVILLAND (*The Heiress*)

Best Supporting Actress: MERCEDES McCAMBRIDGE (*All the King's Men*)

1950

Best Actress: JUDY HOLLIDAY (*Born Yesterday*)

Best Supporting Actress: JOSEPHINE HULL (*Harvey*)

1951

Best Actress: VIVIEN LEIGH (*A Streetcar Named Desire*)

Best Supporting Actress: KIM HUNTER (*A Streetcar Named Desire*)

1952

Best Actress: SHIRLEY BOOTH (*Come Back, Little Sheba*)

Best Supporting Actress: GLORIA GRAHAME (*The Bad and the Beautiful*)

1953

Best Actress: AUDREY HEPBURN (*Roman Holiday*)

Best Supporting Actress: DONNA REED (*From Here to Eternity*)

1954

Best Actress: GRACE KELLY (*The Country Girl*)

Best Supporting Actress: EVA MARIE SAINT (*On the Waterfront*)

1955

Best Actress: ANNA MAGNANI (*The Rose Tattoo*)

Best Supporting Actress: JO VAN FLEET (*East of Eden*)

1956

Best Actress: INGRID BERGMAN (*Anastasia*)

Best Supporting Actress: DOROTHY MALONE (*Written on the Wind*)

1957

Best Actress: JOANNE WOODWARD (*The Three Faces of Eve*)

Best Supporting Actress: MIYOSHI UMEKI (*Sayonara*)

1958

Best Actress: SUSAN HAYWARD (*I Want to Live*)

Best Supporting Actress: WENDY HILLER
(*Separate Tables*)
1959
Best Actress: SIMONE SIGNORET (*Room at the Top*)
Best Supporting Actress: SHELLEY WINTERS (*The Diary of Anne Frank*)
1960
Best Actress: ELIZABETH TAYLOR (*Butterfield 8*)
Best Supporting Actress: SHIRLEY JONES (*Elmer Gantry*)
1961
Best Actress: SOPHIA LOREN (*Two Women*)
Best Supporting Actress: RITA MORENO (*West Side Story*)
1962
Best Actress: ANNE BANCROFT (*The Miracle Worker*)
Best Supporting Actress: PATTY DUKE (*The Miracle Worker*)
1963
Best Actress: PATRICIA NEAL (*Hud*)
Best Supporting Actress: MARGARET RUTHERFORD (*The V.I.P.'s*)
1964
Best Actress: JULIE ANDREWS (*Mary Poppins*)
Best Supporting Actress: LILA KEDROVA (*Zorba the Greek*)
1965
Best Actress: JULIE CHRISTIE (*Darling*)
Best Supporting Actress: SHELLEY WINTERS (*A Patch of Blue*)
1966
Best Actress: ELIZABETH Taylor (*Who's Afraid of Virginia Woolf?*)
Best Supporting Actress: SANDY DENNIS (*Who's Afraid of Virginia Woolf?*)
1967
Best Actress: KATHARINE HEPBURN (*Guess Who's Coming to Dinner*)
Best Supporting Actress: ESTELLE PARSONS (*Bonnie and Clyde*)
1968
Best Actress: KATHARINE HEPBURN (*The Lion in Winter*) and BARBRA STREISAND (*Funny Girl*)

Best Supporting Actress: RUTH GORDON (*Rosemary's Baby*)
1969
Best Actress: MAGGIE SMITH (*The Prime of Miss Jean Brodie*)
Best Supporting Actress: GOLDIE HAWN (*Cactus Flower*)
1970
Best Actress: GLENDA JACKSON (*Women in Love*)
Best Supporting Actress: HELEN HAYES (*Airport*)
1971
Best Actress: JANE FONDA (*Klute*)
Best Supporting Actress: CLORIS LEACHMAN (*The Last Picture Show*)
1972
Best Actress: LIZA MINNELLI (*Cabaret*)
Best Supporting Actress: EILEEN HECKART (*Butterflies Are Free*)
1973
Best Actress: GLENDA JACKSON (*A Touch of Class*)
Best Supporting Actress: TATUM O'NEAL (*Paper Moon*)
1974
Best Actress: ELLEN BURSTYN (*Alice Doesn't Live Here Anymore*)
Best Supporting Actress: INGRID BERGMAN (*Murder on the Orient Express*)
1975
Best Actress: LOUISE FLETCHER (*One Flew Over the Cuckoo's Nest*)
Best Supporting Actress: LEE GRANT (*Shampoo*)
1976
Best Actress: FAYE DUNAWAY (*Network*)
Best Supporting Actress: BEATRICE STRAIGHT (*Network*)
1977
Best Actress: DIANE KEATON (*Annie Hall*)
Best Supporting Actress: VANESSA REDGRAVE (*Julia*)

The Original Peter Pan

Although Salt Lake City-born MAUDE ADAMS (1872–1953) created many roles in her long career in the theater, perhaps her greatest triumph was as Peter Pan in James M. Barrie's play. On stage at five in *Fritz* in San Francisco, she went on to become a child star in *Uncle Tom's Cabin.* Her role as Lady Bobbie in *The Little Minister,* rewritten for her by Barrie, led to performances in other productions of his, including *What Every Woman Knows* and *A Kiss for Cinderella.* A major actress, also celebrated for her roles as the Duke of Reichstadt in *L'Aiglon,* Rosalind in *As You Like It,* Maria in *Twelfth Night,* and Joan of Arc, Maude Adams came out of retirement to tour with Otis Skinner in *The Merchant of Venice* in 1931.

The Divine Duse

ELEONORA DUSE, born in 1858 in Italy, made her American debut as Marguerite Gauthier in Dumas' *Camille* in 1893. Renowned for her many roles in classic— and, for her day, modern— drama, she was the source of inspiration for Gabriele d'Annunzio's *Il Sogno di un Mattino di Primavera.* Eight years before her death in 1924, Eleonora Duse made her only screen appearance, in *Cenere.*

Stage and Screen "Double Vie"

One of history's most renowned actresses of the classical and romantic theater, SARAH BERNHARDT was also one of the first great actresses of cinema—in *La Reine Elizabeth* and *La Dame aux Camélias* in 1911. An illegitimate child of French-Dutch and Jewish parentage, she was born in Paris in 1844. She made her debut at the Théâtre Français (later Comédie Française) in Racine's *Iphigénie en Aulide* in 1862, and later became identified particularly with Racine's *Phaedre,* one of her favorite roles. Leaving the Comédie Française in 1880, she toured widely in Europe and came to the United States six times. She managed the Théâtre de la Renaissance for a period and then bought the Théâtre des Nations, renaming it Théâtre Sarah Bernhardt, and continued to perform even after the amputation of her right leg. A writer, sculptor, and painter as well as noted actress, she was the author of books, plays, and the memoir *Ma Double Vie* (1907). "The incomparable Sarah" was made a Chevalier of the Legion of Honor in 1914. She died in 1923.

First Hollywood Superstar

MARY PICKFORD (born GLADYS MARY SMITH) began a screen career in 1909 as a $5-a-day extra and quickly came to the attention of D. W. Griffith, who turned her into a popular star. Her business acumen, combined with sharp advice from her mother, helped her to force her own salary even higher by refusing to be locked into a contract with any one studio. In 1916 she formed the Mary Pickford Film Corporation, and in 1919, with Griffith, Charlie Chaplin, and Douglas Fairbanks, who in 1920 became her second husband, she formed United Artists. By 1932 she had become one of the richest self-made women in America, with a fortune estimated as high as $50 million. In 1928–29, she won an Oscar for *Coquette* but is better remembered for such little-girl parts as those she played in *Rebecca of Sunnybrook Farm.* She made over two hundred silent films and four "talkies." For some years, Ms. Pickford, long divorced from Fairbanks and married to actor Charles "Buddy" Rogers, has lived in seclusion in the Hollywood she helped to make.

Longest Career

LILLIAN GISH, born in 1893, made her stage debut at the age of five while touring in repertory companies with her younger sister DOROTHY and their mother. The Gishes met MARY PICKFORD (above), who introduced them to D. W. Griffith. The sisters became part of the Griffith company and made their joint screen debut in *An Unseen Enemy* in 1912. By 1914 Lillian had made 20

2-reel films, and performed in the first 4-reeler, *Judith of Bethulia* (1913). She played the ill-fated female lead in *The Birth of a Nation* (1915) and a symbol of eternal motherhood in *Intolerance* (1916). After leaving Griffith in 1921, Lillian Gish had successful roles in *The White Sister* (1923, with Henry King), *La Boheme* (1926, King Vidor), *The Scarlet Letter* (1926, Victor Sjöström), *The Wind* (1928, Victor Sjöström). She directed one film, *Remodeling Her Husband,* starring her sister Dorothy, in 1920. After the talkie *One Romantic Night,* she retired to theater in 1930 but returned to cinema in the early '40s. Lillian Gish was nominated for an Oscar for Best Supporting Actress in *Duel in the Sun* (Vidor) in 1947 and in 1970 was awarded a Special Oscar "for superlative artistry and distinguished contribution to the progress of motion pictures." She had a role in the film *Follow Me, Boys* in 1966, sang and danced in the Broadway production *Musical Jubilee,* (1975), has appeared frequently for D. W. Griffith retrospectives, and in 1978 had a role in the Altman film *A Wedding.*

First Film Actress to Share a Kiss

MAY IRWIN became the first actress in a commercial film to share a kiss (with John Rice in *The Kiss,* 1896) and so provoke the first cries for screen censorship.

Versatile Australian Star

Australian-born JUDITH ANDERSON began her successful acting career in the United States in 1918. Highly acclaimed for her roles in contemporary drama on stage and in film, her most noted roles have been in *Mourning Becomes Electra, Macbeth,* and *Medea.* The second performing artist to be made Dame of the British Empire (the first was NELLIE MELBA, p. 618), in 1960, she toured in *Hamlet* at the age of 71. She made her screen debut in 1933 in *Blood Money*

and was nominated for Best Supporting Actress in *Rebecca* in 1940. Though she remains most associated with the stage, she has made outstanding appearances in *Kings Row* (1942), *Laura* (1944), *Cat on a Hot Tin Roof* (1958), and *A Man Called Horse* (1969).

Shaw's "Gorgeous Dark Lady"

KATHARINE CORNELL (1893–1974), the "gorgeous dark lady," as she was called by George Bernard Shaw, was one of America's outstanding theater actresses during the second quarter of this century. Following early successes in *Little Women* (1919, London), *A Bill of Divorcement* (1921, New York), and *The Green Hat* (1925), she became famous for her role as Elizabeth in *The Barretts of Wimpole Street,* and for *Candida. Romeo and Juliet,* another play included in her road troupe's regular repertory, won her the New York Drama League Award in 1935. She also received many other awards and several honorary doctorates, and appeared in a number of films, the first being *Stage Door Canteen* (1943).

Enigmatic Swede

Legendary star and one of the most enigmatic of all screen personalities, Swedish-born GRETA GARBO had made three films (Erik Petschler's *Peter the Tramp,* in 1922, Mauritz Stiller's *The Saga of Gösta Berling,* in 1924, and G. W. Pabst's *Joyless Street,* in 1925) before arriving in the United States to work for MGM. She was three times nominated for Academy Awards—for *Anna Christie* and *Romance* in 1930, seven years later for *Camille,* and in 1939 for *Ninotchka* —and was presented with a Special Oscar in 1954 "for her unforgettable screen performances." Forever associated with her line in *Grand Hotel* (1932), "I want to be alone," Ms. Garbo gave memorable performances in *A Woman of Affairs* (1929), in *Mata Hari* (1932), *Queen Christina* (1933), and *Anna Karenina* (1935). Her last film was *Two-Faced Woman* in 1941. Born GRETA LOVISA GUSTAFSSON in 1905 of Swedish "peasant stock," she left her apprenticeship in a barber shop to become one of the greatest of film personalities.

Most Oscared Performer

The only actress ever to receive three "Best Actress" Oscars—for *Morning Glory* (1933), *Guess Who's Coming to Dinner* (1967), and *The Lion in Winter* (1968)—KATHARINE HEPBURN also has received more nominations than any other performer. "KATE" was born in Hartford, Connecticut, made her stage debut in *The Czarina* in 1928 upon graduation from Bryn Mawr College, and by 1932 had established herself on Broadway as an Amazon Queen in *The Warrior's Husband* and signed a contract with RKO. Some of her famous roles were in *Bringing up Baby* (1938), *The Philadelphia Story* (1940, with James Stewart and Cary Grant), *Woman of the Year* (1942, with Spencer Tracy), *Adam's Rib* (1949, also with Tracy), and *The African Queen* (1951, with Humphrey Bogart). Her important stage roles have included Katherine in *The Taming of the Shrew*, Portia in *The Merchant of Venice*, Beatrice in *Much Ado About Nothing*, and Cleopatra in *Antony and Cleopatra*. She played Coco CHANEL (see "Women in Fashions and Home Furnishings," p. 240) in the musical *Coco*, and in 1976, at the age of 69, again starred on Broadway, in *A Matter of Gravity*.

First Actress to Win the Life Achievement Award

After almost 50 years in films, BETTE DAVIS "still glows like a star," as *American Film* put it on the occasion of her becoming the first woman to receive the American Film Institute's highest honor, the Life Achievement Award, in 1977. (Previous recipients had been John Ford, James Cagney, Orson Welles, and William Wyler). Ms. Davis, born in 1908 in Lowell, Massachusetts, made her stage debut in a Broadway show, *The Earth Between*, in 1929, followed by her screen debut in 1931 in *Bad Sister* with Universal. Several minor screen roles led to her signing a contract with Warner Brothers. In 1934 she established herself with *Of Human Bondage*, and was featured in *Bordertown* (1935), *Front Page Woman* (1935), and *Dangerous* (1935). The latter brought her an Oscar for Best Actress. Shortly after, a quarrel with Warners and ensuing legal battle became a *cause célèbre*, but when all was settled she returned in 1938 to appear in *Jezebel*, which brought her a second Oscar. Some of her best-known roles were in *Dark Victory* (1939, with George Brent), *Juarez* (1939, with Paul Muni), *Now, Voyager* (1942, with Paul Henreid), *All About Eve* (1950, with Gary Merrill), *The Virgin Queen* (1955, with Richard Todd), *What Ever Happened to Baby Jane?* (1962, with JOAN CRAWFORD), and *Hush . . . Hush, Sweet Charlotte* (1965, with OLIVIA DE HAVILLAND).

Seventy Years A Trouper

HELEN HAYES, born in 1900 in Washington, D.C., made her first stage appearance as Prince Charles in *The Royal Family* when she was five years old and subsequently performed in other child roles in *Little Lord Fauntleroy* and (as both leads) in *The Prince and the Pauper*. Since then she has played in innumerable films and stage productions. Her title role in *Victoria Regina* is remembered as one of her greatest theatrical triumphs; it brought her a Drama League of New York Award in 1936. She won the ANTOINETTE PERRY (Tony) for her performance in *Happy Birthday* in 1947. In 1958 she appeared in *A Touch of the Poet* in the Broadway theater bearing her name, and in 1961 made a world tour with *The Glass Menagerie, The Skin of Our Teeth*, and *The Miracle Worker*. Hollywood gave her an Oscar for her performance in *The Sin of Madelon Claudet* in 1932 and in 1970 the Academy Award for Best Supporting Actress for *Airport*. Other movies in which she has appeared include *Arrowsmith* (1931), *A Farewell to Arms* (1932), *Night Flight* (1934), *What Every Woman Knows* (1943), and many more recent ones. A frequent television performer as well, she won an Emmy in 1952.

A Second Career at Sixty

Long regarded as a brilliant stage performer, EDITH EVANS, born in 1888 in London, was 60 when she made her first screen appearance in 1948 in *The Queen of Spades*. Her theatrical career began in 1912, and she was greatly admired for her magnificent dramatic portrayals in plays by Shakespeare, Chekhov, and Shaw. Considered, with DAME SYBIL THORNDIKE, one of Britain's leading actresses, she was made a Dame Commander of the British Empire in 1946. Her late-life film career lasted for two decades, during which she was nominated for Oscars twice for her performances in *Tom Jones* (1963) and *The Whisperers* (1967); the latter brought her the New York Film Critics Circle Award for Best Actress. She also appeared in *The Importance of Being Earnest* (1951), *The Chalk Garden* (1964), *The Madwoman of Chaillot* (1969), and *David Copperfield* (1970). Dame Edith received a D.Litt. from London University and has been awarded additional honorary doctorates from Cambridge (1951) and Oxford (1954).

Tallulah

Alabamian TALLULAH BANKHEAD (1903–68), most noted for her stage roles in *The Little Foxes* and *The Skin of Our Teeth* (New York Critics Award), also acted in many other plays and appeared occasionally in films, including Cukor's *Tarnished Lady* (1931), Hitchcock's *Lifeboat* (1943), and Ernst Lubitsch's *Royal Scandal* (1945). Her distinctive, husky voice was well known on radio and for a time she had her own TV show. Her autobiography, *Tallulah*, was published in 1952.

Hollywood's Wise-Cracking "Statue of Libido"

MAE WEST made only about a dozen films in the 1930s and early 1940s, but they won her a devoted following. A singer, dancer, and playwright in the 1920s, she made her successful screen debut in 1932 playing opposite George Raft in *Night for Night*. Ms. West wrote her own material, filled with double entendres. Her 1970 comeback in *Myra Breckinridge* earned her the title of "world's oldest sex symbol." The woman with the hour-glass figure and insinuating voice appeared, with her screen make-up on, to have changed very little over the years since George Jean Nathan termed her the "Statue of Libido."

German Actress Who Won the U. S. Medal of Freedom

Spotted by Josef von Sternberg in the revue *Zwei Kravatten* in Berlin in 1929, MARLENE DIETRICH (born in 1901) was cast in his *Morocco* and the historic *Blue Angel* the following year. *The Blue Angel* was an enormous success when it was released in the United States in 1931, and the beautiful blonde with the legs that remained incomparable into her 70s became immensely popular. Fervently anti-Nazi, Ms. Dietrich refused Hitler's order to return to Germany during the war, and entertained Allied troops overseas. Among her many films are *Shanghai Express* (1932), *Desire* (1936, with Gary Cooper), produced by Ernst Lubitsch, *Destry Rides Again* (1939), René Clair's *The Flame of New Orleans* (1941), Alfred Hitchcock's *Stage Fright* (1950), Fritz Lang's *Rancho Notorious* (1952), Stanley Kramer's *Judgment at Nuremberg* (1961), and several others by Von Sternberg. From 1960 on she made world tours as a cabaret entertainer, always singing the wartime ballad "Lili Marlene" she had made her theme song, and visited Germany, where she was warmly greeted. In 1963 she narrated a feature documentary on Hitler, *The Black Fox*. She has been made a Chevalier of the Legion of Honor and decorated with the U. S. Medal of Freedom.

Another Triple Academy-Award Winner

INGRID BERGMAN, born in 1915, in 1939 left her native Sweden where she had begun her film career. David Selznick, who had been impressed by her performance in *Intermezzo* (1936, Molander), cast her in a remake, *Intermezzo: A Love Story,* with Leslie Howard in 1939. With that she became an overnight star in America, and one successful picture followed another: *Casablanca* (1942, nominated for one of the 10 all-time best American films in 1977), *For Whom the Bell Tolls* (1943), and *Gaslight* (1944, with Charles Boyer). The latter won Ingrid Bergman her first Academy Award for Best Actress. Her performance in Hitchcock's *Spellbound* won her the New York Film Critics Award for Best Actress in 1945. She starred in numerous films, including *Stromboli* (1950) and *Europa* (1951), directed by Roberto Rossellini; their open romance while she was still married to her first husband caused an international scandal, and for some time she stayed away from Hollywood. On her return, however, she won an Oscar and the New York Film Critics Award for Best Actress in *Anastasia*. In 1975 she came close if not quite equal to KATHARINE HEPBURN (p. 657), by being named Best Supporting Actress for *Murder on the Orient Express* in the Academy Awards.

Britain's Famed Sister Thespians

Sisters LYNN and VANESSA REDGRAVE, talented daughters of the distinguished British stage and screen actor Sir Michael Redgrave, have had impressive acting careers. Lynn, born in 1943 in London, is best known for her screen performance in *Georgy Girl* (1966), for which she won the New York Film Critics Best Actress Award; since then she has appeared in many other films and on Broadway and in the West End in *My Fat Friend* (1974). Her elder sister Vanessa, born 1937, the more publicized of the two, made her stage debut with her father in *A Touch of the Sun* in 1958 in London, and alternated between roles on stage—notably in *The Prime of Miss Jean Brodie* and *Threepenny Opera*—and on screen. Her first successful film, *Morgan* (1966), was followed by *Blow-Up* (1967), *The Charge of the Light Brigade* and *The Seagull* (both 1968), *Oh! What a Lovely War* (1969), *The Devils* (1971), and *Mary, Queen of Scots* (1971). She won the Oscar for "Best Supporting Actress" for her role in *Julia* (1977), with JANE FONDA (p. 654).

Co-Founder of Théâtre de France

French actress MADELEINE RENAUD, born in 1900, and her husband Jean-Louis Barrault in 1946 founded their own company, Théâtre de France, and produced a wide repertory of plays by Claudel, Molière, Chekhov, Giradoux, and Beckett. They formed a new company in 1968, performing frequently at Théâtre Recamier, and later opened a new theater on the Quai d'Orsay. Madeleine Renaud began her acting career at the Comédie Française in 1923 as Agnes in *L'École des Femmes*. She continued to play classical roles in Molière, Marivaux, Musset, and Shakespeare. She has also appeared in numerous films, receiving Le Grand Prix du Cine in 1934 for *Maria Chapdelaine*. In 1965 she was awarded the rosette of the Chevalier of the Legion of Honor and in 1971 she was the recipient of the Drama Desk Award in the United States for her performance in the stage production of *L'Amante Anglaise*.

Tennessee Williams Wrote *The Rose Tattoo* **for Her**

ANNA MAGNANI (1908–73) had appeared in films for 10 years before her tour de force in Rossellini's *Open City* made her an international star in 1945. Her American debut in *The Rose Tattoo* (1955) in a role written especially for her by Tennessee Williams (she had originally declined to play the part on stage) won her an Oscar in 1955. Two years later she was nominated in the same category for her role in *Wild Is the Wind.* Other films include *Bellissima* (1951, Visconti), *The Golden Coach* (1953, Jean Renoir), *Mamma Roma* (1962, Pier Paolo Pasolini), and *The Secret of Santa Vittoria* (1969, Stanley Kramer). During the 1970s she appeared on an Italian television series with Marcello Mastroianni.

French Actress/Director

"Belle-laide" French actress JEANNE MOREAU, who has worked with a flotilla of first-rank directors—Antonioni, Buñuel, Truffaut, Welles, Renoir, Kazan, Losey, Malle, Brook, Duras, and others —directed her own first screenplay, *Lumière,* at the age of 47 in 1975. Jeanne Moreau, born to an English mother and French restaurateur father, began her career in Paris in 1948, much against her father's wishes and advice. Determined to act, she took her first role at the Comédie Française. By the age of 20 she had made more than 50 films, and in 1952 she joined the Théâtre Populaire, where she co-starred with Gérard Philipe and the company founder Jean Vilar. But not until 1957, with Louis Malle's *Ascenceur Pour l'Echafaud,* did she win fame. Some of her films since then have been *La Notte* (1961, Antonioni), *Jules et Jim* (1962, Truffaut), *La Baie des Anges* (1962, Jacques Demy), *Chère Louise* (1972, Philippe de Broca), and *Mr. Klein* (1977, Alain Delon). Throughout her film career Ms. Moreau has also remained active on the stage and is regarded as one of France's most compelling present-day actresses.

From the Greeks

One of Greece's leading stage and screen stars, IRENE PAPAS began her career in variety shows at 16. She made her screen debut in Greece in 1951 with *Necripolitia* and has appeared in numerous Italian productions. She has been internationally acclaimed for her performances in *The Dead City* (1952), *Tribute to a Bad Man* (1955), *The Guns of Navarone* (1961), *Anne of the Thousand Days* (1970), and the Cacoyannis Euripidean trilogy *Electra* (1962), *The Trojan Women* (1971), and *Iphigenia* (1977), which was distinguished both by her portrayal of Clytemnestra and the first screen appearance of radiant young actress TATIANA PAPAMOUSKOU as Iphigenia. An outspoken Greek patriot like her cohort MELINA MERCOURI (see "Women Activists, Heroes, and Humanitarians, p. 732), she has lived much in exile from her native Greece.

She Set the Pattern for Television Comedy

One of the most energetic, resourceful, and beloved of all American actresses on film and television, LUCILLE BALL (born in 1911) has probably been seen by more world moviegoers and TV watchers than any other performer. (Her old TV shows still run regularly abroad.) Ms. Ball appeared in dozens of B movies and made notable appearances in *The Big Street* (with Henry Fonda, 1942), *Without Love* (1945), *Dubarry Was a Lady* (with Red Skelton, 1943) and *Easy to Wed* (with Keenan Wynn, 1946), before she turned to television in 1951, costarring with her husband Desi Arnaz in "I Love Lucy." The long-lasting, sensationally popular show outlived their marriage both in reruns and as the renamed series, "The Lucy Show" and "Here's Lucy" when she bought out Arnaz after their divorce. More recently, she has made successful film appearances in *Yours, Mine, and*

Ours (1968, with Henry Fonda) and *Mame* (1974). An astute businesswoman as well as a popular entertainer, Ms. Ball was executive president and major stockholder of Desilu, which she sold to Gulf and Western for $17 million. Her value to the TV industry cannot be measured in dollars. As the pioneer performer in the new genre of "sitcoms," she set the pattern for numerous comediennes to follow, including MARY TYLER MOORE, CAROL BURNETT, JEAN STAPLETON, DIAHANN CARROLL, and others.

Political-Minded Hollywood/TV Star

SHIRLEY MACLAINE, who rose to stardom from a chorus line on Broadway, today is active in Democratic politics and the women's movement, the author at 43 of three books, including *You Can Get There from Here* (1975), a description of her trip to the People's Republic of China, and co-director and narrator of a documentary film based on that tour. A four-time Oscar nominee, she also has had her own television series, "Shirley's World." Her films include *The Trouble with Harry* (1956, Alfred Hitchcock), *The Apartment* (1960, Billy Wilder), *Irma la Douce* (1963, Wilder), *Woman Times Seven* (1967, Vittorio de Sica), *Sweet Charity* (1968, Bob Fosse), *The Possession of Joel Delaney* (1971, Hussein), and *The Turning Point* (1977, Herbert Ross), in which she costarred with ANNE BANCROFT.

Antiwar Activist/Actress

In films since 1960, JANE FONDA, daughter of the famous actor Henry Fonda and sister of actor Peter, was nominated for Best Actress in *They Shoot Horses, Don't They* (1969, Sydney Pollack), and won the Oscar for *Klute* (1971). Married to Roger Vadim in 1965, she later divorced him and married antiwar activist Tom Hayden. Herself an outspoken opponent of U.S. involvement in the Vietnam War, she directed and narrated *Introduction to the Enemy*, a documentary account of her visit to Hanoi, in which she attempted to show the North Vietnamese as people, not as the enemy. Also active in the women's movement, she has increasingly combined her convictions with her professional life. Her films include *La Ronde* (1964), *Cat Ballou* (1965), *Barefoot in the Park* (1967), *Barbarella* (1968, Vadim), *Tout Va Bien* (1972, Jean-Luc Godard), *A Doll's House* (1973), *Steelyard Blues* (1973), *Julia* (1977), and *Coming Home*, a Vietnam film (1978). She has been the subject of two documentaries, *Letter to Jane* (1972, Godard and Jean-Pierre Gorin) and *Jane* (1973, MADGE MACKENZIE, for TV). In 1974 she directed a documentary, *Vietnam Journey*, with Haskell Wexler and her husband Tom Hayden.

Award-Winning Norwegian-Born Star

Since her appearance in Ingmar Bergman's *Persona* with BIBI ANDERSSON in 1966, LIV ULLMANN, born in 1939 in Norway, has become an internationally known film star. She continued to appear regularly in Bergman-directed films, won the New York Film Critics Award for *Cries and Whispers* (1973), was nominated for Best Actress for her role in the Swedish production *The Emigrants* (1972, Jan Troell), and won a Hollywood Press Association's Golden Globe. Other films include *The New Land* (1973, sequel to *The Emigrants*), *Scenes from a Marriage* (1974), and *Face to Face* (1975), which won her the Los Angeles Film Critics Award (1976), the New York Film Critics Award (1977), and the National Board of Review of Modern Pictures Award (1977). Also a noted stage actress, she has played in *A Doll's House* (1975, nominated for a Tony), and other productions. Her autobiography, *Changing*, was published to critical acclaim in 1976.

Specialist in Strong Women

British actress GLENDA JACKSON, born in 1938, began her career in amateur theater productions, studied at the Royal Academy in London, and joined the

Royal Shakespeare Company in 1964. She was chosen by director Peter Brook to portray Charlotte Corday in the play *Marat/Sade*. Its success led to a screen version in 1967, and she has since been associated with the image of the strong, independent woman. Her numerous prizes include the New York Film Critics Award and the Academy Award for Best Actress for *Women in Love* in 1969 (Ken Russell), the British Film Academy's Best Actress Award for *Sunday, Bloody Sunday*, a second Oscar for Best Actress in *A Touch of Class*, and two Emmys for her television performance as Queen Elizabeth I. She has also appeared in *The Music Lovers* (1970), *Mary, Queen of Scots* (1972), *The Nelson Affair* (1973), *The Romantic Englishwoman* (1975), *Nasty Habits* (1976), and *House Calls* (1978).

Award-Winning Black Stage/Film/TV Star

Born in 1933 in New York City and raised in East Harlem, CICELY TYSON was a noted Broadway and television actress before winning an Oscar nomination and the National Society of Film Critics Best Actress Award for her screen performance in *Sounder* in 1972. She won her first Vernon Rice Award in 1962 for her performances in the original off-Broadway production of Genet's *The Blacks* and *Moon on a Rainbow Shawl*. Her major television successes include *East Side, West Side* (1963), and *The Autobiography of Miss Jane Pittman* (1974), which was voted Best Drama Special and won Ms. Tyson the Best Actress of the Year Award for a television special. She has made appearances on numerous other TV programs, was instrumental in establishing the Dance Theatre of Harlem, and is a trustee of the American Film Institute and the Human Family Institute, and a member of the board of Urban Gateways, an organization that introduces children to the arts. Ms. Tyson holds honorary doctorates from Atlanta, Loyola, and Lincoln universities and is the recipient of additional awards from the NAACP and the National Council of Negro Women.

Winner of the Cracked Belle Award

LILY TOMLIN, writer-comedienne whose witty repertoire includes the precocious five-year-old Edith Ann, The Tasteful Lady, Fast Talker, and Suzie Sorority, in 1970 was given the Cracked Belle Award and made an honorary member of California's union of telephone operators for Ernestine the switchboard girl. A TV favorite, she appeared on "The Gary Moore Show," Dan Rowan's and Dick Martin's "Laugh-In" (with GOLDIE HAWN), and has appeared on her own specials as well. A strong feminist, Lily Tomlin once walked off "The Dick Cavett Show" because a fellow guest responding to a question about the pets he owned, answered, "I have three horses, three dogs, and a wife." Even earlier, on "Laugh-In," she refused to do jokes that smacked of sexism or racism. Her sensitive portrayal of a white gospel singer in the popular film *Nashville* (1975) earned her an Academy Award nomination. "I never do a character who doesn't like herself," she says. Ms. Tomlin, born in Detroit, studied biology at Wayne State University, where she made her debut in a college variety show. Her recording *This Is a Recording* (1971) won the best comedy album of the year awards of *Cashbox* and *Record World* magazines and the Grammy Award from the National Academy of Recording Arts and Sciences. Her other recordings include "And That's the Truth" and "Modern Scream." She co-starred with Art Carney in *The Late Show* (1976) and has been signed by Universal Pictures to write, produce, and star in two films within the next three years.

Most Discovered Star

Although she was discovered by Kurt Weill-Bertolt Brecht fans off-Broadway in 1954 when she played Lucy in *The*

Threepenny Opera, discovered again by James Joyce fans in 1958 when she welcomed Zero Mostel off-Broadway as the brothel keeper in *Ulysses in Nighttown,* and discovered again when she was awarded a Tony for her performance in *Mame,* BEATRICE ARTHUR never really found fame until she emerged in "Maude" on television. With that role, she arrived in the high Nielsen league.

Polymorph of the Theater

During a long lifetime in the theater, RACHEL CROTHERS, born in 1878 in Illinois to a mother and father who were both doctors, moved from bit player to star, and then from playwright, manager, and producer to philanthropist. Her plays including *He and She* (1911) and *As Husbands Go* (1931) were early feminist statements. Her last play, *Susan and God,* was produced in 1937. Rachel Crothers sponsored many famous actors and actresses and was largely responsible for the stardom of such women as MAXINE ELLIOTT, KATHARINE CORNELL (p. 656) and GERTRUDE LAWRENCE. She remained a vital force in the theater until her death in 1958.

The Woman Behind *Girl Friends*

CLAUDIA WEILL, producer-director of the widely acclaimed feature film *Girl Friends,* written by VICKI POLON, spent three years working on her 1978 success, which was snapped up for world distribution by Warner Brothers. Actual shooting took only six and a half weeks; most of Ms. Weill's time and energy went to raising funds for her independent venture. A 1969 graduate of Radcliffe College who has studied painting in Europe and still photography with Walker Evans at Yale, Claudia Weill, at 31, has behind her several years of experience working on documentary film. *The Other Half of the Sky; A China Memoir,* her 1975 chronicle of the first women's delegation to China, led by SHIRLEY MACLAINE (p. 661), was nominated for an Academy Award. Ms. Weill is under contract to Warner Brothers for two feature productions. She says that she feels "no pressure to stick with women's films . . . Feminism is a point of view you can use on any subject, even a big entertainment film."

Film's "New Woman"

Reporting to the *New York Times* of May 29, 1977, JANE WILSON, a freelance film writer, began her article entitled "Hollywood and the New Woman" with this anecdote about a vice-president for production at one of the major movie studios, who, "speaking slowly and with careful precision," said: "It has emerged in a general way that there is now a marked preference for movies about relationships between people, you can't just have men. Women are people too."

"From such small perceptions, large production schedules grow," Ms. Wilson observed. Twentieth Century-Fox at the time she wrote had Robert Altman's *Three Women* with SHELLEY DUVALL and SISSY SPACEK ready for release, and its upcoming roster included *Julia,* starring JANE FONDA and VANESSA REDGRAVE (pp. 661 and 659), *The Turning Point,* with ANNE BANCROFT and SHIRLEY MACLAINE (p. 661), and SUSAN SARANDON, and JILL CLAYBURGH in the title role of *An Unmarried Woman.*

Ms. Wilson went on to express her dissatisfaction with these films, and with recent TV shows about "liberated women," noting that they "deal with topics which have been heavily worked over by feminists and women in general for some years now." She saw hope, however, that as women become more involved in the writing and directing of movies and television, "we may perhaps expect . . . a greater variety of themes . . . Several new women directors are expected to emerge within the next year, including the Oscar-winning actress LEE GRANT. Ms. Grant got off to a promising directorial start with a tiny grant from the American Film Institute. With her husband, Joseph Feury, serving as producer, she used this grant to partially finance a highly original half-hour movie of Strindberg's enigmatic play *The Stronger*. Now she has been able to arrange private financial backing to make two more movie adaptations of shorter Strindberg plays, and she is developing . . . an adaptation of *The Last Fling* by J. J. Doherty, in which she will direct GOLDIE HAWN."

When Ms. Grant first set out to sell this movie idea about "the first big love relationship in a woman's life" to a group of male studio executives, she was prepared to explain and justify her proposal every inch of the way. "But something astonishing happened," she reports. "As I was talking, I realized that I was surrounded by nodding, assenting heads. They were agreeing with everything I said! They understood!"

Will such enlightenment last? The proof, ultimately, depends on the profit. In the meantime, says Lee Grant, "We must just take our best shot at it. Win, lose, or draw—it's high time this happened!"

OFF-STAGE AND OFF-CAMERA: PRODUCERS, DIRECTORS, WRITERS, AND A CURATOR

Co-Founder and Director of the Group Theatre, Co-Founder of Actors Studio, and Director of ANTA

Broadway producer of musicals *Porgy and Bess, Brigadoon, Paint Your Wagon,* and *One Touch of Venus,* CHERYL CRAWFORD also brought Tennessee Williams' classics, including *Sweet Bird of Youth* and *The Rose Tattoo* (ANTOINETTE PERRY Award, 1951) to the American stage. Born in Akron, Ohio, in 1901, she was in the Theatre Guild in the 1920s, co-founded Group Theatre with Lee Strasberg and Harold Clurman in 1930, and was its director until 1937. Also the founder of the Actors Studio with Elia Kazan and Robert Lewis, the American Repertory Company with EVA LE GALLIENNE and MARGARET WEBSTER in the '40s, and director of the American National Theatre and Academy, she sent many actors and actresses on their way to stardom. Ms. Crawford in 1962 received an honorary doctorate from Smith, her alma mater, and in 1964 was awarded the Brandeis University Achievement Medal. Her autobiography, *One Naked Individual,* was published in 1977.

Broadway's Most Successful Female Angel

Wealthy, Spanish-born Broadway theater producer ADELA HOLZER has backed more than a dozen Broadway shows. Not all have been successful, but *Sherlock Holmes* was, *Sleuth* was, and *Hair* returned nearly $2.5 million on her $57,000 1967 investment. Ms. Holzer, wife of New York shipping executive Peter Holzer, says that the theater "makes her Spanish temperament" come out, but it is by no means the sole source of her wealth. She arrived "nearly penniless" in New York in 1954, but with a business sense acquired as a child in Madrid watching and being instructed by her father, an industrialist. She soon began to build a fortune in real estate, automobiles, farm machinery, commodities, and import-export operations, while also pursuing a doctoral degree in literature at Columbia. Divorced once and widowed once, Ms. Holzer, now in her forties, has involved many acquaintances in her deals, theatrical and otherwise.

Producer/Director/Co-Founder of Arena Stage

In the late 1950s ZELDA FICHANDLER, co-founder with Edward Manguin of the

Arena Stage in Washington, D.C., started planning for the first American theater in many decades to be constructed on a new site. The result was the three-stage theater complex designed by architect Harry Weese on the Potomac channel, completed in 1975. Comprising a theater-in-the-round holding 800 people, a smaller endstage theater holding 500 people, and an intimate cabaret theater holding less than 200 people, the new complex meets differing dramatic needs. Arena Stage and Ms. Fichandler have many distinctions. The company was the first to tour with an American repertory in the Soviet Union; its 1974 premiere of *The Madness of God* was selected for the PBS "Theatre in America" series; and in 1976 it became the first theater company outside of New York to receive the ANTOINETTE PERRY (Tony) Award. American plays premiered at the Arena include *The Great White Hope, Indians, Moonchildren, Pueblo, The Madness of God*, among others, and European playwrights Brecht, Frisch, Ionesco, Grass, Orkeny, and leading Soviet writers have had American premieres of their works at the Arena Stage. On several occasions Ms. Fichandler has also given plays that have failed commercially in New York a "second chance." In addition to her work as producer-director of the Arena Stage, Ms. Fichandler is professor of theater at Boston University, founding member of the American Arts Alliance, delegate to the International Theatre Institute Conference in Moscow in 1973, and frequently appears on nationwide panels. Her personal honors, in addition to those given the company, include the Margo Jones Award (1971), the National Theatre Conference Award (1971), Washingtonian of the Year Award (1972), Brandeis University Creative Arts Award (1974), and the Dickinson College Arts Award (1976). A Phi Beta Kappa graduate in Russian literature from Cornell, Ms. Fichandler earned her M.A. in theater arts at George Washington University and holds honorary doctorates from George Washington, Smith, Georgetown, and Hood College.

Founder of Living Theater

With her husband Julian Beck, JUDITH MALINA launched the revolutionary Living Theater in 1947 and has presented plays all over the world as well as in the living room of her Manhattan apartment. The avant-garde Living Theater introduced such pioneering works as *The Connection* (1959), *In the Jungle of Cities* (1960), *The Brig* (1964), and *Paradise Now* (1968). The troupe, which has collected prizes the world over, made headlines in 1971 when it was jailed in Brazil. Judith Malina, the daughter of a rabbi and an actress, was born in 1926 in Kiel, Germany.

"The Earth Mother"

Founder of La Mama Experimental Theatre Club, ELLEN STEWART, or "the Earth Mother," as she is called by members of her company, started out on New York's Lower East Side in a basement apartment/dress boutique turned cafe theater by night. The original Cafe La Mama, whose stage was the "size of a single bed," was big enough for an audience of 25. *In the Corner of the Morning*, by Michael Locasio, was the first play produced, and Harold Pinter's work was performed for the first time on a New York stage at Cafe La Mama. Due to zoning ordinances, the company was forced to move two times and to be transformed into a nonprofit operation, La Mama Experimental Theatre Club. Ellen Stewart staged more than 200 new plays during the group's first four years, very likely a world record. To broaden the audience and encourage the publication of new playwrights, she took her troupe to Europe. In 1969 Jerzy Grotowski and his Polish Laboratory Theater appeared for the first time in the United States under Mama's sponsorship.

First Woman Film Director

A one-minute film, *La Fée aux Choux* (The Good Fairy in the Cabbage Patch) was, its director ALICE GUY BLACHÉ believed, the first narrative film. (Film historians also credit this record to Georges Méliès and Edwin S. Porter.) Ms. Blaché made it in 1896 while working as Léon Gaumont's secretary. The first woman director and one of the true pioneers of cinema, according to most sources, she directed all films produced by Gaumont until 1905. Alice Blaché was born in 1875 in France and moved to the United States in 1910. Founder and director of the Solax Company on Long Island (later in New Jersey), she supervised more than 300 films starring MAGDA FOY, BLANCHE CORNWALL, Darwin Karr, Vince Burns, MARIAN SWAYNE, CLAIRE WHITNEY, Billy Quirk, Lee Beggs, and Fraunce Fraunholz. Though all of her major Solax Productions have been lost, a half-dozen one-reel films are preserved at the Library of Congress National Film Collection: *Greater Love Hath No Man* (1911), *The Detective's Dog* (1912), *Canned Harmony* (1912), *The Girl in the Armchair* (1912), *A House Divided* (1913), *Matrimony's Speed Limit* (1913). After Solax folded, she directed OLGA PETROVA in her first two films, *The Tigress* (1914) and *The Heart of a Painted Woman* (1915). Ms. Blaché also taught film for a brief period at Columbia University and wrote numerous articles for periodicals. In 1953 she was made a member of the Legion of Honor. She died in 1968.

First American Woman to Direct Films

The first American woman to direct films, elected mayor of Hollywood's Universal City in 1913, and one of the most significant directors of the silent era, LOIS WEBER believed in creating social change through film. Dealing with controversial subjects, she wrote, directed, produced, and appeared in a number of films on marital problems (*What Do Men Want?*, 1921), racial problems (*The Jew's Christmas*, 1913), birth control and abortion (*Where Are My Children?*, 1916), capital punishment (*The People vs. John Doe*, 1916), and prostitution (*Angel of Broadway*, 1927). She also co-starred in many of her films with her husband and co-director, Phillips Smalley. Her last film, *White Heat*, appeared in 1934, five years before her death. An early one, *The Dumb Girl of Portici* (1916), starred ANNA PAVLOVA (p. 639) in her only film.

Winner of Special Academy Award for 62 Years of Film Editing

Many women have been prominent film editors in Hollywood, but the career of MARGARET BOOTH is particularly impressive. She began working with D. W. Griffith in 1919 and then joined Louis B. Mayer at MGM in 1924. In 1937 she became supervising editor of all MGM films produced in U.S. studios as well as in Europe where the company was involved, and remained with MGM until 1968, when she began working on the productions of Ray Shark. In her impressive career of over 55 years, Margaret Booth edited uncounted numbers of films. Notable were *The Bridge of San Luis Rey* (1929), *Bombshell* (1933), *Mutiny on the Bounty* (1935), *Camille* (1936), *The Owl and the Pussycat* (1970). In 1978 she won an honorary Academy Award "for 62 years of especially distinguished service to the motion picture industry as a whole as a film editor."

Avant-Garde French Filmmaker

Associated with the post-World War I avant-garde, GERMAINE DULAC (1882–1942) was part of a radical film group that included Louis Delluc, Abel Gance, Marcel L'Herbier, and others. The best known of her films are *La Fête Espagnole* (1919, script by Louis Delluc) and

La Coquille et le Clergyman (1927, script by Antonin Artaud). Also a journalist and critical essayist of films, she made film newsreels, for Pathé, France Actualités-Gaumont, and Le Cinéma au Service de L'Histoire from 1930 to 1940.

First Compilation Filmmaker

Director of editing of the Soviet Cinema Archive, ESTHER SHUB was one of the early creators of compilation film. By cutting and editing newsreels, she inaugurated a whole new style of montage, and preserved much of early 20th-century Russia on film. In 1927 she wrote and edited *Padenie dinasti Romanovikh,* using footage of the Tsar, covering the years 1912–17 for the anniversary of the February revolution. She also wrote and edited *Velikii Put* to commemorate the October revolution; this provided an invaluable source for her colleague Sergei Eisenstein in the making of his chef d'oeuvre, *October.* She collaborated with Pudovkin on the short film *The Face of the Enemy* in 1941.

First Woman Director of Hollywood Talkies

Her reputation already established during the silent era with *Fashions for Women* (1927), *Ten Modern Commandments* (1927), and *Get Your Man* (1927), DOROTHY ARZNER, born 1900 in California, was one of the major directors of cinema during the transition to sound. In 1929 she directed *Wild Party,* Paramount's first sound film, and she was reportedly the first to conceive the idea of an overhead microphone, dangling it from a fishing pole. Some of her 14 sound films include *Merrily We Go to Hell* (1923), *Christopher Strong* (1933), *Nana* (1934), *The Bride Wore Red* (1937, with JOAN CRAWFORD), *First Comes Courage* (1943, with MERLE OBERON). In early 1975 the Directors Guild of America organized "A Tribute to Dorothy Arzner" in Los Angeles, where Ms. Arzner teaches at UCLA and works on TV commercials.

Twice Winner of Venice Biennale Gold Medals

LENI RIEFENSTAHL, whose reputation was tainted as a Nazi propagandist by *Triumph of the Will,* a film commemorating the Nazi Party Rally in Nürnberg in 1934, achieved world recognition and Venice Biennale gold medals for *The Blue Light* (1932) and *Olympiad* (1938)—the latter a record of the Olympic games of 1936, generally considered a masterpiece. She was cleared of charges of Nazi complicity in 1952, but her role prior to World War II continues to stir controversy. Intrigued by primitive peoples following a visit to Africa in 1956, she was the first white woman to be granted permission by the Sudanese Government to visit the Nuba mountains in Sudan. Her pictorial study of an isolated tribe entitled *The Last of the Nuba,* though praised for its artistic merit and contribution to the field of anthropology, also brought her new criticism for its treatment of people not as human beings but as objects.

First Woman to Receive Guggenheim for Creative Work in Film

A major exponent of experimental film in the post-World War II era and one of the founders of Creative Film Foundation, which encouraged the production of avant-garde films, MAYA DEREN was also among the first directors to distribute her own films. Ms. Deren, who published numerous articles and lectured on campuses across the country, was the first woman to receive a Guggenheim Fellowship for creative work in film and also was awarded a prize at Cannes. Some of her films include *Meshes of the Afternoon* (1943), *At Land* (1944), *Choreography for Camera* (1945), *Ritual in Transfigured Time* (1946), *Meditation on Violence* (1948), and *The Very Eye of Night* (1959). She died in 1961 before her 40th birthday.

From Gangster's Moll to Filmmaker

Prominent during the 1940s in gangster movies, IDA LUPINO turned to directing and producing in 1949. She founded Emerald Productions with her husband, Collier Young, and wrote, directed, produced, and sometimes appeared in a number of films. The first, *Not Wanted*, was followed by others including *Outrage* (1950), *Hard, Fast, and Beautiful* (1951), *Lose and Beware, My Lovely* (1951), *The Bigamist* (1953), and *The Hitchhiker* (1953). Several years working in television followed, until in 1966 she directed *The Trouble with Angels*, starring HAYLEY MILLS, ROSALIND RUSSELL, and GYPSY ROSE LEE.

She Inspired the "New Wave"

AGNÈS VARDA, born in 1928 in Belgium, and raised in southern France, believed when she made her first film that a director should have the same freedoms as a novelist. *La Point Courte*, completed in 1954, was revolutionary for its time. It was not a box office success, but it is regarded as a landmark in film history. Her technique, which counterpointed themes and allowed the viewer to draw his own conclusions, inspired Alain Resnais and other "Nouvelle Vague" ("New Wave") filmmakers. For seven years after *La Pointe Courte* Varda experimented with cinema and produced three prize-winning shorts—one, *Cleo from Five to Seven*, a minute-by-minute study of a dying pop singer awaiting the results of medical tests. *Salut les Cubains* won praise in both France and Cuba, as well as the Bronze Lion award at the 1964 Venice Film Festival. *Le Bonheur* was another success and brought her backing for shorts on the Vietnam War and on the Black Panthers. Unlike her husband, Jacques Demy, who has created such apolitical films as *The Umbrellas of Cherbourg* and *Lola*, Agnès Varda always explores political, social, and intellectual problems. Her latest film, *One Who Sings, the Other Doesn't*, is about women in contemporary society, and she has been working most recently with a film about a family whose life is divided between France and the United States.

Anti-Novelist and Film Director

Novelist (or anti-novelist) and film director MARGUERITE DURAS, born 1914 in Indo-China, lived there to the age of 17. She first became involved in film when she wrote the original script for Alain Resnais' 1959 *Hiroshima, Mon Amour*, backing Resnais' visual imagery with intense dialogue. It received the International Critics Prize at the Cannes Film Festival and the New York Film Critics Award in 1960. In 1960 she collaborated with Gérard Jalot to adapt her novel *Moderato Cantabile* for a film by Peter Brook, and wrote the script of *Une Aussi Longue Absence*, which won her the 1961 Palme d'Or prize at Cannes. She also worked on Jean Chapot's *La Voleuse*, for which she wrote the scenario, and Paul Seban's *La Musica*. In 1969 she wrote the novel and directed the film *Detruire dit-elle*, about the May 1968 student riots in Paris. In her 1972 film, *Nathalie Granger*, essentially nothing happens; instead, the camera slowly penetrates the empty afternoon moments of two women by "staring" at them and focusing on objects. In *The Truck* (1977) she appears with Gerard Depardieu, reading a script of a film in which a woman hitches a ride with a truck driver who is Depardieu—a film within a film.

Leading Czech New Wave Film Director

VERA CHYTILOVA, born in 1929, leading exponent of the Czech New Wave, directed several short films while studying at the Prague Film School: *Villa in the Suburbs* (1959), *Mr. K—Green Street* (1960), and *The Ceiling* (1961). She was awarded a bronze medal at Venice for her documentary *A Bagful of Fleas* (1962). She directed one of the six Czech New Wave films, *Pearls of the Deep,* and has done others including *Sedmikrasky (Daisies,* a feature, 1966), and *Fruit of Paradise* (1969).

Woman of "Boiling Blood"

ARCANGELA FELICE ASSUNTA WERTMULLER VON ELGG SPANOL VON BRAUCHICH-JOB, better known as LINA WERTMULLER, attributes her "boiling blood" (*Time,* February 16, 1976) to her great-great-grandfather, a Swiss baron who is said to have fled to Naples "after slaying a romantic rival in a duel." Her work is strongly marked by her hatred of Fascism and the political climate that dominated her childhood in Italy. Lina Wertmuller attended theater school, and upon graduation in 1951 joined a troupe of puppeteers. In 1962 she met Federico Fellini, who asked her to assist him on his film *8½.* So inspired was she by Fellini's style and his freedom in art that she decided to become a film director herself. Her first film, *The Lizards,* won her a prize at the Locarno Film Festival in 1963. Raising money to produce films was such a problem that she retreated briefly from cinema until she met Giancarlo Giannini, who has been credited by her husband (and publicity manager), sculptor Enrico Job, with relaunching her film career. The themes of machismo, political repression, and middle-class materialism run throughout *The Seduction of Mimi, Love and Anarchy, Swept Away,* and *Seven Beauties,* which followed one another in swift succession. Accused by the *New Yorker*'s PAULINE KAEL (see "Women in Communication," p. 477) for "turning suffering into vaudeville," she has been as vigorously acclaimed by other critics. Known for her white plastic glasses and rings on every finger, she resembles, she herself says, "a crazy gypsy." The 50-or-so-year-old Ms. Wertmuller (she does not admit her age) visited New York in 1978 for the release of *The End of the World in Our Usual Bed on a Night Full of Rain,* starring CANDICE BERGEN (see the Introduction, p. xi).

Underground Female Filmmaker

SHIRLEY CLARKE, born in 1925 in New York, studied dance with the MARTHA GRAHAM dancers (p. 647) directed her first feature, *The Connection,* in 1962, and founded the Film Makers Co-op with Jonas Mekas in New York the same year. By that time she had already made a great impact on the development of underground film in America with her short experimental *Dance in the Sun* (1953), *In Paris Parks* (1954), *Bullfight* (1955), and *Moment in Love* (1957), and as co-director of *Skyscraper* (1959), which won first prize at the Venice Film Festival and an Academy Award nomination. In 1960 she directed the feature *Cool World* and in 1964, at the request of John F. Kennedy and Stewart Udall, the documentary *Robert Frost . . . A Love Letter to the World.* Since her *Portrait of Jason* and *Man in the Polar Region* in 1967, Ms. Clarke has concentrated on video. She appeared in the AGNÈS VARDA (p. 668) film *Lions' Love,* in 1969.

Comedienne/Director

ELAINE MAY is the best known among women directors of Hollywood features, although STEPHANIE ROTHMAN has directed the most—six. Ms. May's feature films have been *A New Leaf* (1971), *The Heartbreak Kid* (1972), and *Mickey and Nicky* (1975). Her personal popularity is, however, based less on her directing than on her appearances on TV and records with Mike Nichols in hilarious comedy skits, which she has written.

Director/Producer of First Labor Film to Win an Oscar

BARBARA J. KOPPLE, director/producer of *Harlan County, U.S.A.,* won the first Oscar ever awarded to a feature-length documentary film about a labor dispute and became the third woman to win an Oscar for directing a documentary film at the Academy of Motion Picture Arts and Sciences 49th awards presentation in March 1977. Ms. Kopple began shooting the film, which was released in 1976, on August 1, 1972, and finished October 10, 1975. During much of that period she lived in the mining community with the miners, who were then engaged in a revolt of the United Mine Workers' rank and file against the administration of the union by W. A. "Tony" Boyle. Though the actual events shaped themselves to form a dramatic story line, the film's impact comes from the lives of people portrayed; Ms. Kopple has said about her work that she tries to let people speak, and tries to be true to what people think. Born in 1946 in New York City, she attended Morris Harvey College, in West Virginia, and Northeastern University. She has worked on more than 27 films, including the sound for *Hearts and Minds* (Peter Davis/Bert Schneider), which won an Oscar for best feature-length documentary for 1975.

From *Nashville* to Cripple Creek

JOAN TEWKESBURY, who wrote the script for Robert Altman's movie *Nashville,* is one of a new breed of star screenwriters. Also a playwright, she wrote *Cowboy Jack Street,* a turn-of-the-century Western with music "about a black man named Tom Dipple, who buys himself a white hope, a boxer who wants to be a cowboy," which ran off-Broadway in late 1977. Its scene was Cripple Creek, Colorado. Ms. Tewkesbury sees a definite connection between her work on film and on stage, although "on film you write to see rather than to hear," she says, and as she did with *Nashville,* she thoroughly explored Cripple Creek, going back into the city's history. Joan Tewkesbury began her career as a dancer and choreographer (she was MARY MARTIN's flying understudy in *Peter*

Pan), then got married and had two children. Gradually, she began returning to the theater, working as a director on location. When she saw *M*A*S*H,* she decided to switch to movies. With no film credentials, she asked Robert Altman for a job. He hired her as script girl on *McCabe and Mrs. Miller.* In 1976 in England, she directed a television documentary about ANNA FREUD (see "Women in Education, the Social Sciences, and Humanities," p. 413), is scheduled to direct the movie version of RITA MAE BROWN's novel, *Ruby Fruit Jungle,* and is looking forward to a triple career as director, screenwriter, and playwright. Now divorced, she lives in Los Angeles with artist Robert Irwin.

Britain's First Female Film Critic, Founder and First Curator of the MOMA Film Library

Founder, curator, and later director of the Museum of Modern Art (MOMA) Film Library (now Department), IRIS BARRY (1895–1969) was reputed to have seen more than 15,000 films in her lifetime. Ms. Barry, born in Birmingham, England, made a profession out of her obsession with the movies and became England's first female film critic, writing for several London newspapers between 1923 and 1930. She founded the London Film Society in 1925 with Lord Bernstein and Ivor Montagu and in 1930 came to the United States, where she and her husband, John Abbott, founded the Film Library at the Museum of Modern Art in New York, thanks to a Rockefeller Foundation Grant. She became its first curator in 1935, director in 1947, and after her retirement in 1950 remained its European representative while residing in the south of France. In 1938 she was a founding member of the International Federation of Film Archives, and held the honorary position of founder-president until her death. She was also an honorary adviser to the department of films and visual education at the United Nations.

America's Leading Woman Dramatist

Playwright and, more recently, autobiographer LILLIAN HELLMAN was immediately established as America's leading woman dramatist with the 1934 Broadway production of her first play *The Children's Hour*. This play, with its then controversial theme of homosexuality, was followed by *The Little Foxes,* a brilliant portrayal of moral decay and greed in the Old South at the turn of the century. It was performed in 1939 and received an Academy Award Nomination as a film in 1941—the year her anti-Nazi play *Watch on the Rhine* was produced and won her the New York Critics Drama Circle Award. The screen production of *Another Part of the Forest* was nominated for an Academy Award in 1946. Other plays written by Ms. Hellman are *The Searching Wind* (1944), *The Autumn Garden* (1951), and *Toys in the Attic* (1960). She is the author of three volumes of memoirs: *An Unfinished Woman* (1969), *Pentimento: A Book of Portraits* (1974), and *Scoundrel Time* (1977). A portion of *Pentimento* has been made into the film *Julia* (see pp. 654 and 663). In 1969 Ms. Hellman received the National Book Award in Arts and Letters and in 1974 was nominated for *Pentimento*. Educated at New York University and Columbia University, she holds honorary doctorates from Wheaton College, Douglass College of Rutgers University, Brandeis University, Smith, NYU, and Yale. She has taught at Yale and MIT.

First Black Playwright to Win New York Drama Critics Circle Award for First Play Written by a Black Woman to Appear on Broadway

LORRAINE HANSBERRY's 1959 drama, *A Raisin in the Sun* (the title was inspired by a phrase in Langston Hughes's poem, "Harlem"), the first play written by a black woman to be staged on Broadway, won her the first New York Drama Critics Circle Award presented to a black dramatist. *The Sign in Sydney Brustein's Window* was completed and produced shortly before her death of cancer, in 1965, at the age of 34. Ms. Hansberry, who was born in Chicago in 1930, was educated at the Art Institute of Chicago, the University of Wisconsin, and in Guadalajara, Mexico.

First Black Woman to Have Film Script Produced

Autobiographer (*I Know Why the Caged Bird Sings,* 1970, and *Gather Together in My Name,* 1974), playwright, and poet, as well as professional performer and songwriter, MAYA ANGELOU was born 1928 in St. Louis, Missouri, and raised in Arkansas. She won a scholarship to the California Labor School in San Francisco, where at 14 she was that city's first female streetcar fare collector. She studied dance with Pearl Primus in New York, became a night-club entertainer, and appeared in *Porgy and Bess* on a State Department-sponsored tour of 22 countries. She also appeared in off-Broadway plays and was northern coordinator of Martin Luther King's Christian Leadership Conference (1960–61). In 1961 she went to Egypt as editor of the English language news-weekly *Observer* and free-lanced for a while in Ghana. In addition to writing such special programs for television as "Blacks, Blues, Black" (10 one-hour 1968 programs), "Assignment America" (six half-hour programs, 1975), "The Legacy" and "The Inheritors" (two Afro-American specials, 1976), Ms. Angelou has written scripts for films and in 1972, with *Georgia, Georgia,* became the first American black woman to have a movie script produced. A member of the Board of Trustees of the American Film Institute since 1975, she also is a member of the Advisory Board of the Women's Prison Association. In 1970 she was nominated for the National Book Award for her autobiographical *Caged Bird* and in 1973 for the Tony Award for her performance in *Look*

Away. The recipient of a scholarship from Yale University in 1970 and a Rockefeller Foundation Scholarship in Italy in 1975, she has received honorary degrees from Smith, Mills, and Lawrence University, and is a member of the faculty of the Center for Advanced Film Studies at Greystone, California.

NOVELISTS, SHORT STORY WRITERS, POETS, AND CRITICS

She Published 45 Stories in Her First Year as a Writer

Pittsburgh-born author of mystery romances, MARY ROBERTS RINEHART published 45 stories in 1903, her first year of writing (necessitated by the loss of a personal fortune in the stock market). Encouraged by her initial success, she went on to write her first two mystery novels, *The Circular Staircase* (1908) and *The Man in Lower Ten* (1909). Her mysteries, though violent, and invariably involving multiple crimes, also contained humor and sentimental love. Her best-known characters, Miss Letitia Carberry (Tish) and Nurse Adams (Miss Pinkerton), reached a wide audience not only through her books but in dozens of films and dramatic productions based on the books—from *The Circular Staircase* (1915 film by Selig, 1953 TV) through *The Bat* (1920 and 1953 films; 1926 and 1930 plays, 1960 TV with HELEN HAYES [p. 657]). In 1958, a year after her death, the Mary Roberts Rinehart Foundation Award was set up in her memory to assist new and unestablished writers.

First Woman to Win Nobel Prize for Literature

SELMA LAGERLÖF was the first woman to receive the Nobel Prize in Literature, in 1909. She was awarded it for a series of novels and short stories, one of which was *Gösta Berling's Saga,* later made into a film with GRETA GARBO (p. 656). Many of her works were based on the legends and folklore of her native province of Värmland in west-central Sweden, and they made her Scandinavia's most popular author since Hans Christian Andersen well before she was chosen for the Nobel. Her strength lay in her colorful writing of folk tales and stories that appealed to adults as well as children; she was also the author of two state-commissioned children's books, *The Wonderful Adventure of Nils* and *Further Adventures of Nils* (1906–7), describing a boy's magical travels on the back of a goose. An early fellowship took her to Italy, and later she visited Egypt and Palestine. She received the Gold Medal of the Swedish Academy in 1904 and became its first woman director in 1914. Uppsala University awarded her an honorary doctorate. She died in 1940 at Mårbacka, her childhood home, which had been sold after her father's death and which she had bought back with Nobel Prize money.

First Woman Member of the Académie Goncourt

French novelist SIDONIE GABRIELLE COLETTE published her first four novels, *Claudine à l'École* (1900), *Claudine à Paris* (1901), *Claudine en Ménage* (1902), and *Claudine S'en Va* (1903), under the pseudonym of her first husband, Henri Gauthier-Villars, who signed his writing "Willy." In 1906, after their divorce, she became an entertainer in a music hall—the subject of later novels, *La Vagabonde* (1910), *L'Entrave* (1913), and *L'Envers du Music-Hall* (1913), done after she left the music hall and married Henri de Jouvenal. Her writing about nature, animals (especially cats), and her mother, considered her most sensitive and beautiful, includes *Dialogues de Bêtes* (1904), published under the name "Colette Willy," *La Paix Chez les Bêtes* (1916). *La Retraite Sentimentale* (1907), and *Les Vrilles de la*

Vigne (1908). Also highly acclaimed were her childhood reminiscences, *La Maison de Claudine* (1923), *La Naissance du Jour* (1928), *Sido* (1929), and *Mes Apprentissages* (1936). In 1916 she wrote a libretto for Ravel's *L'Enfant et les Sortilèges*. Colette was made a Chevalier of the Legion of Honor for her services as a nurse during World War I. Elected a member of the Académie Goncourt in 1945—the first woman so honored—in 1954 she also became the first woman ever to receive a state funeral in France (this despite her two marriages outside the church, her marriage to Henri de Jouvenal ending in divorce in 1924, followed by her marriage to Maurice Goudeket in 1935).

First Woman to Receive Two Pulitzer Prizes

EDITH WHARTON exploited her own background in late 19th-century New York society as a theme in several novels, which she wrote not in New York, but in Paris where she settled permanently in 1907. Her novels reveal the rigid conventionality and emptiness of that society and show her scorn for the social-climbing middle class. *Ethan Frome* (1911), perhaps her best-known work, also reveals her compassion for the lower classes, whose plight she conceived to be similar to that of artists, victimized by established conventions. Her novel *The Age of Innocence* (1920) won her a Pulitzer Prize, and in 1935 *The Old Maid* brought her a second Pulitzer Prize (for drama), making her the first woman to receive the coveted award twice. She was also the first woman to be awarded an honorary doctorate from Yale (1923) and she received the Cross of the Legion of Honor from the French Government for her energetic and devoted work during World War I. When she died in 1937 she was said to have been the recipient of more honors than any other American woman writer.

Norwegian Nobel Prize Writer

SIGRID UNDSET was the daughter of a university professor and archaeologist, and it was from assisting him in his research that she developed a life-long passion for the medieval period. Her vividly realistic novels of Norwegian life include *Gunnar's Daughter* (1909) and *Jenny* (1911). Her masterpiece, the *Kristin Lavransdatter* trilogy, chronicles the life of a devout Norwegian woman of the late 13th and 14th centuries; these books appeared between 1920 and 1922 as *The Bridal Wreath, The Mistress of Husaby,* and *The Cross.* Ms. Undset became a Roman Catholic in 1924, and her conversion is reflected in later works. Her great four-volume novel, *The Master of Hestviken,* also about the Norwegian Middle Ages, appeared in 1925–27. Awarded the Nobel Prize in Literature in 1928, she patterned her personal life on a medieval model, dressing in the style of an early Norse matron and living in a restored house dating from around the year 1000 filled with Norse antiques. Unpopular with the Nazi government of occupied Norway in World War II, and after her 26-year-old son died fighting the Nazis, she fled to Sweden and then came to the United States, where from 1944 to 1945 she lectured and continued writing. Awarded honorary degrees from Rollins College (1942) and Smith College (1943), she also was the first non-royal person to be awarded the Grand Cross of St. Olaf, conferred on her by Norway's King Haakon in 1947, two years before her death.

Early Pulitzer Prize Poet

The lyric verses of SARA TEASDALE, born in 1884 in St. Louis, Missouri, reflect a constant duel between a neurotic attachment to and recoil from her overprotecting parents, but they remain beautiful love poems. The publication of her first volume, *Helen of Troy and Other Poems,* in 1911, won the praise of Louis Untermeyer, and brought her to the literary circle then established in Chicago, where she met poet Vachel Lindsay. Their courtship ended when she married a St. Louis businessman, whom she later divorced in 1929. Her *Love Song* (1917) went through many editions and won her a Pulitzer Prize in 1918. Other works include *Selected Poems* (1930), and *Collected Poems,* published posthumously in 1937. Ms. Teasdale died in 1933 at the age of 48 from an overdose of sleeping pills, two years after Vachel Lindsay's suicide.

Enduring Nebraskan Pulitzer Prize Novelist

Born in Virginia in 1873, nurtured on a ranch near Red Cloud, Nebraska, and finally settling in New York City, where she died in 1947, WILLA CATHER exemplified to her many readers the American search for enduring spiritual values of an agrarian past in the face of the erosion of those values in industrial society. Her novels *O Pioneers!* (1913), *The Song of the Lark* (1915), and *My Ántonia* (1918) were realistic portrayals of people who live close to the land. Later, Willa Cather turned from a preoccupation with 19th-century Midwest America to explore Catholicism in her *Death Comes for the Archbishop* (1927), a novel about French missionaries set in the Southwest, which some regard as her masterpiece, and *Shadows on the Rock* (1931), laid in Quebec. A now less widely read work, *The Old Beauty,* published in 1948, won a Pulitzer Prize. Ms. Cather was the recipient of the Prix Fémina (1933) and the American Academy of Arts and Letters Gold Medal (1944), as well as honorary degrees from numerous universities.

Major Influence on the Modern Novel

English novelist, critic, and essayist VIR-GINIA WOOLF (see also "Women in Education, Social Sciences, and the Humanities," p. 402), whose work has greatly influenced the art of the modern novel,

was a member of the "Bloomsbury" intellectual circle. This included her sister, artist VANESSA BELL, E. M. Forster, J. M. Keynes, Roger Fry, Lytton Strachey, Desmond MacCarthy, and writer and economist Leonard Woolf, whom she married in 1912. In 1917 she and her husband founded the Hogarth Press, which became important in publishing Sigmund Freud, KATHERINE MANSFIELD, T. S. Eliot, and Virginia Woolf herself. Ms. Woolf published two novels, *The Voyage Out* (1915) and *Night and Day* (1919), a collection of short stories, *Monday or Tuesday,* and many critical reviews and essays (collected in *The Common Reader: First Series,* 1925) before writing her much acclaimed novels *Jacob's Room* (1922), *Mrs. Dalloway* (1925), and *To the Lighthouse* (1927). Probing the inner life of her characters, and writing with rich imagery, she treated the themes of love, time, and death. Her later works, *The Waves* (1931) and *Three Guineas* (1938), were less successful, though some critics contend that *Between the Arts,* posthumously published in 1941, is her true masterpiece. Her fear of recurring mental breakdown, from which she had suffered since girlhood, led Virginia Woolf to drown herself in the River Ouse in 1941.

Her Candle Burned at Both Ends

EDNA ST. VINCENT MILLAY, born in 1892, began writing poetry as a child, and at the age of 19, while still a student, published "Renascence," which attracted the attention of the literary public. Her first book, *Renascence and Other Poems,* appeared the year she was graduated from Vassar, 1917, and later she became a romantic symbol of the 1920s' emancipated woman—living in Greenwich Village, writing occasional stories and articles under the pseudonym NANCY BOYD, acting with the Provincetown Players, and writing and publishing verse that proclaimed a woman's right to be as promiscuous as a man. In 1922 she won the Pulitzer Prize for *The Harp-Weaver,* which was included the following year in a book containing some of her most loved and still quoted sonnets. *Fatal Interview,* published in 1931, collected 52 sonnets compared by reviewers of the time to those of Shakespeare and Sir Philip Sydney. Some later poems, more impersonal and less intuitive, displayed her growing concern for contemporary political and social issues (*Make Bright the Arrows,* 1940, and *The Murder of Lidice,* 1942) but others concerned with faded love and her fear of death proved wearisome, and her popularity declined. She died in 1950 at her farm in the Berkshires, in New York State, where she had lived with her husband since their marriage in 1923.

"New" Poet

MARIANNE CRAIG MOORE, first of the group of 20th-century "new" poets (including William Carlos Williams, Kenneth Burke, Wallace Stevens) to be published, received recognition in 1920 when her poem "England" was published in the *Dial.* A year later her first volume, *Poems,* was published without her knowledge in England by friends. *Observations* appeared in 1924 and won her a poetry grant from *Dial,* which continued to publish and praise her writing; in 1926 she became editor of the magazine and continued in that capacity to 1929, when it folded. Ms. Moore, who once said that it had never occurred to her to be a poet, but if her work was considered poetry it was because it could not be categorized as anything else, won the HELEN HAIRE LEVINSON Prize from *Poetry* magazine in 1932 and the Ernest Hartsock Memorial Prize in 1935, for *Selected Poems,* with an introduction by T. S. Eliot. In 1952 her *Collected Poems* won numerous prizes, including a Pulitzer and the National Book Club Award, the Bollingen Prize (1953), and the Gold Medal for Poetry of the National Insti-

tute of Arts and Letters (1953). Ms. Moore was born in St. Louis, Missouri, in 1887, attended school in Carlisle, Pennsylvania, and was graduated from Bryn Mawr in 1909. For several years she was a teacher of commercial subjects at the U. S. Indian School in Carlisle, and from 1921 to 1925 worked as an assistant at the New York Public Library. She died in 1972 in New York City.

Most Widely Translated Writer in the World and Author of the Longest-Running Play in the History of British Theater

World-famous creator of the celebrated Belgian detective Hercule Poirot and the astute Jane Marple, British author AGATHA CHRISTIE during her 55-year literary career wrote 68 novels, more than 100 short stories, 17 plays, a book about her life in the Middle East with her second husband, archaeologist Max Mallowan, and an autobiography published in 1977, the year after her death at 85. Best known for her whodunits, she also wrote several romantic novels under the pseudonym of MARY WESTMACOTT. The most widely translated writer in the English language, her work has appeared in 103 languages and has been frequently adapted for films. Her play *The Mousetrap,* a record-breaker in the history of the British stage, opened in 1952 and had been running continuously to the time of her death. *Witness for the Prosecution* won the New York Drama Critics Circle Award for the best foreign play of the year in 1957. Born in Devon of an American father and English mother, who encouraged her to write, Agatha Miller during World War I married Archibald Christie, father of her only child, Rosalind. She published her first book, *The Mysterious Affair at Styles,* in 1921. In 1956 she was given a CBE and in 1971 named a Dame Commander, Order of the British Empire (DBE). In her autobiography she does not go into the mysterious matter of her disappearance for a period in mid-life, but she does call her Mary Westmacott novel, *Absent in the Spring,* about a woman completely alone for the first time in her life and realizing that she has always had a mistaken image of herself, "an imperative," the one book that "satisfied her completely."

First (and Only) Italian Woman to Receive Nobel Prize for Literature

The first and so far only Italian woman to win the Nobel Prize in Literature in 1926, and the second woman to receive it after SELMA LAGERLÖF (p. 672) in 1909, GRAZIA DELEDDA is little known in Britain and America, largely because much of her work is not available in translation. By 1900, married, living in Rome, and established as one of the most important regionalist writers in Italy, she devoted herself to writing about life in Sardinia, where she was born in 1872. Pessimism and classical tragedy pervade her novels, set mostly in the remote central mountainous area, where poverty, superstition, and violence prevail. Her works include *Dopo il divorzio* (tr. "After the Divorce," 1902), *Elias Portulu* (1903), *Cenere* ("Ashes," 1904), *L'Edera* ("The Ivy," 1906), *Canne al vento* ("Reeds in the Wind," 1913), *Marianna Sirca* (1915), *Les Colpe Altrui* ("The Fault of Others," 1914), and *La Madre* ("The Mother," 1919). Northern Italy became the setting for *Annalena Bilsini* (1928). *Cosima,* published in 1937, a year after her death, is partly autobiographical. She was elected to the Italian Academy in 1926.

Eccentric British Experimentalist in Verse

British poet and critic EDITH SITWELL, born in 1887 the eldest child of an aristocratic family, was a highly eccentric experimenter in verse. Educated privately at Renishaw Park, the family estate for more than 600 years, Ms. Sitwell attracted public attention in 1916 when she became the editor of *Wheels,* an annual anthology to which she and her two brothers, Osbert and Sacheverell, contributed for six years. In 1923 Ms. Sitwell made her premiere poetry recital of *Façade* (music by William Walton), chanting her rhythmic verse from behind a painted curtain with a figure representing a woman with a wide-open mouth and closed eyes. She experimented in a wide spectrum of styles, constantly changing in tone and texture from the mournfully romantic *The Sleeping Beauty* (1924), *Troy Park* (1925), and *Rustic Elegies* (1927) to serious, macabre satire of corruption and cruelty in *Gold Coast Customs* (1929). During the 1930s Ms. Sitwell devoted herself to nonfiction and the writing of critical essays. Her biography of Alexander Pope was published in 1930. Her writing of the 1940s is full of religious imagery (she later converted to Catholicism). Made a Dame of the British Empire in 1954, and awarded the Foyle Prize in 1958, Edith Sitwell was perhaps her own best creative effort, with her mask-like facial makeup and her impressive stature (she was six feet tall) accentuated by flamboyant archaic costumes of extravagantly brocaded silk. She appeared often on BBC before her death in 1964.

Writer of Verse, Plays, Short Stories; Political Activist and Wit

DOROTHY PARKER's ability to level a personal foe or dismiss a literary effort with a rapier-like phrase was the basis of her fame, but she is also remembered for her short stories, plays, and poetry. Convent-educated Ms. Parker's first job was on the editorial staff of *Vogue* in 1916. During the years 1917–22, when she worked for *Vanity Fair,* she helped to found the Hotel Algonquin's famous "Round Table"—luncheon gathering place of Robert Benchley, George S. Kaufman, Robert E. Sherwood, Harold Ross, Peter Arno, EDNA FERBER, Franklin P. Adams, and others. One of the original contributors and (as "Constant Reader") book reviewers for the *New Yorker* from its beginning in 1925, Ms. Parker won the O. Henry Memorial Award in 1929 for her short story "Big Blond" and during the 1930s began writing for film in Hollywood. Active in demonstrations against the execution of Sacco and Vanzetti and in the Joint Anti-Fascist Refugee Committee during the Spanish Civil War and afterward, she was black-listed along with 300 other writers, artists, actors, and professors for her association with what were considered "Communist-front" activities. From 1958 Ms. Parker was a regular contributor of book reviews to *Esquire*. During this period she taught English at Los Angeles State College. In 1944 she ceased to write poetry, considering hers "outdated," although her light verse and couplets ("Men seldom make passes/At girls who wear glasses") had won her an appreciative audience. "I was following in the exquisite footsteps of Miss Edna St. Vincent Millay, unhappily in my own horrible sneakers," she said. Her principal works include *Enough Rope* (1927), *Sunset Gun* (1928), *Death and Taxes* (1931), *Not so Deep as a Well* (1936), *Laments for the Living* (collected stories, 1930), *Here Lies* (1939), and numerous plays and screenplays. Dorothy Parker died in 1967 in Manhattan. She had once suggested for her epitaph "Excuse My Dust" and asked that her gravestone be inscribed, "If you can read this, you've come too close."

Screenwriter/Playwright Who Satirized Hollywood

Gentlemen Prefer Blondes (1925), ANITA LOOS's best-selling novel, a satire on Hollywood society, became a Broadway play starring CAROL CHANNING (1949) and a movie starring MARILYN MONROE (1953). Its sequel, *But Gentlemen Marry Brunettes* (1928), was not nearly as successful. In 1946 Ms. Loos, author meanwhile of innumerable scenarios and screenplays, wrote *Happy*

Birthday especially for HELEN HAYES (p. 657), who was delighted with the part of a demure strait-laced librarian who lets loose in a bar in Newark. In 1972 Ms. Loos collaborated with Helen Hayes to write about their shared admiration for New York in *Twice Over Lightly: New York Then and Now*. Ms. Loos began her professional career by collaborating with John Emerson in 1916, and they were married after early screen projects, including *His Picture in the Paper* (1916, starring Douglas Fairbanks), and collaborated on the writing of *Breaking into the Movies* (1919) and *How to Write Photo Plays* (1921). She also wrote subtitles for several early D. W. Griffith films.

Lord Peter's Midwife

English author of the Lord Peter Wimsey detective novels, DOROTHY SAYERS (1893–1957) still keeps readers and, more recently, TV watchers on the edge of their seats with her bland hero's adventures in *Whose Body* (1923), *Clouds of Witness* (1926), *Strong Poison* (1930), *Have His Carcass* (1932), *Gaudy Night* (1935), and *Busman's Honeymoon* (1938). She also wrote other mystery novels not part of this series, including *Murder Must Advertise* (1933), which drew on her experiences as a copywriter. One of the first women to receive a degree from Oxford in medieval literature, in 1915, Ms. Sayers in a parallel career translated *The Divine Comedy* and published two studies of Dante, wrote religious dramas, among which was *The Man Born to Be King* (1942), serialized in Britain as 12 radio plays, and lectured widely on medieval literature, philosophy, and religion.

Anglo-Irish Novelist Honorary Member of American Academy of Letters

Anglo-Irish writer of short stories and novels ELIZABETH BOWEN, born in 1899 in Dublin, was raised in the family's Cork County mansion, which she immortalized in *Bowen's Court* (1941). It was sold and demolished before her death in 1973, as VICTORIA GLENDENNING movingly describes in her 1978 biography of the author. *Death of the Heart* (1928), a Literary Guild selection in the United States, is today considered Ms. Bowen's most important novel. Others are *The Hotel* (1927), *The House in Paris* (1936), *The Heat of the Day* (1949), and *Eva Trout* (1968), for which in 1970 she was awarded the James Tait Memorial Prize for fiction. She also wrote literary criticism and innumerable book reviews, as well as scripts for television. She lectured in the United States during the 1950s and became an honorary member of the American Academy of Arts and Letters. In 1948 she was made a Commander of the British Empire, and she received honorary doctorates from Trinity College, Dublin (1949), Oxford (1956), and was a member of the Irish Academy of Letters. All her novels are being reissued in paperback, 1978–79.

First American Woman to Win the Nobel Prize in Literature

The daughter of American missionaries who went to China when she was still an infant, PEARL S. BUCK became the first popular interpreter of Chinese culture to Westerners. Her novel *The Good Earth,* published in 1931, won her the Pulitzer Prize, and was later made into a movie. In 1936 she became a member of the National Institute of Arts and Letters and two years later was awarded the Nobel Prize in Literature. Ms. Buck taught English at Nanking University from 1917 to 1924 when her husband, John Lossing Buck, an American missionary, was head of the school's farm-management department, and later taught at National Southeastern University (1925–27) and Chung-Yang University (1928–30). Divorced in 1935, she married John Day, president of her

publishing company, which she had chosen at random out of a handbook. They adopted nine children and from 1941 to 1946 published *Asia Magazine*. In 1949 Pearl Buck founded an adoption agency for Asian-American children, Welcome House, Inc., and in 1964 gave a million dollars to establish the Pearl Buck Foundation to help fatherless Asian-American children. Ms. Buck received her B.A. from Randolph-Macon Women's College, and her M.A. from Cornell, was awarded an honorary M.A. from Yale in 1933 as well as honorary doctorates from several colleges and universities. In addition to *The Good Earth,* she was the author of more than 40 novels and other works, including *Pavilion of Women* (1946), *Peony* (1948), *The Child Who Never Grew* (1951), and *Death in a Castle* (1966). Ms. Buck died in 1973.

Alice B. Toklas' Autobiographer

American writer who emphasized the sounds of words ("A rose is a rose is a rose") over "meaning," GERTRUDE STEIN, born in 1874 in Allegheny, Pennsylvania, pursued her studies at Radcliffe and Johns Hopkins Medical School, but obtained degrees from neither institution, and moved to her famous apartment at 27 Rue de Fleuris in Paris with her brother Leo. Living in Paris from 1903 onward, she acquired an extensive collection of paintings and began a salon for artists and writers. Among her close friends were Matisse, Picasso, Braque, and many of the "Lost Generation" American writers, including Hemingway, Faulkner, and Sherwood Anderson. Her first books, *Three Lives* (1908), *Tender Buttons* (1915), and *The Making of Americans* (1925), were followed by others, including *The Autobiography of Alice B. Toklas* (1933), which tells of her own life through a fictionalized account of ALICE B. TOKLAS, in reality her secretary/companion since 1907 and lifelong lover. In 1934 Gertrude Stein's opera libretto *Four Saints in Three Acts,* with music by Virgil Thomson, was produced in New York. From wartime experiences in Europe she produced several works, including *Brewsie and Willie* (1946), about American GI's in France. Always an experimentalist with language and writing, devoid of emotion, Ms. Stein, a literary "cubist," was more than anything a hostess and collector of people, for whom, said one admirer, she had "an insatiable appetite." Gertrude Stein died in 1946 in Paris.

Her Short Stories Won Both a Pulitzer and the NBA

Short story writer KATHERINE ANNE PORTER, great-great-great-granddaughter of Daniel Boone, born in 1890 in Texas, published her first short story, "Flowering Judas," in 1934. She once said she had thrown out manuscripts "by the trunkful," but those she published, including *Pale Horse, Pale Rider,* a collection of three novelettes (1939), followed by *The Leaning Tower and Other Stories* (1944), established her secure position in the highest ranks of American authors. After a collection of critical essays, *The Days Before* (1952), she devoted herself to the writing of a full-length novel, *Ship of Fools* (1962). Educated in Louisiana and Texas, Ms. Porter has received many honorary doctorates and has taught and lectured in many universities in the United States and abroad. Twice the recipient of Guggenheim Fellowships, in 1931 and 1938, in 1944 she was a Library of Congress Fellow in Regional American Literature, in 1952 a U.S. delegate at the International Festival of Arts in Paris, and has won the New York University Libraries Gold Medal in 1940, the O. Henry Award and the Thoreau Bronze Medal in 1962, and in 1966 both the Pulitzer Prize and the National Book Award for *The Collected Short Stories of Katherine Anne Porter.* She became a member of the American Academy of Arts and Letters in 1967.

Master of the Gothic

English writer of Gothic tales DAPHNE DU MAURIER achieved her first success with the publication of her novel *Jamaica Inn* in 1936. This skillfully written story about smuggling was followed two years later by her most widely read work, *Rebecca,* a romantic Gothic novel set in Ms. Du Maurier's own 17th-century mansion Menabilly in Cornwall. Other well-known writings by Ms. Du Maurier include *The Glassblowers* (1963), *The Flight of the Falcon* (1965), *Kiss Me Again, Stranger* (1952), *The House on the Strand* (1969), *The King's General* (1946), *Frenchman's Creek* (1942), and two successful plays: *The Years Between* (1945) and *September Tide* (1948). Alfred Hitchcock is one of several to have adapted her works to the screen.

Diarist in Search of Identity

Born in 1903 in Paris to a Spanish father and French-Danish mother, both musicians, ANAÏS NIN won fame for her diaries and fiction, and for her friendships with Henry Miller, Antonin Artaud, Otto Rank, Gore Vidal, Lawrence Durrell, and others about whom she writes in *The Diaries of Anaïs Nin,* published over many years. In her early works, which she had printed on her own, she explores a world of dreams and reality, recording her own uninhibited thoughts in an attempt to reveal the life of the mind. They were strongly influenced by her experiences with psychoanalysis, as reflected in *House of Incest* (1936), *Winter of Artifice* (1939), and *Under a Glass Bell* (a collection of short stories, 1944). Ms. Nin trained with Otto Rank, and practiced as an analyst for a brief period, ceasing at the end of five months when she discovered she was "not objective." She experimented with modernist techniques in her *roman fleuve* or continuous novel—*Ladders to Fire* (1946), *Children of the Albatross* (1947), *The Four-Chambered Heart*

(1950), *A Spy in the House of Love* (1954), and *Solar Barque* (1958), later published all together in one volume, *Cities of the Interior,* in 1959. Her theme throughout these works as throughout the diaries, which she started writing at the age of 11 as letters to her father who was estranged from her mother (they were never sent), remains the search for self-identity. She was working on her seventh volume when she died in 1977. Anaïs Nin wrote many other works of criticism and comment, was a member of the National Institute of Arts and Letters, was awarded the Prix Sévigné in 1971, and in 1976 was proposed for a Nobel Prize in Literature by several writers and scholars including Henry Miller, Lawrence Durrell, DAISY ALDEN, LOUISE VARESE, Robert Kirsch, William Goyen, Christopher Isherwood, and others. In 1977 the Anaïs Nin Memorial Fellowship Fund was established after her death with a gift of $10,000 from her publisher and a goal of $100,000 to be spent for annual fellowships in comparative literature for graduate students who possess "scholarly competence" as well as "sensitivity" and "talent."

Anti-Novelist

A leading exponent of the "nouveau roman" or "anti-novel" school, which rejects the traditional form of the novel, NATHALIE SARRAUTE, born in 1902 in Russia, and educated at the Sorbonne and Oxford, began her career not as a writer but as a lawyer, practicing until 1939. The title of her first work, *Tropismes* (1939), refers to the involuntary mental responses that motivate behavior and become the basis of people's lives. *Portrait d'un Inconnu* (tr. *Portrait of a Man Unknown,* 1958) published in 1948 with a preface by Jean-Paul Sartre, was followed in 1953 by *Martereau* (tr. 1958). In the latter the protagonist is unknown and all the reader discovers is what the narrator imagines about him. Her other novels are *Le Planetarium* (1959; tr. *The Planetarium,* 1962); *Les Fruits d'Or* (1963, *The Golden Fruits,* 1965), which won the 1964 International Literary Prize given by 13 publishers all over the world; *Entre la Vie et la Mort* (1968) and *Vous les Entendez?* (1972), in which, by means of a plotless confusion of dialogue and "subconversation," she attempts to reveal "the secret source of existence." Ms. Sarraute also has written philosophical essays on the novel, the most important being *L'Ère du Soupçon* (*Age of Suspicion,* 1956), and plays for radio.

"Urban Poet"

MURIEL RUKEYSER, born in 1913 in New York City, and educated at Vassar and Columbia, has been called an "urban poet" because of her constant use of skyscrapers, machines, and pavement as symbols. While at Vassar she founded a literary review with ELIZABETH BISHOP, MARY MCCARTHY (pp. 688 and 686), and ELEANOR CLARK as a protest against the *Vassar Review*'s policies; later the two magazines merged. Before World War II, Ms. Rukeyser took various jobs in film, the theater, and on theater magazines, and did office work. She took a course in flying at the Roosevelt Aviation School; the literary result, *Theory of Flight,* was selected for publication in 1935 by the Yale Series of Younger Poets, with a foreword by editor Stephen Vincent Benet. In 1936 she went to Spain on the eve of the Civil War to report on the People's Olympiad, a sports event organized in protest against the Nazi-dominated Olympics held that year in Germany. Among her works are *Elegies* (1949), *The Orgy* (a novel, 1965), *The Speed of Darkness* (1968), *29 Poems* (1970), *Breaking Open* (1973), and a play, *The Color of the Day,* produced in Poughkeepsie, New York, in 1966. Since 1967 Ms. Rukeyser has been a member of the Board of Directors, Teachers-Writers Collaborative, in New York. She is the recipient of the Oscar Blumenthal Prize (1940), the Harriet Monroe Award (1941), the National Endowment for the Arts Award (1942), the Levinson Prize (1947), the Eunice Tietjens Memorial Prize (*Poetry, Chicago,* 1962), the Swedish Academy Translation Award (1967), and an honorary doctorate from Rutgers University (1961).

She Only Needed One Novel

Gone With the Wind, her romantic novel set against the crumbling of the Old South, was the only book written by MARGARET MITCHELL. She worked on it over a 10-year period. It sold more than 8 million copies before her death at 49 in 1949, won her a Pulitzer Prize, and was selected as outstanding novel of the year by the American Booksellers Association in 1939, won the first Carl Bohnenberger Memorial Award of the New York Southern Society, and caused Smith College to award its former student an honorary M.A. At its peak the novel sold as many as 50,000 copies in one day, and its 1,037 pages have been translated into dozens of other languages and Braille. In recent years, serious scholars of the Reconstruction in the South have singled it out as giving a true and important picture of that period. The screenplay based on the novel, which is still shown, runs for 220 minutes and for a while was the longest film ever produced. It won several Oscars in various categories and brought lasting fame to VIVIEN LEIGH as Scarlett O'Hara starring opposite Clark Gable as Rhett Butler. HATTIE MCDANIEL was the first black performer to win an Academy Award for Best Supporting Actress as Mammy in the picture. It broke all U.S. movie attendance records and in 1977 on the occasion of the 10th anniversary of the American Film Institute was voted Best American Film.

Spy Story Master

Scottish-American novelist HELEN MACINNES, born in 1907 in Glasgow, started writing her first novel, *Above Suspicion* (1941), set in prewar Nazi Germany, in 1939. Most of her early books deal with World War II themes. She has been praised for her carefully documented descriptions of her international settings. All 16 of her fast-moving thrillers have been translated into many foreign languages, including Arabic, Tamil, Hindi, and Urdu, and many have been made into films, including *Assignment in Brittany* (1942) and *The Venetian Affair* (1963). A New Yorker from 1937, when her husband, Gilbert Highet, was invited to Columbia University to become professor of Latin language and literature, in 1966 she was awarded the Columbia Prize in literature from Iona College, New Rochelle, New York.

The South's Tellers of Tales

Georgia-born author of novels, plays, and short stories, CARSON MCCULLERS enjoyed her first success with the publication of *The Heart Is a Lonely Hunter* (1940), written when she was 23 years old. Her short story, "A Tree, a Rock, a Cloud" was included in the O. Henry Memorial Prize Stories in 1942. *The Member of the Wedding,* written originally as a novel, was later successfully adapted into a play, winning her the New York Drama Critics Circle Award and the Donaldson Award in 1950. In 1961 Edward Albee made a stage adaptation of her short novel written in 1951, *The Ballad of the Sad Cafe.* Other works include her last novel, *Clock Without Hands* (1957), and a volume of children's poetry, *Sweet as a Pickle and Clean as a Pig* (1964). In 1965 Ms. McCullers was awarded the Prize of the Younger Generation from the German newspaper *Die Welt.* Troubled by poor health for many years, Ms. McCullers died in 1967.

Mississippi-born EUDORA WELTY's themes, like those of Carson McCullers, are of loneliness and the grotesque, ambiguity and the eccentric. Her first collection of short stories, *A Curtain of Green*, published in 1941, was widely praised. Five years later she published her first novel, *Delta Wedding*. *The Ponder Heart* (1953), a novella, was later made into a Broadway play. Critics admire her "controlled irony" and sensibility in these and other works including *The Robber Bridegroom* (1942), *The Golden Apples* (short stories, 1949), *The Wide Net* (short stories, 1943), *Selected Stories* (1954), *The Bride of Innisfallen* (short stories, 1955). Educated at Mississippi State College for Women and the University of Wisconsin (B.A. 1929) and the Colorado University School of Advertising (1930–31), Ms. Welty has received several honorary doctorates, was an honorary consultant in American Letters at the Library of Congress, and was elected a member of the American Academy of Arts and Letters in 1971. She won a Howells Medal in 1955, a Brandeis University Creative Arts Award in 1965, and in 1973 won the Pulitzer Prize for her novel *The Optimist's Daughter*.

Another Georgian writer of short stories and novels set in the South, born in 1925 with an incurable crippling disease from which she died before she was 40, FLANNERY O'CONNOR combined her vision of the grotesque and her Catholic orthodoxy with an underlying theme of man's futile flight from God and final redemption. In 1957 she won the O. Henry Award for "Greenleaf" and in 1963 won it again for "Everything that Rises Must Converge." Her other works include *A Good Man Is Hard to Find and Other Stories* (1955), *Wise Blood* (novel, 1952), and *The Violent Bear It Away* (1960). She was posthumously honored with the National Catholic Book Award in 1966 and in 1972 was also posthumously honored with the National Book Award for *The Complete Stories*. Educated at the Women's College of Georgia (A.B. 1945) and the State University of Iowa (M.F.A. 1947), she was awarded hon-

orary doctorates from St. Mary's College in 1962 and from Smith College in 1963.

Denmark's Gothic

So subtle was her writing in *Ways of Retribution* (later retitled *The Angelic Avengers,* 1947), published in Denmark in 1944 under a pseudonym, that the occupying Nazi censors, thinking it merely a Gothic novel, did not grasp the anti-Nazi symbolism the Baroness Blixen of Rungstedlund, ISAK DINESEN, used in it. Her readers did, and it became a bestseller. Known primarily as a Danish writer, though she wrote most often in English, Ms. Dinesen enjoyed her first success with the publication of the fantastic *Seven Gothic Tales* in 1934. Some of her later writing is set in Kenya, where she ran a coffee plantation for many years. Of this, *Out of Africa* (1937) and *Shadows on the Grass* (1961) were well received but she is best remembered as a maker of eerie Gothic stories, especially *Seven Gothic Tales, Winter's Tales* (1942), and *Last Tales* (1957). In 1957 Ms. Dinesen was awarded the Danish Critics Prize and membership in the American Academy of Arts and Letters. She died in 1962 and is buried under a huge tree on her Danish estate, Rungstedlund, which is now a bird sanctuary. The large stone slab reads: KAREN BLIXEN.

First Chilean Awarded Nobel Prize for Literature

Chilean poet LUCILA GODOY ALCAYAGA, born 1889, adopted the nom de plume GABRIELA MISTRAL by combining the names of Gabriele D'Annunzio and Frederic Mistral. In 1945 she was the recipient of the Nobel Prize in Literature —the first Chilean, man or woman, to win the coveted prize (it went to Pablo Neruda in 1971). The daughter of a schoolteacher in the small village of Vicuna, where she was born in 1889, Ms. Alcayaga taught for many years in rural schools before becoming professor of

When poet ADRIENNE RICH won the National Book Award in 1974, she refused it as an individual but accepted it "for all women." (Photo courtesy of W. W. Norton Company, by Thomas Victor)

TONI MORRISON, novelist. Her most recent work, *Song of Solomon*, brought her the National Book Critics Circle Award in 1978—the first time it was given to a black woman writer. (Photo courtesy of Alfred A. Knopf, Inc., by James L. McGuire)

British women suffragists meeting at a country house in England around the turn of the century. (Photo courtesy of the Library of Congress)

In 1916 American suffragists, 5,000 strong, marched on Washington, D.C., urging passage of the 19th Amendment. (Photo courtesy of the Library of Congress)

Election Day!

(Reproduced from the collection of the Library of Congress)

Sole survivor of the National Women's Party, which organized and sponsored the 1916 march, HAZEL HUNKINS HALLINAN is seen here in a 1972 photograph. (Photo by Harry Naltchayan, the *Washington Post*)

Mississippi civil rights leader FANNIE LO[U]
HAMER, like many others who worked f[or]
black equality, later became active in th[e]
anti-Vietnam War movement. She is see[n]
here at a rally for a moratorium on th[e]
war, October 15, 1969. Ms., Hamer died i[n]
1977. (Photo by Stephen Shames, Blac[k]
Star)

ESTHER PETERSON, longtime consumer
activist and at one time head of the
Women's Bureau in the U. S. Department
of Labor. Since 1977 she has been advising
President Carter on consumer problems.

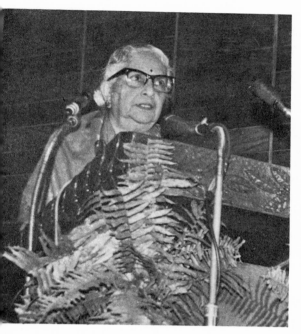

Founder of the Indian Cooperative Union to assist refugees uprooted by the partition of India and Pakistan, KAMALADEVI CHATTOPADHYAY, after rehabilitation was accomplished, redirected the Union to establishing consumer and handloom cooperatives. New Delhi's very successful central Cottage Industries Emporium is the outlet for the latter.

"Out of the rocking chair, into the street!" is the rallying cry for MARGARET E. ("MAGGIE") KUHN's Gray Panthers, an activist group fighting ageism. They have used militant tactics to call attention to such issues as health care and mandatory retirement. Philadelphian Maggie Kuhn is seen above with a young supporter. (Photo courtesy of the Gray Panthers)

"Lady Lindy" AMELIA EARHART, first woman to fly the Atlantic, made the trip first as a passenger aboard a plane piloted by Lou Gordon and Wilmer Stutz in 1928, a year after Charles Lindbergh's transatlantic flight. In May 1932 Ms. Earhart flew the Atlantic solo in a single-engine Lockheed Vega. She was beset by bad weather, her plane's wings coated with ice, forcing her to fly as close as 75 feet above the waves part of the time. Fifteen hours after her departure from Long Island, she landed in a farmer's pasture in Ireland and overnight became a celebrity. In 1937 she disappeared with her plane in the Pacific on an attempted round-the-world flight.

Junior Lieutenant (as she then was) VALENTINA VLADIMIROVNA TERESHKOVA, Piloting the Soviet spaceship *Vostok VI*, she became, on June 16, 1963, the first woman to orbit the earth.

If all goes well, next to follow Russia's cosmonaut TERESHKOVA into space will probably be one or more of these women, the first chosen as astronaut-trainees by the U. S. National Aeronautics and Space Administration (NASA). Pictured in 1978 at the Houston facility as they reported for training are, left to right: MARGARET R. SEDDON, ANNA L. FISHER, JUDITH A. RESNIK, SHANNON W. LUCID, SALLY K. RIDE, and KATHRYN D. SULLIVAN. (Photo courtesy of NASA)

JACQUELINE KENNEDY ONASSIS, widow of President John F. Kennedy and of Aristotle Onassis, one of the world's richest men, is today a New York City resident and book editor. She is pictured above in the early 1960s with her sister, Princess LEE RADZIWILL, on an official trip to India. American Ambassador John Kenneth Galbraith's wife, KITTY GALBRAITH, also accompanies the then President's wife.

Castilian at the Liceo de los Andes, a major school in Santiago, during which time she gained recognition and a literary laurel wreath and medal in the Juegos Florales for her *Sonetos de la Muerte* (Sonnets on Death). She was greatly disturbed by the suicide of her lover when she was a young woman, and her first books of poems reflect this loss, as the suicide of her adopted son later became the subject and theme of much of her work. Between 1922 and 1924 Gabriela Mistral helped in the reorganization of schools in rural Mexico. She also spent a number of years in Europe working for the Institute for Intellectual Cooperation of the League of Nations, was visiting professor at Barnard, Vassar, and Middlebury, 1931–32, and represented her country as a diplomat in Europe, Mexico, Brazil, and the United States. By special law she became a lifelong consul for Chile, in whatever country she wished to live. She died in the United States in 1957, and much of her work remains unpublished.

Poet of Black Urban Life

GWENDOLYN BROOKS published her first poem, "Eventide," at the age of 13, and four years later began submitting poems to *The Defender*, a paper in Chicago, where she has lived most of her life, though she was born in 1917 in Topeka, Kansas. *A Street in Bronzeville*, published in 1945, was the first of many highly acclaimed volumes of her poetry, which effectively reveal the black experience in America. In 1950 with *Annie Allen* she won the Pulitzer Prize for poetry. Her novel, *Maud Martha*, published three years later, concerns the urban life of a young girl in Chicago and is rich in imagery and poetic content. She remains faithful to the theme of the black urban experience in her later poetry, taking a more militant position than she had earlier toward racial problems in her 1968 volume, *In the Mecca*. Educated at Wilson Junior College in Chicago, Ms.

Brooks has received honorary doctorates from Columbia College (1964), Lake Forest College (1965), and Brown University (1974), and has taught at Northeastern Illinois State College, Chicago, and Elmhurst College, Illinois. In 1971 she became Distinguished Professor of the Arts at City College in New York. She won the Friends of Literature Poetry Award in 1963 and the Anisfield-Wolf Award in 1968 and was named Poet Laureate of Illinois in 1969.

Three-Time Stalin Prize Winner

Russian novelist VERA PANOVA started out as a journalist in Rostov-on-Don, where she was born in 1905, became a writer of plays, but felt she could express herself better in the less restricted form of a novel. She recounts her early experiences in her autobiographical novels, *Sentimental 'nyi roman* (1958) and *Vremena Goda* (1953). Her best-known novel, *Sputniki*, published in 1946 (tr. *Travelling Companions*, 1948), inspired by her work on an army hospital train in World War II, won her the first of three Stalin prizes in 1947. The second was awarded for *Kruzhilikha* (1947, tr. *Looking Back*, 1957), which is about factory life during the war. Her third Stalin Prize in 1950 honored *Yasnibereg* (1949), concerning a Soviet farm after the war. She received a public reprimand from the Second Congress of Soviet Writers in 1954 on the basis of her ideology but, despite this, was elected to the executive board of the Congress the same year. Her other works include *Seriozha* (1955, tr. *Times Walked*, 1959) which was made into a film, *A Summer to Remember*. Vera Panova died in 1973.

Co-Founder of "Acmeism"

Russian poet ANNA AKHMATOVA, co-founder with her husband, Nikolai Gumilov, and Osip Mandelstam of "Acmeism," a reaction against symbolism, published six volumes of poetry in this style, including *Evening* (1912),

The Rosary (1914), *Anno Domini MCMXXI* (1922). Her poems of this period, set in contemporary Russia, are nostalgic for the past. For 20 years Ms. Akhmatova was silenced by the revolutionary regime except for some scholarly articles and did not resume publication until 1940. Her "Requiem" poems, some written during this period, did not appear until 1964. During World War II she was permitted to publish in state-sanctioned periodicals and was the author of a much-admired war poem, "Muzhestvo" (Courage). Later called "half nun, half prostitute" by a Soviet cultural leader "because of her preoccupation with religion and love," she was expelled from the Union of Soviet Writers and declared "dangerous and subversive." She lived in misery and did not reappear until after the death of Stalin. In 1963 she refused to condemn radical Soviet writers, reaffirming her independence. She was elected honorary member of the Presidium of the Writers' Union in 1965. Nominated twice for the Nobel Prize, in 1958 and again in 1965 (when it was awarded to Boris Pasternak and Mikhail Sholokov), she won the Taormina Prize for poetry (Catagna, Italy) in 1964. Oxford University awarded her an honorary doctorate in 1965, a year before her death.

The Soviet Union's Most Popular Woman Poet

Idolized in the Soviet Union, BELLA AKHATOVNA AKHMADULINA, born 1937, was married to Yevgeny Yevtushenko from 1955 until 1960, and the two constituted what has been called a first family of Russian poetry. Her sensuous poems reflect the themes of universality and eternity characteristic of great Russian literature; she eschews partisan subjects, saying that "political poetry is not poetry at all, but beautiful poetry is close to people's lives." Her books sell out as soon as they go on sale in the Soviet Union. A collection of her poems trans-lated into English has been published in the United States under the title *Fever,* and she has been inducted into the American Academy of Arts and Letters.

British Novelist of Ancient Greece

British historical novelist MARY RENAULT, born in 1905, became fascinated by ancient Greece while vacationing in Greece during the 1940s and published her first novels when she was still working as a nurse in South Africa. In 1959 she was named a fellow of the Royal Society of Literature. Her well-researched books bring to life Theseus, Phaedra and Hippolytus, Plato, Alexander of Macedon, and many others. The most famous are *The Last of the Wine* (1956), *The King Must Die* (1958), *The Bull from the Sea* (1962), *The Mask of Apollo* (1966), *Fire from Heaven* (1970), and *The Persian Boy* (1973). *The Praise Singer* was published in 1978.

Belgian-born Classicist/Novelist Nominated for French Academy

MARGUERITE YOURCENAR, daughter of a distinguished classics scholar, acquired a love for the ancient world when she was young. Born in 1903 in Brussels of French parentage, she has lived in the United States since 1939 and has written novels, short stories, plays, poems, essays, and translated works by Henry James, VIRGINIA WOOLF (p. 674), the Greek poet Cavafy, and negro spirituals. Among the most admired of her works, set in different times and places, is *Mémoires d'Hadrien* (*Memoirs of Hadrian,* 1951), reflections of the famous Roman emperor as imagined by Ms. Yourcenar, so constructed, documented, and written that the reader must constantly remind himself that this is a novel, not a real memoir; for it she was awarded the Prix Fémina in 1952. Other works include *Alexis ou le Traité du Vain Combat* (1929), set in pre-World War I Austria-

Hungary, and *Dernier du Rêve* (1934), which takes place in Fascist Italy. She was awarded the Page One Award of the Newspaper Guild, New York, in 1955, and the Prix Combat for her essay "Sous Bénéfice d'Inventaire" and other writing in 1963. *L'Oeuvre au Noir,* a novel set in 16th-century Flanders and seen through the eyes of a Renaissance man of high culture, won her the Prix Fémina in 1968. Ms. Yourcenar has taught at colleges and universities in Europe and the United States including Sarah Lawrence, holds an honorary doctorate from Smith (1961), and is a member of the Académie de Belgique (1970). In 1978 she was nominated for membership in the French Academy.

Poet of "Here and Now"

Although poet DENISE LEVERTOV has been living in the United States since her marriage to American novelist Mitchell Goodman, her writing career has its roots in England, where she was born in 1923 of Welsh-Russian Jewish parentage. Her first collection of poems, *Double Image,* published in 1946, reflects the spell of English romanticism, hardly indicative of what was to follow as she was influenced by American poets such as William Carlos Williams and became associated with the Black Mountain group. In 1957, *Here and Now* was published in the Pocket Poets series launched by Lawrence Ferlinghetti, revealing a transformed style, intensified and personal. *Jacob's Ladder* published in 1961, contains a strong mystical element and her preoccupation with political issues shows in *The Sorrow Dance* (1968) about the Vietnam War. In *Footprints* (1972) she returns more to the lyric quality of her earlier poems. Ms. Levertov has taught at a number of American colleges and universities and has been on the editorial staff for poetry of the *Nation.* The recipient of many prizes, including the Harriet Monroe Memorial Prize (1964) and the Morton Dauwen

Zabel Prize (1965, *Poetry,* Chicago), she holds honorary doctorates from Colby College, Waterville, Maine (1970) and the University of Cincinnati (1973).

She Wrote *The Dollmaker*

In 1954 HARRIETTE SIMPSON ARNOW published her moving novel of a woman forced to take her family from the Kentucky hills to Detroit. One of the few novels ever to deal at one and the same time with enduring themes of poverty, urban ugliness (of place and spirit), and a woman's creativity in terms of her family and her art (woodcarving, in the case of Gertie, the dollmaker), it has long been out of print but may be revived, thanks to the new interest in it evoked by the women's movement in the late 1970s. Ms. Arnow, born in 1908, grew up in Burnside, Kentucky, a town, now half under the hundred-mile-long Cumberland Lake, whose early days she describes in *Old Burnside,* a memoir published in 1977. Educated at Berea College and the University of Louisville, she did odd jobs to support her writing and was published in the *Southern Review, Atlantic Monthly, Esquire,* and *Saturday Review.* Married and raising a family, she published her first novel, *Hunter's Horn,* a 1949 best-seller novel, and later wrote *Seedtime on the Cumberland* (1960) and *Flowering of the Cumberland* (1963).

Philosopher / Novelist

Irish-born, British-educated philosopher IRIS MURDOCH did not publish her first novel, *Under the Net* (1954), until the age of 35, but since then she has been a prolific novelist. Critics have found it difficult to characterize her writing, since it fits into no clearly established pattern and has not developed in a steady, comprehensive manner. Existentialism, which has preoccupied her from the time she wrote *Sartre: Romantic Realist* (1953) pervades some of her novels, especially *Under the Net* (1954) and *An*

Unofficial Rose (1962). Other works examine the themes of evil, sado-masochism, homosexuality, love, the Gothic, and so on; despite their apparent lack of continuity, they have been highly praised for their brilliant technique and construction. Ms. Murdoch is a product of Somerville College at Oxford and Newnham College at Cambridge. A university lecturer in philosophy, 1948–63, and since 1963 an honorary fellow at St. Anne's College at Oxford, from 1963 to 1967 she also was a lecturer at the Royal College of Art in London. She is the recipient of the Black Memorial Prize in 1974 and the Whitbread Literary Award in 1974 and is an honorary member of the American Academy of Arts and Letters.

British Feminist-Novelist

British novelist, playwright, and short story writer DORIS LESSING, born in Persia in 1919, lived much of her early life (1924–49) in Rhodesia, which became the setting for many of her works, including *The Grass Is Singing* (1950) and *Going Home* (1957). *The Golden Notebook* (1962) is a sensitive account of a woman's problems (in writing, in particular), of women coming to terms with themselves, and of the relationships between men and women. Her Martha Quest sequence, *Children of Violence*, which she began in 1950 and completed in 1969, is an ambitious series of novels in which she explores the themes of race, war, the political climate of the Cold War, and the struggle against capitalism (for a time, she was a Communist). Ms. Lessing won the Somerset Maugham Award in 1954.

One of "The Group"?

Born in 1912 in Seattle, MARY McCARTHY lost her Jewish mother and Irish Catholic father when she was six during an influenza epidemic. She and her three brothers were brought up with her paternal relatives in Minneapolis, as she recounts in *Memories of a Catholic Girl* (1957). One of the participants while she was an undergraduate at Vassar in the founding of the protest magazine (see MURIEL RUKEYSER, p. 680), she later wrote a novel, *The Group* (1963), an instant best-seller, which traced the experiences of eight Vassar girls from 1933 until the prewar period. Ms. McCarthy began her writing career after college as a book reviewer for the *Nation* and the *New Republic*. Anti-Stalinist (and pro-Trotsky), she later became an editor and drama critic of *Partisan Review*. As a satirist of contemporary American intellectualism—*The Oasis* (1949), *The Groves of Academe* (1952)—Ms. McCarthy has been praised for her sharp wit. Other works include *Venice Observed* (1956), *The Stones of Florence* (1959), *The Company She Keeps* (1957), *Birds of America* (1971), and essays of protest against the Vietnam War. Ms. McCarthy taught at Bard College and at Sarah Lawrence College. She received the *Horizon* Prize in 1949.

British Thriller-Novelist

Since her first novel, *Madame, Will You Talk?* (1956), MARY STEWART has been a writer of best-selling thrillers. They include *Thunder on the Right* (1958), *Nine Coaches Waiting* (1959), *Airs Above the Ground* (1965), and *The Gabriel Hounds* (1967). The recipient of the British Crime Writers Association Award in 1960 for *My Brother Michael*, in 1965 she won the Mystery Writers of America Award for *This Rough Magic*. She also wrote four radio plays, *Lift from a Stranger, Call Me at Ten-Thirty, The Crime of Mr. Murry,* and *The Lord of Langdale* for BBC in 1957–58. *The Moon Spinners* (1962) was made into a Walt Disney movie in 1964 starring HAYLEY MILLS, Eli Wallach, Peter McEnery, JOAN GREENWOOD, IRENE PAPAS (p. 660), and POLA NEGRI. Some of her work has been serialized in *Elle* and *Woman's Journal*. Born in 1916 in Durham, she taught English at the University of Durham, her alma mater, until 1956. She and her husband, Frederick Henry Stewart, live in Scotland where he is head of the Geology Department of the University of Edinburgh. In 1969 she was elected a fellow of the Royal Society of Arts.

The "Confessionalist" Poets

When SYLVIA PLATH took her life in 1963 she was already becoming a legend. Her powerful writing in *The Bell Jar* (1963), a novel that she originally wrote under a pseudonym, recounts a breakdown and suicide attempt, drawing from an experience of a decade earlier. It was published only a month before her death. Her earlier poetry in *Colossus* (1960) was quiet and refined but the system of metaphor and imagery that she constructed developed into the much more violent poetry, some written just a week before her suicide, posthumously published in *Ariel* in 1965 and reflecting her preoccupation with death. Born in 1932 in Boston, Ms. Plath graduated summa cum laude from Smith College and received a Fulbright to study in England at Newnham College, Cambridge, from 1955 to 1957, where she earned her M.A. She was the recipient of many literary prizes including, in 1953, the *Mademoiselle* College Board Contest in fiction. She and her British husband, poet Ted Hughes, were separated in 1962. She had two children. Sylvia Plath is usually identified as a member of the "confessional" school of poetry, along with Robert Lowell and ANNE SEXTON, who also died a suicide in 1974.

"I prefer to think of myself as an imagist who deals with reality and its hard facts," Anne Sexton once noted. Her first collection of poems, *To Bedlam and Part Way Back* (1960), reflects her recovery from a nervous breakdown, what she called "a kind of rebirth at 29." In later works she further explored and confronted her personal feelings and conflicts, often dealing with the pleasures and complexity of love and motherhood. *Live or Die* (1967), considered by many critics her best work, reveals her own inner struggle in intensely sensual language close to speech, sometimes shifting suddenly from the rational to irrational. Ms. Sexton, born in 1928 in Newton, Massachusetts, was educated at Garland College and Radcliffe. A lecturer and professor of creative writing at Boston University from 1970, and a Cranshaw Professor at Colgate University in 1972, she was made an honorary member of Phi Beta Kappa in 1968 and held several honorary doctorates. Her many awards include the Levinson Prize (*Poetry*, Chicago, 1962) and the Shelly Memorial Award and a Pulitzer Prize in 1967.

She Accepted the National Book Award "in the Name of all Women"

While she was still an undergraduate, W. H. Auden chose ADRIENNE RICH to be represented in the Yale Younger Poets series. That first collection, *A Change of World* (1951), with its carefully wrought poems, heavily influenced by Frost, Thomas, Stevens, and Donne is a far cry from the later work exemplified by *Leaflets* (1969) in which she is concerned especially with the student protests of 1968 and the antiwar movement. *The Will to Change* (1971) and *Diving into the Wreck* (1973), which won the National Book Award in 1974, reflect her movement toward "confessional poetry" and are largely concerned with the situation of women—especially women writers. Diction and syntax in these later works become sharper, less concerned with formal elegance than with forcefulness. Ms. Rich rejected the National Book Award as an individual, accepting it with nominees ALICE

WALKER (p. 689) and AUDREY RICH in the name of all women. She is the recipient of numerous other awards including the National Institute of Arts and Letters Award for poetry in 1961 and in 1971 the Shelly Memorial Award of the Poetry Society of America. She has taught at Columbia, Harvard, Swarthmore, the City College of New York and is currently professor of English at Douglass College of Rutgers University. In addition to her poetry, she has written *Of Women Born: Motherhood as Experience and Institution* (1976) and the foreword to the 1977 book *Working It Out: 23 Women Writers, Artists, Scientists, and Scholars Talk About Their Lives and Work*, edited by SARA RUDDICK and PAMELA DANIELS.

First American to Win the Books Abroad/Neustadt International Prize for Literature

Often referred to as an "eye" poet because of her rich visual imagery and individual way of viewing the world, ELIZABETH BISHOP is one of the most honored of all American writers. Though she has been a lecturer in English at Harvard since 1970, she resided for 16 years in Brazil where she translated several Brazilian works into English and worked as an editor and contributing translator for *Anthology of Contemporary Brazilian Poetry* (1972). The poems she wrote while in Brazil appeared first in the *New Yorker* and other magazines and were published with other poems and a short story, "In the Village" in *Questions of Travel* (1965). *Geography III* appeared in 1977. Born in Worcester, Massachusetts, in 1911, Ms. Bishop spent much of her childhood in Nova Scotia, was educated at Vassar (see also MURIEL RUYKEYSER, p. 680). Ms. Bishop has been awarded many prizes and honors, including the Shelly Memorial Award in 1953, the Pulitzer Prize in 1956, the *Partisan Review* Fellowship in 1956, the Amy Lowell Traveling Fellowship in 1957, the Chapel-

brook Fellowship in 1962, the Academy of American Poets Fellowship in 1964, the Rockefeller Fellowship in 1967, the Ingram Merrill Foundation grant in 1969, the National Book Award in 1970, and the $10,000 Books Abroad/Neustadt International Prize for Literature in 1976. She holds honorary doctorates from Smith College, Rutgers University, and Brown University; in 1971 she was named a member of the National Institute of Arts and Letters, Order of Rio Branco (Brazil) and is also a member of the American Academy of Arts and Letters.

Darling or Demon of American Letters?

American novelist, critic, essayist, and film director SUSAN SONTAG published her first book—a novel, *The Benefactor*—in 1963. This was followed by philosophical essays on such varied subjects as film, the French anti-novel, music, art, politics, and pornography, published in numerous periodicals including the *New York Review of Books*, the *New Yorker*, *Partisan Review*, *Commentary*, *Salmagundi*, *Tri-Quarterly*, *Evergreen Review*, *Sight and Sound*, the *Nation*, *Vogue*, *Film Quarterly*, and the *New York Times*. A collection of her essays, *Against Interpretation*, published in 1966, was nominated for a National Book Award for Arts and Letters. Her essay "Trip to Hanoi" was published in 1969 first as a Noonday paperback, and then included in a collection of essays on contemporary thought, in *The Styles of Radical Will*. Ms. Sontag has written short stories that have appeared in many periodicals. Her second novel, *Death Kit* (1967), like her first explores the relationship between dream life and reality. Her 1977 book *On Photography*, in which she describes the act of taking a picture as "something predatory," had a strong critical success. It was followed in 1978 by a collection of stories, *I, etcetera*, and a third collection of essays, *Illness as Metaphor*. Ms. Sontag, fighting against cancer, also has been at work on a new novel. She has written and directed three films: *Duet for Cannibals* (1969), *Brother Carl* (1971), and *Promised Lands* (a documentary, 1974). Ms. Sontag is the recipient of numerous awards, including the *Mademoiselle* Magazine Merit Award in 1964, the George Polk Memorial Award in 1966, and in 1976 the Ingram Merrill Foundation Award in Literature in the Field of American Letters, the Arts and Letters Award of the American Academy of Arts and Letters, and the Brandeis University Creative Arts Award. The 44-year-old New Yorker, sometimes called the "darling," sometimes the "demon" of American letters, attended the University of California at Berkeley, received her B.A. from the University of Chicago, and her M.A. from Harvard. She has also studied at St. Anne's College at Oxford and the University of Paris with the American Association of University Women Fellowship. She has taught at City College, Sarah Lawrence College, and Columbia University, and was writer in residence at Rutgers University.

Henry Miller Praised her *Fear of Flying*

ERICA JONG published two books of verse, *Fruits and Vegetables* (1971) and *Half-Lives* (1973), before she achieved literary renown, popular success, and a measure of notoriety for her novel *Fear of Flying* (1973)—a female picaresque that Henry Miller described as a feminine counterpart of his *Tropic of Cancer,* only "not as bitter and much funnier." She regards it as a serious work about what she terms "unfulfillment" and is a bit annoyed to be known as "the bad girl of American letters or, still worse, a pornographer." Ms. Jong published a second novel, *How to Save Your Own Life,* in 1977. *Half-Lives* won the Alice Faye di Castagnolia Award of the Poetry Society of America and a CAPS (Creative Artists Program Service) award. A third book of verse, *Loveroot* (1975), was selected as a Book-of-the-Month Club alternate, a distinction shared with the works of only two other American poets, Rod McKuen and Robert Frost.

Poet/Novelists of the Black Experience

NIKKI GIOVANNI explores her own identity as a black poet as well as that of blacks in general in deftly handled simple folk and blues rhythms and "Projectionist" verse. Some of her most expressive poems are those written to or focusing on particular individuals. Born in 1943 in Knoxville, Tennessee, Ms. Giovanni published her first two volumes of poetry, *Black Judgment* and *Black Feeling, Black Talk* in 1968 at the age of 25. Two years later *Re: Creation* and *Poem of Angela Yvonne Davis* were published, followed by *My House* in 1972, *Dialogue: James Baldwin and Nikki Giovanni* (1973), and *Poetic Equation: Conversations Between Nikki Giovanni and Margaret Walker* (1974). She has made two recordings, "Truth Is on Its Way" and "Like a Ripple on a Pond"

in 1971 and 1973, and also has written literature for children, including *Spin a Soft Black Song* (1971) and *Ego Tripping and Other Poems for Young Readers* (1973). Ms. Giovanni, who has had a number of awards including the Ford Grant in 1968 and the National Endowment for the Arts Grant in 1969, holds an honorary doctorate from Wilberforce University in Ohio in 1972. She graduated with honors in history in 1967 from Fisk University in Nashville, Tennessee, attended the University of Pennsylvania School of Social Work and Columbia University, and has taught at Livingston College, Rutgers University, 1968–70.

Poet, essayist, lyrical novelist, and magazine columnist ALICE WALKER received the 1976 Front Page Award for Best Magazine Column for her "Beyond the Peacock: The Reconstruction of Flannery O'Connor" review for *Ms.* magazine and the LILLIAN SMITH Award in 1973 for *Revolutionary Petunias & Other Poems*. This collection also was nominated for the National Book Award in 1974. Her other books are *Once* (poems, 1968), *The Third Life of Grange Copeland* (novel, 1970), *Langston Hughes* (biography for children, 1974), and *Meridian* (novel, 1976). *Meridian*, set mostly in the Deep South and New York, is the story of a deserted teen-age mother who volunteers to help in the civil-rights movement and finds her circumscribed life totally changed by it. Ms. Walker, born in 1944 in Eatonton, Georgia, was graduated from Sarah Lawrence College and has been a lecturer in Literature and Writing at Wellesley, the University of Massachusetts, Tongaloo College, and Jackson State College. A staff editor of *Ms.* magazine, Alice Walker also has been a contributing editor to *Southern Voices*, consulting editor for *Freedomways*, and served on the advisory board at *Books*, a New Orleans review in 1973.

First Black Woman to Win the National Book Critics Circle Award

Song of Solomon, her third novel, published in 1977, in 1978 brought TONI MORRISON the distinction of being the first black woman to win the National Book Critics Circle Award. The novel described by *Publishers Weekly* as being "as extraordinary in its imaginative, dramatic fashion as *Roots* was in its own way," followed *The Bluest Eye* (1970) and *Sula* (1974), about which James Baldwin said, "The dry unsparing love which informs this bitter and triumphant testimony causes it to ring and echo down a universal valley, like the sorrow songs." Ms. Morrison, a senior editor at Random House in New York City, was born in 1931 in Lorain, Ohio. She has a B.A. from Howard University and an M.A. from Cornell, and has taught English literature at Texas Southern University and at Howard. The mother of two children, Ms. Morrison has recently begun working only part time as an editor, in order to have more hours free for writing.

THE BEST OF THE WOMEN WRITERS AND ILLUSTRATORS FOR CHILDREN'S BOOKS

Peter Rabbit's Creator

Peter Rabbit, loved by generations of children, was born out of a series of letters written in 1893 by BEATRIX POTTER to the sick child of her former governess. These became the basis of a children's book illustrated with her own watercolors, published in 1902. Beatrix Potter, born in 1866 in London, had a lonely childhood, tempered by her pleasure in small pets and drawing. As she grew older she found herself most comfortable with children. *The Tale of Peter Rabbit*, considered the first "modern picture book," allowing very young children to "read" the pictures, was followed by 22 more Peter Rabbit stories and many others including *The Tailor of Gloucester*

(1903), *The Tale of Squirrel Nutkin* (1903), *The Tale of Benjamin Bunny* (1904), *The Tale of Mrs. Tiggy-Winkle* (1905), *The Tale of the Flopsy Bunnies* and *Ginger and Pickles* (1909), and *The Tale of Mrs. Tittlemouse* (1910). In all of these small-sized books, gentle little animals, dressed like "country folk," come alive in the English countryside of Sawrey, which Ms. Potter knew well. A museum was established at her home, Hill Top, after her death in 1943.

Her Secret Garden Still Blooms

FRANCES ELIZA HODGSON BURNETT, born in 1849 in Manchester, England, moved to a log cabin in Knoxville, Tennessee, with her family at an early age. She published her first of about 40 novels, *Lass o' Lowrie's,* based on her childhood experience in Manchester, to instant success. It was followed by *Editha's Burglar* and *Little Lord Fauntleroy,* her famous tale of a little boy in velvet suits and long curls, which appeared in *St. Nicholas,* a children's magazine, before being published in book form in 1886. Her best-loved book, *The Secret Garden,* the story of a little girl who in making her secret garden "grow and bloom" made herself and her friends "grow and bloom, too," appeared in 1911, followed by *The Lost Prince* (1915).

U.S. Award Winners, Juvenile Literature

The Laura Ingalls Wilder Award (see below):
Clara Ingraham Judson, 1960

Ruth Sawyer Durand, 1965
(E. B. White was the 1970 winner)
Beverly Cleary, 1975

The John Newbery Medal

Awarded annually since 1922 by the Children's Service Division of the American Library Association for the most distinguished contribution to American literature for children. Presentation of the medal, which is for a book published during the preceding year, is made at the annual conference of the ALA at the same time as the Caldecott Medal (below).

Elizabeth Coatsworth, 1931, for *The Cat Who Went to Heaven*

Laura Adams Armer, 1932, for *Waterless Mountain*

Elizabeth Foreman Lewis, 1933, for *Young Fu of the Upper Yangtze*

Cornelia Meigs, 1934, for *Invincible Louisa*

Monica Shannon, 1935, for *Dobry*

Carol Ryrie Brink, 1936, for *Caddie Woodlawn*

Ruth Sawyer, 1937, for *Roller Skates*

Kate Seredy, 1938, for *The White Stag*

Elizabeth Enright, 1939, for *Thimble Summer*

Elizabeth Janet Gray, 1943, for *Adam of the Road*

Esther Forbes, 1944, for *Johnny Tremain: A Novel for Old and Young*

Lois Lenski, 1946, for *Strawberry Girl*

Carolyn Sherwin Bailey, 1947, for *Miss Hickory*

Marguerite Henry, 1949, for *King of the Wind*

Marguerite de Angeli, 1950, for *The Door in the Wall*

Elizabeth Yates, 1951, for *Amos Fortune, Free Man*

Eleanor Estes, 1952, for *Ginger Pye*

Ann Nolan Clark, 1953, for *Secret of the Andes*

Jean Lee Latham, 1956, for *Carry on, Mr. Bowditch*

Virginia Sorensen, 1957, for *Miracles on Maple Hill*

Elizabeth George Speare, 1959, for *The Witch of Blackbird Pond,* and 1962, for *The Bronze Bow*

Madeleine L'Engle, 1963, for *A Wrinkle in Time*

Emily Neville, 1964, for *It's Like This, Cat*

Mala Wojciechowska, 1965, for *Shadow of a Bull*

Elizabeth Borton De Trevino, 1966, for *I, Juan de Pareja*

Irene Hunt, 1967, for *Up a Road Slowly*

Elaine Konigsburg, 1968, for *From the Mixed-Up Files of Mrs. Basil E. Frankweiler*

Betsy Byars, 1971, for *Summer of the Swans*

Jean Craighead George, 1973, for *Julie of the Wolves*

Paula Fox, 1974, for *The Slave Dancer*
Virginia Hamilton, 1975, for *M. C. Higgins, the Great*
Susan Cooper, 1976, for *The Grey King*

Mildred D. Taylor, 1977, for *Roll of Thunder, Hear My Cry*
Katherine Paterson, 1978, for *Bridge to Terabithia*

The Caldecott Medal

Presented since 1938 for the most distinguished American picture book for children. The first award established with the purpose of giving recognition to the illustrator of a book, it was named for the famous English illustrator Randolph Caldecott who, together with KATE GREENAWAY and Walter Crane, began a new era of picture books for children.

Dorothy Lathrop, 1938, for *Animals of the Bible*. Text selected by Helen Dean Fish from the King James Bible.

Ingri (and Edgar) d'Aulaire, 1940, for *Abraham Lincoln*

Virginia Lee Burton, 1943, for *The Little House*

Elizabeth Orton Jones, 1945, for *Prayer for a Child, by* Rachel Field

Maud (and Miska) Petersham, 1946, for *The Rooster Crows*

Berta (and Elmer) Hader, 1949, for *The Big Snow*

Katherine Milhous, 1951, for *The Egg Tree*

Marcia Brown, 1955, for *Cinderella*, and 1962, for *Once a Mouse*

Barbara Cooney, 1959, for *Chanticleer and the Fox*

Marie Hall Ets, 1960, for *Nine Days to Christmas*

Nonny Hogrogian, 1966, for *Always Room for One More*, and 1972, *One Fine Day*

Evaline Ness, 1967, for *Sam, Bangs & Moonshine*

Gail E. Haley, 1971, for *A Story—A Story*

Margot Zemach, 1974, for *Duffy and the Devil*

Diane (and Leo) Dillon, 1976, for *Why Mosquitoes Buzz in People's Ears*, retold by Verna Aardema

Diane (and Leo) Dillon, 1977, for *Ashanti to Zulu: African Traditions*

Her *Little House* Survives

The Little House in the Big Woods, published in 1932 when LAURA INGALLS WILDER was 65 years old, was the first of several children's books recounting her pioneer childhood during the 1870s and 1880s with Ma, Pa, and her three sisters, Mary, Carrie, and Grace. Ms. Wilder's books, including *The Little House on the Prairie* (1935), *Farmer Boy* (1933), *The Banks of Plum Creek* (1937), and *By the Shores of Silver Lake* (1939), paint a vivid picture of the life of American pioneers. In 1954 Ms. Wilder was the first recipient of the Laura Ingalls Wilder Award, created in her honor by the Children's Services Division of the American Library Association. It is awarded every five years "to an author or illustrator whose books published in the United States have over a period of years made a lasting contribution to literature for children" (see above). Ms. Wilder died in 1957. In 1975, her *Little House in the Big Woods* was adapted for television.

She Invented "Tactile" Children's Books

DOROTHY KUNHARDT, born 1901, author and illustrator of children's books, gave them a new dimension in *Pat the Bunny* (1940) with its felt bunny and other objects. Other books by Ms. Kunhardt include *Tickle the Pig, The Telephone Book, Lucky Mrs. Ticklefeather, Junket Is Nice, Now Open the Box,* and *Brave Mr. Buckingham.*

Their Novels and Juveniles Sold Over 1 Million Copies in Hardcover

According to figures compiled by Alice Payne Hackett and James Henry Burke (selected from a list of all books selling more than 750,000 copies in hardcover editions since 1895, as reported in *80 Years of Best Sellers, 1895–1975*, published by R. R. Bowker Co., 1977), the women below in those years sold over a million copies each of their novels and juveniles (crime stories, cookbooks, etiquette books, and other how-tos are not included), exclusive of paperback editions:

Helen Bannerman
  Little Black Sambo (a juvenile), 1899
Gene Stratton Porter
  Freckles, 1904
  The Girl of the Limberlost, 1909
  The Harvester, 1911
  Laddie (a juvenile), 1913
Kate Douglas Wiggin
  Rebecca of Sunnybrook Farm (a juvenile), 1904
Florence Barclay
  The Rosary, 1910
Kathleen Norris
  Mother, 1911
Eleanor H. Porter
  Pollyanna (a juvenile), 1913
  Pollyanna Grows Up (a juvenile), 1915
Elsie E. Egermeier
  Egermeier's Bible Story Book (a juvenile), 1923
Julia Peterkin
  Scarlet Sister Mary, 1928
Pearl S. Buck
  The Good Earth, 1931
Pamela L. Travers
  Mary Poppins (a juvenile), 1934
Margaret Mitchell
  Gone With the Wind, 1936
Daphne du Maurier
  Rebecca, 1938
  Hungry Hill, 1943

  The King's General, 1946
  My Cousin Rachel, 1952
Marguerite Steen
  The Sun Is My Undoing, 1941
Betty Smith
  A Tree Grows in Brooklyn, 1943
Inglis Fletcher
  Lusty Wind for Carolina, 1944
Elizabeth Goudge
  Green Dolphin Street, 1944
Kathleen Winsor
  Forever Amber, 1944
Taylor Caldwell
  This Side of Innocence, 1946
Elizabeth M. Howard
  Before the Sun Goes Down, 1946
Frances Parkinson Keyes
  The River Road, 1946
  Came a Cavalier, 1947
  Dinner at Antoine's, 1948
  Joy Street, 1950
  Steamboat Gothic, 1952
  The Royal Box, 1954
Edna L. Lee
  The Web of Days, 1947
Mary Brinker Post
  Annie Jordan, 1948
Annemarie Selinko
  Desiree, 1953
Laura Ingalls Wilder
  The Little House on the Prairie (a juvenile), 1953 edition
  The Little House in the Big Woods (a juvenile), 1953 edition
Anya Seton
  The Winthrop Woman, 1958
Joan Walsh Anglund
  A Friend Is Someone Who Likes You (a juvenile), 1958
  Love Is a Special Way of Feeling (a juvenile), 1960

16

Women Activists, Heroes, and Humanitarians

By Jean Callahan
(contributing editor-writer)

There are many women, living and dead, whose names should appear in this chapter but who are not represented because of the limitations of space. Some others, contemporary activists, well known in the Women's Movement, do not appear because they specifically asked to be excluded. "Firsts" are tokens, they said. By acknowledging a few outstanding women, they said, we are passively accepting substitutes for true progress toward equality.

But activists, heroes, and humanitarians—particularly female activists, heroes, and humanitarians—are always too busy to give themselves credit. Women need to take time to recognize themselves. This chapter is an attempt to do that for some of them.

There are internationally famous women here, like EMMA GOLDMAN, CORETTA KING, and ELEANOR ROOSEVELT. There are less-well-known activists, like GAIL SINCOTTA, Chicago's one-woman campaign against discriminatory bank practices, and women who are be-

coming better known like JAN PETERSON, founder of the Congress for Neighborhood Women (who in 1977 went to work in the White House).

There are women whose activities are communal—like the Boston Women's Health Collective, twelve women who have worked and sometimes lived together for almost ten years. In 1971 they published Our Bodies, Ourselves, the only health manual in the United States written and produced entirely by women. In 1978 they published Ourselves and Our Children.

There are women who worked for suffrage and women's rights and peace in several nations in the early days of the century. There are women born later who worked for the American civil rights and antiwar movements of the 1960s and '70s, fighting for the freedom of others. There are women in their middle or later years and young women who have been involved in the beginnings and in the continuing development of the women's liberation movement.

There are women from all over the world: DOLORES IBARRURI, "La Pasionaria," Spanish Communist Party leader whose 40-year exile ended with her return to Spain (and election at 81 to Parliament) in 1977 is here; so are Egypt's JIHAN SADAT and India's KAMALADEVI CHATTOPADHYAY.

The women in this chapter range widely in background. Some have risked their lives. They span a broad spectrum politically—from LOUISE DAY HICKS to ANGELA DAVIS. What unites them all is that they are activists. The full impression of their rich and unique stories is that women *are* totally capable of standing up for their rights and the rights of others, of risking themselves in acts of heroism, of struggling day by day in a lifelong movement.

In this chapter, there are women who disagree with each other. Some of them are heroes for me; others far from it. What I respect about each one of them is her spirit and her devotion to whatever it is that she believes in.

JEAN CALLAHAN, *a free-lance writer based in Washington, D.C., has been published in* New Times, Mother Jones, Progressive, *and other magazines. She was involved in the editorial planning and fund-raising for* Washington Newsworks, *a weekly paper for which she also wrote; was a reporter for the* Daily Rag, *an alternative community newspaper in the District of Columbia; and has reported regularly for Pacific News Service. A graduate of Boston College, 1969, with a major in philosophy and minor in English, she was a child welfare caseworker in Wilmington, Delaware, Lynn Massachusetts, and Washington, D.C., 1969–73.*

EARLY FIGHTERS FOR SUFFRAGE, WOMEN'S RIGHTS, AND PEACE

First President of First U.S. Women's Suffrage Organization

SUSAN B. ANTHONY, born at Adams, Massachusetts on February 15, 1820, into a large Quaker family, in 1869 became chairwoman of the executive committee of the National Woman Suffrage Association and in 1892 was elected president—a post she held until her retirement at 80. Throughout her life, Susan B. Anthony fought for woman suffrage, encouraging others to join her fight and building the groundwork for passage of the 19th Amendment in 1920, 14 years after her death on March 13, 1906. In 1872 she lead a group of women to the polls in Rochester, New York, to test their right to enfranchisement under the terms of the 14th Amendment. She was arrested, tried, and sentenced to a fine (which she refused to pay), causing a sensation. Other women followed her example until finally the case was decided against them by the U. S. Supreme Court. Educated in her early years by her father, who conducted a school in their home, she later attended DEBORAH MOULSON's Boarding School near Philadelphia in preparation for a teaching career. After many years of teaching, sometimes for $1.50 a week (then considered good money for a woman), she gave up her career (1850) and devoted herself to the problems of the day. One of her interests was the temperance movement but the greatest was suffrage.

Early Champion of Black Women

FANNY BARRIER WILLIAMS (1855–1944) was born in Brockport, New York, and trained as a schoolteacher. Daughter of a free black family, she was shocked by her first job in the post-Civil War South and came back North to study at the New England Conservatory of Music in Boston and the Washington School of Fine Arts. Married to a lawyer and living in Chicago, she attracted national attention in 1893 by a speech at the World Congress of Representative Women at Chicago's World's Fair Columbian Exposition on "The Intellectual Progress of Colored Women of the United States Since the Emancipation Proclamation"—then only 30 years in the past. Later in the same year she spoke, as successfully, to the World Parliament of Religions, probably the first ecumenical gathering in the United States. In 1895 she became a member of the Chicago Woman's Club, the "only colored," and later became the first woman—and the first black—appointed to the Chicago Library Board.

Second Suffragist President and Co-Founder of the Women's Peace Party

CARRIE CHAPMAN CATT (1859–1947) was graduated from Iowa State College in 1880. By 1883 she was superintendent of schools in Mason City, Iowa, an unusually responsible role for a woman at that time. As a member of the Iowa delegation, she attended the first convention of the newly organized National Woman Suffrage Association and thereafter rose rapidly to the front ranks of the suffrage movement's national leadership. When SUSAN B. ANTHONY retired from the presidency of the Suffrage Association, she chose Ms. Catt as her successor. In January 1915 Carrie Catt, in collaboration with JANE ADDAMS, founded the Women's Peace Party. During World War I, Ms. Catt worked for the cause of pacifism while continuing her struggle for woman's suffrage. At the 1919 convention of the Suffrage Association, she called for the establishment of a League of Women Voters in the states where suffrage had already been won to speed the completion of the work and to enter the field of non-partisan political education. On August 26, 1920, the 19th Amendment was proclaimed as adopted; it is to Carrie Chapman Catt more than any other single figure besides Susan B. Anthony that American women owe their right to vote.

First President of the League of Women Voters

MAUD WOOD PARK (1880–1955) was the first national president of the League of Women Voters. Her interest in woman suffrage began when she was in college at Radcliffe and was stirred by a speech she heard ALICE STONE BLACKWELL give. After her graduation from Radcliffe in 1898, MAUD WOOD married Charles Park, a Boston architect, who died in 1904. In 1900 she helped organize the Massachusetts College Equal Suffrage League. As executive secretary of the Boston Equal Suffrage Association for Good Government for 12 years, she helped organize the first parent-teacher association, secured the first use in Boston of school buildings as community centers, and demonstrated the need for policewomen to protect young women and children in city streets and places of amusement. Ms. Park's genius for legislative strategy led CARRIE CHAPMAN CATT to ask her to direct the congressional work for the suffrage amendment. In 1920 she was elected the first president of the newly formed League of Women Voters. She served for four years in that office and maintained an active involvement in the League long after.

Mother and Daughters Who Led British Woman Suffrage Movement

In 1903 EMMELINE PANKHURST (1858–1928) and her daughters CHRISTABEL (1880–1958) and SYLVIA (1882–1960) Pankhurst, founded Britain's Women's Social and Political Union (WSPU), which quickly developed into a radical organization using militant tactics to lobby for suffrage. Meetings were interrupted. Women marched on the House of Commons, chained themselves to railings, and were repeatedly arrested and imprisoned.

The eldest daughter in a family of 11 children, Emmeline was born in Manchester, England, to parents actively interested in radicalism and reform movements. She was only 14 when her mother took her to her first woman suffrage meeting. In 1879 Emmeline married Richard Marsden Pankhurst, a liberal attorney and advocate of woman suffrage; Dr. Pankhurst died in 1898, leaving his widow with four children. Ms. Pankhurst in 1910 and again in 1911 toured the United States to raise money for her work; on her return from her second trip the offices of the WSPU were raided by the police and she was arrested. In prison, she began a hunger strike and eventually was released. In 1913 she was arrested again and sentenced to three years in prison. Through hunger strikes and other non-violent protests, she managed to stay out of jail for all but 30 days of her sentence, continuing to work for suffrage. Emmeline Pankhurst died in London in June 14, 1928, just after the passage of the second Representation of the People Act, which gave full and equal suffrage to men and women.

Christabel, the elder daughter, qualified as a lawyer but was barred from practice because of her sex. Political strategist of the WSPU from its very beginnings, she led every stage of the militant campaign. When women were granted the vote, she ran for Parliament in the first election in 1918. She lost—but polled more votes than any other woman candidate that year. Created a Dame of the British Empire in 1936, Christabel Pankhurst died in 1958 in Los Angeles.

Sylvia was trained as an artist and dedicated her talents to the WSPU campaign. She became increasingly involved with political and social work among the poorest people of London's East End.

Her socialist sympathies and support of Labour Party candidates went against WSPU policy, and she split with the main branch of the Union. She visited Russia after World War I and strongly supported the Revolution. In the 1930s she supported the cause of Abyssinian independence and eventually settled in Ethiopia. She died in Addis Ababa in 1960 and was given the equivalent of a state funeral.

FLORA MACDONALD DENISON (1867–1921), an early leader in the campaign for woman suffrage in Canada, led an active life as a journalist and worker for women's rights. From 1911 to 1914, she was president of the Canadian Suffrage Association. For several years she wrote a labor column in the *Sunday World,* which was not without influence in winning the vote for women in most of the provinces of Canada in 1918.

Author of the U. S. Equal Rights Amendment

ALICE PAUL, born in 1885 of Quaker parents in Moorestown, New Jersey, died in 1977 still hoping that the Equal Rights Amendment, which she drafted in 1923, three years after woman suffrage was granted, would be ratified. The amendment was meant to be the proper accompaniment to suffrage, and was a principal goal of the National Women's Party, which Ms. Paul founded in 1913. For more than half a century, the author of the ERA, a Swarthmore College graduate, continued her struggle for its passage, often fighting alone when her unflagging energy was not matched by anyone else's. The new wave of feminism in the late 1960s brought the ERA back to the attention of the American public.

Founder of Japan's New Women's Association

Born in 1893, FUSAYE ICHIKAWA in her lifetime has seen fundamental changes as Japan has moved to the emancipation of women; her life has mirrored this transformation. From a village schoolteacher, Ms. Ichikawa became a news reporter, stockbroker's clerk, and labor union worker. In 1918 she was a founder of the pioneering New Women's Association that sought to amend the law prohibiting women from listening to, making, or sponsoring political speeches. In

the 1920s she directed the Women's Committee of the International Labor Organization. In 1931 Miss Ichikawa and co-workers protested fascist trends and addressed themselves to problems created for women by war. Following Japan's surrender at the end of World War II, she was elected leader of the New Japan Women's League, which became the League of Women Voters after woman suffrage was granted. In the 1950s she headed a successful campaign against licensed prostitution and helped found a "Fair and Clean Elections" association to safeguard the franchise. In 1952 she won election as an independent to the upper House of Councilors and served 18 years in the Diet, where she consistently opposed pay raises for members and lived frugally, donating all increases plus a portion of her salary to women's causes. Out of office for three years, she returned to the Diet in 1974, supported by a large following of Japanese women and advocates of political conscience.

Founder of First Puerto Rican Feminist Magazine

In 1910 LUISA CAPETILLO (1880–1922) caused a sensation in Puerto Rico by being the first woman to wear pants in public. That same year, she founded a feminist magazine, *La Mujer,* and finished a book, *My Opinion on the Liberties, Rights, and Obligations of the Puerto Rican Woman,* which was published in 1911. As a young girl in turn-of-the-century Puerto Rico, Luisa Capetillo worked in factories for as little as three cents for a 10-to-12-hour day. She learned to read and write from her father, a construction worker. One of the earliest Puerto Ricans to speak out against U.S. exploitation of island labor, she participated in a 1907 strike at an Arecibo factory and became a member of the Free Federation of Puerto Rican Workers and then a reporter for the labor newspaper, *Workers' Union.*

Founder of Hungarian Feminist-Pacifists

ROSIKA SCHWIMMER was founder and prime mover of the Hungarian *Feministak Egyesulete,* a feminist-pacifist organization instrumental in many of Hungary's social reforms—including suffrage—and, as Hungarian Ambassador to Switzerland, one of the first female diplomats of modern times. When World War I began in Europe, Rosika Schwimmer appealed to Woodrow Wilson to arbitrate a peaceful settlement. That effort failing, she turned to Henry Ford, who agreed to organize an unofficial neutral mediation conference and to send American delegates to Europe on a "peace ship." (U.S. and international criticism thwarted this effort.) In 1920 Ms. Schwimmer fled Hungary, where her life was threatened by the reactionary and anti-Semitic Horthy regime. Eventually, she emigrated to the United States, where her petition for citizenship, in 1926, became a *cause célèbre* when, at the urging of the American Legion, the case was carried to the Supreme Court. The justices ruled against Rosika Schwimmer, supporting the government's contention that her avowed pacifism was incompatible with the naturalization bureau's requirement of willingness to "take up arms in defense of the Constitution." Remaining in America as an alien, she continued to work for world peace until her death in 1948.

First Woman to Receive Nobel Peace Prize

JANE ADDAMS (1860–1935), who was born into a wealthy family, devoted her life to the impoverished and to working for woman suffrage and for peace. In 1931 she became the first woman to receive the Nobel Peace Prize. In 1889, with ELLEN GATES STARR, Jane Addams founded Chicago's famed Hull House, where a system of providing a variety of community services through one center originated. Her work with the poor led her to instigate a wide range of proposals that led to Illinois's first Factory Inspection Act in 1893; the first juvenile court in 1899; the first "Mothers" Pension Act; a law for an eight-hour working day for women; workmen's compensation; and tenement housing regulations. From involvement in 1907 with the cause of woman suffrage, she moved into politics in 1912 to second Theodore Roosevelt's nomination at the Progressive Party convention. When World War I began, she addressed herself exclusively to the cause of peace, organizing and chairing the Woman's Peace Party of the U.S.A. In January 1915, chairing the International Congress of Women at The Hague later that year, and unsuccessfully trying to get President Wilson to mediate between the belligerents. After the war, she became president of the Women's International League for Peace and Freedom. In 1920 she was instrumental in forming the American Civil Liberties Union (ACLU). In a lifetime filled with battles and honors, Ms. Addams had one other notable "first": in 1910 she was the first woman to receive an honorary degree from Yale.

Co-Founder of Women's International League for Peace and Freedom, Nobel Winner

EMILY GREENE BALCH (1867–1961) co-founded the Women's International League for Peace and Freedom with JANE ADDAMS in 1915. She was a delegate to the International Congress of Women at The Hague and secretary of the Women's International League 1919–22. She later became honorary international president of the League. Ms. Balch came to activism from social work; she was a member of the Massachusetts Commission on Industrial Relations from 1908 to 1909. In 1913–14 she was on the Massachusetts Commission on Immigration and from 1914 to 1917 she was on the Boston City Planning Board. For her work with the Women's International League for Peace and Freedom, she received the Nobel Peace Prize in 1946.

Last Survivor of the National Women's Party Founding Members

Eighty-seven-year-old feminist HAZEL HUNKINS HALLINAN has been, since the death of ALICE PAUL (p. 698), the sole survivor of the group who participated in the first campaign of the National

Women's Party in Colorado in 1916. That was the year in which she returned to her hometown of Billings, Montana, after graduation from Vassar and three years of teaching in the chemistry department of the University of Missouri. Determined to practice, not teach, chemistry, she got "stacks of letters," she recalls, assuring her she was qualified but could not be employed because she was a woman. She turned to politics and was soon working at the National Women's Party headquarters in Washington. She took part in the famous 1917 march for suffrage down Pennsylvania Avenue and the peaceful picketing of the White House, was arrested and once jailed. The widow of a former European financial editor for the UPI, mother of four and grandmother of nine, Hazel Hallinan, freckled and sprightly, with bobbed blond hair, has lived for many years in London, where she raises roses and has never stopped working for the worldwide Women's Movement. As vice-president of the Six Point Group, initiated in 1922, she told a *Washington Post* reporter in 1977 that she intended to keep up an ongoing siege of Parliament to get enforcement of England's Equal Pay and Anti-Discrimination Acts, passed in 1975.

THE U.S. CIVIL RIGHTS MOVEMENT

She Sat at the Front of the Bus

On December 1, 1955, seamstress ROSA PARKS refused to "move to the rear" of the Cleveland Avenue bus in downtown Montgomery, Alabama; she was arrested and fined $10. Her action triggered a 381-day bus boycott led by Martin Luther King, Jr., bringing him to national prominence and marking a turning point in the history of black protest. Since 1969 Ms. Parks has been on the staff of Congressman John Conyers (D., Mich.). She lives in Detroit and continues to be an activist.

Founder of Martin Luther King, Jr., Center for Non-Violent Social Change and Leader in Her Own Right

CORETTA SCOTT KING, widow of Dr. Martin Luther King, Jr., has emerged as an eloquent speaker and internationally recognized civil rights leader since the death of her husband. Born in Alabama on April 27, 1927, she attended Antioch College in Ohio. In 1951 she moved to Boston to study voice at the New England Conservatory of Music. While there, she met Martin Luther King, Jr., who was doing graduate work in philosophy at Boston University. They were married in 1953, subsequently moving to Montgomery, Alabama. In 1955 the Kings became national public figures following the Montgomery bus boycott. After her husband's assassination in 1968, Coretta Scott King began plans for the Martin Luther King, Jr., Center for Non-Violent Social Change, which opened in Atlanta, Georgia, in 1971. The Center has a collection of documents and tapes as well as some 3,000 books on the civil rights movement, tracing its history back to 1954. Ms. King is founder and president. In 1969 she traveled to India to accept the Nehru Award for International Understanding on behalf of her husband. In March of that year she became the first woman to preach at St. Paul's Cathedral in London, where she called for "a new ministry of conciliation." In April 1969, she led 200 protesters in a Charleston, South Carolina, march in support of striking hospital workers. She is the author of *My Life with Martin Luther King, Jr.* (1969) and was appointed U.S. representative to the 32nd General Assembly of the United Nations by President Jimmy Carter.

Civil Rights Hero, Co-Founder of the Mississippi Freedom Democratic Party

FANNIE LOU HAMER (1918–77), one of the most powerful leaders of the civil rights movement, first came to national attention in 1964 when the Mississippi Freedom Democratic Party she had helped to found challenged the all-white regular Mississippi delegation to the Democratic National Convention. Although the challenge was not sustained, it did force a walkout of the all-white delegation. Some Freedom Democratic Party delegates were seated in 1968. In 1972 the black-led Freedom Democrats won all the seats, displacing the regular party.

Born the granddaughter of a slave, the youngest of 20 children, Ms. Hamer was sharecropping cotton on a plantation in Sunflower County when the just organized Student Nonviolent Coordinating Committee (SNCC) began working in Mississippi in 1961. The young organizers who poured into Mississippi in those years and the local blacks as well found in Fannie Lou Hamer a source of great spiritual strength and organizing strategy. But she might have stayed in the poverty cycle had she not been politicized by a 1961 operation. She entered the hospital to have a small uterine tumor removed. When she woke up, she found she'd been sterilized. Doctors had given her a hysterectomy. The anger that lingered after that incident prompted her to try to register to vote in 1962, an attempt which got her thrown off the plantation where she had lived for 19 years. By that time she had become a field worker with SNCC and was emerging as one of the greatest movement strategists.

In 1963 she helped set up a network of precinct and political organizations throughout black areas of Mississippi, the forerunner of the Freedom Democratic Party. In 1964 she ran against Congressman Jamie L. Whitten (D., Miss.) in the primary but lost. In 1971 she was elected to the steering committee of the National Women's Political Caucus. In her life, she endured countless threats, a number of jailings, beatings, gunshots into her home, and other reprisals for her commitment to freedom for black people. She became a symbol of unswerving determination to overcome the laws and legacies of segregation. Fannie Lou Hamer died of cancer on March 14, 1977.

First Black Graduate of University of Alabama

Governor George Wallace carried out his 1962 campaign promise when he stood at the University of Alabama's Foster

Hall to bar VIVIAN MALONE and James A. Hood from entering in the autumn of 1963. Despite harassment that ensued after her initial act to desegregate the university, Ms. Malone stayed on to become the first black to graduate from Alabama in 1965.

First Black to Attempt to Desegregate University of Alabama

Seven years before VIVIAN MALONE (above) and James A. Hood accomplished it, AUTHERINE LUCY tried to desegregate the University of Alabama. In 1953 she enrolled in Mills College, part of the university, and after a three-and-a-half-year court fight, won her right to register. Her registration caused a series of violent outbursts in the white community and marked the first time federal and state agencies clashed over the issue of school segregation.

First Black Woman Graduate of the University of Mississippi

CONNIE SLAUGHTER, 30, first black woman to be graduated from the University of Mississippi (1967), was also, while a student there, the first black woman to be elected president of the student body. As a staff attorney for the Lawyers' Committee for Civil Rights and director of the Southern Legal Rights Association, Ms. Slaughter has prepared some of the country's most significant legal briefs. She filed the brief for *Burton v. Williams*—a damage action suit against the state of Mississippi for the wrongful death of two students and the injuring of three others at Jackson State College on May 15, 1970. She lost that case even after an appeal but setbacks and continuing discrimination do not discourage her. "I remain in the legal profession to aid in determining a working definition of 'justice' and 'equality,'" she says.

First Woman President of the Northern Region of the NAACP

MELNEA CASS was the first female president of the Northern Region of the NAACP; the only woman incorporator of Action for Boston Community Development; chairwoman of the Mayor's Committee on Elderly Affairs; Massachusetts' Mother of the Year for 1974; and a former member of the YWCA board of directors. A branch of the Boston YWCA was recently renamed in her honor. Ms. Cass is also president of Roxbury's Council of Elders; on the board of directors of the Roxbury Federation of Neighborhood Centers; and past president of the Massachusetts State Union of Women's Clubs. The "First Lady of Roxbury," as Ms. Cass is affectionately called, holds three honorary doctorates.

Highest-Ranking Woman in the NAACP

MILDRED BOND ROXBOROUGH, assistant director of the NAACP, joined the Association's national office in January 1954; she became its highest-ranking woman in January 1975. Ms. Roxborough, who has served with NAACP branches in more than 40 states and organized the Association's national conventions, has deep roots, in the struggle for human dignity. Her father, Ollie S. Bond, founded the Association's first chapter in Brownsville, Tennessee, seat of Haywood County, in 1938. His efforts to secure voting rights for Negro citizens resulted in his having to flee Brownsville, with his family, on Christmas Eve in 1939. Their home was burned to the ground the same night. Ms. Roxborough, who studied at Howard University and went on to graduate from Washington Square College, New York University, and Columbia University Graduate School, currently lives in New York.

WOMEN'S LIBERATION

First to Write for the Second Sex

In 1949 SIMONE DE BEAUVOIR wrote *The Second Sex* (published in the United States in 1953), a bold and brilliant analysis of women's lot in Western society, which set an important intellectual precedent for the new feminism. "One is not born, but rather becomes a woman," she wrote then. "No biological, psychological, or economic fate determines the figure that the human female presents in society; it is civilization as a whole that produces this creature, intermediate between male and eunuch, which is described as feminine." Born on January 9, 1908, into a cultivated Parisian household, Simone de Beauvoir had by the time she was 15 made up her mind to be an author. In *Memoirs of a Dutiful Daughter* (1958), the first volume of her continuing autobiography, she recalls how, having lost her convent-nurtured childhood faith, she decided that "by writing a work based on my own experience, I would re-create myself and justify my existence. At the same time I would be serving humanity." While studying at the Sorbonne, she met Jean-Paul Sartre and began a deep friendship with him, which has become a model for feminist male-female relationships. One of the leading voices of existentialism, Ms. de Beauvoir's memoirs include *Force of Circumstance* (1965), *A Very Easy Death* (1966), and *All Accounting Made* (1972). In addition to becoming known as Europe's leading feminist, Simone de Beauvoir has stirred up controversy with her provocative commentary on such topics as Communist China (*The Long March,* 1958) and the plight of the elderly (*The Coming of Age,* 1972).

Founder and First President of NOW

BETTY FRIEDAN, born on February 4, 1921, in Peoria, Illinois, is sometimes called "the mother of the new feminist movement." Ms. Friedan might find that title somewhat sexist. But the fact is that this ex-suburban housewife was the first woman to prompt many other women, unfamiliar with the works of earlier feminist writers, to examine their roles in society. With the publication of her influential best-selling book *The Feminine Mystique* (1963), American housewives found themselves described and for the first time read a feminist analysis of the sense of emptiness and the lack of identity they felt. In 1966 Ms. Friedan founded and became the first president of the National Organization for Women (NOW). Although often dismissed by younger, more radical women, NOW has persisted and remains the largest and best-organized of the new feminist groups. On August 26, 1970, Ms. Friedan led the nationwide Women's Strike for Equality, the first large-scale demonstration of feminist protest since the woman suffrage movement. A graduate of Smith College, Ms. Friedan moved to New York in 1942. In 1947 she married Carl Friedan, then a summer stock producer, now an advertising executive. They were divorced in 1969. Betty Friedan stepped down as president of NOW in 1970, but continues to devote much of her energy to feminist causes and to write. Her most recent book, *It Changed My Life,* was published in 1977.

First Black President of NOW and Founder of Black Women for Action

AILEEN HERNANDEZ, one of the original founding members of the National Organization for Women (NOW), succeeded BETTY FRIEDAN as president in

1970. In 1973 Ms. Hernandez founded Black Women for Action, which has filed suits against discriminatory employers, instituted employment opportunity clinics, and helped form a feminist credit union. Operating out of San Francisco, the organization also urges black women to seek political office. Born in Brooklyn, New York, and a graduate of Howard University in Washington, D.C., Ms. Hernandez has had a long involvement in civil rights and labor causes. While working for the International Ladies' Garment Workers' Union (ILGWU) in Los Angeles, she learned a great deal about the plight of Chicanos in America and was invited to tour six South American countries. Appointed head of the Equal Opportunity Commission by Lyndon Johnson in 1965, she resigned after a brief period in office in frustration over bureaucratic lack of progress. As president of NOW, she was concerned to change its image from a middle-class elitism and make the organization more relevant to the needs of working-class women.

Co-Founders of the First Independent U.S. Women's Liberation Group

Denied a forum by male leftists at the National Conference for a New Politics, held in Chicago in September 1967, Chicago feminists JO FREEMAN, SHULAMITH FIRESTONE, HEATHER BOOTH, **and** NAOMI WEISSTEIN **founded the first independent women's caucus organized strictly around women's issues since the fight for suffrage.**

In 1968 Jo Freeman began publishing Voices of Women's Liberation, **the first national newsletter of the new Women's Movement. The author of** The Politics of Women's Liberation **(1975), Freeman is a veteran of the Berkeley free speech movement and former Southern Christian Leadership Conference field worker. She claims to own the world's largest feminist button collection. A professor of political science at the State University of New York, in 1977 she was on a sabbatical at the Brookings Institution in Washington, D.C., studying employment policy as it relates to women.**

Shulamith Firestone, author of The Dialectic of Sex: The Case for Feminist Revolution **(1970), was born in Ottawa, Canada. She studied at the Art Institute of Chicago on scholarship, simultaneously becoming more and more involved in civil rights and antiwar activities before devoting her energies to feminism. Also co-founder, with** PAM ALLEN, **of**

New York Radical Women (the first women's liberation group in New York) and, with ELLEN WILLIS, **of Redstockings, another New York-based women's liberation group, Shulamith Firestone edited** Notes, **a journal of radical feminism, 1968–70.**

From her background in women's, labor, and civil rights organizing, Heather Booth founded the Midwest Academy, a training school for activist leaders and organizers, in 1972. The Academy offers workshops at its headquarters in Chicago and to groups throughout the country. With a special emphasis on training female activists, the Academy is the first and perhaps the only such independent training center in this country. "The Women's Movement has changed the consciousness of a generation," Booth says. "But now we face our strongest test from organized opposition. We must convert our good ideas into viable strategies, our power of sisterhood into concrete activities. With training, we can move from these first steps to victory."

Naomi Weisstein, author of the widely read, influential essay "'Kinder, Küche, Kirche' as Scientific Law: Psychology Constructs the Female" (published in Sisterhood Is Powerful, **edited by** ROBIN MORGAN, **1970), holds a Ph.D. from the University of California at Davis and is a**

professor of psychology at the State University of New York at Buffalo.

Equal Pay Was Her Motive

"I wasn't a feminist; I just wanted more money." That is the way KAREN L. DECROW describes her decision in 1967 to join the National Organization for Women and organize a chapter of the then fledgling group in Syracuse. At the time, she was working for a small publishing house in Syracuse where the men were paid more than the women. "I joined NOW on an issue of equal pay," she says. But as president of NOW from 1974 through 1976, she was paid nothing. Ms. DeCrow was born on December 18, 1937, was graduated from the Medill School of Journalism at Northwestern University in 1959, worked as a journalist for several years, and then enrolled at Syracuse Law School, from which she was graduated in 1972. In January 1969 she and FAITH SEIDENBERG (see "Women in Law and the Justice System," p. 355) were refused service at McSorley's Old Ale House, a hundred-year-old tavern in New York City that had always been an all-male drinking place. With lawyer Seidenberg and under the auspices of NOW, Ms. DeCrow sued McSorley's. On June 25, 1970, Judge Walter R. Mansfield of the District Court of New York ordered the all-male barroom opened to women, declaring that "McSorley's is a public place, not a private club, and the preference of certain of its patrons is not justification for discrimination under the equal protection clause of the U. S. Constitution." Ms. DeCrow turned over the presidency of NOW to ELEANOR SMEAL (see "Women in the Home and Community," p. 120) in 1977.

Creators of the First Women's Health Manual Written Entirely by Women

The Boston Women's Health Book Collective first began working on *Our Bodies, Ourselves* (1971) in the spring of 1969 when they began meeting as a small discussion group. As they shared mystifying medical experiences and their curiosity to know more about how their bodies worked, the twelve women decided to spend their summers researching these topics. The research led to a ten-week course offered in nursery schools, homes, and churches. The course's success led to the first mimeographed, inexpensively bound copies of the book. As its popularity outstripped the means for wider distribution, the collective decided to publish the book commercially. This version—with chapters on anatomy, sexuality, self-defense, birth control, childbearing, and menopause, among others— has become a valuable guidebook for millions of women and has gone through many printings and translations into six foreign languages. The Boston Women's Health Book Collective is still together and in 1978 published *Ourselves and Our Children*.

Author of *The Female Eunuch*

"I'm sick of pretending that some fatuous male's self-important pronouncements are the objects of my undivided attention," says GERMAINE GREER in *The Female Eunuch,* a formative treatise for the new women's liberation movement, which was published in Britain in 1970 and in the United States in 1971. "I refuse to be a female impersonator. I am a woman, not a castrate." Born in Melbourne, Australia, on January 29, 1939, Ms. Greer spent her girlhood in a convent school, took a teaching degree at Melbourne University, did graduate work at the University of Sydney, and moved to England in 1964 on a scholarship to Cambridge, where she earned a Ph.D. Ms. Greer's three-week marriage in 1968 to Paul de Feu, university graduate-turned newsman-turned construction worker, made headlines when De Feu appeared as *Cosmopolitan*'s first nude male center-fold. A professor at the University of Warwick in England, Ms. Greer was a prolific writer in the European press before the publication of *The Female Eunuch*. She began writing articles for the *Listener* and the *Spectator* as well as for such underground journals as the British magazine *Oz* and *Suck*, a newspaper published in Amsterdam which she helped found.

Originator of the First Self-Help Clinic

In 1971 CAROL DOWNER, director of the Feminist Women's Health Center in Los Angeles, started the first women's self-help clinic. "You don't go to a doctor every time you get a cold," she explains. "So why should a woman go to a gynecologist every time she gets a vaginal itch?" Ms. Downer believes that most procedures which take place in the average gynecological office visit are non-medical and could be taken care of by women themselves. If women learned how to examine themselves and each other, she believed, they could learn to recognize and treat vaginal infections and determine pregnancies. Using a plastic speculum, a flashlight, and a mirror, any woman can develop familiarity with her own body. Following the example of Ms. Downer, women all over the country began teaching self-help courses and offering self-help instructions through women's clinics.

Only Mother-Daughter Gynecological Self-Help Team

LOLLY HIRSCH, 55, and her daughter JEANNE, 31, officially teamed up in 1972 to lecture on gynecological self-help and to produce publications that would educate women about their bodies. In 1971, at a convention of the National Organization for Women in Los Angeles, they had met CAROL DOWNER (above) and LORRAINE ROTHMAN, who had just founded a gynecological self-help clinic. Through Carol and Lorraine, the Hirsches developed their interest in self-help demonstrations and launched a series of lectures aimed at showing women what kinds of basic health care they can provide for themselves—becoming the only mother-daughter team to do so.

Founder of *Media Report to Women*

"I decided it was about time we did something about expanding the source of information in the media to portray the *real* us," says DONNA ALLEN, founder of the monthly *Media Report to Women*. "I found that a lot of women were doing things but nobody knew what each other was doing." So in January 1971, Dr. Allen (she has a Ph.D. in history from Howard University) began publishing the useful *Report*. Today 1,500 subscribers find tips on how to set up affirmative action programs, information on the latest legal actions or decisions regarding sex discrimination, news of job openings, of conferences, and of other helpful publications about every form of communication. Dr. Allen, who puts the whole thing together herself with help from a daughter and occasional volunteers, has three daughters, all feminists: MARTHA helps edit the media report; INDRA is editor of "Musica," a newsletter about women and music; and DANA DENSMORE is a writer who was co-founder and editor of *No More Fun & Games,* one of the first radical feminist magazines.

Executive Director of National Women's Education Fund

BETSEY WRIGHT is executive director of the National Women's Education Fund, organized in 1972 to increase the numbers and influence of women in public life by providing programs of political education. NWEF offers practical training, public information, and educational materials to universities, women's organizations, business, labor, and the media. Ms. Wright is also a member of the national advisory council of the National

Women's Political Caucus and the executive board of the Women's Campaign Fund. She served on the Women in Power Committee of the National Commission on the Observance of International Women's Year during 1975 and 1976. Her political experience includes working on numerous local, state, and national campaigns and directing two statewide voter registration drives in her native Texas.

Founder of Center for Women Policy Studies

JANE ROBERTS CHAPMAN is co-director and founder of the Center for Women Policy Studies, a non-profit Washington organization established in 1972 to conduct policy research on selected issues relating to the status of women. An economist, status-of-women specialist, consultant, and experienced panelist and writer, she also served as convener of the Women's National Agenda Task Force on Women and Economic Power (1977).

First President of the Washington, D.C., Chapter of the National Women's Political Caucus

In June 1972 AUDREY COLOM, later to chair the National Women's Political Caucus, was elected president of the D.C. Women's Political Caucus; she was one of the initial organizers of the chapter. Director of women's activities at the Corporation for Public Broadcasting, Ms. Colom, while still under 30, was appointed by President Gerald Ford to the National Commission on the Observance of International Women's Year and chaired its Committee on Child Development. She has written and co-authored handbooks for parents and lay advocates on placements for children with special needs in the District of Columbia, working with the Children's Defense Fund, a public-interest law firm and research group run by MARIAN WRIGHT EDELMAN (p. 728). Ms. Colom also has developed and directed reading programs for

black children in both New York City and Washington, taught in the D.C. public schools, and helped develop the first high school equivalency program for women in the D.C. Women's Detention Center. She was named an Outstanding Young Woman of America in 1976.

President of NOW Legal Defense and Education Fund

Since May 1974 MARY JEAN TULLY has been national president of the NOW Legal Defense and Education Fund, an unpaid volunteer post. In that time she has increased the Fund's capital from $6,000 to $730,000 and has come to be known as the "moneyperson" of the Women's Movement. Fundraiser par excellence, Tully leads seminars on finding money for women's groups and her publications include "Funding the Feminists," in the March/April 1975 issue of *Foundation News.* Tully is a former member of the Financial Development Committee and the International Committee of NOW, as well as editor of *Do It NOW,* the organization's national newsletter. She is married to a corporation executive and is the mother of five children ranging in age from 14 to 25.

Founder of Washington's International Center for Research on Women

IRENE TINKER founded the International Center for Research on Women in 1976 under the aegis of the Federation of Organizations for Professional Women, an umbrella group working for equal opportunities for women in education and the professions, of which she was first president (in 1972). The International Center for Research on Women provides a point of contact for women's research groups around the world and monitors implementation of the Percy Amendment (added to the Foreign Assistance Act of 1973), which requires impact statements on how development will affect women in countries where projects are funded with U.S. monies. Dr. Tinker, who also set up (1973) and continues to head the office of International Science at the American Association for the Advancement of Science, works toward two overlapping goals: the transfer of scientific knowledge and modern institutions to the less-developed countries of the world and equity between peoples in the United States with a particular emphasis on education and employment. An organizer of several UN conferences, Dr. Tinker has been involved in problems of development and the adaptation of institutions since she began advanced studies in London after being graduated from Radcliffe in 1949. She has taught and done research at several universities and been granted fellowships for travel to India and Indonesia.

First Convener of Women's Electoral Lobby of Australia

GAIL RADFORD, born on April 30, 1941, in Melbourne, Australia, was the first convener of the Women's Electoral Lobby in Canberra in 1972. Ms. Radford, a veterinarian, in 1973 was the first woman to be appointed to the National Committee on Discrimination in Employment and Occupation and in 1975 became the first director of Equal Employment Opportunity for the Australian Public Service, a position in which she continues to be active in the women's liberation movement.

Feminist Who Resigned from Australian Government

In October 1975, after two and a half years as special adviser to Australian Prime Minister Edward Gough Whitlam, ELIZABETH ANN REID resigned. She left the office, she said, because she felt unable to deal adequately with real-life conditions of Australian women and believed that the Labour government was insufficiently sensitive to women's problems. A graduate of the Australian National University and of Oxford, and a member of Australian Women's Liberation, the Women's Electoral Lobby, the Association for the Study of Woman and

Society, the Australian Abortion Law Reform Association, and several other women's rights and civil liberties organizations, Ms. Reid taught philosophy in Australia and at Oxford prior to accepting her position with Prime Minister Whitlam.

Leader of Japan's Militant Feminists

MISWO ENOKI, 33-year-old pharmacist, organized the "Pink Panthers" in 1972 and led a fight to legalize birth control pills in Japan that ignited the new wave of Japanese feminism. Ms. Enoki's Pink Panthers wore white military-style uniforms and pink helmets, marched, held sit-ins and protest rallies. Their confrontations focused on demands for women's rights to abortion, equal hiring, equal pay, equitable property settlements and alimony, and easier access to contraceptive pills, which in Japan can only be dispensed as medicine, not as birth control aids, by doctors, most of whom are men. At its height, Ms. Enoki's group included 4,000 members, most of them young single women, but national parliamentary elections in 1977, which saw Ms. Enoki's new Japan Women's Party get only four tenths of 1 per cent of the total popular vote, signaled the collapse of support for radical feminism in this very traditional country. Ms. Enoki, in admitting her at least temporary failure and returning to life as a suburban housewife, said that her group had established a basic awareness of the liberation issue and showed that a woman could be a "determined, assertive fighter" yet remain beautiful and feminine.

Egypt's First Lady Its Foremost Feminist

JIHAN SADAT, wife of Egyptian President Anwar Sadat, is an independent Middle Eastern feminist and social activist. In 1972 she started a welfare project in her husband's native village to raise the standard of living of Egyptian peasants. More recently, she has branched into women's cooperative projects, hospitals, and education programs. She has tried to reform the divorce laws of Egypt, a country where Moslem law allows a man to divorce his wife merely by repeating three times the fact that he is divorcing her, and has called for Islamic monogamy unless the wife permits her husband to take a second wife. She was influential in the passage of a recent Egyptian law providing alimony for divorced wives. "Emancipation of women in Egypt is my beloved thing," Ms. Sadat says.

Head of First Women's Division of the Arab Labor Organization

SAIDA AGREBI was born in Tunis, Tunisia, in 1945. From 1964 to 1968 she attended the University of Tunis, where she was president of the Tunisian National Women's Union, a feminist association. In 1969 she came to the United States with a U. S. Agency for International Development (AID) scholarship to study public health education at the University of Maryland. In 1972 she was named training director for all outreach workers of the Tunisian Family Planning Organization. After a year in this position, she returned to the United States to study for a master's degree in public health at the University of California at Berkeley. In 1976 she was appointed to the Arab League Agency to head the working women committee of the labor organization, which is headquartered in Tunis and represents 21 Arab countries. As head of this committee, Ms. Agrebi is charged with improving conditions and modalities of work for Arab women.

First Arab Radical Feminist

NAWAL EL SAADAWI, M.D., born on October 27, 1930, in Cairo, Egypt, was graduated from the University of Cairo in 1955 and from Columbia University in 1966. She has worked on the staff of the Cairo University Hospital, as a physician in rural areas, as a psychiatrist and novelist. Her book *Woman and Sex,* a psychosocial study, takes a radical perspec-

tive on sexual taboos in Arab society and addresses the political and social factors that oppress women. Because of the feminist nature of her writing, she has encountered much opposition from Arab male leaders. At one time a highly placed bureaucrat, a director in the Ministry of Health and editor of the government-sponsored *Health* magazine, she was dismissed from both of these positions because of her forthright opinions. Dr. Saadawi now lives from writing and lecturing. She is the author of seven novels, four collections of short stories, and four nonfiction texts. The youth of Egypt revere her as a woman who dared to write the "unwritable."

Conveners of the First International Tribunal on Crimes Against Women

The First International Tribunal on Crimes Against Women, which opened at the Palais des Congrès in Brussels, Belgium, on March 8, 1976, was organized by an international coordinating committee that included American activists DIANA E. H. RUSSELL and JUDITH FRIEDLANDER. More than 2,000 women from at least 40 countries participated in this global speak-out, which ended, in keeping with its radical feminist response to the United Nations-declared International Women's Year, on International Women's Day, 1976. Modeled after the spirit of Bertrand Russell's Tribunal Against War Crimes, the women's tribunal heard testimony from the victims of crimes committed against women in the family; by the law; crimes committed against female political prisoners; economic, sexual, and medical crimes against women. The first women's liberation group in Greece, the Greek Women's Union, was formed because of one woman's efforts to get others involved in the tribunal. Refuges for battered women are being set up in Belgium, West Germany, and Norway as a result of the tribunal. Diana Russell, an associate professor of sociology at Mills

College in California, is co-editor of *Crimes Against Women: The Proceedings of the International Tribunal* (1977); her colleague, Judith Fried-lander, is an assistant professor of anthropology at the State University of New York at Purchase.

LATTER-DAY PEACE ADVOCATES

Founder of Women Strike for Peace

DAGMAR WILSON, born in New York City in 1916, moved with her parents to Berlin at the age of three and spent her childhood in Europe as the daughter of an American journalist/foreign correspondent. In 1937 she graduated from London University, Slade School of Fine Arts, and in 1939 returned to the United States to begin working as an artist. While working as a free-lance textile designer in New York City, she began her principal career as an illustrator of children's books. In 1942 she moved to Washington, D.C., with her husband, Christopher B. Wilson, who worked for the British Embassy. Ms. Wilson spent the next several years illustrating books and raising three daughters. In 1959 she became increasingly concerned with nuclear disarmament. "I am not a political animal," she maintains. "But I have always been concerned with war and peace, concerned that human beings live sanely and rationally. For me, it has been less political than of an aesthetic nature, a moral nature." Joining the Committee for a Sane Nuclear Policy (SANE) in 1959, she worked as a lobbyist and designed advertisements for the organization. Then events—the Berlin Wall, the jailing of Bertrand Russell—sparked her to become more active. In the fall of 1961 she organized a few of her female friends from SANE and together they planned the Women Strike for Peace, initially conceived as a one-day demonstration, not an organization. The first demonstration took place on November 1, 1961, and women from 60 cities across the country participated. Immediately an overwhelming response led Ms. Wilson to continue Women Strike for Peace and for the next seven years she remained an antiwar activist as spokeswoman for WSP. Dagmar Wilson lives in Leesburg, Virginia, where she spends much of her time painting landscapes and rural interiors; in September 1976 she held a one-woman show of her work at the National Arboretum in Washington. Some of the books she has illustrated include *Stories to Read to the Very Young* and *Poems to Read to the Very Young*.

Antiwar Broadcaster

From 1958 to 1971 ELSA KNIGHT THOMPSON served first as public affairs director, then as assistant manager and program director of KPFA-FM radio in Berkeley, California, the first listener-sponsored radio station in America. KPFA began broadcasting in 1949, the first station in the Pacifica network, which now includes six stations. Ms. Thompson's leadership drew countless volunteers to KPFA and her programing innovations set a new tone in the developemnt of non-commercial radio. From a background of free speech and civil rights activism, Ms. Thompson became an early opponent of U.S. intervention in Vietnam. In the early 1960s she broadcast information about the Vietnam War that most Americans were not yet ready to believe but came to understand as the war progressed. Her influence extended beyond KPFA to other Pacifica stations through exchange of programs among the stations and by her training of staff members. Ms. Thompson retired from KPFA in September 1971.

Protest Singer

JOAN BAEZ was born on January 9, 1941, on Staten Island to an English-Scotch mother and a Mexican father. Although her family was financially well off, she felt bigotry from her classmates as a young girl because of her Hispanic heritage. While still a teen-ager, Ms. Baez began singing in Cambridge coffee-houses. Her pure soprano voice quickly caught the attention of other folk musicians—Bob Dylan eminent among them—and the public. But, "Music isn't my thing, politics is," Baez told reporters. She devoted herself to non-violent resistance beginning in the early '60s when she became involved with the civil rights movement. Later in that decade, she became one of the foremost opponents of the war in Vietnam. In the late '60s she married David Harris, a war resister who was sentenced to three years in prison for defying the draft in 1969. Harris was released on parole in 1971; he and Ms. Baez were divorced shortly thereafter. Joan Baez continues to support liberal causes, often performing in benefit concerts and placing her politics before her art.

With her sister, MIMI FARINA, and LUCIE ALEXANDER, co-founders of Bread and Roses, which provides free live entertainment for prison inmates, in 1974 she began giving concerts in California institutions, including San Quentin.

Co-Founders of the Irish People's Peace Movement

On August 10, 1976, in Belfast, Northern Ireland, an IRA getaway car, its driver shot through the head by the British soldier whom he had attacked, jumped the curb, crushed to death three young children, and critically injured their mother. Hours later, the mother's sister, MAIREAD CORRIGAN, then a 32-year-old secretary, was on television denouncing the Irish Republican Army—the first Catholic woman in Ulster to dare a challenge to the gunmen. BETTY WILLIAMS, mother of two and wife of a seaman, lived just a few blocks from the place where the tragedy occurred. When she met Mairead Corrigan, these two Catholic women began organizing the People's Peace Movement. Despite their lack of experience, within two weeks they had some 30,000 Protestant and Catholic women marching behind them in Northern Ireland, demanding an end to the violence.

Mairead Corrigan and Betty Williams have suffered death threats and accusations that they are traitors and dupes of the British who will settle for peace at any price. They have also attracted international attention, and raised more than $1 million in contributions from other countries. In 1977 they were awarded the Nobel Peace Prize. A fragile, unprecedented alliance of Ulster's war-weary Protestants and Catholics, the Peace People now have a magazine, two offices, and have been unobtrusively teaching women how to unlock financial and local community support. In an interview in the United States in 1977, Betty Williams said, "I have fabulous hope for Northern Ireland because I can actually see it starting to work . . . Protestant and Catholic [coming] together in a way I'd never [have] thought possible 15 short months ago. . . . The Nobel Peace Prize, I think, has given us the official stamp of approval, that says we mean what we say."

RADICAL POLITICAL ACTIVISTS

American Anarchist

EMMA GOLDMAN (1869–1940) was born in Kovno, Russia; when she was 16, she emigrated to America. One of the most accomplished, magnetic speakers in American history, she lectured extensively on anarchism, the new drama, and the revolt of women. She edited the radical monthly *Mother Earth,* and in 1911 wrote *Anarchism and Other Essays.* She attacked marriage as a "conventional lie" and advocated free love. In 1893 Ms. Goldman was tried, found guilty, and sentenced to a term of one year for urging unemployed workers in Union Square, New York, to steal bread if they could not afford to buy food for their families. In 1901, when President McKinley was assassinated, Emma Goldman was accused of having a connection with the assassination even though she had by this time denounced the use of violence as a tactic. In 1908 she was deprived of her U.S. citizenship and in June 1917 she and Alexander Berkman, another anarchist, were arrested for their leadership of the U.S. opposition to conscription and sentenced to two years in prison. After serving her sentence, Ms. Goldman was deported. For two years she lived in Russia before becoming disillusioned with the emerging totalitarianism there and leaving for Sweden. In 1931 she wrote her autobiography, *Living My Life.* In 1936 she began working against Franco and was raising funds for Spain in Canada in 1940 when she suffered a stroke and died three months later in Toronto.

Eminent Polish Economist-Activist

Throughout her life ROSA LUXEMBURG (1870–1919) struggled to testify personally and intellectually to her convictions. She was one of the founders of the Social Democratic Party of Poland and Lithuania, the leader of the left wing of the SDP of Germany, and a prominent early Marxist economist. Ms. Luxemburg became politically active while she was in high school in Warsaw, Poland, and was forced to flee the country in 1889. She studied political economy in Zurich; her doctoral thesis argued persuasively that the development of industrial capitalism in the Polish kingdom depended heavily on the Russian market and that its political economy would never be more than a part of the czarist economy. Rose Luxemburg was arrested in 1905 when she went back to Warsaw to help the revolutionary movement there. In 1906 she wrote a major work entitled *General Strike, Party, and Trade Unions,* in which she put forward the view that the general strike is the fundamental instrument of the working classes for power. Her most famous economic work, *The Accumulation of Capital* (1913), grew out of lectures she gave at the Berlin School of the SDP and dealt with conditions of economic growth under capitalism. Imprisoned again during World War I for her antimilitary activities in Germany, Ms. Luxemburg devoted her three years in jail to theoretical and journalistic writings. Released in 1918, she immediately joined the German revolution and, with Karl Libknecht, founded the radical Spartacus League and wrote its program. Both were arrested during the civil strife in 1919 and murdered by the soldiers in whose custody they were placed.

First Woman Head of American Communist Party

ELIZABETH GURLEY FLYNN (1890–1964) chaired the American Communist Party from 1961 to her death. She was "the Rebel Girl" ("to the working class . . . a precious pearl") celebrated in the song written by Joe Hill, co-founder with her of the Industrial Workers of the World (IWW) in 1905. Fifteen years old when she began organizing for the IWW, she dropped out of school in 1907 to work full time for the union. Over the next 20 years she participated in many strikes, including the Lawrence, Massachusetts, textile strike of 1912, the Mesabi Range miners strike of 1916, and the Passaic, New Jersey, textile strike of 1926. She worked for the defense of Sacco and Vanzetti, the anarchists who were convicted and executed for murder in Massachusetts, and was a founding member of the American Civil Liberties Union (ACLU) in 1920. In 1940 she was asked to resign from the ACLU because of her Communist Party ties. Although the

Communist Party was formed in the United States in 1919, Ms. Flynn did not join it until 1937. Then she devoted all of her energies to it and rose quickly in the ranks. On March 12, 1961, she became the first woman to chair the National Committee of the American Communist Party. A compelling public speaker, she also wrote a column for the *Daily Worker,* and a number of books including *I Speak My Own Piece: Autobiography of the Rebel Girl* (1955). She died in Moscow in 1964 and her ashes were buried in Waldheim Cemetery in Chicago.

U.S. "China Hand" Foe of Poverty and Class Bias

AGNES SMEDLEY (1894–1950) left home (a poor coal-mining town in Colorado) at 16 and eventually moved to New York City, where she became increasingly involved in left-wing political activity. Late in 1919 she left the United States to spend several years in Berlin with the Indian nationalist leader Virendranath Chattopadhyaya. Her first book, *Daughter of Earth,* a fictionalized autobiography, which is a vivid indictment of poverty and class bias in America, was published in 1929. In 1928 she arrived in China as correspondent for the liberal *Frankfurter Zeitung* and spent most of the rest of her life in China as a foreign correspondent and free-lance writer aligned with the Chinese Communists. In 1936, when Chiang Kai-shek was kidnapped by Manchurian troops, Ms. Smedley was the only Western journalist in Sian at the time; she conducted English-language broadcasts for the Manchurian Tungpei Army until January 1937. Ms. Smedley died in 1950 and is one of only two foreigners buried in the National Revolutionary Martyrs Memorial Park, the People's Republic of China's national cemetery.

Leader of the Spanish Communist Party

Communist leader DOLORES IBARRURI (LA PASIONARIA), **born on December 9, 1895, was one of the most renowned and controversial political figures on the Republican side of the Spanish Civil War. The daughter of a Basque miner, she was among the founders of the Communist Party in Spain in 1920, helped to establish the Popular Front government in 1936, and was known as a spellbinding orator in the Spanish Parliament. After the Civil War broke out in July 1936, she became a driving force behind the Loyalists. Her battle cry, "No pasarán!" ("They shall not pass!"), became their watchword. Ejected from her homeland in March 1939, La Pasionaria lived in exile in the Soviet Union until May 1977, when, after Franco's death, she was allowed to return to Spain. An emotional crowd welcomed Ms. Ibarruri, 81, back to her Basque homeland. In June she was returned to Parliament in the first elections in Spain in 40 years.**

China's Once Most Powerful

CHIANG CHING, wife of the People's Republic of China's late chairman Mao Tse-tung, and leader of the Chinese Cultural Revolution, was the most powerful Communist woman in the world until her husband's death in 1976. A former actress, born in 1913, Ms. Chiang in 1966 was assigned the task of reforming the arts for Mao's Great Proletarian Cultural Revolution. Under her leadership, the arts reflected "pure" revolutionary principles. The Red Detachment of Women, China's famed ballet exemplified Ms. Chiang's ideas about culture: Beauty is nothing in its own right; the arts must deliver revolutionary messages. The aims of the Cultural Revolution were basically established by 1969 and Ms. Chiang faded from prominence. Then, in 1974, she returned to an active role as adviser to the Cultural Revolution Committee of the People's Liberation Army. She continued to exert her influence on Chinese theater, music, literature, and art until, after the death of Mao Tse-tung, she was denounced by an opposing faction and purged—along with comrades in the hardline Maoist faction—from the Communist Party.

First Lady of the Cuban Revolution

WILMA ESPIN, 46-year-old wife of Raul Castro, Fidel's younger brother, became head of the Cuban women's movement in 1959 at Castro's request. She does not see herself as a feminist, insists that there is not and never has been a feminist movement in Cuba, and denounces the U.S. feminist movement. However, under Castro's orders she has promulgated a consciousness of women's equality with the Family Code of "El Código," a ruling that gives the force of law to the division of household labor in Cuba. Born into the upper middle class (her father was vice-director of the Bacardi rum company), Ms. Espin studied chemical engineering at Santiago and later at the Massachusetts Institute of Technology (MIT). She returned to Cuba after Batista's coup d'état and became deeply involved in the revolutionary movement.

Northern Ireland's Firebrand, Youngest Member of the British House of Commons

BERNADETTE DEVLIN, born April 23, 1947, a leader of Northern Ireland's civil rights movement and the youngest member of the British House of Commons, has been variously called a "miniskirted Fidel Castro" and a "Joan of Arc." Her reply: "I am no saint and not even an interesting sinner." The fiery young woman became one of Northern Ireland's twelve members of the British Parliament in April 1969, shortly before her 22nd birthday. She later bore a child out of wedlock. Now married and settled into a parliamentary career, Ms. Devlin believes that Northern Ireland will be racked by turmoil as long as the semiautonomous Ulster government persists in discriminating against the Roman Catholic minority in voting, representation, housing, and employment. She views the situation as a class struggle, however, not as a religious war, and insists that Protestants of the lower economic levels are as much exploited as the predominantly working-class Roman Catholics, who constitute about one third of Northern Ireland's population. "We demand justice for all the Irish," she has said.

African Liberationist

JOSINA ABIATHAR MUTHEMBA was born in 1945 in a southeastern province of Mozambique. One of the few Africans in Mozambique to complete her primary education, Josina dedicated her life to her country's liberation from Portuguese control. At 18, she joined the Liberation Front of Mozambique (FRELIMO). Traveling to Tanzania, the organization's headquarters, she was captured by Rhodesian secret police and imprisoned. Public outcry forced her release and she finally arrived, after being stalled a second time by British authorities, in 1965. In Tanzania, Josina Muthemba was trained by FRELIMO and assigned to organize political education in a women's unit in northern Mozambique. After completing this mission, she joined the women's detachment of the FRELIMO army. She became a commissar of the women's detachment and headed social affairs in the defense department. In 1969 she married Samora Moises Machel, commander of the army, who was later elected president of FRELIMO. In 1970, though seriously ill, Josina Muthemba continued organizing, speaking, and making long marches to hold meetings, train women combatants, and set up orphanages. She was taken to a hospital in Tanzania in 1971, where she died on April 7. At the end, her husband recalls, she "apologized to the doctors for not being able to help them."

Chairperson of the Organization of Afro-American Unity (OAAU)

ELLA MAE COLLINS took over the Organization of Afro-American Unity (OAAU) in 1965 after the death of its founder, her brother Malcolm X. A native of Butler, Georgia, Ms. Collins, a member of the Black Muslims who left the official movement in 1959, still considers herself a Muslim but is not affiliated with any mosque. Before becoming involved with the OAAU, Ms. Collins ran a non-sectarian school in Boston called the Sarah A. Little School for the Preparatory Arts.

Black Militant Communist International Hero

ANGELA YVONNE DAVIS, born on January 26, 1944, in Birmingham, Alabama, the eldest child of public-school-teacher parents, was the subject in the early 1970s of an intensive criminal prosecution and a dramatic defense movement that united the international Left. Ms. Davis did her undergraduate work at Brandeis University, spending her junior year at the University of Paris, where she met and was influenced by Algerian students. In 1963 her radicalization was accelerated by the bombing of a Birmingham Baptist Sunday school, in which four little black girls were killed. Angela knew three of them. Back at Brandeis, her political philosophy was sharpened under the tutelage of Herbert Marcuse, whose Marxist view of contemporary industrial society profoundly affected her thinking. In 1968 she moved to Los Angeles and formally joined the Communist Party. In the spring of 1969 she was hired to teach philosophy at UCLA. That summer an ex-FBI informer exposed her Communist affiliations to the California Board of Regents, who refused to confirm her appointment. Although her classes were some of the most widely attended in the school's history, the Board of Regents declined to renew her contract on the grounds of her allegedly inflammatory speeches in defense of the Soledad Brothers. Then in August 1970 Jonathan Jackson, brother of George Jackson, a Soledad Brother, took over a Marin County courtroom brandishing guns, hoping to take hostages as ransom for the release of his brother and his brother's comrades. In the ensuing shoot-out, two inmates were killed and the district attorney was seriously injured. Three of Jackson's guns were found to be registered to Angela Davis and she was charged with kidnapping, murder, and conspiracy according to California law. She went into hiding, her name was put on the FBI's "10 most wanted" list, and after a two-month, nationwide search, she was captured in a New York City motel on October 13, 1970. The "Free Angela" movement that developed rallied people all over the world to her support. Eventually she was acquitted of all charges against her.

Black Radical Activist

KATHLEEN CLEAVER, wife of former Black Panther Party leader Eldridge Cleaver, and active speaker in her own right, was born in 1945 and grew up in a U. S. Foreign Service family. She traveled extensively in Asia and Africa with her parents, studied at Oberlin and at Barnard College, then worked in the Peace Corps and for the Student National Coordinating Committee. She met Cleaver at a black student conference at Fisk University and married him on December 27, 1967. In 1969 she gave birth to a son named Antonio Maceo after a 19th-century black Cuban revolutionary. Kathleen Cleaver spent two and a half years in Algeria with her exiled husband. Returning to New York in late 1971 to help reorganize the failing East Coast segment of the Black Panther Party, she started a newspaper called *Babylon,* modeled after the California Black Panther Party paper, saying that she hoped to establish a "revolutionary people's communication network."

First Female Head of Black Panther Party

ELAINE BROWN grew up on welfare in a tough Philadelphia ghetto. She once hoped to become a lawyer, but dropped out of Temple University before completing her B.A. In 1968 Ms. Brown joined the Black Panther Party, a group that once consigned woman to "revolutionary servitude." In 1969 she was deputy minister of defense for the Los Angeles chapter. In 1970 she and Eldridge Cleaver represented the party in North Vietnam and North Korea. In the fall of 1971 she accompanied Huey Newton on a trip to China. Her chance to move up in the party hierarchy came early in 1971 when Newton and Cleaver split ideologically, Cleaver was expelled from the party, and she took over as minister of information, a position which made her No. 3 in the leadership. When Newton left the country in 1974, Bobby Seale succeeded him; in 1975, when Seale decided to downplay his party affiliation in order to run for political office, Elaine Brown succeeded him. Huey Newton's return from exile in 1977 sharply underlined the extent of the Black Panthers' ideological shift from its 1960s militancy. Under Newton's leadership, the party called for revolution. Under Elaine Brown's leadership, the party has concentrated on community programs like free-breakfast and free-shoe programs, a medical research clinic, and a senior citizens' self-help program. Ms. Brown has twice run for Oakland city council and lost, but she says optimistically: "We win even if we lose. We reach a lot of people just by running educational campaigns."

THE U.S. ETHNIC MOVEMENT

Founder of First Chicano Welfare Rights Group

In 1967, when California's Medi-Cal health and welfare programs were cut, ALICIA ESCALANTE, originally from El Paso, Texas, became part of the successful "Save Medi-Cal" campaign. Afterward, she formed the East Los Angeles Welfare Rights Organization, the first Chicano welfare rights group. As a result of a sit-in at the Los Angeles Board of Education in October 1968, Alicia was placed on three years' probation. Her confrontations with welfare department heads continued, though, and have resulted in the inclusion of more Chicano administrators, more information in Spanish, and the restoration of previously cut welfare recipients.

First Woman to Chair Board of Mexican-American Legal Defense Educational Fund

GRACIELA OLIVAREZ become first Board chairperson of the Mexican-American Legal Defense Educational Fund shortly after earning the distinction of being the first woman graduate of Notre Dame's law school (in 1970). Before entering law school, she was state antipoverty director in Arizona and afterward ran a food stamp program, became director of the Institute of Social Research and Development of the University of New Mexico, and antipoverty program planning officer for New Mexico governor Jerry Apodaca. In March 1977 she was appointed head of the Community Services Administration (formerly the Office for Economic Opportunity) by President Jimmy Carter. Ms. Olivarez hopes to make the Community Services Administration "the central focus for all poverty-related programs in the federal government."

Jobs for Hispanic Women

ANITA ESPINOSA-LARSEN of Parker, Colorado, 35-year-old mother of two and equal opportunity employment officer for six Western states, founded Hembra

(Female) to improve the lot of Colorado's many Chicano women. Mexican-American women earn the lowest wages (in 1975 their median income was $3,065) and receive the least education in the state. In 1976 Hembra presented free workshops at a Chicano Survival Experience project to help women understand the legislative process and learn job-hunting techniques.

First Chicano to serve as a California Regent

VILMA S. MARTINEZ, 33-year-old civil rights activist, was appointed by Governor Jerry Brown to serve on the California Board of Regents in December 1976. Also the first female president of the Mexican-American Legal Defense Educational Fund, she successfully argued the first equal employment case to be decided by the Supreme Court under the Civil Rights Act, *Phillips* v. *Martin Marietta Corporation* (1971). In 1975 she was declared Mexican-American

Woman of the Year by the Mexican-American Opportunity Foundation in Los Angeles. On June 17, 1976, she became the first woman to receive the national award for Greatest Public Service Performed by an Individual 35 or Under, presented by the American Institute for Public Service, and on April 26, 1977, she received the John D. Rockefeller III Youth Award for 1976 for her vigorous and effective defense of the rights of Mexican-Americans in the Southwest and throughout the country. In May 1977 she was awarded Columbia University's Medal for Excellence in recognition of her professional achievement. A graduate of Columbia University law school in 1967, Ms. Martinez grew up in a poor neighborhood in San Antonio, Texas, and worked her way through the University of Texas. "I never took seriously the notion that because you're a woman, you can't do anything. My culture has a tradition of strong women," Ms. Martinez says.

American Indian Artist/Activist

Popular Indian folk singer and songwriter BUFFY SAINTE-MARIE, born a Plains Cree in Saskatchewan, Canada, in 1941, has been an active speaker and giver of frequent benefit performances and financial support for Indian rights. In 1969 she supported the bid to return Alcatraz Island, site of a federal prison, to native Americans. Ms. Sainte-Marie also is founder of the Nihewan Foundation, which provides scholarships and other aid to Indian students.

Founder/President of Americans for Indian Opportunity

LaDONNA HARRIS was born on a farm in Cotton County, Oklahoma, and was graduated from Walters High School in 1949. She and her husband, former U.S. senator Fred R. Harris, have three chil-

dren. Long an active member of the Comanche Indian tribe, Ms. Harris was reared in the home of her grandparents, where Comanche was the primary language. She is founder and president of Americans for Indian Opportunity, a national non-profit Indian organization based in Albuquerque, New Mexico, whose primary purpose is to work toward improving the quality of life for native Americans. She is also the founder and honorary lifetime president of Oklahomans for Indian Opportunity. She has served as a member of the original National Indian Opportunity Commission and as chairwoman of its committee of urban and off-reservation Indians. In 1967 she was appointed by Sargent Shriver as chair of the Women's National Advisory Council on Poverty. In 1968 she was the recipient jointly with her husband of the Human Rights Award given by the American Jewish Community of New York. In 1973 she was elected as the Outstanding Woman of the Year in the field of human rights by the *Ladies' Home Journal.*

Founder of First Organization of American Indian Women

MARIE COX founded the North American Indian Women's Association, the first national group for Indian women, in August 1970, and was chosen by that group as Outstanding Indian Woman of 1977. She has received much recognition as an Indian leader, including the Indian Leadership Award from the Bureau of Indian Affairs, 1974; Outstanding Citizen of the State of Oklahoma, 1974; and a citation from the Secretary of the Interior in recognition of her outstanding contribution to the better understanding of Indian people in 1974 (she is the only Indian woman who has received this award). Ms. Cox, born in Lawton, Oklahoma, is married to James M. Cox, Sr., chairman of the Comanche tribe. They have been married for 40 years, have one son and two grandchildren. As an advocate for children with special needs, Ms. Cox has been serving since 1972 on the National Action for Foster Children Committee; she is a major signatory to the "Bill of Rights for Foster Children," currently under consideration by Congress.

Founder of American Indian Survival School

LORELEI MEANS, 22, and MADONNA GILBERT, 36, both Lakota (or Sioux) Indians, opened the "We Will Remember" Survival School in 1973 in Rapid City, South Dakota, to offer an educational alternative to Indian children. It is the only Indian-run school that operates without federal funding. With Lorelei's husband, Ted, and his brother Russell Means, Lorelei Means and Madonna Gilbert led the

Oglala Sioux in their armed takeover of Wounded Knee on the Pine Ridge Reservation near Rapid City in February 1973. "I put my life on the line for Indian pride at Wounded Knee," Ms. Means says. "We teach at our school that Indians are fighting for their survival as people." Since the Wounded Knee takeover, both women work regularly in the American Indian Movement (AIM) office, raise funds for the survival school, organize benefits, and care as well for their own children.

Catalyst for Indian Self-Determination

ADA DEER is credited with almost single-handedly getting the U. S. Government to return the land of her Menominee tribe to reservation status. In 1961 the Menominees' forest land was transformed into a Wisconsin county, with all the governmental responsibilities of a county, but without sufficient finances to meet those responsibilities. As head of the Menominee Common Stock and Voting Trust, which administered tribal property, and co-founder of the militant group DRUMS, and after years of work with the National Committee to Save the Menominee People and Forests, which she established in December 1973, Ms. Deer saw the land returned to the Menominees, an event she called a "very significant historical achievement for the grass-roots Indian." The oldest of five children of a Menominee father and a white mother, she lived most of her first 18 years on the reservation in a cabin without electricity or running water. With scholarships, she graduated from the University of Wisconsin, where she was one of 2 Indians among 19,000 students, and from the Columbia University School of Social Work. She has worked as a consultant to a variety of organizations and serves on the boards of several foundations.

ACTIVISTS IN MANY CAUSES

The Temperance Movement's Historic Hatchetwoman

CARRY AMELIA MOORE NATION, born 1846 in Garrard County, Kentucky, in her 50s began a series of saloon-smashing missions, "the hatchetation of joints," as she called it. An imposing, close to 6-foot figure, she invaded saloons with her band of hymn-singing followers, castigating the "rummies" present and swinging her hatchet at bars and tables. Frequently arrested for disturbing the peace, she paid her fines by selling souvenir hatchets. As a young woman she received a teaching certificate from Missouri State Normal School and taught school for a brief period before her father, a prosperous landowner, was ruined by the Civil War and moved to Belton, Missouri. There she met her first husband, Dr. Charles Gloyd, an alcoholic who resisted her efforts to reform him and died, leaving her with a hatred of liquor and its effect on men. Her second husband, David Nation, a lawyer and minister, divorced her for desertion in 1901. By that time, Carry (frequently misspelled as "Carrie") Nation had become deeply involved with the temperance movement, declaring that any property connected with liquor was doomed to destruction. She continued her crusade for many years before poor health finally forced her to retire to the Ozark Mountains in Arkansas. She died in 1911.

Champion of the Poor and First WCTU President in the Philippines

JOSEFA ABIERTAS, Filipina champion of unfortunate women, was born into a poor family in Capiz and became the sole support of her family after losing her father at an early age. With a grandmother, mother, sister, and other relatives, she struggled along on 18 pesos a month, graduated from secondary school at the head of her class, worked for the government in Manila, and graduated second in her class from the Philippine Law School in four years. As a lawyer, she fought for the oppressed, especially the poor, and women, once refusing a well-paid position because the company did not treat its employees fairly. Ms. Abiertas was elected the first president of the Women's Christian Temperance Union in Manila. She died of tuberculosis in 1922, and an orphanage was established in her name in Quezon City in 1930.

Hadassah Founder

Hadassah, the Women's Zionist Organization of America, aimed at fostering Jewish ideals, was founded by HENRIETTA SZOLD in 1912. Originally a group of 38 members worked through chapters in American Jewish communities and sponsored health work in Palestine. In 1918 Ms. Szold expanded Hadassah's activities, organizing a medical unit comprised of a nursing school, clinics, and a hospital, which was established in Palestine (Hadassah is still the sponsor of Israel's only medical college). She was elected the first woman on the World Zionist Executive Board. She established the Szold Foundation for child welfare and education, and in 1933 became director of Youth Aliyah, an organization to rescue and resettle in Palestine young Jewish victims of persecution; 100,000 such youths were saved in Nazi Germany, Eastern Europe, and Russia. Henrietta Szold died in Jerusalem in 1945 at the age of 85. Her organization now claims over 300,000 members.

President of Hadassah Today

As the 15th president of Hadassah, the Women's Zionist Organization of America, ROSE MATZKIN leads the largest activist women's volunteer group in the United States. Ms. Matzkin joined Hadassah in 1934, following family tradition by doing so. Her daughter and now granddaughters are also members. Hadassah has known Ms. Matzkin's leadership in many areas: as president of her local chapter and region, as national chairwoman of American Affairs, national Zionist Affairs chairwoman, national Youth Aliyah chairwoman, and as vice-president. She is also active in the League of Women Voters, the Waterbury (Connecticut) Jewish Federation, the National Council on Soviet Jewry, and many other organizations.

Founder of Women's Division of the American Jewish Congress

LOUISE WATERMAN WISE (1874–1947) was the wife of one of the 20th century's most famous rabbis, Stephen S. Wise, but she made a name on her own. A New Yorker transplanted after marriage to Portland, Oregon, she and Rabbi Wise returned to New York in 1907, where her husband founded the Free Synagogue. In 1916, as a synagogue activity, Ms. Wise formed the Child Adoption Committee, the first adoption service for Jewish orphans. Always an ardent Zionist, Ms. Wise in 1931 formed the Women's Division of the American Jewish Congress, one of the early foes of anti-Semitism and European fascism. When Hitler came to power in 1933, she founded the Congress House for Refugees, which, with two simi-

lar organizations, took in and cared for 3,000 people who fled Nazi Germany in the years before World War II. At the end of the war, she was offered the Order of the British Empire, but refused the honor because of England's refusal to allow Jewish immigration into its then mandated territory of Palestine. Ms. Wise died before Israel became an independent state.

Founder of World's First Birth Control Clinic

Dr. MARIE STOPES (1880–1958) founded what is believed to have been the world's first birth control clinic. The clinic, which she opened in north London in conjunction with her husband, Humphrey Verdon Roe, offered advice to childless women as well as dispensing birth control information to women who wanted it. Dr. Stopes was the author of *Married Love,* a guide to contraception, published in England in 1918. It was banned in the United States as "obscene" until a court suit in 1931 opened the way to an American edition; then it sold over 1 million copies by 1950. A biologist and paleobotanist, Dr. Stopes held two doctoral degrees, one in science from the University of London and one in philosophy from the University of Munich. She was founder and president of the Society for Constructive Birth Control and Racial Progress.

American Birth Control Pioneer

MARGARET HIGGINS SANGER (1883–1966) joined the Socialist Party at the turn of the century and in 1913 began publishing a monthly newsletter, *The Woman Rebel,* in which she introduced the term "birth control" to the American public. Indicted for distributing "obscene" literature through the mails, she fled to Europe. After dismissal of the indictment in 1916, she returned to the United States and opened a birth control clinic on the Lower East Side of New York City. She was arrested for dispensing contraceptive information under a state

law and spent a month in prison. Leaving prison in 1917, Ms. Sanger began a nationwide lecturing tour and launched *The Birth Control Review,* which became, and remained for 23 years, the organ of this movement. In 1922 she visited Japan, the first of several international lecture tours. By 1930, 55 birth control clinics had been established across the United States through the continuing efforts of Margaret Sanger and her associates. In 1927 she spoke at the First World Population Conference in Geneva, Switzerland, and in 1946 helped found the International Planned Parenthood Federation.

Early Advocate of Housing Reform

While living in Puerto Rico with her Navy officer husband, EDITH ELMER WOOD (1871–1945) became convinced that the appalling health problems of the island were directly connected to deplorable housing conditions. When her husband was transferred to Washington just before World War I, she looked closely at housing conditions in the capital and found slums nearly as bad as those in Puerto Rico. Her efforts to improve the situation failed, so in 1917, at age 44, she decided to study housing problems. She went to Columbia University, where she wrote a master's thesis on housing law in Europe; in 1919 she got her Ph.D. from Columbia with a dissertation on American housing. She later did studies on New York tenements, advised the Women's Municipal League of Boston on housing law, and headed the American Association of University Women's housing committee from 1917 until 1929. She was a strong advocate, when the idea was new and unpopular, of government aid to housing and held a number of positions during the New Deal period related to housing, zoning, and urban and regional planning. In 1940 Smith College, from which she had been graduated 50 years earlier, gave her an honorary LL.D.

Founder of Retired Persons Associations

Dr. ETHEL PERCY ANDRUS, founder of the National Retired Teachers Association and the American Association of Retired Persons, and energetic advocate for the elderly, was born in San Francisco in 1884. She received her B.S. from Lewis Institute and became principal of Abraham Lincoln High School in Los Angeles—the first woman high school principal in the state. While teaching, she

received an M.A. (1928) and a Ph.D. (1930) from the University of Southern California. She retired in 1944, becoming director of welfare for the California Retired Teachers Association and lobbying for improved pensions and tax benefits. In 1947 she founded and became president of the NRTA. In 1955 Dr. Andrus scored a major breakthrough: at a time when no private company would insure anyone over 65, she approached 42 companies, finally meeting Leonard Davis, 31-year-old group insurance specialist, who persuaded Continental Casualty to underwrite a test program. In order to make services available to all elderly persons, Dr. Andrus founded the American Association of Retired Persons (membership in 1976 reached 9 million). Soon she added a Pharmacy Service, first of its kind in the country, with low-price medications delivered to members' doors; a Travel Service, first in the country to tailor travel to older tourists; and (in 1963) the Institute of Lifetime Learning, the Retirement Research and Welfare Association, and AARP International. With tireless enthusiasm, Dr. Andrus also lobbied for the elderly and edited four Association journals. She was named National Teacher of the Year (1954) and won a University of Chicago Citation for Public Service as a Useful Citizen (1955) and Freedoms Foundation and Golden Rule Foundation awards (1964). She died of a heart attack in 1967, at the age of 83. In 1973 the University of Southern California joined AARP and NRTA in establishing the $4 million Ethel Percy Andrus Gerontology Center, which includes the nation's first undergraduate school of gerontology.

First Female on Senior Citizens Board

BESSIE GOTTLIEB (1891–1972) was the youngest of 10 children of Romanian parents who emigrated to New York's Lower East Side, where Bessie grew up.

From her parents, she learned humanitarian principles. As a young wife and mother in Chicago, Illinois, she rolled bandages for the Red Cross, helped in the neighborhood kindergarten, and was active in the charitable activities of B'nai B'rith. Widowed in 1947, Ms. Gottlieb then dedicated herself to making life better for her neighbors, particularly the elderly. For a time, she served as vice-president of the Chicago Jewish Community Centers. One of the organizers and the first female Board officer of the National Council of Senior Citizens, she was also one of the first and most vocal of the Medicare advocates, relentlessly devoted to promoting legislation for health insurance for the elderly. On its passage in 1965, President Lyndon B. Johnson invited Bessie Gottlieb to accompany him to Independence, Missouri, where she witnessed the signing of the Medicare law in the presence of former President Harry Truman. As a lobbyist for the elderly, Ms. Gottlieb was indefatigable; she appeared many times as a witness before congressional committees, urging legislation to make life better for senior citizens.

Founder of Gray Panthers

MARGARET E. KUHN, convener of the National Steering Committee of the Gray Panthers, an activist group fighting ageism, which she founded in June 1970, proudly says, "I am an old lady." The Gray Panthers have used militant tactics like sit-ins and picket lines to call attention to such issues as health care and mandatory retirement. "Out of the rocking chair, into the street!" is Ms. Kuhn's rallying cry as she goes about mobilizing the residents of retirement communities and nursing homes. A Philadelphia resident, she also works with other groups in action programs and serves on the boards of the Memorial Society of Philadelphia, the Philadelphia Hearing Society, and the People's Fund. She worked for many years for social justice and peace as associate secretary in the United Presbyterian Office of Church and Society. Before her retirement in 1970, she was employed as coordinator of programs in the United Presbyterian Division of Church and Race. Before that, Ms. Kuhn was a member of the staff of the YWCAs of Cleveland, Ohio, and Germantown (Philadelphia), Pennsylvania, and was on the national staff of the YWCA in New York City. A graduate of Case Western Reserve University, Ms. Kuhn is also former editor of Social Progress (now the Journal of Church and Society) and the author of Let's Get Out There and Do Something About Injustice (1972), a resource book for adult groups in churches. In 1971 Maggie Kuhn on Aging, a dialogue edited by Dieter Hessel, was published.

Founder of Parents Without Partners

"Parents Without Partners: Wouldn't you like to know others in the same position?" JACQUELINE BERNARD and Jim Egleson advertised in February 1957 in the National Guardian, a radical weekly published in New York City. The next week they put the same ad in the New York Post. Thirty replies came in; soon after their first meeting they had a mailing list of 200. In October DOROTHY BARCLAY, then an editor of the New York Times Magazine, mentioned the new organization in an article on divorced and widowed parents and Parents Without Partners received 800 pieces of mail in response. Ms. Bernard believes the response was so high because "up until that point, much was written about how to prevent divorce. But until PWP, no one even wanted to discuss what to do if divorce did come. There was clearly a need for it." Parents Without Partners is now an international organization with 250,000 members in the United States alone. Jacqueline Bernard, who was born in France in 1921, continues as an honorary member of PWP although she has not been active in the organization for years. She is the author of several books including *Journey Toward Freedom: The Story of Sojourner Truth* (Norton, 1967), listed among the American Library Association's "Notable Books for Children." She lives in New York and makes her living as a journalist.

Founder of Japanese Women's Civil Rights and Consumer Organization

Until her death at 78 in 1977, SHIGERI TAKAYAMA, a former journalist who was an early activist for women's rights, remained head of Chifuren, a 6 million-member Japanese women's organization active in civil rights and consumer affairs, which she founded in 1952. One of the founders of the pre-World War II League for the Defense of Women's Rights to Take Part in Government, she became famous in Japan during the war years for her efforts to organize help for the widows of men killed in battle. She later also served in the upper house of the Japanese Parliament, 1965–71.

Founder of Harlem Consumer Education Council

The *New York Times* called her "a perpetually angry, one-woman consumer movement." Busy "telephone militant" FLORENCE M. RICE grew up in orphanages, dropped out of high school, and worked in New York's garment district for 17 years before she was blacklisted for testifying at congressional hearings into discriminatory employment practices. Then in 1964, at 45, she undertook the establishment of the Harlem Consumer Education Council. "Ralph Nader is good for the white middle class," explains Ms. Rice, "but what he does doesn't touch black people." Since 1964 Ms. Rice has been the sole staffer of HCEC,

working with a variety of volunteer helpers. Her main adversaries are Consolidated Edison and the New York Telephone Company; in one long day, Ms. Rice will spend hours on the phone talking with everyone from senior citizens who've had their electricity cut off to corporate executives at Con Ed, the phone company, or department stores. From her storefront office Ms. Rice has counseled more than 20,000 consumers, and she has given testimony at more than 100 federal, state, and city hearings. "I don't see any answers," she says, "except to try and get young people to recognize what I'm doing and get into it. I'm sort of still out here by myself like a pebble in the ocean, but I'd rather be doing this than anything I can think of. Somebody's got to care." Ms. Rice gets occasional donations or small grants for her work, but she lives on the income she receives from taking care of a 99-year-old neighbor in Harlem.

Britain's Leading Consumer Activist

EIRLYS ROBERTS, who founded Britain's non-profit Consumers' Association in 1957 and four years later became editor of its magazine, *Which?*, retired in January 1977. Under her editorship, *Which?* drew reports from 70 part-time shoppers throughout the country; no free samples were accepted for testing (everything tested was bought). Ms. Roberts made special efforts to write simply and clearly so that all readers could understand. With a circulation of nearly 7 million, the magazine is financed by private subscription only. Ms. Roberts has worked not only in journalism but for the British Treasury and military intelligence, with the United Nations in Albania, and in 1973 became part-time director of the European Bureau of Consumer Organizations in Brussels.

Lobbyist Foe of Strip Mining

Co-founder of the National Environmental Policy Center in 1971, LOUISE DUNLAP wanted a strong bill banning strip mining and traveled to the coal fields of Appalachia and the Great Plains to talk to citizens' groups. On her return to Washington she was able to present the views of actual strip mining victims —those who had had huge boulders land in their houses, others whose family cemeteries were devastated. Ms. Dunlap lobbied for strip mining bills, researched and provided data on some 800 proposed amendments, fighting the opposition of the powerful, wealthy energy lobby, and suggested controls that were incorporated in the bill finally signed by President Carter in August 1977, after two vetoes by President Ford.

CAN Consumer Activist

Probably the best-known of the women who founded Consumer Action Now (CAN), environmental lobbying organization, is LOLA REDFORD, who was content to be a mother and the wife of film star Robert Redford for the first 10 years of their marriage but tired of her shadow role. In 1968, after deciding that doing interior decorating for friends was not enough, she met Texan ILENE GOLDMAN, who was also deeply concerned with the health of the environment. They decided that to be effective they needed their own organization and newsletter, and in March 1970 founded CAN. (Subscriptions to the newsletter, on environmental, energy, and later, consumer problems also, paid for their two-room office.) Ms. Redford researches and writes articles on endangered species, pesticides, no-fault insurance; other CAN volunteers inform consumers on packaging and environmental legislation. They lobby in Washington and urge readers to vote for conservationist candidates.

First (and Reappointed) Special Assistant to the President for Consumer Affairs

As special assistant to the President for consumer affairs, consumer activist ESTHER PETERSON (see also "Women in the Labor Movement and Organizations," p. 337) is serving President Carter in the post she was first appointed to in 1964, when it was newly created in the Administration of Lyndon B. Johnson. Earlier, she had served as executive vice-chairwoman of the President's Commission on the Status of Women. Ms. Peterson, who was born in Provo, Utah, on December 9, 1906, became interested in consumer issues through her work as legislative representative for the Amalgamated Clothing Workers of America and the Industrial Union Department of the AFL-CIO. She was appointed director of the Women's Bureau of the Department of Labor by President Kennedy in 1961. In 1970 she joined Giant Food Company as vice-president of consumer programs and consumer adviser to the corporation's president. In that capacity, she spearheaded numerous consumer-related projects.

Westinghouse Symbol Turned Consumer Activist

BETTY FURNESS, a native New Yorker and daughter of a Union Carbide executive, went to Hollywood while she was still in her teens and began a career in motion pictures. During her stint as an actress, she appeared in 35 films before moving back to New York to take up opportunities in the burgeoning television industry. From 1948 to 1960 her name was a household word as she starred in hundreds of live Westinghouse commercials, selling refrigerators and vacuum cleaners. In 1960, while working for Westinghouse, she attended her first national political convention. It sparked her long-time interest in politics. From 1960 to 1964 she hosted political commentary and call-in shows for WABC-TV; "At Your Beck and Call" and "Answering Service" won Betty Furness critical acclaim, including an Emmy in 1963. In 1964 Ms. Furness worked for the Johnson/Humphrey ticket. In 1967

President Johnson appointed her Special Assistant to the President for Consumer Affairs. She left this position in 1970 to serve as chairman and executive director of the New York State Consumer Protection Board until 1973, when she was appointed commissioner of the New York City Department of Consumer Affairs. In 1974 Ms. Furness returned to television to work as a consumer reporter for WNBC-TV News Center, a job she still holds. She is a member of the board of directors of Consumers Union.

First Consumer Activist Assistant Secretary of Agriculture

CAROL TUCKER FOREMAN, 38, former executive director of the Consumer Federation of America and long-time consumer activist, in 1977 was appointed Assistant Secretary of Agriculture for Food and Consumer Services. Ms. Foreman heads the agriculture department's nutrition and feeding programs, which include food stamps and school lunch and breakfast programs; meat and poultry plant inspection; and grading of meat, poultry, fruits, and vegetables. Altogether, she handles $9 billion, two thirds of USDA's total budget. A former lobbyist to the Department of Agriculture, she needs all the tact and skill for which she is noted. As she herself put it on taking up her new post, "I will be an administrator, not a paid advocate. I hope the agency will be more responsive to consumer interests than it has in the past. But I expect to be in an advocacy role with some of the consumers some of the time. Someone said to me the other day, 'I am one of your former friends.'"

Japan's Quiet Foe of Pollution

MICHIKO ISHUMURE became a determined ecologist when "businessmen with no conscience" allowed toxic waste to pollute her community. Minamata was a naturally beautiful fishing and poor farming center at the time that one of Japan's pioneer chemical companies was established there in 1908. Growing into a great chemical complex before and after World War II, the company became the principal employer and dominated local politics. Over the span of a quarter of a century a puzzling "cat's dance disease" spread through Minamata. It caused frenzied cats to drown themselves. Officials ignored the problem even when humans began to be afflicted with a crippling and disfiguring disease that was also often convulsive and fatal. In 1957, Dr. Hajime Hosokawa of Kumamoto University Medical School found that the mysterious disease was a central nervous system disorder resulting from eating fish contaminated by mercury waste discharged into Minamata Bay; his reports were suppressed. Ms. Ishumure quietly sought out the stricken. Her penetrating portrayals of their lives were assembled into a book, *Kukai Jodo (Sea of Suffering)*, published in 1968, which elicited national response. Ostracized by unaffected residents whose living depended on the polluting company, Ms. Ishumure persisted. A second collection of essays was published in 1972 and a book, *Rumin no Miyako (City of Drifters)*, came out in 1973. Finally, the Health and Welfare Ministry in Tokyo began to show interest; belatedly, the chemical industry has begun corrective measures.

California's First Woman Secretary for Resources

CLAIRE DEDRICK was not an environmentalist 10 years ago when she and a few other housewives went to a roadside meeting with the San Mateo County (California) engineer and county supervisors. She had only promised a friend that she'd go to the meeting about building a road and report what happened. After some heated words between the housewives and the officials, an engineer said to one of the women, "Get back in your kitchen, lady, and let me build my road!" That's when Claire Dedrick joined the cause. The road that the engineer wanted to build was a four-lane strip with a 104-foot right of way that would encroach on people's yards, trees, gardens, and homes. Ms. Dedrick and her co-protesters eventually succeeded in minimizing the intrusion. "What made me get involved," she says, "was that the whole process was so undemocratic." Both Ms. Dedrick and her husband Kent became active in various conservation causes as well as local politics. In 1970 she was given the Conservationist of the Year Award by her local chapter of the Sierra Club. In 1971 she became a director of the Sierra Club. Though a scientist by training (she has a doctorate in microbiology), Ms. Dedrick admits to being a politician by nature. In 1976 the Democratic governor of California appointed Claire Dedrick, a Republican, to be secretary for resources for the state.

She Leads Boston's ROAR

LOUISE DAY HICKS has been a vociferous leader of ROAR (Restore Our Alienated Rights), the antibusing movement in Boston, Massachusetts, since 1965, when, as a school board member, she began fighting for repeal of the Racial Imbalance Act. A three-term school committee member and two-term chairwoman, as well as a member of the Boston City Council, she continued to fight school integration until the busing act was implemented in 1974, and in March 1975 she marched at the head of 1,400 anti-busing demonstrators in Washington, D.C. In 1970 Ms. Hicks was elected to the United States House of Representatives, replacing John McCormack. She lost that seat in 1972. As member of the National Organization for Women and a supporter of the Equal Rights Amendment, Louise Day Hicks regards herself as a woman's rightist but not a feminist. She maintains that her antibusing position represents the

feelings of her South Boston white supporters and denies accusations that she is a racist.

First Female President of the National Student Association

Born and raised in Newark, New Jersey, MARGERY ANN TABANKIN, 29, was a fellow of the Saul Alinsky School of Community Organization in Chicago and a 1970 graduate of the University of Wisconsin in Madison with a bachelor's degree in the politics of urban poverty when, in August 1971, she was elected president of the National Student Association. The first woman to head the nationwide organization, she served for a year until she became executive director of the Youth Project, a public charitable organization with a budget of over $2 million, in September 1972. While president of the Youth Project, Ms. Tabankin worked closely with the late Dr. George Wiley, then president of the National Welfare Rights Organization. She was also active in the antiwar movement, and visited American prisoners of war and government officials in North Vietnam. In June 1977 she was chosen to head VISTA (Volunteers in Service to America) by Sam Brown, director of ACTION, the federal agency for volunteer service. At VISTA, she supervises the work of more than 3,900 VISTA volunteers serving throughout the United States to help communities alleviate the causes and effects of poverty.

National Welfare Rights Activist

BEULAH SANDERS was national chairwoman and a member of the executive board of the National Welfare Rights Organization (NWRO) from 1971 until the organization became the Movement for Economic Justice (MEJ) in 1975. Born in North Carolina in 1935, Ms. Sanders moved to New York in 1955. She became active in the New York chapter of NWRO and in October 1969 she spoke before the House Ways and Means Committee, warning that the poor would "disrupt the country" if not given a fair share of the nation's wealth. As

chairwoman of NWRO, Ms. Sanders led boycotts and demonstrations against cuts in welfare payments.

The Three Marias

When MARIA ISABEL BARRENO, MARIA TERESA HORTA, and MARIA VELHO DA COSTA published *The New Portuguese Letters* in the spring of 1972, all three were arrested by the Portuguese authorities on charges of "abuse of the freedom of the press" and "outrage to public decency." The book was banned, and all copies of it were confiscated. Court proceedings against the authors began in October 1972, under the provisions of a new law that made writers, publishers, printers, and distributors legally responsible for the morality of works they put before the Portuguese public. The trial dragged on for many months. During this time the cause of "the three Marias," as they came to be known, was taken up first by women's liberation organizations in many countries and then by international writers' groups. In April 1974 all charges against the authors were dropped and the judge proclaimed *The New Portuguese Letters* a work of literary merit.

Founder of Organization for Battered Wives in England

ERIN PIZZEY founded Women's Aid, a voluntary organization headquartered in London, in 1972; she originally conceived of Women's Aid as an experiment in practical women's liberation. "I joined a women's group but I got tired of people just talking and doing nothing," she says. "I went to the local city council and asked for a house that could serve as an advice center for women—somewhere women could come during the day any time they needed to get away." Ms. Pizzey got a tiny house in Chiswick, a residential suburb of London, from which she operated Women's Aid for two years, quickly realizing that she needed larger quarters to house battered wives who needed places to stay on a temporary basis. In 1974 the organization moved to a rambling Victorian mansion, where abused women get physical protection, legal help, and time to sort things out. The average stay is several weeks.

Symbol of French Pro-Abortion Movement

MICHELE CHEVALIER, born in 1934 on a small farm in the Loire Valley, was herself a single mother. When MARIE-CLAIRE CHEVALIER, the oldest of her three daughters, became pregnant at 16, Michele supported her daughter's decision to seek an abortion. The French law banning abortion was inequitably enforced, mostly against the lower classes. In October 1972 Marie-Claire stood trial for her action; with the help of GISELE HALIMI, a lawyer who founded *Choisir*, French pro-abortion journal, she was acquitted of the charge of having had an illegal abortion. Later that year her

mother was also tried, as an "accomplice." The case was widely publicized. Well-known actresses and writers— among them SIMONE DE BEAUVOIR (p. 703)—testified that they too had had abortions but had never been bothered by the police. Michele Chevalier was given a small fine; the transcripts of both trials were published by *Choisir* and thousands of copies were distributed. Within weeks, doctors were performing free abortions in many major cities. When one doctor was arrested in May 1973, 10,000 people took part in a march demanding repeal of the abortion law, and the chain reaction led to the introduction in the French Parliament of legislation legalizing abortion.

Euthanasia Activist

Dr. OLIVE RUTH RUSSELL, Canadian by birth, is a retired professor emeritus of psychology at Western Maryland College, and it was there that she first became convinced of the necessity for euthanasia legislation. While visiting Rosewood Hospital Center in Owings Mills, Maryland, in the early '60s, she observed children who were so hopelessly deformed and mentally retarded that "there was no chance of their having meaningful, normal lives." A second experience, seeing her own terminally ill mother live for months after she had expressed a desire to end her suffering, strengthened her resolve to campaign for comprehensive legislation at the state level to allow patients who wish to die to receive the help to do so legally from a doctor. Dr. Russell is the author of *Freedom to Die, Moral and Legal Aspects of Euthanasia* (1975). Five states—California, Arkansas, Idaho, Nevada, and New Mexico—have "right to die" bills; Dr. Russell plans to continue her lobbying efforts in Maryland until patients who wish to die are allowed "death with dignity" there.

Founder of the National Organization for Non-Parents

"I never intended to be an activist—I only decided not to have children," says ELLEN PECK, founder of the National Organization for Non-Parents, author of *The Baby Trap* (1971) and co-author (with JUDITH SENDEROWITZ, below) of *Pronatalism: The Myth of Mom and Apple Pie* (1974). Ms. Peck, now 35 and married for 11 years, lives in Baltimore, Maryland. Tired of explaining why she chose not to have children, she founded the organization in 1971. She is also founder of the Consortium on Parenthood Aptitude, and has worked to remove pronatalist influences from publications (even from family planning brochures that say "when" rather than "if" you plan to have children).

First Woman to Be Elected Zero Population Growth President

JUDITH SENDEROWITZ, born on May 25, 1942, in Allentown, Pennsylvania, was elected president of Zero Population Growth in April 1973. Co-author with ELLEN PECK of *Pronatalism,* she is currently director of the organization liaison division of the Population Institute in Washington, D.C.

Co-Founder of Children's Defense Fund

Attorney MARIAN WRIGHT EDELMAN, born in 1939 in Bennettsville, South Carolina, now gives all her time to children's rights. Co-founder in 1973 of the Children's Defense Fund of the Washington Research Project, Inc., she became its first director. The Fund is an advocacy organization that combines research and litigation. Prior to founding the Fund, Ms. Edelman held the position of director at the Center for Law and Education at Harvard University and was a partner in the Washington Research Project of the Southern Center for Public Policy, a public-interest law firm. After graduating from Yale Law School in 1963, Ms. Edelman became staff attorney for the NAACP Legal Defense and Education Fund and in 1964 became director of the NAACP Legal Defense and Education Fund in Jackson, Mississippi. She was the first black woman admitted to the Mississippi bar (1966). She holds three honorary law degrees and is an honorary fellow of the University of Pennsylvania Law School. The wife of Peter B. Edelman, director of New York State's Division for Youth, and mother of three children, Ms. Edelman commutes from upstate New York to spend part of each week in her Washington office.

Fighters for Better TV for Children

Appalled by the commercial television her preschool children were watching, PEGGY CHARREN of Newton, Massachusetts, scheduled a meeting of parents concerned about children's programs and there met free-lance writer EVELYN KAYE SARSON. With LILLIAN AMBROSINO and JUDITH CHALFEN in 1968 they founded Action for Children's Television (ACT) to build pressure on broadcasters by raising public consciousness of the exploitation of children on commercial TV. Seven years later their organization had spread across the country and abroad and boasted seven full-time, five part-time employees and a $300,000 foundation grant. Some results: House and Senate hearings on TV violence and food ads, network action to reduce violence on children's programs, refusal of advertisers to sponsor such violence (ad agency J. Walter Thompson has advised its clients not to), reduction of time devoted to commercials for children by 25 per cent, rejection of ads for medications and vitamins during children's viewing time. ACT continues to research the programs, sponsors conferences, protests ads for sugary foods, offers suggestions for good programs, complains to the Federal Trade Commission, lobbies, and if necessary, goes to court.

Her Death Prompted Nuclear Industry Investigations

On November 13, 1974, KAREN GAY SILKWOOD, 27, was driving alone to a meeting scheduled with an official of the Oil, Chemical, and Atomic Workers Union (OCAW) and a reporter from the New York Times when she was killed in a car crash. An atomic worker in the Kerr-McGee Corporation's Cimarron Facility, a plant near Oklahoma City that manufactured plutonium for nuclear reactors, Ms. Silkwood had been documenting safety infractions at the company: In four years, there had been 17 contamination incidents involving 77 employees, herself among them, and other health and safety violations she had recorded in a notebook that she was bringing to show to the union official and the Times reporter when her car crashed. Her notebook has never been found, and the cause of the accident never determined. These and other circumstances surrounding Ms. Silkwood's death have led many to believe she was murdered. The Cimarron Facility was shut down in December 1974, after five more employees were exposed to radiation; Kerr-McGee never reopened the plant. Karen Silkwood's death prompted Congress to hold hearings in the spring of 1976 into health and safety problems in the nuclear industry.

Founder of the National Congress of Neighborhood Women

JAN PETERSON, 36, founded the National Congress of Neighborhood Women in the fall of 1974 to organize working-class women around issues for the improvement of their neighborhoods and their lives. One hundred fifty activists gathered for the first meeting. Housewives and household workers, secretaries, nuns, and senior citizens found common cause in their concerns about housing, health care, child care, legal and economic assistance, job training, and continuing education. "NCNW tries to change the image of blue-collar women as Edith Bunkers with IQs of 47," says Ms. Peterson. Initially sponsored by the National Center for Urban Ethnic Affairs, NCNW received a $1 million grant from CETA in 1976 to set up a neighborhood-based college in the Italian community of Williamsburg in Brooklyn. The college, which graduated its first class in 1977, credits women academically for their life experiences. Jan Peterson, who grew up in a working-class

Swedish family in Cedarburg, Wisconsin, in 1977 was on the staff of the Public Liaison office of the White House, addressing problems of displaced homemakers, abused wives, and violence in the family.

First to Fight Redlining

GAIL SINCOTTA, 46-year-old Chicago housewife, mother of six, and lifelong community activist, spearheaded the drive against banks' discriminatory practice of refusing home loans in inner-city neighborhoods. Ms. Sincotta is credited with leading the antiredlining forces which prompted President Ford to sign into law a bill (signed January 1976) that prevents banks and other lending institutions from writing off whole neighborhoods as bad risks. A high school graduate who married at 16, Ms. Sincotta is executive director of the National Training and Information Center in Chicago and chairperson of National People's Action, a coalition of over 500 grass-roots community groups throughout the nation.

Co-Founder and First Female Director of People's Lobby

JOYCE KOUPAL, co-founder of People's Lobby in 1968, became national director in 1976 after the death of her husband. People's Lobby, headquartered in Los Angeles, is the organization that was responsible for California's Clean Environment Act of 1972 (defeated at the polls), the California Political Reform Act of 1974 (overwhelmingly passed at the polls), and tax loophole Propositions 5 and 6 (passed at the polls in 1976). The group is currently working with similar organizations throughout the United States. Ms. Koupal, a California native, also helped organize a League of Women Voters chapter in her home state's Placer County and is on the advisory councils of the Friends of the Santa Monica Mountains, Parks, and Seashore; the Women's Clinic; the Environmental Education Group; and Stamp Out Smog. She

was appointed to the Los Angeles County Energy Commission in 1974. In 1973 she was awarded a special teaching credential in the fields of conservation and gerontology in recognition of her work in both fields. She has received the SYLVIA LEVENTHAL Annual Memorial Award for outstanding community service and a certificate of commendation from the Office of the City Attorney of Los Angeles.

Board Member of Gay Rights National Lobby

In September 1976, RONNI B. SMITH was elected to the board of the Gay Rights National Lobby, an organization with both gay and straight members, which has been formed to lobby on a national level for gay civil rights legislation. For the last several years, Ms. Smith has been active in promoting the rights of all women and of Lesbians and homosexual men through legislative reform, administrative change, and coalition building. She is director of special projects for the New York State Division of Human Rights and a member of the Division's Women's Rights Task Force.

Organizer of 1976 Presidential Debates

As chairwoman of the League of Women Voters Education Fund, and president of the League of Women Voters in the United States, RUTH C. CLUSEN spearheaded a successful effort to bring the two major-party presidential candidates together face to face in debates before the national electorate in 1976. The '76 debates marked the first time in 16 years that the nation was offered presidential debates, the first time in history that an incumbent President participated in debates, and the first time in history that vice-presidential candidates participated in such events. In the United States alone, more than 100 million people witnessed the debates. "Americans have signaled their desire to know the substance of the candidates' positions on critical problems," said Ms. Clusen. "They are tired, too, of having these positions handed to them in neat, candidate-controlled packages."

First Woman Food Day Coordinator

BARBARA GOTTLIEB, 23, was national coordinator for Food Day, 1977, the third annual day of education and action on domestic and international food issues held by Washington, D.C.'s Center for Science in the Public Interest, on Thursday, April 21. On the first Food Day, its organizers published a list of "The Terrible 10"—those food companies, foods, and individuals allegedly most responsible for the adulteration of the country's food supply. On Food Day, 1977, Senator Mark Hatfield (R., Ore.) and the Center co-sponsored a conference on Capitol Hill on the underlying causes of world hunger, and a vegetarian dinner, prepared by Food Day organizers, was served at the White House. Besides coordinating Food Day activities in Washington, Ms. Gottlieb orchestrated efforts around the country through contact with thousands of individuals and dozens of groups.

First Female Chairwoman of Common Cause

NAN WATERMAN, 57, of Muscatine, Iowa, succeeded John W. Gardner, the founder of Common Cause, as chairwoman of the Board in April 1977. A Board member since 1971, Ms. Waterman is also vice-president of the national League of Women Voters and heads the League's human resources department. She has been a consultant to several Iowa women's colleges; has served in several capacities in the state government, including the state Commission on Human Rights; and is a member of the National Organization for Women and the National Women's Political Caucus. She is married and has four sons.

Antiapartheid Fighters in South Africa

In the long, and escalating, fight for freedom on the part of South Africa's blacks and "coloureds," women of all racial designations and backgrounds have banded together.

NOMZAMO WINNIE MANDELA is often called the "First Lady" of black South Africa. Wife of jailed nationalist leader Nelson Mandela, she has for some years been a leader in her own right. A statuesque, outspoken woman, regarded as a mother figure by moderate blacks and accepted by most, though not all, radicals, she helped to found the Black Parents' Association in the wake of the 1976 riots in the Johannesburg township of Soweto. Shortly afterward, she was forcibly removed from her home in Soweto and banished to a black slum area in the Orange Free State village of Brandfort, a place she describes as "literally a living grave."

Four white women who went to visit the 43-year-old Ms. Mandela in Brand-fort were sentenced to jail in Johannesburg early in 1978 for their refusal to answer police questions about their visit. They were ILONA KLEINSCHMIDT, 28, JACKIE BOSMAN, 31, BARBARA WAITE, 42, and veteran antiapartheid militant HELEN JOSEPH, 72, who was a banned person for five years and spent nine years under house arrest. The decision of the women to accept jail terms is, one of them said, "terribly important." Blacks "will know there are some whites who will suffer with them."

Another South African white woman, BRIDGET OPPENHEIMER, wife of the world's leading diamond and gold magnate, was moved "to do something" in the wake of the Soweto riots. She formed Women for Peace, a liberal group modeled loosely on its counterpart in Northern Ireland (see p. 711). Assailed by white conservatives and black radicals alike, the members of the group consider themselves to be unaligned—a "continuous high-wire act," according to an organization executive, HELMINE MYBURGH. They do not march ("We don't want to be proscribed—we're much more effective alive than dead") but concentrate on bringing women of different races together in meetings, running a children's program, and making their views felt to the government.

Fiery Greek Actress/Activist/Member of Parliament

After ten years of courageous political activism, most of them spent in forced exile, MELINA MERCOURI, international film star, won a landslide victory in her election to the Greek Parliament in 1977. When a right-wing military junta seized control of Greece in 1967, Ms. Mercouri lashed out at the takeover. She was stripped of her citizenship and spent most of the next seven years in Paris as a political exile from her homeland. Only two days after the junta collapsed in 1974, she flew back to Athens, overjoyed. She lost no time running for Parliament from Athens' port section of Piraeus (which includes the red-light district Ms. Mercouri made famous in her 1960 movie, *Never on Sunday*). She lost her first bid by only nine votes and then won in her second attempt last year. Ms. Mercouri regularly combines show business and politics, directing and starring in productions with strong ideological messages. She and her American-born husband, Jules Dassin, see eye to eye politically and aesthetically and have an unusually productive, creative relationship. Now in her 50s Ms. Mercouri is still in demand as an actress but spends more and more of her time engaged in politics.

HEROES

The Carnegie Medal Winners

The first woman to win a medal from the Carnegie Hero Fund Commission was ERNESTINE F. ATWOOD, a 17-year-old student who was awarded it for saving Harry M. Smith, aged 36, a coachman, from drowning on August 22, 1904. Ms. Atwood dived from a rowboat in Boston Harbor, 200 feet from the shore, and rescued the man from under a float. Her act of heroism was recognized with a silver medal and $500 to be used for educational purposes.

The medals established by Andrew Carnegie on April 15, 1940, are given annually in the United States and Canada for "selfless heroism" to persons who risk their own lives "in an attempt to save the lives of others." Women who have won the medals in recent years have been:

Lois Anderson, 39, housewife. She helped to save Larry E. Haas and others from an impending explosion in Anchorage, Alaska, on October 19, 1964.

Barbara Bruch, 52, housewife. She died saving Laurie A. Hall, 3, from being killed by a runaway truck in Pleasant Valley, Montana, on May 15, 1965.

Edna Roshone, 14, schoolgirl. She saved four young children from suffocation in a fire at Salem, Oregon, on December 5, 1964.

Barbara Mary Michaud, 14, schoolgirl. She saved Anthony Glidden, 10, from drowning at Lakeport, New Hampshire on March 3, 1965.

Dolores J. Carr, 30, housewife. She rescued Robert R. Emery, 40, laborer, from burning at Fowler, Ohio, on October 3, 1965.

Teresa E. Beasley, 15, schoolgirl. She helped to save Mark T. Regan, 10, from drowning at Scarborough, Maine, on August 27, 1965.

Harriet N. Swoboda, 51, housewife. She

died attempting to save Roger D. Byrd, 13, from drowning at Robertsdale, Alabama, on June 4, 1965.

Barbara Lynn Burdette, 14, schoolgirl. She helped to rescue Aaron Shirkey, 10, from burning at Culloden, West Virginia, on August 6, 1965.

Patricia Gail Crawford, 13, schoolgirl. She helped to save Danny McIlveene, 23, student, from drowning at Smackover, Arkansas, on August 28, 1965.

Julie C. Dokken, 17, schoolgirl. She rescued Kenneth Sawatzky, 3, from burning at Assiniboia, Saskatchewan, on August 11, 1964.

Brenda Beth Fagan, 16, schoolgirl. She saved Bedelia Faeder, 73, from suffocation in a fire at Brockville, Ontario, on November 9, 1965.

Gloria Rodriguez, 12, schoolgirl. She died saving Julita Sanchez, 12, from being struck by an automobile in Los Angeles, California, on April 11, 1966.

Louise E. Cannon, 58, boardinghouse operator. She saved Julianna Boulter, 4, from drowning off Prince Edward Island, Canada, on December 6, 1965.

Connie Marie Sorrells, 16, schoolgirl. She helped to save Richard L. Hockersmith from drowning at Dorena, Montana, on July 4, 1966.

Donna Marie Llewellyn, 19, fish packer. She saved Michael O'Neill, 12, from drowning at Georgetown, Prince Edward Island, on August 5, 1965.

Mary M. Rivers, 44, cleaning woman. She rescued Daniel L. Zublena, 4, from burning in Youngstown, Ohio, on May 15, 1966.

Marian E. Bowden, 40, advertising account executive. She saved Maryellen Smith, 30, from drowning at North East, Maryland, on October 3, 1966.

Louise Ann Pedee, 12, schoolgirl. She attempted to save David Nowakowski from drowning at Toledo, Ohio, on December 21, 1965.

Mary L. Buckles, 14, schoolgirl, and Tanja Buckles, 13, schoolgirl. They helped to save Lorena Fornell, 73,

from drowning at New Port Richey, Florida, on September 1, 1966.

Billie Joan Power, 27, market clerk, rescued Ginger Lee Diffie, 3, while she was in a runaway truck at Bisbee, Arizona, on May 19, 1967.

Linda Mary Heath, 19, student. She helped to save Blanche Foltz from drowning at Denver, Colorado, on October 14, 1966.

Anna M. Martuscelli, 68, housewife. She saved Richard Berton, 54, from drowning at Wayland, Massachusetts, on August 13, 1966. Berton, who could not swim, had attempted to retrieve a ball from a large pond and stepped into water beyond his depth. "I am 79 years old and have been saving people all my life," Ms. Martuscelli wrote recently, "so it was a complete surprise when the Foundation presented me with the bronze medal." A first-generation Italian-American, Ms. Martuscelli grew up in South Boston. She lives in Wayland, Massachusetts, now, has been married for 60 years, and has 4 children, 11 grandchildren, and 4 great-grandchildren. At 47, she was paralyzed from the waist down by a stroke. "The doctor said I would never walk again, but I couldn't exist in a wheelchair," she remembers. "After many months of crawling around, I walked again."

Rose Ellen Doane, 34, restaurant hostess. She died trying to save an indeterminate number of persons from burning at Montgomery, Alabama, on February 7, 1967.

Jacquelyn K. Hardin, 16, schoolgirl. She saved Jimmy M. Pippenger, 24, airman, from drowning at Melbourne Beach, Florida, on January 22, 1967.

June E. Roberts, 31, housewife. She helped to save Charles Luongo, 12, from drowning, at Boston, Massachusetts, on July 31, 1967.

Sylvia Jean Mayberry, 27, housewife. She saved Dianne Carr, 4, from suffocation in a fire at Meadville, Pennsylvania, on November 7, 1967.

Virginia Mulcahy, 23, secretary. She rescued Lynn Joy, 21, from assault in New York, New York, on March 1, 1968.

Nancy Anderson, 39, practical nurse. She died saving Mary and John Mobley, ages 8 and 5, from being struck by an automobile at Chester, Pennsylvania, on November 1, 1968.

Donna Jo Adamchick, 17, high school student. She helped to save Suzanne Dillon, 13, and Tracey Fisher, 6, from drowning at Sharpsville, Pennsylvania, on July 12, 1969.

Martha Lunn Thompson, 18, housewife. She saved three young children from burning in a fire at Columbia, Tennessee, on November 21, 1968.

Mayme Lee Barnes, 34, janitor. She saved Antwan, Olde, and Emma Pope, ages 2, 3, and 98 respectively, from burning in a fire at Goldsboro, North Carolina, on June 11, 1969.

Reta Rena Sharp, 12, schoolgirl. She died saving Anthony Cousins, 10, from drowning, at Floral, Arkansas, on January 24, 1970.

Deborah L. Waroe, 13, schoolgirl. She helped to save Denise Croy, 14, from drowning at Portage, Michigan on December 20, 1969.

Kathleen Ann Corrigan, 18, store cashier. She saved Mark Butler, 9, from drowning, at Lakewood, Ohio, on July 4, 1970.

Hazel M. Cromartie, 29, clerk-typist. She saved Melissa and Joseph Gibson, 4 and 5, from suffocating in a fire at San Francisco, California, on August 7, 1969.

Marianne I. Ward, 24, registered nurse. She helped to save Deborah Letourneau, 13, from drowning at Old Orchard Beach, Maine, on June 8, 1969.

Anita M. Thibodeau, 23, registered nurse. She helped to save Deborah Letourneau, 13, from drowning at Old Orchard Beach, Maine, June 8, 1969.

Linda Diana Baker, 13, schoolgirl. She saved John Taylor, Jr., 11, from drowning at Cheboygan, Michigan, on August 30, 1969.

Marilyn M. Hittelman, 32, housewife. She rescued Oliver Paule, 32, insurance salesman, from burning in an automobile accident at Encino, California, on May 6, 1970.

Wava T. Campredon, 70, housewife. She rescued Olive Harris, 64, from an attack by dogs at Santa Fe, New Mexico, on October 28, 1970.

Cynthia Fontes, 18, high school student. She rescued Lois Peralta, 26, from burning when her automobile caught fire at Van Nuys, California, on February 8, 1971.

Shirley Ewen Bayerle, 35, kindergarten teacher. On November 29, 1971, she rescued Joan Hoskey, 40, from a homicidal attack in San Francisco, California.

Jo-Ann Louise Klein, 38. She saved Dennis Killough, 20, from burning at Vacaville, California, on February 18, 1971.

Elinor Plumlee, 28, cocktail waitress. She rescued Robert Bajadjieva, 11 months, from burning in a fire in Las Vegas, Nevada, on November 2, 1971.

Geraldine Modejonge, 14, schoolgirl. She died attempting to save Janet Guenther, 14, from drowning at Parkhill, Ontario, on May 14, 1970.

Naomi Thompson Clinton, 35, housewife. She rescued Harold Martin, 25, truck driver, from burning in a truck accident in Columbia, South Carolina, on October 12, 1972. When Martin's tractor-trailer collided with a truck carrying drums of gasoline, several of which rolled onto the road and caught fire, he was thrown to the pavement amid the flames. Ignoring warnings of an explosion and breaking away from a man who tried to restrain her, Ms. Clinton ran to him, dragged him out of the burning area, and smothered the flames on his clothes with her own body. He recovered from his burns. Ms. Clinton, the mother of three and grandmother of two, left school in the tenth grade.

Diana Joan Stewart, 28, housewife. She helped save Michelle Scara, 3, from drowning at Justice, Illinois, on December 1, 1972.

Carolyn L. Wallace, 27, policewoman. She saved John Wray, 5, from drowning at Big Bear Lake, California, on February 19, 1972.

Betty Rae Manock, 49, housewife. She died attempting to save Terrisa Voepel, 12, from drowning at Charleston, Oregon, on June 3, 1972.

Pamela Anne Stewart, 17, high school student. She saved Todd Nelson, 10, from drowning at Port Edward, British Columbia, on March 24, 1974.

Cynthia M. Gibson, 14, schoolgirl. She died after helping to save Mario Jackson, 4, from drowning at Rock Island, Illinois, on June 28, 1975.

Sarah Lou O'Dell, 31, schoolteacher. She saved an unidentified woman from drowning at Richlands, Virginia, on March 14, 1975.

Jean C. Swedberg, 48, hotel desk clerk. She died helping to save an indeterminate number of persons from burning in a hotel fire at Merritt, British Columbia, on September 3, 1974.

Hero of the German Resistance

When the students in her high school class were ordered to say "Heil Hitler" each morning, HILTGUNT ZASSENHAUS refused. Pressured by school authorities, she thrust her arm through a glass window rather than give the Nazi salute. Five years later, in 1938, having earned a degree in Scandinavian languages, Ms. Zassenhaus was assigned to censor mail going out of Hamburg Prison from resistance fighters to Scandinavia. For her own reasons, she kept meticulous files on the whereabouts of these political prisoners, and her persist-

ence paid off early in 1945 when a prison guard casually mentioned new orders from Hitler that all political prisoners in Germany were to be executed. With the help of a Norwegian minister, Ms. Zassenhaus persuaded Count Folke Bernadotte of the Swedish Red Cross to negotiate with Heinrich Himmler, chief of the SS and the Gestapo, who agreed to release the prisoners if Count Bernadotte could find them. Using Hiltgunt Zassenhaus' files, the Red Cross rescued approximately 1,200 people. Ms. Zassenhaus escaped detection. Now an American citizen, she practices medicine in Baltimore, Maryland. She has written her autobiography, *Walls: Resisting the Third Reich—One Woman's Story* (1974).

Heroic Victim of Nazi Persecution

On August 4, 1944, Nazis raided the attic of an Amsterdam spice warehouse where ANNE FRANK had been hiding with her family for almost 25 months. The attic's inhabitants were removed to concentration camps. At the end of the war, Anne's father returned from Auschwitz only to learn that his wife and two daughters had died in concentration camps. Searching the attic where they had spent their last days of freedom, he found a legacy in Anne's plaid-covered diary, a journal begun on her 13th birthday that chronicled her courage under persecution, her innermost feelings, the hopes and dreams of an exceptional teenage girl. The diary is now available in 40 languages, has been read by 60 million people, and was the inspiration for a painting by Marc Chagall. A statue of her stands just around the corner from where she hid. Millions have made pilgrimages to the attic hiding place of the young girl who wrote: "It's lovely weather outside and I've quite perked up since yesterday. . . . As long as this exists, and I may live to see it, this sunshine, the cloudless skies, while this lasts, I cannot be unhappy."

Filipina Girl Scout Founder Who Died in Prison Camp

JOSEFA LIANES ESCODA (1898–1945), who organized the Girl Scouts of the Philippines and became a hero in World War II, dying as a prisoner of the Japanese, was trained as a teacher. She left teaching in 1922 to become an American Red Cross social worker. She obtained a certificate from the New York School of Social Work and a master's degree in social work from Columbia, both in 1925, founded International House in New York, and met and married Antonio Escoda, with whom she had two children.

Ms. Escoda was an American Red Cross field secretary in the Philippines, 1928–32, and also lectured in sociology from 1927 to 1932. In 1932 she transferred to the Bureau of Health. She became the first national executive secretary for the government-created Girl Scouts in the Philippines. As president of the National Federation of Women's Clubs from 1941 onward, she assisted war prisoners and so angered the Japanese conquerors that they arrested her. Before her death, she became noted for comforting her fellow prisoners. Her husband also died as a war prisoner.

HUMANITARIANS

Founder of the Henry Street Settlement House

LILLIAN D. WALD (1867–1940), public health nurse, settlement leader, and social reformer, was born in Cincinnati, Ohio, and studied at the New York Hospital training school for nurses in 1889–90. In 1891 she enrolled in the Women's Medical College of New York; while still in medical school, she organized home nursing classes for immigrant families on the city's Lower East Side. In 1895 she established the Nurses' Settlement at 265 Henry Street. By 1913 the Henry Street Visiting Nurses Service included 92 nurses making over 200,000 visits annually all over Manhattan and the Bronx. The Henry Street idea spread rapidly, similar programs were set up across the country, and a new profession, public health nursing, was created. Belonging to a generation that produced many eminent social workers, Ms. Wald is among the greatest. Henry Street was the catalyst for many apparently simple ideas of far-reaching social significance.

Settlement House Director

MARY ELIZA McDOWELL (1854–1936) started a career in social work when she was 16. Crowds fleeing the great Chicago Fire of 1871 stopped on the northwest edge of the city near her family home; she got her introduction to social service helping the relief effort. In 1887 she became national organizer for the young women's division of the Women's Christian Temperance Union. In 1890 she joined JANE ADDAMS and ELLEN GATES STARR at Hull House, where she received informal training in settlement house work. Four years later she was chosen to be director of a new experimental settlement house run by the University of Chicago in the stockyard district. Ringed by open garbage pits, the slaughteryards, and "Bubbly Creek," a dead arm of the Chicago River that had become an open sewer, the neighborhood had the worst health record in the city. Ms. McDowell launched a campaign to clean up the area. She made little headway until Upton Sinclair's *The Jungle* (1906) shocked complacent Chicagoans. In 1913 she finally forced the city to form a waste commission and saw the open pits closed. Ms. McDowell set up the first women's union in the stockyards, helped found the Women's Trade Union League in 1903, and played a major role in securing a Women's Bureau within the Department of Labor in 1920. In 1923 she was appointed commissioner of public welfare by Chicago mayor William Dever.

Shaper of Red Cross Volunteer Programs

Successor to CLARA BARTON, who founded the American Red Cross in 1881, MABEL BOARDMAN, born on October 12, 1860, in Cleveland, Ohio, greatly expanded the organization's voluntary services. Under her guidance, the Red Cross became a force in public health nursing, in dietetics, and a leader in lifesaving and first-aid training. She initiated the sale of Christmas Seals in the fight against tuberculosis and worked to organize nurses as a reserve for wartime and disaster service. Always a volunteer, Ms. Boardman held the title of secretary of the American National Red Cross. When offered the organization's highest executive position, she refused it because she felt that the public had more confidence in male executives. In fact, Ms. Boardman ran the agency from 1905 until her retirement in 1944. She died at the age of 85 on March 18, 1946.

Blind Founder of Bangkok School for the Blind

GENEVIEVE CAULFIELD, born in 1888, was blind from infancy. After teaching herself to be independent, she decided at the age of 17 to contribute to international understanding by helping the blind in Asia. In 1923 she arrived in Japan; she first lived with Japanese families to learn their customs and language. Supporting herself by teaching English, she trained blind people to read Braille. When she learned that those without sight in Thailand were considered useless, she spared no effort until the Bangkok School for the Blind was established in 1938. Financed partially from her own savings, the school is now well established and has won regular government and private support. In 1958 she opened an elementary school for the blind in Saigon, Vietnam. Over the years,

she made periodic lecture tours of the United States, sharing with her countrymen what she had learned in her labors in Asia.

Founder of the Rangoon Home for Waifs and Strays

Alarmed by the incidence of crime in her country, Burma's DAW TEE TEE LUCE spent a year studying and coming to know the deserted children who were the perpetrators as well as the victims of crime. Then, on September 1, 1928, she offered a group of street boys a place to live and study; with 19 volunteers, the Home for Waifs and Strays was launched. From that time, she has given abandoned and wayward boys off the streets of Rangoon not only a roof and food but a home and a place in her heart. For over 50 years she provided formal schooling, physical education, and training in useful crafts to as many as 130 boys at a time.

Founder of Community Schools in Hong Kong

ELSIE ELLIOTT, born in 1914 in Great Britain, moved to Hong Kong in 1951. For three years she worked as a Plymouth Brethren missionary in China; in 1954 she opened an urgently needed clinic and school, starting with 30 pupils in an old army tent. For a year, she lived on bread, water, and little else while she developed the school; she now has five Mu Kuang English schools providing kindergarten, primary, and secondary education for some 4,000 poor children. Ms. Elliott lives austerely in one room of a school building and teaches 16 periods a week. At 62, she continues her struggle to improve life for the people of Hong Kong. She is a prolific writer of letters to the editor, speaking out on problems in housing, welfare services, bus service to crowded tenement areas, playgrounds, or licenses for hawkers.

Founder of the Indian Cooperative Union

KAMALADEVI CHATTOPADHYAY, born in 1903 in Mangalore, India, founded the Indian Cooperative Union in 1948 to assist refugees uprooted by partition; the first cooperative, a farm, was formed at Chattarpur, near Delhi. The Union joined in building the new city of Faridabad to rehabilitate 30,000 refugees, providing tools, loans, and direction in a new way of living. When rehabilitation was accomplished, the Union turned to establishing consumer and handloom cooperatives. The central Cottage Industries Emporium in New Delhi developed as a marketing outlet for some 700 cooperatives; through it, designs were introduced, buyers attracted, and products sold in India and internationally. The Indian Cooperative Union has achieved commercial success and has served as a model for the creation of other cooperatives and services to meet the needs of both rural folk and urban craftspeople.

Internationally Admired First Lady Humanist

ANNA ELEANOR ROOSEVELT (1884–1962) was probably voted the world's most admired woman in international polls more often than anyone else. Noted humanitarian, author, UN delegate, and active force in the Democratic Party, Eleanor Roosevelt was hailed by countless numbers as their personal champion in a world first Depression-ridden, then war-torn, and finally maladjusted in the postwar years. She was a symbol of the new role women were to play in the world. Born on October 11, 1884, to Elliott and ANNA HALL ROOSEVELT in New York, she was the niece of Theodore Roosevelt, and distant cousin of Franklin Delano Roosevelt, whom she married on March 17, 1905. In 1921 her husband was struck down with polio; doctors urged her to busy herself with a career in part to encourage him to involve himself again with the world around him. She joined the board of the League of Women Voters and became active in the Women's Trade Union League and in New York State and national committees of the Democratic Party. In the 1930s she became a syndicated news columnist; when she took stands on national and international political issues in her column "My Day" she said so at the risk of much criticism. On March 4, 1933, FDR was inaugurated President. Many Americans who felt that a First Lady should not be so politically opinionated were upset by her continued—indeed, increased—activism, including such moves as her resignation from the DAR when that society refused use of Washington's Constitution Hall to MARIAN ANDERSON (see "Women in the Arts and Entertainment," p. 620). More cheered, however. In 1946 she was elected to chair the Human Rights Commission; she played an important part in drafting the UN's Covenant on Human Rights after being appointed a delegate by Presidents Truman and Kennedy. As a widow, Eleanor Roosevelt became even more active than she had been as a President's wife.

17

Far-Out Women

By Lois Decker O'Neill

"*Far out.*" That wonderful phrase heard so often in the 1960s has no equivalent. Spoken, as it can be, in awe, admiringly, in disbelief, in delight, with a lift of the eyebrow or a shake of the head, we choose it for this final collage of women whose fame, unusual attributes, or singular accomplishments are such that they could not comfortably be confined within any of the preceding chapters.

Farthest Out of All: The First Woman in Space

On June 16, 1963, VALENTINA VLA-DIMIROVNA TERESHKOVA-NIKOLAYEVA, born in 1937 in Soviet Russia's Volga River village of Maslennikovo, became the first woman to orbit the earth in space. The Russian spaceship *Vostok VI*, in which then Junior Lieutenant Tereshkova set her record (not since equaled by any woman of any nationality), completed 48 orbits, having traveled 1.2 mil-

lion miles in 70 hours, 50 minutes. Later that same year the attractive blonde "Valya," as she is known, married fellow cosmonaut Andrian Nikolayev, who in 1962 had orbited the earth 64 times in his ship, *Vostok III*. Valentina Tereshkova was one of three children of a soldier killed in action early in World War II. Her mother was a cotton mill worker. In 1954 the future cosmonaut started work in a tire factory, later switched to join her mother and sister operating looms, and continued her education by correspondence course. In 1959 she became a member of an air sports club and took up parachuting; it was her proficiency in this hobby that led to her acceptance in the cosmonaut training unit for which she volunteered in 1962. The mother of a daughter named ALYOANKA, Valentina Tereshkova-Nikolayeva in an article entitled "Women in Space," written in 1970 for the U.S. journal *Impact of Science on Society*, said, in conclusion, "I believe that a woman should always remain a woman and nothing feminine should be alien to her. At the same time, I strongly feel that no work done by a woman in the field of science or culture or whatever, however vigorous or demanding, can enter into conflict with her ancient 'wonderful mission' [Friedrich Schiller]—to love, to be loved—and with her craving for the bliss of motherhood."

First U.S. Women Astronaut-Trainees

On January 16, 1978, officials of the National Aeronautics and Space Administration announced the names of 35 astronauts who will fly U.S. space shuttles in the 1980s. Among the group named were six women, the first chosen for American space activities. All are in the new "mission specialist" category, and will be trained to conduct scientific, engineering, and medical duties but probably will not pilot the space shuttle. The large number of astronauts chosen reflects NASA's belief that by 1985 it will be launching as many as 60 space shuttles a year, each with up to seven crew members. The women named in 1978 were: Dr. ANNE L. FISHER, 28, of Rancho Palos Verdes, California, a physician; Dr. SHANNON W. LUCID, 35, a biochemist from Oklahoma City who has three small children; Dr. JUDITH A. RESNIK, 28, an electrical engineer for the Xerox Corporation who lives in Redondo Beach, Cali-

fornia; SALLY K. RIDE, 27, a researcher in physics at Stanford University; Dr. MARGARET R. SEDDON of Memphis, a resident in medicine at the Memphis City Hospital; and KATHRYN D. SULLIVAN, 26, of Cupertino, California, who is holder of a recent Ph.D. in geology from Dalhousie University in Halifax, Nova Scotia. One of the women, Dr. Resnik, was interviewed by the Washington Star a few days after the appointments were announced. Asked whether she thought that there might be any particular problems for women in space different from those faced by men, she answered: "I guess the only problems—and I don't see them to be problems; I'm sure they'll be worked out—are just the differences, the hygienic differences. . . . I can't see any responsibilities that couldn't be handled by anyone."

First Woman to Scale Mount Everest

JUNKO TABEI, member and deputy leader of an all-women Japanese expedition, on May 16, 1975, became the first woman in the world to scale the 29,028-foot peak of Mount Everest, in the Nepalese Himalayas, highest mountain on earth. Ms. Tabei, a mother, weighs 94 pounds and stands 4 feet, 11 inches. Shortly after her achievement, she said that she considered herself "just a housewife."

First European Woman to Enter the Forbidden City of Lhasa and other Female Explorers of the Himalayas

French-born ALEXANDRA DAVID-NEEL, an Orientalist and Buddhist scholar who spoke flawless Tibetan, in 1911 became the first woman from the West to interview the Dalai Lama, in Darjeeling, India. Thirteen years later, in 1924, dressed as a peasant Tibetan woman accompanying her lama son (actually her unpaid secretary/student/servant), she entered the Tibetan capital city of Lhasa after an arduous and circuitous trip of many months, largely on foot, from the

Gobi Desert to the China/Tibet border. Her account of this feat in My Journey to Lhasa, written in English and published in 1927, was to become the most popular of more than 20 books she wrote before her death in 1969 at 101 years of age. A rebellious child who asserted herself by frequently running away from her home and nurse and later her convent schools, Alexandra David-Neel made her first trip to the East at the age of 20 on a small inheritance from her godmother.

Until the age of 36 she supported herself as an opera singer in Europe and on tour in Asia. Her unconventional marriage to a distant cousin, Philippe-François Neel, lasted until his death in 1941, although in more than 35 years they spent very little time together.

Alexandra David-Neel is one of five female Himalayan explorers born in the 19th century and living into the 20th, described by LUREE MILLER in her 1976 book *On Top of the World.* The others: Englishwomen NINA MAZUCHELLI, ANNIE TAYLOR, and ISABELLA BIRD BISHOP, and American FANNY BULLOCK WORKMAN, who in 1912 conquered the "world's longest non-polar glacier" in the high Karakorams and was photographed at 21,000 feet carrying a newspaper headlined "Votes for Women."

First Woman to Drive an Automobile Across the United States

A Vassar graduate in the class of 1907, ALICE HUYLER RAMSEY in 1909 was the first woman to drive an automobile across the continent from New York City to San Francisco. In many sections in those days, there were no proper roads. A resident of Covina, California, Ms. Ramsey on her 90th birthday was still driving a car and had never had an accident.

First Woman to Walk Across the United States

Russian-born British citizen Dr. BARBARA MOORE, a health enthusiast who publicized her theories on exercise and diet with lengthy treks in Europe and the United States in the 1950s and '60s, in 1960 at the age of 56 walked across the United States, becoming the first woman known to have done so. It took her 85 days, during which she overcame being hit by a car in Indiana, bad weather in several states, and what she claimed was police harassment in Kansas. Born ANYA

CHERKASOVA, she was one of the first generation of women engineers following the Russian revolution and in 1932 became the Soviet Union's long-distance motorcycling champion. She left Russia in 1939, married an English art teacher from whom she was later separated, and died in London at 73.

First Woman to Sail Solo Across the Atlantic

One of four women among the 125 participants in the Royal Western Single-handed Transatlantic Race in 1976, CLARE FRANCIS was the only one to finish. Despite being battered by 35-foot waves and threatened by icebergs, her 38-foot *Robertson's Golly* reached Newport from Plymouth after 29 days. The final hours went to a quick shampoo and a frantic search for clothes from her gear to fit her new (thinner) figure, sailor Francis reported.

First Woman to Sail Solo Around the World

In June 1978 NAOMI JAMES sailed her sloop, the *Express Crusader,* across the finish line in her home harbor of Dartmouth, England, to become the first woman to complete a round-the-world ocean voyage solo. (A Polish rival several months earlier had completed a solo-round-the-world sail, but she went through the Panama Canal rather than rounding dangerous Cape Horn to make it, as Ms. James did, a strictly ocean sail.) Married two years ago to racing sailor Rob James, she took up sailing because of his love of the sea. She had never skippered a yacht before setting off alone on her record-breaking trip. Her only disappointment, she said, was that she didn't make it nonstop, having had to put in at Cape Town, South Africa, and in the Falkland Islands for repairs Her neighbors planted her garden with summer flowers as a surprise welcome-home present.

Flying Firsts

First Woman and First Person to Parachute Freefall from an Airplane

According to *Air Line Pilot* magazine, July 1976, the man who is usually credited with being the first person to make an intentional freefall parachute jump from an airplane (Leslie Irvin, in 1919) really wasn't. Instead it was a woman, GEORGIA "TINY" BROADWICK, in 1914 in San Diego, California, during demonstrations for the U. S. Army. Ms. Broadwick had been jumping with a static line that automatically opened the chute. On her fourth jump, the line caught momentarily on the tail section of the Martin Trainer from which she was jumping. Afraid that it might tangle again, for her fifth and final flight she cut the line loose and pulled the cord herself while she was falling.

First Woman to Pilot a Jet Plane

According to the Smithsonian Air and Space Museum, it was ANN BAUMGARTNER CARL who in October 1947 became the first woman ever to fly a jet plane, a Bell test aircraft.

First Woman Commander of a Heavy Freight Aircraft

MARIA ATANASSOVA in 1953 was appointed a second pilot in Soviet civil aviation and in 1956 became the first woman commander of the IL-2, IL-4, IL-8, and TU-134 planes. In 1966 she created a sensation at London's Heathrow Airport when she was also the first woman pilot ever to land a passenger aircraft there.

First to Fly Over the North Pole

LOUISE ARNER BOYD (1887–1972), Arctic explorer, geographer, and the first woman councillor of the American Geographical Society (1960), in 1955 was the first woman to make a successful flight over the North Pole and its surrounding areas.

First U.S. Commercial Pilot

In January 1973 Frontier Airlines, the first certified airline in the United States to employ a woman pilot, hired EMILY HOWELL, a flying instructor in Denver who had already qualified as a commercial pilot and in small jets. Eastern and American Airlines followed suit, but their women pilots were soon victims of recession layoffs, while Ms. Howell, a divorcee and mother of a small son, continued to fly for Frontier. The Scandinavian airline SAS was the first Western carrier to hire a woman pilot. Aeroflot, the Soviet airline, is said to have several women pilots on domestic routes.

And First to Cross the Atlantic by Plane, First to Fly It Solo, First To Fly from Hawaii to California, and First to Attempt a Round-the-World Flight

AMELIA EARHART, founder of the famous U.S. women's flying group, the Ninety-Niners, born in 1898 in Atchison, Kansas, was on the last leg of her world flight when, 39 years to the month after her birth, her plane was lost while she was trying to land at Howland Island, a tiny dot in the South Pacific.

"Meely," as her family called her, learned to fly despite their objections. She dropped out of a premed course at Columbia University, took lessons from an early woman flyer, NETA SNOOK, and worked at dozens of odd jobs to support her flying. In 1928, the year after Charles Lindbergh's trans-Atlantic flight, she became the first woman to fly the Atlantic, as a passenger aboard the *Friendship,* piloted by Lou Gordon and Wilmer Stutz. Determined after that trip, more of a publicity stunt than anything else, to make the crossing solo, Amelia Earhart in May 1932 took off in a single-engine red Lockhood Vega (it now hangs in the Smithsonian Air and Space Museum in Washington, and, like Lindy's *Spirit of St. Louis,* looks awfully small).

Carrying with her only a thermos of hot soup, she flew out over the Atlantic, where she was almost immediately beset by bad weather. The plane's wings were coated with ice, forcing her to fly at very low altitudes, sometimes as close as 75 feet above the waves. Fifteen hours after her departure she landed in a farmer's pasture near Londonderry in Ireland and overnight became a celebrity nearly as popular as Lindbergh had been before her.

With the enthusiastic cooperation of her husband, publisher George Putnam, she spent the next few years pushing the barriers of aviation—for women and for all flyers—farther and farther. She flew solo into Mexico and then became the first person to fly nonstop from Mexico to Newark. She was an officer of the Luddington Line, the first airline to provide regular passenger service between New York and Washington. She also lectured, taught, and logged thousands of miles of flying. In 1935 she became the first person to fly from Hawaii to California. The crossing was less eventful than her Atlantic trip had been; she flew steadily at an altitude of between 6,000 and 8,000 feet, maintaining good radio contacts and even listening to the San Francisco Symphony, and landed in Oakland after 18 hours in the air.

Her round-the-world flight, undertaken in a Lockheed Electra with aviator Fred Noonan, began in Oakland in March 1937. The flight was relatively uneventful for most of the trip, although she decided to leave behind the bulky trailing wire antenna, which meant that her radio range extended only about 500 miles. On July 2, an overcast morning, she and Noonan left Lae, New Guinea, heading for Howland Island, about 600 miles north of Samoa. They never arrived.

Years later rumors still circulate as to Amelia Earhart's fate. It has been said that she was on a secret mission for the U. S. Government and was taken prisoner as a spy, possibly executed, by the Japanese, then building up their forces in preparation for their later attack on the United States in the Pacific. She was also reported to be alive and living in mysterious seclusion in New Jersey, guarding the secret of her mysterious South Seas mission. The stories have accumulated and spread, as they do when people become legends.

Her last known communication was recorded in the radio log of a ship just off Howland that July morning in 1937:

7:42 A.M. KHAQQ CALLING ITASCA. WE MUST BE ON YOU BUT CANNOT SEE YOU. BUT GAS IS RUNNING LOW. BEEN UNABLE TO REACH YOU BY RADIO. WE ARE FLYING AT ALTITUDE 1,000 FEET.

Then, at 8:00 a.m.

KHAQQ CALLING ITASCA. WE RECEIVED YOUR SIGNALS BUT UNABLE TO GET A MINIMUM. PLEASE TAKE A BEARING ON US AND ANSWER . . .

That was all. No traces of the plane were ever found.

First Black "Miss Universe"

In 1977 24-year-old JANELLE COMMISSIONG of Trinidad-Tobago became the first black Miss Universe in the 25-year history of the contest. Ms. Commissiong, daughter of a Trinidadian father and Venezuelan mother, was educated as a fashion designer in New York City, and hopes one day to run a chain of boutiques. When the announcement of her victory was made, black singer DIONNE WARWICK, one of the judges, broke into tears, and later said, "I felt as if I had won." Black photographer Gordon Parks described her as having "the classical beauty of black women around the world."

First Woman to Judge a World Heavyweight Fight

When Muhammad Ali won a unanimous 15-round decision in his match with Ear-

n Square Garden,
f the two judges
ʋion nine rounds
va Shain, first
a world heavy

...renghter

ₗ718 New York City opened its fire department to women firefighters, provided they could pass the same tests as men. As early as 1974, Arlington, Virginia, already had Judy Livers on regular duty at its Fire Department Station 4, despite the complaints of other fire-

men's wives because, like the rest of the company, she slept in at the station. Mother of two children and married to a federal firefighter working at Fort Myer, Virginia, Judy Livers failed to lift five 100-pound sandbags off a cart 50 times in 10 minutes the first time she took the test, but tried again and did it in eight minutes. Her husband, Tom, at first opposed her joining the fire department. "We had many discussions, heated and nonheated," he told a reporter. "Finally I realized that she'd made up her mind, and the best thing I could do was keep quiet."

First and Youngest Female Bullfighters

The first woman to become a great bullfighter, Conchita Cintrón, born in 1922 in Chile of American parentage (her father was Puerto Rican and her mother Irish-American), was registered as a U.S. citizen but grew up in Peru, where her family moved when she was a year old. At the age of 12 in Lima she made her first public appearance on horseback as a *rejoneadora* and over the next decade "applied" herself, as the term is, to more than 800 bulls from horseback. At 15, meanwhile, in Mexico, she also appeared for the first time as a *torera,* fighting a bull on foot. She became famous and extremely popular in South America. But in Portugal and Spain she had a long struggle before she was allowed to fight bulls as a *torera* and in France was summoned to court for having "mistreated a domestic animal." (The charge, she said, was insulting to the bull.) In 1949, appearing on horseback in a bull ring in Spain, she defied the rules by dismounting, led the bull through a perfect set of passes, then dropped her sword, choosing not to kill. Two other bullfighters who appeared that afternoon dedicated their bulls to her. She was arrested but pardoned on the spot at the demand of the crowd, then left the ring and never returned. Now in

her mid-50s, Conchita Cintrón lives in Lisbon and is a mother and a writer.

A young woman who has followed more easily in the first *torera*'s disciplined footsteps is Maribel Atienzar of Spain, known to bullfight fans of the present time as La Niña Torera, the "baby bullfighter." She has been fighting since age 14 and by age 17 had killed 35 bulls. At first her mother objected, feeling that the sport was more fitting for Maribo's brother, Palo. But "bullfighting is my life," the daughter insisted. Palo is now La Niña's manager, organizing her bookings in the corridas of Spain.

Youngest U.S. Female Patent Holders

Sisters Teresa and Mary Thompson were eight and nine years old respectively in 1960 when they invented and patented a solar tepee for a science fair project. They called their invention a "Wigwarm." It was based on their experience watching their father build a solar-heated home for the family.

Twelve-year-old Becky Schroeder late one afternoon was waiting impatiently for her mother to return to their parked car in Toledo, Ohio. She had some homework to do. Wouldn't it be great, she thought, if she could write in the dark. That led to her invention, a "glow-in-the-dark writing board," on which she received U.S. Patent no. 3,832,556 in 1974.

Oldest Woman to Receive Oxford M.A.

MABEL PUREFOY FITZGERALD at 100 years of age in 1972 was awarded an honorary degree of Master of the Arts at Oxford University, England. Vice Chancellor Sir Allan Bullock acknowledged that the recognition came a good three quarters of a century late. As a young woman, Ms. Fitzgerald had persuaded the Oxford authorities to let her study physiology. Her work was brilliant, but she was refused a degree on the grounds that the university did not admit women and therefore could not award her a degree. Despite her lack of official credentials, she pursued her career successfully and worked with many of the world's most prominent scientists, dedicating herself to the study of respiration.

Fastest Cube Rooter

SHAKUNTALA DEVI, a mathematical prodigy with inexplicable, untrained abilities, can solve almost any problem involving addition, multiplication, and division in her head in only seconds. She uses "algorithms," mental shortcuts that even she does not understand. Ms. Devi has traveled far from her native Bangalore, India, demonstrating this extraordinary gift. (Others have had it; Isaac Newton was one.) At a New York meeting in 1977 she solved this problem:

Add: 25,842,278
111,201,721
370,247,830
55,511,315
Multiply result by: 9,878

The answer (5,559,369,456,432) came to Ms. Devi in less than 20 seconds.

Most Titled Woman in the World

Spain's Doña MARIA DEL ROSARIO CAYENTA FITZ-JAMES STUART Y SILVA is the most titled woman in the world. The 18th Duchess of Alba, she holds 7 other titles as a duchess, and is 15 times a marchioness and 21 times a countess.

Sole Surviving Shark Kicker

NORMA HANSON is the only woman, or probably person, alive known to have kicked the teeth out of a great white shark. This extraordinary incident occurred when Norma and her husband, Al, were the hard-hat diving act on Catalina Island. She was hanging at about 15 feet and Al was on the bottom when suddenly he spotted a 12-to-15-foot white shark and communicated through their diver's phones: "Norma! Shark going for your legs!" Norma, who couldn't see the shark, drew up her legs and kicked out blindly. Both of her 15-pound steel shoes went straight into the open jaws of the shark. Al, unable to do anything but watch, saw teeth flying left and right. The shark veered off and was never seen again. Norma Hanson has continued to dive commercially.

Chicago-Born Merchandising Heiress, First U.S. Woman Vicereine of India

When Levi Leiter, Pennsylvania-German co-founder of the great Chicago department store, Marshall Field's, moved his family to Washington, D.C., in the 1890s, his beautiful daughter Mary conquered capital society. From Washington she moved on to London, marriage to George Curzon, and in 1898, when her husband was made Viceroy of India, to New Delhi. There, as Vicereine, MARY LEITER CURZON, with an enormous staff of aides and household servants, a dazzling wardrobe, and horses and elephants to ride, became with her husband the direct representative of Queen Victoria in Britain's jewel of empire. As such, she occupied the highest position every held by an American woman overseas. Intelligent as well as lovely looking, Lady Mary Curzon before her early death of peritonitis in

1906, at age 36, was the confidante of prime ministers, presidents, and kings. She was the subject of a biography by Nigel Nicolson published in 1977.

Post Cereal Heiress, First U. S. Ambassador's Wife in U.S.S.R.

At age 27, MARJORIE MERRIWEATHER POST, who died in 1973 at the age of 86, inherited the enormous wealth amassed by her father, C. W. Post, the cereal tycoon. Included were three huge estates—Mar-A-Lago in Palm Beach, Camp Topridge in the New York Adirondacks, and Hillwood, in Washington, D.C. On her own she had built the largest apartment ever on the island of Manhattan—70 rooms—and a 350-foot sailing vessel called the *Sea Cloud,* which she outfitted with tapestries and period furniture. Perhaps the most famous collection among many she made came from Czarist Russia; when she died she owned the largest collection of Fabergé jewels and other Imperial Russian artifacts outside the Soviet Union. She married four times. Her second husband was E. F. Hutton (the father of her actress-daughter DINA MERRILL). Her third was Joseph Davies, President Roosevelt's Ambassador to Stalin. Accompanying Davies, this favored daughter of capitalism became the first ambassador's wife to represent America to the Union of Soviet Socialist Republics.

Three Generations of Indian Superachievers

Lady DHANVANTHI RAMA RAU founded a line of extraordinary Indian women who continue to contribute in several fields and many countries. Herself one of the first Indian women to attend college, she went on to lecture at Presidency College in Madras. After her marriage to a prominent Indian diplomat and politician, she became involved in the world family planning movement, acting as a co-founder of Planned Parenthood International in 1950, and serving as its president for several years. She continues to be involved in this and other educational and social problems in India and elsewhere.

Lady Rama Rau's first daughter, PREMILA WAGLE, born in 1920, was schooled in England and India. In 1960, she started an export business in ready-to-wear clothing called Paville Fashions Private Ltd. The United States is her primary customer. She was named Woman Entrepreneur of the Year for 1976 in India and is adviser to India's UN delegation on import and export quotas.

Premila Wagle's younger sister, novelist SHANTA RAMA RAU, born in 1923, the best-known of the group, attended Wellesley College in the United States and published her first novel while a senior there. More recently, she has been co-author of *A Princess Remembers,* the autobiography of GAYATRI DEVI (the Maharani of Jaipur, another outstanding Indian woman), published in 1976. She also helped her mother with her memoirs, published in 1977.

The third generation is represented by ASHA WAGLE, born in 1944, the first woman to own a London investment business. She attended Oxford University, worked as a financial director at Rothschild's, and left there to found CPI, her own very successful firm.

She Made Millions from Kewpie Dolls

Magazine illustrator and doll designer ROSE CECIL O'NEILL, born in 1874 in Wilkes-Barre, Pennsylvania, began drawing for a living when she was 15. Her work appeared in *Good Housekeeping, Puck,* and other magazines, and she married the editor of *Puck.* The marriage lasted only five years, however. Not long after her divorce in 1907, her "Kewpies" began to be the rage. The *Ladies' Home Journal* gave them a full page, and they were soon all over America in the form of dolls, salt and pepper shakers, on letter paper, buttons, and so on. She made $1.5 million in royalties alone from the products and retired to sculpt, travel, entertain lavishly, and write "Gothics."

She Taught Us All Our Manners

A graduate of Miss Graham's Finishing School for Young Ladies and other private schools in New York City, daughter of a wealthy and socially prominent Baltimore family, EMILY PRICE POST was born in October 1873. Considered a great beauty when she made her 1892 debut, she married Edwin M. Post, a well-to-do banker. He lost his fortune in the 1901 panic, and in 1905 Ms. Post found herself a divorcée with two small children to support. She went to work as a newspaper society reporter until Funk and Wagnall's asked her to do a book on etiquette. The result is the Bible of manners, Emily Post's *Etiquette,* originally titled *Etiquette: The Blue Book of Social Usage* in its 1922 edition. The first such book written for the general public by a woman of high social position, it remained a best seller for many years, and is still in print. In 1931 Emily Post began a radio program and wrote a syndicated column on good taste. In 1938 she published a book on her first love, interior decorating, entitled *The Personality of a House;* it ran to several editions, and was used as a text in schools and colleges. She also wrote *Children Are People* (1940) and *Motor Manners* (1950). Ms. Post died in 1960.

She Cooked and Ate It Right

ADELLE DAVIS, who became the world's best-known advocate of vitamin supplements and natural foods, was born in 1904 on a farm near Lizton, Indiana. Her mother died soon after Adelle's birth, and as a baby she was at first laboriously fed with an eyedropper; this oral deprivation later seemed to Ms. Davis a possible explanation for her interest in nutrition and food. She graduated from Lizton High School in 1923, went on to Purdue, and then to the University of California at Berkeley, where she earned a B.A. in dietetics. An M.S. in biochemistry from Southern California Medical School followed. She worked as a nutrition consultant from 1931 to 1938. By 1938 her reputation was sufficiently well established to lead her to spend all her time writing and lecturing, and later in making TV appearances. She advocated proper cooking, addition of powdered milk and other nutrients to dishes, and the use of meats, especially organ meats ("When under stress, I eat liver for breakfast"), whole grain bread, wheat germ, yogurt, brewer's yeast, organic fruits and vegetables, and—because of the prevalence of refined food in the United States—plentiful vitamin supplements. Her books on nutrition, *Let's Cook It Right* (1947), *Let's Eat Right to Keep Fit* (rev. ed., 1970), *Let's Get Well* (1965), *Let's Have Healthy Children* (1972), and *You Can Get Well* (1972), have sold more than 5 million copies and are still in print today. Ms. Davis was married twice, and adopted two children. In 1927 she was made a fellow of the International College of Applied Nutrition, and in 1972 she received an honorary doctorate from the University of Plano, in Plano, Texas, and a Raymond A. Dart Human Potential Award from the steelworkers of America. She died in 1974.

She Learned from the Sky and the Sea

ANNE MORROW LINDBERGH was the daughter of the U.S. ambassador to Mexico when she met and married, in 1929, America's popular hero, "Lindy." Their life was never tranquil. In 1932 their first child, a two-year-old son, was kidnapped from their home near Hopewell, New Jersey, and murdered. During the trial of the kidnapper the Lindberghs took refuge in Europe to escape the publicity. Lindbergh visited German aviation centers and became impressed with German efficiency. He warned against growing Nazi airpower, but he also embraced a policy of neutrality for the United States; in 1941, under criticism from President Franklin D. Roosevelt, he resigned his commission in the U.S. air corps reserve. Through all this and later traumas that might have defeated a lesser woman, Anne Morrow Lindbergh sought and found a private tranquillity

that eluded her in their public life. A widow since 1974, she has a hard-won serenity that shows in her face and is evoked in the journals and diaries she has kept and published over the years. Her books, which include *North to the Orient* (1935), *Listen! the Wind* (1938), and, most notably, *Gift from the Sea* (1955), share with readers what she learned over the years as her husband's companion on many long flights and in her own explorations of oceans and beaches.

Their Books Have Sold Hundreds of Millions of Copies

ENID BLYTON, British author of more than 400 books for children of all ages, but especially popular with girls 7 to 13, is the third most translated author in the world (after AGATHA CHRISTIE, "Women in the Arts and Entertainment," p. 675, and William Shakespeare). Born in 1900 in London, Ms. Blyton began writing for magazines when she was quite young. Her first book, *Real Fairies,* appeared in 1923, and was followed by a steady succession of others with such titles as *The Naughtiest Girl in School* (1940). Among several series she has created, her Famous Five and Noddy books are especially popular.

Ms. Blyton's closest American counterpart, less widely translated but probably even more widely sold, is HARRIET ADAMS, more familiarly known by her pseudonym CAROLYN KEENE, under which she publishes the Nancy Drew mysteries. (She also writes as LAURA LEE HOPE and under various men's names.) Some 60 million copies of the Nancy Drew series alone have been sold since the girl detective was created by Ms. Adams' father, Edward Stratemeyer, whose syndicate, publishers also of the Hardy Boys, the Rover Boys, the Bobbsey Twins, and Bomba the Jungle Boy, she took over at his death in 1930. Nancy Drew, once praised as a "role model for young feminists" by *Ms.* magazine because of her "resourcefulness and in-

dependence," is, Harriet Adams admitted in 1977 at 84 years of age, her "fiction daughter" and the teen-aged sleuth she herself would "have loved" to have been. But Nancy is "no woman's liberationist," she says.

A Life of Puzzles

ELIZABETH SEELMAN KINGSLEY, born about 1878 in Brooklyn, New York, grew up doing scrambled word puzzles for *St. Nicholas* magazine. After her graduation from Wellesley in 1898 she became an English teacher. When crossword puzzles became a national obsession in the 1920s, Ms. Kingsley decided that "a puzzle which stimulated the imagination and heightened an appreciation of fine literature by reviewing English and American poetry and prose masters would be a puzzle with a goal." She sold her first double-crostic to the *Saturday Review of Literature* in 1934. Her puzzles relied heavily on the works of Shakespeare, Keats, Defoe, and other classics. She utterly ignored Joyce, STEIN, and other modern writers, whose works she did not like.

The Star Behind Brenda

More than 40 years ago while she was still a student at the Chicago Institute of Art, DALE MESSICK created the famous romantic redhead comic-strip character, "Brenda Starr, Reporter." Brenda is everything I'm not," says the twice-divorced Ms. Messick, now past 70, who modeled her character after Hollywood pin-up star RITA HAYWORTH and keeps her alive today as a liberated career woman. In finally marrying Brenda off to her mystery man, Basil St. John, and making the glamour couple parents, Ms. Messick took on a challenge in keeping with common contemporary problems. Brenda must now try to juggle career and home life. Ms. Messick vows that neither retirement nor divorce is in the offing for her long-lasting star reporter.

Her Cartoons Made the *New Yorker* from the Start

HELEN ELNA HOKINSON's gently carica-tured well-endowed ladies—clubwomen, gardeners, shoppers, and presiders over tea tables—graced the pages of the *New Yorker* from its start in 1925. At first the captions were supplied by the editors, later by her collaborator after 1931, James Reid Parker. The topical captions often came from the mouths of presiding officers at club meetings ("It has been moved that our recording secretary send a summary of today's discussion to Mar-shal Tito. Do I hear a second?" "What do you think—should I plunge right into all the Iron Curtain countries or just take up Czechoslovakia?"). They still sting, but Ms. Hokinson's plump, befuddled la-dies were received with real affection. The cartoonist, who was also a painter and ceramics artist, died in 1949 in a plane collision over National Airport in Washington when she was arriving for a scheduled speech at the opening of the Community Chest drive.

Women in Clown Suits

Founder of Le Nouveau Cirque de Paris, and the funny half of a famous clown duo with her husband, ANNIE FRATELLINI is Europe's only prominent woman clown. Ms. Fratellini's school, begun with a French Government grant in 1975, offers basic circus training in dance, mime, acrobatics, music, tra-peze, juggling, tightrope walking, and horseback riding. Ms. Fratellini's daughter also is in the circus, as a tra-peze artist.

By now, a number of young women have been graduated from the Ringling Brothers Circus school for clowns in Florida, but when she joined Ringling Brothers, Barnum and Bailey Circus (as it then was) in 1971, PEGGY LENORE WILLIAMS became the first U.S. woman circus clown. Ms. Williams, who took "PELENORE" for her clown name, makes eleven appearances each show. "One of the most important aspects of my act is my makeup," she says. "I paint a smile on my lips and teardrops under my eyes because, for me, they represent the con-tradictions in life. Some people think clowning is just a fantasy job, but every time I make people laugh, I know that there must also be some sorrow in their lives." Ms. Williams majored in speech pathology at the University of Wisconsin, where she discovered that words were "terribly limited" in communicating to disturbed children. Hence her interest in mime, with which she now enthralls adults and children alike.

Researchers in Human Sexuality

VIRGINIA JOHNSON, in collaboration with her colleague (later to become her hus-band) Dr. William Masters, started it with the ground-breaking study, *Human Sexual Response,* published in 1966, based on work conducted largely in clinics. SHERE HITE, author of the 1977 best-seller, *The Hite Report,* pursued her research via 3,000 replies to questionnaires she devised, editing and interpreting the results on the basis of her graduate work in social history. Her first book deals exclusively with women's sexual responses, but she is now at work on another Hite Report on male sexuality. Eventually, she says, she'd like to write an opera.

"Total Woman"

MARABEL MORGAN, author of the best selling *Total Woman* (1974), grew up "amid a lot of fighting." When her marriage to Charlie Morgan began to be stormy, she turned to the Bible and to her own imagination to help save it. The result has become almost an industry. Ms. Morgan travels the country giving Total Woman courses, and her book has sold over 3 million copies; a successor, *Total Joy* (1977), is on its way to equaling the success of the first book. Ms. Morgan's method is based on three A's: Admire, Adapt, and Appreciate. Husbands are to be treated gently, to be seduced with a variety of cute costumes and little notes like "I crave your body" left in briefcases. "Sex," says Ms. Morgan, 40 (in 1978) to her husband's 38 years of age, and the mother of two daughters, "is as clean and pure as cottage cheese." Graduates of her Total Woman courses include the wives of almost all the Miami Dolphin football team, boxing's Joe Frazier, and golf's Jack Nicklaus.

Solar Countess Who Cooks with the Sun

Countess STELLA ANDRASSY, who holds U.S. patents on nine solar devices, demonstrated how to cook with solar energy at the Smithsonian Institution's Festival of American Folklife in 1977. A resident of Monmouth, New Jersey, the Countess, who was born in Sweden, married a Hungarian diplomat in 1919. In 1945, with three children, one grandchild, and several dogs and horses, they escaped across the Alps when the Russians invaded Hungary. They went first to Sweden and later came to the United States, where Countess Andrassy worked with Dr. MARIA TELKES (see "Women in Science and Technology," p. 189) in New York City for several years. She later worked in Princeton, New Jersey, with Curtiss-Wright's Solar Research Laboratory. Princeton professor Harrison Fraker called her "an incredibly creative and inventive person" in "a world that hasn't listened for nearly 30 years." In 1960 the Andrassys incorporated their own solar research operation, run out of their home basement.

Tradition-Breaking Women Chefs

In Paris, ten tradition-breaking women chefs, excluded from the male chefs' national organization, in 1976 founded the Association des Restauratrices-Cuisinières (ARC). Most of ARC's 50 members are self-taught or learned from mothers or grandmothers. They are now taking apprentices (female only), forego the unbecoming *toque blanche* but wear white smocks over their dresses, and cook by intuition, smell, and taste rather than by recipe and rule. "I have it in my hands," explains GISELE BERGER, ARC president, who runs La Bonne Table in Clichy, a suburb of Paris. The women chefs, who have been widely written up, were inspired to organize by a man, Robert Courtine, restaurant critic for *Le Monde*. He prefers women's cooking.

He Gave Up His Throne for Her

Winston Churchill is said to have written the words. But it was Britain's King Edward VIII who went on radio to tell the world that he was abdicating his throne to marry an American divorcée, WALLIS WARFIELD SIMPSON, of Baltimore, Maryland, "the woman I love." That was in 1937. For many years the Duke and Duchess of Windsor lived principally in France and traveled extensively. Until his death in 1972, they remained stylish leaders of the international set. The Duchess, a widow in her 80s, has recently spent most of her time in Paris.

He Proclaimed Her Queen

ELIZABETH (LISA) HALABY, daughter of Najeeb E. Halaby, the half-Arab longtime head of the U. S. Federal Aviation Administration and later president of Pan American Airways, earned a degree in architecture at Princeton University. In 1976 she accompanied her father to Amman, Jordan, to attend a ceremony turning over a Boeing 747 jetliner to the Royal Jordanian Airlines. Later she went to work designing facilities for the airline. In 1978, in the world's June wedding-of-the-year, Lisa Halaby, 26, married Jordan's King Hussein, 42. Hussein's third wife (he has been twice divorced), Queen ALIA, a Palestinian, was killed in a helicopter crash a year and a half ago. Hussein designated his first two wives (one English-born) princesses. Now he has given Ms. Halaby, whom he married in an Islamic ceremony, the name NUR EL HUSSEIN ("Light of Hussein") and proclaimed her Queen of Jordan.

Working Princess from Philadelphia

GRACE KELLY of the Philadelphia Kellys grew up rich and beautiful. She became a Hollywood star, won an Oscar for *The Country Girl,* (see "Women in the Arts and Entertainment," p. 653) wed Prince Rainier III of Monaco, and gave birth to heir-to-the-throne Prince Albert and his younger and older sisters, STEPHANIE and CAROLINE. Presiding with her husband in dignified fashion over their small kingdom, she is America's only working princess. (HOPE COOKE left Sikkim and her royal husband's state shortly before it became a part of India in 1975.)

The Many Lives of a President's Widow

In the last few years, JACQUELINE BOUVIER KENNEDY ONASSIS, since the days of Camelot on the Potomac one of the world's most admired, written about, and photographed women, has earned new admiration for her work as a New York book editor (first at Viking, now at Doubleday). Her mettle was tested in public and in private by the assassinations of her husband, President John F. Kennedy, and his brother, Robert Kennedy. Later, gossip, slander, and unending curiosity marked her second marriage, to the late Aristotle Onassis, Greek shipping magnate reputed to be one of the wealthiest men of modern times. Through all of this and the subsequent demands of establishing a new existence in Manhattan for herself and her children, CAROLINE and John, she has conducted her extraordinary life with never-failing grace under pressure. A slim, fashionable, smiling woman in her late 40s, she remains as glamorous and competent as she was when, the young wife of a young U.S. President, she charmed and impressed De Gaulle, Nehru, and other heads of governments and ordinary people all over the globe.

The Many Lives of a Superstar

The fame she won as a young girl playing the lead role in *National Velvet* and the Oscars she got for her performances in *Butterfield 8* and *Who's Afraid of Virginia Woolf?* (see "Woman in the Arts and Entertainment," p. 654) have never seemed to mean as much to superstar ELIZABETH TAYLOR HILTON WILDING

TODD FISHER BURTON WARNER as the men in her life, her four children, and, so far, one grandchild. With husband John Warner, she has lately been living and apparently loving a new life. It is centered on the Virginia hunt country, where gentleman-farmer Warner has an estate, their Georgetown house from which they attend many Washington embassy parties, and the political world in which he has ambitions.

Index